Great Britain
&
Ireland
2012

Contents

INTRODUCTION

How to use this guide	4
Commitments	6
Dear reader	7
Classification & awards	8
Facilities & services	10
Prices	11
Informations on localities	12
Plan key	13

AWARDS 2012

Starred establishments	16
Bib Gourmand	22
Bib Hotel	26
Pleasant hotels & guesthouses	28
Pleasant restaurants & pubs	32

FURTHER INFORMATION

Beer and Whisky	38
International dialling codes	972
Index of towns	975
Major Hotel groups	989

TOWNS from A to Z

Great Britain

England	50
Scotland	688
Wales	794

Ireland

Northern Ireland	842
Republic of Ireland	864

MAPS

Distances in miles	992
Great Britain & Ireland in 39 maps	996

How to use this guide

TOURIST INFORMATION

Distances from the main towns, tourist offices, local tourist attractions, means of transport, golf courses and leisure activities...

HOTELS

From 🏨🏨🏨🏨 to 🏠, ⌂:
categories of comfort.
In red 🏨🏨🏨🏨 ... 🏠, ⌂:
the most pleasant.

RESTAURANTS AND PUBS

From XXXXX to X, 🍽: categories of comfort.
In red XXXXX ... X, 🍽:
the most pleasant.

STARS

✿✿✿ Worth a special journey.
✿✿ Worth a detour.
✿ A very good restaurant.

GOOD FOOD AND ACCOMMODATION AT MODERATE PRICES

☺ Bib Gourmand
🍲 Bib Hotel

CAMBRIDGE – Cambs – 504 U27 – pop. 117 717 – Gre
London 55 – Coventry 88 – Ipswich 54 – Leiceste
– Nottingham 88 – Oxford 100
▶ Cambridge Airport: ☏ (01223) 373737, E: 2 m or
▲ The Old Library, Wheeleer St, ☏ (01223) 45758
ℹ Cambridgeshire Moat House Hotel, Bar Hill, ☏
🔞 Town: St John's College AC Y – King's Art Coll
Museum Z M1 – Trinity College Y – Kettle's
⛳ Audley End, S: 13 mi by A1309 – Imperial
on M11

Hotel Gloria
Whitehouse lane, Huntington Rd, CB3 OLX,
– ☏ (01223) 277985 – www.hotelgloria.co
52 rm – ♦ £136 ♦♦ £168/255 – ☕ £7.50
Rest *The Melrose* – Menu £16 (lunch),
♦ Built as a private house in 1852, nov
contemporary rooms include state of t
den and terrace.

Alexander House (Johns)
Midsummer Common, CB4 1HA – Cl
– www.alexanderhouse.com – Cl
1 week spring, Sunday and Mond
Rest – Menu (dinner only and l
Spec. Salad of smoked eel, pig
and pistachios and asparagus.
and mint.
♦ A river Cam idyll. Chic conse
with blissful views over the

The Roasted Pepp
35 Chesterton Rd, CB4 3A
– Closed Christmas-Ne
Rest – (booking essent
♦ Personally run Victor
dishes with mild Asia

at Histon North: 3 m on B

Blue House F
44 High St, CB3 7
– Closed 2 weeks
22 rm – ♦ £38
♦ Red-brick 18
overlooks me
preserves. In

CANTERBURY
London
Felix

OTHER MICHELIN PUBLICATIONS
References for the Michelin map and Green Guide which cover the area.

12A2

LOCATING THE TOWN
Locate the town on the regional map at the end of the guide (map number and coordinates).

QUIET HOTELS
🛏️ Quiet hotel.
🛏️ Very quiet hotel.

LOCATING THE ESTABLISHMENT
Located on the town plan (coordinates and letters giving the location).

Y**a**

DESCRIPTION OF THE ESTABLISHMENT
Atmosphere, style, character and specialities.

PRICES

FACILITIES AND SERVICES

9D2

The MICHELIN guide's commitments

Experienced in quality

Whether it is in Japan, the USA, China or Europe our inspectors use the same criteria to judge the quality of the hotels and restaurants and use the same methods of visiting. The guide can only boast this worldwide reputation thanks to its commitment to the readers and we would like to stress these here:

The MICHELIN guide's commitments:

Anonymous inspections: our inspectors make regular and anonymous visits to hotels and restaurants to gauge the quality of products and services offered to an ordinary customer. They settle their own bill and may then introduce themselves and ask for more information about the establishment. Our readers' comments are also a valuable source of information, which we can then follow up with another visit of our own.

Independence: To remain totally objective for our readers, the selection is made with complete independence. Entry into the guide is free. All decisions are discussed with the Editor and our highest awards are considered at a European level.

Selection and choice: The guide offers a selection of the best hotels and restaurants in every category of comfort and price. This is only possible because all the inspectors rigorously apply the same methods.

Annual updates: All the practical information, the classifications and awards are revised and updated every single year to give the most reliable information possible.

Consistency: The criteria for the classifications are the same in every country covered by the MICHELIN guide.

The sole intention of Michelin is to make your travels both safe and enjoyable.

Dear Reader,

Dear Reader,

Having kept up-to-date with the latest developments in the hotel and restaurant scenes, we are pleased to present this new, improved and updated edition of the Michelin Guide.

Since the very beginning, our ambition has remained the same each year: to accompany you on all of your journeys and to help you choose the best establishments to both stay and eat in, across all categories of comfort and price; whether that's a friendly guesthouse or luxury hotel, a lively gastropub or fine dining restaurant.

To this end, the Michelin Guide is a tried-and-tested travel planner, its primary objective being to provide first-hand experience for you, our readers. All of the establishments selected have been rigorously tested by our team of professional inspectors, who are constantly seeking out new places and continually assessing those already listed.

Every year the guide recognises the best places to eat, by awarding them one ✿, two ✿✿ or three ✿✿✿ stars. These lie at the heart of the selection and highlight the establishments producing the best quality cuisine – in all styles – taking into account the quality of ingredients, creativity, mastery of techniques and flavours, value for money and consistency.

Other symbols to look out for are the Bib Gourmand ☺ and the Bib Hotel 🏨, which point out establishments that represent particularly good value; here you'll be guaranteed excellence but at moderate prices.

We are committed to remaining at the forefront of the culinary world and to meeting the demands of our readers. As such, we are very interested to hear your opinions on the establishments listed in our guide. Please don't hesitate to contact us, as your contributions are invaluable in directing our work and improving the quality of our information.

We continually strive to help you on your journeys.

Thank you for your loyalty and happy travelling with the 2012 edition of the Michelin Guide.

Consult the MICHELIN guide at **www.ViaMichelin.com**
and write to us at:
themichelinguide-gbirl@uk.michelin.com

Classification & awards

CATEGORIES OF COMFORT

The Michelin guide selection lists the best hotels and restaurants in each category of comfort and price. The establishments we choose are classified according to their levels of comfort and, within each category, are listed in order of preference.

🏨🏨🏨	XXXXX	Luxury in the traditional style
🏨🏨	XXXX	Top class comfort
🏨🏨	XXX	Very comfortable
🏨	XX	Comfortable
🏠	X	Quite comfortable
	🍴	Pubs serving good food
↑		Other recommended accommodation (Guesthouses, farmhouses and private homes)
without rest.		This hotel has no restaurant
with rm		This restaurant also offers accommodation

THE AWARDS

To help you make the best choice, some exceptional establishments have been given an award in this year's Guide. They are marked ✿, 🙂, 🍴. For those awarded a Bib Hotel, the mention **"rm"** appears in the description of the establishment.

THE BEST CUISINE

Michelin stars are awarded to establishments serving cuisine, of whatever style, which is of the highest quality. The cuisine is judged on the quality of ingredients, the skill in their preparation, the combination of flavours, the levels of creativity, the value for money and the consistency of culinary standards.
For every restaurant awarded a star we include 3 specialities that are typical of their cooking style. These specific dishes may not always be available.

✿✿✿	**Exceptional cuisine, worth a special journey** One always eats extremely well here, sometimes superbly.
✿✿	**Excellent cooking, worth a detour**
✿	**Very good cooking in its category**

Occasionally "Rising Stars " will feature. These are establishments that we feel have the potential for a higher award. Once they can produce their high standard of cooking on a consistent basis they could me our future stars.

GOOD FOOD AND ACCOMMODATION AT MODERATE PRICES

🙂 **Bib Gourmand**
Establishment offering good quality cuisine for under £28 or €40 in the Republic of Ireland (price of a 3 course meal not including drinks).

Bib Hotel
Establishment offering good levels of comfort and service, with most rooms priced at under £90 or under €115 in the Republic of Ireland (price of a room for 2 people, including breakfast).

PLEASANT HOTELS AND RESTAURANTS

Symbols shown in red indicate particularly pleasant or restful establishments: the character of the building, its décor, the setting, the welcome and services offered may all contribute to this special appeal.

⋔, 🏠 to 🏠🏠🏠🏠 **Pleasant hotels & guesthouses**

🍴, ✗ to ✗✗✗✗✗ **Pleasant restaurants & pubs**

OTHER SPECIAL FEATURES

As well as the categories and awards given to the establishment, Michelin inspectors also make special note of other criteria which can be important when choosing an establishment.

LOCATION

If you are looking for a particularly restful establishment, or one with a special view, look out for the following symbols:

       Quiet hotel
       Very quiet hotel
       Interesting view
       Exceptional view

WINE LIST

If you are looking for an establishment with an excellent wine list, look out for the following symbol:

Particularly interesting wine list
This symbol might cover the list presented by a sommelier in a luxury restaurant or that of a simple pub or restaurant where the owner has a passion for wine. The two lists will offer something exceptional but very different, so beware of comparing them by each other's standards.

SMOKING

In Great Britain and the Republic of Ireland the law prohibits smoking in all pubs, restaurants and hotel public areas.

Facilities & services

30 rm	Number of rooms
	Lift (elevator)
AC	Air conditioning (in all or part of the establishment)
	Fast Internet access in bedrooms
	Wi-fi Internet access in bedrooms
	Establishment at least partly accessible to those of restricted mobility
	Special facilities for children
	Meals served in garden or on terrace
Spa	An extensive facility for relaxation and well-being
	Sauna – Exercise room
	Swimming pool: outdoor or indoor
	Garden – Park
	Tennis court – Golf course and number of holes
	Fishing available to hotel guests. A charge may be made
	Equipped conference room
	Private dining rooms
	Hotel garage (additional charge in most cases)
P	Car park for customers only
	No dogs allowed (in all or part of the establishment)
	Nearest Underground station (in London)
May-October	Dates when open, as indicated by the hotelier

Prices

Prices quoted in this guide were supplied in summer 2011 and apply to low and high seasons. They are subject to alteration if goods and service costs are revised. By supplying the information, hotels and restaurants have undertaken to maintain these rates for our readers.

In some towns, when commercial, cultural or sporting events are taking place the hotel rates are likely to be considerably higher.

Prices are given in £ sterling, except for the Republic of Ireland where euros are quoted.

All accommodation prices include both service and V.A.T. All restaurant prices include V.A.T. Service is also included when an **s** appears after the prices.

Where no **s** is shown, prices may be subject to the addition of a variable service charge which is usually between 10 % - 15 %.

(V.A.T. does not apply in the Channel Islands).

Out of season, certain establishments offer special rates. Ask when booking.

RESERVATION AND DEPOSITS

Some hotels will require a deposit which confirms the commitment of both the customer and the hotelier. Ask the hotelier to provide you with all the terms and conditions applicable to your reservation in their written confirmation.

CREDIT CARDS

Credit cards accepted by the establishment:
AE ⓓ ⓜⓒ VISA American Express – Diners Club – MasterCard – Visa

ROOMS

rm ♦ 50/90	Lowest price 50 and highest price 90 for a comfortable single room
rm ♦♦ 70/120	Lowest price 70 and highest price 120 for a double or twin room for 2 people
rm ⌦ 55/85	Full cooked breakfast (whether taken or not) is included in the price of the room
⌦ 6	Price of breakfast

SHORT BREAKS

Many hotels offer a special rate for a stay of two or more nights which comprises dinner, room and breakfast usually for a minimum of two people. Please enquire at hotel for rates.

RESTAURANT

Set meals: lowest price £13, highest price £28, usually for a 3 course meal. The lowest priced set menu is often only available at lunchtimes.

A la carte meals: the prices represent the range of charges from a simple to an elaborate 3 course meal.

s	Service included
🎭	Restaurants offering lower priced pre and/or post theatre menus

⌂: Dinner in this category of establishment is sometimes communal and meals are not always available every evening. It will generally be a limited menu, served at a ⸺ time, to residents only. Lunch is rarely offered. Many will not be licensed to sell alco

Information on localities

GENERAL INFORMATION

✉ **York**	Postal address
501 M27, ⑩	Michelin map and co-ordinates or fold
🟩 Great Britain	See the Michelin Green Guide Great Britain
pop. 1057	Population
	Source: 2001 Census (Key Statistics for Urban Areas)
	Crown copyright 2004
BX **a**	Letters giving the location of a place on a town plan
🏌18	Golf course and number of holes (handicap sometimes required, telephone reservation strongly advised)
※ ≼	Panoramic view, viewpoint
✈	Airport
🚢	Shipping line (passengers & cars)
🛳	Passenger transport only
🛈	Tourist Information Centre

STANDARD TIME

In winter, standard time throughout the British Isles is Greenwich Mean Time (GMT). In summer, British clocks are advanced by one hour to give British Summer Time (BST). The actual dates are announced annually but always occur over weekends in March and October.

TOURIST INFORMATION

STAR-RATING

★★★	Highly recommended
★★	Recommended
★	Interesting
AC	Admission charge

LOCATION

👁	Sights in town
🧭	On the outskirts
N, S, E, W	The sight lies North, South, East or West of the town
A 22	Take road A 22, indicated by the same symbol on the Guide map
2 mi.	Distance in miles (In the Republic of Ireland kilometres are quoted).

Plan key

Hotels – restaurants

SIGHTS

Place of interest
Interesting place of worship Catholic-Protestant

ROADS

Motorway
Numbered junctions: complete, limited
Dual carriageway with motorway characteristics
Main traffic artery
Primary route (GB) and National route (IRL)
One-way street – Unsuitable for traffic or street subject to restrictions
Pedestrian street – Tramway
Shopping street – Car park – Park and Ride
Gateway – Street passing under arch – Tunnel
Low headroom (16'6" max.) on major through routes
Station and railway
Funicular – Cable-car
Lever bridge – Car ferry

VARIOUS SIGNS

Tourist Information Centre
Church/Place of worship – Mosque – Synagogue
Communications tower or mast – Ruins
Garden, park, wood – Cemetery
Stadium – Racecourse – Golf course
Golf course (with restrictions for visitors) – Skating rink
Outdoor or indoor swimming pool
View – Panorama
Monument – Fountain – Hospital – Covered market
Pleasure boat harbour – Lighthouse
Airport – Underground station – Coach station
Ferry services: passengers and cars
Main post office
Public buildings located by letter:
C H J   County Council Offices – Town Hall – Law Courts
M T U   Museum – Theatre – University, College
POL.   Police (in large towns police headquarters)

LONDON

BRENT WEMBLEY Borough – Area
Borough boundary
Congestion Zone – Charge applies Monday-Friday 07.00-18.00
Nearest Underground station to the hotel or restaurant

Awards 2012

Starred establishments 2012

The colour corresponds to the establishment with the most stars in this location.

London	This location has at least one 3 star restaurant	✼✼✼
Dublin	This location has at least one 2 star restaurant	✼✼
Edinburgh	This location has at least one 1 star restaurant	✼

- Lochinver
- Sleat
- Fort William
- Dalry
- Ballantrae
- Portpatrick
- NORTHERN IRELAND
- Malahide
- Dublin
- REPUBLIC OF IRELAND
- Ardmore
- GUERNSEY
- JERSEY
- La Pulente • St Helier
- ISLES OF SCILLY
- Rock
- Portscatho

SCOTLAND

- Nairn
- **Auchterarder**
- Peat Inn
- Balloch
- Elie
- Edinburgh
- Leith

ENGLAND

- Pooley Bridge
- Windermere
- Ramsgill-in-Nidderdale
- Cartmel
- Oldstead
- Bolton Abbey
- Ilkley
- Langho
- South Dalton
- Birkenhead
- Sheffield
- Chester
- Baslow
- Llandrillo
- **Nottingham**
- Morston
- Clipsham
- Hunstanton
- Montgomery
- Birmingham
- Hambleton
- Ludlow
- Royal Leamington Spa
- Titley
- Winchcombe
- **Cambridge**
- WALES
- Eldersfield
- Upper Slaughter
- Llanddewi *Skirrid*
- **Cheltenham**
- Murcott
- Woburn
- Whitebrook
- **Malmesbury**
- Welwyn Garden City
- Bristol
- Sprigg's Alley
- **Great Milton**
- Colerne
- **Marlow**
- **London**
- Chew Magna
- Shinfield
- Ascot
- Seasalter
- Castle Combe
- Ripley
- Faversham
- Knowstone
- Little Bedwyn
- Bagshot
- Biddenden
- Winchester
- **Bray**
- Cranbrook
- Petersfield
- Bodiam
- **Chagford**
- Dorchester
- Beaulieu
- Emsworth
- Cuckfield
- Torquay
- Ventnor
- Horsham

SHETLAND ISLANDS

ORKNEY ISLANDS

Starred establishments

❀❀❀

→ England

Bray	Fat Duck
Bray	Waterside Inn
London / City of Westminster	Alain Ducasse at The Dorchester
London / Kensington and Chelsea	Gordon Ramsay

❀❀

→ England

Cambridge	Midsummer House
Chagford	Gidleigh Park
Cheltenham	Le Champignon Sauvage
London / City of Westminster	L'Atelier de Joël Robuchon
London / City of Westminster	Le Gavroche
London / City of Westminster	Hibiscus
London / City of Westminster	Hélène Darroze at The Connaught
London / City of Westminster	Marcus Wareing at The Berkeley
London / City of Westminster	Square
London / Kensington and Chelsea	Ledbury
Malmesbury	Whatley Manor
Marlow	Hand and Flowers **N**
Nottingham	Restaurant Sat Bains **N**
Oxford / Great Milton	Le Manoir aux Quat'Saisons
Rock	Restaurant Nathan Outlaw

→ Scotland

Auchterarder	Andrew Fairlie at Gleneagles

→ Republic of Ireland

Dublin	Patrick Guilbaud

→ **N** *New*

→ England

Ascot	Coworth Park **N**
Bagshot	Michael Wignall at The Latymer (at Pennyhill Park Hotel)
Baslow	Fischer's at Baslow Hall
Bath / Colerne	The Park (at Lucknam Park Hotel)
Beaulieu	The Terrace (at Montagu Arms Hotel)
Beverley / South Dalton	Pipe and Glass Inn
Biddenden	West House
Birkenhead	Fraiche
Birmingham	Purnell's
Birmingham	Simpsons
Birmingham	Turners
Blackburn / Langho	Northcote
Blakeney / Morston	Morston Hall
Bodiam	Curlew
Bolton Abbey	Burlington (at Devonshire Arms Country House Hotel)
Bourton-on-the-Water / Upper Slaughter	Lords of the Manor
Bray	Royal Oak
Bristol	Casamia
Castle Combe	Manor House H. and Golf Club
Chester	Simon Radley at The Chester Grosvenor
Chew Magna	Pony and Trap
Chinnor / Sprigg's Alley	Sir Charles Napier **N**
Clipsham	The Olive Branch and Beech House
Cranbrook	Apicius
Cuckfield	Ockenden Manor
Dorchester	Sienna
Eldersfield	Butchers Arms **N**
Emsworth	36 on the Quay
Faversham	Read's
Grange-over-Sands / Cartmel	L'Enclume
Horsham	The Pass (at South Lodge Hotel) **N**
Hunstanton	The Neptune
Ilkley	Box Tree
Jersey / La Pulente	Atlantic
Jersey / St Helier	Bohemia (at Club Hotel and Spa)
Jersey / St Helier	Tassili (at Grand Hotel) **N**
Kington / Titley	The Stagg Inn
London / Bromley	Chapter One
London / Camden	Hakkasan Hanway Place
London / Camden	Pied à Terre
London / City of London	Club Gascon
London / City of London	Rhodes Twenty Four
London / City of Westminster	Amaya
London / City of Westminster	Apsleys

London / City of Westminster	Arbutus
London / City of Westminster	L'Autre Pied
London / City of Westminster	Benares
London / City of Westminster	Dinner by Heston Blumenthal **N**
London / City of Westminster	Galvin at Windows
London / City of Westminster	Gauthier - Soho
London / City of Westminster	Greenhouse
London / City of Westminster	Hakkasan Mayfair **N**
London / City of Westminster	Kai
London / City of Westminster	Locanda Locatelli
London / City of Westminster	Maze
London / City of Westminster	Murano
London / City of Westminster	Nobu (at The Metropolitan Hotel)
London / City of Westminster	Nobu Berkeley St
London / City of Westminster	Pollen Street Social **N**
London / City of Westminster	Pétrus
London / City of Westminster	Quilon
London / City of Westminster	Rhodes W1 (Restaurant)
London / City of Westminster	Semplice
London / City of Westminster	Seven Park Place
London / City of Westminster	Sketch (The Lecture Room and Library)
London / City of Westminster	Tamarind
London / City of Westminster	Texture
London / City of Westminster	Umu
London / City of Westminster	Wild Honey
London / City of Westminster	Yauatcha
London / City of Westminster	Zafferano
London / Hammersmith and Fulham	Harwood Arms
London / Hammersmith and Fulham	River Café
London / Hounslow	La Trompette
London / Islington (Borough of)	North Road **N**
London / Islington (Borough of)	St John (Clerkenwell)
London / Kensington and Chelsea	Kitchen W8
London / Kensington and Chelsea	Rasoi
London / Richmond-upon-Thames	The Glasshouse
London / Richmond-upon-Thames	Petersham Nurseries Café
London / Tower Hamlets	Galvin La Chapelle
London / Tower Hamlets	Viajante
London / Wandsworth (Borough of)	Chez Bruce
Ludlow	Mr Underhill's at Dinham Weir
Marlborough / Little Bedwyn	Harrow at Little Bedwyn
Marlow	Adam Simmonds at Danesfield House
Murcott	Nut Tree
Oakham / Hambleton	Hambleton Hall
Oldstead	Black Swan **N**
Pateley Bridge / Ramsgill-in-Nidderdale	Yorke Arms
Petersfield	JSW
Portscatho	Driftwood **N**

Reading / Shinfield	L'Ortolan
Ripley (Surrey)	Drake's
Royal Leamington Spa	Mallory Court
Sheffield	Old Vicarage
South Molton / Knowstone	The Masons Arms
Torquay	Room in the Elephant
Ullswater / Pooley Bridge	Sharrow Bay Country House
Welwyn Garden City	Auberge du Lac
Whitstable / Seasalter	The Sportsman
Wight (Isle of) / Ventnor	Hambrough
Winchcombe	5 North St
Winchester	The Black Rat
Windermere	Holbeck Ghyll
Woburn	Paris House

→ Scotland

Ballantrae	Glenapp Castle	N
Balloch	Martin Wishart at Loch Lomond (at Cameron House Hotel)	N
Dalry	Braidwoods	
Edinburgh	Castle Terrace	N
Edinburgh	Number One (at Balmoral Hotel)	
Edinburgh	21212	
Edinburgh / Leith	Kitchin	
Edinburgh / Leith	Martin Wishart	
Elie	Sangster's	
Fort William	Inverlochy Castle	
Lochinver	Albannach	
Nairn	Boath House	
Peat Inn	Peat Inn	
Portpatrick	Knockinaam Lodge	
Skye (Isle of) / Sleat	Kinloch Lodgee	

→ Wales

Abergavenny / Llanddewi Skirrid	Walnut Tree	
Llandrillo	Tyddyn Llan	
Monmouth / Whitebrook	Crown at Whitebrook	
Montgomery	The Checkers	N

→ Republic of Ireland

Ardmore	House (at Cliff House Hotel)
Dublin	Chapter One
Dublin	L'Ecrivain
Dublin	Thornton's (at The Fitzwilliam Hotel)
Malahide	Bon Appétitt

Bib Gourmand 2012

• Places with at least one Bib Gourmand establishment.

Bib Gourmand

Good food at moderate prices

→ England

Aldeburgh	Lighthouse
Alderley Edge	The Wizard
Backwell	New Inn
Beaconsfield / Seer Green	Jolly Cricketers
Beverley	Whites
Blackpool / Thornton	Twelve
Bray	Hinds Head
Brighton	Chilli Pickle
Brighton / Hove	Ginger Pig
Brighton / Hove	Meadow
Bristol	Flinty Red **N**
Bristol	Greens' Dining Room
Bruntingthorpe	The Joiners **N**
Bruton	At The Chapel
Burnham Market	Hoste Arms
Bury	Waggon
Bury St Edmunds	Pea Porridge
Cambridge / Little Wilbraham	Hole in the Wall
Clitheroe / Wiswell	Freemasons
Darlington / Hurworth-on-Tees	Bay Horse
Droxford	Bakers Arms
Durham	Bistro 21
East Chisenbury	Red Lion Freehouse
East Haddon	Red Lion **N**
Exeter / Rockbeare	Jack in the Green Inn
Guernsey / St Saviour (Guernsey)	Pavilion
Hastings and St. Leonards	St Clements
Henfield	Ginger Fox
Ingham	Ingham Swan **N**
Itteringham	Walpole Arms
Kelvedon	George and Dragon
Knaresborough / Ferrensby	General Tarleton Inn
Leeds	Piazza by Anthony
London / Brent	Sushi-Say **N**
London / Camden	Bradley's
London / Camden	Giaconda Dining Room
London / Camden	Great Queen Street
London / Camden	Market
London / Camden	Salt Yard
London / City of London	Goldfish City
London / City of London	28°-50°
London / City of Westminster	Al Duca
London / City of Westminster	Bar Trattoria Semplice
London / City of Westminster	Barrafina **N**
London / City of Westminster	Benja Bangkok Table
London / City of Westminster	Bocca di Lupo
London / City of Westminster	da Polpo **N**
London / City of Westminster	Dehesa
London / City of Westminster	Hereford Road
London / City of Westminster	Iberica
London / City of Westminster	Kateh **N**
London / City of Westminster	Koya **N**
London / City of Westminster	Opera Tavern **N**
London / City of Westminster	Polpo
London / City of Westminster	Terroirs
London / City of Westminster	Trishna **N**
London / Hammersmith and Fulham	Azou **N**
London / Hounslow	Charlotte's Bistro
London / Islington (Borough of)	Comptoir Gascon
London / Islington (Borough of)	Drapers Arms

→ **N** *New*

London / Islington (Borough of)	500
London / Islington (Borough of)	Medcalf
London / Islington (Borough of)	Morito
London / Islington (Borough of)	Trullo
London / Lambeth	Canton Arms
London / Lewisham	Chapters
London / Merton	Fox and Grapes N
London / Richmond-upon-Thames	Brown Dog
London / Richmond-upon-Thames	Mango and Silk
London / Richmond-upon-Thames	Simply Thai
London / Southwark (Borough of)	Anchor and Hope
London / Southwark (Borough of)	José N
London / Southwark (Borough of)	Zucca
London / Tower Hamlets	Brawn N
London / Tower Hamlets	Cafe Spice Namaste
London / Tower Hamlets	Galvin Café a Vin
London / Tower Hamlets	St John Bread and Wine N
London / Wandsworth (Borough of)	Triphal N
Masham	Vennell's
Melton Mowbray / Stathern	Red Lion Inn
Millbrook / Freathy	View
Norwich / Stoke Holy Cross	Wildebeest Arms
Oldham	White Hart Inn
Oxford	Anchor N
Oxford	Magdalen Arms
Oxford / Toot Baldon	Mole Inn
Padstow	Rick Stein's Café
Penzance	Untitled by Robert Wright N
Preston Candover	Purefoy Arms
Ramsgate	Age and Sons
Romsey	Three Tuns N
St Ives	Black Rock
Sheffield	Artisan
Stamford	Jim's Yard
Stanton	Leaping Hare
Stockbridge / Longstock	Peat Spade Inn
Stow-on-the-Wold	Old Butchers
Sutton-on-the-Forest	Rose and Crown
Tetbury	Gumstool Inn
Tewkesbury	Owens N
Wells	Old Spot
West Hoathly	Cat Inn
Wimborne St Giles	Bull Inn
Woolhope	Butchers Arms
Wymondham	Berkeley Arms N

→ Scotland

Edinburgh	Dogs
Glasgow	Stravaigin N
Kintyre (Peninsula) / Kilberry	Kilberry Inn
Peebles	Osso
Sorn	Sorn Inn n

→ Wales

Brecon	Felin Fach Griffin N
Cardiff	chai st N
Cardiff	Mint and Mustard N

→ Northern Ireland

Ballyclare	Oregano
Belfast	Cayenne
Holywood	Fontana N
Warrenpoint	Restaurant 23

→ Republic of Ireland

Adare	White Sage
Clonegall	Sha Roe Bistro
Dingle	Chart House
Dublin	Pichet
Dublin	Pig's Ear
Duncannon	Aldridge Lodge
Durrus	Good Things Café
Kinsale	Fishy Fishy Cafe
Lisdoonvarna	Wild Honey Inn
Lismore	O'Brien Chop House
Roundstone	O'Dowd's
Stepaside	Box Tree N

Bib Hotel

Good accommodation at moderate prices

→ England

Aldeburgh / Friston	Old School
Barnard Castle	Homelands
Bodmin	Bokiddick Farm
Bourton-on-the-Water	Coombe House
Bovey Tracey	Brookfield House
Bungay / Earsham	Earsham Park Farm
Bury St Edmunds / Beyton	Manorhouse
Cheddleton	Choir Cottage
Deddington	Old Post House
Devizes / Potterne	Blounts Court Farm
Doddington	Old Vicarage
Earl Stonham	Bays Farm
Eastbourne	Brayscroft
Harrogate / Kettlesing	Knabbs Ash
Hartland	Golden Park
Henfield / Wineham	Frylands
Hexham	West Close House
Holbeach	Pipwell Manor
Kenilworth	Victoria Lodge
Kirkwhelpington	Shieldhall
Leyburn	Clyde House
Longtown	Bessiestown Farm
Morpeth / Longhorsley	Thistleyhaugh Farm
Oxhill	Oxbourne House
Penrith	Brooklands
Pickering	Bramwood
Ripon	Sharow Cross House
Ross-on-Wye / Kerne Bridge	Lumleys
Salisbury / Little Langford	Little Langford Farmhouse
Scarborough	Alexander
Southend-on-Sea	Beaches
Stow-on-the-Wold	Number Nine
Stow-on-the-Wold / Lower Swell	Rectory Farmhouse **N**
Torquay	Colindale
Tynemouth	Martineau
Wallingford	North Moreton House
Wareham	Gold Court House
Warwick	Charter House **N**
Wells / Easton (Somerset)	Beaconsfield Farm
Whitby / Briggswath	Lawns
York	Alexander House

→ Scotland

Anstruther	Spindrift
Auchencairn	Balcary Mews
Ayr	Coila
Ayr	No.26 The Crescent
Ballater	Moorside House
Blairgowrie	Gilmore House
Carnoustie	The Old Manor
Crieff	Merlindale
Dunkeld	Letter Farm
Forres / Dyke	Old Kirk
Glendevon	Tormaukin

 N *New*

Jedburgh	Willow Court
Kingussie	Hermitage
Montrose	36 The Mall
Nairn	Bracadale House
Peebles	Rowanbrae
Perth	Taythorpe
Pitlochry	Dunmurray Lodge
Skye (Isle of) / Broadford	Tigh an Dochais
Skye (Isle of) / Dunvegan	Roskhill House
Stevenston	Ardeer Farm Steading
Stonehaven	Beachgate House **N**
Strathpeffer	Craigvar
Thornhill	Gillbank House
Ullapool	Point Cottage
Wick	The Clachan

→ Wales

Aberaeron	Llys Aero
Betws Garmon	Betws Inn
Colwyn Bay	Rathlin Country House
Dolgellau	Tyddyn Mawr
Llandudno	Abbey Lodge
Llandudno	Lympley Lodge
Llanuwchllyn	Eifionydd
Ruthin	Firgrove
Whitton	Pilleth Oaks **N**

→ Northern Ireland

Bangor	Cairn Bay Lodge
Belfast	Ravenhill House
Crumlin	Caldhame Lodge

→ Republic of Ireland

Ballyvaughan	Drumcreehy House
Bansha	Rathellen House
Carlow	Barrowville Town House **N**
Castlegregory	Shores Country House
Donegal	Ardeevin
Dundalk	Rosemount
Kinsale / Barrells Cross	Rivermount House
Oughterard	Railway Lodge
Oughterard	Waterfall Lodge
Portlaoise	Ivyleigh House **N**
Toormore	Fortview House
Tramore	Glenorney
Wexford	McMenamin's Townhouse **N**

Particularly pleasant hotels & guesthouses

→ England

Dogmersfield	Four Seasons
London / City of Westminster	Berkeley
London / City of Westminster	Claridge's
London / City of Westminster	Connaught
London / City of Westminster	Dorchester
London / City of Westminster	Four Seasons
London / City of Westminster	Mandarin Oriental Hyde Park
London / City of Westminster	Ritz
London / City of Westminster	Savoy
New Milton	Chewton Glen
Oxford / Great Milton	Le Manoir aux Quat' Saisons
Taplow	Cliveden

→ England

Ascot	Coworth Park
Aylesbury	Hartwell House
Bath / Colerne	Lucknam Park
Bourton-on-the-Water / Lower Slaughter	Lower Slaughter Manor
Chagford	Gidleigh Park
Cheltenham	Ellenborough Park
Jersey / St Saviour (Jersey)	Longueville Manor
London / City of Westminster	Goring
London / City of Westminster	One Aldwych
London / City of Westminster	Soho
Lyndhurst	Lime Wood
Malmesbury	Whatley Manor
Newbury	Vineyard at Stockcross
North Bovey	Bovey Castle
Ston Easton	Ston Easton Park

→ Scotland

Ballantrae	Glenapp Castle
Eriska (Isle of)	Isle of Eriska
Fort William	Inverlochy Castle

→ Republic of Ireland

Ballyfin	Ballyfin
Dublin	Merrion
Kenmare	Park
Killarney	Killarney Park

→ England

Abberley	Elms
Amberley	Amberley Castle
Bath	Bath Priory
Beaulieu	Montagu Arms
Bolton Abbey	Devonshire Arms Country House
Bourton-on-the-Water / Upper Slaughter	Lords of the Manor
Broadway	Buckland Manor
Castle Combe	Manor House H. and Golf Club
Dedham	Maison Talbooth
Evershot	Summer Lodge
Gillingham	Stock Hill Country House
Guernsey / St Peter Port	Old Government House H. and Spa
Jersey / La Pulente	Atlantic
London / Camden	Charlotte Street
London / Camden	Covent Garden

London / City of Westminster	Dukes
London / City of Westminster	Halkin
London / City of Westminster	Stafford
London / Kensington and Chelsea	Blakes
London / Kensington and Chelsea	The Capital
London / Kensington and Chelsea	Draycott
London / Kensington and Chelsea	The Milestone
London / Kensington and Chelsea	The Pelham
Newcastle upon Tyne	Jesmond Dene House
Oakham / Hambleton	Hambleton Hall
Reading	Forbury
Royal Leamington Spa	Mallory Court
Scilly (Isles of)	St Martin's on the Isle
Tetbury	Calcot Manor
Ullswater / Pooley Bridge	Sharrow Bay Country House
Winchester / Sparsholt	Lainston House
Windermere / Bowness-on-Windermere	Gilpin H. and Lake House
Yarm	Judges Country House
York	Middlethorpe Halll

→ Scotland

Blairgowrie	Kinloch House
Edinburgh	Prestonfield
Gullane	Greywalls
Torridon	The Torridon

→ Wales

Llandudno	Bodysgallen Hall
Llangammarch Wells and Spa	Lake Country House

→ Republic of Ireland

Ardmore	Cliff House
Ballyvaughan	Gregans Castle
Dublin	Dylan
Gorey (Wexford)	Marlfield House
Mallow	Longueville House

→ England

Ambleside	The Samling
Bath	Queensberry
Bigbury-on-Sea	Burgh Island
Blakeney / Morston	Morston Hall
Brampton	Farlam Hall
Burnham Market	Hoste Arms
Chester	Green Bough
Cirencester / Barnsley	Barnsley House
Cuckfield	Ockenden Manor
Frome	Babington House
Helmsley	Feversham Arms
Horley	Langshott Manor
Lewdown	Lewtrenchard Manor
London / Kensington and Chelsea	Egerton House
London / Kensington and Chelsea	Knightsbridge
London / Kensington and Chelsea	The Levin
London / Kensington and Chelsea	Number Sixteen
Newquay / Mawgan Porth	Scarlet
North Walsham	Beechwood
Orford	Crown and Castle
Portscatho	Driftwood
Rushlake Green	Stone House
St Mawes	Hotel Tresanton
Scilly (Isles of)	Hell Bay
Southampton / Netley Marsh	Hotel TerraVina
Stratford-upon-Avon	Arden
Tavistock / Milton Abbot	Hotel Endsleigh
Torquay / Maidencombe	Orestone Manor
Wareham	Priory
Windermere	Holbeck Ghyll

→ Scotland

Abriachan	Loch Ness Lodge
Achiltibuie	Summer Isles
Arran (Isle of)	Kilmichael Country House
Lochearnhead / Balquhidder	Monachyle Mhor
Nairn	Boath House
Port Appin	Airds
Portpatrick	Knockinaam Lodge
Skye (Isle of) / Sleat	Kinloch Lodge

→ Wales

Llandudno	Osborne House
Machynlleth	Ynyshir Hall
Narberth	Grove
Swansea / Llanrhidian	Fairyhill

→ Republic of Ireland

Ballingarry	Mustard Seed at Echo Lodge
Kinsale	Perryville House

→ England

Ashwater	Blagdon Manor
Bourton-on-the-Water	Dial House
Burnham Market	Vine House
Chillington	whitehouse
Dartmouth / Kingswear	Nonsuch House
Helmsley / Harome	Cross House Lodge
Keswick / Portinscale	Swinside Lodge
Ludlow	De Grey's Town House
Lynton / Martinhoe	Old Rectory
Porlock	Oaks
Salisbury / Teffont Magna	Howard's House

→ Scotland

Kelso / Ednam	Edenwater House
Kirkbean	Cavens
Mull (Isle of) / Tiroran	Tiroran House
Tain / Cadboll	Glenmorangie House

→ Wales

Betws-y-Coed	Tan-y-Foel Country House
Dolgellau	Ffynnon

→ Republic of Ireland

Bagenalstown	Kilgraney Country House
Castlelyons	Ballyvolane House
Dingle	Emlagh Country House
Lahinch	Moy House

→ England

Arnside	Number 43
Ash	Great Weddington
Austwick	Austwick Hall
Beverley	Burton Mount
Blackpool	Number One St Lukes
Bridport / Burton Bradstock	Norburton Hall
Brighton	Kemp Townhouse
Broad Oak	Fairacres
Cheltenham	Thirty Two
Chipping Campden / Broad Campden	Malt House
Clun	Birches Mill
Crackington Haven	Manor Farm
Cranbrook	Cloth Hall Oast
East Hoathly	Old Whyly
Hawkshead / Far Sawrey	West Vale
Haworth	Ashmount Country House
Ivychurch	Olde Moat House
Kendal	Beech House
Kilham	Kilham Hall
Lavenham	Lavenham Priory
Ledbury / Kynaston	Hall End
Lizard	Landewednack House
Marazion / Perranuthnoe	Ednovean Farm
Marazion / St Hilary	Ennys
Moreton-in-Marsh	Old School
North Bovey	Gate House
North Lopham	Church Farm House
Padstow	Treann

Padstow	Treverbyn House
Padstow	Woodlands Country House
Pershore / Eckington	Eckington Manor
Pickering	17 Burgate
Pickering / Levisham	Moorlands Country House
Pillerton Priors	Fulready Manor
Ripon	Sharow Cross House
St Austell / Tregrehan	Anchorage House
Shrewsbury	Pinewood House
Stow-on-the-Wold / Lower Swell	Rectory Farmhouse
Stratford-upon-Avon	Cherry Trees
Tavistock / Chillaton	Tor Cottage
Teignmouth	Thomas Luny House
Thursford Green	Holly Lodge
Warkworth	Roxbro House
Wold Newton	Wold Cottage

➜ Scotland

Ballantrae	Cosses Country House
Bute (Isle of) / Ascog	Balmory Hall
Connel	Ards House
Drumbeg	Blar na Leisg at Drumbeg House
Edinburgh	One Royal Circus
Fort William	Grange
Fortrose	Water's Edge
Grantown-on-Spey	Dulaig
Islay (Isle of) / Ballygrant	Kilmeny
Linlithgow	Arden House
Lochinver	Ruddyglow Park Country House
Mainland (Orkney Islands) / Harray	Holland House
Mull (Isle of) / Gruline	Gruline Home Farm
Skirling	Skirling House
Skye (Isle of) / Bernisdale	Spoons
Strathpeffer	Craigvar
Tain / Nigg	Wemyss House

➜ Wales

Aberaeron	3 Pen Cei
Anglesey (Isle of) / Beaumaris	Cleifiog
Anglesey (Isle of) / Menai Bridge	Neuadd Lwyd
Betws-y-Coed / Penmachno	Penmachno Hall
Dolfor	Old Vicarage
Dolgellau	Tyddyn Mawr
Pwllheli / Boduan	Old Rectory
St Clears	Coedllys Country House

➜ Northern Ireland

Ballintoy	Whitepark House
Dungannon	Grange Lodgel

➜ Republic of Ireland

Castlegregory	Shores Country House
Cong	Ballywarren House
Fethard	Mobarnane House
Kenmare	Sallyport House
Toormore	Fortview House

Particularly pleasant restaurants & pubs

→ **England**

London / City of Westminster	The Ritz Restaurant

→ **England**

Bath / Colerne	The Park (at Lucknam Park Hotel)
Bolton Abbey	Burlington (at Devonshire Arms Country House Hotel)
Bray	Waterside Inn
London / City of Westminster	Hélène Darroze at The Connaught
London / City of Westminster	Marcus Wareing at The Berkeley

→ **Republic of Ireland**

Dublin	Patrick Guilbaud

→ **England**

Baslow	Fischer's at Baslow Hall
Birmingham	Simpsons
Blackburn / Langho	Northcote
Cambridge	Midsummer House
Dedham	Le Talbooth
Faversham	Read's
Ilkley	Box Tree
Lavenham	Great House
London / City of London	Coq d'Argent
London / City of Westminster	Cecconi's
London / City of Westminster	Pétrus
London / City of Westminster	Quo Vadis
London / City of Westminster	The Wolseley
London / Hackney	Boundary
London / Kensington and Chelsea	Bibendum
London / Kensington and Chelsea	The Capital Restaurant (at The Capital Hotel)
London / Tower Hamlets	Galvin La Chapelle

Pateley Bridge / Ramsgill-in-Nidderdale	Yorke Arms
Petersfield	JSW
Reading / Shinfield	L'Ortolan
Skipton / Hetton	Angel Inn and Barn Lodgings
Ston Easton	Sorrel (at Ston Easton Park Hotel)
Welwyn Garden City	Auberge du Lac
Winteringham	Winteringham Fields
Woburn	Paris House

➜ Scotland

Edinburgh	21212
Peat Inn	Peat Inn
St Andrews	Seafood

➜ Wales

Llandrillo	Tyddyn Llan

➜ England

Alkham	Marquis
Arlingham	Old Passage Inn
Bath / Colerne	Brasserie (at Lucknam Park Hotel)
Bildeston	Bildeston Crown
Brockenhurst	The Pig
Burnham Market	Hoste Arms
Bury St Edmunds	Maison Bleue
Cheltenham	Daffodil
Grange-over-Sands / Cartmel	L'Enclume
Grantham / Great Gonerby	Harry's Place
Grantham / Hough-on-the-Hill	Brownlow Arms
Kibworth Beauchamp	Firenze
Kirkby Lonsdale	Hipping Hall
London / Camden	Mon Plaisir
London / City of Westminster	Le Café Anglais
London / City of Westminster	Clos Maggiore
London / City of Westminster	J. Sheekey
London / City of Westminster	Rules
London / City of Westminster	Wild Honey
London / Hammersmith and Fulham	River Café
Ludlow	Mr Underhill's at Dinham Weir
Malmesbury	Le Mazot (at Whatley Manor Hotel)
Newquay / Watergate Bay	Fifteen Cornwall
Padstow	Paul Ainsworth at No.6
Padstow	The Seafood
St Mawes	Restaurant Tresanton (at Hotel Tresanton)
Sark	La Sablonnerie
Stanton	Leaping Hare
Yeovil / Barwick	Little Barwick House

➜ Scotland

Kingussie	Cross at Kingussie
Lochinver	Albannach
Skye (Isle of) / Dunvegan	Three Chimneys and The House Over-By

→ Wales

Abergavenny	Hardwick
Caernarfon / Llandwrog	Rhiwafallen
Pwllheli	Plas Bodegroes

→ Republic of Ireland

Aran Islands / Inishmaan	Inis Meáin Restaurant and Suites
Celbridge	La Serre
Clogheen	Old Convent
Dublin	Locks Brasserie
Dunfanaghy	Mill
Dunkineely	Castle Murray House
Durrus	Blairscove House

→ England

Ashburton	Agaric
Bournemouth	West Beach
Bray / Bray Marina	Riverside Brasserie
Jersey / Gorey (Channel Islands)	Sumas
Jersey / Green Island	Green Island
Jersey / St Brelades Bay	Oyster Box
London / City of Westminster	L'Atelier de Joël Robuchon
London / City of Westminster	Bocca di Lupo
London / City of Westminster	Dehesa
London / City of Westminster	J. Sheekey Oyster Bar
London / Islington	Comptoir Gascon
London / Islington	Trullo
London / Kensington and Chelsea	Bibendum Oyster Bar
London / Richmond-upon-Thames	Petersham Nurseries Café
London / Southwark	Oxo Tower Brasserie
London / Southwark	Zucca
Mousehole	Cornish Range
St Ives	Porthminster Beach Cafe
Shaldon	ODE
Stow-on-the-Wold / Daylesford	Café at Daylesford Organic
Studland	Shell Bay
Summercourt	Viners
West Malling	Swan

→ Scotland

Kingairloch	Boathouse and Steadings
Perth / Stanley	Apron Stage
Thurso / Scrabster	The Captain's Galley

→ Republic of Ireland

Barna	O'Grady's on the Pier
Dingle	Chart House
Kinsale	Fishy Fishy Cafe

→ England

Alton / Lower Froyle	The Anchor Inn
Ambleside	Drunken Duck Inn
Barnard Castle / Romaldkirk	Rose and Crown
Bath / Combe Hay	Wheatsheaf
Baughurst	Wellington Arms
Beverley / South Dalton	Pipe and Glass Inn
Bolnhurst	Plough at Bolnhurst
Bray	Hinds Head
Burford / Swinbrook	Swan Inn
Cambridge / Little Wilbraham	Hole in the Wall
Chichester / Chilgrove	Fish House
Chichester / East Lavant	The Royal Oak Inn
Cirencester / Barnsley	Village Pub
Cirencester / Sapperton	Bell
Clipsham	The Olive Branch and Beech House
Clitheroe / Wiswell	Freemasons
East Garston	Queen's Arms
Helmsley / Harome	Star Inn
Kendal / Crosthwaite	Punch Bowl Inn
Keyston	Pheasant
Lydford	Dartmoor Inn
Marlow	Hand and Flowers
Mistley	Mistley Thorn
Old Warden	Hare and Hounds
Oldstead	Black Swan
Oxford / Fyfield	White Hart
Skipton / Hetton	Angel Inn
South Molton / Knowstone	The Masons Arms
Stockbridge / Longstock	Peat Spade Inn
Stoke-by-Nayland	Crown
Stow-on-the-Wold / Nether Westcote	Feathered Nest
Sutton-on-the-Forest	Rose and Crown
Tarr Steps	Tarr Farm Inn
Windermere / Troutbeck	Queen's Head
Woolhope	Butchers Arms

→ Wales

Aberaeron	Harbourmaster
Brecon	Felin Fach Griffin
Skenfrith	Bell at Skenfrith

→ Republic of Ireland

Kinsale	Toddies at The Bulman

Further information

Beer...

It's no exaggeration to say that beer and its consumption has pretty much defined popular conception of the British character for hundreds of years. From humble alehouse, via ubiquitous urban tavern, to agreeable coaching inn – all manner of drinking establishments have lined the British highway and byway since medieval times. As an example of the popularity of the properties of ale, by the fourteenth century there were over 350 taverns in London alone, while exactly 400 years ago you could have wandered round the capital's Square Mile and found over a thousand alehouses.

The quality of the beverage proffered to thirsty customers has varied as much as the fixtures and fittings but, generally speaking, the production of beer has followed a time-honoured recipe of four ingredients: barley, hops, yeast and water. The perfect pint begins with barley - the classic beer-making grain - and a clean, plentiful water supply coming together in a maltings, creating sugar for fermentation. The result looks like thin porridge; this boiling sludge is then filtered to a brown, hazy liquid called sweet wort.

Malt imparts sweetness to a beer and so, to give it balance, the addition of hops provides a bitter element to the mix. The hops need to be boiled to release their bitterness; it's at this point the true process of brewing is enacted. Eventually, the 'hopped wort' is cooled and filtered, in preparation for the key operation: fermentation. To ferment the beer, the brewers' little miracle-worker – yeast – is added to the fermentation vessels. Yeast is a living micro-organism, and its great claim to fame (apart from filling jars of Marmite!) is being able to convert the sugars into alcohol, carbon dioxide gas and a host of subtle flavours. With real ale, a secondary fermentation takes place when the finished product is safely ensconced in its barrel or cask, a process known as conditioning which happens before it leaves the brewery, and later, as it lies in the pub cellar. The final link in the chain is the publican, who (hopefully) oversees that decent pint gushing enticingly from the hand pump!

... and Whisky

Translated from the Gaelic term 'water of life', whisky depends for its very existence on the classic qualities of H2O. The local water supply dictates the nature of your glass of whisky; above and beyond that, the characteristics of the drink itself can range from spicy and aromatic to stylish and fruity, from light and fragrant to seaweedy and peaty. The classic Scotch whisky - only produced in the ideal natural environment of Scotland - makes full use of plentiful water supplies: barley is steeped in water for two to three days to turn it into malt, and then dried in a kiln traditionally fuelled by peat, before being ground in a mill.

The milled malt is called grist, and when hot water is added, the mixture is fed into a mash tun. This is where the sugars from malting dissolve, and the resulting solution – wort – oozes through the floor of the tun, to be passed into large wooden or stainless steel vessels. Add yeast, and fermentation occurs, with the sugars turning to alcohol. By now, this looks something like beer, but when it's distilled – a two-pronged process in which condensing vapours are captured - any resemblance to ale is long gone! By the time the different parts of the distillation are gathered together and redistilled, the resultant liquid – the new-make whisky – is ready to spend the next three years (by law) in oak casks maturing: the wood enhances the final aroma and flavour. Whisky makers enjoy a certain pact with the heavens: as the liquid matures, some of it evaporates into the ether, and this is known as the 'Angels' Share'…

Irish whiskey (note the extra 'e') differs slightly from the Scottish version, and not just in the spelling. It's traditionally made from cereals, and peat is hardly ever used in the malting process, so there's a lack of the smoky, earthy characteristics found over the Irish Sea. It's also encouraged to sit around for a much longer time: the maturation period is seven years, more than twice that of Scotch.

The Michelin Adventure

It all started with rubber balls! This was the product made by a small company based in Clermont-Ferrand that André and Edouard Michelin inherited, back in 1880. The brothers quickly saw the potential for a new means of transport and their first success was the invention of detachable pneumatic tyres for bicycles. However, the automobile was to provide the greatest scope for their creative talents. Throughout the 20th century, Michelin never ceased developing and creating ever more reliable and high-performance tyres, not only for vehicles ranging from trucks to F1 but also for underground transit systems and aeroplanes.

From early on, Michelin provided its customers with tools and services to facilitate mobility and make travelling a more pleasurable and more frequent experience. As early as 1900, the Michelin Guide supplied motorists with a host of useful information related to vehicle maintenance, accommodation and restaurants, and was to become a benchmark for good food. At the same time, the Travel Information Bureau offered travellers personalised tips and itineraries.

The publication of the first collection of roadmaps, in 1910, was an instant hit! In 1926, the first regional guide to France was published, devoted to the principal sites of Brittany, and before long each region of France had its own Green Guide. The collection was later extended to more far-flung destinations, including New York in 1968 and Taiwan in 2011.

In the 21st century, with the growth of digital technology, the challenge for Michelin maps and guides is to continue to develop alongside the company's tyre activities. Now, as before, Michelin is committed to improving the mobility of travellers.

MICHELIN TODAY

WORLD NUMBER ONE TYRE MANUFACTURER
- 70 production sites in 18 countries
- 111,000 employees from all cultures and on every continent
- 6,000 people employed in research and development

Moving for a world

Moving forward means developing tyres with better road grip and shorter braking distances, whatever the state of the road.

CORRECT TYRE PRESSURE

RIGHT PRESSURE

- Safety
- Longevity
- Optimum fuel consumption

-0,5 bar

- Durability reduced by 20% (- 8,000 km)

-1 bar

- Risk of blowouts
- Increased fuel consumption
- Longer braking distances on wet surfaces

forward together
where mobility is safer

It also involves helping motorists take care of their safety and their tyres. To do so, Michelin organises "Fill Up With Air" campaigns all over the world to remind us that correct tyre pressure is vital.

WEAR

DETECTING TYRE WEAR

The legal minimum depth of tyre tread is 1.6mm.

Tyre manufacturers equip their tyres with tread wear indicators, which are small blocks of rubber moulded into the base of the main grooves at a depth of 1.6mm.

Tyres are the only point of contact between vehicle and road.

The photo below shows the actual contact zone.

NEW TYRE

WORN TYRE
(1,6 mm tread)

If the tread depth is less than 1.6mm, tyres are considered to be worn and dangerous on wet surfaces.

Moving forward means sustainable mobility

INNOVATION AND THE ENVIRONMENT

By 2050, Michelin aims to cut the quantity of raw materials used in its tyre manufacturing process by half and to have developed renewable energy in its facilities. The design of MICHELIN tyres has already saved billions of litres of fuel and, by extension, billions of tonnes of CO_2.

Similarly, Michelin prints its maps and guides on paper produced from sustainably managed forests and is diversifying its publishing media by offering digital solutions to make travelling easier, more fuel efficient and more enjoyable!

The group's whole-hearted commitment to eco-design on a daily basis is demonstrated by ISO 14001 certification.

Like you, Michelin is committed to preserving our planet.

Chat with Bibendum

Go to
www.michelin.com/corporate/fr
Find out more about Michelin's
history and the latest news.

QUIZ

Michelin develops tyres for all types of vehicles. See if you can match the right tyre with the right vehicle…

Solution: A-6 / B-4 / C-2 / D-1 / E-3 / F-7 / G-5

Great Britain

England
Channel Islands · Isle of Man

ABBERLEY – Worcestershire – 503 M27 – pop. 654 – ✉ Worcester 18 B2
▶ London 137 mi – Birmingham 21 mi – Worcester 13 mi

Elms
West : 2 mi on A 443 ✉ WR6 6AT – ✆ (01299) 896 666
– www.theelmshotel.co.uk
23 rm (dinner included) – †£ 200/315 ††£ 330/510
Rest *Brooke Room* – see restaurant listing
Rest *Pear Terrace* – Carte £ 22/25
♦ Impressive Queen Anne house built in 1710. Inside, modern colours and fabrics blend seamlessly with traditional furnishings. Bedrooms are split between the house and old stables, and most boast pleasant country views. Choice of modern fine dining, or snacks and more traditional dishes in informal Pear Terrace – that latter set within an impressive spa. Child friendly.

Brooke Room – at Elms Hotel
West : 2 mi on A 443 ✉ WR6 6AT – ✆ (01299) 896 666
– www.theelmshotel.co.uk
Rest – Menu £ 21/49 – Carte £ 17/49
♦ Fine dining room set in an impressive Queen Anne house designed by Sir Gilbert White in 1710. Straightforward menu offers dishes of a modern persuasion. Homemade goat's cheese is a feature.

ABBOTSBURY – Dorset – 503 M32 – pop. 422 3 B3
▶ London 146 mi – Bournemouth 44 mi – Exeter 50 mi – Weymouth 10 mi
◉ Town★★ – Chesil Beach★★ – Swannery★ **AC** – Sub-Tropical Gardens★ **AC**
◉ St Catherine's Chapel★, 0.5 mi uphill (30 mn rtn on foot). Maiden Castle★★ (≤★)
NE : 7.5 m

Abbey House without rest
Church St ✉ DT3 4JJ – ✆ (01305) 871 330 – www.theabbeyhouse.co.uk
– March-November
5 rm – †£ 110 ††£ 110
♦ Historic stone house; part-15C abbey infirmary. Garden holds a unique Benedictine water mill. Breakfast room with low beamed ceiling and fireplace. Cosy bedrooms.

ABINGDON – Oxfordshire – 503 Q28 – pop. 36 010 ▍Great Britain 10 B2
▶ London 64 mi – Oxford 6 mi – Reading 25 mi
▬ from Abingdon Bridge to Oxford (Salter Bros. Ltd) 2 daily (summer only)
🛈 Abbey Close ✆ (01235) 52 27 11, www.abingdon.gov.uk
▣ Drayton Park Drayton Steventon Rd, ✆ (01235) 55 06 07
◉ Town★ – County Hall★

at Marcham West : 3 mi on A 415

Rafters without rest
Abingdon Rd, on A 415 ✉ OX13 6NU – ✆ (01865) 391 298
– www.bnb-rafters.co.uk
4 rm – †£ 52/85 ††£ 120
♦ Modern, well-equipped bedrooms; the superior room, with luxury bathroom and balcony, is best. Friendly owner offers substantial, locally sourced breakfast. Massage chair for relaxation.

ABINGER COMMON – Surrey – 504 S30 7 D2
▶ London 32 mi – Croydon 26 mi – Barnet 62 mi – Ealing 44 mi

Abinger Hatch
Abinger Ln ✉ RH5 6HZ – ✆ (01306) 730 737 – www.theabingerhatch.com
Rest – Menu £ 15 (weekdays) – Carte £ 22/31
♦ Set in prime walking country, this attractive 18C inn has been lovingly restored and now oozes country gentility. The bar is the best spot to enjoy the flavoursome country cooking, from lamb pie to gooseberry fool. Hampers available.

ABINGER HAMMER – Surrey – 504 S30   7 C2
▶ London 35 mi – Brighton 40 mi – Dover 91 mi – Portsmouth 50 mi

XX Drakes on the Pond
Dorking Rd, on A 25 ✉ *RH5 6SA* – ℰ *(01306) 731 174*
– *www.drakesonthepond.com – Closed 2 weeks August, Christmas-New Year, Sunday and Monday*
Rest – Menu £ 26 (lunch) – Carte £ 42/53

♦ Long-standing neighbourhood restaurant – formerly a cowshed – run by husband and wife: he cooks, she leads front of house. Long, narrow room with bright walls. Simply presented, classic dishes.

ALDEBURGH – Suffolk – 504 Y27 – pop. 2 654   15 D3
▶ London 97 mi – Ipswich 24 mi – Norwich 41 mi
🛈 152 High St ℰ (01728) 45 36 37, www.aldeburgh-uk.com
ThorpenessHotel and Golf Course Thorpeness, ℰ (01728) 45 21 76

Wentworth
Wentworth Rd. ✉ *IP15 5BD* – ℰ *(01728) 452 312*
– *www.wentworth-aldeburgh.com*
35 rm – †£ 92/132 ††£ 150/170
Rest – Menu £ 15/24 – Carte lunch £ 21/30

♦ Carefully furnished, traditional seaside hotel; coast view bedrooms are equipped with binoculars and all have a copy of 'Orlando the Marmalade Cat'; a story set in the area. Formal dining room offers mix of brasserie and classic dishes.

Brudenell
The Parade ✉ *IP15 5BU* – ℰ *(01728) 452 071* – *www.brudenellhotel.co.uk*
44 rm – †£ 80/159 ††£ 147/314   **Rest** – Carte £ 23/34

♦ Contemporary hotel situated right on the beach, with a relaxed ambience and superb sea views. Bedrooms feature modern bathrooms and up-to-date facilities. Informal, split-level bar/restaurant offers an accessible menu of modern classics to suit every taste.

X Lighthouse
77 High St ✉ *IP15 5AU* – ℰ *(01728) 453 377* – *www.lighthouserestaurant.co.uk*
– *Closed lunch 1 January and lunch 26 December*
Rest – (booking essential) Carte £ 20/31

♦ Busy, unpretentious bistro boasts a wealth of Suffolk produce from local meats to Aldeburgh cod and potted shrimps. Rustic, flavoured dishes with strong Mediterranean influences. Good choice of wines, amiable service and a warm, relaxing ambience.

at Friston Northwest : 4 mi by A 1094 on B 1121 – ✉ Aldeburgh

Old School without rest
✉ *IP17 1NP* – ℰ *(01728) 688 173* – *www.fristonoldschool.co.uk*
3 rm – †£ 60/72 ††£ 80

♦ Red-brick former school house with pleasant gardens. Good-sized bedrooms boast attractive furnishings, modern bathrooms and nice views. Communal breakfasts include a 'Full Suffolk', locally smoked kippers and milk from the nearby dairy. Run by lovely owners.

ALDERLEY EDGE – Cheshire East – 502 N24 – pop. 5 280   20 B3
▶ London 187 mi – Chester 34 mi – Manchester 14 mi – Stoke-on-Trent 25 mi
Wilmslow Mobberley Great Warford, ℰ (01565) 87 21 48

Alderley Edge
Macclesfield Rd ✉ *SK9 7BJ* – ℰ *(01625) 583 033* – *www.alderleyedgehotel.com*
– *Closed 25-26 December*
49 rm – †£ 90/130 ††£ 145/180, ⊇ £ 18 – 1 suite
Rest *Alderley* – see restaurant listing

♦ Well-run, early Victorian country house in affluent village. Smart landscaped gardens; compact, fairly formal interior. Modern, leather-furnished guest areas. More classically styled bedrooms.

ALDERLEY EDGE

Alderley – at Alderley Edge Hotel
☒ SK9 7BJ – ℰ (01625) 583 033 – www.alderleyedgehotel.com
– Closed 25-26 December and Sunday dinner
Rest – Menu £ 24/35 – Carte approx. £ 46
♦ Formal restaurant with full-length windows and long-standing reputation. Modern British menus display some interesting combinations and unusual twists. Good value lunch and daily evening menus.

The Wizard
Macclesfield Rd, Southeast : 1.25 mi on B 5087 ☒ SK10 4UB – ℰ (01625) 584 000
– www.ainscoughs.co.uk – Closed 25 December
Rest – Carte £ 25/38
♦ Characterful, dog-friendly, 200 year old pub with flag floors, wood beams and open fires. Seasonal menu of traditional dishes, including pub favourites and the occasional Mediterranean influence. Small tapas-style plates provide nibbles for drinkers.

ALDERNEY – Alderney – **503** Q33 – pop. 2 400 – see Channel Islands

---

ALDFIELD – North Yorkshire – **502** P21 – see Ripon

ALFRISTON – East Sussex – **504** U31 – pop. 1 721 – ☒ Polegate   8 A3

▶ London 66 mi – Eastbourne 9 mi – Lewes 10 mi – Newhaven 8 mi

Moonrakers with rm
High St ☒ BN25 5TD – ℰ (01323) 871 199 – www.moonrakersrestaurant.co.uk
– Closed January, Sunday dinner, Monday and Tuesday
1 rm ☐ – ♦ £ 155/215   **Rest** – (booking essential) Menu £ 19/35
♦ Charming 16C cottage with heavy beams, inglenook fireplace and lovely terrace. Interesting dishes display classic flavour combinations with modern twists. Ingredients are handled with care. A stylish, beamed bedroom with sitting room occupies the first floor.

Wingrove House with rm
High St ☒ BN26 5TD – ℰ (01323) 870 276 – www.wingrovehousealfriston.com
– Closed 25 December
5 rm ☐ – ♦ £ 95 ♦♦ £ 155
Rest – (closed Sunday dinner in winter) Carte £ 21/30
♦ Imposing colonial-style house; personally run, with relaxed, informal feel. Spacious, contemporary brasserie, wood-floored lounge and pleasant terrace. Modern menu of brasserie dishes served by a bright team. Understated, stylish bedrooms; some with balconies.

George Inn with rm
High St ☒ BN26 5SY – ℰ (01323) 870 319 – www.thegeorge-alfriston.com
– Closed 25-26 December
6 rm ☐ – ♦ £ 75/90 ♦♦ £ 125/145   **Rest** – Carte £ 24/32
♦ Characterful 14C stone and timber pub in a delightful village on the Southdown Way. Menu offers sharing boards and restaurant-style dishes, with pub classics appearing as specials. Comfy, simply furnished bedrooms; Bob Hall, with its 13C murals, is the best.

ALKHAM – Kent – **504** X30 – pop. 607   9 D2

▶ London 72 mi – Bexley 61 mi

Marquis with rm
Alkham Valley Rd ☒ CT15 7DF – ℰ (01304) 873 410
– www.themarquisatalkham.co.uk – Closed Monday lunch
10 rm ☐ – ♦ £ 145/185 ♦♦ £ 145/235   **Rest** – Menu £ 23/43
♦ Fashionable former pub with smart bar, stylish dining room and relaxed atmosphere. Accomplished cooking features classical combinations with original touches; portions are generous and presentation is modern. A six course tasting menu is available. Chic, sexy bedrooms boast luxurious bathrooms.

ALNWICK – Northumberland – **501** O17 – pop. 7 767 – Great Britain — 24 B2

- London 320 mi – Edinburgh 86 mi – Newcastle upon Tyne 34 mi
- 2 The Shambles, *(01665) 510 6 65, www.visitalnwick.org.uk*
- Swansfield Park, *(01665) 60 26 32*
- Town ★ - Castle ★★ **AC**
- Dunstanburgh Castle ★ **AC**, NE : 8 mi by B 1340 and Dunstan rd (last 2.5 mi on foot)

Greycroft without rest
Croft Pl, via Prudhoe St ⊠ NE66 1XU – (01665) 602 127 – www.greycroft.co.uk – Closed Christmas
6 rm – †£60 ††£110

♦ Quiet 19C house, 5min walk from Alnwick castle. Bedrooms individually decorated to a high standard, including a delightful family room. Breakfast in airy conservatory overlooking walled garden. Hospitable owners.

Aln House without rest
South Rd, Southeast : 0.75 mi by B 6346 on Newcastle rd ⊠ NE66 2NZ – (01665) 602 265 – www.alnhouse.co.uk – Closed 24-26 December
6 rm – †£55/80 ††£80/95

♦ Semi-detached Edwardian house with mature front and rear gardens, close to the castle and town centre. Homely lounge enhanced by personal touches. Individually appointed, immaculately kept bedrooms with smart bold feature walls.

Blackmore's with rm
24 Bondgate Without ⊠ NE66 1PN – (01665) 602 395 – www.blackmoresofalnwick.com – Closed 25 December
14 rm – †£50/100 ††£115/135   **Rest** – Carte £18/24 **s**

♦ 18C stone building with modern, open-plan interior and central bar. Bistro serves menu of mainly pub classics; first floor restaurant, with interesting display of clocks, offers more ambitious fare. Well-kept, contemporary bedrooms in chocolate tones.

at North Charlton North : 6.75 mi by A 1 – ⊠ Alnwick

North Charlton Farm without rest
⊠ NE67 5HP – (01665) 579 443 – www.northcharltonfarm.co.uk – Closed Christmas
3 rm – †£80 ††£80

♦ Attractive house on working farm with agricultural museum. Offers traditional accommodation. Each bedroom is individually decorated and has countryside views.

at Chathill North : 8.75 mi by A 1 off B 6347

Doxford Hall H. and Spa
⊠ NE67 5DN – (01665) 589 700 – www.doxfordhall.com
30 rm – †£150 ††£175 – 1 suite
Rest *George Runciman* – Menu £25 (lunch) – Carte dinner £37/50

♦ 18C house with recent extensions, well-appointed spa and immaculately kept formal gardens. Spacious bedrooms, styled to complement original house; all have mod cons including flat screens, while impressive feature beds add a sense of luxury. Interesting modern cuisine served in formal dining room.

ALSTONEFIELD – Staffordshire – **504** O24 – pop. 274 — 19 C1

- London 157 mi – Birmingham 66 mi – Liverpool 77 mi – Leeds 88 mi

George
⊠ DE6 2FX – (01335) 310 205 – www.thegeorgeatalstonefield.com – Closed 25 December
Rest – Carte £20/39

♦ Simply furnished, family-run pub with roaring fire and relaxed, cosy atmosphere. Daily changing menus offer well-priced, down-to-earth dishes; good 'on toast' section at lunch.

ALTON – Hampshire – **504** R30 – pop. 16 051　　6 B2

▶ London 53 mi – Reading 24 mi – Southampton 29 mi – Winchester 18 mi
🛈 7 Cross and Pillory Lane ℰ (01420) 8 84 48, www.visit-hampshire.co.uk
⛳ Old Odiham Rd, ℰ (01420) 8 20 42

at Lower Froyle Northeast : 4.5 mi by A 31

The Anchor Inn with rm
✉ GU34 4NA – ℰ (01420) 23 261 – www.anchorinnatlowerfroyle.co.uk – Closed 25 December
5 rm – †£ 90/130 ††£ 120/150　**Rest** – Carte £ 27/35
♦ Part-whitewashed, part-tile hung 14C building in pretty countryside, boasting low beams, open fires and bric-a-brac aplenty. Good-sized menus offer classic pub dishes with a refined edge; cooking is hearty and flavoursome. Bedrooms are fittingly characterful.

ALTRINCHAM – Greater Manchester – **502** N23 – pop. 40 695　　20 B3

▶ London 191 mi – Chester 30 mi – Liverpool 30 mi – Manchester 8 mi
🛈 20 Stamford New Rd ℰ (0161) 912 59 31, www.altrincham.org.uk
⛳ Altrincham Municipal Timperley Stockport Rd, ℰ (0161) 928 07 61
⛳ Dunham Forest Oldfield Lane, ℰ (0161) 928 26 05
⛳ Ringway Hale Barns Hale Mount, ℰ (0161) 980 26 30

Victoria
29 Stamford St ✉ WA14 1EX – ℰ (0161) 613 18 55 – Closed 1 January, 26 December and Sunday dinner
Rest – Carte £ 24/33
♦ Traditional looking pub in a quiet part of town, with flowers on the windowsills, a few pavement tables and an appealing, single-roomed interior with a wooden bar at its centre. Menu offers light bites and classics with a modern twist.

at Little Bollington Southwest : 3.25 mi on A 56 – ✉ Altrincham

Ash Farm without rest
Park Ln ✉ WA14 4TJ – ℰ (0161) 929 92 90 – www.ashfarm.co.uk
– Closed 22 December-2 January
3 rm – †£ 49/61 ††£ 77/86
♦ 18C former farmhouse with large garden, modern pine-furnished breakfast room and comfy, boho lounge. Traditional, antique-furnished bedrooms have a pleasant country house style. Friendly owners.

ALVESTON – Warwickshire – **504** O/P27 – see Stratford-upon-Avon

AMBERLEY – West Sussex – **504** S31 – pop. 525 – ✉ Arundel　　7 C2

▐ Great Britain
▶ London 56 mi – Brighton 31 mi – Portsmouth 31 mi
◉ Bignor Roman Villa (mosaics★) **AC**, NW : 3.5 mi by B 2139 via Bury

Amberley Castle
Southwest : 0.5 mi on B 2139 ✉ BN18 9LT – ℰ (01798) 831 992
– www.amberleycastle.co.uk
13 rm – †£ 230/285 ††£ 465/520 – 6 suites
Rest Queen's Room – see restaurant listing
♦ Stunning 12C castle displaying original stonework, battlements and evidence of a moat. Charming grounds with lovely gardens, lakes and a croquet lawn, matched inside by a characterful array of rooms packed with armour and heraldic antiques. Sumptuous bedrooms boast spa baths and a palpable sense of history.

Queen's Room – at Amberley Castle Hotel
Southwest : 0.5 mi on B 2139 ✉ BN18 9LT – ℰ (01798) 831 992
– www.amberleycastle.co.uk
Rest – (booking essential) Menu £ 33/63
♦ Elegant dining room with a barrel-vaulted ceiling, lancet windows and an open fire, set within a stunning 12C castle. Ambitious modern menu; dishes are complex and arrive artfully presented.

AMBLESIDE – Cumbria – **502** L20 – pop. 3 064 – Great Britain — 21 A2

▶ London 278 mi – Carlisle 47 mi – Kendal 14 mi
🛈 Market Cross ✆ (015394) 3 25 82, www.amblesideonline.co.uk
◉ Lake Windermere★★ – Dove Cottage, Grasmere★ **AC** AY **A** – Brockhole National Park Centre★ **AC**, SE : 3 mi by A 591 AZ. Wrynose Pass★★, W : 7.5 mi by A 593 AY – Hard Knott Pass★★, W : 10 mi by A 593 AY

Plan on next page

The Samling
Ambleside Rd, South : 1.5 mi on A 591 ✉ *LA23 1LR –* ✆ *(015394) 31 922*
– www.thesamlinghotel.co.uk
9 rm – †£ 175/265 ††£ 190/280 – 2 suites
Rest – *(booking essential for non-residents)* Menu £ 35/60
♦ Located on the hillside, with a lovely lake outlook and fantastic views from the hot tub. Highly individual bedrooms range from classical and characterful to bold and eye-catching; all boast excellent facilities. Intimate dining room, with attentive, structured service.

Lakes Lodge without rest
Lake Rd ✉ *LA22 0DB –* ✆ *(015394) 33 240 – www.lakeslodge.co.uk*
– Closed 19-27 December   AZ**s**
16 rm – †£ 60/130 ††£ 75/150
♦ Three-storey townhouse on the roadside. Modern, stylish bedrooms with bright fabrics and compact bathrooms; great views from number 10. Newer basement rooms boast wall-sized Lakeland images.

Riverside without rest
Under Loughrigg ✉ *LA22 9LJ –* ✆ *(015394) 32 395*
– www.riverside-at-ambleside.co.uk – Closed 12 December-31 January
6 rm – †£ 65/98 ††£ 85/116   BY**s**
♦ Homely, mid-Victorian slate house with steep lawned garden and fire-lit lounge; set in a peaceful riverside road. Bedroom 2 with its four-poster and double-aspect views is best. Lovely owners.

Red Bank without rest
Wansfell Rd ✉ *LA22 0EG –* ✆ *(015394) 34 637 – www.red-bank.co.uk*
3 rm – †£ 60/70 ††£ 80/100   AZ**r**
♦ Well-maintained guest house close to centre of town. Small seating area with wood burning stove; breakfast room overlooks the garden. 3 colour-themed bedrooms with compact, modern bathrooms.

Log House with rm
Lake Rd ✉ *LA22 0DN –* ✆ *(015394) 31 077 – www.loghouse.co.uk*
– Closed 3 January-1 February, 25-26 December and Monday
3 rm – †£ 60/93 ††£ 60/93   **Rest** – *(dinner only)* Carte £ 25/39   BY**v**
♦ Attractive cream-painted log cabin, imported from Norway over 100 years ago as a studio for artist Alfred Heaton Cooper. Modern, Mediterranean-influenced menus; sit in the raised rear area. Simple bedrooms – Room 1 is most characterful; Room 3 has the best view.

Drunken Duck Inn with rm
Barngates, Southwest : 3 mi by A 593 and B 5286 on Tarn Hows rd
✉ *LA22 0NG –* ✆ *(01539) 436 347 – www.drunkenduckinn.co.uk*
– Closed 25 December
17 rm – †£ 117/150 ††£ 230/295
Rest – *(booking essential)* Carte £ 22/46
♦ Attractive pub in beautiful Lakeland countryside with fire-lit bar and two formal, linen-laid dining rooms. Simple lunches and elaborate dinners with prices to match; generous cooking and attentive service. Ales brewed on-site. Boutique, country house bedrooms – some with patios, all with squashy beds and country views.

AMBLESIDE			King St	AZ	13	Smithy Brow	AZ	23
			Lake Rd	AZ				
Borrans Rd	BY	2	Market Pl.	AZ	14	**GRASMERE**		
Cheapside	AZ	4	North Rd	AZ	17			
Church St	AZ	6	Old Lake Rd	AZ	20	Broadgate	BZ	3
Compston St	AZ	8	St Mary's			Easedale Rd	BZ	10
Kelsick Rd	AZ	12	Lane	AZ	22	Swan Lane	AY	24

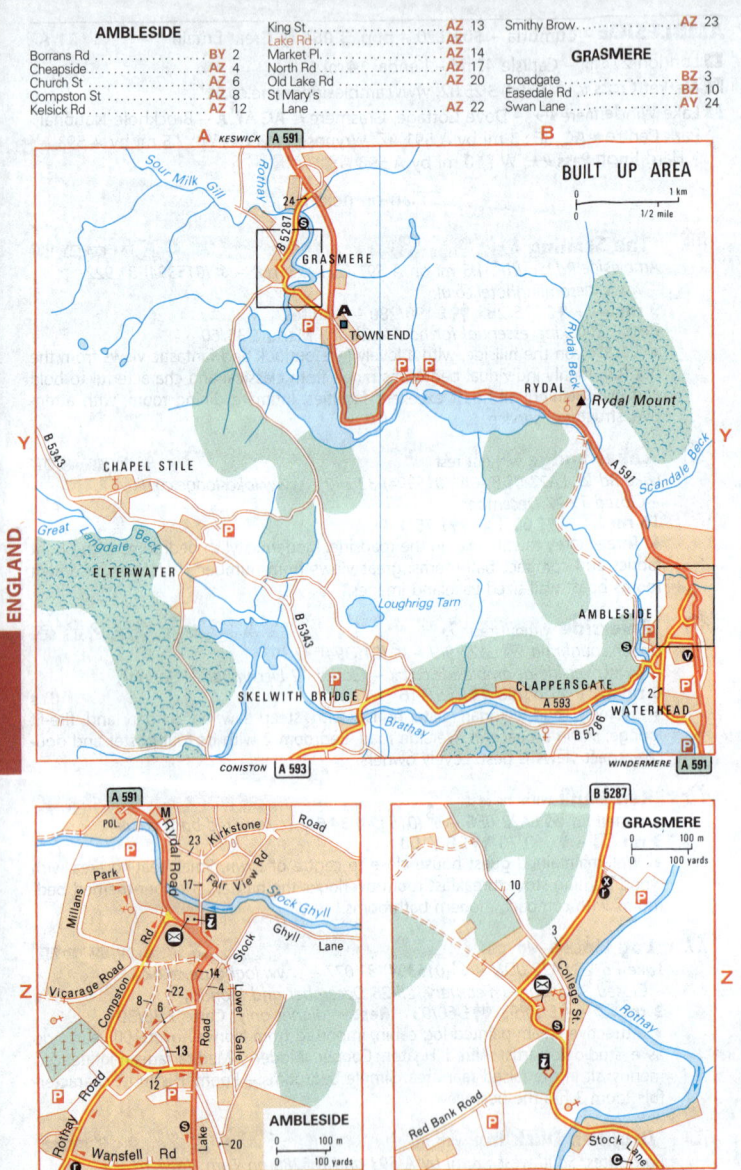

AMERSHAM (Old Town) – Buckinghamshire – 504 S29 11 D2
– pop. 21 470

▶ London 29 mi – Aylesbury 16 mi – Oxford 33 mi

🛈 Little Chalfont Lodge Lane, ✆ (01494) 76 48 77

AMERSHAM (Old Town)

Artichoke
9 Market Sq ⊠ HP7 0DF – ℰ (01494) 726 611 – www.artichokerestaurant.co.uk
– Closed 2 weeks late August, 1 week Christmas, Sunday and Monday
Rest – (booking essential at dinner) Menu £ 25/44 – Carte lunch £ 33/46
♦ 16C red-brick house in a picturesque town, with an artichoke etched on its window. A narrow beamed room with cream-painted walls and polished tables leads through to a more modern extension. Ambitious modern dishes arrive nicely presented.

Gilbey's
⊠ HP7 0DF – ℰ (01494) 727 242 – www.gilbeygroup.com
Rest – (booking essential) Menu £ 24 (weekdays) – Carte £ 30/43
♦ Part of a former 17C school, this busy neighbourhood restaurant is cosy and informal with modern artwork on walls. Eclectic range of British cooking with global influences.

AMPLEFORTH – North Yorkshire – 502 Q21 – see Helmsley

ANSTEY – Hertfordshire – 504 Q25   12 B2
▶ London 38 mi – Croydon 71 mi – Barnet 35 mi – Ealing 47 mi

Anstey Grove Barn without rest
East : 0.5 mi on Meesden rd ⊠ SG9 0BJ – ℰ (01763) 848 828
– www.ansteygrovebarn.co.uk
6 rm ⊡ – †£ 65 ††£ 80
♦ Converted barn on what was once a working pig farm. Simply furnished, homely bedrooms named after breeds of pig; the best is Old Yorkshire with its four-poster and roll-top bath.

APPLEBY-IN-WESTMORLAND – Cumbria – 502 M20 – pop. 2 862   21 B2
▶ London 285 mi – Carlisle 33 mi – Kendal 24 mi – Middlesbrough 58 mi
🛈 Boroughgate ℰ (017683) 5 11 77, www.visitcumbria.com
🛈 Appleby Brackenber Moor, ℰ (017683) 5 14 32

Appleby Manor Country House
Roman Rd, East : 1 mi by B 6542 and Station Rd
⊠ CA16 6JB – ℰ (017683) 51 571 – www.applebymanor.co.uk – Closed Christmas
31 rm ⊡ – †£ 95/100 ††£ 150/250 **Rest** – Carte £ 27/36 **s**
♦ Family-run, Victorian gentleman's residence with mature gardens and more recent extensions. Spacious, traditionally styled guest areas; small leisure suite. Bedrooms in original house are the most characterful. Two-roomed, formal restaurant offers classical menus.

Tufton Arms
Market Sq ⊠ CA16 6XA – ℰ (017683) 51 593 – www.tuftonarmshotel.co.uk
– Closed 24-27 December
20 rm ⊡ – †£ 77/95 ††£ 130/210
Rest – Menu £ 30 (dinner) – Carte £ 18/33
♦ 16C former coaching inn in traditional market town boasts contemporary interior; chic, comfortable bedrooms in bold colours. Fishing, shooting and stalking can be arranged. Easy-going menu served in modern dining room.

APPLEDORE – Devon – 503 H30 – pop. 2 187   2 C1
▶ London 228 mi – Barnstaple 12 mi – Exeter 46 mi – Plymouth 61 mi
◉ Town ★

West Farm without rest
Irsha St, West : 0.25 mi ⊠ EX39 1RY – ℰ (01237) 425 269 – Closed Christmas-New Year
3 rm ⊡ – †£ 67 ††£ 100
♦ 17C house, boasting particularly pleasant garden at the back, in a charming little coastal village. Delightfully appointed sitting room. Bedrooms feel comfortable and homely.

APPLETREEWICK – North Yorkshire – 502 O21 — 22 B2

▶ London 236 mi – Harrogate 25 mi – Skipton 11 mi

Knowles Lodge without rest
South : 1 mi on Bolton Abbey rd ⊠ BD23 6DQ – ℰ (01756) 720 228
– www.knowleslodge.com
4 rm – †£ 60 ††£ 100
♦ Unusual Canadian ranch-house style guesthouse, clad in timber and sited in quiet dales location. Large sitting room with fine outlook. Cosy bedrooms have garden views.

ARKHOLME – Lancashire — 20 A1

▶ London 254 mi – Birmingham 140 mi – Liverpool 71 mi – Leeds 99 mi

Redwell Inn
Southwest : 1 mi on B 6254 ⊠ LA6 1BQ – ℰ (015242) 21 240
– www.redwellinnarkholme.co.uk
Rest – (booking advisable) Menu £ 16 (lunch) – Carte £ 16/39
♦ Attractive 16C stone inn with rustic bar and more formal dining room. Son cooks while mum and dad look after front of house. Menus offer something for everyone, from nibbles such as a homemade Scotch egg with HP sauce to a classic fish pie.

ARLINGHAM – Gloucestershire – 503 M28 – pop. 377 – ⊠ Gloucester — 4 C1

▶ London 120 mi – Birmingham 69 mi – Bristol 34 mi – Gloucester 16 mi

Old Passage Inn with rm
Passage Rd, West : 0.75 mi ⊠ GL2 7JR – ℰ (01452) 740 547
– www.theoldpassageinn.com – Closed 25-26 December and Monday
3 rm – †£ 60/110 ††£ 80/140, ⊇ £ 8
Rest – Seafood – Menu £ 20 (weekdays) – Carte £ 34/55
♦ Sweet, green painted former inn by the River Severn – its terrace is a great place to watch the famous Severn Bore. Bright yellow décor, red tiled floors and eye-catching local art for sale. Good-sized seafood menus offer simply prepared dishes of top notch produce. Well-equipped modern bedrooms boast pleasant views.

ARMSCOTE – Warwickshire – 504 P27 — 19 C3

▶ London 91 mi – Birmingham 36 mi – Oxford 38 mi

Willow Corner without rest
⊠ CV37 8DE – ℰ (01608) 682 391 – www.willowcorner.co.uk – Restricted opening in winter
3 rm ⊇ – †£ 50/65 ††£ 70/85
♦ Cream-washed cottage in a small village, with low-beamed guest areas and homely décor. Original features include mullioned windows and a stable door. Cottagey bedrooms boast good facilities and thoughtful touches.

ARNSIDE – Cumbria – 502 L21 – pop. 2 301 — 21 A3

▶ London 257 mi – Liverpool 74 mi – Manchester 69 mi – Bradford 97 mi

Number 43
43 The Promenade ⊠ LA5 0AA – ℰ (01524) 762 761 – www.no43.org.uk
6 rm ⊇ – †£ 100 ††£ 185   **Rest** – Menu £ 23
♦ Stylishly converted Victorian townhouse boasting superb estuary and fell views. Contemporary bedrooms with smart bathrooms, quality furnishings and good facilities. Comfy, open-plan lounge and dining room. Home-cooked meals by arrangement; lighter sharing platters every evening. Have breakfast on glass-enclosed terrace.

ARUNDEL – West Sussex – 504 S31 – pop. 3 297 ▮ Great Britain — 7 C2

▶ London 58 mi – Brighton 21 mi – Southampton 41 mi – Worthing 9 mi
🛈 61 High St ℰ (01903) 88 22 68, www.arundel.org.uk
◉ Castle ★★ **AC**

ARUNDEL

XX **Town House** with rm
65 High St ⌷ BN18 9AJ – ✆ (01903) 883 847 – www.thetownhouse.co.uk
– Closed 2 weeks February, 2 weeks October, 25-26 December, 1 January, Sunday and Monday
4 rm – †£ 75 ††£ 130   **Rest** – Menu £ 20/30
♦ Early 17C house displaying original sugar glass windows and impressive Renaissance ceiling with gilded walnut panelling. Smartly laid, intimate dining room. Confidently executed, tried-and-tested dishes with a classical base. Modern, well-equipped bedrooms.

at Burpham Northeast : 3 mi by A 27 – ⌷ Arundel

Burpham Country House
The Street ⌷ BN18 9RJ – ✆ (01903) 882 160 – www.burphamcountryhouse.com
– Closed January and 25-26 December
9 rm – †£ 80/95 ††£ 120/140
Rest – *(closed Sunday and Monday) (dinner only)* Carte £ 25/31
♦ Reputedly a hunting lodge for the Duke of Norfolk, this tranquil hotel constitutes the ideal 'stress remedy break'. Calm, pastel-coloured bedrooms overlook exquisite gardens. Seasonal menu of classic dishes served in dining room and conservatory.

George and Dragon
Main St ⌷ BN18 9RR – ✆ (01903) 883 131 – www.gdinn.co.uk
Rest – Carte £ 25/46
♦ It's all in the name: a good old-fashioned English pub with a rustic bar, linen-clad dining room and relaxed feel. Cooking features British classics, old pub favourites and daily specials.

ENGLAND

ASCOT – Windsor and Maidenhead – **504** R29 – **pop. 15 761**   **11 D3**
▶ London 36 mi – Reading 15 mi
▣ Mill Ride Ascot, ✆ (01344) 88 67 77

Coworth Park
London Rd, East : 2.75 mi on A 329 ⌷ SL5 7SE
– ✆ (01344) 876 600 – www.coworthpark.com
57 rm – †£ 195/500 ††£ 195/500, ⌑ £ 25 – 13 suites
Rest *Barn* – see restaurant listing
Rest *John Campbell at Coworth Park* – Menu £ 30 (weekday lunch)/60
Spec. Duck with cherries and water chestnuts. Halibut with oyster, chorizo and seaweed. Hay chocolate mousse with rose and blood orange sorbets.
♦ 17C property set in 246 acres and boasting its own championship polo pitches. Comfortable, stylish guest areas; superb spa. Beautiful bedrooms feature bespoke furniture, marble bathrooms and a high level of facilities. Fine dining restaurant serves inventive cooking with plenty of original touches.

XX **Ascot Oriental**
East : 2.25 mi on A 329 ⌷ SL5 0PU – ✆ (01344) 621 877
– www.ascotoriental.com – Closed 25-26 December
Rest – Chinese – Menu £ 29 – Carte £ 32/47
♦ Professionally run restaurant with calming décor. Extensive menu combines old customer favourites with newer, more original dishes; excellent Cantonese choices. Clean, flavoursome cooking.

XX **Barn** – at Coworth Park Hotel
London Rd, East : 2.75 mi on A 329 ⌷ SL5 7SE – ✆ (01344) 876 600
– www.coworthpark.com
Rest – Carte £ 30/35
♦ An informal alternative to the fine dining restaurant, this buzzy, rustic room's floor-to-ceiling windows let in plenty of light and offer views over the fields. Menu offers classics like steak and fish and chips.

ASCOT

Ascot Grill
6 Hermitage Par, High St ⊠ SL5 7HE – ℰ (01344) 622 285 – www.ascotgrill.co.uk
– Closed 25-26 December, 1 January and Sunday
Rest – Menu £ 16 (lunch) – Carte £ 21/52
• Set at the end of a 1950s shopping parade. Slick interior with leather, silk and velvet furnishings; floor-to-ceiling windows open onto a pleasant pavement terrace. Wide-ranging modern grill menu offers seafood, steak and vegetarian dishes.

ASENBY – North Yorkshire – see Thirsk

ASH – Kent – 504 X30   9 D2
▶ London 70 mi – Canterbury 9 mi – Dover 15 mi

Great Weddington
Northeast : 0.5 mi by A 257 on Weddington rd ⊠ CT3 2AR – ℰ (01304) 813 407
– www.greatweddington.co.uk – Closed Christmas-New Year
4 rm ⊇ – †£ 75/95 ††£ 100/125 **Rest** – Menu £ 40
• Charming Regency country house, ideally located for Canterbury and Dover. Well appointed drawing room and terrace. Thoughtfully furnished, carefully co-ordinated rooms. Communal dining room; owner an avid cook.

ASHBOURNE – Derbyshire – 502 O24 – pop. 5 020 ▍Great Britain   16 A2
▶ London 146 mi – Birmingham 47 mi – Manchester 48 mi – Nottingham 33 mi
🛈 13 Market Pl ℰ (01335) 34 36 66, www.visitpeakdistrict.com
◉ Dovedale★★ (Ilam Rock★) NW : 6 mi by A 515

Callow Hall
Mappleton Rd, West : 0.75 mi by Union St (off Market Pl) ⊠ DE6 2AA
– ℰ (01335) 300 900 – www.callowhall.co.uk
15 rm ⊇ – †£ 140 ††£ 190 – 1 suite **Rest** – Menu £ 25/45 – Carte £ 37/43
• Victorian country house in 44 acres of gardens, fields and woodland. Individually styled bedrooms boast original features, well-appointed bathrooms and quality fabrics and furnishings. Daily changing menus feature local produce and tasty home-smoked salmon.

dining room
33 St Johns St ⊠ DE6 1GP – ℰ (01335) 300 666
– www.thediningroomashbourne.co.uk – Closed Sunday-Wednesday
Rest – (dinner only) (booking essential) Menu £ 40/48
• Modern, stylish décor blends agreeably with period features including a cast iron range and 17C salt safe. Well-sourced, seasonal ingredients inform intricate modern dishes on 8 or 16 course tasting menus.

ASHBURTON – Devon – 503 I32 – pop. 3 309   2 C2
▶ London 220 mi – Exeter 20 mi – Plymouth 25 mi
◉ Dartmoor National Park★★

Agaric with rm
30 and 36 North St ⊠ TQ13 7QD – ℰ (01364) 654 478
– www.agaricrestaurant.co.uk – Closed first 2 weeks August, 2 weeks Christmas, Sunday-Tuesday and Saturday lunch
4 rm ⊇ – †£ 50/65 ††£ 130 **Rest** – (booking essential) Carte £ 32/39
• 200 year-old house, selling home-made jams, fudge and olives. Relaxed neighbourhood restaurant using a blend of cooking styles. Very stylish, individually themed bedrooms.

ASHFORD – Kent – 504 W30 – pop. 58 936   9 C2
▶ London 56 mi – Canterbury 14 mi – Dover 24 mi – Hastings 30 mi
Access Channel Tunnel : Eurostar information and reservations ℰ (08705) 186186
🛈 18 The Churchyard ℰ (01233) 62 91 65, www.visitheartofkent.com

ASHFORD

Eastwell Manor
Eastwell Park, Boughton Lees, North : 3 mi by A 28 on A 251
✉ TN25 4HR – ⌂ (01233) 213 000 – www.eastwellmanor.co.uk
20 rm – †£ 190 ††£ 295 – 22 suites – ††£ 445
Rest *Manor* – Menu £ 20/27 – Carte approx. £ 50
Rest *Pavilion* – ⌂ (01233) 213 100 – Carte £ 21/31
♦ Impressive manor house with Tudor origins, surrounded by manicured gardens and extensive parkland. Rebuilt in 1926 following a fire but some superb plaster ceilings and stone fireplaces remain. Characterful guest areas and luxurious bedrooms. Sizeable spa and golf course. Choice of wood-panelled restaurant complete with pianist or more casual brasserie and terrace.

ASHFORD-IN-THE-WATER – Derbyshire – 502 O24 – see Bakewell

ASHPRINGTON – Devon – 503 J32 – see Totnes

ASHWATER – Devon – 503 H31   2 C2
▶ London 218 mi – Bude 16 mi – Virginstow 3 mi

Blagdon Manor
Northwest : 2 mi by Holsworthy rd on Blagdon rd ✉ EX21 5DF – ⌂ (01409) 211 224 – www.blagdon.com – Closed January, Monday and Tuesday
7 rm – †£ 85 ††£ 195   **Rest** – (booking essential) Menu £ 20/38
♦ Proudly run former farmhouse in peaceful, rural location. Modern country house bedrooms, spotlessly kept, named after surrounding villages. Library, lounges and flag-floored bar. Classically-based cooking with a modern touch, served in dining room with conservatory extension.

ASKRIGG – North Yorkshire – 502 N21 – pop. 1 002 – ✉ Leyburn   22 A1
▶ London 251 mi – Kendal 32 mi – Leeds 70 mi – Newcastle upon Tyne 70 mi

Yorebridge House
Bainbridge, West : 1 mi ✉ DL8 3EE – ⌂ (01969) 652 060
– www.yorebridgehouse.com
11 rm – †£ 225 ††£ 250
Rest – (booking essential for non residents) Menu £ 45 (dinner) – Carte £ 23/45
♦ Lovingly restored former school with warm, hospitable owners. Modern, stylish and comfortable interior. Individually designed bedrooms, some with hot tubs. Locally sourced produce in relaxing dining room.

ASTON CANTLOW – Warwickshire – 503 O27 – pop. 1 843   19 C3
▫ Great Britain
▶ London 106 mi – Birmingham 20 mi – Stratford-upon-Avon 5 mi
◉ Mary Arden's House ★ AC, SE : 2 mi by Wilmcote Lane and Aston Cantlow Rd

King's Head
21 Bearley Rd ✉ B95 6HY – ⌂ (01789) 488 242 – www.thekh.co.uk – *Closed 25 December and Sunday dinner*
Rest – Carte £ 22/31
♦ Characterful black and white timbered, part 15C inn, set in a picturesque village. Seasonal menus feature traditional pub dishes, with local meats and fish to the fore. Regular duck suppers.

ASTON ROWANT – Oxfordshire – 504 R28 – pop. 2 512   11 C2
▶ London 45 mi – Coventry 69 mi

Lambert Arms
London Rd, on A 40 ✉ OX49 5SB – ⌂ (01844) 351 496
– www.bespokehotels.com
42 rm – †£ 79/119 ††£ 109/129, ⌂ £ 7   **Rest** – Carte £ 20/37
♦ Traditional, half-timbered roadside inn with large mews extension to rear. Bedrooms are split between the two; newer mews rooms are spacious, modern and ideal for business travellers. Rustic bar and restaurant serve accessible, pub-style dishes. Cheery staff.

ASTON TIRROLD – Oxfordshire — 10 B3
▶ London 58 mi – Reading 16 mi – Streatley 4 mi

Sweet Olive at The Chequers Inn
Baker St ⊠ OX11 9DD – ℘ (01235) 851 272 – www.sweet-olive.com
– Closed 3 weeks February, 2 weeks July, Sunday dinner and Wednesday
Rest – *(booking essential)* Carte £ 25/35
♦ Red-brick Victorian pub at heart of the village; cosy, welcoming and popular with the locals. Gallic owners offer French-influenced menu and interesting selection of fine wines.

ATCHAM – Shropshire – 503 L25 – see Shrewsbury

ATTLEBOROUGH – Norfolk – 504 X26 – pop. 6 530 — 15 C2
▶ London 101 mi – Norwich 19 mi – Ipswich 42 mi – Peterborough 87 mi

Mulberry Tree with rm
Station Rd ⊠ NR17 2AS – ℘ (01953) 452 124 – www.the-mulberry-tree.co.uk
– Closed 24 December-2 January and Sunday
5 rm ☐ – †£ 75 ††£ 100 **Rest** – Carte £ 27/34
♦ Contemporary bar/restaurant set in imposing brick-built property with pleasant terrace and bowling green. Bar menu popular at lunch. À la carte offers attractively presented, globally influenced, modern dishes. Stylish, very comfortable bedrooms.

AUGHTON – Lancashire – 502 L23 – pop. 8 342 — 20 A2
▶ London 217 mi – Liverpool 13 mi – Manchester 40 mi – Bradford 68 mi

Swan Inn with rm
2 Springfield Rd ⊠ L39 6ST – ℘ (01695) 421 450 – www.mpwtheswan.co.uk
12 rm ☐ – †£ 50/70 ††£ 60/140
Rest – Menu £ 16/20 (weekday dinner) – Carte approx. £ 25
♦ Sizeable, smartly refurbished restaurant with linen-laid tables; its walls decorated with cartoons from Marco Pierre White's private collection. Accessible menu of modern British cooking with some locally influenced dishes. Stylish, contemporary bedrooms.

AUSTWICK – North Yorkshire – 502 M21 – pop. 467 — 22 A2
– ⊠ Lancaster (lancs.).
▶ London 259 mi – Kendal 28 mi – Lancaster 20 mi – Leeds 46 mi

Traddock
⊠ LA2 8BY – ℘ (015242) 51 224 – www.thetraddock.co.uk
12 rm ☐ – †£ 85/105 ††£ 145/185
Rest – *(booking essential for non-residents)* Carte £ 22/35
♦ Georgian country house – formerly a private residence – named after an old horse trading paddock. Modern interior with bright, airy lounges. Bedrooms boast feature beds, rural views and roll-top baths. Formal dining room serves modern versions of old classics.

Austwick Hall
Southeast : 0.5 mi on Townend Ln ⊠ LA2 8BS – ℘ (015242) 51 794
– www.austwickhall.co.uk
5 rm ☐ – †£ 170 ††£ 185 **Rest** – Menu £ 29
♦ Characterful house in a delightful village on the edge of the dales and surrounded by tiered gardens and woodland. Spacious, antique-furnished bedrooms; one with a roll-top bath affording views down the garden. Nothing is too much trouble for the friendly owners. Tea on arrival. Dinner includes a local cheese selection.

Wood View without rest
The Green ⊠ LA2 8BB – ℘ (015242) 51 190 – www.woodviewbandb.com
– Restricted opening in winter
5 rm ☐ – †£ 48/55 ††£ 84
♦ In a charming spot on the village green, the cottage dates back to 17C with many of the original features still in place including exposed rafters in several bedrooms.

AXMINSTER – Devon – **503** L31 – pop. 4 952   **2** D2
▶ London 156 mi – Exeter 27 mi – Lyme Regis 5 mi – Taunton 22 mi
◎ Lyme Regis★ – The Cobb★, SE : 5.5 mi by A 35 and A 3070

✕ River Cottage Canteen   VISA ⦿
Trinity Sq ✉ EX13 5AN – ☏ (01297) 631 715 – www.rivercottage.net – Closed dinner Sunday and Monday
Rest – Carte £ 19/44
♦ Busy restaurant, deli and coffee shop owned by Hugh Fearnley-Whittingstall. Simple, industrial-style room with mismatched furniture. Blackboards change twice-daily, offering gutsy, flavoursome country cooking and showcasing local produce.

AYLESBURY – Buckinghamshire – **504** R28 – pop. 69 021   **11** C2
🟩 Great Britain
▶ London 46 mi – Birmingham 72 mi – Northampton 37 mi – Oxford 22 mi
🛈 Kings Head Passage off Market Square ☏ (01296) 33 05 59, www.visitbuckinghamshire.org
⛳ Weston Turville New Rd, ☏ (01296) 42 40 84
⛳ Aylesbury Golf Centre Bierton Hulcott Lane, ☏ (01296) 39 36 44
◎ Waddesdon Manor★★, NW : 5.5 mi by A 41 – Chiltern Hills★

🏛 Hartwell House   VISA ⦿ AE
Oxford Rd, Southwest : 2 mi on A 418 ✉ HP17 8NR – ☏ (01296) 747 444 – www.hartwell-house.com
36 rm ⊋ – †£ 160/200 ††£ 260 – 10 suites
Rest *Soane* – Menu £ 23/33 – Carte dinner £ 43/53 **s**
♦ Where Louis XVIII, exiled King of France, was once resident. Impressive palatial house in 90 acres of parkland, boasting luxurious lounges, ornate furnishings and magnificent, antique-filled bedrooms. Restaurant offers good value lunches and traditional country house cooking.

ENGLAND

AYLESFORD – Kent – **504** V30   **8** B1
▶ London 37 mi – Maidstone 3 mi – Rochester 8 mi

✕✕✕ Hengist   AC ⇔ VISA ⦿ AE ①
7-9 High St ✉ ME20 7AX – ☏ (01622) 719 273 – www.hengistrestaurant.co.uk – Closed Monday
Rest – Menu £ 15 (lunch) – Carte £ 32/38
♦ Converted 16C town house, elegantly appointed throughout, with bonus of exposed rafters and smart private dining room upstairs. Accomplished modern cooking with seasonal base.

AYLSHAM – Norfolk – **504** X25 – pop. 5 504   **15** D1
▶ London 128 mi – Norwich 13 mi – Ipswich 57 mi – Stevenage 105 mi

↑ Old Pump House *without rest*   P VISA ⦿
2 Holman Rd ✉ NR11 6BY – ☏ (01263) 733 789 – www.theoldpumphouse.com – Closed Christmas
5 rm ⊋ – †£ 80/98 ††£ 98/120
♦ Well-run Georgian house with the original village water pump still standing outside. Tastefully furnished throughout: bedrooms boast fine reproduction oak furniture – one boasts a four-poster. The owners have a passion for antiques and art.

AYNHO – Northamptonshire – **504** Q28 – pop. 632   **16** B3
▶ London 73 mi – Birmingham 66 mi – Leicester 62 mi – Coventry 48 mi

🏨 Cartwright   P VISA ⦿ AE
1-5 Croughton Rd ✉ OX17 3BE – ☏ (01869) 811 885 – www.oxfordshire-hotels.co.uk
21 rm ⊋ – †£ 80/120 ††£ 140/150   **Rest** – Menu £ 17/21 – Carte £ 21/34
♦ Modernised 16C inn, ideally placed for Silverstone and Bicester Village. Spacious bedrooms come with complimentary wi-fi and are split between main house and rear conversion. Dining is an informal affair, with a seasonal menu of robust dishes.

AYOT ST LAWRENCE – Hertfordshire – see Welwyn

AYSGARTH – North Yorkshire – 502 O21 — 22 A1
▶ London 249 mi – Ripon 28 mi – York 56 mi

George and Dragon Inn with rm
✉ DL8 3AD – ☎ (01969) 663 358 – www.georgeanddragonaysgarth.co.uk
– Closed 2 weeks January
7 rm – †£ 40/55 ††£ 80/90 **Rest** – Menu £ 13 (lunch) – Carte £ 20/30
♦ Laid-back coaching inn set in the National Park, close to the breathtaking River Ure waterfalls. Unfussy pub classics include plenty of local meats, game and proper old-fashioned puddings. Comfy, individually styled bedrooms; some with whirlpool baths.

BABBACOMBE – Torbay – 503 J32 – see Torquay

BACKWELL – North Somerset – 503 L29 – pop. 5 455 — 3 B2
▶ London 127 mi – Bristol 9 mi – Cardiff 48 mi – Swansea 83 mi

New Inn
86 West Town Rd ✉ BS48 3BE – ☎ (01275) 462 199
– www.newinn-backwell.co.uk – Closed 2 weeks January, 25-26 December, Sunday dinner and Monday
Rest – Menu £ 16/24 – Carte £ 27/40
♦ Pretty 18C stone pub with warm farmhouse feel, welcoming open-fired bar and more formal dining area with 'tea room' atmosphere. Cooking is in a stylishly modern vein, featuring appealing menus of precisely prepared, elegant dishes and interesting side plates.

BAGSHOT – Surrey – 504 R29 – pop. 5 247 — 7 C1
▶ London 37 mi – Reading 17 mi – Southampton 49 mi
🛈 Windlesham Grove End, ☎ (01276) 45 22 20

Pennyhill Park
London Rd, Southwest : 1 mi on A 30 ✉ GU19 5EU – ☎ (01276) 471 774
– www.exclusivehotels.co.uk
112 rm – †£ 195/295 ††£ 295, ⊒ £ 21 – 11 suites
Rest *Michael Wignall at The Latymer* ☆
Rest *Brasserie* – see restaurant listing
♦ Impressive 19C manor house set in 123 acres. Classical guest areas display modern touches; spacious bedrooms boast period furnishings and great views. Have afternoon tea in the comfy lounge before heading for one of the best spas in Europe.

Michael Wignall at The Latymer – at Pennyhill Park Hotel
London Rd, Southwest : 1 mi on A30 ✉ GU19 5EU
– ☎ (01276) 486 156 – www.exclusivehotels.co.uk
– Closed 1-16 January, Sunday, Monday, lunch Tuesday and Saturday
Rest – (booking essential) Menu £ 34/60
Spec. Poached chicken, smoked eel and horseradish emulsion. Saddle of rabbit and glazed veal belly with butternut squash purée. Poached pear, liquorice ice cream and crisp pear cannelloni.
♦ Elegant hotel dining room with oak-clad walls, glass-enclosed chef's table, quality place settings and formal service. Cooking is careful, precise and uses only top quality ingredients. The menu is concise and offers ambitious, original dishes that are full of flavour.

Brasserie – at Pennyhill Park Hotel
London Rd, Southwest : 1 mi on A 30 ✉ GU19 5EU – ☎ (01276) 471 774
– www.exclusivehotels.co.uk – Closed Saturday lunch
Rest – (buffet lunch) Carte £ 34/48
♦ Spacious hotel dining room set in an impressive 19C manor house that lies within 123 acres of grounds. Stylish, modern décor with doors opening out onto the garden. Appealing brasserie menu.

BAKEWELL – Derbyshire – 502 O24 – pop. 3 676 – Great Britain 16 A1

- London 160 mi – Derby 26 mi – Manchester 37 mi – Nottingham 33 mi
- Bridge St (01629) 81 65 58, www.peakdistrict.gov.uk
- Chatsworth ★★★ (Park and Garden ★★★) **AC**, NE : 2.5 mi by A 619 – Haddon Hall ★★ **AC**, SE : 2 mi by A 6

at Ashford-in-the-Water Northwest : 1.75 mi by A 6 and A 6020 – ⊠ Bakewell

Riverside House
Fennel St ⊠ DE45 1QF – (01629) 814 275 – www.riversidehousehotel.co.uk
14 rm ⊇ – †£ 155 ††£ 195
Rest *Riverside Room* – Menu £ 15/45

♦ Homely former shooting lodge with gardens running down to the river. Cosy open-fired bar and elegant drawing room. Well-furnished bedrooms with good extras – some have views, some in the wing open onto a terrace. Classical dining takes place over several rooms.

River Cottage without rest
Buxton Rd ⊠ DE45 1QP – (01629) 813 327 – www.rivercottageashford.co.uk
4 rm ⊇ – †£ 80/95 ††£ 100/135

♦ Traditional stone cottage by the River Wye, with delightful gardens and terrace. Bedrooms blend modern furnishings and antique furniture. Complimentary wines and afternoon tea.

BALSALL COMMON – West Midlands – see Coventry

BAMBURGH – Northumberland – 501 O17 – pop. 582 – Great Britain 24 B1

- London 337 mi – Edinburgh 77 mi – Newcastle upon Tyne 51 mi
- Castle ★ **AC**

Lord Crewe Arms
Front St ⊠ NE69 7BL – (01668) 214 243 – www.lordcrewe.co.uk
– *February-October*
17 rm ⊇ – †£ 65/105 ††£ 85/150
Rest – *(bar lunch)* Carte £ 16/35

♦ Privately owned, 17C former coaching inn, in the shadow of the Norman castle. Spacious, comfy lounge and contemporary bedrooms. Characterful, beamed bar is more rustic in style and offers a traditional menu.

at Waren Mill West : 2.75 mi on B 1342 – ⊠ Belford

Waren House
⊠ NE70 7EE – (01668) 214 581 – www.warenhousehotel.co.uk
12 rm (dinner included) ⊇ – †£ 110/150 ††£ 190/235 – 3 suites
Rest – *(dinner only)* Menu £ 35

♦ Personally run, antique-furnished country house set in beautiful, tranquil gardens. Bedrooms, named after the owners' family members, mix classic and modern styles: some have four-posters and coastal views. Formal dining room boasts ornate ceiling; menus showcase local ingredients.

BAMPTON – Devon – 503 J31 – pop. 1 617 2 D1

- London 189 mi – Exeter 18 mi – Minehead 21 mi – Taunton 15 mi

Bark House
Oakfordbridge, West : 3 mi by B 3227 on A 396 ⊠ EX16 9HZ – (01398) 351 236 – www.thebarkhouse.co.uk – Closed 1 week January and 1 week November
6 rm ⊇ – †£ 54/64 ††£ 70/100
Rest – *(closed Monday) (dinner only and Sunday lunch) (booking essential for non-residents)* Menu £ 22

♦ Simple, homely hotel; formerly used as a wood store for the local tannery. Bedrooms boast contemporary fabrics and modern bathrooms. One leads to a small garden; another has a balcony. Honest home cooking, coupled with good bin ends from the owner's wine business.

BAMPTON

Quarrymans Rest with rm
Briton St ⊠ EX16 9LN – ℰ (01398) 331 480 – www.thequarrymansrest.co.uk
– Closed 25 December and Sunday dinner
3 rm ⊑ – ♦£ 55/65 ♦♦£ 65/85   **Rest** – Carte £ 23/31 **s**
- 17C inn with relaxed, open-fired bar/lounge and more formal, intimate restaurant. Locally sourced produce to the fore on seasonal menu of tried-and-tested classics, with the occasional Asian influence. Clean, fresh, uncluttered bedrooms.

BANBURY – Oxfordshire – 503 P27 – pop. 43 867 – Great Britain   10 B1

▶ London 76 mi – Birmingham 40 mi – Coventry 25 mi – Oxford 23 mi
🛈 Spiceball Park Rd ℰ (01295) 25 98 55, www.visitnorthoxfordshire.com
⛳ Cherwell Edge Chacombe, ℰ (01295) 71 15 91
◉ Upton House★ **AC**, NW : 7 mi by A 422

at Sibford Gower West : 8 mi by B 4035 – ⊠ Banbury

Wykham Arms
Temple Mill Rd. ⊠ OX15 5RX – ℰ (01295) 788 808 – www.wykhamarms.co.uk
– Closed Monday except bank holidays
Rest – Carte £ 23/31
- Thatched stone pub set down country lanes in a small village. Featuring local produce, menus range from bar snacks and lights bites to the full 3 courses. Good range of wines by the glass.

BARNARD CASTLE – Durham – 502 O20 – pop. 6 714 – Great Britain   24 A3

▶ London 258 mi – Carlisle 63 mi – Leeds 68 mi – Middlesbrough 31 mi
🛈 Flatts Rd ℰ (01833) 69 09 09, www.teesdalediscovery.com
⛳ Harmire Rd, ℰ (01833) 63 83 55
◉ Bowes Museum★ **AC**
◉ Raby Castle★ **AC**, NE : 6.5 mi by A 688

Homelands
85 Galgate ⊠ DL12 8ES – ℰ (01833) 638 757
– www.homelandsguesthouse.co.uk – Closed 25 September-2 October and 15 December-15 January
5 rm ⊑ – ♦£ 43/67 ♦♦£ 78   **Rest** – Menu £ 20
- Victorian terraced house on the main road through the town, just a short drive from Raby Castle. Immaculately maintained interior with cosy lounge. Individually furnished bedrooms are compact but well-priced; four are in the house, the fifth, at the end of a long, mature rear garden. Home-cooked dinners by arrangement.

at Greta Bridge Southeast : 4.5 mi off A 66 – ⊠ Barnard Castle

Morritt
⊠ DL12 9SE – ℰ (01833) 627 232 – www.themorritt.co.uk
27 rm ⊑ – ♦£ 110/120 ♦♦£ 179/200
Rest *Morritt* – see restaurant listing
Rest *Bistro/Bar* – Carte approx. £ 23
- Personally run, 19C former coaching inn displaying a pleasant mix of old and new. Individually designed bedrooms blend contemporary décor with antique furnishings, and boast four-posters or other interesting bedsteads. Oak panelled restaurant serves modern menu; all-day snacks offered in the bistro and bar.

Morritt – at Morritt Hotel
⊠ DL12 9SE – ℰ (01833) 627 232 – www.themorritt.co.uk
Rest – Carte £ 30/35
- Smart oak-panelled dining room with dark wood beams and a lovely parquet floor, set within a charming coaching inn. Modern menu relies on local ingredients and dishes arrive well-presented.

BARNARD CASTLE

at Hutton Magna Southeast : 7.25 mi by A 66

Oak Tree Inn
DL11 7HH – ℰ (01833) 627 371 – Closed 24-27 December, 31 December, 1 January and Monday
Rest – (dinner only) (booking essential) Carte £ 27/34

♦ Small but charming whitewashed pub consisting of a single room. Run by a husband and wife team; he cooks, while she serves. Cooking is hearty and flavoursome with a rustic French feel.

at Romaldkirk Northwest : 6 mi by A 67 on B 6277 – ✉ Barnard Castle

Rose and Crown with rm
DL12 9EB – ℰ (01833) 650 213 – www.rose-and-crown.co.uk – Closed 24-26 December
12 rm – †£ 95/125 ††£ 135/185
Rest – Carte £ 22/33 **s**
Rest *The Restaurant* – (dinner only and Sunday lunch) Menu £ 19/35 **s**

♦ Quintessential 18C English inn with atmospheric bar and horse brasses; set by a Saxon church and surrounded by three village greens. Both bar and rear brasserie serve classical fare; more formal restaurant offers seasonally changing four course dinner menu. Bedrooms boast designer décor, flat screen TVs and Bose radios.

BARNSLEY – Gloucestershire – **503** O28 – see Cirencester

BARRASFORD – Northumberland   24 A2

▶ London 309 mi – Newcastle upon Tyne 29 mi – Sunderland 42 mi – Middlesbrough 66 mi

Barrasford Arms with rm
NE48 4AA – ℰ (01434) 681 237 – www.barrasfordarms.co.uk – Closed January, 25-26 December, Monday February-March, Sunday dinner, Monday lunch and bank holidays
7 rm – †£ 50/65 ††£ 85
Rest – Menu £ 16 (weekday lunch) – Carte £ 22/30

♦ Close to Kielder Water and Hadrian's Wall, this personally run 19C stone inn has a traditional, homely atmosphere. Pub classics served at lunch; more substantial dishes at dinner. Modern, comfortable bedrooms.

BARTON-ON-SEA – Hampshire – **503** P31   6 A3

▶ London 108 mi – Bournemouth 11 mi – Southampton 24 mi – Winchester 35 mi

✕✕ Pebble Beach with rm
Marine Dr ✉ BH25 7DZ – ℰ (01425) 627 777 – www.pebblebeach-uk.com
4 rm – †£ 70 ††£ 100, ⊇ £ 6.50   **Rest** – Seafood – Carte £ 17/41

♦ Large, split-level restaurant with open-plan kitchen, fish tank and white baby grand piano. Metal-furnished terrace boasts impressive Solent and Isle of Wight views. Extensive, seasonally changing menus centred around local seafood. Good-sized, homely bedrooms.

BARWICK – Somerset – **503** M31 – see Yeovil

BASHALL EAVES – Lancashire – **502** M23 – see Clitheroe

BASLOW – Derbyshire – **502** P24 – pop. 1 184 – ✉ Bakewell   16 A1
Great Britain

▶ London 161 mi – Derby 27 mi – Manchester 35 mi – Sheffield 13 mi
◉ Chatsworth ★★★ (Park and Garden ★★★) **AC**

BASLOW

Cavendish
Church Ln, on A 619 – DE45 1SP – ℰ (01246) 582 311
– www.cavendish-hotel.net
23 rm – †£ 140/154 ††£ 177/230, ⊇ £ 18.90 – 1 suite
Rest *The Gallery* – see restaurant listing
Rest *Garden Room* – Carte £ 26/31

♦ Elegant hotel on the Chatsworth Estate, boasting lovely parkland views. Bedrooms have a cosy, country house feel and a slightly contemporary edge. Some of the furniture and paintings come from Chatsworth House. Formal restaurant serves traditional menus; Garden Room offers all-day dining and afternoon teas.

Fischer's at Baslow Hall with rm
Calver Rd, on A 623 – DE45 1RR – ℰ (01246) 583 259
– www.fischers-baslowhall.co.uk – Closed 25-26 and 31 December
10 rm ⊇ – †£ 105/145 ††£ 155/225 – 1 suite
Rest – (closed Sunday dinner to non-residents and Monday lunch) (booking essential) Menu £ 34/72
Spec. Deep-fried crab in kadaif pastry, caramelised pork belly and Pedro Ximenez vinegar. Goosnargh duck à l'orange. English strawberries three ways with a camomile tea panna cotta.

♦ Edwardian manor house with impressive formal grounds and walled vegetable garden. Classically based and accomplished cooking, with the occasional modern twist, uses much local produce. Comfortable bedrooms in main house; garden rooms larger.

The Gallery – at Cavendish Hotel
Church Ln, on A 619 – DE45 1SP – ℰ (01246) 582 311
– www.cavendish-hotel.net
Rest – Menu £ 41

♦ Fine dining restaurant in an elegant hotel on the Chatsworth Estate, which boasts views out across the parkland. Dishes have a traditional base but presentation and techniques are more modern.

Rowley's
Church St – DE45 1RY – ℰ (01246) 583 880 – www.rowleysrestaurant.co.uk
– Closed Sunday dinner
Rest – (booking advisable) Menu £ 26 (lunch) – Carte £ 26/35

♦ Contemporary restaurant and bar set over two floors; downstairs with view of open plan kitchen. Modern menu, with produce sourced from in and around Peak District.

BASSENTHWAITE – Cumbria – **501** K19 – pop. 433   **21** A2
▶ London 300 mi – Carlisle 24 mi – Keswick 7 mi

Pheasant
Southwest : 3.25 mi by B 5291 on Wythop Mill Rd – CA13 9YE – ℰ (017687) 76 234 – www.the-pheasant.co.uk – Closed 24-25 December
15 rm ⊇ – †£ 90/125 ††£ 150/250
Rest *Bistro at The Pheasant* – Carte £ 22/33
Rest *Dining Room* – (dinner only and Sunday lunch) Menu £ 35

♦ 16C whitewashed coaching inn with hugely characterful bars, comfy lounge and traditional styled bedrooms – some with lovely country views. Home-cooked dishes in laid-back, oak-furnished Bistro. Daily changing menu and garden outlook in more formal Dining Room.

Overwater Hall
Northeast : 2.5 mi by Uldale rd on Overwater rd – CA7 1HH
– ℰ (017687) 76 566 – www.overwaterhall.co.uk – Closed 2-16 January
11 rm (dinner included) ⊇ – †£ 110/170 ††£ 220/300
Rest – (closed Monday lunch) Menu £ 48 (dinner) – Carte lunch £ 24/31

♦ Castellated Georgian manor house built in 1811, set in 18 acres of mature gardens. Three good-sized lounges, one with a bar. Large, boldly patterned bedrooms with rich fabrics and good quality bathrooms. Formal dining room offers a traditional country house menu.

BATH

See city maps on following pages

4 C2

© Ingolf Pompe/Hemis.fr

Bath and North East Somerset – pop. 80 488 – 503 M29 – 504 M29 – Great Britain
▶ London 119 – Bristol 13 – Southampton 63 – Taunton 49

🛈 Tourist Information
Abbey Chambers, Abbey Church Yard, ✆(0906) 711 20 00, www.visitbath.co.uk

Golf Courses
- Tracy Park Wick Bath Rd, ✆(0117) 9 37 18 00
- Lansdown, ✆(01225) 42 21 38
- Entry Hill, ✆(01225) 83 42 48

◉ SIGHTS

In the town : City★★★ • Royal Crescent★★★ AV • The Circus★★★ AV • Museum of Costume★★★ AC AV M7 • Roman Baths★★ AC BX D • Holburne Museum★★ AC Y M5 • Pump Room★ BX B • Assembly Rooms★★ AV • Bath Abbey★ BX • Pulteney Bridge★ BV • Lansdown Crescent★★ Y • Camden Crescent★ Y

On the outskirts : American Museum at Claverton★★ AC E : 3 mi by A 36 Y

In the surrounding area : Corsham Court★★ AC, NE : 8.5 mi by A 4 • Dyrham Park★ AC, N : 6.5 mi by A 4 and A 46

🏨 **Royal Crescent**
16 Royal Cres ⌧ BA1 2LS – ✆(01225) 823 333 – www.royalcrescent.co.uk
35 rm – ††£ 199/595 – 10 suites   AV**a**
Rest *Dower House* – see restaurant listing
♦ Professionally run townhouse in sweeping Georgian crescent, boasting smart fire-lit entrance, period drawing room/library and stylish spa. Elegant Georgian bedrooms display antiques.

🏨 **Bath Spa**
Sydney Rd ⌧ BA2 6JF – ✆(0844) 879 91 06 – www.macdonaldhotels.co.uk
118 rm – †£ 153/215 ††£ 153/320, ⌧ £ 18 – 11 suites   Y**z**
Rest *Vellore* – (dinner only) (booking essential) Carte £ 40/50
Rest *Alfresco* – (lunch only and dinner Friday-Saturday) Carte £ 26/33
♦ Impressive 19C mansion in mature gardens, with newer wing. Period lounges and contemporary bedrooms; full butler service in Imperial Suites. Superb spa. Impressive, formal Georgian dining room with Corinthian columns. Informal Alfresco offers classic grill menu.

Bath Priory
Weston Rd ✉ *BA1 2XT* – ℰ *(01225) 331 922* – *www.thebathpriory.co.uk*
27 rm 🛏 – 🛌 £ 430/645   **Yc**
Rest – Menu £ 35/75 ⊗⊗
♦ Impressive Georgian house with mature gardens, classical guest areas, sumptuous sitting room and smart spa. Luxurious bedrooms blend the traditional and the modern. Designer bathrooms. Two dining rooms; the smaller more romantic, the larger more modern. Ambitious cooking uses some unexpected combinations.

Homewood Park
Abbey Ln, Hinton Charterhouse, Southeast : 6.5 mi on A 36 ✉ *BA2 7TB* – ℰ *(01225) 723 731* – *www.homewoodpark.co.uk*
19 rm 🛏 – 🛌 £ 215 🛌 £ 255 – 2 suites
Rest – Menu £ 22/55 s
♦ Remotely set country house with fashionable interior. Charming guest areas – many boasting open fires – and contemporary bedrooms with bold colour schemes. Superb spa and treatment facilities. Dining split between 3 rooms. Modern dishes are stylishly presented.

Queensberry
Russel St ✉ *BA1 2QF* – ℰ *(01225) 447 928* – *www.thequeensberry.co.uk*
29 rm – 🛌 £ 135/195 🛌 £ 135/480, 🛏 £ 15   **AVx**
Rest *Olive Tree* – see restaurant listing
♦ Long-standing Georgian townhouse in the city centre, run by a friendly well-versed team. Guest areas include a snug lounge, well-appointed sitting rooms and a bar, all with a contemporary feel. Funky, individually designed bedrooms have nice designer touches, plasma TVs, digital radios and a host of extras.

Street	Ref		Street	Ref		Street	Ref
Ambury	BX 2		Green St	BV 21		Pierrepont St	BX 39
Argyle St	BV 3		Guinea Lane	BV 23		Quiet St	BV 40
Bennett St	AV 4		Henry St	BX 24		Russel St	AV 42
Bridge St	BVX 6		Lower Borough Walls	BX 26		Southgate Shopping Centre	BX
Broad Quay	BX 7		Milsom St	ABV		Southgate St	BX 43
Chapel Row	AVX 9		Monmouth Pl	AVX 28		Terrace Walk	BX 46
Charles St	AX 10		Monmouth St	AX 30		Union St	BX 47
Charlotte St	AV 12		New Bond St	BV 31		Upper Borough Walls	BX 48
Cheap St	BX 13		New Orchard St	BX 32		Westgate Buildings	AX 49
Churchill Bridge	BX 14		Nile St	AV 34		Westgate St	ABX 50
Circus Pl	AV 16		Northgate St	BVX 35		Wood St	AV 52
Gay St	AV		Old Bond St	BX 36		York St	BX 53
Grand Parade	BX 17		Orange Grove	BX 38			
Great Stanhope St	AV 18						

Dukes

Great Pulteney St ✉ BA2 4DN – ☏ (01225) 787 960 – www.dukesbath.co.uk

BVn

13 rm ⊑ – † £ 99/123 †† £ 139/179 – 4 suites
Rest *Cavendish* – Menu £ 10 (lunch) – Carte £ 24/45

♦ Welcoming Palladian-style townhouse with period furnishings and plenty of charm. Bedrooms, named after famous Dukes, feature bold prints, heavy fabrics and antiques; some have four-posters. Dining room opens onto a patio area and offers a modern, formal menu.

A good night's sleep without spending a fortune? Look for Bib Hotel 🏨.

BATH

Oldfields without rest
102 Wells Rd ⊠ BA2 3AL – ℰ (01225) 317 984 – www.oldfields.co.uk – Closed 24-25 December
16 rm ⊇ – †£ 55/70 ††£ 65/170   **Z u**

♦ Spaciously elegant Victorian house with comfy, well-furnished drawing room, breakfast room boasting 'Bath rooftops' view and bedrooms that exude a high standard of comfort.

Apsley House without rest
141 Newbridge Hill ⊠ BA1 3PT – ℰ (01225) 336 966 – www.apsley-house.co.uk – Closed 24-25 December
12 rm ⊇ – †£ 125/150 ††£ 175/200   **Y x**

♦ Built for the Duke of Wellington and staffed with the unobtrusive calm of an English private house. Spacious individual rooms; two open onto a peaceful, mature rear garden.

Cheriton House without rest
9 Upper Oldfield Pk ⊠ BA2 3JX – ℰ (01225) 429 862 – www.cheritonhouse.co.uk
12 rm ⊇ – †£ 60/95 ††£ 85/165   **Z u**

♦ Immaculately kept house with 19C origins, run by very charming hosts. Comfortable, sizeable rooms and lounge, with some fine tiled fireplaces. Breakfast in the conservatory.

Dorian House without rest
1 Upper Oldfield Pk ⊠ BA2 3JX – ℰ (01225) 426 336 – www.dorianhouse.co.uk – Closed 24-25 December
13 rm ⊇ – †£ 69/99 ††£ 99/165   **Z u**

♦ Charming 19C house featuring original stained glass. Music-related memorabilia in reception. Well-appointed bedrooms display good attention to detail; some are Victorian in style, others more modern. Delightful conservatory breakfast room.

Villa Magdala without rest
Henrietta Rd ⊠ BA2 6LX – ℰ (01225) 466 329 – www.villamagdala.co.uk – Closed 1 week Christmas
18 rm ⊇ – †£ 110/130 ††£ 130/150   **BV r**

♦ Named after Napier's 1868 victory. Well-equipped rooms, floral furnishings; carefully preserved ornate balustrade and showpiece bedroom with four-poster and chaise longue.

One Three Nine without rest
139 Wells Rd ⊠ BA2 3AL – ℰ (01225) 314 769 – www.139bath.co.uk – Closed 24-25 December
10 rm ⊇ – †£ 65/170 ††£ 75/180   **Z r**

♦ Unassuming Victorian building conceals the chic, bold décor of a stylish boutique hotel. Individually styled bedrooms may include four-posters or spa baths. Excellent terrace breakfast.

Lavender House without rest
17 Bloomfield Pk, (off Bloomfield Rd) ⊠ BA2 2BY – ℰ (01225) 314 500 – www.lavenderhouse-bath.com
4 rm ⊇ – †£ 65 ††£ 90/120   **Z s**

♦ Edwardian house hidden way from the town centre, in a residential area. Snug sitting room and pleasant breakfast room boasting a characterful 17C sideboard. Comfortable bedrooms have delightful designer wallpapers and nice extra touches.

Athole House without rest
33 Upper Oldfield Pk ⊠ BA2 3JX – ℰ (01225) 320 000 – www.atholehouse.co.uk
4 rm ⊇ – †£ 70/100 ††£ 100/130   **Z i**

♦ Spacious, bay windowed Victorian guesthouse with large garden, away from city centre. Bright breakfast room; conservatory lounge. Light, airy, contemporary bedrooms.

BATH

🕱🕱🕱🕱 Dower House – at Royal Crescent Hotel
16 Royal Cres ✉ BA1 2LS – ℰ (01225) 823 333 – www.royalcrescent.co.uk
Rest – Menu £ 28/56 🕸

AV**a**

♦ Plush, contemporary dining room with swish bar, spacious lounge and lovely garden. Creative, seasonal cooking is underpinned by a French base. Attentive, understated service.

🕱🕱 Olive Tree – at Queensberry Hotel
Russel St ✉ BA1 2QF – ℰ (01225) 447 928 – www.thequeensberry.co.uk
– Closed Monday lunch
Rest – Menu £ 23 (lunch) – Carte £ 44/59

AV**x**

♦ Stylish restaurant set within an established boutique townhouse hotel. Split into two rooms, with elegantly laid tables and contemporary artwork hung on the walls. Modern menus display Mediterranean influences. Pleasant team.

🕱 Bistro La Barrique
31 Barton St ✉ BA1 1HG – ℰ (01225) 463 861 – www.bistrolabarrique.co.uk
– Closed 25-26 December, 1 January, second week January and Sunday October-April
Rest – French – Carte £ 21/27

AX**a**

♦ Unpretentious bistro-style restaurant, with sheltered courtyard for terrace dining. Small, good value menu of 'petits plats'; classic French dishes with some Mediterranean twists.

🕱 Casanis
4 Saville Row ✉ BA1 2QP – ℰ (01225) 780 055 – www.casanis.co.uk
– Closed 25-26 December, 1 week January, 1 week August, Sunday and Monday
Rest – French – *(booking essential)* Menu £ 19 (lunch) – Carte £ 27/38

AV**n**

♦ Sweet French bistro set in an elegant Georgian building near the Assembly Rooms. Exposed wooden floors, clothed tables and a tiny rear courtyard. Skilful cooking of classic French dishes.

🍺 Marlborough Tavern
35 Marlborough Buildings ✉ BA1 2LY – ℰ (01225) 423 731
– www.marlborough-tavern.com – Closed 25 December
Rest – *(booking advisable)* Menu £ 15 (lunch) – Carte £ 26/34

AV**z**

♦ Spacious, modern pub next to the park and Royal Crescent, boasting funky flock wallpaper, scrubbed wooden floors and local artwork. Unfussy, hearty, classical dishes use very local produce.

🍺 White Hart
Widcombe Hill ✉ BA2 6AA – ℰ (01225) 338 053 – www.whitehartbath.co.uk
– Closed 25-26 December, Sunday dinner and bank holidays
Rest – *(booking essential at dinner)* Carte £ 13/29

Z**o**

♦ Appealing pub on south east edge of the city centre, with a local following and a neighbourhood feel. Generous portions of hearty cooking; smaller tapas plates also popular.

at Box Northeast : 4.75 mi on A 4 - **Y** – ✉ Bath

🍺 The Northey
Bath Rd ✉ SN13 8AE – ℰ (01225) 742 333 – www.ohhcompany.co.uk
– Closed 25-26 December
Rest – Carte £ 22/30

♦ Traditional-looking, family-run stone coaching inn with open-plan interior, large dining room and vast bar. Appealing monthly menus feature unfussy, seasonal British dishes; fish is a strength.

BATH

at Colerne Northeast : 6.5 mi by A 4 - Y - Batheaston rd and Bannerdown Rd – ✉ Chippenham

Luckham Park
North : 0.5 mi on Marshfield rd ✉ SN14 8AZ – ☎ (01225) 742 777
– www.lucknampark.co.uk
36 rm – †£315 ††£495, 🍴 £22 – 5 suites
Rest *The Park* ❀ **Rest** *Brasserie* – see restaurant listing
♦ Grand Palladian mansion with tree-lined drive, rich décor, luxurious furnishings and sumptuous fabrics. Top class facilities include impressive spa complex and renowned equestrian centre. Extremely comfortable bedrooms.

The Park – at Lucknam Park Hotel
North : 0.5 mi on Marshfield rd ✉ SN14 8AZ – ☎ (01225) 742 777
– www.lucknampark.co.uk – Closed Sunday dinner
Rest – (dinner only and Sunday lunch) (booking essential) Menu £70
Spec. Poached langoustines, potato mousse, asparagus and caviar. Loin of lamb with crushed peas, morels and garlic. Cannelloni of lemon, summer berries and crème fraîche sorbet.
♦ Located within an impressive mansion, an opulent dining room with skilled, amiable service and a knowledgeable kitchen team. Classical menus display modern European influences, with dishes expertly crafted from locally sourced farm produce.

Brasserie – at Lucknam Park Hotel
North : 0.5 mi on Marshfield rd ✉ SN14 8AZ – ☎ (01225) 742 777
– www.lucknampark.co.uk – Closed 25-26 December and 1 January
Rest – Menu £21 (lunch) – Carte £33/53
♦ Linen-laid brasserie in state-of-the-art spa complex, boasting spacious bar-lounge and airy dining room with full-length windows. Precise, modern cooking in well-judged combinations; healthy options available. BBQs on the terrace in summer. Clued-up service.

at Monkton Combe Southeast : 4.5 mi by A 36 - Y – ✉ Bath

Wheelwrights Arms with rm
Church Ln ✉ BA2 7HB – ☎ (01225) 722 287 – www.wheelwrightsarms.co.uk
7 rm 🍴 – †£85/95 ††£150 **Rest** – Carte £22/30 **s**
♦ Charming 18C former carpenter's workshop in a sleepy little village, displaying exposed stone walls, parquet floors and open fires. Wide-ranging, traditional menus; mainly fish specials. Individually designed bedrooms are modern with rustic overtones.

at Combe Hay Southwest : 5 mi by A 367 – ✉ Bath

Wheatsheaf with rm
✉ BA2 7EG – ☎ (01225) 833 504 – www.wheatsheafcombehay.com – Closed 1 week January, 24-25 December, Sunday dinner and Monday except bank holidays
3 rm 🍴 – †£120 ††£150 **Rest** – Carte £23/37
♦ A modern take on the classical country pub; remotely set in a pretty village, with chic styling, open fires, comfy sofas and a relaxed atmosphere. Contemporary presentation of flavourful, seasonal dishes. Spacious, modern bedrooms boast a quality feel.

BATTLE – East Sussex – **504** V31 – pop. 5 190 🏴 Great Britain 8 B3

▶ London 55 mi – Brighton 34 mi – Folkestone 43 mi – Maidstone 30 mi
ℹ Battle and Bexhill TIC, Battle Abbey, High St ☎ (01424) 77 37 21, www.battle-sussex.co.uk
◉ Town★ – Abbey and Site of the Battle of Hastings★ **AC**

BATTLE

Nobles ✕✕
17 High St ⊠ TN33 0AE – ℰ *(01424) 774 422 –* www.noblesrestaurant.co.uk
– Closed Sunday dinner and bank holidays
Rest – Menu £ 15 (weekday lunch) – Carte £ 24/39
♦ Simple, tasteful eatery with terrace, in heart of historical high street. Regularly changing menus offer unfussy classical dishes of local, seasonal produce, with the occasional twist.

BAUGHURST – Hampshire   6 B1
▶ London 61 mi – Camberley 28 mi – Farnborough 27 mi

Wellington Arms
Baughurst Rd, Southwest : 0.5 mi ⊠ RG26 5LP – ℰ *(0118) 982 01 10*
– www.thewellingtonarms.com *– Closed Sunday dinner*
Rest *– (booking essential)* Menu £ 19 (weekday lunch) – Carte £ 18/34
♦ Smart, cream pub boasting its own pigs, chickens, bees, herb beds and vegetable gardens. Produce is strictly local and home-grown/reared/made. Blackboard menus feature 6 dishes per course, which are replaced as produce runs out. Cooking is generous and satisfying.

BEACONSFIELD – Buckinghamshire – 504 S29 – pop. 12 292   11 D3
▶ London 26 mi – Aylesbury 19 mi – Oxford 32 mi
🄱 Beaconsfield Seer Green, ℰ (01494) 67 65 45

Crazy Bear
73 Wycombe End ⊠ HP9 1LX – ℰ *(01494) 673 086*
– www.crazybeargroup.co.uk
10 rm – †£ 345 ††£ 430, ⚌ £ 19.50
Rest *Thai* **Rest** *English* – see restaurant listing
♦ Unique hotel with sumptuous, over-the-top style and plush, idiosyncratic furnishings. Moody, masculine bedrooms blend original features with rich fabrics and leather; copper baths fill from the ceiling. Flamboyant bars and Thai or English restaurant – with caviar and expensive wines, the sky's the limit.

English ✕✕ – at Crazy Bear Hotel
73 Wycombe End ⊠ HP9 1LX – ℰ *(01494) 673 086*
– www.crazybeargroup.co.uk
Rest *– (booking advisable)* Menu £ 19 (lunch) – Carte £ 31/59
♦ Lavishly styled restaurant in a truly theatrical hotel. Flamboyant, sumptuous furnishings and a unique, quirky style. Extensive menus rely on specialist suppliers and their own farm produce.

Thai ✕✕ – at Crazy Bear Hotel
73 Wycombe End ⊠ HP9 1LX – ℰ *(01494) 673 086 –* www.crazybeargroup.co.uk
Rest – Thai *– (dinner only) (booking essential)* Carte £ 29/36
♦ Chicly decorated hotel restaurant boasting chandeliers, flock wallpapers, snakeskin handrails and studded leather chairs. Thai dishes dominate although influences are drawn from all over Asia.

at Seer Green Northeast : 2.5 mi by A 355 – ⊠ Buckinghamshire

Jolly Cricketers
24 Chalfont Rd ⊠ HP9 2YG – ℰ *(01494) 676 308 – Closed 2 weeks January, Sunday dinner and Monday*
Rest *– (booking advisable)* Carte £ 23/39
♦ Charming Victorian pub filled with a host of cricketing memorabilia; even the menu is divided into 'Openers, Main Play and Lower Order'. Warming open fire and friendly staff. Appealing cooking pleasingly balances a selection of classics with more modern choices.

BEACONSFIELD

at Wooburn Common Southwest : 3.5 mi by A 40 – ✉ Beaconsfield

Chequers Inn
Kiln Ln, Southwest : 1 mi on Bourne End rd ✉ *HP10 0JQ* – ✆ *(01628) 529 575*
– *www.chequers-inn.com* – *Closed 25 December and 1 January*
17 rm – †£ 100 ††£ 108, ⌑ £ 9.95   **Rest** – Menu £ 18/26 – Carte £ 28/39
♦ Attractive 17C red-brick former inn: family-owned and run since 1975. Cosy beamed bar and spacious, leather-furnished lounge. Good-sized bedrooms boast flat screen TVs and wi-fi. Choice of bar snacks, or more ambitious dishes in the clothed rear restaurant.

BEAMHURST – Staffordshire – see Uttoxeter

BEAMINSTER – Dorset – 503 L31 – pop. 2 791   3 B3
▶ London 154 mi – Exeter 45 mi – Taunton 30 mi – Weymouth 29 mi
⛳ Chedington Court South Perrott, ✆ (01935) 89 14 13

BridgeHouse
3 Prout Bridge ✉ *DT8 3AY* – ✆ *(01308) 862 200* – *www.bridge-house.co.uk*
14 rm ⌑ – †£ 86/150 ††£ 180/215
Rest – Menu £ 25 (lunch) – Carte dinner £ 30/44
♦ Hugely characterful 13C former priest's house, with newer extensions. Traditionally furnished, flag-floored lounges boast inglenook fireplaces. Mix of classical and modern bedrooms. Linen-laid restaurant with conservatory and terrace offers brasserie-style menu.

Wild Garlic
4 The Square ✉ *DT8 3AS* – ✆ *(01308) 861 446* – *www.thewildgarlic.co.uk*
– *Closed 25-26 December, 1 January and Sunday-Tuesday*
Rest – *(booking essential)* Menu £ 22 (lunch) **s** – Carte £ 31/41 **s**
♦ Pretty, rustic restaurant in charming town; ask for a window table overlooking the square. Run by 2009 Masterchef winner, who is a keen forager. Appealing menu supplemented by blackboard specials.

BEARSTED – Kent – 504 V30 – see Maidstone

BEAULIEU – Hampshire – 503 P31 – pop. 726 – ✉ Brockenhurst   6 B2
▌Great Britain
▶ London 102 mi – Bournemouth 24 mi – Southampton 13 mi – Winchester 23 mi
◉ Town★★ - National Motor Museum★★ AC
◉ Buckler's Hard★ (Maritime Museum★ AC) SE : 2 m

Montagu Arms
Palace Ln ✉ *SO42 7ZL* – ✆ *(01590) 612 324* – *www.montaguarmshotel.co.uk*
18 rm ⌑ – †£ 140/160 ††£ 198 – 4 suites
Rest *The Terrace* ✿ **Rest** *Monty's Inn* – see restaurant listing
♦ Well-run 18C inn which boasts a characterful parquet-floored reception and wood-panelled lounge. Lovely rear gardens are overlooked by a wicker-furnished conservatory and paved terrace. Traditional country house style bedrooms successfully marry antique furniture with modern facilities. Good level of service.

The Terrace – at Montagu Arms Hotel
Palace Ln ✉ *SO42 7ZL* – ✆ *(01590) 612 324* – *www.montaguarmshotel.co.uk*
– *Closed Tuesday lunch and Monday*
Rest – Menu £ 25 (lunch) – Carte dinner £ 63/69
Spec. Cannelloni of braised rabbit with glazed spring vegetables and black pudding. Honey roast duck with smoked pecans, tamarind and date purée. Passion fruit and white chocolate cheesecake.
♦ Traditional country house dining room with wood-panelled lounge. Good-sized, linen-laid tables; polite, efficient service. Lovely garden outlook from terrace. Precisely prepared, top quality produce used in refined, classically based dishes with modern touches.

BEAULIEU

Monty's Inn – at Montagu Arms Hotel
Palace Ln ⊠ SO42 7ZL – ℰ (01590) 612 324 – www.montaguarmshotel.co.uk
Rest – Carte £ 25/38
• Set within a large red-brick inn in a pleasant town, an informal hotel restaurant serving home-cooked classics. Meats are free range and from nearby farms; eggs are from their own chickens.

BEELEY – Derbyshire – pop. 165   16 B1

▶ London 160 mi – Derby 26 mi – Matlock 5 mi

Devonshire Arms with rm
Devonshire Sq ⊠ DE4 2NR – ℰ (01629) 733 259 – www.devonshirebeeley.co.uk
8 rm ⊇ – †£ 114/134 ††£ 197/217   **Rest** – Carte £ 19/35
• Stone inn close to Chatsworth House and owned by the Estate. Rustic bar; modern extension with lovely views. Unusual starters followed by classics and daily 'market' dishes. Tasty afternoon teas. Beamed bedrooms in main house; larger, brighter rooms next door.

BELCHFORD – Lincolnshire – 502 T24 – ⊠ Horncastle   17 C1

▶ London 169 mi – Horncastle 5 mi – Lincoln 28 mi

Blue Bell Inn
1 Main Rd ⊠ LN9 6LQ – ℰ (01507) 533 602 – Closed 2 weeks mid-January
Rest – Carte £ 20/27
• A traditionally styled whitewashed pub, popular with walkers on the Viking Way. Numerous blackboard menus list sandwiches, pub favourites and more ambitious choices.

BELFORD – Northumberland – 501 O17 – pop. 1 177   24 A1

▶ London 335 mi – Edinburgh 71 mi – Newcastle upon Tyne 49 mi
▣ Belford South Rd, ℰ (01668) 21 33 23

Market Cross without rest
1 Church St ⊠ NE70 7LS – ℰ (01668) 213 013 – www.marketcross.net
4 rm ⊇ – †£ 50/80 ††£ 80/110
• 200 year-old stone house in rural town centre. Warmly decorated lounge, homely touches in tasteful bedrooms. Wide, locally inspired breakfast choice in cosy pine surroundings.

BELPER – Derbyshire – 502 P24 – pop. 21 938   16 B2

▶ London 141 mi – Birmingham 59 mi – Leicester 40 mi – Manchester 55 mi

at Shottle Northwest : 4 mi by A 517 – ⊠ Belper

Dannah Farm Country House without rest
Bowmans Lane, North : 0.25 mi by Alport rd ⊠ DE56 2DR
– ℰ (01773) 550 273 – www.dannah.co.uk – Closed 24-26 December
4 rm ⊇ – †£ 79/110 ††£ 165/210 – 4 suites
• Family-run converted farmhouse - part of a working farm. Spacious, contemporary bedrooms are diverse in style; the two level Studio suite includes hot tub and spiral staircase.

BENENDEN – Kent – 504 V30   8 B2

▶ London 55 mi – Croydon 49 mi – Barnet 81 mi – Ealing 85 mi

Ramsden Farm without rest
Dingleden Ln, Southeast : 1 mi by B 2086 ⊠ TN17 4JT – ℰ (01580) 240 203
– www.ramsdenfarmcottage.co.uk
3 rm ⊇ – †£ 70/120 ††£ 85/120
• Attractive clapperboard house with modern styling, a refreshingly relaxed air and fine countryside views. Spacious, up-to-date bedrooms; luxurious, modern bathrooms with underfloor heating.

BEPTON – West Sussex – see Midhurst

BERKHAMSTED – Hertfordshire – **504** S28 – pop. 18 800   12 A2
🟩 Great Britain

▶ London 34 mi – Aylesbury 14 mi – St Albans 11 mi

◉ Whipsnade Wild Animal Park★ **AC**, N : 9.5 mi on A 4251, B 4506 and B 4540

✕✕ The Gatsby   VISA ⦾ AE
97 High St ✉ HP4 2DG – ℰ (01442) 870 403 – www.thegatsby.net
– Closed 25-26 December
Rest – Menu £ 21 (lunch) – Carte £ 32/44

♦ Charming cinema built in 1938 and sympathetically converted to incorporate a trendy art deco bar and glamorous restaurant. Dine among elegant columns and ornate plasterwork. Menus offer detailed, classically based dishes with modern twists.

BERWICK-UPON-TWEED – Northumberland – **501** O16   24 A1
– pop. 13 031 🟩 Great Britain

▶ London 349 mi – Edinburgh 57 mi – Newcastle upon Tyne 63 mi

ℹ 106 Marygate ℰ (01289) 33 07 33, www.visitnorthumberland.com

⛳ Goswick, ℰ (01289) 38 72 56

⛳ Magdalene Fields, ℰ (01289) 30 61 30

◉ Town★★ - Walls★

◉ Foulden★, NW : 5 mi – Paxton House (Chippendale furniture★) **AC**, W : 5 mi by A 6105, A 1 and B 6461. St Abb's Head★★ (⇐★), NW : 12 mi by A 1, A 1107 and B 6438 - SW : Tweed Valley★★ – Eyemouth Museum★ **AC**, N : 7.5 mi by A 1 and A 1107 – Holy Island★ (Priory ruins★ **AC**, Lindisfarne Castle★ **AC**), SE : 9 mi by A 1167 and A 1 – Manderston★ (stables★), W : 13 mi by A 6105 - Ladykirk (Kirk o'Steil★), SW : 8.5 mi by A 698 and B 6470

✕ 1 Sallyport with rm   📶 VISA ⦾ AE ⓘ
1 Sallyport, off Bridge St ✉ TD15 1EZ – ℰ (01289) 308 827
– www.sallyport.co.uk
6 rm ⊇ – †£ 85 ††£ 150   **Rest** – Carte £ 19/31 **s**

♦ Pair of listed 17C houses on a cobbled alley, in the older part of town. All-day café-cum-bistro with cake and pastry counter. Bright, modern restaurant with vivid fabrics and polished tables. Daily changing menus have a classical base. Funky, boutique bedrooms feature interesting modern artwork and extras.

BEVERLEY – East Riding of Yorkshire – **502** S22 – pop. 29 110   23 D2
– ✉ Kingston-Upon-Hull 🟩 Great Britain

▶ London 188 mi – Kingston-upon-Hull 8 mi – Leeds 52 mi – York 29 mi

ℹ 34 Butcher Row ℰ (01482) 86 74 30, www.yorkshire.com

⛳ The Westwood, ℰ (01482) 86 87 57

◉ Town★ - Minster★★ – St Mary's Church★

⌂ Burton Mount without rest   🚗 ⌀ P VISA ⦾
Malton Rd, Cherry Burton , Northwest : 2.75 mi by A 164, B 1248 on Leconfield rd
✉ HU17 7RA – ℰ (01964) 550 541 – www.burtonmount.co.uk
5 rm ⊇ – †£ 64 ††£ 91

♦ Homely, red-brick house overlooking large, mature gardens. Dining room boasts French windows opening onto the terrace. Comfy bedrooms display heavy fabrics and dark wood furniture. Good breakfasts; dinners of well sourced local produce cooked on the Aga.

✕✕ Whites with rm   VISA ⦾
12a North Bar Without ✉ HU17 7AB – ℰ (01482) 866 121
– www.whitesrestaurant.co.uk – Closed 1 week Christmas, 1 week August, Sunday and Monday
4 rm ⊇ – †£ 100 ††£ 125
Rest – (booking advisable) Menu £ 18/28 – Carte dinner £ 33/37

♦ Small, friendly restaurant beside the old city walls, its plain décor contrasting nicely with black wood tables and eye-catching glass art. Good value weekday set menu uses lesser-known cuts; à la carte offers more complex dishes. Smart, modern bedrooms, some with bespoke furniture; rooftop terrace breakfast.

BEVERLEY

at Tickton Northeast : 3.5 mi by A 1035 – ✉ Kingston-Upon-Hull

Tickton Grange
✉ HU17 9SH – ✆ (01964) 543 666 – www.beverleyticktongrange.co.uk
21 rm ⊆ – †£ 95 ††£ 140
Rest *Champagne* – Menu £ 25/35
◆ Warm, welcoming, family-run hotel. Bedrooms blend Georgian and contemporary architecture, and display antique and period-inspired furniture. Richly swagged fabrics and open fires in an inviting lounge. Dine in Georgian style; large bay windows look onto the lawn.

at South Dalton Northwest : 5 mi by A 164 and B 1248 – ✉ Beverley

Pipe and Glass Inn (James Mackenzie) with rm
West End ✉ HU17 7PN – ✆ (01430) 810 246
– www.pipeandglass.co.uk – Closed 2 weeks January,
25 December, Sunday dinner and Monday except bank holidays
2 rm – †£ 140 ††£ 160   **Rest** – Carte £ 34/45
Spec. Wild rabbit, langoustine and Jerusalem artichoke crumble, pickled girolle salad. Rump of lamb with a 'Hotch Potch' of spring vegetables, pearl barley and crispy mutton belly. Lemon verbena posset, East Yorkshire sugar cakes
◆ Warm, bustling and inviting pub, personally run by experienced owners. Generous portions of carefully executed, flavourful cooking with judicious use of local, seasonal and traceable produce. Luxury, designer bedrooms boast all mod cons and have their own patios overlooking estate woodland. Breakfast served in bedrooms.

ENGLAND

BEYTON – Suffolk – **504** W27 – see Bury St Edmunds

BIBURY – Gloucestershire – **503** O28 – pop. 570 – ✉ Cirencester   **4 D1**
▌ Great Britain
▶ London 86 mi – Gloucester 26 mi – Oxford 30 mi
◉ Village ★

Swan
✉ GL7 5NW – ✆ (01285) 740 695 – www.cotswold-inns-hotels.co.uk/swan
18 rm ⊆ – †£ 140/200 ††£ 160/280 – 4 suites
Rest *Café Swan* – see restaurant listing
Rest *Gallery* – (dinner only) Menu £ 33 – Carte £ 28/35
◆ Ivy-clad former coaching inn with private garden and trout stream, set in a delightful village. Cosy lounges and clubby, leather-furnished bar. Mix of cottagey character and contemporary touches in bedrooms; the best are in the annexes, opt for a duplex suite. Choice of formal restaurant or relaxed brasserie.

Café Swan – at Swan Hotel
✉ GL7 5NW – ✆ (01285) 740 695 – www.cotswold-inns-hotels.co.uk/swan
Rest – Carte £ 28/35
◆ Set in a delightful Cotswold village, a relaxed, modern brasserie within a 17C coaching inn. Lovely flagstone courtyard complete with water fountain. Menu of light bites and brasserie dishes.

Cotteswold House without rest
Arlington, on B 4425 ✉ GL7 5ND – ✆ (01285) 740 609
– www.cotteswoldhouse.net
3 rm ⊆ – †£ 55 ††£ 75
◆ Set in a pleasant garden outside the picturesque village. Homely, spotless and modestly priced bedrooms, comprehensively remodelled behind a Victorian façade. Friendly, welcoming owner.

BIDDENDEN – Kent – **504** V30 – pop. 2 205 ▌ Great Britain   **9 C2**
▶ London 52 mi – Ashford 13 mi – Maidstone 16 mi
◉ Bodiam Castle ★★, S : 10 mi by A 262, A 229 and B 2244 – Sissinghurst Garden ★,
W : 3 mi by A 262 – Battle Abbey ★, S : 20 mi by A 262, A 229, A 21 and A 2100

79

BIDDENDEN

Barclay Farmhouse without rest
Woolpack Corner, South : 0.5 mi by A 262 on Benenden rd ✉ TN27 8BQ
– ℰ (01580) 292 626 – www.barclayfarmhouse.co.uk
3 rm ☑ – †£ 65 ††£ 90

♦ Set in an acre of pleasant garden: well-priced, very comfortable accommodation with fine French oak flooring and furniture. Inventive breakfasts in the barn conversion.

West House (Graham Garrett)
28 High St ✉ TN27 8AH – ℰ (01580) 291 341
– www.thewesthouserestaurant.co.uk – Closed Christmas-New Year, 2 weeks summer, Saturday lunch, Sunday dinner and Monday
Rest – Menu £ 25/38
Spec. Grilled calves tongue, salt-baked beetroot and smoked anchovy dressing. Slow-cooked pork belly, sherry soaked prunes, cauliflower and chorizo. White chocolate and honeycomb parfait with dark chocolate sorbet.

♦ Pretty part-16C former weavers' cottages in picturesque village. Charming beamed interior with inglenook and modern artwork. Concise seasonal menu; confident and technically skilled cooking allows the ingredients to shine.

The Three Chimneys
Hareplain Rd, West : 1.5 mi by A 262 ✉ TN27 8LW – ℰ (01580) 291 472
– www.thethreechimneys.co.uk – Closed 25 and dinner 31 December
Rest – (booking essential) Carte £ 25/36

♦ Delightful pub with charming terrace and garden, dating back to 1420 and boasting a roaring fire, dimly lit low-beamed rooms and an old world feel. Largely British dishes and nursery puddings.

BIGBURY – Devon – 503 I33   2 C3
▶ London 195 mi – Exeter 41 mi – Plymouth 22 mi
◉ Kingsbridge★, E : 13 mi by B 3392 and A 379

Oyster Shack
Milburn Orchard Farm, Stakes Hill, East : 1 mi on Easton rd ✉ TQ7 4BE
– ℰ (01548) 810 876 – www.oystershack.co.uk – Closed 3 January-2 February
Rest – Seafood – (booking essential) Carte £ 30/35

♦ Eccentric venue; half a lovely covered terrace, decorated with fishing nets. Seafood, particularly local oyster dishes; classic and modern dishes using the freshest produce.

BIGBURY-ON-SEA – Devon – 503 I33 – pop. 600 – ✉ Kingsbridge   2 C3
▶ London 196 mi – Exeter 42 mi – Plymouth 23 mi

Burgh Island
South : 0.5 mi by sea tractor ✉ TQ7 4BG – ℰ (01548) 810 514
– www.burghisland.com
15 rm (dinner included) ☑ – †£ 300/460 ††£ 620 – 10 suites
Rest – (dinner only and Sunday lunch) (booking essential for non-residents) Menu £ 60

♦ Unique Grade II listed 1930s country house in private island setting: stylishly romantic art deco interior. Charmingly individual rooms with views: some have fantastic style. Ballroom dining: dress in black tie. Owners pride themselves on accomplished cooking.

Henley
Folly Hill ✉ TQ7 4AR – ℰ (01548) 810 240 – www.thehenleyhotel.co.uk
– April-October
5 rm ☑ – †£ 80 ††£ 144
Rest – (dinner only) (booking essential for non-residents) Menu £ 36

♦ Charming hotel with superb views over Burgh Island and Bolt Tail. Homely lounge, wicker-furnished conservatory and comfy bedrooms that cross New England and English Country styles; Room 2 boasts double-aspect views. Concise, unfussy dinners use local ingredients.

BILDESTON – Suffolk – 504 W27   15 C3
▶ London 85 mi – Bury St Edmunds 18 mi – Ipswich 15 mi

※※ **Bildeston Crown** with rm
104 High St ⊠ IP7 7EB – ℰ (01449) 740 510 – www.thebildestoncrown.co.uk
– Closed dinner 25-26 December and 1 January
12 rm ⊇ – ♦£ 70/150 ♦♦£ 150/250
Rest – Menu £ 24 (lunch) – Carte £ 33/45
♦ Old beamed inn with lovely courtyard. Stylish, modern interior with 2 bars, a smart lounge and formal restaurant; warm colours and open fires feature. Choose from classics, an ambitious à la carte or tasting menu. Elaborate, artistic cooking. Luxurious bedrooms boast bold colours, designer furniture and chic bathrooms.

BIRKENHEAD – Merseyside – 502 K23 – pop. 83 729   20 A3
▶ London 222 mi – Liverpool 2 mi
Access Mersey Tunnels (toll)
⛴ to Liverpool and Wallasey (Mersey Ferries) frequent services daily
⛳ Arrowe Park Woodchurch, ℰ (0151) 677 15 27
⛳ Prenton Golf Links Rd, ℰ (0151) 609 34 26

Plan : see Liverpool p. 3

※※※ **Fraiche** (Marc Wilkinson)
❀ 11 Rose Mount, Oxton, Southwest : 2.25 mi by A 552 and B 5151 ⊠ CH43 5SG
– ℰ (0151) 652 29 14 – www.restaurantfraiche.com – Closed 25 December, 1-7 July, Monday and Tuesday
Rest – (dinner only and lunch Friday-Saturday) (booking essential)
Menu £ 27/65
Spec. Arctic char, yuzu jelly and watermelon. Anjou pigeon, textures of artichoke and pickled mushrooms. Rhubarb and celery sorbet, vanilla mousse and wild strawberries.
♦ Stylish, sophisticated restaurant displaying interesting glass friezes. Choice of 3 set menus. Creative, modern dishes use excellent quality ingredients from around the globe. Unusual combinations; impressive presentation. Knowledgeable, personable service.

ENGLAND

BIRMINGHAM

See city maps on following pages

19 C2

West Midlands – pop. 942 766 – 503 O26 – 504 O26 – Great Britain

London 122 – Bristol 91 – Liverpool 103 – Manchester 86

Tourist Information

150 New St ℘(0121) 202 50 00, www.visitbirmingham.com

Airport

Birmingham International Airport : ℘(0844) 576 6000, E : 6 ½ m. by A 45 DU

Golf Courses

Edgbaston Church Rd, ℘(0121) 454 17 36

Hilltop Handsworth Park Lane, ℘(0121) 554 44 63

Hatchford Brook Sheldon Coventry Rd, ℘(0121) 743 98 21

SIGHTS

In the town : City★ • Museum and Art Gallery★★ LYM2 • Barber Institute of Fine Arts★★ EXU

On the outskirts : Aston Hall★★ FVM

In the surrounding area : Black Country Museum★, Dudley, NW : 10 mi by A 456 and A 4123 AU • Bournville★, SW : 4 mi on A 38 and A 441

INDEX OF STREET NAMES IN BIRMINGHAM

Addison Rd . . . . **FX**
Albert St . . . . **MY** 2
Alcester Rd . . . . **FX**
Aldridge Rd . . . . **FV**
Alum Rock Rd . . . . **GV**
Aston Church Rd . . . . **GV**
Aston Expressway . . . . **FV**
Aston Lane . . . . **FV**
Aston St . . . . **MY**
Bath Row . . . . **KZ**
Bearwood Rd . . . . **EV**
Birchfield Rd . . . . **FV**
Bishopsgate St . . . . **KZ**
Booth St . . . . **EV**
Bordesley Green . . . . **GV**
Bordesley Green Rd . . . . **GV**
Boulton Rd . . . . **EV**
Bowyer Rd . . . . **GV**
Bradford Rd . . . . **HV**
Brindley Pl. . . . . **KZ**
Bristol Rd . . . . **EFX**
Bristol St. . . . . **LZ**
Broad St . . . . **KLZ**
Bromford Lane . . . . **GV**
Bromford Rd. . . . . **HV**
Brookvale Rd. . . . . **FV**
Brook Lane . . . . **GX**
Browning St. . . . . **JZ**
Bull Ring Centre. . . . . **MZ**
Bull St. . . . . **MY** 3
Calthorpe Rd . . . . **FX** 14
Cambridge St . . . . **KYZ** 8
Camden St . . . . **JKY**
Camp Hill . . . . **FX** 15
Cape Hill . . . . **EV**
Caroline St. . . . . **KLY**
Carver St . . . . **KY**
Cattell Rd . . . . **GV**
Centenary Square. . . . . **KZ**
Chapel St . . . . **MY** 30
Charlotte St . . . . **KLY**
Chester Rd . . . . **HV**
Church Lane . . . . **EV**
Church Rd EDGBASTON. . . . **FX**
Church Rd SHELDON . . . . . **HX**
Church Rd YARDLEY. . . . . . . **HX**
Church St . . . . **LY**
City Rd. . . . . **EV**
Clement St . . . . **KY**
Coleshill Rd. . . . . **HV**
College Rd . . . . **GX**
Colmore Circus . . . . **MY**
Colmore Row . . . . **LY**
Commercial St. . . . . **LZ**
Constitution Hill . . . . **LY**
Cope St . . . . **JY**
Corporation St. . . . . **FV** 20
Court Oak Rd . . . . **EX**
Coventry Rd . . . . **GHX**
Cox St. . . . . **LY**
Cregoe St . . . . **LZ**
Dale End. . . . . **MY** 21
Darmouth Middleway . . . . . **FV** 22
Digbeth . . . . **FV** 24
Dudley Park Rd . . . . **GX** 25
Dudley Rd . . . . **EV**
Edgbaston Rd . . . . **FX**
Edgbaston Shopping Centre . . **JZ**
Edmund St. . . . . **LY**
Eyre St . . . . **JY**
Fiveways . . . . **JZ**
Fiveways Shopping Centre . . **KZ**
Fordhouse Lane . . . . **FX**
Fox Hollies Rd . . . . **GX**
Francis Rd . . . . **JZ**
Frederick St. . . . . **KY**
Freeth St . . . . **JY**
George St . . . . **KY**
George St West . . . . **JY** 19
Gilby Rd . . . . **JZ**
Golden Hillock Rd . . . . **GX**
Graham St. . . . . **KY**

Granville St . . . . **KLZ**
Gravelly Hill. . . . . **GV**
Great Charles St . . . . **LY**
Great Tindal St . . . . **JZ** 18
Grosvenor St West . . . . **JKZ**
Haden Way . . . . **FX**
Hagley Rd . . . . **JZ**
Hall St . . . . **KY** 29
Hampstead Rd . . . . **FV**
Harborne Lane . . . . **EX**
Harborne Park Rd . . . . **EX**
Harborne Rd . . . . **EX**
Heath St . . . . **EV**
Highfield Rd . . . . **GX**
Highfield Rd SALTLEY. . . . . . **GV**
Highgate Rd . . . . **FX**
High St . . . . **MZ**
High St ASTON. . . . . **FV**
High St BORDESLEY . . . . . . **FX**
High St HARBORNE . . . . **EX**
High St KING'S HEATH . . . . **FX**
High St SALTLEY. . . . . **GV** 31
High St SMETHWICK . . . . . . **EV**
Hill St . . . . **LZ**
Hob's Moat Rd. . . . . **HX**
Hockley Circus . . . . **FV**
Holliday St . . . . **KLZ**
Holloway Circus . . . . **LZ** 32
Holloway Head . . . . **LZ**
Holyhead Rd . . . . **EV**
Horse Fair . . . . **LZ** 29
Hurst St . . . . **MZ**
Icknield Port Rd. . . . . **EV**
Icknield St . . . . **JKY**
Island Rd . . . . **EV**
Islington Row Middleway . . . **KZ** 34
James Watt Queensway . . . . **MY** 35
Jennen's Rd. . . . . **MY** 36
Kingsbury Rd . . . . **HV**
King Edwards Rd . . . . **JY** 98
Ladywell Walk . . . . **MZ** 37
Ladywood Circus . . . . **JZ**
Ladywood Middleway . . . . . **JYZ**
Ladywood Rd . . . . **JZ**
Lancaster Circus . . . . **MY** 39
Lancaster St. . . . . **MY** 41
Lawley St. . . . . **FV** 40
Ledseam St . . . . **JYZ**
Lee Bank Middleway . . . . . . **FX** 42
Legge Lane . . . . **KY** 52
Lichfield Rd . . . . **FV**
Linden Rd . . . . **EX**
Livery St . . . . **LY**
Lodge Rd. . . . . **EV**
Lordswood Rd . . . . **EX**
Lozells Rd. . . . . **FV**
Ludgate Hill . . . . **LY**
Martineau Place Shopping
  Centre . . . . **MY**
Masshouse Circus . . . . **MY**
Metchley Lane . . . . **EX**
Minories Shopping
  Centre . . . . **MY**
Moat Lane . . . . **MZ** 44
Moor St Queensway . . . . . **MYZ** 46
Morville St . . . . **JZ** 65
Moseley Rd. . . . . **FX**
Navigation St . . . . **LZ** 49
Nechell's Parkway . . . . **FV** 50
Newhall Hill . . . . **KY** 69
Newhall St. . . . . **MY**
Newport Rd . . . . **HV**
Newton St. . . . . **MY** 53
New John St West . . . . **FV**
New St . . . . **LMZ**
New Town Row . . . . **FV** 54
Norfolk Rd . . . . **EX**
Nursery Rd . . . . **EX** 55
Oak Tree Lane. . . . . **EX**
Olton Bd East. . . . . **GX**
Oxhill Rd . . . . **EV**
Paradise Circus . . . . **LYZ** 56

Paradise Forum Shopping
  Centre . . . . **LYZ**
Park St . . . . **MYZ**
Pershore Rd . . . . **FX**
Pershore St . . . . **MZ**
Portland Rd . . . . **EV**
Princip St . . . . **MY**
Priory Queensway. . . . . **MY** 59
Priory Rd . . . . **FX**
Rabone Lane. . . . . **EV**
Richmond Rd . . . . **HX**
Robin Hood Lane . . . . **GX**
Rolfe St . . . . **EV**
Rookery Rd . . . . **FV**
Rotton Park Rd . . . . **EV**
Ruston St. . . . . **JZ**
Ryland St . . . . **JKZ**
St. Chads Queensway . . . . . **MY** 63
St Paul's Square. . . . . **LY**
St Vincent St . . . . **JKZ**
St Vincent St West . . . . **JZ**
St Chads Circus . . . . **LY** 62
St Marks Crescent. . . . . **JY**
St Martin's Circus . . . . **MZ** 64
Salisbury Rd . . . . **FX**
Saltley Rd . . . . **GV** 66
Sandon Rd . . . . **EV**
Sandy Lane . . . . **FX** 10
Sand Pits Parade. . . . . **KY**
Severn St . . . . **LZ**
Shadwell St . . . . **LMY** 70
Shaftmoor Lane . . . . **GX**
Sheaf Lane . . . . **HX**
Sheepcote St . . . . **KZ**
Sheldon Heath Rd . . . . **HX**
Shirley Rd . . . . **GX**
Smallbrook Queensway . . . **LMZ** 71
Small Heath Highway . . . . . **GX**
Snow Hill Queensway . . . . **LMY** 73
Soho Rd. . . . . **EV**
Solihull Lane . . . . **GX** 74
Spring Hill. . . . . **JY**
Spring Hill Circus . . . . **JY**
Station Rd . . . . **HV**
Stechford Lane. . . . . **HV**
Steelhouse Lane . . . . **MY**
Stockfield Rd . . . . **GX**
Stoney La. MOSELEY. . . . . . **GX**
Stoney La. YARDLEY. . . . . . . **HX**
Stour St . . . . **JY**
Stratford Rd . . . . **GX**
Suffolk St . . . . **LZ**
Summer Hill Rd . . . . **JKY** 76
Summer Hill St . . . . **KY** 93
Summer Row . . . . **KY** 77
Temple Row . . . . **MY** 80
The Row . . . . **MZ**
Tyburn Rd . . . . **GHV**
Vicarage Rd . . . . **FX**
Victoria Rd . . . . **FV**
Victoria Square. . . . . **LZ**
Villa Rd . . . . **FV**
Wagon Lane . . . . **HX**
Wake Green Rd . . . . **FX**
Warstone Lane . . . . **KY**
Warwick Rd . . . . **GX**
Washwood Heath Rd . . . . . . **GV**
Waterloo St . . . . **LY** 84
Watery Lane . . . . **FV** 85
Wellington Rd . . . . **FV**
Westfield Rd . . . . **EX**
Westley Rd. . . . . **GX** 87
Wheeley's Lane . . . . **KZ** 88
Whittall St. . . . . **MY**
William St . . . . **KZ** 97
Winson Green Rd. . . . . **EV**
Witton Lane . . . . **FV**
Witton Rd . . . . **FV**
Wood End Rd. . . . . **GV**
Wyse St. . . . . **KY**
Yardley Rd. . . . . **HX**
Yardley Wood Rd. . . . . **GX**

ENGLAND

BIRMINGHAM AND WOLVERHAMPTON

Ablewell St	CT	2
Bilston Rd	BT	3
Cape Hill	CU	6
Dudley Rd	CU	8
Dudley St	BT	12
Harborne Park Rd	CU	33
Merry Hill	AU	
New Rd	BT	19
North High St	DT	21
Wednesbury Rd	BT	27
Wellington Rd	AT	29

85

BIRMINGHAM

Calthorpe Rd	FX 14
Camp Hill	FX 15
Corporation St	FV 20
Darmouth Middleway	FV 22
Digbeth	FV 24
Dudley Park Rd	GX 25
High St SALTLEY	GV 31
Jennen's Rd	FV 36
Lawley St	FV 40
Lee Bank Middleway	FX 42
Nechell's Parkway	FV 50
New Town Row	FV 54
Nursery Rd	EX 55
Saltley Rd	GV 66
Sandy Lane	FX 10
Solihull Lane	GX 74
Watery Lane	FV 85
Westley Rd	GX 87

87

Street	Ref	Street	Ref	Street	Ref
Albert St	MY 2	George St West	JY 19	Ladywell Walk	MZ 37
Bull Ring Centre	MZ	Great Tindal St	JZ 18	Lancaster Circus	MY 39
Bull St	MY 3	Hall St	KY 29	Lancaster St	MY 41
Cambridge St	KYZ 8	Holloway Circus	LZ 32	Legge Lane	KY 52
Chapel St	MY 30	Horse Fair	LZ 28	Martineau Place Shopping Centre	MY
Corporation St	MYZ	Islington Row Middleway	KZ 34	Minories Shopping Centre	MY
Dale End	MY 21	James Watt Queensway	MY 35	Moat Lane	MZ 44
Edgbaston Shopping Centre	JZ	Jennen's Rd.	MY 36	Moor St Queensway	MYZ 46
Fiveways Shopping Centre	KZ	King Edwards Rd	JY 98		

Street	Grid Ref		Street	Grid Ref		Street	Grid Ref
Morville St	JZ 65		Priory Queensway	MY 59		Summer Hill Rd	JKY 76
Navigation St	LZ 49		St. Chads Queensway	MY 63		Summer Hill St	KY 93
Newhall Hill	KY 69		St Chads Circus	LY 62		Summer Row	KY 77
Newton St	MY 53		St Martin's Circus	MZ 64		Temple Row	MY 80
New St	LMZ		Shadwell St	LMY 70		Waterloo St	LY 84
Paradise Circus	LYZ 56		Smallbrook Queensway	LMZ 71		Wheeley's Lane	KZ 88
Paradise Forum Shopping Centre	LYZ		Snow Hill Queensway	LMY 73		William St	KZ 97

BIRMINGHAM

Hyatt Regency
2 Bridge St ⊠ B1 2JZ – ℰ (0121) 643 12 34
– www.birmingham.regency.hyatt.com
KZ**a**
315 rm – †£ 95/219 ††£ 95/219, ⊆ £ 18 – 4 suites
Rest *Aria* – Menu £ 15 (weekday lunch)/20 – Carte £ 25/41

• Striking mirrored exterior. Glass enclosed lifts offer panoramic views. Sizeable rooms with floor to ceiling windows. Covered link with International Convention Centre. Contemporary style restaurant in central atrium; modish cooking.

Malmaison
Mailbox, 1 Wharfside St ⊠ B1 1RD – ℰ (0121) 246 50 00
– www.malmaison.com
LZ**e**
184 rm – †£ 150/180 ††£ 150/295, ⊆ £ 15 – 1 suite
Rest *Brasserie* – see restaurant listing

• One of the few new-build Malmaisons, set next to designer clothes and homeware shops on the site of the old Royal Mail sorting office. Contemporary, dark-hued bedrooms; the suite has a mini-cinema. Small spa offers good range of treatments.

Hotel Du Vin
25 Church St ⊠ B3 2NR – ℰ (0121) 200 06 00 – www.hotelduvin.com
66 rm – †£ 99/170 ††£ 99/170, ⊆ £ 14.50
LY**e**
Rest *Bistro* – see restaurant listing

• Characterful former eye hospital in a relaxed, boutique style. Richly hued bedrooms named after wine companies and estates; one suite boasts an 8 foot bed, 2 roll-top baths and a gym. Small cellar bar/pub and comfy Bubble Bar for champagne.

Mint
1 Brunswick Sq, Brindley Pl ⊠ B1 2HW – ℰ (0121) 643 10 03
– www.minthotel.com
KZ**b**
238 rm – †£ 225 ††£ 225, ⊆ £ 14
Rest *City Café* – ℰ (0121) 633 63 00 – Menu £ 15/20 – Carte £ 24/33

• In heart of vibrant Brindley Place; the spacious atrium with bright rugs and blond wood sets the tone for equally stylish bedrooms. Corporate friendly with many meeting rooms. Eat in restaurant, terrace or bar.

Simpsons (Andreas Antona) with rm
20 Highfield Rd, Edgbaston ⊠ B15 3DU – ℰ (0121) 454 34 34
– www.simpsonsrestaurant.co.uk – Closed 25-26 December and bank holidays
4 rm – †£ 160 ††£ 225
EX**e**
Rest – Contemporary – *(closed Sunday dinner)* Menu £ 35/38
– Carte £ 47/54

Spec. Seared scallops, lime beurre noisette and borage. Fillet of Aberdeenshire beef, braised short rib. Macaé chocolate and praline mousse.

• Smart Georgian mansion with stylish lounges, pleasant garden terrace and summer house. Tables are well-spaced; service is formal and efficient. Classical menu displays Mediterranean influences, contemporary twists and excellent produce. Spacious bedrooms boast French country styling.

Purnell's (Glynn Purnell)
55 Cornwall St ⊠ B3 2DH – ℰ (0121) 212 97 99 – www.purnellsrestaurant.com
– Closed 1-14 August, 1 week Easter, 1 week Christmas, Saturday lunch,
Sunday and Monday
LY**b**
Rest – Modern – Menu £ 26/46

Spec. Poached egg yolk with smoked haddock, cornflakes, milk foam and curry oil. Daube of beef, English lettuce and leeks, fondue of leeks and crème fraîche. Warm dark chocolate mousse and torte, mango sorbet.

• Passionately run, stylish restaurant in sizeable red-brick property with large lounge. Refined and modern cooking displays plenty of original and individual touches. The tasting menus are particularly innovative in style.

Opus

54 Cornwall St ✉ B3 2DE – ℘ (0121) 200 2323 – www.opusrestaurant.co.uk
– Closed 24 December-early January, Saturday lunch, Sunday and bank holidays
Rest – Modern – Menu £ 25 – Carte £ 30/42   LY**z**

♦ Set in the heart of the financial district; its name means 'hard work'. Floor-to-ceiling windows, cocktail bar and chef's table. Daily changing modern menus of precisely prepared, wholesome dishes.

Asha's

12-22 Newhall St ✉ B3 3LX – ℘ (0121) 200 27 67 – www.ashasuk.co.uk – Closed lunch Saturday and Sunday   LY**m**
Rest – Indian – Menu £ 13/25 – Carte £ 26/48

♦ Smart restaurant with delightful décor and vivid artwork. Owned by renowned artiste/gourmet Asha Bhosle. Authentic North West Indian cuisine cooked by chefs originally from that region.

Edmunds

6 Central Sq, Brindley Pl ✉ B1 2JB – ℘ (0121) 633 49 44
– www.edmundsrestaurant.co.uk – Closed 1 week January, 1 week April, 2 weeks summer, Saturday lunch, Sunday and Monday   KZ**x**
Rest – Modern European – Menu £ 20/43

♦ Formal restaurant in heart of city. Smart interior with neutral décor and modern lighting. Immaculately laid tables boast fine china and glassware. Smart, attentive staff.

Carters of Moseley

2c St Mary's Row, Wake Green Rd ✉ B13 9EZ – ℘ (0121) 449 8885
– www.cartersofmoseley.co.uk – Closed 26-31 December, 31 July-16 August, Sunday dinner and Monday   FX**a**
Rest – (booking advisable) Menu £ 18 (lunch and early dinner)
– Carte £ 32/47 **s**

♦ Smart suburban conversion with dark banquette seating, black ash tables, large wine wall and neighbourhood bistro feel. Modern British cooking relies largely on Cornish ingredients; afternoon tea – on Saturdays – is done very well.

Turners (Richard Turner)

69 High St, Harborne ✉ B17 9NS – ℘ (0121) 426 44 40
– www.turnersofharborne.com – Closed Sunday and Monday   EX**a**
Rest – Modern – (booking essential) Menu £ 30/60
Spec. Confit leg and rillette of rabbit, crayfish and vanilla. Roast veal, sweetbreads, cheek and white asparagus. Strawberry Arctic roll.

♦ Neat neighbourhood restaurant in suburban parade, with wood panels, etched mirrors and velvet chairs. Menus offer refined, flavoursome dishes of accomplished, classical cooking with modern touches; only tasting menus are offered Saturday night. Formal, structured service.

Loves

The Glasshouse, Canal Sq ✉ B16 8FL – ℘ (0121) 454 51 51
– www.loves-restaurant.co.uk – Closed 2 weeks January, 2 weeks Easter, 2 weeks August, Sunday and Monday   JZ**a**
Rest – Inventive – Menu £ 25/43

♦ Situated on the ground floor of an apartment block on the canal basin, with spacious, contemporary interior and smartly laid tables. Cooking uses modern techniques and presentation.

Lasan

3-4 Dakota Buildings, James St, St Pauls Sq ✉ B3 1SD – ℘ (0121) 212 36 64
– www.lasangroup.com – Closed 25 December and Saturday lunch
Rest – Indian – Carte £ 40/56   KY**a**

♦ Jewellery quarter restaurant of sophistication and style; good quality ingredients allow the clarity of the spices to shine through in this well-run Indian establishment.

BIRMINGHAM

XX **Bank**
4 Brindley Pl ⊠ B1 2JB – ℰ *(0121) 633 44 66 – www.bankrestaurants.com*
– Closed 26 December and 1 January
KZu
Rest – Modern – Menu £ 15 (lunch and early dinner) – Carte £ 27/39
♦ Well-run, contemporary bar-restaurant. Striking glass squares hang from the dining room ceiling, its full-length windows overlooking the canal and terrace. Eclectic seasonal menu with weekly specials and influences from Asia and the Med.

XX **Bistro** – at Hotel Du Vin
25 Church St ⊠ B3 2NR – ℰ *(0121) 200 06 00 – www.hotelduvin.com*
Rest – French – Carte £ 21/34
LYe
♦ Classically styled hotel restaurant in striking 19C former eye hospital. Walls are filled with wine-related memorabilia and there's a hidden courtyard. French bistro menu; extensive wine list.

XX **Brasserie** – at Malmaison Hotel
Mailbox, 1 Wharfside St ⊠ B1 1RD – ℰ *(0121) 246 50 00 – www.malmaison.com*
Rest – British – Menu £ 18 (lunch) – Carte £ 29/41
LZe
♦ Bustling hotel brasserie that's particularly popular with lunchtime shoppers and local workers. Simple, rustic British menu. Private dining and wine tasting rooms ideal for corporate clients.

> Undecided between two equivalent establishments in the same town? Within each category, establishments are classified in our order of preference: the best first.

BISHOP'S STORTFORD – Hertfordshire – 504 U28 – pop. 35 325   12 B2
▌ Great Britain
▶ London 34 mi – Cambridge 27 mi – Chelmsford 19 mi – Colchester 33 mi
✈ Stansted Airport : ℰ (0844) 3351803, NE : 3.5 m
ℹ 2 Market Square ℰ (01279) 65 58 31, www.bishopsstortford.org
◉ Audley End★★ **AC**, N : 11 mi by B 1383

X **Lemon Tree**
14-16 Water Ln ⊠ CM23 2LB – ℰ *(01279) 757 788 – www.lemontree.co.uk*
– Closed 25-27 December, 1 January, Sunday dinner and bank holidays
Rest – Menu £ 20 (weekday dinner) – Carte £ 27/46
♦ Friendly little restaurant in a 200 year old house, hidden in the town centre. Characterful interior with comfy bar-lounge and several beamed dining areas. Seasonal menus offer a good choice of unfussy, classical dishes; good value lunch.

BISHOPSTONE – Swindon – 503 P29 – see Swindon

BLACKBURN – Blackburn with Darwen – 502 M22 – pop. 105 085   20 B2
▶ London 228 mi – Leeds 47 mi – Liverpool 39 mi – Manchester 24 mi
ℹ 50-54 Church St ℰ (01254) 68 80 40, www.visitblackburn.co.uk
⛳ Pleasington, ℰ (01254) 20 21 77
⛳ Wilpshire 72 Whalley Rd, ℰ (01254) 24 82 60
⛳ Great Harwood Harwood Bar, Whalley Rd, ℰ (01254) 88 43 91

🍴 **Clog & Billycock**
Billinge End Rd, Pleasington, West : 2 mi by A 677 ⊠ BB2 6QB
– ℰ *(01254) 201 163 – www.theclogandbillycock.com – Closed 25 December*
Rest – Carte £ 20/33
♦ Spacious, modern, open-plan pub. Extensive menus offer plenty of choice and display a strong Lancastrian slant; cooking is rustic and generous. Most produce is sourced from within 20 miles.

BLACKBURN

at Langho North : 4.5 mi on A 666 – ✉ Whalley

Northcote (Nigel Haworth) with rm
Northcote Rd, North : 0.5 mi on A 59 at junction with A 666 ✉ BB6 8BE
– ℰ (01254) 240 555 – www.northcote.com – Closed 25 December
14 rm ⌑ – †£ 185/225 ††£ 220/270
Rest – Menu £ 25 (weekday lunch) – Carte £ 42/66 ℬℬ
Spec. Roast halibut with Lancashire cheese fondue and bacon tempura. New season's lamb with asparagus, tomato and a mint relish. Roast pineapple and Eccles cake ice cream
♦ Smartly refurbished restaurant in red-brick Victorian house. Traceability and food miles are all-important to this team, with regional ingredients and local suppliers the stars of the show; some produce travelling only a few metres from their own organic gardens. Elegant, contemporary bedrooms boast designer touches.

at Mellor Northwest : 3.25 mi by A 677 – ✉ Blackburn

Stanley House
Southwest : 0.75 mi by A 677 and Further Lane ✉ BB2 7NP – ℰ (01254) 769 200
– www.stanleyhouse.co.uk
12 rm ⌑ – †£ 155/180 ††£ 185/285
Rest *Grill on the Hill* – (closed Sunday dinner and Monday) (dinner only and Sunday lunch) Carte £ 25/44
♦ Attractive 17C manor house boasting superb countryside views and stylish, individually designed bedrooms; some featuring original beams or mullioned windows. Old farmhouse building houses the function rooms, a casual bar-lounge and terrace. Grill restaurant affords great views over the grounds to the coast.

Millstone
Church Ln ✉ BB2 7JR – ℰ (01254) 813 333 – www.millstonehotel.com
22 rm ⌑ – †£ 99 ††£ 125 – 1 suite **Rest** – Carte £ 25/34
♦ Attractive sandstone former coaching inn set in a quiet village. Pub-style bar with log fire and comfy sofas. Cosy, well-kept bedrooms have matching floral patterns and good modern facilities. Traditional wood-panelled dining room offers accessible menu.

BLACKPOOL – Blackpool – **502** K22 – pop. 142 283 🟩 Great Britain   **20** A2

▶ London 246 mi – Leeds 88 mi – Liverpool 56 mi – Manchester 51 mi
✈ Blackpool Airport : ℰ (0844) 4827171, S : 3 mi by A 584
🛈 1 Clifton St ℰ (01253) 47 82 22, www.visitblackpool.com
⛳ Blackpool Park North Park Drive, ℰ (01253) 39 79 16
⛳ Poulton-le-Fylde Breck Rd, Myrtle Farm, ℰ (01253) 89 24 44
◉ Tower★ **AC** AY **A**

Plan on next page

Number One South Beach
4 Harrowside West ✉ FY4 1NW – ℰ (01253) 343 900
– www.numberonehotels.com   BZ**v**
13 rm ⌑ – †£ 81/145 ††£ 125/155 – 1 suite
Rest – (dinner only and Sunday lunch) Carte £ 21/27
♦ Modernised hotel set back off promenade. Contemporary interior with stylish, boldly coloured bedrooms; two with four-posters. Superb bathrooms boast whirlpool baths and TVs. Interesting menus are largely made up of free range, organic and fair trade produce.

Number One St Lukes without rest
1 St Lukes Rd ✉ FY4 2EL – ℰ (01253) 343 901 – www.numberoneblackpool.com
3 rm ⌑ – †£ 70/120 ††£ 100/130   AZ**a**
♦ Engagingly run, enticingly stylish guesthouse. The good value nature of the establishment is further enhanced by an elegant breakfast room and luxuriously appointed bedrooms.

BLACKPOOL

Abingdon St.	AY	2
Adelaide St	AY	3
Ansdell Rd	BZ	4
Blackpool Old Rd	BY	5
Burlington Rd West	AZ	6
Caunce St	AY	7
Central Drive	BZ	
Cherry Tree Rd	BZ	9
Church St	AY	
Clifton St	AY	12
Condor Grove	BZ	13
Cookson St	AY	14
Deansgate	AY	15
Garstang Rd West	BY	16
George St	AY	17
Grange Rd	BY	19
Grasmere Rd	BZ	20
Grosvenor St	AY	21
High St	AY	22
Hornby Rd	BY	
Hounds Hill Centre	AY	
King St	AY	23
Lark Hill St	AY	24
New Bonny St	AY	25
North Park Drive	BY	26
Pleasant St	AY	27
Plymouth Rd	BZ	28
Poulton Rd	BY	29
Queen's Promenade	BY	
Reads Ave	BZ	32
Rigby Rd	BZ	33
Seaside Way	BZ	34
South King St	AY	35
South Park Drive	BZ	36
Talbot Square	AY	39
Topping St	AY	40
Westcliffe Drive	BY	41

94

at Thornton Northeast : 5.5 mi by A 584 - BY - on B 5412 – ✉ Blackpool

Twelve
VISA ☉ AE

Marsh Mill, Fleetwood Rd North, North : 0.5 mi on A 585 ✉ FY5 4JZ – ✆ (01253) 821 212 – www.twelve-restaurant.co.uk – Closed first 2 weeks January and Monday
Rest – (dinner only and Sunday lunch) Menu £ 28 – Carte £ 30/48
♦ Spacious restaurant where brick walls, exposed pipework and grey beams contribute to a slightly industrial feel. Passionately run by dynamic owner and friendly team. Good value menus offer interesting, well-executed modern dishes with the odd innovative touch.

BLAKENEY – Norfolk – **504** X25 – pop. 1 628 – ✉ Holt   15 C1

▶ London 127 mi – King's Lynn 37 mi – Norwich 28 mi

Blakeney
The Quay ✉ NR25 7NE – ✆ (01263) 740 797 – www.blakeneyhotel.co.uk
63 rm (dinner included) – †£ 134/219 ††£ 292/318
Rest – (closed to non-residents 24-28 December dinner and 31 December-1 January) Menu £ 28 – Carte lunch £ 20/25
♦ Traditional, privately owned hotel in a great quayside location, affording views over the estuary and salt marshes. Various comfortable lounges and bar with subtle modern touches. Individually designed bedrooms, some with balconies or sea views. Formal dining room offers good outlook and a wide-ranging menu.

Blakeney House without rest
High St ✉ NR25 7NX – ✆ (01263) 740 561 – www.blakeneyhouse.com
– Closed Christmas and 1 week early January
8 rm – †£ 80/95 ††£ 120/150
♦ Substantial Victorian house tucked away in a tranquil spot on the High Street. Spacious, individually decorated, up-to-date bedrooms. Pleasant breakfast room with garden views.

Moorings
AC VISA ☉

High St ✉ NR25 7NA – ✆ (01263) 740 054 – www.blakeney-moorings.co.uk
– Closed 3 weeks January, Tuesday-Thursday November-March, Sunday except bank holidays and Monday dinner
Rest – (light lunch) (booking essential) Carte £ 26/36
♦ Bright village bistro near the quayside, offering popular light lunches. Classical dinner menu boasts unfussy, seasonal dishes, including game and local seafood. Tasty puddings.

White Horse with rm
4 High St ✉ NR25 7AL – ✆ (01263) 740 574 – www.blakeneywhitehorse.co.uk
– Closed 25 December
9 rm – †£ 50/80 ††£ 70/140   **Rest** – (booking advisable) Carte £ 20/34
♦ Brick and flint former coaching inn set by the harbour. Traditional, hearty pub favourites on lunch menu. Evening à la carte features seasonal dishes and some interesting combinations. Modern bedrooms come in various shapes and sizes.

at Cley next the Sea East : 1.5 mi on A 149 – ✉ Holt

Cley Windmill
The Quay ✉ NR25 7RP – ✆ (01263) 740 209 – www.cleywindmill.co.uk
8 rm – †£ 189 ††£ 189
Rest – (dinner only) (booking essential to non residents) Menu £ 33
♦ Restored 18C redbrick windmill in salt marshes with a viewing gallery: a bird-watcher's paradise. Neatly kept rooms, full of character, in the mill, stable and boatshed. Flagstoned dining room; communal table.

BLAKENEY

at Wiveton South : 1 mi by A149 on Wiveton Rd

Wiveton Bell with rm
Blakeney Rd ⊠ *NR25 7TL –* ℰ *(01263) 740 101 – www.wivetonbell.com – Closed 25 December*
4 rm ⊑ – †£ 90/140 ††£ 90/140   **Rest** – *(booking essential)* Carte £ 21/29
♦ Characterful pub with colourful garden; surrounded by salt marshes and nature reserves. Comfy, modern bar and airy conservatory. Menus offer traditional British dishes with some international influences. Charming bedrooms come with a tuck-box for breakfast in bed.

at Morston West : 1.5 mi on A 149 – ⊠ Holt

Morston Hall (Galton Blackiston)
The Street ⊠ *NR25 7AA –* ℰ *(01263) 741 041 – www.morstonhall.com*
– Closed 1-27 January and 24-26 December
13 rm (dinner included) ⊑ – †£ 200/230 ††£ 350/380
Rest – *(dinner only and Sunday lunch) (booking essential) (set menu only)*
Menu £ 60
Spec. Ox tongue and broad bean purée with petit pois and shallot jus. Canon of lamb with sweetbreads and wild garlic jus. Black cherry sorbet with morello consommé, nougatine and pistachios.
♦ Attractive country house with manicured gardens and antique-filled guest areas. Annexed bedrooms are largest, most luxurious and display subtle contemporary touches. Formal 4 course daily menu offers well-balanced, local, seasonal dishes. Cooking is classical, sophisticated and exhibits a delicate, modern touch.

BLANDFORD FORUM – Dorset – 503 N31 – pop. 9 854   4 C3

▶ London 124 mi – Bournemouth 17 mi – Dorchester 17 mi – Salisbury 24 mi
🛈 1 Greyhound Yard ℰ (01258) 45 47 70, www.visit-dorset.org.uk
🏌 Ashley Wood Wimbourne Rd, ℰ (01258) 45 22 53
◉ Town ★
⦿ Kingston Lacy ★★ **AC**, SE : 5.5 mi by B 3082 – Royal Signals Museum ★, NE : 2 mi by B 3082. Milton Abbas ★, SW : 8 mi by A 354 – Sturminster Newton ★, NW : 8 mi by A 357

Portman Lodge without rest
Whitecliff Mill St ⊠ *DT11 7BP –* ℰ *(01258) 453 727 – www.portmanlodge.co.uk*
– Closed 2 weeks spring and Christmas
3 rm ⊑ – †£ 60 ††£ 70
♦ Red-brick guesthouse boasting many original Victorian features. Guest areas display artefacts from the owners' travels. Plush breakfast room or terrace dining in summer. Classical bedrooms.

at Farnham Northeast : 7.5 mi by A 354 – ⊠ Blandford Forum

Farnham Farm House without rest
North : 1 mi by Shaftesbury rd ⊠ *DT11 8DG –* ℰ *(01725) 516 254 – www.farnhamfarmhouse.co.uk – Closed 25-26 December*
3 rm ⊑ – †£ 70 ††£ 90
♦ Attractive farmhouse in peaceful location. Homely, individually furnished bedrooms with country views. Swimming pool and therapy centre on site. Breakfast features local produce; picnics available.

Museum Inn with rm
⊠ *DT11 8DE –* ℰ *(01725) 516 261 – www.museuminn.co.uk*
8 rm ⊑ – †£ 110 ††£ 165   **Rest** – *(bookings not accepted)* Carte £ 30/34
♦ Part-thatched 17C country pub, in a picture postcard village. Menu offers British classics with a Mediterranean edge; cooking is seasonal, unfussy and local. Bedrooms range from small and cottagey, to spacious with a four-poster.

BLEDINGTON – Gloucestershire – 503 P28 – see Stow-on-the-Wold

BLETSOE – Bedford – **504** S27   **12** A1

▶ London 65 mi – Croydon 102 mi – Barnet 54 mi – Ealing 63 mi

Bourne End Farm without rest
North : 1.5 mi by A 6 on Bourne End rd ✉ MK44 1QS – ✆ (01234) 783 184
– www.bourneendfarm.co.uk
3 rm – †£ 60/80 ††£ 85/90
♦ Spotless house in over 400 acres of arable farmland; comfortable, simply furnished bedrooms with showers; cosy lounge and charming hosts. Communal farm breakfast in dining room.

BLOCKLEY – Gloucestershire – **503** O27 – pop. 1 668   **4** D1
– ✉ Moreton-In-Marsh

▶ London 91 mi – Birmingham 39 mi – Oxford 34 mi

Lower Brook House
Lower St ✉ GL56 9DS – ✆ (01386) 700 286 – www.lowerbrookhouse.com
– Closed 16-27 December
6 rm – †£ 80/190 ††£ 80/190
Rest – (closed Sunday) (dinner only) Carte £ 25/33
♦ Personally run, adjoining 17C Cotswold stone cottages with large inglenooks, exposed beams and flagged floors. Hugely characterful and stylish from every aspect. Individually appointed bedrooms take on a more contemporary style. Imaginative evening menus of local Cotswold produce.

BODIAM – East Sussex – **504** V30 🇬🇧 Great Britain   **8** B2

▶ London 58 mi – Cranbrook 7 mi – Hastings 13 mi
◉ Castle ★★
◉ Battle Abbey ★, S : 10 mi by B 2244, B 2089, A 21 and minor rd – Rye ★★, SW : 13 mi by A 268

Curlew
Junction Rd, Northwest : 1.5 mi at junction with B 2244 ✉ TN32 5UY
– ✆ (01580) 861 394 – www.thecurlewrestaurant.co.uk – Closed 2 weeks January and Monday
Rest – British – Menu £ 21 (lunch) – Carte £ 29/35
Spec. Double-baked cheese soufflé. Jacob's ladder, beef dripping potatoes and coleslaw. Douglas fir pine parfait, chocolate sorbet.
♦ Stylish restaurant with laid-back lounge, cow motif wallpaper and bespoke leather banquettes. Concise British menu offers accomplished, classically based dishes, interpreted in modern ways. Preparation is careful, execution is precise and presentation is appealing.

BODMIN – Cornwall – **503** F32 – pop. 12 778   **1** B2

▶ London 270 mi – Newquay 18 mi – Plymouth 32 mi – Truro 23 mi
ℹ Mount Folly ✆ (01208) 7 66 16, www.bodminlive.com
◉ St Petroc Church ★
◉ Bodmin Moor ★★ – Lanhydrock ★★, S : 3 mi by B 3269 – Blisland ★ (Church ★), N : 5.5 mi by A 30 and minor roads – Pencarrow ★, NW : 4 mi by A 389 and minor roads – Cardinham (Church ★), NE : 4 mi by A 30 and minor rd – St Mabyn (Church ★), N : 5.5 mi by A 389, B 3266 and minor rd. St Tudy ★, N : 7 mi by A 389, B 3266 and minor rd

Trehellas House
Washaway, Northwest : 3 mi on A 389 ✉ PL30 3AD – ✆ (01208) 72 700
– www.trehellashouse.co.uk
12 rm – †£ 47/76 ††£ 75/180
Rest – (closed Monday lunch) Menu £ 15 (lunch) – Carte £ 26/38 **s**
♦ Relaxed, personally run country house with keen owners. Bedrooms divided between main house and converted stable. Cosy and cottagey feel without being chintzy. Traditional cooking; venison a speciality.

Bokiddick Farm without rest

Lanivet, South : 5 mi by A 30 following signs for Lanhydrock and Bokiddick
✉ PL30 5HP – ℘ (01208) 831 481 – www.bokiddickfarm.co.uk – *Closed Christmas*
5 rm – †£ 45/50 ††£ 70/80

◆ Traditional farmhouse on a working dairy farm, where you are guaranteed a very warm welcome. Homely, spotlessly kept bedrooms with fridges – 3 in the main house; 2 larger rooms in the old barn. Hearty breakfasts taken overlooking the garden. Cream tea on arrival.

BOLNHURST – Bedford   12 A1

▶ London 64 mi – Bedford 8 mi – St Neots 7 mi

Plough at Bolnhurst
Kimbolton Rd, South : 0.5 mi on B 660 ✉ MK44 2EX – ℘ (01234) 376 274
– www.bolnhurst.com – *Closed 2 weeks January, Sunday dinner and Monday*
Rest – Menu £ 19/25 – Carte £ 27/37

◆ Smart, cosy whitewashed pub with rustic bar, modern restaurant, lovely garden and bustling atmosphere. Menus change with the seasons but always feature a 28-day aged Aberdeenshire steak selection, strong Mediterranean influences and good old fashioned puddings.

BOLTON ABBEY – North Yorkshire – 502 O22 – pop. 117   22 B2
– ✉ Skipton ▮ Great Britain

▶ London 216 mi – Harrogate 18 mi – Leeds 23 mi – Skipton 6 mi

◉ Bolton Priory★ **AC**

Devonshire Arms Country House
✉ BD23 6AJ – ℘ (01756) 710 441
– www.devonshirehotels.co.uk
38 rm (dinner included) – †£ 206/249 ††£ 249/332 – 2 suites
Rest *Burlington* ❀ **Rest** *Brasserie* – see restaurant listing

◆ Fine period coaching inn, with antique-furnished guest areas and vast art collection. Compact bedrooms in extension, recently refurbished in bright, contemporary country house style. Refurbishment to continue in main house. Good spa and leisure. Smooth service.

Burlington – at Devonshire Arms Country House Hotel
✉ BD23 6AJ – ℘ (01756) 710 441
– www.devonshirehotels.co.uk – *Closed Monday*
Rest – *(dinner only and Sunday lunch) (booking essential)* Menu £ 65
Spec. Scallops with celeriac and smoked eel. Lamb with broccoli purée, goat's cheese and tomato. Caramelised apple with blackcurrant sorbet and Calvados cream.

◆ Elegant, antique-filled dining room with polished tables and oil paintings. Structured, formal service. Ambitious, creative cooking captures modern trends; elaborate dishes are artistically presented, displaying the chef's obvious passion.

Brasserie – at Devonshire Arms Country House Hotel
✉ BD23 6AJ – ℘ (01756) 710 710
– www.devonshirehotels.co.uk
Rest – Carte £ 23/31

◆ A contrast to the restaurant in atmosphere and design. This is a modern, vividly decorated brasserie; the kitchen produces carefully prepared, satisfying brasserie favourites.

BOLTON-BY-BOWLAND – Lancashire – 502 M/N22 ▮ Great Britain   20 B2

▶ London 246 mi – Blackburn 17 mi – Skipton 15 mi

◉ Skipton - Castle★, E : 12 mi by A 59 – Bolton Priory★, E : 17 mi by A 59

BOLTON-BY-BOWLAND

Middle Flass Lodge
Settle Rd, North : 2.5 mi by Clitheroe rd on Settle rd ✉ BB7 4NY
– ☎ (01200) 447 259 – www.middleflasslodge.co.uk
7 rm ⚏ – †£ 45/52 ††£ 68/75 **Rest** – Menu £ 30
♦ Friendly, welcoming owners in a delightfully located barn conversion. Plenty of beams add to rustic effect. Pleasantly decorated, comfy rooms with countryside outlook. Blackboard's eclectic menu boasts local, seasonal backbone.

BONCHURCH – Isle of Wight – **504** P32 – see Wight (Isle of)

BORDON – Hampshire   **504** R 30
▶ London 54 mi – Croydon 57 mi – Barnet 67 mi – Ealing 49 mi

Groomes
Frith End, North : 2.75 mi by A 325 on Frith End Sand Pit rd ✉ GU35 0QR
– ☎ (01420) 489 858 – www.groomes.co.uk
7 rm ⚏ – †£ 90 ††£ 150 **Rest** – Carte £ 28/39
♦ Former farmhouse set in 185 acres, with lawned gardens and wood-furnished terrace. Good-sized bedrooms boast modern facilities; some have free-standing roll-top baths. Two tables of six for communal dining; set menus of home-cooked dishes make use of local produce.

BOREHAM – Essex – **504** V27 – see Chelmsford

BOROUGHBRIDGE – North Yorkshire – **502** P21 – pop. 3 311   **22** B2
▶ London 215 mi – Leeds 19 mi – Middlesbrough 36 mi – York 16 mi
🛈 2 Fishergate ☎ (01423) 323 3 73, www.boroughbridge.org.uk

thediningroom
20 St James's Sq ✉ YO51 9AR – ☎ (01423) 326 426
– www.thediningroomonline.co.uk – Closed 26 December, 1 January, Sunday dinner and Monday
Rest – (dinner only and Sunday lunch) (booking essential) Menu £ 30
♦ Characterful, bow-fronted cottage with courtyard terrace. Modern lounge-bar and intimate beamed restaurant. Set price menu offers hearty, boldly flavoured, Mediterranean-influenced dishes.

at Roecliffe West : 1 mi

Crown Inn with rm
✉ YO51 9LY – ☎ (01423) 322 300 – www.crowninnroecliffe.com – Closed Sunday dinner
4 rm ⚏ – †£ 82/97 ††£ 114/120 **Rest** – Carte £ 25/30
♦ Smart 16C inn with stylish country interior, set by a delightful village green. Good-sized menus offer a nice balance of meat and fish, and a dedicated 'meat free' selection. Well-chosen wine list. Smart bedrooms with antique-style furnishings and feature beds.

BOSCASTLE – Cornwall – **503** F31   **1** B2
▶ London 260 mi – Bude 14 mi – Exeter 59 mi – Plymouth 43 mi
◉ Village ★
◉ Poundstock Church ★ – Tintagel Old Post Office ★

Boscastle House without rest
Tintagel Rd, South : 0.75 mi on B 3263 ✉ PL35 0AS – ☎ (01840) 250 654
– www.boscastlehouse.com – Closed 2 weeks Christmas
6 rm ⚏ – †£ 90 ††£ 120
♦ Modern styling in a detached Victorian house. Bedrooms are light and spacious, with roll-top baths and walk-in showers. Hearty breakfasts, cream teas and a calm, relaxing air.

BOSCASTLE

⌂ **Trerosewill Farm** without rest
Paradise, South : 1 mi off B 3263 ✉ *PL35 0BL* – ✆ *(01840) 250 545*
– *www.trerosewill.co.uk* – *April-September*
9 rm ⌂ – †£ 58/82 ††£ 92/108
♦ Modern guesthouse on 50 acre working farm, affording fine views of the coast and close to good clifftop walks. Conservatory breakfast room. Bedrooms in matching patterns, some with jacuzzis.

⌂ **Old Rectory** without rest
St Juliot, Northeast : 2.5 mi by B 3263 ✉ *PL35 0BT* – ✆ *(01840) 250 225*
– *www.stjuliot.com* – *Restricted opening in winter*
4 rm ⌂ – †£ 35/70 ††£ 80/98
♦ Lovely house with beautiful Victorian walled garden, originally built for the rector of St Juliot's church. Characterful bedrooms; one with a courtyard, another with a four-poster. Breakfasts use garden produce. Thomas Hardy once stayed.

BOSHAM – West Sussex – 504 R31 – see Chichester

BOSTON SPA – West Yorkshire – 502 P22 – pop. 5 952   22 B2

▶ London 127 mi – Harrogate 12 mi – Leeds 12 mi – York 16 mi

⌂ **Four Gables** without rest
Oaks Ln, West : 0.25 mi by A 659 ✉ *LS23 6DS* – ✆ *(01937) 845 592*
– *www.fourgables.co.uk* – *Closed Christmas-New Year*
4 rm ⌂ – †£ 60 ††£ 83/93
♦ Down a quiet private road, a Grade II listed Arts and Crafts house with period fireplaces, stripped oak and terracotta tile floors. Traditional, individually decorated rooms. Manicured garden.

Guesthouses ⌂ don't provide the same level of service as hotels. They are often characterised by a warm welcome and a décor which reflects the owner's personality. Those shown in red ⌂ are particularly pleasant.

BOUGHTON MONCHELSEA – Kent – pop. 2 863   8 B2

▶ London 46 mi – Southend-on-Sea 60 mi – Basildon 48 mi – Maidstone 4 mi

XX **Mulberry Tree**
Hermitage Lane, South : 1.5 mi by Park Lane and East Hall Hill ✉ *ME17 4DA*
– ✆ *(01622) 749 082* – *www.themulberrytreekent.co.uk* – *Closed first 2 weeks January, Sunday dinner and Monday*
Rest – Menu £ 18 (weekdays) – Carte £ 28/35
♦ Remotely located restaurant with stylish bold design, smart bar, large terrace and screened kitchen footage. Modern British menus provide a good choice of confidently prepared, accomplished dishes crafted from well-sourced ingredients.

BOURN – Cambridgeshire – 504 T27 – pop. 1 764   14 A3

▶ London 58 mi – Croydon 87 mi – Barnet 44 mi – Ealing 57 mi

ID **Willow Tree**
29 High St ✉ *CB23 2SQ* – ✆ *(01954) 719 775* – *www.thewillowtreebourn.com*
Rest – Carte £ 18/38
♦ Quirky pub with life-sized cow model in the garden and gilt mirrors, chandeliers and Louis XV style furniture inside. Menus range from old pub classics to much more ambitious modern dishes.

BOURNEMOUTH – Bournemouth – 503 O31 – pop. 158 955   4 D3

▶ London 114 mi – Bristol 76 mi – Southampton 34 mi
✈ Bournemouth (Hurn) Airport : ℰ (01202) 364000, N : 5 mi by Hurn - DV
🛈 Westover Rd ℰ (0845) 0 51 17 00, www.bournemouth.co.uk
⛳ Queens Park Queens Park West Drive, ℰ (01202) 30 26 11
⛳ Meyrick Park Central Drive, ℰ (01202) 78 60 00
👁 Compton Acres★★ (English Garden ⩽★★★) **AC** AX – Russell-Cotes Art Gallery and Museum★★ **AC** DZ **M1** - Shelley Rooms **AC** EX **M2**
🌍 Poole★, W : 4 mi by A 338 – Brownsea Island★ (Baden-Powell Stone ⩽★★) **AC**, by boat from Sandbanks BX or Poole Quay – Christchurch★ (Priory Church★) E : 4.5 mi on A 35. Corfe Castle★, SW : 18 mi by A 35 and A 351 – Lulworth Cove★ (Blue Pool★) W : 8 mi of Corfe Castle by B 3070 – Swanage★, E : 5 mi from Corfe Castle by A 351

Plans on following pages

🏨 Bournemouth Highcliff Marriott
St Michael's Rd, West Cliff ✉ *BH2 5DU*
– ℰ *(01202) 557 702 – www.bournemouthhighcliffmarriott.co.uk*   CZ**z**
157 rm – †£ 150 ††£ 170 – 3 suites
Rest *Highcliff Grill* – see restaurant listing
• Set on the clifftop, this grand old seaside hotel has a funicular linking it directly to the beach. Smart guest areas and airy modern bedrooms; some with lovely sea views. Leisure club boasts a tennis court and indoor and outdoor pools.

🏨 Miramar
19 Grove Rd, East Overcliff ✉ *BH1 3AL* – ℰ *(01202) 556 581*
– *www.miramar-bournemouth.com*   DZ**u**
43 rm (dinner included) – †£ 52/111 ††£ 104/212 **Rest** – Menu £ 19/31
• Along the handsome lines of a grand Edwardian villa, with award winning gardens. Large, well-cared for bedrooms – a few with curved balconies – have bright, modern décor. Pleasant sun terrace faces the sea. Dining room offers a good outlook and a traditional menu.

🏨 Green House
4 Grove Rd ✉ *BH1 3AX* – ℰ *(01202) 498 900 – www.thegreenhousehotel.com*
32 rm – †£ 99/180 ††£ 155/240   DZ**n**
Rest *Green Room* – see restaurant listing
• Bright, eco-friendly hotel, set in a small Victorian property and run by an enthusiastic team. Contemporary interior features reclaimed and eco-furnishings, including chairs made from old video game consoles and vegetable ink wallpapers.

🏠 Urban Beach
23 Argyll Rd ✉ *BH5 1EB* – ℰ *(01202) 301 509 – www.urbanbeach.co.uk*
12 rm – †£ 72 ††£ 174/180 **Rest** – Carte £ 28/37   DX**a**
• Laid-back hotel with large decked terrace, set close to the beach and town. Unremarkable exterior hides spacious designer bedrooms and stylish, luxury bathrooms. Small reception is located in the trendy bar/bistro. Large menu of modern classics and steaks.

XXX Highcliff Grill – at Bournemouth Highcliff Marriott Hotel
St Michael's Rd, West Cliff ✉ *BH2 5DU* – ℰ *(01202)*
557 702 – www.bournemouthhighcliffmarriott.co.uk   CZ**z**
Rest – *(dinner only and Sunday lunch)* Carte £ 27/49 **s**
• Stylish grill restaurant set within a landmark hotel on the clifftop and offering superb sea views. Modern steak and seafood orientated menu; dishes arrive well-presented and in a modern vein.

XX Edge
2 Studland Rd, (4th Floor) ✉ *BH4 8JA* – ℰ *(01202) 757 007*
– *www.edgerestaurant.co.uk*   CX**s**
Rest – Carte £ 30/44
• Stylish, trendy restaurant on top floor of apartment block, with floor to ceiling windows and excellent views. Seafood-based menu; modern dishes styled on classic combinations.

BOURNEMOUTH AND POOLE

Street	Ref
Archway Rd	BX 2
Banks Rd	BX 4
Boscombe Overcliff Rd	EX 6
Boscombe Spa Rd	DX 7
Branksome Wood Rd	CY 9
Chessel Ave	EX 10
Clarendon Rd	CX 13
Commercial Rd	CY 13
Compton Ave	BX 14
Cranleigh Rd	EV 16
Durley Rd	CZ 17
Ensbury Park Rd	CV 19
Exeter Rd	CDZ 20
Fernside Rd	ABX 21
Fir Vale Rd	DY 23
Gervis Pl	DY 24
Gloucester Rd	EV 26
Hampshire Centre	DV
Hinton Rd	DZ 27
Lansdowne Rd	DY 30
Lansdowne (The)	DY 28
Leven Ave	CX 31
Longfleet Rd	BX 32
Madeira Rd	DY 34
Manor Rd	EY 35
Meyrick Rd	EYZ 36
Old Christchurch Rd	DY
Old Wareham Rd	BV 39
Parkstone Rd	BX 40
Pinecliff Rd	CX 42
Post Office Rd	CY 43
Priory Rd	CZ 45
Queen's Rd	CX 46
Richmond Hill	CY 47
Richmond Park Rd	DV 48
Russell Cotes Rd	DZ 49
St Michael's Rd	CZ 51
St Paul's Rd	EY 52
St Peter's Rd	DY 53
St Stephen's Rd	CY 55
St Swithuns Rd South	EV 56
Seabourne Rd	EV 57
Seamoor Rd	CY 58
Sea View Rd	BV 59
Southbourne Grove	EX 61
Southbourne Overcliff Drive	EX 62
Sovereign Shopping Centre	EX
Square (The)	CY 63
Suffolk Rd	CY 64
Surrey Rd	CY 66
Triangle (The)	CY 67
Upper Hinton Rd	DZ 68
Wessex Way	CY 70
Western Rd	CX 73
Westover Rd	DZ 75
West Cliff Promenade	CZ 71

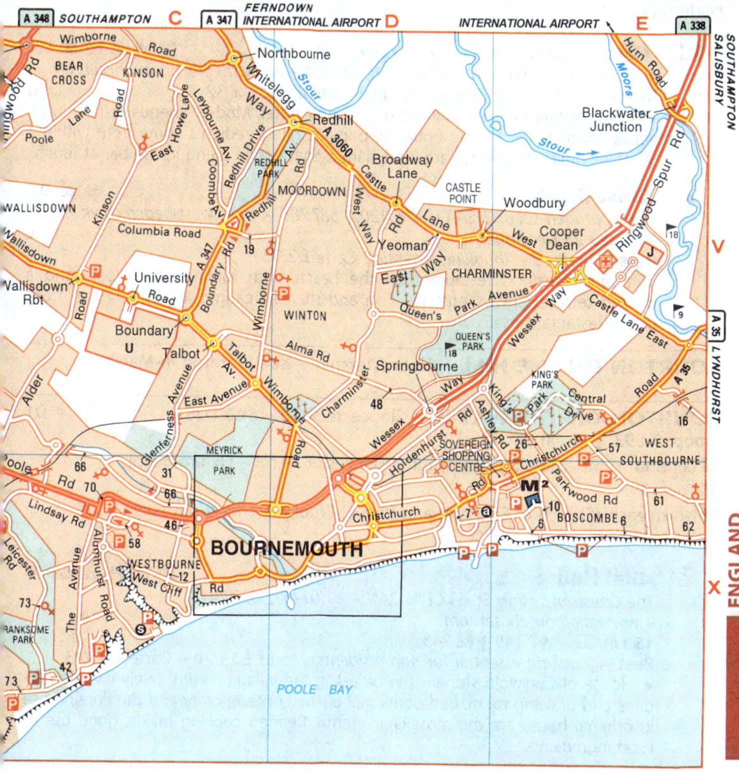

A 348 SOUTHAMPTON
C
A 347
FERNDOWN INTERNATIONAL AIRPORT
D
INTERNATIONAL AIRPORT
E
A 338
SOUTHAMPTON SALISBURY
Wimborne Road
BEAR CROSS
KINSON
Northbourne
Whitelegg Way
Stour
Moors
Hurn Road
Blackwater Junction
Stour
Redhill
A 3060
Poole Lane
Road
East Howe Lane
Leybourne Av.
Redhill Drive
REDHILL PARK
Broadway Lane
Castle Rd
CASTLE POINT
Woodbury
Spur Rd
Ringwood
WALLISDOWN
Kinson
Coombe Av.
Redhill
MOORDOWN
West Way
Yeoman
Lane
West
Cooper Dean
Columbia Road
Wallisdown
19
Wimborne
East Way
CHARMINSTER
V
Wallisdown Rbt
University Road
A 347
Boundary Rd
WINTON
Queen's Park Avenue
Wessex Way
Castle Lane East
Road
Boundary
U
Talbot
Talbot Av.
Alma Rd
QUEEN'S PARK
A 35
LYNDHURST
Alder
Avenue
East Avenue
Wimborne Road
Charminster
Springbourne
Way
KING'S PARK
King's Park
Central Drive
Road
A 35
16
48
Glenferness
Wessex
Ashley Rd
Holdenhurst Rd
SOVEREIGN SHOPPING CENTRE
26
Christchurch
57
WEST SOUTHBOURNE
MEYRICK PARK
Poole Rd
66
70
31
66
Lindsay Rd
Leicester Rd
Alumhurst Road
The Avenue
58
46
Christchurch
7
M²
10
Parkwood Rd
BOSCOMBE
61
6
62
BOURNEMOUTH
WESTBOURNE
West Cliff Rd
12
73
BRANKSOME PARK
42
73
X
POOLE BAY

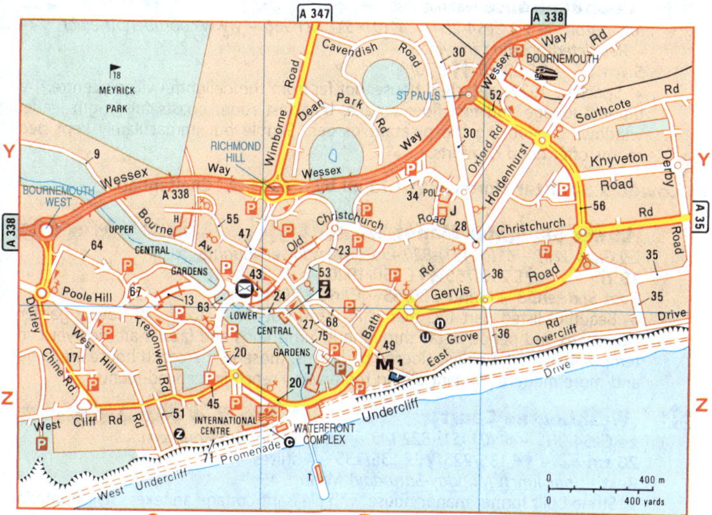

A 347
A 338
Cavendish Road
30
Wessex Way Rd
BOURNEMOUTH
MEYRICK PARK
Wimborne Road
Dean Park Rd
ST PAULS
52
Rd
Southcote
Y
9
RICHMOND HILL
Way
30
Oxford Rd
Holdenhurst
Derby Road
Knyveton Road
Y
BOURNEMOUTH WEST
Wessex Way
A 338
Wessex
34
POL
J
Rd
56
A 35
H
Bourne Av.
55
47
Christchurch Road
28
Christchurch Rd
A 338
UPPER CENTRAL GARDENS
64
Old
23
Rd
35
43
53
36
Road
Poole Hill
67
13
63
24
Gervis
35
Drive
LOWER CENTRAL GARDENS
27
68
75
Bath
Grove
36
Rd
Overcliff
Durley Chine Rd.
West Hill
Tregonwell Rd
17
20
49
M¹
East
Drive
T
20
Z
Z
West Cliff Rd
Rd
51
45
INTERNATIONAL CENTRE
WATERFRONT COMPLEX
Undercliff
71
Promenade
West Undercliff
0 400 m
0 400 yards
C
D
E

ENGLAND

Green Room – at Green House Hotel
4 Grove Rd ⌂ BH1 3AX – ℰ (01202) 498 900 – www.thegreenhousehotel.com
Rest – *(light lunch Monday-Saturday)* Carte approx. £ 32   DZ**n**
• Large restaurant set within an eco-friendly hotel. Modern menus display innovative touches; the tasting option is popular. All ingredients come from within a 50 miles radius and wines are biodynamic. Snack-style menu in the bar at lunch.

West Beach
Pier Approach ⌂ BH2 5AA – ℰ (01202) 587 785 – www.west-beach.co.uk
– Closed 25 December   DZ**c**
Rest – Seafood – *(booking essential)* Carte £ 23/57
• Popular seafood restaurant on the beach, with folding glass doors and a decked terrace. Always bustling. Fish and shellfish caught locally; some in front of the restaurant itself.

BOURTON ON THE HILL – Gloucestershire – see Moreton-in-Marsh

BOURTON-ON-THE-WATER – Gloucestershire – 503 O28   4 D1
– pop. 3 093 ▌Great Britain
▶ London 91 mi – Birmingham 47 mi – Gloucester 24 mi – Oxford 36 mi
▣ Town ★
▣ Northleach (Church of SS. Peter and Paul ★, Wool Merchants' Brasses ★), SW : 5 mi by A 429

Dial House
The Chestnuts, High St ⌂ GL54 2AN – ℰ (01451) 822 244
– www.dialhousehotel.com
15 rm ⌂ – †£ 145 ††£ 245
Rest – *(booking essential for non-residents)* Menu £ 15/20 – Carte £ 31/43
• House of Cotswold stone – the oldest in the village – with lovely lawned gardens and drawing room. Bedrooms mix of the contemporary and the floral; those in original house are the most characterful. Refined cooking makes good use of local ingredients.

Coombe House without rest
Rissington Rd ⌂ GL54 2DT – ℰ (01451) 821 966 – www.coombehouse.net
– Restricted opening in winter
5 rm ⌂ – †£ 50/60 ††£ 70/90
• Spacious 1920s detached house, not far from the delightful village centre. Traditional lounge and first floor terrace; breakfast room boasts full-length leaded windows overlooking the pleasant garden. Simple but immaculately kept bedrooms offer good comforts.

at Lower Slaughter Northwest : 1.75 mi by A 429 – ⌂ Cheltenham

Lower Slaughter Manor
⌂ GL54 2HP – ℰ (01451) 820 456 – www.lowerslaughter.co.uk
19 rm ⌂ – †£ 250/765 ††£ 250/1020
Rest *Sixteen58* – Menu £ 39/65 – Carte £ 29/49
• Beautiful listed part-17C manor in warm Cotswold stone with lovely garden. Open fires and period detail throughout; furnishings and fabrics are rich yet contemporary. Smart, boldly coloured bedrooms; those in the coach house are larger and more modern. Elegant dining room with French-influenced menu.

Washbourne Court
⌂ GL54 2HS – ℰ (01451) 822 143 – www.washbournecourt.co.uk
26 rm ⌂ – †£ 135/225 ††£ 135/235 – 4 suites
Rest – *(bar lunch Monday-Saturday)* Menu £ 45
• Stone-built former manor house with pleasant cottage annexes. Stylish interior boasts marble floored reception, contemporary bedrooms, comfy lounges and low-beamed bar with terrace. Local produce a feature in the dark wood-furnished dining room.

BOURTON-ON-THE-WATER

at Upper Slaughter Northwest : 2.5 mi by A 429 – ✉ Bourton-On-The-Water

Lords of the Manor
✉ GL54 2JD – ☎ (01451) 820 243 – www.lordsofthemanor.com
24 rm – †£ 195 ††£ 195/380 – 2 suites
Rest – (dinner only and Sunday lunch) (booking essential for non-residents)
Menu £ 65
Spec. Crab lasagne with coriander, fennel and crab bisque. Rib and cheek of beef, snails, ceps and red wine sauce. Raspberry soufflé, Eton mess and raspberry ripple ice cream.
♦ Charming and attractive 17C former rectory set in pretty Cotswold village, with neat and mature gardens. Comfortable sitting rooms and subtly contemporary bedrooms. Formal dining room where the classically based cooking is given a modern twist.

BOVEY TRACEY – Devon – **503** I32 – pop. 4 514 – ✉ Newton Abbot   2 C2
▶ London 214 mi – Exeter 14 mi – Plymouth 32 mi
🏌 Stover Bovey Rd, Newton Abbot, ☎ (01626) 35 24 60
◉ St Peter, St Paul and St Thomas of Canterbury Church ★
◉ Dartmoor National Park ★★

Brookfield House without rest
Challabrook Ln, Southwest : 0.75 mi by Brimley rd ✉ TQ13 9DF – ☎ (01626) 836 181 – www.brookfield-house.com – February-November
3 rm – †£ 51/55 ††£ 72/80
♦ Early Edwardian house on a peaceful part of town. Set behind electric gates, in two acres of attractive gardens, it has a simple, classically styled interior and large, immaculately appointed bedrooms; popular 'Iris' catches the sun all day.

BOWLAND BRIDGE – Cumbria – ✉ Cumbria   21 A2_3
▶ London 269 mi – Liverpool 86 mi – Preston 48 mi – Blackpool 60 mi

Hare & Hounds with rm
✉ LA11 6NN – ☎ (015395) 68 333 – www.hareandhoundsbowlandbridge.co.uk
3 rm – †£ 80 ††£ 100
Rest – Carte £ 22/27
♦ Charming 17C Lakeland pub in a delightful village. Large front terrace leads through into a rustic, open-fired inner hung with old village photos and hop bines. Menus offer typical, hearty favourites and most produce is locally sourced. Bedrooms are well-equipped and elegant; some boast roll-top baths.

BOWNESS-ON-WINDERMERE – Cumbria – **502** L20 – see Windermere

BOX – Bath & North East Somerset – **503** N29 – see Bath

BRADFIELD – Essex – see Mistley

BRADFORD-ON-AVON – Wiltshire – **503** N29 – pop. 9 072   4 C2
▶ London 118 mi – Bristol 24 mi – Salisbury 35 mi – Swindon 33 mi
🛈 50 St Margarets St ☎ (01225) 86 57 97, www.bradfordonavon.co.uk
◉ Town ★★ - Saxon Church of St Lawrence ★★ – Tithe Barn ★ – Bridge ★
◉ Great Chalfield Manor ★ (All Saints ★) **AC**, NE : 3 mi by B 3109 – Westwood Manor ★ **AC**, S : 1.5 mi by B 3109 – Top Rank Tory (≤ ★). Bath ★★★, NW : 7.5 mi by A 363 and A 4 – Corsham Court ★★ **AC**, NE : 6.5 mi by B 3109 and A 4

BRADFORD-ON-AVON

Woolley Grange
Woolley Green, Northeast : 0.75 mi by B 3107 on Woolley St ✉ BA15 1TX
– ✆ (01225) 864 705 – www.woolleygrangehotel.co.uk
19 rm – †£ 120/227 ††£ 315/395 – 7 suites **Rest** – Menu £ 20/43
♦ Modern art, period furniture: innumerable charming details spread through the rooms of a beautiful Jacobean manor. This is a hotel very much geared to families. Classic British cooking in restaurant, conservatory or terrace.

Bradford Old Windmill
4 Masons Lane, on A 363 ✉ BA15 1QN – ✆ (01225) 866 842
– www.bradfordoldwindmill.co.uk – March-October
3 rm – †£ 70/105 ††£ 80/125 **Rest** – Menu £ 25 s
♦ 1807 windmill in redressed local stone; Gothic windows and restored bridge. Rooms and circular lounge, stacked with books and curios, share a homely, unaffected quirkiness. Flavourful vegetarian menus.

at Holt East : 2 mi on B 3107 – ✉ Bradford-On-Avon

Tollgate Inn with rm
Ham Grn ✉ BA14 6PX – ✆ (01225) 782 326 – www.tollgateholt.co.uk – Closed Sunday dinner and Monday
4 rm – †£ 60/110 ††£ 110
Rest – (booking essential) Menu £ 20 (weekday lunch) – Carte £ 23/35
♦ 16C pub featuring a cosy, fire-lit bar, two traditional dining rooms and a delightful terrace and garden. Daily changing menu focuses on local produce, with light bites at lunch and more robust dishes at dinner. Comfortable, thoughtfully appointed bedrooms.

BRADWELL – 504 O24 – pop. 1 728 – ✉ Derbyshire   16 A1
▶ London 170 mi – Birmingham 99 mi – Liverpool 66 mi – Leeds 48 mi

Samuel Fox with rm
Stretfield Rd ✉ S33 9JT – ✆ (01433) 621 562 – www.samuelfox.co.uk
4 rm – †£ 75 ††£ 115 **Rest** – Menu £ 15 (lunch) – Carte £ 19/29
♦ Smart, stone-built inn with the fresh, light feel of a French bistro. Set price lunch menu and evening à la carte offer simple, flavourful dishes, with game in the winter and fish specials in the summer. Efficient, cheery service. Comfortable modern bedrooms.

BRAITHWAITE – Cumbria – 502 K20 – see Keswick

BRAMFIELD – Suffolk – 504 Y27 – pop. 1 778 – ✉ Ipswich   15 D2
▶ London 215 mi – Ipswich 27 mi – Norwich 28 mi

Queen's Head
The Street ✉ IP19 9HT – ✆ (01986) 784 214 – www.queensheadbramfield.co.uk
– Closed 25 December
Rest – Carte £ 21/30
♦ Characterful, personally run, cream-washed pub set in the heart of a small village. Local, seasonal produce informs the classical daily menu; organic ingredients are used where possible.

BRAMPFORD SPEKE – Devon   2 D2
▶ London 184 mi – Cardiff 110 mi – Plymouth 50 mi – Torbay 29 mi

Lazy Toad Inn
✉ EX5 5DP – ✆ (01392) 841 591 – www.thelazytoad@btinternet.com – Closed 3 weeks January, Sunday dinner, Monday and bank holidays
Rest – Carte £ 24/29
♦ Sweet little pub with cobbled courtyard, which uses vegetables from its own polytunnel and lambs raised in its smallholding. Homemade pork scratchings in the bar; cooking displays some Asian influences – even the pak choi is homegrown.

BRAMPTON – Cumbria – 501 L19 – pop. 3 965 – Great Britain 21 B1

▶ London 317 mi – Carlisle 9 mi – Newcastle upon Tyne 49 mi
🛈 Market Pl ☏ (016977) 34 33, www.visitcumbria.com
🐟 Talkin Tarn, ☏ (016977) 22 55
🏛 Hadrian's Wall★★, NW : by A 6077

Farlam Hall
Southeast : 2.75 mi on A 689 ✉ CA8 2NG – ☏ (016977) 46 234
– www.farlamhall.co.uk – Closed 4-18 January and 25-30 December
12 rm (dinner included) – ♦£ 160/190 ♦♦£ 360
Rest – (dinner only) (booking essential for non-residents) Menu £ 45

♦ Long-standing, family-owned Victorian country house. Comfortable guest areas overlook ornamental gardens and lake. Traditionally decorated bedrooms boast Bose radios and flat screen TVs. Fine, formal dining in sumptuous restaurant. Attentive, pristine service.

BRANCASTER STAITHE – Norfolk 15 C1

▶ London 131 mi – King's Lynn 25 mi – Boston 57 mi – East Dereham 27 mi

White Horse with rm
✉ PE31 8BY – ☏ (01485) 210 262 – www.whitehorsebrancaster.co.uk
15 rm – ♦£ 77/97 ♦♦£ 96/134 **Rest** – (booking essential) Carte £ 22/28

♦ Elevated position affords beautiful coastal views from rear conservatory and terrace, while landscaped front terrace boasts parasols, heaters and lights. Varied menu with local seafood. Up-to-date, comfortable bedrooms.

Jolly Sailors
✉ PE31 8BJ – ☏ (01485) 210 314 – www.jollysailorsbrancaster.co.uk
Rest – Carte £ 17/23 s

♦ Characterful, rustic pub with welcoming open fire. Simple menu ranges from light bites such as a ploughman's, to freshly made pizzas and pub classics; all followed by tasty nursery puddings.

BRAY – Windsor and Maidenhead – 504 R29 – pop. 8 121 11 C3
– ✉ Maidenhead

▶ London 34 mi – Reading 13 mi

Plan : see Maidenhead

Waterside Inn (Alain Roux) with rm
Ferry Rd ✉ SL6 2AT – ☏ (01628) 620 691 – www.waterside-inn.co.uk – Closed 26 December-2 February X s
9 rm – ♦£ 210/450 ♦♦£ 210/450 – 2 suites
Rest – French – (closed Tuesday except dinner June-August and Monday) (booking essential) Menu £ 58/148 – Carte £ 112/161
Spec. Tronçonnettes de homard poêlées minute au Porto blanc. Filets de lapereau grillés, sauce à l' armagnac et aux marrons glacés. Péché Gourmand selon "Alain" et "Michel".

♦ Few restaurants can match this glorious setting on the Thames, with the terrace an enchanting spot for an aperitif. Enjoy classic French cuisine, prepared with great care, in elegant surroundings. Service is charming and expertly organised. Luxurious bedrooms are spacious and chic.

Fat Duck (Heston Blumenthal)
High St ✉ SL6 2AQ – ☏ (01628) 580 333 – www.fatduck.co.uk – Closed 2 weeks Christmas-New Year, Sunday dinner and Monday X e
Rest – (booking essential 2 months in advance) (set menu only) Menu £ 160
Spec. Mock turtle soup. 'Sound of the Sea'. Black Forest gâteau with kirsch ice cream.

♦ Low-beamed, converted pub where history and science combine in an exciting, innovative alchemy of contrasting flavours and textures. It's very stimulating and involving; the attentive team are on hand to guide you through the experience.

BRAY

Caldesi in Campagna
Old Mill Ln ⊠ SL6 2BG – ℰ (01628) 788 500 – www.caldesi.com – Closed Sunday dinner and Monday

Rest – Italian – Menu £ 20 (lunch) – Carte £ 21/37

♦ Welcoming former pub with smart interior, conservatory and decked garden with wood fired oven. Flavoursome Italian cooking displays Ligurian, Tuscan and Sicilian influences.

Hinds Head
High St ⊠ SL6 2AB – ℰ (01628) 626 151 – www.hindsheadhotel.co.uk – Closed 25-26 December and Sunday dinner

Rest – *(booking essential)* Menu £ 28 – Carte £ 32/48

♦ Set at the heart of a pretty village. Dark panelling and log fires provide a characterful, almost medieval feel. Food is down-to-earth, with classic, comforting dishes and traditional desserts. Dishes are fiercely British and big on flavour; rich, simple and satisfying.

Royal Oak
Paley Street, Southwest : 3.5 mi by A 308, A 330 on B 3024 ⊠ SL6 3JN – ℰ (01628) 620 541 – www.theroyaloakpaleystreet.com – Closed Sunday dinner

Rest – Menu £ 23 (weekday lunch) – Carte £ 41/61

Spec. Lasagne of rabbit with wild mushrooms and chervil. Roast turbot with samphire, cockles and mussels. Yorkshire rhubarb trifle.

♦ A warm and welcoming beamed dining pub, with service that gets the tone just right. The menu champions British produce and is very appealing. This is skilled, confident cooking which sensibly avoids over-elaboration; game is handled deftly.

Crown
High St ⊠ SL6 2AH – ℰ (01628) 621 936 – www.thecrownatbray.co.uk

Rest – Carte £ 21/35

♦ Charmingly restored 16C building, formerly 2 cottages and a bike shop. Dark oak columns and low beams in the bar; lighter cottage style dining room. Cooking is robust, flavoursome and British.

at Bray Marina Southeast : 2 mi by B 3208, A 308 - X - on Monkey Island Lane – ⊠ Bray-On-Thames

Riverside Brasserie
(follow road through the marina) ⊠ SL6 2EB – ℰ (01628) 780 553 – www.riversidebrasserie.co.uk – April-September

Rest – *(booking essential)* Carte £ 37/52

♦ Marina boathouse, idyllically set on the banks of the Thames. Very simply appointed interior and decked terrace. Inventive cooking in informal, busy and buzzy surroundings.

BRAYE – 503 Q33 – see Channel Islands (Alderney)

BRAY MARINA – Buckinghamshire – see Bray

BREARTON – North Yorkshire – pop. 141   22 B2

▶ London 216 mi – Leeds 23 mi – Sheffield 67 mi – Manchester 77 mi

Malt Shovel
Main St ⊠ HG3 3BX – ℰ (01423) 862 929 – www.themaltshovelbrearton.co.uk – Closed 25 December, 1 January, Monday, Tuesday and dinner Sunday

Rest – Carte £ 20/40

♦ Quirky, shabby-chic pub run by the Bleikers, who also own the famous smokehouse. Classical dishes with continental flavours; lots of smoked seasonal produce. Tapas-style small plates at lunch.

BREEDON ON THE HILL – Leicestershire – pop. 958 — 16 B2
– ✉ Castle Donington

▶ London 121 mi – Birmingham 35 mi – Sheffield 57 mi – Manchester 95 mi

Three Horseshoes Inn
44-46 Main St ✉ DE73 8AN – ℰ (01332) 695 129 – www.thehorseshoes.com
– Closed 25-26 December, 1 January and Sunday dinner
Rest – Carte £ 20/39
♦ Large, highly characterful, whitewashed pub with numerous interlinking rooms, cosy fires and pleasant terrace. Blackboard menus display robust, classical dishes of flavoursome, seasonal produce.

BRENTWOOD – Essex – 504 V29 – pop. 47 593 — 13 C2
▶ London 22 mi – Chelmsford 11 mi – Southend-on-Sea 21 mi
ℹ 44 High St ℰ (01277) 20 03 00, www.visitessex.com
⛳ Bentley G. & C.C. Ongar Rd, ℰ (01277) 37 31 79
⛳ Warley Park Little Warley Magpie Lane, ℰ (01277) 22 48 91

Marygreen Manor
London Rd, Southwest : 1.25 mi on A 1023 ✉ CM14 4NR – ℰ (01277) 225 252
– www.marygreenmanor.co.uk
44 rm – †£ 160 ††£ 160, ⛳ £ 15
Rest *Tudors* – Menu £ 18/42
♦ Mock-Tudor house with 15C origins; once owned by a servant of Catherine of Aragon. Charming open-fired rooms, ornate plaster ceilings and carved wood panelling. Bedrooms split between the house and courtyard; the former, more characterful. Rustic, formal restaurant offers elaborate, classically based dishes.

BRIDGNORTH – Shropshire – 502 M26 – pop. 11 891 ▮ Great Britain — 18 B2
▶ London 146 mi – Birmingham 26 mi – Shrewsbury 20 mi – Worcester 29 mi
ℹ Listley St ℰ (01746) 76 32 57, www.visitbridgnorth.co.uk
⛳ Stanley Lane, ℰ (01746) 76 33 15
◉ Ironbridge Gorge Museum★★ **AC** (The Iron Bridge★★ - Coalport China Museum★★ - Blists Hill Open Air Museum★★ - Museum of the Gorge and Visitor Centre★) NW : 8 mi by B 4373

at Worfield Northeast : 4 mi by A 454 – ✉ Bridgnorth

Old Vicarage
✉ WV15 5JZ – ℰ (01746) 716 497 – www.oldvicarageworfield.com
14 rm ⛳ – †£ 73/85 ††£ 120/175
Rest – *(closed Sunday dinner) (booking essential)* Menu £ 22/39 – Carte £ 35/43
♦ Antiques, rare prints and rustic pottery: a personally run Edwardian parsonage in a rural setting with thoughtfully appointed bedrooms, some in the coach house. Delightful orangery dining room overlooking garden; modern British cooking.

BRIDPORT – Dorset – 503 L31 – pop. 12 977 — 3 B3
▶ London 150 mi – Exeter 38 mi – Taunton 33 mi – Weymouth 19 mi
ℹ 47 South St ℰ (01308) 42 49 01, www.visit-dorset.org.uk
⛳ Bridport and West Dorset West Bay East Cliff, ℰ (01308) 42 25 97
◉ Mapperton Gardens★, N : 4 mi by A 3066 and minor rd. Lyme Regis★ - The Cobb★, W : 11 mi by A 35 and A 3052

Roundham House *without rest*
Roundham Gdns, West Bay Rd, South : 1 mi by B 3157 ✉ DT6 4BD
– ℰ (01308) 422 753 – www.roundhamhouse.co.uk – May-October
8 rm ⛳ – †£ 58/93 ††£ 125
♦ Sizeable Edwardian house displaying rich colours and period furnishings. Comfy lounge; modern bedrooms with bold feature walls and good comforts. Elevated position offers pleasant country views.

BRIDPORT

Riverside
West Bay, South : 1.75 mi by B 3157 – DT6 4EZ – ℘ (01308) 422 011 – www.thefishrestaurant-westbay.co.uk – Closed 2 December-10 February, Sunday dinner and Monday except bank holidays
Rest – Seafood – *(booking essential)* Menu £ 26 (weekday lunch) – Carte £ 30/60
♦ Long-standing seafood restaurant with harbour views; accessed via a bridge. Good value daily menu offers extremely fresh, straightforward dishes crafted from local produce. Plenty of choice.

Bull with rm
34 East St – DT6 3LF – ℘ (01308) 422 878 – www.thebullhotel.co.uk
19 rm – †£ 85/175 ††£ 175/195 **Rest** – Carte £ 25/40
♦ Boutique, Regency style inn displaying an eclectic mix of period features and chic, contemporary décor. Local meats and Lyme Bay fish are showcased in classic brasserie dishes. Uniquely styled, modern bedrooms boast bold feature walls and stylish bathrooms.

at Burton Bradstock Southeast : 2 mi by B 3157

Norburton Hall without rest
Shipton Ln – DT6 4NQ – ℘ (01308) 897 007 – www.norburtonhall.com
3 rm – †£ 110/190 ††£ 110/220
♦ Spacious Edwardian Arts and Crafts house with coastal views and 6 acres of mature grounds. Woodwork, ornate carvings and period furniture abound; classical bedrooms, modern shower rooms.

BRIGGSWATH – North Yorkshire – **502** S20 – see Whitby

BRIGHOUSE – West Yorkshire – **502** O22 – pop. 32 360 **22** B2
▶ London 213 mi – Bradford 12 mi – Burnley 28 mi – Leeds 15 mi
🏌 Crow Nest Park Hove Edge Coach Rd, ℘ (01484) 40 11 21

Brook's
6 Bradford Rd – HD6 1RW – ℘ (01484) 715 284 – www.brooks-restaurant.co.uk – Closed 10 days January, 10 days summer and Sunday
Rest – *(dinner only)* Menu £ 20 (weekdays) – Carte £ 20/31
♦ Long-standing, very personally run restaurant, where eclectic art fills the walls. Pleasant wine bar and upstairs lounge. Robust, tasty, interesting dishes; kangaroo and zebra sometimes feature.

BRIGHTON AND HOVE – Brighton and Hove – **504** T31 **8** A3
– pop. 127 035   Great Britain
▶ London 53 mi – Portsmouth 48 mi – Southampton 61 mi
✈ Shoreham Airport : ℘ (01273) 467373, W : 8 mi by A 27 AV
🛈 Royal Pavilion Shops ℘ (01273) 29 25 95, www.visitbrighton.com
🏌 East Brighton Roedean Rd, ℘ (01273) 60 48 38
🏌 The Dyke Devil's Dyke Rd, Devil's Dyke, ℘ (01273) 85 72 96
🏌 Hollingbury Park Ditchling Rd, ℘ (01273) 55 20 10
🏌 Waterhall Waterhall Rd, ℘ (01273) 50 86 58
◎ Town★★ - Royal Pavilion★★★ **AC** CZ – Seafront★★ – The Lanes★ BCZ – St Bartholomew's★ **AC** CX **B**
◉ Devil's Dyke (≤★) NW : 5 mi by Dyke Rd (B 2121) BY

Plans on following pages

BRIGHTON AND HOVE

Hotel du Vin
2-6 Ship St ⊠ BN1 1AD – ℘ (01273) 718 588 – www.hotelduvin.com
49 rm – ✝£ 110/190 ✝✝£ 140/250, ⊇ £ 15 CZ**a**
Rest *Bistro* – see restaurant listing
• Set on the promenade and made up of various different buildings; the oldest being a 17C former arts club. Cavernous bar-lounge with gothic style and mezzanine lounge with terrace. Comfy, contemporary bedrooms; some in their next door pub.

Drakes
43-44 Marine Par ⊠ BN2 1PE – ℘ (01273) 696 934 – www.drakesofbrighton.com
20 rm – ✝£ 115/145 ✝✝£ 225/275, ⊇ £ 12.50 CZ**u**
Rest *Restaurant* – see restaurant listing
• Pair of 18C townhouses on the promenade. Stylish, modern interior with cocktail bar. Chic bedrooms boast bamboo flooring, wooden feature walls, good mod cons and wet rooms; city or sea views.

Myhotel Brighton without rest
17 Jubilee St ⊠ BN1 1GE – ℘ (01273) 900 300 – www.myhotels.com
80 rm – ✝£ 160 ✝✝£ 160, ⊇ £ 9.50 CY**z**
• Contemporary glass cube, set in the heart of town. Whacky, designer interior with relaxed vibe and stylish bar. Quirky, minimalist bedrooms boast the latest technological extras.

Kemp Townhouse without rest
21 Atlingworth St ⊠ BN2 1PL – ℘ (01273) 681 400
– www.kemptownhousebrighton.com CZ**n**
9 rm – ✝£ 75/95 ✝✝£ 95/215
• Stylish, very personally run 19C townhouse. Bedrooms have an uncluttered, classic style and compact wet rooms; those facing the front are larger and more comfortable. 2 four-posters.

Paskins without rest
18-19 Charlotte St ⊠ BN2 1AG – ℘ (01273) 601 203 – www.paskins.co.uk
19 rm ⊇ – ✝£ 55/75 ✝✝£ 95/105 CV**e**
• Quirky, personally run guesthouse. Small, modern bedrooms are simply furnished and well-kept. Showers only – to save water – and eco-toiletries. Organic breakfast features homemade sausages.

brightonwave without rest
10 Madeira Pl ⊠ BN2 1TN – ℘ (01273) 676 794 – www.brightonwave.com
– Closed 25-26 December CZ**s**
8 rm ⊇ – ✝£ 65/120 ✝✝£ 100/175
• Personally run Victorian townhouse featuring ever-changing artwork. Contemporary bedrooms: the front facing and garden rooms are the largest and most comfortable. One modern four-poster.

Restaurant – at Drakes Hotel
43-44 Marine Par ⊠ BN2 1PE – ℘ (01273) 696 934
– www.therestaurantatdrakes.co.uk CZ**u**
Rest – *(booking advisable)* Menu £ 40
• Set in hotel basement, this cool, contemporary eatery conveys a soft, moody atmosphere. The menus present a good balanced choice of modern British dishes with Gallic twists.

Gingerman
21A Norfolk Sq ⊠ BN1 2PD – ℘ (01273) 326 688
– www.gingermanrestaurants.com – Closed 25 December, 2 weeks in winter and Monday BZ**i**
Rest – *(booking essential)* Menu £ 18/32
• Tucked away off the promenade; French and Mediterranean flavours to the fore in a confident, affordable, modern repertoire: genuine neighbourhood feel.

BRIGHTON AND HOVE

Adelaide Crescent	AY 2
Brunswick Pl.	AY 3
Brunswick Square	AYZ 4
Carlton Terrace	AV 5
Chatham Pl.	BX 6
Churchill Square Shopping Centre	BYZ
Denmark Rd.	BY 7
Eastern Rd.	CV 9
East St.	CZ 8
George St.	AV 10
Gladstone Terrace	CX 12
Gloucester Pl.	CX 13
Gloucester Rd.	CX 14
Goldsmid Rd.	BX 15
Grand Junction Rd.	CZ 16
Hollingbury Park Ave.	BV 17
Hollingdean Rd.	CV 18
Hove St.	AV 19
London Rd.	CX
Marlborough Pl.	CY 21
Montpelier Pl.	BY 22
North St.	CZ
Old Steine	CZ 23
Pavilion Parade	CY 26
Richmond Pl.	CY 27
Richmond Terrace	CX 28
St George's Pl.	CY 30
St Peter's Pl.	CX 31
Terminus Rd.	BCX 32
Upper Lewes Rd.	CX 33
Warren Rd.	CV 37
Waterloo Pl.	CX 39
Wellington Rd.	AV 40
Western Rd.	ABY
York Pl.	CY 42

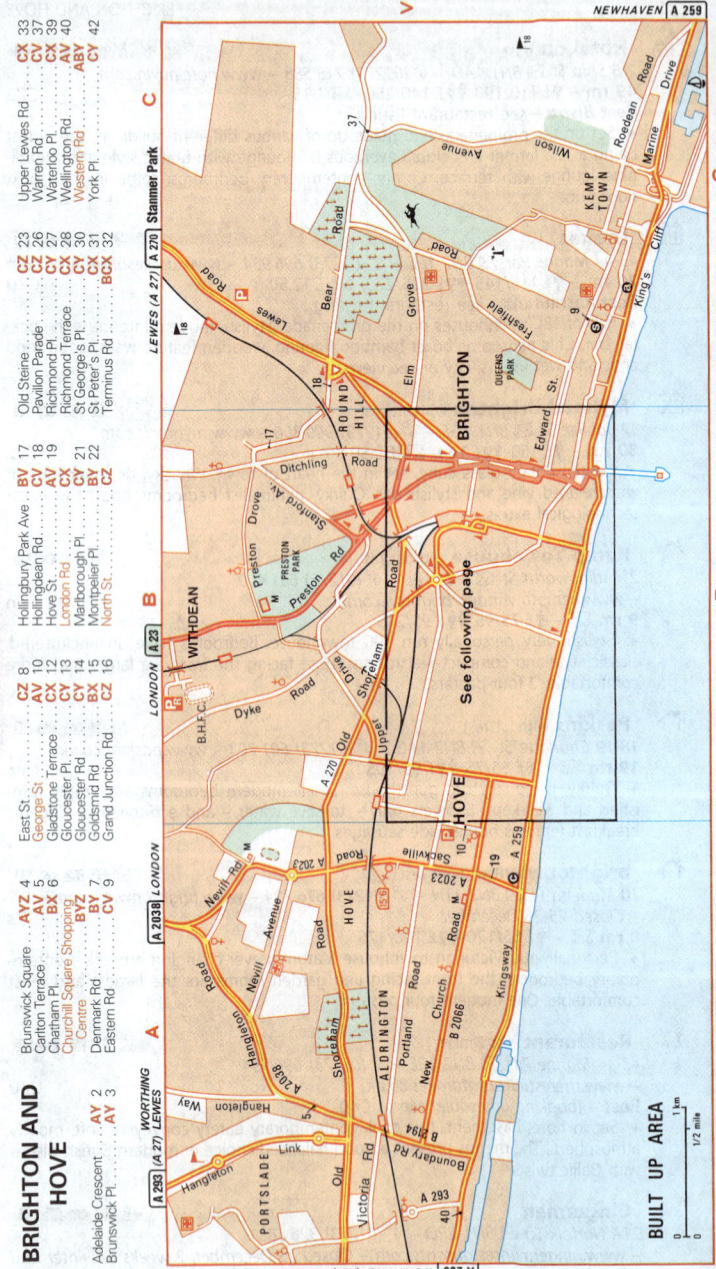

ENGLAND

BUILT UP AREA

BRIGHTON AND HOVE

Terre à Terre
71 East St ⊠ BN1 1HQ – ℰ (01273) 729 051 – www.terreaterre.co.uk
– Closed 25-26 December and Monday in winter CZe
Rest – Vegetarian – *(booking essential)* Menu £ 30 (lunch) – Carte £ 24/32

♦ Relaxed, friendly restaurant decorated in warm burgundy colours. Appealing menu of tasty, original vegetarian dishes which include items from Japan, China and South America. Generous portions.

Sam's of Sevendials
1 Buckingham Pl ⊠ BN1 3TD – ℰ (01273) 885 555
– www.samsofsevendials.co.uk – Closed 25 December and Sunday dinner
Rest – Menu £ 14 (weekday lunch) – Carte £ 21/32 BXa

♦ Former bank on street corner: the vault now acts as function room. Light, airy feel with high ceiling. Modern menus with local ingredients admirably to fore. Good value lunch.

Due South
139 King's Rd Arches ⊠ BN1 2FN – ℰ (01273) 821 218 – www.duesouth.co.uk
– Closed 25-26 December BZx
Rest – Menu £ 20 (lunch) – Carte £ 22/39

♦ Set beside the beach, with pleasant arch interior: the best tables upstairs facing a half-moon window and overlooking sea. Modern, seafood-based menus rely on local and organic produce.

Sam's of Brighton
1 Paston Pl ⊠ BN2 1HA – ℰ (01273) 676 222 – www.samsofbrighton.co.uk
– Closed 25 December CVa
Rest – Menu £ 14 (lunch and early dinner) – Carte £ 22/33

♦ Simple neighbourhood eatery boasting three enormous candelabras. Simple menu of classical, seasonal dishes. Early brunch on offer at the weekend and a concise à la carte at noon.

Chilli Pickle
17 Jubilee St ⊠ BN1 1GE – ℰ (01273) 900 383 – www.thechillipickle.com
– Closed 25 December CYz
Rest – Indian – Carte £ 17/37

♦ Simple, relaxed restaurant with passionate chef, buzzy vibe and friendly, welcoming service. Oft-changing menu of tasty, thoughtfully prepared, authentic Indian dishes, with delicate spicing and good quality ingredients. Great selection of beers and teas.

Riddle and Finns
12b Meeting House Ln ⊠ BN1 1HB – ℰ (01273) 323 008
– www.riddleandfinns.co.uk CZi
Rest – Seafood – Carte £ 35/70

♦ Informal and simply decorated, with white tiles, bar stools and high, marble-topped tables for communal dining. Well-executed, classical seafood dishes; polite, attentive service.

Blenio Bistro
87-93 Dyke Rd ⊠ BN1 3JE – ℰ (01273) 220 220 – www.bleniobistro.com
– Closed 2 weeks late June-early July, Monday and Tuesday BXc
Rest – Carte £ 29/34

♦ Friendly, passionately run neighbourhood bistro. Simply furnished, with exposed brick, food-related art and pleasant terrace. Regularly changing menu ranges from snacks to the full 3 courses.

Bistro – at Hotel du Vin
2-6 Ship St ⊠ BN1 1AD – ℰ (01273) 718 588 – www.hotelduvin.com
Rest – *(booking essential)* Carte £ 25/37 CZa

♦ Relaxed brasserie located within a part-17C, part-gothic hotel on the promenade; in summer, make for the hidden courtyard. Extensive wine list accompanies a menu of British brasserie classics.

The Ginger Dog

12 College Pl – BN2 1HN – ℘ (01273) 620 990
– www.gingermanrestaurants.com – Closed 25 December
Rest – Carte £ 18/30

CV**s**

♦ Warm and welcoming shabby-chic pub; part of the growing local 'Ginger' empire. Fresh produce is to the fore on the menu, which is mostly in a British vein but with the odd nod to Italy.

at Hove

Meadow

64 Western Rd – BN3 2JQ – ℘ (01273) 721 182
– www.themeadowrestaurant.co.uk – Closed 24-31 December, Sunday dinner
and Monday
Rest – Carte £ 22/34

AY**o**

♦ Airy, split-level dining room with small shop. Its name symbolises the chef's vision to support local producers – the 'grass roots' of the restaurant. Beasts are bought in whole; some items are from his parents' garden or foraged for. Unfussy, British cooking.

Graze

42 Western Rd – BN3 1JD – ℘ (01273) 823 707 – www.graze-restaurant.co.uk
– Closed 1 January
Rest – Menu £ 32

AY**z**

♦ Lively neighbourhood eatery with quirky, informal feel. Cooking is elaborate and adventurous: good value midweek menu; 7 course tapas-style tasting menu must be ordered in advance for lunch.

Ginger Pig

3 Hove St – BN3 2TR – ℘ (01273) 736 123 – www.gingermanrestaurants.com
– Closed 25 December
Rest – Carte £ 24/34

AV**c**

♦ Smart building by the seafront – formerly a hotel – boasting a mortar ship relief and beautifully restored revolving door. Menus offer precise, flavoursome British dishes and vegetarians are well-catered for. Great value set menus. Service copes well under pressure.

BRISTOL

See city maps on following pages

4 C2

© Bernd Tschaker/imagebroker/Age fotostock

City of Bristol – pop. 420 556 – **503** M29 – **504** M29 – Great Britain

London 121 – Birmingham 91

Tourist Information

Harbourside (0333) 321 01 01, www.visitbristol.co.uk

Airport

Bristol Airport : (0871) 334 4444, SW : 7 m. by A 38 **AX**

Bridge

Severn Bridge (toll)

Golf Courses

Short Lodge GC Carsons Rd, (0117) 956 55 01
Clifton Beggar Clifton Bush Lane, Failand, (01275) 39 34 74

SIGHTS

In the town

City★★ • St Mary Redcliffe★★ **DZ** • At-Bristol★★ **CZ** • Brandon Hill★★ **AX** • Georgian House★★ **AX K** • Bristol Museum★★ **CZ M3** • Brunel's ss Great Britain and Maritime Heritage Centre★ **AC AX S2** • The Old City★ **CYZ** : Theatre Royal★★ **CZ T** • Merchant Seamen's Almshouses★ **CZ Q** • St Stephen's Church★ **CY S1** • St John the Baptist★ **CY** • College Green★ **CYZ** • City Museum and Art Gallery★ **AX M1**

On the outskirts

Clifton★★ **AX** • Clifton Suspension Bridge★★ (toll) • RC Cathedral of St Peter and St Paul★ **F1** • Bristol Zoological Gardens★★ **AC**

In the surrounding area

Bath★★★, SE : 13 mi by A 4 **BX**

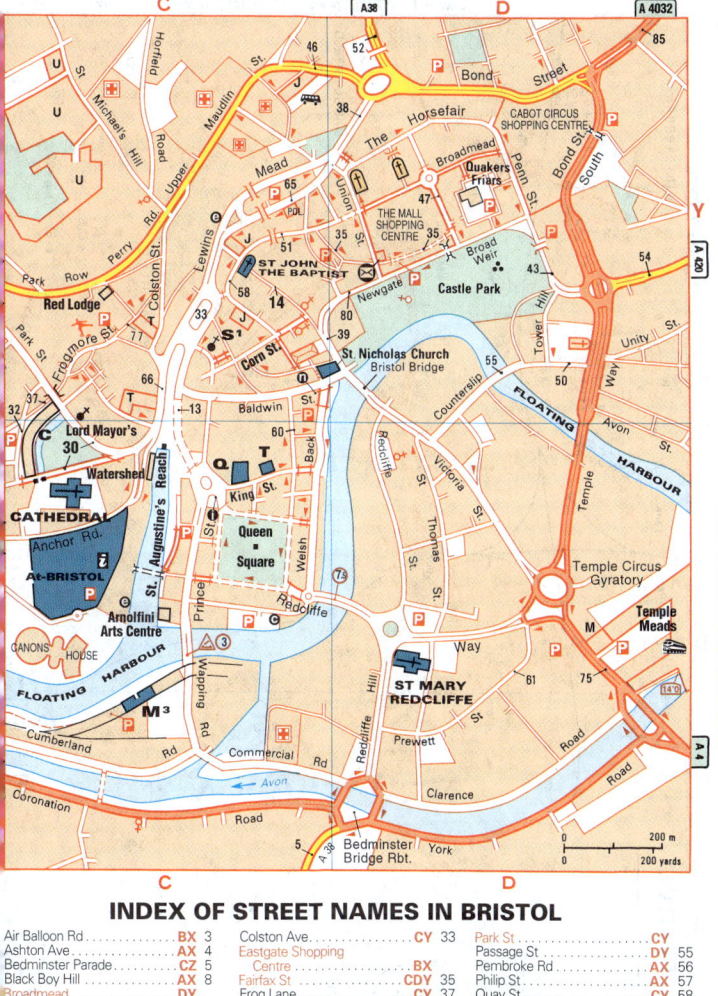

INDEX OF STREET NAMES IN BRISTOL

Air Balloon Rd . . . . **BX** 3	Colston Ave. . . . . **CY** 33	Park St . . . . **CY**
Ashton Ave . . . . **AX** 4	Eastgate Shopping	Passage St . . . . **DY** 55
Bedminster Parade . . . . **CZ** 5	Centre . . . . **BX**	Pembroke Rd . . . . **AX** 56
Black Boy Hill . . . . **AX** 8	Fairfax St . . . . **CDY** 35	Philip St . . . . **AX** 57
Broadmead . . . . **DY**	Frog Lane . . . . **CY** 37	Quay St . . . . **CY** 58
Broad Quay . . . . **CYZ** 13	Haymarket . . . . **DY** 38	Queen Charlotte
Broad St. . . . . **CY** 14	High St . . . . **CDY** 39	St . . . . **CZ** 60
Brunel Way . . . . **AX** 16	Horse Fair (The) . . . . **DY**	Redcliffe Mead Lane . . . . **DZ** 61
Cabot Circus Shopping Centre **DY**	Lawrence Hill . . . . **BX** 41	Regent St . . . . **AX** 62
Canford Rd . . . . **AV** 17	Lodge Hill . . . . **BX** 42	Royal York Crescent. . . . . **AX** 63
Cassel Rd . . . . **BV** 18	Lower Castle St . . . . **DY** 43	Rupert St . . . . **CY** 65
Cheltenham Rd . . . . **AX** 20	Malago Rd . . . . **AX** 44	St Augustine's Parade . . . . . **CY** 66
Church School Rd. . . . . **BX** 21	Mall (The) . . . . **DY**	Sheene Rd . . . . **AX** 67
Clarence Rd . . . . **BX** 22	Marlborough St . . . . **CDY** 46	Sion Hill . . . . **AX** 70
Cliff House Rd . . . . **AX** 24	Merchant St . . . . **DY** 47	Stokes Croft . . . . **AX** 72
Clifton Down Rd . . . . **AX** 25	Nags Head Hill . . . . **BX** 49	Summerhill Rd . . . . **BX** 73
Clifton Hill . . . . **AX** 26	Narrow Plain . . . . **DY** 50	Temple Gate . . . . **DZ** 75
Clifton Park . . . . **AX** 28	Nelson St . . . . **CY** 51	Thicket Rd . . . . **BV** 76
Clouds Hill Rd . . . . **BX** 29	New Foundland St . . . . **DY** 85	Trenchard St . . . . **CY** 77
College Green . . . . **CZ** 30	North St . . . . **DY** 52	Victoria St . . . . **BV** 79
College St . . . . **CYZ** 32	Old Market St . . . . **DY** 54	Wine St . . . . **DY** 80

117

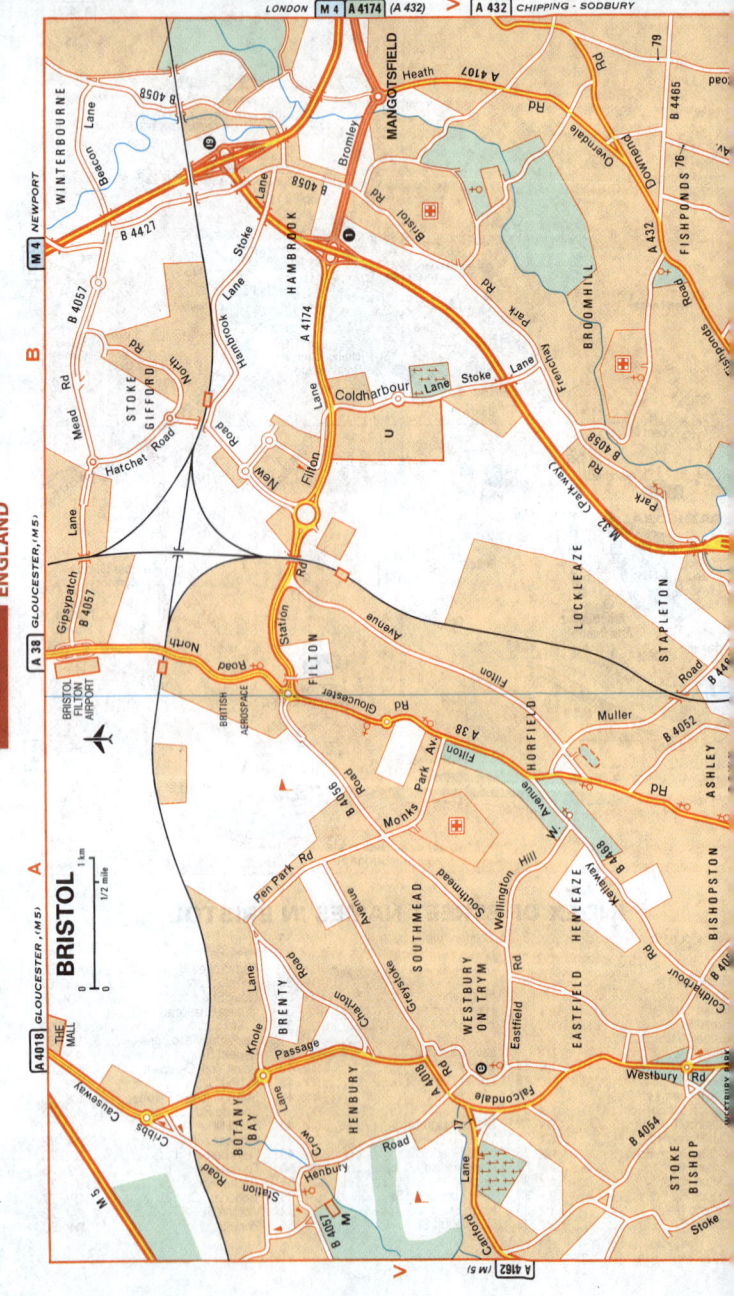

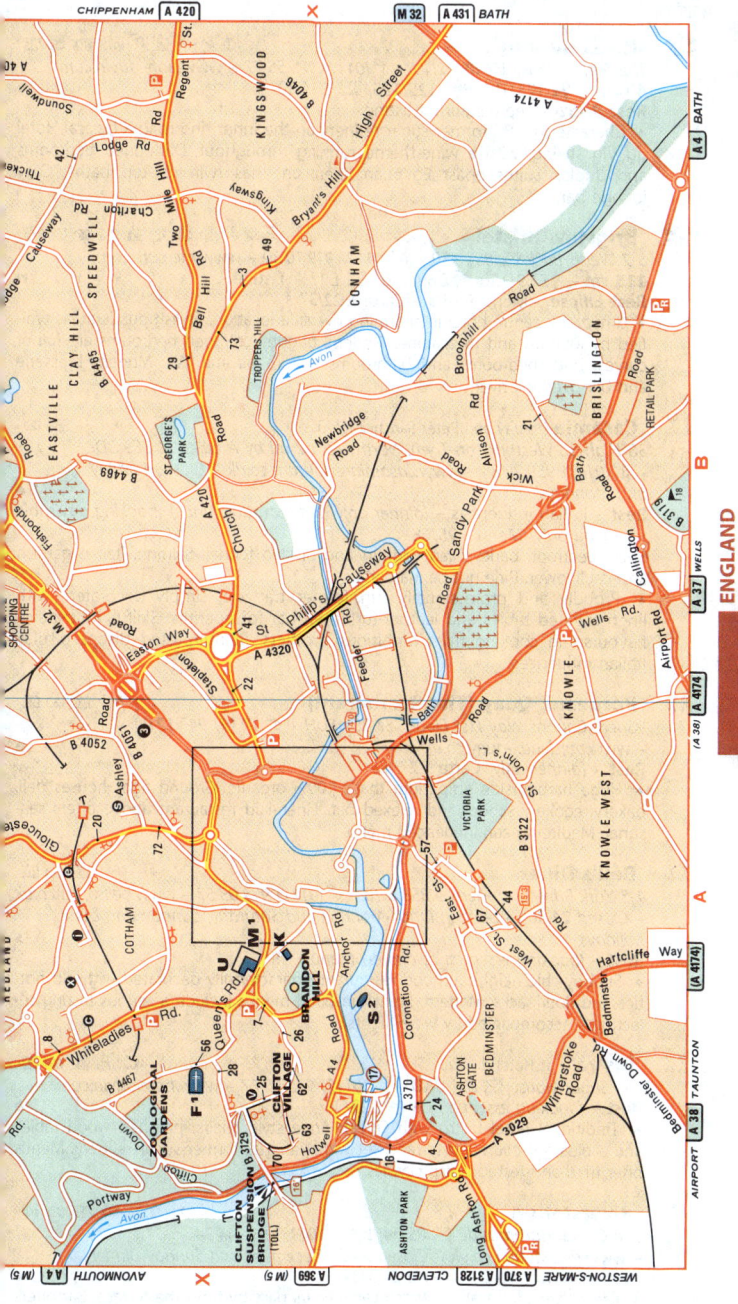

BRISTOL

Hotel du Vin
The Sugar House ⊠ *BS1 2NU* – ℰ *(0117) 925 55 77* – *www.hotelduvin.com*
40 rm – †£ 125/195 ††£ 125/195, ⊇ £ 14.50
CYe
Rest *Bistro* – see restaurant listing
♦ Characterful 18C former sugar refinery on the inner ring road. Classical Hotel du Vin styling, with a wine-theme running throughout. Dark-hued bedrooms and duplex suites boast Egyptian linen; one has twin roll-top baths. Cosy lounge bar.

Brigstow Bristol
5-7 Welsh Back ⊠ *BS1 4SP* – ℰ *(0117) 929 10 30* – *www.mercure.com*
115 rm – †£ 69/150 ††£ 69/150, ⊇ £ 17 – 1 suite
CYn
Rest *Ellipse* – Menu £ 18 **s** – Carte £ 22/37 **s**
♦ Smart city centre hotel in charming riverside location. Stylish public areas typified by lounges and mezzanine. Modern, brightly coloured bedrooms are full of curves: both bedrooms and bathrooms feature plasma TVs. Modern brasserie and bar overlook river.

Casamia (Jonray and Peter Sanchez-Iglesias)
38 High St, Westbury-on-Trym, Northwest : 2 mi by A 4018 ⊠ *BS9 3DZ*
– ℰ *(0117) 959 28 84* – *www.casamiarestaurant.co.uk* – *Closed Sunday and Monday*
AVe
Rest – Italian influences – *(dinner only and Saturday lunch) (booking advisable set menu only)* Menu £ 25/68
Spec. Beetroot, barley, iced yoghurt and pickled fennel. Salmon, Italian garnish and cauliflower. Pine nut panna cotta.
♦ Proudly and professionally run former trattoria; simply decorated, with linen-covered tables and leather-furnished bar for aperitifs. Skilful, innovative, flavoursome cooking from ambitious brothers. Reinterpreted dishes display Italian influences.

Bordeaux Quay (The Restaurant)
VShed, Canons Way (1st Floor) ⊠ *BS1 5UH* – ℰ *(0117) 943 12 00*
– *www.bordeaux-quay.co.uk*
CZe
Rest – *(dinner only)* Carte £ 27/42
♦ Huge harbourside emporium that's 100% organic. Ground floor houses deli, bakery, cookery school and relaxed bar. Linen-laid restaurant above offers seasonal, Mediterranean-influenced menu.

Bell's Diner
1-3 York Rd, Montpelier ⊠ *BS6 5QB* – ℰ *(0117) 924 03 57* – *www.bellsdiner.co.uk*
– *Closed 24-30 December, lunch Monday and Saturday, Sunday and bank holidays*
AXs
Rest – *(booking essential at dinner)* Menu £ 38
♦ Shabby-chic neighbourhood restaurant, characterfully decorated with old bottles and flour sacks. Modern, French-inspired menus include a serious tasting selection – accompanied by wine flights.

Bistro – at Hotel du Vin
The Sugar House ⊠ *BS1 2NU* – ℰ *(0117) 925 55 77* – *www.hotelduvin.com*
Rest – *(booking essential)* Carte £ 22/38
CYe
♦ Traditional hotel bistro with Queen Anne style chairs, polished wood tables and a pleasant courtyard terrace, set within an 18C former sugar refinery. Menus offer tried-and-tested bistro classics.

Riverstation
The Grove, Harbourside ⊠ *BS1 4RB* – ℰ *(0117) 914 44 34*
– *www.riverstation.co.uk* – *Closed 24-26 December and Sunday dinner*
Rest – Menu £ 16/20 – Carte £ 25/34
CZc
♦ Great riverside location: watch canal boats pass by from the terrace. Bar offers all day dining with breakfast, brunch and meze plates. Upstairs café offers more substantial modern European fare.

Rockfish Grill

128 Whiteladies Rd ✉ *BS8 2RS* – ✆ *(0117) 973 73 84* – *www.rockfishgrill.co.uk*
– *Closed 25-29 December, 1 January, Monday and Sunday dinner* AX**c**
Rest – Seafood – *(booking essential)* Carte £ 24/39

♦ Well-run and busy, with polite, friendly service. Daily changing menus focus on fresh, simply prepared fish and seafood, cooked in the charcoal josper oven. Owners' fishmongers is adjacent.

Culinaria

1 Chandos Rd, Redland ✉ *BS6 6PG* – ✆ *(0117) 973 79 99*
– *www.culinariabristol.co.uk* – *Closed 2 weeks summer, 1 week spring, 1 week autumn, 1 week Christmas and Sunday-Wednesday* AX**x**
Rest – Menu £ 20 (lunch) – Carte £ 28/35

♦ Combined deli and eatery; the personally run diner is informal with lots of light and space. Sound cooking behind a collection of Mediterranean, English and French dishes.

Flinty Red

34 Cotham Hill ✉ *BS6 6LA* – ✆ *(0117) 923 87 55* – *www.flintyred.co.uk*
– *Closed 1 January, last week August, 25-28 December, Monday lunch and Sunday* AX**n**
Rest – Mediterranean – Carte £ 20/30

♦ Combined effort of two couples; one pair are independent wine merchants, the other, chefs. Simple, rustic interior and friendly, knowledgeable team. Concise daily menu of Mediterranean small plates. Unfussy cooking relies on quality local produce and features well-used, lesser-known cuts. Tempting wine list.

Greens' Dining Room

25 Zetland Rd ✉ *BS6 7AH* – ✆ *(0117) 924 64 37* – *www.greensdiningroom.com*
– *Closed 1 week Christmas, Sunday and Monday* AX**e**
Rest – *(booking essential)* Carte £ 19/31

♦ Family-run neighbourhood eatery set in residential area, with an intimate, homely interior and a convivial atmosphere. Good value, daily changing menu; unfussy, Italian-influenced dishes rely on natural flavours and carefully sourced produce. Chatty service.

Albion Public House and Dining Rooms

Boyces Ave, Clifton Village ✉ *BS8 4AA* – ✆ *(0117) 973 35 22*
– *www.thealbionclifton.co.uk* – *Closed 25 December and Monday lunch*
Rest – *(booking essential)* Menu £ 31 (dinner) – Carte £ 31/40 AX**v**

♦ Trendy Grade II listed pub at the heart of the village. Unfussy, highly seasonal menu changes twice a day; everything is homemade. BBQs held on the pleasant terrace every Sunday evening.

Kensington Arms

35-37 Stanley Rd ✉ *BS6 6NP* – ✆ *(0117) 944 64 44*
– *www.thekensingtonarms.co.uk* – *Closed 25-26 December and Sunday dinner*
Rest – Carte £ 29/37 AX**i**

♦ Welcoming neighbourhood pub with traditional bar, impressive high-ceilinged dining room and charming Victorian style. Menus change every two months and have a strong British and seasonal base.

Robin Hood's Retreat

197 Gloucester Rd ✉ *BS7 8BG* – ✆ *(0117) 924 86 39*
– *www.robinhoodsretreat.co.uk* – *Closed 25 December* AX**a**
Rest – *(booking advisable at dinner)* Menu £ 14 (lunch) – Carte £ 25/33

♦ Red-brick, Victorian pub in busy part of city, with characterful bar and relaxed atmosphere. Daily changing menus offer hearty, flavourful interpretations of British classics.

BROAD CAMPDEN – Gloucestershire – see Chipping Campden

BROAD OAK - East Sussex - 504 V31

8 B3

▶ London 62 mi – Hastings 8 mi – Rye 7 mi

Fairacres without rest
Udimore Rd, on B 2089 ✉ TN31 6DG – ✆ (01424) 883 236
– www.fairacresrye.co.uk – Closed Christmas-New Year
3 rm – †£ 56/70 ††£ 88/110
- Listed 17C cottage in picture-postcard pink. Big breakfasts under low beams. Individual rooms: one overlooks superb magnolia tree in garden. All have many thoughtful extras.

BROADSTAIRS - Kent - 504 Y29 - pop. 22 712

9 D1

▶ London 77 mi – Canterbury 18 mi – Ramsgate 2 mi

Belvedere Place without rest
Belvedere Rd. ✉ CT10 1PF – ✆ (01843) 579 850 – www.belvedereplace.co.uk
5 rm – †£ 120 ††£ 180
- Centrally located Georgian house with charming owner, green credentials and eclectic, individual style. Bohemian, shabby-chic lounge boasts a retro football table. Spacious bedrooms mix modern facilities with older antique furnishings.

Burrow House without rest
Granville Rd ✉ CT10 1QD – ✆ (01843) 601 817 – www.burrowhouse.com
4 rm – †£ 80/95 ††£ 95/175
- Tastefully restored and subtly modernised Victorian house close to seafront. Bedrooms blend contemporary décor and fine antique furniture. Gourmet dinners by arrangement. Substantial breakfasts.

BROADWAY - Worcestershire - 503 O27 - pop. 2 496 ▮ Great Britain

19 C3

▶ London 93 mi – Birmingham 36 mi – Cheltenham 15 mi – Oxford 38 mi
🛈 1 Cotswold Court ✆ (01386) 85 29 37, www.broadway-cotswolds.co.uk
◉ Town ★
◉ Country Park (Broadway Tower ❄ ★★★), SE : 2 mi by A 44 – Snowshill Manor ★ (Terrace Garden ★), **AC**, S : 2.5 m

Buckland Manor
✉ WR12 7LY – ✆ (01386) 852 626 – www.bucklandmanor.com
14 rm – †£ 195/290 ††£ 495/515
Rest – (booking essential for non-residents) Menu £ 23 (lunch)
– Carte £ 37/55
- Secluded part 13C country house with beautiful gardens. Individually furnished bedrooms boast high degree of luxury. Fine service throughout as old-world serenity prevails. Restaurant boasts elegant crystal, fine china and smooth service.

Lygon Arms
High St ✉ WR12 7DU – ✆ (01386) 852 255
– www.barcelo-hotels.co.uk/lygonarms
72 rm – †£ 104/265 ††£ 144/305 – 6 suites
Rest Goblets – see restaurant listing
Rest Great Hall – (closed Saturday lunch) Carte £ 35/57 s
- Superbly enticing, quintessentially English coaching inn with many 16C architectural details in its panelled, beamed interiors, and in rooms that Charles I and Cromwell once stayed in. Refined dining amongst baronial splendours, including a minstrels' gallery.

Broadway
The Green ✉ WR12 7AA – ✆ (01386) 852 401 – www.cotswold-inns-hotels.co.uk
19 rm – †£ 115/155 ††£ 155/215
Rest Courtyard – Menu £ 13/28 – Carte £ 22/31
- Characterful 16C inn set on the green in the heart of the village; originally an abbot's retreat. Classically styled guest areas. Crisp, light colour schemes in more modern bedrooms. Timbered, horse racing themed bar. Modern British cooking and good value lunches.

BROADWAY

Olive Branch without rest
78 High St ⊠ WR12 7AJ – ✆ *(01386) 853 440*
– www.theolivebranch-broadway.com
8 rm – †£ 55/85 ††£ 88/110
♦ Welcoming guesthouse run by experienced husband and wife team; formerly a 1950s staging post. Pleasantly cluttered bedrooms with thoughtful extras – one has a small veranda. Rustic, characterful dining room with homemade cakes at breakfast.

Windrush House without rest
Station Rd ⊠ WR12 7DE – ✆ *(01386) 853 577 – www.windrushhouse.com*
– Closed January and Christmas
5 rm – †£ 75 ††£ 90
♦ Fresh, modern guesthouse with landscaped garden, set in a picturesque village. Comfortable lounge. Light, airy bedrooms come with homemade biscuits; some boast wrought iron beds.

Russell's with rm
20 High St ⊠ WR12 7DT – ✆ *(01386) 853 555 – www.russellsofbroadway.co.uk*
– Closed Sunday dinner
7 rm – †£ 80/98 ††£ 245/300 **Rest** – Menu £ 16 (lunch) – Carte £ 26/36
♦ Behind the splendid Cotswold stone façade lies a stylish modern restaurant with terrace front and rear. Seasonally influenced, regularly changing menus. Smart, comfy bedrooms.

Goblets – at Lygon Arms Hotel
High St ⊠ WR12 7DU – ✆ *(01386) 854 418*
– www.barcleo-hotels.co.uk/lygonarms.co.uk – Closed Monday
Rest – *(booking essential)* Carte £ 22/28 **s**
♦ Characterfully firelit in rustic dark oak. Modern dining room at front more atmospheric than one to rear. Menus of light, tasty, seasonal dishes offered.

ENGLAND

BROCKENHURST – Hampshire – 503 P31 – pop. 2 865 ▐ Great Britain   6 A2
▶ London 99 mi – Bournemouth 17 mi – Southampton 14 mi – Winchester 27 mi
▣ Brockenhurst Manor Sway Rd, ✆ (01590) 62 33 32
▣ New Forest★★ (Rhinefield Ornamental Drive★★, Bolderwood Ornamental Drive★★)

Rhinefield House
Rhinefield Rd, Northwest : 3 mi ⊠ SO42 7QB – ✆ *(01590) 625 600*
– www.rhinefieldhousehotel.co.uk
50 rm – †£ 99/255 ††£ 109/265 – 1 suite
Rest *Armada* – *(dinner only and Sunday lunch)* Menu £ 36 – Carte £ 48/58
Rest *The Brasserie* – Carte £ 25/48
♦ Impressive country house with ornamental pond, parterres and yew maze, in 40 acres of tranquil forest parkland. Period features include ornate wood carvings. Contemporary bedrooms boast the latest mod cons; rooms in the original house are more characterful. Fine dining in Armada. Relaxed Brasserie with terrace.

New Park Manor
Lyndhurst Rd, North : 1.5 mi on A 337 ⊠ SO42 7QH – ✆ *(01590) 623 467*
– www.newparkmanorhotel.co.uk
24 rm (dinner included) – †£ 120/220 ††£ 190/255
Rest *The Stag* – Menu £ 20/43 **s**
♦ Extended, elegantly proportioned former hunting lodge built by Charles II on his return from France. Classic bedrooms in the main house; those in the Forest Wing are more contemporary. Candlelit fine dining.

BROCKENHURST

Cloud
Meerut Rd ⊠ SO42 7TD – ℰ (01590) 622 165 – www.cloudhotel.co.uk
– Closed 27 December-13 January
18 rm – †£ 81/170 ††£ 162/176
Rest *Encore* – Menu £ 18/30
- Well-kept hotel made up of four cottages, set on the edge of a pretty New Forest town; photos attest to the owner's past as a tiller girl. Neat, tidy bedrooms. Busy, linen-laid restaurant with conservatory extension and theatrical theme; traditional menus.

Cottage Lodge without rest
Sway Rd ⊠ SO42 7SH – ℰ (01590) 622 296 – www.cottagelodge.co.uk – Closed Christmas
15 rm – †£ 80/100 ††£ 140/160
- 350 year old former forester's cottage in the heart of the village: proudly run by welcoming owner. Low oak-beamed ceiling, cosy snug bar and large, neatly appointed rooms.

The Pig with rm
Beaulieu Rd, East : 1 mi on B 3055 ⊠ SO42 7QL – ℰ (01590) 622 354
– www.thepighotel.co.uk
26 rm – †£ 125/175 ††£ 175/225, ⊇ £ 15 **Rest** – Menu £ 20/30
- Georgian house in 14 acres of mature gardens, in charming New Forest setting. Relaxed dining, where the kitchen makes good use of local produce. Keen, attentive service. Stylish, modern lounges; attractive terraces. Spacious, contemporary bedrooms offer a good level of facilities.

Thatched Cottage with rm
16 Brookley Rd ⊠ SO42 7RR – ℰ (01590) 623 090 – www.thatchedcottage.co.uk
6 rm – †£ 30/90 ††£ 140, ⊇ £ 10
Rest – *(closed Sunday dinner, Monday and Tuesday) (booking essential)* Menu £ 29 – Carte £ 21/29
- Long-standing restaurant set in traditional, very individually styled 17C farmhouse, with wood-furnished terrace and open kitchen. Classic dishes on locally sourced menu. Cottage-style bedrooms.

BROCKTON – Shropshire – see Much Wenlock

BROMESWELL – Suffolk – see Woodbridge

BROMFIELD – Shropshire – 503 L26 – see Ludlow

BROUGHTON GIFFORD – Wiltshire
4 C2
▶ London 109 mi – Bristol 31 mi – Cardiff 64 mi – Southampton 81 mi

Fox
The Street ⊠ SN12 8PN – ℰ (01225) 782 949
– www.thefox-broughtongifford.co.uk – Closed 25 December, 1 January, Sunday dinner and Monday
Rest – *(booking essential at weekends)* Menu £ 18 (lunch) – Carte £ 24/39
- Raising the profile of this pub, both locally and farther afield, has been a labour of love for its young owner. Cooking is simple, unfussy and fresh, using what's in the garden: salad leaves, fruits, chickens and pigs.

BRUNDALL – Norfolk – 504 Y26 – pop. 5 832
15 D2
▶ London 118 mi – Great Yarmouth 15 mi – Norwich 8 mi

Lavender House
39 The Street ⊠ NR13 5AA – ℰ (01603) 712 215 – www.lavenderhouse.co.uk
– Closed 26 December-8 January, Sunday dinner, Monday and Tuesday
Rest – *(dinner only and Sunday lunch) (booking advisable)* Menu £ 40
- Characterful low-ceilinged thatched cottage with comfy lounge and bar, cosy dining rooms and impressive 8-seater table in kitchen. Original monthly menus display interesting modern twists.

BRUNTINGTHORPE – Leicestershire — Great Britain   16 B3
▶ London 96 mi – Leicester 10 mi – Market Harborough 15 mi
◉ Leicester - Museum and Art Gallery★, Guildhall★ and St Mary de Castro Church★, N : 11 mi by minor rd and A 5199

The Joiners
Church Walk ✉ LE17 5QH – ✆ (0116) 247 82 58 – www.thejoinersarms.co.uk
– Closed Sunday dinner and Monday
Rest – (booking essential) Menu £ 14 (lunch) – Carte £ 26/30
♦ Neat and tidy whitewashed pub with characterful interior. Good value menus offer a mix of refined pub classics and brasserie-style dishes, cooked and presented in a straightforward manner.

BRUSHFORD – Somerset – 503 J30 – see Dulverton

BRUTON – Somerset – 503 M30 – pop. 2 982   4 C2
▶ London 118 mi – Bristol 27 mi – Bournemouth 44 mi – Salisbury 35 mi
◉ Stourhead★★★ AC, W : 8 mi by B 3081

At The Chapel
High St ✉ BA10 0AE – ✆ (01749) 814 070 – www.atthechapel.co.uk
– Closed Sunday dinner
Rest – Carte £ 21/32
♦ Stylish, informal restaurant in former 18C chapel, with bakery to one side and wine shop to the other. Well-priced, daily menus offer rustic, Mediterranean-influenced dishes; wood-fired breads, pizzas and cakes a speciality. Friendly team.

BRYHER – 503 A/B34 – see Scilly (Isles of)

BUCKDEN – Cambridgeshire – 504 T27 – pop. 2 385 – ✉ Huntingdon   14 A2
▶ London 65 mi – Bedford 15 mi – Cambridge 20 mi – Northampton 31 mi

George
High St ✉ PE19 5XA – ✆ (01480) 812 300 – www.thegeorgebuckden.com
12 rm ☑ – †£ 100/120 ††£ 150
Rest *Brasserie* – see restaurant listing
♦ Delightfully restored former 19C coaching inn with stylish, contemporary look, typified by leather tub chairs and sofas. Smart bedrooms are all named after famous Georges.

Brasserie – at George Hotel
High St ✉ PE19 5XA – ✆ (01480) 812 300 – www.thegeorgebuckden.com
Rest – Menu £ 18 (lunch) – Carte dinner £ 27/42
♦ Spacious, modern brasserie serving a range of dishes, from traditional English game to coq au vin and even tempura of squid. French windows lead to a courtyard, creating an airy feel.

BUCKHORN WESTON – Dorset   4 C3
▶ London 117 mi – Poole 36 mi – Bath 33 mi – Weymouth 37 mi

Stapleton Arms with rm
Church Hill ✉ SP8 5HS – ✆ (01963) 370 396 – www.thestapletonarms.com
– Closed 25-26 December
4 rm ☑ – †£ 72/96 ††£ 90/120   **Rest** – Carte £ 21/28
♦ Stylish, shabby-chic pub with elegant dining room; muddy boots, dogs and children are all welcome. Wide-ranging menu offers traditional choices with some Mediterranean touches. Spacious, contemporary bedrooms – some boast underfloor heating.

BUCKINGHAM – Buckinghamshire – 503 Q27 – pop. 12 512   11 C1
Great Britain
▶ London 64 mi – Birmingham 61 mi – Northampton 20 mi – Oxford 25 mi
⛳ Silverstone Stowe Silverstone Rd, ✆ (01280) 85 00 05
⛳ Tingewick Rd, ✆ (01280) 81 55 66
◉ Stowe Gardens★★, NW : 3 mi by minor rd. Claydon House★ AC, S : 8 mi by A 413

BUCKINGHAM

Villiers
3 Castle St ⊠ MK18 1BS – ☏ (01280) 822 444 – www.oxfordshire-hotels.co.uk
49 rm ⊇ – †£ 130/160 ††£ 170/180 – 3 suites
Rest *Villiers* – (closed dinner 25 December) Menu £ 17/21
– Carte dinner £ 29/34

♦ Professionally run hotel on central street. Spacious, bedrooms vary in style: some boasting original beams and eaves; all equally comfy with large, well-kept bathrooms. Modern restaurant offers appealing British menu. Locals often pop in to the lounges for coffee.

BUCKLAND MARSH – Oxfordshire – pop. 2 243   10 A2
▶ London 76 mi – Faringdon 4 mi – Oxford 15 mi

Trout at Tadpole Bridge with rm
⊠ SN7 8RF – ☏ (01367) 870 382 – www.troutinn.co.uk – Closed 25-26 December and Sunday dinner November-March
6 rm ⊇ – †£ 70/80 ††£ 120/150   **Rest** – Carte £ 22/34

♦ Smart pub with attractive garden leading down to the Thames. Concise menu consists of classic Gallic dishes with contemporary touches; seafood and game often feature as specials. Comfy bedrooms exceed expectations. Private moorings available.

BUCKLAND NEWTON – Dorset – 503 M31 – pop. 618   4 C3
▶ London 214 mi

Gaggle of Geese
⊠ DT2 7BS – ☏ (01300) 345 249 – www.thegaggle.co.uk – Closed 25 December
Rest – Carte £ 19/27

♦ Shabby-chic pub with skittle alley and relaxed, boho feel. Vegetable garden, orchard and paddocks supply the kitchen; hearty pub dishes but refined presentation. Hosts regular village events.

BUDE – Cornwall – 503 G31 – pop. 3 681   1 B2
▶ London 252 mi – Exeter 51 mi – Plymouth 50 mi – Truro 53 mi
🛈 The Crescent ☏ (01288) 35 42 40, www.visitbude.info
⛳ Burn View, ☏ (01288) 35 20 06
👁 The Breakwater★★ – Compass Point (≤★)
🌀 Poughill★ (church★★), N : 2.5 mi – E : Tamar River★★ – Kilkhampton (Church★), NE : 5.5 mi by A 39 – Stratton (Church★), E : 1.5 mi – Launcells (Church★), E : 3 mi by A 3072 – Marhamchurch (St Morwenne's Church★), SE : 2.5 mi by A 39 – Poundstock★ (≤★★, church★, guildhouse★), S : 4.5 mi by A 39. Morwenstow (cliffs★★, church★), N : 8.5 mi by A 39 and minor roads - Jacobstow (Church★), S : 7 mi by A 39

Falcon
Breakwater Rd ⊠ EX23 8SD – ☏ (01288) 352 005 – www.falconhotel.com
– Closed 25 December
29 rm ⊇ – †£ 65/83 ††£ 130/140 – 1 suite
Rest – (bar lunch Monday-Saturday) Carte £ 21/30 s

♦ An imposing, personally run hotel with the proudly traditional character of a bygone age. Contemporary and classic blend in bedrooms. Separate private garden. Formal dining.

XX Sea Fever
Summerleaze Cres. ⊠ EX23 8HJ – ☏ (01288) 352 893 – www.sea-fever.co.uk
– Closed 2 weeks January-February, 1 week November, Sunday and Monday
Rest – Menu £ 24 – Carte £ 26/33

♦ Modern hotel restaurant with striking black, white and grey flowered wallpaper and purple, brushed velvet banquettes. Choice of classics on the à la carte, more ambitious dishes on the tasting menu or a mix of the two on the set selection.

BUDLEIGH SALTERTON – Devon – **503** K32 – pop. 4 801   **2** D2
▶ London 182 mi – Exeter 16 mi – Plymouth 55 mi
🛈 Fore St ✆ (01395) 44 52 75, www.visitbudleigh.com
🏌 East Devon Links Rd, Budleigh Salterton, ✆ (01395) 44 33 70
◉ East Budleigh (Church★), N : 2.5 mi by A 376 – Bicton★ (Gardens★) **AC**, N : 3 mi by A 376

Long Range
5 Vales Rd, by Raleigh Rd ✉ EX9 6HS – ✆ (01395) 443 321
– www.thelongrangehotel.co.uk – *Restricted opening in winter*
9 rm – ♦£ 60/80 ♦♦£ 100/112   **Rest** – Carte £ 19/30
♦ Homely and unassuming guesthouse, personally run in quiet residential street. Sun lounge with bright aspect, overlooking broad lawn and neat borders. Simple, unfussy rooms. Tasty, locally sourced dishes in a comfy dining room.

BUNBURY – **502** M24 – pop. 1 308 – ✉ Tarporley   **20** A3
▶ London 183 mi – Birmingham 68 mi – Liverpool 39 mi – Sheffield 87 mi

Yew Tree Inn
Long Ln, Spurstow ✉ CW6 9RD – ✆ (01829) 260 274
– www.theyewtreebunbury.com
Rest – Carte £ 23/28
♦ Attractive part red brick, part black and white timbered pub with central bar and smaller rustic rooms surrounding it. Extensive menus offer local and home-made produce. Regular themed events.

BUNGAY – Suffolk – **504** Y26 – pop. 4 895 Great Britain   **15** D2
▶ London 108 mi – Beccles 6 mi – Ipswich 38 mi
◉ Norwich★★ – Cathedral★★, Castle Museum★, Market Place★, NW : 15 mi by B 1332 and A 146

Castle Inn with rm
35 Earsham St ✉ NR35 1AF – ✆ (01986) 892 283 – www.thecastleinn.net
– *Closed 25 December*
4 rm – ♦£ 70 ♦♦£ 100
Rest – *(closed Sunday dinner)* Menu £ 19 (lunch) – Carte £ 20/30
♦ Sky-blue pub with open-plan dining area and intimate rear bar. Fresh, simple and seasonal country based cooking; the Innkeeper's platter of local produce is a perennial favourite. Tasty homemade cakes and cookies on display. Homely, comfortable bedrooms.

at Earsham Southwest : 3 mi by A 144 and A 143 – ✉ Bungay

Earsham Park Farm without rest
Old Railway Rd, on A 143 ✉ NR35 2AQ – ✆ (01986) 892 180
– www.earsham-parkfarm.co.uk
4 rm – ♦£ 51/61 ♦♦£ 82/102
♦ Appealing red-brick farmhouse on a working farm. Country-style interior displays sculptures and stencilling by the charming owner. Individually furnished bedrooms boast attractive furnishings. Extensive breakfasts include their own homemade bacon and sausages.

BURCOMBE – Wiltshire – see Salisbury

BURFORD – Oxfordshire – **503** P28 – pop. 1 171   **10** A2
▶ London 76 mi – Birmingham 55 mi – Gloucester 32 mi – Oxford 20 mi
🛈 Sheep St ✆ (01993) 82 35 58, www.burfordcotswolds.co.uk
🏌 Burford Golf Club, ✆ (01993) 82 25 83

Bay Tree
Sheep St ✉ OX18 4LW – ✆ (01993) 822 791
– www.cotswold-inns-hotels.co.uk/bay-tree
18 rm – ♦£ 120/130 ♦♦£ 170/210 – 3 suites
Rest – Menu £ 16/32 – Carte £ 24/31
♦ Characterful, creeper-clad 16C house with coaching inn style, antique furnishings and original features. Two front lounges with vast stone fireplaces. Comfortable bedrooms. Light, airy restaurant overlooking beautiful landscaped garden.

BURFORD

Burford House
99 High St ⊠ OX18 4QA – ℰ (01993) 823 151 – www.burfordhouse.co.uk
8 rm ⊇ – **†** £ 128/193 **††** £ 165/205
Rest – *(closed Sunday) (lunch only and dinner Thursday-Saturday)*
Menu £ 17/36 – Carte approx. £ 20
♦ Characterful 17C B&W timbered townhouse. Lounge and garden room have a subtle, contemporary edge, while comfy, individually decorated bedrooms are more traditional in style. Good breakfasts, homely lunches and gourmet dinners in informal restaurant.

Cotland House without rest
Fulbrook Hill, Fulbrook, Northeast : 0.5 mi on A 361 ⊠ OX18 4BH – ℰ (01993) 822 382 – www.cotlandhouse.com
4 rm ⊇ – **†** £ 70 **††** £ 75/95
♦ Bright, modern house in Cotswold stone; its cool, light décor tinged with Gallic style. Neatly kept by friendly owner, with candles, magazines, fresh flowers and top-name toiletries.

Lamb Inn with rm
Sheep St ⊠ OX18 4LR – ℰ (01993) 823 155 – www.cotswold-inns-hotels.co.uk
17 rm ⊇ – **†** £ 155 **††** £ 270 **Rest** – Menu £ 25/39 – Carte £ 25/38
♦ 15C weavers' cottage set in a charming town. Bar offers light bites and afternoon tea; the restaurant, a daily market and set menu. Ambitious cooking is robust and classically based. Bedrooms are cosy; Rosie has its own garden.

Highway Inn with rm
117 High St ⊠ OX18 4RG – ℰ (01993) 823 661 – www.thehighwayinn.co.uk
– Closed first 2 weeks January and 25-26 December
9 rm ⊇ – **†** £ 79/99 **††** £ 89/140 **Rest** – Carte £ 24/34
♦ Characterful, personally run beamed inn dating from 1480. Simple, honest cooking of pub classics, with an emphasis on local produce; tasty nursery puddings. Classic, cosy bedrooms.

Carpenter's Arms
Fulbrook Hill, Northeast : 0.5 mi on A 361 ⊠ OX18 4BH – ℰ (01993) 823 275 – www.thecarpentersarmsfulbrook.com
Rest – Menu £ 17 (lunch) – Carte £ 21/27
♦ Its unassuming outer appearance gives little clue as the warm, inviting style within. Expect robust and competitively prices dishes, from grilled chops to cod with chickpea stew. Personally run.

at Swinbrook East : 2.75 mi by A 40 – ⊠ Burford

Swan Inn with rm
⊠ OX18 4DY – ℰ (01993) 823 339 – www.theswannswinbrook.co.uk
– Closed 25-26 December
6 rm ⊇ – **†** £ 80/120 **††** £ 120 **Rest** – Carte £ 20/35
♦ Wisteria-clad, honey-coloured pub on the riverbank boasting a lovely garden filled with fruit trees. Charming interior displays an open oak frame and exposed stone walls hung with old photos. Daily menu features the latest local produce and a modern take on older recipes. Well-appointed bedrooms have a luxurious feel.

BURLTON – Shropshire – ⊠ Shrewsbury   18 B1
▶ London 235 mi – Shrewsbury 10 mi – Wrexham 20 mi

Burlton Inn with rm
⊠ SY4 5TB – ℰ (01939) 270 284 – www.burltoninn.com – Closed 25 December
6 rm ⊇ – **†** £ 85 **††** £ 105 **Rest** – *(closed Sunday dinner)* Carte £ 21/30
♦ Characterful 18C whitewashed inn with pleasant terrace and pretty fountain. Keenly priced menus feature unfussy classical cooking, with lighter snacks at lunch and more adventurous dishes in the evening. Neat, wood-furnished bedrooms boast large bathrooms.

BURNHAM MARKET – Norfolk – **504** W25 – pop. 898 – Great Britain   **15** C1

► London 128 mi – Cambridge 71 mi – Norwich 36 mi
Lambourne Dromore Rd, ℰ (01628) 66 67 55
Holkham Hall ★★ **AC**, E : 3 mi by B 1155

Hoste Arms
The Green ⊠ *PE31 8HD* – ℰ *(01328) 738 777* – www.hostearms.co.uk
34 rm – †£ 192/210 ††£ 261/281 – 1 suite
Rest *Hoste Arms* – see restaurant listing

• Extended 17C inn, in the heart of a pretty village. Stylish, comfortable bedrooms boast a high level of facilities and include the eye-catching Zulu wing with its South African themed décor. Smart beauty and wellness spa features treatment rooms and a relaxing outdoor seating area.

Vine House without rest
The Green ⊠ *PE31 8HD* – ℰ *(01328) 738 777*
– www.vinehouseboutiquehotel.co.uk
6 rm – †£ 149/232 ††£ 213/298 – 1 suite

• Stylish, comfortable and elegant rooms with great bathrooms at this extended Georgian house. Evening butler service for drinks. Reception and meals at Hoste Arms opposite.

Railway Inn without rest
Creake Rd ⊠ *PE31 8HD* – ℰ *(01328) 738 777* – www.hostearms.co.uk
8 rm – †£ 80/141 ††£ 97/152

• Former station house with derelict platform and carriage to rear. Stylish, contemporary bedrooms boast bold feature walls, modern furniture, retro fittings and good facilities.

Hoste Arms
The Green ⊠ *PE31 8HD* – ℰ *(01328) 738 777* – www.hostearms.co.uk
Rest – (booking advisable) Carte £ 25/30

• Extensive restaurant offering a choice of dining areas, including a rustic bar, informal conservatory and Moroccan garden. Classically based menus feature global influences, with an emphasis on local produce. Friendly, polite service.

BURNHAM-ON-CROUCH – Essex – **504** W29   **13** D2

► London 53 mi – Croydon 58 mi – Barnet 61 mi – Ealing 74 mi

Contented Sole
80 High St ⊠ *CM0 8AA* – ℰ *(01621) 786 900* – www.contentedsole.co.uk
– Closed 26 December-18 January, Sunday dinner and Tuesday
Rest – Menu £ 22 (weekdays) – Carte £ 33/43

• 18C house that's been a draw for diners since the '60s. Traditional interior with old beams and oak panelling. Unfussy cooking uses flavourful seasonal ingredients in familiar combinations.

BURNSALL – North Yorkshire – **502** O21 – pop. 108 – ⊠ Skipton   **22** A2

► London 223 mi – Bradford 26 mi – Leeds 29 mi

Devonshire Fell
⊠ *BD23 6BT* – ℰ *(01756) 729 000* – www.devonshirefell.co.uk
10 rm – †£ 103/144 ††£ 144/196 – 2 suites
Rest – (light lunch Monday-Saturday) Carte £ 26/42

• Stone-built hotel – once a club for 19C mill owners – decorated with bold colours and striking, contemporary artwork. Spacious bedrooms boast dale views. Formal, linen-clad conservatory and more funky, modern brasserie; wide-ranging, modern menu.

Red Lion with rm
⊠ *BD23 6BU* – ℰ *(01756) 720 204* – www.redlion.co.uk
21 rm – †£ 70/90 ††£ 113/158 – 4 suites   **Rest** – Carte £ 20/37

• Appealing stone inn on the riverbank with cosy bar, laid-back lounge and formally dressed dining room. Extensive menus offer local meat/fish/game, pub favourites and daily specials. Classic bedrooms have modern overtones; the annexe rooms are more contemporary.

BURPHAM – West Sussex – **504** S30 – see Arundel

BURRINGTON – Devon – 503 I31 – pop. 533 2 C1
London 260 mi – Barnstaple 14 mi – Exeter 28 mi – Taunton 50 mi

Northcote Manor
Northwest : 2 mi on A 377 – EX37 9LZ – ℰ (01769) 560 501 – www.northcotemanor.co.uk
14 rm – †£ 110/170 ††£ 160/215 – 1 suite
Rest – *(booking essential)* Menu £ 42 (dinner) – Carte £ 20/34
♦ Creeper-clad hall in the Torr Valley, dating from 1716. Fine fabrics and antiques in elegant, individually styled rooms; attention to well-judged detail lends air of idyllic calm. Country house restaurant features eye-catching murals.

BURTON BRADSTOCK – Dorset – 503 L31 – see Bridport

BURTON-UPON-TRENT – Staffordshire – 502 O25 – pop. 43 784 19 C1
London 128 mi – Birmingham 29 mi – Leicester 27 mi – Nottingham 27 mi
Market Place ℰ (01283) 50 80 00, www.eaststaffsbc.gov.uk
Branston G. & C.C. Burton Rd, ℰ (01283) 52 83 20
Craythorne Stretton Craythorne Rd, ℰ (01283) 56 43 29

at Stretton Northwest : 3.25 mi by A 5121 (A 38 Derby) – Burton-Upon-Trent

Dovecliff Hall
Dovecliff Rd – DE13 0DJ – ℰ (01283) 531 818 – www.dovecliffhallhotel.co.uk
15 rm – †£ 99 ††£ 120
Rest – *(closed Sunday dinner)* Menu £ 19/22 – Carte £ 30/43
♦ Imposing, listed 1790s house with lovely gardens and spacious rooms, nestling in an elevated position above the Trent. Airy bedrooms, most boasting garden vistas. Formal dining rooms in restaurant and delightful orangery.

BURY – Greater Manchester – 502 N23 – pop. 60 718 20 B2
London 211 mi – Leeds 45 mi – Liverpool 35 mi – Manchester 9 mi
Market St ℰ (0161) 253 51 11, www.visitbury.com
Greenmount, ℰ (01204) 88 37 12

Waggon
131 Bury and Rochdale Old Rd, Birtle, East : 2 mi on B 6222 – BL9 6UE – ℰ (01706) 622 955 – www.thewaggonatbirtle.com – Closed 26 December-2 January, 2 weeks summer, Monday and Tuesday
Rest – *(dinner only and lunch Thursday, Friday and Sunday)* Menu £ 17 (lunch and weekday dinner) – Carte £ 24/36
♦ Unprepossessing façade hides a pleasantly decorated eatery with good value, no-nonsense cooking featuring a decidedly strong Lancashire base and the famous Bury Black Pudding.

BURY ST EDMUNDS – Suffolk – 504 W27 – pop. 36 218 15 C2
Great Britain
London 79 mi – Cambridge 27 mi – Ipswich 26 mi – Norwich 41 mi
6 Angel Hill ℰ (01284) 76 46 67, www.visit-burystedmunds.co.uk
The Suffolk Golf and Spa Hotel Fornham St Genevieve, ℰ (01284) 70 67 77
Town★ - Abbey and Cathedral★
Ickworth House★ **AC**, SW : 3 mi by A 143

Angel
3 Angel Hill – IP33 1LT – ℰ (01284) 714 000 – www.theangel.co.uk
73 rm – †£ 115/130 ††£ 130/220 – 1 suite
Rest *Eaterie* – see restaurant listing
♦ 15C coaching inn with attractive creeper-clad Georgian façade, set opposite Abbey Gardens. Relaxed, contemporary interior with open-fired lounge. No two bedrooms are the same; some are modern in style, others are classic four-poster suites.

BURY ST EDMUNDS

Ounce House without rest
Northgate St – IP33 1HP – ℰ (01284) 761 779 – www.ouncehouse.co.uk
5 rm – †£ 85/95 ††£ 130/135
♦ Two 1870s houses knocked together; well furnished with Victorian elegance. Spacious, individually styled bedrooms; well-chosen antiques contribute to a characterful interior.

Maison Bleue
30-31 Churchgate St – IP33 1RG – ℰ (01284) 760 623 – www.maisonbleue.co.uk
– Closed 3 weeks January, 2 weeks summer, Sunday and Monday
Rest – Seafood – Menu £ 20/32 – Carte £ 29/43
♦ 17C glass-fronted house with blue canopies, set in the heart of town. Chic, pastel grey colour scheme with modern landscapes. Well-presented cooking displays classic French roots, with fish the main element of the monthly changing menu. Formal, efficient service.

Pea Porridge
28-29 Cannon St – IP33 1JR – ℰ (01284) 700 200 – www.peaporridge.co.uk
– Closed last week December, first week January, 2 weeks summer, Sunday and Monday
Rest – (booking advisable) Menu £ 16 (weekday dinner) – Carte £ 26/30
♦ Charming restaurant in cosy 19C brick cottage – a former bakery – well run by husband and wife team. Tasty, seasonal, country-style cooking with a strong Mediterranean bias. Great value lunch menus. Biodynamic and organic old world wines. Efficient service.

Eaterie – at Angel Hotel
3 Angel Hill – IP33 1LT – ℰ (01284) 714 000 – www.theangel.co.uk
Rest – Menu £ 18 (lunch) – Carte £ 27/45
♦ Informal bistro in an attractive 15C coaching inn, where Dickens once stayed. Bright room boasts a long bar and modern artwork. Accessible menu offers modern European brasserie-style dishes.

at Ixworth Northeast : 7 mi by A 143 – ⊠ Bury St Edmunds

Theobalds
68 High St – IP31 2HJ – ℰ (01359) 231 707 – www.theobaldsrestaurant.co.uk
– Closed 1 week early summer, Monday and dinner Sunday
Rest – (dinner only and lunch Sunday and Friday) Menu £ 29 – Carte £ 31/36
♦ Beamed part 16C cottage with a cosy firelit lounge. Friendly service and well-judged seasonal menus combine heartwarming favourites and contemporary dishes.

at Beyton East : 6 mi by A 14 – ⊠ Bury St Edmunds

Manorhouse without rest
The Green – IP30 9AF – ℰ (01359) 270 960 – www.beyton.com
4 rm – †£ 50/60 ††£ 73/80
♦ Attractive, part-15C Suffolk longhouse with large rear garden, overlooking the village green. Cosy beamed lounge-cum-breakfast room with huge fireplace, sofas and individual dining tables. Spacious, understated bedrooms have a rustic feel; 2 are in the old barn.

at Whepstead South : 4.5 mi by A 143 on B 1066

The White Horse
Rede Rd – IP29 4SS – ℰ (01284) 735 760 – www.whitehorsewhepstead.co.uk
– Closed 1 week in January, 25-26 December and Sunday dinner
Rest – Carte £ 12/20
♦ Cheerfully run 17C village pub; choose between a characterful beamed room and the brighter Gallery with local artists' work. The kitchen's strength lies in the more conventional dishes.

BURY ST EDMUNDS

at Horringer Southwest : 3 mi on A 143 – ✉ Bury St Edmunds

Ickworth
✉ IP29 5QE – ✆ (01284) 735 350 – www.ickworthhotel.co.uk
26 rm ☐ – †£ 110/310 ††£ 120/345 – 12 suites
Rest *Fredericks* – (dinner only) Menu £ 43 **s**
Rest *Conservatory* – Carte £ 25/36

♦ Family-orientated hotel set in the east wing of a grand 200 year old mansion: formerly home to the Marquise of Bristol and now owned by the National Trust. Set in 1,800 acres it boasts three airy drawing rooms and comfy bedrooms with views. Smart Fredericks overlooks gardens. Casual dining in impressive former orangery.

BUSHEY – Hertfordshire – 504 S29 – pop. 17 001   12 A2

▶ London 18 mi – Luton 21 mi – Watford 3 mi
🏌 Bushey Hall Bushey Hall Drive, ✆ (01923) 22 22 53
🏌 Bushey G. & C.C. High St, ✆ (020) 8950 22 83

Plan : see Greater London (North-West) 1

Alpine
135 High Rd ✉ WD23 1JA – ✆ (020) 8950 2024
– www.thealpinerestaurant.co.uk – Closed 26-27 December, dinner 25 December and Monday
Rest – Italian – Menu £ 17/24 – Carte £ 30/35   **BTc**

♦ Long-standing family restaurant with low lighting, bold wallpaper and contemporary fabrics. Honest Italian menu displays influences from Sicily and Emilia-Romagna, ranging from family classics to more modern interpretations; homemade pasta.

BUTTERMERE – Cumbria – 502 K20 – pop. 139 – ✉ Cockermouth   21 A2

▶ London 306 mi – Carlisle 35 mi – Kendal 43 mi

Wood House
Northwest : 0.5 mi on B 5289 ✉ CA13 9XA – ✆ (017687) 70 208
– www.wdhse.co.uk – April-October
3 rm ☐ – †£ 70 ††£ 110   **Rest** – Menu £ 29 **s**

♦ 16C house in a wonderfully serene lakeside setting with stunning views. Well-appointed lounge; antique furnished bedrooms. Meals cooked on the Aga using fresh seasonal, local ingredients and served family-style around an antique table.

BUXHALL – Suffolk – see Stowmarket

BUXTON – Derbyshire – 502 O24 – pop. 20 836   16 A1

▶ London 172 mi – Derby 38 mi – Manchester 25 mi – Stoke-on-Trent 24 mi
ℹ The Cultural Quarter ✆ (01298) 2 51 06, www.visitbuxton.co.uk
🏌 Buxton and High Peak Townend, ✆ (01298) 2 62 63

Buxton's Victorian without rest
3A Broad Walk ✉ SK17 6JE – ✆ (01298) 78 759 – www.buxtonvictorian.co.uk
– Closed Christmas-New Year
7 rm ☐ – †£ 54/70 ††£ 94/100

♦ Charming Victorian house built in 1860 for the Duke of Devonshire. Cosy lounge and breakfast room with views over boating lake and bandstand. Bedrooms boast period furniture.

Grendon without rest
Bishops Ln., Southeast : 0.75 mi by A 53 ✉ SK17 6UN – ✆ (01298) 78 831
– www.grendonguesthouse.co.uk – Closed January
5 rm ☐ – †£ 50/70 ††£ 80/95

♦ Cosy Edwardian house on edge of town, built for a wealthy mill owner in the 1900s, with period features and pleasant gardens. Comfortable, traditionally furnished bedrooms.

CALLINGTON – Cornwall – 503 H32 – pop. 4 048 2 C2
▶ London 237 mi – Exeter 53 mi – Plymouth 15 mi – Truro 46 mi

XX Langmans VISA ⊚ AE
3 Church St ✉ PL17 7RE – ℰ (01579) 384 933 – www.langmansrestaurant.co.uk – Closed Sunday-Wednesday
Rest – *(dinner only) (booking essential) (set menu only)* Menu £ 38
♦ Quaint double-fronted shop conversion; run by husband and wife team. Pre-dinner drinks in lounge followed by 6 course tasting menu in rear dining room. Refined, precise cooking.

CALLOW HILL – Worcestershire 19 C3
▶ London 120 mi – Birmingham 26 mi – Coventry 35 mi – Wolverhampton 27 mi

Royal Forester with rm
✉ DY14 9XW – ℰ (01299) 266 286 – www.royalforesterinn.co.uk
7 rm ⊑ – †£ 55 ††£ 79
Rest – Menu £ 15 (weekdays) – Carte dinner £ 24/38
♦ Pub dating from 1411; rustic dining room, relaxed atmosphere and bright, contemporary bar with grand piano. Simple, flavourful cooking and informative, bi-monthly menu. Fresh, modern, food-themed bedrooms; Aubergine, Pear and Cherry are the largest.

CALNE – Wiltshire – 503 O29 – pop. 13 789 4 C2
▶ London 91 mi – Bristol 33 mi – Southampton 63 mi – Swindon 17 mi
◉ Bowood House★ **AC**, (Library ≤★) SW : 2 mi by A 4 – Avebury★★ (The Stones★, Church★) E : 6 mi by A 4

Bowood
Derry Hill, West : 3 mi by A 4 on Derry Hill rd ✉ SN11 9PQ – ℰ (01249) 822 228 – www.bowood-hotel.co.uk
43 rm ⊑ – †£ 155/205 ††£ 175/285
Rest *Shelburne* – *(dinner only and Sunday lunch)* Carte £ 28/50
Rest *Clubhouse Brasserie* – Menu £ 25 (dinner) – Carte lunch £ 19/40
♦ Smart, professionally run, purpose-built hotel in grounds of Lord and Lady Lansdowne's Estate. Contemporary country house styling. Spacious bedrooms; some with balconies. Modern British cooking in formal Shelburne, with attractive terrace. Brasserie menu in golf clubhouse.

CAMBER – E. Sussex – 504 W31 – see Rye

CAMBRIDGE – Cambridgeshire – 504 U27 – pop. 117 010 14 B3
🟩 Great Britain
▶ London 55 mi – Coventry 88 mi – Ipswich 54 mi – Kingston-upon-Hull 137 mi
✈ Cambridge City Airport : ℰ (01223) 373765, E : 2 mi on A 1303 X
🛈 Paes Hill ℰ (0871) 2 26 80 06, www.visitcambridge.org
🏨 Cambridge Menzies Hotel Bar Hill, ℰ (01954) 78 00 98
◉ Town★★★ – St John's College★★★ **AC** Y – King's College★★ (King's College Chapel★★★) Z The Backs★★ YZ – Fitzwilliam Museum★★ Z **M1** – Trinity College★★ Y – Clare College★ Z **B** – Kettle's Yard★ Y **M2** – Queen's College★ **AC** Z
◉ Audley End★★, S : 13 mi on Trumpington Rd, A 1309, A 1301 and B 1383 – Imperial War Museum★, Duxford, S : 9 mi on M 11

Plan on next page

Hotel du Vin
15-19 Trumpington St ✉ CB2 1QA – ℰ (01223) 227 330 – www.hotelduvin.com
41 rm – †£ 150/220 ††£ 150/380, ⊑ £ 15 Z**e**
Rest *Bistro* – see restaurant listing
♦ Row of ex-university owned 18C houses; now a smart, stylish hotel. Contemporary bedrooms feature wine theme; 'Brown Brothers' comes with its own cinema. Relaxing, clubby bar.

CAMBRIDGE

Street	Grid	No.
Bridge St	Y	2
Coldham's Lane	X	5
Corn Exchange St.	Z	6
Downing St	Z	7
Free School Lane	Z	12
Grafton Centre	Y	
Hobson St	Y	14
King's Parade	Z	15
Lion Yard Centre	Z	
Madingley Rd	X	16
Magdalene St	Y	17
Market Hill	YZ	18
Market St	Y	19
Milton Rd		20
Newmarket Rd	Y	21
Northampton St	Y	22
Parker St	Z	23
Peas Hill	Z	25
Pembroke St	Z	26
Petty Cury	Z	27
Rose Crescent	Z	28
St Andrew's St	Z	30
St John's St	Z	31
Short St	Z	32
Sidney St	Y	34
Trinity St	Y	36
Trumpington Rd	Z	37
Wheeler St	Z	39

COLLEGES

College	Grid	Letter
Christ's	Y	A
Churchill	X	B
Clare	Z	B
Clare Hall	X	N
Corpus Christi	Z	D
Darwin	Z	G¹
Downing	Z	E¹
Emmanuel	Z	F
Fitzwilliam	X	G
Gonville and Caius	Y	G²
Hugues Hall	Z	K
Jesus	Y	K
King's	Z	
Lucy Cavendish	Y	O¹
Magdalene	Y	N
Newnham	X	E²
New Hall	X	D
Pembroke	Z	N
Peterhouse	Z	O²
Queen's	Z	
Robinson	X	K
St Catharine's	Z	R
St Edmund's House	Y	U
St John's	Y	
Selwyn	X	F
Sidney Sussex	Y	P
Trinity	Y	
Trinity Hall	Y	V
Wolfson	X	U

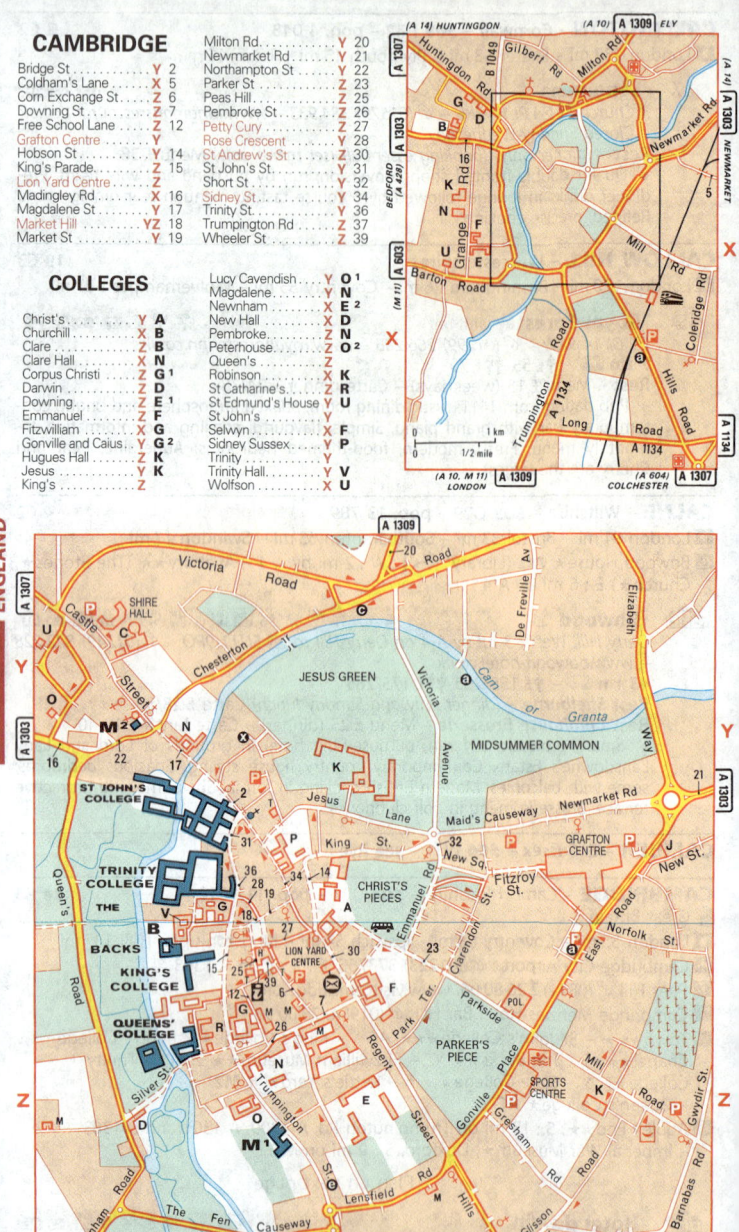

Hotel Felix

Whitehouse Ln, Huntingdon Rd, Northwest : 1.5 mi by A 1307 – CB3 0LX
– ℰ (01223) 277 977 – www.hotelfelix.co.uk
52 rm – †£ 160 ††£ 295, ⌑ £ 8
Rest *Graffiti* – see restaurant listing

♦ Set in 3 acres of gardens, a substantial Victorian mansion that was once a private house. Stylish, contemporary lounge and bar hung with modern art. Large, comfortable, boutique bedrooms with good mod cons; only four are in the main house.

Varsity

Thompson's Ln – CB5 8AQ – ℰ (01223) 306 030 – www.thevarsityhotel.co.uk
46 rm ⌑ – †£ 160/180 ††£ 160/180 – 2 suites   Yx
Rest *River Bar* – Carte £ 21/38 s

♦ Boutique hotel on banks of the River Cam. Smart spa, stylish roof terrace and tranquil lounge with complimentary drinks. Bedrooms with designer bathrooms; some boast coffee machines, fresh orchids and balconies. Informal restaurant.

Midsummer House (Daniel Clifford)

Midsummer Common – CB4 1HA – ℰ (01223) 369 299
– www.midsummerhouse.co.uk – Closed 2 weeks December, Sunday, Monday and lunch Tuesday   Ya
Rest – Menu £ 40/75
Spec. Seared scallop, celeriac, truffle, Granny Smith and caramel. Rack of lamb, courgette and basil purée, essence of lovage. Mango and Douglas fir cream, white chocolate cookies.

♦ Charming and idyllic location beside the River Cam; conservatory dining with fresh, bright feel. Visually impressive dishes reveal cooking that is confidently crafted; flavours are clear and pronounced. Tasting menu only Fri/Sat. Service is formal and well-timed.

Alimentum

152-154 Hills Rd – CB2 8PB – ℰ (01223) 413 000
– www.restaurantalimentum.co.uk – Closed 23-30 December, Sunday May-Oct and bank holidays   Xa
Rest – Menu £ 20 (lunch and early dinner)/40

♦ Sleek, stylish restaurant with striking red and black décor and spacious cocktail bar. Modern menu has French base; dishes are clean and unfussy with some innovative touches.

Restaurant 22

22 Chesterton Rd – CB4 3AX – ℰ (01223) 351 880 – www.restaurant22.co.uk
– Closed 24 December-2 January, Sunday and Monday   Yc
Rest – (booking essential) Menu £ 30

♦ Converted Victorian house with distinctive dining room decorated in rich colours. Monthly changing classical menu; tasty, good value French-influenced dishes. Formal service.

Bistro – at Hotel du Vin

15-19 Trumpington St – CB2 1QA – ℰ (01223) 227 330 – www.hotelduvin.com
Rest – Menu £ 20 (lunch) – Carte £ 25/46   Ze

♦ Spacious brasserie with black banquettes and walls filled with wine memorabilia. Classic dishes presented in a modern style, with French undertones. Relaxed, buzzy ambience.

Graffiti – at Hotel Felix

Whitehouse Ln, Huntingdon Rd, Northwest : 1.5 mi by A 1307 – CB3 0LX
– ℰ (01223) 277 977 – www.hotelfelix.co.uk
Rest – Menu £ 18 (lunch) – Carte £ 25/39

♦ Dark wood furnished restaurant hung with contemporary art. Cosy fire for colder months and south facing terrace the perfect spot in summer. Interesting modern menu with Mediterranean twists.

CAMBRIDGE

Cotto
183 East Rd ⌧ CB1 1BG – ✆ (01223) 302 010 – www.cottocambridge.co.uk
– Closed August, 25 December-10 January, Sunday, Monday, dinner
Tuesday-Wednesday and Saturday lunch

Za

Rest – (booking essential) Menu £ 40 (dinner) s – Carte lunch £ 24/36 s
- By day, a café serving homemade pastries, platters and snacks. By night, a restaurant with large illuminated canvases and a weekly set menu of well-prepared, classically based dishes that showcase excellent ingredients. Very personally run.

at Histon North : 3 mi on B 1049 - X – ⌧ Cambridge

Phoenix
20 The Green ⌧ CB4 9JA – ✆ (01223) 233 766 – Closed 25-26 December
Rest – Chinese – Menu £ 20/28 – Carte £ 44/72
- Popular Chinese restaurant in former pub on village green. Comfortable, homely inner. Polite, smartly attired staff. Vast menu with plenty of Peking and Sichuan favourites.

at Horningsea Northeast : 4 mi by A 1303 - X - and B 1047 on Horningsea rd – ⌧ Cambridge

Crown and Punchbowl with rm
High St ⌧ CB25 9JG – ✆ (01223) 860 643 – www.thecrownandpunchbowl.co.uk
– Closed 26 December-1 January, dinner Sunday and bank holiday Monday
5 rm ⌧ – †£ 75 ††£ 95   **Rest** – Carte £ 25/33
- Homely dining pub with relaxed service. Dishes display European influences and arrive in a mix of classic and more ambitious styles. Daily fish specials and a mix and match sausage board. Simple, tidy bedrooms are handy for the airport.

at Little Wilbraham East : 7.25 mi by A 1303 - X – ⌧ Cambridge

Hole in the Wall
2 High St ⌧ CB21 5JY – ✆ (01223) 812 282 – www.the-holeinthewall.com
– Closed 2 weeks January, 2 weeks September-October, Sunday dinner and Monday except lunch on bank holidays
Rest – Carte £ 23/29
- Characterful 15C pub with sympathetically designed extension, set well off the beaten track. Beamed ceilings feature throughout and there's a large brick fireplace with wood burning stove. Traditionally prepared local produce; satisfying, flavoursome dishes.

at Madingley West : 4.5 mi by A 1303 - X – ⌧ Cambridge

Three Horseshoes
High St ⌧ CB23 8AB – ✆ (01954) 210 221
– www.threehorseshoesmadingley.com
Rest – (booking advisable) Carte £ 22/38
- Attractive thatched pub with bustling atmosphere. Concise bar menu and daily changing, Italian à la carte, featuring straightforward combinations and fresh, tasty dishes.

CAMPSEA ASH – Suffolk   15 D3
▶ London 101 mi – Norwich 46 mi – Southend-on-Sea 76 mi – Ipswich 16 mi

Old Rectory
Station Rd ⌧ IP13 0PU – ✆ (01728) 746 524 – www.theoldrectorysuffolk.com
– Closed 25 December-2 Jan
7 rm ⌧ – †£ 75 ††£ 120/140
Rest – (closed Saturday and Sunday) (dinner only) (set menu only) Menu £ 30
- Former Georgian rectory; now a stylish hotel with attractive gardens. Contemporary bedrooms; Oak is the most luxurious. Striking dining room with open fire. Dinner served on an ad hoc basis, so arrange when booking. Set 3 course menu; accomplished home cooking.

CANTERBURY – Kent – 504 X30 – pop. 41 784 Great Britain   9 D2

▶ London 59 mi – Brighton 76 mi – Dover 15 mi – Maidstone 28 mi
🛈 Buttermarket ✆ (01227) 37 81 00, www.canterbury.co.uk
◉ City ★★★ - Cathedral ★★★ Y - St Augustine's Abbey ★★ AC YZ K – King's School ★ Y - Mercery Lane ★ Y 12 - Christ Church Gate ★ Y D – Museum of Canterbury ★ AC Y M1 - St Martin's Church ★ Y N – West Gate Towers ★ AC Y R

🏠 Abode Canterbury

30-33 High St ✉ CT1 2RX - ✆ (01227) 766 266
– www.michaelcaines.com Ya
72 rm – ♂£ 99/155 ♂♂£ 99/155, ☐ £ 14 – 1 suite
Rest *Michael Caines* – see restaurant listing
♦ Centrally located former coaching inn; heavily beamed, yet with a stylish, modern, boutique feel. Contemporary bedrooms, comfortable champagne bar and atmospheric first floor lounge.

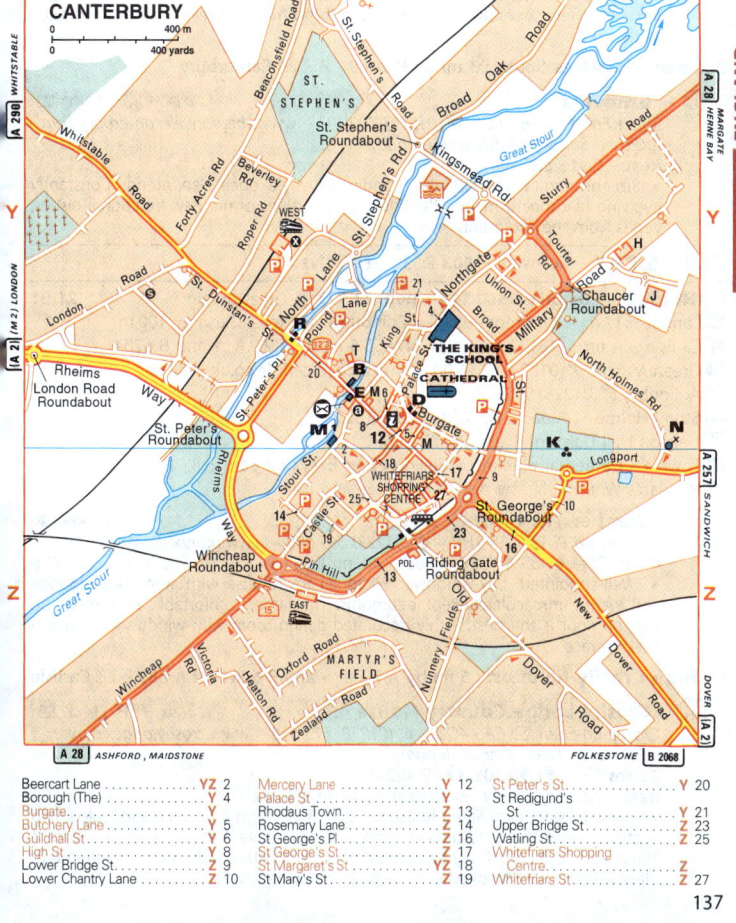

Beercart Lane	YZ 2	Mercery Lane	Y 12	St Peter's St	Y 20
Borough (The)	Y 4	Palace St	Y	St Redigund's St	Y 21
Burgate	Y	Rhodaus Town	Z 13	Upper Bridge St	Z 23
Butchery Lane	Y 5	Rosemary Lane	Y 14	Watling St	Z 25
Guildhall St	Y 6	St George's St	Z 16	Whitefriars Shopping Centre	Z
High St	Y 8	St George's Pl	Z 17	Whitefriars St	Z 27
Lower Bridge St	Z 9	St Margaret's St	YZ 18		
Lower Chantry Lane	Z 10	St Mary's St	Z 19		

CANTERBURY

↑ **Magnolia House** without rest
36 St Dunstan's Terr. ⊠ CT2 8AX – ℰ (01227) 765 121
– www.magnoliahousecanterbury.co.uk – Closed 25-26 December
6 rm ⊋ – ♦£ 55/70 ♦♦£ 125   Ys

♦ Creamwashed Georgian house in residential area close to town. Lounge is filled with local information; breakfast room overlooks the walled garden. Neat, tidy bedrooms offer good facilities, including flat screen TVs, CD players and fridges.

✕✕ **Michael Caines** – at Abode Canterbury Hotel
High St ⊠ CT1 2RX – ℰ (01227) 826 684 – www.michaelcaines.com – Closed
Sunday dinner   Ya
Rest – Menu £ 14 (lunch) – Carte £ 37/47

♦ Enjoy a glass of Champagne in smart bar before repairing to the upmarket restaurant to enjoy modern British cooking utilising a variety of styles and classical techniques.

✕ **Goods Shed**
Station Rd West, St Dunstans ⊠ CT2 8AN – ℰ (01227) 459 153
– www.thegoodsshed.net – Closed 25 December, 1 January, Sunday dinner and
Monday   Yx
Rest – Carte £ 27/30

♦ Once derelict railway shed, now a farmers' market that's open all day. Its eating area offers superbly fresh produce with no frills and real flavours very much to the fore.

at Lower Hardres South : 3 mi on B 2068 - Z – ⊠ Canterbury

🍺 **Granville**
Street End ⊠ CT4 7AL – ℰ (01227) 700 402 – www.thegranvillecanterbury.com
– Closed Sunday dinner and Monday
Rest – Carte £ 21/34

♦ Sizeable, family-run pub with Scandinavian-style, open-plan interior. Constantly evolving blackboard menu offers generous portions of unfussy, traditional dishes; veg is from the allotment.

CARBIS BAY – Cornwall – **503** D33 – see St Ives

CARLISLE – Cumbria – **501** L19 – pop. 71 773 ▌Great Britain   **21** B1

▶ London 317 mi – Blackpool 95 mi – Edinburgh 101 mi – Glasgow 100 mi
✈ Carlisle Airport ℰ (01228) 573641, NW : 5.5 mi by A 7 - BY - and B 6264
🛈 Green Market ℰ (01228) 62 56 00, www.discovercarlisle.co.uk
⛳ Aglionby, ℰ (01228) 51 30 29
⛳ Stony Holme St Aidan's Rd, ℰ (01228) 62 55 11
⛳ Dalston Hall Dalston, ℰ (01228) 71 01 65
◉ Town★ - Cathedral★ (Painted Ceiling★) AY **E** – Tithe Barn★ BY **A**
◉ Hadrian's Wall★★, N : by A 7 AY

↑ **Number Thirty One**
31 Howard Pl ⊠ CA1 1HR – ℰ (01228) 597 080 – www.number31.co.uk
4 rm ⊋ – ♦£ 65 ♦♦£ 90   **Rest** – Menu £ 25   BYa

♦ Well-appointed, bay-windowed Victorian townhouse with sumptuous lounge and warm, immaculately-kept bedrooms. The large, comfortable Red Room on the top floor is the best. Richly decorated dining room with window onto plant-filled terrace.

at High Crosby Northeast : 5 mi by A 7 - BY - and B 6264 off A 689 – ⊠ Carlisle

🏨 **Crosby Lodge Country House** ⊛
Crosby-on-Eden ⊠ CA6 4QZ – ℰ (01228) 573 618 – www.crosbylodge.co.uk
– Closed 25 December-10 January
11 rm ⊋ – ♦£ 90/105 ♦♦£ 200/250
Rest – (Sunday dinner residents only) Carte £ 36/52

♦ Grade II listed, castellated house built in 1802. Warm ambience and welcoming hostess. Traditionally furnished lounge. Comfortable bedrooms with pleasant countryside outlook. Richly coloured dining room with polished brass around fireplace. Classic, homecooked food includes renowned sweet trolley.

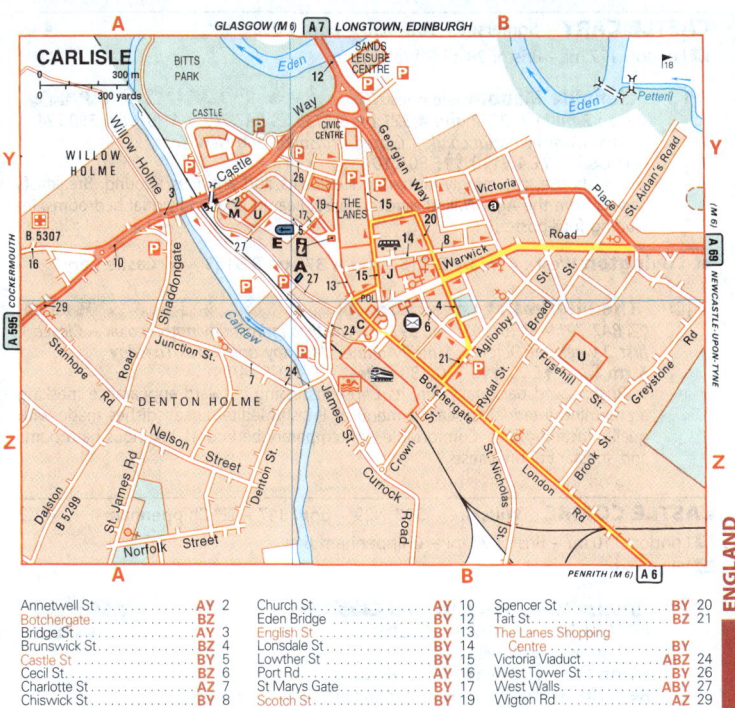

Annetwell St	AY 2	Church St	AY 10	Spencer St	BY 20
Botchergate	BZ	Eden Bridge	BY 12	Tait St	BZ 21
Bridge St	AY 3	English St	BY 13	The Lanes Shopping Centre	BY
Brunswick St	BZ 4	Lonsdale St	BY 14	Victoria Viaduct	ABZ 24
Castle St	BY 5	Lowther St	BY 15	West Tower St	BY 26
Cecil St	BZ 6	Port Rd	AY 16	West Walls	ABY 27
Charlotte St	AZ 7	St Marys Gate	BY 17	Wigton Rd	AZ 29
Chiswick St	BY 8	Scotch St	BY 19		

CARLTON HUSTHWAITE – North Yorkshire – 502 Q21   22 B2

▶ London 230 mi – Leeds 51 mi – Middlesbrough 32 mi – York 20 mi

Carlton Bore   P VISA ⊚

✉ YO7 2BW – ☏ (01845) 501 265 – www.carltonbore.co.uk – Closed first 2 weeks January

Rest – Menu £ 16 (lunch) – Carte £ 23/32

♦ Characterful 17C stone inn offering appealing menu of well-priced, generously proportioned pub favourites. Three brightly decorated rooms and a warm, welcoming atmosphere.

CARLTON-IN-COVERDALE – North Yorkshire – 502 O21 – see Middleham

CARLYON BAY – Cornwall – 503 F33 – see St Austell

CARTHORPE – North Yorkshire   22 B1

▶ London 228 mi – Leeds 49 mi – Middlesbrough 40 mi – York 34 mi

Fox and Hounds   P VISA ⊚

✉ DL8 2LG – ☏ (01845) 567 433 – www.foxandhoundscarthorpe.co.uk – Closed 25 December, first week January and Monday

Rest – Menu £ 17 (weekdays) – Carte £ 21/32

♦ Family run, ivy-clad stone pub with a real sense of history. Menus offer a huge array of choice, with meats from the local butcher, flour milled nearby and produce from the village dairy.

CARTMEL – Cumbria – 502 L21 – see Grange-over-Sands

CASTLE CARY – Somerset – 503 M30 – pop. 3 056 4 C2
▶ London 127 mi – Bristol 28 mi – Wells 13 mi

Clanville Manor without rest
West : 2 mi by B 3152 and A 371 on B 3153 ✉ BA7 7PJ – ℰ (01963) 350 124
– www.clanvillemanor.co.uk – *Closed Christmas and New Year*
4 rm ⌂ – †£ 40/110 ††£ 80/110
◆ 18C house, charmingly cluttered. Heirlooms and antiques abound. Breakfasts served from the Aga. Walled garden boasts heated pool. Individual bedrooms, including four-poster.

at Lovington *West : 4 mi by B 3152 and A 371 on B 3153* – ✉ Castle Cary

The Pilgrims at Lovington with rm
✉ BA7 7PT – ℰ (01963) 240 597 – www.thepilgrimsatlovington.co.uk – *Closed first 2 weeks of October, Sunday dinner, Monday and lunch Tuesday*
5 rm ⌂ – †£ 90 ††£ 120/130 **Rest** – Carte £ 24/39
◆ Pristine and personally run; its unprepossessing outward appearance masking a charming interior. Appealing menu of British/Mediterranean dishes made with quality local produce. Comfortable, contemporary bedrooms, luxurious bathrooms and substantial breakfasts.

CASTLE COMBE – Wiltshire – 503 N29 – pop. 347 – ✉ Chippenham 4 C2
▶ London 110 mi – Bristol 23 mi – Chippenham 6 mi
◉ Village ★★

Manor House H. and Golf Club
✉ SN14 7HR – ℰ (01249) 782 206
– www.exclusivehotels.co.uk
44 rm ⌂ – †£ 255 ††£ 255 – 4 suites
Rest *The Bybrook* – *(closed Monday lunch)* Menu £ 30/60
Spec. Seared scallops with cauliflower purée and agrodolce dressing. Slow cooked loin of veal, braised red cabbage and sweetbreads. Baked apple terrine, apple doughnut and date ice cream
◆ Fine period manor house in 365 acres of formal gardens and parkland. Interior exudes immense charm and style, with oak panelling and a host of open-fired lounges. Uniquely styled, luxurious bedrooms; many in the courtyard. Large dining room offers refined, carefully prepared dishes with a classical base. Slick service.

Castle Inn
✉ SN14 7HN – ℰ (01249) 783 030 – www.castle-inn.info – *Closed 25 December*
11 rm ⌂ – †£ 80/165 ††£ 195 **Rest** – *(bar lunch)* Carte £ 24/34
◆ A hostelry dating back to the 12C in the middle of a delightful and historic village. Wooden beams and much character throughout. Breakfast in conservatory. Large and varied menu served in rustic bar.

CASTLE EDEN – Durham 24 B3
▶ London 265 mi – Sunderland 15 mi – Newcastle upon Tyne 28 mi
– Middlesbrough 18 mi

Castle Eden Inn
Stockton Rd ✉ TS27 4SD – ℰ (01429) 835 137 – www.castleedeninn.com
Rest – Carte £ 22/31
◆ A substantial building with a modern interior. The large, stylish bar and elegant dining room share the same extensive menu, which offers everything from shepherds pie to local oysters, and uses trusted regional suppliers.

CATEL/CASTEL – 503 P33 – see Channel Islands (Guernsey)

CAUNTON – Nottinghamshire – 502 R24 – see Newark-on-Trent

CERNE ABBAS – Dorset – 503 M31   4 C3

▶ London 132 mi – Bristol - 60 mi – Cardiff 115 mi – Southampton 58 mi

New Inn
*14 Long St ⊠ DT2 7JF – ℰ (01300) 341 274 – www.newinncerneabbas.com
– Restricted opening in winter*
Rest – Carte £ 21/29
♦ Sizeable pub set in picture postcard village, with exposed beams, decked terrace and vast garden. Freshly prepared, traditional dishes make good use of locally sourced produce.

CHADDESLEY CORBETT – Worcestershire – 503 N26 – see Kidderminster

CHADWICK END – West Midlands – 503 O26   19 C2

▶ London 106 mi – Birmingham 13 mi – Leicester 40 mi – Stratford-upon-Avon 16 mi

Orange Tree
*Warwick Rd, on A 4141 ⊠ B93 0BN – ℰ (01564) 785 364
– www.lovelypubs.co.uk – Closed 25 December and Sunday dinner*
Rest – *(booking essential)* Menu £ 16 (lunch and early dinner) – Carte £ 17/36
♦ Large, contemporary pub with neat gardens, spacious terrace and buzzing atmosphere. Wide-ranging menu offers several dishes in two sizes, with tasty spit roast chicken a speciality.

CHAGFORD – Devon – 503 I31 – pop. 1 417   2 C2

▶ London 218 mi – Exeter 17 mi – Plymouth 27 mi
ⓖ Dartmoor National Park★★

Gidleigh Park (Michael Caines)
❀❀
*Northwest : 2 mi by Gidleigh Rd ⊠ TQ13 8HH
– ℰ (01647) 432 367 – www.gidleigh.com*
23 rm ⊑ – †£ 300 ††£ 525 – 1 suite
Rest – *(booking essential)* Menu £ 52/110
Spec. Salmon with Oscietra caviar, salmon jelly and Greek yoghurt vinaigrette. Salt cod, crab, chorizo, samphire and lemon purée. Caramel and cardamom parfait, milk chocolate mousse and cardamom foam.
♦ Lovingly restored and extremely comfortable Arts and Crafts house set in 100 acres. Luxurious bedrooms boast impressive bathrooms; some have a balcony. Formal restaurant, where classical French menus showcase skilfully prepared, quality local produce. Tasting menu for Michael Caines' signature dishes.

22 Mill Street with rm
22 Mill St ⊠ TQ13 8AW – ℰ (01647) 432 244 – www.22millst.com
2 rm – †£ 90/119 ††£ 99/149, ⊑ £ 10
Rest – *(booking essential)* Menu £ 22/42
♦ Smart, intimate restaurant on high street of scenic village, right in the heart of Dartmoor. Fresh and unfussy, with formally laid tables. An array of modern menus offer simply cooked, seasonal classics. Comfortable, rustic-style bedrooms.

at Sandypark Northeast : 2.25 mi on A 382 – ⊠ Chagford

Mill End
on A 382 ⊠ TQ13 8JN – ℰ (01647) 432 282 – www.millendhotel.com – Closed 4-19 January
13 rm ⊑ – †£ 75 ††£ 130/160 – 1 suite   **Rest** – *(dinner only)* Menu £ 40
♦ Well-maintained house with pleasant gardens; its comfy, antique-furnished lounge retaining a traditional charm. Classically styled bedrooms in original house; larger, more modern rooms in extension. A modern take on the classics in the bright, linen-laid restaurant.

Parford Well without rest
on Drewsteignton rd ⊠ TQ13 8JW – ℰ (01647) 433 353 – www.parfordwell.co.uk
3 rm ⊑ – †£ 50/90 ††£ 90/95
♦ Tastefully maintained with superbly tended gardens. Elegant sitting room has plenty of books and French windows to garden. Two breakfast rooms. Homely, immaculate bedrooms.

CHAGFORD

at Easton Northeast : 1.5 mi on A 382 – ✉ Chagford

Easton Court without rest 🐾 P VISA ⊕
Easton Cross ✉ TQ13 8JL – ℰ (01647) 433 469 – www.easton.co.uk
5 rm ⊇ – †£ 60/70 ††£ 80/85
◆ Well appointed accommodation and a high ceilinged lounge overlooking the immaculate gardens. Home made marmalade a speciality. Friendly atmosphere.

CHANNEL ISLANDS – 503 L/M33

ALDERNEY – Alderney – 503 M32 5 B1
✈ Aurigny Air Services ℰ (01481) 822886
ℹ States Office, Island Hall, Royal Connaught Sq ℰ (01481) 822 8 11, www.visitalderney.com
◉ Braye Bay★ – Mannez Garenne (≤★ from Quesnard Lighthouse) – Telegraph Bay★ – Vallee des Trois Vaux★ – Clonque Bay★

BRAYE – Alderney 5 B1

Braye Beach ≤ 🐾 rm, P VISA ⊕ AE ①
✉ GY9 3XT – ℰ (01481) 824 300 – www.brayebeach.com
27 rm ⊇ – †£ 80/190 ††£ 100/260 **Rest** – Carte £ 18/32 s
◆ Smart, contemporary hotel set on edge of beach. Vaulted basement houses a series of lounges and a 19-seat cinema. Modern European cooking with a subtle seafood slant.

GUERNSEY – Guernsey – 503 L32 – pop. 58 867 5 A2
✈ Guernsey Airport ℰ (01481) 237766, Aurigny Air ℰ (01481) 822 886
⛴ from St Peter Port to France (St Malo) and Jersey (St Helier) (Condor Ferries Ltd) 2 weekly – from St Peter Port to France (Dielette) (Manche Iles Express) (summer only) (60 mn) – from St Peter Port to Herm (Herm Seaway) (25 mn) – from St Peter Port to Sark (Isle of Sark Shipping Co. Ltd) (45 mn) – from St Peter Port to Jersey (St Helier) (HD Ferries) (1hr) – from St Peter Port to Jersey (St Helier) (Condor Ferries Ltd) daily
⛴ from St Peter Port to France (St Malo) and Jersey (St Helier) (Condor Ferries Ltd) – from St Peter Port to Jersey (St Helier) and Weymouth (Condor Ferries Ltd)
ℹ North Esplanade ℰ (01481) 72 35 52, www.visitguernsey.com
◉ Island★ – Pezeries Point★★ – Icart Point★★ – Côbo Bay★★ – St Martin's Point★★ – St Apolline's Chapel★ – Vale Castle★ – Fort Doyle★ – La Gran'mere du Chimquiere★ – Rocquaine Bay★ – Jerbourg Point★

CATEL/CASTEL – Guernsey 5 A2

Cobo Bay ≤ 🐾 AC rest, P VISA ⊕ AE
Cobo Coast Rd ✉ GY5 7HB – ℰ (01481) 257 102 – www.cobobayhotel.com
– *Closed January-February*
34 rm ⊇ – †£ 49/120 ††£ 69/190
Rest – Menu £ 29 (dinner) – Carte lunch £ 22/31
◆ Modern hotel on sandy Cobo Bay; an ideal location for families. The rooms are pleasant with bright décor and some have the delightful addition of seaview balconies. Romantic dining with views of sunsets.

FERMAIN BAY – Guernsey 5 A2

Fermain Valley ≤ 🐾 P VISA ⊕ AE
Fermain Ln ✉ GY1 1ZZ – ℰ (01481) 235 666 – www.fermainvalley.com
45 rm ⊇ – †£ 131/183 ††£ 175/245
Rest *Valley* – see restaurant listing
◆ Stylish, comfortable hotel with beautiful gardens, hidden in a picturesque valley and affording pleasant bay views through the trees. Well-equipped bedrooms are widely dispersed; 'Gold' rooms boast balconies. Colonial-style bar and lounge.

CHANNEL ISLANDS - Guernsey

XX **Valley** – at Fermain Valley Hotel
Fermain Ln ⊠ GY1 1ZZ – ℰ (01481) 235 666 – www.fermainvalley.com
Rest – Menu £ 25 **s** – Carte £ 25/36 **s**
♦ Informal hotel restaurant with beautiful multi-level terrace and lovely sea views. Accessible menu offers fresh fish and simple grills. A fine array of Beken yacht photos hang on the walls.

KINGS MILLS – Guernsey   5 A2

Fleur du Jardin with rm
Grand Moulins ⊠ GY5 7JT – ℰ (01481) 257 996 – www.fleurdujardin.com
17 rm ⊡ – †£ 65/89 ††£ 90/138 – 1 suite   **Rest** – Carte £ 21/27
♦ Attractive inn with stylish terrace, lovely landscaped gardens and several charming, adjoining rustic rooms. Menu ranges from homemade burgers to sea bass and tasty island seafood specials. Stylish New England themed bedrooms; there's even a heated outdoor pool.

ST MARTIN – Guernsey – pop. 6 267   5 A2

 St Peter Port 2 mi

Bella Luce ⌂
La Fosse ⊠ GY4 6EB – ℰ (01481) 238 764 – www.bellalucehotel.com – Closed 2-16 January
23 rm ⊡ – †£ 112/132 ††£ 140/320
Rest *Bella Luce* – Menu £ 25 – Carte dinner £ 27/39
♦ Originally a Norman manor house; with a cosy beamed bar, cellar-like lounge and stylish, intimate interior featuring voluptuous velvets. Opulent bedrooms boast modern bathrooms. Pleasant gardens with pool. Bella Luce offers an eclectic array of modern dishes.

La Barbarie ⌂
Saints Bay ⊠ GY4 6ES – ℰ (01481) 235 217 – www.labarbariehotel.com
– March-October
26 rm ⊡ – †£ 65/82 ††£ 79/114 – 1 suite   **Rest** – (bar lunch) Carte £ 30/37
♦ Stone-built former priory with a welcoming, cottagey style. Characterful bar; well-kept pool and terrace. Bedrooms are traditional and comfortable. Seafood a speciality.

XX **Auberge**
Jerbourg Rd ⊠ GY4 6BH – ℰ (01481) 238 485 – www.theauberge.gg – Closed 24 December-1 February and Sunday dinner
Rest – (booking essential) Menu £ 19 (dinner) – Carte £ 27/45
♦ Superbly located informal modern restaurant, with attractive terrace boasting tranquil sea and island views. Artistic dishes display bold flavours. Quality island-caught fish is a favourite.

ST PETER PORT – Guernsey   5 A2

Rohais St Pierre Park, ℰ (01481) 72 70 39
Town★★ - St Peter's Church★ Z – Hauteville House★ **AC** Z – Castle Cornet★ (⇐★) **AC** Z
Saumarez Park★ (Guernsey Folk Museum★), W : 2 mi by road to Catel Z – Little Chapel★, SW : 2.25 mi by Mount Durand road Z

Plan on next page

 Old Government House H. & Spa
St Ann's Pl ⊠ GY1 2NU – ℰ (01481)
724 921 – www.theoghhotel.com   Ya
61 rm ⊡ – †£ 143/215 ††£ 180/280 – 1 suite
Rest *Governors* – (dinner only) (booking essential) Menu £ 45 – Carte £ 35/48
Rest *Brasserie* – ℰ (01481) 738 604 – Carte £ 28/46
♦ Fine 18C building; classically furnished, with many of its original features restored. Glorious ballroom, well-equipped spa and individually styled bedrooms with modern bathrooms. Intimate fine dining in Governors, where ambitious cooking has a French base. Smart yet informal Brasserie, with delightful outside terrace.

ST PETER PORT

Street	Ref		Street	Ref		Street	Ref
Ann's Place	Y 3		Forest Lane	Y 12		Quay (The)	Z 19
Beauregard Lane	Y 4		Fountain Street	Z 13		St-George's Esplanade	Y 20
Bordage	Z 5		High Street	Z 14		St-James Street	Z 22
Charroterie	Z 7		Market Street	Z 15		Smith Street	Z 23
College Street	YZ 8		North Esplanade	YZ 16		South	
Cornet Street	Z 9		Pollet	Y 18		Esplanade	Z 25

✕✕ Nautique

Quay Steps ✉ *GY1 2LE –* ✆ *(01481) 721 714 – www.lenautiquerestaurant.co.uk*
– Closed Saturday lunch and Sunday   Zr

Rest – Menu £ 19 (lunch) – Carte £ 31/39

♦ Quayside former warehouse with pleasant marina view and characterful, nautically themed interior; ask for a window seat. Large menu of generously sized, classic dishes, with fish a feature.

✕✕ Pier 17

Albert Pier ✉ *GY1 1AD –* ✆ *(01481) 720 823 – www.pier17restaurant.com*
– Closed Sunday   Zx

Rest – Carte £ 26/32

♦ Set at the end of a substantial stone pier in the centre of Guernsey harbour. Conservatory extension affords superb water views and the two terraces catch the last of the suns rays. Traditionally based, seasonal dishes.

CHANNEL ISLANDS - Guernsey

Swan Inn
St Julian's Ave ⊠ GY1 1WA – ℰ (01481) 728 969 – Closed 25 December and Sunday
Rest – Carte £ 12/18
Yx
♦ Smart Victorian pub with bottle-green façade, traditional styling and good value early week menu. Choose hearty, satisfying dishes in the bar or more ambitious fare in the dining room.

ST SAVIOUR – Guernsey   5 A2
▶ St Peter Port 4 mi

Farmhouse
Route des Bas Courtils ⊠ GY7 9YF – ℰ (01481) 264 181 – www.thefarmhouse.gg
14 rm ⊇ – †£ 109/145 ††£ 109/265
Rest – Menu £ 25 – Carte dinner £ 21/42
♦ Former farm restyled in boutique vein. Stylish, sumptuous bedrooms with high-tech amenities; bathrooms with heated floors. Pleasant garden and pool; terrace and kitchen garden. Contemporary cooking with international edge uses island's finest produce in eclectic ways.

Pavilion
Le Gron ⊠ GY7 9RN – ℰ (01481) 264 165 – www.thepavilion.co.gg – Closed 2 weeks January, Christmas and Monday in winter
Rest – (lunch only and dinner Friday-Saturday) Menu £ 23 – Carte £ 20/28 **s**
♦ Farmhouse-style restaurant displaying exposed stone and beams. Menus offer something for everyone, from tea and cakes to full 3 courses. Fresh, simple, intelligent cooking. Desserts a must.

ENGLAND

HERM – Herm – 503 M33   5 A2
🚢 to Guernsey (St Peter Port) (Herm Seaway) (20 mn)
◉ Le Grand Monceau★

White House
⊠ GY1 3HR – ℰ (01481) 750 075 – www.herm.com – April-7 October
40 rm (dinner included) ⊇ – †£ 79/144 ††£ 158/292
Rest *Conservatory* – (booking essential) Menu £ 20/28 – Carte £ 40/50
Rest *Ship Inn* – (booking advisable) Carte £ 16/29
♦ Hotel with real country house feel: the beach extends to the door. Guernsey and Jethou can be viewed from the lounge. Attractive rooms. Formal Conservatory with seafood emphasis. Relaxed Ship Inn.

JERSEY – C.I. – 503 L33 – pop. 85 150   5 B2
✈ States of Jersey Airport : ℰ (01534) 446 000
🚢 from St Helier to France (St Malo) (Condor Ferries Ltd) (summer only) – from St Helier to France (St Malo) (Condor Ferries Ltd) 3 weekly - from Gorey to France (Carteret) (Manche Iles Express) (summer only) (60mn) – from St Helier to Guernsey (St Peter Port) (Condor Ferries Ltd) (50 mn) – from St Helier to Guernsey (St Peter Port) (Condor Ferries Ltd) daily
🚢 from St Helier to France (St Malo) and Guernsey (St Peter Port) (Condor Ferries Ltd) – from St Helier to Sark (Condor Ferries Ltd) (50 mn) – from St Helier to Guernsey (St Peter Port) and Weymouth (Condor Ferries Ltd)
🛈 St Helier ℰ (01534) 44 88 77, www.jersey.com
◉ Island★★ - Jersey Zoo★★ **AC** – Jersey Museum★ - Eric Young Orchid Foundation★ – St Catherine's Bay★ (≤★★) – Grosnez Point★ - Devil's Hole★ – St Matthews Church, Millbrook (glasswork★) – La Hougue Bie★ (Neolithic tomb★ **AC**) - Waterworks Valley – Hamptonne Country Life Museum★ – St Catherine's Bay★ (≤★★) – Noirmont Point★

GOREY – Saint Martin   5 B2
▶ St Helier 4 mi
◉ Mont Orgueil Castle★ (≤★★) **AC** – Jersey Pottery★

145

CHANNEL ISLANDS - Jersey

Moorings
Gorey Pier ⊠ *JE3 6EW* – ℰ *(01534) 853 633* – *www.themooringshotel.com*
15 rm – †£ 58/109 ††£ 115/150 **Rest** – Menu £ 17/23 – Carte £ 30/46
• Located at the base of Gorey Castle, overlooking the waterfront, once the heart of the oyster fishing industry. Well-priced; the first floor bedrooms have terraces. Pleasant decked area at front of restaurant.

Sumas
Gorey Hill ⊠ *JE3 6ET* – ℰ *(01534) 853 291* – *www.sumasrestaurant.com*
– *Closed 23 December-20 January and dinner Sunday*
Rest – *(booking essential)* Menu £ 20 *(weekdays)* – Carte £ 34/39
• One of the best known eateries on the island, set overlooking the harbour. Huge sliding glass doors and small heated terrace. Good value lunch and early evening menu. Local produce includes fresh island seafood; unfussy cooking displays Mediterranean influences.

Castle Green
La Route de la Cote ⊠ *JE3 6DR* – ℰ *(01534) 840 218*
– *www.castlegreenjersey.co.uk* – *Closed 25 December, 1 January and Sunday dinner*
Rest – Carte £ 22/34
• Relaxed, friendly restaurant above Gorey Harbour, with decked terrace and southerly sea panorama. Accessible menu of modern classics, with plenty of Mediterranean dishes and fish specials.

Bass and Lobster
Gorey Coast Rd ⊠ *JE3 6EU* – ℰ *(01534) 859 590* – *www.bassandlobster.com*
– *Closed Monday lunch and Sunday*
Rest – Menu £ 13/16 – Carte £ 27/43
• Bright, modern 'foodhouse' close to the beach. Seasonal island produce; fresh, tasty seafood and shellfish dominate the menu. Fantastic oysters; good value lunches. Smooth, effective service.

GREEN ISLAND – Saint Clement   5 B2

Green Island
St Clement ⊠ *JE2 6LS* – ℰ *(01534) 857 787* – *www.greenisland.je* – *Closed 23 December-3 January, Sunday dinner and Monday*
Rest – Mediterranean – *(booking essential)* Menu £ 19/24 – Carte £ 32/45
• Charming, personally run restaurant with terrace and seaside kiosk. Internationally influenced dishes and seafood specials showcase island produce. Flavours are bold and perfectly judged.

GROUVILLE – Grouville   5 B2
▶ St Helier 3 mi

Cafe Poste
La Rue de la ville ès Renauds ⊠ *JE3 9FY* – ℰ *(01534) 859 696*
– *www.cafeposte.co.uk* – *Closed 14 November-1 December, Monday and Tuesday*
Rest – Carte £ 22/41
• Popular neighbourhood restaurant – formerly a post office – with French country themed interior and cosy fire in winter. Eclectic menus include plenty of well-crafted seafood creations.

ROZEL BAY – Saint Martin   5 B2
▶ St Helier 6 mi

Chateau La Chaire
Rozel Valley ⊠ *JE3 6AJ* – ℰ *(01534) 863 354* – *www.chateau-la-chaire.co.uk*
12 rm – †£ 85/130 ††£ 95/255 – 2 suites **Rest** – Menu £ 15/43
• Impressive 19C country house and gardens; drawing room features original plaster ceiling. More contemporary bedrooms blend chic styling with period furniture; Room 2 has a delightful balcony. Conservatory dining room with popular terrace; good use of island ingredients.

CHANNEL ISLANDS - Jersey

St Aubin – Saint Brelade   5 B2
▶ St Helier 4 mi

Somerville
Mont du Boulevard, South : 0.75 mi via harbour ✉ JE3 8AD – ✆ (01534) 741 226
– www.dolanhotels.com
56 rm ⌧ – †£ 56/176 ††£ 99/219
Rest *Tides* – Menu £ 16/30 **s** – Carte £ 38/45 **s**
♦ Grand 19C hotel in stunning position above the town, with superb view over St Aubin Bay. Stylish public areas and bright bedrooms. The dining room features subtle, contemporary styling; most tables offer a view. Modern menus, with lobster specials in season.

Panorama without rest
La Rue du Crocquet ✉ JE3 8BZ – ✆ (01534) 742 429
– www.panoramajersey.com – Mid-April to October
14 rm ⌧ – †£ 60/120 ††£ 120/160
♦ Charming, personally run and immaculately kept hotel offering stunning bay and castle views and an extraordinary collection of teapots. Individually decorated bedrooms and comprehensive breakfasts.

St Brelade's Bay – Saint Brelade   5 B2
▶ St Helier 6 mi
◉ Fishermen's Chapel (frescoes ★)

L'Horizon
✉ JE3 8EF – ✆ (01534) 743 101 – www.handpickedhotels.co.uk/lhorizon
99 rm ⌧ – †£ 90/175 ††£ 180/290 – 7 suites
Rest *Grill* **Rest** *Brasserie* – see restaurant listing
♦ Long-standing hotel located right on the beachfront and boasting stunning views out over the bay. Luxurious interior with extensive guest areas and subtle modern styling. Choose a deluxe bedroom, as they come with balconies and sea views.

St Brelade's Bay
La Route de la Baie ✉ JE3 8EF – ✆ (01534) 746 141
– www.stbreladesbayhotel.com
80 rm ⌧ – †£ 88/179 ††£ 206/364 – 5 suites
Rest *Bay* – (closed Monday and Tuesday lunch) Menu £ 17/30 – Carte £ 27/40
♦ Traditional seafront hotel boasting charming gardens filled with tropical plants and superb panoramic views across the bay. Original parquet floors and ornate plaster ceilings blend nicely with a modernised lounge and contemporary bedrooms. Formal restaurant offers impressive sea view and a classical menu.

Grill – at L'Horizon Hotel
✉ JE3 8EF – ✆ (01534) 743 101 – www.handpicked.co.uk/lhorizon – Closed Sunday and Monday
Rest – (dinner only) Menu £ 45
♦ Stylish restaurant with a formal atmosphere, located inside a long-standing hotel which boasts lovely views across the bay. Modern British menu with a focus on fresh, locally caught seafood.

Oyster Box
La Route de la Baie ✉ JE3 8EF – ✆ (01534) 743 311 – www.oysterbox.co.uk
– Closed 25-26 December, 1 January and dinner Sunday-Monday October-April
Rest – (booking essential) Carte £ 26/36
♦ Glass-fronted eatery with pleasant heated terrace, set on the promenade and affording superb views over St Brelade's Bay. Stylish, airy interior hung with sail cloths and fishermen's floats. Laid-back, friendly service. Accessible seasonal menu features plenty of fish and shellfish; oysters are a speciality.

Brasserie – at L'Horizon Hotel
✉ JE3 8EF – ✆ (01534) 494 413 – www.handpicked.co.uk/lhorizon
Rest – Menu £ 25/33
♦ Informal brasserie in a well-established beachfront hotel. A delightful terrace provides the perfect spot when the sun is shining. Extensive, accessible menu offers something for everyone.

CHANNEL ISLANDS - Jersey

Crab Shack
La Route de la Baie ✉ JE3 8EF – ✆ (01534) 744 611
– www.crabshackjersey.co.uk – Closed 25-26 December, 1 January and Monday dinner except bank holidays
Rest *– (booking advisable) Carte £ 19/26*

♦ Scaled down version of next door Oyster Box, superbly sited on the beachfront. Choose a cosy booth or bench outside; relaxed, family friendly atmosphere. Prime island produce features in accessible modern dishes, with seafood a speciality.

ST HELIER – Saint Helier 5 B2

Jersey Museum★ **AC** Z - Elizabeth Castle (≤★) **AC** Z – Fort Regent (≤★ **AC**) Z

St Peter's Valley - German Underground Hospital★ **AC**, NW : 4 mi by A 1, A 11 St Peter's Valley rd and C 112

Grand
The Esplanade ✉ JE2 3QA – ✆ (01534) 722 301 – www.grandjersey.com
117 rm ⊇ – †£ 125/225 ††£ 215/225 – 6 suites   **Yu**
Rest *Tassili* ✿ – see restaurant listing
Rest *Victoria's* – (dinner only) Menu £ 25 – Carte £ 25/44

♦ Welcoming Victorian hotel with large terrace, overlooking St Aubin's Bay. Stylish, modern interior with chic champagne bar, well-equipped spa and corporate cinema. Contemporary bedrooms in bold colours; some with balconies and sea views. Fine dining in sophisticated Tassili; Mediterranean menu in Victoria's.

Club Hotel & Spa
Green St ✉ JE2 4UH – ✆ (01534) 876 500 – www.theclubjersey.com – Closed 24-30 December   **Ze**
44 rm – †£ 99/215 ††£ 99/215, ⊇ £ 7.50 – 2 suites
Rest *Bohemia* ✿ – see restaurant listing

♦ Well-run, fresh, modern hotel with pleasant poolside terrace. Bedrooms differ considerably but all are sleek and contemporary with good amenities and luxurious bathrooms.

Royal Yacht
Weighbridge ✉ JE2 3NF – ✆ (01534) 720 511 – www.theroyalyacht.com
109 rm ⊇ – †£ 140 ††£ 230 – 2 suites   **Zb**
Rest *Sirocco* – (dinner only and Sunday lunch) Menu £ 25 – Carte £ 39/60
Rest *Grill* – (closed 25 December) Carte £ 13/29

♦ Set overlooking the harbour, with contemporary interior and splendid spa. The most spacious bedrooms look to the harbour; the quietest over the inner courtyard; suites feature hot tubs. Formal dining in first floor Sirocco, with its enviable view and Mediterranean menu. Nautical style in Grill, with steaks a speciality.

Eulah Country House *without rest*
Mont Cochon, Northwest : 2 mi by A 1 on B 27 ✉ JE2 3JA – ✆ (01534) 626 626
– www.eulah.co.uk – Closed 20 December-4 January
9 rm ⊇ – †£ 145/185 ††£ 170/230

♦ Informally run Edwardian country house proves pleasantly unconventional. Stylish combined lounge and breakfast room, luxurious bedrooms and superb views of St Aubin's Bay.

Bohemia – *at Club Hotel & Spa*
Green St ✉ JE2 4UH – ✆ (01534) 880 588 – www.bohemiajersey.com – Closed 24-30 December, Sunday and lunch bank holiday Mondays   **Ze**
Rest – Menu £ 24/55
Spec. Curry salted scallops with coconut dhal, onion bhaji and apple salad. Lamb with minted peas, goat's cheese and honeycomb. Valrhona dark chocolate tart with raspberries and tarragon ice cream.

♦ This stylish restaurant has been extended to include a chef's table. Comfy bar and very attentive serving team. Top quality produce is showcased in cooking that is well-judged and clever, without being gimmicky. Good choice of wines by the glass.

ST HELIER

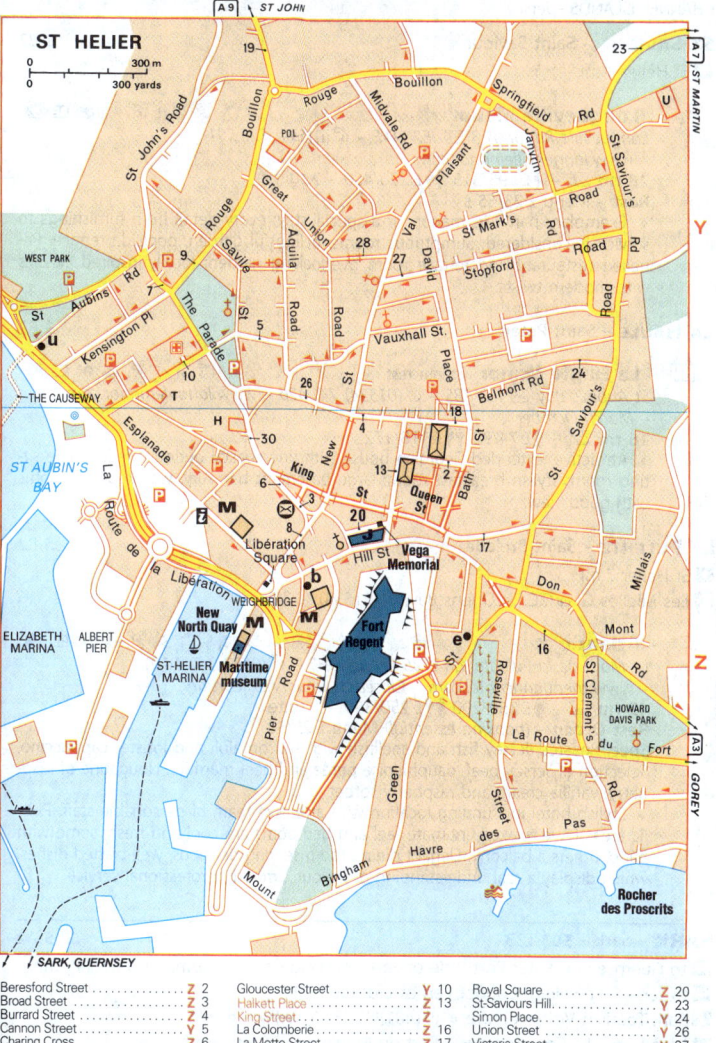

Beresford Street	Z 2	Gloucester Street	Y 10	Royal Square	Z 20
Broad Street	Z 3	Halkett Place	Z 13	St-Saviours Hill	Z 23
Burrard Street	Z 4	King Street	Z	Simon Place	Y 24
Cannon Street	Y 5	La Colomberie	Z 16	Union Street	Z 26
Charing Cross	Z 6	La Motte Street	Z 17	Victoria Street	Y 27
Cheapside	Y 7	Minden Place	Z 18	Windsor Road	Y 28
Conway Street	Z 8	Queen Street	Z	York Street	Y 30
Elizabeth Place	Y 9	Queen's Road	Y 19		

Tassili – at Grand Hotel

The Esplanade ✉ JE4 8WD – ✆ (01534) 722 301 – www.grandjersey.com
– Closed Sunday and Monday

Rest – *(dinner only) (booking essential)* Carte £ 49/85

Spec. Lobster 'Caesar' salad with shellfish linguini. Quail with boudin noir, foie gras and cauliflower cheese. Banana cake with lime jelly, coconut cream and piña colada sorbet.

♦ Small, sophisticated hotel restaurant. Intimate atmosphere with aubergine colour scheme and vibrant artwork. Accomplished, innovative modern cooking uses local island produce in precisely executed, interesting and visually impressive combinations. Proud, knowledgeable service.

CHANNEL ISLANDS - Jersey

St Saviour – Saint Saviour 5 B2
▶ St Helier 1 mi

Longueville Manor
Longueville Rd, on A 3 ✉ JE2 7WF – ℘ (01534) 725 501
– www.longuevillemanor.com
28 rm – †£ 195/315 ††£ 220/460 – 2 suites
Rest – Menu £ 25/55 s

♦ Exemplary part 13C manor for a special stay; every detail from furnishings to service is considered. Sumptuous rooms, delightful garden, poolside terrace. Panelled restaurant and terrace room overlooking garden; locally-inspired classics with modern twists.

La Haule – Saint Peter 5 B2

La Haule Manor without rest
St Aubin's Bay ✉ JE3 8BS – ℘ (01534) 741 426 – www.lahaulemanor.com
– March-October
16 rm – †£ 74/92 ††£ 118/172

♦ Attractive, extended Georgian house with fine coastal outlook. Period style sitting room; stylish breakfast room; large basement bar. Airy, well-kept bedrooms with good view.

La Pulente – Saint Brelade 5 B2
▶ St Helier 7 mi
⛳ Les Mielles G. & C.C. St Ouens Bay, ℘ (01534) 48 27 87

Atlantic
Le Mont de la Pulente, on B 35 ✉ JE3 8HE – ℘ (01534) 744 101
– www.theatlantichotel.com – Closed 3 January-2 February
49 rm – †£ 150/200 ††£ 250/350 – 1 suite
Rest Ocean – (booking essential) Menu £ 25/50
Spec. Roasted Jersey fish and shellfish with saffron aioli and lobster cappuccino. Selection of Jersey beef, dauphinoise purée and beef marmite. Nougatine of raspberry, vanilla cream and raspberry sorbet.

♦ Stylish hotel in stunning location with attentive team of personable staff. Public areas have relaxed, intimate feel and bedrooms are cool and fresh; some with patio, others a balcony. Elegant dining room serving delicious, well-crafted dishes, which display a real understanding of flavour. Smooth, professional service.

SARK – Sark – 503 L33 5 A2
⛴ to Guernsey (St Peter Port) (Isle of Sark Shipping Co. Ltd) (summer only) (45 mn)
⛴ to Jersey (St Helier) (Condor Ferries Ltd) (50 mn)
🛈 Sark Tourism Visitor Centre ℘ (01481) 83 23 45, www.sark.info
◉ Island ★★ – La Coupée ★★★ – Port du Moulin ★★ – Creux Harbour ★
– La Seigneurie ★ **AC** – Pilcher Monument ★ – Hog's Back ★

Sablonnerie with rm
Little Sark ✉ GY9 0SD – ℘ (01481) 832 061 – www.lasablonnerie.com
– mid-April-mid-October
20 rm (dinner included) – †£ 70/218 ††£ 139/290 – 2 suites
Rest – (booking essential) Menu £ 30 – Carte £ 25/37

♦ Charming, whitewashed 16C former farmhouse with beautiful gardens. Cosy, beamed interior with a comfortable lounge for aperitifs. Regularly changing, five course menu offers a classic style of cooking using produce from their own farm. Prompt service. Neat, tidy bedrooms; Room 14, in the former stables, is the best.

CHANNEL TUNNEL – Kent – 504 X30 – see Folkestone

CHAPEL-EN-LE-FRITH – Derbyshire – 504 O24 – pop. 6 581   16 A1
▶ London 175 mi – Sheffield 27 mi – Manchester 21 mi – Stoke-on-Trent 34 mi

⌂ **High Croft** without rest
Manchester Rd, West : 0.75 mi on B 5470 ✉ *SK23 9UH* – ✆ *(01298) 814 843*
– *www.highcroft-guesthouse.co.uk*
4 rm – †£ 65 ††£ 85/105
• Edwardian house with Arts and Crafts features and lovely mature garden. Comfortable bedrooms overlook surrounding hills and valleys; Atholl suite – a four-poster with tub – is best.

CHARLTON – West Sussex – 504 R31 – see Chichester

CHARMOUTH – Dorset – 503 L31 – pop. 1 497 – ✉ Bridport   3 B3
▶ London 157 mi – Dorchester 22 mi – Exeter 31 mi – Taunton 27 mi

⌂ **White House**
2 Hillside, The Street ✉ *DT6 6PJ* – ✆ *(01297) 560 411*
– *www.whitehousehotel.com* – *Restricted opening in winter*
6 rm – †£ 60/90 ††£ 90/120   **Rest** – *(dinner only)* Menu £ 35
• Gleaming white Regency villa close to the Jurassic Coast, personally run by a friendly couple. Bedrooms feature cast iron/sleigh beds and flat screen TVs. Comfortable sitting room in period style. More modern, wood-furnished dining room; classic menus.

⌂ **Abbots House** without rest
The Street ✉ *DT6 6QF* – ✆ *(01297) 560 339* – *www.abbotshouse.co.uk* – *Closed last 2 weeks December and January*
3 rm – †£ 120 ††£ 120
• Dating back to 1480 – originally an annexe of Forde Abbey. Cosy beamed, panelled lounge; conservatory breakfast room overlooks well-tended gardens and a working model railway. Spacious, stylish bedrooms offer homemade treats and a memento.

CHATHILL – Northumberland – see Alnwick

CHATTON – Northumberland – 502 O17 – pop. 438   24 A1
▶ London 336 mi – Sunderland 63 mi – Newcastle upon Tyne 52 mi
– South Shields 57 mi

⌂ **Chatton Park House** without rest
(East : 5 mi on B 6348 , Wooler rd.) ✉ *NE66 5RA* – ✆ *(01688) 215 507*
– *www.chattonpark.com* – *Closed 23-26 and 31 December and 1 January*
3 rm – †£ 100/110 ††£ 150/170 – 1 suite
• Fine period house built in the 1750s, set in 4 acres of formal gardens and mature grounds. Smart parquet-floored hallway, huge, open-fired sitting room and airy breakfast room. Spacious bedrooms blend modern décor with original features.

CHEDDLETON – Staffordshire – 502 N24 – pop. 2 719 – ✉ Leek   19 C1
▶ London 125 mi – Birmingham 48 mi – Derby 33 mi – Manchester 42 mi

⌂ **Choir Cottage** without rest
Ostlers Lane, via Hollow Lane, (opposite Red Lion on A 520) ✉ *ST13 7HS*
– ✆ *(01538) 360 561* – *www.choircottage.co.uk*
3 rm – †£ 65/69 ††£ 79/90
• 17C stone cottage, once owned by the church and let to the needy, with the rent paying for new choir gowns. Smart, modern guest areas. 2 four-poster bedrooms in the old cottage; 1 more contemporary room in a newer building. All boast private outdoor seating.

CHELMSFORD – Essex – 504 V28 – pop. 99 962   13 C2
▶ London 33 mi – Cambridge 46 mi – Ipswich 40 mi – Southend-on-Sea 19 mi
ℹ Unit 3, Dukes Walk, Duke St ✆ (01245) 28 34 00, www.chelmsford.gov.uk

CHELMSFORD

XX Barda
30-32 Broomfield Rd ⊠ CM1 1SW – ℰ (01245) 357 799
– www.barda-restaurant.com – Closed Sunday and Monday
Rest – Menu £ 18 – Carte £ 26/35

• Keenly run, contemporary restaurant with a large decked terrace. Simple, flavoursome dishes on offer at lunchtimes; more interesting, international cooking with modern touches at dinner.

at Boreham Northeast : 3.5 mi on B 1137 (Springfield Rd)

Lion Inn
Main Rd ⊠ CM3 3JA – ℰ (01245) 394 900 – www.lioninnhotel.co.uk – Closed 26 December
15 rm ⊇ – †£ 89 ††£ 150 **Rest** – Carte £ 22/30

• Keenly run, extended former pub with eco-friendly credentials and a French feel. Soundproofed bedrooms blend contemporary fabrics with reproduction furniture. Large open-plan lounge/brasserie with buzzy atmosphere; short menu of appealing, pub-style dishes.

CHELTENHAM – Gloucestershire – 503 N28 – pop. 104 968   4 C1
Great Britain

▶ London 99 mi – Birmingham 48 mi – Bristol 40 mi – Gloucester 9 mi
🛈 77 Promenade ℰ (01242) 52 28 78, www.visitcheltenham.com
⛳ Cleeve Hill, ℰ (01242) 67 20 25
⛳ Cotswold Hills Ullenwood, ℰ (01242) 51 52 64
◎ Town★
◉ Sudeley Castle★ (Paintings★) **AC**, NE : 7 mi by B 4632 A

Ellenborough Park
Southam, Northeast : 2.75 mi on B 4632 ⊠ GL52 3NH
– ℰ (01242) 545 454 – www.ellenboroughpark.com   AXa
62 rm ⊇ – †£ 240 ††£ 850
Rest *Beaufort Rest Tudor Club Brasserie* – see restaurant listing

• Part-16C, part-timbered manor house, with stone conversions, an understated, Indian-themed spa and large grounds stretching down to the racecourse. Beautifully furnished guest areas have an elegant, classical style; Nina Campbell designed bedrooms boast superb bathrooms, the latest mod cons and plenty of extras. Excellent levels of service from a smartly attired team.

Hotel du Vin
Parabola Rd ⊠ GL50 3AQ – ℰ (01242) 588 450 – www.hotelduvin.com
48 rm – †£ 135/190 ††£ 135/190, ⊇ £ 14 – 1 suite   BYc
Rest *Bistro* – see restaurant listing

• Attractive Regency house in an affluent residential area next to the Ladies College. Shabby-chic styling with leather-furnished bar and comfy lounge. Individually designed, well-equipped, wine-themed bedrooms; some with baths in the room.

Montpellier Chapter
Bayshill Rd ⊠ GL50 3AS – ℰ (01242) 527 788 – www.chapterhotels.com
61 rm – †£ 125 ††£ 440, ⊇ £ 10   BZr
Rest – Menu £ 15 (lunch) – Carte £ 25/36

• Extended Regency townhouse with retro lounges and large conservatory. Light wood furnished bedrooms come with Nespresso machines, complimentary mini bars and in-room info on an iPod touch. Dine on British dishes at marble-topped tables or on one of two terraces.

Hotel
38 Evesham Rd ⊠ GL52 2AH – ℰ (01242) 518 898 – www.thehoteluk.co.uk
12 rm – †£ 155/495 ††£ 155/495, ⊇ £ 19   CYr
Rest *Parkers* – see restaurant listing

• Stylish, modern hotel displaying bold, contemporary colours and striking furniture. Black marble floored reception, comfortable lounge and smart bar. Bedrooms – named after dukes and dignitaries – boast chic styling, good modern facilities and smart bathrooms.

CHELTENHAM

Berkeley St	CYZ 4	Keynsham Rd		CZ
Clarence St	CY 6	Knapp Rd		BY
Crescent Terrace	BY 7	Montpellier Ave		BZ 17
Deep St	AX 9	Montpellier Walk		BZ 18
Dunalley St	CY 10	North St		CY 20
Henrietta St	CY 13	Norwood Rd		BCY
High St	BCY	Oriel Rd		BZ 21
High St PRESTBURY	AX 14	Pittville St		CZ 22
		Portland St		CY 26
Regent Arcade Shopping Centre		Promenade (The)		CY 27
Regent St	CY 29			
Rodney Rd	CY 30			
Royal Well Rd	BCY 32			
St James St	CY 33			
St Johns Ave	CY 34			
St Margaret's Rd	CY 35			
Sandford Mill Rd	CY 36			
Sandford Terrace	CZ 37			
Winchcombe St	CY 38			

ENGLAND

CHELTENHAM

Beaumont House without rest
56 Shurdington Rd – GL53 0JE – ℰ *(01242) 223 311 – www.bhhotel.co.uk*
16 rm – †£ 79/85 ††£ 170/249
AXu
- Keenly run Georgian house with comfy drawing room and bar; breakfast room overlooks lawned garden. Refurbished bedrooms are stylish and contemporary with excellent bathrooms.

Lypiatt House without rest
Lypiatt Rd – GL50 2QW – ℰ *(01242) 224 994 – www.staylypiatt.co.uk*
10 rm – †£ 78/95 ††£ 95/130
BZc
- A privately owned, serene Victorian house with friendly service. Bedrooms on the top floor with dormer roof tend to be smaller than those on the other floors. Soft, pale colours.

Butlers without rest
Western Rd – GL50 3RN – ℰ *(01242) 570 771 – www.butlers-hotel.co.uk*
9 rm – †£ 55/65 ††£ 95/155
BYv
- Personally managed hotel where bedrooms constitute a peaceful haven with stylish drapes and canopies. Rooms named after famous butlers; some overlook wooded garden to rear.

Thirty Two without rest
32 Imperial Sq – GL50 1QZ – ℰ *(01242) 771 110 – www.thirtytwoltd.com*
– Closed 25-26 December
3 rm – †£ 155 ††£ 155, ⊐ £ 10 – 1 suite
BZe
- Immaculate Regency house overlooking grassy city square. Stylish, beautifully appointed bedrooms with furniture designed by owner; superb bathrooms. Excellent facilities and extra touches.

Hanover House without rest
65 St George's Rd – GL50 3DU – ℰ *(01242) 541 297 – www.hanoverhouse.org*
– Closed one week Christmas and Easter
3 rm ⊐ – †£ 70 ††£ 100
BYu
- Early Victorian townhouse, perfectly located for seeing the city. Comfortable family lounge filled with books and portraits; spacious, tastefully furnished bedrooms. Organic breakfasts.

Georgian House without rest
77 Montpellier Terr – GL50 1XA – ℰ *(01242) 515 577 – www.georgianhouse.net*
– Closed 19 December-3 January
3 rm ⊐ – †£ 70/85 ††£ 85/115
BZs
- Smart, terraced Georgian house, hospitably run, in sought-after Montpellier area. Good-sized bedrooms decorated in authentic period style. Comfy, elegant communal rooms.

Le Champignon Sauvage (David Everitt-Matthias)
24-28 Suffolk Rd – GL50 2AQ – ℰ *(01242) 573 449*
– www.lechampignonsauvage.com – Closed 3 weeks June, 10 days Christmas, Sunday and Monday
BZa
Rest – Menu £ 32 (lunch and weekday dinner)/60
Spec. Dexter beef tartare and corned beef, wasabi cream. Winchcombe venison, salt and burdock baked golden beetroot, roasted quince. Rhubarb poached with hibiscus, mascarpone cream, gin and tonic sorbet.
- Firmly established restaurant with professional service from a well-versed team. Confident, accomplished cooking is underscored by a classical base but dishes have personality and are visually impressive. Some ingredients are foraged for by the chef.

Lumière
Clarence Par – GL50 3PA – ℰ *(01242) 222 200 – www.lumiere.cc*
– Closed 2 weeks January, 2 weeks summer, Tuesday lunch, Sunday and Monday
Rest – (booking essential) Menu £ 25/45
BCYz
- Elegant, comfortable and personally run restaurant, decorated in chic browns and leather. Cooking is modern, original and inventive, and makes excellent use of local suppliers.

CHELTENHAM

XXX Beaufort – at Ellenborough Park Hotel
Southam, Northeast : 2.75 mi on B 4632 – GL52 3NH – ℰ (01242) 545 454 – www.ellenboroughpark.com – Closed Sunday dinner and Monday lunch
Rest – Menu £ 24/50 **s** AX**a**
♦ Formal dining room in a part-16C, part-timbered manor house, displaying original stone fireplaces, stained glass windows and dark wood panelling. Classical menu relies on local ingredients.

XX Daffodil
18-20 Suffolk Par – GL50 2AE – ℰ (01242) 700 055 – www.thedaffodil.com – Closed 1-14 January, 25 December and Sunday BZ**u**
Rest – Menu £ 16 (lunch and early dinner) – Carte £ 24/45
♦ Originally a 1920s art deco cinema, now a very pleasant restaurant with its kitchen in the former screen area and a stylish lounge in what was the old balcony. Brasserie-style dishes display worldwide influences. Service is attentive.

XX Parkers – at The Hotel
38 Evesham Rd – GL52 2AH – ℰ (01242) 518 898 – www.thehoteluk.co.uk
Rest – Menu £ 20/40 – Carte £ 41/57 CY**r**
♦ Smart, stylish restaurant with plain walls, minimalist styling and bright pink, brushed velvet chairs. French-based menus make good use of local produce. Pleasant enclosed rear terrace.

XX Curry Corner
133 Fairview Rd – GL52 2EX – ℰ (01242) 528 449 – www.thecurrycorner.com – Closed 25 December, lunch Friday and Monday except bank holiday
Rest – Bangladeshi – Menu £ 20 (lunch) – Carte £ 35/51 CY**a**
♦ Long-standing, family run restaurant in smart Regency townhouse. Authentic, flavoursome dishes from across India, Persia and Bangladesh. Imported spices are ground and roasted every morning.

XX Tudor Club Brasserie – at Ellenborough Park Hotel
Southam, Northeast : 2.75 mi on B 4632 – GL52 3NH – ℰ (01242) 545 454 – www.ellenboroughpark.com AX**a**
Rest – Carte £ 22/37 **s**
♦ Informal brasserie with low timbered ceiling and wood-clad walls, set within a part-16C, part-timbered manor house. Décor incorporates a sports and 'Cresta Run' theme. Classic brasserie dishes.

XX Bistro – at Hotel du Vin
Parabola Rd – GL50 3AQ – ℰ (01242) 588 450 – www.hotelduvin.com
Rest – Menu £ 18 (lunch) – Carte £ 25/36 BY**c**
♦ Bistro-style restaurant in an attractive Regency hotel. Eye-catching chandelier made from wine glasses; paved terrace for warmers days. Classical French menu accompanied by a good wine list.

X Royal Well Tavern
5 Royal Well Pl – GL50 3DN – ℰ (01242) 221 212 – www.theroyalwelltavern.com – Closed 25 December and Sunday dinner
Rest – Menu £ 13 (lunch and early dinner) – Carte £ 27/32 BY**e**
♦ Tucked away in side street close to theatre. Bustling contemporary eatery; a fusion of gentleman's club and brasserie. Rustic modern menu of carefully prepared dishes; many in two sizes.

X Brosh
8 Suffolk Par Montpellier – GL50 2AB – ℰ (01242) 227 277 – www.broshrestaurant.co.uk – Closed Christmas and New Year BZ**o**
Rest – Mediterranean – *(dinner only)* Carte £ 16/37
♦ Keenly run restaurant with atmospheric interior: dimmed lights and flickering candles in the evening make for a great vibe. Eastern Mediterranean and Middle Eastern cooking features mezze.

CHELTENHAM

at Cleeve Hill Northeast : 4 mi on B 4632 – AX – ✉ Cheltenham

Cleeve Hill without rest
✉ GL52 3PR – ✆ (01242) 672 052 – www.cleevehill-hotel.co.uk
10 rm – †£ 50/98 ††£ 85/120
♦ Edwardian house in elevated spot; most bedrooms have views across Cleeve Common and the Malvern Hills. Breakfast room is in the conservatory; admire the landscape over coffee.

Malvern View with rm
✉ GL52 3PR – ✆ (01242) 672 017 – www.malvernview.com
– Closed 26 December-14 January, Sunday and Monday
6 rm – †£ 55/75 ††£ 80/130 **Rest** – Carte £ 26/36
♦ Sandstone house with views out across the Malvern countryside towards Cleeve Hill. Concise menu of classically based dishes; hearty, flavoursome cooking. Boutique-style bedrooms boast bold feature walls and modern facilities; Room 1 is the largest. Friendly service.

at Shurdington Southwest : 3.75 mi on A 46 – AX – ✉ Cheltenham

Greenway
✉ GL51 4UG – ✆ (01242) 862 352 – www.thegreenway.co.uk
16 rm – †£ 125/250 ††£ 125/420 – 1 suite **Rest** – Menu £ 26/53
♦ Ivy-clad Elizabethan manor house set in large grounds and peaceful lawned gardens. Spacious, classically styled lounges and drawing rooms. Bedrooms have a typical country house feel. Smart spa facility. Garden and lily pond on view from formal restaurant.

CHERITON FITZPAINE – 503 J31 – ✉ Devon — 2 C2

▶ London 182 mi – Cardiff 108 mi – Plymouth 59 mi – Swansea 144 mi

Devon Wine School
Redyeates Farm, North : 0.75 mi by Way Rd turning left down unmarked road after Redyeates cross roads. ✉ EX17 4HG – ✆ (01363) 866 742
– www.devonwineschool.co.uk – Closed 2 weeks July
5 rm – ††£ 85/100 **Rest** – Menu £ 35
♦ Delightful 17C farmhouse in idyllic rural spot; offering residential wine school run by a Master of Wine. Fresh, modern bedrooms; Saint Amour has its own private terrace and roll-top bath. Set dinner menu served at large table in vaulted barn.

CHESTER – Cheshire West and Chester – 502 L24 – pop. 80 624 — 20 A3
Great Britain

▶ London 207 mi – Birkenhead 7 mi – Birmingham 91 mi – Liverpool 21 mi
ℹ Vicars Lane ✆ (01244) 40 21 11, www.visitchester.com
⛳ Upton-by-Chester Upton Lane, ✆ (01244) 38 11 83
⛳ Curzon Park, ✆ (01244) 67 77 60
◉ City★★ – The Rows★★ B – Cathedral★ B – City Walls★ B
◉ Chester Zoo★ AC, N : 3 mi by A 5116

Plans on following pages

Chester Grosvenor
Eastgate ✉ CH1 1LT – ✆ (01244) 324 024 – www.chestergrosvenor.com
– Closed 25-26 December Ba
76 rm – †£ 230 ††£ 360, ☐ £ 25 – 4 suites
Rest *Simon Radley at Chester Grosvenor* **Rest** *Brasserie* – see restaurant listing
♦ 19C hotel with grand black and white timbered façade; set close to the cathedral and historic city centre. Lavish interior displays rich décor, impressive antiques and luxurious bedrooms.

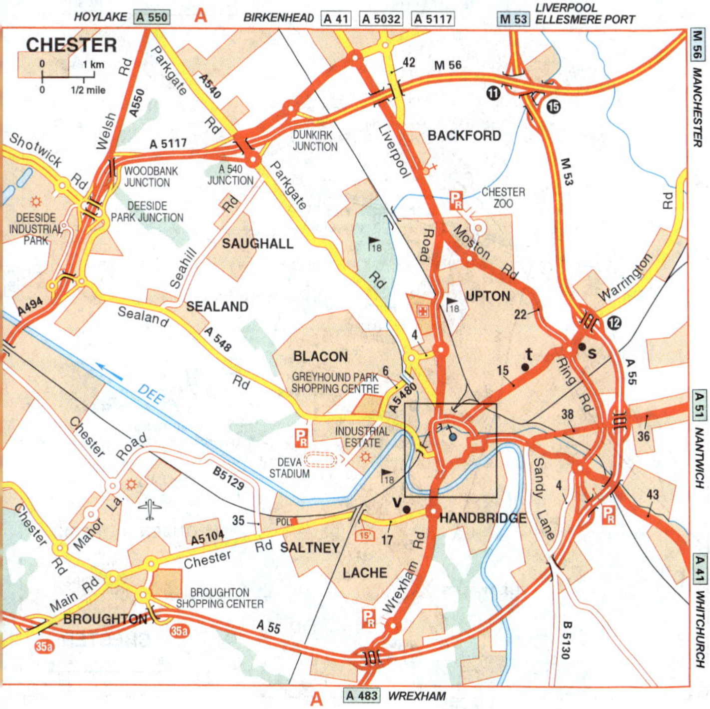

Caldy Valley Rd . . . . **A** 4	Hoole Rd . . . . **A** 15	Tarvin Rd . . . . **A** 36
Countess Way . . . . **A** 5	Hough Green . . . . **A** 17	Vicar's Cross
Deva Link . . . . **A** 6	Long Lane . . . . **A** 22	Rd . . . . **A** 38
Greyhound Park	Saltney Ferry	Whitby Lane . . . . **A** 42
Shopping Centre . . . . **A**	Rd . . . . **A** 35	Whitchurch Rd . . . . **A** 43

Doubletree by Hilton Chester

As

Warrington Rd, Northeast : 2 mi on A 56 ✉ CH2 3PD
– ℘ (01244) 408 800 – www.doubletree-hilton.co.uk/chester
140 rm – †£ 79/190 ††£ 79/230, ⊇ £ 13
Rest – Menu £ 20 (dinner) **s** – Carte £ 22/32 **s**
Rest *Marco Pierre White Steakhouse Bar & Grill* – Beef specialities –
℘ (01244) 408 830 *(closed Sunday dinner) (dinner only and Sunday lunch)*
Carte £ 33/52

♦ Smart, stylish hotel offering sleek, spacious bedrooms with super king-sized beds, bright white décor and modern facilities. State-of-the-art conference facilities. Superb spa with well-equipped leisure club. Modern steakhouse set in 18C manor house. Informal brasserie.

Abode Chester

Bz

Grosvenor Rd ✉ CH1 2DJ – ℘ (01244) 347 000 – www.abodehotels.co.uk
85 rm – †£ 99/195 ††£ 99/550, ⊇ £ 14
Rest *Michael Caines* – see restaurant listing
Rest *MC Café Bar & Grill* – Carte £ 19/31

♦ Imposing modern hotel opposite the castle and the racecourse; a short walk into the city. Four categories of bedroom; Enviable and Fabulous are the best. Ask for a room with a racecourse view. Ground floor MC Café Grill & Bar offers a modern brasserie menu.

Boughton	B 2	Handbridge	B 13	Pepper St.	B 30
Bridge St	B 3	Little St John St.	B 19	Pierpoint Lane	B 31
Eastgate St	B 7	Liverpool Rd	B 21	St John St	B 32
Forum Shopping centre	B	Lower Bridge St	B 23	St Martins Way	B 33
Frodsham St	B 9	Nicholas St.	B 25	Vicar's Lane	B 40
Grosvenor Park Rd	B 10	Northgate St	B 26	Watergate
Grosvenor St	B 12	Parkgate Rd.	B 28	St	B

Green Bough
60 Hoole Rd, on A 56 ✉ CH2 3NL – ℰ (01244) 326 241 – www.greenbough.co.uk – Closed 1 January, 25 and 31 December

At

12 rm – †£95/125 ††£195/245 – 3 suites

Rest *Olive Tree* – see restaurant listing

♦ Red-brick Victorian house on the edge of the city. Comfortable, homely lounge with over 50 whiskies behind the bar. Bedrooms vary greatly in their décor, from traditional country house styling to bold contemporary designs – all with a high level of facilities and extra touches. Polite, friendly service.

Dragonfly without rest
94 Watergate St ✉ CH1 2LF – ℰ (01244) 346 740 – www.hoteldragonfly.com

Br

7 rm – †£170 ††£170, ⊇ £10

♦ Stylish boutique townhouse. Georgian cornicing and flag/parquet floors blend with contemporary art and chic black breakfast tables. Spacious, modern bedrooms boast iPod docks and huge showers.

Mitchell's of Chester without rest
28 Hough Grn, Southwest : 1 mi by A 483 on A 5104 ✉ CH4 8JQ – ℰ (01244) 679 004 – www.mitchellsofchester.com – Closed 21-29 December

Av

7 rm – †£40/80 ††£65/90

♦ Large Victorian house, attractively restored and privately run. Homely breakfast room; lounge comes complete with parrot. Individually decorated bedrooms continue Victoriana feel.

CHESTER

XXXX Simon Radley at Chester Grosvenor
Eastgate ✉ *CH1 1LT* – ℰ *(01244) 324 024* – *www.chestergrosvenor.com*
– *Closed January-February, 25-26 December, Sunday and Monday*
Rest – *(dinner only)* Menu £69
B a

Spec. Pigeon pie, cep duxelle and velouté of truffles. Noisette butter poached skate, wild garlic and langoustines. Manjari chocolate with pistachio cream, almond milk ice and rose jelly.

• Smart restaurant with fabric-covered walls, plush furnishings, stylish cocktail lounge and formal, detailed service. Quality ingredients come together in sophisticated dishes that boast creative, innovative touches. Attractive, modern presentation.

XX Michael Caines – at Abode Chester Hotel
Grosvenor Rd, (Fifth Floor) ✉ *CH1 2DJ* – ℰ *(01244) 405 820*
– *www.michaelcaines.com* – *Closed Sunday*
Rest – Menu £14 (lunch) – Carte £27/47
B z

• Fashionable spot for city dining, located on fifth floor of hotel. Menus combine a French base with a modern edge; try the tasting menu to fully appreciate the flavourful, artistic cooking.

XX Brasserie – at Chester Grosvenor Hotel
Eastgate ✉ *CH1 1LT* – ℰ *(01244) 324 024* – *www.chestergrosvenor.com*
– *Closed January- February and 25-26 December*
Rest – Carte £33/53
B a

• Attractive, classically styled Parisian brasserie with hand-painted glass skylight and pleasant buzzy ambience. Menus feature traditional British, French and Mediterranean dishes.

XX Oddfellows with rm
20 Lower Bridge St ✉ *CH1 1RS* – ℰ *(01244) 400 001* – *www.oddfellows.biz*
4 rm – †£115/250 ††£115/250, ⚏ £13
Rest – Carte £24/41 **s**
B c

• Quirky, uniquely styled 17C house with impressive façade. Atmospheric restaurant and stylish bar; Bedouin tents in garden. Modern British dishes come with wine recommendations. Well-equipped bedrooms have eccentric, modern style; some boast double roll-top baths.

XX Olive Tree – at Green Bough Hotel
60 Hoole Rd, on A 56 ✉ *CH2 3NL* – ℰ *(01244) 326 241* – *www.greenbough.co.uk*
– *Closed 1 January, 25 and 31 December*
Rest – *(dinner only)* Menu £25 – Carte £38/45
A t

• Stylish, two-roomed fine dining restaurant; it's décor inspired by Italy. Mediterranean-based menus use local, seasonal ingredients. Start with canapés in the lounge or on the rooftop garden.

X Joseph Benjamin
134-140 Northgate St ✉ *CH1 2HT* – ℰ *(01244) 344 295*
– *www.josephbenjamin.co.uk* – *Closed Monday*
Rest – *(lunch only and dinner Thursday -Saturday) (booking essential)*
Carte £24/33
B u

• Bistro, deli and cookshop, named after its two passionate owners. Simple, light décor mirrors the style of cooking. Monthly menu of well-judged, satisfying dishes and tasty homemade pastries.

XX Upstairs at the Grill
70 Watergate St ✉ *CH1 2LA* – ℰ *(01244) 344 883* – *www.upstairsatthegrill.com*
– *Closed 25 December*
Rest – Beef specialities – *(dinner only and lunch Friday-Sunday)* Carte £22/34
B n

• Unique, buzzy restaurant adorned with cow paraphernalia. Prime quality steaks – including rib-eye, sirloin, chateaubriand and rare breeds – come with expert guidance. Clubby cocktail bar.

CHESTER

1539
The Racecourse ✉ CH1 2LY – ✆ (01244) 304 611 – www.restaurant1539.co.uk
– Closed Sunday dinner
B e
Rest – Carte £ 23/33
• Stylish and spacious modern brasserie set in a stand of the racecourse, with smartly furnished, decked terraces and panoramic views. Modern British cooking makes use of local produce.

CHESTERFIELD – Derbyshire – 502 P24 – pop. 70 260 – Great Britain 16 B1

▶ London 152 mi – Derby 24 mi – Nottingham 25 mi – Sheffield 12 mi

🏌 Grassmoor North Wingfield Rd, ✆ (01246) 85 60 44

🏛 Bolsover Castle★ **AC**, E : 5 mi by A 632

Non Solo Vino
417 Chatsworth Rd, Brampton ✉ S40 3AD – ✆ (01246) 276 760
– www.nonsolovino.co.uk – Closed 25 December, 1 January, Sunday dinner and Monday
Rest – Italian – Menu £ 20 (lunch) – Carte £ 25/44
• Originally a wine shop specialising in Italian wines, now also incorporates a bright, contemporary restaurant. Adventurous, modern cooking features Italian classics with a twist. Unsurprisingly, offers an interesting, well-priced wine list.

CHESTER-LE-STREET – Durham – 502 P19 – pop. 36 049 24 B2

▶ London 275 mi – Durham 7 mi – Newcastle upon Tyne 8 mi

🏌 Lumley Park, ✆ (0191) 388 32 18

🏌 Roseberry Grange Grange Villa, ✆ (0191) 370 06 60

Lumley Castle
East : 1 mi on B 1284 ✉ DH3 4NX – ✆ (0191) 389 11 11
– www.lumleycastle.com – Closed 24-27 December
73 rm ⚏ – ♦£ 69/145 ♦♦£ 115/250 – 1 suite
Rest *Black Knight* – (closed Saturday lunch) Carte £ 25/46
• Norman castle, without additions, underscoring its uniqueness. Rich, gothic interiors of carved wood, chandeliers, statues, tapestries, rugs. Rooms imbued with atmosphere. Restaurant offers classical dishes with an original twist.

CHEW MAGNA – Bath and North East Somerset – 503 M29 4 C2
– pop. 1 187

▶ London 128 mi – Bristol 9 mi – Cardiff 52 mi – Bournemouth 89 mi

Pony & Trap (Josh Eggleton)
❀
Knowle Hill, Newtown, South : 1.25 mi on Bishop Stuttard rd ✉ BS40 8TQ
– ✆ (01275) 332 627 – www.theponyandtrap.co.uk – Closed Sunday dinner in winter and Monday except bank holidays
Rest – (booking essential) Carte £ 19/36
Spec. Scallops with hodge podge, parsnip purée and apple salad. Pressed breast of lamb, sweetbreads and sautéed liver with aubergine salad and red wine sauce. Cardamom panna cotta, layered chocolate mousse cake and macerated strawberries.
• Cosy whitewashed pub in a tiny hamlet; its oversized dining room windows offering lovely country views. Twice-daily menu of extremely fresh, seasonal produce, including locally sourced, hung and smoked meats and fish. Classical cooking with clean, clear flavours.

Bear & Swan
13 South Par ✉ BS40 8SL – ✆ (01275) 331 100 – www.bearandswan.co.uk
– Closed Sunday dinner
Rest – Carte £ 22/35
• Well-established village pub with delightful open-fired bar, candlelit dining room and loyal local following. Choice of fresh, homemade British pub classics or more European-influenced dishes.

CHICHESTER – West Sussex – 504 R31 – pop. 27 477 – Great Britain   7 C2

▶ London 69 mi – Brighton 31 mi – Portsmouth 18 mi – Southampton 30 mi
🛈 29a South St ℰ (01243) 77 58 88, www.visitchichester.org
🏌 Goodwood Kennel Hill, ℰ (01243) 75 51 33
🏌 Chichester Golf Centre Hunston Village, ℰ (01243) 53 38 33

◉ City★★ – Cathedral★★ BZ A – St Mary's Hospital★ BY D – Pallant House★ AC BZ M

◉ Fishbourne Roman Palace★★ (mosaics★) AC AZ R. Weald and Downland Open Air Museum★★ AC, N : 6 mi by A 286 AY

Ship
57 North St ⬛ PO19 1NH – ℰ (01243) 778 000 – www.theshiphotel.net
36 rm ⬜ – ♦£ 88/110 ♦♦£ 110/135   BYs
Rest – Menu £ 18 – Carte £ 23/29

♦ Grade II listed building, formerly home to one of Nelson's men. Some Georgian and Regency features remain, including a cantilevered wrought iron staircase. Stylish, contemporary bedrooms. Airy brasserie with modern menu; meat and game from nearby estate.

Brasserie Blanc
Richmond House, The Square ⬛ PO19 7SJ – ℰ (01243) 534 200
– www.brasserieblanc.com – Closed 25 December   BZz
Rest – French – Menu £ 14/16 – Carte £ 18/38

♦ Classically styled brasserie with lovely terrace, tucked away in a modern cobbled square. Impressive open-kitchen and display of artisan provisions for sale. Tasty, rustic French cooking.

Comme ça
67 Broyle Rd, on A 286 ⬛ PO19 6BD – ℰ (01243) 788 724
– www.commeca.co.uk – Closed 1 week Christmas-New Year, Sunday dinner and Monday   AYc
Rest – French – Menu £ 25/35

♦ Stalwart of the local dining scene for many years. Classical French cooking ministered by Normand chef. Family lunches on Sundays; good value pre-theatre menu. Eat in the airy conservatory.

ENGLAND

CHICHESTER

Birdham Rd. . . . . AZ 2	Kingsham Rd . . . . BZ 13	St Paul's Rd . . . . BY 27
Bognor Rd . . . . AZ 3	Lavant Rd . . . . AY 14	Sherborne Rd . . . . AZ 28
Chapel St . . . . BY 6	Little London . . . . BY 15	Southgate . . . . BZ 29
Chartres (Av. de) . . . . BZ 7	Market Rd . . . . BZ 16	South Pallant . . . . BZ 31
Chichester Arundel Rd. . . AY 8	Northgate . . . . BY 17	South St . . . . BZ
East Pallant . . . . BZ 9	North Pallant . . . . BZ 19	Spitalfield Lane . . . . BY 32
East St. BZ	North St . . . . BYZ	Stockbridge Rd. . . . . AZ 33
Florence Rd . . . . AZ 10	Oaklands Way . . . . BY 18	Tower St . . . . BY 35
Hornet (The) . . . . BZ 12	St Jame's St . . . . AZ 21	Via Ravenna . . . . AZ 37
	St John's St . . . . BZ 23	Westhampnett
	St Martin's Square . . . . . . BY 24	Rd . . . . AYZ 38
	St Pancras . . . . BY 25	West Pallant . . . . BZ 39

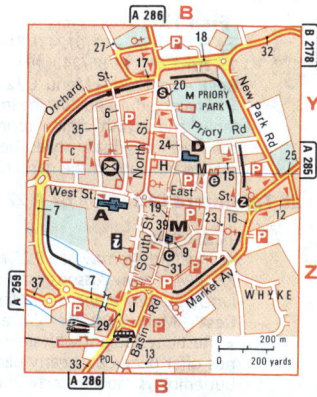

CHICHESTER

Field and Fork at Pallant House Gallery
9 North Pallant ⊠ PO19 1TJ – ℰ (01243) 770 827 – www.fieldandfork.co.uk
– Closed 25 December, Monday and dinner Sunday, Tuesday and Wednesday
Rest – Menu £ 22/25 – Carte £ 20/34

BZ**c**

♦ Modern restaurant in striking Queen Anne building, with delightful courtyard and adjoining art gallery. Light dishes at lunch; more formal dinner menu. Fresh, seasonal produce used with care.

at Mid Lavant North : 2 mi on A286

Rooks Hill without rest
Lavant Rd ⊠ PO18 0BQ – ℰ (01243) 528 400 – www.rookshill.co.uk – Closed 26 December-8 January
3 rm ⊑ – †£ 85/135 ††£ 135/175

♦ Charming Grade II listed guesthouse with mix of contemporary styling and original features. Breakfast room opens into lovely terrace/garden. Well appointed bedrooms with attractive bathrooms. Large buffet breakfast.

Earl of March
⊠ PO18 0BQ – ℰ (01243) 533 993 – www.theearlofmarch.com – Closed Sunday dinner
Rest – Menu £ 23 (early dinner) **s** – Carte £ 30/39 **s**

♦ 18C inn with perfect blend of country character and contemporary styling. Terrace with amazing views of the South Downs. Good quality, seasonal produce used in classic British dishes.

at East Lavant North : 2.5 mi off A 286 - AY – ⊠ Chichester

The Royal Oak Inn with rm
Pook Ln ⊠ PO18 0AX – ℰ (01243) 527 434 – www.royaloakeastlavant.co.uk
8 rm ⊑ – †£ 110/185 ††£ 185/275
Rest – (closed 25 December) Menu £ 21 (lunch) – Carte £ 25/47

♦ 18C whitewashed inn with rustic, laid-back feel; arrive early for a spot by the fire. Cooking is fairly refined but steaks play an important role. There are interesting vegetarian options, a good cheese selection and plenty of wines by the glass. Spacious bedrooms are comfy and well-equipped; breakfast is a treat.

at Charlton North : 6.25 mi by A 286 - AY – ⊠ Chichester

Fox Goes Free
⊠ PO18 0HU – ℰ (01243) 811 461 – www.thefoxgoesfree.com
Rest – Carte £ 21/32

♦ Charming 17C flint pub with lovely South Downs outlook, pleasant garden and many original features. Dishes range from simple pub classics to more substantial local offerings; some to share.

at Chilgrove North : 6.5 mi by A 286 on B 2141

Fish House with rm
⊠ PO18 9HX – ℰ (01243) 519 444 – www.thefishhouse.co.uk
15 rm ⊑ – †£ 85/240 ††£ 150/240
Rest – Seafood – Menu £ 22 (lunch) – Carte £ 28/60

♦ Characterful and low beamed, with marble topped bar, oyster counter, fish tanks and stylish dining room. Classical seafood à la carte with international touches. Individually styled bedrooms boast espresso machines, iPod docks and private hot tubs in the garden.

at Tangmere East : 2 mi by A 27 - AY – ⊠ Chichester

Cassons
Arundel Rd, Northwest : 0.25 mi off A 27 (westbound) ⊠ PO18 0DU – ℰ (01243) 773 294 – www.cassonsrestaurant.co.uk – Closed 26-30 December, Tuesday lunch, Sunday dinner and Monday
Rest – Menu £ 20/31 – Carte £ 39/50

♦ Rustic restaurant with linen-laid tables and exposed brick walls. Set price menus offer generous, hearty dishes with bold flavours. Cooking is classically based but employs modern techniques.

CHICHESTER

at Sidlesham South : 5 mi on B 2145 - AZ

Landseer House without rest
Cow Ln, South : 1.5 mi by B2145 and Keynor Lane ✉ PO20 7LN – ✆ (01243) 641 525 – www.landseerhouse.co.uk
6 rm ⌧ – †£ 80 ††£ 175
♦ Delightful guesthouse with large conservatory and unusual furniture; set in 4½ acres of gardens by a nature reserve and harbour. Two bedrooms in the courtyard. Views to the Isle of Wight.

Crab and Lobster with rm
Mill Ln ✉ PO20 7NB – ✆ (01243) 641 233 – www.crab-lobster.co.uk
4 rm ⌧ – †£ 80 ††£ 180
Rest – (booking advisable) Menu £ 22 (weekday lunch) – Carte £ 28/51
♦ Historic inn, superbly located on a nature reserve, with pretty gardens and a light, relaxed feel. Seasonal menu focuses on seafood. Very comfortable bedrooms have a modern, minimalist style; one has its own garden and an open fired stove.

at Bosham West : 4 mi by A 259 - AZ – ✉ Chichester

Millstream
Bosham Ln ✉ PO18 8HL – ✆ (01243) 573 234 – www.millstream-hotel.com
32 rm ⌧ – †£ 85/129 ††£ 149/169 – 3 suites
Rest – Menu £ 25/33 – Carte £ 25/43
♦ Attractive hotel with a pretty garden that backs onto a stream bobbing with ducks. Cosy bedrooms display individually co-ordinated fabric furnishings, sandwash fitted furniture and large windows. Seasonal, daily changing menus.

at Funtington Northwest : 4.75 mi by B 2178 - AY - on B 2146 – ✉ Chichester

Hallidays
Watery Ln ✉ PO18 9LF – ✆ (01243) 575 331 – www.hallidays.info – Closed 1 week spring, 2 weeks summer, Saturday lunch, Sunday dinner, Monday and Tuesday
Rest – Menu £ 21/26 – Carte £ 28/34
♦ A row of part-13C thatched cottages; confident and keen chef delivers a lively medley of frequently changing menus. Modern meals sit alongside classics; local produce plays a key role.

ENGLAND

CHIDDINGFOLD – Surrey – 504 S30 – pop. 2 128   7 C2
▶ London 47 mi – Guildford 10 mi – Haslemere 5 mi

Swan Inn with rm
Petworth Rd ✉ GU8 4TY – ✆ (01428) 684 688
– www.theswaninnchiddingfold.com
10 rm ⌧ – ††£ 100/125 **Rest** – Carte £ 22/29
♦ Elegant tile-hung pub with 200 year old history and up-to-date interior. Local Surrey set pop in for crab cakes or the 'terrine of the day' at lunch; à la carte changes daily, depending on the latest local produce available. Bedrooms are cool and contemporary.

CHIEVELEY – West Berkshire – 503 Q29   10 B3
▶ London 60 mi – Newbury 5 mi – Swindon 25 mi

Crab at Chievely with rm
The Square, West : 2.5mi by School Rd on B 4494 ✉ RG20 8UE – ✆ (01635) 247 550 – www.chieveley.com
13 rm ⌧ – †£ 195 ††£ 195/215
Rest – Seafood – Menu £ 20 (lunch) – Carte £ 35/70
♦ Thatched former inn, a characterful venue, located on a country road lined with wheat fields. Atmospheric restaurant is filled with seafaring memorabilia and offers a seafood-orientated menu. Highly original bedrooms are themed around famous hotels.

CHILGROVE – West Sussex – 504 R31 – see Chichester

CHILLATON – Devon – 503 H32 – see Tavistock

CHILLINGTON – Devon – 503 I33

2 C3

► London 217 mi – Plymouth 26 mi – Torbay 20 mi – Torquay 22 mi

whitehouse

✉ TQ7 2JX – ✆ (01548) 580 505 – www.whitehousedevon.com – *Closed 3-31 January*
6 rm ☐ – †£ 160/180 ††£ 180/250
Rest – *(booking advisable for non residents)* Carte £ 25/38
♦ Sizeable Georgian house with modern furnishings, relaxed atmosphere and beautiful gardens. Sumptuous, well appointed bedrooms, with large baths and handmade toiletries. Lovely dining room with casual, airy feel and appealing menu.

CHINNOR – Oxfordshire – 504 R28 – pop. 5 407 ▌Great Britain

11 C2

► London 45 mi – Oxford 19 mi
◉ Ridgeway Path★★

at Sprigg's Alley Southeast : 2.5 mi by Bledlow Ridge rd – ✉ Chinnor

Sir Charles Napier

✉ OX39 4BX – ✆ (01494) 483 011 – www.sircharlesnapier.co.uk – *Closed 24-26 December, Sunday dinner and Monday except bank holidays*
Rest – *(booking advisable)* Menu £ 25 (weekdays) – Carte £ 35/51
Spec. Scallops with salt cod brandade, sweet and sour lentils. Duck breast and pithivier with carrot purée, rhubarb and ginger. Vanilla yoghurt, citrus jelly and honeycomb.
♦ Attractive flint pub in a small hillside hamlet, with a hint of eccentricity in its decoration. Pleasant terrace and delightful gardens for summer; log fires and candlelight in winter. Polished and boldly flavoured French based dishes are prepared with obvious skill. Gem of a wine list.

CHIPPENHAM – Wiltshire – 503 N29 – pop. 33 189

4 C2

► London 106 mi – Bristol 27 mi – Southampton 64 mi – Swindon 21 mi
🛈 Market Place ✆ (01249) 66 59 70, www.visitwiltshire.co.uk
🅿 Monkton Park (Par Three), ✆ (01249) 65 39 28
◉ Yelde Hall★
◉ Corsham Court★★ **AC**, SW : 4 mi by A 4 – Sheldon Manor★ **AC**, W : 1.5 mi by A 420 – Biddestone★, W : 3.5 mi – Bowood House★ **AC** (Library ≤★) SE : 5 mi by A 4 and A 342. Castle Combe★★, NW : 6 mi by A 420 and B 4039

at Stanton St Quintin North : 5 mi by A 429 – ✉ Chippenham

Stanton Manor

✉ SN14 6DQ – ✆ (01666) 837 552 – www.stantonmanor.co.uk
23 rm ☐ – †£ 180 ††£ 180   **Rest** – Menu £ 20/28
♦ Extended 19C manor in formal gardens; popular as a wedding venue. Appealing range of bedrooms, geared to corporate market; the deluxe rooms considerably better than the standards. Elegant restaurant uses produce from the garden.

CHIPPING CAMPDEN – Gloucestershire – 503 O27 – pop. 1 943

4 D1

▌Great Britain
► London 93 mi – Cheltenham 21 mi – Oxford 37 mi – Stratford-upon-Avon 12 mi
🛈 Old Police Station ✆ (01386) 84 12 06, www.chippingcampdenonline.org
◉ Town★
◉ Hidcote Manor Garden★★ **AC**, NE : 2.5 m

Cotswold House H. and Spa

The Square ✉ GL55 6AN – ✆ (01386) 840 330 – www.cotswoldhouse.com
25 rm ☐ – †£ 500 ††£ 500 – 3 suites
Rest *Hicks'* – see restaurant listing
Rest *Juliana's* – *(closed Sunday-Wednesday) (dinner only)* Menu £ 50
♦ Enviably stylish Regency townhouse with graceful spiral staircase winding upwards to luxurious rooms, some very modern, boasting every mod con imaginable. Chic spa and impressive service. Formal though stylish Juliana's for accomplished cooking with an original style.

CHIPPING CAMPDEN

Kings
The Square ⊠ *GL55 6AW –* ℰ *(01386) 840 256 – www.kingscampden.co.uk*
19 rm ⊇ – †£ 97/115 ††£145/175
Rest *Kings* – see restaurant listing
♦ Beautiful Cotswold stone townhouse with stylish, boutique interior. Bedrooms in the main house mix antiques with modern facilities and some boast sleigh beds; rooms in the cottage at the end of the garden are more contemporary.

Seymour House without rest
High St ⊠ *GL55 6AG –* ℰ *(01386) 840 064 – www.seymourhousebandb.co.uk*
– Closed Christmas-New Year
4 rm ⊇ – †£ 90 ††£ 120/140
♦ Welcoming Cotswold stone house with early 18C origins. Spacious hall, homely lounge and good-sized bedrooms with modern facilities – 3 are in the eaves. Lovely garden and breakfast terrace.

Staddlestones without rest
7 Aston Rd, North : 0.5 mi by B 4081 on B 4035 ⊠ *GL55 6HR –* ℰ *(01386) 849 288 – www.staddle-stones.com*
3 rm ⊇ – †£ 65 ††£ 85
♦ Attractive sandstone war veteran's cottage. Individually decorated bedrooms with high level of facilities; large annexed suite boasts comfy lounge and country views. Afternoon tea on arrival.

Kings – at Kings Hotel
The Square ⊠ *GL55 6AW –* ℰ *(01386) 840 256 – www.kingscampden.co.uk*
Rest – Menu £ 30 – Carte £ 18/29
♦ Appealing restaurant in a stylish boutique townhouse. Rustic interior boasts exposed stone walls, wooden beams and a large inglenook fireplace. Modern British menus use top quality ingredients and dishes are refined and flavoursome.

Hicks' – at Cotswold House H. and Spa
The Square ⊠ *GL55 6AN –* ℰ *(01386) 840 330 – www.cotswoldhouse.com*
Rest – *(booking essential)* Carte £ 19/50
♦ Named after a local benefactor. Open all day serving locals and residents from a varied modern menu. Morning coffees, afternoon teas and homemade cake available. Booking essential.

Eight Bells Inn with rm
Church St ⊠ *GL55 6JG –* ℰ *(01386) 840 371 – www.eightbellsinn.co.uk – Closed 25 December*
7 rm ⊇ – †£ 60/95 ††£ 125 **Rest** – Carte £ 23/34
♦ 14C pub close to the historic high street in an old wool merchant's town. Cooking is traditionally British – pies are the real thing, puddings are comforting and specials are just that, so arrive early. Bedrooms combine plenty of character with good mod cons.

at Mickleton North : 3.25 mi by B 4035 and B 4081 on B 4632
– ⊠ Chipping Campden

Three Ways House
⊠ *GL55 6SB –* ℰ *(01386) 438 429 – www.threewayshousehotel.com*
48 rm ⊇ – †£ 85/125 ††£ 145/240
Rest – *(bar lunch Monday-Saturday)* Menu £ 37
♦ Built in 1870 and renowned as the home of the Pudding Club. Two types of bedroom, split between the original house and modern block; all are very comfy and modern – opt for one of the pudding-themed rooms. Informal bar-cum-brasserie boasts antique tiled floor. Formal arcaded dining room offers weekly menu.

Nineveh Farm without rest
Southwest : 0.75 mi by B 4632 on B 4081 ⊠ *GL55 6PS –* ℰ *(01386) 438 923*
– www.stayinthecotswolds.co.uk
6 rm ⊇ – †£ 65/85 ††£ 75/95
♦ Georgian farmhouse in pleasant garden. Warm welcome; local information in residents' lounge. Comfortable rooms with view in main house or with French windows in garden house.

CHIPPING CAMPDEN

at Ebrington East : 2 mi by B 4035

Ebrington Arms with rm
✉ GL55 6NH – ✆ (01386) 593 223 – www.theebringtonarms.co.uk
3 mn ⌑ – †£ 95/105 ††£ 110/120 **Rest** – Carte £ 21/31
♦ Proper village local with beamed, flag-floored bar at its hub, set in charming chocolate box village. Robust, traditional dishes use local ingredients and up-to-date techniques. Bedrooms have country views; Room 3, with four-poster bed and luxury bathroom, is best.

at Paxford Southeast : 3 mi by B 4035 – ✉ Chipping Campden

Churchill Arms with rm
✉ GL55 6XH – ✆ (01386) 594 000 – www.thechurchillarms.com – Closed 25 December
4 rm ⌑ – †£ 60/75 ††£ 80/95 **Rest** – (bookings not accepted) Carte £ 20/36
♦ Traditional stone inn set in a lovely location, boasting homely, rustic interior and great views. Cooking displays a real mix of influences, from pub classics to more restaurant-style dishes. Cosy bedrooms with good outlooks – can be noisy before closing time.

at Broad Campden South : 1.25 mi by B 4081 – ✉ Chipping Campden

Malt House without rest
✉ GL55 6UU – ✆ (01386) 840 295 – www.malt-house.co.uk – Closed Christmas-New Year
7 rm ⌑ – †£ 95 ††£ 165
♦ For a rare experience of the countryside idyll, this 16C malting house is a must. Cut flowers from the gardens on view in bedrooms decked out in fabrics to delight the eye.

at Weston Subedge Northwest : 3 mi by B 4081, B 4035 on B 4632

Seagrave Arms with rm
Friday St ✉ GL55 6QH – ✆ (01386) 840 192 – www.seagravearms.co.uk – Closed first week January and Monday
6 rm ⌑ – †£ 95/115 ††£ 95/115 **Rest** – Carte £ 26/32
♦ Part Georgian coach house that's been attractively refurbished. Compact but cosy, with open-fired bar, wood-furnished dining rooms and polite, formal service. Concise menu of ambitious, complex, restaurant-style dishes. Stylish, modern bedrooms are well-equipped.

CHIPPING NORTON – Oxfordshire – 503 P28 – pop. 5 688   10 A1
▶ London 77 mi – Oxford 22 mi – Stow-on-the-Wold 9 mi

Wild Thyme
10 New St ✉ OX7 5LJ – ✆ (01608) 645 060 – www.wildthymerestaurant.co.uk – Closed 2 weeks January, 1 week Spring, Sunday and Monday
Rest – (booking advisable) Carte £ 25/39
♦ Friendly little restaurant off the high street with rustic scrubbed tables and tiny courtyard garden. Wholesome regional British cooking with Mediterranean influences; tasty homemade breads.

Masons Arms
Banbury Rd, Swerford, Northeast : 5 mi on A 361 ✉ OX7 4AP – ✆ (01608) 683 212 – www.masons-arms.com – Closed Sunday dinner
Rest – Menu £ 15 (lunch) – Carte £ 20/30
♦ Stone-built inn with vast garden and pleasant countryside views. Good value menus display an eclectic mix of straightforward dishes, ranging from the traditional to the more exotic. All produce is traceable, meats are rare breed and breads/desserts are homemade.

CHORLEY – Lancashire – 502 M23 – pop. 33 424   20 A2
▶ London 222 – Blackpool 30 – Liverpool 33 – Manchester 26
▣ Duxbury Park Duxbury Hall Rd, ✆ (01257) 26 53 80
▣ Shaw Hill Hotel G. & C.C. Whittle-le-Woods Preston Rd, ✆ (01257) 26 92 21

Red Cat

Blackburn Rd, Whittle-Le-Woods, Northeast : 2.5 mi on A 674 ✉ PR6 8LL
– ℰ (01257) 263 966 – www.theredcat.co.uk
Rest – Menu £ 22 (lunch) – Carte £ 29/45

◆ Restored pub with original beams, stone walls and brick fireplaces. Unfussy, modern dishes display good ingredients and sound cooking in well presented, classic combinations.

CHORLTON-CUM-HARDY – Greater Manchester – 502 N23 – see Manchester

CHRISTCHURCH – Dorset – 503 O31 – pop. 40 208 4 D3

▶ London 111 mi – Bournemouth 6 mi – Salisbury 26 mi – Southampton 24 mi
🛈 49 High St ℰ (01202) 47 17 80, www.visitchristchurch.info
▣ Highcliffe Castle Highcliffe-on-Sea 107 Lymington Rd, ℰ (01425) 27 29 53
▣ Riverside Ave, ℰ (01202) 43 64 36
◉ Town★ - Priory★
◉ Hengistbury Head★ (≤★★) SW : 4.5 mi by A 35 and B 3059

Christchurch Harbour

95 Mudeford, East : 2 mi ✉ BH23 3NT
– ℰ (01202) 483 434 – www.christchurch-harbour-hotel.co.uk
64 rm – †£ 120/190 ††£ 130/290
Rest *Jetty* – see restaurant listing
Rest – Menu £ 18 (lunch) – Carte £ 28/37

◆ Busy hotel in a great spot, with pleasant drinks terrace and chic spa. Contemporary styling and plush bedrooms; choose between 'Inland' or 'Harbour'; the latter boasting either a balcony or terrace. Restaurant offers classically based cuisine.

Captain's Club

Wick Ferry, Wick Ln ✉ BH23 1HU – ℰ (01202) 475 111
– www.captainsclubhotel.com
17 rm – †£ 169 ††£ 199, ⟂ £ 16 – 12 suites
Rest *Tides* – see restaurant listing

◆ Eye-catching hotel displaying striking art deco and nautical influences. Floor to ceiling windows throughout; attractive river views. Sleek, unfussy bedrooms and suites. Stylish spa.

Kings

18 Castle St ✉ BH23 1DT – ℰ (01202) 588 933
– www.thekings-christchurch.co.uk
20 rm (dinner included) ⟂ – †£ 105/155 ††£ 115/165
Rest *Jacks* – Menu £ 16 (lunch) – Carte £ 21/35

◆ Lovingly restored late 17C former coaching inn, in the heart of the town, overlooking the priory, ruins and bowling green. Pretty, boutique style and well-appointed, contemporary bedrooms. Appealing ground floor bar and brasserie.

Druid House without rest

26 Sopers Ln ✉ BH23 1JE – ℰ (01202) 485 615 – www.druid-house.co.uk
9 rm ⟂ – †£ 40/80 ††£ 70/110

◆ Bright, fresh inner in contrast to its exterior. Modern, slightly kitsch breakfast room; light, airy conservatory sitting room and smart bar. Spacious bedrooms, two with balconies.

Jetty – at Christchurch Harbour Hotel

95 Mudeford, East : 2 mi ✉ BH23 3NT – ℰ (01202) 483 434
– www.christchurch-harbour-hotel.co.uk
Rest – Menu £ 22 (lunch) – Carte £ 28/53

◆ Contemporary, eco-friendly restaurant in a fantastic waterside setting. Local, seasonal produce includes crabs from just over the bay. Tasty specials are cooked on the josper charcoal grill.

CHRISTCHURCH

Tides – at Captain's Club Hotel
Wick Ferry, Wick Ln ⊠ BH23 1HU – ℰ (01202) 475 111 – www.captainsclubhotel.com
Rest – Menu £ 19/26 – Carte £ 22/44
• Stylish restaurant with water feature wall, oversized windows and river views. Modern, well judged cooking offers a wide choice, good combinations and some unusual formats.

Splinters
12 Church St ⊠ BH23 1BW – ℰ (01202) 483 454 – www.splinters.uk.com – Closed 1-10 January, Sunday and Monday
Rest – Menu £ 17/27 – Carte £ 27/39
• Family-run restaurant in cobbled street with bar, lounge and several cosy, characterful rooms; one with intimate booths. Unfussy, classical cooking uses good ingredients. Interesting wine list.

CHURCH ENSTONE – Oxfordshire – ⊠ Chipping Norton   10 B1

▶ London 72 mi – Banbury 13 mi – Oxford 38 mi

Crown Inn
Mill Ln ⊠ OX7 4NN – ℰ (01608) 677 262 – Closed 25-26 December, 1 January and Sunday dinner
Rest – Carte £ 19/29
• 17C inn set among pretty stone houses in a picturesque village. Meat, fruit and veg come from local farms and seafood is a speciality. Lunch offers pub favourites; tasty puddings are homemade.

CHURCH STRETTON – Shropshire – 502 L26 – pop. 3 841   18 B2
▌ Great Britain

▶ London 166 mi – Birmingham 46 mi – Hereford 39 mi – Shrewsbury 14 mi

🏌 Trevor Hill, ℰ (01694) 72 22 81

◉ Wenlock Edge★, E : by B 4371

Studio
⊠ SY6 6BY – ℰ (01694) 722 672 – www.thestudiorestaurant.net – Closed 3 weeks January, 1 week spring, 1 week autumn, Christmas-New Year and Sunday-Tuesday
Rest – (dinner only) Menu £ 29
• Personally run former art studio; walls enhanced by local artwork. Pleasant rear terrace for sunny lunches. Tried-and-tested dishes: much care taken over local produce.

CIRENCESTER – Gloucestershire – 503 O28 – pop. 15 861   4 D1
▌ Great Britain

▶ London 97 mi – Bristol 37 mi – Gloucester 19 mi – Oxford 37 mi

🛈 Corinium Museum Park Street ℰ (01285) 65 41 80, www.cirencester.gov.uk

🏌 Bagendon Cheltenham Rd, ℰ (01285) 65 24 65

◉ Town★ – Church of St John the Baptist★ – Corinium Museum★ (Mosaic pavements★) **AC**

◉ Fairford : Church of St Mary★ (stained glass windows★★) E : 7 mi by A 417

No 12 without rest
12 Park St ⊠ GL7 2BW – ℰ (01285) 640 232 – www.no12cirencester.co.uk
4 rm ⊇ – †£ 70 ††£ 95/110
• 16C property with Georgian façade, in the centre of a historic Roman town. Delightful rear walled garden. Excellent organic breakfast. Stylish rooms charmingly blend old and new.

Old Brewhouse without rest
7 London Rd ⊠ GL7 2PU – ℰ (01285) 656 099 – www.theoldbrewhouse.com
10 rm ⊇ – †£ 56 ††£ 68
• 17C former brewhouse in busy central spot, with characterful cluttered interior. Cottage-style bedrooms – most with wrought iron beds – or more modern rooms in the extension, set around a small courtyard. Two stone-faced breakfast rooms.

CIRENCESTER

Made by Bob
Unit 6, The Corn Hall, 26 Market Pl – GL7 2NY – ℰ (01285) 641 818
– www.foodmadebybob.com – Closed 25-26 December, 1 January and Sunday
Rest – (lunch only and dinner Thursday-Friday) Carte £ 27/37

• Large deli crammed with produce and an informal eatery boasting an open kitchen. Everything is homemade or locally sourced, from tasty breakfasts and light lunches to more structured dinners.

at Barnsley Northeast : 4 mi by A 429 on B 4425 – ⊠ Cirencester

Barnsley House
⊠ GL7 5EE – ℰ (01285) 740 000 – www.barnsleyhouse.com
11 rm – †£ 247 ††£ 265/495 – 7 suites
Rest – Menu £ 24 (lunch) – Carte £ 29/47

• Impressive 17C Cotswold manor house. Contemporary interior, with hi-tech bedrooms; largest and most modern in annexed courtyard. Well-kept gardens, hydrotherapy pool, cinema. Dining room has pleasant outlook. Modern, interesting menus.

Village Pub with rm
⊠ GL7 5EF – ℰ (01285) 740 421 – www.thevillagepub.co.uk
6 rm – †£ 95/150 ††£ 95/150   **Rest** – Carte £ 24/31

• Stylish pub with open fires and cosy feel. Appealing, daily changing menu of modern British dishes, with irresistible nibbles, locally sourced meats, charcuterie from Highgrove and comforting desserts. Individually decorated bedrooms; Six has a four-poster.

at Sapperton West : 5 mi by A 419 – ⊠ Cirencester

Bell
⊠ GL7 6LE – ℰ (01285) 760 298 – www.foodatthebell.co.uk – Closed 25 December and Sunday dinner November-March
Rest – Carte £ 24/35

• Charming pub in a pretty village. Wide-ranging, daily changing menu and seafood specials take on a refined yet rustic style, relying on local and regional produce. Interesting wine list.

CLANFIELD – Oxfordshire – 503 P28 – pop. 1 709   10 A2
London 75 mi – Oxford 24 mi – Swindon 16 mi

Cotswold Plough
Bourton Rd, (on A 4095) ⊠ OX18 2RB – ℰ (01367) 810 222
– www.cotswoldploughhotel.com – Closed 24-28 December
11 rm – †£ 89 ††£ 175
Rest Restaurant – see restaurant listing

• Charming hotel with delightful stone façade, located in the heart of a pretty village. Serene lounge with period fireplace. Comfortable, characterful bedrooms with a modern touch.

Restaurant – at Cotswold Plough Hotel
Bourton Rd, (on A 4095) ⊠ OX18 2RB – ℰ (01367) 810 222
– www.cotswoldploughhotel.com – Closed 24-28 December
Rest – Menu £ 13 (lunch) – Carte £ 22/31

• Accomplished modern cooking; strong on fish and game. Dining over several rooms at polished tables; pre and post-prandial drinks by the fire. Friendly, informal service.

CLAVERING – Essex – 504 U28 – pop. 1 663 – ⊠ Saffron Walden   12 B2
London 44 mi – Cambridge 25 mi – Colchester 44 mi – Luton 29 mi

Cricketers with rm
⊠ CB11 4QT – ℰ (01799) 550 442 – www.thecricketers.co.uk – Closed 25-26 December
14 rm – †£ 68 ††£ 95/115   **Rest** – Carte £ 24/34

• Attractive whitewashed pub exuding old-world charm. Straightforward cooking is precise and flavoursome. Local produce is key – all veg comes from their son Jamie Oliver's garden. Simple modern bedrooms in courtyard, more traditional rooms in the pavilion.

CLEARWELL – Gloucestershire
4 C1

▶ London 138 mi – Birmingham 85 mi – Bristol 31 mi – Cardiff 46 mi

Tudor Farmhouse
High St ✉ GL16 8JS – ℰ (01594) 833 046 – www.tudorfarmhousehotel.co.uk
– Closed 24-27 December
20 rm – †£ 85/95 ††£ 100/175
Rest – Menu £ 34 (dinner) – Carte lunch £ 18/32
♦ Converted farm buildings in the heart of the Forest of Dean. Character bedrooms in original farmhouse feature beams, uneven floors and antique furniture. More modern bedrooms in two outbuildings. Restaurant offers classic, French-influenced dishes with a twist.

CLEEVE HILL – Gloucestershire – **503** N28 – see Cheltenham

CLENT – Worcestershire – **504** N26 ▮ Great Britain
19 C2

▶ London 127 mi – Birmingham 12 mi – Hagley 2 mi

◉ Black Country Museum★, N : 7 mi by A 491 and A 4036 – Birmingham★ - Museum and Art Gallery★★, Aston Hall★★, NE : 10 mi by A 491 and A 456

Bell & Cross
Holy Cross, West : 0.5 mi off A 491 (northbound carriageway) (Bromsgrove rd)
✉ DY9 9QL – ℰ (01562) 730 319 – www.bellandcrossclent.co.uk – Closed 25 December and dinner 26, 31 December, 1 January and Sunday
Rest – Menu £ 17 (weekdays) – Carte £ 21/31
♦ Charming pub down a maze of lanes, with colourful window boxes and country views. Light bites and pub classics at lunch; more ambitious dishes at dinner. Influences range from Asia to the Med.

CLEY-NEXT-THE-SEA – Norfolk – **504** X25 – see Blakeney

CLIFTON – Cumbria – **502** L20 – see Penrith

CLIPSHAM – Rutland
17 C2

▶ London 101 mi – Leicester 35 mi – Coventry 72 mi – Nottingham 38 mi

The Olive Branch & Beech House (Sean Hope) with rm
Main St ✉ LE15 7SH – ℰ (01780) 410 355
– www.theolivebranchpub.com
6 rm – †£ 98/118 ††£ 175/205
Rest – *(booking essential)* Menu £ 21/28 – Carte £ 25/41
Spec. Warm salad of honey and mustard chicken, olives and lemon. Whole baked sea bass, chickpea and chorizo caponata. Sticky toffee pudding, vanilla ice cream.
♦ Characterful, rustic pub with charming garden, which really captures the heart of the local community. Well-prepared, classically based dishes are flavoursome and robust, and display plenty of respect for fresh, local ingredients. Stylish bedrooms include a host of extras and the homemade breakfasts are a delight.

CLITHEROE – Lancashire – **502** M22 – pop. 14 697
20 B2

▶ London 64 mi – Blackpool 35 mi – Manchester 31 mi
🛈 Church Walk ℰ (01200) 42 55 66, www.visitlancashire.com
🚉 Whalley Rd, ℰ (01200) 42 26 18

Heathcotes Grill & Bar
Ethos House, York St. ✉ BB7 2DL – ℰ (01200) 452 440
– www.heathcotesgrillandbar.co.uk – Closed Sunday and Monday
Rest – Menu £ 14 (lunch and early dinner) – Carte approx. £ 25
♦ Stylish split-level restaurant with contemporary lighting, open kitchen and smart horseshoe bar. Good value menus offer classics with a modern touch, and local meats/fish from the wood grill.

CLITHEROE

at Grindleton Northeast : 3 mi by A 671

Duke of York Inn
Brow Top ⊠ BB7 4QR – ℰ (01200) 441 266 – www.dukeofyorkgrindleton.com
– Closed 25 December, Monday except bank holidays and Tuesday following bank holidays
Rest – Menu £ 14 – Carte £ 24/39
• Ivy-clad pub in the heart of the Trough of Bowland, with views to Pendle Hill. Rustic bar and light, contemporary dining room. Good choice on seasonal menu, with plenty of regional dishes.

at Wiswell South : 3.75 mi by A 671

Freemasons
8 Vicarage Fold ⊠ BB7 9DF – ℰ (01254) 822 218
– www.freemasonswiswell.co.uk – Closed Monday except bank holidays
Rest – Menu £ 17 (weekdays) – Carte £ 28/46
• Delightful pub, hidden away on a narrow lane. Flag floors, low beams and open fires downstairs; elegant, antique-furnished dining rooms upstairs. Interesting menu features modern versions of traditional pub dishes. Skilful cooking, with clear flavours. Charming service.

at Bashall Eaves Northwest : 3 mi by B6243

Red Pump Inn with rm
Clitheroe Rd ⊠ BB7 3DA – ℰ (01254) 826 227 – www.theredpumpinn.co.uk
– Closed 2 weeks January and Monday except bank holidays
3 rm ⊠ – †£ 75/95 ††£ 95/115
Rest – Menu £ 15 (weekdays) – Carte £ 18/28
• One of the oldest pubs in the Ribble Valley, with traditional restaurant, rustic bar and charming fire-lit snug. Local produce features on seasonal menus, with game a speciality. Spacious bedrooms boast good facilities and views of Pendle Hill or Longridge Fell.

CLOVELLY – Devon – **503** G31 – pop. 439 – ⊠ Bideford   **1** B1
▶ London 241 mi – Barnstaple 18 mi – Exeter 52 mi – Penzance 92 mi
◉ Village ★★
☒ SW : Tamar River ★★. Hartland : Hartland Church ★ - Hartland Quay ★ (viewpoint ★★) – Hartland Point ≼ ★★★, W : 6.5 mi by B 3237 and B 3248 – Morwenstow (Church ★, cliffs ★★), SW : 11.5 mi by A 39

Red Lion
The Quay ⊠ EX39 5TF – ℰ (01237) 431 237 – www.clovelly.co.uk
11 rm (dinner included) ⊠ – †£ 112/115 ††£ 188/198
Rest – (dinner only) Menu £ 30
• Cosy little hotel/inn on the quayside; a superb location. All rooms enjoy sea and harbour views and are dressed in soft, understated colours, providing a smart resting place. Simple dining room looks out to harbour.

CLUN – Shropshire – **503** K26   **18** A2
▶ London 173 mi – Church Stretton 16 mi – Ludlow 16 mi

Birches Mill without rest
Northwest : 3 mi by A 488, Bicton rd, Mainstone rd and Burlow rd ⊠ SY7 8NL
– ℰ (01588) 640 409 – www.birchesmill.co.uk – April-October
3 rm ⊠ – †£ 72/82 ††£ 82/92
• High quality comforts in remote former corn mill: interior has characterful 17C/18C structures. Flagged lounge with lovely inglenook. Simple but tastefully decorated rooms.

COCKERMOUTH – Cumbria – **501** J20 – pop. 7 446   **21** A2
▶ London 306 mi – Carlisle 25 mi – Keswick 13 mi
ℹ Market St ℰ (01900) 82 26 34, www.cockermouth.org.uk
◧ Embleton, ℰ (017687) 7 62 23

COCKERMOUTH

at Lorton Southeast : 4.25 mi by B 5292 – ✉ Cockermouth

Winder Hall Country House
on B 5289 ✉ CA13 9UP – ✆ (01900) 85 107 – www.winderhall.co.uk
7 rm – †£ 170/185 ††£ 170/185
Rest – (booking essential for non-residents) Menu £ 25/35 s
♦ Part-Jacobean manor house with mullioned windows and tranquil garden. Comfortable lounge and high quality bedrooms retain rich history of house and include two four-posters. Oak panelled dining room overlooks garden. Local produce well-used in homemade dishes. Relaxed, friendly service.

New House Farm
South : 1.25 mi on B 5289 ✉ CA13 9UU – ✆ (01900) 85 404
– www.newhouse-farm.com
5 rm – †£ 50/90 ††£ 99/160 **Rest** – Menu £ 30
♦ Very well appointed, richly decorated guesthouse with hot tub in garden. Sumptuous bedrooms; one with double jacuzzi, two with four-posters. Fine furnishings and roll-top baths. Aga-cooked breakfasts and home-cooked evening meals. Tea rooms just next door.

Old Vicarage
Church Ln, North : 0.5 mi by B 5289 on Lorton Church rd ✉ CA13 9UN
– ✆ (01900) 85 656 – www.oldvicarage.co.uk – Restricted opening in winter
8 rm – †£ 80/135 ††£ 135 **Rest** – Menu £ 32
♦ Well-kept Victorian house in beautiful countryside spot. Comfortable lounge and hospitable owners. Sympathetically modernised bedrooms; four-postered Room 1 is the best. Dining room offers lovely fell views and home-cooked, local produce.

COCKLEFORD – Gloucestershire – ✉ Cheltenham   4 C1
▶ London 95 mi – Bristol 48 mi – Cheltenham 7 mi

The Green Dragon Inn with rm
✉ GL53 9NW – ✆ (01242) 870 271 – www.green-dragon-inn.co.uk – Closed dinner 25-26 December and 1 January
9 rm – †£ 70 ††£ 95 **Rest** – (booking essential) Carte £ 26/32
♦ Characterful stone pub with huge open fires and carved mice hidden in the woodwork – the hallmark of designer Robert 'Mouseman' Thompson. Hearty lunches; unusual starters; generous, meaty mains. Simple, modern bedrooms; one boasts a super king-sized bed.

COGGESHALL – Essex – 504 W28 – pop. 3 919 – ✉ Colchester   13 C2
▶ London 49 mi – Braintree 6 mi – Chelmsford 16 mi – Colchester 9 mi

Baumanns Brasserie
4-6 Stoneham St ✉ CO6 1TT – ✆ (01376) 561 453
– www.baumannsbrasserie.co.uk – Closed first 2 weeks January, Monday and Tuesday
Rest – Menu £ 15/24 – Carte £ 28/36
♦ Characterful 16C building, its walls packed with pictures and prints. Tasty cooking, made using local produce, brings out classic flavour combinations. Speedy service.

at Pattiswick Northwest : 3 mi by A 120 (Braintree Rd) – ✉ Coggeshall

Compasses at Pattiswick
Compasses Rd ✉ CM77 8BG – ✆ (01376) 561 322
– www.thegreatpubcompany.co.uk
Rest – Carte £ 23/30
♦ Smart, rural pub with cheery service. Cooking is simple and honest, with plenty of effort put into sourcing local ingredients. Pheasant is from local shoots and venison from the woods behind.

COLERNE – Wiltshire – 503 M29 – see Bath (Bath & North East Somerset)

COLN ST ALDWYNS – Gloucestershire – 503 O28 – pop. 260   4 D1
– ✉ Cirencester
▶ London 101 mi – Bristol 53 mi – Gloucester 20 mi – Oxford 28 mi

COLN ST ALDWYNS

New Inn at Coln
✉ GL7 5AN – ✆ (01285) 750 651 – www.new-inn.co.uk
14 rm ⊇ – †£ 130/150 ††£ 170
Rest – *(bar lunch) (booking essential for non-residents)* Carte £ 24/35
♦ Charming 16C foliage-clad coaching inn, in a delightful little village. Characterful guest areas and bold modern bedrooms – some with exposed beams, stone walls or brass beds; those in the extension are quieter, with country views. Extensive list of bar meals or more formal menu in contemporary restaurant.

COLSTON BASSETT – Nottinghamshire – 502 R25 – pop. 239   16 B2
– ✉ Nottingham
▶ London 129 mi – Leicester 23 mi – Lincoln 40 mi – Nottingham 15 mi

The Martins Arms
School Ln ✉ NG12 3FD – ✆ (01949) 81 361 – www.themartinsarms.co.uk
– Closed dinner 25 December and Sunday dinner
Rest – Carte £ 27/33
♦ Creeper-clad pub in charming village, with cosy, fire-lit bar and period furnished dining rooms. Menu has strong masculine base, with the occasional Italian influence or global flavour.

COLTISHALL – Norfolk – 504 Y25 – pop. 2 161 – ✉ Norwich   15 D1
▪ Great Britain
▶ London 133 mi – Norwich 8 mi
◉ Norfolk Broads★

Norfolk Mead ⚜
✉ NR12 7DN – ✆ (01603) 737 531 – www.norfolkmead.co.uk – Closed 25-26 December
13 rm ⊇ – †£ 75 ††£ 150
Rest – *(closed Saturday lunch, Sunday dinner and Monday)* Menu £ 20 (lunch)
– Carte £ 25/35
♦ Restful 18C manor with an otter lake and gardens leading down to the River Bure. Bedrooms are individually colour-themed. Room 7 boasts a jacuzzi and lovely views. Candlelit restaurant looks out over the grounds.

COLTON – North Yorkshire – see Tadcaster

COLWALL – Herefordshire – see Great Malvern

COLYFORD – Devon – 503 K31 – ✉ Colyton ▪ Great Britain   2 D2
▶ London 168 mi – Exeter 21 mi – Taunton 30 mi – Torquay 46 mi
◉ Colyton★ (Church★), N : 1 mi on B 3161 – Axmouth (≤★), S : 1 mi by A 3052 and B 3172

Swallows Eaves
Swan Hill Rd ✉ EX24 6QJ – ✆ (01297) 553 184 – www.swallowseaves.co.uk
8 rm ⊇ – †£ 48/90 ††£ 90/110
Rest *Reeds* – *(closed Sunday and Monday lunch)* Menu £ 28 (dinner)
– Carte lunch £ 18/26
♦ Unusual grey shale-coated 1920s house, with views from some rooms over the Axe Valley; listen out for birdsong on the marshes. Fully refurbished guest areas – bedrooms and bathrooms to follow. Menus feature locally sourced meats, fish and vegetables.

COMBE HAY – Bath and North East Somerset – see Bath

CONEYTHORPE – North Yorkshire – see Knaresborough

CONGLETON – Cheshire East – 502 N24 – pop. 25 400 ▪ Great Britain   20 B3
▶ London 183 mi – Liverpool 50 mi – Manchester 25 mi – Sheffield 46 mi
🛈 High St ✆ (01260) 27 10 95, www.cheshirepeakdistrict.com
◉ Biddulph Rd, ✆ (01260) 27 35 40
◉ Little Moreton Hall★★ **AC**, SW : 3 mi by A 34

CONGLETON

Pecks
Newcastle Rd, Moreton, South : 2.75 mi on A 34 ✉ CW12 4SB – ✆ (01260) 275 161 – www.pecksrest.co.uk – Closed 25-30 December, Sunday dinner and Monday
Rest – Menu £ 21 (lunch) – Carte £ 24/44
♦ Airy, modish restaurant with unique style. À la carte lunch; monthly changing 5/7 course set dinner at 8pm sharp. Traditional homemade dishes use good produce and arrive in generous portions.

L'Endroit
70-72 Lawton St ✉ CW12 1RS – ✆ (01260) 299 548 – www.lendroit.co.uk – Closed 2 weeks February-March, 1 week June, 1 week September, Sunday, Monday and lunch Saturday
Rest – French – Menu £ 12 (lunch) – Carte £ 22/29
♦ Welcoming restaurant with warm décor, upmarket bistro-style and small patio. Seasonally changing à la carte displays tasty, well-done dishes with strong French undertones. Good value lunch.

CONSTABLE BURTON – North Yorkshire – **502** O21 – see Leyburn

CONSTANTINE BAY – Cornwall – **503** E32 – see Padstow

COOKHAM – Windsor and Maidenhead – **504** R29 – pop. 5 304   **11** C3
– ✉ Maidenhead ▮ Great Britain
▶ London 32 mi – High Wycombe 7 mi – Oxford 31 mi – Reading 16 mi
⛴ to Marlow, Maidenhead and Windsor (Salter Bros. Ltd) (summer only)
◉ Stanley Spencer Gallery★ **AC**

White Oak
Pound Ln ✉ SL6 9QE – ✆ (01628) 523 043 – www.thewhiteoak.co.uk – Closed dinner Sunday and bank holidays
Rest – Menu £ 19 (weekdays) – Carte £ 25/29
♦ Smart, contemporary pub with neutral hues and lovely terrace. Straightforward pub-style dishes feature quality meats and unfussy accompaniments, and include tasty sharing boards and assiettes.

COOKHAM DEAN – Windsor and Maidenhead ▮ Great Britain   **11** C3
▶ London 32 mi – High Wycombe 7 mi – Oxford 31 mi – Reading 16 mi
◉ Windsor Castle★★★, Eton★★ and Windsor★, S : 5 mi by B 4447, A 4 (westbound) and A 308

Sanctum on the Green
The Old Cricket Common ✉ SL6 9NZ – ✆ (01628) 482 638 – www.sanctumonthegreen.com
9 rm ⌑ – †£ 120 ††£ 160/220
Rest – (booking essential) Menu £ 20 – Carte £ 26/41
♦ Part-timbered, part red-brick property with large terraces and heated outdoor pool, hidden away in a quiet village. Contemporary furnishings contrast with old beams. Stylish, boutique bedrooms come in bold colours. Two lounges, smart dining room and conservatory; classic dishes arrive in a modern style.

CORBRIDGE – Northumberland – **501** N19 – pop. 2 800   **24** A2
▮ Great Britain
▶ London 300 mi – Hexham 3 mi – Newcastle upon Tyne 18 mi
🛈 Hill St ✆ (01434) 63 28 15, www.thisiscorbridge.co.uk
◉ Hadrian's Wall★★, N : 3 mi by A 68 – Corstopitum★ **AC**, NW : 0.5 m

CORBRIDGE

🍺 Duke of Wellington with rm
Newton, East : 3 mi by A 6350 and A 69 ✉ *NE43 7UL* – ℘ *(01661) 844 446*
– *www.thedukeofwellingtoninn.co.uk*
7 rm ⌑ – ♦£ 90/100 ♦♦£ 120/135
Rest – *(booking advisable)* Carte £ 22/32 **s**
- A single track leads to this remote inn, which is reported to be the county's oldest licensed premises, dating from the early 1600s. Rescued by a local, it's now a smart, modern pub offering good food – try the local lamb or roe deer for dinner. Stylish, luxurious bedrooms.

at Great Whittington North : 5.5 mi by A 68 off B 6318 – ✉ Corbridge

🍺 Queens Head Inn
✉ *NE19 2HP* – ℘ *(01434) 672 267* – *www.the-queens-head-inn.co.uk* – *Closed Sunday dinner, Monday and Tuesday*
Rest – Carte £ 17/33
- Dating from 1615, with cosy bar and bric à brac filled dining room. Menu offers everything from stotties to duck spring rolls, with lamb and beef from farm next door. Friendly service.

CORFE CASTLE – Dorset – 503 N32 – pop. 1 335 – ✉ Wareham   4 C3
▶ London 129 mi – Bournemouth 18 mi – Weymouth 23 mi
◉ Castle★ (≤★★) **AC**

🏨 Mortons House
45 East St ✉ *BH20 5EE* – ℘ *(01929) 480 988* – *www.mortonshouse.co.uk*
19 rm ⌑ – ♦£ 80/100 ♦♦£ 150/160 – 2 suites
Rest – Menu £ 38 – Carte lunch £ 25/37
- Elizabethan manor built in the shape of an "E" in the Queen's honour. Wood-panelled drawing room. Range of different bedrooms, some themed: the Victoria room boasts an original Victorian bath. Traditional, formal dining room offers views out over the courtyard.

CORNHILL-ON-TWEED – Northumberland – 501 N17 – pop. 317   24 A1
▌Scotland
▶ London 345 mi – Edinburgh 49 mi – Newcastle upon Tyne 59 mi
◉ Ladykirk (Kirk o'Steil★), NE : 6 mi by A 698 and B 6470

🏨 Tillmouth Park
Northeast : 2.5 mi on A 698 ✉ *TD12 4UU* – ℘ *(01890) 882 255*
– *www.tillmouthpark.co.uk* – *Closed 2 January-29 March*
14 rm ⌑ – ♦£ 79/205 ♦♦£ 225
Rest *Library* – *(dinner only and Sunday lunch)* Carte £ 20/44
- Traditional 19C country house in 15 acres of grounds; set in prime shooting/-fishing country. Welcoming interior with characterful stained glass and grand staircases. Spacious bedrooms boast modern bathrooms. Wood-panelled restaurant serves à la carte dinners and a set lunch on Sunday.

🏠 Coach House
Crookham, East : 4 mi on A 697 ✉ *TD12 4TD* – ℘ *(01890) 820 293*
– *www.coachhousecrookham.com* – *February-November*
11 rm ⌑ – ♦£ 50/70 ♦♦£ 88/110
Rest – *(dinner only)* *(booking essential for non-residents)* Menu £ 24
- Keenly run, small hotel set around a courtyard, converted from a collection of old farm buildings, including a 1680s dower house. Lounge with honesty bar in stable block; where the bedrooms are larger and more modern. Cosy breakfast/-dining room in original house.

CORSE LAWN – Worcestershire – see Tewkesbury (Glos.)

CORTON DENHAM – Somerset – 504 M31 – pop. 210 – ✉ Sherborne 4 C3
▶ London 123 mi – Bristol 36 mi – Cardiff 110 mi – Southampton 84 mi

Queens Arms with rm
✉ DT9 4LR – ✆ (01963) 220 317 – www.thequeensarms.com
5 rm – †£ 75/95 ††£ 95/120 **Rest** – (booking advisable) Carte £ 22/28
♦ Charming 18C stone pub run by an enthusiastic owner, who takes care not to out-price the locals. Lunch focuses on one or two hearty courses, while the evening menu offers a more formal three course selection. Bedrooms are charming, well-appointed and good value.

COTEBROOK – Cheshire West and Chester – see Tarporley

COVENTRY – West Midlands – 503 P26 – pop. 267 755 ▮ Great Britain 19 D2
▶ London 100 mi – Birmingham 18 mi – Bristol 96 mi – Leicester 24 mi
🛈 Priory Street ✆ (024) 7622 72 64, www.visitcoventry.co.uk
🏨 Windmill Village Allesley Birmingham Rd, ✆ (024) 7640 40 41
Sphinx Sphinx Drive, ✆ (024) 7645 13 61
◉ City★ – Cathedral★★★ **AC** – Old Cathedral★ – Museum of British Road Transport★ **AC**

at Shilton Northeast : 6.75 mi by A 4600 – on B 4065 – ✉ Coventry

Barnacle Hall without rest
Shilton Ln., West : 1 mi by B 4029 following signs for garden centre ✉ CV7 9LH
– ✆ (024) 7661 2629 – www.barnaclehall.co.uk – Closed 24 December-2 January
3 rm ⊡ – †£ 35/45 ††£ 65/75
♦ Interesting part-16C farmhouse in rural location. Westerly facing 18C stone façade; remainder 16/17C. Beamed rooms have countryside outlook and farmhouse style furnishings.

at Balsall Common West : 6.75 mi by B 4101 – ✉ Coventry

White Horse
Kenilworth Rd ✉ CV7 7DT – ✆ (01676) 533 207 – www.thewhitehorseatbc.co.uk
Rest – Carte £ 22/30
♦ Striking black and white timbered pub with decked terrace, spacious modern interior and paved rear dining area. Easy-to-read menus display British pub classics and some Mediterranean influences.

COVERACK – Cornwall – 503 E33 1 A3
▶ London 300 mi – Penzance 25 mi – Truro 27 mi

Bay
North Corner ✉ TR12 6TF – ✆ (01326) 280 464 – www.thebayhotel.co.uk
– Closed 1-22 December and 3 January-29 February
13 rm (dinner included) ⊡ – †£ 88/150 ††£ 210/240 – 2 suites
Rest – (bar lunch) Menu £ 30
♦ Imposing Victorian country house located in a pretty fishing village and boasting views over the bay. Homely lounge and bar. Spotless, modern bedrooms with a slight New England style. Dining room and conservatory offer classical daily menu and fish specials.

COWLEY – Gloucestershire – 504 N28 4 C1
▶ London 105 mi – Swindon 28 mi – Gloucester 14 mi – Cheltenham 6 mi

Cowley Manor ⟫
✉ GL53 9NL – ✆ (01242) 870 900 – www.cowleymanor.com
22 rm ⊡ – †£ 150/250 ††£ 150/595 – 8 suites **Rest** – Carte £ 25/38
♦ Impressive Regency house. 55 acres; beautiful gardens. Retro interior, bold colours, obscure fittings, excellent mod cons. Stylish bedrooms, some with balconies/lake views, most with huge bathrooms. Spa, 2 pools and sun terrace. Semi-formal restaurant with paved terrace serves classic British dishes.

COWSHILL – Durham – 502 N19 24 A3
▶ London 295 mi – Newcastle upon Tyne 42 mi – Stanhope 10 mi
– Wolsingham 16 mi

COWSHILL

Low Cornriggs Farm
Weardale, Northwest : 0.75 mi on A 689 ✉ *DL13 1AQ –* ✆ *(01388) 537 600*
– www.cornriggsfarm.co.uk – Closed 24-26 December, 31 December and 1 January
3 rm – †£ 44 ††£ 64 **Rest** – Menu £ 18 **s**
♦ Stone-built 300 year-old farmhouse boasting some superb views over Teesdale. Conservatory dining room for summer use. Cosy, pine-furnished bedrooms. Beamed dining room offers hearty, home-cooked, organic dishes.

CRACKINGTON HAVEN – Cornwall – 503 G31 – ✉ Bude 1 B2
▶ London 262 mi – Bude 11 mi – Plymouth 44 mi – Truro 42 mi
Poundstock★ (≼★★, church★, guildhouse★), NE : 5.5 mi by A 39 – Jacobstow (Church★), E : 3.5 m

Manor Farm without rest
Southeast : 1.25 mi by Boscastle rd taking left turn onto Church Park Rd after 1 mi then taking first right onto unmarked lane ✉ *EX23 0JW*
– ✆ *(01840) 230 304 – Closed 25 December*
3 rm – †£ 45 ††£ 80
♦ Appears in the Domesday Book and belonged to William the Conqueror's half brother. A lovely manor in beautifully manicured grounds. Affable owner and comfortable rooms.

CRANBROOK – Kent – 504 V30 – pop. 4 225 ▌Great Britain 8 B2
▶ London 53 mi – Hastings 19 mi – Maidstone 15 mi
🛈 Stone St ✆(01580) 71 25 38, www.cranbrook.org
Sissinghurst Castle★ **AC**, NE : 2.5 mi by A 229 and A 262

Cloth Hall Oast
Coursehorn Ln, East : 1 mi by Tenterden rd ✉ *TN17 3NR –* ✆ *(01580) 712 220*
– www.clothhalloast.co.uk – Closed Christmas
3 rm – †£ 55/70 ††£ 125 **Rest** – Menu £ 25
♦ Superbly restored oast house that was rebuilt in 2001. Antiques, family photos and fine artwork fill the drawing room. Bedrooms are well-equipped but retain some original character; one boasts a splendid four-poster bed. Communal breakfasts and dinners at an antique table, set below restored rafters in the main hall.

XX Apicius (Tim Johnson)
ಟಿ *23 Stone St* ✉ *TN17 3HE –* ✆ *(01580) 714 666 – www.restaurant-apicius.co.uk*
– Closed 2 weeks August, 2 weeks Christmas-New Year, Saturday lunch, Sunday dinner, Monday and Tuesday
Rest – Menu £ 30/36
Spec. Ham hock ballotine, spring pea velouté and foie gras mousse. Roast fillet of halibut, ceps and artichokes. Poached white peach, lavender infused savarin and vanilla ice cream.
♦ Named after Roman author of world's first cookbook. Cosy interior mixes original features with modern style. Passionate, well balanced, precise cooking uses local ingredients.

at Sissinghurst Northeast : 1.75 mi by B 2189 on A 262 – ✉ Cranbrook

X Rankins
The Street, on A 262 ✉ *TN17 2JH –* ✆ *(01580) 713 964*
– www.rankinsrestaurant.com – Closed Monday, Tuesday and bank holidays
Rest – *(dinner only and Sunday lunch) (booking essential)* Carte £ 26/35
♦ Well-run village restaurant, immaculately kept by knowledgeable, personable owners. Concise set menus display hearty, traditional dishes with the odd Mediterranean touch. Desserts a speciality.

CRAYKE – North Yorkshire – see Easingwold

CRICKLADE – Wiltshire – 503 O29 — 4 D1
▶ London 89 mi – Birmingham 86 mi – Bristol 54 mi – Cardiff 87 mi

Red Lion with rm
74 High St ⊠ SN6 6DD – ℰ (01793) 750 776 – Closed Sunday Dinner
5 rm ⌑ – †£75 ††£75   **Rest** – *(booking essential)* Carte £ 21/33
♦ Very charming 17C pub, just off the Thames path. 9 real ales and 30 speciality beers in the low-beamed bar; beer pairings for every dish in the airy dining room. Classical cooking uses extremely local produce. Comfortable bedrooms are located in the old stables.

CROCKERTON – Wiltshire – see Warminster

CROFT-ON-TEES – North Yorkshire – 502 P20 – see Darlington

CROPSTON – Leicestershire – 502 Q25 — 16 B2
▶ London 106 mi – Birmingham 49 mi – Sheffield 67 mi – Leicester 6 mi

Horseshoe Cottage Farm
Roecliffe Rd, Hallgates, Northwest : 1 mi on Woodhouse Eaves rd ⊠ LE7 7HQ – ℰ (0116) 235 00 38 – www.horseshoecottagefarm.com
3 rm ⌑ – †£63 ††£95   **Rest** – Menu £ 21
♦ Extended farmhouse in pleasant countryside location beside Bradgate Country Park. Comfortable lounge; homely touches in spacious, traditional bedrooms. Home-cooked food in communal dining room; local produce well used, including some from the vegetable garden.

CROSTHWAITE – Cumbria – 502 L21 – see Kendal

CRUDWELL – Wiltshire – 503 N29 – see Malmesbury

CUCKFIELD – West Sussex – 504 T30 – pop. 3 266 — 7 D2
▶ London 40 mi – Brighton 15 mi

Ockenden Manor
⊠ RH17 5LD – ℰ (01444) 416 111 – www.ockenden-manor.co.uk
25 rm ⌑ – †£124 ††£400 – **3 suites**
Rest – *(booking essential at lunch)* Menu £ 28/55
Spec. English asparagus, boudin blanc, chicken oysters and morels. Sea bass, wild leaf garlic gnocchi, tomato fondue and razor clam gratin. Strawberry millefeuille.
♦ Part-Elizabethan manor house dating back to the 16C, set in 9 acres of parkland and boasting pleasant South Downs views. Elegant open-fired sitting room, cosy wood-panelled bar and antique-furnished bedrooms. Contemporary orangery dining room opens onto the gardens and offers refined seasonal cooking with well-balanced flavours and good attention to detail.

Cuckoo
1 Broad St ⊠ RH17 5LJ – ℰ (01444) 414 184 – www.cuckoorestaurant.co.uk – Closed 1 week January, 1 week late August, Saturday lunch, Sunday dinner and Monday
Rest – Menu £ 19 (lunch) – Carte £ 27/31
♦ Charming 17C cottage in heart of pretty village, with log fire, fresh flowers, personable owner and informal ambience. Tasty, modern British cooking uses fresh, seasonal produce.

CUDDINGTON – Buckinghamshire – 503 M24 ◾ Great Britain — 11 C2
▶ London 48 mi – Aylesbury 6 mi – Oxford 17 mi
◉ Waddesdon Manor ★★ **AC**, NE : 6 mi via Cuddington Hill, Cannon's Hill, Waddesdon Hill and A 41

Crown
Aylesbury Rd ⊠ HP18 0BB – ℰ (01844) 292 222
– www.thecrowncuddington.co.uk – Closed Sunday dinner
Rest – Carte £ 20/30
♦ Attractive thatched pub with traditional styling, welcoming atmosphere and friendly team. Seasonal menus display hearty comfort food in the winter and lighter dishes in the summer.

CURY – Cornwall – **503** E33 – see Helston

CUTNALL GREEN – Worcestershire – **503** N27 – see Droitwich Spa

DARGATE – Kent – see Faversham

DARLEY – North Yorkshire – **502** O21   **22** B2

▶ London 217 mi – Harrogate 8 mi – Ripon 16 mi

Cold Cotes without rest
Cold Cotes Rd, Felliscliffe, South : 2 mi by Kettlesing rd, going straight over crossroads and on Harrogate rd ✉ *HG3 2LW* – ✆ *(01423) 770 937*
– www.coldcotes.com
6 rm ⏚ – †£ 50/60 ††£ 87/99

♦ Remotely set former farmhouse in colourful, well-tended gardens; the owners love gardening and run a small plant nursery. Smart bedrooms provide good comforts; those in the house are small suites, those in the barn conversion are open-plan.

DARLEY ABBEY – Derby – **502** P25 – see Derby

DARLINGTON – Darlington – **502** P20 – pop. 86 082   **22** B1

▶ London 251 mi – Leeds 61 mi – Middlesbrough 14 mi
– Newcastle upon Tyne 35 mi

✈ Teesside Airport : ✆ (08712) 242426, E : 6 mi by A 67

🛈 Horsemarket ✆ (01325) 38 86 66, www.visitdarlington.com

⛳ Blackwell Grange Briar Close, ✆ (01325) 46 44 58

⛳ Stressholme Snipe Lane, ✆ (01325) 46 10 02

at Croft-on-Tees South : 4.25 mi on A 167 – ✉ Darlington

Clow Beck House
Monk End Farm, West : 0.75 mi by A 167 off Barton rd ✉ *DL2 2SW* – ✆ *(01325) 721 075 – www.clowbeckhouse.co.uk – Closed 24 December-3 January*
13 rm ⏚ – †£ 85 ††£ 135
Rest – *(dinner only) (residents only)* Carte £ 28/39 **s**

♦ Collection of converted farm buildings not far from the River Tees. Welcoming owners and homely interior. Immaculately kept, tastefully furnished bedrooms come with iPod docks, bathrobes and chocolates. Home-cooked dinners with a puzzle supplied while you wait.

at Hurworth-on-Tees South : 5.5 mi by A 167

Rockliffe Hall
✉ DL2 2DU – ✆ (01325) 729 999 – www.rockliffehall.com
60 rm ⏚ – †£ 165/275 ††£ 165/440
Rest *Kenny Atkinson at The Orangery* – see restaurant listing
Rest *Waterhouse Bistro* – Menu £ 28 **s** – Carte £ 27/29 **s**
Rest *Clubhouse* – Menu £ 28 **s** – Carte £ 20/25 **s**

♦ Impressive red-brick property in 376 acres of grounds, boasting a championship golf course, state-of-the-art leisure facilities and spa. Grand guest areas and characterful bedrooms in original Victorian house; modern bedrooms in extensions. Bright, airy bistro offers light, modern dishes. The Clubhouse is aimed at golfers and ranges from sandwiches to Sunday lunch.

Kenny Atkinson at The Orangery – at Rockliffe Hall Hotel
✉ DL2 2DU – ✆ (01325) 729 999
– www.rockliffehall.com – Closed Sunday
Rest – *(dinner only)* Menu £ 48/70 **s**

♦ Restored Victorian orangery set within an impressive hotel, boasting a formal bar and spacious dining room with well-spaced tables and views over the golf course. Complex cooking displays modern techniques. Live piano music accompanies.

DARLINGTON

Bay Horse
45 The Green ✉ *DL2 2AA* – ✆ *(01325) 720 663*
– *www.thebayhorsehurworth.com* – *Closed Sunday dinner*
Rest – Menu £ 17 (lunch) – Carte £ 25/33
♦ Smart village pub with pleasant terrace and gardens. Wide-ranging menu offers largely hearty classics; presentation ranges from simple and rustic to more modern and intricate.

at Headlam Northwest : 8 mi by A 67 – ✉ Gainford

Headlam Hall
✉ *DL2 3HA* – ✆ *(01325) 730 238* – *www.headlamhall.co.uk*
– *Closed 24-26 December*
36 rm – †£ 95 ††£ 145 – 4 suites **Rest** – Carte £ 26/40
♦ Part-Georgian, part-Jacobean manor house in a delightful, secluded countryside setting, with charming walled gardens. Period interior furnishings and antiques. Good leisure facilities. Country house restaurant in four distinctively decorated rooms.

at Summerhouse Northwest : 7.5 mi on B 6279

Raby Hunt with rm
✉ *DL2 3UD* – ✆ *(01325) 374 237* – *www.rabyhuntrestaurant.co.uk* – *Closed 1 week spring, 1 week autumn, 25-26 December, 1 January, Sunday dinner and Monday-Wednesday lunch*
2 rm – †£ 70/110 ††£ 110
Rest – *(booking advisable)* Menu £ 18 (lunch) – Carte £ 31/44
♦ Pleasant inn located in a rural hamlet, now a family-run restaurant with elegant dining room, small bar and walls decorated with local art. Self-taught chef creates a weekly changing menu of complex, ambitious dishes. Comfy bedrooms have a cosy, homely feel.

DARTMOUTH – Devon – **503** J32 – pop. 6 008   **2** C3
▶ London 236 mi – Exeter 36 mi – Plymouth 35 mi
🛈 Mayor's Ave ✆(01803) 83 42 24, www.discoverdartmouth.com
◉ Town★★ (≤★) - Old Town - Butterwalk★ - Dartmouth Castle (≤★★★) **AC**
◉ Start Point (≤★), S : 13 mi (including 1 mi on foot)

Dart Marina
Sandquay ✉ *TQ6 9PH* – ✆ *(01803) 832 580* – *www.dartmarina.com*
49 rm ⌂ – †£ 119/170 ††£ 140/200
Rest *River Restaurant* – see restaurant listing
Rest *Wildfire* – Carte £ 31/42 **s**
♦ Modern, laid-back hotel converted from an old boat works and chandlery. Smart, contemporary bedrooms boast lovely outlooks over either river or marina; many also boast balconies. Small spa and leisure centre. Formal restaurant or more casual brasserie specialising in steaks, which opens out onto a terrace.

Royal Castle
11 The Quay ✉ *TQ6 9PS* – ✆ *(01803) 833 033* – *www.royalcastle.co.uk*
25 rm ⌂ – †£ 100/110 ††£ 190/210 **Rest** – Carte £ 25/34
♦ Modernised 15C coaching inn: once two buildings, now joined by a smart glass atrium. Boldly coloured bedrooms with good comforts – some have jacuzzi baths. Two bars: one for drinkers only, one serving all-day dishes. Restaurant offers modern takes on old classics.

Seahorse
5 South Embankment ✉ *TQ6 9BH* – ✆ *(01803) 835 147*
– *www.seahorserestaurant.co.uk* – *Closed Monday, Sunday dinner and Tuesday lunch*
Rest – Seafood – *(booking essential)* Menu £ 20 (lunch and early dinner)
– Carte £ 32/46
♦ Picturesque location overlooking estuary/harbour; some al fresco tables. Classic bistro dishes with strong seafood slant; cooked in charcoal oven. Twice daily menu; simplicity is key.

DARTMOUTH

XX Angelique with rm
2 South Embankment ⊠ TQ6 9BH – ℰ (01803) 839 425
– www.angeliquedartmouth.co.uk – Closed Sunday dinner, Tuesday lunch and Monday
7 rm – †£ 85/125 ††£ 95/125 **Rest** – Menu £ 29/56
♦ Split-level, wood-furnished restaurant with open kitchen and lovely estuary outlook; all tables share the view. Attractively presented dishes showcase local produce: choose from a set selection, concise à la carte or fish tasting menu. Large bedrooms, 5mins down the road, take on a modern, boutique style.

XX River Restaurant – at Dart Marina Hotel
Sandquay ⊠ TQ6 9PH – ℰ (01803) 832 580 – www.dartmarina.com
Rest – (dinner only and Sunday lunch) Menu £ 17/33
♦ Stylish, linen-clad restaurant overlooking the river; popular with those mooring their boats in the marina. Menu offers modern versions of old classics and showcases local, seasonal produce.

X Jan and Freddies Brasserie
10 Fairfax Pl ⊠ TQ6 9AD – ℰ (01803) 832 491
– www.janandfreddiesbrasserie.co.uk – Closed January and Sunday except before bank holidays
Rest – (booking advisable) Carte £ 18/35
♦ Bright, stylish brasserie in the town centre, with welcoming service and a personal touch. Menus are classically based, with dishes crafted from local, seasonal produce.

X Annabelles Kitchen
24 South Embankment ⊠ TQ6 9BB – ℰ (01803) 833 540
– www.annabelleskitchen.co.uk – Closed 2 weeks February, 1 week November, Sunday, Monday and lunch Tuesday
Rest – (booking essential) Carte £ 26/33
♦ Occupying a prime estuary facing spot is this laid-back little eatery, run by a husband and wife team. Their philosophy is based around sourcing local and seasonal ingredients and keeping the dishes simple.

If you are looking for particularly pleasant accommodation, book a hotel shown in red : ⭡, ... 🏨.

at Kingswear East : via lower ferry – ⊠ Dartmouth

🏠 Nonsuch House
Church Hill, from lower ferry take first right onto Church Hill before Steam Packet Inn ⊠ TQ6 0BX – ℰ (01803) 752 829 – www.nonsuch-house.co.uk
4 rm – †£ 100/125 ††£ 125/150
Rest – (closed Tuesday, Wednesday and Saturday) (dinner only) (residents only) Menu £ 38 **s**
♦ Charming Edwardian house run by friendly, hands-on owners; and boasting lovely views over the castle, town and sea. Bright Mediterranean style décor blends nicely with original features. Spacious, well-appointed bedrooms – one has a small balcony. Local, seasonal cooking in conservatory dining room.

at Strete Southwest : 4 mi on A 379 – ⊠ Dartmouth

🍴 Kings Arms
Dartmouth Rd ⊠ TQ6 0RW – ℰ (01803) 770 377
– www.kingsarms-dartmouth.co.uk – Closed Sunday dinner and Monday in winter
Rest – Carte £ 20/34
♦ Dour exterior hides gem of a pub serving wide-ranging menu with focus on seafood; locally caught, simply cooked and very tasty. Delightful rear garden with fantastic coastal views.

DATCHWORTH – Hertfordshire – 504 T28 — 12 B2

▶ London 31 mi – Luton 15 mi – Stevenage 6 mi

Coltsfoot Country Retreat
Coltsfoot Ln, Bulls Grn, South : 0.75 mi by Bramford Rd ✉ *SG3 6SB –* ℰ *(01438) 212 800 – www.coltsfoot.com*
15 rm – †£110 ††£135
Rest – *(closed Sunday) (dinner only) (booking essential)* Menu £33 – Carte £25/50

• Stylish hotel, once a working farm, in 40 rural acres. Lounge bar with log-burning stove. Comfortable, rustic bedrooms spread around the central courtyard: some boast terraces; No.15 was where the prize bull was once kept. Main barn houses restaurant. Concise modern menus employ good seasonal produce.

Tilbury
Watton Rd ✉ *SG3 6TB –* ℰ *(01438) 815 550 – www.thetilbury.co.uk – Closed Sunday dinner*
Rest – Menu £18 (lunch) – Carte £25/33

• Local, seasonal produce leads the way at Paul Bloxham's pub. Menus change regularly and feature a real mix of dishes, from classical steaks to adventurous stuffed lobster and scallop sea bass.

DAVENTRY – Northamptonshire – 504 Q27 – pop. 21 731 — 16 B3

▶ London 79 mi – Coventry 23 mi – Leicester 31 mi – Northampton 13 mi

🛈 Norton Rd, ℰ (01327) 70 28 29
🏌 Hellidon Lakes H. & C.C. Hellidon, ℰ (01327) 26 25 50
🏌 Staverton Park Staverton, ℰ (01327) 30 20 00

Fawsley Hall
Fawsley, South : 6.5 mi by A 45 off A 361 ✉ *NN11 3BA –* ℰ *(01327) 892 000 – www.fawsleyhall.com*
56 rm ⌂ – †£185 ††£355 – 2 suites
Rest *Equilibrium* **Rest** *Bess's Brasserie* – see restaurant listing

• Set in 2,000 peaceful acres, a luxurious Tudor manor house boasting Georgian and Victorian wings. Cavernous grand hall and exclusive leisure club/spa. Well-appointed bedrooms vary from wing to wing: most characterful are in the main house.

Equilibrium – at Fawsley Hall Hotel
Fawsley, South : 6.5 mi by A 45 off A 361 ✉ *NN11 3BA –* ℰ *(01327) 892 000 – www.fawsleyhall.com – Closed Sunday and Monday*
Rest – *(dinner only) (booking essential)* Carte £34/46

• Spread over two characterful rooms, an intimate hotel restaurant set within a grand Tudor manor house. European menu offers both traditional combinations and dishes with more innovative touches.

Bess's Brasserie – at Fawsley Hall Hotel
Fawsley, South : 6.5 mi by A 45 off A 361 ✉ *NN11 3BA –* ℰ *(01327) 892 000 – www.fawsleyhall.com*
Rest – Carte £21/35

• Situated in the heart of an impressive manor house, a smart yet informal hotel dining room boasting an impressive stone fireplace. Menu offers brasserie classics; some in a choice of dish size.

at Staverton Southwest : 2.75 mi by A 45 off A 425 – ✉ Daventry

Colledges House
Oakham Ln, off Glebe Ln ✉ *NN11 6JQ –* ℰ *(01327) 702 737 – www.colledgeshouse.co.uk*
4 rm ⌂ – †£68/70 ††£98/106 **Rest** – Menu £32

• Part 17C house in a quiet village. Full of charm with antiques, curios, portraits and an inglenook fireplace. Homely bedrooms are in the main house and an adjacent cottage. Evening meals served at elegant oak table.

DAYLESFORD – Gloucestershire – 503 O28 – See Stow-on-the-Wold

DEAL – Kent – **504** Y30 – pop. 29 248   9 D2
▶ London 78 mi – Canterbury 19 mi – Dover 8 mi – Margate 16 mi
ℹ 129 High St ℰ (01304) 36 95 76, www.deal.gov.uk
🏌 Walmer & Kingsdown Kingsdown The Leas, ℰ (01304) 37 32 56

🏠 Dunkerley's
19 Beach St ✉ *CT14 7AH* – ℰ *(01304) 375 016 – www.dunkerleys.co.uk*
16 rm – †£ 70/80 ††£ 100/150
Rest *Restaurant* – see restaurant listing
♦ The hotel faces the beach and the Channel. Bedrooms are comfortably furnished and the principal rooms have jacuzzis. Comfortable bar offers a lighter menu than the restaurant.

🏠 Number One *without rest*
1 Ranelagh Rd ✉ *CT14 7BG* – ℰ *(01304) 364 459*
– www.numberonebandb.co.uk
4 rm – †£ 80 ††£ 100
♦ Former boarding house close to the promenade, refurbished in a contemporary style. Understated bedrooms boast bold feature wallpaper, luxury bathrooms, fine bed linen and stimulating art.

✕✕ Restaurant – at Dunkerley's Hotel
19 Beach St ✉ *CT14 7AH* – ℰ *(01304) 375 016 – www.dunkerleys.co.uk*
– Closed Sunday dinner and Monday
Rest – Seafood – Menu £ 16/28
♦ With views of the Channel, the restaurant is best known for preparing locally caught seafood, although non-seafood options are also available. Wide ranging wine list.

at Worth Northwest : 5 mi by A 258

🏠 Solley Farm House *without rest*
The Street ✉ *CT14 0DG* – ℰ *(01304) 613 701 – www.solleyfarmhouse.co.uk*
3 rm – †£ 85/90 ††£ 120/130
♦ 300 year old house, overlooking the village pond and church. Full of character and charm, with a very welcoming owner. Organic breakfasts served on the terrace in summer.

DEDDINGTON – Oxfordshire – **503** Q28 – pop. 1 595   10 B1
▶ London 72 mi – Birmingham 46 mi – Coventry 33 mi – Oxford 18 mi

🏠 Old Post House *without rest*
New St, on A4260 ✉ *OX15 0SP* – ℰ *(01869) 338 978 – www.oldposthouse.co.uk*
3 rm – †£ 60 ††£ 85
♦ Charming 17C sandstone house with mullioned windows and beautiful walled garden. Comfy, open-fired lounge and spacious, classically styled bedrooms. Outdoor pool by prior arrangement. Tea and cake on arrival; tasty Aga-cooked breakfasts and homemade preserves.

DEDHAM – Essex – **504** W28 – pop. 1 847 – ✉ Colchester   13 D2
▌ Great Britain
▶ London 63 mi – Chelmsford 30 mi – Colchester 8 mi – Ipswich 12 mi
◎ Stour Valley★ – Flatford Mill★, E : 6 mi by B 1029, A 12 and B 1070

🏨 Maison Talbooth
Stratford Rd, West : 0.5 mi ✉ *CO7 6HN* – ℰ *(01206) 322 367*
– www.milsomhotels.com
12 rm – †£ 200 ††£ 405
Rest *Le Talbooth* – see restaurant listing
♦ Quiet, Victorian country house with intimate atmosphere, lawned gardens and views over river valley. Some rooms are smart and contemporary, others more traditional in style.

DEDHAM

Milsoms
Stratford Rd, West : 0.75 mi ✉ CO7 6HW – ℰ (01206) 322795
– www.milsomhotels.com
15 rm – †£117 ††£184, ⌑ £16
Rest – *(bookings not accepted)* Carte £21/41

• Modern hotel overlooking Constable's Dedham Vale with attractive garden and stylish lounge. Bright, airy and welcoming rooms feature unfussy décor and modern colours. Likeably modish, wood-floored bistro.

Le Talbooth
Gun Hill, West : 0.5 mi ✉ CO7 6HP – ℰ (01206) 323 150
– www.milsomhotels.com – Closed Sunday dinner October-June
Rest – Menu £29 (lunch) – Carte £39/57 ❀❀

• Part Tudor house in attractive riverside setting. Exposed beams and real fires contribute to the traditional atmosphere. Menus combine the classic and the more modern. Well chosen wine list.

Sun Inn with rm
High St ✉ CO7 6DF – ℰ (01206) 323 351 – www.thesuninndedham.com
– Closed 25-26 December
5 rm ⌑ – †£65/110 ††£75/160
Rest – Menu £15 (weekdays) – Carte £25/35

• Sunny-coloured pub in idyllic village location. Italian-themed à la carte features simple, tasty dishes. Bar board menu offers sandwiches, terrines and tarts. Contemporary bedrooms.

DENHAM – Buckinghamshire – 504 S29 – pop. 2 269 – Great Britain   11 D3

▶ London 20 mi – Buckingham 42 mi – Oxford 41 mi
◉ Windsor Castle ★★★, Eton ★★ and Windsor ★, S : 10 mi by A 412

Swan Inn
Village Rd ✉ UB9 5BH – ℰ (01895) 832 085 – www.swaninndenham.co.uk
– Closed 25-26 December
Rest – *(booking essential)* Carte £23/28

• Wisteria-clad, red-brick Georgian pub with pleasant terrace and gardens. Menus change with the seasons and offer plenty of interest; sides are appealing and pudding is a must.

DERBY – Derby – 502 P25 – pop. 247 530 – Great Britain   16 B2

▶ London 132 mi – Birmingham 40 mi – Coventry 49 mi – Leicester 29 mi
✈ Nottingham East Midlands Airport, Castle Donington : ℰ (0871) 919 9000, SE : 12 mi by A 6 X
🛈 Market Pl ℰ (01332) 25 58 02, www.visitderby.co.uk
▣ Sinfin Wilmore Rd, ℰ (01332) 76 63 23
▣ Mickleover Uttoxeter Rd, ℰ (01332) 51 60 11
▣ Kedleston Park Quardon Kedlston, ℰ (01332) 84 00 35
▣ Breadsall Priory H. & C.C. Morley Moor Rd, ℰ (01332) 83 61 06
▣ Allestree Park Allestree Allestree Hall, ℰ (01332) 55 06 16
◉ City ★ – Museum and Art Gallery ★ (Collection of Derby Porcelain ★) YZ **M1** – Royal Crown Derby Museum ★ **AC** Z **M2**
◉ Kedleston Hall ★★ **AC**, NW : 4.5 mi by Kedleston Rd X

Cathedral Quarter
16 St. Marys Gate ✉ DE1 3JR – ℰ (01332) 546 080 – www.finessecollection.com
38 rm ⌑ – †£60/120 ††£80/200   Y**x**
Rest *Opulence* – *(closed Sunday dinner and Monday)* Menu £16/20
– Carte £27/41

• Boutique-style hotel retaining original features like mosaic floors and marble pillars. Bedrooms vary in size but all are furnished in a contemporary style with pastel shades. First floor Opulence boasts wood panelling and a 10-seater chef's table. Modern menus.

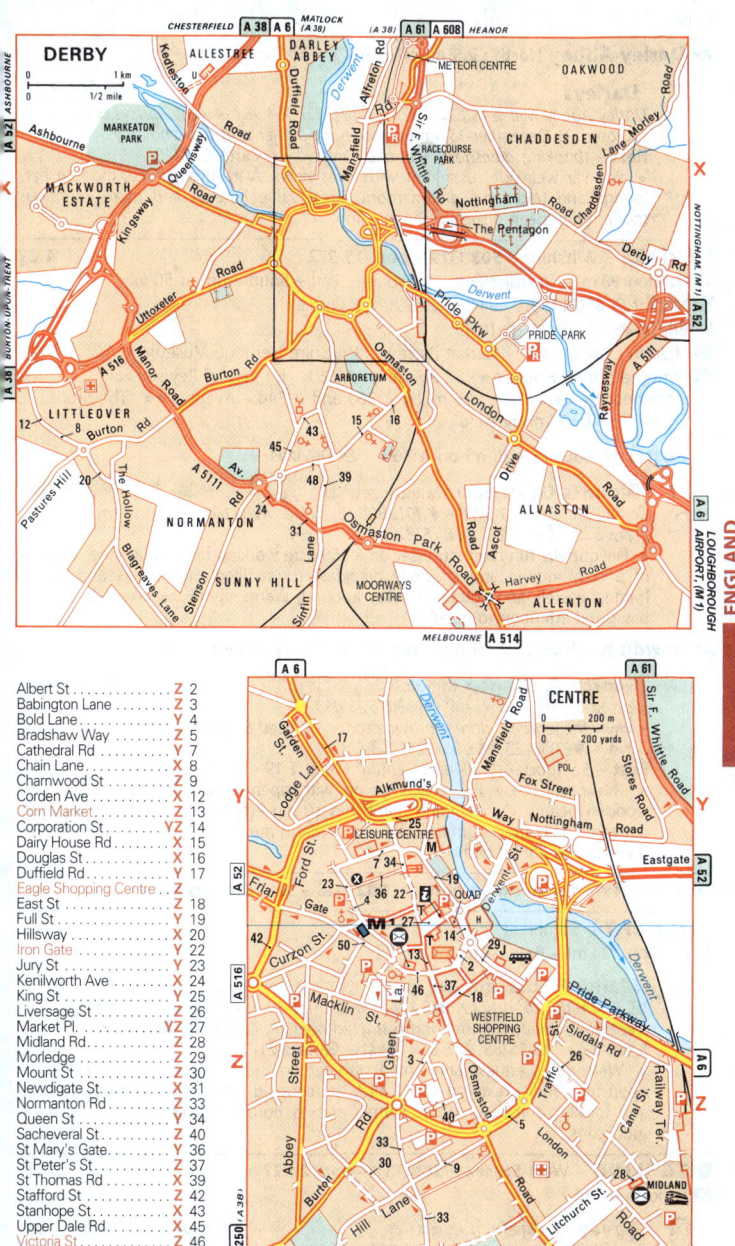

DERBY

Albert St	Z 2
Babington Lane	Z 3
Bold Lane	Y 4
Bradshaw Way	Z 5
Cathedral Rd	Y 7
Chain Lane	X 8
Charnwood St	Z 9
Corden Ave	X 12
Corn Market	Z 13
Corporation St	YZ 14
Dairy House Rd	X 15
Douglas St	Z 16
Duffield Rd	Y 17
Eagle Shopping Centre	Z
East St	Z 18
Full St	Y 19
Hillsway	X 20
Iron Gate	Y 22
Jury St	Y 23
Kenilworth Ave	X 24
King St	Y 25
Liversage St	Z 26
Market Pl.	YZ 27
Midland Rd	Z 28
Morledge	Z 29
Mount St	Z 30
Newdigate St	Z 31
Normanton Rd	Z 33
Queen St	Y 34
Sacheveral St	Z 40
St Mary's Gate	Y 36
St Peter's St	Z 37
St Thomas Rd	X 39
Stafford St	Z 42
Stanhope St	X 43
Upper Dale Rd	X 45
Victoria St	Z 46
Walbrook Rd	X 48
Wardwick	Z 50

DERBY

at Darley Abbey North : 2.5 mi off A 6 - X - ✉ Derby

XX Darleys
Darley Abbey Mill ✉ DE22 1DZ – ℘ (01332) 364 987 – www.darleys.com
– Closed 25 December-15 January, Sunday dinner and bank holidays
Rest *– (booking advisable)* Menu £ 20 (lunch) – Carte £ 33/46
♦ Popular weir-side restaurant with river views. Attractive terrace, modern bar-lounge and traditional dining room. Great value lunches and more ambitious modern European dishes in the evening.

DEVIZES – Wiltshire – **503** O29 – pop. 15 272   4 C2

▶ London 98 mi – Bristol 38 mi – Salisbury 25 mi – Southampton 50 mi
🛈 Market Pl ℘ (01380) 72 94 08, www.devizes.org.uk
⛳ Erlestoke, ℘ (01380) 83 10 69
◉ St John's Church★★ – Market Place★ – Wiltshire Heritage Museum★ **AC**
◉ Potterne (Porch House★★) S : 2.5 mi by A 360 – E : Vale of Pewsey★. Stonehenge★★★ **AC**, SE : 16 mi by A 360 and A 344 – Avebury★★ (The Stones★, Church★) NE : 7 mi by A 361

at Potterne South : 2.25 mi on A 360 – ✉ Devizes

⌂ Blounts Court Farm *without rest*
Coxhill Ln ✉ SN10 5PH – ℘ (01380) 727 180 – www.blountscourtfarm.co.uk
3 rm ☐ – † £ 45/82 †† £ 75/82
♦ Delightfully run farmhouse set on a 150 acre working farm. Snug inner consists of a cosy lounge and spacious breakfast room filled with clocks and curios; framed pastels and country photos abound. Warm, comfy, well-kept bedrooms pay good attention to detail.

at Rowde Northwest : 2 mi by A 361 on A 342 – ✉ Devizes

🏠 George & Dragon *with rm*
High St ✉ SN10 2PN – ℘ (01380) 723 053
– www.thegeorgeanddragonrowde.co.uk – Closed Sunday dinner
3 rm – † £ 85/125 †† £ 85/125, ☐ £ 8
Rest – Seafood *– (booking essential)* Menu £ 19 – Carte £ 21/39
♦ Rustic and cosy 16C coaching inn with open fires, solid stone floors and wooden beams. Oft-changing menu has strong emphasis on seafood, with fish delivered daily from Cornwall. Old-world charm meets modern facilities in the individually designed bedrooms.

DIDSBURY – Greater Manchester – **502** N23 – see Manchester

DITCHEAT – Somerset   4 C2
▶ London 124 mi – Bath 29 mi

🏠 Manor House Inn *with rm*
✉ BA4 6RB – ℘ (01749) 860 276 – www.manorhouseinn.co.uk – Closed 25 December, Sunday dinner and restricted opening Christmas-New Year
3 rm ☐ – † £ 55/85 †† £ 85   **Rest** – Carte £ 21/31
♦ Welcoming, equestrian-themed pub set on the Somerset Levels. Traditional open fires and a restored skittle alley are coupled with honest classical cooking and locally sourced produce. Former stables house cosy bedrooms with good mod cons.

DITCHLING – West Sussex – **504** T31 – pop. 2 027   7 D2
▶ London 47 mi

⌂ Tovey Lodge *without rest*
Underhill Ln, South : 1 mi by B 2112 off Ditchling Beacon rd ✉ BN6 8XE
– ℘ (08456) 120 544 – www.sussexcountryholidays.co.uk
5 rm ☐ – † £ 110/150 †† £ 125/165
♦ Luxuriously appointed, keenly run house with mature gardens and pleasant views. Bedrooms boast modern technology and luxurious bathrooms; Maple, with its balcony, is the best.

DODDINGTON – Kent – **504** W30   9 C2

▶ London 50 mi – Croydon 51 mi – Barnet 73 mi – Ealing 87 mi

Old Vicarage without rest
Church Hill ⊠ *ME9 0BD –* ℰ *(01795) 886 136*
– www.oldvicaragedoddington.co.uk – Closed 24 December-2 January
3 rm – †£ 58/65 ††£ 79/89

♦ Grade II listed former vicarage for the 12C church, where wooden beams, exposed stone and period features blend with modern furnishings. Impressive hall, comfy lounge and striking antique dining table. Large bedrooms boast coffee machines and Bose sound systems.

DOGMERSFIELD – Hampshire   7 C1

▶ London 44 mi – Farnham 6 mi – Fleet 2 mi

Four Seasons
Dogmersfield Park, Chalky Ln ⊠ *RG27 8TD –* ℰ *(01252) 853 000 – www.fourseasons.com/hampshire*
111 rm – †£ 195/265 ††£ 195/265, ⊇ £ 25 – 22 suites
Rest *Seasons* – *(closed dinner Sunday and Monday) (dinner only and Sunday lunch)* Carte £ 45/70

♦ Part Georgian splendour in extensive woodlands; many original features in situ. Superb spa facilities: vast selection of leisure pursuits. Luxurious, highly equipped bedrooms. Restaurant has thoroughly modish, relaxing feel.

DONCASTER – South Yorkshire – **502** Q23 – pop. 67 977   23 C3

▶ London 173 mi – Kingston-upon-Hull 46 mi – Leeds 30 mi – Nottingham 46 mi
✈ Robin Hood Airport : ℰ *(0871) 220 2210, SE : 7m off A638*
🛈 38-40 High St ℰ *(01302) 734 309, www.visitdoncaster.com*
🏌 Doncaster Town Moor Belle Vue Bawtry Rd, ℰ *(01302) 53 37 78*
🏌 Crookhill Park Conisborough, ℰ *(01709) 86 29 79*
🏌 Wheatley Amthorpe Rd, ℰ *(01302) 83 16 55*
🏌 Owston Park Owston Owston Lane, Carcroft, ℰ *(01302) 33 08 21*

Mount Pleasant
Great North Rd, Southeast : 6 mi on A 638 ⊠ *DN11 0HW –* ℰ *(01302) 868 696 – www.mountpleasant.co.uk*
54 rm ⊇ – †£ 79/99 ††£ 99/169 – 2 suites
Rest *Garden* – Carte £ 27/41

♦ Well-run, privately owned hotel with spacious inner. Comfortable, individually styled bedrooms: one with a five-poster bed; some with jacuzzi baths or saunas. Pleasant wellness centre and treatment rooms. Large formal dining room offers extensive, classical menu.

DONHEAD-ST-ANDREW – Wiltshire – **503** N30   4 C3

▶ London 115 mi – Bournemouth 34 mi – Poole 32 mi – Bath 37 mi

Forester Inn
Lower St ⊠ *SP7 9EE –* ℰ *(01747) 828 038*
– www.theforesterdonheadstandrews.co.uk – Closed Sunday dinner
Rest – Menu £ 19 (weekdays) – Carte £ 23/31

♦ Gloriously rustic 13C thatched pub. Menus display a strong seafood base, with constantly changing Brixham fish and a set 3 course selection. Charcuterie and tapas dishes on offer in the bar.

DORCHESTER – Dorset – **503** M31 – pop. 17 861   4 C3

▶ London 135 mi – Bournemouth 27 mi – Exeter 53 mi – Southampton 53 mi
🛈 11 Antelope Walk, ℰ *(01305) 26 79 92, www.visit-dorchester.co.uk*
🏌 Came Down, ℰ *(01305) 81 34 94*
◉ Town★ - Dorset County Museum★ **AC**
⊙ Maiden Castle★★ (≤★) SW : 2.5 mi – Puddletown Church★, NE : 5.5 mi by A 35. Moreton Church★★, E : 7.5 mi – Bere Regis★ (St John the Baptist Church★ - Roof★★) NE : 11 mi by A 35 – Athelhampton House★ **AC**, NE : 6.5 mi by A 35 - Cerne Abbas★, N : 7 mi by A 352 – Milton Abbas★, NE : 12 mi on A 354 and by-road

DORCHESTER

🏠 **Yalbury Cottage** 🚗 📶 **P** 𝗩𝗜𝗦𝗔 ⓜ
Lower Bockhampton, East : 3.75 mi by A 35 ✉ *DT2 8PZ* – 📞 *(01305) 262 382* – *www.yalburycottage.com* – *Closed 23-27 December*
8 rm 🍽 – 👤£ 70/85 👥£ 100/115
Rest – *(closed Sunday and Monday to non-residents) (dinner only)* Menu £ 36
♦ Welcoming thatched cottage with a small garden, set in a quiet hamlet. Characterful beamed lounge with a gas-fire. Modern, comfortable bedrooms are located in the extension. Linen-clad dining room offers a set menu; most produce is sourced from within nine miles.

🏠 **Little Court** without rest 🚗 🏊 ❀ ❀ 📶 **P** 𝗩𝗜𝗦𝗔 ⓜ
5 Westleaze, Charminster, North : 1 mi by A 37, turning right at Loders garage ✉ *DT2 9PZ* – 📞 *(01305) 261 576* – *www.littlecourt.net*
8 rm 🍽 – 👤£ 99 👥£ 99/109
♦ Lutyens style house boasting Edwardian wood/brickwork, leaded windows and mature gardens with a pool and tennis court. Bedrooms display original features and modern furnishings; one four-poster.

XX **Sienna** (Russell Brown) 𝗔𝗖 𝗩𝗜𝗦𝗔 ⓜ
❀
36 High West St ✉ *DT1 1UP* – 📞 *(01305) 250 022* – *www.siennarestaurant.co.uk* – *Closed 2 weeks spring, 2 weeks autumn, Sunday and Monday*
Rest – *(booking essential)* Menu £ 29/43
Spec. Veal with white beans and pickled carrots. Fillet of brill with scallops, Jersey Royals and asparagus. Selvatica chocolate tasting plate.
♦ Small high street restaurant with frosted glass façade, intimate interior and smartly laid tables. Choice of concise à la carte or 6 course tasting menu. Precise cooking uses top quality local produce and classic flavour combinations. Polite, measured service.

at Winterbourne Steepleton West : 4.75 mi by B 3150 and A 35 on B 3159 – ✉ **Dorchester**

🏠 **Old Rectory** without rest 🚗 ❀ **P**
✉ *DT2 9LG* – 📞 *(01305) 889 468* – *www.theoldrectorybandb.co.uk* – *Closed 1 week Christmas*
4 rm 🍽 – 👤£ 60 👥£ 100
♦ Attractive house in pretty village; cross the brook and enter mature gardens. Comfy lounge and conservatory breakfast room. Immaculate bedrooms with homely, modern décor and smart bathrooms.

DORRIDGE – West Midlands – **503** O26 – ✉ Birmingham   **19** C2
▶ London 109 mi – Birmingham 11 mi – Warwick 11 mi

XX **Forest** with rm 🍽 𝗔𝗖 rest, 📶 🛁 **P** 𝗩𝗜𝗦𝗔 ⓜ 𝗔𝗘
25 Station Approach ✉ *B93 8JA* – 📞 *(01564) 772 120* – *www.forest-hotel.com* – *Closed 25 December and Sunday dinner*
12 rm – 👤£ 95 👥£ 125 **Rest** – Menu £ 16 (weekdays) – Carte £ 21/29
♦ Attractive red-brick and timber former pub with a busy ambience. Food is its backbone: modern classics served in stylish bar and restaurant. Cool, modern bedrooms.

DOUGLAS – Douglas – **502** G21 – **see Man (Isle of)**

DOVER – Kent – **504** Y30 – pop. 35 338 ▌Great Britain   **9** D2
▶ London 76 mi – Brighton 84 mi
🚢 to France (Calais) (P & O Stena Line) frequent services daily (1 h 15 mn) – to France (Calais) (SeaFrance S.A.) frequent services daily (1 h 30 mn) – to France (Boulogne) (SpeedFerries) 3-5 daily (50 mn)
🅘 Biggin 📞 (01304) 20 51 08, www.whitecliffscountry.org.uk
◉ Castle★★ **AC** Y
◉ White Cliffs, Langdon Cliffs, NE : 1 mi on A 2 **Z** and A 258

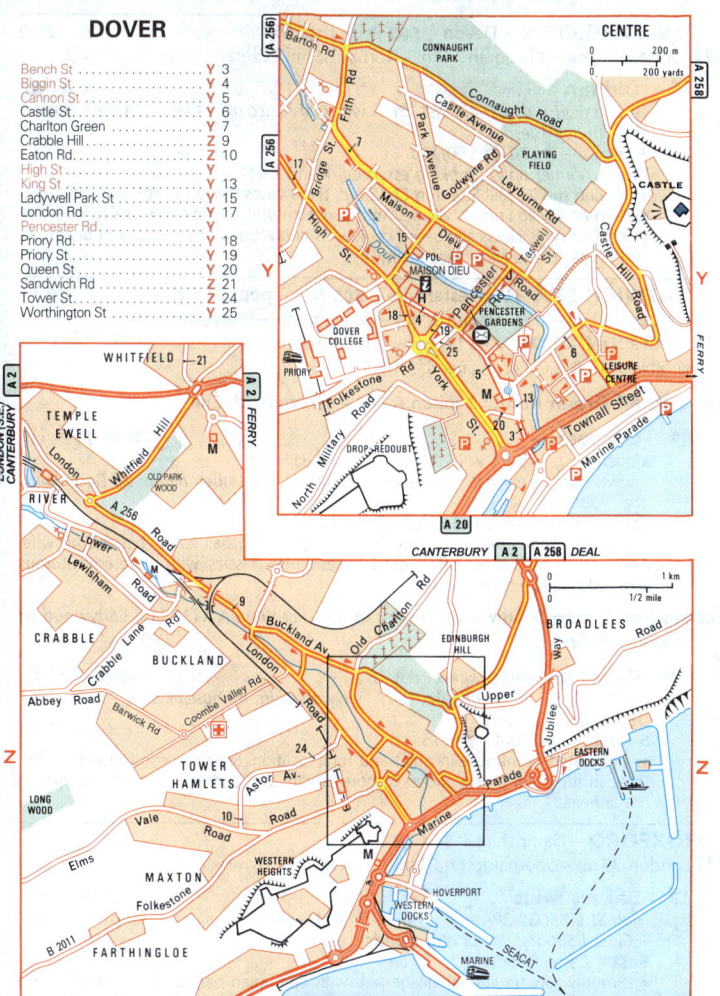

at St Margaret's at Cliffe Northeast : 4 mi by A 258 - Z - ✉ Dover

Wallett's Court Country House
West Cliffe, Northwest : 0.75 mi on Dover rd ✉ CT15 6EW
– ✆ (01304) 852 424 – www.wallettscourt.com – Closed 24-26 December
17 rm ☕ – ‡£ 90/150 ‡‡ £ 150/290
Rest *The Restaurant* – *(dinner only and Sunday lunch)* Menu £ 22/40
♦ Heavily beamed 17C country house with characterful lounge and comfy bar. Four-poster bedrooms in main house; rustic rooms in annexes; most luxurious rooms above pleasant spa. Atmospheric restaurant with smartly laid tables offers ambitious, original, modern menu.

DOWNTON – Hampshire – **503** P31 – see Lymington

DREWSTEIGNTON – Devon – 503 I31 – pop. 668 — 2 C2
▶ London 190 mi – Plymouth 56 mi – Torbay 35 mi – Exeter 15 mi

Old Inn with rm
✉ EX6 6QR – ✆ (01647) 281 276 – www.old-inn.co.uk – Closed 2 weeks winter and Sunday-Tuesday
3 rm – †£ 70 ††£ 90/100
Rest – (dinner only) (booking essential) Menu £ 43
◆ Having run 22 Mill Street in Chagford, the owners moved to this delightful cottage in an idyllic English village. Anthea is a natural hostess and clearly loves the place; Duncan's classically based cooking is gutsy, boldly flavoured and generous, and his set menu sings seasonality.

DROITWICH SPA – Worcestershire – 503 N27 – pop. 22 585 — 19 C3
▶ London 129 mi – Birmingham 20 mi – Bristol 66 mi – Worcester 6 mi
🛈 Victoria Sq ✆ (01905) 77 43 12, www.cotswolds.info
Droitwich G. & C.C. Ford Lane, ✆ (01905) 77 43 44

at Cutnall Green North : 3 mi on A 442 – ✉ Droitwich Spa

Chequers
Kidderminster Rd ✉ WR9 0PJ – ✆ (01299) 851 292
– www.chequerscutnallgreen.co.uk – Closed 25 December, dinner 26 December and 1 January
Rest – Menu £ 17 (weekdays) – Carte £ 21/30
◆ Cosy roadside pub, run by the former England football team chef and his wife. Asian-influenced menus offer light bites and pub classics, with more adventurous fish and offal-based specials.

at Hadley Heath Southwest : 4 mi by Ombersley Way, A 4133 and Ladywood rd – ✉ Droitwich Spa

Old Farmhouse without rest
✉ WR9 0AR – ✆ (01905) 620 837 – www.theoldfarmhouse.uk.com – Closed 25 December-1 February
5 rm – †£ 40/45 ††£ 75
◆ Converted farmhouse in quiet and rural location. Spacious comfortable rooms, three in the main house and two, more private and perhaps suited to families, in the annexe.

DROXFORD – Hampshire – 504 Q31 — 6 B2
▶ London 79 mi – Southampton 21 mi – Portsmouth 16 mi – Basingstoke 37 mi

Bakers Arms
High St ✉ SO32 3PA – ✆ (01489) 877 533 – www.thebakersarmsdroxford.com
– Closed Sunday dinner and Monday
Rest – Carte £ 25/31
◆ Proudly run, traditional village pub with open-plan bar, Chesterfield sofas and roaring log fire; decorative beer adverts, Victorian photographs and stag heads. Unfussy, filling dishes rely on locally sourced produce. Friendly, polite service. Local ales.

DRY DODDINGTON – Lincolnshire – see Grantham

DULVERTON – Somerset – 503 J30 – pop. 1 870 — 3 A2
▶ London 198 mi – Barnstaple 27 mi – Exeter 26 mi – Minehead 18 mi
◉ Village ★
◉ Exmoor National Park ★★ - Tarr Steps ★★, NW : 6 mi by B 3223

Woods
4 Banks Sq ✉ TA22 9BU – ✆ (01398) 324 007 – Closed dinner 1 January and 26 December
Rest – Carte £ 16/25
◆ Delightful pub displaying charming décor and smart hand-made furniture. Regularly changing, classical Gallic menu uses both French and local, traceable produce; meat is from the owner's farm.

DULVERTON

at Brushford South : 1.75 mi on B 3222 – ✉ Dulverton

↑ Three Acres Country House without rest
✉ TA22 9AR – ✆ (01398) 323 730 – www.threeacrescountryhouse.co.uk
6 rm ⬜ – †£ 75 ††£ 120
♦ Remotely set guesthouse boasting nearly 3 acres of mature gardens/parkland. Comfy lounge, small bar, pine-furnished breakfast room and pleasant terrace. Large, cosy bedrooms with country views.

DUNSTER – Somerset – **503** J30 – pop. 848   **3** A2
▶ London 185 mi – Minehead 3 mi – Taunton 23 mi
◎ Town★★ - Castle★★ **AC** (upper rooms ≤★) - Water Mill★ **AC**
- St George's Church★ - Dovecote★

↑ Exmoor House without rest
12 West St ✉ TA24 6SN – ✆ (01643) 821 268 – www.exmoorhousedunster.co.uk
– March-25 December
6 rm ⬜ – †£ 50 ††£ 85
♦ Terraced Georgian house on the main street of a historic town; run by warm, welcoming owners. Comfy, chintzy lounge and spacious pine-furnished breakfast room. Cosy, well-kept bedrooms.

DURHAM – Durham – **501** P19 – pop. 42 100 ▮ Great Britain   **24** B3
▶ London 267 mi – Leeds 77 mi – Middlesbrough 23 mi
– Newcastle upon Tyne 20 mi
ℹ 2 Millennium Pl ✆ (0191) 384 37 20, www.thisisdurham.com
⛳ Mount Oswald South Rd, ✆ (0191) 386 75 27
◎ City★★★ - Cathedral★★★ (Nave★★★, Chapel of the Nine Altars★★★, Sanctuary Knocker★) B – Oriental Museum★★ **AC** (at Durham University by A 167) B – City and Riverside (Prebends' Bridge ≤★★ A, Framwellgate Bridge ≤★★ B)
– Monastic Buildings (Cathedral Treasury★, Central Tower ≤★) B
– Castle★ (Norman chapel★) **AC** B
◉ Hartlepool Historic Quay★, SE : 14 mi by A 181, A 19 and A 179

Plan on next page

🏠 Farnley Tower
The Avenue ✉ DH1 4DX – ✆ (0191) 375 00 11 – www.farnley-tower.co.uk
13 rm ⬜ – †£ 65/75 ††£ 85/95   A**c**
Rest *Gourmet Spot* – ✆ (0191) 384 66 55 *(closed Sunday-Monday) (dinner only)* Menu £ 25/38
♦ Spacious Victorian house in quiet residential area close to city centre. Modern, airy, well-equipped bedrooms with a good degree of comfort. Gourmet Spot, stylish and slick in black granite and leather, serves original, modern cuisine.

↑ Cathedral View Town House without rest
212 Lower Gilesgate ✉ DH1 1QN – ✆ (0191) 386 95 66
– www.cathedralview.com – Closed 24 December-4 January   B**n**
6 rm ⬜ – †£ 70/100 ††£ 90/125
♦ Cosy, welcoming, Georgian townhouse with terraced garden, set in the older part of the city near the centre. Attractive breakfast room with good views; extensive menu includes daily specials. Spacious, individually named rooms.

↑ Castle View without rest
4 Crossgate ✉ DH1 4PS – ✆ (0191) 386 88 52 – www.castle-view.co.uk
– Closed 15 December-10 January   A**e**
6 rm ⬜ – †£ 55/70 ††£ 80/90
♦ Attractive Georgian townhouse set beside a Norman castle, off a steep cobbled hill, reputedly once the vicarage to adjacent church. Have breakfast on the terrace in summer. Individually furnished bedrooms.

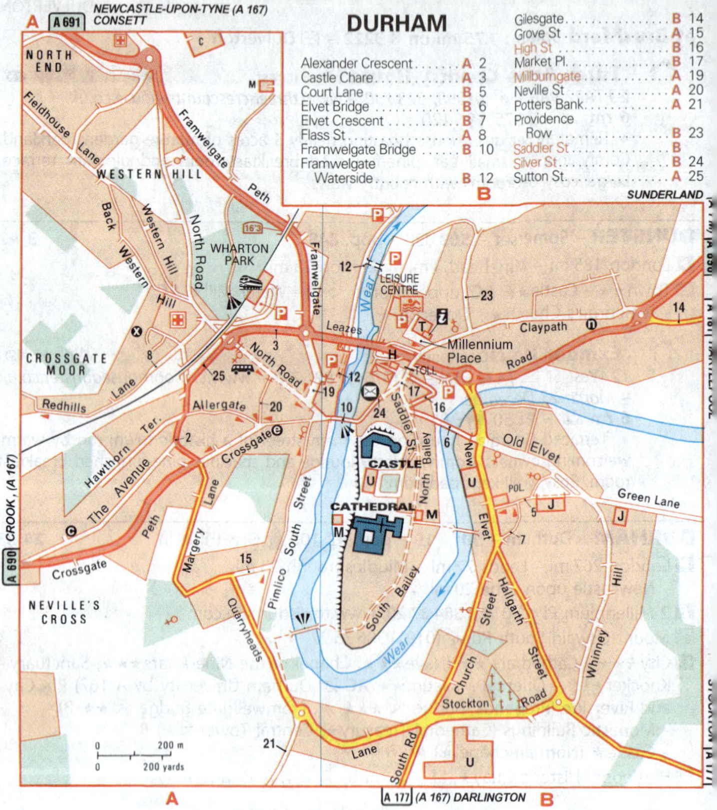
DURHAM
NEWCASTLE-UPON-TYNE (A 167) CONSETT
A 691
Alexander Crescent A 2
Castle Chare A 3
Court Lane B 5
Elvet Bridge B 6
Elvet Crescent B 7
Flass St A 8
Framwelgate Bridge B 10
Framwelgate Waterside B 12
Gilesgate B 14
Grove St A 15
High St B 16
Market Pl. B 17
Millburngate A 19
Neville St A 20
Potters Bank A 21
Providence Row B 23
Saddler St B
Silver St B 24
Sutton St. A 25
SUNDERLAND
NORTH END
WESTERN HILL
WHARTON PARK
CROSSGATE MOOR
NEVILLE'S CROSS
LEISURE CENTRE
Millennium Place
CASTLE
CATHEDRAL
Claypath
Old Elvet
Green Lane
CROOK, (A 167)
A 690
A 177 (A 167) DARLINGTON
STOCKTON
0 200 m
0 200 yards

ENGLAND

Finbarr's

Waddington St, Flass Vale ✉ DH1 4BG – ✆ (0191) 370 9999 – www.finbarrsrestaurant.co.uk **Ax**

Rest – *(booking advisable)* Menu £ 17 (lunch) – Carte £ 22/45

◆ Hidden in a hotel outside the city and leased by the owner. Spacious modern dining room with monochrome photos and well-spaced, smartly laid tables. Modern, bi-monthly menus display strong French influences. Smooth, professional service.

Bistro 21

Aykley Heads House, Aykley Heads, Northwest : 1.5 mi by A 691 and B 6532 ✉ DH1 5TS – ✆ (0191) 384 43 54 – www.bistrotwentyone.co.uk – Closed Sunday and bank holidays

Rest – *(booking essential)* Menu £ 19 (weekdays) – Carte £ 23/44

◆ Popular restaurant in former stables of 17C villa, with French farmhouse styling and enclosed courtyard. Fresh, uncomplicated cooking; neatly presented classics. Good value lunch/midweek menu.

Enjoy good food without spending a fortune! Look out for the Bib Gourmand symbol to find restaurants offering fine cuisine at special prices !

EARL STONHAM – Suffolk – 504 X27 — 15 C3
▶ London 91 mi – Ipswich 12 mi – Colchester 33 mi – Clacton-on-Sea 38 mi

Bays Farm without rest
Forward Grn, Northwest : 1 mi by A1120 on Broad Green Rd ⊠ IP14 5HU
– ℰ (01449) 711 286 – www.baysfarmsuffolk.co.uk
4 rm – †£ 50/100 ††£ 60/110
♦ 17C farmhouse with kitchen garden, set in 4 attractive acres. Characterful interior with comfy lounge and beamed dining room. Individually styled bedrooms; annexed 'Hayloft' is the most luxurious. Communal breakfasts of local produce and homemade bread and jam.

EARSHAM – Norfolk – 504 Y26 – see Bungay

EASINGWOLD – North Yorkshire – 502 Q21 – pop. 3 975 – ⊠ York — 23 C2
▶ London 217 mi – Leeds 38 mi – Middlesbrough 37 mi – York 14 mi
🛈 Chapel Lane ℰ (01347) 82 15 30, www.visit-easingwold.com
Stillington Rd, ℰ (01347) 82 24 74

Old Vicarage without rest
Market Pl ⊠ YO61 3AL – ℰ (01347) 821 015
– www.oldvicarage-easingwold.co.uk – Closed 2 weeks Christmas-New Year
4 rm – †£ 80/85 ††£ 100/105
♦ Spacious, part Georgian country house with walled rose garden and adjacent croquet lawn. Immaculately kept throughout with fine period antiques in the elegant sitting room.

at Crayke East : 2 mi on Helmsley Rd – ⊠ York

Durham Ox with rm
Westway ⊠ YO61 4TE – ℰ (01347) 821 506 – www.thedurhamox.com – Closed 25 December
5 rm – †£ 80 ††£ 100 **Rest** – (booking essential) Carte £ 24/35
♦ 300 year old, family run pub set in a sleepy hamlet. Regularly changing à la carte features hearty dishes of fresh seafood, local meats, Crayke game and tasty spit-roast chicken. Bedrooms are set in old farm cottages; some are suites, some have jacuzzis.

EAST CHILTINGTON – East Sussex – see Lewes

EAST CHISENBURY – Wiltshire — 4 D2
▶ London 92 mi – Bristol 51 mi – Southampton 53 mi – Reading 51 mi

Red Lion Freehouse
⊠ SN9 6AQ – ℰ (01980) 671 124 – www.redlionfreehouse.com
Rest – (booking advisable) Menu £ 18 (lunch) – Carte £ 25/33
♦ Delightful thatched pub with exposed beams, wood burner and a pretty garden. Enthusiastic owners cook pleasingly down-to-earth dishes, precisely composed and packed with flavour. Daily changing, seasonal à la carte, great value lunch menu and Sunday roasts.

EAST END – Hampshire – see Lymington

EAST GARSTON – West Berkshire — 10 B3
▶ London 69 mi – Bristol 58 mi

Queen's Arms with rm
⊠ RG17 7ET – ℰ (01488) 648 757 – www.queensarmshotel.co.uk – Closed 25 December
8 rm – †£ 90/130 ††£ 120/130 **Rest** – Carte £ 22/32
♦ A quintessentially English inn with an atmospheric, antique-furnished bar, which celebrates country pursuits. Rustic British dishes might include shepherd's pie or rib-eye steak; the lunch menu is particularly good value. Superb bedrooms and a generous breakfast.

EAST GRINSTEAD – West Sussex – 504 T30 – pop. 26 222 — 7 D2
▶ London 48 mi – Brighton 30 mi – Eastbourne 32 mi – Lewes 21 mi
Copthorne Borers Arm Rd, ℰ (01342) 71 25 08

EAST GRINSTEAD

Gravetye Manor
Vowels Ln, Southwest : 4.5 mi by B 2110 taking second turn left towards West Hoathly ⊠ RH19 4LJ – ✆ (01342) 810 567 – www.gravetyemanor.co.uk
18 rm – †£ 200 ††£ 240/550
Rest – (booking essential) Menu £ 25/37 – Carte approx. £ 55
• Elizabethan manor house surrounded by 35 acres of gardens and 1,000 acres of forestry land. Wood-panelled guest areas display heavy fabrics. Traditionally appointed bedrooms boast large beds. Afternoon tea and all day dining in lounges. Classical dining room.

EAST HADDON – Northamptonshire
16 B3
▶ London 76 mi – Birmingham 47 mi – Leicester 32 mi – Coventry 34 mi

Red Lion with rm
Main St ⊠ NN6 8BU – ✆ (01604) 770 223 – www.redlioneasthaddon.co.uk
5 rm – †£ 80 ††£ 95/120 **Rest** – (closed Sunday dinner) Carte £ 20/26
• Thatched, honey-stone inn set in an attractive village and boasting pretty gardens and a pleasing mix of exposed wood and slate. With the chef and owner both having worked at Rhodes 24, food is taken seriously, and menus offer upgraded pub classics. Warm, welcoming bedrooms; one in the adjacent 18C cottage.

EAST HENDRED – Oxfordshire – 503 P29 – see Wantage

EAST HOATHLY – East Sussex – 504 U31 – pop. 1 206
8 B3
▶ London 60 mi – Brighton 16 mi – Eastbourne 13 mi – Hastings 25 mi

Old Whyly
London Rd, Northwest : 0.5 mi, turning right after post box on right, taking centre gravel drive after approx. 400 metres ⊠ BN8 6EL – ✆ (01825) 840 216 – www.oldwhyly.co.uk
3 rm – †£ 73/95 ††£ 135 **Rest** – Menu £ 33
• Charming red-brick house built in 1760, set in beautiful grounds and very personally run by its delightful owner. Guest areas mix the classic and the contemporary. Bedrooms are individually designed around a theme: choose from Tulip, French or Chinese. Stylish, minimalist dining room with homemade yoghurts and jams at breakfast and daily changing 3 course dinners.

EAST KENNETT – Wiltshire – see Marlborough

EAST LAVANT – West Sussex – see Chichester

EAST WITTON – North Yorkshire – 502 O21 – ⊠ Leyburn
22 B1
▶ London 238 mi – Leeds 45 mi – Middlesbrough 30 mi – York 39 mi

Blue Lion with rm
⊠ DL8 4SN – ✆ (01969) 624 273 – www.thebluelion.co.uk
15 rm – †£ 70 ††£ 145 **Rest** – (booking essential) Carte £ 23/44 s
• Charming, characterful countryside pub. Daily-changing menu features a tasty mix of classic and modern dishes, all with seasonality and traceability at their core. Bedrooms – in the pub and outbuildings – are warm and cosy.

EASTBOURNE – East Sussex – 504 U31 – pop. 106 562 ▌Great Britain
8 B3
▶ London 68 mi – Brighton 25 mi – Dover 61 mi – Maidstone 49 mi
🛈 Cornfield Rd ✆ (01323) 41 54 50, www.visiteastbourne.com
▣ Royal Eastbourne Paradise Drive, ✆ (01323) 74 40 45
▣ Eastbourne Downs East Dean Rd, ✆ (01323) 72 08 27
▣ Eastbourne Golfing Park Lottbridge Drove, ✆ (01323) 52 04 00
◉ Seafront ★
◉ Beachy Head ★★★, SW : 3 mi by B 2103 Z

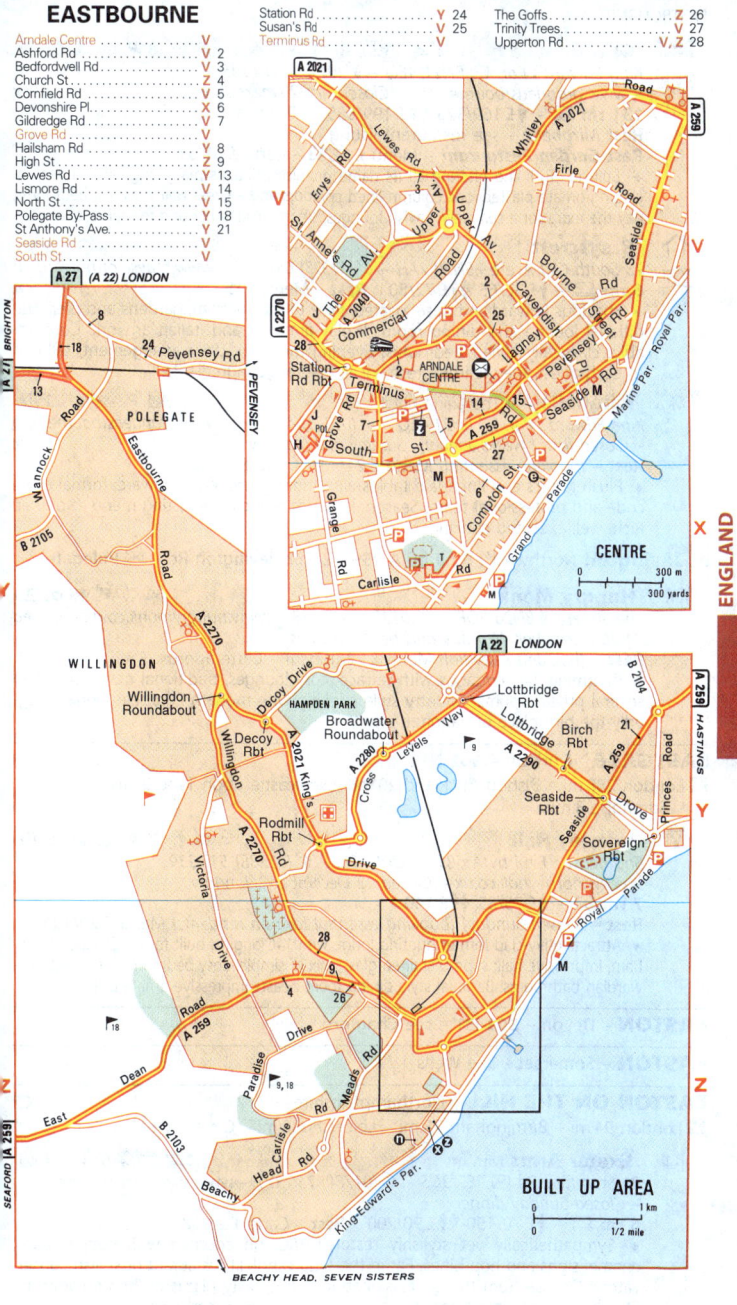

EASTBOURNE

Grand
King Edward's Par. ⊠ BN21 4EQ – ℰ (01323) 412 345
– www.grandeastbourne.com – Closed first 2 weeks January   Zx
131 rm ⊇ – †£ 169/525 ††£ 199/555 – 10 suites
Rest *Mirabelle* – see restaurant listing
Rest *Garden Restaurant* – Menu £ 22/38 – Carte £ 31/63
• Built in 1871 and offering all its name promises. Retains many original features, including ornate plasterwork, column-lined corridors and a Great Hall. Classical bedrooms; pay the extra for a sea view. Lavish lounges, smart cocktail bar and formal restaurant.

Brayscroft
13 South Cliff Ave ⊠ BN20 7AH – ℰ (01323) 647 005 – www.brayscrofthotel.co.uk
6 rm ⊇ – †£ 36/65 ††£ 72/80   **Rest** – Menu £ 15   Zn
• Spacious Edwardian house located close to the seafront, gardens and pier. Traditional lounge and dining room display antiques and Italian artwork. Comfortable, classically styled bedrooms. Evening meals by daily arrangement; tailored to each guest, they feature fresh, local, free range ingredients.

Mirabelle – at The Grand Hotel
King Edward's Par. ⊠ BN21 4EQ – ℰ (01323) 435 066 – www.grandeastbourne.com
– Closed first 2 weeks January, Sunday and Monday   Zx
Rest – *(booking essential)* Menu £ 24/40 – Carte £ 40/65
• Plush fabrics and linen-laid tables with monogrammed silverware; formal dress code and professional team. Seasonal classics or 6 course tasting menu at dinner. Rich, well-executed cooking.

at Jevington Northwest : 6 mi by A 259 - **Z** - on Jevington Rd - ⊠ Polegate

Hungry Monk
The Street ⊠ BN26 5QF – ℰ (01323) 482 178 – www.hungrymonk.co.uk – Closed 24-26 December, Monday and bank holidays
Rest – *(booking essential)* Menu £ 22 (lunch) – Carte approx. £ 35
• Charming 14C cottages with terrace, cosy lounges, traditional main room and several private rooms. Country style cooking with modern European edge. Allegedly the birthplace of banoffee pie.

EASTGATE – Durham – **502** N19   24 A3
▶ London 288 mi – Bishop Auckland 20 mi – Newcastle upon Tyne 35 mi
– Stanhope 3 mi

Horsley Hall
Southeast : 1 mi by A 689 ⊠ DL13 2LJ – ℰ (01388) 517 239
– www.horsleyhall.co.uk – Closed 22 December-2 January
7 rm ⊇ – †£ 75/85 ††£ 140
Rest – *(closed Sunday) (booking essential for non residents)* Menu £ 20/30
• Attractive ivy-clad former hunting lodge with 14C origins, built for the Bishop of Durham. Impressive hall; superb stained glass; mix of simple, cosy bedrooms – two with Edwardian bathrooms. Baronial style dining room boasts impressive ornate ceiling.

EASTON – Devon – **503** I31 – see Chagford

EASTON – Somerset – see Wells

EASTON ON THE HILL – Northamptonshire   17 C2
▶ London 94 mi – Birmingham 75 mi – Leicester 30 mi – Coventry 61 mi

Exeter Arms with rm
21 Stamford Rd ⊠ PE9 3NS – ℰ (01780) 756 321 – www.theexeterarms.net
– Closed Sunday dinner
6 rm ⊇ – †£ 70/150 ††£ 90/200   **Rest** – Carte £ 23/38
• Sympathetically yet stylishly restored 18C inn adorned with copper pans, enamel signs and hop bines. Eat in the snug candlelit restaurant or stylish conservatory. Choose from the chef's signature dishes, tasty pizzas or 'home comforts'. Stylish, well-appointed bedrooms boast smart modern bathrooms.

EBRINGTON – Gloucestershire – **504** O27 – see Chipping Campden

ECCLESTON – Lancashire – 502 L23 – pop. 4 708
20 A2

▶ London 219 mi – Birmingham 103 mi – Liverpool 29 mi – Preston 11 mi

Parr Hall Farm without rest
Parr Ln. ⊠ PR7 5SL – ℰ (01257) 451 917 – www.parrhallfarm.com
10 rm – †£ 40 ††£ 70

♦ Welcoming, red-brick former farmhouse. Low-beamed, pine-furnished breakfast room. Bedrooms, located in the adjacent barn conversion, boast country style fabrics and modern bathrooms.

ECKINGTON – Derbyshire – 502 P24 – pop. 16 684
16 B1

▶ London 155 mi – Leeds 49 mi – Sheffield 10 mi – Manchester 58 mi

Inn at Troway
Snowdon Ln, Southeast : 7.5 mi by A 6135, B 6052 and B 6056 ⊠ S21 5RU – ℰ (01246) 290 751 – www.relaxeatanddrink.co.uk
Rest – (booking advisable) Menu £ 15 (lunch and early dinner) – Carte £ 19/36

♦ Early Victorian pub in picturesque location with delightful countryside views. Hearty, satisfying dishes on wide-ranging menu. Fine selection of local ales; helpful local staff.

ECKINGTON – Worcestershire – 504 N27 – see Pershore

EDINGTON – Wiltshire – 503 N30
4 C2

▶ London 105 mi – Bristol 43 mi – Cardiff 76 mi – Southampton 64 mi

Paulet Arms with rm
47 Westbury Rd ⊠ BA13 4PG – ℰ (01380) 830 940 – www.pauletarms.co.uk
– Closed Sunday dinner and Monday
3 rm – †£ 80/110 ††£ 150/185, ⊇ £ 12.95
Rest – Menu £ 13 (lunch) – Carte £ 24/35

♦ Some Americans buy football clubs – in this small village, one bought a pub and then spent a fortune doing it up. Lunch is best enjoyed in the bar; dinner is quite a formal affair but the cooking is skilled and the ingredients clearly top-notch. Smart, boutique-style bedrooms.

EGHAM – Surrey – 504 S29 – pop. 27 666
7 C1

▶ London 29 mi – Reading 21 mi

Great Fosters
Stroude Rd, South : 1.25 mi by B 388 ⊠ TW20 9UR – ℰ (01784) 433 822
– www.greatfosters.co.uk
41 rm – †£ 135/215 ††£ 215, ⊇ £ 19.50 – 2 suites
Rest *Oak Room* – see restaurant listing

♦ Elizabethan mansion built as a hunting lodge for Henry VIII. Charming inner with original features; spacious guest areas offer lovely garden views. Medieval-style bedrooms boast feature beds.

Monsoon
20 High St ⊠ TW20 9DT – ℰ (01784) 432 141
– www.monsoonrestaurantegham.co.uk
Rest – Indian – Carte £ 12/22

♦ Smart, stylish restaurant that prides itself on immaculate upkeep and personable service. Contemporary artwork enlivens the walls. Freshly cooked, authentic Indian dishes.

Oak Room – at Great Fosters Hotel
Stroude Rd, South : 1.25 mi by B 388 ⊠ TW20 9UR – ℰ (01784) 433 822
– www.greatfosters.co.uk – Closed Saturday lunch
Rest – Menu £ 27/56

♦ Spacious 16C oak-framed dining room with cosy bar and delightful terrace. Charming period features, immaculately laid tables and formal service. Skilful, modern cooking; complex combinations.

ELDERSFIELD – Worcestershire 18 B3
▶ London 124 mi – Birmingham 63 mi – Liverpool 145 mi – Bristol 52 mi

Butchers Arms (James Winter)
Lime Street, Southeast : 1 mi ✉ GL19 4NX – ✆ (01452) 840 381
– www.thebutchersarms.net – Closed 2 weeks early January, 2 weeks late August, Sunday dinner September-May, Tuesday lunch and Monday
Rest – (booking essential) Carte £ 34/43
Spec. Middle White pig's cheek with crackling and Bramley apples. Fillet of beef with foie gras and wild mushrooms. Orange marmalade pudding with Drambuie custard.

♦ Pleasant red-brick pub with a traditional feel, run by a husband and wife team, where everyone comes for the great atmosphere and the terrific food. Everything from bread to ice cream is homemade; the cooking is clever and dishes full of flavour. But hurry, only 25 diners can be accommodated.

ELLAND – West Yorkshire – 502 O22 – pop. 14 554 – ✉ Halifax 22 B3
▶ London 204 mi – Bradford 12 mi – Burnley 29 mi – Leeds 17 mi
Hullen Edge Hammerstones Leach Lane, ✆ (01422) 37 25 05

La Cachette
31 Huddersfield Rd ✉ HX5 9AW – ✆ (01422) 378 833
– www.lacachette-elland.com – Closed 2 weeks August, 26 December-9 January, Sunday and bank holidays
Rest – Menu £ 22 (dinner) – Carte £ 23/38

♦ Long-standing, well-run bistro. Spacious bar and dining rooms display Gallic décor and memorabilia. Extensive choice from daily/weekly menus and specials. Classical, seasonal French cooking.

ELTISLEY – Cambridgeshire – 507 T27 14 A3
▶ London 70 mi – Leicester 62 mi

Eltisley
2 The Green ✉ PE19 6TG – ✆ (01480) 880 308 – www.theeltisley.co.uk
– Closed Monday in winter and Sunday dinner
Rest – Carte £ 22/37

♦ Chic and stylish gastropub beside a village green. Simple, unfussy cooking relies on quality, local produce to speak for itself; everything from starters to desserts is homemade.

ELTON – Cambridgeshire – 504 S26 14 A2
▶ London 84 mi – Peterborough 11 mi – Bedford 40 mi – Kettering 24 mi

Crown Inn with rm
8 Duck St ✉ PE8 6RQ – ✆ (01832) 280 232 – www.thecrowninn.org
– Closed Sunday dinner and Monday lunch
5 rm ⚂ – †£ 65 ††£ 95 **Rest** – Carte £ 21/26

♦ 17C honey-stone pub in a delightful country parish, with thatched roof, cosy inglenook and laid-back feel. Extensive menus offer British classics and some Mediterranean influences. Smart, individually styled bedrooms – some with feature beds or roll-top baths.

ELY – Cambridgeshire – 504 U26 – pop. 13 954 – Great Britain 14 B2
▶ London 74 mi – Cambridge 16 mi – Norwich 60 mi
🛈 29 St Mary's St ✆ (01353) 66 20 62, www.visitely.org.uk
107 Cambridge Rd, ✆ (01353) 66 27 51
◉ Cathedral★★ **AC**
◉ Wicken Fen★, SE : 9 mi by A 10 and A 1123

Boathouse
5-5a Annesdale ✉ CB7 4BN – ✆ (01353) 664 388 – www.theboathouseely.co.uk
– Closed Christmas
Rest – Menu £ 19 (weekdays) – Carte £ 22/32

♦ A riverside setting makes for charming ambience: bag a table on the terrace if you can. Inside there's a display of old Oxford and Cambridge oars. Worldwide menus benefit from numerous creative touches.

at Little Thetford South : 2.75 mi by A 10 – ✉ Ely

Springfields without rest
Ely Rd, North : 0.5 mi on A 10 ✉ *CB6 3HJ* – ℰ *(01353) 663 637 – Closed 10 days Christmas- New Year*
3 rm ⊑ – †£ 55 ††£ 75
♦ Welcoming, curio-filled bungalow in pleasant gardens; a perfect home from home. Immaculately kept bedrooms are decorated around colour themes and boast tea trays laid with Wedgwood and Minton China. Take breakfast among the Cranberry Glass collection or in the courtyard.

at Sutton Gault West : 8 mi by A 142 off B 1381 – ✉ Ely

Anchor Inn with rm
✉ *CB6 2BD* – ℰ *(01353) 778 537 – www.anchor-inn-restaurant.co.uk*
4 rm ⊑ – †£ 89/99 ††£ 115/155
Rest – Menu £ 18 (weekday lunch) – Carte £ 25/34
♦ Riverside pub dating back to 1650 and the creation of the Hundred Foot Wash. Tempting menu complemented by daily fish specials. For a pleasant river outlook head for the wood-panelled rooms to the front of the bar. Neat, pine-furnished bedrooms include two suites; one with river views.

EMSWORTH – Hampshire – **504** R31 – pop. 18 310   6 B2
▶ London 75 mi – Brighton 37 mi – Portsmouth 10 mi – Southampton 22 mi

36 on the Quay (Ramon Farthing) with rm
47 South St, The Quay ✉ *PO10 7EG* – ℰ *(01243) 375 592*
– *www.36onthequay.co.uk – Closed 2 weeks January, 1 week May, 1 week November, 24-26 December, Sunday and Monday*
6 rm – †£ 75/90 ††£ 100/110 **Rest** – *(booking essential)* Menu £ 29/55
Spec. Duck egg, lentils and duck liver torchon with truffle dressing. Turbot and shrimps with parsley sauce and bacon foam. Dark chocolate cube with banana ice cream
♦ Long-standing quayside restaurant run by experienced chef-owner. Elegant bar-lounge and intimate linen-laid restaurant in neutral hues. Concise à la carte of well-executed, classical dishes in flavoursome, tried-and-tested combinations. Contemporary bedrooms with good comforts; be ready to order breakfast at check-in.

Fat Olives
30 South St ✉ *PO10 7EH* – ℰ *(01243) 377 914 – www.fatolives.co.uk – Closed 2 weeks late June, 1 week Christmas, 1 week spring, Sunday and Monday*
Rest – *(booking essential)* Menu £ 20 (lunch) – Carte £ 29/41
♦ Small terraced house with a welcoming ambience. Simply decorated with wood floor and rough plaster walls. Tasty modern British menu and, yes, fat olives are available!

EPSOM – Surrey – **504** T30 – pop. 64 493   7 D1
▶ London 17 mi – Guildford 16 mi
🏌 Longdown Lane South Epsom Downs, ℰ (01372) 72 16 66
🏌 Horton Park G & C.C. Hook Rd, ℰ (020) 8393 84 00

Chalk Lane
Chalk Ln., Southwest : 0.5 mi by A 24 and Woodcote Rd ✉ *KT18 7BB*
– ℰ *(01372) 721 179 – www.chalklanehotel.com*
22 rm ⊑ – †£ 90/145 ††£ 135/200
Rest – *(closed Saturday lunch)* Menu £ 19 (lunch) – Carte £ 30/43
♦ At the foot of the Epsom Downs and near to the racecourse. Quality furnishings throughout; the neatly kept bedrooms are most comfortable. Smart, modern dining room.

EPSOM

✕✕ Le Raj

211 Fir Tree Rd, Epsom Downs, Southeast : 2mi by B 289 and B 284 on B 291
✉ KT17 3LB – ℘ (01737) 371 371 – www.lerajrestaurant.co.uk
Rest – Bangladeshi – Carte £ 30/51

♦ Original, interesting menu makes good use of fresh ingredients and brings a modern style to traditional Bangladeshi cuisine. Smart, vibrant, contemporary interior décor.

ERMINGTON – Devon – 503 I32

2 C2

▶ London 216 mi – Plymouth 11 mi – Salcombe 15 mi

✕✕ Plantation House with rm

Totnes Rd, Southwest : 0.5 mi on A 3121 ✉ PL21 9NS – ℘ (01548) 831 100
– www.plantationhousehotel.co.uk
8 rm ⊇ – †£ 69/105 ††£ 180/230
Rest – *(dinner only) (booking essential for non-residents)* Menu £ 38 **s**

♦ Appealing, converted Georgian rectory with smart gardens and terraced seating area. Personally run. Sound cooking of locally sourced ingredients. Individually styled bedrooms.

ETTINGTON – Warwickshire – 504 P27 – pop. 953

19 C3

▶ London 95 mi – Birmingham 41 mi – Leicester 48 mi – Coventry 23 mi

🍺 Chequers Inn

91 Banbury Rd ✉ CV37 7SR – ℘ (01789) 740 387
– www.the-chequers-ettington.co.uk – Closed Sunday dinner and Monday
Rest – Carte £ 24/34

♦ Chandeliers, brushed velvet furniture and Regency chairs set at chequered tables mean that this is not your typical pub. Menu offers a broad international style, ranging from British classics to Asian-inspired dishes.

EVERSHOT – Dorset – 503 M31 – pop. 225 – ✉ Dorchester

4 C3

▶ London 149 mi – Bournemouth 39 mi – Dorchester 12 mi – Salisbury 53 mi

🏨 Summer Lodge

9 Fore St ✉ DT2 0JR – ℘ (01935) 482 000
– www.summerlodgehotel.com
20 rm ⊇ – †£ 235/365 ††£ 330/390 – 4 suites
Rest *The Restaurant* – *(booking essential to non residents)* Menu £ 25/40
– Carte dinner £ 48/67

♦ Attractive former dower house in mature gardens. Country house style guest areas display heavy fabrics and antiques. Individually designed bedrooms boast quality furnishings and marble bathrooms. Exclusive glass-built wellness centre. Formal dining room and conservatory offer classical cuisine. Smart, effective service.

🏠 Acorn Inn

28 Fore St ✉ DT2 0JW – ℘ (01935) 83 228 – www.acorn-inn.co.uk
10 rm ⊇ – †£ 79/109 ††£ 99/189 **Rest** – Carte £ 23/36

♦ Historic inn mentioned in 'Tess of the d'Urbervilles'. Individually styled bedrooms boast fabric-covered walls, good facilities and modern bathrooms. Guest areas include a characterful residents' lounge, a locals bar with skittle alley and a classical restaurant.

🏠 Wooden Cabbage

East Chelborough, West : 3.25 mi by Beaminster rd and Chelborough rd on East Chelborough rd ✉ DT2 0QA – ℘ (01935) 83 362 – www.woodencabbage.co.uk
– Restricted opening in winter
3 rm ⊇ – †£ 75 ††£ 100 **Rest** – Menu £ 30

♦ Attractive former gamekeeper's cottage. Spacious guest areas include a cosy dining room used in winter and an airy conservatory used in summer. Pretty bedrooms boast good facilities and lovely countryside views. Meals (by arrangement) feature home-grown produce.

EXETER – Devon – 503 J31 – pop. 109 247

2 D2

- London 201 mi – Bournemouth 83 mi – Bristol 83 mi – Plymouth 46 mi
- Exeter Airport : ℰ (01392) 367433, E : 5 mi by A 30 **V**
- Princesshay ℰ (01392) 66 57 00, www.discoverexeter.ne
- Downes Crediton Hookway, ℰ (01363) 77 30 25
- City★★ – Cathedral★★ **Z** – Royal Albert Memorial Museum★ **Y**
- Killerton★★ **AC**, NE : 7 mi by B 3181 **V** – Ottery St Mary★ (St Mary's★) E : 12 mi by B 3183 – **Y** – A 30 and B 3174 – Crediton (Holy Cross Church★), NW : 9 mi by A 377

Abode Exeter

Cathedral Yard ⊠ EX1 1HD – ℰ (01392) 319 955 – www.abodehotels.co.uk
52 rm – †£95/225, ††£95/225, ⊑ £13.50 – 1 suite   **Yz**
Rest *Michael Caines* – see restaurant listing

♦ Georgian-style frontage; located on the doorstep of the cathedral. Boutique style hotel with a very modern, stylish interior. Understated bedrooms feature good mod cons.

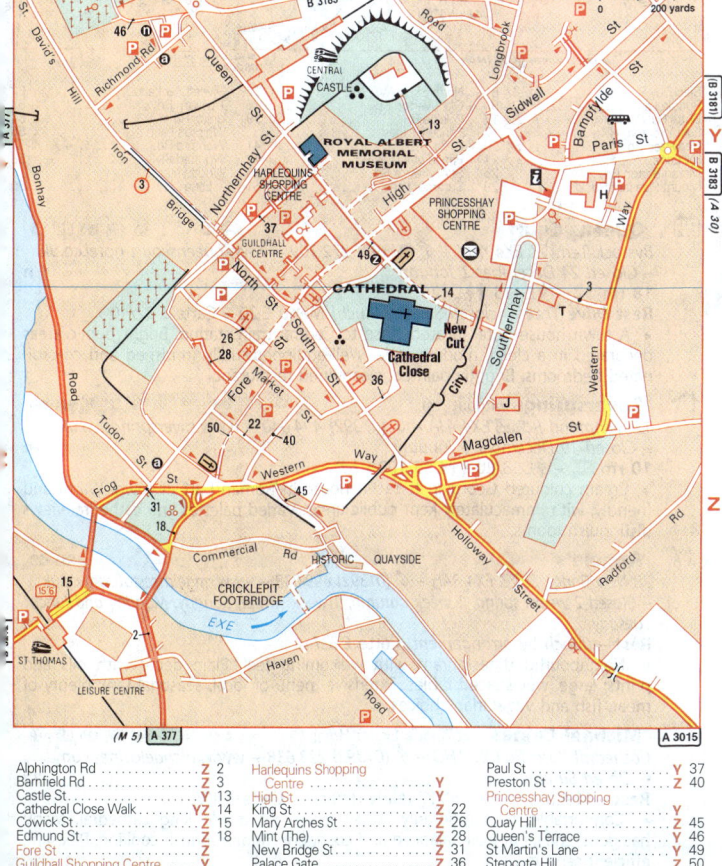

Alphington Rd .... Z 2	Harlequins Shopping Centre .... Y	Paul St .... Y 37
Barnfield Rd .... Z 3	High St .... Y	Preston St .... Z 40
Castle St .... Y 13	King St .... Z 22	Princesshay Shopping Centre .... Y
Cathedral Close Walk .... YZ 14	Mary Arches St .... Z 26	Quay Hill .... Z 45
Cowick St .... Z 15	Mint (The) .... Z 28	Queen's Terrace .... Y 46
Edmund St .... Z 18	New Bridge St .... Z 31	St Martin's Lane .... Y 49
Fore St .... Z	Palace Gate .... Z 36	Stepcote Hill .... Z 50
Guildhall Shopping Centre .... Y		

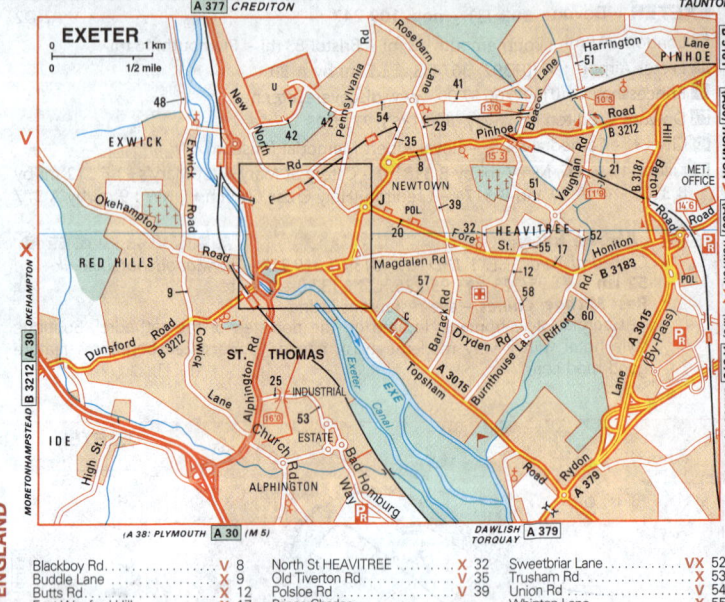

Blackboy Rd. . . . . V 8	North St HEAVITREE . . . . X 32	Sweetbriar Lane . . . . VX 52
Buddle Lane . . . . V 9	Old Tiverton Rd. . . . . X 35	Trusham Rd. . . . . X 53
Butts Rd. X 12	Polsloe Rd. . . . . V 39	Union Rd . . . . V 54
East Wonford Hill . . . . X 17	Prince Charles	Whipton Lane . . . . X 55
Heavitree Rd. . . . . VX 20	Rd. . . . . X 41	Wonford Rd. . . . . X 57
Hill Lane . . . . V 21	Prince of Wales Rd . . . . V 42	Wonford St . . . . X 58
Marsh Barton Rd. . . . . X 25	St Andrew's Rd. . . . . V 48	Woodwater
Mount Pleasant Rd . . . . V 29	Summer Lane . . . . V 51	Lane . . . . X 60

Queens Court

Bystock Terr. ⊠ *EX4 4HY –* ℘ *(01392) 272 709 – www.queenscourt-hotel.co.uk*
– Closed 24 December-2 January Yn

18 rm ⊠ – †£ 115 ††£ 125

Rest *Olive Tree –* (closed Sunday lunch) Menu £ 20 – Carte £ 32/40

♦ A town house hotel located close to Central train station. Bright public areas decorated in a clean, modern style. Well-equipped, tidily furnished and co-ordinated bedrooms. Brightly painted, clean-lined restaurant.

Silversprings without rest

12 Richmond Rd ⊠ *EX4 4JA –* ℘ *(01392) 494 040 – www.silversprings.co.uk*
– Closed 19 December-1 January Ya

10 rm ⊠ – †£ 58/80 ††£ 85/100

♦ Cream coloured Georgian terraced house in Roman part of town. Warm and friendly, with immaculately kept public areas. Varied palettes and cathedral views distinguish rooms.

Angela's

38 New Bridge St ⊠ *EX4 3AH –* ℘ *(01392) 499 038 – www.angelasrestaurant.co.uk*
– Closed 2 weeks spring, 1 week autumn, 1 week winter, Sunday, Monday and lunch Tuesday Za

Rest *–* (lunch by arrangement) Carte £ 33/45

♦ Neighbourhood restaurant with welcoming feel. Plain décor with oils and prints; large, well-spaced tables. Extensive menu of local, seasonal fare; plenty of meat, fish and vegetarian choices.

Michael Caines – at Abode Exeter Hotel

Cathedral Yard ⊠ *EX1 1HD –* ℘ *(01392) 223 638 – www.michaelcaines.com*
– Closed Sunday Yz

Rest – Menu £ 14 (lunch)/17 (early dinner) – Carte £ 47/51

♦ Comfortable, contemporarily stylish restaurant overlooking cathedral. Menu has good choice of well-balanced and confident modern British cooking. Pleasant, efficient service.

EXETER

at Rockbeare East : 7.5 mi by A 30 - V – ✉ Exeter

Jack in the Green Inn
*London Rd ✉ EX5 2EE – ℰ (01404) 822 240 – www.jackinthegreen.uk.com
– Closed 25 December-6 January*
Rest – Menu £ 25 – Carte £ 33/42

♦ Unassuming whitewashed pub with warm, welcoming interior. They support local producers and cooking is taken seriously. Extensive menus feature fresh fish specials; and bread, veg and water are satisfyingly free of charge. Jazz evenings take place in summer.

at Kenton Southeast : 7 mi by A 3015 - X - on A 379 – ✉ Exeter

Rodean
*The Triangle ✉ EX6 8LS – ℰ (01626) 890 195 – www.rodeanrestaurant.co.uk
– Closed Sunday dinner and Monday*
Rest – *(dinner only and Sunday lunch) (booking advisable)* Menu £ 19
– Carte £ 28/37

♦ Family-run, early-20C butchers shop in pretty spot. Bar area for pre-prandials. Restaurant in two rooms with beams and local photos. Menus employ good use of local ingredients.

EXFORD – Somerset – 503 J30 — 3 A2

▶ London 193 mi – Exeter 41 mi – Minehead 14 mi – Taunton 33 mi
◉ Church★
◉ Exmoor National Park★★

Crown
✉ TA24 7PP – ℰ (01643) 831 554 – www.crownhotelexmoor.co.uk
16 rm ⌑ – †£ 69/100 ††£ 119/139
Rest – *(dinner only)* Menu £ 35 – Carte £ 23/33

♦ Attractive 17C, family-run coaching inn with delightful terrace and water garden to rear. Relaxed, cosy interior filled with country prints. Comfy, modern bedrooms with bold décor. Large bar serves snacks. Formal dining room offers traditional, seasonal dishes.

EXTON – Devon – 503 J30 — 2 D2

▶ London 176 mi – Exmouth 4 mi – Topsham 3 mi

Puffing Billy
Station Rd ✉ EX3 0PR – ℰ (01392) 877 888 – www.thepuffingbilly.co.uk – Closed 25 December and Sunday dinner January-15 February
Rest – Carte £ 25/28

♦ Spacious, modern pub with stylish bar, formal dining room and efficient, welcoming service. Menus offer something for everyone, covering the traditional, the regional and the international.

FAIRFORD – Gloucestershire – 503 O28 – pop. 2 960 ▌ Great Britain — 4 D1

▶ London 88 mi – Cirencester 9 mi – Oxford 29 mi
◉ Church of St Mary★ (Stained glass windows★★)
◉ Cirencester★ - Church of St John the Baptist★ - Corinium Museum★ (Mosaic Pavements★), W : 9 mi on A 429, A 435, Spitalgate Lane and Dollar St – Swindon - Great Railway Museum★ **AC** - Railway Village Museum★ **AC**, S : 17 mi on A 419, A 4312, A 4259 and B 4289

Allium
*1 London St, Market Pl ✉ GL7 4AH – ℰ (01285) 712 200
– www.restaurantallium.co.uk – Closed 23 December-7 January, Sunday and Monday*
Rest – Menu £ 26/43

♦ Unassuming neighbourhood restaurant with stylish lounge and bar. Contemporary, boldly patterned wallpapers and mood lighting. Original, modern set menus showcase seasonal, local produce in complex dishes; excellent presentation.

FALMOUTH – Cornwall – 503 E33 – pop. 21 635   1 A3

▶ London 308 mi – Penzance 26 mi – Plymouth 65 mi – Truro 11 mi
🛈 Prince of Wales Pier ℰ (01326) 31 23 00, www.discoverfalmouth.co.uk
⛳ Swanpool Rd, ℰ (01326) 31 12 62
⛳ Budock Vean Hotel Mawnan Smith, ℰ (01326) 25 21 02
◉ Town★ – Pendennis Castle★ (≤★★) **AC** B
◉ Glendurgan Garden★★ **AC** - Trebah Garden★, SW : 4.5 mi by Swanpool Rd A – Mawnan Parish Church★ (≤★★) S : 4 mi by Swanpool Rd A – Cruise along Helford River★. Trelissick★★ (≤★★) NW : 13 mi by A 39 and B 3289 A – Carn Brea (≤★★) NW : 10 mi by A 393 A – Gweek (Setting★, Seal Sanctuary★) SW : 8 mi by A 39 and Treverva rd – Wendron (Poldark Mine★) **AC**, SW : 12.5 mi by A 39 - A - and A 394

Greenbank
Harbourside ⊠ *TR11 2SR* – ℰ *(01326) 312 440* – *www.greenbank-hotel.co.uk*
59 rm ⌕ – †£95/165 ††£185/235 – 1 suite   **Aa**
Rest *Harbourside* – Carte £ 28/34
♦ 17C former coaching inn where flagstone floors and a sweeping staircase contrast with bold, modern colours and contemporary furnishings. Spacious, light wood bedrooms; some overlook the harbour. All day restaurant serves local, seasonal produce and fresh seafood.

St Michael's H & Spa
Gyllyngvase Beach ⊠ *TR11 4NB* – ℰ *(01326) 312 707*
– *www.stmichaelshotel.co.uk*   **Bc**
61 rm ⌕ – †£60/105 ††£120/290
Rest *Flying Fish* – see restaurant listing
♦ Contemporary hotel with a nautical theme running throughout, from the reception desk 'boat' and portholes in the guest areas to the New England style bedrooms – some of which boast balconies and sea views. Modern leisure club and spa.

Dolvean House without rest
50 Melvill Rd ⊠ *TR11 4DQ* – ℰ *(01326) 313 658* – *www.dolvean.co.uk* – *Closed first 2 weeks November and 22-28 December*   **Bn**
10 rm ⌕ – †£39/66 ††£77/98
♦ Smart cream property with local books and guides in parlour: exceptionally good detail wherever you look. Elegant, neatly laid breakfast room. Bright, well-kept bedrooms.

Chelsea House without rest
2 Emslie Rd ⊠ *TR11 4BG* – ℰ *(01326) 212 230* – *www.chelseahousehotel.com*
9 rm ⌕ – †£45/50 ††£60/110   **Be**
♦ Large Victorian house in quiet residential area with partial sea-view at front. Neat breakfast room; well-appointed bedrooms, three with their own balconies.

Prospect House without rest
1 Church Rd, Penryn, Northwest : 2 mi by A 39 on B 3292 ⊠ *TR10 8DA*
– ℰ *(01326) 373 198* – *www.prospecthouse-penryn.co.uk*
3 rm ⌕ – †£40/45 ††£70/75
♦ Large Georgian guesthouse on Penryn River, set within a walled garden and run by a welcoming owner. Super breakfasts with local produce in abundance. Individually styled bedrooms.

✂ Bistro de la Mer
28 Arwenack St ⊠ *TR11 3JB* – ℰ *(01326) 316 509* – *www.bistrodelamer.com*
– *Closed 2 weeks November, 1 week March, 1 January, 25-26 December, Sunday and Monday except dinner April-September*   **Br**
Rest – Menu £ 18 (lunch) – Carte £ 24/40
♦ Modest bistro with a subtle Mediterranean feel, set over two floors and decorated in sunny seaside colours of yellow and blue. Extensive seafood-oriented menu; honest cooking.

FALMOUTH

Samphire
36 Arwenack St ⊠ TR11 3JF – ℰ (01326) 210 759 – www.samphire-falmouth.co.uk
Rest – Carte £ 27/39   **Bx**

• Informal restaurant situated in the heart of town, with oversized windows looking onto the street. Appealing seasonal menu includes plenty of fresh local seafood and tasty Sunday roasts. Attentive service.

Flying Fish – at St Michael's Hotel & Spa
Gyllyngvase Beach ⊠ TR11 4NB – ℰ (01326) 312 707
– www.stmichaelshotel.co.uk   **Bc**
Rest – Menu £ 28 (dinner) – Carte lunch £ 21/29

• Glass-fronted hotel restaurant in shades of blue, looking down sloping gardens towards the bay. Snacks served in the daytime; concise à la carte supplemented by daily specials in the evening.

Rick Stein's Seafood Bar
Discovery Quay (1st floor) ⊠ TR11 3XA – ℰ (01326) 330 053
– www.rickstein.com – Closed Monday lunch in winter and Sunday
Rest – Seafood – Carte £ 19/21   **Ba**

• Head upstairs for keenly priced and very fresh hot or cold 'tapas', which blends British and Spanish influences and uses prime local seafood. Grab a table or watch the kitchen action from a seat at the counter; and don't miss dessert.

at Maenporth Beach South : 3.75 mi by Pennance Rd

Cove
Maenporth Beach ⊠ TR11 5HN – ℰ (01326) 251 136 – www.thecovemaenporth.co.uk
Rest – Carte £ 30/35

• Within a modern building overlooking the beach and cove. Concise menu with daily specials; bright, unfussy cooking, with the occasional Asian note. Young, enthusiastic service.

FARNBOROUGH – Hampshire – 504 R30 – pop. 57 147   7 C1

▶ London 41 mi – Reading 17 mi – Southampton 44 mi – Winchester 33 mi
🛈 Southwood Ively Rd, ℰ (01252) 54 87 00

Aviator
Farnborough Rd, Southwest : 1 mi on A 325 ⊠ GU14 6EL – ℰ (01252) 555 890
– www.aviatorfarnborough.co.uk
169 rm – †£ 205/245 ††£ 205/375, ⊇ £ 16
Rest *Brasserie* – see restaurant listing

• Eye-catching, modern hotel overlooking Farnborough Airport and boasting an unusual circular atrium, a smart first-floor lounge-bar and a small deli. Sleek, good-sized bedrooms feature light wood, modern facilities and fully tiled bathrooms.

Brasserie – at Aviator Hotel
Farnborough Rd, Southwest : 1 mi on A 325 ⊠ GU14 6EL – ℰ (01252) 555 890
– www.aviatorfarnborough.co.uk
Rest – Menu £ 21 (lunch) **s** – Carte £ 30/46 **s**

• Stylish brasserie within an eye-catching hotel that overlooks the airport. Contemporary surroundings provide the perfect backdrop for modern, visually appealing dishes of seasonal produce.

FARNHAM – Dorset – 503 N31 – see Blandford Forum

FARNINGHAM – Kent – 504 U29   8 B1

▶ London 22 mi – Dartford 7 mi – Maidstone 20 mi

Beesfield Farm without rest
Beesfield Lane, off A 225 ⊠ DA4 0LA – ℰ (01322) 863 900
– www.beesfieldfarm.co.uk – Closed 25 December
3 rm ⊇ – †£ 65/70 ††£ 80/90

• Peaceful valley setting, with attractive garden. Exudes character: oldest part is 400 year-old Kentish longhouse. Comfy sitting room; bedrooms boast beams and garden outlook.

FAR SAWREY – Cumbria – **502** L20 – see Hawkshead

FAVERSHAM – Kent – **504** W30 – pop. 18 222   9 C1
▶ London 52 mi – Dover 26 mi – Maidstone 21 mi – Margate 25 mi
🛈 13 Preston St ✆ (01795) 53 45 42, www.faversham.org

XXX **Read's** (David Pitchford) with rm
❀
Macknade Manor, Canterbury Rd, East : 1 mi on A 2 ✉ ME13 8XE – ✆ (01795)
535 344 – www.reads.com – Closed 2 weeks early September, 1 week early
January, 25-26 December, Sunday and Monday
6 rm ⊑ – ✝£ 125/185 ✝✝£ 165/195   **Rest** – Menu £ 25/58
Spec. Fillet of smoked eel, new potato salad and crispy bacon. Lamb four ways.
Rhubarb soufflé with rhubarb ripple ice cream.
♦ Elegant red-brick house with beautiful grounds and traditionally furnished dining rooms. Confident, well-presented, classically based dishes make the best of local produce, including fruit, vegetables and herbs from the walled garden. Comfortable, well-kept bedrooms, tastefully decorated in a country house style.

at Dargate East : 6 mi by A 2 off A 299 – ✉ Kent

🍺 **Dove**
Plum Pudding Ln ✉ ME13 9HB – ✆ (01227) 751 360
– www.thedoveinndargate.co.uk – Closed 1 week February, Sunday dinner and Monday
Rest – (booking advisable at weekends) Carte £ 18/34
♦ Attractive Victorian pub with well-tended gardens and cosy rooms. Weekday menus offer enticing nibbles, pub classics and specials. Concise Friday and Saturday menus are much more ambitious.

at Oare Northwest : 2.5 mi by A2 off B2045 – ✉ Kent

🍺 **Three Mariners**
2 Church Rd ✉ ME13 0QA – ✆ (01795) 533 633
– www.thethreemarinersoare.co.uk – Closed Sunday dinner
Rest – (closed 25 December) Menu £ 17 (weekdays) – Carte £ 25/32
♦ Welcoming 500 year old pub set by a small marina in a sleepy hamlet, boasting pleasant marsh views. Constantly evolving menus offer an appealing mix of carefully prepared, flavoursome dishes.

FELIXKIRK – North Yorkshire – **502** Q21 – see Thirsk

FERMAIN BAY – **503** L33 – see Channel Islands (Guernsey)

FERNHURST – West Sussex – **504** R30   7 C2
▶ London 50 mi – Brighton 40 mi – Southampton 46 mi

XX **Wheeler's at The King's Arms** with rm
Midhurst Rd, South : 1 mi on A286 ✉ GU27 3HA – ✆ (01428)
652 005 – www.wheelerskingsarms.com
6 rm ⊑ – ✝£ 110 ✝✝£ 120   **Rest** – Menu £ 20 – Carte £ 26/36
♦ Attractive stone-built former pub with pleasant garden and professional, attentive service. Spacious, linen-laid restaurant boasts velvet curtains, open fire and cartoon prints. Extensive menu offers Marco Pierre White classics. Simple, compact, modern bedrooms.

FERRENSBY – North Yorkshire – see Knaresborough

FLAUNDEN – Hertfordshire – pop. 5 468   12 A2
▶ London 35 mi – Reading 43 mi – Luton 23 mi – Milton Keynes 42 mi

🍺 **Bricklayers Arms**
Hogpits Bottom ✉ HP3 0PH – ✆ (01442) 833 322 – www.bricklayersarms.com
– Closed 25 December
Rest – Carte £ 26/39
♦ Smart pub tucked away in a small hamlet. There are no snacks, just traditional, hearty, French-inspired dishes and old-school puddings. Wine list is a labour of love, featuring boutique Australian wines.

FLETCHING – East Sussex – **504** U30/3 – pop. 1 722
8 A2

▶ London 45 mi – Brighton 20 mi – Eastbourne 24 mi – Maidstone 20 mi

Griffin Inn with rm
✉ TN22 3SS – ℰ (01825) 722 890 – www.thegriffininn.co.uk – *Closed 25 December*
13 rm ⊒ – †£ 60/80 ††£ 145
Rest – *(meals in bar Sunday dinner)* Carte £ 20/27

♦ Hugely characterful brick coaching inn, under the same ownership for over 30 years. Various rooms and sizeable garden/terrace with wood burning oven for summer BBQs. British and Italian classics. Individually decorated bedrooms accessed via narrow, sloping corridors.

FOLKESTONE – Kent – **504** X30 – pop. 45 273 ▌Great Britain
9 D2

▶ London 76 mi – Brighton 76 mi – Dover 8 mi – Maidstone 33 mi
Access Channel Tunnel : Eurotunnel information and reservations ℰ (08705) 353535
ℹ Bouverie Place Shopping Centre ℰ (01303) 25 85 94, www.discoverfolkestone.co.uk
◉ The Leas★ (≤★) Z

Relish without rest
4 Augusta Gardens ✉ CT20 2RR – ℰ (01303) 850 952 – www.hotelrelish.co.uk
– *Closed 22 December-2 January*
Zn
10 rm ⊒ – †£ 69/95 ††£ 105/145

♦ Large Regency townhouse overlooking private parkland. Stylish black canopy covered entrance; modish furnishings. Handy food and drink area at foot of stairs. Light, airy bedrooms.

Rocksalt with rm
4-5 Fish Market ✉ CT19 6AA – ℰ (01303) 468 843
– www.rocksaltfolkestone.co.uk – *Closed Sunday dinner and Monday*
Zx
4 rm – †£ 75/85 ††£ 85/100
Rest – Menu £ 18 (weekday lunch) – Carte £ 22/55

♦ Set within a stylish harbourfront eco-building affording lovely sea views. Smart cantilevered dining room with full-length windows opening onto a terrace; semi open air bar upstairs. Menus mix seafood and local meats; veg is from their farm. Nearby, bedrooms boast antique beds, Egyptian linen and wet rooms.

FORDINGBRIDGE – Hampshire – **503** O31 – pop. 5 755
6 A2

▶ London 101 mi – Bournemouth 17 mi – Salisbury 11 mi – Southampton 22 mi
ℹ Salisbury St ℰ (01425) 65 45 60, www.visit-hampshire.co.uk

at Stuckton Southeast : 1 mi by B 3078 – ✉ Fordingbridge

Three Lions
Stuckton Rd ✉ SP6 2HF – ℰ (01425) 652 489
– www.thethreelionsrestaurant.co.uk – *Closed last 2 weeks February*
7 rm – †£ 69/79 ††£ 80/125, ⊒ £ 8.75
Rest – *(closed Sunday dinner and Monday)* Menu £ 25 (weekday lunch)
– Carte £ 35/45

♦ Traditional pine-furnished former farmhouse on quiet rural lane. Pleasant bedrooms are located among various adjoining buildings. Blackboard offers well-presented dishes with classical undertones – which can be more elaborate than descriptions imply.

FOREST GREEN – Surrey – pop. 1 843 – ✉ Dorking
7 D2

▶ London 34 mi – Guildford 13 mi – Horsham 10 mi

Parrot Inn
✉ RH5 5RZ – ℰ (01306) 621 339 – www.theparrot.co.uk – *Closed 25 December and Sunday dinner*
Rest – Carte £ 20/31

♦ Traditional 17C pub set on the village green. Well-priced, generously proportioned dishes use produce from the pub's own farm. Homemade bread, cheese, cakes and preserves for sale.

FOLKESTONE

shley Ave	X 3
ack Bull Rd	X, Y 4
ouverie Pl.	Z 6
adstone Rd	Y 8
nterbury Rd	X 9
astle Rd	X 12
heriton High St.	X 14
heriton Pl.	Z 13
herry Garden Lane	X 15
fton Crescent	X 16
fton Rd.	Z 17
rlocks (The)	Y 20
rl's Ave	X 21
ace Hill	Y 22
uildhall St	YZ 23
rbour App. Rd.	Z 25
rbour St	Z 24
nghorne Gardens	Z 27
anor Rd	Z 28
arine Terrace	Z 29
ddelburg Sq.	Z 30
orth St.	Y 32
d High St.	YZ
nd Hill Rd	X 33
dnor Bridge Rd	Y 34
membrance (Rd of)	Z 35
ndezvous St	Z 37
land Pl.	Y 38
ndgate High St	Y 39
ndgate Rd	Z
orncliffe Rd.	Y 41
ekiln Lane	Y 42
ntine St.	Y
nity Gardens	Z 43
ctoria Grove	Y 45
est Terrace	Z 47

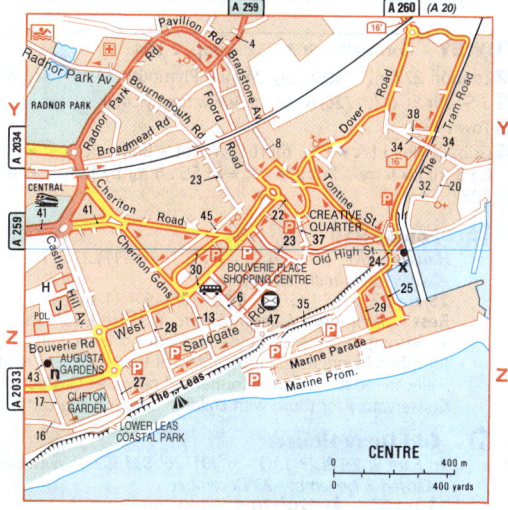

Fancy a last minute break?
Check hotel websites to take advantage of price promotions.

FOREST ROW – East Sussex – 504 U30 – pop. 3 623   8 A2

London 35 mi – Brighton 26 mi – Eastbourne 30 mi – Maidstone 32 mi
Royal Ashdown Forest Forest Row, Chapel Lane, (01342) 82 20 18

FOREST ROW

Ashdown Park
Colemans Hatch Rd, South : 3.25 mi by A 22 ✉ RH18 5JR
– ℰ (01342) 824 988 – www.ashdownpark.com
94 rm ⊑ – †£ 140/160 ††£ 240/300 – 5 suites
Rest *Anderida* – Menu £ 25/39 – Carte £ 43/52
• Impressive Victorian building in extensive parkland. Luxury country house interior boasts grand staircases, impressive halls and open-fired lounges. Huge bedrooms display antiques and feature beds. Formal restaurant offers classical cooking and good estate views.

FORTON – Lancashire – 502 M25 ▮ Great Britain 20 A1

▶ London 236 mi – Blackpool 18 mi – Manchester 45 mi
◉ Lancaster - Castle★, N : 5.5 mi by A 6

Bay Horse Inn with rm
Bay Horse Ln, North : 1.25 mi by A 6 on Quernmore rd ✉ LA2 0HR – ℰ (01524) 791 204 – www.bayhorseinn.com – Closed Sunday dinner and Monday except bank holidays
2 rm ⊑ – †£ 75/89 ††£ 75/89   **Rest** – Menu £ 22 (lunch) **s** – Carte £ 22/36 **s**
• Cosy pub in a pleasant rural location, with characterful interior and attractive terrace. Seasonal, locally sourced produce is crafted into a mix of classic and modern dishes. Beautifully appointed bedrooms are housed in the nearby corn store.

FOTHERINGHAY Northants – 504 S26 – see Oundle

FOWEY – Cornwall – 503 G32 – pop. 2 064 1 B2

▶ London 277 mi – Newquay 24 mi – Plymouth 34 mi – Truro 22 mi
ℹ 5 South St ℰ (01726) 83 36 16, www.fowey.co.uk
◉ Town★★
◉ Gribbin Head (≤★★) 6 mi rtn on foot – Bodinnick (≤★★) - Lanteglos Church★, E : 5 mi by ferry – Polruan (≤★★) SE : 6 mi by ferry – Polkerris★, W : 2 mi by A 3082

Fowey Hall
*Hanson Drive, West : 0.5 mi off A 3082 ✉ PL23 1ET – ℰ (01726) 833 866
– www.foweyhallhotel.co.uk*
25 rm ⊑ – †£ 145/230 ††£ 170/245 – 11 suites
Rest – *(light lunch Monday-Saturday)* Carte £ 23/43 **s**
• Striking 19C manor house overlooking town, with ornate library and period-furnished lounge/billiard room. Mix of traditional and modern bedrooms. Families well-catered for; trendy, informal feel pervades. Oak-panelled restaurant for adults. Conservatory for those with children. Classical à la carte has modern touches.

Old Quay House
*28 Fore St ✉ PL23 1AQ – ℰ (01726) 833 302 – www.theoldquayhouse.com
– Closed 7 November-23 December*
11 rm ⊑ – †£ 120/170 ††£ 140/340
Rest – *(closed lunch October-April)* Carte £ 35/52
• Friendly boutique hotel, run by experienced owner. Stylish interior has black and white theme; great outlook from terrace. Bedrooms range from small standard to penthouse – some have balconies and water views. Chic, informal bar-cum-restaurant with modern menu.

✂ Bistro
24 Fore St. ✉ PL23 1AQ – ℰ (01726) 832 322 – www.tiffinsbistro.co.uk – Closed 25 December and 1 January
Rest – Menu £ 19 – Carte £ 23/30
• Former deli; now a relaxed, cosy, all day eatery. Upstairs restaurant open in evening. Modern European dishes range from sandwiches and pizza to bouillabaisse and beef Bourguignon.

FOWEY

at Golant North : 3 mi by B 3269 – ✉ Fowey

Cormorant ⌘
✉ PL23 1LL – ℰ (01726) 833 426 – www.cormoranthotel.co.uk
14 rm ⌑ – †£ 80/170 ††£ 160/200
Rest – (closed lunch Monday and Tuesday) (booking essential for non residents) Menu £ 30 (dinner) – Carte (except dinner in winter) £ 29/45
● Well-run hotel in superb waterside position. At only one room deep, all its bedrooms overlook the estuary; superior rooms boast balconies. Lounge, bar and formal, linen-laid restaurant. Appealing seasonal menus feature local meats and interesting seafood dishes.

FREATHY – Cornwall – see Millbrook

FRESSINGFIELD – Suffolk – **504** X26   **15** D2
▶ London 104 mi – Ipswich 34 mi – Lowestoft 27 mi

Fox & Goose Inn
Church Rd ✉ IP21 5PB – ℰ (01379) 586 247 – www.foxandgoose.net – Closed 1 week early January, 25-30 December and Monday
Rest – (booking advisable) Menu £ 18 (lunch) – Carte £ 29/36
● Attractive 16C pub opposite the duck pond, with wooden beams, open fireplaces and pleasant terrace. Classic pub dishes and local cask ales. More modern, original dishes in upstairs restaurant.

FRILSHAM – West Berkshire – see Yattendon

FRISTON – Suffolk – see Aldeburgh

FRITHSDEN – Hertfordshire – see Hemel Hempstead

FRITTON – Norfolk   **15** D2
▶ London 133 mi – Great Yarmouth 8 mi – Norwich 19 mi

Fritton House ⌘
Church Ln ✉ NR31 9HA – ℰ (01493) 484 008 – www.adnams.co.uk
8 rm ⌑ – †£ 120/140 ††£ 120/140 – 1 suite   **Rest** – Carte £ 13/32
● Attractive 15C former coaching inn with period features, at the heart of the Somerleyton Estate. Cosy drawing room. Stylish bedrooms with old beams and modern bathrooms. Rustic bar and dining area with terrace. Pub dishes at lunch; restaurant fare at dinner.

FROGGATT EDGE – Derbyshire – **502** P24   **16** A1
▶ London 167 mi – Bakewell 6 mi – Sheffield 11 mi

Chequers Inn with rm
on A 625 ✉ S32 3ZJ – ℰ (01433) 630 231 – www.chequers-froggatt.com
– Closed 25 December
5 rm ⌑ – †£ 77/102 ††£ 77/102   **Rest** – Carte £ 24/30
● Traditional 16C inn built right into the stone boulders of Froggat Edge and boasting a direct path up to the peak. Cooking is unfussy, tasty and largely classical, with more imaginative specials. Bedrooms are comfy; the one to the rear is quietest and best.

FROME – Somerset – **503** M/N30 – pop. 24 171   **4** C2
▶ London 118 mi – Bristol 24 mi – Southampton 52 mi – Swindon 44 mi

Babington House ⌘
Babington, Northwest : 6.5 mi by A 362 on Vobster rd
✉ BA11 3RW – ℰ (01373) 812 266 – www.babingtonhouse.co.uk
32 rm – ††£ 190/720, ⌑ £ 16
Rest *Orangery* – Carte £ 27/32
● Country house with a vivid difference: Georgian exterior; cool, fashionable inner, with a laid-back, bohemian feel. Good health club, children's play area and even a cinema. Modern, understated bedrooms. Large conservatory dining room with solid stone floor; appealing Mediterranean menu.

ENGLAND

FULLER STREET – Essex – **504** V28 – pop. 50   13 C2

▶ London 52 mi

Square & Compasses
✉ CM3 2BB – ☏ (01245) 361 477 – www.thesquareandcompasses.co.uk – Closed 1 January
Rest – (closed 25-26 December and Sunday dinner) (booking essential)
Carte £ 20/26
♦ Charming little pub with low beams, wood burning stoves and character aplenty. Unfussy menus of freshly made pub classics and unashamedly traditional puddings; daily blackboards offer locally shot game and fish caught nearby. Friendly team.

FULMER – **504**   11 D3

▶ London 21 mi – Croydon 49 mi – Barnet 30 mi – Ealing 13 mi

Black Horse
Windmill Rd ✉ SL3 6HD – ☏ (01753) 663 183 – www.blackhorsefulmer.co.uk – Closed 25-26 December
Rest – Carte £ 23/28
♦ 17C whitewashed inn set in a chocolate box village. Characterful beamed bar with log fire and dining room overlooking the gardens. Gutsy modern dishes; seasonality and provenance paramount.

FUNTINGTON – West Sussex – **504** R31 – see Chichester

FYFIELD – Oxfordshire – see Oxford

GATESHEAD – Tyne and Wear – **501** P19 – pop. 78 403 Great Britain   24 B2

▶ London 282 mi – Durham 16 mi – Middlesbrough 38 mi – Newcastle upon Tyne 1 mi

Access Tyne Tunnel (toll)

🛈 Prince Consort Rd ☏ (0191) 433 84 20, www.newcastlegateshead.com

⛳ Ravensworth Wrekenton Angel View, Long Bank, ☏ (0191) 487 60 14

⛳ Heworth Gingling Gate, ☏ (0191) 469 98 32

◉ Beamish : North of England Open Air Museum★★ **AC**, SW : 6 mi by A 692 and A 6076 BX

Plan : see Newcastle upon Tyne

Stables Lodge without rest
South Farm, Lamesley, Southwest : 5 mi by A 167 and Belle Vue Bank on A 692
✉ NE11 0ET – ☏ (0191) 492 17 56 – www.thestableslodge.co.uk
4 rm ⌁ – ♦£ 65/74 ♦♦£ 85/138
♦ Rustic and cosy former farmhouse, just off the A1. Individually decorated, very comfortable bedrooms; the Red Room is the most luxurious; the Garden Room has its own hot tub.

Six
Baltic Centre for Contemporary Art, Gateshead Quays, South Shore Rd
✉ NE8 3BA – ☏ (0191) 440 49 48 – www.sixbaltic.com – Closed 25 December, 1 January and Sunday dinner   BX**x**
Rest – Menu £ 18 (lunch) – Carte £ 32/41
♦ Fantastic location on top floor of Baltic Centre; floor to ceiling windows afford views of city's skyline, the Tyne and the Millennium Bridge. Modern brasserie, with a menu to match.

GATESHEAD

at Low Fell South : 2 mi on A 167 - **BX** - ✉ Gateshead

   Eslington Villa
8 Station Rd, West : 0.75 mi by Belle Vue Bank, turning left at T junction, right at roundabout then taking first right turn ✉ *NE9 6DR –* ℰ *(0191) 487 60 17*
– www.eslingtonvilla.co.uk – Closed 25-26 December
18 rm – †£ 80 ††£ 100/120
Rest – *(closed Saturday lunch and Sunday dinner)* Menu £ 19/27
♦ Well-run, stylish, privately owned hotel 10 minutes' drive from city centre. Nicely furnished lounge bar leads from smart reception. Attractively styled, modern bedrooms. Classical dining room and conservatory; wide-ranging, traditional menu with modern twists.

GEORGE GREEN – Buckinghamshire   11 D3
▶ London 23

Pinewood
Wexham Park Ln, Uxbridge Rd, on A 412 ✉ *SL3 6AP –* ℰ *(01753) 896 400*
– www.pinewoodhotel.co.uk – Closed 25-28 December
49 rm – †£ 65/145 ††£ 95/155
Rest *Eden* – Carte £ 24/35 **s**
♦ Located on the A412 close to Slough; ideal for those on business or on a trip to Legoland. Functional, modern rooms with some flair. Modern dishes with a twist in Eden.

GERRARDS CROSS – Buckinghamshire – 504 S29   11 D3
▶ London 22 mi – Birmingham 106 mi – Bristol 112 mi – Cardiff 145 mi

Three Oaks
Austenwood Rd, Northwest : 0.75 mi by A 413 on Gold Hill rd ✉ *SL9 8NL*
– ℰ *(01753) 899 016 – www.thethreeoaksgx.co.uk – Closed dinner Sunday and bank holidays*
Rest – Menu £ 19 (lunch) – Carte £ 24/38
♦ Revamped pub with reconditioned furniture to add a lived-in look. Two dining rooms; choose the brighter one overlooking the terrace and garden. Bright young service and satisfying cooking that sticks to the tried-and-tested.

GILLINGHAM – Dorset – 503 N30 – pop. 8 630   4 C3
▶ London 116 mi – Bournemouth 34 mi – Bristol 46 mi – Southampton 52 mi
🄖 Stourhead★★★ **AC**, N : 9 mi by B 3092, B 3095 and B 3092

   Stock Hill Country House
Stock Hill, West : 1.5 mi on B 3081 ✉ *SP8 5NR –* ℰ *(01747) 823 626*
– www.stockhillhouse.co.uk
8 rm (dinner included) – †£ 130/180 ††£ 260/325
Rest – *(booking essential)* Menu £ 30/40
♦ Well-run Georgian country house with later extensions, in attractive, mature grounds. Classical lounges boast heavy fabrics and antiques. Bedrooms, in the main house and stables, are a mix of cottagey and contemporary country house styles; all have good facilities. Formal, two-roomed restaurant with own kitchen garden.

GITTISHAM – Devon – 503 K31 – see Honiton

GODSHILL – Isle of Wight – 504 Q32 – see Wight (Isle of)

GOLANT Cornwall – Cornwall – 503 G32 – see Fowey

GOLDSBOROUGH – North Yorkshire – see Whitby

GOREY – 503 P33 – see Channel Islands (Jersey)

GORING – Oxfordshire – 503 Q29 – pop. 4 193 🇬🇧 Great Britain   10 B3
▶ London 56 mi – Oxford 16 mi – Reading 12 mi
🄖 Ridgeway Path★★

GORING

XX Leatherne Bottel
The Bridleway, North : 1.5 mi by B 4009 ⊠ RG8 0HS – ℰ *(01491) 872 667*
– www.leathernebottel.co.uk – Closed Sunday dinner
Rest *– (booking essential)* Menu £ 20 (lunch) – Carte £ 35/46

♦ Delightful Thameside restaurant with lovely summer terrace. Menus fuse traditional recipes with interesting, modern combinations. Leaves picked fresh from garden. Impressive Chablis selection.

GORRAN HAVEN – Cornwall – 503 F33   1 B3
▶ London 260 mi – Plymouth 53 mi – Torbay 80 mi – Torquay 83 mi

Llawnroc
Chute Ln ⊠ PL26 6NU – ℰ *(01726) 843 461 – www.thellawnrochotel.co.uk*
18 rm ☐ – †£ 96/208 ††£ 120/260 **Rest** *– (bar lunch)* Menu £ 43

♦ Unpretentious boutique hotel built around The Gwineas pub; enjoy tea on the terrific terrace, fish in the pub or more intimate meals in the main dining room. Plenty of contemporary design touches to the boldly coloured, well-equipped bedrooms. A hotel popular with families.

GOVETON – Devon – 503 I33 – see Kingsbridge

GRANGE-OVER-SANDS – Cumbria – 502 L21 – pop. 4 835   21 A3
🟩 Great Britain
▶ London 268 mi – Kendal 13 mi – Lancaster 24 mi
🅘 Main St ℰ (015395) 3 40 26, www.grange-over-sands.com
🅘 Meathop Rd, ℰ (015395) 3 31 80
🅖 Cartmel Priory★, NW : 3 mi

Netherwood
Lindale Rd ⊠ LA11 6ET – ℰ *(015395) 32 552 – www.netherwood-hotel.co.uk*
34 rm ☐ – †£ 75/85 ††£ 120/160 **Rest** – Menu £ 18/34

♦ Impressive castellated mansion on the hillside, affording lovely bay views. Traditional guest areas display wood panelling and original features. Simple, well-maintained bedrooms; more contemporary rooms in outbuildings. Formal dining comes with great outlook.

Clare House
Park Rd ⊠ LA11 7HQ – ℰ *(015395) 33 026 – www.clarehousehotel.co.uk – 27 March-9 November*
18 rm (dinner included) ☐ – †£ 86/159 ††£ 172/182
Rest *– (dinner only and Sunday lunch) (booking essential for non-residents)*
Menu £ 36

♦ Family-run Victorian house set in lovely gardens, overlooking Morecambe Bay. Two classical sitting rooms. Stylish, boldly coloured bedrooms in main house; smaller, simpler rooms with balconies in wing. Smart, modern dining room offers traditional daily menus.

---

at Cartmel Northwest : 3 mi – ⊠ Grange-Over-Sands

XX L'Enclume (Simon Rogan) with rm
Cavendish St ⊠ LA11 6PZ – ℰ *(015395) 36 362 – www.lenclume.co.uk*
12 rm ☐ – †£ 69 ††£ 159/199
Rest *– (closed lunch Monday-Tuesday) (booking essential)* Menu £ 25 (lunch)
– Carte £ 69/89
Spec. Vintage potatoes with onion ashes, lovage and sorrel. Native lobster in pig skin, grilled wild leeks and sea purslane. Coniston oatmeal stout ice cream with apple, sweet bracken and malt.

♦ Stone-built former blacksmiths in an attractive little village, run by a friendly team. Refined, original cooking uses modern techniques and is underpinned by a classical style. Flavours are clean and clear, and home-grown or foraged produce features highly. Choice of 8 or 13 course menu. Smart, traditionally styled bedrooms are spread about the village.

GRANGE-OVER-SANDS

XX **Rogan and Company** VISA ⦿
The Square ✉ *LA11 6QD* – ☏ *(015395) 35 917* – *www.roganandcompany.co.uk*
– *Closed Monday in low season*
Rest – Carte £ 24/39
♦ Converted cottage by lovely stream; informal cousin to L'Enclume. Stylish, split-level interior with sofas, polished tables and high bar seating. Extensive menus of locally sourced produce.

GRANTHAM – Lincolnshire – **502** S25 – pop. 34 592 ▌Great Britain — 17 C2

▶ London 113 mi – Leicester 31 mi – Lincoln 29 mi – Nottingham 24 mi
i St Peter's Hill ☏ (01476) 40 61 66, www.granthamuk.com
Belton Park Londonthorpe Rd, Belton Lane, ☏ (01476) 56 73 99
De Vere Belton Woods H., ☏ (01476) 59 32 00
◉ St Wulfram's Church ★
◉ Belton House ★ **AC**, N : 2.5 mi by A 607. Belvoir Castle ★★ **AC**, W : 6 mi by A 607

at Hough-on-the-Hill North : 6.75 mi by A 607 – ✉ Grantham

XX **Brownlow Arms** with rm 🛜 AC rest, ⟨ʼ¹⟩ P VISA ⦿
High Rd ✉ *NG32 2AZ* – ☏ *(01400) 250 234*
4 rm ⇌ – ♦£ 65 ♦♦£ 98
Rest – *(closed Sunday dinner and Monday) (dinner only and Sunday lunch)*
Carte £ 28/40
♦ Characterful former shooting lodge for the nearby Belton Estate, with wood-panelled walls and large open fireplaces. Lengthy menu and specials list offer classically based dishes with modern presentation. Lovely terrace and friendly service. Delightful bedrooms are furnished with contemporary fabrics and period pieces.

at Harlaxton Southwest : 2.5 mi on A 607 – ✉ Grantham

ID **Gregory** 🛜 P VISA ⦿
The Drift, Southwest : 2 mi by A 607 ✉ *NG32 1AD* – ☏ *(01476) 577 076*
– *www.thegregory.co.uk* – *Closed dinner 25-26 December and 1 January*
Rest – Carte £ 21/33
♦ Roadside community pub with spacious dining room and smaller lounge, both with very modern feel. Pub classics dominate the menu, with steaks, pies and old-fashioned puddings.

at Woolsthorpe-by-Belvoir West : 7.5 mi by A 607 – ✉ Grantham

ID **Chequers** with rm 🚗 🛜 P VISA ⦿ AE
Main St ✉ *NG32 1LU* – ☏ *(01476) 870 701* – *www.chequersinn.net* – *Closed dinner 25-26 December and 1 January*
4 rm ⇌ – ♦£ 50 ♦♦£ 70   **Rest** – Menu £ 17 (weekdays) – Carte £ 21/33
♦ Cosy, open-fired pub in a quaint village owned by the Belvoir Estate, and backing onto the local cricket pitch. Simple homemade and local offerings at lunch, supplemented by steaks and game at dinner. Crisply furnished, modern bedrooms located in the old stables.

at Great Gonerby Northwest : 2 mi on B 1174 – ✉ Grantham

XX **Harry's Place** P VISA ⦿
17 High St ✉ *NG31 8JS* – ☏ *(01476) 561 780* – *Closed 1 week August, 25-30 December, Sunday, Monday and bank holidays*
Rest – *(booking essential)* Carte £ 55/66
♦ Long-standing, intimate restaurant consisting of just three tables; run by dedicated and delightful husband and wife team. Warm, welcoming feel, with fresh flowers, candles and antiques. Classically based, hand-written menus offer two choices per course.

ENGLAND

215

GRANTHAM

at Dry Doddington Northwest : 11 mi by B 1174 and A 1

Wheatsheaf Inn
Main St ✉ NG23 5HU – ℰ (01400) 281 458 – www.wheatsheaf-pub.co.uk
– Closed Monday except bank holidays
Rest – Menu £ 15 (lunch) – Carte £ 23/28
♦ Smartly kept pub overlooking a pretty green, with cosy bar, laid-back restaurant and small courtyard. Simple, unfussy light bites lunch menu; more ambitious à la carte with evening specials.

GRASMERE – Cumbria – 502 K20 – ✉ Ambleside ∎ Great Britain 21 A2

▶ London 282 mi – Carlisle 43 mi – Kendal 18 mi
👁 Dove Cottage★ **AC** AY **A**
🅶 Lake Windermere★★, SE : by A 591 AZ

Plans : see Ambleside

Rothay Garden
Broadgate ✉ LA22 9RJ – ℰ (01539) 435 334 – www.rothaygarden.com
30 rm ⌑ – †£ 103/108 ††£ 185/195   AYs
Rest – Menu 40 (dinner) **s** – Carte £ 29/38 **s**
♦ Old Lakeland house with gardens leading to river and stylish, contemporary inner. Boldly coloured lounges. Contemporary bedrooms with good facilities: choose those with patios or the loft suites. Neat, linen-laid dining room has lovely outlook and modern menu.

Moss Grove Organic without rest
✉ LA22 9SW – ℰ (015394) 35 251 – www.mossgrove.com – Closed 25-26 December   BZs
11 rm ⌑ – †£ 99/114 ††£ 114/129
♦ Large house with stylish, modern interior, which features some reclaimed furnishings. Sizeable bedrooms boast feature walls: several have four-posters; one has a hot tub. Organic breakfasts.

Grasmere
Broadgate ✉ LA22 9TA – ℰ (015394) 35 277 – www.grasmerehotel.co.uk
– Closed January   BZr
13 rm ⌑ – †£ 55/63 ††£ 110/126 – 1 suite
Rest – *(dinner only) (booking essential for non-residents)* Menu £ 30 **s**
♦ Small Victorian house close to the village centre, with the River Rothay running through the garden. Traditionally styled lounge and bar. Similarly classical bedrooms, with colourful fabrics adding a modern touch. Pine-roofed dining room overlooks the garden.

Oak Bank
Broadgate ✉ LA22 9TA – ℰ (015394) 35 217 – www.lakedistricthotel.co.uk
– Closed 2-26 January and weekdays 12 November-26 December   BZx
14 rm (dinner included) ⌑ – †£ 84/102 ††£ 150/192
Rest *Restaurant* – see restaurant listing
♦ Victorian house with pretty rear garden, set on the edge of a famous village. Relax beside a converted range in the sitting room or open-fire in the lounge-bar. Stylish, modern bedrooms boast comfortable beds and contemporary furnishings.

Lake View Country House without rest
Lake View Dr ✉ LA22 9TD – ℰ (015394) 35 384 – www.lakeview-grasmere.com
4 rm ⌑ – ††£ 102/112   BZc
♦ Traditional country house run by an enthusiastic owner. Cosy, homely bedrooms display some antiques; two rooms have spa baths. Linen-laid breakfast room. Yoghurts and compotes are homemade.

GRASMERE

XX Restaurant – at Oak Bank Hotel
Broadgate ⊠ *LA22 9TA –* ℰ *(015394) 35 217 – www.lakedistricthotel.co.uk*
– Closed 2-26 January and weekdays 12 November-26 December **BZx**
Rest *– (dinner only)* Menu £ 28

♦ Split-roomed hotel restaurant in a Victorian house, with pleasant conservatory extension overlooking the garden. Concise daily menu features interesting modern dishes crafted from local, seasonal produce. Puddings are classically based.

GRASSINGTON – North Yorkshire – 502 O21 – pop. 1 102   22 A2
– ⊠ Skipton

▶ London 240 mi – Bradford 30 mi – Burnley 28 mi – Leeds 37 mi
ℹ National Park Centre, Colvend, Hebden Rd ℰ (01756) 75 16 90, www.grassington.uk.com

Ashfield House
Summers Fold, off Main St ⊠ *BD23 5AE –* ℰ *(01756) 752 584*
– www.ashfieldhouse.co.uk
8 rm ⊑ – †£ 85/120 ††£ 96/136
Rest *– (closed Sunday in winter) (dinner only) (booking essential for non-residents)* Menu £ 36

♦ Bright, cheery hotel with larger-than-life owner. Cosy beams and flag floors blend well with Mediterranean colours in the bedrooms. Split-level rear cottage boasts spiral staircase and terrace. Modern menus rely on local produce; vegetarian dishes a speciality.

Grassington Lodge without rest
8 Wood Ln ⊠ *BD23 5LU –* ℰ *(01756) 752 518 – www.grassingtonlodge.co.uk*
12 rm ⊑ – †£ 70/95 ††£ 80/160

♦ Georgian stone house set on a cobbled street close to the square. Fresh, modern inner with comfy lounge, bar and smart terrace. Neat bedrooms: those in the eaves are the best. Good extras.

XX Grassington House with rm
5 The Square ⊠ *BD23 5AQ –* ℰ *(01756) 752 406*
– www.grassingtonhousehotel.co.uk
9 rm ⊑ – †£ 90 ††£ 125   **Rest** – Menu £ 17 (lunch) – Carte £ 29/41

♦ Georgian house with large bar-lounge and two-roomed restaurant; one a conservatory with grand piano. Delightful service. Classical menu displays Mediterranean touches and includes home-bred pork. Smart, modern bedrooms. Breakfast offers home-cured bacon/sausages.

GREAT DUNMOW – Essex – 504 V28 – pop. 5 943   13 C2

▶ London 42 mi – Cambridge 27 mi – Chelmsford 13 mi – Colchester 24 mi

XXX Starr with rm
Market Pl ⊠ *CM6 1AX –* ℰ *(01371) 874 321 – www.the-starr.co.uk – Closed 27-31 December and 2-5 January*
8 rm ⊑ – †£ 60/90 ††£ 95/120
Rest *– (closed Sunday dinner and Monday)* Menu £ 40 (dinner) – Carte lunch £ 39/49

♦ Former 15C pub with rustic bar and fire. Characterful restaurant has exposed beams and conservatory. Strong, interesting cooking, traditionally inspired. Smart bedrooms.

X Square 1
15 High St. ⊠ *CM6 1AB –* ℰ *(01371) 859 922 – www.square1restaurant.co.uk*
– Closed 25-26 December and Sunday dinner
Rest – Menu £ 13 (lunch) – Carte £ 23/37

♦ Pretty little whitewashed building; once a 14C monastic reading room. Much original character remains in the form of exposed beams and low ceilings – which contrast with vibrant modern art. Unfussy monthly menu has Mediterranean leanings.

at Great Easton North : 2.75 mi by B 184

Green Man
Mile End Green, Northeast : 1 mi by B 184 on Mile End Green rd ⊠ *CM6 2DN*
– ℰ *(01371) 852 285* – *www.thegreenmanrestaurant.com* – *Closed two weeks January, Monday and Tuesday*
Rest – *(closed Sunday dinner)* Carte £ 25/38

♦ Contemporary pub, 20 minutes from Stansted Airport. Dishes are more of a restaurant than pub persuasion, and are coupled with attentive, assured service. Terrace and garden overlook fields.

GREAT EASTON – Essex – **504** U28 – see Great Dunmow

GREAT GONERBY – Lincolnshire – **502** S25 – see Grantham

GREAT MALVERN – Worcestershire – **503** N27 – pop. 35 588   **18** B3

▣ London 127 mi – Birmingham 34 mi – Cardiff 66 mi – Gloucester 24 mi
🛈 21 Church St ℰ (01684) 89 22 89, www.great-malvern.co.uk

Bredon House without rest
34 Worcester Rd ⊠ *WR14 4AA* – ℰ *(01684) 566 990* – *www.bredonhouse.co.uk*
10 rm ☑ – †£ 55/75 ††£ 90/110   Ba

♦ Elegant, Grade II listed Regency house with spectacular views. Personable owners make breakfast a special event. Most of the individually styled rooms enjoy the fine vista.

Cotford
51 Graham Rd ⊠ *WR14 2HU* – ℰ *(01684) 572 427* – *www.cotfordhotel.co.uk*
15 rm ☑ – †£ 65/79 ††£ 125   Bs
Rest *L'Amuse Bouche* – *(dinner only and Sunday lunch)* Menu £ 30

♦ Recently refurbished Victorian gothic stone building in landscaped gardens; built in 1851 for the Bishop of Worcester. Modern but homely guest areas; cosy bedrooms. Contemporary dining room with garden views; seasonal menu of local, organic produce.

at Guarlford East : 2.5 mi on B 4211

Plough and Harrow
Rhydd Rd, East : 0.5 mi on B 4211 ⊠ *WR13 6NY* – ℰ *(01684) 310 453*
– *www.theploughandharrow.co.uk* – *Closed 1 week spring,1 week autumn, 25-26 December, 1 January, Sunday dinner and Monday*
Rest – Carte £ 21/36

♦ Passionately run pub set off the beaten track. Light lunches; short evening à la carte; simpler midweek bar snacks. Seasonality is key and much of the fruit/veg comes from their garden.

at Malvern Wells South : 2 mi on A 449 – ⊠ Malvern

Cottage in the Wood
Holywell Rd ⊠ *WR14 4LG* – ℰ *(01684) 588 860* – *www.cottageinthewood.co.uk*
30 rm ☑ – †£ 79/121 ††£ 99/198   **Rest** – Carte £ 22/37 s   Az

♦ Three detached properties with woodland behind, superbly set and boasting amazing views down the valley. Smart, good-sized bedrooms boast modern soft furnishings; most rooms have views. Cosy bar-lounge. Bright restaurant with full-length windows and modern menu.

at Colwall Southwest : 3 mi on B 4218 – ⊠ Great Malvern

Colwall Park
⊠ *WR13 6QG* – ℰ *(01684) 540 000* – *www.colwall.co.uk*
21 rm ☑ – †£ 85/100 ††£ 125/135 – 1 suite   Av
Rest *Seasons* – *(booking essential at lunch)* Menu £ 25 – Carte £ 22/35

♦ Passionately run, part red-brick, part black and white timbered house with lovely gardens, nestled in the Malvern Hills. Pleasant lounges. Comfy bedrooms range from traditional to more contemporary styles. Brasserie menu available in bar or linen-laid restaurant.

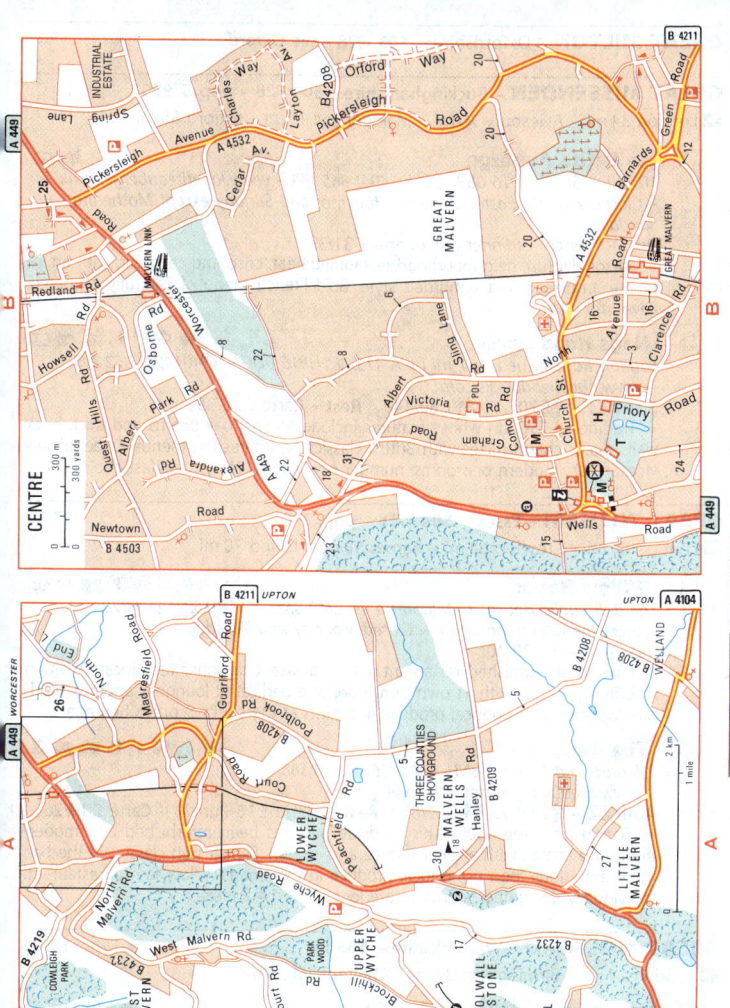

GREAT MALVERN

Street	Grid
Albert Rd South	B 3
Blackmore Park Rd.	A 5
Church St.	B
Clerkenwell Crescent	B 6
Cockshot Rd	B 8
Court Rd	A 12
Croft Bank	A 13
Happy Valley off St Ann's Rd	B 15
Imperial Rd	B 16
Jubilee Drive	A 17
Lygon Bank	B 18
Madresfield Rd	B 20
Moorlands Rd	B 22
North Malvern Rd	B 23
Orchard Rd	B 24
Richmond Rd	B 25
Townsend Way	A 26
Upper Welland Rd	A 27
Walwyn Rd	A, B 29
Wells Rd.	B 30
Zetland Rd	B 31

219

GREAT MILTON – Oxfordshire – **503** Q28 – see Oxford

GREAT MISSENDEN – Buckinghamshire – **504** R28 – pop. 7 980 **11** C2
▶ London 34 mi – Aylesbury 10 mi – Maidenhead 19 mi – Oxford 35 mi

La Petite Auberge
107 High St ✉ HP16 0BB – ℘ (01494) 865 370 – www.lapetiteauberge.co.uk
– Closed 2 weeks Easter, 2 weeks Christmas and Sunday except Mothering Sunday
Rest – French – *(dinner only)* Carte £ 31/39
♦ Personally run, neighbourhood restaurant; neat, crisp and candlelit, with an intimate ambience and unhurried style. Bold French menu of carefully prepared, flavourful dishes.

Nags Head with rm
London Rd, Southeast : 1 mi by A 413. ✉ HP16 0DG – ℘ (01494) 862 200
– www.nagsheadbucks.com
5 rm – †£ 70/130 ††£ 80/140 **Rest** – Carte £ 25/35
♦ Traditional 15C inn whose features include original oak beams and thick brick walls. Gallic charm mixes with British classics on interesting menus. Cheerful service. Stylish, modern bedrooms; number one is best. Tasty breakfast choice.

GREAT TOTHAM – Essex – **504** W28 – pop. 720 **13** C2
▶ London 59 mi – Croydon 64 mi – Barnet 58 mi – Ealing 70 mi

Willow Room
The Bull Public House, 2 Maldon Rd ✉ CM9 8NH – ℘ (01621) 894 020
– www.thewillowroom.co.uk – Closed Monday and Tuesday
Rest – Menu £ 20/40
♦ Luxuriously furnished restaurant with a pleasant designer feel, located within 'The Bull' pub but with its own front door and dedicated lounge. Elaborate, modern cooking relies on local produce and hints at the chef's Scottish heritage.

The Bull with rm
2 Maldon Rd ✉ CM9 8NH – ℘ (01621) 893 385
– www.thebullatgreattotham.co.uk
4 rm – †£ 59/75 ††£ 69/85 **Rest** – Menu £ 16 (lunch) – Carte £ 19/26
♦ Dating from the 1500s, this roadside pub has been refurbished and modernised and comes with a great terrace and garden. Expect pub classics in the bar; more ambitious food using local produce in the smart 'Willow Room' restaurant. Individually decorated bedrooms are located in the annexe.

GREAT WOLFORD – Warwickshire – **503** P27 **19** C3
▶ London 84 mi – Birmingham 37 mi – Cheltenham 26 mi

Fox & Hounds Inn with rm
✉ CV36 5NQ – ℘ (01608) 674 220 – www.thefoxandhoundsinn.com
– Closed first two weeks January, Sunday dinner and Monday
3 rm – †£ 60 ††£ 90 **Rest** – Carte £ 17/32
♦ Cosy, characterful, family-run country inn with traditional interior, low beams, hop bines and a large inglenook. Daily blackboard menus display rustic pub dishes of local, seasonal produce. Simple, pine-furnished bedrooms offer pleasant country views.

GREAT YARMOUTH – Norfolk – **504** Z26 – pop. 58 032 **15** D2
Great Britain
▶ London 126 mi – Cambridge 81 mi – Ipswich 53 mi – Norwich 20 mi
🛈 25 Marine Parade ℘ (01493) 84 63 45, www.great-yarmouth.co.uk
⛳ Gorleston Warren Rd, ℘ (01493) 66 19 11
⛳ Beach House Caister-on-Sea, Great Yarmouth & Caister, ℘ (01493) 72 86 99
◉ Norfolk Broads ★

GREAT YARMOUTH

XX Andover House with rm
28-30 Camperdown ⊠ NR30 3JB – ℰ (01493) 843 490
– www.andoverhouse.co.uk – Closed 23-30 December and Sunday dinner
16 rm ⊆ – †£ 67/89 ††£ 89/99 – 4 suites
Rest – *(dinner only) (residents only Sunday and Monday)* Menu £ 27 **s**
– Carte £ 27/48 **s**

• Modernised, listed Victorian property with a crisp, chic style and friendly, well-drilled service. Constantly evolving à la carte of modern, well-presented and accomplished dishes, with the occasional Asian touch. Simple, modern bedrooms; some with four-posters, some with large bay windows.

XX Seafood
85 North Quay ⊠ NR30 1JF – ℰ (01493) 856 009 – www.theseafood.co.uk
– Closed 2 weeks Christmas, last 2 weeks May, Saturday lunch, Sunday and bank holidays
Rest – Seafood – Menu £ 20 (lunch) – Carte £ 26/49

• Long-standing restaurant on the edge of town, run by friendly owners. Traditional interior boasts intimate booths, a lobster tank and fresh fish display. Reliable, classical seafood dishes.

GREAT WHITTINGTON – Northumberland – **501** O18 – see Corbridge

GREEN ISLAND – **503** P33 – see Channel Islands (Jersey)

GREETHAM – Rutland — **17** C2

▶ London 101 mi – Birmingham 86 mi – Liverpool 164 mi – Leeds 98 mi

Wheatsheaf Inn
1 Stretton Rd ⊠ LE15 7NP – ℰ (01572) 812 325
– www.wheatsheaf-greetham.co.uk – Closed first 2 weeks January, Monday except bank holidays and Sunday dinner
Rest – Carte £ 19/30

• The aroma of fresh bread is the first thing you notice at this simple, family-friendly country pub. Robust modern cooking comes with hints of the Med; cheaper cuts keep prices sensible and desserts are a must. Run by a charming couple.

GRETA BRIDGE – Durham – **502** O20 – see Barnard Castle

GRIMSTON – Norfolk – **504** V25 – see King's Lynn

GRINDLETON – Lancashire – **502** M22 – see Clitheroe

GRINSHILL – Shropshire – **503** L25 – see Shrewsbury

GROUVILLE – **503** M33 – pop. 4 658 – see Channel Islands (Jersey)

GUARLFORD – Worcestershire – see Great Malvern

GUERNSEY – Guernsey – **503** O/P33 – pop. 58 867 – see Channel Islands

GUILDFORD – Surrey – **504** S30 – pop. 68 601 ▮ Great Britain — **7** C1

▶ London 33 mi – Brighton 43 mi – Reading 27 mi – Southampton 49 mi

🛈 14 Tunsgate ℰ (01483) 44 43 33, www.guildford.gov.uk

◉ Clandon Park★★, E : 3 mi by A 246 Z – Hatchlands Park★, E : 6 mi by A 246 Z. Painshill★★, Cobham, NE : 10 m – Polesden Lacey★, E : 13 mi by A 246 Z and minor rd

Plan on next page

GUILDFORD

Bedford Rd	Y	2
Bridge St	Y	3
Castle St	Y	5
Chertsey St	Y	6
Commercial Rd	Y	8
Eastgate Gardens	Y	9
Friary Bridge	Y	12
Friary Centre	Y	
High St	Y	
Ladymead	Z	13
Leapale Lane	Y	15
Leapale Rd	Y	16
Leas Rd	Y	17
Market St	Y	18
Mary Rd	Y	19
Middle St	Z	20
Millbrook	Y	21
New Inn Lane	Z	22
North St	Y	
One Tree Hill Rd.	Y	24
Onslow St	Y	25
Park St	Y	27
Quarry St	Y	28
Stoughton Rd.	Z	30
Trood's Lane	Z	31
Tunsgate	Y	33
Tunsgate Shopping Centre	Y	
Warwick's Bench	Y	34
Woodbridge Rd	Z	37

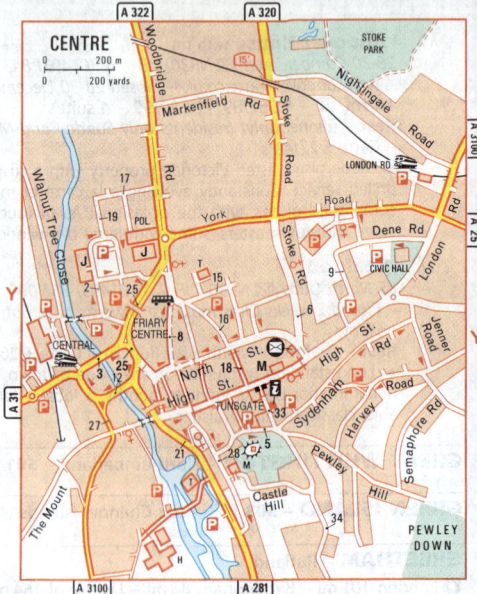

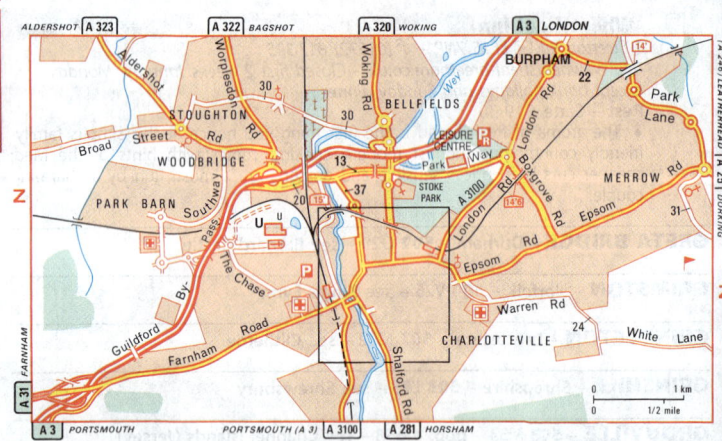

at Shere East : 6.75 mi by A 246 off A 25 - Z - ✉ Guildford

XX Kinghams   P VISA ◎ AE ①

Gomshall Ln ✉ GU5 9HE – ℰ (01483) 202 168
– www.kinghams-restaurant.co.uk – Closed 25 December-5 January, Sunday dinner and Monday
Rest – (booking essential) Menu £ 23 (weekday lunch) – Carte £ 26/39
♦ Popular restaurant in 17C cottage, set in an appealing village. Daily blackboard menu and fish specials are particularly good value. Adventurous modern menus feature bold combinations.

GULVAL – Cornwall – **503** D33 – see Penzance

HADLEIGH – Suffolk – **504** W27 – pop. 7 124 — **15** C3

▶ London 72 mi – Cambridge 49 mi – Colchester 17 mi – Ipswich 10 mi
🛈 29 High St ℰ (01473) 82 37 78, www.suffolktouristguide.com

↑ Edge Hall without rest
2 High St. ⊠ IP7 5AP – ℰ (01473) 822 458 – www.edgehall.co.uk – Closed 23-29 December
6 rm ⌸ – †£ 50/60 ††£ 85/99
• One of the oldest houses in the town (1590), with a Georgian façade. Spacious, comfy bedrooms are traditionally furnished, as are the communal areas. Very well-kept gardens.

HADLEY HEATH – Worcestershire – see Droitwich Spa

HALFORD – Warwickshire – **503** P27 – pop. 301 — **19** C3

▶ London 94 mi – Oxford 43 mi – Stratford-upon-Avon 8 mi

↑ Old Manor House without rest
Queens St ⊠ CV36 5BT – ℰ (01789) 740 264 – www.oldmanor-halford.co.uk – Closed 25-27 December
3 rm ⌸ – †£ 65 ††£ 90/100
• Characterful house in pretty little village, well-located for Stratford and the Cotswolds. Spacious garden next to the River Stour. Well-appointed drawing room and atmospheric bedrooms with rich fabrics.

HALFWAY BRIDGE – West Sussex – **504** R31 – see Petworth

HALIFAX – West Yorkshire – **502** O22 – pop. 83 570 — **22** B2

▶ London 205 mi – Bradford 8 mi – Burnley 21 mi – Leeds 15 mi
🛈 Piece Hall ℰ (01422) 36 87 25, www.visitcalderdale.com
⛳ Halifax Bradley Hall Holywell Green, ℰ (01422) 37 41 08
⛳ Halifax West End Highroad Well Paddock Lane, ℰ (01422) 34 18 78
⛳ Ryburn Sowerby Bridge Norland, ℰ (01422) 83 13 55
⛳ Lightcliffe Knowle Top Rd, ℰ (01422) 20 24 59
⛳ Ogden Union Lane, ℰ (01422) 24 41 71

✕✕ Design House
Dean Clough (Gate 5) ⊠ HX3 5AX – ℰ (01422) 383 242
– www.designhouserestaurant.co.uk – Closed 26 December-8 January, Saturday lunch, Sunday and bank holiday Mondays
Rest – Carte £ 22/37 **s**
• Long-standing restaurant in converted mill complex. Striking interior with subtle blue hues; smart team offer warm welcome. Extensive menus of precise, tasty, classical and more modern dishes.

🍴 Shibden Mill Inn with rm
Shibden Mill Fold ⊠ HX3 7UL – ℰ (01422) 365 840 – www.shibdenmillinn.com – Closed dinner 25-26 December and 1 January
11 rm ⌸ – †£ 105 ††£ 123   **Rest** – Menu £ 13 (lunch) **s** – Carte £ 28/33 **s**
• Charming whitewashed country inn – formerly a corn mill – set in the valley. Extensive menu ranges from the traditional to the more modern. Events include fortnightly 'guinea pig' nights. Individually appointed bedrooms are comfy and cosy.

HALTWHISTLE – Northumberland – **501** M19 – pop. 3 811 — **24** A2
🇬🇧 Great Britain

▶ London 335 mi – Carlisle 22 mi – Newcastle upon Tyne 37 mi
🛈 Station Rd ℰ (01434) 32 20 02, www.visitnorthumberland.com
⛳ Wallend Farm Greenhead, ℰ (01697) 74 73 67
◎ Hadrian's Wall★★, N : 4.5 mi by A 6079 – Housesteads★★ **AC**, NE : 6 mi by B 6318 – Roman Army Museum★ **AC**, NW : 5 mi by A 69 and B 6318 – Vindolanda (Museum★) **AC**, NE : 5 mi by A 69 – Steel Rig (≤★) NE : 5.5 mi by B 6318

HALTWHISTLE

Centre of Britain
Main St ⊠ NE49 0BH – ℰ (01434) 322 422 – www.centre-of-britain.org.uk
12 rm – †£ 59/79 ††£ 90/110   **Rest** – Menu £ 18/20 – Carte £ 19/30
• Attractive hotel on busy main street. The oldest part, a pele tower, dates from the 16C. Comfy modern interior incorporates original architectural features. Bedrooms 3 and 9 boast saunas, while chalet rooms are popular with walkers, cyclists and guests with dogs. Glass-roofed restaurant with light, airy feel.

Ashcroft without rest
Lantys Lonnen ⊠ NE49 0DA – ℰ (01434) 320 213
– www.ashcroftguesthouse.co.uk – Closed 25 December
9 rm – †£ 50/90 ††£ 70/135
• Imposing Victorian house, formerly a vicarage, with beautifully kept gardens. Family run and attractively furnished throughout creating a welcoming atmosphere. Large bedrooms.

HAMBLE-LE-RICE – Hampshire – **503** Q31 – see Southampton

HAMBLETON – Rutland – see Oakham

HAMPTON IN ARDEN – West Midlands – **504** O26 – pop. 1 655   **19** C2
▶ London 113 mi – Birmingham 15 mi – Leicester 39 mi – Coventry 11 mi

Hampton Manor
Shadowbrook Ln ⊠ B92 0EN – ℰ (01675) 446 080 – www.hamptonmanor.eu
– Closed 25 December
11 rm – †£ 140 ††£ 140, ⊇ £ 15 – 1 suite
Rest *Peel's Restaurant by Martyn Pearn* – see restaurant listing
• Early Victorian manor house in 45 acres; built for grandson of Sir Robert Peel. Contemporary décor blends with characterful plasterwork and wood panelling; bedrooms boast mod cons.

Peel's Restaurant by Martyn Pearn – at Hampton Manor Hotel
Shadowbrook Ln. ⊠ B92 0EN – ℰ (01675) 446 080
– www.peelsrestaurant.co.uk – Closed 25 December, Sunday dinner and Monday lunch
Rest – Menu £ 19/40
• Contemporary dining room situated in former stable courtyard, with slate floor, glass roof and floor-to-ceiling windows. Modern style menus; bold, gutsy flavours. Formal service.

HAMPTON POYLE – Oxfordshire – pop. 106   **10** B2
▶ London 68 mi – Birmingham 72 mi – Barnet 71 mi – Ealing 57 mi

Bell at Hampton Poyle with rm
11 Oxford Rd. ⊠ OX5 2QD – ℰ (01865) 376 242
– www.thebellathamptonpoyle.co.uk
9 rm – †£ 140 ††£ 140   **Rest** – Menu £ 18 – Carte £ 23/31
• Almost Mediterranean in its style, with a very visual kitchen that includes a wood burning oven. Menu offers everything from mezze and charcuterie boards to pub staples and seafood. Bright, fresh bedrooms are located above the bar and in a cottage.

HARLAXTON – Lincolnshire – **502** S25 – see Grantham

HAROME – North Yorkshire – see Helmsley

HARROGATE – North Yorkshire – 502 P22 – pop. 66 178

22 B2

Great Britain

- London 211 mi – Bradford 18 mi – Leeds 15 mi – Newcastle upon Tyne 76 mi
- Crescent Rd ℘ (01423) 53 73 00, www.harrogate.gov.uk
- Forest Lane Head, ℘ (01423) 86 31 58
- Pannal Follifoot Rd, ℘ (01423) 87 26 28
- Oakdale, ℘ (01423) 56 71 62
- Crimple Valley Hookstone Wood Rd, ℘ (01423) 88 34 85
- Town ★
- Fountains Abbey ★★★ **AC** :- Studley Royal **AC** (≤ ★ from Anne Boleyn's Seat) - Fountains Hall (Fa 0.5ade ★), N : 13 mi by A 61 and B 6265 AY – Harewood House ★★ (The Gallery ★) **AC**, S : 7.5 mi by A 61 BZ

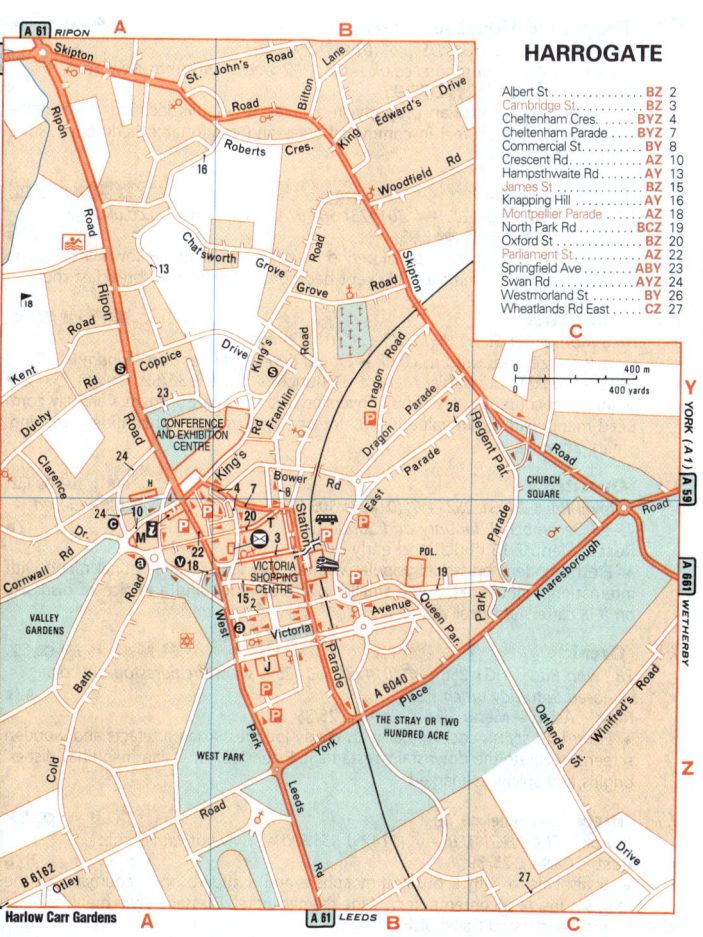

HARROGATE

Albert St.	BZ	2
Cambridge St.	BZ	3
Cheltenham Cres.	BYZ	4
Cheltenham Parade	BYZ	7
Commercial St.	BY	8
Crescent Rd.	AZ	10
Hampsthwaite Rd	AY	13
James St	BZ	15
Knapping Hill	AY	16
Montpellier Parade	AZ	18
North Park Rd	BCZ	19
Oxford St	BZ	20
Parliament St.	AZ	22
Springfield Ave	ABY	23
Swan Rd	AYZ	24
Westmorland St	BY	26
Wheatlands Rd East	CZ	27

HARROGATE

Rudding Park
Rudding Park, Follifoot, Southeast : 3.75 mi by A 661 ⊠ HG3 1JH
– ℰ (01423) 871 350 – www.ruddingpark.co.uk
85 rm ⊆ – †£ 105/150 ††£ 126/490 – 5 suites
Rest *Clocktower* – see restaurant listing

• Grade I listed Georgian manor house and Victorian church, set in 250 acres of mature grounds. Modern lounges and bars are located mainly in the newer extensions. The most luxurious bedrooms boast media hubs and touch lighting. Small spa.

Hotel du Vin
Prospect Pl ⊠ HG1 1LB – ℰ (01423) 856 800 – www.hotelduvin.com
48 rm – †£ 85/170 ††£ 125/190, ⊆ £ 14.50
Rest *Bistro* – see restaurant listing   BZ**a**

• Smart, modern hotel set in a terrace of Georgian houses and overlooking a pleasant green. Boutique-style interior with wine-themed décor. Contemporary bedrooms; two run the length of the attic and boast huge bathrooms. Small basement spa.

Brookfield House *without rest*
5 Alexandra Rd ⊠ HG1 5JS – ℰ (01423) 506 646
– www.brookfieldhousehotel.co.uk – Closed 2 weeks Christmas-New Year
6 rm ⊆ – †£ 60/75 ††£ 75/95   BY**s**

• Family owned Victorian property in a quiet, residential location close to the town centre. Homely feel in communal areas and comfortable bedrooms with a mix of styles.

Bijou *without rest*
17 Ripon Rd ⊠ HG1 2JL – ℰ (01423) 567 974 – www.thebijou.co.uk
10 rm – †£ 55/85 ††£ 95   AY**s**

• As the name suggests, a small period house, in the centre of town close to the Convention Centre. Immaculately kept bedrooms; elegantly set breakfast room.

Van Zeller
No.8 Montpellier St ⊠ HG1 2TQ – ℰ (01423) 508 762
– www.vanzellerrestaurants.co.uk – Closed Sunday dinner and Monday
Rest – (booking advisable) Menu £ 21 (lunch) – Carte £ 36/52   AZ**v**

• Intimate, contemporary shop conversion in trendy part of town. Carefully compiled menu, with good value lunch; unfussy, well-crafted and confident cooking. Smart, attentive staff.

Quantro
3 Royal Par ⊠ HG1 2SZ – ℰ (01423) 503 034 – www.quantro.co.uk – Closed 25-26 December, 1 January and Sunday   AZ**a**
Rest – Menu £ 15 (lunch and early dinner) – Carte £ 27/31

• Fresh, modern brasserie; popular with all. Keenly priced, seasonal menu with international influences. Some smaller plates at lunch and a choice of dish size on à la carte suits local workers.

Orchid
28 Swan Rd ⊠ HG1 2SE – ℰ (01423) 560 425 – www.orchidrestaurant.co.uk
– Closed Saturday lunch   AZ**c**
Rest – Asian – Menu £ 14 – Carte £ 25/39

• Enter into stylish cocktail bar with comfy lounges. Asian artefacts and wooden screens decorate the downstairs restaurant. Extensive pan-Asian menu has dishes' origins and spiciness marked.

Bistro – *at Hotel du Vin*
Prospect Pl ⊠ HG1 1LB – ℰ (01423) 856 800 – www.hotelduvin.com
Rest – Carte £ 25/39 ⊛   BZ**a**

• Stylish bistro with a buzzy atmosphere and a superb open courtyard to the rear, set inside a contemporary, wine-themed hotel. Brasserie-style menu focuses largely on classical Gallic dishes.

HARROGATE

Clocktower – at Rudding Park Hotel
Rudding Park, Follifoot, Southeast : 3.75 mi by A 661 – ⊠ HG3 1JH – ℰ (01423) 871 350 – www.ruddingpark.co.uk
Rest – Menu £ 35 **s** – Carte £ 36/54 **s**

♦ Chic, contemporary hotel dining room with an impressive chandelier at its centre. Set in the old stables, the room is named after a clock that hangs above it. Extensive array of modern dishes.

at Kettlesing West : 6.5 mi by A 59 - AY – ⊠ Harrogate

Knabbs Ash without rest
Skipton Rd, on A 59 – ⊠ HG3 2LT – ℰ (01423) 771 040 – www.knabbsash.co.uk
3 rm – †£ 55/60 ††£ 80/90

♦ Welcoming, stone-built farmhouse set on a smallholding overlooking Knabbs Moor. Comfy, cosy lounge and pine-furnished breakfast room. Light, airy bedrooms have plain walls, modern fabrics and a complimentary decanter of sherry. Spacious gardens and grounds.

HARTINGTON – Derbyshire – 502 O24 – pop. 1 604 – ⊠ Buxton   16 A1
▶ London 168 mi – Derby 36 mi – Manchester 40 mi – Sheffield 34 mi

Biggin Hall
Biggin, Southeast : 2 mi by B 5054 – ⊠ SK17 ODH – ℰ (01298) 84 451 – www.bigginhall.co.uk
20 rm – †£ 70/126 ††£ 126/136
Rest – (booking essential) Menu £ 12/20 – Carte £ 16/18

♦ Characterful house with traditional, rustic appeal. Many guests follow the Tissington Trail: bike storage and picnics are offered. Classical, low-beamed bedrooms in main house; brighter rooms in the barns. Pleasant garden views from dining room. Homely cooking.

HARTLAND – Devon – 503 G31   1 B1
▶ London 221 mi – Bude 15 mi – Clovelly 4 mi

Golden Park without rest
Southwest : 5 mi following signs for Elmscott and Bude – ⊠ EX39 6EP – ℰ (01237) 441 254 – www.goldenpark.co.uk – Closed Christmas-New Year and restricted opening in winter
3 rm – †£ 65/75 ††£ 75/95

♦ Part-17C farmhouse a stone's throw from the rugged North Devon coastline, in an Area of Outstanding Natural Beauty. Characterful interior with comfy garden room, oak-beamed drawing room and garden/coastal views. Smartly decorated bedrooms, one with a slipper bath.

Hart Inn
The Square – ⊠ EX39 6BL – ℰ (01237) 441 474 – www.thehartinn.com – Closed 1 week Spring, Sunday dinner and Monday
Rest – Carte £ 15/24

♦ Part 14 and 16C coaching inn with rustic, homely interior. Regularly changing menu features some Scandinavian influences but produce remains seasonal and local; generous portions.

HARWELL – Oxfordshire – 503 Q29 – pop. 2 015   10 B3
▶ London 64 mi – Oxford 16 mi – Reading 18 mi – Swindon 22 mi

Kingswell
Reading Rd, East : 0.75 mi on A 417 – ⊠ OX11 0LZ – ℰ (01235) 833 043 – www.kingswell-hotel.com
20 rm – †£ 99/103 ††£ 115/130 **Rest** – Menu £ 15/22 – Carte £ 22/34

♦ Large red-brick hotel located on the south Oxfordshire Downs. Convenient for Didcot rail and Oxford. Spacious, uniform, traditional bedrooms and pubby public areas. Classic menus served in traditional dining room.

HARWICH – Essex – 504 X28 – pop. 20 130   13 D2

▶ London 78 mi – Chelmsford 41 mi – Colchester 20 mi – Ipswich 23 mi
⛴ to Denmark (Esbjerg) (DFDS Seaways A/S) 3-4 weekly (20 h) – to The Netherlands (Hook of Holland) (Stena Line) 2 daily (3 h 30 mn)
🛈 Parkeston ✆ (01255) 50 61 39, www.touruk.co.uk
🅿 Parkeston Station Rd, ✆ (01255) 50 36 16

Pier at Harwich
The Quay ✉ CO12 3HH – ✆ (01255) 241 212 – www.milsomhotels.com
14 rm ☐ – †£ 112 ††£ 210
Rest *Harbourside* – see restaurant listing
Rest *Ha'Penny Pier* – Carte £ 20/35
♦ Victorian hotel in a pleasant quayside spot – built to accommodate rail travellers waiting to board their cruise liners and an ideal place to stay if you're catching the ferry. Stylish New England style bedrooms; some boast port views. Smart seafood restaurant or casual all-day dining overlooking the pier.

Harbourside – at Pier at Harwich Hotel
The Quay ✉ CO12 3HH – ✆ (01255) 241 212 – www.milsomhotels.com
Rest – Seafood – Menu £ 25 (lunch) – Carte £ 31/57 **s**
♦ Comfortable hotel dining room boasting crisp linen-laid tables and attractive port and North Sea views. Seafood-orientated menu offers everything from the traditional to the more contemporary.

HASTINGS and ST LEONARDS – East Sussex – 504 V31   8 B3
– pop. 85 828

▶ London 65 mi – Brighton 37 mi – Folkestone 37 mi – Maidstone 34 mi
🛈 Town Hall, Queen's Sq, Priory Meadow ✆ (0845) 2 74 10 01, www.hastingschoice.co.uk
🅿 Beauport Park Golf Course St Leonards-on-Sea Battle Rd, ✆ (01424) 85 42 45

Zanzibar
9 Eversfield Pl ✉ TN37 6BY – ✆ (01424) 460 109 – www.zanzibarhotel.co.uk
8 rm ☐ – †£ 89/99 ††£ 155/245   AZc
Rest *Pier Nine* – Menu £ 17 (lunch) – Carte £ 25/32
♦ Stylish boutique hotel in a Victorian townhouse, with large lounge and communal breakfast room. Named and themed after places the owner has visited, bedrooms are furnished to a high standard, with intimate lighting, good mod cons and smart bathrooms. Concise seasonal menu of North African inspired dishes.

Hastings House without rest
9 Warrior Sq. ✉ TN37 6BA – ✆ (01424) 422 709 – www.hastingshouse.co.uk
8 rm ☐ – †£ 80/110 ††£ 99/150   AZu
♦ Stylish, modern and very comfortable guesthouse just off the promenade; personally run by hospitable owners. Rooms 3, 5 and 7 are the best choice for their size and sea views.

Webbe's Rock-a-Nore
1 Rock-a-Nore ✉ TN34 3DW – ✆ (01424) 721 650
– www.webbesrestaurants.co.uk – Closed 24-26 December and 2-16 January
Rest – Seafood – Carte £ 23/46   BYx
♦ Bright, contemporary restaurant with horseshoe counter and open kitchen, in an enviable position across the beach from the fishing Stade. Unsurprisingly fresh fish and seafood.

St Clements
3 Mercatoria, St Leonards on Sea ✉ TN38 0EB – ✆ (01424) 200 355
– www.stclementsrestaurant.co.uk – Closed Sunday dinner and Monday
Rest – Menu £ 19/27 – Carte £ 26/34   AZa
♦ Pleasant neighbourhood restaurant with striking local artwork hung on plain walls. Comprehensive a la carte and concise, good value lunch and midweek menus. Tasty modern European cooking is unfussy with a rustic edge. Fresh fish from Hastings plays a key role.

HASTINGS ST. LEONARDS

Albert Rd .... **BZ** 3	Denmark Pl. .... **BZ** 13	Priory Meadow Shopping
Bourne (The)........ **BY** 4	Dorset Pl. .... **BZ** 15	Centre .... **BZ**
Cambridge Gardens .... **BZ** 5	Gensing Rd........... **AZ** 16	Queen's Rd........... **BZ**
Castle Hill Rd .... **BZ** 8	George St .... **BY** 18	Robertson St .... **BZ** 27
Castle St .... **BZ** 7	Grosvenor Crescent .... **AY** 19	Rock-a-Nore Rd ...... **BY** 30
Cornwallis Gardens.... **BZ** 9	Harold Pl............ **BZ** 20	St Helen's Park Rd .... **BY** 31
Cornwallis Terrace .... **BZ** 10	Havelock Rd .... **BZ** 21	Sedlescombe Rd South .. **AY** 32
	King's Rd .... **AZ** 22	Silchester Rd .... **AZ** 33
	London Rd .... **AZ**	Warrior Square .... **BZ** 34
	Marine Court .... **BZ** 23	Wellington Pl......... **BZ** 35
	Middle St .... **BZ** 24	Wellington Square .... **BZ** 36
	Norman Rd.......... **AZ**	White Rock Road ..... **BZ** 38

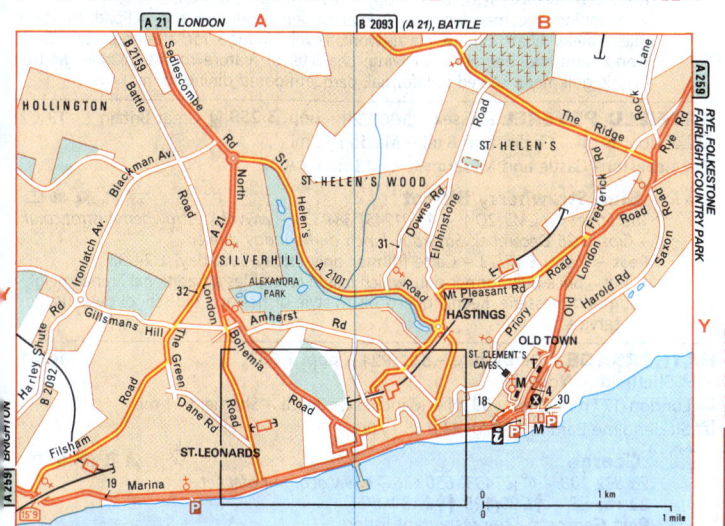

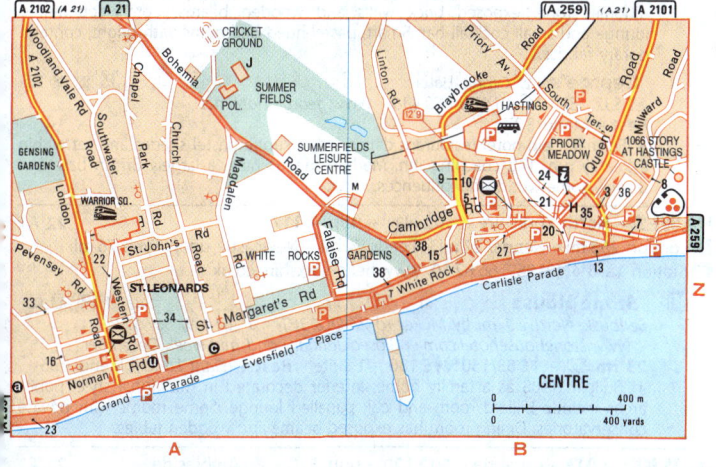

Good food at moderate prices? Look for the Bib Gourmand

HATCH BEAUCHAMP – Somerset – *503* K30 – see Taunton

HATFIELD HEATH – Essex – **504** U28 – pop. 1 514 — 12 B2
– ✉ Bishop'S Stortford
▶ London 33 mi – Birmingham 130 mi – Croydon 53 mi – Barnet 31 mi

Down Hall Country House
South : 1.5 mi by Matching Ln.
✉ CM22 7AS – ☎ (01279) 731 441 – www.downhall.co.uk
99 rm – †£ 69/109 ††£ 99/209
Rest *Grill Room* – (closed Saturday lunch) Menu £ 30 – Carte £ 36/44
♦ Stunning 19C mansion with formal gardens, fountain and helipad. Classical guest areas boast ornate plasterwork. Lovely lounge for afternoon tea. Dark wood furnished bedrooms in wing; characterful feature rooms in main house. Classic grill menu served in informal, parquet-floored dining room.

HATFIELD PEVEREL – Essex – **504** V28 – pop. 3 258 — Great Britain — 13 C2
▶ London 39 mi – Chelmsford 8 mi – Maldon 12 mi
ⓒ Colchester - Castle and Museum★, E : 13 mi by A 12

Blue Strawberry Bistrot
The Street ✉ CM3 2DW – ☎ (01245) 381 333 – www.bluestrawberrybistrot.co.uk
– Closed 26 December, Saturday lunch and Sunday dinner
Rest – Menu £ 17/23 – Carte (dinner only Friday-Saturday) £ 24/33
♦ Busy, brick-built former pub, which inside resembles a traditional French neighbourhood brasserie. Keenly priced bistro-style dishes and old-school desserts. Polite service.

HATHERSAGE – Derbyshire – **502** P24 – pop. 1 582 — 16 A1
– ✉ Sheffield (s. Yorks.)
▶ London 177 mi – Derby 39 mi – Manchester 34 mi – Sheffield 11 mi
🏌 Sickleholme Bamford, ☎ (01433) 65 13 06

George
✉ S32 1BB – ☎ (01433) 650 436 – www.george-hotel.net
22 rm – †£ 99/125 ††£ 139/175
Rest *George's* – see restaurant listing
♦ Keenly run 14C coaching inn where modern furnishings blend nicely with traditional stone, exposed brick walls and wooden beams. Comfy, open-fired lounge and small cocktail bar. Smart, pastel-hued bedrooms with bright, contemporary fabrics.

George's – at George Hotel
✉ S32 1BB – ☎ (01433) 650 436 – www.george-hotel.net
Rest – Menu £ 37
♦ Formally laid hotel restaurant decorated in subtle pastel shades and set within a keenly run, 14C coaching inn. Modern menus have a largely British base but display some worldwide influences.

HAWES – North Yorkshire – **502** N21 – pop. 1 117 — 22 A1
▶ London 253 mi – Kendal 27 mi – Leeds 72 mi – Newcastle upon Tyne 76 mi
ⓘ Station Yard ☎ (01969) 66 62 10, www.hello-yorkshire.co.uk

Stone House
Sedbusk, North : 1 mi by Muker rd ✉ DL8 3PT – ☎ (01969) 667 571
– www.stonehousehotel.com – Closed January and mid-week December
23 rm ☐ – †£ 63/150 ††£ 180 – 1 suite **Rest** – (Light Lunch) Menu £ 35
♦ Built in 1908 as a family home. Interior decorated in traditional style; public areas include billiard room and oak panelled lounge. Some rooms with private conservatories. Dining room has exposed beams and wooden tables.

HAWKSHEAD – Cumbria – **502** L20 – pop. 570 – ✉ Ambleside — 21 A2
Great Britain
▶ London 283 mi – Carlisle 52 mi – Kendal 19 mi
ⓘ Main Street ☎ (015394) 3 69 46, www.hawksheadtouristinfo.org.uk
◉ Village★
ⓒ Lake Windermere★★ – Coniston Water★ (Brantwood★, on east side),
SW : by B 5285

HAWKSHEAD

at Far Sawrey Southeast : 2.5 mi on B 5285 – ✉ Ambleside

West Vale without rest
✉ LA22 0LQ – ℰ (015394) 42817 – www.westvalecountryhouse.co.uk – Closed 25-26 December and restricted opening 3 January-4 February
7 rm – †£ 90/130 ††£ 120/175
♦ Welcoming slate house boasting lovely countryside views; run by keen owners. Two comfy lounges and a smart country house style room for hearty breakfasts. Good-sized bedrooms with warm, comfy, boutique style. Tea and cake on arrival, and plenty of extra touches.

HAWNBY – North Yorkshire – 502 Q21 – ✉ Helmsley 23 C1

▶ London 245 mi – Middlesbrough 27 mi – Newcastle upon Tyne 69 mi – York 30 mi

Inn at Hawnby
✉ YO62 5QS – ℰ (01439) 798 202 – www.innathawnby.co.uk – Closed 25 December
9 rm – †£ 69/79 ††£ 99 **Rest** – Carte £ 24/32
♦ Homely inn set in a very rural spot in prime walking and shooting country. Classically styled bedrooms are split between the house and barn, and boast good linens and home comforts. Simplicity is key. Pub-style dishes at lunch; more substantial, classical dinners.

at Laskill Northeast : 2.25 mi by Osmotherley rd – ✉ Hawnby

Laskill Country House
Easterside ✉ YO62 5NB – ℰ (01439) 798 265 – www.laskillcountryhouse.co.uk – Closed 24-25 December
3 rm – †£ 45/60 ††£ 120 **Rest** – Menu £ 25
♦ Delightful manor-style house in popular shooting/walking area. Comfy lounge; small function suite. Good-sized bedrooms with countryside views. Communal dining; wholesome home-cooked meals, with meat from the family's farms.

HAWORTH – West Yorkshire – 502 O22 – pop. 6 078 – ✉ Keighley 22 A2
Great Britain

▶ London 213 mi – Burnley 22 mi – Leeds 22 mi – Manchester 34 mi
🛈 2-4 West Lane ℰ (01535) 64 23 29, www.haworth-village.org.uk
◉ Bront Parsonage Museum**AC**

Ashmount Country House without rest
Mytholmes Ln ✉ BD22 8EZ – ℰ (01535) 645 726
– www.ashmounthaworth.co.uk
10 rm – †£ 50/80 ††£ 75/245
♦ Built in 1870 by the physician to the Brontë sisters, this refurbished guesthouse has extremely comfortable, period-furnished bedrooms and state-of-the-art bathrooms; some rooms even have their own outdoor hot tubs.

Old Registry without rest
2-6 Main St ✉ BD22 8DA – ℰ (01535) 646 503
– www.theoldregistryhaworth.co.uk – Closed 24-26 December
9 rm – †£ 55/80 ††£ 100/120
♦ Stone former registrar's office on cobbled main street. Individually themed bedrooms boast rich fabrics and antiques: 5 are feature rooms; some have four-posters. Breakfast of local produce.

Weaver's with rm
15 West Ln ✉ BD22 8DU – ℰ (01535) 643 822 – www.weaverssmallhotel.co.uk
– Closed 21 December-7 January, Saturday lunch, Sunday and Monday
3 rm – †£ 65/75 ††£ 110/120 **Rest** – Menu £ 19 (lunch) – Carte £ 24/35
♦ Charming former weavers' cottages at the top of a cobbled street. Characterful, cluttered lounge with ornaments, artefacts and informal atmosphere. Wide-ranging menus have a strong northern base. Warm, welcoming bedrooms.

HAYDON BRIDGE – Northumberland – 501 N19 – see Hexham

HAYLING ISLAND – Hampshire – **504** R31 – pop. 14 842 — **6** B3

▶ London 77 mi – Brighton 45 mi – Southampton 28 mi
🛈 Seven Seafront, www.hayling.co.uk
⛳ Links Lane, ✆ (023) 9246 44 46

⌂ **Cockle Warren Cottage** without rest
36 Seafront ✉ *PO11 9HL* – ✆ *(023) 9246 4961* – *www.cocklewarren.co.uk*
6 rm – **†**£ 49/59 **††**£ 70/89
♦ Pleasant cottage with welcoming owner, set just across the road from the beach. Comfortable, well-kept bedrooms; 1 and 4 have sea views. Conservatory breakfast room and terrace overlook pool.

HAYWARDS HEATH – West Sussex – **504** T31 – pop. 29 110 — **7** D2
🟩 Great Britain

▶ London 41 mi – Brighton 16 mi
⛳ Lindfield East Mascalls Lane, ✆ (01444) 48 44 67
🟢 Sheffield Park Garden★, E : 5 mi on A 272 and A 275

XX **Jeremy's at Borde Hill**
Borde Hill Gdns, North : 1.75 mi by B 2028 on Balcombe Rd ✉ *RH16 1XP* – ✆ *(01444) 441 102* – *www.jeremysrestaurant.com* – *Closed 1-14 January, Monday except lunch on bank holidays and Sunday dinner*
Rest – Menu £ 18 (weekday lunch) – Carte £ 29/39
♦ Converted 19C stables with delightful views to Victorian walled garden. Contemporary interior with modern art. Confident, vibrant cooking in a light Mediterranean style.

HEADLAM – Durham – **502** O20 – see Darlington

HEBDEN BRIDGE – West Yorkshire – **502** N22 – pop. 4 086 — **22** A2
– ✉ West Yorkshire

▶ London 223 mi – Burnley 13 mi – Leeds 24 mi – Manchester 25 mi
🛈 1 Bridge Gate ✆ (01422) 84 38 31, www.hebdenbridge.co.uk
🟢 Great Mount Wadsworth, ✆ (01422) 84 28 96

⌂ **Holme House** without rest
New Road ✉ *HX7 8AD* – ✆ *(01422) 847 588*
– *www.holmehousehebdenbridge.co.uk*
3 rm – **†**£ 65 **††**£ 78/90
♦ Late Georgian house in town centre with gated parking and neat garden. Smart, comfortable, well furnished rooms. Bedrooms boast excellent facilities and spacious bathrooms.

HEDDON ON THE WALL – Northumberland — **24** A2

▶ London 288 mi – Blaydon 7 mi – Newcastle upon Tyne 8 mi

🏠 **Close House**
Southwest : 2.25 mi by B 6528 ✉ *NE15 0HT* – ✆ *(01661) 852 255*
– *www.closehouse.co.uk*
31 rm ⊡ – **†**£ 150/260 **††**£ 150/260
Rest *Bewickes* – ✆ (01661) 835 099 – Menu £ 22/33 – Carte dinner £ 30/46
♦ Stunning Georgian mansion in 300 acres of mature grounds that stretch to the river. Original features blend with modern décor; front bedrooms have views, those to rear are more contemporary. Stylish restaurant offers interesting modern cooking and intimate air.

HEDLEY ON THE HILL – Northumberland — **24** A2

▶ London 293 mi – Newcastle upon Tyne 16 mi – Sunderland 26 mi
– South Shields 26 mi

Feathers Inn

✉ NE43 7SW – ✆ (01661) 843 607 – www.thefeathers.net
Rest – *(closed first 2 weeks in January, Sunday dinner and Mondays except bank holidays)* Carte £ 20/29

♦ Traditional stone inn set on a steep hill, offering daily changing menu of hearty British classics, cooked using carefully sourced, regional produce. Relaxed, friendly atmosphere.

HELMSLEY – **North Yorkshire** – **502** Q21 – **pop. 1 559** Great Britain **23** C1

▶ London 239 mi – Leeds 51 mi – Middlesbrough 28 mi – York 24 mi
🛈 Castlegate ✆ (01439) 77 01 73, www.yorkshire.com
Ampleforth College Castle Drive, Gilling East, ✆ (01439) 78 82 12
Rievaulx Abbey★★ **AC**, NW : 2.5 mi by B 1257

Black Swan

Market Pl ✉ *YO62 5BJ* – ✆ *(01439) 770 466* – *www.blackswan-helmsley.co.uk*
42 rm ⊇ – †£ 92/182 ††£ 132/197 – 3 suites
Rest *The Rutland Room* – see restaurant listing

♦ One of the best known coaching inns in the country, dating back to the 16C and overlooking the historic marketplace. Charming interior with beams, modern lounge-bar and all-day tea shop. Most characterful bedrooms in the original building.

Feversham Arms

on B 1257 ✉ *YO62 5AG* – ✆ *(01439) 770 766* – *www.fevershamarmshotel.com*
17 rm (dinner included) ⊇ – †£ 193 ††£ 330 – 16 suites
Rest *Conservatory* – Menu £ 45 (dinner) – Carte lunch £ 33/41

♦ Former coaching inn; its stone façade concealing a surprisingly modern interior. Muted colours and quality fabrics feature throughout. Comfortable bedrooms have a quiet, restful nature; some overlook the swimming pool. Superb spa facility. Warm, red décor in airy, glass-roofed restaurant; modern brasserie-style menu.

No.54 without rest

54 Bondgate ✉ *YO62 5EZ* – ✆ *(01439) 771 533* – *www.no54.co.uk* – *Closed Christmas and New Year*
3 rm ⊇ – †£ 55 ††£ 110

♦ Victorian terraced cottage, formerly the village vet's. Charming owner. Bedrooms are strong point: set around flagged courtyard, they're airy, bright and very well-equipped.

Carlton Lodge without rest

Bondgate ✉ *YO62 5EY* – ✆ *(01439) 770 557* – *www.carlton-lodge.com*
8 rm ⊇ – †£ 50/70 ††£ 85/95

♦ Late 19C house set just out of town. Homely and traditional air to the décor in the communal areas and the bedrooms, some of which have period features. Cosy breakfast room.

The Rutland Room – at Black Swan Hotel

Market Pl ✉ *YO62 5BJ* – ✆ *(01439) 770 466* – *www.blackswan-helmsley.co.uk*
Rest – (dinner only and Sunday lunch) Menu £ 33 – Carte £ 33/52

♦ Fine dining restaurant with a subtle, modern style, set within a historic 16C coaching inn. Concise à la carte and daily specials consist of classically based dishes with some modern twists.

at Harome Southeast : 2.75 mi by A 170 – ✉ York

Pheasant

✉ *YO62 5JG* – ✆ *(01439) 771 241* – *www.thepheasanthotel.com*
12 rm (dinner included) ⊇ – †£ 105/145 ††£ 210 – 2 suites
Rest – *(booking essential for non residents)* Menu £ 29/36 – Carte £ 36/44

♦ Ivy-clad hotel in picturesque hamlet with a duck pond and mill stream close by. Under the same ownership as The Star Inn. Charmingly decorated public areas; comfy, up-to-date bedrooms. Formal restaurant and conservatory; choose from array of fresh, modern menus.

HELMSLEY

Cross House Lodge
✉ YO62 5JE – ✆ (01439) 770 397 – www.thestaratharome.co.uk
11 rm – †£ 150 ††£ 150/240
Rest *Star Inn* – see restaurant listing
♦ Converted farm buildings set opposite a pub, in a pretty village. Open-plan, split-level lounge. Ultra-stylish, super-smart bedrooms in either the main building or local cottages.

Star Inn
High St ✉ YO62 5JE – ✆ (01439) 770 397 – www.thestaratharome.co.uk
– Closed Monday lunch, Sunday dinner and bank holidays
Rest – (booking essential) Menu £ 25 – Carte £ 35/55
♦ Charming 14C thatched pub with cosy bar and two dining rooms: one traditional; one more modern and boasting a chef's table. Pub-style dishes are rooted in tradition but use modern techniques. Herbs and vegetables come straight from the kitchen garden.

at Ampleforth Southwest : 4.5 mi by A 170 off B 1257 – ✉ Helmsley

Shallowdale House
West : 0.5 mi ✉ YO62 4DY – ✆ (01439) 788 325 – www.shallowdalehouse.co.uk
– Closed Christmas-New Year
3 rm – †£ 80/105 ††£ 100/125 **Rest** – Menu £ 38
♦ Modern guesthouse affording spectacular views of the Howardian Hills; an area of outstanding beauty. Spacious rooms boast large picture windows to make the most of the scenery. A warm, relaxed atmosphere pervades. 4 course, home-cooked evening meals.

at Scawton West : 8.5 mi by A 170 – ✉ Helmsley

Hare Inn
✉ YO7 2HG – ✆ (01845) 597 769 – www.thehareinn.co.uk – Closed 25 December, Sunday dinner and Monday
Rest – Carte £ 23/34
♦ Warm, inviting and busy pub, parts of which date from 13C; in a remote setting, close to Rievaulx Abbey. Satisfying local food, with meat from Masham and poultry from Pateley Bridge.

HELPERBY – North Yorkshire – 502 Q21   22 B2
▶ London 220 mi – Leeds 36 mi – Sheffield 70 mi – Manchester 81 mi

Oak Tree Inn with rm
Raskelf Rd. ✉ YO61 2PH – ✆ (01423) 789 189 – www.theoaktreehelperby.com
6 rm – †£ 120 ††£ 150 **Rest** – Carte £ 19/29
♦ A pub of two halves, with a large bar, tap room, two snugs and a smarter dining room. Menus offer hearty, generous dishes using ingredients from small local suppliers. Everything is homemade and combinations are familiar and comforting. Smart, modern bedrooms come with 'Yorkie' bars and Jacuzzi baths.

HELSTON – Cornwall – 503 E33 – pop. 10 578   1 A3
▶ London 306 mi – Falmouth 13 mi – Penzance 14 mi – Truro 17 mi
◉ The Flora Day Furry Dance★★
◉ Lizard Peninsula★ – Gunwalloe Fishing Cove★, S : 4 mi by A 3083 and minor rd
- Culdrose (Flambards Village Theme Park★), SE : 1 mi - Wendron (Poldark Mine★), NE : 2.5 mi by B 3297 – Gweek (Seal Sanctuary★), E : 4 mi by A 394 and minor rd

Nansloe Manor
Meneage Rd, South : 1.5 mi on A 3083 ✉ TR13 0SB – ✆ (01326) 558 400
– www.nansloe-manor.co.uk – Closed 2 weeks January
15 rm (dinner included) – †£ 230/285 ††£ 275/335
Rest – (closed Sunday and Monday) Menu £ 19 (lunch) – Carte £ 30/39
♦ Restored Georgian Manor House set in 4 acres. Handmade French furniture, pastel décor and airy, continental feel. Subtly elegant bedrooms; some with balcony/terrace/views. Menus make use of produce from garden; classic combinations are presented in a contemporary style.

HELSTON

at Trelowarren Southeast : 4 mi by A 394 and A 3083 on B 3293 – ✉ Helston

New Yard
Trelowarren Estate ✉ *TR12 6AF –* ✆ *(01326) 221 595 – www.trelowarren.com*
– Closed October-May, Sunday dinner, Monday and Tuesday
Rest *– (booking advisable at dinner)* Menu £ 21/27 – Carte £ 29/44
♦ Converted stable yard adjoining a craft gallery. Large, simply furnished dining room opens onto a terrace. Dinner offers elaborate seasonal menus of locally inspired dishes; lunch is simpler.

at Cury South : 5 mi by A394 off A3083

Colvennor Farmhouse *without rest*
✉ *TR12 7BJ –* ✆ *(01326) 241 208 – www.colvennorfarmhouse.com*
3 rm ⊡ – †£ 47/48 ††£ 68/70
♦ Part-17C farmhouse in a peaceful location, boasting a lovely mature garden and vegetable patch to the rear. Homely lounge features a wood burning stove. Simple, wood-furnished bedrooms are of a reasonable size. Linen-laid breakfast room.

HEMEL HEMPSTEAD – Hertfordshire – **504** S28 – pop. 83 118   **12** A2
Great Britain

▶ London 30 mi – Aylesbury 16 mi – Luton 10 mi – Northampton 46 mi
🏌 Little Hay Golf Complex Bovingdon Box Lane, ✆ (01442) 83 37 98
🏌 Boxmoor 18 Box Lane, ✆ (01442) 24 24 34
◉ Whipsnade Wild Animal Park★

Restaurant 65
65 High St (Old Town) ✉ *HP1 3AF –* ✆ *(01442) 239 010*
– www.restaurant65.com – Closed 1 week January, 1 week July, Saturday lunch, Sunday dinner and Monday
Rest *– (booking advisable)* Menu £ 19/27
♦ Charming 17C building in old part of town; snug restaurant with white walls, black beams and homely, relaxed feel. Well executed modern British cooking with a classical base.

at Frithsden Northwest : 4.5 mi by A 4146 – ✉ Hemel Hempstead

Alford Arms
✉ *HP1 3DD –* ✆ *(01442) 864 480 – www.alfordarmsfrithsden.co.uk – Closed 25-26 December*
Rest – Carte £ 22/28
♦ Attractive Victorian pub overlooking the village green. Traditional British menu follows the seasons: salads and fish in summer, game and comfort dishes in winter. Good classical desserts.

HEMINGFORD GREY – Cambridgeshire – **504** T27 – see Huntingdon

---

HENFIELD – West Sussex – **504** T31 – pop. 4 527   **7** D2
▶ London 47 mi – Brighton 10 mi – Worthing 11 mi

Ginger Fox
Albourne, Southwest 3 mi on A281 ✉ *BN6 9EA –* ✆ *(01273) 857 888*
– www.gingermanrestaurants.com – Closed 25 December
Rest – Carte £ 18/30
♦ Characterful 17C inn with thatched roof, wooden beams and open fires. Cooking is skilful, with a real country flavour. Tasty, unfussy dishes and popular vegetarian tasting plate. Favoured by families, with children's menu, spacious garden and slides.

ENGLAND

HENFIELD

at Wineham Northeast : 3.5 mi by A 281 and B 2116 on Wineham Lane – ✉ Henfield

Frylands without rest
West : 0.25 mi taking left turn at telephone box ✉ BN5 9BP – ℘ (01403) 710 214 – www.frylands.co.uk – *Closed 20 December-2 January*
3 rm – ♦£ 35/40 ♦♦£ 60/65
♦ Part-Elizabethan farmhouse with outdoor swimming pool and 250 acres of woods, farmland and fishing ponds. Bedrooms exude charm and character with homely furnishings and original features. Fresh home-cooked breakfasts feature local produce. Very charming owner.

HENLADE – Somerset – see Taunton

HENLEY – West Sussex – see Midhurst

HENLEY-IN-ARDEN – Warwickshire – **503** O27 – pop. **2 797**   **19** C3

▶ London 104 mi – Birmingham 15 mi – Stratford-upon-Avon 8 mi – Warwick 8 mi

Crabmill
Preston Bagot, Claverdon, East : 1 mi on A 4189 ✉ B95 5EE – ℘ (01926) 843 342 – www.thecrabmill.co.uk – *Closed Sunday dinner*
Rest – *(booking essential)* Carte £ 21/33
♦ Characterful timbered pub with various beamed rooms and peaceful terrace and garden. Good-sized menu offers modern Mediterranean-influenced dishes, with lighter bites available during the day.

HENLEY-ON-THAMES – Oxfordshire – **504** R29 – pop. **10 513**   **11** C3

▶ London 40 mi – Oxford 23 mi – Reading 9 mi

⛴ to Reading (Salter Bros. Ltd) (summer only) daily (2 h 15 mn) – to Marlow (Salter Bros. Ltd) (summer only) daily (2 h 15 mn)

ℹ Market Place ℘ (01491) 57 80 34, www.henley-on-thames.org

⛳ Huntercombe Nuffield, ℘ (01491) 64 12 07

Hotel du Vin
New St. ✉ RG9 2BP – ℘ (01491) 848 400 – www.hotelduvin.com
41 rm – ♦£ 125/205 ♦♦£ 125/205, ⚏ £ 14.50 – 2 suites
Rest *Bistro* – see restaurant listing
♦ Characterful 1857 building that was formerly the Breakspear Brewery. Stylish bedrooms include airy doubles and duplex suites: one features two roll-top tubs and a great view of the church; others boast heated balconies and outdoor baths.

Falaise House without rest
37 Market Pl ✉ RG9 2AA – ℘ (01491) 573 388 – www.falaisehouse.com – *Closed Christmas*
6 rm ⚏ – ♦£ 85 ♦♦£ 115
♦ Very well located 18C house boasting stylish, luxury bedrooms; some with chaises longues. Good breakfast choice includes homemade preserves and smoked salmon, cooked to order.

Bistro – at Hotel du Vin
New St. ✉ RG9 2BP – ℘ (01491) 848 400 – www.hotelduvin.com
Rest – Carte £ 28/39
♦ Classical French bistro in a characterful former brewery building dating back to 1857. Menus are formed around traditional Gallic dishes. Excellent wine list offers the choice of over 700 bins.

Parisien
50 Bell St ✉ RG9 2BG – ℘ (01491) 571 115 – www.leparisienrestaurant.co.uk – *Closed Sunday dinner*
Rest – French – *(booking advisable)* Menu £ 20/23 – Carte £ 33/46
♦ Welcoming French bistro with clothed tables, modern artwork and a private dining room overlooking the walled garden terrace. Experienced chef creates seasonal menus of timeless French classics; presentation displays a light, modern touch.

HENLEY-ON-THAMES

Luscombes at The Golden Ball
Lower Assendon, Northwest : 0.75 mi by A 4130 on B 480 ✉ *RG9 6AH*
– ☎ *(01491) 574 157 – www.luscombes.co.uk*
Rest – Carte £ 29/45
♦ Cosy restaurant, popular with locals, serving modern menu of tasty, simply cooked dishes. Smiley, attentive service. Lighter lunches, homemade preserves and afternoon cream teas.

at Lower Shiplake South : 2 mi by A 4155 – ✉ Henley-On-Thames

Crowsley House
Crowsley Rd ✉ *RG9 3JT –* ☎ *(01189) 406 708 – www.crowsleyhouse.co.uk*
3 rm – †£ 125 ††£ 150, ⊇ £ 10 **Rest** – Menu £ 30
♦ Discreet guest house in secluded conservation area; two lively cats come as part of the family. Pristine, well-equipped bedrooms boast contemporary bathrooms. Breakfast is an extensive continental affair, with freshly baked pastries. Gourmet meals by arrangement.

at Shiplake Row South : 3.5mi. by A 4155 by Peppard rd and Binfield Heath rd

Orwells
Shiplake Row ✉ *RG9 4DP –* ☎ *(01189) 403 673 – www.orwellsatshiplake.co.uk*
– *Closed first 2 weeks January, first 2 weeks September, 1 week April, Sunday dinner and Monday except bank holidays*
Rest – Menu £ 16 (lunch) – Carte £ 25/53
♦ Dating from the 18C and named after George Orwell, who spent his childhood in the area. Contemporary interior divided into three: the bar, conservatory and 'fine dining' room. Modern cooking, with a 'use local' ethos. More elaborate dishes at dinner in The Room.

ENGLAND

HEPWORTH – West Yorkshire – see Holmfirth

HEREFORD – Herefordshire – **503** L27 – pop. 55 213 ▌Great Britain **18** B3

▶ London 133 mi – Birmingham 51 mi – Cardiff 56 mi
🛈 1 King St ☎ (01432) 26 84 30, www.visitherefordshire.co.uk
🏌 Raven's Causeway Wormsley, ☎ (01432) 83 02 19
🏌 Belmont Lodge Belmont Ruckhall Lane, ☎ (01432) 35 26 66
🏌 Hereford Municipal Holmer Rd, ☎ (01432) 34 43 76
🏌 Burghill Valley Burghill Tillington Rd, ☎ (01432) 76 04 56
◉ City★ - Cathedral★★ (Mappa Mundi★) A **A** – Old House★ A **B**
◉ Kilpeck (Church of SS. Mary and David★★) SW : 8 mi by A 465 B

Plan on next page

Brandon Lodge without rest
Ross Rd, South : 1.75 mi on A 49 ✉ *HR2 8BH –* ☎ *(01432) 355 621*
– www.brandonlodge.co.uk
10 rm ⊇ – †£ 45/50 ††£ 60/68
♦ A good value hotel with 18C origins, charmingly overseen by owner. Bedrooms in main building or adjacent annexe: all are spacious, boasting a cheery warmth and good facilities.

Stewing Pot
17 Church St ✉ *HR1 2LR –* ☎ *(01432) 265 233 – www.stewingpot.co.uk – Closed 25-26 December, Sunday and Monday* A**a**
Rest – (booking essential at dinner) Menu £ 17 (lunch) – Carte £ 25/36
♦ Neighbourhood eatery tucked away down a narrow street, with plain décor and simple, homely furnishings. Taking on a bistro style, cooking is classical and reliably tasty.

HEREFORD

Aubrey St	**A** 3
Berrington St	**A** 5
Blueschool St.	**A** 6
Broad St	**A** 7
Church St	**A** 12
Commercial Rd	**A** 14
Commercial St.	**A** 13
Eign St	**B** 16
Greyfriars Bridge	**A** 17
Hampton Park Rd	**B** 18
High St.	**A** 19
High Town	**A** 20
King St	**A** 23
Maylord Orchards Shopping Centre	**A**
Newmarket St.	**A** 25
Newtown Rd	**B** 26
St Ethelbert St.	**A** 28
St Nicholas St	**A** 29
Union St	**A** 32

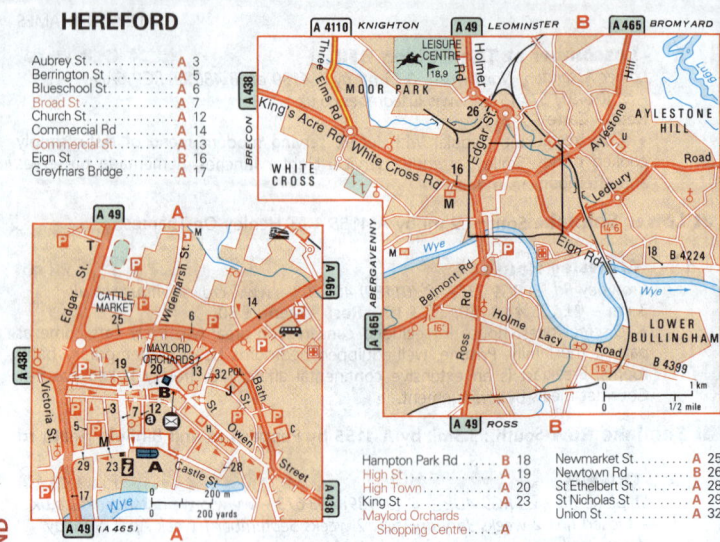

at Winforton Northwest : 15 mi on A 438 – ✉ Hereford

Winforton Court without rest
✉ HR3 6EA – ☎ (01544) 328 498 – www.winfortoncourt.co.uk – Closed 20-28 December
3 rm – ♦£ 73/83 ♦♦£ 88/110
♦ Wonderfully characterful 16C house used as a circuit court by "Hanging" Judge Jeffries. Exudes personality with exposed beams, thick walls and uneven floors. Rustic bedrooms.

HERM – Herm – 503 P33 – pop. 60 – see Channel Islands

HERNE BAY – Kent – 504 X29 – pop. 34 747   9 D1
▶ London 65 mi – Croydon 68 mi – Bromley 59 mi – Enfield 80 mi

Le Petit Poisson
Pier Approach, Central Par. ✉ CT6 5JN – ☎ (01227) 361 199
– www.lepetitpoisson.co.uk – Closed Sunday dinner and Monday except bank holidays when closed Tuesday
Rest – Seafood – Carte £ 23/29
♦ Sweet whitewashed building with small terrace, overlooking the pier. Split-level interior boasts flag floors, exposed brick and eye-catching mosaic art. Concise, constantly evolving blackboard menus consist of tasty, unfussy seafood dishes.

HERSTMONCEUX – East Sussex – 504 U31 – pop. 3 898   8 B3
▶ London 63 mi – Eastbourne 12 mi – Hastings 14 mi – Lewes 16 mi

Sundial
Gardner St ✉ BN27 4LA – ☎ (01323) 832 217 – www.sundialrestaurant.co.uk
– Closed 2 weeks January, Sunday dinner and Monday
Rest – French – Menu £ 24/40
♦ Converted 16C cottage retaining leaded windows and beamed ceiling. Comfy dining room. Seasonal menus offer rich, classical French dishes; the chateaubriand for two must be ordered in advance.

at Wartling Southeast : 3.75 mi by A 271 on Wartling rd – ✉ Herstmonceux

Wartling Place
✉ BN27 1RY – ☏ (01323) 832 590 – www.wartlingplace.co.uk
4 rm ⊡ – †£ 75/89 ††£ 145/165   **Rest** – Menu £ 35
♦ Part Georgian house with three acres of gardens, sited in the village. Pleasantly furnished, with some antiques; two of the rooms have four-poster beds. Breakfast is taken communally at an antique table in the dining room. Dinner by arrangement.

HESSLE – East Riding of Yorkshire – **502** S22 – see Kingston-upon-Hull

HETTON – North Yorkshire – **502** N21 – see Skipton

HEXHAM – Northumberland – **501** N19 – pop. 10 682 Great Britain   24 A2

▶ London 304 mi – Carlisle 37 mi – Newcastle upon Tyne 21 mi
🛈 Wentworth Car Park ☏ (01434) 65 22 20, www.visitnorthumberland.com
🏌 Spital Park, ☏ (01434) 60 30 72
🏌 De Vere Slaley Hall Slaley, ☏ (01434) 67 31 54
🏌 Tynedale Tyne Green, ☏ (01434) 60 81 54
◉ Abbey★ (Saxon Crypt★★, Leschman chantry★)
◎ Hadrian's Wall★★, N : 4.5 mi by A 6079. Housesteads★★, NW : 12.5 mi by A 6079 and B 6318

Hallbank without rest
Hallgate ✉ NE46 1XA – ☏ (01434) 605 567 – www.hallbankguesthouse.com
7 rm ⊡ – †£ 50/80 ††£ 70/120
♦ Set right in the heart of town, in the shadow of the 14C Gaol; formerly two separate houses, now an L-shaped guesthouse with an almost medieval feel. Fair-sized bedrooms offer a good level of comforts and are immaculately kept.

West Close House without rest
Hextol Ter, Southwest : 0.5 mi by B 6305 ✉ NE46 2AD – ☏ (01434) 603 307
– Restricted opening December-February
3 rm ⊡ – †£ 33/49 ††£ 65/66
♦ Detached house hidden down a private road. Immensely peaceful – from the well-maintained, Zen-like garden featuring lots of bamboo, to the cosy, immaculately kept interior boasting plenty of polished wood. Snug breakfast room with window seating and breakfast to order; keenly priced, comfortable bedrooms.

Bouchon
4-6 Gilesgate ✉ NE46 3NJ – ☏ (01434) 609 943 – www.bouchonbistrot.co.uk
– Closed 24-26 December, Sunday, Monday and bank holidays
Rest – French – Menu £ 16 (lunch and early dinner) – Carte £ 22/33
♦ Fiercely French restaurant in the centre of town. Simply styled ground floor with bar and plush intimate first floor dining room with opulent purple furnishings. Tasty, neatly presented, authentic French cooking and a Gallic team.

Rat Inn
Anick, Northeast : 1.5 mi signposted off A 69 roundabout ✉ NE46 4LN
– ☏ (01434) 602 814 – www.theratinn.com – Closed Sunday dinner and Monday except bank holidays lunch
Rest – Carte £ 21/31
♦ Traditional pub with an open range and pleasant Tyne Valley views. Daily changing blackboard menu features wholesome pub classics, as well as some more ambitious dishes – including some for two.

HEXHAM

at Slaley Southeast : 5.5 mi by B 6306 – ✉ Hexham

Slaley Hall
Southeast : 2.25 mi ✉ NE47 0BX – ℰ (01434) 673 350
– www.deverehotels.com
135 rm ⊇ – †£79/179 ††£99/219 – 7 suites
Rest *Hadrian's Brasserie* – see restaurant listing
Rest *Dukes Grill* – (dinner only) Menu £ 26 – Carte £ 28/94
Rest *Claret Jug* – Carte £ 24/40
• Extended Edwardian manor house set in 1,000 acres and boasting two championship golf courses, a spa and extensive leisure facilities. Spacious, stylish guest areas. Largely classical bedrooms, with 'Double Deluxe' being more contemporary. Classical dishes served in formal, cosy Duke's; Brasserie menu in Hadrian's; British favourites offered in clubby Claret Jug.

Hadrian's Brasserie – at Slaley Hall Hotel
Southeast : 2.25 mi ✉ NE47 0BX – ℰ (01434) 673 350 – www.devere.co.uk
Rest – (dinner only) Menu £ 26 – Carte £ 26/48
• Large brasserie set within an extended Edwardian manor house in a spacious country leisure resort. À la carte and set menu offer classically based dishes crafted from locally sourced produce.

at Haydon Bridge West : 7.5 mi on A 69 – ✉ Hexham

Langley Castle
Langley-on-Tyne, South : 2 mi by A 69 on A 686 ✉ NE47 5LU
– ℰ (01434) 688 888 – www.langleycastle.com
27 rm ⊇ – †£120/210 ††£149/275   **Rest** – Menu £ 16/40
• Stunning 14C castle in 12 acres. Stone walls, tapestries and heraldic shields give baronial feel. Luxurious bedrooms exhibit period features; some have window seats or four-posters. Stable rooms are simpler. Dining room offers adventurous, seasonally influenced menu.

HEYTESBURY – Wiltshire – 503 N30 – see Warminster

HIGHCLERE – Hampshire – 503 P29 – pop. 2 409 – ✉ Newbury   6 B1

▶ London 69 mi – Newbury 5 mi – Reading 25 mi

Yew Tree with rm
Hollington Cross, Andover Rd., South : 1 mi on A 343 ✉ RG20 9SE – ℰ (01635) 253 360 – www.theyewtree.net – Closed dinner 25-26 December
7 rm ⊇ – †£120 ††£120   **Rest** – Menu £ 20 (lunch) – Carte £ 30/41
• Characterful 17C whitewashed inn with wood-furnished terrace, rustic beamed interior, three linen-laid dining rooms and a marble-topped bar. Classical cooking mixes pub and restaurant style dishes. Service is structured. Smart, modern bedrooms boast wet rooms.

HIGHCLIFFE – Dorset – 503 O31   4 D3

▶ London 112 mi – Bournemouth 10 mi – Salisbury 21 mi – Southampton 26 mi

Lord Bute
179-185 Lymington Rd ✉ BH23 4JS – ℰ (01425) 278 884 – www.lordbute.co.uk
11 rm ⊇ – †£105 ††£115 – 2 suites
Rest – (closed Sunday dinner and Monday) Menu £ 17/33 – Carte £ 21/36
• Modern, purpose-built property with a warm, contemporary style. Light, airy conservatory lounge with terrace. Comfortable, well-appointed bedrooms boast bold colours, safes and spa baths. Smart, formal restaurant hosts occasional cabaret or jazz evenings.

HIGH CROSBY – Cumbria – see Carlisle

HIGHER BURWARDSLEY – Cheshire West and Chester – see Tattenhall

HINDON – Wiltshire – 503 N30 – pop. 493   4 C2
▶ London 103 mi – Shaftesbury 7 mi – Warminster 10 mi

Lamb Inn with rm
High St ✉ SP3 6DP – ✆ (01747) 820 573 – www.lambathindon.co.uk
19 rm – †£ 95/120 ††£ 120/180, ⌂ £ 10 **Rest** – Carte £ 20/35
- Scottish-themed 13C inn with cosy, characterful rooms featuring deep red walls, inglenook fireplaces and antique furniture. Appealing menu blends local produce and traditional Scottish dishes with a few Mediterranean specials. Smart bedrooms; some four-posters.

HINDRINGHAM – Norfolk   15 C1
▶ London 118 mi – Fakenham 8 mi – Holt 8 mi

Field House without rest
Moorgate Rd ✉ NR21 0PT – ✆ (01328) 878 726
– www.fieldhousehindringham.co.uk – Closed 20 December-1 February
3 rm ⌂ – †£ 70/75 ††£ 90/110
- Well-kept flint stone house with pretty garden and summer house. Pristine lounge with books and magazines. Extensive breakfast menus. Carefully co-ordinated rooms with extras.

HINTLESHAM – Suffolk – 504 X27 – see Ipswich

HINTON ST GEORGE – Somerset   3 B3
▶ London 138 mi – Taunton 21 mi – Weymouth 41 mi – Yeovil 13 mi

Lord Poulett Arms with rm
High St ✉ TA17 8SE – ✆ (01460) 73 149 – www.lordpoulettarms.com – Closed 25-26 December and 1 January
4 rm ⌂ – †£ 60/65 ††£ 85/95 **Rest** – Carte £ 20/38
- Charming pub with lavender-framed terrace, boules pitch, secret garden and detailed, candlelit country interior. Local, seasonal produce informs an interesting menu that's rooted firmly in the Med. Smart, stylish bedrooms boast roll-top or slipper baths.

HISTON – Cambridgeshire – 504 U27 – see Cambridge

HITCHIN – Hertfordshire – 504 T28 – pop. 33 352   12 A2
▶ London 40 mi – Bedford 14 mi – Cambridge 26 mi – Luton 9 mi

Radcliffe Arms
31 Walsworth Rd ✉ SG4 9ST – ✆ (01462) 456 111 – www.radcliffearms.com
Rest – Carte £ 27/42
- True neighbourhood pub with central bar, gravity fed ales and a good spirit and wine selection. Tasty cooking focuses on well-presented, restaurant-style dishes. Breakfast is served from 8am.

HOCKLEY HEATH – West Midlands – 503 O26 – pop. 1 525   19 C2
– ✉ Solihull
▶ London 117 mi – Birmingham 11 mi – Coventry 17 mi

Nuthurst Grange Country House
Nuthurst Grange Ln, South : 0.75 mi by A 3400 ✉ B94 5NL – ✆ (01564) 783 972
– www.nuthurst-grange.co.uk
19 rm ⌂ – †£ 95/132 ††£ 110/165
Rest *Kingswood* – see restaurant listing
- Attractive part-Edwardian former farmhouse, next to the M40. Ground and first floor bedrooms boast four-posters; second floor rooms are more modern. Self-contained function suite has two chapels, a minstrel's gallery and walled herb garden.

Kingswood – at Nuthurst Grange Country House Hotel
Nuthurst Grange Ln, South : 0.75 mi by A 3400 ✉ B94 5NL – ✆ (01564) 783 972
– www.nuthurst-grange.co.uk
Rest – (closed Saturday lunch and Sunday dinner) Menu £ 25/45
- Traditional hotel dining room with formal ambience and country house style décor. Seasonal, classically based menus display innovative modern touches, ranging from 2 courses at lunch to 7 at dinner. Influences come from throughout Europe.

HOLBEACH – Lincolnshire – **502** U25 – pop. 7 247   **17** D2
▶ London 117 mi – Kingston-upon-Hull 81 mi – Norwich 62 mi – Nottingham 60 mi

Pipwell Manor without rest
Washway Rd, Saracen's Head, Northwest : 1.5 mi by A 17 ✉ *PE12 8AY* – ☏ *(01406) 423 119*
4 rm – †£ 40 ††£ 60

♦ Charming Georgian manor set close to The Wash, on the site of an old Cistercian Grange. Homely guest areas and traditional country bedrooms with fresh, modern touches. A warm welcome is guaranteed, with cake served on arrival. Miniature railway in the garden.

HOLFORD – Somerset – **503** K30 – pop. 307 – ✉ Bridgwater   **3** B2
Great Britain

▶ London 171 mi – Bristol 48 mi – Minehead 15 mi – Taunton 22 mi
◉ Stogursey Priory Church★★, W : 4.5 mi

Combe House
Southwest : 0.75 mi by Youth Hostel rd ✉ *TA5 1RZ* – ☏ *(01278) 741 382*
– *www.combehouse.co.uk*
18 rm – †£ 85/115 ††£ 145/165   **Rest** – Carte £ 20/35

♦ Smart country house with lovely garden, in a secluded wooded valley. Stylish, modern interior boasts a pleasant spa. Bright bedrooms feature contemporary fabrics and white furniture. Split-level restaurant offers classical cooking with a modern edge.

HOLKHAM – Norfolk – **504** W25   **15** C1
▶ London 124 mi – King's Lynn 32 mi – Norwich 39 mi

Victoria
Park Rd. ✉ *NR23 1RG* – ☏ *(01328) 711 008* – *www.holkham.co.uk*
10 rm – †£ 90/130 ††£ 130/185
Rest *The Restaurant* – see restaurant listing

♦ Extended flint farmhouse boasting country outlook and large lawned gardens. Characterful, shabby-chic interior with individually styled bedrooms; some furniture from Indian sub-continent.

The Restaurant – at The Victoria Hotel
Park Rd ✉ *NR23 1RG* – ☏ *(01328) 711 008* – *www.holkham.co.uk*
Rest – Menu £ 24 (weekend lunch) – Carte £ 30/42

♦ Choice of 2 colonial-style dining rooms, conservatory or wood-furnished terrace. Seasonally evolving menus have unfussy, brasserie style: local produce to the fore. Friendly, attentive service.

HOLMFIRTH – West Yorkshire – **502** O23 – pop. 21 979   **22** B3
▶ London 187 mi – Leeds 35 mi – Sheffield 32 mi – Manchester 25 mi

Sunnybank
78 Upperthong Ln, West : 0.5 mi by A 6024 ✉ *HD9 3BQ* – ☏ *(01484) 684 857*
– *www.sunnybankguesthouse.co.uk*
5 rm – †£ 60 ††£ 70/100   **Rest** – Menu £ 25

♦ Attractive Victorian house with lovely gardens, hidden away down a narrow road. Mix of period and modern furnishings; smart art deco piano in the lounge. Cosy bedrooms have a personal touch – those in the courtyard are slightly more modern. Oak panelled dining room features local produce and valley views.

at Hepworth Southeast : 2 mi by A 635 off B 6106

Butchers Arms
38 Towngate ✉ *HD9 1TE* – ☏ *(01484) 682 361* – *www.thebutchersarms.co.uk*
Rest – (booking essential) Menu £ 17 (weekday lunch) – Carte £ 33/45

♦ Stone inn with delightful terraces, hidden on the fringes of a sleepy hamlet. A huge array of menus offer robust, country dishes. All produce is from within 75 miles; most from even closer.

HOLT – Wiltshire – **503** – see Bradford-on-Avon

HOLT – Norfolk – **504** X25 – pop. 3 550

15 C1

▶ London 124 mi – King's Lynn 34 mi – Norwich 22 mi

Byfords
Shirehall Plain ✉ NR25 6BG – ℰ (01263) 711 400 – www.byfords.org.uk
16 rm – †£ 115 ††£ 190   **Rest** – Carte £ 26/36

• Flint-fronted Grade II listed house that boasts something different: a well-stocked deli; rustic cellar café; and stunning rooms, with great bathrooms and under-floor heating.

HOLTON – Somerset – **503** M30 – pop. 225

4 C3

▶ London 117 mi – Bristol 35 mi – Cardiff 111 mi – Southampton 76 mi

Old Inn
✉ BA9 8AR – ℰ (01963) 32 002 – www.theoldinnrestaurant.co.uk
Rest – Carte £ 26/40

• The owner of nearby Clinger Farm always fancied being a chef but instead bought this 400 year old pub, added a large restaurant and now delights in seeing the kitchen make good use of his produce; the Josper grill is the star of the show.

HONITON – Devon – **503** K31 – pop. 11 213

2 D2

▶ London 186 mi – Exeter 17 mi – Southampton 93 mi – Taunton 18 mi

🛈 Lace Walk Car Park ℰ (01404) 4 37 16, www.honiton.com

◉ All Hallows Museum ★ **AC**

◉ Ottery St Mary★ (St Mary's★) SW : 5 mi by A 30 and B 3177. Faraway Countryside Park (≤★) **AC**, SE : 6.5 mi by A 375 and B 3174

Holt
178 High St ✉ EX14 1LA – ℰ (01404) 47 707 – www.theholt-honiton.com
– Closed 2 January, 25-26 December, Sunday and Monday
Rest – Carte £ 25/29

• Rustic family-run pub providing a 'distinctive and sustainable taste of Devon'. Regularly changing menu of regional and homemade produce; local ales from the family brewery.

Railway
Queen St ✉ EX14 1HE – ℰ (01404) 47 976 – www.therailwayhoniton.co.uk
– Closed 25-26 December, Sunday and Monday
Rest – Carte £ 25/34

• Smart, modern town centre pub offering authentic Italian cooking at affordable prices, including homemade pasta, brick-fired pizzas and steaks. Eclectic wine list. Weekly film club.

at Gittisham Southwest : 3 mi by A 30 – ✉ Honiton

Combe House
✉ EX14 3AD – ℰ (01404) 540 400 – www.combehousedevon.com
– Closed 3-18 January
13 rm – †£ 169/179 ††£ 199 – 3 suites
Rest – (booking essential for non-residents) Menu £ 33/49

• Listed Elizabethan mansion set in glorious Devon countryside. Impressive Great Hall. Individually designed, stylish bedrooms with fine antiques and roaring fires. Unfussy cooking makes good use of local produce. Friendly service.

HOOK – Hampshire – **504** R30 – pop. 6 471 – ✉ Basingstoke

6 B1

▶ London 47 mi – Oxford 39 mi – Reading 13 mi – Southampton 31 mi

Tylney Hall
Rotherwick , Northwest : 2.5 mi by A30 and Newnham rd on Ridge Ln
✉ RG27 9AZ – ℰ (01256) 764 881 – www.tylneyhall.co.uk
103 rm – †£ 190 ††£ 220 – 9 suites
Rest *Oak Room* – Menu £ 25/40 – Carte approx. £ 50

• Grand and beautifully restored 19C mansion in delightful, extensive Gertrude Jekyll gardens. Country house rooms, some with private conservatories or suites over two floors. Classically English dining room with oak panelling and garden views.

HOOK

Old House at Home
Newnham Green – RG27 9AH – ℘ (01256) 762 222 – Closed 25 December and dinner Sunday and bank holidays
Rest – *(booking advisable)* Menu £ 18 – Carte £ 26/34
♦ Mid-19C former post office tucked away in the corner of a lovely green. Main room split in two, with open fires on both sides; the old bar is cosier. Refined, measured, modern seasonal dishes.

Hogget
London Rd, (at the junction of A 30 and A 287) – RG27 9JJ – ℘ (01256) 763 009 – www.hogget.co.uk – Closed 25-26 December and Sunday dinner
Rest – Carte £ 30/36
♦ Located at junction of A30 and A287. Wholesome, honest cooking; sensibly priced dishes, made using local produce: pie and mash or steak and chips through to crab cake or calves liver.

HOPE – Derbyshire – 502 O23 – ⊠ Sheffield 16 A1

▶ London 180 mi – Derby 50 mi – Manchester 31 mi – Sheffield 15 mi

Losehill House
Lose Hill Ln, Edale Rd, North : 1 mi by Edale Rd – S33 6AF – ℘ (01433) 621 219 – www.losehillhouse.co.uk
21 rm – †£ 140/160 ††£ 160/265   **Rest** – Menu £ 17/38
♦ Comfortable, well-kept hotel with a bright, airy, modern feel. Open-plan lounge and bar. Small pool, sauna and outdoor hot tub. Bedrooms all have a view. Formally laid restaurant with superb views up to Win Hill; modern-style dishes, with cheese a speciality.

Underleigh House without rest
Losehill Ln, Hope Valley, North : 1 mi by Edale Rd – S33 6AF – ℘ (01433) 621 372 – www.underleighhouse.co.uk – Closed 1-25 February, Christmas and New Year
5 rm – †£ 70 ††£ 90/105
♦ Converted Victorian property, rurally located and personally run; well situated for the Peak District. Countryside views and a welcoming country ambience.

HORLEY – Surrey – 504 T30 – pop. 22 582 7 D2

▶ London 27 mi – Brighton 26 mi – Royal Tunbridge Wells 22 mi

Langshott Manor
Langshott, North : 0.5 mi by A 23 turning right at Chequers H. onto Ladbroke Rd – RH6 9LN – ℘ (01293) 786 680 – www.langshottmanor.com
21 rm – †£ 150/180 ††£ 180/600 – 1 suite
Rest *Mulberry* – see restaurant listing
♦ Characterful manor house dating back to 1540 and set amidst roses, vines and ponds. Traditional exterior contrasts with contemporary furnishings. Bedrooms are split between the manor and three mews houses: many feature fireplaces or four-posters and one has a patio terrace. Smart marble and granite bathrooms.

Mulberry – at Langshott Manor Hotel
Langshott, North : 0.5 mi by A 23 turning right at Chequers H. onto Ladbroke Rd – RH6 9LN – ℘ (01293) 786 680 – www.langshottmanor.com
Rest – *(booking essential)* Menu £ 20/44 – Carte £ 24/63
♦ Smart hotel dining room set within a charming manor house, which part-dates back to 1540. Good choice of modern, well-presented dishes from the set menu, à la carte or evening tasting menu.

HORNCASTLE – Lincolnshire – 502 T24 – pop. 6 090 17 C1

▶ London 143 mi – Lincoln 22 mi – Nottingham 62 mi
i Wharf Rd ℘ (01507) 60 11 11, www.horncastleuk.com

HORNCASTLE

※※ **Magpies** with rm   AC rest, VISA ⦿
71-75 East St ⌷ LN9 6AA – ℰ (01507) 527 004 – www.magpiesrestaurant.co.uk
– Closed 27 December-11 January, Saturday lunch, Monday and Tuesday
3 rm ⌑ – †£ 110 ††£ 130
Rest – Menu £ 42 (dinner) – Carte (lunch) £ 30/32
♦ Formerly three 18C cottages, now a cosy, family-run restaurant. Hearty, classically based dishes arrive attractively presented, with tasty homemade breads to start and mini-assiettes to finish. Quarterly wine dinners are a feature. Bedrooms have floral feature walls and a free-standing bath or double sinks.

HORNDON-ON-THE-HILL – Thurrock – **504** V29 – pop. 1 612   **13** C3
▶ London 25 mi – Chelmsford 22 mi – Maidstone 34 mi – Southend-on-Sea 16 mi

🛏 **Bell** with rm   📶 ⁞ P VISA ⦿ AE
High Rd ⌷ SS17 8LD – ℰ (01375) 642 463 – www.bell-inn.co.uk – Closed 25-26 December and bank holiday Mondays
15 rm – †£ 60 ††£ 85/100, ⌑ £ 9.50   **Rest** – Carte £ 22/37
♦ 15C coaching inn, run by the same family for 50 years. Cooking is a step above your usual pub fare, displaying classically based dishes with some modern touches. Pub bedrooms are styled after Victorian mistresses; those in Hill House display thoughtful extras.

HORNINGSEA – Cambridgeshire – see Cambridge

HORNINGSHAM – Wiltshire – **504** N30 – see Warminster

HORN'S CROSS – Devon – **503** H31 – ⌷ Bideford ▮ Great Britain   **2** C1
▶ London 222 mi – Barnstaple 15 mi – Exeter 46 mi
◉ Clovelly★★, W : 6.5 mi on A 39 and B 3237 – Bideford : Bridge★★ – Burton Art Gallery★ **AC** – Lundy Island★★ (by ferry), NE : 7 mi on a 39 and B 3235 – Hartland : Hartland Church★ - Hartland Quay★ (❋★★) – Hartland Point ⌕★★★, W : 9 mi on A 39 and B 3248 – Great Torrington (Dartington Crystal★ **AC**), SE : 15 mi on A 39 and A 386 – Rosemoor★, SE : 16 mi on A 39, A 386 and B 3220

⌂ **Roundhouse** without rest   ⎈ ※ P VISA ⦿ ⓘ
West : 1 mi on A 39 ⌷ EX39 5DN – ℰ (01237) 451 687
– www.the-round-house.co.uk
3 rm ⌑ – †£ 40/50 ††£ 65
♦ Located on site of 13C corn mill, this friendly guesthouse offers cream teas on arrival. Spacious lounge and good quality breakfasts. Comfy, clean, well-kept bedrooms.

HORRINGER – Suffolk – **504** W27 – see Bury St Edmunds

HORSHAM – West Sussex – **504** T30 – pop. 47 804   **7** D2
▶ London 39 mi – Brighton 23 mi – Guildford 20 mi – Lewes 25 mi
ℹ 9 Causeway ℰ (01403) 21 16 61, www.horsham.gov.uk
⛳ Mannings Heath Fullers, Hammerpond Rd, Mannings Heath, ℰ (01403) 21 02 28

🏨 **South Lodge** ⌘   ⌕ ⎈ ⓓ ⛳ ※ 🖼 ⎊ ⁞ ⌲ P VISA ⦿ AE ⓘ
Brighton Rd, Lower Beeding, Southeast : 5 mi on A 281 ⌷ RH13 6PS – ℰ (01403) 891 711 – www.exclusivehotels.co.uk
85 rm ⌑ – †£ 260 ††£ 260 – 4 suites
Rest *The Pass*❀ – see restaurant listing
Rest *Camellia Country Kitchen* – (booking essential for non-residents)
Menu £ 22/35 – Carte £ 29/47
♦ Victorian mansion set in 93 acres, with period furnishings, heavy panelled walls and corporate feel. Traditional bedrooms in the main house and more contemporary rooms in the wing; some suites boasts jacuzzis or terraces. Relaxed Camellia Country Kitchen or live kitchen action in The Pass.

ENGLAND

245

HORSHAM

XX The Pass – at South Lodge Hotel
Brighton Rd, Lower Beeding, Southeast : 5 mi on A 281 – ✉ RH13 6PS
– ☏ (01403) 891 711 – www.southlodgehotels.co.uk
Rest – *(closed Monday and Tuesday)* Menu £ 25/70
Spec. Squab pigeon, orange and parfait. Gigha halibut with baby gem, parsley and clams. Honey cheesecake, lemon thyme and lavender.
• A unique experience and ideal for those for whom a chef's table is not enough. You sit and watch all the action in the hotel's main kitchen, while the central station cooks for you. Expect modern, intricate and balanced dishes, with well-thought-out combinations.

XX Restaurant Tristan
Stans Way, off East St – ✉ RH12 1HU – ☏ (01403) 255 688
– www.restauranttristan.co.uk – Closed 2 weeks late July-early August, 25 December-7 January, Sunday and Monday
Rest – Menu £ 18/38
• First floor restaurant in characterful 16C beamed house. Cooking is seasonal but also elaborate in style and the kitchen is a fan of modern techniques. Service is smooth and effective.

at Rowhook Northwest : 4 mi by A 264 and A 281 off A 29 – ✉ Horsham

Chequers Inn
✉ RH12 3PY – ☏ (01403) 790 480 – Closed 25 December and Sunday dinner
Rest – Carte £ 21/35
• Part-15C inn with a charming open-fired, stone-floored bar and unusual corrugated dining room extension. Chef-owner grows, forages for or shoots the majority of his produce. Classical menus.

HOUGH-ON-THE-HILL – Lincolnshire – see Grantham

HOVE – Brighton and Hove – **504** T31 – see Brighton and Hove

HOVERINGHAM – Nottinghamshire – pop. 308   16 B2
▶ London 135 mi – Birmingham 77 mi – Leeds 74 mi – Sheffield 57 mi

Reindeer Inn
Main St – ✉ NG14 7JR – ☏ (01159) 663 629 – www.thereindeerinn.com – Closed 1 week May, 1 week October, Tuesday lunch, Sunday dinner and Monday
Rest – Menu £ 10 (lunch) – Carte £ 25/36
• Characterful country inn set next to a cricket pitch, with beams, open fire and a cosy, relaxed atmosphere. Popular with locals. Well-priced menus offer mainly classical dishes.

HUDDERSFIELD – West Yorkshire – **502** O23 – pop. 146 234   22 B3
▶ London 191 mi – Bradford 11 mi – Leeds 15 mi – Manchester 25 mi
🛈 Princes Alexandra Walk ☏ (01484) 22 32 00, www.huddersfieldonline.org.uk
⛳ Bradley Park Bradley Rd, ☏ (01484) 22 37 72
⛳ Woodsome Hall Fenay Bridge, ☏ (01484) 60 29 71
⛳ Outlane Slack Lane, Off New Hey Rd, ☏ (01422) 37 47 62
⛳ Meltham Thick Hollins Hall, ☏ (01484) 85 02 27
⛳ Fixby Hall Lightridge Rd, ☏ (01484) 42 62 03
⛳ Crosland Heath Felks Stile Rd, ☏ (01484) 65 32 16

at Thunder Bridge Southeast : 5.75 mi by A 629 – ✉ Huddersfield

Woodman Inn with rm
✉ HD8 0PX – ☏ (01484) 605 778 – www.woodman-inn.co.uk – Closed 25-26 December
12 rm – †£ 48/68 ††£ 74/85   **Rest** – Carte £ 21/34 s
• Traditional 19C pub set in a small hamlet in the valley. The classic British menus are extensive and change with the seasons. Lunch is simple and hearty, dinner more ambitious. Nearby cottage bedrooms are simple but well-kept.

at Shelley Southeast : 6.25 mi by A 629 - on B 6116 – ✉ Huddersfield

Three Acres
Roydhouse, Northeast : 1.5 mi on Flockton rd ✉ *HD8 8LR* – ☎ *(01484) 602 606*
– www.3acres.com – Closed 1 January
14 rm ⊡ – †£ 83/105 ††£ 125 – 2 suites
Rest – *(booking essential)* Carte £ 30/43

♦ Well-established stone inn, set in a pleasant rural location. Two smart meeting rooms. Bedrooms are warm, modern and comfortable; those in the annexe are the most spacious. Agreeably busy restaurant with open fires: fish dishes prepared at open seafood bar.

HULLBRIDGE – Essex   13 C2_3
▶ London 40 mi – Croydon 46 mi – Barnet 50 mi – Ealing 63 mi

Anchor
Ferry Rd ✉ *SS5 6ND* – ☎ *(01702) 230 777* – *www.theanchorhullbridge.co.uk*
– Closed 25 December
Rest – Carte £ 21/35

♦ Modern, informal, open-plan restaurant with pleasant terrace, sleek bar and lots of windows to take in the river views. Accessible, seasonal British menu; more adventurous specials at dinner.

HUNNINGHAM – Warwickshire – pop. 190   19 D3
▶ London 94 mi – Birmingham 36 mi – Liverpool 129 mi – Leeds 125 mi

Red Lion
Main St ✉ *CV33 9DY* – ☎ *(01926) 632 715* – *www.redlionhunningham.co.uk*
Rest – Carte £ 19/34

♦ Charming, part-17C timbered inn set by the River Lemm and displaying over 300 framed American comics and a ceiling-mounted air pipe for delivering orders. Daily menu offers well-crafted, unfussy pub fare, with the occasional modern touch.

HUNSDON – Hertfordshire   12 B2
▶ London 26 mi – Bishop's Stortford 8 mi – Harlow 7 mi

Fox and Hounds
2 High St ✉ *SG12 8NH* – ☎ *(01279) 843 999*
– www.foxandhounds-hunsdon.co.uk – Closed 26 December, Sunday dinner and Monday
Rest – Menu £ 17 (weekdays) – Carte £ 26/35

♦ Sizeable pub with rustic bar, cookery book filled dining room, large garden and terrace. Short menus offer unfussy, simply prepared dishes in a range of different styles; portions are generous.

HUNSTANTON – Norfolk – 502 V25 – pop. 4 505   14 B1
▶ London 120 mi – Cambridge 60 mi – Norwich 45 mi
🛈 The Green ☎ (01485) 53 26 10, www.hunstanton-info.com
 Golf Course Rd, ☎ (01485) 53 28 11

The Neptune (Kevin Mangeolles) with rm
85 Old Hunstanton Rd, Old Hunstanton, Northeast : 1.5 mi on A 149
✉ *PE36 6HZ* – ☎ *(01485) 532 122* – *www.theneptune.co.uk – Closed Monday*
6 rm (dinner included) ⊡ – †£ 125/150 ††£ 210/225
Rest – *(dinner only and Sunday lunch)* Menu £ 30/52
Spec. Asparagus with sweetcorn custard and deep-fried hen's egg. Lamb loin with sweetbread and tongue, Epoisses mash. Strawberry parfait, compressed strawberries and Campari jelly

♦ Very personally run, attractive, red-brick former pub. New England style interior boasts rattan-furnished bar and dining room with large nautical photographs. Constantly evolving menu relies on the latest local produce available. Presentation is modern; service is relaxed and efficient. Simple, comfortable bedrooms.

HUNSTANTON

at Thornham Northeast : 4.5 mi on A 149

Orange Tree with rm
High St ⊠ PE36 6LY – ℘ *(01485) 512 213*
– www.theorangetreethornham.co.uk
6 rm ⊑ – †£ 65/110 ††£ 85/110
Rest – Carte £ 25/35 **s**

♦ Gregarious staff ensure a warm welcome at this 17C inn; even your dog will be offered a snack in the bar. Menu in the contemporary restaurant covers all bases and several countries. Compact but modern bedrooms also available.

HUNTINGDON – Cambridgeshire – 504 T26 – pop. 20 600   14 A2

▶ London 69 mi – Bedford 21 mi – Cambridge 16 mi

🛈 St. Mary's St ℘ (01480) 38 85 88, www.visithuntingdonshire.org

⛳ Hemingford Abbots Cambridge Rd, New Farm Lodge, ℘ (01480) 49 50 00

Old Bridge
1 High St ⊠ PE29 3TQ – ℘ *(01480) 424 300 – www.huntsbridge.com*
24 rm ⊑ – †£ 99/150 ††£ 150/240
Rest *Terrace* – see restaurant listing

♦ Long-standing, family-owned riverside hotel with small wine shop in reception: one owner is a Master of Wine. Contemporary bedrooms feature plenty of fabrics and spacious bathrooms.

Terrace – at Old Bridge Hotel
1 High St ⊠ PE29 3TQ – ℘ *(01480) 424 300 – www.huntsbridge.com*
Rest – Menu £ 20 (lunch) – Carte £ 30/39 **s**

♦ Choose between formal wood-panelled dining room and more casual conservatory with terrace. Menus change every two days and feature traditional dishes with some Mediterranean influences.

at Wyton East : 2.5 mi by B 1514 off A 1123

Magdalene House without rest
Huntingdon Rd ⊠ PE28 2AD – ℘ *(01480) 465 011*
– www.magdalene-house.co.uk
3 rm – †£ 78 ††£ 88/98

♦ Modern barn conversion in grounds of attractive 17C thatched house once owned by Magdalene College. Spacious bedrooms with good level of extras. Continental breakfast is taken in your room.

at Hemingford Grey Southeast : 5 mi by A 1198 off A 14 – ⊠ Huntingdon

Cock
47 High St ⊠ PE28 9BJ – ℘ *(01480) 463 609 – www.thecockhemingford.co.uk*
Rest – (booking essential) Carte £ 26/35

♦ Homely 17C country pub with spacious dining room, run by an experienced team. Tried-and-tested pub cooking offers good value lunches, daily fish specials and a mix and match sausage board.

HUNWORTH – Norfolk   15 C1

▶ London 129 mi – Norwich 25 mi – East Dereham 17 mi – Taverham 19 mi

Hunny Bell
The Green ⊠ NR24 2AA – ℘ *(01263) 712 300 – www.hunnybell.co.uk*
Rest – Carte £ 25/34

♦ Sympathetically renovated 18C whitewashed pub with smart country interior. Appealing menu of sophisticated pub classics crafted from local, seasonal produce; even the bar snacks are homemade.

HURLEY – Windsor and Maidenhead – pop. 1 712   11 C3
▶ London 35 mi – Maidenhead 5 mi – Reading 18 mi

Olde Bell Inn
High St ⌧ *SL6 5LX* – ✆ *(01628) 825 881* – *www.theoldebell.co.uk* – *Closed 25-26 December*
47 rm – †£ 109/400 ††£ 109/400 – 1 suite
Rest *Restaurant* – see restaurant listing

♦ Part-12C timbered inn close to the Thames. Charming rear gardens with outside bar, rotisserie and BBQ. Characterful bedrooms in contemporary, minimalist style; all have rocking chairs, sheepskin rugs and good extras. Lovely open-fired bar.

Restaurant – at Olde Bell Inn
High St ⌧ *SL6 5LX* – ✆ *(01628) 825 881* – *www.theoldebell.co.uk* – *Closed 25-26 December*
Rest – *(closed Sunday dinner and bank holiday Monday dinner)* Menu £ 17 – Carte £ 31/34

♦ Heavily timbered dining room within a part-12C inn, boasting wood-panelling, tiled floors and shabby-chic furnishings. Interesting seasonal menus with a rustic base; much of the produce is from the kitchen garden. Pleasant summer terrace.

Black Boys Inn with rm
Henley Rd, Southwest : 1.5 mi on A 4130 ⌧ *SL6 5NQ* – ✆ *(01628) 824 212*
– *www.blackboysinn.co.uk*
8 rm – †£ 75/88 ††£ 120/150
Rest – *(closed Sunday dinner)* Menu £ 15 (lunch) – Carte £ 26/42

♦ Rustic restaurant in 16C former pub with exposed beams and wood burning stove. Experienced owners are avid Francophiles and the concise, traditional French menu reflects this. Polite service. Clean, unfussy bedrooms with thoughtful extras such as books.

HURSTBOURNE TARRANT – Hampshire – 503 P30 – pop. 700   6 B1
– ⌧ Andover
▶ London 77 mi – Bristol 77 mi – Oxford 38 mi – Southampton 33 mi

Esseborne Manor
Northeast : 1.5 mi on A 343 ⌧ *SP11 0ER* – ✆ *(01264) 736 444*
– *www.esseborne-manor.co.uk*
19 rm – †£ 89/109 ††£ 89/240
Rest – Menu £ 17/25 **s** – Carte dinner approx. £ 35 **s**

♦ 100 year old country house in attractive grounds with herb garden. Smart, well-appointed bedrooms, some in the garden cottages. Ferndown room boasts a spa bath and private patio. Long, narrow dining room with large windows.

HURSTPIERPOINT – 504 T31 – pop. 6 264   7 D2
▶ London 45 mi – Croydon 35 mi – Barnet 87 mi – Ealing 69 mi

Fig Tree
120 High St ⌧ *BN6 9PX* – ✆ *(01273) 832 183* – *www.figtreerestaurant.co.uk*
– *Closed 2 weeks January, Tuesday lunch, Sunday dinner and Monday*
Rest – Menu £ 19/23 – Carte £ 25/39

♦ Attractive Victorian house in pretty high street, with striking Gothic arched bay window and small terrace. Carefully priced menus showcase local, seasonal ingredients. Loyal local following.

HURWORTH-ON-TEES – Darlington – 502 P20 – see Darlington

HUTTON-LE-HOLE – North Yorkshire – 502 R21 – pop. 162   23 C1
▶ London 244 mi – Scarborough 27 mi – York 33 mi

Burnley House without rest
⌧ *YO62 6UA* – ✆ *(01751) 417 548* – *www.burnleyhouse.co.uk* – *March-November*
6 rm – †£ 60 ††£ 80/95

♦ Attractive part 16C, part Georgian house, Grade II listed in a picturesque Moors village. Brown trout in beck winding through garden. Simple, individually styled bedrooms.

HUTTON MAGNA – Durham – see Barnard Castle

ICKLESHAM – East Sussex – 504 V/W31 9 C3
▶ London 66 mi – Brighton 42 mi – Hastings 7 mi

Manor Farm Oast
Windmill Ln, South : 0.5 mi ⊠ TN36 4WL – ℰ (01424) 813787
– www.manorfarmoast.co.uk – Closed 26 February-26 March and Christmas-New Year
3 rm ⊇ – †£ 85/105 ††£ 105 **Rest** – Menu £ 32
♦ 19C former oast house retaining original features and surrounded by orchards. Welcoming beamed lounge with open fire. One of the comfy bedrooms is completely round. Home-cooked menus in circular dining room.

IDEN GREEN – Kent – 504 V30 8 B2
▶ London 55 mi – Croydon 49 mi – Barnet 81 mi – Ealing 85 mi

Waters End Farm without rest
Standen St, Southeast : 1.25 mi ⊠ TN17 4LA – ℰ (01580) 850 731
– www.watersendfarm.co.uk – March-October
5 rm ⊇ – †£ 95/135 ††£ 95/135
♦ Characterful part-timbered, part-brick house, set in 43 peaceful acres. Bedrooms – in converted barns – boast heavy wood furniture and modern facilities. Huge mural of the house in the breakfast room or eat outside on the terrace in summer.

ILFRACOMBE – Devon – 503 H30 – pop. 10 490 ▮ Great Britain 2 C1
▶ London 218 mi – Barnstaple 13 mi – Exeter 53 mi
ⓒ Mortehoe★★ : St Mary's Church - Morte Point★, SW : 5.5 mi on B 3343 – Lundy Island★★ (by ferry). Braunton : St Brannock's Church★, Braunton Burrows★, S : 8 mi on A 361 – Barnstaple★ : Bridge★, S : 12 mi on A 3123, B 3230, A 39, A 361 and B 3233

Hampton's without rest
Excelsior Villas, Torrs Pk. ⊠ EX34 8AZ – ℰ (01271) 864 246
– www.thehamptonshotel.co.uk
6 rm ⊇ – †£ 75/110 ††£ 80/110
♦ Imposing Victorian villa with individual, bohemian style. Open-plan lounge and breakfast room with honesty bar and DVDs. Well-equipped, individually styled bedrooms are designed by the friendly owner; those to the front boast rooftop views.

Gendarmerie
63 Fore St ⊠ EX34 9ED – ℰ (01271) 865 984 – Closed November, Tuesday-Wednesday October-March and Monday
Rest – *(dinner only) (booking advisable)* Menu £ 27
♦ Simple little restaurant with intimate, candlelit interior, tucked away on a side street and very personally run by a husband and wife team. Concise, daily changing menu showcases market produce in precise, skilfully executed combinations.

ILKLEY – West Yorkshire – 502 O22 – pop. 13 472 22 B2
▶ London 210 mi – Bradford 13 mi – Harrogate 17 mi – Leeds 16 mi
🛈 Station Rd ℰ (01943) 60 23 19, www.visitbradford.com
▦ Myddleton, ℰ (01943) 60 72 77

Box Tree (Simon Gueller)
37 Church St, on A 65 ⊠ LS29 9DR – ℰ (01943) 608 484 – www.theboxtree.co.uk
– Closed 1-6 January, 27-30 December, Sunday dinner and Monday
Rest – *(dinner only and lunch Friday-Sunday)* Menu £ 25/55
Spec. Ballotine of salmon with herb fromage blanc. Squab pigeon 'en vessie' peas, baby onions and pancetta. Passion fruit soufflé with a hot passion fruit sauce.
♦ Iconic restaurant in a charming 18C sandstone cottage. Plush sitting area with semi-gilded ceiling and fine antiques. Two main dining rooms laid with quality tableware. Confident, classical cooking is precise and skilful, with a strong French bias. Preparations are straightforward and let the ingredients shine through.

ILMINGTON – Warwickshire – **504** O27 – Great Britain — **19** C3

► London 91 mi – Birmingham 31 mi – Oxford 34 mi – Stratford-upon-Avon 9 mi
◉ Hidcote Manor Garden★★, SW : 2 mi by minor rd – Chipping Campden★★, SW : 4 mi by minor rd

Folly Farm Cottage
Back St ⊠ *CV36 4LJ* – ℰ *(01608) 682 425* – *www.follyfarm.co.uk*
3 rm ⊇ – †£ 65 ††£ 88 **Rest** – Menu £ 20
♦ Cosy, characterful cottage in small village, with friendly owners and lovely garden. Beams and heavy drapes abound. Bedrooms are named after garden plants; some have four-posters or whirlpool baths. Simple home-cooked dinners.

Howard Arms with rm
Lower Green ⊠ *CV36 4LT* – ℰ *(01608) 682 226* – *www.howardarms.com*
8 rm ⊇ – †£ 85 ††£ 155 **Rest** – Carte £ 21/29
♦ Delightful 17C Cotswold stone inn, on a peaceful village green. Choice of beamed bar with inglenook fireplace, raised-level dining room and lovely terrace. Dishes are hearty and British-based. Warm, cosy bedrooms; those in the extension are more contemporary.

INGHAM – Norfolk – **504** W27 – pop. 376 — **15** D1

► London 139 mi – Norwich 25 mi – Ipswich 65 mi – Lowestoft 30 mi

Ingham Swan
Sea Palling Rd ⊠ *NR12 9AB* – ℰ *(01692) 581 099* – *www.theinghamswan.co.uk*
– Closed 25-26 December
Rest – *(booking essential at dinner)* Menu £ 19/28 **s** – Carte £ 22/41 **s**
♦ Cosy, attractive, thatched 14C pub in the shadow of an 11C church; equally characterful beamed interior. Quite complex dishes use plenty of ingredients, albeit in classic combinations.

INGLETON – North Yorkshire – **502** M21 – pop. 1 641 — **22** A2
– ⊠ Carnforth (lancs.)

► London 266 mi – Kendal 21 mi – Lancaster 18 mi – Leeds 53 mi

Riverside Lodge
24 Main St ⊠ *LA6 3HJ* – ℰ *(015242) 41 359* – *www.riversideingleton.co.uk*
– Closed 24-25 December
8 rm ⊇ – †£ 42 ††£ 64 **Rest** – Menu £ 17 **s**
♦ Pleasant 19C house close to famous pot-holing caves. Informal gardens. Cosy sitting room and homely bedrooms. Conservatory dining room with great views across Yorkshire Dales.

IPSWICH – Suffolk – **504** X27 – pop. 145 708 – Great Britain — **15** C3

► London 76 mi – Norwich 43 mi
🛈 St Stephens Lane ℰ (01473) 25 80 70, www.visit-ipswich.com
▪ Rushmere Rushmere Heath, ℰ (01473) 72 56 48
▪ Purdis Heath Bucklesham Rd, ℰ (01473) 72 89 41
▪ Fynn Valley Witnesham, ℰ (01473) 78 52 67
◉ Sutton Hoo★, NE : 12 mi by A 12 Y and B 1083 from Woodbridge

Plan on next page

Salthouse Harbour
1 Neptune Quay ⊠ *IP4 1AX* – ℰ *(01473) 226 789* – *www.salthouseharbour.co.uk*
68 rm ⊇ – †£ 125 ††£ 140/220 – 2 suites **X a**
Rest *Eaterie* – see restaurant listing
♦ Old quayside salt warehouse boasting a modern extension and attractive marina views. Boutique bedrooms: some with exposed brick walls, others with chaise longues or copper slipper baths; ask for one with a balcony overlooking the marina.

IPSWICH

Argyle St.	X	2
Back Hamlet	Z	3
Birkfield Drive	X	5
Bond St.	X	6
Bridgwater Rd.	X	7
Buttermarket Centre	X	9
Carr St.	X	10
Chevallier St.	Y	13
College St.	X	15
Corn Hill	X	16
Dogs Head St.	X	18
Ellenbrook Rd.	Z	19
Falcon St.	X	21
Fore Hamlet	Z	22
Franciscan Way	X	24
Friars St.	X	25
Grey Friars Rd.	X	26
Grove Lane	YZ	28
Handford Rd.	X, Y	30
Lloyds Ave	X	31
Lower Orwell St.	X	32
Northgate St.	X	33
Orwell Pl.	X	34
Quadling St.	X	35
Queen St.	X	37
St Helen's St.	X, Y	39
St Margarets St.	X	40
St Nicholas St.	X	41
St Peter's St.	X	42
Salthouse St.	X	43
Silent St.	X	46
Tavern St.	X	47
Tower Ramparts Centre	X	47
Upper Orwell St.	X	49
Waterworks St.	X	51
Westgate St.	X	52
Wolsey St.	X	53
Yarmouth Rd.	Y	54

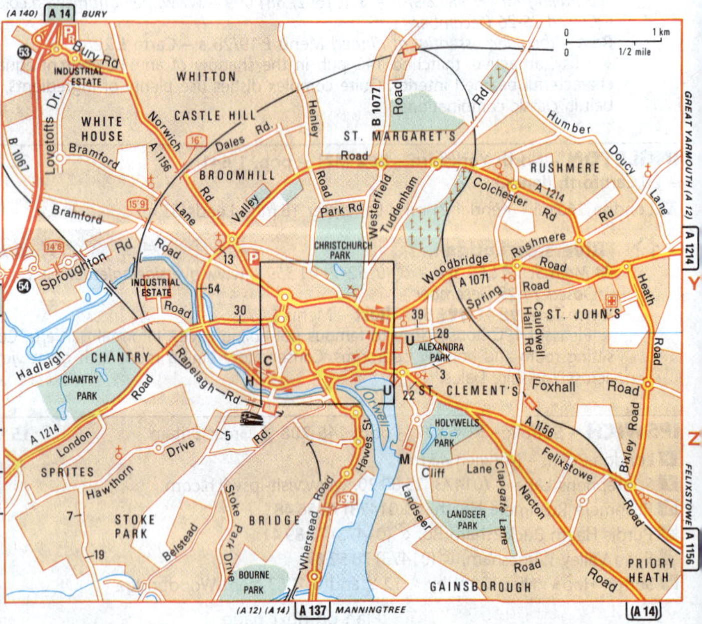

Guesthouses don't provide the same level of service as hotels. They are often characterised by a warm welcome and a décor which reflects the owner's personality. Those shown in red are particularly pleasant.

Kesgrave Hall

Hall Rd, East : 4.75 mi by A 1214 on Bealings rd ✉ *IP5 2PU –* ✆ *(01473) 333 471*
– www.kesgravehall.com
22 rm – †£ 184 ††£ 230/245, ⊇ £ 16 – 1 suite
Rest – Carte £ 23/42

♦ White Georgian house with large lawned gardens and impressive terrace. Stylish lounges have relaxed, urban-chic feel. Large, luxurious bedrooms boast quality furnishings, modern facilities and stylish bathrooms. Busy informal dining room offers European menu.

Eaterie – at Salthouse Harbour Hotel

1 Neptune Quay ✉ *IP4 1AX –* ✆ *(01473) 226 789 – www.salthouseharbour.co.uk*
Rest – Menu £ 18 (lunch) – Carte £ 27/45 **Xa**

♦ Informal hotel restaurant within an old salt warehouse. Exposed brick and wood floors contrast with contemporary black booths and a stylish bar. Modern menu displays Mediterranean influences.

at Hintlesham West : 5 mi by A 1214 on A 1071 - Y - ✉ Ipswich

Hintlesham Hall

✉ *IP8 3NS –* ✆ *(01473) 652 334 – www.hintleshamhall.com*
30 rm ⊇ – †£ 150 ††£ 160 – 3 suites
Rest – Menu £ 34/45 **s**

♦ Impressive Georgian manor house with 16C roots; original features such as ornate plasterwork and gold leaf inlaid cornicing remain. Grand bedrooms in main house; cosy courtyard rooms – some with terraces. Vast dining room offers both classical and modern dishes.

IRBY – Merseyside – 502 K23 20 A3

▶ London 212 mi – Liverpool 12 mi – Manchester 46 mi – Stoke-on-Trent 56 mi

Da Piero

5 Mill Hill Rd ✉ *CH61 4UB –* ✆ *(0151) 648 73 73 – www.dapiero.co.uk – Closed 2 weeks September, 1 week January, Sunday and Monday*
Rest – Italian – *(dinner only) (booking essential)* Carte £ 23/49

♦ Family-owned and run restaurant with homely, understated décor and intimate, pleasant feel. Carefully prepared, classical Italian cooking, with lots of rustic Sicilian dishes.

IRONBRIDGE – Telford and Wrekin – 503 M26 – pop. 1 560 18 B2
Great Britain

▶ London 135 mi – Birmingham 36 mi – Shrewsbury 18 mi

◉ Ironbridge Gorge Museum★★ **AC** (The Iron Bridge★★, Coalport China Museum★★, Blists Hill Open Air Museum★★, Museum of the Gorge and Visitor Centre★)

Library House without rest

11 Severn Bank ✉ *TF8 7AN –* ✆ *(01952) 432 299 – www.libraryhouse.com*
– Closed 24-30 December
4 rm ⊇ – †£ 70 ††£ 100

♦ Nicely hidden, albeit tricky to find, guesthouse with rear terrace. Homely sitting room. Cottage style breakfast room. Compact, comfy rooms, with a touch of style about them.

Restaurant Severn

33 High St. ✉ *TF8 7AG –* ✆ *(01952) 432 233 – www.restaurantsevern.co.uk*
– Closed 2 weeks January, 2 weeks August, Sunday dinner, Monday and Tuesday
Rest – *(dinner only and Sunday lunch) (booking essential)* Menu £ 19/29

♦ Close to the Severn and world heritage site 'Ironbridge'. Pleasant, light and airy dining room with a real family feel. Experienced owners cook tasty, classically based dishes.

IRONBRIDGE

🍴 **da Vinci** VISA ◎◎
26 High St ⊠ TF8 7AD – ℰ (01952) 432 250
– www.davinci-restaurant-ironbridge.co.uk – Closed Christmas-New Year, 1 week spring, 1 week autumn, Sunday and Monday
Rest – Italian – *(dinner only) (booking essential)* Carte £ 17/37
♦ Keenly run osteria in conservation village. Split-level dining with warm décor and simple, rustic style. Italian chef sources produce from his homeland. Authentic cooking; Tuscan specialities.

ISLE OF MAN – I.O.M. – **502** G21 – see Man (Isle of)

ITTERINGHAM – Norfolk – **504** X25 – ⊠ Aylsham   **15** C1

▶ London 126 mi – Cromer 11 mi – Norwich 17 mi

🛏 **Walpole Arms**   🚗 🍴 P VISA ◎◎
The Common ⊠ NR11 7AR – ℰ (01263) 587 258 – www.thewalpolearms.co.uk
– Closed 25 December and Sunday dinner
Rest – Carte £ 20/31
♦ 18C inn with characterful beamed bar and more formal restaurant. Interesting, Mediterranean-influenced menu is made up of generous, well-prepared dishes and appealing daily specials. The pork belly with Mediterranean vegetables is a firm favourite with the locals.

IVYCHURCH – Kent – **504** W30 – 🟩 Great Britain   **9** C2

▶ London 67 mi – Ashford 11 mi – Rye 10 mi

◉ Rye Old Town★★ : Mermaid St★ - St Mary's Church (≤★), SW : 9 mi on A 2070 and A 259

🏠 **Olde Moat House** without rest   🚗 ✍ 📡 P VISA ◎◎
Northwest : 0.75 mi on B 2070 ⊠ TN29 0AZ – ℰ (01797) 344 700
– www.oldemoathouse.co.uk
3 rm ⊒ – †£ 50/60 ††£ 70/110
♦ Blissfully characterful guesthouse with 15C origins, set in over three acres, encircled by small moat. Beamed sitting room with inglenook. Individual, homely styled rooms.

IXWORTH – Suffolk – **504** W27 – see Bury St Edmunds

JERSEY – C.I. – **503** O/P33 – pop. 85 150 – see Channel Islands

---

JEVINGTON – East Sussex – **504** U31 – see Eastbourne

KEGWORTH – Leicestershire – **502** Q25 – pop. 3 338 – 🟩 Great Britain   **16** B2

▶ London 123 mi – Leicester 18 mi – Loughborough 6 mi – Nottingham 13 mi

◉ Calke Abbey★, SW : 7 mi by A 6 (northbound) and A 453 (southbound) – Derby★ - Museum and Art Gallery★, Royal Crown Derby Museum★, NW : 9 mi by A 50 – Nottingham Castle Museum★, N : 11 mi by A 453 and A 52

🏠 **Kegworth House** without rest   🚗 ✍ 📡 P VISA ◎◎ AE
42 High St ⊠ DE74 2DA – ℰ (01509) 672 575 – www.kegworthhouse.co.uk
– Closed Christmas and New Year
11 rm ⊒ – †£ 90/180 ††£ 140/250
♦ Georgian manor house in village, secluded in walled garden. Fine interior with original decorative features. Individually-decorated bedrooms of charm and character.

KELSALE – Suffolk – **504** Y27 – pop. 1 309 – ⊠ Saxmundham   **15** D3

▶ London 103 mi – Cambridge 68 mi – Ipswich 23 mi – Norwich 37 mi

🏠 **Mile Hill Barn** without rest   🚗 ✍ P
North Green, North : 1.5 mi on A 12 ⊠ IP17 2RG – ℰ (01728) 668 519
– www.mile-hill-barn.co.uk
3 rm ⊒ – †£ 60/75 ††£ 85/95
♦ Traditional 15C Suffolk barn in landscaped gardens. Tea on arrival in impressive raftered lounge. Bedrooms boast feature beds and modern bathrooms. Cosy breakfast room; Aga-cooked breakfasts.

KELVEDON – Essex – **504** W28 – pop. 4 593   13 C2
▶ London 56 mi

George & Dragon
Cogglshall Rd, Northwest : 2 mi on B 1024 ✉ *CO5 9PL* – ℘ *(01376) 561 797*
– *www.georgeanddragonkelvedon.co.uk* – *Closed 25 December-2 January, Sunday and Monday*
Rest – Carte £ 25/30
♦ Clean, bright, welcoming restaurant with a sleek, contemporary style, encompassing topiary planters, marble tiled floors, antique mirrors, and art deco pictures and statuettes. Simple, well-priced menu with locally caught fish specials. Pretty terrace.

KENDAL – Cumbria – **502** L21 – pop. 28 030 Great Britain   21 B2
▶ London 270 mi – Bradford 64 mi – Burnley 63 mi – Carlisle 49 mi
🛈 Highgate ℘ (01539) 79 75 16, www.golakes.co.uk
🏌 The Heights, ℘ (01539) 72 34 99
◉ Levens Hall and Garden★ **AC**, S : 4.5 mi by A 591, A 590 and A 6. Lake Windermere★★, NW : 8 mi by A 5284 and A 591

Beech House *without rest*
40 Greenside, by All Hallows Lane ✉ *LA9 4LD* – ℘ *(01539) 720 385*
– *www.beechhouse-kendal.co.uk* – *Closed 1 week Christmas*
6 rm ⊑ – †£ 60/75 ††£ 80/100
♦ Pretty three-storey Georgian house set just out of town. Small honesty bar. Modern, open-plan lounge with comfy sofas and communal breakfast tables. Bright, airy, pine-furnished bedrooms come with complimentary cake and up-to-date bathrooms. Welcoming owners.

Newmoon
129 Highgate ✉ *LA9 4EN* – ℘ *(01539) 729 254*
– *www.newmoonrestaurant.co.uk* – *Closed 1-7 January, 25-26 December, Sunday and Monday*
Rest – *(booking advisable)* Carte £ 23/29
♦ Smart, high street restaurant with ground floor bar, intimate, beamed dining room and a loyal local following. The owner's Turkish heritage is reflected in the menu, which has a strong Mediterranean base; dishes are fresh and colourful.

at Sizergh Southwest : 3 mi by A 591 – ✉ Kendal

Strickland Arms
✉ *LA8 8DZ* – ℘ *(01539) 561 010* – *www.thestricklandarms.com* – *Closed 25 December*
Rest – Carte £ 20/28
♦ Former coach house for next door Sizergh Castle. Sizeable interior with characterful, shabby-chic feel. Menus feature classical pub dishes, with daily specials on the board. Regular events.

at Crosthwaite West : 5.25 mi by All Hallows Lane – ✉ Kendal

Punch Bowl Inn *with rm*
✉ *LA8 8HR* – ℘ *(01539) 568 237* – *www.the-punchbowl.co.uk*
9 rm ⊑ – †£ 120 ††£ 305 **Rest** – Carte £ 21/39
♦ Charming 17C inn set in the picturesque Lyth Valley, boasting cosy fires, exposed wooden beams and trailing hop bines. Choice of rustic bar or formal restaurant, which offer interesting takes on old favourites at lunch and more ambitious dishes at dinner. Luxury bedrooms boast quality linens and roll-top baths.

KENILWORTH – Warwickshire – **503** P26 – pop. 22 218 Great Britain   19 C2
▶ London 102 mi – Birmingham 19 mi – Coventry 5 mi – Leicester 32 mi
🛈 11 Smalley Pl ℘ (01926) 74 89 00, www.kenilworthweb.co.uk
◉ Castle★ **AC**

KENILWORTH

Victoria Lodge without rest

180 Warwick Rd ⊠ CV8 1HU – ℰ (01926) 512 020
– www.victorialodgekenilworth.co.uk – Closed 2 weeks Christmas-New Year
10 rm ⊇ – †£ 50/65 ††£ 82
♦ Keenly and proudly run red-brick house with comfortable lounge and linen-laid breakfast room. Immaculately kept, colourfully decorated bedrooms come with complimentary mineral water and fresh milk; some rooms boast balconies or patios. Excellent breakfasts.

Bosquet
97a Warwick Rd ⊠ CV8 1HP – ℰ (01926) 852 463
– www.restaurantbosquet.co.uk – Closed 2 weeks July-August, 1 week Christmas, Sunday and Monday
Rest – French – (dinner only and lunch by arrangement) Menu £ 33
– Carte £ 36/42
♦ Contemporary feel to this established restaurant with wooden floors, well-spaced tables and stylish leather chairs. Confident, well-informed cooking displays a classical French base.

Beef
11 Warwick Rd ⊠ CV8 1HD – ℰ (01926) 863 311 – www.beef.uk.com – Closed 1 week Christmas-New Year, 1 week Easter, 22 August-5 September, Sunday dinner and bank holidays
Rest – Beef specialities – Menu £ 20 (lunch) – Carte £ 24/38
♦ Rustic restaurant boasting exposed brickwork, slate floors and quirky cowhide banquettes. Menus offer robust, hearty dishes; mainly Scottish steaks cooked on the charcoal grill and cuts of beef from American, Argentinean or Wagyū cattle.

KENTON – Devon – **503** J31 – see Exeter

KERNE BRIDGE – Herefordshire – **503** M28 – see Ross-on-Wye

KESSINGLAND – Suffolk – pop. 4 211   **15** D2
▶ London 126 mi – Norwich 28 mi – Ipswich 40 mi – Colchester 66 mi

Old Rectory
157 Church Rd ⊠ NR33 7SQ – ℰ (01502) 742 188 – www.bandblowestoft.co.uk
– Closed 17 December-2 January
3 rm ⊇ – †£ 62 ††£ 94   **Rest** – Menu £ 22 s
♦ 1834 rectory retaining original character, a short walk from the beach. Individually furnished bedrooms boast antique furniture and feature beds. Beautiful gardens. Choice of dishes offered at dinner; locally sourced produce includes their own vegetables and eggs.

KESWICK – Cumbria – **502** K20 – pop. 4 984   Great Britain   **21** A2
▶ London 294 mi – Carlisle 31 mi – Kendal 30 mi
ℹ Market Sq. ℰ (017687) 7 26 45, www.keswick.org
Threlkeld Hall, ℰ (017687) 7 93 24
Derwentwater★ X – Thirlmere (Castlerigg Stone Circle★), E : 1.5 mi X A

Lairbeck
Vicarage Hill ⊠ CA12 5QB – ℰ (017687) 73 373
– www.lairbeckhotel-keswick.co.uk – Closed Christmas-New Year and restricted opening 9 November-10 March
                                                                                 Xa
14 rm ⊇ – †£ 61/107 ††£ 126   **Rest** – (dinner only) Menu £ 24 s
♦ Attractive Victorian house in the suburbs, its mature garden boasting a huge Sequoia Redwood. Original barley-twist staircase, galleried landing and comfy bar-lounge. Bedrooms come in a mix of styles; some have lovely views. Daily menu in pleasant dining room.

KESWICK

Bank St	Z	2
Borrowdale Rd	Z	3
Brackenrigg Drive	Z	5
Brundholme Rd	X	6
Chestnut Hill	X	8
Church St	Z	10
Crosthwaite Rd	X	12
Derwent St	Z	13
High Hill	Z	14
Main St	Z	
Manor Brow	X	17
Market Square	Z	18
Museum Square	Z	19
Otley Rd	Z	20
Park Horse Yard	Z	21
Police Station Court	Z	22
Ratcliffe Pl.	Z	23
St Herbert St	Z	24
Standish St	Z	25
Station St	Z	26
The Crescent	Z	27
The Hawthorns	Y	29
The Headlands	Z	31
Tithebarn St	Z	32

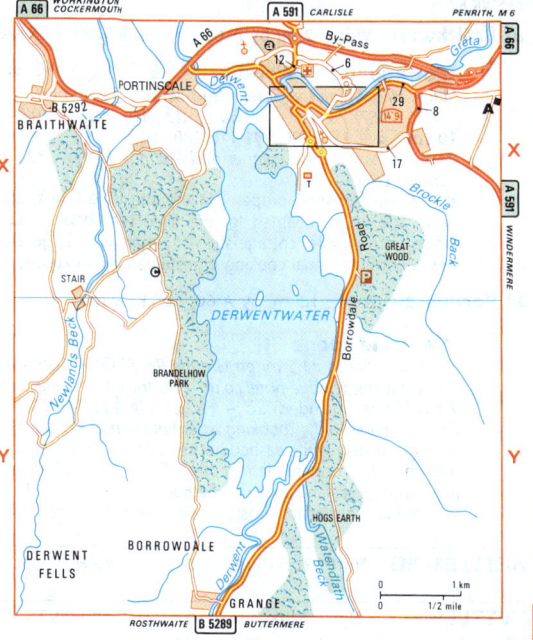

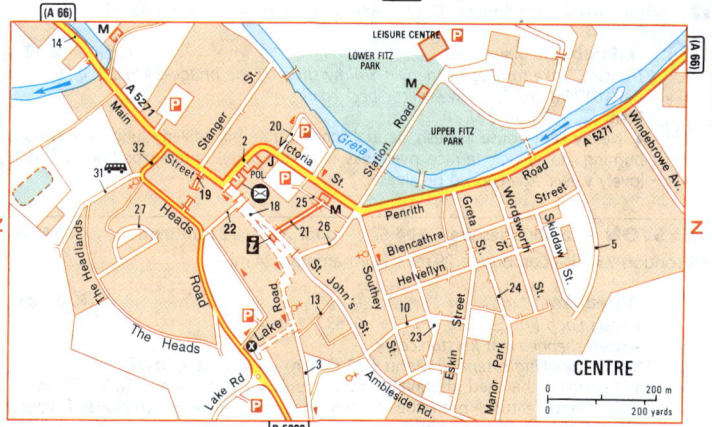

CENTRE

Morrel's

34 Lake Rd ⌨ CA12 5DQ – ✆ (017687) 72 666
– www.morrels.co.uk
– Closed 2 weeks January, 25-26 December and Monday

Zx

Rest – *(dinner only)* Carte £ 24/33

♦ Popular local eatery with scrubbed wood flooring, etched glass dividers and large, colourful canvasses. Seasonally changing dishes have subtle Mediterranean influences; some come in two sizes.

KESWICK

at Braithwaite West : 2 mi by A 66 - X - on B 5292 – ✉ Keswick

Cottage in the Wood
Magic Hill, Whinlatter Forest, Northwest : 1.75 mi on B 5292 ✉ *CA12 5TW*
– ✆ *(017687) 78 409* – *www.thecottageinthewood.co.uk* – *Closed January*
10 rm – †£ 80/90 ††£ 110/180
Rest – *(closed Sunday dinner and Monday)* Menu £ 32 (dinner) **s** – Carte lunch approx. £ 19
♦ 17C whitewashed property in mountainside forest, affording excellent views down the valley. Beamed lounge filled with books and ornaments. Bedrooms range from simple, cottage-style to smart with large beds, roll-top baths and views. Local, seasonal cooking in restaurant; airy extension offers superb outlook.

at Portinscale West : 1.5 mi by A 66 – ✉ Keswick

Swinside Lodge
Newlands, South : 1.5 mi on Grange Rd ✉ *CA12 5UE* – ✆ *(017687) 72 948*
– *www.swinsidelodge-hotel.co.uk* – *Restricted opening January & December*
7 rm (dinner included) – †£ 124/144 ††£ 248/296   **Xc**
Rest – *(dinner only) (booking essential for non-residents)* Menu £ 45 **s**
♦ Immaculately whitewashed house in countryside location, boasting lovely views over the fells. Local info in reception. Two small, traditional country house lounges filled with books and antiques. Bedrooms are more modern in style. Formal, linen-laid dining room offers classical daily menus and house party atmosphere.

KETTLESING – North Yorkshire – **502** P21 – see Harrogate

KETTLEWELL – North Yorkshire – **502** N21 – pop. 297   **22** A2

▶ London 246 mi – Darlington 42 mi – Harrogate 30 mi – Lancaster 42 mi

Littlebeck without rest
The Grn., take turning at the Old Smithy shop by the bridge ✉ *BD23 5RD*
– ✆ *(01756) 760 378* – *www.little-beck.co.uk*
3 rm – †£ 50 ††£ 78
♦ Neatly kept house in fresh, neutral tones. Large, book-filled lounge with wood burning stove; rear terrace overlooks stream. Comfy, unfussy bedrooms boast lovely views. Aga-cooked breakfasts.

KEYSTON – Cambridgeshire – **504** S26 – pop. 257 – ✉ Huntingdon   **14** A2

▶ London 75 mi – Cambridge 29 mi – Northampton 24 mi

Pheasant
Village Loop Rd. ✉ *PE28 0RE* – ✆ *(01832) 710 241*
– *www.thepheasant-keyston.co.uk*
Rest – *(booking essential)* Menu £ 22 (lunch) – Carte £ 28/40
♦ Charming thatched 'destination dining' pub set in a sleepy hamlet. Seasonal daily menu features both the classics and some more international flavours – and a good selection of offal.

KIBWORTH BEAUCHAMP – Leicestershire – **504** Q/R26   **16** B2
– pop. 3 550 – ✉ Leicester

▶ London 85 mi – Birmingham 49 mi – Leicester 6 mi – Northampton 17 mi

Firenze
9 Station St ✉ *LE8 0LN* – ✆ *(0116) 279 62 60* – *www.firenze.co.uk* – *Closed 1 week Christmas-New Year, Sunday, Monday and bank holidays*
Rest – Italian – *(booking essential)* Menu £ 23 (weekdays) – Carte £ 23/40
♦ Smart neighbourhood restaurant displaying colourful modern fabrics and Mediterranean artwork. Extensive à la carte and tasting menus offer authentic Italian dishes; good value lunch.

KIBWORTH HARCOURT Leics. – Leicestershire – **504** R26 — **16** B2

▶ London 101 mi – Leicester 9 mi – Coventry 36 mi – Nottingham 41 mi

Boboli
88 Main St ⊠ LE8 0NQ – ℘ (0116) 279 33 03 – www.bobolirestaurant.co.uk
– Closed 25-26 December
Rest – Italian – Menu £ 17 (lunch) – Carte £ 19/35
♦ Stylish Italian restaurant named after gardens in Florence. Fresh, simple and seasonally-changing cooking with bold flavours. Affordable wines and cheery, prompt service.

KIDDERMINSTER – Worcestershire – **503** N26 – pop. 55 348 — **18** B2

▶ London 139 mi – Birmingham 17 mi – Shrewsbury 34 mi – Worcester 15 mi

at Chaddesley Corbett Southeast : 4.5 mi by A 448 – ⊠ Kidderminster

Brockencote Hall
on A 448 ⊠ DY10 4PY – ℘ (01562) 777 876 – www.brockencotehall.com
17 rm – †£ 96 ††£ 190
Rest *Restaurant* – see restaurant listing
♦ Keenly run, 19C mansion with long driveway leading past a lake, croquet lawn and grazing sheep. Classic guest areas. Spacious, well-equipped bedrooms: some in annexe; some with great park views.

Restaurant – at Brockencote Hall Hotel
on A 448 ⊠ DY10 4PY – ℘ (01562) 777 876 – www.brockencotehall.com
Rest – Menu £ 26/40 **s** – Carte £ 45/55 **s**
♦ Well-run restaurant with cocktail bar and conservatory. Large, airy dining room with French windows opening onto a terrace. Skilfully prepared, flavoursome modern dishes have a classical base.

ENGLAND

KILHAM – East Riding of Yorkshire – **502** S21 — **23** D2

▶ London 225 mi – Leeds 63 mi – Sheffield 75 mi – Manchester 108 mi

Kilham Hall
Driffield Rd, South : 0.25 mi ⊠ YO25 4SP – ℘ (01262) 420 466
– www.kilhamhall.co.uk – March-October
3 rm – †£ 100/110 ††£ 120/170 **Rest** – Menu £ 33
♦ Attractive Victorian house with croquet lawn, tennis court and small heated pool. Stylish guest areas boast heavy fabrics and bespoke furniture; spacious bedrooms mix the modern and classic. Charming owner offers homemade scones on arrival. Substantial communal breakfasts; home-cooked dinners by arrangement.

Don't confuse the couvert rating ✗ with the stars ✿ !
Couverts defines comfort and service, while stars are awarded for the best cuisine across all categories of comfort.

KINGHAM – Oxfordshire – **503** P28 – pop. 1 434 — **10** A1

▶ London 81 mi – Gloucester 32 mi – Oxford 25 mi

Mill House
⊠ OX7 6UH – ℘ (01608) 658 188 – www.millhousehotel.co.uk
23 rm – †£ 70/80 ††£ 110/130 **Rest** – Menu £ 18/35 – Carte £ 22/30
♦ Privately run house in 10 acres of lawned gardens with a brook flowing through the grounds. Spacious lounge with comfortable armchairs and books. Comfortable, traditionally styled bedrooms. Modern décor suffuses restaurant.

KINGHAM

Moat End without rest
The Moat, by West St ✉ *OX7 6XZ* – ✆ *(01608) 658 090* – *www.moatend.co.uk*
– Closed Christmas and New Year
3 rm – †£ 60/70 ††£ 80
• Cosy converted barn with garden, ponies and countryside views; luxury breakfasts include eggs from own hens. Neatly kept, compact rooms. Friendly owner has wealth of local knowledge.

Kingham Plough with rm
The Green ✉ *OX7 6YD* – ✆ *(01608) 658 327* – *www.thekinghamplough.co.uk*
– Closed 25 December
7 rm – †£ 75/130 ††£ 130
Rest – Carte £ 27/40
• Rustic, laid-back pub and restaurant located on the green in an unspoilt Cotswold village; run by a friendly team and experienced chef-owner. Menus mix modern, gutsy pub dishes with a few more ambitious offerings, and evolve as new ingredients arrive. Comfy bedrooms await: 2 and 4, in the main building, are best.

Tollgate Inn with rm
Church St ✉ *OX7 6YA* – ✆ *(01608) 658 389* – *www.thetollgate.com*
– Closed Sunday dinner and Monday
9 rm – †£ 70/75 ††£ 100
Rest – Carte £ 20/35
• Grade II listed inn in centre of unspoiled village. Easy-going lunch menu; more ambitious evening à la carte. Comfy seating and inglenooks, plus popular front terrace. Immaculately kept bedrooms have a warm, bright feel.

KING'S LYNN – Norfolk – **502** V25 – pop. 43 119 – Great Britain — 14 B1

▶ London 103 mi – Cambridge 45 mi – Leicester 75 mi – Norwich 44 mi

🛈 Purfleet Quay ✆ (01553) 76 30 44, www.kingslynnonline.com

🛇 Eagles Tilney All Saints School Rd, ✆ (01553) 82 71 47

◉ Houghton Hall★★ **AC**, NE : 14.5 mi by A 148 – Four Fenland Churches★ (Terrington St Clement, Walpole St Peter, West Walton, Walsoken) SW : by A 47

Bankhouse
King's Staithe Sq ✉ *PE30 1RD* – ✆ *(01553) 660 492* – *www.thebankhouse.co.uk*
11 rm – †£ 80/120 ††£ 100/150
Rest – Carte £ 21/29
• Grade II listed Georgian house by the River Ouse. Comfortable bedrooms in various shapes and sizes: all have good facilities and excellent bathrooms; some have a pleasant outlook. Stylish, contemporary bar and brasserie.

at Grimston East : 6.25 mi by A 148 – ✉ King'S Lynn

Congham Hall
Lynn Rd. ✉ *PE32 1AH* – ✆ *(01485) 600 250*
– *www.conghamhallhotel.co.uk*
13 rm – †£ 106/185 ††£ 135/395 – 1 suite
Rest *Orangery* – Menu £ 22 – Carte £ 41/49
• Part-Georgian country house with neat lawns and formal flower garden. Comfy lounges and small bar with terrace. Well-appointed bedrooms offer pleasant views. Currently undergoing an extension project. Good service from smartly attired staff. Restaurant offers classical menu; kitchen and herb garden produce features.

KINGS MILLS – see Channel Islands (Guernsey)

KINGSBRIDGE – Devon – **503** I33 – pop. 5 521　　　　　　　　　　　　2 C3

▶ London 236 mi – Exeter 36 mi - Plymouth 24 mi – Torquay 21 mi
☗ Thurlestone, ✆ (01548) 56 04 05
◉ Town★ – Boat Trip to Salcombe★★ **AC**
◉ Prawle Point (≼★★★) SE : 10 mi around coast by A 379

at Goveton Northeast : 2.5 mi by A 381 – ✉ Kingsbridge

Buckland-Tout-Saints ⚘

Goveton, Northeast : 2.5 mi by A 381 ✉ *TQ7 2DS –* ✆ *(01548) 853 055*
– www.tout-saints.co.uk – Closed 3-19 January
14 rm ⊇ – ♦£ 125/205 ♦♦£ 165/205 – 2 suites
Rest – Menu £ 20/39

♦ Immaculate, impressive Queen Anne mansion with neat lawned gardens in rural location. Wood panelled lounge; all other areas full of antiques. Well-furnished bedrooms. Accomplished cooking in beautiful wood-panelled country house restaurant.

KINGSKERSWELL – Devon – **503** J32 – pop. 4 624 – ✉ Torquay　　　　2 C2

▶ London 199 mi – Exeter 18 mi – Torquay 4 mi

Bickley Mill Inn with rm

Stoneycombe, West : 2 mi by Stoneycombe rd. ✉ *TQ12 5LN –* ✆ *(01803) 873 201*
– www.bickleymill.co.uk – Closed 23-30 December
12 rm ⊇ – ♦£ 65/85 ♦♦£ 80/130
Rest – Carte £ 18/25

♦ Modern-looking former flour mill with huge decked terrace and gardens built into the rocks. Menus are simple, traditional and keenly priced; Brixham market fish features in the specials. Individually designed bedrooms are bold and stylish; two are in the eaves.

KINGSTON BAGPUIZE – Oxfordshire – **503** P28 – see Oxford

KINGSTON-UPON-HULL – Kingston upon Hull – **502** S22　　　　23 D2
– pop. 265 615 ▌Great Britain

▶ London 183 mi – Leeds 61 mi – Nottingham 94 mi – Sheffield 68 mi
Access Humber Bridge (toll)
✈ Humberside Airport : ✆ (01652) 688456, S : 19 mi by A 63
⛴ to The Netherlands (Rotterdam) (P & O North Sea Ferries) daily (11 h) – to Belgium (Zeebrugge) (P & O North Sea Ferries) 3-4 weekly (13 h 45 mn)
🛈 1 Paragon St ✆ (01482) 22 35 59, www.hull.touristinformationguide.co.uk
☗ Springhead Park Willerby Rd, ✆ (01482) 65 63 09
☗ Sutton Park Salthouse Rd, ✆ (01482) 37 42 42
◉ Burton Constable★ **AC**, NE : 9 mi by A 165 and B 1238 Z

Plan on next page

Boars Nest

22-24 Princes Ave, Northwest : 1 mi by Ferensway off West Spring Bank Rd
✉ *HU5 3QA –* ✆ *(01482) 445 577 – www.theboarsnesthull.com*　　Zx
Rest – Menu £ 12/23 – Carte £ 20/28

♦ Rustic restaurant, formerly part-butcher's shop, with tiles/meats hooks still in situ. 3 main dining areas and upstairs lounge. Simple, classical English dishes use local, seasonal produce.

at Hessle Southwest : 2 mi by A 63 – ✉ Kingston-Upon-Hull

Artisan

22 The Weir ✉ *HU13 0RU –* ✆ *(01482) 644 906 – www.artisanrestaurant.com*
– Closed first 2 weeks January, Sunday and bank holiday Mondays
Rest – *(dinner only) (booking essential) (lunch by arrangement)* Menu £ 50

♦ Intimate restaurant with plush, homely interior, run by a passionate husband and wife team. Classical French and Italian influenced set menus with local ingredients to the fore.

KINGSTON-UPON-HULL

Bond St	X	3
Carr Lane	Y	
Commercial Rd	X	8
County Rd North	Z	9
Dock Office Row	X	10
Dock St	X	12
Fairfax Ave	Z	13
Ferensway	XY	14
George St	X	
Grimston St	X	15
Humber Dock St	Y	16
Jameson St	X	17
Jarratt St	X	18
Kingston Retail Park	Y	
King Edward St	X	19
Lowgate	Y	23
Market Pl.	Y	24
Maybury Rd	Z	25
Paragon St	X	29
Princes Quay Shopping Centre	Y	
Prince's Ave	Z	31
Prince's Dock St	Y	32
Prospect Shopping Centre	X	
Prospect St	X	
Queen St	X	35
Queen's Dock Ave	X	36
Queen's Rd	X	33
Reform St	X	37
Sculcoates Bridge	X	42
Southcoates Ave	Z	43
Southcoates Lane	X	44
Waterhouse Lane	X	47
Whitefriargate	Y	49
Wilberforce Drive	X	50
Worship St	X	52

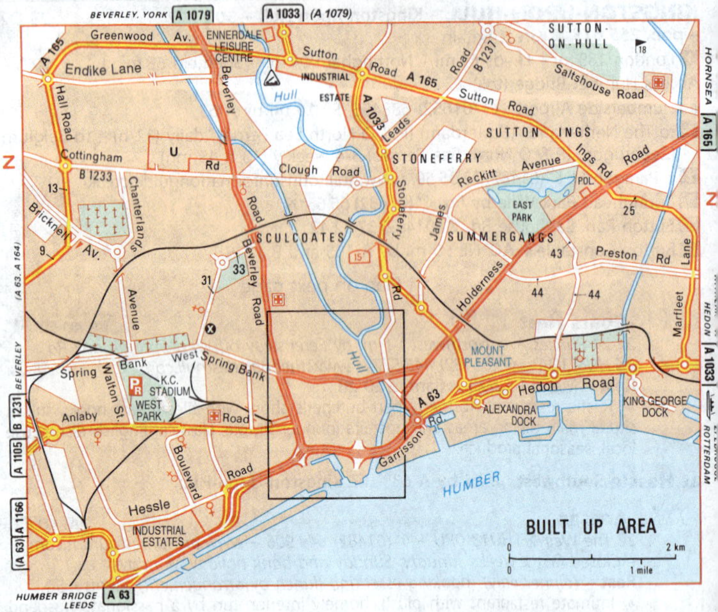

ENGLAND

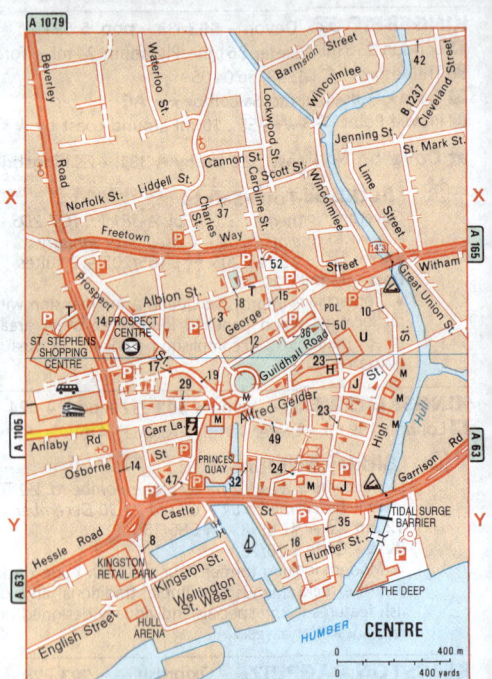

KINGSWEAR – Devon – 503 J32 – see Dartmouth

KINGTON – Herefordshire – 503 K27 – pop. 2 597   18 A3
▶ London 152 mi – Birmingham 61 mi – Hereford 19 mi – Shrewsbury 54 mi

at Titley Northeast : 3.5 mi on B 4355 – ✉ Kington

The Stagg Inn (Steve Reynolds) with rm
✉ HR5 3RL – ☎ (01544) 230 221 – www.thestagg.co.uk – Closed 2 weeks between January and February, first 2 weeks in November, 25-26 December, Sunday dinner and Monday
6 rm – †£ 65/70 ††£ 100/150 **Rest** – (booking essential) Carte £ 29/34
Spec. Scallops and parsnip purée. Fillet of beef with garlic butter. 3 crème brûlées of vanilla, elderflower and lemon.
♦ Part-medieval, part-Victorian pub with delightfully cosy interior. Straightforward cooking uses classically based recipes and relies on careful preparation and top quality produce. Menus are short, simple and to the point; dishes are truly satisfying. Bedrooms in the pub can be noisy; opt for one in the old vicarage.

KIRKBY FLEETHAM – North Yorkshire – 502 P20 – pop. 556   22 B1
▶ London 234 mi – Liverpool 124 mi – Leeds 53 mi – Sheffield 84 mi

Black Horse Inn with rm
Lumley Ln ✉ DL7 0SH – ☎ (01609) 749 010
– www.blackhorsekirkbyfleetham.com
7 rm – †£ 75 ††£ 75 **Rest** – (closed Sunday dinner) Carte £ 21/32
♦ Subtly modernised 18C pub with original beams, smart new flagged floor, candlelit bar and rear dining room. Menu ranges from tasty sharing boards to flavoursome British classics that are a step above your usual pub fare. Stylish bedrooms come with good comforts and designer bathrooms.

KIRKBY LONSDALE – Cumbria – 502 M21 – pop. 2 076   21 B3
– ✉ Carnforth (lancs.)
▶ London 259 mi – Carlisle 62 mi – Kendal 13 mi – Lancaster 17 mi
🏌 Scaleber Lane Barbon, ☎ (015242) 7 63 66
🏌 Casterton Sedbergh Rd, ☎ (015242) 7 15 92

Hipping Hall with rm
Southeast : 2.5 mi on A 65 ✉ LA6 2JJ – ☎ (015242) 71 187
– www.hippinghall.com – Closed 2-5 January
9 rm (dinner included) – †£ 248 ††£ 330
Rest – (dinner only and lunch Saturday-Sunday) Menu £ 30/50
♦ Charming part-15/16C house set in mature grounds; with attractive medieval-style restaurant, minstrels gallery and well-spaced tables laid with quality tableware. Concise, modern menus; polite service. Comfy, boldly papered lounges and well-appointed, stark white bedrooms featuring thick carpets and modern bathrooms.

Sun Inn with rm
6 Market St ✉ LA6 2AU – ☎ (015242) 71 965 – www.sun-inn.info – Closed Monday lunch
11 rm – †£ 72/92 ††£ 102/154
Rest – Menu £ 20 (lunch) – Carte £ 29/34
♦ 17C inn in busy market town with lively locals bar and rustically refurbished restaurant. Tempting bar nibbles and tasty, seasonal dishes made with locally sourced produce. Good quality linen in modern, immaculately kept bedrooms.

at Lupton Northwest : 4.75 mi on A 65 – 502 L21

Plough with rm
Cow Brow ✉ LA6 1PJ – ☎ (015395) 67 700 – www.theploughatlupton.co.uk
5 rm – †£ 100/140 ††£ 115/195, ⊇ £ 7.50 **Rest** – Carte £ 18/29
♦ Homely pub with antique tables and comfy sofas, set on the main road from the Lake District to North Yorkshire. Choose grills or a selection of small plates to mix and match with enticing sides. Smart, individually styled bedrooms complete the picture.

KIRKBY STEPHEN – Cumbria – 502 M20 – pop. 1 832 — 21 B2
▶ London 296 mi – Carlisle 46 mi – Darlington 37 mi – Kendal 28 mi

Augill Castle
Northeast : 4.5 mi by A 685 ✉ *CA17 4DE* – ✆ *(01768) 341 937*
– www.stayincastle.com
12 rm – †£ 80/100 ††£ 180   **Rest** – *(dinner only)* Menu £ 40

♦ Carefully restored Victorian folly in neo-Gothic style with extensive gardens; fine antiques and curios abound. Comfy music room and library. Individually decorated bedrooms. Expansive dining room with ornate ceiling and Spode tableware.

at Ravenstonedale Southwest : 5 mi by A 685

Black Swan with rm
✉ *CA17 4NG* – ✆ *(01539) 623 204* – *www.blackswanhotel.com* – *Closed 25 December*
15 rm – †£ 60/125 ††£ 75/125   **Rest** – Carte £ 18/29

♦ Set in a remote village, a part-Victorian, family-run pub with a huge garden and babbling beck. Menus feature filling pub classics, supplemented by restaurant-style specials in the evening. Cosy, antique-furnished bedrooms; one is more modern and boasts a four-poster.

KIRKBYMOORSIDE – North Yorkshire – 502 R21 – pop. 2 595 — 23 C1
▶ London 244 mi – Leeds 61 mi – Scarborough 26 mi – York 33 mi
🏛 Manor Vale, ✆ (01751) 43 15 25

Brickfields Farm without rest
Kirby Mills, East : 0.75 mi by A 170 on Kirby Mills Industrial Estate rd
✉ *YO62 6NS* – ✆ *(01751) 433 074* – *www.brickfieldsfarm.co.uk*
7 rm – †£ 125 ††£ 125

♦ Attractive red-brick farmhouse with most of its bedrooms in converted outbuildings; one boasts a four-poster. Simple, modern comforts and traditional character. Conservatory breakfast room.

Cornmill without rest
Kirby Mills, East : 0.5 mi by A 170 ✉ *YO62 6NP* – ✆ *(01751) 432 000*
– www.kirbymills.co.uk
5 rm – †£ 55/75 ††£ 100/105

♦ Charming 18C cornmill with pleasant courtyard. Spacious, rustic bedrooms set in the old farmhouse and stables. Characterful dining room with mill race running beneath a glass panel.

KIRKWHELPINGTON – Northumberland – 501 N/O18 – pop. 353 — 24 A2
– ✉ Morpeth 🟩 Great Britain
▶ London 305 mi – Carlisle 46 mi – Newcastle upon Tyne 20 mi
🟩 Wallington House ★, AC, E : 3.5 mi by A 696 and B 6342

Shieldhall
Wallington, Southeast : 2.5 mi by A 696 on B 6342 ✉ *NE61 4AQ* – ✆ *(01830) 540 387* – *www.shieldhallguesthouse.co.uk* – *Closed Christmas-New Year*
4 rm – †£ 60/78 ††£ 96   **Rest** – Menu £ 28

♦ Early 17C farmhouse and outbuildings, where Capability Brown's uncle once lived. Mix of rustic and country house guest areas; library-lounge boasts garden views. Individually styled bedrooms, with furniture handmade by the owner. Beamed, flag-floored dining room offers classical British dishes and Aga-cooked breakfasts.

KIRTLINGTON – Oxfordshire – 503 Q28 — 10 B2
▶ London 70 mi – Bicester 11 mi – Oxford 16 mi

Dashwood
South Green, Heyford Rd ✉ *OX5 3HJ* – ✆ *(01869) 352 707*
– www.thedashwood.co.uk
12 rm – †£ 85 ††£ 115/160   **Rest** – *(closed Sunday)* Carte £ 26/38

♦ Grade II listed 16C building in local soft stone. Lounge with comfy leather armchairs. Bedrooms, boasting super contemporary décor, divided between main building and barn. Exposed stone dining room: impressive menus with modern European slant.

KNARESBOROUGH – North Yorkshire – **502** P21 – pop. 13 380   **22** B2

London 217 – Bradford 21 – Harrogate 3 – Leeds 18
Market Pl, (01423) 86 68 86, www.knaresborough.co.uk
Boroughbridge Rd, (01423) 86 26 90

Newton House without rest
5-7 York Pl ⊠ HG5 0AD – (01423) 863 539 – www.newtonhouseyorkshire.com
– Closed 1 week Christmas
11 rm ⊒ – †£ 55/85 ††£ 95/120

♦ Extended mid-18C house boasts homely lounge with soft suites and smart, comfortable, individually decorated bedrooms; those on the first floor and in the annexe are larger.

at Ferrensby Northeast : 3 mi on A 6055

General Tarleton Inn with rm
Boroughbridge Rd ⊠ HG5 0PZ – (01423) 340 284 – www.generaltarleton.co.uk
13 rm ⊒ – †£ 75/137 ††£ 129/150   **Rest** – Carte £ 25/36

♦ This 18C coaching inn has several dining areas inside and out. The menu has a strong seasonal Yorkshire base and features well-priced, tasty dishes and classics aplenty. Bedrooms are comfortable and well-kept.

at Coneythorpe Northeast : 4.75 mi by A 59

Tiger Inn
⊠ HG5 0RY – (01423) 863 632 – www.tiger-inn.co.uk – Closed 25 December
Rest – (booking advisable) Carte £ 20/30

♦ Popular, family-owned pub with bustling atmosphere, particularly in the front bar. Monthly changing menu of pub classics, supplemented by fish specials; hearty, substantial cooking.

KNOWSTONE – Devon – see South Molton

KNUTSFORD – Cheshire East – **502** M24 – pop. 12 656   **20** B3

London 187 mi – Chester 25 mi – Liverpool 33 mi – Manchester 18 mi
Toft Rd, (01565) 63 26 11, www.virtual-knutsford.co.uk

Belle Epoque Brasserie with rm
60 King St ⊠ WA16 6DT – (01565) 633 060 – www.thebelleepoque.com
7 rm ⊒ – †£ 95 ††£ 115
Rest – (closed Sunday dinner) Menu £ 18 – Carte £ 26/56

♦ Bustling brasserie with art nouveau décor. Traditional and modern dishes with international touches use local produce. Contemporary style bedrooms boast modern facilities.

at Mobberley Northeast : 2.5 mi by A 537 on B 5085 – ⊠ Knutsford

Hinton without rest
Town Lane, on B 5085 ⊠ WA16 7HH – (01565) 873 484
– www.thehinton.co.uk
6 rm ⊒ – †£ 53 ††£ 65

♦ Welcoming cream-washed guesthouse on the main road through the village. Traditional sitting room with velvet sofas. Comfy, well-kept bedrooms have a homely style and offer good facilities.

at Lower Peover Southwest : 3.25 mi by A 50 on B 5081

Bells of Peover
The Cobbles ⊠ WA16 9PZ – (01565) 722 269
Rest – Carte £ 21/42

♦ Refurbished 16C former coaching inn whose regulars once included Generals Eisenhower and Patton. Offers a range of options: from appealing snacks in the bar, to 'fine dining' upstairs.

KNUTSFORD

at Lach Dennis Southwest : 7 mi by A 50 and B 5081 on B 5082 – ✉ Knutsford

Duke of Portland
Penny's Ln ✉ *CW9 8SY* – ✆ *(01606) 46 264* – *www.dukeofportland.com*
Rest – Menu £ 17 – Carte £ 19/30
♦ Village inn on main road; most popular place to dine is smart, contemporary room housing stag's head. Lengthy menu offers simply prepared dishes of carefully sourced, local produce.

KYNASTON – Herefordshire – see Ledbury

LACH DENNIS – Cheshire West and Chester – see Knutsford

LACOCK – Wiltshire – **503** N29 – pop. 1 068 – ✉ Chippenham **4 C2**
▶ London 109 mi – Bath 16 mi – Bristol 30 mi – Chippenham 3 mi
◉ Village★★ - Lacock Abbey★ **AC** – High St★, St Cyriac★, Fox Talbot Museum of Photography★ **AC**

At The Sign of the Angel
6 Church St ✉ *SN15 2LB* – ✆ *(01249) 730 230* – *www.lacock.co.uk* – Closed 25-28 December
11 rm ☐ – †£ 85 ††£ 129/159
Rest – *(closed Monday lunch except bank holidays)* Menu £ 19/23 – Carte £ 27/35
♦ Delightful 15C inn with beamed ceilings and open fires, located in charming 15C National Trust village. Traditional, antique-furnished bedrooms offer modern amenities; Room 5 is particularly pleasant and light. Classic country cooking uses home-grown produce.

LA HAULE – **503** L33 – see Channel Islands (Jersey)

LAMBOURN WOODLANDS – West Berkshire **10 A3**
▶ London 70 mi – Birmingham 112 mi – Bristol 59 mi – Cardiff 92 mi

Hare
Ermin St ✉ *RG17 7SD* – ✆ *(01488) 71 386* – *www.thehererestaurant.co.uk*
Rest – *(booking essential)* Menu £ 28 (lunch) – Carte £ 30/40
♦ Extended red-brick former pub with terrace, gazebo and chicken coop. Small bar, lounge and three smart dining areas with long banquettes. Daytime snack menu supplements set menus and an evening à la carte. Classical, country house cooking.

LANCASTER – Lancashire – **502** L21 – pop. 45 952 ▮ Great Britain **20 A1**
▶ London 252 mi – Blackpool 26 mi – Bradford 62 mi – Burnley 44 mi
ℹ Meeting House Lane ✆ (01524) 58 23 94, www.visitlancashire.com
▦ Ashton Hall Ashton-with-Stodday, ✆ (01524) 75 20 90
▦ Lansil Caton Rd, ✆ (01524) 3 92 69
◉ Castle★ **AC**

Ashton
Wyresdale Rd, Southeast : 1.25 mi by A 6 on Clitheroe rd ✉ *LA1 3JJ* – ✆ *(01524) 68 460* – *www.theashtonlancaster.com*
5 rm ☐ – †£ 98/128 ††£ 128/175 **Rest** – Menu £ 35 **s**
♦ Georgian house in lawned gardens; personally run by friendly owner. Good-sized bedrooms are decorated in bold colours and feature a blend of modern and antique furniture. Small, informal dining room; home-cooked comfort food makes good use of local produce.

Borough
3 Dalton Sq ✉ *LA1 1PP* – ✆ *(01524) 64 170* – *www.theboroughlancaster.co.uk* – Closed 25 December
Rest – Carte £ 19/32
♦ Characterful pub set on cobbled square. Hearty, filling dishes use regional produce; DIY deli boards are popular. Local bitters and some unusual bottled beers. Regular comedy nights.

LANGAR – Nottinghamshire – 502 R25   16 B2
▶ London 132 mi – Boston 45 mi – Leicester 25 mi – Lincoln 37 mi

Langar Hall
⊠ NG13 9HG – ℰ (01949) 860 559 – www.langarhall.co.uk
11 rm – †£ 95/140 ††£185/195 – 1 suite
Rest – Menu £ 25/30 – Carte £ 33/41
♦ Georgian manor in pastoral setting, next to early English church; overlooks park, medieval fishponds. Antique filled rooms named after people featuring in house's history. Elegant, candlelit, pillared dining room.

LANGHO – Lancashire – 502 M22 – see Blackburn

LANGPORT – Somerset – 503 L30 – pop. 2 851   3 B3
▶ London 134 mi – Weston-super-Mare 31 mi – Taunton 15 mi – Yeovil 16 mi

Parsonage
Mulchelney, South : 2 mi on Muchelney Pottery rd ⊠ TA10 ODL – ℰ (01458) 259 058 – www.parsonagesomerset.co.uk – Closed Christmas and New Year
3 rm – †£ 53 ††£ 95 **Rest** – Menu £ 30
♦ Traditional Somerset longhouse in charming setting with airy, well-kept country bedrooms and lovely rear garden. Delightful hosts dine with their guests at family style meals crafted from fresh, local ingredients. Al fresco breakfast in summer.

LANGTHWAITE – North Yorkshire – 502 O20 – see Reeth

LA PULENTE – 503 P33 – see Channel Islands (Jersey)

LAPWORTH – Warwickshire – pop. 2 100   19 C2
▶ London 108 mi – Birmingham 23 mi – Leicester 47 mi – Coventry 19 mi

Boot Inn
Old Warwick Rd ⊠ B94 6JU – ℰ (01564) 782 464 – www.bootinnlapworth.co.uk – Closed dinner 25 December and dinner 1 January
Rest – (booking essential) Menu £ 16 (weekdays) – Carte £ 26/38
♦ Buzzy large red-brick pub close to the M40, boasting a large terrace, traditional bar and modern first floor restaurant. Dishes vary from simple bar snacks to sophisticated specials and sharing plates.

LASKILL – North Yorkshire – 502 Q21 – see Hawnby

LASTINGHAM – North Yorkshire – 502 R21 – pop. 87 – ⊠ York   23 C1
▶ London 244 mi – Scarborough 26 mi – York 32 mi

Lastingham Grange
⊠ YO62 6TH – ℰ (01751) 417 345 – www.lastinghamgrange.com
– March-November
11 rm – †£ 95/135 ††£ 150/200
Rest – Menu £ 40 (dinner) – Carte lunch £ 25/34
♦ A delightfully traditional country house atmosphere prevails throughout this extended, pleasantly old-fashioned, 17C farmhouse. Lovely gardens; well-appointed bedrooms. Dining room with rustic fare and rose garden view.

LAVENHAM – Suffolk – 504 W27 – pop. 1 231 – ⊠ Sudbury   15 C3
 Great Britain
▶ London 66 mi – Cambridge 39 mi – Colchester 22 mi – Ipswich 19 mi
🛈 Lady St ℰ(01787) 24 82 07, www.discoverlavenham.co.uk
◉ Town★★ – Church of St Peter and St Paul★

Swan
High St ⊠ CO10 9QA – ℰ (01787) 247 477 – www.theswanatlavenham.co.uk
42 rm (dinner included) – †£ 130/180 ††£ 250 – 3 suites
Rest Gallery – Menu £ 22/36 **s** – Carte dinner £ 41/50 **s**
♦ Characterful, 15C former coaching inn with superbly atmospheric baronial bar. Beamed, individually decorated bedrooms boast a subtle contemporary style. The Gallery, with its timbered roof and minstrels' gallery, offers a modern British menu. Live piano at weekends.

LAVENHAM

Lavenham Priory without rest
Water St. ⊠ CO10 9RW – ℰ (01787) 247 404 – www.lavenhampriory.co.uk
– Closed Christmas-New Year
6 rm ⊡ – †£ 92 ††£ 166
♦ Part-13C, Grade I listed priory in a historic town, with gorgeous garden and mini parterre. Characterful interior features a vast inglenook fireplace, Elizabethan murals and a Jacobean staircase. Cosy lounge and atmospheric dining room. Heavily beamed bedrooms with feature beds and roll-top or slipper baths.

Great House with rm
Market Pl. ⊠ CO10 9QZ – ℰ (01787) 247 431 – www.greathouse.co.uk – Closed 3 weeks January, 2 weeks summer, Sunday dinner, Monday and lunch Tuesday
3 rm – †£ 95 ††£ 155/195, ⊡ £ 15 – 2 suites
Rest – French – Menu £ 21 (weekday lunch) – Carte dinner £ 32/46
♦ Impressive Georgian façade conceals 14C timbered house with eye-catching modern art and heated rear terrace. Classical French cooking displays modern twists. Service is well-paced and attentive. Contemporary, country house bedrooms boast old beams and modern hues.

LAWHITTON – Cornwall
2 C2
▶ London 221 mi – Bristol 136 mi – Cardiff 156 mi – Plymouth 26 mi

Primrose Cottage without rest
Southeast : 1.25 mi on B 3362 ⊠ PL15 9PE – ℰ (01566) 773 645
– www.primrosecottagesuites.co.uk – Closed Christmas
3 rm ⊡ – †£ 70/90 ††£ 110/130
♦ Part-18C house with friendly owner and lovely gardens leading down to the river. Good-sized bedrooms boast their own entrances, separate sitting rooms and afford great country views. Complimentary wine and homemade cakes; light suppers available in your room.

LEDBURY – Herefordshire – 503 M27 – pop. 8 491
18 B3
▶ London 119 mi – Hereford 14 mi – Newport 46 mi – Worcester 16 mi

Feathers
High St ⊠ HR8 1DS – ℰ (01531) 635 266 – www.feathers-ledbury.co.uk
19 rm ⊡ – †£ 125 ††£ 235 – 3 suites
Rest *Quills* – (dinner only Friday-Saturday and lunch Sunday) Menu £ 22 (dinner) – Carte £ 24/36
Rest *Fuggles* – Menu £ 22 (dinner) – Carte £ 24/36
♦ Modernised 16C black and white timbered coaching inn; a clever blend of old and new. Comfortable bedrooms; Lanark House suites more contemporary in style. Linen-clad Quills boasts chandeliers. Fuggles is more informal. Modern, seasonally changing menus.

at Kynaston West : 6.5 mi by A 449, A 4172 and Aylton rd on Much Marcle rd.
– ⊠ Ledbury

Hall End without rest
⊠ HR8 2PD – ℰ (01531) 670 225 – www.hallendhouse.com – Closed Christmas-New Year
3 rm ⊡ – †£ 60 ††£ 100
♦ Lovingly restored, personally run, part Georgian home and livery stable in the countryside. Relax in the orangery and, suitably reposed, retire to lavishly furnished bedrooms.

at Trumpet Northwest : 3.25 mi on A 438 – ⊠ Ledbury

Verzon House
Hereford Rd ⊠ HR8 2PZ – ℰ (01531) 670 381 – www.verzonhouse.com – Closed 2-9 January
8 rm ⊡ – †£ 90/135 ††£ 125/170 **Rest** – (light lunch) Carte £ 28/42
♦ Pleasantly restored Georgian house with delightful terrace. Modern bedrooms are named after cider apples; most have countryside views. There is a midweek, set price 4 course Italian menu and an à la carte of modern, mostly English dishes. Tapas only at lunchtime.

LEEDS

See city maps on following pages   22 B2

West Yorkshire – pop. 440 954 – 502 P22 – Great Britain
London 204 – Liverpool 75 – Manchester 43 – Newcastle upon Tyne 95

Tourist Information

City Station (0113) 242 52 42, www.visitleeds.co.uk

Airport

Leeds-Bradford Airport : (0113) 250 9696, NW : 8 m. by A 65 and A 658 BT

Golf Courses

Temple Newsam Halton Temple Newsam Rd, (0113) 264 56 24
Gotts Park Armley Armley Ridge Rd, (0113) 234 20 19
Middleton Park Middleton Ring Rd, Beeston Park, (0113) 270 04 49

PRACTICAL INFORMATION

SIGHTS

In the town : City★ • Royal Armouries Museum★★★ GZ • City Art Gallery★ AC GYM

On the outskirts : Kirkstall Abbey★ AC, NW : 3 mi by A 65 GY • Temple Newsam★ AC, E : 5 mi by A 64 and A 63 CUD

In the surrounding area : Harewood House★★ AC, N : 8 mi by A 61 CT • Nostell Priory★, SE : 18 mi by A 61 and A 638 • Yorkshire Sculpture Park★, S : 20 mi by M 1 to junction 38 and 1 mi north off A 637 • Brodsworth Hall★, SE : 25 mi by M 1 to junction 40, A 638 and minor rd (right) in Upton

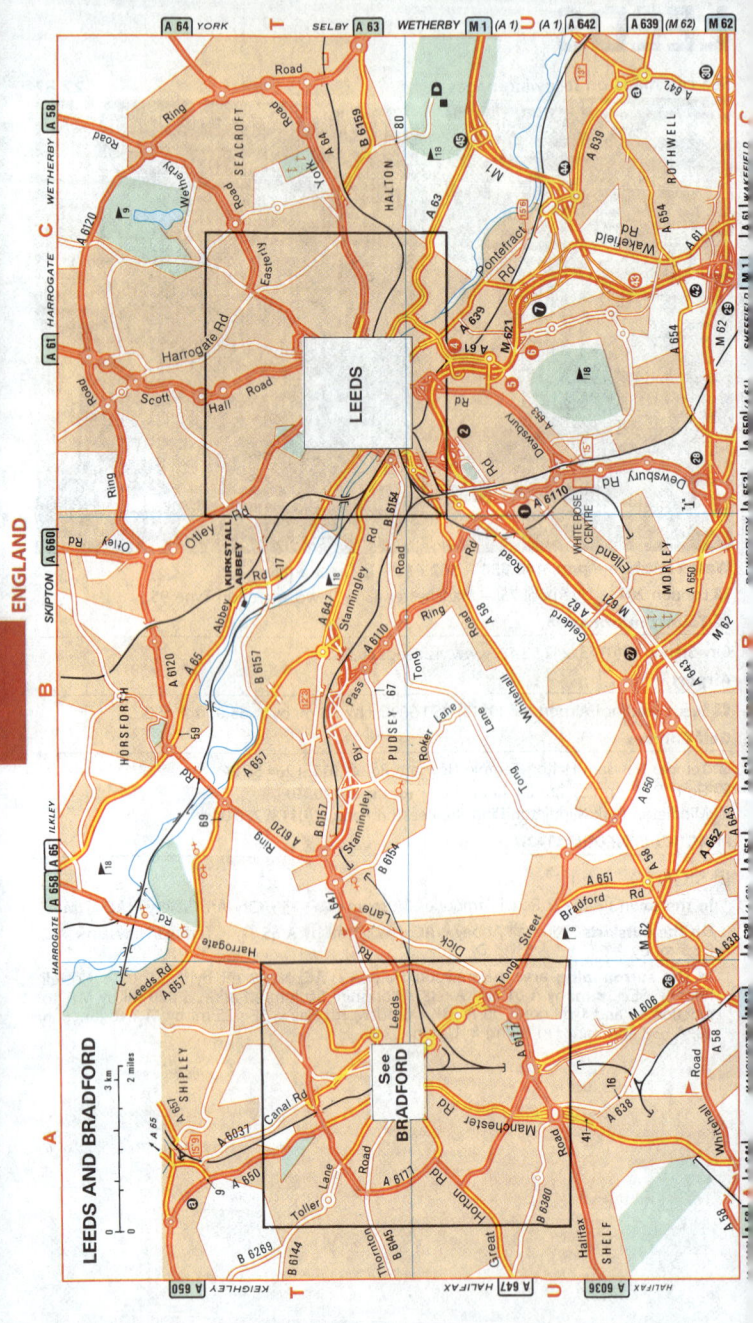

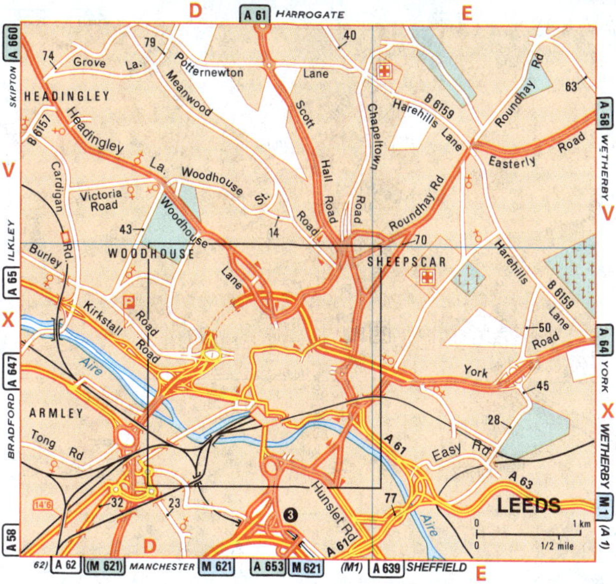

Street	Ref
dford Rd.	AT 9
nbridge Rd	DV 14
ckheaton Rd	AU 16
mmercial Rd.	BT 17
nestic St	DX 23
t Park Parade	EX 28
derd Rd	DX 32
rogate Rd	DV 40
Huddersfield Rd.	AU 41
Hyde Park Rd	AV 43
Ivy St	EX 45
Lupton Ave	EX 51
New Rd Side	BT 59
Oakwood Lane	EV 63
Pudsey Rd.	BT 67
Rodley Lane	BV 69
Roseville Rd	EVX 70
Shaw Lane	DV 74
South Accommodation Rd	EX 77
Stainbeck Rd	DV 79
Templenewsam Rd	CT 80
White Rose Centre	CU

Malmaison

1 Swinegate ⊠ LS1 4AG – ℘ (0113) 398 10 00 – www.malmaison.com
99 rm – †£ 79/170 ††£ 79/170, ⊇ £ 14.50 – 1 suite   GZn
Rest – Menu £ 30 (weekdays) – Carte £ 24/38

♦ Relaxed, contemporary hotel hides behind imposing Victorian exterior. Vibrantly and individually decorated rooms are stylishly furnished, with modern facilities to the fore. Dine in modern interpretation of a French brasserie.

Quebecs without rest

9 Quebec St ⊠ LS1 2HA – ℘ (0113) 244 89 89 – www.quebechotel.co.uk
– Closed 25 December   FZa
43 rm – †£ 75/115 ††£ 75/115, ⊇ £ 14.95 – 2 suites

♦ 19C former Liberal Club, now a modish, intimate boutique hotel. Original features include oak staircase and stained glass window depicting Yorkshire cities. Stylish bedrooms.

42 The Calls

42 The Calls ⊠ LS2 7EW – ℘ (0113) 244 00 99 – www.42thecalls.co.uk
– Closed 3 days Christmas   GZz
38 rm – †£ 85/175 ††£ 125/195, ⊇ £ 15 – 3 suites
Rest *Brasserie Forty 4* – see restaurant listing

♦ Converted 18C quayside grain mill retaining many of its original workings. Well-equipped, comfortable bedrooms offer a host of extras; those facing the river are the best.

The sun's out? Then enjoy eating outside on the terrace:

LEEDS

Aire St. ... FZ 2	East Parade ... FGZ 27	New York Rd. ... GY 6
Albion St ... GZ 3	Hanover Way ... FY 38	Park Lane ... FY 6
Boar Lane ... GZ 4	Headrow Centre ... GZ 39	Queen St ... FZ 6
Bond St ... GZ 8	Headrow (The) ... GY	St John's Centre ... GY
Bowman Lane ... GZ 9	Infirmary St ... GZ 44	St Paul's St. ... FZ
Bridge St ... GY 10	King St ... FZ 46	St Peter's St. ... GZ
Briggate ... GZ	Kirkgate ... GZ 48	Sheepscar St South ... GY
City Square ... GZ 15	Lands Lane ... GZ 49	Skinner Lane ... GY
Commercial St ... GZ 18	Leeds Shopping Plaza ... GZ 50	South Parade ... FGZ
Cookridge St. ... GY 19	Marsh Lane ... GZ 52	Trinity St Shopping Centre ... GZ
County Arcade ... GZ 20	Meadow Lane ... GZ 53	Victoria Rd. ... GZ
Cross Stamford St. ... GY 21	Merrion Centre ... GY	Wade Lane ... GY
Crown Point Rd ... GZ 22	Merrion St. ... GY 54	Waterloo St. ... GZ
Dock St ... GZ 23	Merrion Way ... GY 55	Wellington Rd ... FZ
Duncan St ... GZ 25	Millennium Square ... GY 56	Westgate ... FZ
Eastgate ... GZ 31	New Briggate ... GY 57	West St ... FZ

New Ellington
FZx

23-25 York Pl. ✉ LS1 2EY - ☎ (0113) 204 21 50 - www.thenewellington.com
– Closed 25-26 December

33 rm – ✝ £ 89/125 ✝✝ £ 89/125, ☕ £ 11.50 – 1 suite
Rest – *(closed Sunday dinner)* Menu £ 19 – Carte dinner £ 29/36

♦ Purpose-built hotel with striking interior. Comfy lounge displays boldly coloured furnishings and is split in two by the cocktail bar. Funky bedrooms boast good facilities and mosaic-tiled bathrooms, and you can borrow ipods and games consoles. Chic, intimate basement brasserie offers modern British cooking.

Prices quoted after the symbol ✝ refer to the lowest rate in low season followed by the highest rate in high season, for a single room.
The same principle applies to the symbol ✝✝ for a double room.

LEEDS

XXX Anthony's
19 Boar Ln ⊠ LS1 6EA – ℘ *(0113) 245 59 22 – www.anthonysrestaurant.co.uk
– Closed 25 December-3 January, Sunday and Monday*   GZ**a**
Rest – *(booking essential)* Menu £ 24/45

♦ Family-run, basement restaurant offering immaculately laid tables and formal service from a well-versed team. Creative cooking features modern techniques and some interesting combinations.

XX Brasserie Forty 4 – at 42 The Calls Hotel
44 The Calls ⊠ LS2 7EW – ℘ *(0113) 234 32 32 – www.brasserie44.com – Closed Sunday and bank holidays except Good Friday*   GZ**z**
Rest – Carte £ 26/31

♦ Former riverside warehouse with minimalist dining room and stylish bar which exudes atmosphere of buzzy informality. Smokehouse and chargrilled options in an eclectic range of dishes.

XX Piazza by Anthony
The Corn Exchange ⊠ LS1 7BR – ℘ *(0113) 247 09 95
– www.anthonysrestaurant.co.uk – Closed 25-26 December and 1 January*
Rest – Carte £ 23/33   GZ**b**

♦ Located on the ground floor of the historic former Corn Exchange; large open dining room in the centre, with meeting rooms, private dining areas and artisanal food shops surrounding. Wide-ranging menu of tasty European dishes. Outstanding breads in the bakery.

XX Foundry
1 Saw Mill Yard, Round Foundry ⊠ LS11 5WH – ℘ *(0113) 245 03 90
– www.thefoundrywinebar.co.uk – Closed 26 December, Saturday lunch and Sunday*
Rest – Menu £ 16 (lunch) – Carte £ 20/26   FZ**b**

♦ Set in a building once joined to the foundry and mills, with vaulted ceiling, ornate bar and French bistro feel. Classical menus feature hearty, robust comfort dishes and extensive daily specials.

XX Fourth Floor – at Harvey Nichols
107-111 Briggate ⊠ LS1 6AZ – ℘ *(0113) 204 80 00 – www.harveynichols.com
– Closed 25 December, 1 January, Easter Sunday and dinner Sunday-Monday*
Rest – Menu £ 20 – Carte £ 26/35   GZ**s**

♦ Bright, contemporary dining room on the top floor of this chic store; watch the chefs prepare tasty, modern, globally influenced dishes. Pleasant service from a smartly attired team.

ENGLAND

LEICESTER – Leicester – 502 Q26 – pop. 296 594 ▌Great Britain   16 B2

▶ London 107 mi – Birmingham 43 mi – Coventry 24 mi – Nottingham 26 mi
🛧 East Midlands Airport, Castle Donington : ℘ (0871) 9199000 NW : 22 mi by A 50 - AX - and M 1
🛈 7-9 Every St ℘ (0844) 888 51 81, www.goleicestershire.com
⛳ Leicestershire Evington Lane, ℘ (0116) 273 88 25
⛳ Western Park Scudamore Rd, ℘ (0116) 287 52 11
⛳ Humberstone Heights Gipsy Lane, ℘ (0116) 299 55 70
⛳ Oadby Leicester Road Racecourse, ℘ (0116) 270 02 15
⛳ Blaby Lutterworth Rd, ℘ (0116) 278 48 04
◉ Guildhall ★ BY **B** – Museum and Art Gallery ★ CY **M3** – St Mary de Castro Church ★ BY **D**
◉ National Space Centre ★ N : 2 mi by A 6 - AX - turning east into Corporation Rd and right into Exploration Drive

Plans on following pages

🏨 Leicester Marriott
Smith Way, Grove Park, Enderby, Southwest : 4 mi by A 5460 off A 563 at junction 21 of M1 ⊠ LE19 1SW – ℘ *(0116) 282 01 00 – www.leicestermarriott.co.uk*
226 rm – ♦£ 139 ♦♦£ 139, ⊑ £ 15.95 – 1 suite   AY**z**
Rest – *(dinner only and Sunday lunch)* Menu £ 23 – Carte approx. £ 23

♦ Purpose-built hotel on a suburban business park. Stylish open-plan guest areas include an atrium lounge and informal café in the lobby. Uniform bedrooms boast a good level of facilities. Smart executive lounge and excellent leisure club. East meets West in restaurant; choice of buffet or eclectic à la carte.

LEICESTER

Belgrave Rd	**CX**
Belvoir St	**CY** 5
Bishop St	**CY** 7
Blackbird Rd	**BX** 8
Braunstone Gate	**BY** 12
Cank St	**BCY** 15
Causeway Lane	**BX** 16
Church Gate	**BCX**
East Bond St	**BCX** 19
Fleet St	**CY** 20
Gallowtree Gate	**CY** 24
Great Central St	**BX** 27
Haymarket Shopping Centre	**CX**
High St	**BXY**
Hinckley Rd	**BY** 30
Horsefair St	**CY** 31
Humberstone Gate	**CX** 33
Humberstone Rd	**CX** 34
Infirmary Rd	**BCY** 36
Lee St	**CX** 39
Market St	**CY** 42
Market (The)	**CY** 43
Millstone Lane	**BY** 45
Narborough Rd North	**BY** 46
Newarke (The)	**BY** 47
Peacock Lane	**BY** 50
St Georges Retail Park	**CX**
St Augustine Rd	**BY** 51
St Martin's	**BY** 55
St Nicholas Circle	**BY** 57
Shires Shopping Centre (The)	**BX**
Southgate St	**BY** 63
Sparkenhoe St	**CX** 65
Swain St	**CY** 67
Welford Pl	**CY** 72
Western Boulevard	**BY** 74

Belmont
De Montfort St. ⌧ LE1 7GR – ℰ (0116) 254 47 73 – www.belmonthotel.co.uk
– Closed 26-29 December   **CYc**
74 rm ⌑ – †£ 79/99 ††£ 99/109 – 1 suite
Rest *Cherry's* – see restaurant listing
♦ Friendly, family-run hotel in a city suburb, made up of a collection of houses – each with its own classical style. Spacious guest areas and contemporary bar. Bedrooms vary in shape and size but all are modern and offer good facilities.

Hotel Maiyango
13-21 St. Nicholas Pl ⌧ LE1 4LD – ℰ (0116) 251 88 98 – www.maiyango.com
– Closed 25-26 December   **BYa**
13 rm – †£ 163/186 ††£ 163/186, ⌑ £ 7.95 – 1 suite
Rest *Maiyango* – see restaurant listing
♦ Privately owned city centre hotel in a 150 year old shoe factory. Stylish interior with a trendy bar opening onto a terrace overlooking the rooftops. Spacious, individually designed bedrooms boast bespoke wood furniture and a colonial feel.

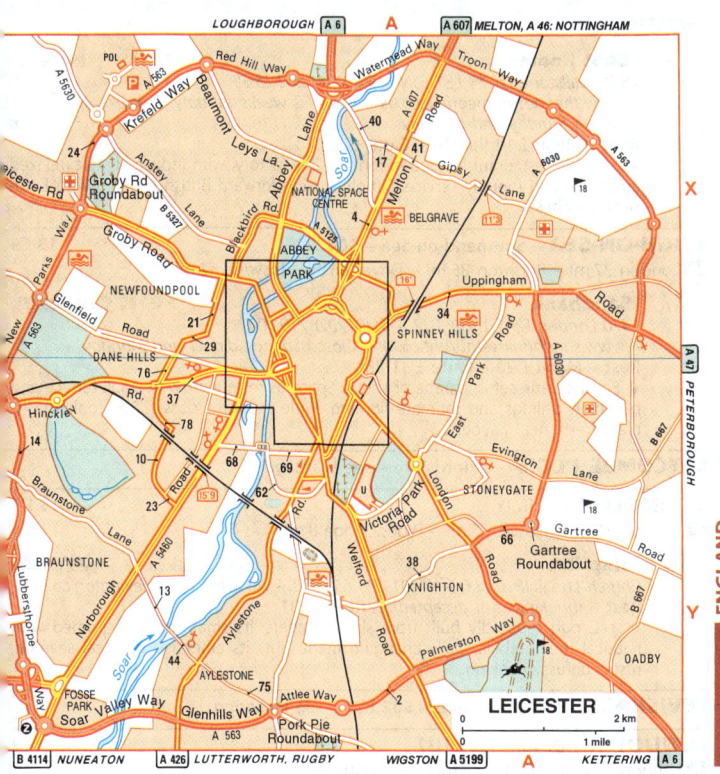

quith Way	AY 2	Glenfrith Way	AX 24	Raw Dykes		
lgrave Rd	AX 4	Henley Rd.	AX 29	Rd.	AY	62
aunstone Ave	AY 10	Humberstone Rd	AX 34	Stoughton Rd	AY	66
aunstone Lane East	AY 13	King Richards Rd	AY 37	Upperton Rd	AY	68
aunstone Way	AY 14	Knighton Rd	AY 38	Walnut St	AY	69
ecketts Rd	AY 17	Loughborough Rd	AY 40	Wigston Lane	AY	75
sse Rd North	AX 21	Marfitt St	AX 41	Woodville Rd.	AY	76
lhurst Ave	AY 23	Middleton St	AY 44	Wyngate Drive	AY	78

Chutney Ivy
41 Halford Rd ⊠ LE1 1TR – ℰ (0116) 251 1889 – www.chutneyivy.com
– Closed 25-26 December, Saturday lunch and Sunday CY**x**
Rest – Indian – Menu £ 7/13 – Carte £ 20/39

♦ Keenly run warehouse conversion with smart, industrial feel. Menus mix modern and classical dishes, with influences coming from Hyderabad, Goa and Bengal. Floor-to-ceiling windows open onto the pavement and there's a popular basement bar.

Maiyango – at Hotel Maiyango
13-21 St. Nicholas Pl ⊠ LE1 4LD – ℰ (0116) 251 88 98 – www.maiyango.com
– Closed 25-26 December BY**a**
Rest – (closed Sunday lunch) Menu £ 19/29

♦ Glass-fronted restaurant in a stylish hotel. Dark wood, round booths and silk drapes create a Moorish feel. Refined cooking uses local and allotment produce, and is Mediterranean and Asian-led.

Cherry's – at Belmont Hotel
De Montfort St. ⊠ LE1 7GR – ℰ (0116) 254 47 73 – www.belmonthotel.co.uk
– Closed 26-29 December, Saturday lunch and Sunday dinner CY**c**
Rest – Menu £ 21 – Carte £ 21/38

♦ Formal restaurant in a friendly, family-run hotel. Wide-ranging menus are classically based; choose from a 3-choice set menu or 4 course à la carte. Seasonal cooking has a Mediterranean edge.

LEICESTER

Boot Room
VISA ◎◎ AE
26-29 Millstone Ln ✉ LE1 5JN – ℰ (0116) 262 25 55
– www.thebootroomeaterie.co.uk – Closed 2 weeks January, 2 weeks
summer, Sunday and Monday
BYx
Rest – Menu £ 14 (lunch) – Carte £ 20/31
♦ Sizeable restaurant located in former shoe factory, with industrial style, relaxed ambience and friendly service. Simple, straightforward British cooking with European touches.

LEIGH-ON-SEA – Southend-on-Sea – 504 W29
13 C3

▶ London 37 mi – Brighton 85 mi – Dover 86 mi – Ipswich 57 mi

Sandbank
1470 London Rd ✉ SS9 2UR – ℰ (01702) 719 000
– www.sandbankrestaurant.co.uk – Closed Sunday dinner and Monday
Rest – Menu £ 20 – Carte £ 31/38
♦ Former bank set in parade of shops. Spacious restaurant with small terrace and bar, high ceilings and intimate lighting. Wide menu of classic '80s cooking displays fresh, neat flavours.

LETCOMBE REGIS – Oxfordshire – see Wantage

LEVINGTON – Suffolk
15 D3

▶ London 75 mi – Ipswich 5 mi – Woodbridge 8 mi

Ship Inn
Church Ln ✉ IP10 0LQ – ℰ (01473) 659 573 – www.theshipinnlevington.co.uk
Rest – (bookings not accepted) Carte £ 22/31
♦ 14C pub reputedly built from ships' timbers; its small rooms crammed with nautical memorabilia. Daily changing menu puts its emphasis on local seafood; rustic, unfussy cooking.

LEVISHAM – North Yorkshire – 502 R21 – see Pickering

LEWDOWN – Devon – 503 H32
2 C2

▶ London 238 mi – Exeter 37 mi – Plymouth 29 mi

◎ Lydford★★, E : 4 m. Launceston★ - Castle★ (≤★) St Mary Magdalene★,
W : 8 mi by A 30 and A 388

Lewtrenchard Manor
South : 0.75 mi by Lewtrenchard rd ✉ EX20 4PN – ℰ (01566) 783 222
– www.lewtrenchard.co.uk
13 rm – †£ 175/205 ††£ 275/305 – 1 suite
Rest – (booking essential for non-residents) Menu £ 24/51
♦ Historic country house where Jacobean architecture blends with smart, contemporary styling. Characterful main house bedrooms; those in coach house more modern. Unique private dining concept, Purple Carrot: watch chefs at work. Traditional dining in formal restaurant; classically based menu utilises home-grown produce.

LEWES – East Sussex – 504 U31 – pop. 15 988 – Great Britain
8 A3

▶ London 53 mi – Brighton 8 mi – Hastings 29 mi – Maidstone 43 mi

🛈 187 High St ℰ (01273) 48 34 48, www.enjoysussex.info

⛳ Chapel Hill, ℰ (01273) 47 32 45

◉ Town★ (High St★, Keere St★) – Castle★ (≤★) **AC**

◎ Sheffield Park Garden★ **AC**, N : 9.5 mi by A 275

Shelleys
High St ✉ BN7 1XS – ℰ (01273) 472 361 – www.the-shelleys.co.uk
18 rm – †£ 130/234 ††£ 160/306 – 1 suite
Rest – Menu £ 30 (lunch) – Carte £ 36/50
♦ Formerly an inn, and before that, a private house dating back to 1577 – owned by the great poet's family. Spacious, classically styled bedrooms include a four-poster and suite with garden views. Smart restaurant overlooks the lawns.

LEWES

Millers without rest
134 High St ⊠ BN7 1XS – ℰ (01273) 475 631
– www.millersbedandbreakfast.com – Closed 18 December-5 January and 4-6 November
3 rm ⊇ – †£ 85 ††£ 95
◆ Characterful, small family home in a row of 16C houses that lead to the high street. Appealing personal feel in the individual bedrooms with books, trinkets and knick-knacks.

Real Eating Company
18 Cliffe High St ⊠ BN7 2AJ – ℰ (01273) 402 650 – www.real-eating.co.uk
– Closed 25 December, Sunday and Monday dinner
Rest – Carte £ 23/34
◆ Light lunches in buzzy atmosphere; more intimate at dinner. Fresh seasonal, local produce cooked in unfussy style to create honest, tasty dishes, including plenty of British favourites.

at East Chiltington Northwest : 5.5 mi by A 275 and B 2116 off Novington Lane – ⊠ Lewes

Jolly Sportsman
Chapel Ln ⊠ BN7 3BA – ℰ (01273) 890 400 – www.thejollysportsman.com
– Closed 25-26 December
Rest – (booking essential) Menu £ 16 (lunch) – Carte £ 27/35
◆ Set in a small hamlet, a grey clapperboard pub that's popular with the locals. Plenty of choice, including interesting bar bites, good value set menus and a rustic, European-based à la carte.

LEYBURN – North Yorkshire – 502 O21 – pop. 1 844   22 B1
▶ London 251 mi – Darlington 25 mi – Kendal 43 mi – Leeds 53 mi
ℹ Railway St ℰ (01748) 82 87 47, www.hello-yorkshire.co.uk

Clyde House without rest
5 Railway St ⊠ DL8 5AY – ℰ (01969) 623 941 – www.clydehouse.com – Closed 8-21 January
6 rm ⊇ – †£ 55 ††£ 80
◆ 18C former coaching inn, refurbished to a high standard, with fresh, bright, modern styling. Bedrooms are spacious with high ceilings; those in former stables are smaller but boast exposed beams. Hearty Yorkshire breakfasts served in smart, open-plan kitchen.

Sandpiper Inn with rm
Market Pl ⊠ DL8 5AT – ℰ (01969) 622 206 – www.sandpiperinn.co.uk – Closed Monday
2 rm ⊇ – †£ 75/80 ††£ 85/90   **Rest** – Carte £ 22/35 s
◆ Charming 16C inn just off the square in busy market town. Frequently changing blackboard menus feature fine local produce; simpler dishes and sandwiches at lunchtime. Pleasant bedrooms have a homely feel.

at Constable Burton East : 3.5 mi on A 684 – ⊠ Leyburn

Wyvill Arms with rm
⊠ DL8 5LH – ℰ (01677) 450 581 – www.thewyvillarms.co.uk – Closed Monday except bank holidays
3 rm ⊇ – †£ 60 ††£ 80   **Rest** – Carte £ 20/33 s
◆ Intimate, ivy-clad stone pub with pleasant gardens, formerly an 18C farmhouse. Menus offer plenty of choice and feature local, traceable produce in carefully prepared, classical dishes. Simple, well-kept bedrooms.

LICHFIELD – Staffordshire – 502 O25 – pop. 28 435   Great Britain   19 C2
▶ London 128 mi – Birmingham 16 mi – Derby 23 mi – Stoke-on-Trent 30 mi
ℹ Castle Dyke ℰ (01543) 41 21 12, www.visitlichfield.co.uk
Lichfield Golf and Country Club Elmhurst, ℰ (01543) 41 73 33
◉ City ★ - Cathedral ★★ AC

LICHFIELD

Chandlers Grande Brasserie
AC VISA ⓪
Corn Exchange, Conduit St ✉ *WS13 6JU* – ☏ *(01543) 416688*
– www.chandlersrestaurant.co.uk – Closed 26 December, 2-9 January, 1 May and 27 August
Rest – Menu £ 15 (weekday lunch) – Carte £ 25/37
♦ Hexagonal building in heart of the city, with spacious, wood-floored restaurant and mezzanine floor for more intimate dining. Menus offer a mix of classic and Mediterranean dishes.

LIFTON – Devon – 503 H32 – pop. 964
2 C2

▶ London 238 mi – Bude 24 mi – Exeter 37 mi – Launceston 4 mi

Launceston★ - Castle★ (≤★) St Mary Magdalene★, W : 4.5 mi by A 30 and A 388

Arundell Arms
Fore St ✉ *PL16 0AA* – ☏ *(01566) 784666* – *www.arundellarms.com*
23 rm ⊇ – ♦£ 98/118 ♦♦£ 175/199 **Rest** – Menu £ 20/43
♦ Roadside former coaching inn with access to 20 miles of the Tamar River for fishing. Comfortable, characterful bedrooms. Smart bar and restaurant; the latter with views over the garden and terrace. Light lunches available in bar. Classic menus in restaurant.

LINCOLN – Lincolnshire – 502 S24 – pop. 86958 ▌Great Britain
17 C1

▶ London 140 mi – Bradford 81 mi – Cambridge 94 mi – Kingston-upon-Hull 44 mi

✈ Humberside Airport : ☏ (01652) 688456, N : 32 mi by A 15 - Y - M 180 and A 18

🛈 Britain & London Visitor Centre 9 Castle Hill ☏ (01522) 87 32 13, www.lincolntourism.co.uk

Carholme Carholme Rd, ☏ (01522) 52 37 25

◉ City★★ - Cathedral and Precincts★★★ AC Y – High Bridge★★ Z 9 – Usher Gallery★ AC YZ M1 – Jew's House★ Y – Castle★ AC Y

Doddington Hall★ AC, W : 6 mi by B 1003 - Z - and B 1190. Gainsborough Old Hall★ AC, NW : 19 mi by A 57 - Z - and A 156

Charlotte House
The Lawns, Union Rd ✉ *LN1 3BJ* – ☏ *(01522) 541 000*
– www.charlottehouselincoln.com   Yv
14 rm – ♦£ 175 ♦♦£ 235, ⊇ £ 10 – 6 suites
Rest – (dinner only and Sunday lunch) Carte £ 29/42
♦ Set next to a castle, a stylish and contemporary converted Georgian building with 8 acres of grounds, super-cool, comfy bedrooms and luxurious bathrooms. Free town transfers. Dine at linen-laid tables in smart, glass-fronted restaurant.

Bailhouse without rest
34 Bailgate ✉ *LN1 3AP* – ☏ *(01522) 541 000* – *www.bailhouse.co.uk*
10 rm – ♦♦£ 69/225, ⊇ £ 10   Yc
♦ Beautiful 14C building with 19C additions. Intimate, relaxing feel enhanced by unobtrusive service, enclosed garden, and rooms oozing charm, some with 14C exposed beams.

St Clements Lodge without rest
21 Langworthgate ✉ *LN2 4AD* – ☏ *(01522) 521 532*
– www.stclementslodge.co.uk   Yu
3 rm ⊇ – ♦£ 50 ♦♦£ 68
♦ A good value house in a convenient location, a short walk from the sights. Run by hospitable owners who keep three large, pleasantly decorated bedrooms.

Wig & Mitre
AC VISA ⓪ AE ①
30-32 Steep Hill ✉ *LN2 1LU* – ☏ *(01522) 535 190* – *www.wigandmitre.com*
Rest – Menu £ 16 – Carte £ 21/30   Yr
♦ Well-established pub with a cosy bar, period dining rooms and an airy beamed restaurant. Classical dishes display some global influences; breakfasts are hearty. Over 50 wines by the glass.

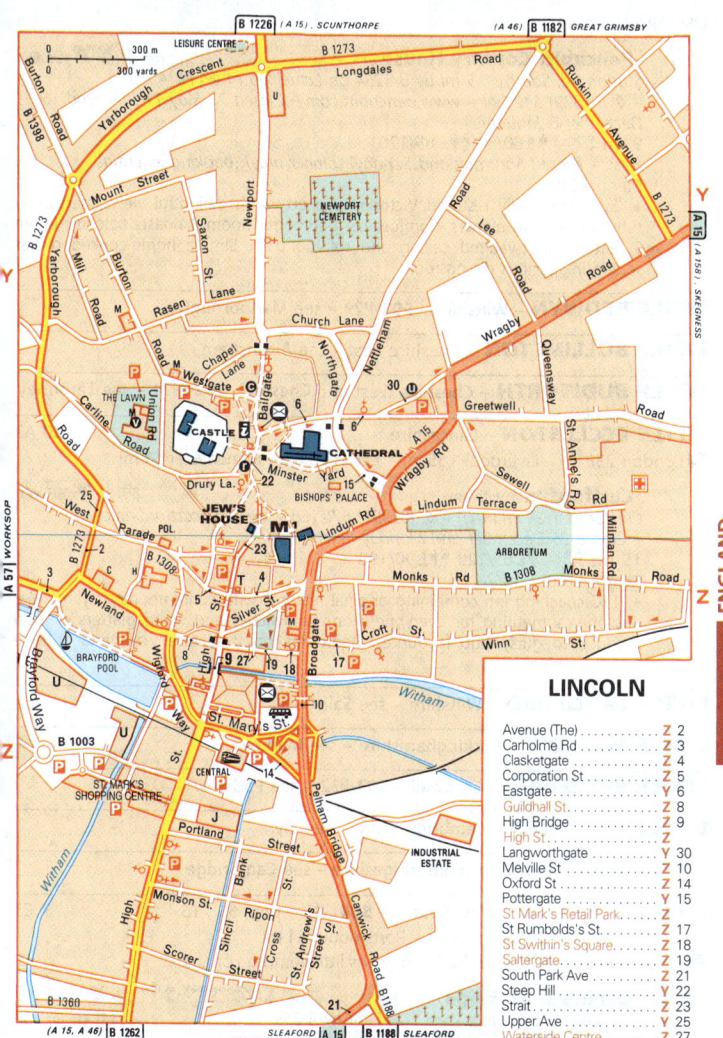

LINCOLN

Avenue (The)	Z	2
Carholme Rd	Z	3
Clasketgate	Z	4
Corporation St	Z	5
Eastgate	Y	6
Guildhall St	Z	8
High Bridge	Z	9
High St	Z	
Langworthgate	Y	30
Melville St	Z	10
Oxford St	Z	14
Pottergate	Y	15
St Mark's Retail Park	Z	
St Rumbolds's St.	Z	17
St Swithin's Square	Z	18
Saltergate	Z	19
South Park Ave	Z	21
Steep Hill	Y	22
Strait	Z	23
Upper Ave	Y	25
Waterside Centre	Z	27

LISKEARD – Cornwall – 503 G32 – pop. 8 478   1 B2

▶ London 261 mi – Exeter 59 mi – Plymouth 19 mi – Truro 37 mi

◉ Church★

◉ Lanhydrock★★, W : 11.5 mi by A 38 and A 390 – NW : Bodmin Moor★★
- St Endellion Church★★ - Altarnun Church★ - St Breward Church★
- Blisland★ (church★) - Camelford★ - Cardinham Church★ - Michaelstow Church★ - St Kew★ (church★) - St Mabyn Church★ - St Neot★ (Parish Church★★) - St Sidwell's, Laneast★ - St Teath Church★ - St Tudy★ – Launceston★
- Castle★ (≤★) St Mary Magdalene★, NE : 19 mi by A 390 and A 388

LISKEARD

Pencubitt Country House
Station Rd, South : 0.5 mi by B 3254 on Lamellion rd ✉ PL14 4EB
– ℰ (01579) 342 694 – www.pencubitt.com – Closed 27 May-11 June and 16 December-6 January
9 rm ⌑ – †£ 60/80 ††£ 85/120
Rest – *(closed Saturday and Sunday) (dinner only) (booking essential)*
Menu £ 30 **s**
• Sympathetically restored Victorian property with delightful views, personally run by charming owners. Comfortable bedrooms; Room 3 boasts balcony; Room 9 features part-vaulted ceiling and roll-top bath. Simple home-cooked dishes served in spacious dining room.

LITTLE BEDWYN – Wiltshire – **503** P29 – see Marlborough

LITTLE BOLLINGTON – Cheshire East – see Altrincham

LITTLE BUDWORTH – Cheshire West and Chester – **502** M24 – see Tarporley

LITTLE ECCLESTON – Lancashire   **20** A2
▶ London 238 mi – Liverpool - 55 mi – Leeds 83 mi – Manchester 51 mi

Cartford Inn with rm
Cartford Ln ✉ PR3 0YP – ℰ (01995) 670 166 – www.thecartfordinn.co.uk
– Closed 25 December and Monday lunch
15 rm ⌑ – †£ 65/120 ††£ 90/190
Rest – Carte £ 18/28
• 17C coaching inn combining original features with contemporary styling. Menus offer something for everyone; from sandwiches and wood platters of local produce to gutsy pub favourites. Bedrooms boast feature walls and antique French furniture.

LITTLE LANGFORD – Wiltshire – see Salisbury

LITTLE MARLOW – Buckinghamshire – see Marlow

LITTLE PETHERICK – Cornwall – **503** F32 – see Padstow

LITTLE THETFORD – Cambridgeshire – see Ely

LITTLE WILBRAHAM – Cambridgeshire – see Cambridge

LITTLEHAMPTON – West Sussex – **504** S31 – pop. 55 716   **7** C3
▶ London 64 mi – Brighton 18 mi – Portsmouth 31 mi
🛈 63-65 Surrey St ℰ (01903) 72 18 66, www.littlehampton.org.uk

Bailiffscourt & Spa
Climping St, Climping, West : 2.75 mi by A 259
✉ BN17 5RW – ℰ (01903) 723 511 – www.hshotels.co.uk
39 rm (dinner included) ⌑ – †£ 248/263 ††£ 450/470
Rest – Menu £ 22/50
• Charming, reconstructed medieval manor in immaculate gardens. Bedrooms are split between the house and outbuildings; the newer rooms in the grounds are more suited to families. Beautiful spa facility. Classic country house cooking served in formal dining room.

Amberley Court without rest
Crookthorn Ln, Climping, West : 1.75 mi by B 2187 off A 259 ✉ BN17 5SN
– ℰ (01903) 725 131 – Closed 25 December
5 rm ⌑ – †£ 55/79 ††£ 79/89
• Converted farm barn with a tidy, homely atmosphere. Exposed beams, flourishing plants and a warm welcome. Clean, modern, simply decorated bedrooms; some are in the grounds.

LIVERPOOL

See city maps on following pages

20 A3

Merseyside – pop. 452 773 – 502 L23 – 503 L23 – Great Britain

▶ London 219 – Birmingham 103 – Leeds 75 – Manchester 35

Tourist Information

36-38 Whitechapel ℰ (0151) 233 24 59, www.visitliverpool.com

Airport

Liverpool John Lennon Airport: ℰ (0871) 521 8484, SE: 6 m. by A 561 BX

Ferries and Shipping Lines

to Birkenhead and Wallasey (Mersey Ferries) frequent services daily.
to Isle of Man (Douglas) (Isle of Man Steam Packet Co. Ltd) 2 daily (2h 30 mn) - to Dublin (P & O Irish Sea) 1-2 daily (8h).

Tunnel

Mersey Tunnels (toll) AX

Golf Courses

Allerton Municipal Allerton Rd, ℰ (0151) 428 10 46
Liverpool Municipal Kirby Ingoe Lane, ℰ (0151) 546 54 35

SIGHTS

In the town : City★ • The Walker★★ DY M3 • Liverpool Cathedral★★ EZ • Metropolitan Cathedral of Christ the King★★EY • Albert Dock★CZ

In the surrounding area : Speke Hall★ AC, SE : 8 mi by A 561 BX

ENGLAND

LIVERPOOL

Aintree Lane	BV	2
Aintree Rd.	AV	3
Allerton Rd.	AX	5
Bailey Drive	AV	7
Belmont Rd.	BX	8
Borough Rd.	AX	11
Bowring Park Rd.	BX	12
Breck Rd.	BX	13
Brewster St.	ABX	14
Bridge Rd.	AV	16
Broad Green Rd.	BX	18
Calderstones Rd.	BX	21
Chester St.	AX	24
Church St.	DY	
Commercial Rd.	AV	29
Copple House Lane	BV	33
County Rd.	BX	34
Croxteth Hall Lane	BV	37
Croxteth Rd.	BX	39
Durning Rd.	BX	42
Dwerry House Lane	BV	43
Elmswood Rd.	BX	44
Gainsborough Rd.	BX	50
Great Howard St.	AX, CY	56
Holt Rd.	BX	61
Hornby Rd.	AV	64
Kirkdale Rd.	AV	71
Linacre Rd.	AV	74
Lodge Lane	BX	79
Low Hill	ABX	82
Melrose Rd.	AV	

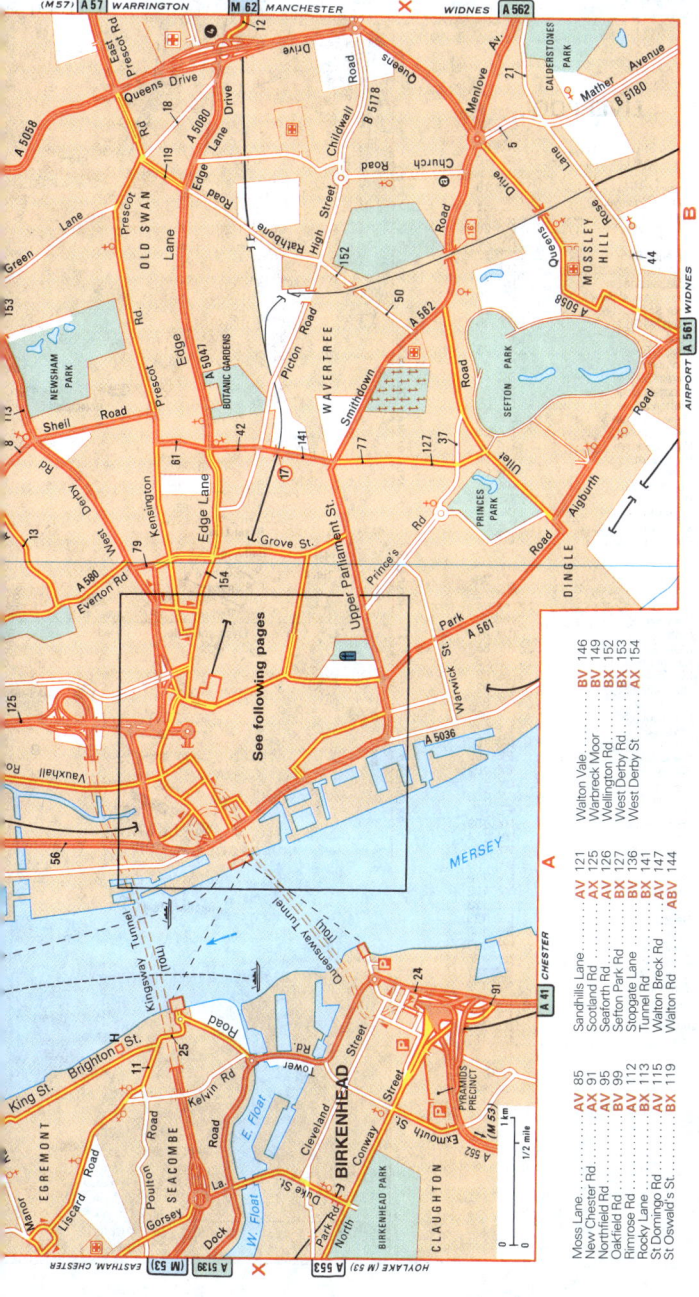

LIVERPOOL

Street	Ref	No
Argyle St	DZ	6
Blackburne Pl.	EZ	10
Bold St.	DZ	
Brunswick Rd	EY	19
Canada Boulevard	CYZ	22
Canning Pl.	CZ	23
Churchill Way	DY	26
Church St	DY	
Clarence St	EYZ	27
Clayton Square Shopping Centre	DY	
College Lane	DZ	28
Commutation Row	DY	30
Cook St	CY	32
Crosshall St	DY	36
Daulby St	EY	40
Erskine St	EY	45
Fontenoy St	DY	48
Forrest St	DZ	49
George's Dock Lane	CY	51
Grafton St	DZ	53
Great Charlotte St	DY	54
Great Howard St	DY	56
Hatton Garden	DY	57
Haymarket	DY	58
Hood St	DY	62
Houghton St	DY	65
Huskisson St	EZ	66
James St	CY	68
King Edward St	CY	69
Knight St	EZ	72
Leece St	EZ	73
Lime St	DY	
Liver St	CZ	76
London Rd	DEY	
Lord St	CDY	
Mansfield St	DEY	80
Mathew St	CDY	81
Moss St	EY	86
Mount St	EZ	88
Myrtle St	EZ	89
Newington St	DZ	92
New Quay	CY	93
North John St	CY	96
Norton St	EY	97
Parker St	DY	103
Prescot St	EY	105
Prince's Rd	EZ	107
Queen Square	DY	
Ranelagh St	DY	108
Renshaw St	DEZ	
Richmond St	DY	109
Roe St	DY	114
St James Pl.	EZ	117
St John's Centre	DY	
St John's Lane	DY	118
School Lane	DYZ	122
Scotland Pl.	DY	123
Sefton St	DZ	129
Seymour St	EY	130
Skelhorne St	DY	133
Stanley St	CDY	135
Suffolk St	DZ	137
Tarleton St	DY	139
Victoria St	DY	143
Water St	CY	150
William Brown St	DY	156
York St	DZ	157

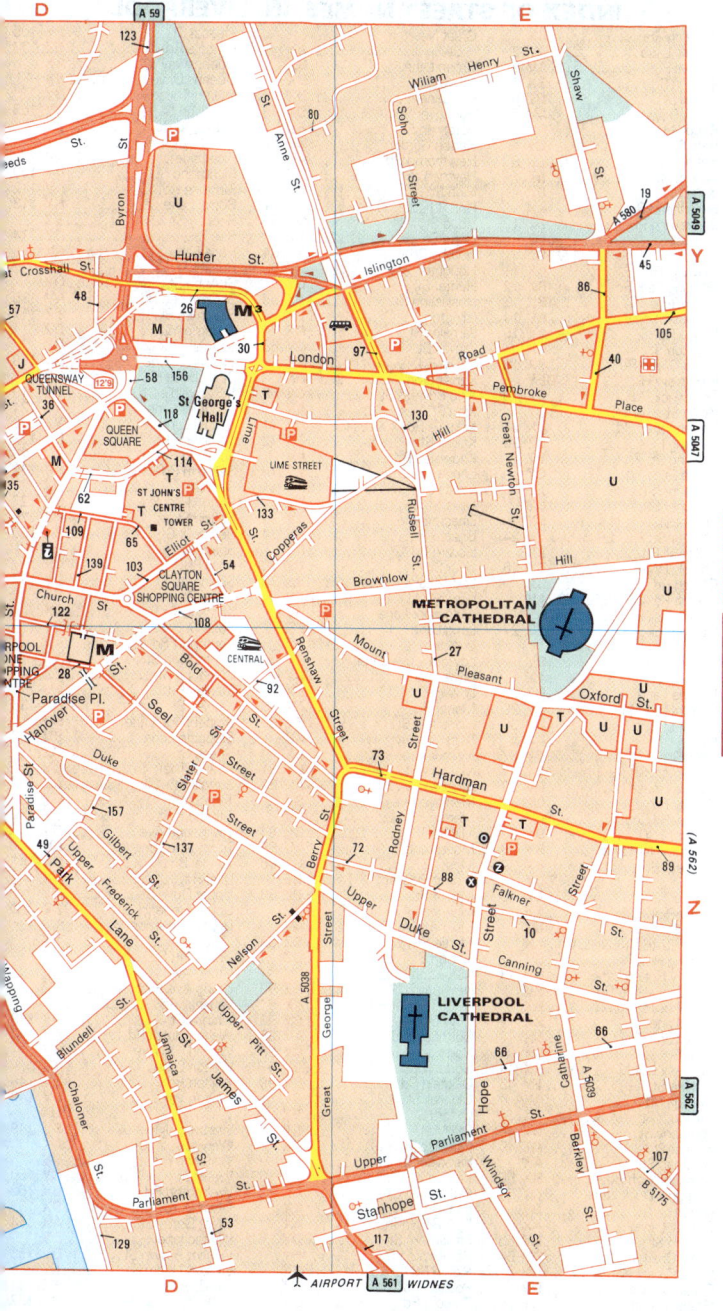

INDEX OF STREET NAMES IN LIVERPOOL

Street	Grid	#
Aigburth Rd.	BX	
Aintree Lane	BV	2
Aintree Rd.	AV	3
Allerton Rd	BX	5
Argyle St	DZ	6
Bailey Drive	AV	7
Balliol Rd	AV	
Bath St	CY	
Belmont Rd	BX	8
Berkley St	EZ	
Berry St	DZ	
Birkenhead Rd	AX	
Blackburne Pl.	EZ	10
Blundell St	DZ	
Bold St.	DZ	
Borough Rd	AX	11
Bowring Park Rd	BX	12
Breck Rd	ABX	
Brewster St	AV	14
Bridge Rd	AV	16
Brighton St	AX	
Broad Green Rd	BX	18
Brownlow Hill	DEY	
Brunswick Rd	EY	19
Byron St	DY	
Calderstones Rd.	BX	21
Canning Pl.	CZ	23
Canning St.	EZ	
Castle St	CY	
Catharine St	EZ	
Chaloner St	DZ	
Chapel St.	CY	
Chester St	AX	24
Childwall Rd	BX	
Churchill Way	DY	26
Church Rd.	BX	
Church Rd (LITHERLAND)	AV	
Church St	DY	
Clarence St.	EYZ	27
Clayton Square Shopping Centre	DY	
Cleveland St	AX	
College Lane	DZ	28
Commercial Rd.	AV	29
Commutation Row	DY	30
Conway St	AX	
Cook St	CY	32
Copperas Hill	DEY	
Copple House La	BV	33
County Rd.	AV	34
Crosby Rd South	AV	
Crosshall St.	DY	36
Croxteth Hall Lane	BV	39
Croxteth Rd	BX	37
Dale St	CDY	
Daulby St.	EY	40
Derby Rd.	AV	
Duke St	DZ	
Duke St. (BIRKENHEAD)	AX	
Durning Rd	BX	42
Dwerry House Lane	BV	43
East Lancashire Rd	BV	
East Prescot Rd	BX	
Edge Lane	BX	
Edge Lane Drive	BX	
Elliot St	DY	
Elmswood Rd.	BX	44
Erskine St	EY	45
Everton Rd	AX	
Exmouth St	AX	
Fontenoy St	DY	48
Forrest St	DZ	49
Freeman St.	AV	
Gainsborough Rd.	BX	50
George's Dock Lane.	CY	51
Gilbert St	DZ	
Gorsey Lane	AX	
Grafton St	DZ	53
Great Charlotte St	DY	54
Great Crosshall St	DY	
Great George St	DY	
Great Howard St.	CY	56
Great Newton St	EY	
Green Lane	BX	
Grove St	BX	
Hall Lane	BX	
Hannover St	DZ	
Hardman St	EZ	
Hatton Garden	DY	57
Hawthorne Rd	AV	
Haymarket	DY	58
High St	BX	
Holt Rd	BX	61
Hood St	DY	62
Hope St	EZ	
Hornby Rd.	AV	64
Houghton St.	DY	65
Hunter St	DY	
Huskisson St.	EZ	66
Islington	EY	
Jamaica St.	DZ	
James St.	CY	68
Kelvin St	AX	
Kensington	BX	
King Edward St.	CY	69
King St	AX	
Kirkdale Rd	AV	71
Knight St	EZ	72
Knowsley Rd	AV	
Leece St	EZ	73
Leeds St	CDY	
Lime St	DY	
Linacre Lane	AV	
Linacre Rd	AV	74
Liscard Rd.	AX	
Liver St	CZ	76
Lodge Lane	BX	77
London Rd.	DEY	
Longmoor Lane	BV	
Long Lane	BV	
Lord St	CDY	
Lower House Lane	BV	
Lower Lane	BV	
Low Hill	ABX	79
Manor Rd	AX	
Mansfield St.	DEY	80
Marsh Lane	AV	
Mather Ave.	BX	
Mathew St.	CDY	81
Melrose Rd.	AV	82
Menlove Ave	BV	
Merton Rd	AV	
Mill Bank	BV	84
Moss Lane	AV	85
Moss St.	EY	86
Mount Pleasant.	EZ	
Mount St	EZ	88
Muirhead Ave	BV	
Muirhead Ave East.	BV	
Myrtle St	EZ	89
Nelson St	DZ	
Netherton Way	AV	
Newington St	DZ	92
New Chester Rd	AX	91
New Quay	CY	93
Northfield Rd	AV	95
North John St	CY	96
Norton St.	EY	97
Oakfield Rd	BV	99
Old Hall St.	CY	
Oxford St	EZ	
Pall Mall	CY	
Paradise Pl	DZ	
Paradise St	DZ	
Parker St.	DY	103
Park Lane	DZ	
Park Rd	AX	
Park Rd North	AX	
Parliament St	DZ	
Pembroke Pl.	EY	
Picton Rd	BX	
Poulton Rd	AX	
Prescot Rd	BX	
Prescot St	EY	105
Prince's Rd	EZ	107
Queensway	AX	
Queens Drive	BX	
Queen Square	DY	
Ranelagh St	DY	108
Rathbone Rd.	BX	
Renshaw St.	DEZ	
Rice Lane	AV	
Richmond St	DY	109
Rimrose Rd.	AV	112
Rocky Lane	BX	113
Rodney St	EZ	
Roe St	DY	114
Rose Lane	BX	
Russel St.	EY	
St Anne St	DY	
St Domingo Rd.	AV	115
St James Pl.	EZ	117
St James St	DZ	
St John's Centre.	DY	
St John's Lane	DY	118
St Nicholas Pl.	CY	
St Oswald's St	BX	119
Sandhills Lane.	AV	121
School Lane	DYZ	122
Scotland Pl.	DY	123
Scotland Rd	AX	125
Seaforth Rd.	AV	126
Seel St.	DZ	
Sefton Park Rd.	BX	127
Sefton St.	DZ	129
Seymour St.	EY	130
Shaw St.	EY	
Sheil Rd.	BX	
Skelhorne St.	DY	133
Slater St.	DZ	
Smithdown Rd	BX	
Soho St	AV	
Southport Rd	AV	
South John St.	CYZ	
Stanhope St.	EZ	
Stanley Rd.	AV	
Stanley St.	CDY	135
Stonebridge Lane.	BV	
Stopgate Lane	BV	136
Strand St	CZ	
Strand (The).	CY	
Suffolk St.	DZ	137
Tarleton St.	DY	139
Tithebarn St.	CY	
Townsend Ave.	BV	
Townsend Lane	BV	
Tunnel Rd.	BX	141
Ullet Rd.	BX	
Upper Duke St	EZ	
Upper Frederick St	DZ	
Upper Parliament St	EZ	
Upper Pitt St	DZ	
Utting Ave.	AV	
Utting Ave East	BV	
Vauxhall Rd.	CY	
Victoria St	DY	143
Walton Breck Rd.	AV	147
Walton Hall Ave	BV	
Walton Lane	AV	
Walton Rd	ABV	144
Walton Vale.	BV	146
Wapping	CDZ	
Warbreck Moor	BV	149
Warwick	AX	
Waterloo Rd	CY	
Water St	CY	150
Wellington Rd.	BX	152
West Derby Rd.	BX	153
West Derby St	AX	154
Whitechapel	DY	
William Brown St	DY	156
William Henry St.	EY	
Windsor St.	EZ	
York St.	DZ	157

ENGLAND

LIVERPOOL

Hilton
3 Thomas Steers Way ✉ *L1 8LW –* ✆ *(0151) 708 42 00*
– www.hilton.co.uk/liverpool CZ**x**
204 rm – †£ 99/149 ††£ 109/159, ⊇ £ 14.95 – 11 suites
Rest *Exchange* – Menu £ 25 (dinner) – Carte lunch £ 15/27

• Spacious, light-filled hotel in waterfront location, with the latest in modern styling and facilities. Floor to ceiling windows in bedrooms. Trendy cocktail bar, good conference facilities and well-equipped gym. Accessible menu of international dishes in Exchange.

Malmaison
7 William Jessop Way, Princes Dock ✉ *L3 1QZ –* ✆ *(0151) 229 50 00*
– www.malmaison-liverpool.com CY**n**
130 rm – †£ 175 ††£ 175, ⊇ £ 14.50 – 2 suites
Rest *Brasserie* – see restaurant listing

• Contemporary hotel with striking stone and black glass façade, set overlooking the marina. Stylish bedrooms are decorated in sensuous purple or orange tones and boast sunken baths; two are football-themed suites. Sexy, sophisticated bar.

Hope Street
40 Hope St ✉ *L1 9DA –* ✆ *(0151) 709 30 00 – www.hopestreethotel.co.uk*
80 rm – †£ 89/180 ††£ 89/180, ⊇ £ 16.50 – 9 suites EZ**o**
Rest *London Carriage Works* – see restaurant listing

• Former carriage works; now a modern, boutique hotel. Stylish, minimalist bedrooms boast stark white walls and underfloor heating; top floor loft suites have stunning skyline views. Trendy bar open Thurs-Sat.

Hard Days Night
Central Buildings, North John St ✉ *L2 6RR –* ✆ *(0151) 236 19 64*
– www.harddaysnighthotel.com CY**i**
110 rm – †£ 110/275 ††£ 110/275, ⊇ £ 15.95 – 2 suites
Rest *Blakes* – *(closed Sunday and Monday)* Menu £ 14 (lunch) **s**
– Carte £ 34/49 **s**

• Unique Beatles themed hotel; their story recounted in artwork from doorstep to rooftop, with every room featuring original works. Suites styled around Lennon and McCartney. Blakes, named after designer of Sgt. Pepper album cover, features modern brasserie menu.

Racquet Club
Hargreaves Buildings, 5 Chapel St ✉ *L3 9AG –* ✆ *(0151) 236 66 76*
– www.racquetclub.org – Closed first week January, 25 December and bank holidays CY**e**
8 rm – †£ 60/100 ††£ 60/100, ⊇ £ 12
Rest *Ziba* – see restaurant listing

• Ornate Victorian building, formerly a Shipping Agency office and then a gentleman's club, boasting a grand façade and bohemian style. Bedrooms differ greatly in both layout and décor but most feature antique furniture and eclectic art.

XXX Panoramic
West Tower (34th floor), Brook St ✉ *L3 9PJ –* ✆ *(0151) 236 55 34*
– www.panoramicliverpool.com – Closed 25-26 December, Sunday dinner and bank holidays CY**r**
Rest – Menu £ 20 (lunch) – Carte approx. £ 40

• On 34th floor of city's highest building; a stylish glass skyscraper with 360° views. Clothed tables, formal service; intimate dinners. Creative, ambitious cooking; excellent value lunch.

XX 60 Hope Street
60 Hope St ✉ *L1 9BZ –* ✆ *(0151) 707 60 60 – www.60hopestreet.com – Closed Sunday dinner and bank holidays* EZ**x**
Rest – Menu £ 27 – Carte £ 41/52

• Attractive Grade II listed Georgian house concealing well-established modern brasserie with bold feature walls and informal basement wine bar. Interesting regional dishes provide good value.

LIVERPOOL

XX London Carriage Works – at Hope Street Hotel
40 Hope St ⊠ L1 9DA – ℰ (0151) 705 22 22
– www.thelondoncarriageworks.co.uk
EZ**o**
Rest – Menu £ 20 (lunch and early dinner) – Carte £ 23/52
♦ Spacious, open-plan brasserie dominated by impressive glass sculpture, with long bar, squashy sofas and relaxed ambience. Modern European brasserie dishes focus on local ingredients.

XX Spire
1 Church Rd ⊠ L15 9EA – ℰ (0151) 734 50 40 – www.spirerestaurant.co.uk
– Closed first 2 weeks January and lunch Saturday-Monday
BX**a**
Rest – Menu £ 13 (lunch) – Carte dinner £ 28/37
♦ Simple neighbourhood restaurant set in the Penny Lane area of the city. Good value, understated menus offer regional and modern European dishes. Tasty modern cooking; friendly service.

XX Ziba – at Racquet Club Hotel
Hargreaves Buildings, 5 Chapel St ⊠ L3 9AG – ℰ (0151) 236 66 76
– www.racquetclub.org – Closed first week January, 25 December, Saturday lunch, Sunday and bank holidays
CY**e**
Rest – Carte £ 18/28 **s**
♦ Airy, linen-clad restaurant with large arched windows, in a slightly quirky, bohemian-style hotel. Eclectic menu offers British dishes with a twist; many ingredients are from the family farm.

XX Brasserie – at Malmaison Hotel
7 William Jessop Way, Princes Dock ⊠ L3 1QZ – ℰ (0151) 229 50 00
– www.malmaison-liverpool.com
CY**n**
Rest – Menu £ 15 (lunch) – Carte £ 26/40
♦ Industrial-style brasserie with exposed ceiling ducts, Liverpool pop art and a stylish chef's table, set in a modern waterfront hotel. Extensive menu offers classic British brasserie dishes.

X Host
31 Hope St ⊠ L1 9HX – ℰ (0151) 708 58 31 – www.ho-st.co.uk – Closed 25 December and 1 January
EZ**z**
Rest – South-East Asian – Carte £ 17/26
♦ Lively place with trendy bar and informal dining area of refectory-style tables. Wide range of Asian-inspired dishes, including Chinese, Japanese, Thai and Vietnamese. Good desserts.

X Maritime Dining Room
Merseyside Maritime Museum, (4th Floor) ⊠ L3 4AQ – ℰ (0151) 478 40 56
– www.liverpoolmuseums.org.uk – Closed 25-26 December
CZ**c**
Rest – (lunch only) Carte £ 17/19
♦ Located on top floor of the superb maritime museum, with views over the famous Albert Dock. Seasonally changing menu of hearty, rustic British classics, with the occasional modern twist.

LIZARD – Cornwall – 503 E34
1 A3

London 326 mi – Penzance 24 mi – Truro 29 mi

☼ Lizard Peninsula★ - Mullion Cove★★ (Church★) - Kynance Cove★★ - Cadgwith★ - Coverack★ - Cury★ (Church★) - Gunwalloe Fishing Cove★ - St Keverne (Church★) - Landewednack★ (Church★) – Mawgan-in-Meneage (Church★) - Ruan Minor (Church★) - St Anthony-in-Meneage★

⌂ Landewednack House
Church Cove, East : 1 mi by A 3083 ⊠ TR12 7PQ – ℰ (01326) 290 877
– www.landewednackhouse.com
6 rm ⊇ – †£ 55/85 ††£ 130/190
Rest – Menu £ 38 **s**
♦ Part 17C former rectory and garden, overlooking Church Cove. Smart interiors stylishly furnished with antiques. Diners encouraged to discuss menus: best local produce to hand.

LONDON

See city maps on following pages

12 B3

– Great Britain

Tourist Information

Black Rd (020) 8846 90 00, www.visitlondon.com

Airports

- **Heathrow** 0844 335 1801 **12** AX Terminal: Bus and Coach services run regularly, each day from Victoria. By Rail: Heathrow Express and Connect from Paddington Underground, daily every 20 minutes.
- **Gatwick** 0844 335 1802 **13**: by A23 EZ and M23 - Terminal: Coach services from Victoria Coach Station run regularly each day. By Rail: Gatwick Express from Victoria Underground, daily every 15 minutes. Southern Trains every 15 minutes from Victoria, London Bridge and Clapham Junction
- **London City Airport** (020) 7646 0088 **11** HV
- **Stansted**, at Bishop's Stortford 0844 335 1803, NE: 34m **11** by M11 JT and A120.

British Airways, Ticket sales and reservations, Paddington Station London, W2, 08700 8509 8500 **36** BX

Medical Emergencies

To contact a doctor for first aid, emergency medical advice and chemists night service: 07000 372255.
Accident & Emergency: dial 999 for Ambulance, Police or Fire Services.

Shopping

Most stores are found in Oxford Street (Selfridges, M & S), Regent Street (Hamleys, Libertys) and Knightsbridge (Harrods, Harvey Nichols). Open usually Monday to Saturday 9 am to 6 pm. Some open later (8 pm) once a week; Knightsbridge Wednesday, Oxford Street and Regent Street Thursday. Other areas worth visiting include Jermyn Street and Savile Row (mens outfitters), Bond Street (jewellers and haute couture).

Theatres

The "West End" has many major theatre performances and can generally be found around Shaftesbury Avenue. A half-price ticket booth is located in Leicester Square and is open Monday to Saturday 1 pm to 6.30 pm, Sunday and matinée days 12 noon to 6.30 pm. Restrictions apply.

Tipping

When a service charge is included in a bill it is not necessary to tip extra. If service is not included a discretionary 10% is normal.

LONDON

Travel

As driving in London is difficult, it is advisable to take the Underground, a bus or taxi. Taxis can be hailed when the amber light is illuminated.

Congestion Charging

The congestion charge is £10 per day on all vehicles (except motor cycles and exempt vehicles) entering the central zone between 7.00 am and 6.00 pm - Monday to Friday except on Bank Holidays.

Payment can be made in advance, on the day, by post, on the Internet, by telephone (0845 900 1234) or at retail outlets.

A charge of up to £100 will be made for non-payment.

Further information is available on the Transport for London website - www.tfl.gov.uk

Localities outside the Greater London limits are listed alphabetically throughout the guide.

SIGHTS

Historical Buildings and Monuments

Palace of Westminster★★★ 39ALX • Tower of London★★★ • London Eye★★★ ※ 32 AMV •Banqueting House★★ 31ALV • Buckingham Palace★★ 38AIX • Kensington Palace★★ 27ABV • Lincoln's Inn★★ 32AMT • Lloyds Building★★ 34ARU • Royal Hospital Chelsea★★ 37AGZ • St James's Palace★★ 30AJV • Somerset House★★ 32AMU • South Bank Arts Centre★★ 32AMV • Spencer House★★ 30AIV • The Temple★★ 32ANU • Tower Bridge★★ 34ASV • Albert Memorial★ Gray's Inn★ 32AMV • Guildhall★ 33AQT • Shakespeare's Globe★ 33APV• London Bridge★ 34ARV • Mansion House★ 33AQV • The Monument★※ 34ARU • Old Admiralty★ 31AKV • Royal Albert Hall★ 36ADX • Royal Exchange★ 34ARU • Royal Opera House★ 31ALU • Theatre Royal★ 31AKV

Churches in the City

St Paul's Cathedral★★★ ≤ 33APU •St Bartholomew the Great★★ 33APT • Temple Church★★ 32ANU • All Hallows-by-the-Tower★ 34ARU • St Giles Cripplegate★ 33AQT • St Helen Bishopgate★ 34ART

Other Churches

Westminster Abbey★★★ 39ALX • Southwark Cathedral★★ 33AQV • Queens Chapel★ 39AJV • St James's★ 30AJV • St Margaret's★ 39ALX • St Martin-in-the-Fields★ 31ALV

Parks

Regent's Park★★★ 11QZC • Hyde Park★ 29AFV • Kensington Gardens★★ 28 ACV • St James's Park★★31AKV

Streets and Squares

The City★★★ 33AQT •Burlington Arcade★ 30 AIV • Covent Garden★★ 31ALU • The Mall★★ 31AKV • Piccadilly★ 30AIV - Trafalgar Square★★ 31AKV • Whitehall★★ 31 ALV• Bond Street★ 30 AIU • Jermyn Street★ 30AJV • Leicester Square★ 31AKU • Piccadilly Circus★ 31AJU • Shepherd Market★ 30AHV • Victoria Embankment Gardens★ 31ALV

Museums

British Museum★★★ 31AKL • Imperial War Museum★★★ 40ANY • National Gallery★★★ 31AKV • Science Museum★★★ 36ADX • Tate Britain★★★ 39ALY • Victoria and Albert Museum★★★ 36ADY • Wallace Collection★★★ 29AGT • Somerset House★★ 32AMU • Museum of London★★ 33APT • National Portrait Gallery★★ 31AKU • Natural History Museum★★ 36ADY • Sir John Soane's Museum★★ 32AMT • Tate Modern★★ ≤ 33APV• Madame Tussaud's Waxworks★ 17QZD

Outer London

Brentford 5BX Syon Park★★

Chiswick 6CV Chiswick Mall★★• Chiswick House★ **D** • Hogarth's House★ **E**

Greenwich 7 and **8** GHV Cutty Sark★★ G**VF** •National Maritime Museum★★ GV**M**^{2} • Royal Naval College★★ GV**G** • The Park and Old Royal Observatory★ HV**K**

Hampstead Kenwood House★★ **2** EUP •Fenton House★★ **11**PZA

Kew 6 CX Royal Botanic Gardens★★★

Kingston upon Thames 5BY Hampton Court Palace★★★

Hendon★ 2 Royal Air Force Museum★★ CT**M**^{3}

Hounslow 5BV Osterley Park★★

Richmond 5 and **6** CX Richmond Park★★※CX •Ham House★★ BX**V**

Twickenham 5BX Marble Hill House★ **Z** • Strawberry Hill★ **A**

The maps in this section of the Guide are based upon the Ordnance Survey of Great Britain with the permission of the Controller of Her Majesty's Stationery Office. © Crown Copyright 100000247

Alphabetical index of hotels

A		page
Amsterdam		405
Andaz Liverpool Street		378
Arch		445
Aster House		410
Athenaeum		434

B		page
Baglioni		406
B + B Belgravia		464
Beaufort		399
Berkeley		430
Bermondsey Square		418
Bingham		415
Blakes		409
Bloomsbury		371
Brown's		434

C		page
The Cadogan		398
Cannizaro House		414
The Capital		398
Cavendish		452
Chancery Court		376
Charlotte Street		371
Chesterfield		434
Claridge's		433
Colonnade Town House		428
Connaught		433
Corinthia		463
Covent Garden		371
The Cranley		410
Crowne Plaza London - St James		463

D		page
Dean Street Townhouse		454
Dorchester		433
Draycott		398
Dukes		451
Durrants		445

E		page
Egerton House		398

F		page
51 Buckingham Gate		463
41		463
Four Seasons (Canary Wharf)		422
Four Seasons (Mayfair)		433

G		page
The Gore		410
Goring		463
Grosvenor House		434

H		page
Halkin		430
Hart House		446
Haymarket		451
Hazlitt's		454
The Hempel		427
High Road House		391
Hilton London Green Park		435
Hilton London Heathrow Airport		390
Hilton London Tower Bridge		417
The Hoxton		385
Hyatt Regency London-The Churchill		445

I		page
InterContinental		433

J		page
Jumeirah Carlton Tower		397
Jumeirah Lowndes		430

K		page
K + K George		405
Knightsbridge		398

L		page
Lancaster London		427
The Landmark London		444
Lanesborough		430

LONDON

Hotel		Page
Langham	🏨	444
The Levin	🏨	398
London Bridge	🏨	418
London Heathrow Marriott	🏨	390
London Hilton	🏨	433
London Marriott H. County Hall	🏨	413
London Marriott H. Grosvenor Square	🏨	435
London Marriott H. Park Lane	🏨	434
London Syon Park	🏨	390
Lord Milner	🏨	464

M — page

Malmaison	🏨	393
Mandarin Oriental Hyde Park	🏨	432
Mandeville	🏨	445
Marble Arch by Montcalm	🏨	446
Mayflower	🏨	405
Metropolitan	🏨	434
The Milestone	🏨	405
Montague on the Gardens	🏨	371
Montcalm	🏨	445
Montcalm London City at The Brewery	🏨	378
Moran	🏨	391

N — page

New Linden	🏨	428
Novotel London St. Pancras	🏨	375
Number Sixteen	🏨	409
No. Ten Manchester Street	🏨	445

O — page

One Aldwych	🏨	460

P — page

The Pelham	🏨	409
Petersham	🏨	415
The Portobello	🏨	408

R — page

Ritz	🏨	451
The Rockwell	🏨	410
The Rookery	🏨	393
Royal Garden	🏨	405
Royal Park	🏨	428
The Rubens at The Palace	🏨	463
Rushmore	🏨	405

S — page

St Ermin's	🏨	463
St James's Hotel and Club	🏨	451
St Martins Lane	🏨	460
St Pancras Renaissance	🏨	377
Sanctum Soho	🏨	454
Sanderson	🏨	445
Savoy	🏨	460
Sheraton Park Tower	🏨	398
The Sloane Square	🏨	399
Sofitel	🏨	390
Soho	🏨	454
Stafford	🏨	451
Sumner	🏨	446
Sydney House	🏨	399

T — page

Threadneedles	🏨	378
Tophams	🏨	464
Town Hall	🏨	421
Twenty Nevern Square	🏨	405

V — page

Verta	🏨	426

W — page

Westbury	🏨	434
W London	🏨	454
Wyndham Grand	🏨	397

Z — page

Zetter	🏨	395

Alphabetical index of restaurants

A

		page
L'Absinthe	X	377
A Cena	XX	417
Admiral Codrington	🍴	404
Alain Ducasse at The Dorchester	XXXXX ✿✿✿	435
Albert's Table	XX	383
Al Borgo	XX	416
Al Duca	X ✿	453
Alloro	XX	441
Almeida	XX	396
Amaranto	XXX	438
Amaya	XXX ✿	431
Amico Bio	X	382
Anchor and Hope	🍴 ✿	421
Angelus	XX	428
Anglesea Arms	🍴	388
L'Anima	XXX	386
Apsleys	XXX ✿	431
Aqua Kyoto	XX	456
Aqua Nueva	XXX	455
Arbutus	X ✿	457
Archipelago	XX	373
Asadal	XX	376
Asia de Cuba	XX	462
Assaggi	X	429
L'Atelier de Joël Robuchon	X ✿✿	462
Aubaine (South Kensington)	X	411
Aubaine (Mayfair)	X	444
Au Lac	X	396
Automat	X	444
L'Autre Pied	XX ✿	447
Avalon	🍴	425
L'Aventure	XX	449
Avenue	XX	453
Avista	XXX	439
Avventura	X	421
Awana	XXX	400
Axis	XXX	460
Azou	X ✿	388

B

		page
Babylon	XX	406
Baltic	XX	420
Bangkok	X	411
Bank	XX	466
Baozi Inn	X	459
Bar Battu	X	383
Barbecoa	XX	381
Bar Boulud	XX	432
Il Baretto	X	450
Barnsbury	🍴	397
Barrafina	X ✿	458
Barrica	X	374
Barshu	X	458
Bar Trattoria Semplice	X ✿	443
Ba Shan	X	459
Bedford and Strand	X	462
Beijing Dumpling	X	459
Bellamy's	XX	440
Belvedere	XXX	406
Benares	XXX ✿	437
Benja Bangkok Table	X ✿	457
Bennett	XX	425
Bentley's (Grill)	XXX	439
Bentley's (Oyster Bar)	X	444
Bibendum	XXX	399
Bibendum Oyster Bar	X	403
Bingham Restaurant	XX	416
Bistro Aix	X	388
Bistro du Vin (Clerkenwell)	X	394
Bistro du Vin (Soho)	X	457
Bistro Fifteen	XX	411
Bistro K	XX	411
Bistrot Bruno Loubet	X	395
Bleeding Heart	XX	376
Bluebird	XX	401
Blue Elephant	XX	387
Blueprint Café	X	418
Bobbin	🍴	413
Bob Bob Ricard	XX	456
Bocca di Lupo	X ✿	457
Boisdale	XX	465
Boisdale of Bishopsgate	XX	381
Bolingbroke	🍴	426
Bollo	🍴	384
Bombay Brasserie	XXX	410
Bonds	XXX	379
The Botanist	XX	402
Le Boudin Blanc	X	444
Boundary	XXX	386
Bradley's	XX ✿	377
Brasserie James	X	425
Brasserie Max	XX	373
Brasserie Vacherin	X	421
Brawn	X ✿	422
Brew Wharf	X	421

295

LONDON

Name		Page
Brown Dog	🍺 ☺	415
Brula	XX	417
Brumus	XX	453
Brunello	XX	408
Builders Arms	🍺	404
Bull and Last	🍺	375
Bumpkin (North Kensington)	X	409
Bumpkin (South Kensington)	X	411
Butlers Wharf Chop House	X	419

C

Name		Page
Cadogan Arms	🍺	404
Le Café Anglais	XX	428
Cafe at Sotheby's	XX	443
Cafe Luc	XX	448
Cafe Spice Namaste	XX ☺	424
Caffé Caldesi	X	450
Cambio de Tercio	XX	411
Cannizaro House	XX	414
Canonbury Kitchen	X	393
Cantina Del Ponte	X	419
Cantina Vinopolis	X	420
Cantinetta	X	427
Canton Arms	🍺 ☺	413
The Capital Restaurant	XXX	399
Capote y Toros	X	412
Le Caprice	XX	452
Caravan	X	396
Casa Batavia	XX	407
Casa Malevo	X	429
Cassis	XX	410
Cassoulet	XX	383
Cat and Mutton	🍺	385
Catch	XX	382
Cây Tre	X	459
Cecconi's	XXX	436
Cellar Gascon	X	382
Le Cercle	XX	401
Chabrot	X	432
Chada	XX	425
Chada Chada	X	450
Champor-Champor	X	419
The Chancery	XX	380
Chapter One	XXX ✿	370
Chapters	XX ☺	414
Charlotte's Bistro	XX ☺	391
Charlotte's Place	X	384
Chelsea Brasserie	XX	402
Chelsea Ram	🍺	404
Cheneston's	XX	407
Chez Bruce	XX ✿	427
China Tang	XXXX	436
Chisou	X	443
Chiswell Street Dining Rooms	XX	382
Chutney Mary	XXX	400
Cibo	XX	408
Cicada	X	395
Cigala	X	374
Cigalon	XX	381
The Cinnamon Club	XXX	464
Cinnamon Kitchen	XX	380
Clarke's	XX	406
Clerkenwell Kitchen	X	396
Clissold Arms	🍺	389
Clos Maggiore	XX	461
Club Gascon	XX ✿	379
La Cocotte	X	375
Le Colombier	XX	401
Colony	XX	448
Comptoir Gascon	X ☺	394
Cookbook Café	XX	443
Coq d'Argent	XXX	379
Corrigan's Mayfair	XXX	439
Crabtree	🍺	388

D

Name		Page
Daphne's	XX	401
da Polpo	X ☺	462
Dartmouth Castle	🍺	388
Dean Street Townhouse Restaurant	XX	455
Dehesa	X ☺	458
Le Deuxième	XX	461
Les Deux Salons	XX	461
Devonshire Arms	🍺	392
Dinings	X	450
Dinner by Heston Blumenthal	XXX ✿	432
Dock Kitchen	X	409
Dockmaster's House	XXX	422
Dolada	XX	441
Drapers Arms	🍺 ☺	397
Duke of Sussex	🍺	384

E

Name		Page
E and O	XX	409
Ebury	🍺	466
Ebury Wine Bar	XX	466
Edera	XX	409
Eight over Eight	XX	401
Eighty-Six	XX	402
Eleven Park Walk	XXX	400
El Pirata De Tapas	X	429
Engineer	🍺	377

296

Enoteca Turi	XX	426
Entrée	X	426
Eriki	XX	378
L'Etranger	XX	410

F page

Fakhreldine	XX	442
Fellow	ID	397
Fifteen London	X	385
Fifth Floor	XXX	399
Fig Bistro	X	392
Fino	XX	372
500	X ✿	392
5 Pollen St	XX	440
Floridita	XX	456
Forge	XX	461
Fox and Grapes	ID ✿	414
Foxtrot Oscar	X	403
Franco's	XX	452
French Kitchen	X	376
The French Table	XX	412
Friends	XX	389

G page

Galoupet	XX	403
Galvin at Windows	XXXX ✿	436
Galvin Bistrot de Luxe	XX	447
Galvin Café a Vin	X ✿	424
Galvin La Chapelle	XXX ✿	423
Garrison	ID	419
Gauthier - Soho	XXX ✿	455
Le Gavroche	XXXX ✿✿	435
Geales	X	403
Giaconda Dining Room	X ✿	374
Gilbert Scott	XX	377
The Glasshouse	XX ✿	415
Goldfish	X	375
Goldfish City	X ✿	383
Good Earth	XX	402
Goodman	XX	441
Goodman City	XX	382
Gordon Ramsay	XXXX ✿✿✿	399
Gordon Ramsay at Claridge's	XXXX	436
Goring	XXX	465
Grazing Goat	ID	450
Great Eastern Dining Room	XX	385
Great Queen Street	X ✿	376
Green	ID	396
Greenhouse	XXX ✿	437
The Grill	XXX	438
Gun	ID	423

H page

Hakkasan Hanway Place	XX ✿	372
Hakkasan Mayfair	XX ✿	440
Haozhan	XX	456
Harrison's	X	425
Harwood Arms	ID ✿	387
Havelock Tavern	ID	388
Hawksmoor (Seven Dials)	X	462
Hawksmoor (Spitalfields)	X	423
Hélène Darroze at The Connaught	XXXX ✿✿	435
Henry Root	X	403
Hereford Road	X ✿	429
Hibiscus	XXX ✿✿	437
High Road Brasserie	X	391
High Timber	XX	382
Hix (Selfridges)	X	450
HIX at The Albemarle	XXX	438
Hix (Soho)	X	458
Hix Oyster and Chop House	X	394
House	ID	393
Hoxton Grill	X	385
Hush	XX	442

I page

Iberica	XX ✿	448
Il Convivio	XX	465
Ilia	XX	402
Imli	X	459
Imperial China	XXX	455
Incanto	XX	389
Incognico	XX	372
Indian Zilla	XX	415
Indian Zing	XX	387
Inn the Park	X	453
Inside	XX	384
Island	XX	428
The Ivy	XXX	460

J page

Joe's	XX	403
José	X ✿	419
J. Sheekey	XX	461
J. Sheekey Oyster Bar	X	462
Junction Tavern	ID	378
JW Steakhouse	XX	442

K page

Kai	XXX ✿	438
Kateh	X ✿	429

LONDON

Kennington Tandoori	XX	413
Kensington Place	X	408
Kenza	XX	380
Kew Grill	XX	415
Kiku	XX	443
Kings Head	ID	417
Kiraku	X	384
Kitchen W8	XX ✿	406
Koffmann's	XxX	431
Kopapa	X	373
Koya	X ⊛	459
Kyashii	XX	461

L — page

Lamberts	X	425
Larder	X	393
Larrik	ID	451
Latium	XxX	446
Launceston Place	XxX	406
Ledbury	XxX ✿✿	408
Lena	XX	386
Levant	XX	448
Light House	X	414
Lobster Pot	X	413
Locanda Locatelli	XxX ✿	446
Lola Rojo	X	426
Lots Road Pub and Dining Room	ID	404
Luc's Brasserie	XX	381
Lutyens	XxX	379

M — page

Magdala	ID	375
Magdalen	XX	418
Malabar	XX	408
Mango and Silk	X ⊛	417
Manicomio (City of London)	XX	381
Manicomio (Chelsea)	X	403
Manson	XX	386
Mao Tai	XX	386
Marco	XX	402
Marcus Wareing at The Berkeley	XxxX ✿✿	430
Market	X ⊛	374
Massimo	XxX	465
Matsuba	X	416
Matsuri - St James's	XX	453
Maze	XX ✿	440
Maze Grill	XX	441
Medcalf	X ⊛	395
Medlar	XX	401
Mennula	X	373
The Mercer	XX	381
Metrogusto	X	426
Le Metro	X	404
Mews of Mayfair	XX	442
Michael Nadra	XX	391
Min Jiang	XxX	406
Mint Leaf	XX	453
Mint Leaf Lounge	XX	380
The Modern Pantry	X	395
Momo	XX	443
Mon Plaisir	XX	372
The Montagu	XX	449
Morgan Arms	ID	422
Morgan M	XX	392
Morito	X ⊛	395
Moro	X	395
Moti Mahal	XX	376
Mr Chow	XX	432
Murano	XxX ✿	437
My dining room	ID	387

N — page

Nahm	XX	431
Narrow	ID	423
The National Dining Rooms	X	454
1901	XxX	379
Nipa	XX	428
Nobu (at The Metropolitan Hotel)	XX ✿	440
Nobu Berkeley St	XX ✿	440
Nopi	X	457
Northall	XxX	465
Northgate	ID	397
North Road	XX ✿	394
Notting Hill Brasserie	XX	408
Noura Brasserie	XX	431

O — page

Odette's	XX	377
Olivo	X	466
Olivomare	X	466
190 Queensgate	X	412
One-O-One	XxX	400
Only Running Footman	ID	444
Opera Tavern	XX ⊛	461
Orange	ID	466
Orrery	XxX	447
Oscar	XX	373
Osteria Dell' Angolo	XX	466
Ottolenghi	X	397
Owl and Pussycat	ID	424
Oxo Tower	XxX	419
Oxo Tower Brasserie	X	420
Ozer	XX	447

P		page
Painted Heron	XX	402
Palmerston	🍴	413
Pantechnicon	🍴	432
Paradise by way of Kensal Green	🍴	370
Paramount	X	373
Pasha	XX	411
Paternoster Chop House	X	382
Patterson's	XX	441
Pearl	XxX	376
Pearl Liang	XX	428
Peasant	🍴	396
Petersham Nurseries Café	X ✿	416
Pétrus	XxX ✿	431
Phoenix	🍴	404
Phoenix Palace	XX	449
Pied à Terre	XxX ✿	372
Pig's Ear	🍴	404
Plateau	XX	423
Plum Valley	XX	456
Poissonnerie de l'Avenue	XX	401
Pollen Street Social	XX ✿	441
Polpetto	X	458
Polpo	X 🙂	458
Le Pont de la Tour	XxX	418
Portman	🍴	451
Portrait	X	454
Prince Alfred and Formosa Dining Room	🍴	429
Prince Arthur	🍴	385
Prince of Wales	🍴	427
Princess of Shoreditch	🍴	386
Princess Victoria	🍴	388
The Providores	XX	448

Q		page
Quadrato	XxX	422
Quaglino's	XX	453
Queens Pub and Dining Room	🍴	389
Quilon	XxX ✿	464
Quince	XX	441
Quo Vadis	XxX	455

R		page
Racine	XX	401
Ransome's Dock	X	425
Rasa Samudra	XX	373
Rasoi	XX ✿	400
Red Fort	XxX	455
Redhook	XX	393
Red n Hot	XX	375
Refuel	XX	457
Restaurant at St Paul's Cathedral	X	383
Rétro Bistrot	XX	416
Retsina	X	371
Rhodes Twenty Four	XxX ✿	379
Rhodes W1 Brasserie	XX	447
Rhodes W1 (Restaurant)	XxxX ✿	446
Rib Room	XxX	400
Riding House Café	X	449
Ritz Restaurant	XxXxX	452
Riva	X	415
River Café	XX ✿	387
River Room	XxX	460
Rivington Grill (Greenwich)	X	385
Rivington Grill (Shoreditch)	X	386
Roast	XX	420
Roganic	XX	448
Roka	XX	372
Roka Canary Wharf	XX	423
Roots at N1	XX	392
Rose and Crown	XX	389
Roussillon	XxX	464
Roux at Parliament Square	XxX	464
Roux at the Landau	XxX	446
Royal China	XX	448
Rules	XX	461

S		page
St John (Soho)	X	457
St John (Clerkenwell)	X ✿	394
St John Bread and Wine	X 🙂	424
St John's Tavern	🍴	392
Sake No Hana	XX	452
Salt Yard	X 🙂	374
Salusbury	🍴	370
Sam's Brasserie	X	391
Sands End	🍴	387
Santini	XxX	465
Sardo	XX	372
Sartoria	XxX	439
Sauterelle	XX	380
Savoy Grill	XxxX	460
Scott's	XxX	438
Semplice	XX ✿	439
Seven Park Place	XxX ✿	452
Seventeen	XX	407

LONDON

Name		Page
Shepherd's	XxX	465
Simply Thai	X 🌿	416
Singapore Garden	XX	377
Sketch (The Gallery)	XX	442
Sketch (The Lecture Room and Library)	XxxX ✤	436
Skylon	XxX	413
Smith's of Wapping	XX	424
Sonny's	XX	414
Spice Market	XX	456
Spuntino	X	459
Square	XxxX ✤✤	436
Suka	XX	449
Sumosan	XX	442
Sushi-Say	X 🌿	370
Swagat	X	416

T

Name		page
Tamarind	XxX ✤	438
Tandis	X	371
Tangawizi	X	417
Tapas Brindisa (London Bridge)	X	420
Tapas Brindisa (Soho)	X	458
Tate Modern (Restaurant)	X	420
Tempo	XX	442
Tendido Cero	X	411
Tendido Cuatro	X	387
Terroirs	X 🌿	462
Texture	XX ✤	447
Theo Randall	XxX	438
Thomas Cubitt	🍴	466
Timo	XX	407
Tinello	XX	465
Tom Ilić	X	426
Tom's Kitchen	X	403
Toto's	XxX	400
Trinity	XX	412
Triphal	X 🌿	427
Trishna	X 🌿	449
Les Trois Garcons	XX	423
La Trompette	XxX ✤	391
Trullo	X 🌿	393
Tsunami (Bloomsbury)	X	374
Tsunami (Clapham)	X	412
28°-50°	X 🌿	383

U

Name		page
Umu	XxX ✤	437
Upstairs	XX	412

V

Name		page
Le Vacherin	XX	384
Vanilla Black	XX	380
Vasco and Piero's Pavilion	XX	456
Veeraswamy	XX	443
Verru	XX	448
Viajante	XX ✤	422
Victoria	🍴	417
Village East	X	418
Vinoteca (Regent's Park and Marylebone)	X	450
Vinoteca (Clerkenwell)	X	394
Vivat Bacchus	XX	380
Vivat Bacchus London Bridge	X	419

W

Name		page
The Wallace	X	449
Walnut	X	378
Wapping Food	X	424
Warrington	🍴	429
Waterway	🍴	430
Well	🍴	396
Wells	🍴	375
Whitechapel Gallery Dining Room	X	424
The White Swan	XX	381
Whits	XX	407
Wild Honey	XX ✤	439
Winter Garden	XX	449
The Wolseley	XxX	452
Wright Brothers	X	420
Wright Brothers Soho	X	458

X

Name		page
Xian	XX	370
XO	XX	371

Y

Name		page
Yalla Yalla	X	450
Yashin	XX	407
Yauatcha	XX ✤	455
York and Albany	XX	374

Z

Name		page
Zafferano	XxX ✤	431
Zaika	XX	407
Zayna	XX	447
Zen Oriental	X	390
Zucca	X 🌿	418
Zuma	XX	432

Starred Restaurants

✽✽✽

		page
Alain Ducasse at The Dorchester	XxXxX	435
Gordon Ramsay	XxX	399

✽✽

		page
L'Atelier de Joël Robuchon	X	462
Le Gavroche	XxX	435
Hélène Darroze at The Connaught	XxX	435
Hibiscus	XxX	437
Ledbury	XxX	408
Marcus Wareing at The Berkeley	XxX	430
Square	XxX	436

✽

		page			page
Amaya	XxX	431	Nobu Berkeley St	XX	440
Apsleys	XxXxX	431	North Road N	XX	394
Arbutus	X	457	Petersham Nurseries Café	X	416
L'Autre Pied	XX	447	Pétrus	XxX	431
Benares	XxX	437	Pied à Terre	XxX	372
Chapter One	XxX	370	Pollen Street Social N	XX	441
Chez Bruce	XX	427	Quilon	XxX	464
Club Gascon	XX	379	Rasoi	XX	400
Dinner by Heston Blumenthal N	XxX	432	Rhodes Twenty Four	XxX	379
Galvin at Windows	XxXxX	436	Rhodes W1 (Restaurant)	XxXxX	446
Galvin La Chapelle	XxX	423	River Café	XX	387
Gauthier - Soho	XxX	455	St John (Clerkenwell)	X	394
The Glasshouse	XX	415	Semplice	XX	439
Greenhouse	XxX	437	Seven Park Place	XxX	452
Hakkasan Hanway Place	XX	372	Sketch (The Lecture Room and Library)	XxXxX	436
Hakkasan Mayfair N	XX	440	Tamarind	XxX	438
Harwood Arms	🍴	387	Texture	XX	447
Kai	XxX	438	La Trompette	XxX	391
Kitchen W8	XX	406	Umu	XxX	437
Locanda Locatelli	XxX	446	Viajante	XX	422
Maze	XX	440	Wild Honey	XX	439
Murano	XxX	437	Yauatcha	XX	455
Nobu (at The Metropolitan Hotel)	XX	440	Zafferano	XxX	431

LONDON

Bib Gourmand
Good food at moderate prices

		page
Al Duca	X	453
Anchor and Hope	ID	421
Azou N	X	388
Barrafina N	X	458
Bar Trattoria Semplice	X	443
Benja Bangkok Table	X	457
Bocca di Lupo	X	457
Bradley's	XX	377
Brawn N	X	422
Brown Dog	ID	415
Cafe Spice Namaste	XX	424
Canton Arms	ID	413
Chapters	XX	414
Charlotte's Bistro	XX	391
Comptoir Gascon	X	394
da Polpo N	X	462
Dehesa	X	458
Drapers Arms	ID	397
500	X	392
Fox and Grapes N	ID	414
Galvin Café a Vin	X	424
Giaconda Dining Room	X	374
Goldfish City	X	383
Great Queen Street	X	376
Hereford Road	X	429
Iberica	XX	448
José N	X	419
Kateh N	X	429
Koya N	X	459
Mango and Silk	X	417
Market	X	374
Medcalf	X	395
Morito	X	395
Opera Tavern N	XX	461
Polpo	X	458
St John Bread and Wine N	X	424
Salt Yard	X	374
Simply Thai	X	416
Sushi-Say N	X	370
Terroirs	X	462
Triphal N	X	427
Trishna N	X	449
Trullo	X	393
28°-50°	X	383
Zucca	X	418

Particularly pleasant hotels

🏨🏨🏨	page
Berkeley	430
Claridge's	433
Connaught	433
Dorchester	433
Four Seasons (Mayfair)	433
Mandarin Oriental Hyde Park	432
Ritz	451
Savoy	460

🏨🏨	page
Goring	463
One Aldwych	460
Soho	454

🏨	page
Blakes	409
The Capital	398
Charlotte Street	371
Covent Garden	371
Draycott	398
Dukes	451
Halkin	430
The Milestone	405
The Pelham	409
Stafford	451

🏠	page
Egerton House	398
Knightsbridge	398
The Levin	398
Number Sixteen	409

Particularly pleasant restaurants

XXXXX	page
Ritz Restaurant	452

XXXX	page
Hélène Darroze at The Connaught	435
Marcus Wareing at The Berkeley	430

XXX	page
Bibendum	399
Boundary	386
The Capital Restaurant	399
Cecconi's	436
Coq d'Argent	379
Galvin La Chapelle	423
Pétrus	431
Quo Vadis	455
The Wolseley	452

XX	page
Le Café Anglais	428
Clos Maggiore	461
J. Sheekey	461
Mon Plaisir	372
River Café	387
Rules	461
Wild Honey	439

X	page
L'Atelier de Joël Robuchon	462
Bibendum Oyster Bar	403
Bocca di Lupo	457
Comptoir Gascon	394
Dehesa	458
J. Sheekey Oyster Bar	462
Oxo Tower Brasserie	420
Petersham Nurseries Café	416
Trullo	393
Zucca	418

Restaurants by cuisine type

American

		page
Automat	X	444
Hoxton Grill	X	385
Spuntino	X	459

Argentinian

		page
Casa Malevo	X	429

Asian

		page
Asia de Cuba	XX	462
Champor-Champor	X	419
Cicada	X	395
E and O	XX	409
Eight over Eight	XX	401
Goldfish	X	375
Goldfish City	X 🕭	383
Great Eastern Dining Room	XX	385
Singapore Garden	XX	377
Spice Market	XX	456
XO	XX	371
Zen Oriental	X	390

Asian influences

		page
Galoupet	XX	403
Kopapa	X	373
Suka	XX	449

Beef specialities

		page
Goodman	XX	441
Goodman City	XX	382
Hawksmoor (Seven Dials)	X	462
Hawksmoor (Spitalfields)	X	423
JW Steakhouse	XX	442
Kew Grill	XX	415
Maze Grill	XX	441
Redhook	XX	393

British

		page
Anchor and Hope	🍴🕭	421
Anglesea Arms	🍴	388
Bedford and Strand	X	462
Bennett	XX	425
Bentley's (Grill)	XXX	439
Bluebird	XX	401
Bolingbroke	🍴	426
Builders Arms	🍴	404
Bull and Last	🍴	375
Bumpkin (North Kensington)	X	409
Bumpkin (South Kensington)	X	411
Butlers Wharf Chop House	X	419
Cadogan Arms	🍴	404
Cannizaro House	XX	414
Canton Arms	🍴🕭	413
Cat and Mutton	🍴	385
Chelsea Ram	🍴	404
Cheneston's	XX	407
Chiswell Street Dining Rooms	XX	382
Corrigan's Mayfair	XXX	439
Dean Street Townhouse Restaurant	XX	455
Dinner by Heston Blumental	XXX ✤	432
Drapers Arms	🍴🕭	397
Engineer	🍴	377
Fox and Grapes	🍴🕭	414
Gilbert Scott	XX	377
Goring	XXX	465
Great Queen Street	X 🕭	376
Green	🍴	396
The Grill	XXX	438
Harwood Arms	🍴 ✤	387
Hereford Road	X 🕭	429
HIX at the Albemarle	XXX	438
Hix (Soho)	X	458
Hix Oyster and Chop House	X	394
Inn the Park	X	453
Magdalen	XX	418
Market	X 🕭	374
Medcalf	X 🕭	395
The Montagu	XX	449
The National Dining Rooms	X	454
Northall	XXX	465
190 Queensgate	X	412
Owl and Pussycat	🍴	424
Paradise by way of Kensal Green	🍴	370
Paternoster Chop House	X	382
Peasant	🍴	396
Prince Arthur	🍴	385
Prince of Wales	🍴	427

LONDON

Queens Pub and Dining Room	⌑	389
Quo Vadis	XxX	455
Ransome's Dock	X	425
Restaurant at St Paul's Cathedral	X	383
Rhodes Twenty Four	XxX✿	379
Rib Room	XxX	400
Rivington Grill (Greenwich)	X	385
Rivington Grill (Shoreditch)	X	386
Roast	XX	420
Rules	XX	461
St John (Soho)	X	457
St John (Clerkenwell)	X✿	394
St John Bread and Wine	X☺	424
Sands End	⌑	387
Savoy Grill	XxXx	460
Shepherd's	XxX	465
Tate Modern (Restaurant)	X	420
Victoria	⌑	417
Well	⌑	396
Wells	⌑	375

Chinese — page

Baozi Inn	X	459
Barshu	X	458
Ba Shan	X	459
Beijing Dumpling	X	459
China Tang	XxXx	436
Good Earth	XX	402
Hakkasan Hanway Place	XX✿	372
Hakkasan Mayfair	XX✿	440
Haozhan	XX	456
Imperial China	XxX	455
Kai	XxX✿	438
Mao Tai	XX	386
Min Jiang	XxX	406
Mr Chow	XX	432
Pearl Liang	XX	428
Phoenix Palace	XX	449
Plum Valley	XX	456
Red n Hot	XX	375
Royal China	XX	448
Seventeen	XX	407
Xian	XX	370
Yauatcha	XX✿	455

Eastern European — page

Baltic	XX	420

French — page

L'Absinthe	X	377
Alain Ducasse at The Dorchester	XxXxX ✿✿✿	435
Almeida	XX	396
Angelus	XX	428
L'Atelier de Joël Robuchon	X✿✿	462
Aubaine (South Kensington)	X	411
Aubaine (Mayfair)	X	444
L'Aventure	XX	449
Bar Battu	X	383
Bar Boulud	XX	432
Bellamy's	XX	440
Bibendum	XxX	399
Bistro Aix	X	388
Bistro K	XX	411
Bistrot Bruno Loubet	X	395
Bleeding Heart	XX	376
Le Boudin Blanc	X	444
Boundary	XxX	386
Brasserie Vacherin	X	421
Brula	XX	417
The Capital Restaurant	XxX	399
Cassis	XX	410
Cassoulet	XX	383
Cellar Gascon	X	382
Le Cercle	XX	401
Chabrot	X	432
Chelsea Brasserie	XX	402
Chez Bruce	XX✿	427
Cigalon	XX	381
Clos Maggiore	XX	461
Club Gascon	XX✿	379
La Cocotte	X	375
Le Colombier	XX	401
Comptoir Gascon	X☺	394
Coq d'Argent	XxX	379
Les Deux Salons	XX	461
French Kitchen	X	376
Galvin at Windows	XxXx✿	436
Galvin Bistrot de Luxe	XX	447
Galvin Café a Vin	X☺	424
Galvin La Chapelle	XxX✿	423
Gauthier - Soho	XxX✿	455
Le Gavroche	XxXx✿✿	435
Gordon Ramsay	XxXx✿✿✿	399
Hélène Darroze at The Connaught	XxXx✿✿	435
Henry Root	X	403
Koffmann's	XxX	431
Lobster Pot	X	413
Luc's Brasserie	XX	381

Marcus Wareing at The Berkeley	XxXX 🏵🏵	430
Mon Plaisir	XX	372
Morgan M	XX	392
My dining room	🍽	387
1901	XX	379
Notting Hill Brasserie	XX	408
Pearl	XxX	376
Le Pont de la Tour	XxX	418
Racine	XX	401
Rétro Bistrot	XX	416
Rhodes W1 (Restaurant)	XxXX 🏵	446
Roussillon	XxX	464
Roux at Parliament Square	XxX	464
Roux at the Landau	XxX	446
Sauterelle	XX	380
Sketch (The Lecture Room and Library)	XxxX 🏵	436
Square	XxxX 🏵🏵	436
Terroirs	X 🅐	462
Tom's Kitchen	X	403
Les Trois Garcons	XX	423
28°-50°	X 🅐	383
Le Vacherin	XX	384
The Wallace	X	449

Greek · page

Retsina	X	371

Grills · page

Barbecoa	XX	381

Indian · page

Amaya	XxX 🏵	431
Benares	XxX 🏵	437
Bombay Brasserie	XxxX	410
Cafe Spice Namaste	XX 🅐	424
Chutney Mary	XxX	400
The Cinnamon Club	XxX	464
Cinnamon Kitchen	XX	380
Colony	XX	448
Dockmaster's House	XxX	422
Eriki	XX	378
Imli	X	459
Indian Zilla	XX	415
Indian Zing	XX	387
Kennington Tandoori	XX	413
Malabar	XX	408
Mango and Silk	X 🅐	417
Mint Leaf	XX	453
Mint Leaf Lounge	XX	380
Moti Mahal	XX	376

LONDON

Painted Heron	XX	402
Quilon	XxX 🏵	464
Rasa Samudra	XX	373
Rasoi	XxX 🏵	400
Red Fort	XxX	455
Roots at N1	XX	392
Swagat	X	416
Tamarind	XxX 🏵	438
Tangawizi	X	417
Triphal	X 🅐	427
Trishna	X 🅐	449
Veeraswamy	XX	443
Zaika	XX	407
Zayna	XX	447

Innovative · page

Archipelago	XX	373
L'Etranger	XX	410
Greenhouse	XxX 🏵	437
Hibiscus	XxX 🏵🏵	437
Maze	XX 🏵	440
Pied à Terre	XxX 🏵	372
Pollen Street Social	XX 🏵	441
The Providores	XX	448
Roganic	XX	448
Texture	XX 🏵	447
Trinity	XX	412
Viajante	XX 🏵	422

International · page

Caravan	X	396
The Ivy	XxX	460
Light House	X	414
The Modern Pantry	X	395
Nopi	X	457
Sketch (The Gallery)	XX	442

Italian · page

A Cena	XX	417
Al Borgo	XX	416
Al Duca	X 🅐	453
Alloro	XX	441
Amaranto	XxX	438
L' Anima	XxX	386
Apsleys	XxxX 🏵	431
Assaggi	X	429
Avista	XxX	439
Avventura	X	421
Il Baretto	X	450
Bar Trattoria Semplice	X 🅐	443
Bocca di Lupo	X 🅐	457
Brunello	XX	408
Caffé Caldesi	X	450

LONDON

Restaurant		Page
Canonbury Kitchen	X	393
Cantina Del Ponte	X	419
Cantinetta	X	427
Casa Batavia	XX	407
Cecconi's	XXX	436
Cibo	XX	408
Daphne's	XX	401
da Polpo	X 🙂	462
Dolada	XX	441
Edera	XX	409
Eleven Park Walk	XXX	400
Enoteca Turi	XX	426
Fifteen London	X	385
500	X 🙂	392
5 Pollen St	XX	440
Franco's	XX	452
Il Convivio	XX	465
Ilia	XX	402
Incanto	XX	389
Latium	XXX	446
Lena	XX	386
Locanda Locatelli	XXX ✽	446
Manicomio (City of London)	XX	381
Manicomio (Chelsea)	X	403
Massimo	XXX	465
Mennula	X	373
Metrogusto	X	426
Olivo	X	466
Osteria Dell' Angolo	XX	466
Polpetto	X	458
Polpo	X 🙂	458
Quadrato	XXX	422
Riva	X	415
River Café	XX ✽	387
Salusbury	🍽	370
Santini	XXX	465
Sardo	XX	372
Sartoria	XXX	439
Semplice	XX ✽	439
Tempo	XX	442
Theo Randall	XXX	438
Timo	XX	407
Tinello	XX	465
Toto's	XXX	400
Trullo	X 🙂	393
Vasco and Piero's Pavilion	XX	456
Zafferano	XXX ✽	431
Zucca	X 🙂	418

Italian influences

		page
Murano	XXX ✽	437

Petersham Nurseries Café	X ✽	416
Whitechapel Gallery Dining Room	X	424

Italian vegetarian

		page
Amico Bio	X	382

Japanese

		page
Aqua Kyoto	XX	456
Chisou	X	443
Dinings	X	450
Kiku	XX	443
Kiraku	X	384
Koya	X 🙂	459
Kyashii	XX	461
Matsuba	X	416
Matsuri - St James's	XX	453
Nobu (at The Metropolitan Hotel)	XX ✽	440
Nobu Berkeley St	XX ✽	440
Roka	XX	372
Roka Canary Wharf	XX	423
Sake No Hana	XX	452
Sumosan	XX	442
Sushi-Say	X 🙂	370
Tsunami (Bloomsbury)	X	374
Tsunami (Clapham)	X	412
Umu	XXX ✽	437
Yashin	XX	407
Zuma	XX	432

Korean

		page
Asadal	XX	376

Latin American

		page
Floridita	XX	456

Lebanese

		page
Fakhreldine	XX	442
Kenza	XX	380
Levant	XX	448
Noura Brasserie	XX	431
Yalla Yalla	X	450

Malaysian

		page
Awana	XXX	400

Mediterranean

		page
Brawn	X 🙂	422

LONDON

Cantina Vinopolis	✗	420
Dartmouth Castle	🍴	388
Dehesa	✗ 😊	458
Dock Kitchen	✗	409
Duke of Sussex	🍴	384
The French Table	✗✗	412
Harrison's	✗	425
Le Metro	✗	404
Moro	✗	395
Northgate	🍴	397
Opera Tavern	✗✗ 😊	461
Ottolenghi	✗	397
Salt Yard	✗ 😊	374
Sam's Brasserie	✗	391
Winter Garden	✗✗	449

Modern European — page

Admiral Codrington	🍴	404
Albert's Table	✗✗	383
Arbutus	✗ ✿	457
L'Autre Pied	✗✗ ✿	447
Avenue	✗✗	453
Axis	✗✗✗	460
Babylon	✗✗	406
Bank	✗✗	466
Belvedere	✗✗✗	406
Bingham Restaurant	✗✗	416
Bistro du Vin (Clerkenwell)	✗	394
Bistro du Vin (Soho)	✗	457
Bistro Fifteen	✗✗	411
Blueprint Café	✗	418
Bonds	✗✗✗	379
The Botanist	✗✗	402
Bradley's	✗✗ 😊	377
Brasserie James	✗	425
Brasserie Max	✗✗	373
Brumus	✗✗	453
Le Café Anglais	✗✗	428
Cafe at Sotheby's	✗✗	443
Cafe Luc	✗✗	448
Le Caprice	✗✗	452
The Chancery	✗✗	380
Chapter One	✗✗✗ ✿	370
Chapters	✗✗ 😊	414
Charlotte's Bistro	✗✗ 😊	391
Charlotte's Place	✗	384
Clarke's	✗✗	406
Clerkenwell Kitchen	✗	396
Clissold Arms	🍴	389
Crabtree	🍴	388
Le Deuxième	✗✗	461
Devonshire Arms	🍴	392
Ebury	🍴	466
Ebury Wine Bar	✗✗	466
Eighty-Six	✗✗	402
Entrée	✗	426
Fellow	🍴	397
Fifth Floor	✗✗✗	399
Fig Bistro	✗	392
Forge	✗✗	461
Friends	✗✗	389
Giaconda Dining Room	✗ 😊	374
The Glasshouse	✗✗ ✿	415
Gordon Ramsay at Claridge's	✗✗✗✗	436
High Timber	✗✗	382
Hix (Selfridges)	✗	450
House	🍴	393
Hush	✗✗	442
Incognico	✗✗	372
Inside	✗✗	384
Island	✗✗	428
Joe's	✗✗	403
Junction Tavern	🍴	378
Kensington Place	✗	408
Kings Head	🍴	417
Kitchen W8	✗✗ ✿	406
Larder	✗	393
Launceston Place	✗✗✗	406
Ledbury	✗✗✗ ✿✿	408
Lutyens	✗✗✗	379
Magdala	🍴	375
Manson	✗✗	386
Medlar	✗✗	401
The Mercer	✗✗	381
Mews of Mayfair	✗✗	442
Michael Nadra	✗✗	391
North Road	✗✗ ✿	394
Odette's	✗✗	377
Orange	🍴	466
Orrery	✗✗✗	447
Oscar	✗✗	373
Oxo Tower	✗✗✗	419
Oxo Tower Brasserie	✗	420
Paramount	✗	373
Patterson's	✗✗	441
Pétrus	✗✗✗ ✿	431
Phoenix	🍴	404
Plateau	✗✗	423
Portman	🍴	451
Portrait	✗	454
Prince Alfred and Formosa Dining Room	🍴	429
Quaglino's	✗✗	453
Refuel	✗✗	457
Rhodes W1 Brasserie	✗✗	447

LONDON

Riding House Café	X	449
River Room	XX	460
Rose and Crown	XX	389
St. John's Tavern	ID	392
Seven Park Place	XXX ✿	452
Skylon	XXX	413
Sonny's	XX	414
Thomas Cubitt	ID	466
La Trompette	XXX ✿	391
Upstairs	XX	412
Verru	XX	448
Village East	X	418
Vinoteca (Regent's Park and Marylebone)	X	450
Vinoteca (Clerkenwell)	X	394
Wapping Food	X	424
Warrington	ID	429
Waterway	ID	430
The White Swan	XX	381
Whits	XX	407
Wild Honey	XX ✿	439
The Wolseley	XXX	452
York and Albany	XX	374

Moroccan   page

Momo	XX	443
Pasha	XX	411

North African   page

Azou	X ☺	388

Persian   page

Kateh	X ☺	429
Tandis	X	371

Scottish   page

Boisdale	XX	465
Boisdale of Bishopsgate	XX	381

Seafood   page

Bentley's (Oyster Bar)	X	444
Bibendum Oyster Bar	X	403
Catch	XX	382
Geales	X	403
J. Sheekey	XX	461
J. Sheekey Oyster Bar	X	462
Olivomare	X	466
One-O-One	XXX	400
Poissonnerie de l'Avenue	XX	401
Scott's	XXX	438
Smith's of Wapping	XX	424
Wright Brothers	X	420
Wright Brothers Soho	X	458

Spanish   page

Aqua Nueva	XXX	455
Barrafina	X ☺	458
Barrica	X	374
Cambio de Tercio	XX	411
Capote y Toros	X	412
Cigala	X	374
El Pirata De Tapas	X	429
Fino	XX	372
Iberica	XX ☺	448
José	X ☺	419
Lola Rojo	X	426
Morito	X ☺	395
Tapas Brindisa (London Bridge)	X	420
Tapas Brindisa (Soho)	X	458
Tendido Cero	X	411
Tendido Cuatro	X	387

Thai   page

Bangkok	X	411
Benja Bangkok Table	X ☺	457
Blue Elephant	XX	387
Chada	XX	425
Chada Chada	X	450
Nahm	XX	431
Nipa	XX	428
Simply Thai	X ☺	416

Traditional   page

Barnsbury	ID	397
Bobbin	ID	413
Bob Bob Ricard	XX	456
Bollo	ID	384
Brew Wharf	X	421
Cookbook Café	XX	443
Foxtrot Oscar	X	403
Grazing Goat	ID	450
Havelock Tavern	ID	388
High Road Brasserie	X	391
Lamberts	X	425
Larrik	ID	451
Lots Road Pub and Dining Room	ID	404
Marco	XX	402
Only Running Footman	ID	444

310

Palmerston	🍴🍺	413
Pig's Ear	🍴🍺	404
Princess of Shoreditch	🍴🍺	386
Princess Victoria	🍴🍺	388
Ritz Restaurant	XxXxX	452
Tom Ilić	X	426
Vivat Bacchus	XX	380
Vivat Bacchus London Bridge	X	419
Walnut	X	378

Turkish page
| Ozer | XX | 447 |
| Quince | XX | 441 |

Vegetarian page
| Vanilla Black | XX | 380 |

Vietnamese page
| Au Lac | X | 396 |
| Cây Tre | X | 459 |

Outside dining

Admiral Codrington	🍴🍺	404
Al Borgo	XX	416
Amaranto	XxX	438
Anchor and Hope	🍴🍺 ⊛	421
Anglesea Arms	🍴🍺	388
Aubaine (Mayfair)	X	444
Avalon	🍴🍺	425
L'Aventure	XX	449
Babylon	XX	406
Bank	XX	466
Barnsbury	🍴🍺	397
Bar Trattoria Semplice	X ⊛	443
Belvedere	XxX	406
Bennett	XX	425
Bentley's (Oyster Bar)	X	444
Bingham Restaurant	XX	416
Bistro K	XX	411
Bistrot Bruno Loubet	X	395
Bleeding Heart	XX	376
Bobbin	🍴🍺	413
Boisdale	XX	465
Bolingbroke	🍴🍺	426
Bollo	🍴🍺	384
Le Boudin Blanc	X	444
Brasserie James	X	425
Brew Wharf	X	421
Brown Dog	🍴🍺 ⊛	415
Bull and Last	🍴🍺	375
Butlers Wharf Chop House	X	419
Cantina Del Ponte	X	419
Cantinetta	X	427
Canton Arms	🍴🍺 ⊛	413
Cecconi's	XxX	436
Chapters	XX ⊛	414
Charlotte's Place	X	384
Cicada	X	395
Cigala	X	374
Cinnamon Kitchen	XX	380
Clerkenwell Kitchen	X	396
Clissold Arms	🍴🍺	389
Coq d'Argent	XxX	379
Crabtree	🍴🍺	388
Dartmouth Castle	🍴🍺	388
Dean Street Townhouse Restaurant	XX	455
Dehesa	X ⊛	458
Devonshire Arms	🍴🍺	392
Drapers Arms	🍴🍺 ⊛	397
Duke of Sussex	🍴🍺	384
Engineer	🍴🍺	377
Fig Bistro	X	392
French Kitchen	X	376
Galvin Café a Vin	X ⊛	424
Galvin La Chapelle	XxX ⊛	423
Green	🍴🍺	396
Gun	🍴🍺	423
Havelock Tavern	🍴🍺	388
Henry Root	X	403
High Road Brasserie	X	391
High Timber	XX	382
Hix Oyster and Chop House	X	394
House	🍴🍺	393
Hush	XX	442
Indian Zing	XX	387
Inn the Park	X	453
Junction Tavern	🍴🍺	378
Kateh	X ⊛	429
Kings Head	🍴🍺	417
Ledbury	XxX ⊛⊛	408
Lola Rojo	X	426
Magdala	🍴🍺	375
Manicomio (Chelsea)	X	403
Medcalf	X ⊛	395

LONDON

Medlar	XX	401
The Modern Pantry	X	395
Momo	XX	443
Morgan Arms	ID	422
My dining room	ID	387
Narrow	ID	423
Northgate	ID	397
Odette's	XX	377
Olivomare	X	466
Orrery	XxX	447
Oscar	XX	373
Oxo Tower	XxX	419
Oxo Tower Brasserie	X	420
Painted Heron	XX	402
Paternoster Chop House	X	382
Petersham Nurseries Café	X ✿	416
Phoenix	ID	404
Plateau	XX	423
Le Pont de la Tour	XxX	418
Princess Victoria	ID	388
Quadrato	XxX	422
Queens Pub and Dining Room	ID	389
Ransome's Dock	X	425
Ritz Restaurant	XxXxX	452
River Café	XX ✿	387
Rose and Crown	XX	389
St John's Tavern	ID	392
Sands End	ID	387
Santini	XxX	465
Toto's	XxX	400
La Trompette	XxX ✿	391
Victoria	ID	417
Wapping Food	X	424
Waterway	ID	430
Well	ID	396
Wells	ID	375
Wright Brothers Soho	X	458
York and Albany	XX	374

Restaurants open late

Time of last orders in brackets

Arbutus (23.30)	X ✿	457
L'Atelier de Joël Robuchon (00.00)	X ✿✿	462
Automat (23.45)	X	444
Bentley's (Grill) (23.45)	XxX	439
Bentley's (Oyster Bar) (00.00)	X	444
Boisdale (23.15)	XX	465
Bombay Brasserie (23.30)	XxxX	410
Brasserie Max (00.00)	XX	373
Brumus (00.00)	XX	453
Cambio de Tercio (23.30)	XX	411
Le Caprice (00.00)	XX	452
Casa Batavia (23.15)	XX	407
Cecconi's (23.30)	XxX	436
China Tang (00.00)	XxxX	436
Chutney Mary (23.30)	XxX	400
Cinnamon Kitchen (23.15)	XX	380
Daphne's (23.15)	XX	401
da Polpo (23.15)	X ⓐ	462
Dean Street Townhouse Restaurant (23.30)	XX	455
Le Deuxième (00.00)	XX	461
Eighty-Six (23.45)	XX	402
Eleven Park Walk (00.00)	XxX	400
Fakhreldine (23.15)	XX	442
Forge (00.00)	XX	461

Hakkasan Hanway Place (23.30)	XX ✿	372
Hakkasan Mayfair (00.00)	XX ✿	440
Haozhan (02.00)	XX	456
Imperial China (00.00)	XxX	455
The Ivy (23.30)	XxX	460
J. Sheekey (00.00)	XX	461
J. Sheekey Oyster Bar (00.00)	X	462
Levant (23.30)	XX	448
Malabar (23.30)	XX	408
Mao Tai (23.30)	XX	386
Mon Plaisir (23.15)	XX	372
Moro (23.45)	X	395
Mr Chow (23.50)	XX	432
Nobu Berkeley St (23.30)	XX ✿	440
Noura Brasserie (23.30)	XX	431
190 Queensgate (23.30)	X	412
Opera Tavern (23.30)	XX ⊛	461
Oscar (00.00)	XX	373
Ozer (23.30)	XX	447
Paramount (23.30)	X	373
Phoenix Palace (23.15)	XX	449
Plum Valley (00.00)	XX	456
Poissonnerie de l'Avenue (23.30)	XX	401
Red Fort (23.30)	XxX	455
St John (Soho) (02.00)	X	457
St John (Clerkenwell) (23.45)	X ✿	394
Singapore Garden (23.15)	XX	377
Sketch (The Gallery) (00.30)	XX	442
Spice Market (23.30)	XX	456
Spuntino (00.00)	X	459
Sumosan (23.30)	XX	442
Theo Randall (23.15)	XxX	438
Toto's (23.30)	XxX	400
The Wolseley (23.45)	XxX	452
Yauatcha (23.30)	XX ✿	455
Zafferano (23.30)	XxX ✿	431

LONDON

Restaurants open on Sunday

Name	Symbol	Page
L'Absinthe	X	377
Admiral Codrington	🍴	404
Amaya	XXX ❀	431
Angelus	XX	428
Anglesea Arms	🍴	388
Apsleys	XXXX ❀	431
Aqua Kyoto	XX	456
Aqua Nueva	XXX	455
Arbutus	X ❀	457
Asia de Cuba	XX	462
Aubaine (South Kensington)	X	411
Au Lac	X	396
Automat	X	444
Avalon	🍴	425
Awana	XXX	400
Azou	X 🌿	388
Baltic	XX	420
Baozi Inn	X	459
Barbecoa	XX	381
Bar Boulud	XX	432
Il Baretto	X	450
Barnsbury	🍴	397
Barrafina	X 🌿	458
Barshu	X	458
Bar Trattoria Semplice	X 🌿	443
Ba Shan	X	459
Beijing Dumpling	X	459
Benares	XXX ❀	437
Benja Bangkok Table	X 🌿	457
Bentley's (Grill)	XXX	439
Bentley's (Oyster Bar)	X	444
Bibendum	XXX	399
Bibendum Oyster Bar	X	403
Bistro Aix	X	388
Bistro du Vin (Clerkenwell)	X	394
Bistro Fifteen	XX	411
Bistrot Bruno Loubet	X	395
Bluebird	XX	401
Blue Elephant	XX	387
Bolingbroke	🍴	426
Bollo	🍴	384
Bombay Brasserie	XXXX	410
The Botanist	XX	402
Le Boudin Blanc	X	444
Brasserie James	X	425
Brasserie Max	XX	373
Brasserie Vacherin	X	421
Brown Dog	🍴 🌿	415
Brumus	XX	453
Brunello	XX	408
Builders Arms	🍴	404
Bull and Last	🍴	375
Bumpkin (North Kensington)	X	409
Bumpkin (South Kensington)	X	411
Butlers Wharf Chop House	X	419
Cadogan Arms	🍴	404
Le Café Anglais	XX	428
Cafe Luc	XX	448
Caffè Caldesi	X	450
Cambio de Tercio	XX	411
Canonbury Kitchen	X	393
Cantina Del Ponte	X	419
Cantina Vinopolis	X	420
Le Caprice	XX	452
Casa Batavia	XX	407
Cassis	XX	410
Cassoulet	XX	383
Cây Tre	XX	459
Cecconi's	XXX	436
Chabrot	X	432
Chapter One	XXX ❀	370
Chapters	XX 🌿	414
Charlotte's Bistro	XX 🌿	391
Charlotte's Place	XX	384
Chez Bruce	XX ❀	427
China Tang	XXXX	436
Chiswell Street Dining Rooms	XX	382
Chutney Mary	XXX	400
Cibo	XX	408
Cigala	X	374
Clissold Arms	🍴	389
Clos Maggiore	XX	461
Le Colombier	XX	401
Colony	XX	448
Corrigan's Mayfair	XXX	439
Crabtree	🍴	388
Daphne's	XX	401
da Polpo	X 🌿	462
Dartmouth Castle	🍴	388
Dean Street Townhouse Restaurant	XX	455
Le Deuxième	XX	461
Les Deux Salons	XX	461
Devonshire Arms	🍴	392
Dinner by Heston Blumenthal	XXX ❀	432
Drapers Arms	🍴 🌿	397
Duke of Sussex	🍴	384

314

LONDON

Name	Symbol	Page
E and O	XX	409
Ebury	ID	466
Ebury Wine Bar	XX	466
Edera	XX	409
Eight over Eight	XX	401
Eleven Park Walk	XxX	400
El Pirata De Tapas	X	429
Engineer	ID	377
Entrée	X	426
Eriki	XX	378
L'Etranger	XX	410
Fakhreldine	XX	442
Fifteen London	X	385
Forge	XX	461
Fox and Grapes	ID ☺	414
Foxtrot Oscar	X	403
French Kitchen	X	376
Galvin Bistrot de Luxe	XX	447
Galvin Café a Vin	X ☺	424
Galvin La Chapelle	XxX ✽	423
Garrison	ID	419
Geales	X	403
Gilbert Scott	XX	377
The Glasshouse	XX ✽	415
Goldfish	X	375
Good Earth	XX	402
Gordon Ramsay at Claridge's	XxxX	436
Grazing Goat	ID	450
Great Queen Street	X ☺	376
Green	ID	396
Gun	ID	423
Hakkasan Hanway Place	XX ✽	372
Hakkasan Mayfair	XX ✽	440
Haozhan	XX	456
Harrison's	X	425
Harwood Arms	ID ✽	387
Havelock Tavern	ID	388
Henry Root	X	403
Hereford Road	X ☺	429
High Road Brasserie	X	391
Hix (Selfridges)	X	450
HIX at The Albemarle	XxX	438
Hix (Soho)	X	458
Hix Oyster and Chop House	X	394
House	ID	393
Hoxton Grill	X	385
Ilia	XX	402
Imli	X	459
Imperial China	XxX	455
Incognico	XX	372
Indian Zilla	XX	415
Indian Zing	XX	387
Inn the Park	X	453
Island	XX	428
The Ivy	XxX	460
J. Sheekey	XX	461
J. Sheekey Oyster Bar	X	462
Junction Tavern	ID	378
Kai	XxX ✽	438
Kateh	X ☺	429
Kew Grill	XX	415
Kings Head	ID	417
Kiraku	X	384
Kitchen W8	XX ✽	406
Koffmann's	XxX	431
Kopapa	X	373
Koya	X ☺	459
Larrik	ID	451
Launceston Place	XxX	406
Ledbury	XxX ✽✽	408
Levant	XX	448
Locanda Locatelli	XxX ✽	446
Lola Rojo	X	426
Lots Road Pub and Dining Room	ID	404
Magdala	ID	375
Malabar	XX	408
Manicomio (Chelsea)	X	403
Mao Tai	XX	386
Matsuri - St James's	XX	453
Maze	XX ✽	440
Maze Grill	XX	441
Mennula	X	373
Mews of Mayfair	XX	442
Min Jiang	XxX	406
The Modern Pantry	X	395
Morgan Arms	ID	422
Mr Chow	XX	432
My dining room	ID	387
Narrow	ID	423
The National Dining Rooms	X	454
Nobu (at The Metropolitan Hotel)	XX ✽	440
Nopi	X	457
Northgate	ID	397
Notting Hill Brasserie	XX	408
Noura Brasserie	XX	431
Odette's	XX	377
Olivomare	X	466
Indigo	XX	460
190 Queensgate	X	412
One-O-One	XxX	400
Only Running Footman	ID	444
Orange	ID	466
Orrery	XxX	447
Oscar	XX	373
Owl and Pussycat	ID	424

LONDON

Name	Rating	Page
Oxo Tower	XxX	419
Oxo Tower Brasserie	X	420
Ozer	XX	447
Painted Heron	XX	402
Palmerston	ID	413
Pantechnicon	ID	432
Paradise by way of Kensal Green	ID	370
Pasha	XX	411
Pearl Liang	XX	428
Peasant	ID	396
Petersham Nurseries Café	X ✿	416
Phoenix	ID	404
Phoenix Palace	XX	449
Pig's Ear	ID	404
Plum Valley	XX	456
Poissonnerie de l'Avenue	XX	401
Le Pont de la Tour	XxX	418
Portman	ID	451
Portrait	X	454
Prince Alfred and Formosa Dining Room	ID	429
Prince Arthur	ID	385
Prince of Wales	ID	427
Princess of Shoreditch	ID	386
Princess Victoria	ID	388
The Providores	XX	448
Quadrato	XxX	422
Queens Pub and Dining Room	ID	389
Quilon	XxX ✿	464
Racine	XX	401
Rasoi	XX ✿	400
Red n Hot	XX	375
Restaurant at St Paul's Cathedral	X	383
Restaurant at The Petersham	XxX	415
Retsina	X	371
Rhodes W1 Brasserie	XX	447
Riding House Café	X	449
Ritz Restaurant	XxXxX	452
Riva	X	415
River Room	XxX	460
Rivington Grill (Greenwich)	X	385
Rivington Grill (Shoreditch)	X	386
Roka	XX	372
Royal China	XX	448
Rules	XX	461
St John (Soho)	X	457
St John Bread and Wine	X ☺	424
St John's Tavern	ID	392
Salusbury	ID	370
Sam's Brasserie	X	391
Sands End	ID	387
Savoy Grill	XxXx	460
Scott's	XX	438
Shepherd's	XX	465
Simply Thai	X ☺	416
Singapore Garden	XX	377
Spice Market	XX	456
Spuntino	X	459
St Ermin's	XX	463
St Pancras Renaissance	X	377
Sushi-Say	X ☺	370
Swagat	X	416
Tamarind	XxX ✿	438
Tandis	X	371
Tangawizi	X	417
Tapas Brindisa (London Bridge)	X	420
Tapas Brindisa (Soho)	X	458
Tate Modern (Restaurant)	X	420
Tendido Cero	X	411
Tendido Cuatro	X	387
Thomas Cubitt	ID	466
Tom's Kitchen	X	403
Toto's	XX	400
Triphal	X ☺	427
Trishna	X ☺	449
La Trompette	XxX ✿	391
Tsunami (Clapham)	X	412
Veeraswamy	XX	443
Verru	XX	448
Viajante	XX ✿	422
Victoria	ID	417
Village East	X	418
The Wallace	X	449
Warrington	ID	429
Waterway	ID	430
Well	ID	396
Wells	ID	375
Wild Honey	XX ✿	439
The Wolseley	XxX	452
Wright Brothers	X	420
Wright Brothers Soho	X	458
XO	XX	371
Yauatcha	XX ✿	455
York and Albany	XX	374
Zafferano	XxX ✿	431
Zaika	XX	407
Zayna	XX	447
Zuma	XX	432

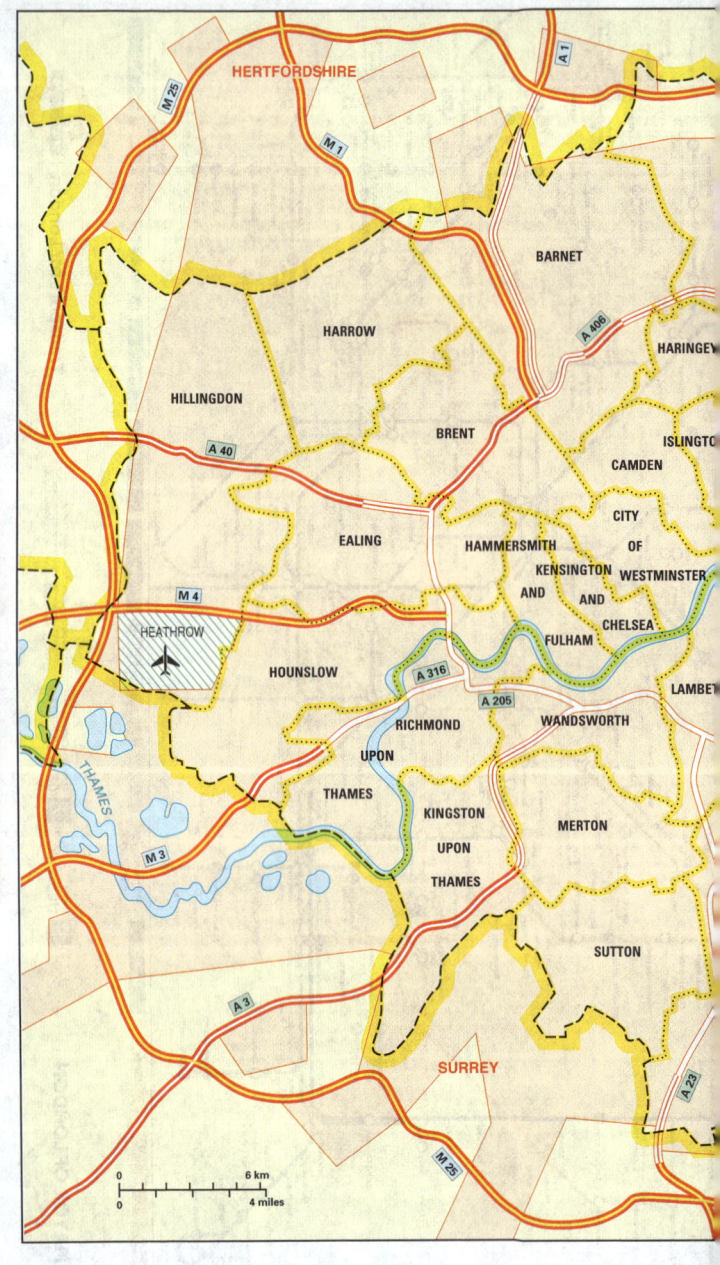

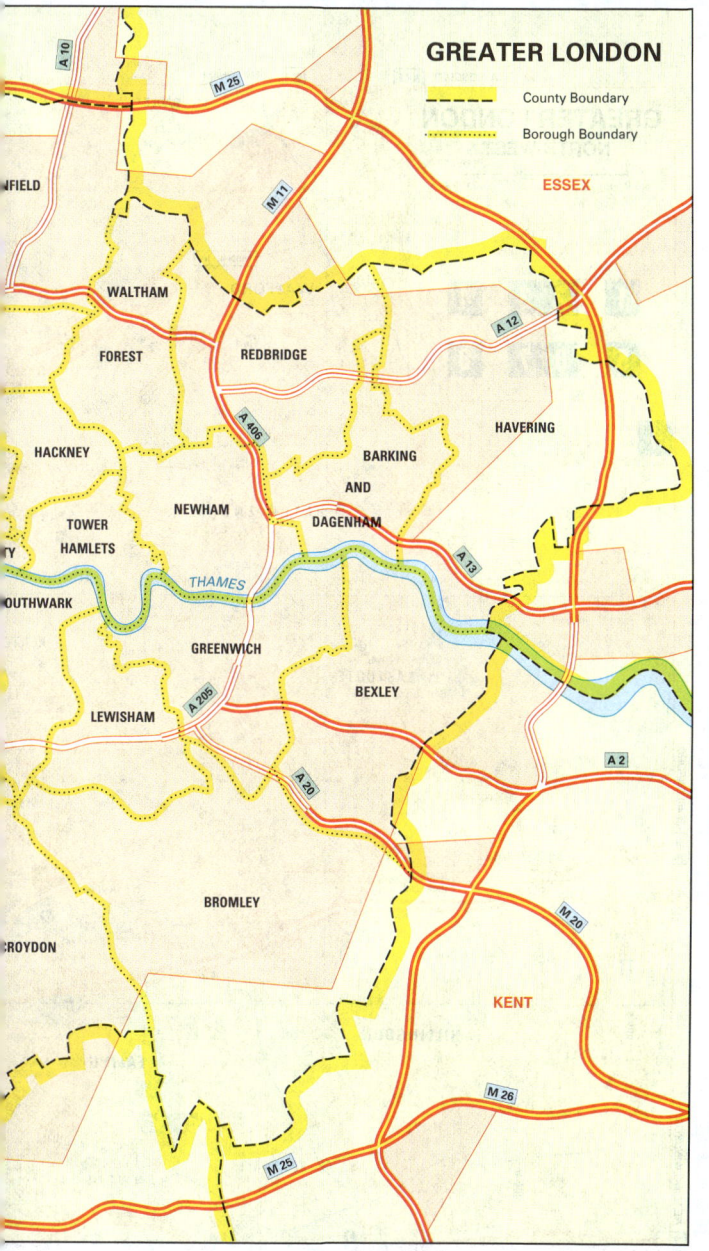

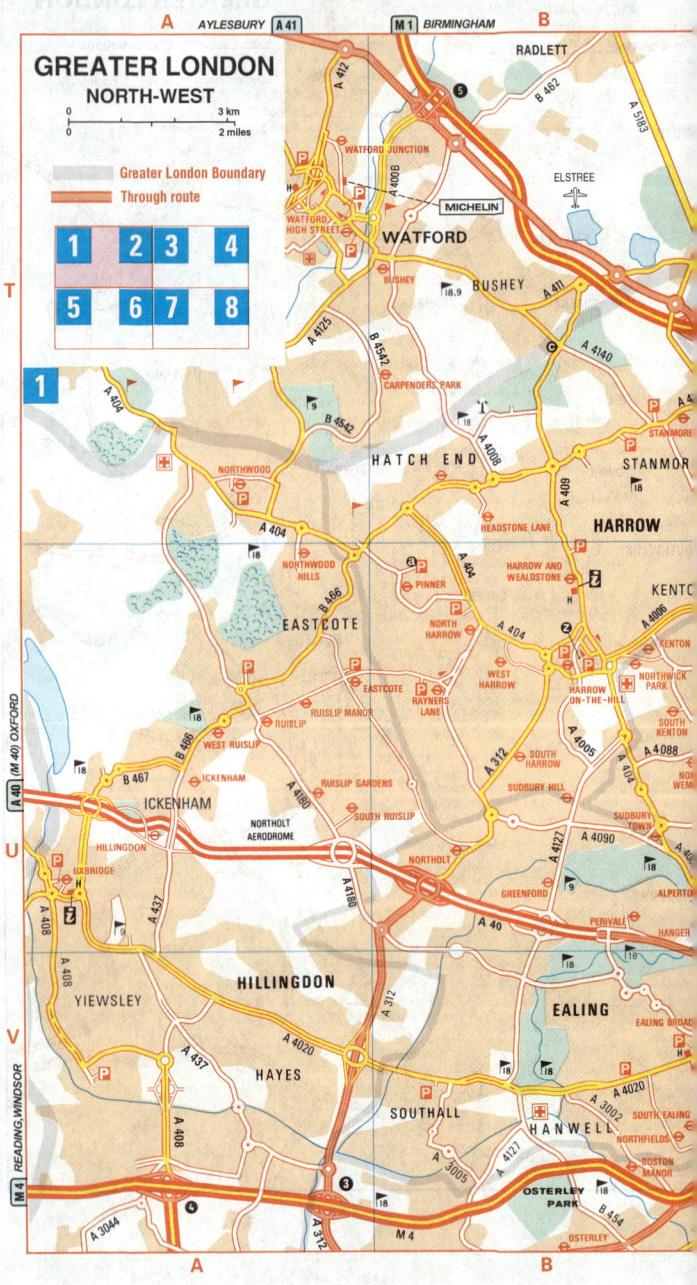

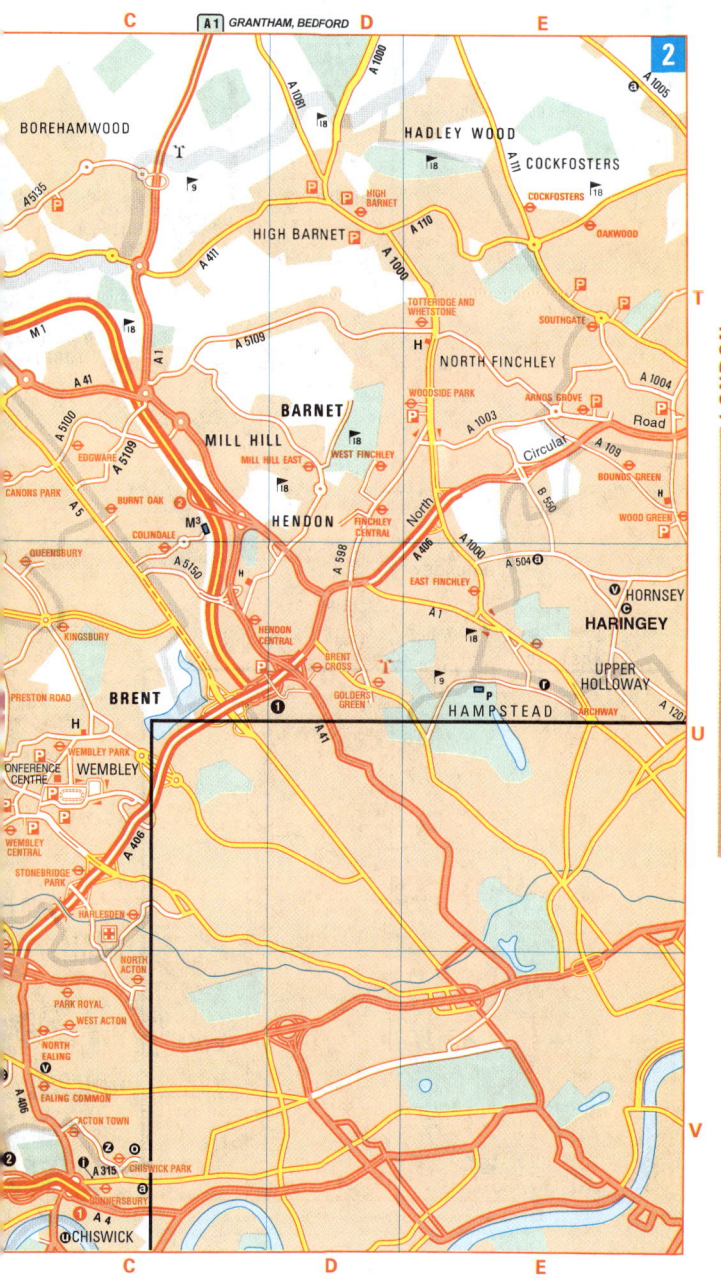

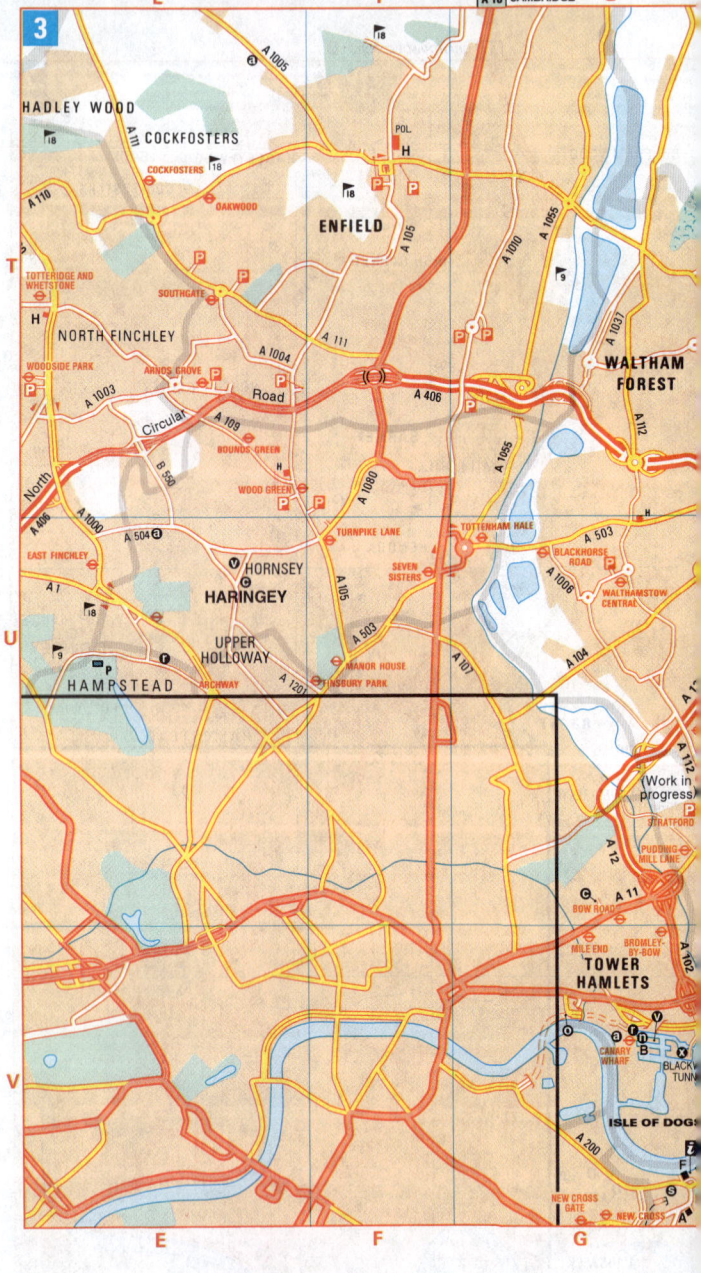

GREATER LONDON
NORTH-EAST

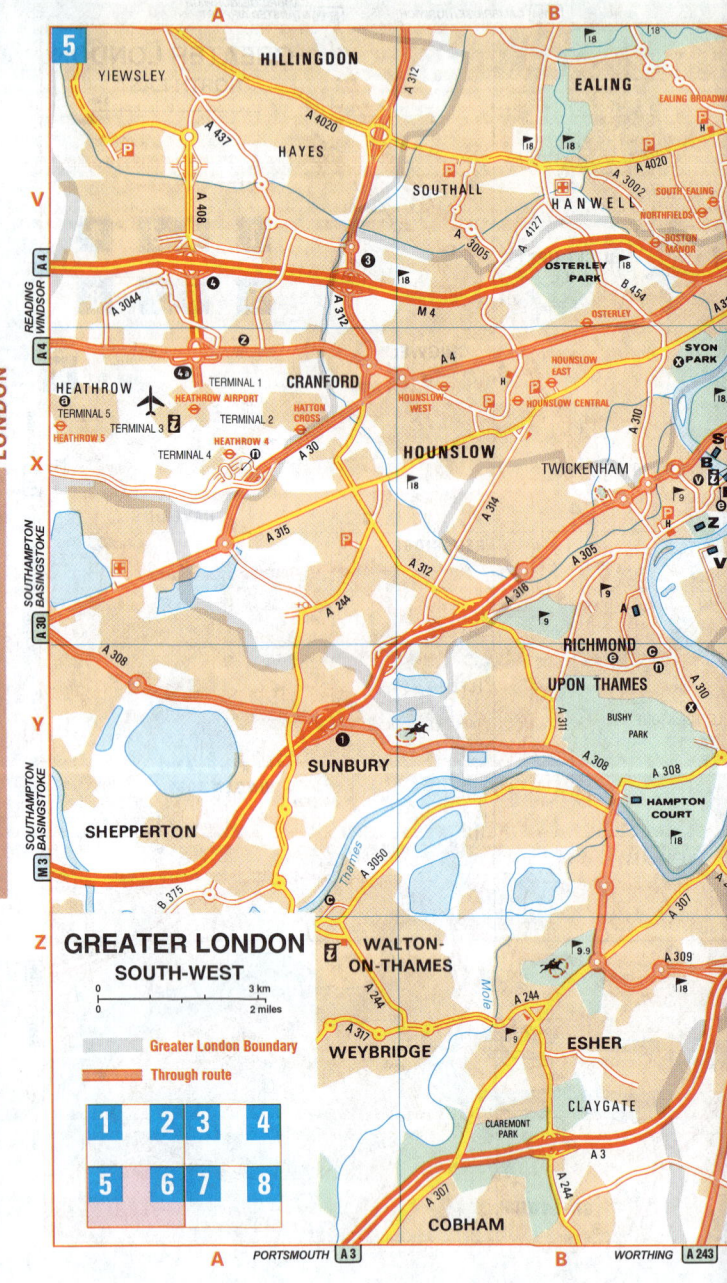

325

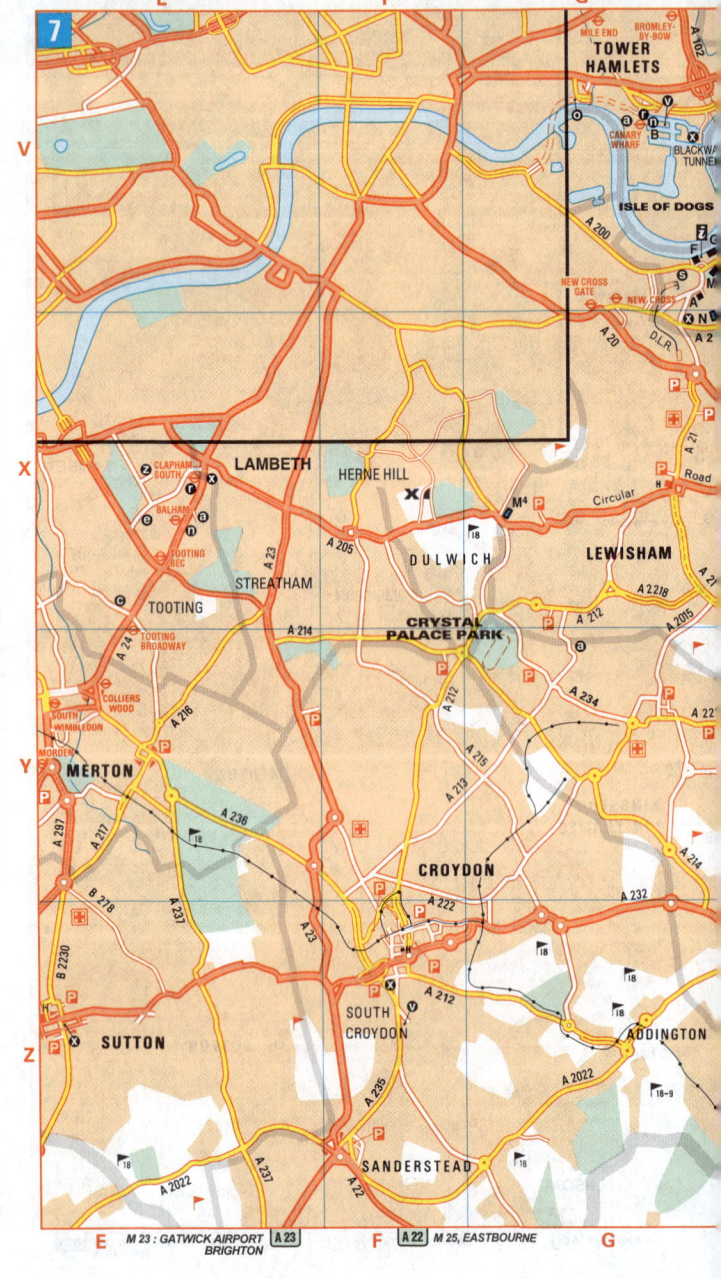

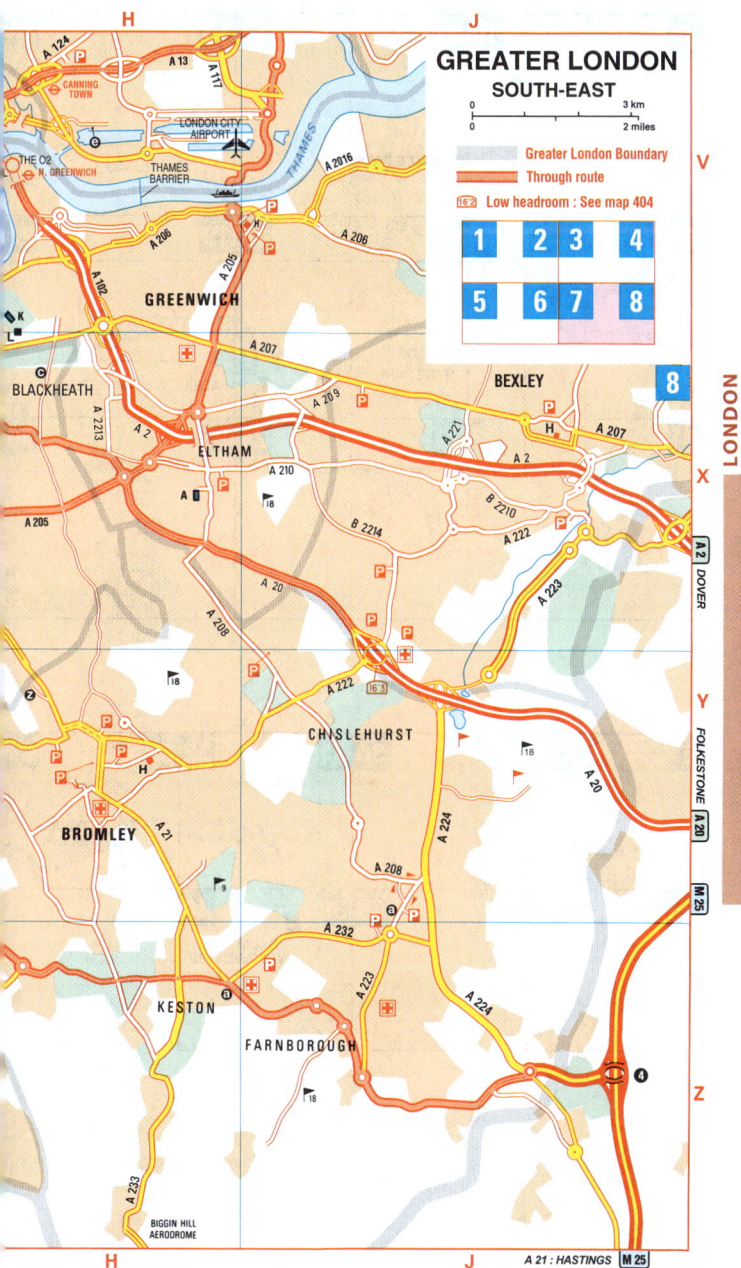

9
10
11
12
13
14
REGENT'S PARK
15
16
17
18
19
20
TOWER
BRIDGE
HYDE PARK
PALACE OF WESTMINSTER
21
22
23
24
25
26
THAMES

27
28
29
30
31
32
33
34
THAMES
TOWER
BRIDGE
HYDE PARK
35
36
37
38
39
40
PALACE OF
WESTMINSTER

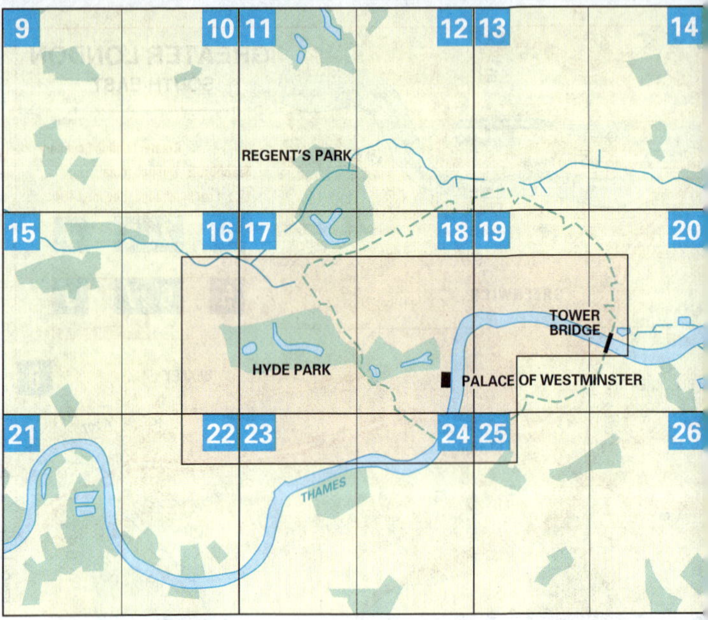

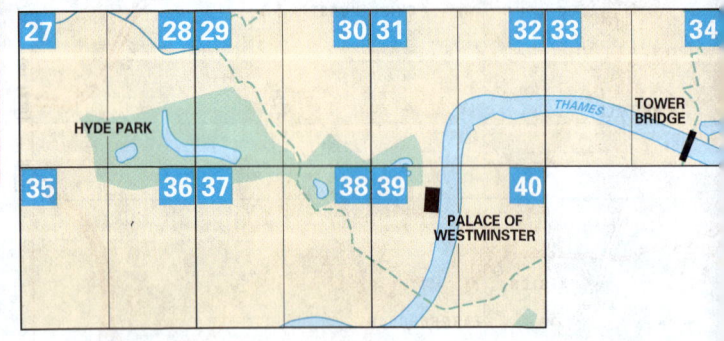

INDEX OF STREET NAMES IN LONDON CENTRE

PLAN 09

Street	Plan	Grid	
cton Lane	9	KZB	
ll Souls Ave	9	LZB	
nson Rd	9	LZA	
athurst Gardens	9	LZB	
rondesbury Park	9	LZB	
rook Rd	9	KZA	
urnley Rd	9	KZA	
hamberlayne Rd	9	LZB	
hapter Rd BRENT	9	KZB	
hurch Rd BRENT	9	KZB	
lifford Gardens	9	LZA	
oles Green Rd	9	LZA	
ollege Rd	9	LZB	
raven Park	9	KZB	351
raven Park Rd	9	KZB	352
rest Rd	9	KZA	
ricklewood Broadway	9	LZA	
enzil Rd	9	KZA	
ollis Hill Lane	9	KZA	
onnington Rd	9	LZB	
oyle Gardens	9	LZB	
udden Hill Lane	9	KZA	
dgware Rd BRENT	9	LZA	
urness Rd	9	KZB	
arding Rd	9	LZB	
arlesden Rd	9	KZB	
arley Rd	9	KZB	
awthorn Rd	9	LZB	357
eber Rd	9	LZA	
igh Rd BRENT	9	KZB	
igh St	9	KZB	
endal Rd	9	LZA	
ongstone Ave	9	KZB	196
lanor Park Rd	9	KZB	
lora Rd	9	LZA	
lortimer Rd	9	LZC	
lount Pleasant Rd	9	LZB	
leasden Lane	9	KZA	
orth Circular Rd	9	KZA	
orth Park Ave	9	LZA	
eter Ave	9	LZB	
ound Lane	9	KZB	
oundwood Rd	9	KZB	
herrick Green Rd	9	LZB	
idmouth Rd	9	LZB	
neyd Rd	9	LZA	
anfield Ave	9	KZA	
Valm Lane	9	LZB	
Vrottesley Rd	9	KZB	

PLAN 10

Street	Plan	Grid	
sford Rd	10	MZA	425
venue ((The) BRENT)	10	MZB	
ylestone Rd	10	MZB	
elsize Rd	10	NZB	
roadhurst Gardens	10	OZB	
rondesbury Villas	10	NZB	
ambridge Rd	10	NZB	335
arlton Vale	10	NZB	
avendish Ave	10	MZB	
hatsworth Rd BRENT	10	MZB	
hevening Rd	10	MZB	
hichele Rd	10	MZA	
hristchurch Ave	10	MZA	
laremont Rd	10	MZA	
rediton Hill	10	NZA	
ricklewood Lane	10	MZA	
yne Rd	10	MZB	
rognal Lane	10	NZA	
ascony Rd	10	NZB	
reville Pl	10	OZB	
arvist Rd	10	MZB	
eath Drive	10	NZA	
Hendon Way	10	MZA	
Hermitage Lane	10	NZA	
Iverson Rd	10	NZB	
Kilburn High Rd	10	NZB	
Kilburn Lane	10	MZB	
Kilburn Park Rd	10	NZC	
Kingswood Ave	10	MZB	
Lichfield Rd	10	MZA	
Lyndale Ave	10	NZA	
Mapesbury Rd	10	MZB	
Mill Lane	10	MZA	
Milman Rd	10	MZB	
Oxford Rd	10	NZB	336
Platt's Lane	10	NZA	
Priory Rd	10	NZB	
Quex Rd	10	NZB	
Randolph Ave	10	OZC	
Redington Rd	10	NZA	
Salusbury Rd	10	MZB	
Shoot Up Hill	10	MZA	
Teignmouth Rd	10	MZA	
Tiverton Rd	10	MZB	
Vale (The BARNET)	10	MZA	
Westbere Rd	10	MZA	
West End Lane	10	NZA	
West Heath Rd	10	NZA	
Willesden Lane	10	MZB	

PLAN 11

Street	Plan	Grid	
Abbey Rd	11	PZB	
Abercorn Pl	11	PZB	277
Acacia Rd	11	PZB	
Adelaide Rd	11	OZB	
Agincourt Rd	11	QZA	362
Akenside Rd	11	PZA	22
Allitsen Rd	11	PZB	
Arkwright Rd	11	OZA	
Avenue Rd	11	PZA	
Belsize Ave	11	PZA	
Belsize Lane	11	PZB	
Belsize Park	11	PZB	19
Belsize Park Gardens	11	PZB	
Boundary Rd	11	OZB	
Canfield Gardens	11	OZB	
Carlton Hill	11	OZB	
Chalk Farm Rd	11	QZB	
Charlbert St	11	PZB	79
Circus Rd	11	PZB	
Constantine Rd	11	QZA	106
Downshire Hill	11	PZA	139
East Heath Rd	11	PZA	
Elsworthy Rd	11	PZB	
England's Lane	11	PZA	323
Eton Ave	11	PZB	
Fairfax Rd	11	PZB	
Fairhazel Gardens	11	OZB	
Finchley Rd	11	PZB	
Fitzjohn's Ave	11	PZA	
Fleet Rd	11	QZA	
Frognal	11	PZA	
Frognal Rise	11	PZA	171
Gayton Rd	11	PZA	324
Gloucester Ave	11	QZB	
Greencroft Gardens	11	OZB	
Grove End Rd	11	PZC	
Hamilton Terrace	11	OZB	
Hampstead Grove	11	PZA	208
Hampstead High St	11	PZA	209
Haverstock Hill	11	QZB	
Heath St	11	PZA	
Hollybush Hill	11	PZA	227
Keat's Grove	11	PZA	236
King Henry's Rd	11	PZB	297
Lancaster Grove	11	PZB	
Lawn Rd	11	QZA	
Loudoun Rd	11	PZB	
Lower Terrace	11	OZA	
Lyndhurst Rd	11	PZA	
Maida Vale	11	OZB	
Malden Rd	11	QZA	
Mansfield Rd	11	QZA	
Marlborough Pl	11	PZB	
Nassington Rd	11	QZA	
Netherhall Gardens	11	PZA	
New End Square	11	PZA	305
North End Way	11	PZA	
Nutley Terrace	11	PZB	
Ordnance Hill	11	PZA	
Ornan Rd	11	PZA	
Outer Circle	11	QZB	
Parkhill Rd	11	QZA	
Parliament Hill	11	QZA	
Pond St	11	PZA	
Primrose Hill Rd	11	QZB	
Prince Albert Rd	11	QZB	
Prince of Wales Rd	11	QZB	
Queen's Grove	11	PZB	
Regent's Park Rd	11	QZB	
Hosslyn Hill	11	PZA	
St John's Wood Park	11	PZB	379
St. John's Wood High St.	11	PZB	29
Savernake Rd	11	QZA	
Southampton Rd	11	QZA	
South End Rd	11	PZA	
South Hill	11	PZA	390
Spaniards Rd	11	PZA	
Wellington Rd	11	PZB	
Well Walk	11	PZA	
Willoughby Rd	11	PZA	479
Willow Rd	11	PZA	

PLAN 12

Street	Plan	Grid	
Agar Grove	12	SZB	
Albany St	12	RZB	
Bartholomew Rd	12	RZB	16
Brewery Rd	12	SZB	
Busby Pl	12	RZB	
Camden High St	12	RZB	
Camden Rd	12	RZB	
Camden St	12	RZB	
Carleton Rd	12	SZA	
Chetwynd Rd	12	RZA	
Copenhagen St	12	SZB	
Crowndale Rd	12	RZB	
Dalmeny Ave	12	SZA	
Dalmeny Rd	12	RZA	
Dartmouth Park Hill	12	RZA	
Delancey St	12	RZB	
Eversholt St	12	SZC	
Fortess Rd	12	RZA	
Gaisford St	12	RZA	
Hampstead Rd	12	RZB	
Highgate Rd	12	RZA	
Hillmarton Rd	12	SZA	
Holloway Rd	12	SZA	
Hornssey Rd	12	SZA	
Hungerford Rd	12	SZA	
Islip St	12	RZA	
Junction Rd	12	RZA	
Kentish Town Rd	12	RZB	
Lady Margaret Rd	12	RZA	
Leighton Rd	12	RZA	
Market Rd	12	SZB	
Midland Rd	12	SZB	
North Rd	12	SZB	
Ossulton St	12	SZC	
Pancras Rd	12	SZB	
Parkhurst Rd	12	SZA	
Parkway	12	RZB	
Park Village East	12	RZB	
Patshull Rd	12	RZB	
Pratt St	12	RZB	
Randolph St	12	RZB	366
Royal College St	12	RZB	
St Pancras Way	12	RZB	
Spring Pl	12	RZA	
Swains Lane	12	RZA	

Street	Plan	Grid	Ref
Swinton St	12	TZC	417
Tollington Park	12	TZA	
Tollington Way	12	SZA	
Torriano Ave	12	SZA	
Tufnell Park Rd	12	SZA	
Wharfdale Rd	12	SZB	455
Willes Rd	12	RZB	
York Way	12	SZB	

PLAN 13

Street	Plan	Grid	Ref
Albion Rd	13	VZA	
Amwell St	13	UZC	
Ardilaun Rd	13	VZA	333
Balls Pond Rd	13	VZB	
Barnsbury Rd	13	UZB	
Barnsbury St	13	UZB	
Benwell Rd	13	UZA	
Blackstock Rd	13	UZA	
Bride St	13	UZB	
Brownswood Rd	13	UZA	
Caledonian Rd	13	TZA	
Calshot St	13	TZB	
Camden Passage	13	UZB	70
Canonbury Rd	13	UZB	
Canonbury Square	13	UZB	
Chapel Market	13	UZB	78
Clissold Crescent	13	VZA	
Clissold Rd	13	VZA	
Downham Rd	13	VZB	
Drayton Park	13	UZA	
Eagle Wharf Rd	13	VZB	
East Rd	13	VZC	
Englefield Rd	13	VZB	
Essex Rd	13	VZB	
Fonthill Rd	13	UZA	
Gillespie Rd	13	UZA	
Green Lanes	13	VZA	
Grosvenor Ave	13	VZB	
Halliford St	13	VZB	
Hemingford Rd	13	UZB	
Highbury Grove	13	UZA	
Highbury Hill	13	UZA	
Highbury New Park	13	VZA	
Highbury Park	13	UZA	
Highbury Pl	13	UZA	
Hyde Rd	13	VZB	235
Isledon Rd	13	UZA	
Liverpool Rd	13	UZB	
Lordship Park	13	VZA	
Lordship Rd	13	VZA	
Mackenzie Rd	13	TZB	
Matthias Rd	13	VZA	
Mildmay Park	13	VZA	
Mildmay Rd	13	VZA	
Mountgrove Rd	13	UZA	
New North Rd	13	VZB	
Offord Rd	13	TZB	
Penn St	13	VZB	343
Pentonville Rd	13	TZB	
Penton Rise	13	TZB	344
Penton St	13	TZB	345
Petherton Rd	13	VZA	
Pitfield St	13	VZC	
Poole St	13	VZB	350
Prebend St	13	VZB	
Queen's Drive	13	VZA	
Richmond Ave	13	TZB	
Riversdale Rd	13	VZA	
Roman Way	13	TZB	
St Paul's Rd	13	VZB	
St Peter's St	13	UZB	
St Thomas's Rd	13	UZA	
Seven Sisters Rd	13	TZA	
Shepherdess Walk	13	VZB	
Southgate Rd	13	VZB	
Spencer St	13	UZC	398
Stoke Newington Church St	13	VZA	
Thornhill Rd	13	UZB	
Upper St	13	UZB	
Westbourne Rd	13	UZB	56
Westland Pl	13	VZC	478
Wharf Rd	13	VZB	

PLAN 14

Street	Plan	Grid	Ref
Albion Drive	14	XZB	
Amhurst Rd	14	XZA	
Barbauld Rd	14	XZA	
Barretts Grove	14	XZA	
Bishop's Way	14	YZB	
Boleyn Rd	14	XZA	
Bonner Rd	14	YZB	
Bouverie Rd	14	XZA	
Brooke Rd	14	XZA	
Canrobert St	14	YZC	
Cassland Rd	14	YZB	
Cecilia Rd	14	XZA	
Chatsworth Rd HACKNEY	14	YZA	
Clapton Way	14	YZA	
Cleveleys Rd	14	YZA	
Clifden Rd	14	YZA	
Columbia Rd	14	XZC	
Cricketfield Rd	14	YZA	378
Dalston Lane	14	XZA	
De Beauvoir Rd	14	XZB	
Downs Park Rd	14	XZA	
Downs Rd	14	YZA	
Evering Rd	14	XZA	
Forest Rd	14	XZA	
Frampton Park Rd	14	YZB	
Graham Rd	14	XZB	
Hackney Rd	14	XZC	
Homerton High St	14	YZB	
Hoxton St	14	XZC	
Kenninghall Rd	14	XZA	
Kingsland Rd	14	XZB	
King Henry's Walk	14	XZA	337
Kyverdale Rd	14	XZA	
Lansdowne Drive	14	YZB	
Lea Bridge Rd	14	YZA	
Lower Clapton Rd	14	YZA	
Mare St	14	YZB	
Maury Rd	14	XZA	
Median Rd	14	YZA	
Middleton Rd	14	XZB	
Millfields Rd	14	YZA	
Morning Lane	14	YZB	
Mount Pleasant Hill	14	YZA	
Nevill Rd	14	XZA	
Northwold Rd	14	XZA	
Nuttall St	14	XZB	
Old Bethnal Green Rd	14	XZC	
Old Ford Rd	14	YZC	
Pembury Rd	14	YZA	
Powerscroft Rd	14	YZA	
Pownall Drive	14	XZB	
Prince George Rd	14	XZA	
Pritchard's Rd	14	YZB	
Queensbridge Rd	14	XZB	
Rectory Rd	14	XZA	
Richmond Rd	14	XZB	
Ridley Rd	14	XZA	
Sandringham Rd	14	XZA	
Sewardstone Rd	14	YZB	
Shacklewell Lane	14	XZA	
Sheep Lane	14	YZB	
Stoke Newington High St	14	YZA	
Upper Clapton Rd	14	YZA	
Victoria Park Rd	14	YZB	
Walford Rd	14	XZA	
Warner Pl	14	XZB	
Well St	14	YZB	
Whiston Rd	14	XZB	
Whitmore Rd	14	XZB	464

PLAN 15

Street	Plan	Grid	Ref
Abinger Rd	15	KZE	
Ashfield Rd	15	KZE	
Askew Rd	15	KZE	
Avenue (The EALING)	15	KZE	
Barlby Rd	15	LZD	
Bienheim Rd	15	LZE	
Bloemfontein Rd	15	LZE	
Brackenbury Rd	15	LZE	
Brassie Ave	15	KZD	
Bromyard Ave	15	KZE	
Bryony Rd	15	KZE	
Cobbold Rd	15	KZE	
Coningham Rd	15	LZE	
Davisville Rd	15	KZE	46
Du Cane Rd	15	KZD	
East Acton Lane	15	KZE	
Emlyn Rd	15	KZE	
Fairway (The)	15	KZD	
Goldhowk Rd	15	LZE	
Hammersmith Grove	15	LZE	
Highlever Rd	15	LZD	
Larden Rd	15	KZE	
Lime Grove	15	LZE	
Old Oak Common Lane	15	KZD	
Old Oak Lane	15	KZC	
Old Oak Rd	15	KZE	
Paddenswick Rd	15	LZE	
Percy Rd	15	LZD	
St Quintin Ave	15	LZD	
Sawley Rd	15	KZE	
Serubs Lane	15	KZE	
Sheperd's Bush Green	15	LZE	45
Shepherd's Bush Rd	15	LZF	
South Africa Rd	15	LZE	
Stamford Brook Rd	15	KZE	38
Steventon Rd	15	KZE	
Uxbridge Rd	15	LZE	
Vale (The EALING)	15	KZE	
Victoria Rd	15	KZD	
Western Ave	15	KZD	
Westway	15	LZD	
Wingate Rd	15	LZE	46
Wood Lane	15	LZD	
Wormholt Rd	15	KZE	
Wulfstan St	15	KZD	
Yew Tree Rd	15	KZE	

PLAN 16

Street	Plan	Grid	Ref
Abbotsbury Rd	16	MZE	
Addison Ave	16	MZE	
Addison Crescent	16	MZE	3
Addison Rd	16	MZE	
Blythe Rd	16	MZE	
Bravington Rd	16	MZC	
Chesterton Rd	16	MZD	
Chippenham Rd	16	NZD	34
Clarendon Rd	16	MZE	
Cornwall Crescent	16	MZD	10
Delaware Rd	16	NZD	
Elgin Ave	16	NZD	
Fernhead Rd	16	NZC	
Fifth Ave	16	MZC	
Golborne Rd	16	MZD	
Holland Park	16	MZE	
Holland Park Gardens	16	MZE	22
Holland Rd	16	MZE	
Holland Villas Rd	16	MZE	
Kensal Rd	16	MZD	
Ladbroke Grove	16	MZD	
Lancaster Rd	16	MZD	
Lansdowne Walk	16	MZE	33
Lauderdale Rd	16	OZD	
Masbro Rd	16	MZE	
Olympia Way	16	MZE	32

Street	Plan	Grid	Ref
Oxford Gardens	16	MZD	
Royal Crescent	16	MZE	371
St Ann's Rd	16	MZE	
St Mark's Rd	16	MZD	
Shirland Rd	16	NZD	
Sinclair Rd	16	MZE	
Sixth Ave	16	MZC	
Sutherland Ave	16	NZD	
Walterton Rd	16	NZD	347
Warwick Ave	16	OZD	
West Cross Route	16	MZE	

PLAN 17

Street	Plan	Grid	Ref
Allsop Pl.	17	QZD	4
Blomfield Rd	17	OZD	
Broadley St	17	PZD	
Clifton Gardens	17	PZD	
Frampton St	17	PZD	
Hall Rd	17	PZC	
Lisson Grove	17	PZD	
Maida Ave	17	PZD	
North Carriage Drive	17	PZE	
Park Rd	17	QZD	
Rossmore Rd	17	QZD	
St John's Wood Rd	17	PZD	
Warrington Crescent	17	OZD	348

PLAN 18

Street	Plan	Grid	Ref
Bernard St	18	SZD	25
Chester Rd	18	RZC	
Euston Rd	18	RZD	
Fitzroy Square	18	RZD	
Great Ormond St	18	SZD	
Guilford St	18	SZD	
Herbrand St	18	SZD	218
Hunter St	18	SZD	233
Judd St	18	SZC	
Park Crescent	18	RZD	28
Robert St	18	RZC	
Russell Square	18	SZD	
Sidmouth St	18	SZD	385
Tavistock Pl.	18	SZD	
Tavistock Square	18	SZD	409
Upper Woburn Pl.	18	SZD	432
Woburn Pl.	18	SZD	

PLAN 19

Street	Plan	Grid	Ref
Bath St	19	VZC	
Beech St	19	VZD	
Borough Rd	19	UZE	
Bowling Green Lane	19	UZD	43
Bunhill Row	19	VZD	
Calthorpe St	19	TZD	65
Central St	19	VZC	
Chiswell St	19	VZD	
City Rd	19	VZC	
Clerkenwell Rd	19	UZD	474
Corporation Row	19	UZD	110
Dufferin St	19	VZD	141
Elephant and Castle Shopping Centre	19	UZF	
Falmouth Rd	19	VZE	
Fann St	19	VZD	166
Goswell Rd	19	UZC	
Great Dover St	19	VZE	
Harper Rd	19	VZE	
King's Cross Rd	19	TZC	
Lever St	19	VZC	
Lloyd Baker St	19	UZC	265
Long Lane SOUTHWARK	19	VZE	
Merrick Square	19	VZE	
Moreland St	19	VZC	293
Myddelton St	19	UZC	296
Newington Causeway	19	VZE	307
New Kent Rd	19	VZF	
Old St	19	VZD	
Paul St	19	VZD	
Percival St	19	UZD	
Pilgrimage St	19	VZE	349
Rosebery Ave	19	UZD	
St John St	19	UZC	
Suffolk St	19	VZE	
Tabard St	19	VZE	408
Trinity Church Square	19	VZE	
Trinity St	19	VZE	
Whitecross St	19	VZD	
Worship St	19	VZD	

PLAN 20

Street	Plan	Grid	Ref
Abbey St	20	XZE	
Appold St	20	XZD	5
Back Church Rd	20	XZD	
Bermondsey St	20	XZE	
Bethnal Green Rd	20	YZD	
Bigland St	20	YZD	
Brady St	20	YZD	
Brick Lane	20	XZD	
Brunel St	20	YZE	
Cable St	20	YZD	
Cambridge Heath Rd	20	YZD	
Cannon Street Rd	20	YZD	
Cavell St	20	YZD	
Cephas St	20	YZD	
Cheshire St	20	XZD	
Christian St	20	YZD	
Clements Rd	20	YZE	
Club Row	20	XZD	
Commercial Rd	20	YZD	
Curtain Rd	20	XZD	126
Dock St	20	XZD	
Drummond Rd	20	YZE	
Fielgate St	20	YZD	
Globe Rd	20	YZC	
Grange Rd	20	XZE	
Great Eastern St	20	XZD	192
Highway (The)	20	YZE	
Jamaica Rd	20	YZE	
Jubilee St	20	YZD	
Lower Rd	20	YZE	
Luke St	20	XZD	
Mile End Rd	20	YZD	
New Rd	20	YZD	
Old Montague St	20	XZF	
Pages Walk	20	XZF	
Redman's Rd	20	YZD	
Roman Rd	20	YZC	
Rovel Rd	20	YZE	75
Salter Rd	20	YZE	
Sclater St	20	XZD	470
Shoreditch High St	20	XZD	384
Sidney St	20	YZD	
Spa Rd	20	XZE	
Stepney Way	20	YZD	
Surrey Quay's Rd	20	YZE	377
Tarling St	20	YZD	
Thomas Moore St	20	XZE	365
Turin St	20	XZC	
Vallance Rd	20	YZD	
Vaughan Way	20	XZE	
Wapping High St	20	YZE	
Wapping Lane	20	YZE	
Wapping Wall	20	YZE	
Whitechapel Rd	20	XZD	

PLAN 21

Street	Plan	Grid	Ref
Banin St	21	LZF	
Barnes High St	21	KZH	404
Bath Rd	21	KZF	
Brook Green	21	LZF	
Burlington Lane	21	KZG	
Castelnau	21	LZG	
Chancellor's Rd	21	LZG	21
Chiswick High Rd	21	KZG	
Chiswick Lane	21	KZG	
Chiswick Mall	21	KZG	
Church Rd RICHMOND UPON THAMES	21	KZH	
Dailing Rd	21	LZF	13
Devonshire Rd	21	KZG	
Dorchester Grove	21	KZG	402
Dover House Rd	21	LZH	
Erpingham Rd	21	LZH	
Ferry Rd	21	KZG	
Glenthorne Rd	21	LZF	
Great West Rd	21	KZG	
Gwendolen Ave	21	LZH	
Hammersmith Bridge	21	LZG	
Hammersmith Bridge Rd	21	LZG	431
Hertford Ave	21	KZH	
Hotham Rd	21	LZH	
Howards Lane	21	LZH	
King St HAMMERSMITH	21	KZG	
Lonsdale Rd	21	KZG	
Lower Richmond Rd	21	LZH	
Mill Hill Rd	21	LZH	
Prebend Gardens	21	KZF	
Priory Lane	21	LZH	
Queen's Ride Lower	21	LZH	
Rainville Rd	21	LZG	
Rannoch Rd	21	LZG	
Rocks Lane	21	LZH	
Roehampton Lane	21	LZH	
Station Rd	21	KZG	
Stevenage Rd	21	LZG	
Suffolk Rd	21	KZG	
Talgarth Rd	21	LZG	
Terrace (The)	21	KZH	
Turnham Green Terrace	21	KZG	389
Upper Richmond Rd	21	LZH	
Upper Richmond Rd West	21	KZH	
Verdun Rd	21	KZH	
Vine Rd	21	LZH	
White Hart Lane	21	KZH	

PLAN 22

Street	Plan	Grid	Ref
Armoury Way	22	NZH	7
Bagley's Lane	22	OZH	
Baron's Court Rd	22	MZG	
Bishops Rd	22	MZG	
Bishop's Park Rd	22	MZH	
Broomhouse Lane	22	NZH	
Carnwath Rd	22	NZH	
Charlwood Rd	22	MZH	
Clancarty Rd	22	NZH	
Crabtree Lane	22	MZG	164
Dawes Rd	22	MZG	
Disraeli Rd	22	MZG	
Edith Rd	22	MZG	
Estcourt Rd	22	MZG	203
Fairfield St	22	OZH	165
Fawe Park Rd	22	MZH	
Filmer Rd	22	MZG	
Finlay St	22	MZH	
Fulham High St	22	MZH	172
Fulham Palace Rd	22	MZG	
Gliddon Rd	22	MZG	182
Greyhound Rd	22	MZG	
Gunterstone Rd	22	MZG	
Halford Rd	22	NZG	
Hammersmith Rd	22	MZG	
Harwood Rd	22	NZG	
Hugon Rd	22	NZH	
Hurlingham Rd	22	NZH	
Munster Rd	22	MZG	
Musard Rd	22	MZG	
New King's Rd	22	NZH	
Oakhill Rd	22	NZH	

Street	Plan	Grid	Ref
Oxford Rd WANDSWORTH	22	MZH	
Parsons Green Lane	22	NZG	
Peterborough Rd	22	NZH	
Putney Bridge	22	MZH	
Putney Bridge Rd	22	MZH	
Putney High St	22	MZH	
Putney Hill	22	MZH	358
Queensmill Rd	22	MZG	450
Rylston Rd	22	MZG	
St Dunstan's Rd	22	MZG	
Star Rd	22	MZG	
Stephendale Rd	22	OZH	
Studdridge St	22	NZH	
Swandon Way	22	OZH	
Vanston Pl	22	NZG	207
Wandsworth Bridge	22	OZH	437
Wandsworth Bridge Rd	22	NZH	
West Cromwell Rd	22	NZG	
Woodlaw Rd	22	MZG	

PLAN 23

Street	Plan	Grid	Ref
Albert Bridge	23	QZB	
Albert Bridge Rd	23	QZG	
Avenue (The)	23	QZG	
Battersea Bridge	23	PZG	
Battersea Bridge Rd	23	PZG	
Battersea Church Rd	23	PZG	
Battersea Park Rd	23	QZH	
Battersea Rise	23	PZH	
Cambridge Rd BATTERSEA	23	QZH	449
Carriage Drive East	23	QZG	
Carriage Drive North	23	QZG	
Carriage Drive South	23	QZG	
Cheyne Walk	23	PZG	
Clapham Common West Side	23	QZH	92
East Hill	23	PZG	155
Edith Grove	23	PZG	
Elspeth Rd	23	QZH	
Falcon Rd	23	PZH	
Gowrie Rd	23	QZH	
Gunter Grove	23	OZG	202
Imperial Rd	23	OZG	
Latchmere Rd	23	QZH	
Lavender Hill	23	QZH	
Lombard Rd	23	PZH	266
Lots Rd	23	OZG	
Marney Rd	23	QZH	
Northcote Rd	23	QZH	
North Side	23	PZH	316
Parade (The)	23	QZG	
Parkgate Rd	23	QZG	
Plough Rd	23	PZH	
Prince of Wales Drive	23	QZG	
St John's Hill	23	PZH	
St John's Rd	23	QZH	
Surrey Lane	23	PZH	
Townmead Rd	23	OZH	
Trinity Rd	23	PZH	441
Vicarage Crescent	23	PZH	433
Westbridge Rd	23	PZG	
York Rd WANDSWORTH	23	PZH	

PLAN 24

Street	Plan	Grid	Ref
Acre Lane	24	SZH	
Bedford Rd	24	SZH	
Binfield Rd	24	SZH	
Bridgefoot	24	SZG	49
Cedars Rd	24	RZH	
Clapham Common North Side	24	RZH	428
Clapham High St	24	SZH	
Clapham Manor St	24	SZH	
Clapham Park Hill	24	SZH	
Crescent Lane	24	SZH	
Fentiman Rd	24	TZG	
Jeffrey's Rd	24	SZH	
King's Ave	24	SZH	
Landor Rd	24	SZH	
Landsdowne Way	24	SZG	
Larkhall Lane	24	SZH	
Lingham St	24	SZH	
Long Rd	24	RZH	
Miles St	24	SZG	290
North St	24	RZH	
Old Town	24	RZH	426
Park Rd LAMBETH	24	SZH	
Queenstown Rd	24	RZH	
Queen's Circus	24	RZG	361
Rectory Grove	24	RZH	
Silverthorne Rd	24	RZH	
Triangle Place	24	SZH	
Union Rd	24	SZH	
Voltaire Rd	24	SZH	436
Wandsworth Rd	24	SZG	
Wilkinson St	24	TZG	420

PLAN 25

Street	Plan	Grid	Ref
Akerman Rd	25	UZH	
Albany Rd	25	VZG	
Angell Drive	25	UZH	
Atlantic Rd	25	UZH	
Barrington Rd	25	UZH	
Benhill Rd	25	VZG	
Brixton Hill	25	UZH	
Brixton Rd	25	UZH	
Calais St	25	UZG	
Caldwell St	25	UZG	
Camberwell Grove	25	VZH	
Camberwell New Rd	25	UZG	
Camberwell Rd	25	VZG	
Carew St	25	VZH	
Champion Park	25	VZH	
Chapter Rd	25	UZG	
Church St Camberwell	25	VZG	
Clapham Rd	25	TZH	
Coldharbour Lane	25	UZH	
Comber Grove	25	VZG	
Denmark Hill	25	VZH	
Denmark Rd	25	VZH	
Dorset Rd	25	TZG	
East St	25	VZG	
Edmund St	25	VZG	
Effra Rd	25	UZH	
Elephant Rd	25	VZF	163
Elmington Rd	25	VZG	
Fawnbrake Ave	25	VZH	
Ferndene Rd	25	VZH	
Flint St	25	VZG	
Flodden Rd	25	VZG	
Foxley Rd	25	UZG	
Groveway	25	UZG	
Grove Lane	25	VZH	
Harleyford St	25	UZG	211
Herne Hill	25	VZH	
Herne Hill Rd	25	VZH	
Heygate St	25	VZF	
John Ruskin St	25	VZG	
Kellett Rd	25	UZH	
Knatchbull Rd	25	UZH	
Lilford Rd	25	UZH	
Lomond Grove	25	VZG	
Lothian Rd	25	UZG	
Loughborough Rd	25	UZH	
Manor Pl	25	VZG	
Milkwood Rd	25	VZH	
Minet Rd	25	UZH	
Mostyn Rd	25	UZH	
Newington Butts	25	UZF	306
New Church Rd	25	VZG	
Penton Pl	25	UZG	
Portland St	25	VZG	
Railton Rd	25	UZH	
Red Post Hill	25	VZH	
Rodney Rd	25	VZF	
Shakespeare Rd	25	UZH	
Sidney Rd	25	TZH	
Southampton Way	25	VZG	
Stocwell Park Rd	25	TZH	
Stocwell Rd	25	TZH	
Sunray Ave	25	VZH	
Thurlow St	25	VZG	
Vassall Rd	25	UZG	
Walworth Rd	25	VZG	
Warner Rd	25	VZG	
Wells Way	25	VZG	
Wiltshire Rd	25	UZH	
Wyndham Rd	25	VZG	

PLAN 26

Street	Plan	Grid	Ref
Ady's Rd	26	XZH	
Asylum Rd	26	YZG	
Avondale Rise	26	XZH	
Avonley Rd	26	YZG	
Barry Rd	26	YZH	
Bellenden Rd	26	XZH	
Bird In Bush Rd	26	YZG	
Carlton Grove	26	YZG	
Catlin St	26	YZG	
Cheltenham Rd	26	YZG	
Clayton Rd	26	YZG	
Clifton Way	26	YZG	
Cobourg Rd	26	XZG	
Commercial Way	26	XZG	
Consort Rd	26	YZH	
Coopers Rd	26	XZG	
Copeland Rd	26	YZH	
Crystal Palace Rd	26	XZH	
Dalwood St	26	XZG	
Dog Kennel Hill	26	XZH	
Dunton Rd	26	XZG	
East Dulwich Grove	26	XZH	
East Dulwich Rd	26	XZH	
Evelina Rd	26	YZH	
Galleywall Rd	26	YZG	
Glengall Rd	26	XZG	
Grove Hill Rd	26	XZH	
Grove Vale	26	XZH	
Hanover Park	26	YZH	
Havil St	26	XZG	
Heaton Rd	26	YZH	
Hollydale Rd	26	YZH	
Ilderton Rd	26	YZG	
Kender St	26	YZG	
Lausanne Rd	26	YZG	
Linden Grove	26	YZH	
Lordship Lane	26	XZH	
Lyndhurst Grove	26	XZH	
Lyndhurst Way	26	XZH	
Lynton Rd	26	YZG	
Mandela Way	26	XZF	
Marlborough Grove	26	XZG	
Mc Neil Rd	26	XZG	
Meeting House Lane	26	YZG	
Melbourne Grove	26	XZH	
Naylord Rd	26	YZG	
Neate St	26	XZG	
Nunhead Grove	26	YZH	
Nunhead Lane	26	YZH	
Oglander Rd	26	YZH	
Old Kent Rd	26	XZG	
Peckham Hill St	26	XZG	
Peckham Park Rd	26	XZG	
Peckham Rd	26	XZH	
Peckham Rye	26	XZH	
Pomeroy St	26	YZG	
Pytchley Rd	26	XZH	
Queens Rd	26	YZH	
Raymouth Rd	26	YZF	
Reverdy Rd	26	XZG	
Rolls Rd	26	XZG	

Rotherhithe New Rd	**26**	**YZG**
Rye Lane	**26**	**XZH**
St George's Way	**26**	**YZG**
St James Rd	**26**	**YZG**
Shenley Rd	**26**	**YZG**
Southwark Park Rd	**26**	**XZF**
Stuart Rd	**26**	**YZH**
Summer Rd	**26**	**YZG**
Surrey Canal Rd	**26**	**YZG**
Trafalgar Ave	**26**	**YZG**
Verney Rd	**26**	**YZG**
Willowbrook Rd	**26**	**YZG**
Willow Walk	**26**	**XZF**
Waldind Rd	**26**	**XZF** 369

PLAN 27

Artesian Rd	**27**	**AAU**
Aubrey Walk	**27**	**AAV**
Bark Pl	**27**	**ABU**
Bayswater Rd	**27**	**ABU**
Bedford Gardens	**27**	**AAV**
Bishop's Bridge Rd.	**27**	**ABT**
Bourne Terrace	**27**	**ABT**
Broad Walk (The)	**27**	**ABV**
Campden Grove	**27**	**AAV**
Campden Hill Rd	**27**	**AAV**
Campden Hill Square	**27**	**AAV**
Chepstow Crescent	**27**	**AAU** 84
Chepstow Pl	**27**	**AAU**
Chepstow Rd	**27**	**AAT**
Chepstow Villas	**27**	**AAU**
Colville Rd	**27**	**AAU**
Colville Terrace	**27**	**AAU**
Dawson Pl	**27**	**AAU**
Garway Rd	**27**	**ABU**
Gloucester Terrace	**27**	**ABT**
Great Western Rd	**27**	**AAT**
Harrow Rd	**27**	**ABT**
Hereford Rd	**27**	**ABU**
Holland Park Ave	**27**	**AAV**
Inverness Terrace	**27**	**ABU**
Kensington Church St	**27**	**AAV**
Kensington Gardens Square	**27**	**ABU**
Kensington Palace Gardens	**27**	**ABV**
Kensington Park Rd	**27**	**AAV**
Kensington Pl	**27**	**AAV**
Ladbroke Rd	**27**	**AAV**
Ladbroke Square	**27**	**AAV**
Ledbury Rd	**27**	**AAT**
Leinster Square	**27**	**ABU**
Linden Gardens	**27**	**AAU**
Moscow Rd	**27**	**ABU**
Newton Rd	**27**	**ABT**
Notting Hill Gate	**27**	**AAV**
Orme Court	**27**	**ABU** 328
Ossington St	**27**	**ABU**
Palace Court	**27**	**ABU**
Palace Gardens Terrace	**27**	**ABV**
Palace Green	**27**	**ABV**
Pembridge Crescent	**27**	**AAU**
Pembridge Gardens	**27**	**AAU**
Pembridge Rd	**27**	**AAU**
Pembridge Square	**27**	**AAU**
Pembridge Villas	**27**	**AAU**
Porchester Gardens	**27**	**ABU**
Porchester Rd	**27**	**ABT**
Porchester Square	**27**	**ABT** 197
Portobello Rd	**27**	**AAU**
Queensborough Terrace	**27**	**ABU**
Queensway	**27**	**ABU**
St Luke's Rd	**27**	**AAT**
St Petersburgh Pl.	**27**	**AAU**
Sheffield Terrace	**27**	**AAV**
Talbot Rd	**27**	**AAT**
Tavistock Rd	**27**	**AAT**
Uxbridge St	**27**	**AAV**
Westbourne Gardens	**27**	**ABT**
Westbourne Grove	**27**	**AAU**
Westbourne Park Rd	**27**	**AAT**
Westbourne Park Villas	**27**	**ABT**

PLAN 28

Chilworth St	**28**	**ACU**
Church St	**28**	**ADT**
Cleveland Square	**28**	**ACU**
Cleveland Terrace	**28**	**ACT**
Craven Hill	**28**	**ACU**
Craven Rd	**28**	**ACU**
Craven Terrace	**28**	**ACU**
Devonshire Terrace	**28**	**ACU** 136
Eastbourne Terrace	**28**	**ACT**
Edgware Rd	**28**	**ADT**
Gloucester Square	**28**	**ADU**
Hyde Park Gardens	**28**	**ADU**
Lancaster Gate	**28**	**ACU**
Lancaster Terrace	**28**	**ADU** 257
Leinster Gardens	**28**	**ACU**
Leinster Terrace	**28**	**ACU**
London St	**28**	**ADT**
Norfolk Pl	**28**	**ADT**
North Wharf Rd	**28**	**ADT**
Orsett Terrace	**28**	**ACT**
Porchester Terrace	**28**	**ACU**
Praed St	**28**	**ADU**
Queen Anne's Gate	**28**	**ACU** 94
Queen's Gardens	**28**	**ACU**
Radnor Pl	**28**	**ADT**
Ring (The)	**28**	**ADV**
Sale Place	**28**	**AET**
South Wharf Rd	**28**	**ADT**
Spring St	**28**	**ADU**
Stanhope Terrace	**28**	**ADU** 158
Sussex Gardens	**28**	**ADU**
Sussex Pl	**28**	**ADU**
Sussex Square	**28**	**ADU**
Westbourne Crescent	**28**	**ADU** 448
Westbourne St	**28**	**ADU**
Westbourne Terrace	**28**	**ACT**
Westbourne Terrace Rd	**28**	**ACT** 452

PLAN 29

Albion St	**29**	**AFU**
Aybrook St	**29**	**AGT**
Baker St	**29**	**AGT**
Bell St	**29**	**AET**
Blandford St	**29**	**AGT**
Bryanston Pl	**29**	**AFT**
Bryanston Square	**29**	**AFT** 14
Bryanston St	**29**	**AFU**
Cambridge Square	**29**	**AFU** 67
Chapel St	**29**	**AET**
Chiltern St	**29**	**AGT**
Clarendon Pl	**29**	**AEU** 93
Connaught Square	**29**	**AFU**
Connaught St	**29**	**AFU**
Crawford Pl	**29**	**AFT**
Crawford St	**29**	**AFT**
Culross St	**29**	**AGU**
Dorset St	**29**	**AGT**
Dunraven St	**29**	**AGU** 149
Enford St	**29**	**AFT**
George St	**29**	**AFT**
Gloucester Pl	**29**	**AGT**
Granville Pl	**29**	**AGU** 476
Great Cumberland Pl	**29**	**AGU**
Green St	**29**	**AGU**
Harcourt St	**29**	**AFT**
Harrowby St	**29**	**AFT**
Hyde Park Square	**29**	**AEU**
Hyde Park St	**29**	**AEU**
Kendal St	**29**	**AFU**
Lees Pl	**29**	**AGU**
Manchester Square	**29**	**AGT** 281
Manchester St	**29**	**AGT**
Marble Arch	**29**	**AGU**
Marylebone Rd	**29**	**AFT**
Montagu Pl	**29**	**AFT**
Montagu Square	**29**	**AGT** 90
Mount St	**29**	**AGV**
Norfolk Crescent	**29**	**AFT**
North Audley St	**29**	**AGU** 314
North Row	**29**	**AGU**
Old Marylebone Rd	**29**	**AFT**
Orchard St	**29**	**AGU**
Oxford Square	**29**	**AFU** 332
Oxford St	**29**	**AGU**
Paddington St	**29**	**AGT**
Park Lane	**29**	**AGU**
Park St MAYFAIR	**29**	**AGU**
Portman Square	**29**	**AGT**
Portman St	**29**	**AGU**
Reeves Mews	**29**	**AGV** 103
Rotten Row	**29**	**AEV**
Serpentine Rd	**29**	**AFV**
Seymour St	**29**	**AFU**
Shouldham St	**29**	**AFT**
Southwick St	**29**	**AET** 156
Stanhope Pl	**29**	**AFU** 400
Upper Berkeley St	**29**	**AFU**
Upper Brook St	**29**	**AGU**
Upper Grosvenor St	**29**	**AGU**
Upper Montagu St	**29**	**AFT**
Wigmore St	**29**	**AGU**
Woods Mews	**29**	**AGU**
York St	**29**	**AFT**

PLAN 30

Adam's Row	**30**	**AHU**
Albemarle St	**30**	**AIU** 225
Aldford St	**30**	**AHV** 2
Argyll St	**30**	**AIU**
Arlington St	**30**	**AIV** 6
Avery Row	**30**	**AHU** 12
Beak St	**30**	**AIU**
Berkeley Square	**30**	**AHU**
Berkeley St	**30**	**AIV**
Binney St	**30**	**AHU**
Bolton St	**30**	**AIV**
Brick St	**30**	**AHV**
Brook St	**30**	**AHU**
Brook's Mews	**30**	**AHU**
Bruton St	**30**	**AIU**
Burlington Arcade	**30**	**AIV**
Bury St	**30**	**AIV**
Carlos Pl	**30**	**AHU** 35
Carnaby St	**30**	**AIU**
Cavendish Square	**30**	**AHT**
Chandos St	**30**	**AIT** 36
Charles St	**30**	**AHV**
Cleveland St	**30**	**AIT**
Clifford St	**30**	**AIU** 38
Conduit St	**30**	**AIU**
Cork St	**30**	**AIU**
Curzon St	**30**	**AHV**
Davies St	**30**	**AHU**
Deanery St	**30**	**AHV** 132
Devonshire St	**30**	**AHT** 48
Dover St	**30**	**AIV**
Duke St	**30**	**AHU**
Duke St ST. JAMES.	**30**	**AIV**
Eastcastle St	**30**	**AIT**
Farm St MAYFAIR	**30**	**AHV**
Foley St	**30**	**AIT**
Gilbert St	**30**	**AHU**
Grafton St	**30**	**AIU** 62
Great Castle St	**30**	**AIT** 189
Great Marlborough St	**30**	**AIU**

Street	Plan	Grid	Ref
Great Portland St	30	AIT	
Great Titchfield St	30	AIT	
Grosvenor Square	30	AHU	
Grosvenor St	30	AHU	
Half Moon St	30	AHV	81
Hamilton Pl	30	AHV	205
Hanover Square	30	AIU	
Hanover St	30	AIU	
Harley St WESTMINSTER	30	AHT	
Hay's Mews	30	AHV	
Henrietta Pl	30	AHT	
Hertford St	30	AHV	
Hill St	30	AHV	
Holles St	30	AIT	
Howland St	30	AIT	232
James St	30	AHT	
Kingly St	30	AIU	
King St ST. JAMES'S	30	AIV	
Langham Pl	30	AIT	
Little Portland St	30	AIT	228
Maddox St	30	AIU	
Margaret St	30	AIT	
Market Pl	30	AIT	286
Marshall St	30	AIU	
Marylebone High St	30	AHT	
Marylebone Lane	30	AHT	287
Mortimer St	30	AIT	
Mount Row	30	AHU	
New Bond St	30	AHU	
New Cavendish St	30	AHT	
Old Bond St	30	AIV	
Old Burlington St	30	AIU	322
Old Park Lane	30	AHV	
Oxford Circus	30	AIT	
Piccadilly	30	AHV	
Piccadilly Arcade	30	AIV	
Poland St	30	AIT	
Portland Pl	30	AIT	
Princes St	30	AQU	
Queen Anne St	30	AHT	
Queen's Walk	30	AIV	
Regent St	30	AIT	
Sackville St	30	AIU	
St George St	30	AIU	
St James's Pl	30	AIV	116
St James's St	30	AIV	
Savile Row	30	AIU	
Shepherd Market	30	AHV	
Shepherd St	30	AHV	153
South Audley St	30	AHU	
South Molton St	30	AHU	
South St	30	AHV	
Stratton St	30	AIV	168
Thayer St	30	AHT	413
Tilney St	30	AHV	421
Vere St	30	AHU	
Vigo St	30	AIU	
Waverton St	30	AHV	178
Weighouse St	30	AHU	184
Welbeck St	30	AHT	
Wells St	30	AIT	
Weymouth St	30	AHT	
Wimpole St	30	AHT	

PLAN 31

Street	Plan	Grid	Ref
Adam St	31	ALU	
Bateman St	31	AKU	18
Bayley St	31	AKT	260
Bedfordbury	31	ALU	243
Bedford Square	31	AKT	
Bedford St	31	ALU	
Berner's St	31	AJT	
Berwick St	31	AJT	26
Bloomsbury Square	31	ALT	
Bloomsbury St	31	AKT	
Bloomsbury Way	31	ALT	9
Boswell St	31	ALT	
Bow St	31	ALU	
Brewer St	31	AJU	
Broadwick St	31	AJU	
Bury St	31	ALT	
Cambridge Circus	31	AKU	
Carlton Gardens	31	AJV	74
Carlton House Terrace	31	AKV	
Carting Lane	31	ALU	245
Chandos Pl	31	ALU	
Charing Cross	31	ALV	
Charing Cross Rd	31	AKT	
Charles II St	31	AKV	
Charlotte St	31	AJT	
Cherries St	31	AKT	256
Cockspur St	31	AKV	39
Coventry St	31	AKU	
Cranbourn St	31	AKU	115
Craven St	31	ALV	
Dean St	31	AJT	
Denman St	31	AJU	133
Denmark St	31	AKT	134
Drury Lane	31	ALT	
Duke of York St	31	AJV	143
Duncannon St	31	ALV	147
D'Arblay St	31	AJU	
Earlham St	31	AKU	
Endell St	31	ALT	
Exeter St	31	ALU	
Floral St	31	ALU	
Frith St	31	AKU	
Garrick St	31	ALU	
Gerrard St	31	AKU	174
Glasshouse St SOHO	31	AJU	179
Golden Jubilee Bridge	31	ALV	
Golden Square	31	AJU	
Goodge St	31	AJT	
Gower St	31	AKT	
Great Queen St	31	ALT	
Great Russell St	31	AKT	
Great Windmill St	31	AJU	261
Greek St	31	AKU	
Hanway St	31	AKT	210
Haymarket	31	AKU	
Henrietta St	31	ALU	217
Horse Guards Ave	31	ALV	
Horse Guards Rd	31	AKV	
James St SOHO	31	ALU	
Jermyn St	31	AJV	
John Adam St	31	ALV	238
Kingsway	31	ALT	
King St STRAND	31	ALU	
Leicester Square	31	AKU	
Lexington St	31	AJU	
Lisle St	31	AKU	
Long Acre	31	ALU	
Macklin St	31	ALT	
Maiden Lane	31	ALU	83
Mall (The)	31	AKV	
Monmouth St	31	ALU	88
Museum St	31	ALT	
Neal St	31	ALU	
Newman St	31	AJT	
Newton St	31	ALT	
New Oxford St	31	AKT	
New Row	31	ALU	
Noel St	31	AJU	
Northumberland Ave	31	ALV	
Old Compton St	31	AKU	
Old Gloucester St	31	ALT	
Orange St	31	AKV	
Pall Mall	31	AJV	
Panton St	31	AKU	
Parker St	31	ALT	
Percy St	31	AJT	
Piccadilly Circus	31	AJU	
Richmond Terrace	31	ALV	234
Romilly St	31	AKU	368
Royal Opera Arcade	31	AKV	
Rupert St	31	AKU	
Russell St	31	ALU	
St Giles Circus	31	AKT	
St Giles High St	31	AKT	
St James's Square	31	AJV	
St Martins Lane	31	ALU	
Savoy Pl	31	ALU	
Shaftesbury Ave	31	ALU	
Shelton St	31	ALU	
Shorts Gardens	31	ALU	
Soho Square	31	AKT	
Southampton Row	31	ALT	473
Southampton St	31	ALU	388
Store St	31	AKT	
Strand	31	ALV	
Tavistock St	31	ALU	
Tottenham Court Rd	31	AJT	
Trafalgar Square	31	AKV	
Upper St Martin's Lane	31	ALU	430
Villiers St	31	ALV	
Wardour St	31	AJU	
Warwick St	31	AJU	444
Waterloo Pl	31	AKV	
Wellington St	31	ALU	187
Whitcomb St	31	AKU	191
Whitehall	31	ALV	
Whitehall Court	31	ALV	460
Whitehall Pl	31	ALV	
Wild St	31	ALU	
William IV St	31	ALV	467

PLAN 32

Street	Plan	Grid	Ref
Aldwych	32	AMU	
Arundel St	32	AMU	
Bedford Row	32	AMT	
Belvedere Rd	32	AMV	
Bouverie St	32	ANU	
Bream's Buildings	32	ANT	47
Carey St	32	AMU	
Chancery Lane	32	AMT	
Charterhouse St	32	ANT	
Cornwall Rd	32	ANV	
Cut (The)	32	ANV	
Essex St	32	AMU	
Farringdon Rd	32	ANT	
Fetter Lane	32	ANT	
Fleet St	32	ANU	
Furnival St	32	ANT	278
Gray's Inn Rd	32	ANT	
Greville St	32	ANT	
Halton Garden	32	ANT	
Hatfields	32	ANV	
High Holborn	32	AMT	
Holborn	32	ANT	
Holborn Viaduct	32	ANT	
John Carpenter St	32	ANT	17
Kemble St	32	AMU	
Lancaster Pl	32	AMU	
Leather Lane	32	ANT	
Lincoln's Inn Fields	32	AMT	
New Fetter Lane	32	ANT	
New Square	32	AMT	
New St Square	32	ANT	283
Portugal St	32	AMU	
Procter St	32	AMT	273
Red Lion Square	32	AMT	
Red Lion St	32	AMT	
Roupel St	32	ANV	
St Andrews St	32	ANT	373
St Bride St	32	ANT	378
Sardinia St	32	AMT	38
Savoy St	32	AMU	276
Serle St	32	AMT	
Shoe Lane	32	ANT	
Stamford St	32	ANV	
Surrey St	32	AMU	178
Temple Ave	32	ANU	
Temple Pl	32	AMU	

334

Street	Plan	Grid	Ref
Theobald's Rd	32	AMT	
Tudor St	32	ANU	
Upper Ground	32	AMU	
Victoria Embankment	32	AMU	
Waterloo Bridge	32	AMV	
Waterloo Rd	32	ANV	

PLAN 33

Street	Plan	Grid	Ref
Aldersgate St	33	APT	
Bankside	33	APV	291
Basinghall St	33	AQT	
Blackfriars Bridge	33	AOU	
Blackfriars Rd	33	AOV	
Borough High St	33	APU	
Bow Lane	33	AQU	
Cannon St	33	AQU	
Charterhouse Square	33	APT	475
Cheapside	33	AQU	
Cowcross St	33	AOT	113
Ewer St	33	APV	
Farringdon St	33	AOT	
Finsbury Square	33	AQT	310
Fore St	33	AQT	
Foster Lane	33	APT	
Giltspur St	33	AOT	
Great Guilford St	33	APV	
Great Suffolk St	33	APV	
Gresham St	33	AQT	
John St	33	APT	299
King Edward St	33	APT	247
King St CITY OF LONDON	33	AQU	
Limeburner Lane	33	AOT	298
Little Britain	33	APT	264
London Wall	33	APT	
Long Lane CITY	33	APT	
Lothbury	33	AQT	
Ludgate Hill	33	AOU	
Millennium Bridge	33	APU	
Montague St	33	APT	292
Moorgate	33	AQT	
Moor Lane	33	AQT	
Nelson Square	33	AOV	
Newcomen St	33	AQV	
Newgate St	33	APT	
New Bridge St	33	AOU	
New Change	33	APU	
Old Bailey	33	AOT	
Old Jewry	33	AQT	
Park St SOUTHWARK	33	APV	
Paternoster Square	33	APV	
Poultry	33	AQU	
Princes St	33	AQU	
Queen St	33	AQU	
Queen Street Pl	33	AQU	301
Queen Victoria St	33	APU	
Redcross Way	33	APV	
Ropemaker St	33	AQT	
St Martin's-le-Grand	33	APT	380
St Paul's Churchyard	33	APV	
St Swithin's Lane	33	AQU	308
St Thomas St	33	AQV	
Silk St	33	AQT	
Southwark Bridge	33	AQV	
Southwark Bridge Rd	33	AQV	
Southwark St	33	APV	
Stoney St	33	AQV	
Sumner St	33	APV	169
Union St	33	AOV	
Upper Thames St	33	AQU	
Walbrook Crescent	33	AQU	304
Warwick Lane	33	APT	294
West Smithfield	33	AOT	
Wood St	33	AQT	

PLAN 34

Street	Plan	Grid	Ref
Aldgate High St	34	ASU	
Bell Lane	34	AST	
Bevis Marks	34	ART	34
Bishopsgate	34	ART	
Blomfield St	34	ART	
Braham St	34	ASU	
Brick Lane	34	AST	
Broadgate	34	AST	
Brushfield St	34	AST	
Byward St	34	ARU	
Camomile St	34	ART	71
Commercial St	34	AST	
Coopers Row	34	ASU	318
Cornhill	34	ARU	309
Crucifix Lane	34	ARV	125
Druid St	34	ARV	
Duke St Hill	34	ARV	
Duke's Pl	34	AST	145
Eastcheap	34	ARU	
East Smithfield	34	ASU	
Eldon St	34	ART	
Fenchurch St	34	ARU	
Finsbury Circus	34	ART	
Fish Street Hill	34	ARU	319
Gainford St	34	ASV	
Goodman's Yard	34	ASU	
Goulston St	34	AST	
Gracechurch St	34	ARU	
Great Tower St	34	ARU	
Harrow Pl	34	AST	317
Hay's Galleria Shopping Centre	34	ARV	
Houndsditch	34	ART	
King William St	34	ARU	250
Leadenhall St	34	ARU	
Leman St	34	ASU	
Liverpool St	34	ART	
Lloyd's Ave	34	ASU	
Lombard St	34	ARU	268
London Bridge	34	ARV	
Lower Thames St	34	ARU	
Mansell St	34	ASU	
Mark Lane	34	ARU	
Middlesex St	34	AST	
Minories	34	ASU	
New St	34	ART	
Old Broad St	34	ART	
Pepys St	34	ASU	
Prescot St	34	ASU	
Princelet St	34	AST	
Princes St	34	AQU	
Royal Mint Rd	34	ASU	
St Botolph St	34	AST	
St Mary Axe	34	ART	
Shad Thames	34	ASV	
Shorter St	34	ASU	
Snows Fields	34	ARV	386
South Pl	34	ART	391
Spital Square	34	AST	399
Sun St	34	ART	
Sun Street Passage	34	ART	
Threadneedle St	34	ARU	
Throgmorton Ave	34	ART	
Throgmorton St	34	ART	418
Tooley St	34	ARV	
Tower Bridge	34	ASV	
Tower Bridge Approach	34	ASV	
Tower Bridge Rd	34	ASV	
Tower Hill	34	ASU	
Wentworth St	34	AST	
Weston St	34	ARV	188
Whitechapel High St	34	AST	
Wilson St	34	ART	
Wormwood St	34	ART	472

PLAN 35

Street	Plan	Grid	Ref
Abingdon Rd	35	AAX	
Argyll Rd	35	AAX	
Barkston Gardens	35	ABY	
Bolton Gardens	35	ABZ	
Bramham Gardens	35	ABY	
Campden Hill Rd	35	AAX	
Collingham Gardens	35	ABY	99
Collingham Rd	35	ABY	101
Cornwall Gardens	35	ABY	
Courtfield Gardens	35	ABY	
Cromwell Crescent	35	AAY	119
Cromwell Rd	35	AAY	
Eardley Crescent	35	AAZ	151
Earl's Court Gardens	35	ABY	
Earl's Court Rd	35	AAY	
Earl's Court Square	35	ABZ	
Edwardes Square	35	AAY	
Finborough Rd	35	ABZ	
Holland St	35	AAX	
Holland Walk	35	AAX	
Hornton St	35	AAX	
Ifield Rd	35	ABZ	
Kensington Court	35	ABX	241
Kensington Court Pl	35	ABX	242
Kensington High St	35	AAX	
Kensington Rd	35	ABX	
Kensington Square	35	ABX	
Kenway Rd	35	ABY	
Knaresborough Pl	35	ABY	
Lexham Gardens	35	ABY	
Lillie Rd	35	AAZ	
Logan Pl	35	AAY	
Longridge Rd	35	AAY	
Marloes Rd	35	ABX	
Melbury Rd	35	AAX	
Nevern Pl	35	AAY	
Nevern Square	35	AAY	
North End Rd	35	AAZ	
Old Brompton Rd	35	ABZ	
Pembroke Gardens	35	AAY	342
Pembroke Rd	35	AAY	
Penywern Rd	35	ABZ	
Philbeach Gardens	35	AAZ	
Phillimore Gardens	35	AAX	
Redcliffe Gardens	35	ABZ	
Redcliffe Square	35	ABZ	
St Albans Grove	35	ABX	
Scarsdale Villas	35	AAY	
Seagrave Rd	35	AAZ	
Templeton Pl	35	AAY	410
Trebovir Rd	35	AAZ	
Warwick Gardens	35	AAY	
Warwick Rd	35	AAY	
Young St	35	ABX	

PLAN 36

Street	Plan	Grid	Ref
Ashburn Pl	36	ACY	
Beaufort St	36	ADZ	
Bina Gardens	36	ACY	
Boltons (The)	36	ACZ	
Bute St	36	ADY	59
Cale St	36	ADZ	
Carlyle Square	36	ADZ	
Cathcart Rd	36	ACZ	
Chelsea Square	36	ADZ	
Courtfield Rd	36	ACY	
Cranley Gardens	36	ACZ	
Cranley Pl	36	ADY	215
Cromwell Pl	36	ADY	120
De Vere Gardens	36	ACX	
Dovehouse St	36	ADZ	
Drayton Gardens	36	ACZ	
Elm Park Gardens	36	ADZ	
Elm Park Rd	36	ADZ	
Elvaston Pl	36	ACX	
Evelyn Gardens	36	ACZ	
Exhibition Rd	36	ADX	
Flower Walk	36	ACX	
Foulis Terrace	36	ADZ	170
Fulham Rd	36	ADZ	
Gilston Rd	36	ACZ	
Glendower Pl	36	ADY	180

Street	Plan	Grid	Ref
Gloucester Rd	36	ACX	
Grenville Pl	36	ACY	
Harcourt Terrace	36	ACY	477
Harrington Gardens	36	ACY	
Harrington Rd	36	ADY	
Hollywood Rd	36	ACZ	
Hyde Park Gate	36	ACX	
Kensington Gore	36	ACX	
King's Rd	36	ADZ	
Launceston Pl	36	ACX	259
Little Boltons (The)	36	ACZ	
Manresa Rd	36	ADZ	
Neville Terrace	36	ADZ	300
Old Church St	36	ADZ	
Onslow Gardens	36	ADZ	
Onslow Square	36	ADY	
Palace Gate	36	ACX	
Park Walk	36	ACZ	
Pelham St	36	ADY	
Prince Consort Rd	36	ADX	
Prince's Gardens	36	ADX	356
Queensberry Pl	36	ADY	360
Queen's Gate	36	ACX	
Queen's Gate Gardens	36	ACY	198
Queen's Gate Pl	36	ACY	363
Queen's Gate Terrace	36	ACX	
Redcliffe Rd	36	ACZ	
Roland Gardens	36	ACZ	
South Parade	36	ADZ	
Stanhope Gardens	36	ACY	
Sumner Pl	36	ADY	
Sydney Pl	36	ADY	405
Thurloe Pl	36	ADY	
Thurloe Square	36	ADY	
Tregunter Rd	36	ACZ	
Vale (The)	36	ADZ	
Victoria Grove	36	ACX	
Victoria Rd KENSINGTON	36	ACX	
Wetherby Gardens	36	ACY	

PLAN 37

Street	Plan	Grid	Ref
Basil St	37	AFX	
Beauchamp Pl	37	AFX	
Belgrave Square	37	AGX	
Bourne St	37	AGY	
Bray Pl	37	AFY	45
Britten St	37	AEZ	
Brompton Rd	37	AFX	
Cadogan Gardens	37	AGY	23
Cadogan Gate	37	AGY	220
Cadogan Pl	37	AGY	
Cadogan Square	37	AGY	
Cadogan St	37	AFY	
Carriage Rd (The)	37	AFX	
Chelsea Bridge Rd	37	AGZ	
Chelsea Embankment	37	AGZ	
Chelsea Manor St	37	AFZ	
Cheltenham Terrace	37	AGZ	
Chesham Pl	37	AGX	
Chesham St	37	AGY	
Chester Row	37	AGY	
Cheval Pl	37	AFX	
Christchurch St	37	AFZ	
Draycott Ave	37	AFY	
Draycott Pl	37	AFY	
Eaton Pl	37	AGY	
Egerton Gardens	37	AFY	160
Egerton Gardens Mews	37	AFY	162
Egerton Terrace	37	AFY	161
Elystan Pl	37	AFZ	
Elystan St	37	AEY	
Ennismore Gardens	37	AEX	
Flood St	37	AFZ	
Franklin's Row	37	AGZ	
Glebe Pl	37	AEZ	
Grosvenor Crescent	37	AGX	
Hans Crescent	37	AFX	
Hans Pl	37	AFX	
Hans Rd	37	AFX	
Harriet St	37	AGX	214
Hasker St	37	AFY	
Holbein Mews	37	AGZ	223
Holbein Pl	37	AGY	
Ixworth Pl	37	AEY	
Jubilee Pl	37	AFZ	
Knightsbridge	37	AFX	
Lennox Gardens	37	AFY	
Lennox Gardens Mews	37	AFY	263
Lower Sloane St	37	AGY	
Lowndes Square	37	AGX	
Lowndes St	37	AGX	
Lyall St	37	AGY	
Markham St	37	AFZ	
Milner St	37	AFY	
Montpelier Square	37	AFX	
Montpelier St	37	AFX	
Moore St	37	AFY	
Mossop St	37	AFY	
Oakley St	37	AFZ	
Ormonde Gate	37	AGZ	329
Pimlico Rd	37	AGZ	
Pont St	37	AFY	
Radnor Walk	37	AFZ	
Rawlings St	37	AFY	
Redesdale St	37	AFZ	367
Royal Hospital Rd	37	AFZ	
Rutland Gate	37	AEX	
St Leonard's Terrace	37	AGZ	
Shawfield St	37	AFZ	
Sloane Ave	37	AFY	
Sloane Square	37	AGY	
Sloane St	37	AGX	
Smith St	37	AFZ	
South Terrace	37	AEY	
Sydney St	37	AEZ	
Symons St	37	AGY	407
Tedworth Square	37	AFZ	
Tite St	37	AFZ	
Trevor Pl	37	AFX	
Trevor Square	37	AFX	
Walton St	37	AFY	
West Halkin St	37	AGX	
Whiteheads	37	AFY	
William St	37	AFX	468
Wilton Pl	37	AGX	

PLAN 38

Street	Plan	Grid	Ref
Alderney St	38	AIY	
Belgrave Pl	38	AHX	
Belgrave Rd	38	AIY	
Birdcage Walk	38	AIX	
Bressenden Pl	38	AIX	
Buckingham Gate	38	AIX	
Buckingham Palace Rd	38	AHY	
Carlisle Pl	38	AIY	
Castle Lane	38	AIX	
Chapel St BELGRAVIA	38	AHX	
Charlwood St	38	AIZ	
Chelsea Bridge	38	AHZ	
Chester Square	38	AHY	
Chester St	38	AHX	
Churchill Gardens Rd	38	AIZ	
Clarendon St	38	AIZ	
Constitution Hill	38	AHX	
Cumberland St	38	AIZ	
Denbigh St	38	AIZ	
Duke of Wellington Pl	38	AHX	142
Eaton Square	38	AHY	
Ebury Bridge	38	AHZ	
Ebury Bridge Rd	38	AHZ	
Ebury St	38	AHY	
Eccleston Bridge	38	AHY	157
Eccleston Square	38	AIY	
Eccleston St	38	AHY	
Elizabeth St	38	AHY	
Francis St	38	AIY	
Gillingham St	38	AIY	
Gloucester St	38	AIZ	
Grosvenor Gardens	38	AHX	
Grosvenor Pl	38	AHX	
Grosvenor Rd	38	AHZ	
Guildhouse St	38	AIY	201
Halkin St	38	AHX	
Hobart Pl	38	AHX	
Hudson's Pl	38	AIY	
Hugh St	38	AIY	
Lower Belgrave St	38	AHY	
Lower Grosvenor Pl	38	AIX	274
Lupus St	38	AIZ	
Palace St	38	AIX	
St George's Drive	38	AIY	
South Eaton Pl	38	AHY	
Sutherland St	38	AHZ	
Terminus Pl	38	AIY	412
Upper Belgrave St	38	AHX	
Vauxhall Bridge Rd	38	AIY	
Victoria St	38	AIX	
Warwick Square	38	AIY	
Warwick Way	38	AHZ	
Wilton Rd	38	AIY	
Wilton St	38	AHX	

PLAN 39

Street	Plan	Grid	Ref
Abingdon St	39	AKY	
Albert Embankment	39	ALY	
Artillery Row	39	AJX	8
Atterbury St	39	ALZ	
Aylesford St	39	AKZ	
Bessborough Gardens	39	AKZ	
Bessborough St	39	AKZ	30
Bridge St	39	ALX	
Broad Sanctuary	39	ALX	52
Caxton St	39	AJX	
Chichester St	39	AJZ	
Claverton St	39	AJZ	
Dolphin Square	39	AJZ	
Douglas St	39	AKY	
Erasmus St	39	AKY	
Glasshouse St LAMBETH	39	ALZ	108
Great College St	39	ALX	
Great George St	39	AKX	193
Great Peter St	39	AKY	
Great Smith St	39	AKX	
Greencoat Pl	39	AJY	
Greycoat Pl	39	AJY	200
Greycoat St	39	AJY	
Horseferry Rd	39	AKY	
Howick Pl	39	AJY	
John Islip St	39	AKZ	
King Charles St	39	ALX	
Lambeth Bridge	39	ALY	
Marsham St	39	AKY	
Millbank	39	ALZ	
Monck St	39	AKY	
Montpelier Walk	37	AFX	
Moreton St	39	AJZ	
Nine Elms Lane	39	AKZ	
Old Pye St	39	AKX	
Page St	39	AKY	
Palmer St	39	AJX	
Parliament Square	39	ALX	
Parliament St	39	ALX	
Parry St	39	ALZ	341
Petty France	39	AJX	
Ponsonby Pl	39	AKZ	
Rampayne St	39	AKZ	

Regency St . . . . **39 AKY**	Brook Drive . . . . **40 ANY**	Lambeth Rd **40AMY**
Rochester Row. . . . . **39 AJY**	Chester Way. . . . . . . **40 ANY**	Lambeth Walk **40AMY**
St Anne's St . . . . **39 AKX**	Clayton St . . . . **40 ANZ**	London Rd . . . . **40 AOX**
St George's Square . **39 AJZ**	Cleaver St . . . . **40 ANZ**	Lower Marsh **40AMX**
South Lambeth Rd. . **39 ALZ** 154	Cooks St . . . . **40 AOZ**	Newburn St . . . . **40 AMZ**
Storeys Gate . . . . **39 AKX**	Courtenay St. . . . . . . **40 AMZ**	Pearman St . . . . **40 ANX**
Tachbrook St. . . . . . . **39 AJY**	Dante Rd. . . . . **40 AOY**	Ravensdon St . . . . . . **40 ANZ** 219
Thirleby Rd . . . . **39 AJY** 416	De Laune St . . . . **40 ANZ**	Renfrew Rd . . . . **40 ANY**
Thorney St. . . . . **39 ALY**	Durham St. . . . . **40 AMZ** 150	St George's Rd . . . . . **40 ANX**
Tinworth St . . . . **39 ALZ** 129	Fitzalan St **40AMY**	Sancroft St . . . . **40 AMZ**
Tothill St. . . . . **39 AKX**	Garden Row . . . . **40 AOX** 173	Stannary St . . . . **40 ANZ**
Tufton St . . . . **39 AKX**	Harleyford Rd **40AMZ**	Tyers St. . . . . **40 AMZ**
Vauxhall Bridge . . . . . **39 ALZ**	Hayles St. . . . . **40 AOY**	Vauxhall St. . . . . **40 AMZ**
Vincent Square . . . . . **39 AJY**	Hercules Rd **40AMX**	Vauxhall Walk . . . . . . **40 AMZ**
Vincent St . . . . **39 AKY**	Johnathan St. . . . . . . **40 AMZ**	Walcot Square . . . . . **40 ANY**
Westminster Bridge. **39 ALX**	Juxon St **40AMY**	Walnut Tree Walk. . . **40AMY**
	Kennington Lane . . . **40 AMZ**	Webber St. . . . . **40 ANY**
PLAN 40	Kennington Oval . . . . **40 AMZ**	Westminster Bridge
Baylis Rd . . . . **40 ANX**	Kennington Rd . . . . . **40 ANX**	Rd **40AMX**
Black Prince Rd. **40AMY**	Kennington Park Rd **40 ANZ**	West Square. . . . . . . **40 AOY**
Braganza St . . . . **40 AOZ**	Lambeth High St . . . **40AMY**	Wincoot St . . . . **40 ANY**
	Lambeth Palace Rd . **40AMX**	York Rd **40AMX**

9

LONDON

BRENT

Brent Reservoir
North Circular Road (A 406)
Neasden Junction
Tanfield Avenue
Crest Road
Brook Rd
Coles Green Rd
Edgware Rd (A 5)
Cricklewood
Dollis Hill Lane
Gladstone Park
Mora Rd
Sneyd Rd
Heber Rd
Neasden Lane
Dudden Hill (A 4088)
Neasden
Kendal Rd
Anson Road
Park Ave North
Burnley Road
Sherrick Green Rd
Dollis Hill
Denzil Road
Chapter Road
WILLESDEN GREEN
Willesden Green
High Road
Pound Lane
High Road (A 407)
Walm Lane
Brondesbury
Roundwood Road
Willesden Cemetery
Peter Ave
Sidmouth Rd
KILBURN
Church Road
Roundwood Park
Harlesden Road
Donnington Road
Mount Pleasant
Chamberlayne
A 404
Manor Park Rd
Doyle
Hardinge Rd
College Rd
Acton Lane
High Street
Wrottesley Road
Furness Road
All Souls Ave
Bathurst Gdns
Clifford Gdns
Harley Road
Willesden Junction
Oak Lane
Harrow Road
Kensal Green
Mortimer
A 404

482
351
352
196
357
480

K   L
ZA
ZB
ZC
15

338

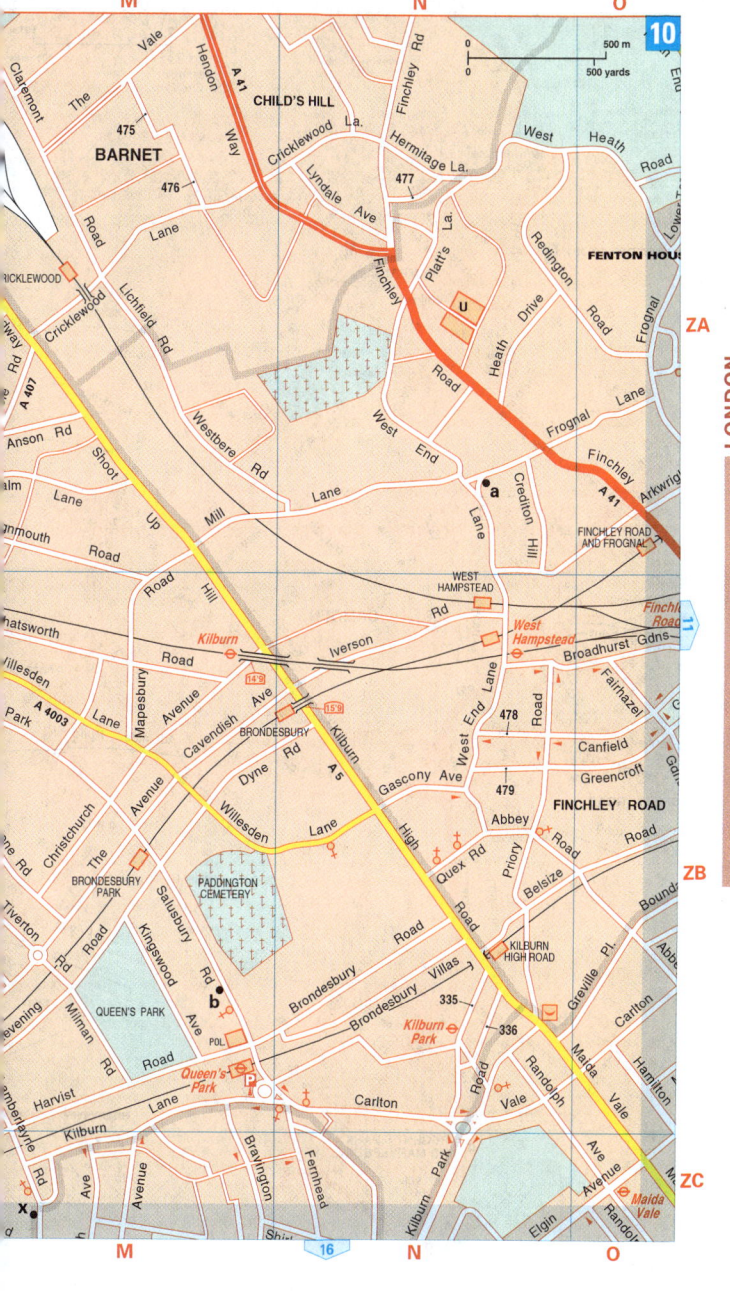

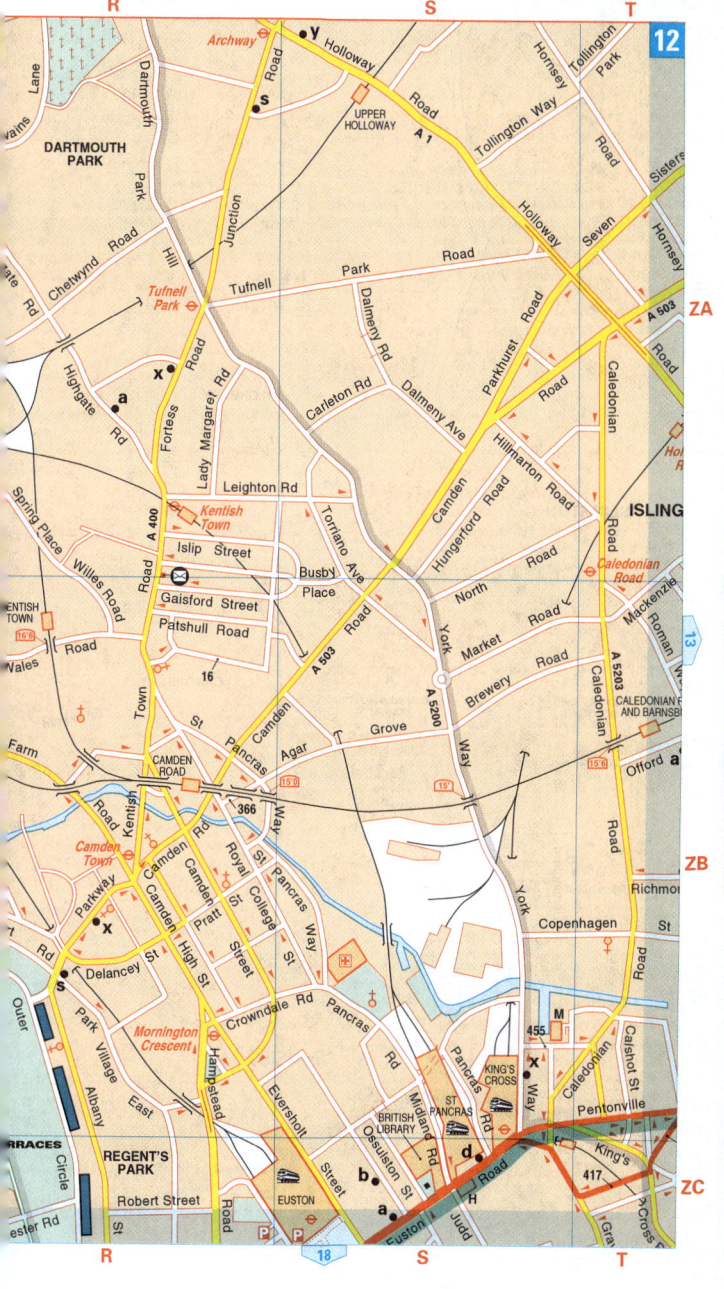

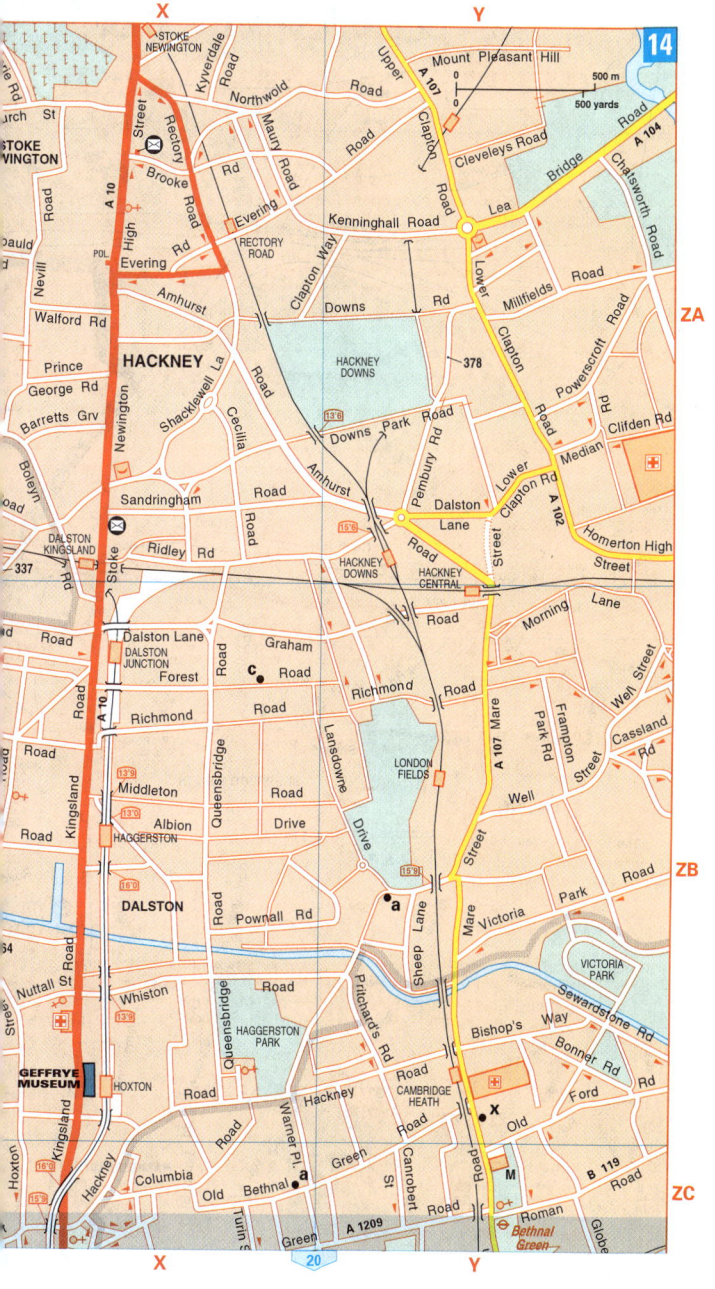

15

LONDON

ZC / ZD / ZE / ZF
K / L

Willesden Junction
Oak Lane
Harrow Road
A 404 Kensal Green
Mortimer
Kensal Gre...
Harro...

500 m
500 yards

Victoria Rd
Old Oak
Grand Union Canal
A 219
KENSAL GREEN CEMETERY

12'6

15'9

WORMWOOD SCRUBS
Scrubs Lane
Barby
St Qu...
Highlever Road
14'6

The Fairway
Brassie Ave
Western Ave
Wulfstan Street
East Acton
Common Lane
Du
Cane Road
Wood Lane

Westway A 40 Westway
A 219
White City

East Acton Lane
Bromyard Avenue
Ashfield Rd
Old Oak Road
Yew Tree Rd
Steventon Rd
Bryony Road
Wormholt Road
Sawley Road
Bloemfontein Road
South Africa Road
LOFTUS ROAD STADIUM
BBC
Wood Lane
WHITE
WEST
SHOP
CEN

EALING
The Vale
Uxbridge Road
A 4020 • a
SHEPHERD'S BUSH
Uxbridge Road
Shepherd's Bush Market
Wood Lane

Larden Road
Askew Road
Percy Road
Coningham Road
454
Lime Grove
Goldhawk Road
15'9
Goldhawk Road

Cobbold Road
462
Goldhawk Road
Brackenbury Rd
Hammersmith
10'8

The Blenheim Avenue
Emlyn Rd
Abinger Road
387
Goldhawk Road A 402
463 • c
Paddenswick Rd

RAVENSCOURT PARK
Banim St
HAMMERSMITH

ZF
Bath Road
Preben Gdns
Stamford Brook
14'6
Goldhawk Road
12'6
Ravenscourt Park
13
Glenthorne Rd
• e
Hammersmith
Shepherd's...
Turnham Green

K / L
21

344

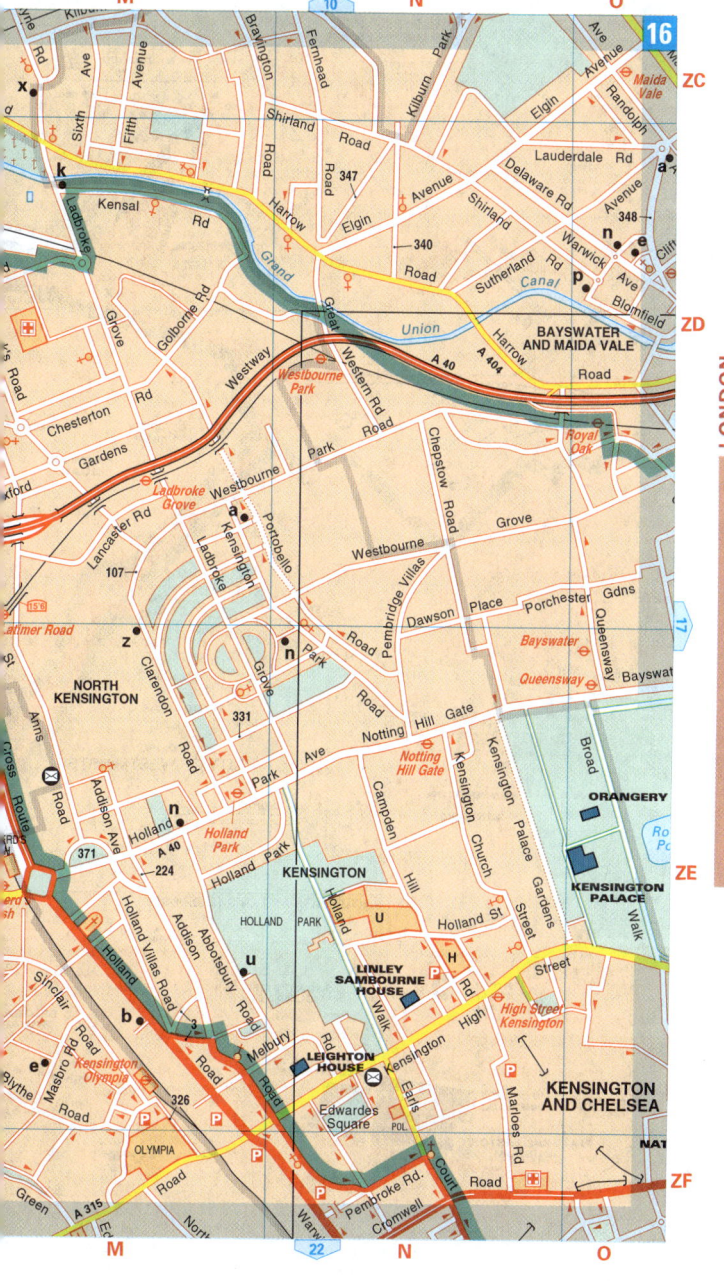

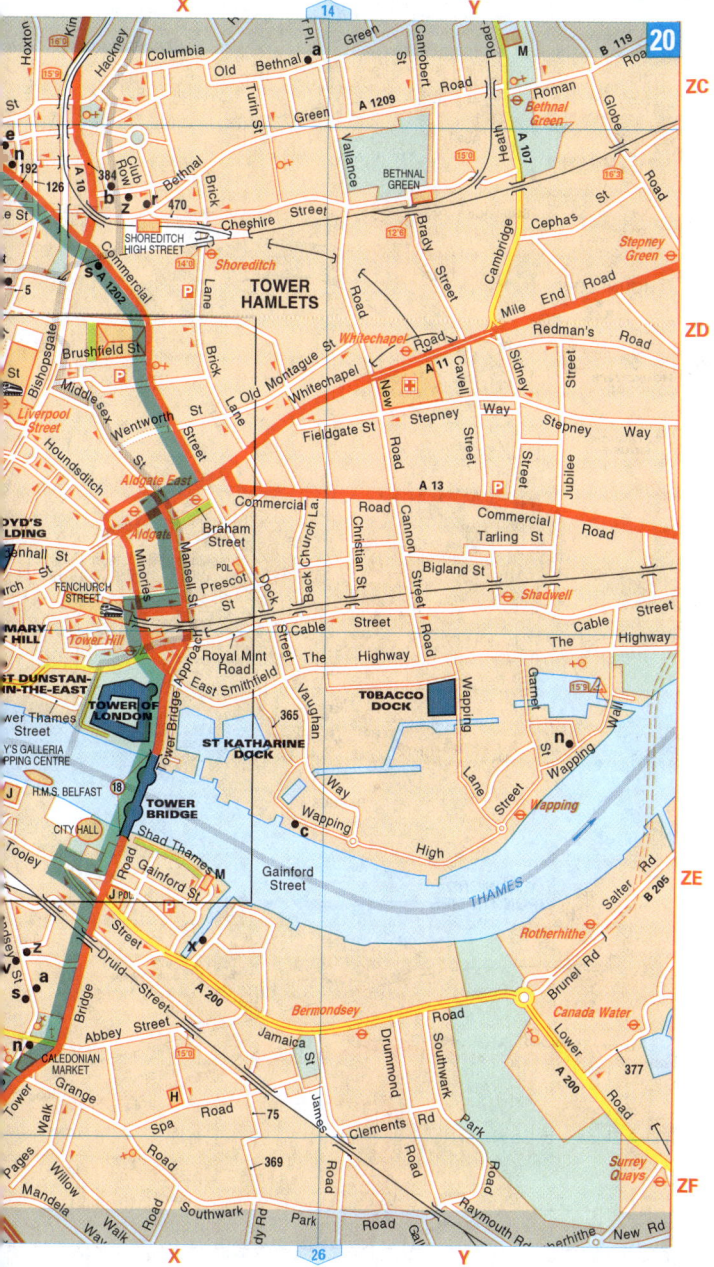

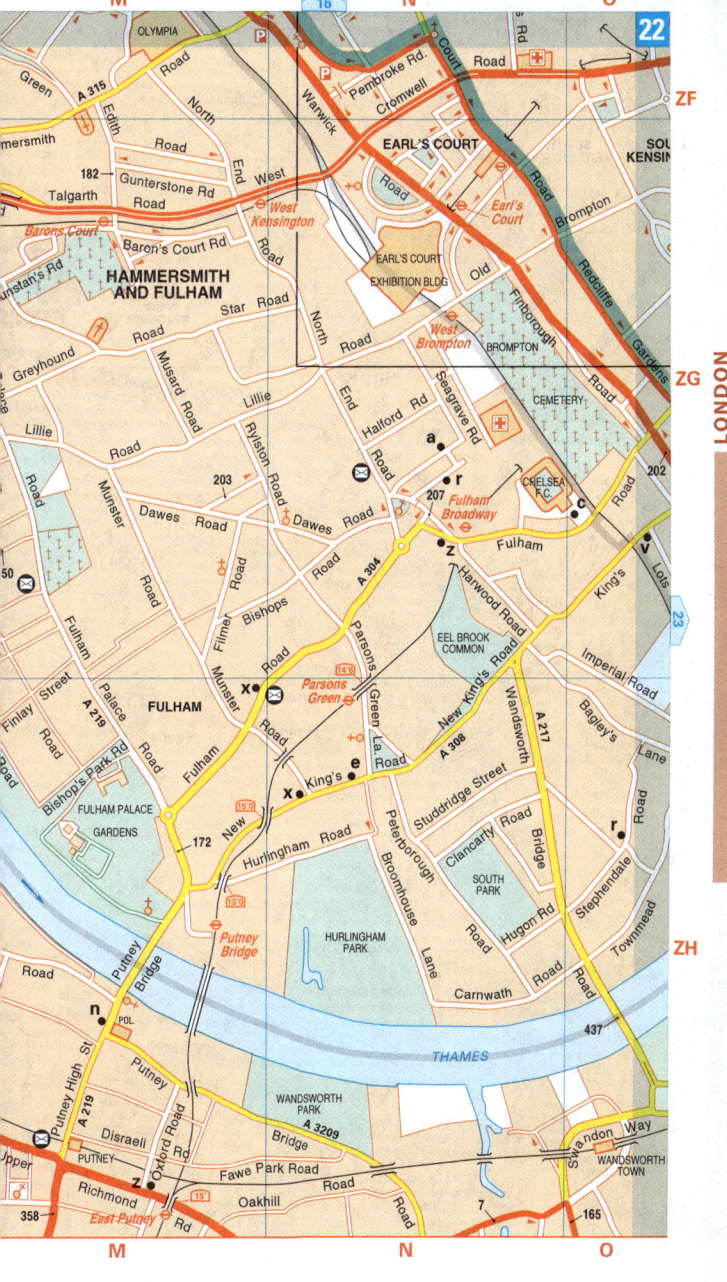

25

LONDON

KENNINGTON, Lambeth High St, Fitzalan Street, Walk, Brook Drive, IMPERIAL WAR MUSEUM, Hayles, ELEPHANT AND CASTLE SHOPPING CENTRE, New Kent Road, A 201, WALWORTH

Black, Vauxhall Walk, Lambeth, Tyers St, Prince Rd, Newburn St, Vauxhall St, Kennington Road, Chester Way, A 3204 Kennington Lane, Kennington Park Road, Penton Place, Heygate St, 163, Rodney Rd, Flint St, East St, Walworth, East Street, Portland Street

Harleyford Rd, Kennington, Clayton St, A 23, A 3, Braganza St, Manor Pl, Chapter Rd, Albany Rd

THE OVAL, Oval, 211, Oval, KENNINGTON PARK, Camberwell, Ruskin, Bethwin Rd, New Church Rd, BURGESS PARK, Southampton, Edmund St, Lomond Gro, Elmington, Benhill

Dorset Rd, 420, Road, Caldwell St, Brixton Road, Vassall Road, Foxley Rd, John Ruskin St, New Wyndham St, Comber Gro, Road, Grove Lane

Way, Clapham, Stockwell Park Rd, **LAMBETH**, Mostyn Road, Aketeman, Knatchbull, Lothian Rd, Calais St, Flodden Rd, A 202 Road, Warner Road, Denmark Road, Church Street Camberwell

Stockwell, Sidney Rd, Groveway, Loughborough Rd, Loughborough Rd, Lilford Rd, Carew St, Minet Rd, Denmark Rd, Denmark Hill, DENMARK HILL, Champion Park

Brixton Road, Wiltshire Road, Angell Dr, Barrington Rd, LOUGHBOROUGH JUNCTION, Coldharbour Lane, Herne Hill, RUSKIN PARK, Ferndene Rd

Brixton, A 2217 Coldharbour Lane, Shakespeare Road, Milkwood Road, Fawnbrake Avenue, Herne Hill, Red Post Hill, Denmark Hill, Sunray Avenue, A 215

Acre Lane, Kellett Rd, Elfra Rd, Railton Road, Brixton Hill, Atlantic Rd

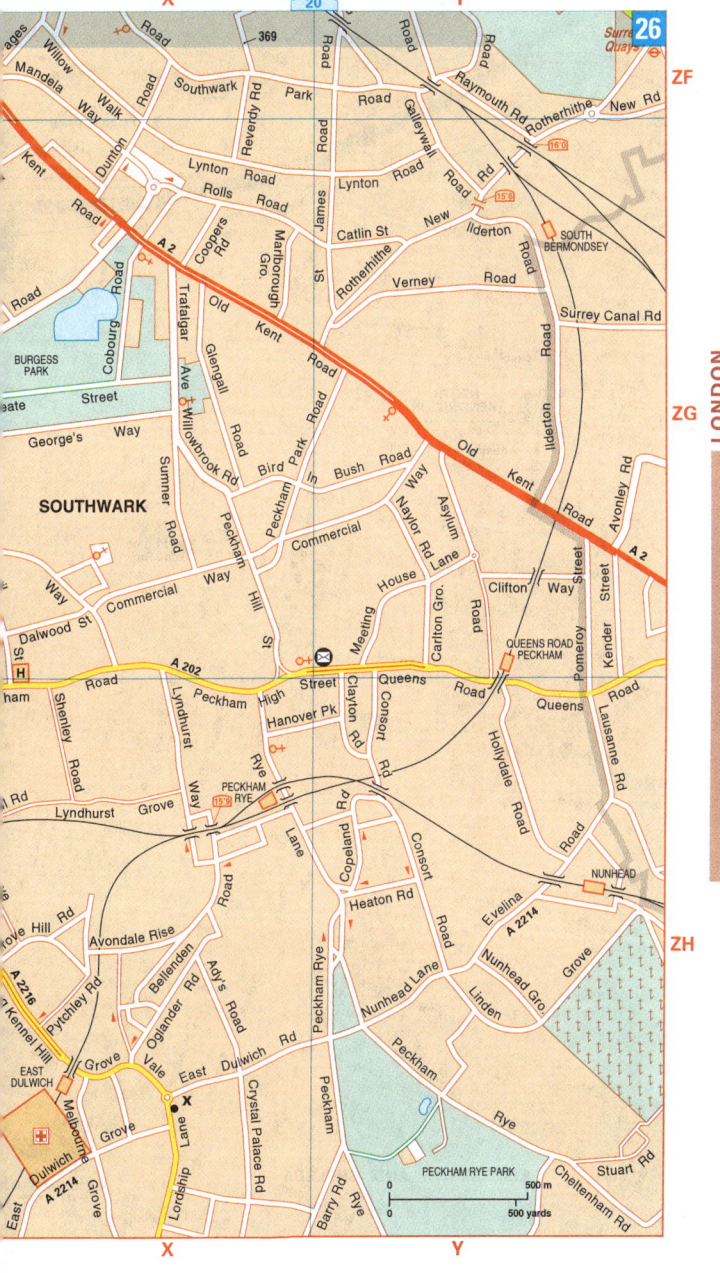

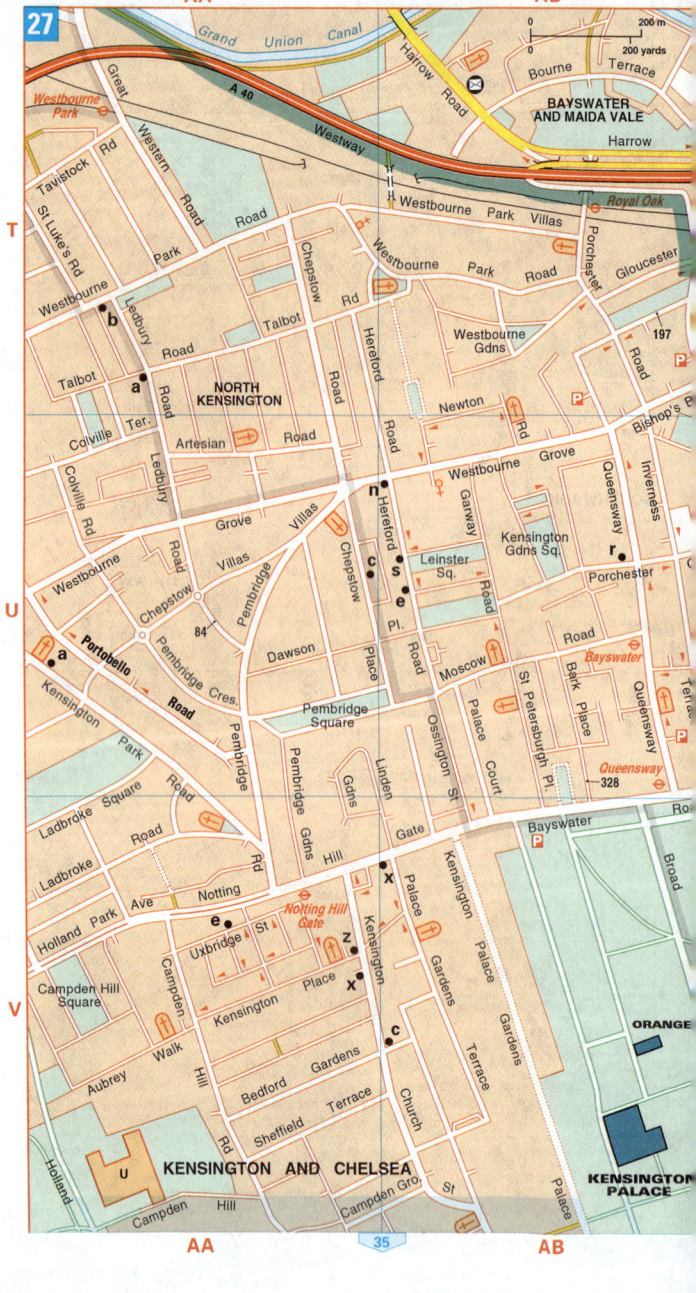

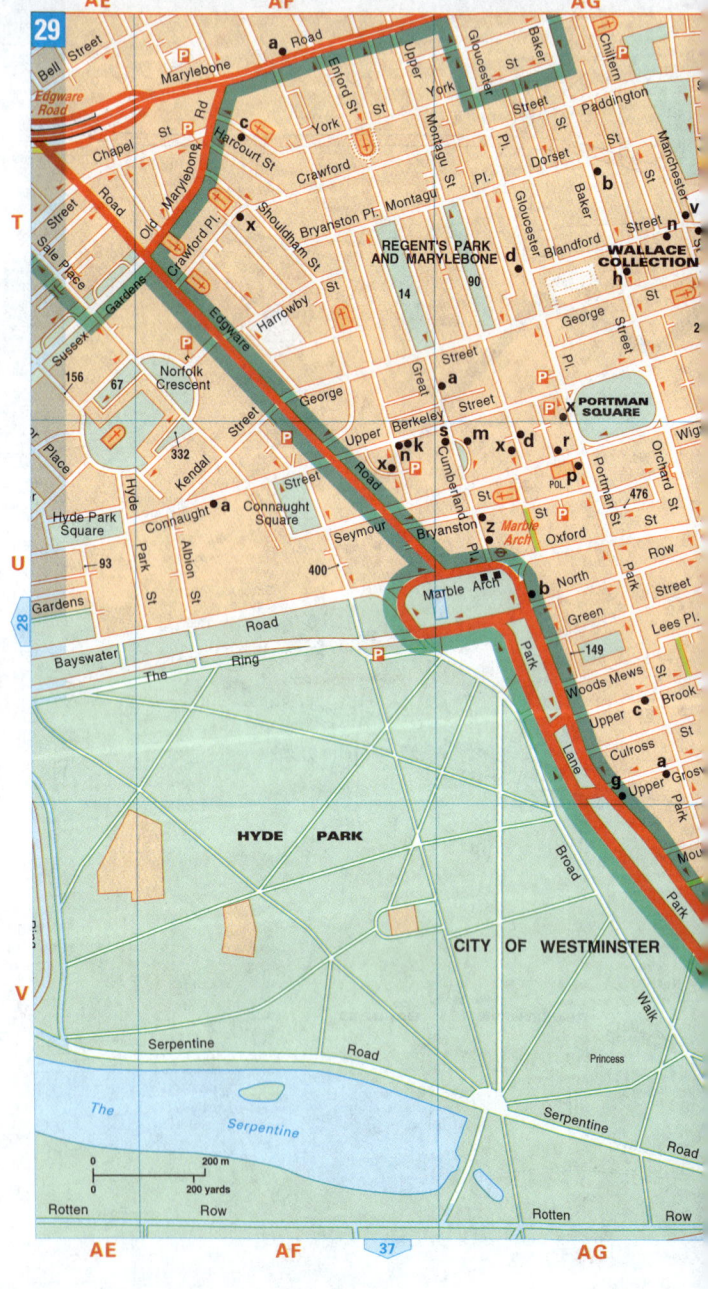

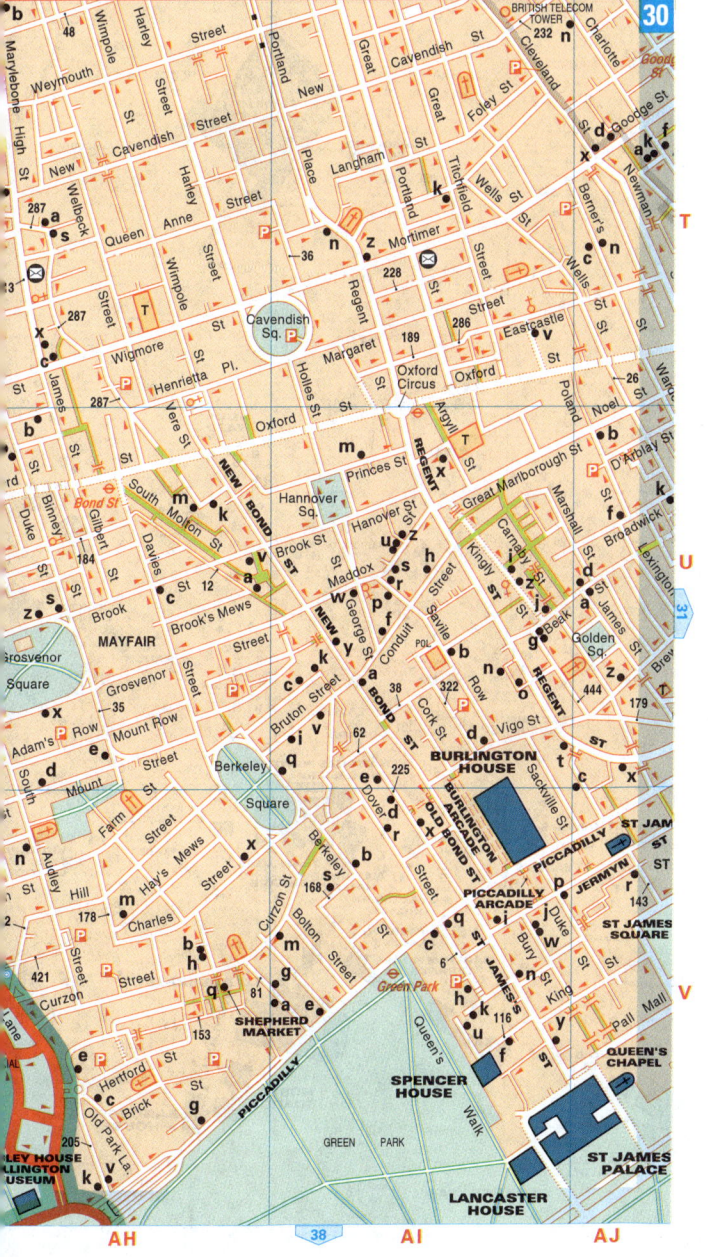

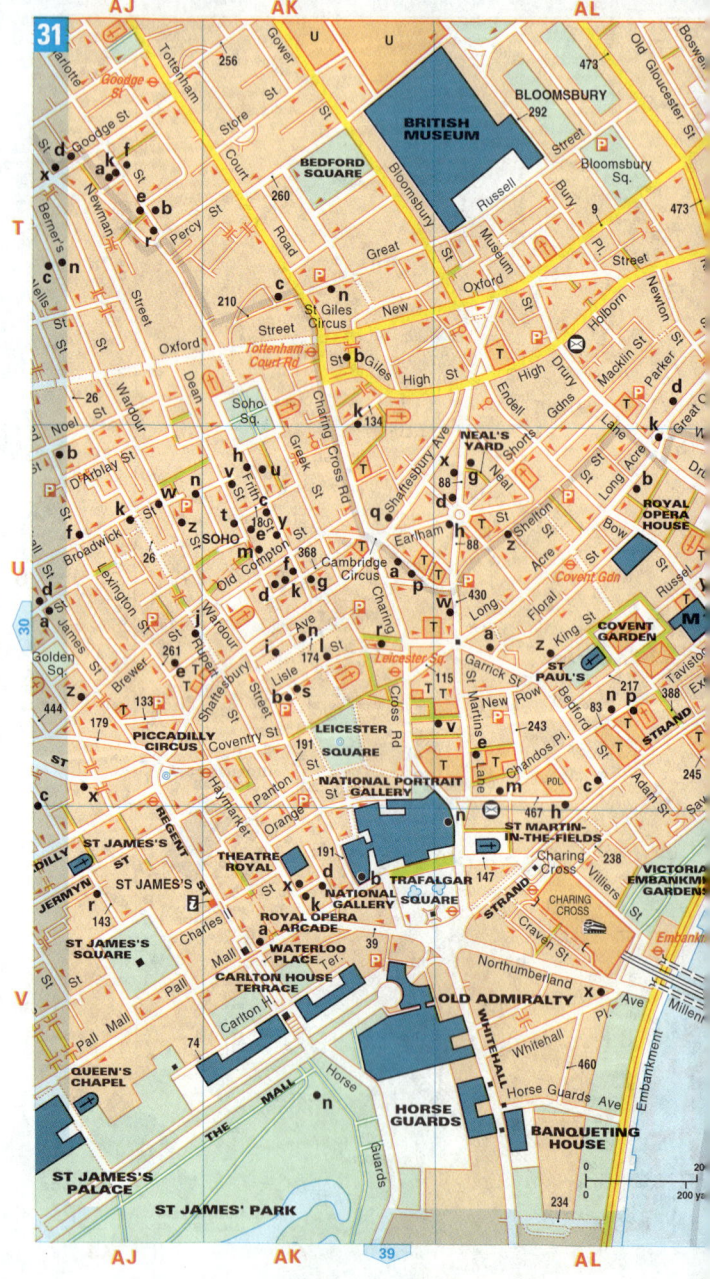

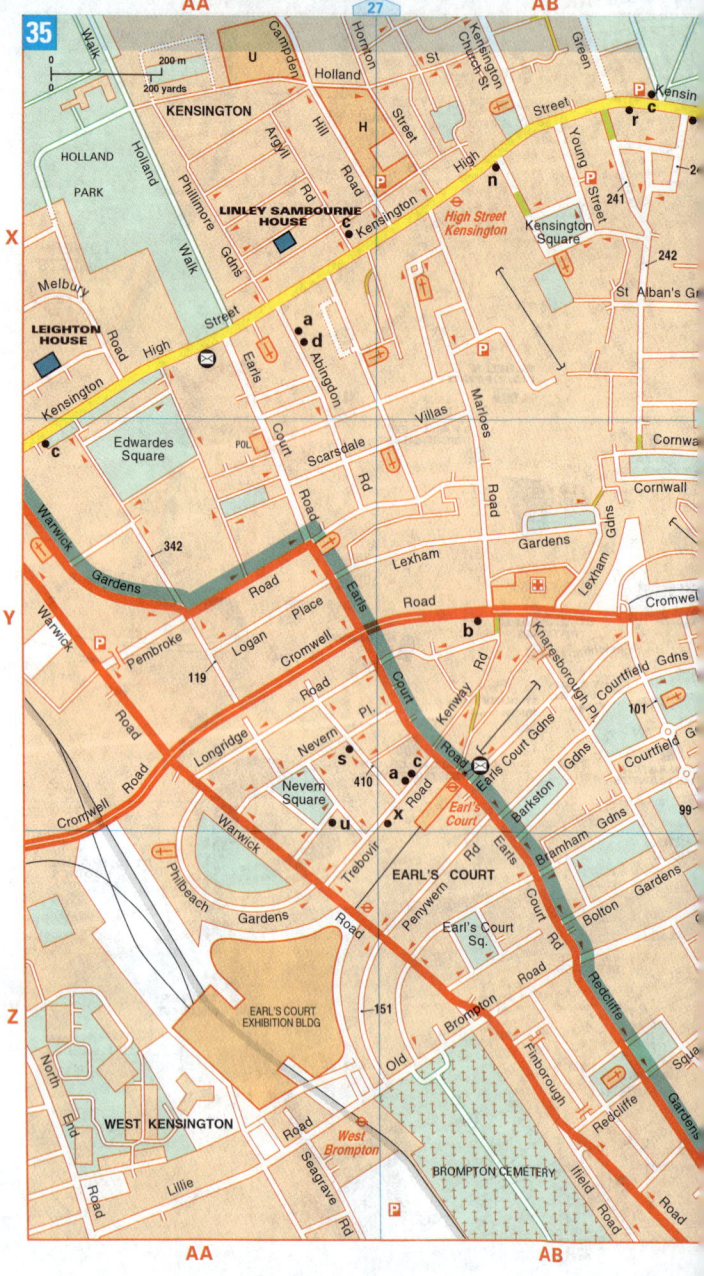

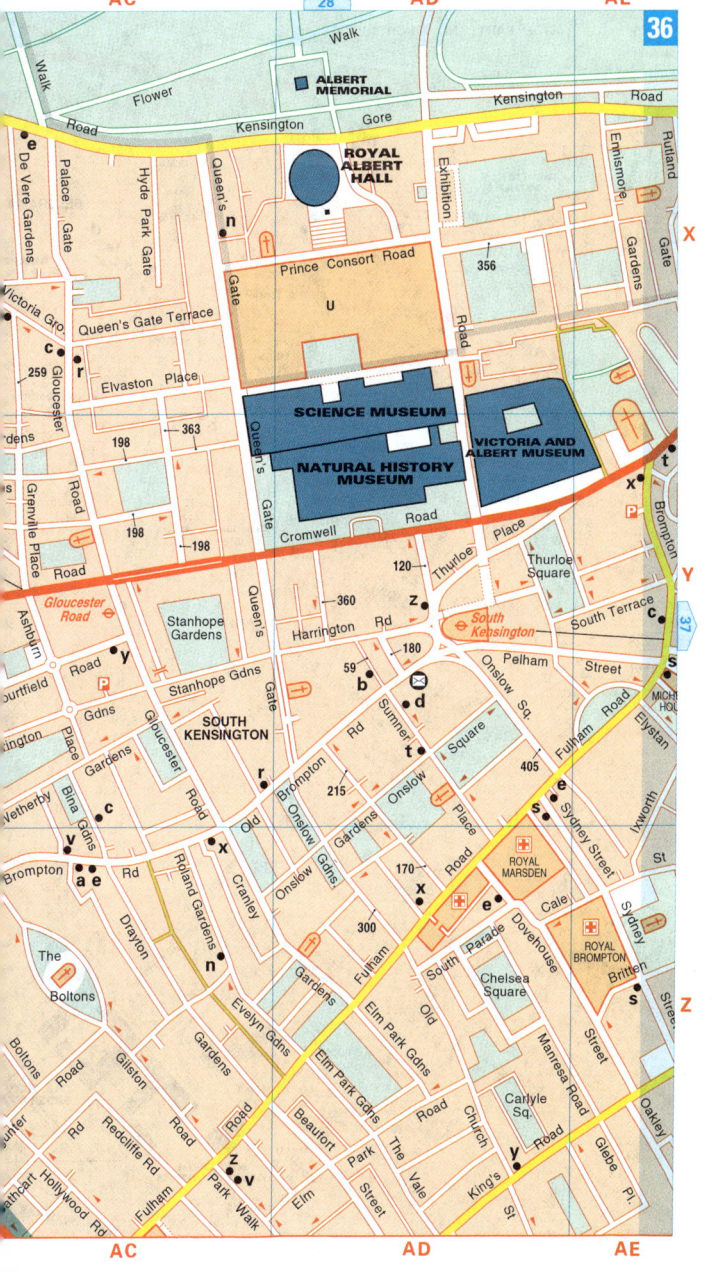

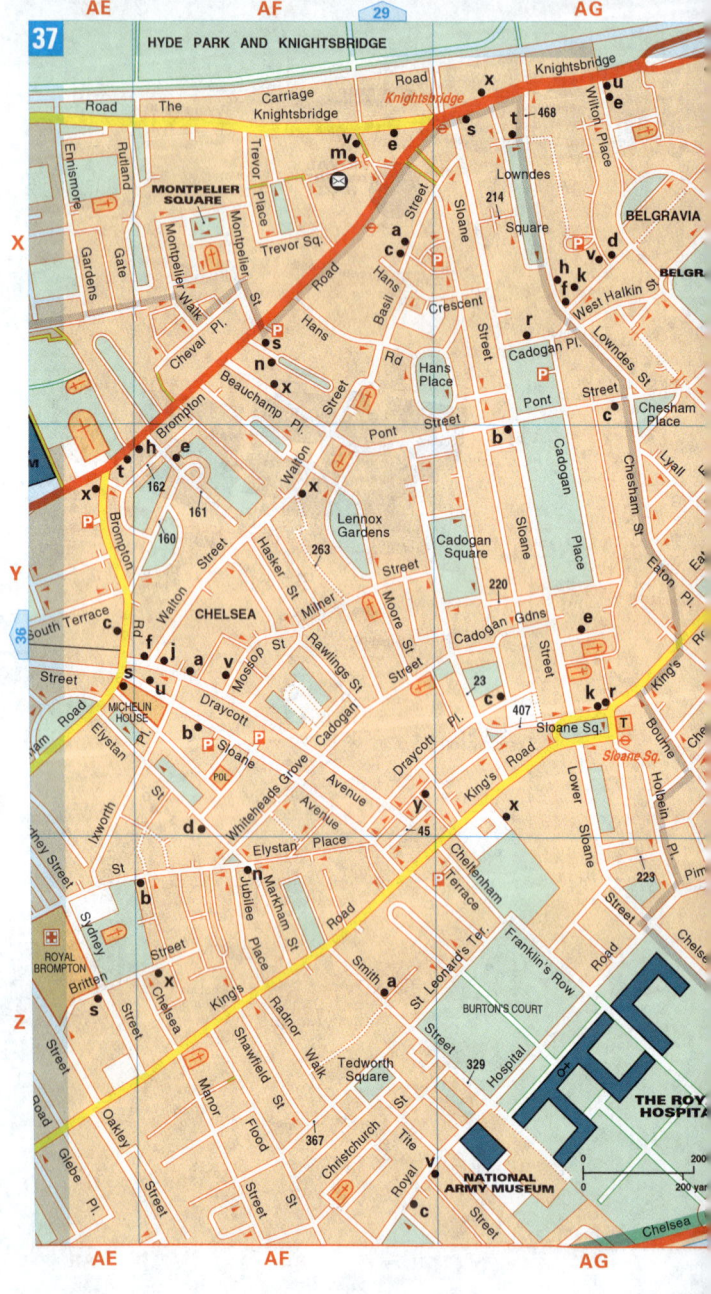

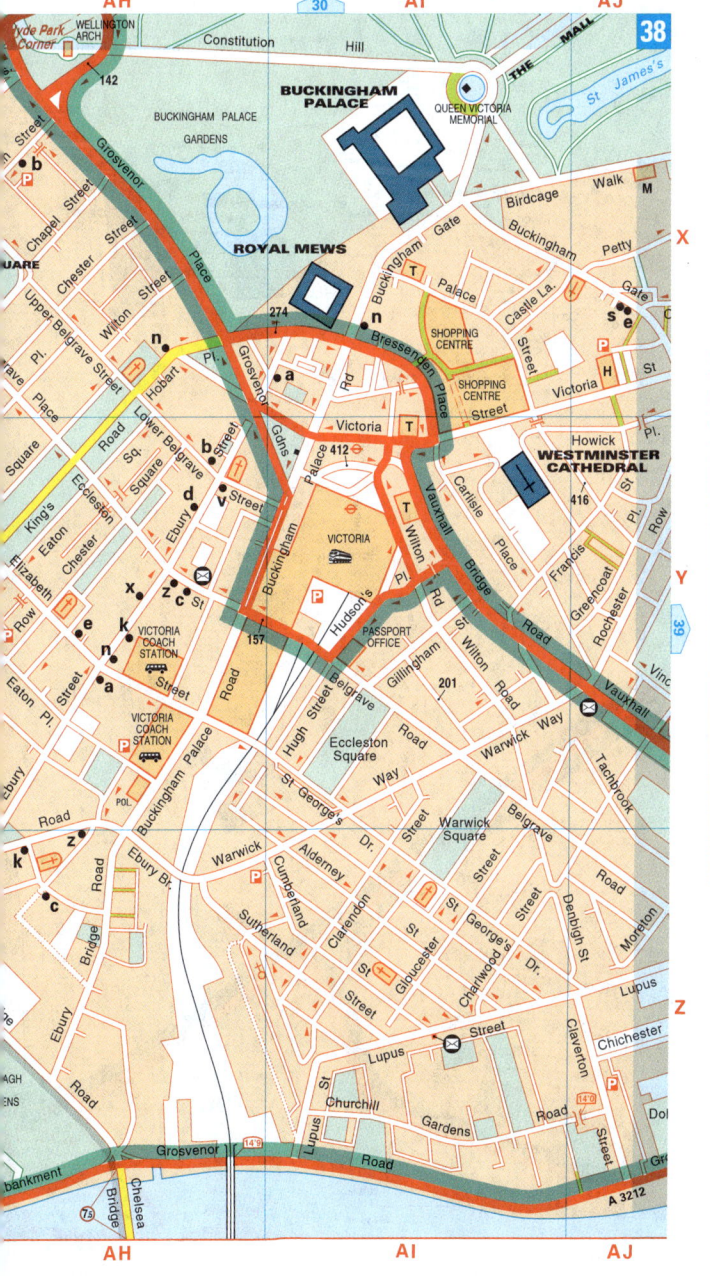

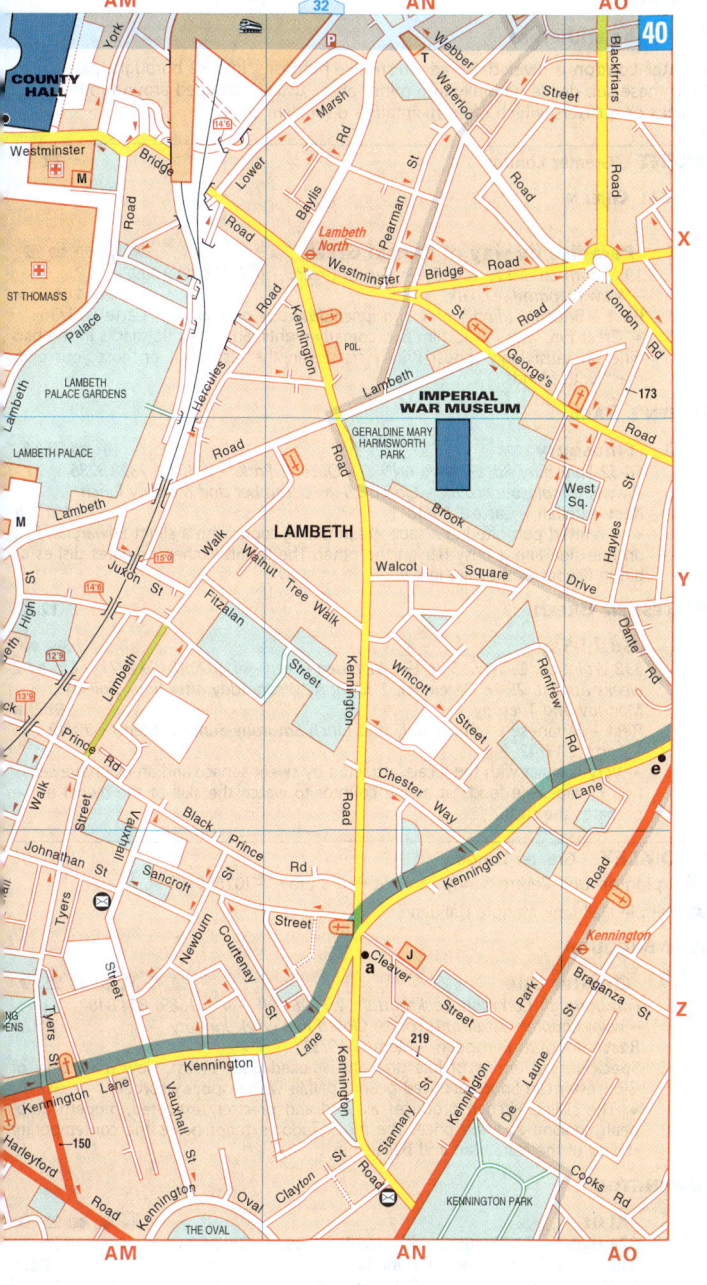

LONDON

Boroughs and areas

Greater London is divided, for administrative purposes, into 32 boroughs plus **the City:** these sub-divide naturally into minor areas, usually grouped around former villages or quarters, which often maintain a distinctive character.

BRENT – Greater London   12 A3

KENSAL GREEN

🍽 **Paradise by way of Kensal Green**   AC ✧ VISA ⊚ ⓘ
19 Kilburn Ln. ⊠ W10 4AE ⊖ Kensal Green. – ℰ (020) 8969 0098
– www.theparadise.co.uk   **10**MZ**Cx**
Rest – British – *(dinner only and lunch Saturday and Sunday)* Carte £ 21/36
♦ Great fun, with music, film and comedy nights. Share terrific snacks in the bar; dine on satisfyingly robust British classics in the restaurant or 'host your own roast' with friends.

QUEEN'S PARK

🍽 **Salusbury**   VISA ⊚ AE ⓘ
50-52 Salusbury Rd. ⊠ NW6 6NN ⊖ Queen's Park. – ℰ (020) 7328 3286
– www.thesalusbury.co.uk – Closed 25-26 December and Monday lunch
Rest – Italian – Carte £ 20/30   **10**MZ**Bb**
♦ A refitted pub offering a sage green dining room with a slight Edwardian feel on one side and a busy bar on the other. The Italian kitchen prepares dishes as big in flavour as they are in size.

WILLESDEN GREEN   12 B3

✕ **Sushi-Say**   VISA ⊚

33B Walm Ln. ⊠ NW2 5SH ⊖ Willesden Green – ℰ (020) 8459 2971 – Closed 2 weeks August, 25-26 December, 1 January, Wednesday after bank holidays, Monday and Tuesday   **9**LZ**Ba**
Rest – Japanese – *(dinner only and lunch Saturday-Sunday)* Menu £ 20/42
– Carte £ 17/42
♦ Very popular with the locals, attracted by sweet service and an extensive selection of Japanese food. Sit at the counter to watch the skill of the owner as he prepares the sushi.

BROMLEY – Greater London   12 B3

🏌 Orpington Golf Centre Sandy Lane, St Paul's Cray, ℰ (01689) 83 96 77
🏌 Magpie Hall lane Magpie Hall lane

FARNBOROUGH

✕✕✕ **Chapter One**   AC ✧ P VISA ⊚ AE ⓘ

Farnborough Common, Locksbottom ⊠ BR6 8NF – ℰ (01689) 854 848
– www.chaptersrestaurants.com – Closed first week January
Rest – Modern European – Menu £ 19/35   **8**HZ**a**
Spec. Pressed terrine of foie gras and smoked duck breast. Slow roast belly of Gloucester Old Spot pork. Iced peanut parfait with raspberry sorbet.
♦ The skilled kitchen produces assured and precisely executed, modern European cooking at a fair price. The mock Tudor exterior belies the contemporary styling of the restaurant and bar within.

ORPINGTON

✕✕ **Xian**   AC VISA ⊚ AE ⓘ
324 High St. ⊠ BR6 0NG – ℰ (01689) 871 881 – Closed 2 weeks April, 25-26 December, Sunday lunch and Monday   **8**JY**a**
Rest – Chinese – Menu £ 10/17 – Carte £ 19/26
♦ Modern, marbled interior with oriental artefacts make this personally run Chinese restaurant a firm favourite with locals. Look out for the Peking specialities.

CAMDEN – Greater London

BELSIZE PARK

XO
29 Belsize Ln. – NW3 5AS – Belsize Park – ℘ (020) 7433 0888
– www.rickerrestaurants.com/xo – Closed 25-26 December and 1 January
Rest – Asian – Menu £ 15 (lunch) – Carte £ 23/33

• Busy bar behind which is a slick and stylish dining room. Vibrant atmosphere; popular with all the good-looking locals. Japanese, Korean, Thai and Chinese cooking; dishes are best shared.

Retsina
48-50 Belsize Ln – NW3 5AR – Belsize Park – ℘ (020) 7431 5855
– www.retsina-london.com – Closed 25-26 December, 1 January, Monday lunch and bank holidays
Rest – Greek – Menu £ 20 (lunch) – Carte £ 20/47

• Family-run restaurant whose unapologetically traditional menu offers all the Greek classics but the grill and souvla are the stars of the show. Service and atmosphere are both relaxed and friendly.

Tandis
73 Haverstock Hill – NW3 4SL – Chalk Farm – ℘ (020) 7586 8079
– www.tandisrestaurant.com – Closed 25 December
Rest – Persian – Carte £ 20/30

• Enticing Iranian food comes in the form of invigorating 'koresht' stews and succulent 'kababs', along with specialities such as 'sabzi polo' and 'kashke bademjaan'. Contemporary décor.

BLOOMSBURY

Covent Garden
10 Monmouth St. – WC2H 9HB – Covent Garden – ℘ (020) 7806 1000
– www.coventgardenhotel.co.uk
56 rm – † £ 300 †† £ 426, ⊇ £ 21 – 2 suites
Rest *Brasserie Max* – see restaurant listing

• Popular with those of a theatrical bent. Boldly designed, stylish bedrooms, with technology discreetly concealed. Boasts a very comfortable first floor oak-panelled drawing room with its own honesty bar.

Charlotte Street
15 Charlotte St. – W1T 1RJ – Goodge Street – ℘ (020) 7806 2000
– www.charlottestreethotel.co.uk
48 rm – † £ 288 †† £ 396, ⊇ £ 20 – 4 suites
Rest *Oscar* – see restaurant listing

• Stylish interior designed with a charming and understated English feel. Impeccably kept and individually decorated bedrooms. In-house screening room is popular with the local advertising execs.

Montague on the Gardens
15 Montague St. – WC1B 5BJ – Holborn – ℘ (020) 7637 1001 – www.montaguehotel.com
94 rm – † £ 174/330 †† £ 198/330, ⊇ £ 16.50 – 6 suites
Rest *Blue Door Bistro* – English – Menu £ 25 – Carte £ 28/59

• A traditional but elegant British feel to this period townhouse; its clubby bar and conservatory overlook a secluded garden. Individually decorated bedrooms. Bistro divided between two small, pretty rooms.

Bloomsbury
16-22 Gt Russell St – WC1B 3NN – Tottenham Court Road – ℘ (020) 7347 1000 – www.doylecollection.com/bloomsbury
153 rm – † £ 450 †† £ 468, ⊇ £ 21
Rest *Landseer* – (closed lunch Saturday and Sunday) Menu £ 25 (dinner) – Carte £ 35/57

• Neo-Georgian building by Edward Lutyens, built for YMCA in 1929. Refurbished in 2009 and now comes with a smart, comfortable interior, from the lobby to the bedrooms. Restaurant with largely British menu.

CAMDEN

Pied à Terre
XXX ✿

34 Charlotte St ✉ W1T 2NH ⊖ Goodge Street – ✆ (020) 7636 1178
– www.pied-a-terre.co.uk – Closed last week December, first week January, Saturday lunch and Sunday
Rest – Innovative – Menu £ 30/75

31AJTf

Spec. Pressed terrine of foie gras and smoked eel with wasabi vinaigrette. Poached lobster with confit pineapple and pata negra. Millefeuille 'Peach Melba'.

♦ 2011 saw a change at this 20 year veteran of Charlotte Street. Shane Osborn sailed into the sunset and in his place as head chef came Marcus Eaves from L'Autre Pied. The menu is an appealing read and the cooking remains ambitious in its reach and elaborate in its execution.

Hakkasan Hanway Place
XX ✿

8 Hanway Pl. ✉ W1T 1HD ⊖ Tottenham Court Road – ✆ (020) 7927 7000
– www.hakkasan.com – Closed 24-25 December

31AKTc

Rest – Chinese – Carte £ 40/89

Spec. Peking duck with Royal Beluga caviar. Roasted silver cod. Jivara hazelnut bomb.

♦ Cool and seductive subterranean restaurant, with an air of exclusivity. Innovation and originality have been added to the Cantonese base to create dishes with zip and depth. Lunchtime dim sum is a highlight.

Mon Plaisir
XX

19-21 Monmouth St. ✉ WC2H 9DD ⊖ Covent Garden – ✆ (020) 7836 7243
– www.monplaisir.co.uk – Closed Christmas-New Year, Sunday and bank holidays

31ALUg

Rest – French – Menu £ 19 (lunch and early dinner) – Carte £ 30/41

♦ This proud French institution opened in the 1940s. Enjoy satisfyingly authentic classics in any of the four contrasting rooms, full of Gallic charm; the bar was salvaged from a Lyonnais brothel.

Incognico
XX

117 Shaftesbury Ave. ✉ WC2H 8AD ⊖ Tottenham Court Road – ✆ (020) 7836 8866 – www.incognico.com – Closed Sunday and bank holidays
Rest – Modern European – Menu £ 25 (lunch) – Carte £ 29/38

31AKUq

♦ Comfortable, smartly dressed restaurant with dark wood and brown leather lending a masculine, clubby feel. Influences from France and Italy inform the cooking from a capable kitchen.

Roka
XX

37 Charlotte St ✉ W1T 1RR ⊖ Goodge Street – ✆ (020) 7580 6464
– www.rokarestaurant.com – Closed 24-26 December

31AJTk

Rest – Japanese – Carte £ 35/65

♦ Bright, atmospheric interior of teak and oak; bustling and trendy feel. Contemporary touches added to Japanese dishes; try specialities from the on-view Robata grill. Capable and chatty service.

Fino
XX

33 Charlotte St. (entrance on Rathbone St.) ✉ W1T 1RR ⊖ Goodge Street
– ✆ (020) 7813 8010 – www.finorestaurant.com – Closed Saturday lunch, Sunday and bank holidays

31AJTa

Rest – Spanish – Menu £ 18 (lunch) – Carte £ 21/49

♦ Seafood is handled especially well in this lively, quite smart and smoothly run basement tapas restaurant. Sensibly divided menu, with dishes designed for sharing. Youthful, helpful service.

Sardo
XX

45 Grafton Way ✉ W1T 5DQ ⊖ Warren Street – ✆ (020) 7387 2521
– www.sardo-restaurant.com – Closed Christmas, Saturday lunch and Sunday
Rest – Italian – Carte £ 26/34

18RZDc

♦ Expect a warm and welcoming atmosphere at this simply decorated Italian restaurant, with plenty of regulars and friendly service. Sardinian specialities and seasonal specials are the highlights.

CAMDEN

XX **Archipelago** VISA ◎◎ AE ①
110 Whitfield St. ⊠ W1T 5ED ⊖ Goodge Street – ℰ (020) 7383 3346
– www.archipelago-restaurant.co.uk – Closed 24-27 December, Saturday
lunch, Sunday and bank holidays   **18**RZD**c**
Rest – Innovative – Carte £ 28/38
♦ Eccentrically decorated in the style of an overflowing bazaar. Asian influence to the equally exotic and highly unusual menu which could include crocodile, zebra, wildebeest and even scorpion.

XX **Brasserie Max** – at Covent Garden Hotel   AC ⇔ VISA ◎◎ AE ①
10 Monmouth St. ⊠ WC2H 9HB ⊖ Covent Garden – ℰ (020) 7806 1000
– www.firmdalehotels.com   **31**ALU**x**
Rest – Modern European – (booking essential) Menu £ 24/25 – Carte £ 35/54
♦ It's not just shoppers and theatregoers who appreciate this stylish brasserie. Its international menu, grilled specialities, Sunday brunches and afternoon teas have widespread appeal.

XX **Oscar** – at Charlotte Street Hotel   AC VISA ◎◎ AE ①
15 Charlotte St. ⊠ W1T 1RJ ⊖ Goodge Street – ℰ (020) 7907 4005
– www.charlottestreethotel.co.uk   **31**AJT**e**
Rest – Modern European – Menu £ 23/25 – Carte £ 33/56
♦ Its terrace spills out onto Charlotte Street, full of those enjoying cocktails and sharing platters, while inside is awash with colour. Grilled meats are a highlight of the large menu.

XX **Rasa Samudra**   VISA ◎◎ AE
5 Charlotte St. ⊠ W1T 1RE ⊖ Goodge Street – ℰ (020) 7637 0222
– www.rasarestaurants.com – Closed 25 December-1 January, lunch Sunday and bank holidays   **31**AJT**r**
Rest – Indian – Menu £ 23/30 – Carte £ 22/32
♦ Its bright pink hue makes it easy to spot. Specialises in the southwest region of Kerala so expect fish, vegetarian dishes and plenty of coconut and have the pre-meal snacks. Well meaning service.

X **Mennula**   AC ⇔ VISA ◎◎ AE ①
10 Charlotte St. ⊠ W1T 2LT ⊖ Goodge Street – ℰ (020) 7363 2833
– www.mennula.com – Closed 1 week Christmas, Saturday lunch and bank holidays   **31**AJT**b**
Rest – Italian – Menu £ 20 (lunch and early dinner) – Carte approx. £ 30
♦ Sicilian specialities provide the highlights at this enthusiastically run Italian restaurant, whose name means 'almond'. Compact but bright, crisply decorated room; ask for one of the booths.

X **Paramount**   ⇐ AC ⇔ VISA ◎◎ AE
Centre Point (31st floor) 101-103 New Oxford St. ⊠ WC1A 1DD
⊖ Tottenham Court Road – ℰ (020) 7420 2900 – www.paramount.uk.net
– Closed 25-26 December and Sunday dinner   **31**AKT**b**
Rest – Modern European – Menu £ 24 (lunch and early dinner) – Carte £ 30/46
♦ Worth the palaver of getting into this Grade II listed building: the views are terrific and this is a fun, keenly run restaurant. Ambitious and quite elaborate cooking; champagne bar one floor up.

X **Kopapa**   AC ⇔ VISA ◎◎ AE
32-34 Monmouth St ⊠ WC2H 9HA ⊖ Covent Garden – ℰ (020) 7240 6076
– www.kopapa.co.uk – Closed 25 December   **31**ALU**h**
Rest – Asian influences – (booking advisable) Menu £ 25 (lunch and early dinner) – Carte £ 24/34
♦ Kopapa, a Maori word for a gathering, is Peter Gordon's just-drop-in-anytime place. It's cramped but fun, with breakfast morphing into all-day dining. It's the 'fusion'-inspired tapas that will give your taste buds the best workout.

CAMDEN

Giaconda Dining Room
9 Denmark St. ⊠ WC2H 8LS ⊖ Tottenham Court Road – ℘ (020) 7240 3334
– www.giacondadining.com – Closed 3 weeks August, 2 weeks Easter, 2 weeks Christmas-New Year, Saturday lunch, Sunday, Monday and bank holidays
Rest – Modern European – *(booking essential)* Carte £ 22/30   **31**AKT**k**

• Aussie owners run a small, fun and very busy place in an unprepossessing location. The very well priced menu offers an appealing mix of gutsy, confident, no-nonsense food, with French and Italian influences.

Salt Yard
54 Goodge St. ⊠ W1T 4NA ⊖ Goodge Street – ℘ (020) 7637 0657
– www.saltyard.co.uk – Closed 24 December-4 January, Saturday lunch and Sunday   **31**AJT**d**
Rest – Mediterranean – Carte approx. £ 20

• Ground floor bar and buzzy basement restaurant specialising in good value plates of tasty Italian and Spanish dishes, ideal for sharing; charcuterie a speciality. Super wine list.

Cigala
54 Lamb's Conduit St. ⊠ WC1N 3LW ⊖ Russell Square – ℘ (020) 7405 1717
– www.cigala.co.uk   **19**TZD**a**
Rest – Spanish – *(booking essential)* Menu £ 18 (lunch) – Carte £ 24/32

• Spanish restaurant on corner of attractive street. Simply furnished; open-plan kitchen. Robust Iberian cooking, with some dishes designed for sharing; interesting drinks list.

Tsunami
93 Charlotte St. ⊠ W1T 4PY ⊖ Goodge Street – ℘ (020) 7637 0050
– www.tsunamirestaurant.co.uk – Closed Saturday lunch and Sunday
Rest – Japanese – Carte £ 30/38 **s**   **30**AIT**n**

• Sister to the original in Clapham. Sweet, pretty place, with lacquered walls, floral motif and moody lighting. Contemporary Japanese cuisine is carefully prepared and sensibly priced.

Barrica
62 Goodge St ⊠ W1T 4NE ⊖ Goodge Street – ℘ (020) 7436 9448
– www.barrica.co.uk – Closed 25-26 December, 1 January, Sunday and bank holidays   **31**AJT**x**
Rest – Spanish – *(booking essential)* Carte £ 18/20

• Lively, noisy and warmly decorated tapas bar. Authentic dishes come with plenty of flavour and are complemented by a thoughtfully compiled Spanish wine list. Busy front bar.

CAMDEN TOWN

York & Albany with rm
127-129 Parkway ⊠ NW1 7PS ⊖ Camden Town – ℘ (020) 7388 3344
– www.gordonramsay.com/yorkandalbany   **12**RZB**s**
10 rm – †£ 168/186 ††£ 168/348, ⊡ £ 12
Rest – Modern European – *(booking essential)* Carte £ 25/38

• 1820s John Nash former coaching inn, now part of Gordon Ramsay's empire. Smart bar and informal dining; lower level offers kitchen views. Cooking is refined without being fussy, and influences are European. Comfortable, individually decorated bedrooms.

Market
43 Parkway ⊠ NW1 7PN ⊖ Camden Town – ℘ (020) 7267 9700
– www.marketrestaurant.co.uk – Closed 25 December-3 January ,Sunday dinner and bank holidays   **12**RZB**x**
Rest – British – *(booking essential)* Carte £ 25/34

• Market fresh produce used to create satisfying and refreshingly matter of fact British dishes, at excellent prices that entice plenty of passers-by. Appealing décor of exposed brick walls, old school chairs and zinc-topped tables.

DARTMOUTH PARK

Bull and Last
168 Highgate Rd ✉ NW5 1QS ⊖ Tufnell Park. – ℰ (020) 7267 3641
– www.thebullandlast.co.uk – Closed 24- 25 December
12RZA**a**
Rest – British – *(booking essential)* Carte £ 27/33
• A busy Victorian pub with plenty of charm and character; the upstairs is a little quieter. Cooking is muscular, satisfying and reflects the time of year; charcuterie is a speciality.

EUSTON

Novotel London St. Pancras
100-110 Euston Rd. ✉ NW1 2AJ ⊖ Euston – ℰ (020) 7666 9000 – www.novotel.com
18SZC**a**
309 rm – †£ 350 ††£ 350, ☲ £ 14.95 – 3 suites
Rest – *(bar lunch Saturday, Sunday and bank holidays)* Menu £ 19/23 – Carte £ 30/48
• Halfway between Euston and Kings Cross, this hotel has good-sized bedrooms for London and those on the higher floors enjoy views over the city. Good business amenities. International menu and buffet breakfast.

Red n Hot
37 Chalton St ✉ NW1 1JD ⊖ Euston – ℰ (020) 7388 0808
– www.rednhotgroup.com – Closed 25 December
12SZC**b**
Rest – Chinese – Carte £ 15/19
• The clue is in the name! The fiery pepper dominates the extensive selection of Sichuan specialities that make good use of freshwater fish and poultry. Simpler lunchtime menu includes hotpots.

HAMPSTEAD

Goldfish
82 Hampstead High St ✉ NW3 1RE ⊖ Hampstead – ℰ (020) 7794 6666
– www.restaurantprivilege.com
11PZA**z**
Rest – Asian – Carte approx. £ 40
• Sweet little place, divided into three differently decorated rooms. Mix of Chinese and other Asian countries; chef also adds own creations. Well-priced lunch menu, including popular weekend dim sum.

La Cocotte
85b Fleet Rd ✉ NW3 2QY ⊖ Belsize Park – ℰ (020) 7433 3317
– www.la-cocotte.co.uk – Closed Sunday dinner, Monday and lunch Tuesday-Thursday
11QZA**a**
Rest – French – Menu £ 13 (lunch) – Carte £ 21/31
• The decorative clichés are countered by affable, self-deprecating service at this busy, unpretentious bistro. Expect bourgeois classics, with slow-cooked dishes in shallow iron pots a highlight.

Wells
30 Well Walk ✉ NW3 1BX ⊖ Hampstead. – ℰ (020) 7794 3785
– www.thewellshampstead.co.uk
11PZA**v**
Rest – British – Carte £ 28/38
• Part country pub, part city sophisticate; busy ground floor, with more sedate upstairs restaurant. Cooking is hearty in flavour and sophisticated in look, with a pleasing British edge.

Magdala
2A South Hill Park ✉ NW3 2SB ⊖ Belsize Park. – ℰ (020) 7435 2503
– www.the-magdala.com
11PZA**s**
Rest – Modern European – Carte £ 22/30
• Uncomplicated pub food but prepared with care; some dishes designed for sharing. Relaxed, locals pub on the edge of the Heath, with countryside feel. Upstairs room used at weekends.

CAMDEN

HATTON GARDEN

Bleeding Heart
Bleeding Heart Yard, off Greville St. ✉ EC1N 8SJ ⊖ Farringdon – ℰ (020) 7242 8238 – www.bleedingheart.co.uk – Closed Christmas-New Year, Saturday and Sunday
32ANT**e**
Rest – French – *(booking essential)* Menu £ 25 (lunch) **s** – Carte £ 28/43 **s**

♦ Dickensian yard plays host to this atmospheric, candlelit restaurant; popular with those from The City. Classic French cuisine is the draw, with service that's formal but has personality. Wines from owners' New Zealand estate.

HOLBORN

Chancery Court
252 High Holborn ✉ WC1V 7EN ⊖ Holborn – ℰ (020) 7829 9888 – www.chancerycourt.com
32AMT**a**
354 rm – †£ 264/366 ††£ 264/366, ⊑ £ 26 – 2 suites
Rest *Pearl* – see restaurant listing

♦ Striking former Pearl Assurance HQ, built in 1914, now an imposing place to stay. Impressive marbled lobby and grand central courtyard. Decent sized bedrooms with comprehensive modern facilities.

Pearl – at Chancery Court Hotel
252 High Holborn ✉ WC1V 7EN ⊖ Holborn – ℰ (020) 7829 7000 – www.pearl-restaurant.com – Closed 2 weeks August, Sunday and bank holidays
32AMT**a**
Rest – French – Menu £ 30/60

♦ Impressive former banking hall, with walls clad in Italian marble and Corinthian columns. Waiters provide efficient service at well-spaced tables; cooking shows originality.

Asadal
227 High Holborn ✉ WC1V 7DA ⊖ Holborn – ℰ (020) 7430 9006 – www.asadal.co.uk – Closed 25-26 December, 1 January and Sunday lunch
Rest – Korean – Menu £ 14/20 – Carte £ 17/31
31ALT**n**

♦ Sharing is the key in this busy basement, where you'll be oblivious to its unprepossessing location. Hotpots, dumplings and barbeques are the highlights from the easy-to-follow menu. Staff cope well with the evening rush.

Moti Mahal
45 Great Queen St. ✉ WC2B 5AA ⊖ Holborn – ℰ (020) 7240 9329 – www.motimahal-uk.com – Closed Christmas, Sunday and lunch Saturday and bank holidays
31ALU**k**
Rest – Indian – Carte £ 37/46

♦ Restaurant is split between a bright, busy ground floor and more intimate basement. Specialities follow the Grand Trunk Road, stretching from Bengal to the North West and the Pakistan border.

Great Queen Street
32 Great Queen St ✉ WC2B 5AA ⊖ Holborn – ℰ (020) 7242 0622 – Closed Christmas-New Year and bank holidays
31ALT**d**
Rest – British – *(booking essential)* Carte £ 25/30

♦ The menu is a model of British understatement and is dictated by the seasons; the cooking, confident and satisfying with laudable prices and generous portions. Lively atmosphere and enthusiastic service.

French Kitchen
95-97 High Holborn ✉ WC1V 6LF ⊖ Holborn – ℰ (020) 7242 4580 – www.french-kitchen.co.uk – Closed 25 December
32AMT**k**
Rest – French – Carte £ 20/32

♦ Open all day and offering everything from breakfast and afternoon tea to pizza, charcuterie and comforting French classics. Large, animated room with a rustic feel and friendly service.

CAMDEN

PRIMROSE HILL

Odette's
130 Regent's Park Rd. ⊠ NW1 8XL ⊖ Chalk Farm – ℰ (020) 7586 8569
– www.odettesprimrosehill.com – Closed 1 week Christmas **11**QZB**b**
Rest – Modern European – Menu £ 20 (lunch and early dinner) – Carte £ 31/51
♦ A local institution that has recently lightened up. Warm and inviting interior, with chatty but organised service. Robust and quite elaborate cooking, with chef-owner passionate about his Welsh roots.

L'Absinthe
40 Chalcot Rd ⊠ NW1 8LS ⊖ Chalk Farm – ℰ (020) 7483 4848
– www.labsinthe.co.uk – Closed August, Christmas and Monday **11**QZB**s**
Rest – French – Menu £ 13 (lunch) – Carte £ 22/34
♦ Lively and enthusiastically run French bistro, with tightly packed tables, spread over two floors. All the favourites, from Lyonnais salad to duck confit. Commendably priced French wine list.

Engineer
65 Gloucester Ave ⊠ NW1 8JH ⊖ Chalk Farm. – ℰ (020) 7722 0950
– www.the-engineer.com – Closed 1 week Christmas **12**RZB**a**
Rest – British – Carte £ 26/44
♦ Grade II listed pub with Italianate façade. Divided between bar and restaurant, with a popular garden terrace at the back. Confident, wholesome cooking; suppliers name-checked on the menu.

ST PANCRAS

St Pancras Renaissance
Euston Rd ⊠ NW1 2AR ⊖ King's Cross St. Pancras
– ℰ (020) 7941 3540 – www.stpancrasrenaissance.co.uk **12**SZC**d**
207 rm – †£ 390 ††£ 390/1140, ⊇ £ 17 – 38 suites
Rest *Gilbert Scott* – see restaurant listing
Rest *Booking Office* – British – Carte £ 27/40
♦ This Gothic jewel, built in 1873 as the Midland Grand hotel and now finally restored, reopened in 2011 under the Marriott brand. Former taxi rank now the spacious lobby and all-day dining is in the old Booking Office. Corridors and staircases evoke the past; bedrooms are a little more functional.

Gilbert Scott – at St Pancras Renaissance Hotel
Euston Rd ⊠ NW1 2AR ⊖ King's Cross St. Pancras – ℰ (020) 7278 3888
– www.thegilbertscott.co.uk **12**SZC**d**
Rest – British – Carte £ 32/70
♦ Run under the aegis of Marcus Wareing and named after the architect of this Gothic masterpiece, the restaurant has the look of a Grand Salon but the buzz of a brasserie. It celebrates the UK's many regional and historic specialities.

SWISS COTTAGE

Bradley's
25 Winchester Rd. ⊠ NW3 3NR ⊖ Swiss Cottage – ℰ (020) 7722 3457
– www.bradleysnw3.co.uk – Closed Saturday lunch and Sunday dinner
Rest – Modern European – Menu £ 18/25 – Carte £ 30/40 **11**PZB**e**
♦ A stalwart of the local dining scene and ideal for visitors to the nearby Hampstead Theatre. The thoughtfully compiled and competitively priced set menus of mostly classical cooking draw in plenty of regulars.

Singapore Garden
83 Fairfax Rd. ⊠ NW6 4DY ⊖ Swiss Cottage – ℰ (020) 7328 5314
– www.singaporegarden.co.uk – Closed 24-28 December **11**PZB**x**
Rest – Asian – Menu £ 30 (dinner) – Carte £ 31/52
♦ A smart, bright and comfortable room, with endearingly enthusiastic service. Your best bet is to pick vibrant and zesty dishes from the list of Singaporean and Malaysian specialities.

CAMDEN

XX Eriki
4-6 Northways Par, Finchley Rd ⊠ NW3 5EN ⊖ Swiss Cottage – ℰ (020) 7722 0606 – www.eriki.co.uk – Closed Saturday lunch
11PZBu
Rest – Indian – Menu £ 20 (dinner) – Carte £ 27/35

♦ The menu offers an invigorating gastronomic tour of all parts of India; vegetarians will be in clover. Vividly coloured, comfortable room with fine tapestries; well-meaning service and lots of regulars.

TUFNELL PARK

Junction Tavern
101 Fortess Rd ⊠ NW5 1AG ⊖ Tufnell Park. – ℰ (020) 7485 9400 – www.junctiontavern.co.uk – Closed 24-26 December and 1 January
Rest – Modern European – Carte £ 23/31
12RZAx

♦ Sizeable pub with striking matt black façade. Dining room on one side, along with conservatory and busy bar. Well-balanced menu; flavoursome cooking. Interesting and regularly changing guest beers.

WEST HAMPSTEAD

X Walnut
280 West End Ln., Fortune Grn. ⊠ NW6 1LJ ⊖ West Hampstead – ℰ (020) 7794 7772 – www.walnutwalnut.com – Closed Sunday and Monday
Rest – Traditional – (dinner only) Carte £ 24/38
10NZAa

♦ Eco-aware chef-owner in his raised, open kitchen offers classical cooking, where game and fish are the specialities. Relaxed and informal corner restaurant, with plenty of local regulars.

CITY OF LONDON – Greater London
12 B3

Andaz Liverpool Street
40 Liverpool St. ⊠ EC2M 7QN ⊖ Liverpool Street – ℰ (020) 7961 1234 – www.andazdining.com
34ARTt
264 rm – †£ 144/516 ††£ 372/600, ⊇ £ 22 – 3 suites
Rest *1901* – see restaurant listing
Rest *Catch* – see restaurant listing
Rest *Miyako* – Japanese – ℰ (020) 7618 7100 *(closed Saturday lunch and Sunday) (booking essential)* Carte £ 23/52

♦ A contemporary and stylish interior hides behind the classic Victorian façade. Bright and spacious bedrooms with state-of-the-art facilities. Various dining options include Miyako, a compact Japanese restaurant, and a traditional pub.

Threadneedles
5 Threadneedle St. ⊠ EC2R 8AY ⊖ Bank – ℰ (020) 7657 8080 – www.theetoncollection.com
34ARUy
68 rm – †£ 222/414 ††£ 294/546, ⊇ £ 23 – 1 suite
Rest *Bonds* – see restaurant listing

♦ A converted bank, dating from 1856, with a stunning stained-glass cupola in the lounge. Bedrooms are very stylish and individual featuring CD players and Egyptian cotton sheets.

Montcalm London City at The Brewery
52 Chiswell St ⊠ EC1Y 4SD ⊖ Moorgate – ℰ (020) 7614 0100 – www.themontcalmlondoncity.co.uk
19VZDr
220 rm – †£ 300/540 ††£ 300/540, ⊇ £ 20 – 18 suites
Rest *Chiswell Street Dining Rooms* – see restaurant listing

♦ The majority of the contemporary rooms are in the original part of the Whitbread Brewery, built in 1752; ask for a quieter room overlooking the courtyard, or one of the 25 found in one of the 4 restored Georgian townhouses across the road.

CITY OF LONDON

XXX Rhodes Twenty Four
Tower 42, (24th floor) 25 Old Broad St. — EC2N 1HQ — Liverpool Street
– ℰ (020) 7877 7703 – www.rhodes24.co.uk – Closed Christmas-New Year,
Saturday, Sunday and bank holidays **34ARTv**
Rest – British – Carte £ 45/65
Spec. Scallop raviolo with buttered samphire. Steamed mutton and onion suet pudding with carrots. Warm chocolate pudding, passion fruit sorbet.
♦ Prepare for security checks at Tower 42 before taking the lift up to its 24th floor; the views will be worth it. The unmistakeable signature of Gary Rhodes is writ large on the menu: seasonal dishes of a pleasingly British persuasion.

XXX Coq d'Argent
1 Poultry — EC2R 8EJ — Bank – ℰ (020) 7395 5000 – www.coqdargent.co.uk
– Closed 25-27 December, 1 January, Saturday lunch, Sunday dinner and bank holidays **33AQUc**
Rest – French – (booking essential) Menu £ 32 (lunch) – Carte £ 36/45
♦ Resembling the bow of a ship; with a busy bar, terrace and formal garden providing commanding views over the Square Mile. Slick, well run, modern restaurant; appealing shellfish counter.

XXX 1901 – at Andaz Liverpool Street Hotel
Liverpool St. — EC2M 7QN — Liverpool Street – ℰ (020) 7618 7000
– www.andaz.com – Closed Saturday lunch, Sunday and bank holidays
Rest – French – Menu £ 25 (lunch) – Carte £ 32/52 **34ARTt**
♦ An impressive and imposing room, with an eye-catching cupola, cocktail bar and cheese and wine room. Kitchen makes proud use of British ingredients in refined and skilled cooking.

XXX Bonds – at Threadneedles Hotel
5 Threadneedle St. — EC2R 8AY — Bank – ℰ (020) 7657 8088
– www.theetoncollection.com – Closed Saturday, Sunday and Bank Holidays
Rest – Modern European – Menu £ 23 (lunch and early dinner) **34ARUy**
– Carte £ 37/51
♦ Former banking hall from the 1850s, with pillars, marble and panelling. Experienced kitchen produces dishes with bold flavours; fish from Newhaven and slow-cooked meats the specialities.

XXX Lutyens
85 Fleet St. — EC4Y 1AE — St Paul's – ℰ (020) 7583 8385
– www.lutyens-restaurant.com – Closed 1 week Christmas, Saturday, Sunday and bank holidays **32ANUc**
Rest – Modern European – Menu £ 40 (dinner) – Carte £ 40/55
♦ The unmistakable hand of Sir Terence Conran: timeless and understated good looks mixed with functionality and an appealing Anglo-French menu with plenty of classics that include fruits de mer.

XX Club Gascon (Pascal Aussignac)
57 West Smithfield — EC1A 9DS — Barbican – ℰ (020) 7796 0600
– www.clubgascon.com – Closed Christmas - New Year, Saturday lunch, Sunday and bank holidays **33APTz**
Rest – French – (booking essential) Menu £ 29 (lunch) – Carte £ 50/69
Spec. Line-caught mackerel, pine, abalone and oyster sorbet. Charolais beef variation, caviar and ox sauce. Turrón, sweet foie gras, Baileys, baby meringues and passion fruit.
♦ The gastronomy of Gascony and France's southwest are the starting points but the assured and intensely flavoured cooking also pushes at the boundaries. Marble and huge floral displays create suitably atmospheric surroundings.

CITY OF LONDON

XX The Chancery
9 Cursitor St ✉ EC4A 1LL ⊖ Chancery Lane – ℰ (020) 7831 4000
– www.thechancery.co.uk – Closed 24 December-4 January, Saturday lunch and Sunday
32ANT**a**
Rest – Modern European – Menu £ 35
♦ Cosy restaurant and basement bar, near the Law Courts, with contemporary interior and intimate feel. Quality ingredients put to good use in accomplished, modern dishes.

XX Mint Leaf Lounge
12 Angel Ct., Lothbury ✉ EC2R 7HB ⊖ Bank – ℰ (020) 7600 0992
– www.mintleaflounge.com – Closed 25-26 December, Saturday, Sunday and bank holidays
33AQT**b**
Rest – Indian – Menu £ 18 (lunch and early dinner) – Carte £ 38/60
♦ Sister branch to the original in St James's. Slick and stylish, with busy bar. Well paced service of carefully prepared contemporary Indian food, with many of the influences from the south.

XX Vivat Bacchus
47 Farringdon St (basement) ✉ EC4A 4LL ⊖ Farringdon – ℰ (020) 7353 2648
– www.vivatbacchus.co.uk – Closed 25 December, 1 January, Saturday, Sunday and bank holidays
32ANT**c**
Rest – Traditional – Menu £ 18 – Carte £ 28/60
♦ Platters and tapas served in the large bar; more intimate basement restaurant for meat dishes and South African specialities. Hugely impressive wine list with five cellars of wine.

XX Vanilla Black
17-18 Tooks Ct. ✉ EC4A 1LB ⊖ Chancery Lane – ℰ (020) 7242 2622
– www.vanillablack.co.uk – Closed 2 weeks Christmas-New Year, Saturday lunch and Sunday
32ANT**x**
Rest – Vegetarian – Menu £ 24/33
♦ Proving that vegetarian food can be flavoursome and satisfying, with a menu that is varied and imaginative. This is a well run, friendly restaurant with understated décor, run by a husband and wife team.

XX Cinnamon Kitchen
9 Devonshire Sq ✉ EC2M 4YL ⊖ Liverpool Street – ℰ (020) 7626 5000
– www.cinnamon-kitchen.com – Closed Saturday lunch, Sunday and bank holidays
34ART**e**
Rest – Indian – Menu £ 18/22 – Carte £ 31/56
♦ Sister to The Cinnamon Club. Contemporary Indian cooking, with punchy flavours and arresting presentation. Sprightly service in large, modern surroundings. Watch the action from the Tandoor Bar.

XX Kenza
10 Devonshire Sq. ✉ EC2M 4YP ⊖ Liverpool Street – ℰ (020) 7929 5533
– www.kenza-restaurant.com – Closed Saturday lunch, Sunday and bank holidays
34ART**c**
Rest – Lebanese – Carte £ 26/33
♦ Exotic basement restaurant, with lamps, carvings, pumping music and nightly belly dancing. Lebanese and Moroccan cooking are the menu influences and the cooking is authentic and accurate.

XX Sauterelle
The Royal Exchange ✉ EC3V 3LR ⊖ Bank – ℰ (020) 7618 2483
– www.sauterelle-restaurant.co.uk – Closed Saturday, Sunday and bank holidays,
Rest – French – Menu £ 24 – Carte £ 35/53
33AQU**a**
♦ Impressive location on the mezzanine floor of The Royal Exchange; ask for a table looking down over the Grand Café. A largely French inspired contemporary menu makes good use of luxury ingredients.

CITY OF LONDON

XX Cigalon
115 Chancery Ln ⊠ WC2A 1PP ⊖ Chancery Lane – ℘ (020) 7242 8373
– www.cigalon.co.uk – Closed 24 December-3 January, Saturday, Sunday and bank holidays
32ANUx
Rest – French – Menu £ 25 (lunch) – Carte £ 26/31
♦ Pays homage to the food and wine of Provence, in an appropriately bright space that was a once an auction house. All the classics are here, from bouillabaisse to pieds et paquets. Busy bar in the cellar.

XX The Mercer
34 Threadneedle St ⊠ EC2R 8AY ⊖ Bank – ℘ (020) 7628 0001
– www.themercer.co.uk – Closed 25 December, Saturday, Sunday and bank holidays
34ARUx
Rest – Modern European – Carte £ 28/37
♦ Converted bank, with airy feel thanks to high ceilings and large windows. Brasserie style menu with appealing mix of classics and comfort food. Huge choice of wines available by glass or carafe.

XX Boisdale of Bishopsgate
Swedeland Crt., 202 Bishopsgate ⊠ EC2M 4NR ⊖ Liverpool Street
– ℘ (020) 7283 1763 – www.boisdale.co.uk – Closed 25 December-2 January, Saturday, Sunday and bank holidays
34ARTa
Rest – Scottish – Carte £ 28/52
♦ Through ground floor bar, serving oysters and champagne, to brick vaulted basement with red and tartan décor. Menu featuring Scottish produce. Live jazz most evenings.

XX The White Swan
108 Fetter Lane ⊠ EC4A 1ES ⊖ Chancery Lane – ℘ (020) 7242 9696
– www.thewhiteswanlondon.com – Closed 25-26 December, Saturday, Sunday and bank holidays
32ANTn
Rest – Modern European – Menu £ 30 (lunch) – Carte £ 28/34
♦ Smart dining room above pub just off Fleet Street: mirrored ceilings, colourful paintings on walls. Modern, daily changing menus, are good value for the heart of London.

XX Manicomio
6 Gutter Ln. ⊠ EC2V 8AS ⊖ St Paul's – ℘ (020) 7726 5010
– www.manicomio.co.uk – Closed 1 week Christmas, Saturday, Sunday and bank holidays
33APTs
Rest – Italian – Carte £ 31/54
♦ Second branch to follow the first in Chelsea. Regional Italian fare, with top-notch ingredients. Bright and fresh first floor restaurant, with deli-café on the ground floor and bar on top floor.

XX Luc's Brasserie
17-22 Leadenhall Market ⊠ EC3V 1LR ⊖ Bank – ℘ (020) 7621 0666
– www.lucsbrasserie.com – Closed 23 December-3 January, Saturday, Sunday and bank holidays
34ARUv
Rest – French – (lunch only and dinner Tuesday-Thursday) (booking essential at lunch) Menu £ 20 – Carte £ 27/42
♦ Looks down on the Victorian splendour of Leadenhall Market. First appeared in 1890 but re-invigorated this century. The menu is a paean to all things French and every classic dish is there.

XX Barbecoa
20 New Change Passage ⊠ EC4M 9AG ⊖ St. Paul's – ℘ (020) 3005 8555
– www.barbecoa.com
33APUv
Rest – Grills – (booking essential) Carte £ 28/45
♦ American chef Adam Perry Lane, in collaboration with our own Jamie Oliver, shows us what barbecuing is all about. The prime meats, butchered in-house, are cooked to perfection; go for the pulled pork shoulder with cornbread on the side.

High Timber

8 High Timber St. ✉ EC4V 3PA ⊖ Mansion House – ✆ (020) 7248 1777
– www.hightimber.com – Closed 25 December-4 January, Saturday, Sunday and bank holidays
33APU**b**
Rest – Modern European – Menu £ 19 (lunch) – Carte £ 25/55

♦ Rustic look to the room, despite being in a modern block, offering river views. Great wine cellar, with large choice from South Africa, the owners' homeland. Cumbrian steaks the speciality.

Goodman City

11 Old Jewry ✉ EC2R 8DU ⊖ Bank – ✆ (020) 7600 8220
– www.goodmanrestaurants.com – Closed Saturday, Sunday and bank holidays
Rest – Beef specialities – Menu £ 21 (lunch) – Carte £ 48/68
33AQU**s**

♦ Steaks, cut to order, are the stars of the show at this sister to the Mayfair original. Choose corn-fed, wet-matured USDA beef or Scottish and Irish grass-fed; plenty of side dishes available too.

Chiswell Street Dining Rooms – at Montcalm London City Hotel

56 Chiswell St ✉ EC1Y 4SA ⊖ Moorgate – ✆ (020) 7614 0177 – www.chiswellstreetdining.com
19VZD**r**
Rest – British – Carte £ 30/52

♦ The Martin brothers used their Botanist restaurant as the model for this corner of the old Whitbread brewery. The cocktail bar comes alive at night. Makes good use of British produce, especially fish from nearby Billingsgate.

Catch – at Andaz Liverpool Street Hotel

40 Liverpool St. ✉ EC2M 7QN ⊖ Liverpool Street – ✆ (020) 7618 7200
– www.andazdining.com – Closed Saturday and Sunday
34ART**t**
Rest – Seafood – Carte £ 34/60

♦ The seafood counter forms the striking centrepiece at Catch, which is located in what was once the lobby of this Victorian hotel. You decide on the cooking method for the catch of the day.

Amico Bio

44 Cloth Fair ✉ EC1A 7JQ ⊖ Barbican – ✆ (0207) 600 77 78
– www.amicobio.co.uk – Closed 25 December, Saturday lunch, Sunday and bank holidays
33APT**v**
Rest – Italian vegetarian – Carte £ 21/26

♦ Simple little place owned by an experienced chef and his cousin; the organic produce comes from the family farm in Capua and the combination of flavours remain true to their upbringing in Campania.

Paternoster Chop House

Warwick Ct., Paternoster Sq. ✉ EC4M 7DX ⊖ St Paul's – ✆ (020) 7029 9400
– www.paternosterchophouse.com – Closed 24 December-1 January, Saturday, Sunday dinner and bank holidays
33APT**x**
Rest – British – Menu £ 27 – Carte £ 32/57

♦ Appropriately British menu in a restaurant lying in the shadow of St Paul's Cathedral. Large, open room with full-length windows; busy bar attached. Kitchen uses thoughtfully sourced produce.

Cellar Gascon

59 West Smithfield ✉ EC1A 9DS ⊖ Barbican – ✆ (020) 7600 7561
– www.cellargascon.com – Closed 22 December-4 January, Saturday, Sunday and bank holidays
33APT**c**
Rest – French – (booking essential at lunch) Carte £ 14/19

♦ It's not unlike a smart tapas bar and the monthly changing menu has plenty of treats: pâtés, rillettes, hams, cheeses and even some salads for the virtuous; but the Toulouse sausages and the Gascony pie stand out.

CITY OF LONDON

28°-50°

140 Fetter Ln ✉ EC4A 1BT ⊖ Temple – ✆ (020) 7242 8877 – www.2850.co.uk
– Closed Saturday, Sunday and bank holidays
Rest – French – Menu £ 22 (lunch) – Carte £ 26/30

32ANUs

♦ Subterranean wine bar and informal restaurant, from the same owners as Texture. Robust, mostly French dishes accompany a thoughtfully assembled wine list, with much choice by the glass.

Restaurant at St Paul's Cathedral

St Paul's Churchyard ✉ EC4M 8AD ⊖ St. Paul's – ✆ (020) 7248 2469
– www.restaurantatstpauls.co.uk – Closed 25 December
Rest – British – (lunch only) (booking advisable) Menu £ 26

33APUs

♦ Tucked away in a corner of the crypt of Sir Christopher Wren's 17C masterpiece. The kitchen prepares everything from scratch and celebrates all things British, including drinks.

Bar Battu

48 Gresham St ✉ EC2V 7AY ⊖ Bank – ✆ (020) 7036 6100
– www.barbattu.com – Closed 24 December-2 January, Saturday, Sunday and bank holidays
Rest – French – Menu £ 20 – Carte £ 24/38

33AQTx

♦ Captures the zeitgeist with its bare brick interior and appealing menu of small plates and rustic main courses. It is also a self-styled 'natural wine bar' and features unfiltered wines made from organically grown grapes.

Goldfish City

46 Gresham St. ✉ EC2V 7AY ⊖ Bank – ✆ (020) 7726 0308
– www.goldfish-resaturant.co.uk – Closed Saturday, Sunday and bank holidays
Rest – Asian – (booking advisable) Carte £ 19/30

33AQUx

♦ Busy at lunch thanks to the selection of well-priced steamed dim sum. Balanced main menu mixes the classic with the modern. Spread over three floors, with discreet décor and helpful service.

LONDON

CROYDON – Greater London

12 B3

SOUTH CROYDON

Cassoulet

18 Selsdon Rd. ✉ CR2 6PA – ✆ (020) 8633 1818 – www.lecassoulet.co.uk
– Closed 25-26 December
Rest – French – Menu £ 19/30

7FZv

♦ Evolving, seasonal set menus offer a range of traditional and more modern French dishes, with wider choice at dinner. Chic and elegant interior; carefully run, with attentive service.

Albert's Table

49b South End ✉ CR0 1BF – ✆ (020) 8680 2010 – www.albertstable.co.uk
– Closed Sunday dinner and Monday
Rest – Modern European – Menu £ 20/32

7FZx

♦ The accomplished cooking defined by its well-judged flavours is somewhat at odds with the decoration, which is a touch sparse. The owner-chef has an impressive pedigree and his restaurant, named after his grandfather, deserves to succeed.

EALING – Greater London

12 A3

West Middlesex Southall Greenford Rd, ✆ (020) 8574 34 50

Horsenden Hill Woodland Rise

EALING

ACTON GREEN

✗✗ Le Vacherin
76-77 South Par. ✉ W4 5LF ⊖ Chiswick Park – ☎ (020) 8742 2121
– www.levacherin.com – Closed 25 December and Sunday dinner
Rest – French – *(dinner only and lunch Saturday-Sunday)*
Menu £ 20 (weekdays)/35 – Carte £ 20/40

6CVo

♦ Authentic feel to this comfortable brasserie, with its brown leather banquette seating, mirrors and belle époque prints. French classics from snails to duck confit; beef is a speciality.

🍺 Bollo
13-15 Bollo Ln. ✉ W4 5LR ⊖ Chiswick Park. – ☎ (020) 8994 6037
– www.thebollohouse.co.uk
Rest – Traditional – Carte £ 20/31

6CVz

♦ Large Victorian pub with original glass cupola and oak panelling. Menu is a mix of generous pub classics and dishes with a southern Mediterranean influence. Look out for quiz nights and promotions.

🍺 Duke of Sussex
75 South Par. ✉ W4 5LF ⊖ Chiswick Park. – ☎ (020) 8742 8801
– www.realpubs.co.uk – Closed dinner 25 December and Monday lunch
Rest – Mediterranean – Carte £ 23/28

6CVo

♦ Bustling Victorian pub, whose striking dining room was once a variety theatre complete with proscenium arch. Stick to the Spanish dishes; stews and cured meats are the specialities. BYO on Mondays.

EALING

✗ Charlotte's Place
16 St Matthew's Rd. ✉ W5 3JT ⊖ Ealing Common – ☎ (020) 8567 7541
– www.charlottes.co.uk – Closed 26 December-4 January
Rest – Modern European – Menu £ 16/26 (early dinner) – Carte £ 28/32

2CVc

♦ Warmly run neighbourhood restaurant opposite the Common; divided between bright ground floor room and cosier downstairs. Menu mixes British and Mediterranean influences. Planning to move to another site in Ealing as we went to print.

✗ Kiraku
8 Station Par., Uxbridge Rd. ✉ W5 3LD ⊖ Ealing Common – ☎ (020) 8992 2848 – www.kiraku.co.uk – Closed 10 days Christmas-New Year, 10 days August, Tuesday following bank holidays and Monday
Rest – Japanese – Carte £ 17/33

2CVv

♦ The name of this cute little Japanese restaurant means 'relax and enjoy'; easy with such charming service. Extensive menu includes zensai, skewers, noodles, rice dishes and assorted sushi.

GREENWICH – Greater London

12 B3

✗✗ Inside
19 Greenwich South St. ✉ SE10 8NW ⊖ Greenwich (DLR) – ☎ (020) 8265 5060
– www.insiderestaurant.co.uk – Closed 24 December-2 January, Sunday dinner and Monday
Rest – Modern European – Menu £ 18 (weekday lunch)/23 – Carte dinner £ 21/26

7GXx

♦ Inside is tidy, comfortable and uncluttered, although it does take a few diners to generate an atmosphere. On offer is a well-priced set menu, with quite elaborate, largely European cooking.

GREENWICH

Rivington Grill
178 Greenwich High Rd. ⊠ SE10 8NN ↔ Greenwich (DLR) – ℘ (020) 8293 9270 – www.rivingtongreenwich.co.uk – Closed 25-26 December, Monday and lunch Tuesday-Wednesday
7GV**s**
Rest – British – Carte £ 25/39
- Part of the Picturehouse complex; 21C rustic interior with closely set tables. Firmly English menus in bar and galleried restaurant. Banquets and market breakfasts on offer.

HACKNEY – Greater London 12 B3

HACKNEY

Cat & Mutton
76 Broadway Mkt. ⊠ E8 4QJ ↔ Bethnal Green. – ℘ (020) 7254 5599 – www.catandmutton.co.uk – Closed 25-26 December and Sunday dinner
Rest – British – Menu £ 15 (dinner) – Carte £ 24/34 **14**YZB**a**
- The pub's lived-in look, music and relaxed vibe attract a young, local crowd. Satisfying pub food, from a weekly changing menu, delivers on flavour. Regular quiz nights and art classes.

Prince Arthur
95 Forest Rd. ⊠ E8 3BH ↔ Bethnal Green. – ℘ (020) 7249 9996 – www.theprincearthurlondonfields.com – Closed 25-26 December **14**XZB**c**
Rest – British – (dinner only and lunch Saturday-Sunday) Carte £ 26/41
- An intimate local pub for local people, with plenty of character. Unpretentious and heart-warming menu, with classics like a pint of prawns and cottage pie; filling puddings.

HOXTON

The Hoxton
81 Great Eastern St. ⊠ EC2A 3HU ↔ Old Street – ℘ (020) 7550 1000 – www.hoxtonhotels.com **20**XZD**x**
208 rm – †£ 70/358, ††£ 70/358, ⊇ £ 12
Rest *Hoxton Grill* – see restaurant listing
- Urban lodge: industrial styled, clean lined modernism. "No rip-offs" mantra: cheap phone rate, free internet, complimentary 'lite Pret' breakfast. Carefully considered rooms and an appealing laid-back vibe.

Great Eastern Dining Room
54 Great Eastern St ⊠ EC2A 3QR ↔ Old Street – ℘ (020) 7613 4545 – www.rickerrestaurants.com – Closed Saturday lunch and Sunday
Rest – Asian – Menu £ 20 (lunch and early dinner) **20**XZD**n**
– Carte £ 22/39
- Half the place is a bar that's heaving in the evening. Dining area has candle-lit tables, contemporary chandeliers, and carefully prepared, seriously tasty pan-Asian cooking.

Fifteen London
15 Westland Pl. ⊠ N1 7LP ↔ Old Street – ℘ (020) 3375 1515 – www.fifteen.net – Closed 24-26 December **13**VZC**c**
Rest – Italian – (booking essential) Menu £ 30 (lunch) – Carte dinner £ 29/48
- Original branch of Jamie Oliver's charitable restaurants; run by trainees alongside full-time staff. Buzzy ground floor trattoria; more formal basement restaurant. Tasty, seasonal Italian food.

Hoxton Grill – at The Hoxton Hotel
81 Great Eastern St. ⊠ EC2A 3HU ↔ Old Street – ℘ (020) 7550 1000 – www.hoxtonhotels.com **20**XZD**x**
Rest – American – Carte £ 28/44
- A young, hip crowd has colonised this large, open-plan space which comes with a discernible New York feel. Burgers, salads, steaks and smoothies keep the open kitchen busy all day.

HACKNEY

SHOREDITCH

XXX Boundary with rm
2-4 Boundary St. ✉ E2 7DD – Old Street – ☏ (020) 7729 1051
– www.theboundary.co.uk – Closed Sunday dinner
12 rm – †£ 192 ††£ 192, ☐ £ 10 – 5 suites
Rest – French – *(dinner only and lunch Saturday-Sunday)* Menu £ 25 (lunch)
– Carte £ 28/56

20XZDb

◆ Sir Terence Conran has taken a warehouse and created a 'caff' with a bakery and shop, a rooftop terrace and a stylish, good-looking French restaurant serving plenty of cross-Channel classics. Comfy and individual bedrooms.

XXX L' Anima
1 Snowden St. ✉ EC2A 2DQ – Liverpool Street – ☏ (0207) 422 70 00
– www.lanima.co.uk – Closed 25 December, Saturday lunch, Sunday and bank holidays
Rest – Italian – *(booking essential)* Menu £ 37 (lunch) – Carte £ 35/63

20XZDa

◆ Very handsome room, with limestone and leather creating a sophisticated, glamorous environment. Appealing menu is a mix of Italian classics and less familiar dishes, with the emphasis firmly on flavour. Service is smooth and personable.

XX Lena
66 Great Eastern St. ✉ EC2A 3JT – Old Street – ☏ (020) 7739 5714
– www.lenarestaurant.com – Closed 25 December, 1 January and Sunday lunch
Rest – Italian – Menu £ 14 (lunch) – Carte £ 21/34

20XZDc

◆ Named after the owner's mother and eclectically decorated using leather, wood, plastic and ceramics. Menu looks to southern Italy for influences. Live jazz in the stylish bar at weekends.

X Rivington Grill
28-30 Rivington St. ✉ EC2A 3DZ – Old Street – ☏ (020) 7729 7053
– www.rivingtonshoreditch.co.uk – Closed 25-26 December
Rest – British – Carte £ 26/48

20XZDe

◆ Very appealing 'back to basics' British menu, with plenty of comforting classics including a section 'on toast'. This converted warehouse is popular with the local community of artists.

🍺 Princess of Shoreditch
76-78 Paul St. ✉ EC2A 4NE – Old Street. – ☏ (020) 7729 9270
– www.theprincessofshoreditch.com – Closed 24-26 December
Rest – Traditional – Menu £ 18 (lunch) – Carte £ 25/32

19VZDa

◆ Pies and platters in the busy ground floor bar; more ambitious but still flavoursome European-influenced cooking in the calmer upstairs room. Friendly service a feature.

HAMMERSMITH and FULHAM – Greater London   12 B3

FULHAM

XX Mao Tai
58 New Kings Rd., Parsons Green ✉ SW6 4LS – Parsons Green
– ☏ (020) 7731 2520 – www.maotai.co.uk – Closed 25-27 December
Rest – Chinese – *(dinner only and Sunday lunch)* Carte £ 31/55

22NZHe

◆ Influences from across China inform the modern menu of this stylish, long-standing Chinese restaurant. Divided into two rooms; the front section with the cocktail bar is the more animated.

XX Manson
676 Fulham Rd. ✉ SW6 5SA – Parsons Green – ☏ (020) 7384 9559
– www.mansonrestaurant.co.uk – Closed 25-26 December and Sunday dinner
Rest – British – *(booking advisable)* Menu £ 18 (lunch and early dinner) – Carte £ 26/36

22MZHx

◆ Slight Left Bank aesthetic, with smoked mirrors and 1930s French street lamps. Pleasant, breezy service. Cooking also has a French bias and displays more sophistication than one expects.

HAMMERSMITH and FULHAM

XX Blue Elephant
4-6 Fulham Broadway ⊠ SW6 1AA ⊖ Fulham Broadway – ℰ (020) 7385 6595
– www.blueelephant.com – Closed 24-27 December and 1 January
Rest – Thai – *(booking essential)* Menu £ 20/37 – Carte £ 42/60   **22**NZG**z**

♦ A London institution, with a gloriously unrestrained décor of plants, streams and bridges. Carefully prepared dishes from across Thailand. Curries are a strength and service is well-meaning.

X Tendido Cuatro
108-110 New Kings Road ⊠ SW6 4LY ⊖ Parsons Green – ℰ (020) 7371 5147
– www.cambiodetercio.co.uk   **22**NZH**x**
Rest – Spanish – Carte £ 21/49

♦ Along with tapas, the speciality is paella. Designed for a hungry two, they vary from seafood to quail and chorizo; cuttlefish ink to vegetarian. Vivid colours used with abandon deck out the busy room.

🍺 Harwood Arms ✥
Walham Grove ⊠ SW6 1QP ⊖ Fulham Broadway. – ℰ (020) 7386 1847
– www.harwoodarms.com – Closed 26-29 August, 25-28 December, 1 January and Monday lunch   **22**NZG**a**
Rest – British – *(booking essential)* Carte £ 30/34 ✥
Spec. Rabbit, prune and bacon faggots with celeriac purée and Horn of Plenty mushrooms. Glazed Aylesbury duck leg and Douglas fir sausage with a beetroot tart. Chilled rice pudding, strawberries and Grasmere gingerbread.

♦ Its reputation may have spread like wildfire but this remains a proper, down-to-earth pub that just happens to serve really good food. The cooking is very seasonal, proudly British, full of flavour and doesn't seem out of place in this environment. Service is suitably relaxed and friendly.

🍺 My dining room
18 Farm Ln ⊠ SW6 1PP ⊖ Fulham Broadway. – ℰ (020) 7381 3331
– www.mydiningroom.net   **22**NZG**r**
Rest – French – Menu £ 14/20 – Carte £ 21/37

♦ A modern bar, a chic dining room and a French owner; this is truly a gastropub of our time. There's plenty of choice from the French rustic menu and lots of wines served by the glass.

🍺 Sands End
135-137 Stephendale Rd. ⊠ SW6 2PR ⊖ Fulham Broadway. – ℰ (020) 7731 7823 – www.thesandsend.co.uk – Closed 25-26 December   **22**OZH**r**
Rest – British – *(booking advisable)* Carte £ 32/42

♦ Cosy, warm and welcoming little corner pub, offering appealing bar snacks and a thoughtfully put-together menu with a British bias. Game is handled deftly and ingredients are well-sourced.

HAMMERSMITH

XX River Café (Ruth Rogers) ✥
Thames Wharf, Rainville Rd ⊠ W6 9HA ⊖ Barons Court – ℰ (020) 7386 4200
– www.rivercafe.co.uk – Closed Christmas, Sunday dinner and bank holidays
Rest – Italian – *(booking essential)* Carte £ 49/78 ✥   **21**LZG**v**
Spec. Crab linguini. Sea bass baked in salt with salsa verde. Chocolate Nemesis.

♦ It's all about the natural flavours of some superlative ingredients. The on-view kitchen with its wood-fired oven dominates the stylish riverside room; the contagiously effervescent atmosphere is helped along by very charming service.

XX Indian Zing
236 King St. ⊠ W6 0RF ⊖ Ravenscourt Park – ℰ (020) 8748 5959
– www.indianzing.co.uk – Closed dinner 25 December   **21**LZG**a**
Rest – Indian – Menu £ 15 (lunch) – Carte £ 25/35

♦ The enthusiastic chef-owner offers well-judged, flavoursome and quite refined Indian cooking from across all parts of the country. Colourful surroundings; keen, if slightly disorganised, service.

HAMMERSMITH and FULHAM

Azou
375 King St. ⊠ W6 9NJ ⊖ Stamford Brook – ℘ (020) 8563 7266
– www.azou.co.uk – Closed 25 December, 1 January and bank holidays
Rest – North African – *(dinner only and lunch Saturday-Sunday)*
(booking essential) Carte £ 23/35

21KZGu

♦ Silks, lanterns and rugs add to the atmosphere of this personally run, North African restaurant. Most come for the excellent tajines, with triple steamed couscous. Much is designed for sharing.

Anglesea Arms
35 Wingate Rd. ⊠ W6 0UR ⊖ Ravenscourt Park. – ℘ (020) 8749 1291
– www.anglesea-arms.com – Closed 25-27 December
Rest – British – *(bookings not accepted)* Carte £ 20/52

15LZEc

♦ Busy wood-panelled bar; brighter, calmer rear dining room with part-glass roof and exposed kitchen. Regularly changing blackboard menu; expect robust cooking with a strong British bias.

Havelock Tavern
57 Masbro Rd., Brook Grn. ⊠ W14 0LS ⊖ Kensington Olympia. – ℘ (020) 7603 5374 – www.havelocktavern.com – Closed 25-26 December
Rest – Traditional – *(bookings not accepted)* Carte £ 21/30 **s**

16MZEe

♦ Warm, friendly and atmospheric pub with easygoing service and pleasantly mixed clientele. Blackboard menu offers robust, satisfying pub food. Arrive early if you don't want to wait for a table.

Dartmouth Castle
26 Glenthorne Rd. ⊠ W6 0LS ⊖ Hammersmith. – ℘ (020) 8748 3614
– www.thedartmouthcastle.co.uk – Closed 24 December-2 January and Saturday lunch
Rest – Mediterranean – Carte £ 18/31

21LZFe

♦ The Mediterranean exerts quite an influence on the large menu at this popular, welcoming and traditional pub. Spread over two levels but the ground floor is the more atmospheric.

Crabtree
4 Rainville Rd. ⊠ W6 9HA ⊖ Barons Court. – ℘ (020) 7385 3929
– www.thecrabtreeW6.co.uk
Rest – Modern European – Carte £ 24/34

21LZGx

♦ With a beer garden for 200 and a separate dining room terrace, this Victorian pub makes great use of its riverside location. Parfaits and terrines are highlights but Veggies are also considered.

SHEPHERD'S BUSH

Princess Victoria
217 Uxbridge Rd. ⊠ W12 9DH ⊖ Shepherd's Bush. – ℘ (020) 8749 5886
– www.princessvictoria.co.uk – Closed 24-28 December
Rest – Traditional – Menu £ 13 (lunch) – Carte £ 21/34

15KZEa

♦ Magnificent Victorian gin palace, with original plasterwork. The kitchen knows its butchery; pork board, homemade sausages and terrines all feature. Excellent wine list, with over 350 bottles.

HARINGEY – Greater London
12 B3

CROUCH END

Bistro Aix
54 Topsfield Par., Tottenham Ln. ⊠ N8 8PT – ℘ (020) 8340 6346
– www.bistroaix.co.uk – Closed 1 January
Rest – French – *(dinner only and lunch Saturday-Sunday)* Carte £ 23/32

3EUv

♦ Dressers, cabinets and contemporary artwork lend an authentic Gallic edge to this bustling bistro. Traditionally prepared French classics are the highlights of an extensive menu.

Queens Pub and Dining Room

26 Broadway Par. ⊠ N8 9DE – ℘ (020) 8340 2031
– www.thequeenscrouchend.co.uk   **3EUc**
Rest – British – Carte £ 24/29

• Striking example of a classic Victorian pub, from the original mahogany panelling to the stained glass windows and ornate ceiling. Traditional British comfort dishes are the highlights of the menu.

FORTIS GREEN

Clissold Arms

105 Fortis Green ⊠ N2 9HR ⊖ East Finchley. – ℘ (020) 8444 4224
– www.clissoldarms.co.uk   **3EUa**
Rest – Modern European – Carte £ 18/30

• Reputedly the venue for The Kinks' first gig. Now modernised throughout, with a large rear terrace. Interesting menus, with terrines, whole sea bass and 28-day aged steaks the specialities.

HIGHGATE

Rose and Crown

86 Highgate High St. ⊠ N6 5HX ⊖ Archway – ℘ (020) 8340 0770
– www.roseandcrownhighgate.co.uk – Closed Sunday dinner and Monday lunch
Rest – Modern European – Menu £ 15/18 – Carte £ 26/34   **2EUi**

• Converted pub, smartly kitted out but not overly formal thanks to genial staff. Seasonally changing, European-influenced cooking, with competitively priced weekly-changing set menu.

A restaurant name printed in red denotes a Rising Star - an establishment showing great potential. It is in line for a higher award: a star or an additional star. They are included in the list of starred establishments at the beginning of the guide.

HARROW – Greater London   12 A3

HARROW ON THE HILL

Incanto

41 High St. ⊠ HA1 3HT ⊖ Harrow on the Hill – ℘ (020) 8426 6767
– www.incanto.co.uk – Closed 25-26 December, 1 January, Easter
Sunday, Monday and dinner Sunday   **1BUz**
Rest – Italian – Menu £ 22/24 – Carte £ 29/45

• Within Grade II former post office; split-level restaurant to rear of well stocked deli. Well-paced service; Southern Italian bias to the rustic cooking, with quality produce to the fore.

PINNER

Friends

11 High St. ⊠ HA5 5PJ ⊖ Pinner – ℘ (020) 8866 0286
– www.friendsrestaurant.co.uk – Closed Sunday dinner, Monday and bank
holidays   **1BUa**
Rest – Modern European – Menu £ 25/33

• Pretty beamed cottage, with some parts dating back 400 years. Inside, a welcoming glow from the log fire; personal service from owners and a fresh, regularly-changing menu.

HILLINGDON – Greater London 12 A3
Haste Hill Northwood The Drive, ✆ (01923) 82 52 24

HEATHROW AIRPORT

Sofitel
Terminal 5, Heathrow Airport ✉ TW6 2GD ⊖ Heathrow Terminal 5
– ✆ (020) 8757 7777 – www.sofitel.com
578 rm – †£ 155/475 ††£ 155/475, ⊇ £ 21 – 27 suites
5AXa
Rest *La Belle Époque* – French – Menu £ 26 – Carte £ 27/39
Rest *Vivre* – Menu £ 25 (dinner) – Carte £ 26/50
♦ Smart and well-run contemporary hotel, opened in 2008. Designed around a series of atriums, with direct access to T5. Crisply decorated, comfortable bedrooms with luxurious bathrooms. Choice of restaurant: international or classical French cuisine.

Hilton London Heathrow Airport
Terminal 4 ✉ TW6 3AF ⊖ Heathrow Terminal 4
– ✆ (020) 8759 7755 – www.hilton.co.uk/heathrow
355 rm ⊇ – †£ 197/329 ††£ 251/395 – 5 suites
5AXn
Rest *Zen Oriental* – see restaurant listing
Rest *Aromi* – (closed lunch Saturday, Sunday and bank holidays) (buffet lunch) Menu £ 21/29 – Carte £ 29/54
♦ Group hotel with a striking modern exterior and linked to Terminal 4 by a covered walkway. Good-sized bedrooms, with contemporary styled suites. Casual dining in Aromi which occupies part of the vast atrium.

London Heathrow Marriott
Bath Rd., Hayes ✉ UB3 5AN ⊖ Heathrow Terminal 1,2,3
– ✆ (020) 8990 1100 – www.londonheathrowmarriott.co.uk
391 rm – †£ 202 ††£ 202, ⊇ £ 17.95 – 2 suites
5AXz
Rest *Tuscany* – Italian – (dinner only) Carte £ 31/49
Rest *Allie's grille* – Menu £ 13 (lunch) – Carte £ 30/49
♦ Built at the end of 20C, this modern, comfortable hotel is centred around a large atrium, with comprehensive business facilities: there is an exclusive Executive floor. Italian cuisine in bright and convivial Tuscany. Grill favourites in Allie's.

✗ **Zen Oriental** – at Hilton London Heathrow Airport Hotel
Terminal 4 ✉ TW6 3AF ⊖ Heathrow Terminal 4
– ✆ (020) 8564 9609 – www.hilton.co.uk/heathrow – Closed 25-26 December
Rest – Asian – Menu £ 34/47 – Carte £ 27/50
5AXn
♦ With its appealing menu of classics and capable service, Zen Oriental has long been a favourite at the Hilton. Popular for business lunches; the atmosphere is more relaxed at dinner.

HOUNSLOW – Greater London 12 A3
ℹ High St ✆ (0845) 456 29 29, www.hounslow.inuklocal.co.uk
Wyke Green Isleworth Syon Lane, ✆ (020) 8560 87 77
Airlinks Southall Lane, ✆ (020) 8561 14 18
Hounslow Heath, Staines Rd, ✆ (020) 8570 52 71

BRENTFORD

London Syon Park
Park Rd. ✉ TW7 6AZ – ✆ (020) 7870 777
– www.londonsyonpark.com
5BXx
136 rm – †£ 478 ††£ 478, ⊇ £ 18.50 – 1 suite
Rest *Capability* – Menu £ 22 (lunch) – Carte £ 32/48
♦ Opened in 2011, no expense was spared with this purpose-built, resort-style hotel. It's in the grounds of Syon House, home to the Duke and Duchess of Northumberland, and run by Hilton under their Waldorf Astoria brand. Ask for a room overlooking the walled garden. British produce features in the restaurant.

CHISWICK

Moran
626 Chiswick High Rd. ⌂ *W4 5RY* – *Gunnersbury* – ✆ *(020) 8996 5200*
– *www.moranhotels.com*
123 rm – †£ 230 ††£ 230/335, ☕ £ 10
Rest *Napa* – Menu £ 17/25 **s** – Carte £ 30/39 **s**

♦ Converted office block with all-glass exterior, midway between Heathrow and West End. Decorated in a restrained contemporary style with bright and airy bedrooms. Two-tiered restaurant with terrace and modern menu.

High Road House
162 Chiswick High Rd ⌂ *W4 1PR* – *Turnham Green* – ✆ *(020) 8742 7474*
– *www.highroadhouse.co.uk*
14 rm – ††£ 105/195, ☕ £ 10.50
Rest *High Road Brasserie* – see restaurant listing

♦ Cool, sleek hotel and club, the latter a slick place to lounge around or play games. Light, bright bedrooms with crisp linen. A carefully appointed, fairly-priced destination.

La Trompette
5-7 Devonshire Rd ⌂ *W4 2EU* – *Turnham Green* – ✆ *(020) 8747 1836*
– *www.latrompette.co.uk* – Closed 24-26 December
Rest – Modern European – *(booking essential)* Menu £ 26/40
Spec. Scallops with pea purée, hispi cabbage and bayonne ham. Corn-fed chicken with morel ragoût, shallots, broad beans and macaroni. Strawberry shortbread and sorbet with Chantilly cream.

♦ Enthusiastically run and smart neighbourhood restaurant, sister to Chez Bruce. Small front terrace and light, comfortable interior. Balanced menu and confident kitchen produce robust, spirited dishes. Wine list varied in price and geography.

Michael Nadra
6-8 Elliott Rd. ⌂ *W4 1PE* – *Turnham Green* – ✆ *(020) 8742 0766*
– *www.restaurant-michaelnadra.co.uk* – Closed Sunday dinner and Monday
Rest – Modern European – Menu £ 24/35

♦ Enough regulars now appreciate the chef-owner's well-judged cooking for him to finally put his own name above the door of this intimate, friendly restaurant. Balanced and sensibly priced menu.

Charlotte's Bistro
6 Turnham Green Terr ⌂ *W4 1QP* – *Turnham Green* – ✆ *(020) 8742 3590*
– *www.charlottes.co.uk*
Rest – Modern European – *(booking advisable)* Menu £ 16/26 (early dinner) – Carte £ 28/31

♦ A pleasant, unpretentious bistro; run by a friendly team, with a well-priced menu of flavoursome, well prepared dishes of largely European provenance. Little sister to Charlotte's Place in Ealing.

High Road Brasserie – at High Road House Hotel
162 Chiswick High Rd. ⌂ *W4 1PR* – *Turnham Green* – ✆ *(020) 8742 7474*
– *www.highroadhouse.co.uk*
Rest – Traditional – *(booking essential)* Menu £ 16 (lunch) – Carte £ 20/42

♦ Authentic brasserie, with mirrors, panelling and art deco lighting. Despite the high volume of customers, the classic dishes are prepared with care and staff cope well with being busy.

Sam's Brasserie
11 Barley Mow Passage ⌂ *W4 4PH* – *Turnham Green* – ✆ *(020) 8987 0555*
– *www.samsbrasserie.co.uk* – Closed 23-28 December
Rest – Mediterranean – Menu £ 17 (weekday lunch)/19 (weekday dinner) – Carte £ 29/35

♦ A former Sanderson wallpaper mill, now a bustling, fun brasserie with Sir Peter Blake artwork adding to the hip feel. Appealing, modern menu; satisfying dishes deliver on flavour. Look out for regular Soul and Jazz evenings.

HOUNSLOW

🛏️ Devonshire Arms   🍴 VISA ⓪

126 Devonshire Rd ✉ W4 2JJ ⊖ Turnham Green. – ☏ (020) 8742 2302
– www.devonshirearmspub.com   **21**KZG**x**
Rest – Modern European – *(booking advisable)* Carte £ 20/25

◆ Those behind the Drapers Arms in Islington are now at the helm of this characterful local and it's had a makeover true to its Edwardian roots. The menu changes twice daily; dishes are vibrant and appealing, with influences from the Med.

ISLINGTON – Greater London   **12** B3

ARCHWAY

🍴 500   VISA ⓪ AE

782 Holloway Rd ✉ N19 3JH ⊖ Archway – ☏ (020) 7272 3406
– www.500restaurant.co.uk – Closed 2 weeks summer, 2 weeks Christmas-New Year and lunch Monday-Thursday   **12**SZA**y**
Rest – Italian – *(booking essential)* Carte £ 21/25

◆ Small, fun and well-priced Italian that's always busy. Good pastas and bread; the veal chop and rabbit are specialities. The passion of the ebullient owner and keen chef are evident.

🛏️ St John's Tavern   🍴 VISA ⓪ AE

91 Junction Rd ✉ N19 5QU ⊖ Archway. – ☏ (020) 7272 1587
– www.stjohnstavern.com – Closed 25-26 December and 1 January
Rest – Modern – *(dinner only and lunch Friday-Sunday) (booking advisable at dinner)* Carte £ 24/33   **12**RZA**s**

◆ Daily changing menu in the dining room at the back of the pub. Cosy atmosphere, with dark colours and fireplace. Rustic cooking from open kitchen and blackboard menu.

BARNSBURY

🍴🍴 Morgan M   A/C VISA ⓪ ⓪

489 Liverpool Rd. ✉ N7 8NS ⊖ Highbury & Islington – ☏ (020) 7609 3560
– www.morganm.com – Closed 24-30 December, Monday, Sunday dinner and lunch Tuesday and Saturday   **13**UZA**a**
Rest – French – Menu £ 29/43

◆ Classic, full flavoured French dishes, seasonal specialities and a separate vegetarian menu ensures a loyal crowd of regulars at this formally run restaurant, set within a converted pub.

🍴🍴 Roots at N1   A/C VISA ⓪

115 Hemingford Rd ✉ N1 1BZ ⊖ Caledonian Road – ☏ (020) 7697 4488
– www.rootsatn1.com – Closed 25-26 December and Monday   **13**UZB**d**
Rest – Indian – *(dinner only) (booking essential)* Menu £ 23 – Carte £ 25/39

◆ Opening their own place was the dream of these three friends from India. Their warm, friendly restaurant is known for its refreshingly short menu; tandoori lamb chops and Rogan Josh are the highlights.

🍴 Fig Bistro   🍴 VISA ⓪ ⓪

169 Hemingford Rd. ✉ N1 1DA ⊖ Caledonian Road – ☏ (020) 7609 3009
– www.figbistro.co.uk – Closed 25-26, 31 December, 1 January and Sunday dinner   **13**UZB**a**
Rest – Modern European – *(dinner only and Sunday lunch)* Carte £ 19/31

◆ Charming service and flavoursome cooking displaying a degree of refinement belie the 'bistro' name. The compact candlelit room is appealingly frayed and the atmosphere very welcoming.

ISLINGTON

CANONBURY

Trullo
300-302 St Paul's Rd. ✉ N1 2LH ⊖ Highbury & Islington – ℰ (020) 7226 2733
– www.trullorestaurant.com – Closed 23 December-2 January, Sunday dinner and Monday
13UZB**t**
Rest – Italian – *(dinner only and lunch Saturday-Sunday) (booking essential)*
Carte £ 25/32

♦ Great value Italian food that delivers on flavour ensures that this friendly and relaxed restaurant is always full of contented diners. Terrific antipasti and the charcoal grill dishes are favourites.

Canonbury Kitchen
19 Canonbury Ln ✉ N1 2AS ⊖ Highbury & Islington – ℰ (0207) 226 97 91
– www.canonburykitchen.com – Closed Monday
13UZB**c**
Rest – Italian – *(dinner only and lunch Saturday-Sunday)* Carte £ 24/31

♦ A bright, local Italian with seating for just 40; exposed brick walls and painted floorboards add to the fresh feel. The kitchen keeps things simple and the menu pricing is prudent.

House
63-69 Canonbury Rd ✉ N1 2DG ⊖ Highbury & Islington. – ℰ (020) 7704 7410
– www.thehouse.islington.com – Closed Monday except bank holidays
Rest – Modern European – Carte £ 20/30
13UZB**h**

♦ A smart looking pub with an attractive terrace; but one that still feels like a genuine local. The cooking is crisp and confident and there's an emphasis on good quality, organic ingredients.

CLERKENWELL

Malmaison
18-21 Charterhouse Sq ✉ EC1M 6AH ⊖ Barbican – ℰ (020) 7012 3700
– www.malmaison.com
19UZD**q**
97 rm – ♦£ 282/390 ♦♦£ 318/570, ☕ £ 18.50
Rest *Brasserie* – *(closed Saturday lunch)* Carte £ 29/41

♦ Striking early 20C red-brick building overlooking pleasant square. Stylish, comfy public areas. Bedrooms in vivid, bold colours, with plenty of extra touches. Modern brasserie employing meats from Smithfield.

The Rookery without rest
12 Peters Ln, Cowcross St ✉ EC1M 6DS ⊖ Barbican – ℰ (020) 7336 0931
– www.rookeryhotel.com – Closed 24-26 December
32 rm – ♦£ 222/282 ♦♦£ 246/282, ☕ £ 11.95 – 1 suite
33AOT**p**

♦ A row of charmingly restored 18C houses. Wood panelling, stone-flagged flooring, open fires and antique furniture. Highly individual bedrooms, with Victorian bathrooms.

Larder
91-93 St John St. ✉ EC1M 4NU ⊖ Farringdon – ℰ (020) 7608 1558
– www.thelarderrestaurant.com – Closed 23 December-3 January, Saturday lunch, Sunday and bank holidays
19UZD**f**
Rest – Modern European – Menu £ 15 (lunch) – Carte £ 26/37

♦ Large, glass-fronted restaurant with stark, noisy, industrial feel and own bakery selling breads and pastries. Unfussy food has an English accent with some European influences.

Redhook
89 Turnmill St ✉ EC1M 5QU ⊖ Farringdon – ℰ (020) 7065 6800
– www.redhooklondon.com – Closed Easter, 25 December, Saturday lunch and Sunday
19UZD**a**
Rest – Beef specialities – *(booking advisable at dinner)* Menu £ 18 (lunch)
– Carte £ 24/41

♦ Brooklyn comes to Clerkenwell in the shape of this American-style restaurant specialising in seafood and steaks. Bare brick walls, booths and a faux industrial aesthetic add to the New York feel.

ISLINGTON

North Road (Christoffer Hruskova)
*69-73 St John St ⊠ EC1M 4AN ⊖ Farringdon – ℰ (020) 3217 0033
– www.nrrestaurant.com – Closed 23 December- 2 January, Saturday lunch and Sunday* **19UZDh**
Rest – Modern European – Menu £ 20 (lunch) – Carte £ 32/41
Spec. Scallops with sea buckthorn, malt bread and wild herbs. Whey-poached turbot, asparagus and green strawberries. Yoghurt 'in textures and temperatures'.
- Owner-chef's Danish roots are evident in his clean, crisp cooking, which uses sous-vide techniques, little or no butter or cream and is fully respectful of the seasons. Coolly designed, elegantly understated room provides the ideal backdrop.

St John
*26 St John St ⊠ EC1M 4AY ⊖ Farringdon – ℰ (020) 3301 8069
– www.stjohnrestaurant.com – Closed Christmas-New Year, Saturday lunch, Sunday dinner and bank holidays,* **33APTk**
Rest – British – *(booking essential)* Carte £ 26/44
Spec. Roast bone marrow and parsley salad with toasted bread and wet salt. Braised rabbit, peas and bacon. Ginger loaf and butterscotch sauce with vanilla ice cream.
- 'Nose to tail eating' is how they describe their cooking at this busy, bright, converted 19C smokehouse. Strong on offal, game and unusual cuts; gloriously British, highly seasonal, appealingly simple and very satisfying.

Comptoir Gascon
*61-63 Charterhouse St. ⊠ EC1M 6HJ ⊖ Farringdon – ℰ (020) 7608 0851
– www.comptoirgascon.com – Closed 24 December-4 January, Sunday and Monday* **33AOTa**
Rest – French – *(booking essential)* Carte £ 24/36
- Buzzy restaurant; sister to Club Gascon. Rustic and satisfying specialities from the SW of France include wine, cheese, bread and especially duck. Further produce on display to take home.

Bistro du Vin
*40 St John St ⊠ EC1M 4DL ⊖ Farringdon – ℰ (020) 7490 9230
– www.bistroduvinandbar.com* **33APTt**
Rest – Modern European – Carte £ 26/45
- They've nailed the bistro aesthetic and oenologists will be in clover, so there's no arguing with the name. Beef dishes are the stand outs – dry-cured in-house and cooked in a Josper grill.

Hix Oyster and Chop House
*36-37 Greenhill Rents ⊠ EC1M 6BN ⊖ Farringdon
– ℰ (020) 7017 1930 – www.hixoysterandchophouse.co.uk
– Closed 25-29 December* **33AOTe**
Rest – British – Menu £ 18 (lunch and early dinner) – Carte £ 26/50
- Appropriately utilitarian surroundings put the focus on seasonal and often underused British ingredients. Cooking is satisfying and unfussy, with plenty of oysters and aged beef served on the bone.

Vinoteca
*7 St John St. ⊠ EC1M 4AA ⊖ Farringdon – ℰ (020) 7253 8786
– www.vinoteca.co.uk – Closed Christmas-New Year, Sunday and bank holidays*
Rest – Modern European – *(bookings not accepted at dinner)* **33APTa**
Carte £ 27/35
- This cosy and passionately run 'bar and wine shop' is always busy and full of life. Thrilling wine list is constantly evolving; the classic and vibrant dishes are the ideal accompaniment.

FINSBURY

Zetter
St John's Sq., 86-88 Clerkenwell Rd. — EC1M 5RJ — Farringdon
– (020) 7324 4444 – www.thezetter.com
72 rm – †£ 222 ††£ 222/480, ☕ £ 9.50   **19**UZD**s**
Rest *Bistrot Bruno Loubet* – see restaurant listing
♦ A trendy and discreet converted 19C warehouse with well-equipped bedrooms that come with pleasant touches, such as Penguin paperbacks. The more idiosyncratic Zetter Townhouse across the square is used as an overflow.

Bistrot Bruno Loubet – at Zetter Hotel
St John's Sq., 86-88 Clerkenwell Rd. — EC1M 5RJ — Farringdon
– (020) 7324 4455 – www.bistrotbrunoloubet.com – Closed 25-26 December
Rest – French – *(booking advisable)* Carte £ 30/40   **19**UZD**s**
♦ Having made his name in the early '90s, Bruno Loubet's London return was much anticipated. His flavoursome regional French cooking proves a good fit for this busy, bright restaurant at the Zetter hotel.

Moro
34-36 Exmouth Mkt — EC1R 4QE — Farringdon – (020) 7833 8336
– www.moro.co.uk – Closed Christmas-New Year and Sunday   **19**UZD**m**
Rest – Mediterranean – *(booking essential)* Carte £ 29/36
♦ Daily changing menu an eclectic mix of Mediterranean, Moroccan and Spanish. Friendly T-shirted staff. Informal surroundings with bare tables and a large zinc bar.

Medcalf
40 Exmouth Mkt. — EC1R 4QE — Farringdon – (020) 7833 3533
– www.medcalfbar.co.uk – Closed 31 December-3 January, Sunday dinner and bank holidays   **19**UZD**m**
Rest – British – *(booking essential)* Carte £ 24/32
♦ Bustling, no-frills former butcher's shop with lively atmosphere. Satisfying robust cooking, with the emphasis on seasonal, British ingredients. Good range of beer and wine by the glass.

Cicada
132-134 St John St. — EC1V 4JT — Farringdon – (020) 7608 1550
– www.rickerrestaurants.com – Closed 25 December, 1 January, Saturday lunch and Sunday   **19**UZD**d**
Rest – Asian – Carte £ 24/34
♦ Set in a culinary hotbed, this buzzy restaurant and vibrant bar is spacious, lively and popular for its south east Asian dishes. You can even just pop in for one course and a beer.

The Modern Pantry
47-48 St John's Sq. — EC1V 4JJ — Farringdon – (020) 7553 9210
– www.themodernpantry.co.uk – Closed 25-26 December and 29 August
Rest – International – *(booking advisable)* Carte £ 35/39   **19**UZD**k**
♦ Fusion cooking that uses complementary flavours to create vibrant, zesty dishes. The simple, crisp ground floor of this Georgian building has the buzz; upstairs is more intimate. Clued-up service.

Morito
32 Exmouth Mkt — EC1R 4QE — Farringdon – (020) 7278 7007 – Closed Christmas-New Year, Sunday and bank holidays   **19**UZD**b**
Rest – Spanish – Carte approx. £ 21
♦ From the owners of next door Moro comes this authentic and appealingly down to earth little tapas bar. Seven or eight dishes between two should suffice but over-ordering is easy and won't break the bank.

ISLINGTON

Caravan ✗
*11-13 Exmouth Mkt ⊠ EC1R 4QD ⊖ Farringdon – ℰ (020) 7833 8115
– www.caravanonexmouth.co.uk – Closed Christmas-New Year and dinner Sunday*
19UZD**c**

Rest – International – *(booking advisable)* Carte £ 24/31

♦ A discernible Antipodean vibe pervades this casual eatery, from the laid-back charm of the service to the kitchen's confident combining of unusual flavours. Cooking is influenced by owner's travels – hence the name.

Clerkenwell Kitchen ✗
*27-31 Clerkenwell Cl ⊠ EC1R 0AT ⊖ Farringdon – ℰ (020) 7101 9959
– www.theclerkenwellkitchen.co.uk – Closed Christmas-New Year, Saturday, Sunday and bank holidays*
19UZD**v**

Rest – Modern European – *(lunch only) (booking advisable)* Carte approx. £ 19

♦ The owner of this simple, friendly, tucked away eatery worked with Hugh Fearnley-Whittingstall and is committed to sustainability. Daily changing, well-sourced produce; fresh, flavoursome cooking.

Green 🍴
*29 Clerkenwell Gn ⊠ EC1R 0DU ⊖ Farringdon. – ℰ (020) 7490 8010
– www.thegreenec1.co.uk – Closed 25-30 December*
19UZD**z**

Rest – British – Carte £ 24/34

♦ The building dates from 1580 and became a tavern in 1720. Appetising and imaginative bar snacks on the ground floor; intimate upstairs dining room for fresh, seasonal and unfussy cooking.

Peasant 🍴
*240 St John St ⊠ EC1V 4PH ⊖ Farringdon. – ℰ (020) 7336 7726
– www.thepeasant.co.uk – Closed 25 December-1 January and bank holidays except Good Friday*
19UZD**e**

Rest – British – *(booking essential)* Carte £ 23/30

♦ This handsome Victorian pub was at the vanguard of the gastropub movement. Busy bar with its tiles and mosaics; upstairs for a less frantic environment and wholesome British cooking.

Well 🍴
*180 St John St ⊠ EC1V 4JY ⊖ Farringdon. – ℰ (020) 7251 9363
– www.downthewell.com – Closed 25-26 December*
19UZD**x**

Rest – British – Carte £ 23/33

♦ Compact pub with sliding glass doors and popular pavement benches. Modern dishes range from potted shrimps to foie gras and chicken liver parfait. Classic puddings; splendid cheeses.

HIGHBURY

Au Lac ✗
*82 Highbury Park ⊠ N5 2XE ⊖ Arsenal – ℰ (020) 7704 9187
– Closed 1-2 January and 24-26 December*
13UZA**b**

Rest – Vietnamese – *(dinner only and lunch Thursday-Friday)* Carte £ 10/23

♦ Cosy Vietnamese restaurant, with brightly coloured walls and painted fans. Large menus with authentic dishes usefully highlighted. Fresh flavours; good value.

ISLINGTON

Almeida ✗✗
*30 Almeida St. ⊠ N1 1AD ⊖ Angel – ℰ (020) 7354 4777
– www.almeida-restaurant.co.uk – Closed Sunday dinner and Monday lunch*

Rest – French – Menu £ 19/34 – Carte £ 35/55
13UZB**r**

♦ Crisply decorated restaurant dating from 1891. Classically inspired menus with plenty of choice; good value lunch. Interesting French regional wines. Overwhelmingly busy pre/post theatre.

ISLINGTON

Ottolenghi
287 Upper St. ✉ N1 2TZ – Highbury & Islington – ℘ (020) 7288 1454
– www.ottolenghi.co.uk – Closed 25-26 December, dinner Sunday and bank holidays
13UZB**k**
Rest – Mediterranean – *(booking essential)* Carte £ 20/45
♦ This attractive deli morphs into a little restaurant at night, with communal tables and chatty service. Fresh, flavoursome dishes with influences from across all parts of the Med.

Drapers Arms
44 Barnsbury St ✉ N1 1ER – Highbury & Islington. – ℘ (020) 7619 0348
– www.thedrapersarms.com
13UZB**x**
Rest – British – *(booking advisable at dinner)* Carte £ 24/32
♦ Expect satisfying and robust British cooking at this handsome Georgian pub. Prices are kept at reasonable levels for both the appealingly understated menu and the wine list. The ground floor is more fun than the upstairs room.

Barnsbury
209-211 Liverpool Rd ✉ N1 1LX – Highbury & Islington. – ℘ (020) 7607 5519
– www.thebarnsbury.co.uk – Closed 24-26 December
13UZB**v**
Rest – Traditional – *(dinner only and lunch Friday-Sunday)* Carte £ 20/35
♦ Expect generous portions of gutsy cooking at this genuine neighbourhood pub, with friendly and attentive service. Sit in the more atmospheric bar rather than in the dining area at the back.

Northgate
113 Southgate Rd ✉ N1 3JS – Dalston Kingsland (rail). – ℘ (020) 7359 7392
– Closed 1 January
13VZB**a**
Rest – Mediterranean – *(dinner only and lunch Saturday-Sunday)* Carte £ 20/29
♦ Cavernous corner pub; busy front bar with tables laid for dining at the back. Large blackboard menu lists mostly Mediterranean-influenced dishes with the emphasis on flavour. Relaxed service.

KING'S CROSS

Fellow
24 York Way ✉ N1 9AA – King's Cross St Pancras. – ℘ (020) 7833 4395
– www.thefellow.co.uk – Closed 25 December and Sunday dinner
12SZB**x**
Rest – Modern European – Carte £ 26/33
♦ Busy, atmospheric pub close to the station with a youthful, local clientele. Confident cooking on the ground floor displays a lightness of touch; boisterous upstairs cocktail bar.

KENSINGTON and CHELSEA (Royal Borough of)   12 B3
– Greater London

CHELSEA

Jumeirah Carlton Tower
Cadogan Pl. ✉ SW1X 9PY – Knightsbridge – ℘ (020) 7235 1234 – www.jumeirahcarltontower.com
37AGX**r**
186 rm – †£ 276/900 ††£ 276/900, ⊇ £ 37 – 30 suites
Rest *Rib Room* – see restaurant listing
♦ Imposing international hotel overlooking a leafy square and just yards from all the swanky boutiques. Well-equipped rooftop health club has great views. Generously proportioned bedrooms boast every conceivable facility.

Wyndham Grand
Chelsea Harbour ✉ SW10 0XG – Imperial Wharf (rail)
– ℘ (020) 7823 3000 – www.wyndhamgrandlondon.co.uk
23PZG**k**
158 suites – ††£ 192/425, ⊇ £ 23
Rest *Chelsea Riverside Brasserie* – Carte £ 25/43
♦ Modern, all-suite hotel within an exclusive marina and retail development. Many of the spacious and well-appointed rooms have balconies and views across the Thames. Modern restaurant overlooks the harbour.

KENSINGTON and CHELSEA

Sheraton Park Tower
101 Knightsbridge ✉ *SW1X 7RN* ⊖ *Knightsbridge* – ✆ *(020) 7235 8050*
– www.luxurycollection.com/parktowerlondon
275 rm – †£ 516/642 ††£ 516/774, ⌑ £ 26 – 5 suites **37**AGX**t**
Rest *One-O-One* – see restaurant listing

• Built in the 1970s in a unique cylindrical shape. Well-equipped bedrooms are all identical in size. Top floor executive rooms have commanding views of Hyde Park and City.

The Capital
22-24 Basil St. ✉ *SW3 1AT* ⊖ *Knightsbridge* – ✆ *(020) 7589 5171*
– www.capitalhotel.co.uk
49 rm – †£ 294/420 ††£ 294/420, ⌑ £ 19.50 – 1 suite **37**AFX**a**
Rest *The Capital Restaurant* – see restaurant listing

• In 2011 this thoroughly British hotel celebrated 40 years under the same private ownership. Immaculately kept bedrooms from a number of different designers, a discreet atmosphere and conscientious, attentive service are the hallmarks.

Draycott
26 Cadogan Gdns. ✉ *SW3 2RP* ⊖ *Sloane Square* – ✆ *(020) 7730 6466*
– www.draycotthotel.com
24 rm – †£ 168/312 ††£ 282/312, ⌑ £ 20.95 – 11 suites **37**AGY**c**
Rest – (room service only)

• Charming 19C house with elegant sitting room overlooking tranquil garden for afternoon tea. Bedrooms are individually decorated in a country house style and are named after writers or actors.

The Cadogan
75 Sloane St ✉ *SW1X 9SG* ⊖ *Knightsbridge* – ✆ *(020) 7235 7141*
– www.cadogan.com
64 rm – †£ 478 ††£ 538, ⌑ £ 27.50 **37**AGY**b**
Rest *Langtry's* – (closed Sunday dinner) Menu £ 20 – Carte £ 28/58

• An Edwardian townhouse, made famous by two former residents – Oscar Wilde and Lillie Langtry. Quiet drawing room for afternoon tea; bedrooms are varied and comfortable. Restaurant offers a traditional menu.

Knightsbridge
10 Beaufort Gdns ✉ *SW3 1PT* ⊖ *Knightsbridge* – ✆ *(020) 7584 6300*
– www.knightsbridgehotel.com
44 rm – †£ 216/276 ††£ 384/774, ⌑ £ 19 **Rest** – (room service only) **37**AFX**s**

• Attractively furnished townhouse with a very stylish, discreet feel. Every bedroom is immaculately appointed and has an individuality of its own; fine detailing throughout.

Egerton House
17-19 Egerton Terr. ✉ *SW3 2BX* ⊖ *South Kensington* – ✆ *(020) 7589 2412*
– www.egertonhousehotel.com
27 rm – †£ 336/408 ††£ 420/732, ⌑ £ 29.50 – 1 suite **37**AFY**e**
Rest – (room service only)

• Compact but comfortable townhouse in a very good location, well maintained throughout and owned by the Red Carnation group. High levels of personal service make the hotel stand out.

The Levin
28 Basil St. ✉ *SW3 1AS* ⊖ *Knightsbridge* – ✆ *(020) 7589 6286*
– www.thelevinhotel.co.uk
12 rm – †£ 300/384 ††£ 300/384 **37**AFX**c**
Rest *Le Metro* – see restaurant listing

• A discreet townhouse and sister to The Capital hotel next door. Impressive façade, contemporary interior and comfortable bedrooms in subtle art deco style, boasting marvellous champagne mini bars.

KENSINGTON and CHELSEA

Beaufort
33 Beaufort Gdns ✉ SW3 1PP ⊖ Knightsbridge – ✆ (020) 7584 5252
– www.thebeaufort.co.uk   **37**AFX**n**
29 rm – †£ 216/360 ††£ 288/600, ☕ £ 16   **Rest** – *(room service only)*
♦ A vast collection of English floral watercolours adorn this 19C townhouse in a useful location. Modern and co-ordinated rooms. Tariff includes all drinks and afternoon tea.

Sydney House *without rest*
9-11 Sydney St. ✉ SW3 6PU ⊖ South Kensington – ✆ (020) 7376 7711
– www.sydneyhousechelsea.com – Closed 25-26 December   **36**ADY**s**
21 rm – †£ 125/225 ††£ 155/255, ☕ £ 12.95
♦ Stylish and compact Georgian townhouse made brighter through plenty of mirrors and light wood. Thoughtfully designed bedrooms; Room 43 has its own terrace. Part of the Abode group.

The Sloane Square
7-12 Sloane Sq. ✉ SW1W 8EG ⊖ Sloane Square – ✆ (020) 7896 9988
– www.sloanesquarehotel.co.uk   **37**AGY**k**
102 rm – †£ 234/288 ††£ 288/448, ☕ £ 16
Rest *Chelsea Brasserie* – see restaurant listing
♦ Well-placed, red-brick hotel boasts bright, contemporary décor. Stylish, co-ordinated bedrooms, with laptops; library of DVDs and games available. Rooms at the back are slightly quieter.

Gordon Ramsay
68-69 Royal Hospital Rd. ✉ SW3 4HP ⊖ Sloane Square – ✆ (020) 7352 4441
– www.gordonramsay.com – Closed Christmas, Saturday and Sunday
Rest – French – *(booking essential)* Menu £ 45/90   **37**AFZ**c**
Spec. Ravioli of lobster, langoustine and salmon with a lemongrass and chervil velouté. Best end of lamb with confit breast, braised shank and a navarin of spring vegetables. Granny Smith parfait with a blackberry foam, honeycomb and cider sorbet.
♦ Head Chef Clare Smyth has brought a lighter, more instinctive style to the cooking while still delivering on the Gordon Ramsay classics. The elegant simplicity of the room exudes calmness; service is equally composed and well-organised.

Bibendum
Michelin House, 81 Fulham Rd. ✉ SW3 6RD ⊖ South Kensington – ✆ (020) 7581 5817 – www.bibendum.co.uk – Closed 24-26 December and 1 January
Rest – French – Menu £ 30 (lunch) – Carte £ 36/63   **37**AEY**s**
♦ Has maintained a loyal following for over 20 years, with its French food that comes with a British accent. Located on the 1st floor of a London landmark – Michelin's former HQ, dating from 1911.

The Capital Restaurant – *at The Capital Hotel*
22-24 Basil St. ✉ SW3 1AT ⊖ Knightsbridge – ✆ (020) 7591 1202
– www.capitalhotel.co.uk   **37**AFX**a**
Rest – French – *(booking essential)* Menu £ 30 (lunch) – Carte £ 46/70
♦ Elegant surroundings, formal service and elaborately presented, classic cuisine have featured at the family-owned Capital for many years. It is also known for its superlative wine list.

Fifth Floor – *at Harvey Nichols*
109-125 Knightsbridge ✉ SW1X 7RJ ⊖ Knightsbridge – ✆ (020) 7235 5250
– www.harveynichols.com – Closed Easter Sunday, 25 December and Sunday dinner   **37**AGX**s**
Rest – Modern European – Carte £ 35/55
♦ Modern cooking with influences kept mostly from within Europe. Stylish and elegant, tent-like room with sophisticated bar attached; reached via its own elevator. Prompt service.

KENSINGTON and CHELSEA

XXX Toto's
Walton House, Walton St. ✉ *SW3 2JH* ⊖ *Knightsbridge* – ✆ *(020) 7589 0075*
– Closed 25-27 December **37AFYx**
Rest – Italian – *(booking essential at dinner)* Menu £ 23 (lunch) – Carte £ 35/47
♦ A long standing Chelsea institution, with old school service and plenty of local regulars who add to the discreet atmosphere. Familiar and satisfying dishes, with homemade pasta the highlight.

XXX Awana
85 Sloane Ave. ✉ *SW3 3DX* ⊖ *South Kensington* – ✆ *(020) 7584 8880*
– www.awana.co.uk – Closed 25-26 December, 1 January and dinner 24 December **37AFYb**
Rest – Malaysian – *(booking essential)* Menu £ 15 (lunch) – Carte £ 24/58
♦ Smart and stylish restaurant showcasing Malaysia's rich culinary diversity. The 'Malaysian Journey' menu provides a good introduction. If without a booking, consider sitting at the Satay Bar.

XXX Chutney Mary
535 King's Rd. ✉ *SW10 0SZ* ⊖ *Fulham Broadway* – ✆ *(020) 7351 3113*
– www.realindianfood.com – Closed dinner 25 December **22OZGv**
Rest – Indian – *(dinner only and lunch Saturday-Sunday)* Menu £ 22 (weekdays) – Carte £ 38/53
♦ Soft lighting and sepia etchings hold sway at this forever popular restaurant. Extensive menu of specialities from all corners of India. Complementary wine list.

XXX One-O-One – at Sheraton Park Tower Hotel
101 Knightsbridge ✉ *SW1X 7RN* ⊖ *Knightsbridge* – ✆ *(020) 7290 7101*
– www.oneoonerestaurant.com **37AGXt**
Rest – Seafood – Menu £ 22 (lunch) – Carte £ 55/75
♦ Smart ground floor restaurant; lacking a little in atmosphere but the seafood is good. Much of the produce from Brittany and Norway; don't miss the King crab legs. Small tasting plates also offered.

XXX Eleven Park Walk
11 Park Walk ✉ *SW10 0AJ* ⊖ *South Kensington* – ✆ *(020) 7352 3449*
– www.11parkwalk.co.uk – Closed 25 December **36ACZz**
Rest – Italian – Carte £ 34/58
♦ What was Aubergine is now a sophisticated Italian; its menu traverses the country but it is the Sardinian specialities that shine. It attracts an equally smart set who appreciate the polished service.

XXX Rib Room – at Jumeirah Carlton Tower Hotel
Cadogan Pl. ✉ *SW1X 9PY* ⊖ *Knightsbridge* – ✆ *(020) 7235 1234*
– www.jumeirahcarltontower.com **37AGXr**
Rest – British – Menu £ 36/50 – Carte £ 61/88
♦ Rib of Aberdeen Angus, steaks and other classic British dishes attract a prosperous, international crowd; few of whom appear to have a beef with the prices at this swish veteran.

XX Rasoi (Vineet Bhatia) ✿
10 Lincoln St ✉ *SW3 2TS* ⊖ *Sloane Square* – ✆ *(020) 7225 1881*
– www.rasoirestaurant.co.uk – Closed 25-26 December and Saturday lunch
Rest – Indian – Menu £ 27/59 – Carte £ 59/85 **37AFYy**
Spec. Tandoori lobster with chilli and wasabi, lentil and lobster soup. Smoked rack of lamb with biryani khichdi. Chocolate craving platter.
♦ Vineet Bhatia proves that Indian food can be just as open to interpretation as other cuisines. You'll find his exotically decorated yet intimate dining room sitting somewhat incongruously within an archetypal Chelsea townhouse.

KENSINGTON and CHELSEA

XX Le Colombier
VISA ◎ AE
145 Dovehouse St. ⊠ SW3 6LB ⊖ South Kensington – ℰ (020) 7351 1155
– www.le-colombier-restaurant.co.uk **36ADZe**
Rest – French – Menu £ 27 (lunch) – Carte £ 32/51

♦ Proudly Gallic corner restaurant in an affluent residential area. Attractive enclosed terrace. Bright and cheerful surroundings and service of traditional French cooking.

XX Racine
AC 🅥 VISA ◎ AE
239 Brompton Rd ⊠ SW3 2EP ⊖ South Kensington – ℰ (020) 7584 4477
– www.racine-restaurant.com – Closed Christmas **37AEYt**
Rest – French – Menu £ 18 (lunch and early dinner) – Carte £ 30/55

♦ An authentic feel to this French brasserie, with dark leather seats, wood floors and mirrors. The menu provides a roll-call of classic regional specialities, from steak tartare to fruits de mer.

XX Medlar
🍴 AC ⇔ VISA ◎ AE
438 King's Rd ⊠ SW10 0LJ ⊖ Sloane Square – ℰ (020) 7349 1900
– www.medlarrestaurant.co.uk – Closed Sunday dinner and Monday
Rest – Modern European – Menu £ 25/38 **23PZGx**

♦ Two young owners have created a charming local spot; David provides warm but unobtrusive service; Joe, a Chez Bruce alumnus, concentrates on matching flavours. His set menu showcases cooking with a French base but a lighter touch.

XX Daphne's
AC ⇔ VISA ◎ AE ①
112 Draycott Ave. ⊠ SW3 3AE ⊖ South Kensington – ℰ (020) 7589 4257
– www.daphnes-restaurant.co.uk – Closed 25-26 December **37AFYj**
Rest – Italian – (booking essential) Menu £ 20 (lunch and early dinner) – Carte £ 30/46

♦ Established over 40 years ago and a Chelsea institution with 'celebrity' following. Reliable formula of tried and tested Italian classics in a room with a warm, Tuscan feel.

XX Poissonnerie de l'Avenue
AC ⇔ VISA ◎ AE ①
82 Sloane Ave. ⊠ SW3 3DZ ⊖ South Kensington – ℰ (020) 7589 2457
– www.poissonneriedelavenue.com – Closed Easter and 25-26 December
Rest – Seafood – Menu £ 30 (lunch) – Carte £ 31/48 **37AFYu**

♦ A smart, personally run, wood-panelled Chelsea institution since 1946. Its extensive choice of carefully prepared, traditional seafood dishes attracts a smart and loyal following.

XX Eight over Eight
AC ⇔ VISA ◎ AE ①
392 King's Rd ⊠ SW3 5UZ ⊖ Gloucester Road – ℰ (020) 7349 9934
– www.rickerrestaurants.com – Closed 25-28 December **23PZGn**
Rest – Asian – Carte £ 24/50

♦ Reopened in 2010 after a fire, with a slightly plusher feel; still as popular as ever with the fashionable crowds. Influences stretch across South East Asia and dishes are designed for sharing.

XX Bluebird
AC 🅥 ⇔ VISA ◎ AE ①
350 King's Rd. ⊠ SW3 5UU ⊖ Sloane Square – ℰ (020) 7559 1000
– www.bluebird-restaurant.co.uk **23PZGn**
Rest – British – Menu £ 25 – Carte £ 26/49

♦ Former industrial space incorporates everything from a wine store to a private members club. Large, buzzy restaurant champions British produce in an appealing menu that has something for everyone.

XX Le Cercle
AC VISA ◎ AE ①
1 Wilbraham Pl. ⊠ SW1X 9AE ⊖ Sloane Square – ℰ (020) 7901 9999
– www.lecercle.co.uk – Closed 25 December, Sunday, Monday and bank holidays
Rest – French – Menu £ 15 (lunch) – Carte £ 28/31 **37AGYe**

♦ Deep basement location made into a fashionable spot, with drapes and high ceilings; comes alive more at dinner. Order three or four small plates of the delicate French cooking per person.

KENSINGTON and CHELSEA

XX Painted Heron
112 Cheyne Walk ⊠ SW10 0DJ ⊖ Gloucester Road – ℰ (020) 7351 5232
– www.thepaintedheron.com – Closed 25 December   **23 PZG d**
Rest – Indian – *(dinner only and lunch Saturday-Sunday)* Menu £ 20/35
– Carte £ 30/38
♦ Well-supported locally and quite formally run Indian restaurant. Nooks and crannies create an intimate atmosphere. Fish and game dishes are the highlight of the contemporary Indian cooking.

XX Eighty-Six
86 Fulham Rd, (1st Floor) ⊠ SW3 6HR ⊖ South Kensington
– ℰ (020) 7052 9620 – www.86restaurant.co.uk – Closed Sunday and Monday
Rest – Modern European – *(dinner only)* Menu £ 41   **36 ADZ x**
♦ A mix of baroque, rococo and bling are used to create a gilded jewel for young movers and shakers. The menu roams around Europe but the best dishes are the simpler ones that use British ingredients.

XX Ilia
96 Draycott Ave. ⊠ SW3 3AD ⊖ South Kensington – ℰ (020) 7225 2555
– www.ilia-london.com   **37 AFY a**
Rest – Italian – Carte £ 29/47
♦ Formerly a French restaurant but its owner decided to try Italian. Bewildering array of dishes but at least there's something for everyone and the cooking is capable. Cool, fresh room; best tables by the French windows.

XX Marco
Stamford Bridge, Fulham Rd. ⊠ SW6 1HS ⊖ Fulham Broadway
– ℰ (020) 7915 2929 – www.marcorestaurant.org
– Closed 2 weeks July-August, 25 December, Sunday and Monday   **22 OZG c**
Rest – Traditional – *(dinner only)(booking advisable)* Carte £ 31/59
♦ Marco Pierre White's brasserie at Chelsea Football Club offers an appealing range of classics, from British favourites to satisfying French and Italian fare; puddings are a highlight. Comfortable and well-run room.

XX Good Earth
233 Brompton Rd. ⊠ SW3 2EP ⊖ Knightsbridge
– ℰ (020) 7584 3658 – www.goodearthgroup.co.uk
– Closed 23-31 December   **37 AFY h**
Rest – Chinese – Menu £ 12/30 – Carte £ 21/36
♦ The basement is busier and more popular than the ground floor. Extensive menu makes good use of quality ingredients and offers appealing choice between classic and more unusual dishes.

XX The Botanist
7 Sloane Sq ⊠ SW1W 8EE ⊖ Sloane Square – ℰ (020) 7730 0077
– www.thebotanistsloanesquare.com – Closed 25-26 December   **37 AGY r**
Rest – Modern European – Carte £ 31/51
♦ Pass through the busy bar to get to the stylish and comfortable restaurant with its warm and vibrant atmosphere. Appealing and accessible menu delivers unfussy and satisfying dishes.

XX Chelsea Brasserie – at The Sloane Square Hotel
7-12 Sloane Sq. ⊠ SW1W 8EG ⊖ Sloane Square
– ℰ (020) 7896 9988 – www.sloanesquarehotel.co.uk
– Closed Sunday dinner   **37 AGY k**
Rest – French – Menu £ 25 (lunch and early dinner) – Carte £ 33/40
♦ You pass through the busy bar to get to the smartly lit brasserie, with exposed brick, mirrors and tiles. Cooking has a strong French base. Good value theatre menu and brisk service.

KENSINGTON and CHELSEA

Joe's

126 Draycott Ave ⊠ SW3 3AH ⊖ South Kensington – ℘ (020) 7225 2217
– www.joseph.co.uk – Closed 25 December, Easter Sunday and dinner
Sunday-Monday   37AFYf
Rest – Modern European – Menu £ 17 (lunch) – Carte £ 24/37
♦ Back in the '80s when the only thing bigger than the hair were the shoulder pads, Joe's was the place to be seen. It's now fashionable once again and its appealing, fortnightly changing menu comes with Mediterranean overtones.

Galoupet

13 Beauchamp Pl ⊠ SW13 1NQ ⊖ Knightsbridge – ℘ (020) 7036 3600
– www.galoupet.co.uk – Closed 25 December   37AFXx
Rest – Asian influences – Carte £ 35/50
♦ The 'Enomatic' wine dispensers are a clue that wine plays an important part here; indeed, the owners have a vineyard in Provence. Dishes fuse the East with the Med and offer pleasant contrasting textures and a refreshing vitality.

Bibendum Oyster Bar

Michelin House, 81 Fulham Rd. ⊠ SW3 6RD ⊖ South Kensington
– ℘ (020) 7589 1480 – www.bibendum.co.uk – Closed 24-26 December and 1 January
Rest – Seafood – (bookings not accepted) Carte £ 21/35   37AEYs
♦ Oysters, potted shrimps and fruits de mer are the highlights at this continental-style café, with its mosaic floor and colourful ceramic tiles. Wine list includes 460ml pots.

Foxtrot Oscar

79 Royal Hospital Rd. ⊠ SW3 4HN ⊖ Sloane Square – ℘ (020) 7352 4448
– www.gordonramsay.com – Closed 25 December   37AFZv
Rest – Traditional – (booking essential) Menu £ 22 (lunch) – Carte £ 26/33
♦ Gordon Ramsay's least known restaurant has a relaxed, local feel, with celebrity photographs adorning its burgundy walls. Bistro cooking, with the Foxtrot Burger a highlight.

Henry Root

9 Park Walk ⊠ SW10 0AJ ⊖ South Kensington – ℘ (020) 7552 7040
– www.thehenryroot.com – Closed 25-27 December   36ACZz
Rest – French – (booking advisable) Menu £ 13 (lunch) – Carte £ 24/34
♦ William Donaldson satirised many of the good and the great on his day through the letters of his alter ego, Henry Root. His name lives on in this cheery local spot, with its appealing menu that includes small plates and charcuterie.

Manicomio

85 Duke of York Sq., King's Rd. ⊠ SW3 4LY ⊖ Sloane Square
– ℘ (020) 7730 3366 – www.manicomio.co.uk – Closed 1 January, 24-26 and
31 December   37AGYx
Rest – Italian – Carte £ 31/43
♦ Modern, busy Italian, popular with shoppers and visitors to the Saatchi Gallery; the simplest dishes are the best ones. The terrific terrace fills quickly. Next door is their café and deli.

Tom's Kitchen

27 Cale St. ⊠ SW3 3QP ⊖ South Kensington – ℘ (020) 7349 0202
– www.tomskitchen.co.uk   37AFZb
Rest – French – Carte £ 29/50
♦ A converted pub, whose white tiles and mirrors help to give it an industrial feel. Appealing and wholesome dishes come in man-sized portions. The eponymous Tom is Tom Aikens.

Geales

1 Cale St. ⊠ SW3 3QT ⊖ South Kensington – ℘ (020) 7965 0555
– www.geales.com – Closed 25-26 December, 1 January and Monday lunch
Rest – Seafood – Carte £ 28/36   37AFZn
♦ Fish and chips are the main draw at this cosy, warmly run and sweetly decorated spot. Other choices can include fish pie and soft shell crab tempura, along with wholesome, homemade puddings.

KENSINGTON and CHELSEA

Le Metro – at The Levin Hotel
28 Basil St. ✉ *SW3 1AS* ⊖ *Knightsbridge* – ✆ *(020) 7589 6286*
– *www.thelevinhotel.co.uk – Closed Sunday dinner*   **37AFX c**
Rest – Mediterranean – Carte £ 25/30

♦ Open all day and for those in the know, Le Metro is a useful and secretive little spot next to Harrods. Pop in for the pie or pasta of the week or a bellini and a croque monsieur.

Admiral Codrington
17 Mossop St ✉ *SW3 2LY* ⊖ *South Kensington.* – ✆ *(020) 7581 0005*
– *www.theadmiralcodrington.com – Closed 25-26 December*   **37AFY v**
Rest – Modern European – Carte £ 23/43

♦ A Chelsea institution, with popular bar in the evenings and a separate, smart restaurant with retractable roof. The menu covers all bases and mixes British classics with European influences.

Chelsea Ram
32 Burnaby St ✉ *SW10 0PL* ⊖ *Fulham Broadway.* – ✆ *(020) 7351 4008*
– *Closed Sunday dinner*   **23PZG r**
Rest – British – Carte £ 22/26 s

♦ A warm, welcoming and relaxed pub surrounded by residential streets, with a loyal local following. Expect proper 'pub grub' where the portions are generous and the prices fair.

Cadogan Arms
298 King's Rd ✉ *SW3 5UG* ⊖ *South Kensington.* – ✆ *(020) 7352 6500*
– *www.thecadoganarmschelsea.com – Closed 25-26 December*   **36ADZ y**
Rest – British – *(booking advisable at dinner)* Carte £ 24/33

♦ Part of the Martin Brothers bourgeoning pub group. This is a proper pub, with billiard tables upstairs and a gusty, full-on menu. Stuffed and mounted animals stare down as you eat.

Builders Arms
13 Britten St ✉ *SW3 3TY* ⊖ *South Kensington.* – ✆ *(020) 7349 9040*
– *www.geronimo-inns.co.uk*   **37AFZ x**
Rest – British – *(bookings not accepted)* Carte £ 22/34

♦ Smart looking and busy pub for the Chelsea set; drinkers are welcomed as much as diners. Cooking reveals the effort put into sourcing decent ingredients; rib of beef for two is a favourite. Thoughtfully compiled wine list.

Pig's Ear
35 Old Church St ✉ *SW3 5BS* ⊖ *Sloane Square.* – ✆ *(020) 7352 2908*
– *www.thepigsear.com*   **23PZG v**
Rest – Traditional – Carte £ 15/25

♦ Honest pub, with rough-and-ready ground floor bar for lunch; more intimate, wood-panelled upstairs dining-room for dinner. Robust, confident and satisfying cooking with a classical bent.

Phoenix
23 Smith St. ✉ *SW3 4EE* ⊖ *Sloane Square.* – ✆ *(020) 7730 9182*
– *www.geronimo-inns.co.uk/thepheonix – Closed 25 December*   **37AFZ a**
Rest – Modern European – Carte £ 21/34

♦ Friendly, conscientiously run Chelsea local, where satisfying and carefully prepared pub classics are served in the roomy, civilised bar or in the warm, comfortable dining room at the back.

Lots Road Pub & Dining Room
114 Lots Rd ✉ *SW10 0RJ* ⊖ *Fulham Broadway.* – ✆ *(020) 7352 6645*
– *www.lotsroadpub.com*   **23PZG b**
Rest – Traditional – Carte £ 20/30

♦ Lively semicircular shaped pub, close to Chelsea Harbour. Hearty and satisfying classics, from mussels to Perthshire côte de boeuf and a tart of the day. Staff keep things bright and cheery.

KENSINGTON and CHELSEA

EARL'S COURT

K + K George
1-15 Templeton Pl. ✉ SW5 9NB ⊖ Earl's Court – ℰ (020) 7598 8700
– www.kkhotels.com   35AAYs
154 rm – †£ 140/300 ††£ 150/336 **Rest** – Carte £ 21/42 s
♦ Five converted 19C houses overlooking large rear garden. Scandinavian-style rooms with low beds, white walls and light wood furniture. Breakfast room has the garden view. Informal dining in the bar.

Twenty Nevern Square without rest
20 Nevern Sq. ✉ SW5 9PD ⊖ Earl's Court – ℰ (020) 7565 9555
– www.twentynevernsquare.co.uk   35AAYu
20 rm – †£ 115/180 ††£ 220/250, ⊇ £ 9
♦ In an attractive Victorian garden square, an individually designed, privately owned townhouse. Original pieces of furniture and some bedrooms with their own terrace.

Mayflower without rest
26-28 Trebovir Rd. ✉ SW5 9NJ ⊖ Earl's Court – ℰ (020) 7370 0991
– www.mayflowerhotel.co.uk   35ABYx
43 rm – †£ 120/130 ††£ 120/130, ⊇ £ 10 – 4 suites
♦ Conveniently placed, friendly establishment with a secluded rear breakfast terrace and basement breakfast room. Individually styled bedrooms with Asian influence.

Amsterdam without rest
7-9 Trebovir Rd. ✉ SW5 9LS ⊖ Earl's Court – ℰ (020) 7370 2814
– www.amsterdam-hotel.com   35ABYc
19 rm – †£ 86/99 ††£ 108/120, ⊇ £ 3 – 8 suites
♦ Basement breakfast room and a small secluded garden. The brightly decorated bedrooms are light and airy. Some have smart wood floors; some boast their own balcony.

Rushmore without rest
11 Trebovir Rd. ✉ SW5 9LS ⊖ Earl's Court – ℰ (020) 7370 3839
– www.rushmore-hotel.co.uk   35ABYa
22 rm – †£ 89/109 ††£ 129/199
♦ Behind its Victorian façade lies a hotel popular with tourists. Individually decorated bedrooms in a variety of shapes and sizes. Piazza-style conservatory breakfast room.

KENSINGTON

Royal Garden
2-24 Kensington High St. ✉ W8 4PT ⊖ High Street Kensington – ℰ (020) 7937 8000 – www.royalgardenhotel.co.uk   35ABXc
372 rm – †£ 360 ††£ 408, ⊇ £ 23.50 – 22 suites
Rest *Min Jiang* – see restaurant listing
Rest *Park Terrace* – ℰ (020) 7361 0602 – Menu £ 20/33
♦ A tall, modern hotel with many of its rooms enjoying enviable views over the adjacent Kensington Gardens. All the modern amenities and services, with well-drilled staff. Bright, spacious Park Terrace offers British, Asian and modern European cuisine.

The Milestone
1-2 Kensington Ct. ✉ W8 5DL ⊖ High Street Kensington – ℰ (020) 7917 1000
– www.milestonehotel.com   35ABXu
56 rm – †£ 360/534 ††£ 420/594, ⊇ £ 29.50 – 6 suites
Rest *Cheneston's* – see restaurant listing
♦ Elegant hotel with decorative Victorian façade and English feel. Charming oak-panelled lounge and snug bar. Meticulously decorated bedrooms with period detail. The enthusiasm of the staff also sets it apart.

KENSINGTON and CHELSEA

Baglioni
60 Hyde Park Gate ⊠ SW7 5BB ⊖ High Street Kensington – ℰ (020) 7368 5700 – www.baglionihotels.com
52 rm – †£ 311/474 ††£ 347/546, ⌚ £ 29 – 15 suites
36ACXe
Rest *Brunello* – see restaurant listing

• Opposite Kensington Palace and no escaping the fact that this is an Italian owned hotel. The interior is bold and ornate and there's a trendy basement bar. Stylish bedrooms have a masculine feel and boast impressive facilities.

Launceston Place
1a Launceston Pl. ⊠ W8 5RL ⊖ Gloucester Road – ℰ (020) 7937 6912 – www.launcestonplace-restaurant.co.uk – Closed 24-30 December, Monday lunch and dinner bank holiday Mondays
36ACXa
Rest – Modern European – Menu £ 22/45

• Its most recent reincarnation, with its dark walls and moody lighting, still attracts plenty of locals. Cooking is original, deftly executed and uses ingredients largely from the British Isles.

Min Jiang – at Royal Garden Hotel
Royal Garden Hotel (10th Floor), 2-24 Kensington High St. ⊠ W8 4PT ⊖ High Street Kensington – ℰ (020) 7361 1988 – www.minjiang.co.uk
Rest – Chinese – Menu £ 17/50 – Carte approx. £ 48
35ABXc

• A comfortable Chinese restaurant looking down over Kensington Gardens from its 10th floor location. Most provinces of China are represented on the menu but the main speciality is the Beijing duck.

Belvedere
Holland House, off Abbotsbury Rd. ⊠ W8 6LU ⊖ Holland Park – ℰ (020) 7602 1238 – www.belvedererestaurant.co.uk – Closed Sunday dinner
Rest – Modern European – Menu £ 20 (weekday lunch) – Carte £ 28/44
16MZEu

• Former 19C orangery in a delightful position in the middle of the park. On two floors with a bar and balcony terrace and decorated with huge vases of flowers. Modern take on classic dishes.

Kitchen W8
11-13 Abingdon Rd ⊠ W8 6AH ⊖ High Street Kensington – ℰ (020) 7937 0120 – www.kitchenw8.com – Closed bank holidays
35AAXa
Rest – Modern European – Menu £ 20 (lunch) – Carte £ 33/47
Spec. Sauté of lamb sweetbreads and tongue with garlic, parsley and morels. Fillet of halibut with wild garlic and meat vinaigrette. Salted chocolate parfait with malt ice cream.

• Smart, comfortable restaurant which is not as casual as its name implies, but which does have a pleasant, neighbourhood feel. Skilled kitchen produces balanced dishes free of showiness, with the emphasis on flavour.

Babylon – at The Roof Gardens
99 Kensington High St (entrance on Derry St) ⊠ W8 5SA ⊖ High Street Kensington – ℰ (020) 7368 3993 – www.roofgardens.virgin.com – Closed 24-30 December, 1-2 January and Sunday dinner
35ABXn
Rest – Modern European – Menu £ 23 (lunch) – Carte £ 33/47

• Situated on the roof of this pleasant London building affording attractive views of the London skyline. Stylish modern décor in keeping with the contemporary, British cooking.

Clarke's
124 Kensington Church St. ⊠ W8 4BH ⊖ Notting Hill Gate – ℰ (020) 7221 9225 – www.sallyclarke.com – Closed Christmas-New Year, Sunday dinner and bank holidays
27ABVc
Rest – Modern European – *(booking advisable)* Menu £ 41 (dinner) – Carte £ 33/46

• Forever popular restaurant, serving a choice of dishes boasting trademark fresh, seasonal ingredients and Sally Clarke's famed lightness of touch. Has enjoyed a loyal local following for over 25 years.

KENSINGTON and CHELSEA

XX Yashin
[AC] [VISA] [CO] [AE]

1A Argyll Rd. ⊠ W8 7DB ⊖ High Street Kensington – ℰ (020) 7938 1536
– www.yashinsushi.com – Closed first and third Monday in month, 25 and 31
December, and 1 January
35AAXc

Rest – Japanese – *(booking essential)* Carte £ 41/90

♦ Ask for a counter seat to watch the chefs prepare the sushi; choose 8, 11 or 15 pieces, to be served together. The quality of fish is clear; tiny garnishes and the odd bit of searing add originality.

XX Casa Batavia
[AC] ⇔ [VISA] [CO] [AE]

135 Kensington Church St ⊠ W8 7LP ⊖ Notting Hill Gate – ℰ (020) 7221 7348
– www.casabatavia.com
27AAVx

Rest – Italian – *(booking advisable)* Menu £ 22 (lunch) – Carte £ 24/37

♦ Intimate restaurant opened in 2011 by an experienced restaurateur and a chef from Turin. The refined cooking of Piedmont is the main influence; look out for ricotta crostino, potted rabbit with hazelnuts and, of course, panna cotta.

XX Zaika
[AC] [VISA] [CO] [AE] [①]

1 Kensington High St. ⊠ W8 5NP ⊖ High Street Kensington – ℰ (020)
7795 6533 – www.zaika-restaurant.co.uk – Closed 25-26 December, 1-2 January
and Monday lunch
35ABXr

Rest – Indian – Menu £ 25 (lunch) – Carte £ 30/45

♦ The smell of incense is one clue that the days of this being a bank are long gone; bright colours offset the high ceiling and wood panelling. The cooking is original and sophisticated but at times the spicing can lack a degree of subtlety.

XX Whits
[AC] [VISA] [CO] [AE]

21 Abingdon Rd. ⊠ W8 6AH ⊖ High Street Kensington – ℰ (020) 7938 1122
– www.whits.co.uk – Closed 1 week August, Sunday and Monday
35AAXd

Rest – Modern European – *(dinner only)* Menu £ 24 – Carte £ 31/40

♦ Run by friendly owner. Bar runs length of lower level. Most diners migrate upstairs with its modish artwork and intimate tables. Modern cooking with generous portions.

XX Timo
[AC] [VISA] [CO] [AE]

343 Kensington High St. ⊠ W8 6NW ⊖ High Street Kensington – ℰ (020)
7603 3888 – www.timorestaurant.net – Closed Christmas, Sunday and bank holidays
35AAYc

Rest – Italian – *(booking advisable)* Menu £ 18 (lunch and early dinner)
– Carte £ 30/40

♦ Comfortable and comforting neighbourhood Italian restaurant, with careful and reliable cooking. Service is smart and conscientious and is undertaken under the watchful eye of the owner.

XX Seventeen
[AC] ⇔ [VISA] [CO] [AE] [①]

17 Notting Hill Gate ⊠ W11 3JQ ⊖ Notting Hill Gate – ℰ (020) 7985 0006
– www.seventeen-london.co.uk
27ABVx

Rest – Chinese – Menu £ 12/21 – Carte £ 18/45

♦ Stylishly kitted out, intimate and moodily lit Chinese restaurant on two floors. The kitchen, behind an eye-catching glass wall, specialises in authentic Sichuan and Shanghainese delicacies.

XX Cheneston's – at The Milestone Hotel
[AC] [VISA] [CO] [AE] [①]

1-2 Kensington Ct. ⊠ W8 5DL ⊖ High Street Kensington – ℰ (020) 7917 1000
– www.milestonehotel.com
35ABXu

Rest – British – *(booking essential for non-residents)* Menu £ 30 (lunch)
– Carte £ 51/63 ⌘

♦ The Milestone is an elegant Victorian hotel and her restaurant is equally decorous and includes a charming little oratory. Expect refined British cooking and a superior wine list.

KENSINGTON and CHELSEA

Brunello – at Baglioni Hotel
60 Hyde Park Gate ⊠ SW7 5BB ⊖ High Street Kensington – ℰ (020) 7368 5900 – www.baglionihotels.com
36ACXe
Rest – Italian – Menu £ 28/33 – Carte £ 45/66

♦ The Baglioni hotel's ground floor bar, lounge and restaurant all merge into one in a heady mix of grey, gold and glass. The menu traverses all parts of Italy and uses prime ingredients.

Cibo
3 Russell Gdns ⊠ W14 8EZ ⊖ Kensington Olympia – ℰ (020) 7371 6271 – www.ciborestaurant.net – Closed 1 week Christmas and bank holidays
Rest – Italian – Menu £ 25 – Carte £ 23/37
16MZEb

♦ Long-standing neighbourhood Italian with local following. More space at the back of the room. Robust, satisfying cooking; the huge grilled shellfish and seafood platter a speciality.

Malabar
27 Uxbridge St. ⊠ W8 7TQ ⊖ Notting Hill Gate – ℰ (020) 7727 8800 – www.malabar-restaurant.co.uk – Closed 1 week Christmas
27AAVe
Rest – Indian – (buffet lunch Sunday) Menu £ 25 s – Carte £ 26/41 s

♦ Opened in 1983 in a residential Notting Hill street, but keeps up its appearance, remaining fresh and good-looking. Balanced menu of carefully prepared and sensibly priced Indian dishes.

Kensington Place
201-209 Kensington Church St. ⊠ W8 7LX ⊖ Notting Hill Gate – ℰ (020) 7727 3184 – www.kensingtonplace-restaurant.co.uk – Closed Sunday dinner and Monday lunch
27AAVz
Rest – Modern European – Menu £ 20/25

♦ Opened in 1987 as a big, boisterous, brasserie; these days a little less noisy but it remains well run. Competitively priced set menu offers a wide choice of modern European dishes.

NORTH KENSINGTON

The Portobello without rest
22 Stanley Gdns. ⊠ W11 2NG ⊖ Notting Hill Gate – ℰ (020) 7727 2777 – www.portobellohotel.co.uk – Closed 24-29 December
16NZEn
21 rm – †£ 174/234 ††£ 252/378, ☐ £ 20

♦ An attractive Victorian townhouse in an elegant terrace. Original and theatrical décor. Circular beds, half-testers, Victorian baths: no two bedrooms are the same.

Ledbury (Brett Graham)
127 Ledbury Rd. ⊠ W11 2AQ ⊖ Notting Hill Gate – ℰ (020) 7792 9090 – www.theledbury.com – Closed 24-26 December, August bank holiday and Monday lunch
27AATa
Rest – Modern European – Menu £ 34/70

Spec. Buffalo milk curd, truffle toast and grilled onion broth. Loin and shoulder of lamb, black sugar and garlic glazed aubergine. Whipped ewe's milk yoghurt with berries, verbena meringues and beignets.

♦ Elegant, understated surroundings with professional, well-organised service but it still has a neighbourhood feel. Highly skilled kitchen with an inherent understanding of flavour; great ingredients, especially game in season.

Notting Hill Brasserie
92 Kensington Park Rd ⊠ W11 2PN ⊖ Notting Hill Gate – ℰ (020) 7229 4481 – www.nottinghillbrasserie.com
27AAUa
Rest – French – Menu £ 20 (weekday lunch) – Carte £ 43/61

♦ More formal than the name suggests and housed within a row of attractive Edwardian townhouses. Menu provides large choice of carefully constructed and quite elaborate dishes. Nightly live jazz.

KENSINGTON and CHELSEA

Edera
148 Holland Park Ave. – W11 4UE – Holland Park – ℰ (020) 7221 6090
– www.edera.co.uk   **16**MZE**n**
Rest – Italian – Carte £ 37/54

♦ Warm and comfortable neighbourhood restaurant with plenty of local regulars and efficient, well-marshalled service. Robust cooking has a subtle Sardinian accent and comes in generous portions.

E&O
14 Blenheim Cres. – W11 1NN – Ladbroke Grove – ℰ (020) 7229 5454
– www.rickerrestaurants.com – Closed 25-26 December and 1 January
Rest – Asian – Menu £ 19 (lunch) – Carte £ 23/54   **16**MZD**a**

♦ Mean, moody and cool and that's just the customers. Sophisticated, chic and noisy, thanks to contented groups of diners. Menus scour the Far East, with dishes designed for sharing.

Dock Kitchen
Portobello Dock, 342-344 Ladbroke Grove – W10 5BU – Ladbroke Grove
– ℰ (020) 8962 1610 – www.dockkitchen.co.uk – Closed last week August, 24 December-5 January and Sunday dinner   **16**MZD**k**
Rest – Mediterranean – Menu £ 19 (lunch) – Carte £ 26/37

♦ What started as a 'pop-up' became a permanent feature in this open-plan former Victorian goods yard. The chef's peregrinations inform his cooking, which relies on simple, natural flavours.

Bumpkin
209 Westbourne Park Rd – W11 1EA – Westbourne Park – ℰ (020) 7243 9818
– www.bumpkinuk.com   **27**AAT**b**
Rest – British – Carte £ 29/37

♦ Converted pea-green pub with casual, clubby feel and wholesome philosophy of cooking seasonal, carefully sourced and organic food. The same modern Mediterranean-influenced menu is served on both floors.

SOUTH KENSINGTON

The Pelham
15 Cromwell Pl – SW7 2LA – South Kensington – ℰ (020) 7589 8288
– www.pelhamhotel.co.uk   **36**ADY**z**
51 rm – †£ 216/300 ††£ 324/399, ⊑ £ 17.50 – 1 suite
Rest *Bistro Fifteen* – see restaurant listing

♦ Immaculately kept, with willing staff and a discreet atmosphere. Decoratively it's a mix of English country house and city town house, with a panelled sitting room and library with honesty bar.

Blakes
33 Roland Gdns. – SW7 3PF – Gloucester Road – ℰ (020) 7370 6701
– www.blakeshotels.com   **36**ACZ**n**
33 rm – †£ 234/594 ††£ 390/654, ⊑ £ 19.50 – 8 suites
Rest – Menu £ 23 (lunch) – Carte £ 49/73

♦ Behind the Victorian façade lies one of London's first 'boutique' hotels. Dramatic, bold and eclectic décor, with oriental influences and antiques from around the globe. Fashionable restaurant with bamboo and black walls.

Number Sixteen
16 Sumner Pl. – SW7 3EG – South Kensington – ℰ (020) 7589 5232
– www.numbersixteenhotel.co.uk   **36**ADY**d**
42 rm – †£ 156/210 ††£ 258, ⊑ £ 18.50   **Rest** – (room service only)

♦ Enticingly refurbished 19C town houses in smart area. Discreet entrance, comfy sitting room and charming breakfast terrace. Bedrooms in English country house style.

409

KENSINGTON and CHELSEA

The Cranley

10 Bina Gdns. ✉ SW5 0LA ⊖ Gloucester Road – ℰ (020) 7373 0123
– www.thecranley.com
36ACYc
38 rm – ♦£ 192/300 ♦♦£ 240/312, ⊊ £ 17.95 – 1 suite
Rest – (room service only)

• Delightful Regency townhouse combines charm and period details with modern comforts and technology. Individually styled bedrooms; some with four-posters. Breakfast served in bedrooms.

The Rockwell

181-183 Cromwell Rd. ✉ SW5 0SF ⊖ Earl's Court – ℰ (020) 7244 2000
– www.therockwell.com
35ABYb
40 rm (dinner included) – ♦£ 140/220 ♦♦£ 200/260, ⊊ £ 9.50
Rest – Menu £ 48 (dinner) – Carte £ 27/40

• Two Victorian houses with open, modern lobby and secluded, south-facing garden terrace. Bedrooms come in bold warm colours; 'Garden Rooms' have their own patios. Small dining room offers easy menu of modern European staples.

The Gore

190 Queen's Gate ✉ SW7 5EX ⊖ Gloucester Road – ℰ (020) 7584 6601
– www.gorehotel.com
36ACXn
50 rm – ♦£ 174/198 ♦♦£ 174/528, ⊊ £ 17.50
Rest *190 Queensgate* – see restaurant listing

• Idiosyncratic, hip Victorian house whose narrow lobby is covered with pictures and prints. Individually styled bedrooms have plenty of character and charming bathrooms. The closest hotel to Royal Albert Hall.

Aster House without rest

3 Sumner Pl. ✉ SW7 3EE ⊖ South Kensington – ℰ (020) 7581 5888
– www.asterhouse.com
36ADYt
13 rm – ♦£ 96/180 ♦♦£ 162/300

• End of terrace Victorian house with a pretty little rear garden and first floor conservatory. Ground floor rooms available. Useful location for visiting many tourist attractions.

Bombay Brasserie

Courtfield Rd. ✉ SW7 4QH ⊖ Gloucester Road – ℰ (020) 7370 4040
– www.bombaybrasserielondon.com – Closed 25-26 December
36ACYy
Rest – Indian – (booking advisable at dinner) Menu £ 22 (lunch)
– Carte £ 31/43

• Plush new look for this well-run, well-known and comfortable Indian restaurant; very smart bar and conservatory with a show kitchen. More creative dishes now sit alongside the more traditional.

Cassis

232-236 Brompton Rd. ✉ SW3 2BB ⊖ South Kensington – ℰ (020) 7581 1101
– www.cassisbistro.co.uk – Closed 25 December
36AEYx
Rest – French – Menu £ 20 (weekday lunch) – Carte £ 26/51 ⊗

• The colours and aromas of southern France come to south Ken at this crisply stylish Provençal 'bistro'. Start with some 'petites bouchées' such as classic barbajuans or pissaladière; follow up with authentic bouillabaisse or daube of beef.

L'Etranger

36 Gloucester Rd. ✉ SW7 4QT ⊖ Gloucester Road – ℰ (020) 7584 1118
– www.circagroupltd.co.uk
36ACXc
Rest – Innovative – (booking essential) Menu £ 24 (lunch) – Carte dinner
£ 41/53 ⊗

• Eclectic menu mixes French dishes with techniques and flavours from Japanese cooking. Impressive wine and sake lists. Moody and atmospheric room; ask for a corner table.

KENSINGTON and CHELSEA

XX Pasha
1 Gloucester Rd. ✉ *SW7 4PP* ⊖ *Gloucester Road* – ✆ *(020) 7589 7969*
– www.pasha-restaurant.co.uk – Closed 25-26 December   **36**ACX**r**
Rest – Moroccan – Menu £ 20/30 – Carte £ 27/33
♦ Relax over ground floor cocktails, then descend to mosaic floored restaurant where the rose-petal strewn tables are the ideal accompaniment to tasty Moroccan home cooking.

XX Bistro K
117-119 Old Brompton Rd. ✉ *SW7 3RN* ⊖ *Gloucester Road* – ✆ *(020)*
7373 7774 – www.bistro-k.co.uk – Closed Sunday and Monday   **36**ACZ**x**
Rest – French – Menu £ 15 (lunch) – Carte £ 36/46
♦ More formal than the name would suggest and the cooking is more delicate and sophisticated. The surroundings are bright and contemporary and the front terrace is an appealing spot.

XX Cambio de Tercio
163 Old Brompton Rd. ✉ *SW5 0LJ* ⊖ *Gloucester Road* – ✆ *(020) 7244 8970*
– www.cambiodetercio.co.uk – Closed 25 December   **36**ACZ**a**
Rest – Spanish – Carte £ 30/54 **s**
♦ Good ingredients and authentic Spanish flavours; desserts are more contemporary. Choose tapas or regular menu. Service improves the more you visit. Owner also has tapas bar across the road.

XX Bistro Fifteen – at The Pelham Hotel
15 Cromwell Pl ✉ *SW7 2LA* ⊖ *South Kensington* – ✆ *(020) 7589 8288*
– www.pelhamhotel.co.uk   **36**ADY**z**
Rest – Modern European – Menu £ 18 (lunch and early dinner)
– Carte £ 26/41
♦ This concealed little basement bistro offers respite from the plethora of chain restaurants in these parts. It has a sweet, intimate feel and a menu of European and British dishes.

X Bumpkin
102 Old Brompton Rd. ✉ *SW7 3RD* ⊖ *Gloucester Road* – ✆ *(020) 7341 0802*
– www.bumpkinuk.com   **36**ACY**r**
Rest – British – Carte £ 30/37
♦ Sister to the Notting Hill original with the same pub-like informality and friendly service. The kitchen champions British seasonal produce; the simpler dishes are the best ones.

X Aubaine
260-262 Brompton Rd. ✉ *SW3 2AS* ⊖ *South Kensington* – ✆ *(020) 7052 0100*
– www.aubaine.co.uk   **37**AEY**c**
Rest – French – Carte £ 22/52
♦ 'Boulangerie, patisserie, restaurant'. Pass the bakery aromas to an all-day eatery with 'distressed' country feel. Well-judged menus range from croque monsieur to coq au vin.

X Bangkok
9 Bute St ✉ *SW7 3EY* ⊖ *South Kensington* – ✆ *(020) 7584 8529*
– www.bankokrestaurant.co.uk – Closed 24 December-2 January and Sunday
Rest – Thai – Carte £ 19/26   **36**ADY**b**
♦ This simple Thai bistro has been a popular local haunt for nearly 40 years. Guests can watch the chefs at work, preparing inexpensive and authentic dishes from the succinct menu.

X Tendido Cero
174 Old Brompton Rd. ✉ *SW5 0BA* ⊖ *Gloucester Road* – ✆ *(020) 7370 3685*
– www.cambiodetercio.co.uk – Closed 25 December   **36**ACZ**v**
Rest – Spanish – Carte £ 30/34
♦ Highlights at this busy tapas bar include Galician octopus, white bean stew with chorizo and pork cheeks with potato purée. There are also some unusual dishes, like the mini 'hamburger' made with sardines.

KENSINGTON and CHELSEA

Capote y Toros
157 Old Brompton Road ⊠ SW5 0LJ ⊖ Gloucester Road – ℘ (020) 7373 0567
– www.cambiodetercio.co.uk – Closed Sunday and Monday
Rest – Spanish – (dinner only) Carte £ 19/32

36ACZv

♦ Expect to queue at this compact and vividly coloured spot which celebrates sherry, tapas, ham...and bullfighting. Sherry is the star; those as yet unmoved by this most underappreciated of wines will be dazzled by the huge variety.

190 Queensgate – at The Gore Hotel
190 Queen's Gate ⊠ SW7 5EX ⊖ Gloucester Road – ℘ (020) 7584 6601
– www.gorehotel.com
Rest – British – (booking essential) Menu £ 20/24 – Carte £ 29/42

36ACXn

♦ This is the nearest restaurant to the Royal Albert Hall so it's busiest early or late evening. Bright, bustling bistro atmosphere with an appealing and accessible menu to match.

KINGSTON UPON THAMES – Greater London   12 A3
Hampton Court Palace Hampton Wick, ℘ (020) 8977 24 23

SURBITON

The French Table
85 Maple Rd ⊠ KT6 4AW – ℘ (020) 8399 2365 – www.thefrenchtable.co.uk
– Closed 2 weeks summer, 25 December, Sunday dinner and Monday
Rest – Mediterranean – Menu £ 23 (lunch) – Carte dinner
£ 25/42

6CYa

♦ Husband and wife team run this lively local. Expect zesty and satisfying French-Mediterranean cooking; learn how with Saturday morning cookery lessons. They also run the bakery next door.

LAMBETH – Greater London   12 B3

BRIXTON

Upstairs
89b Acre Ln. ⊠ SW2 5TN ⊖ Clapham North – ℘ (020) 7733 8855
– www.upstairslondon.com – Closed 24 December-9 January, 8-18 April, 19 August-4 September, Sunday and Monday
Rest – Modern European – (dinner only) Menu £ 32

24SZHb

♦ Uncomplicated, easy to eat and flavoursome cooking from a concise but balanced and well-priced set menu. First floor bar, second floor dining room – look for the buzzer next to Opus coffee shop.

CLAPHAM COMMON

Trinity
4 The Polygon ⊠ SW4 0JG ⊖ Clapham Common – ℘ (020) 7622 1199
– www.trinityrestaurant.co.uk – Closed 24-30 December, Monday lunch and Sunday dinner
Rest – Innovative – Menu £ 20 (lunch) – Carte £ 31/47

24RZHa

♦ Smartly decorated and smoothly run neighbourhood restaurant; ask for a table by the windows in summer. Sophisticated cooking displays some innovative combinations. Good value lunch menu.

Tsunami
Unit 3, 5-7 Voltaire Rd ⊠ SW4 6DQ ⊖ Clapham North – ℘ (020) 7978 1610
– www.tsunamirestaurant.co.uk – Closed 24-26 December
Rest – Japanese – (dinner only and lunch Saturday-Sunday) Carte £ 23/45

24SZHa

♦ Stylish and lively surroundings in which to enjoy innovative and original, modern Japanese food. The restaurant enjoys a large, local following and there's a second branch in Charlotte Street.

Bobbin

1-3 Lillieshall Rd ✉ SW4 OLN ⊖ Clapham Common. – ✆ (020) 7738 8953
– www.thebobbinclapham.com **24**RZH**x**
Rest – Traditional – Carte £ 19/27

♦ In a quiet residential street which, combined with its warm service, cosy bar and the Wednesday Quiz night, makes it feel like a proper local. Expect charcuterie boards to share along with wholesome seasonal cooking.

EAST DULWICH

Palmerston

91 Lordship Ln ✉ SE22 8EP ⊖ East Dulwich (rail). – ✆ (020) 8693 1629
– www.thepalmerston.net **26**XZH**x**
Rest – Traditional – Menu £ 16 (lunch) – Carte £ 25/32

♦ Full of atmosphere and attracting a range of ages, thanks to the engaging staff and good food on offer. Menus evolve monthly and mix classics with the more modern; look out for the well-priced weekday menu.

KENNINGTON

Kennington Tandoori

313 Kennington Rd ✉ SE11 4QE ⊖ Kennington – ✆ (020) 7735 9247
– www.kenningtontandoori.com **40**ANZ**a**
Rest – Indian – *(booking advisable)* Menu £ 18/28 – Carte £ 22/40

♦ Known as KT, the Hoque family's longstanding Indian restaurant was reinvigorated a couple of years ago when their son Kowsar took over. This stylish spot has a familiar menu of classics but what sets it apart is the skilled execution.

Lobster Pot

3 Kennington Ln. ✉ SE11 4RG ⊖ Kennington – ✆ (020) 7582 5556
– www.lobsterpotrestaurant.co.uk – Closed 24 December-3 January,
Sunday and Monday **40**AOY**e**
Rest – French – Carte £ 38/53

♦ Family-run, with exuberant décor of fish tanks, portholes and even the sound of seagulls. Classic seafood menu with fruits de mer, plenty of oysters and daily specials. Good crêpes too.

SOUTHBANK

London Marriott H. County Hall

Westminster Bridge Rd ✉ SE1 7PB ⊖ Westminster
– ✆ (020) 7928 5200 – www.marriottcountyhall.com **40**AMX**a**
195 rm – †£ 448 ††£ 448, ⊇ £ 21 – 5 suites
Rest *County Hall* – ✆ (020) 7902 8000 – Carte £ 29/41

♦ Occupying the historic County Hall building. Many of the spacious and comfortable bedrooms enjoy river and Parliament outlook. Impressive leisure facilities. World famous views from restaurant.

Skylon

1 Southbank Centre, Belvedere Rd ✉ SE1 8XX ⊖ Waterloo – ✆ (020) 7654 7800
– www.skylon-restaurant.co.uk – Closed 25 December and Sunday dinner
Rest – Modern European – Menu £ 29/45 **32**AMV**a**

♦ Ask for a window table here at the Royal Festival Hall. Informal grill-style operation on one side, a more formal and expensive restaurant on the other, with a busy cocktail bar in the middle.

STOCKWELL

Canton Arms

177 South Lambeth Rd ✉ SW8 1XP ⊖ Stockwell. – ✆ (020) 7582 8710
– www.cantonarms.com – Closed Christmas-New Year, Monday lunch, Sunday
dinner and bank holidays **24**SZG**a**
Rest – British – Carte £ 19/27

♦ An appreciative crowd of all ages come for the earthy, robust and seasonal British dishes which suit the relaxed environment of this pub so well. Staff are attentive and knowledgeable.

LEWISHAM – Greater London　　　　　　　　　　　　　　　　　　　12 B3
BLACKHEATH

Chapters
43-45 Montpelier Vale ⊠ SE3 0TJ – ℰ (020) 8333 2666
– www.chaptersrestaurants.com – Closed 2-3 January　　　　　　　　8HX c
Rest – Modern European – Carte £ 19/35

♦ A contemporary and bustling all day brasserie and bar at the top of town. Large, appealingly priced menu with British and Mediterranean influences, with meats cooked over charcoal a speciality.

MERTON – Greater London　　　　　　　　　　　　　　　　　　　　12 B3
WIMBLEDON

Cannizaro House
West Side, Wimbledon Common ⊠ SW19 4UE ⊖ Wimbledon
– ℰ (020) 8879 1464 – www.cannizarohouse.com　　　　　　　　　　6DXY x
44 rm – †£ 222/594 ††£ 222/594 – 2 suites
Rest *Cannizaro House* – see restaurant listing

♦ Part-Georgian mansion in charming spot overlooking Wimbledon Common. Modern bedrooms; funky suites; 'Sophia Johnson' has lovely balcony overlooking the park. Local artists' work decorates.

Cannizaro House
West Side, Wimbledon Common ⊠ SW19 4UE ⊖ Wimbledon
– ℰ (020) 8879 1464 – www.cannizarohouse.com　　　　　　　　　　6DXY x
Rest – British – Menu £ 30 – Carte £ 33/40

♦ London offers a huge choice of dining options, and that includes a Georgian mansion in 34 acres of parkland. Here, in the restaurant of the renovated Cannizaro House, British produce is celebrated.

Light House
75-77 Ridgway ⊠ SW19 4ST ⊖ Wimbledon – ℰ (020) 8944 6338
– www.lighthousewimbledon.com – Closed 25-26 December, 1 January and Sunday dinner　　　　　　　　　　　　　　　　　　　　　　　　　　6DY n
Rest – International – Menu £ 15 (lunch) – Carte £ 23/32

♦ The robust and flavoursome Italian dishes provide the highlights of the menu. This large, well lit room attracts plenty of locals and the service remains calm and cheery.

Fox and Grapes with rm
9 Camp Rd. ⊠ SW19 4UN ⊖ Wimbledon. – ℰ (020) 8619 1300
– www.foxandgrapeswimbledon.co.uk – Closed 25 December　　　　6DX v
3 rm – †£ 125 ††£ 125, ⊇ £ 12.50
Rest – British – *(booking advisable)* Menu £ 20 (lunch) – Carte £ 26/38

♦ Owned by Claude Bosi, chef-owner of Hibiscus, and run by Cedric, his brother. They may be French but they know about 'proper' pub food, from Cumberland sausages and prawn cocktail to wild boar scotch egg. Three cosy bedrooms also available.

RICHMOND-UPON-THAMES – Greater London　　　　　　　　　　　12 B3
🛈 Whittaker Ave ℰ (020) 8940 91 25, www.visitrichmond.co.uk
🏌 Richmond Park Roehampton Gate, ℰ (020) 8876 32 05
🏌 Sudbrook Park

BARNES

Sonny's
94 Church Rd ⊠ SW13 0DQ – ℰ (020) 8748 0393 – www.sonnys.co.uk – Closed Sunday dinner and bank holidays　　　　　　　　　　　　　　　21KZH x
Rest – Modern European – Menu £ 17/20 (midweek) – Carte £ 23/35

♦ Long-established neighbourhood spot which successfully combines its role as deli, café and restaurant. The latter's menus are full of seasonal goodness and the service is warm and attentive.

RICHMOND-UPON-THAMES

XX Indian Zilla
2-3 Rocks Ln. ⊠ SW13 0DB – ℘ (020) 8878 3989 – www.indianzilla.co.uk
Rest – Indian – Menu £ 15 (lunch) – Carte £ 27/36   **21**LZH**k**
♦ Bright, and contemporary restaurant with attentive, friendly service. Modern menu includes a few classics; the authentic, fully-flavoured dishes display a lightness of touch.

X Riva
169 Church Rd. ⊠ SW13 9HR – ℘ (020) 8748 0434 – Closed 3 weeks August, 10 days Christmas-New Year, Saturday lunch and bank holidays   **21**LZH**a**
Rest – Italian – Carte £ 32/56
♦ A restaurant built on customer loyalty; the regulars are showered with attention from the eponymous owner. Gutsy, no-nonsense dishes, full of flavour. Interesting all-Italian wine list.

Brown Dog
28 Cross St ⊠ SW13 0AP – Barnes Bridge (Rail) – ℘ (020) 8392 2200
– www.thebrowndog.co.uk – Closed 25-26 December   **21**KZH**b**
Rest – Carte £ 20/30
♦ Pretty Victorian pub with a genuine neighbourhood feel; snug bar, intimate dining room and a look that combines the traditional with the modern. Concise, balanced menu delivers commendably priced dishes that display a deft touch.

KEW

XX The Glasshouse
14 Station Par. ⊠ TW9 3PZ – Kew Gardens – ℘ (020) 8940 6777
– www.glasshouserestaurant.co.uk – Closed 24-26 December and 1 January
Rest – Modern European – Menu £ 26/40   **6**CX**z**
Spec. Sashimi of sea bass, wasabi mayonnaise and shrimp beignet. Roast pollock, wild garlic velouté, morels and leeks. Lemon tart with custard ice cream.
♦ Bright and relaxed interior, with a palpable sense of neighbourhood. Balanced and seasonally informed dishes are full of flavour, from a varied and appealing menu influenced mostly by Europe. Service is pleasant and unflappable.

XX Kew Grill
10b Kew Grn. ⊠ TW9 3BH – Kew Gardens – ℘ (020) 8948 4433
– www.awtrestaurants.com – Closed Monday lunch   **6**CV**u**
Rest – Beef specialities – (booking essential) Menu £ 15 (weekday lunch)
– Carte £ 29/49
♦ Just off Kew Green, this long, narrow restaurant has a Mediterranean style and feel. Grilled specialities employ top-rate ingredients: the beef is hung for 35 days.

RICHMOND

Petersham

Nightingale Ln. ⊠ TW10 6UZ – Richmond – ℘ (020) 8940 7471
– www.petershamhotel.co.uk   **6**CX**c**
59 rm – †£ 135 ††£ 175/185 – 1 suite
Rest *Restaurant at The Petersham* – ℘ (020) 8939 1084 – Menu £ 26/39
– Carte dinner £ 31/52
♦ Extended over the years, a fine example of Victorian Gothic architecture, with Portland stone and self-supporting staircase. The most comfortable bedrooms overlook the Thames. Formal restaurant in which to enjoy a mix of classic and modern cooking; ask for a window table for terrific park and river views.

Bingham
61-63 Petersham Rd. ⊠ TW10 6UT – Richmond – ℘ (020) 8940 0902
– www.thebingham.co.uk – Closed first week January   **6**CX**c**
15 rm – †£ 215/360 ††£ 240/360, £ 15
Rest *Bingham Restaurant* – see restaurant listing
♦ A pair of conjoined and restored Georgian townhouses; a short walk from Richmond centre. Ask for a room overlooking the river and garden. Contemporary styled bedrooms; some with four-posters.

RICHMOND-UPON-THAMES

XX Bingham Restaurant – at Bingham Hotel
61-63 Petersham Rd. ✉ TW10 6UT ⊖ Richmond – ℰ (020) 8940 0902
– www.thebingham.co.uk – Closed first week January and Sunday dinner
Rest – Modern European – Menu £ 26/55   6CXc

♦ Charming spot, especially if you've arrived on foot from along the river; dine on the balcony overlooking the garden or in the more traditional dining room. There's a modern style to the cooking and dishes are visually impressive.

X Petersham Nurseries Café
Church Ln (off Petersham Rd) ✉ TW10 7AG – ℰ (020) 8605 3627
– www.petershamnurseries.com – Closed 24-29 December and Monday
Rest – Italian influences – (lunch only) (booking advisable)   6CXx
Carte £ 45/61
Spec. Crab salad with nam jim sauce and mixed cress. Sea bass fillet with spinach, fresh chilli and preserved lemon dressing. Chocolate mousse with ginger caramel and Jersey cream.

♦ The Café is outside on sunny days and in a greenhouse the rest of the time; leave your best shoes at home! The food's all about natural flavours and fresh, vibrant ingredients; its earthiness seems so right when you're eating among plants and flowers.

X Matsuba
10 Red Lion St ✉ TW9 1RW ⊖ Richmond – ℰ (020) 8605 3513 – Closed 25-26 December, 1 January and Sunday   6CXn
Rest – Japanese – Carte £ 40/45

♦ Family-run Japanese restaurant with just 11 tables; understated but well-kept appearance. Extensive menu offers wide range of Japanese dishes, along with bulgogi, a Korean barbecue dish.

X Swagat
86 Hill Rise ✉ TW10 6UB ⊖ Richmond – ℰ (0208) 940 75 57
– www.swagatindiancuisine.co.uk – Closed 25-26 December,
1 January and Sunday   6CXi
Rest – Indian – (dinner only) Menu £ 30 – Carte £ 22/34

♦ Well-meaning service and an appealing menu have made this Indian restaurant popular with locals so it's worth booking. Plenty of classics and vegetarian choices; try the less familiar.

TEDDINGTON

XX Rétro Bistrot
114-116 High St ✉ TW11 8JB – ℰ (0208) 977 22 39 – www.retrobistrot.co.uk
– Closed first 2 weeks August, first 10 days January, Sunday dinner and Monday
Rest – French – Menu £ 14/23 – Carte £ 23/41   5BYn

♦ There's substance as well as style to this French bistrot. The classic bourgeois cuisine is prepared with innate skill; service is warm and effusive and the slick decoration conducive to merrymaking.

XX Al Borgo
3 Church Rd. ✉ TW11 8PF – ℰ (020) 8943 4456 – www.alborgo.co.uk – Closed Sunday and bank holidays   5BYe
Rest – Italian – Carte approx. £ 35

♦ A refreshingly unpretentious and keenly run Italian restaurant that exudes warmth and bonhomie. Homemade focaccia and pasta are the highlights. Look out too for seasonal offerings such as the black truffle menu.

X Simply Thai
196 Kingston Rd. ✉ TW11 9JD – ℰ (020) 8943 9747
– www.simplythai-restaurant.co.uk – Closed 25-26 December and Monday
Rest – Thai – (dinner only) Menu £ 25 – Carte £ 23/34   5BYx

♦ Extremely busy local Thai restaurant; the owner does all the cooking and her passion is clear. New creations sit alongside classics on the large menu. Prices are competitive; service can sometimes struggle to keep up.

RICHMOND-UPON-THAMES

Kings Head
123 High St — TW11 8HG – ℘ (020) 3166 2900 – www.whitebrasserie.com
Rest – Modern European – Menu £ 14/16 – Carte £ 19/26   **5**BY**c**

♦ Britain has its pubs and France its brasseries; The King's Head does its bit for the entente cordiale by combining both. Have a drink in the front bar, then enjoy rustic classics in the rear brasserie.

TWICKENHAM

A Cena
418 Richmond Rd. — TW1 2EB ⇄ Richmond – ℘ (020) 8288 0108
– www.acena.co.uk – Closed 25-26 December, Sunday dinner and Monday lunch
Rest – Italian – Carte £ 30/36   **5**BX**e**

♦ Rustic and quite intimate feel to this well-run neighbourhood Italian restaurant. Appealing, seasonal menu covers most of Italy and the generously sized dishes are full of flavour.

Brula
43 Crown Rd., St Margarets — TW1 3EJ – ℘ (020) 8892 0602 – www.brula.co.uk
– Closed 26-30 December and Sunday dinner   **5**BX**v**
Rest – French – (booking essential) Menu £ 18 (lunch) – Carte £ 22/36

♦ Traditional in look, with its mirrors and chandeliers but friendly service and popular with the locals. They come for the good value, well-crafted cooking, which is largely French but now comes with a few Spanish and Italian influences.

Tangawizi
406 Richmond Rd., Richmond Bridge — TW1 2EB ⇄ Richmond – ℘ (020) 8891 3737 – www.tangawizi.co.uk – Closed 25-26 December and 1 January
Rest – Indian – (dinner only and Sunday lunch) Carte £ 15/31   **5**BX**e**

♦ Name means Ginger in Swahili. Sleek décor in warm purple with subtle Indian touches. Well-priced, nicely balanced, slowly evolving menus take their influence from north India.

EAST SHEEN

Mango & Silk
199 Upper Richmond Rd. West — SW14 8 QT – ℘ (020) 8876 6220
– www.mangoandsilk.co.uk – Closed 25 December and Monday   **21**KZH**k**
Rest – Indian – (dinner only and buffet lunch Sunday) Carte £ 20/23

♦ An air of calm pervades the restaurant, thanks to the charming owner. Udit Sarkhel is the chef and his cooking is as expertly crafted as ever. The generous prices make over-ordering the easy option.

Victoria with rm
10 West Temple Sheen — SW14 7RT ⇄ Mortlake (Rail). – ℘ (020) 8876 4238
– www.thevictoria.net   **6**CX**u**
7 rm – †£ 115 ††£ 125, ⊑ £ 8   **Rest** – British – Carte £ 28/30

♦ Beautifully restored pub, eat in the relaxed bar or more formal conservatory overlooking the terrace; this is a genuine local that plays its part in the community and the kitchen takes its sourcing seriously. Simple bedrooms available.

SOUTHWARK – Greater London   **12** B3

🛈 Level 2, Tate Modern, Bankside ℘ (020) 7401 52 66, www.visitlondon.com

BERMONDSEY

Hilton London Tower Bridge
5 More London, Tooley St. — SE1 2BY ⇄ London Bridge
– ℘ (020) 3002 4300 – www.hilton.co.uk/towerbridge   **34**ARV**e**
245 rm – †£ 598 ††£ 598, ⊑ £ 22.50   **Rest** – Carte £ 35/45

♦ Usefully located new-style Hilton hotel with boldly decorated open-plan lobby. Contemporary bedrooms boast well-designed features; 4 floors of executive rooms. Dine on classics and comfort food in restaurant with outdoor seating.

SOUTHWARK

Bermondsey Square

Bermondsey Sq, Tower Bridge Rd ✉ SE1 3UN ⊖ London Bridge
– ℘ (020) 7378 2450 – www.bermondseysquarehotel.co.uk
79 rm – †£ 130/250 ††£ 130/600, ⚍ £ 11
20XZE**n**
Rest *Alfie's* – English – Carte £ 24/31

♦ Opened in 2009 in hip, regenerated square. Cleverly designed hotel, with subtle '60s influence and fun feel. Well-equipped bedrooms, including four loft suites. English menu in Alfie's makes good use of local food markets.

London Bridge

8-18 London Bridge St ✉ SE1 9SG ⊖ London Bridge – ℘ (020) 7855 2200
– www.londonbridgehotel.com
138 rm – †£ 358 ††£ 358, ⚍ £ 17 – 3 suites
33AQV**a**
Rest *Londinium* – *(closed Sunday lunch)* Carte £ 28/43

♦ In one of the oldest parts of London, independently owned with an ornate façade dating from 1915. Modern interior with classically decorated bedrooms and an impressive gym. Londinium for brasserie dining.

Le Pont de la Tour

36d Shad Thames, Butlers Wharf ✉ SE1 2YE ⊖ London Bridge
– ℘ (020) 7403 8403 – www.lepontdelatour.co.uk
34ASV**c**
Rest – French – Menu £ 32/45

♦ Providing, since 1991, seasonal French cooking, an urbane atmosphere and a wonderful riverside location, with views of Tower Bridge. Simpler dishes served in the livelier cocktail bar and grill.

Magdalen

152 Tooley St. ✉ SE1 2TU ⊖ London Bridge – ℘ (020) 7403 1342
– www.magdalenrestaurant.co.uk – Closed 24 December-5 January, 15-30
August, Saturday lunch, Sunday and bank holidays
34ARV**b**
Rest – British – Menu £ 19 (lunch) – Carte £ 30/40

♦ The clever sourcing and confident British cooking will leave you satisfied. Add genial service, an affordable lunch menu and a food-friendly wine list and you have the favourite restaurant of many.

Zucca

184 Bermondsey St ✉ SE1 3TQ ⊖ Borough – ℘ (020) 7378 6809
– www.zuccalondon.com – Closed 24 December-10 January, Easter, Sunday
dinner and Monday
20XZE**s**
Rest – Italian – *(booking essential at dinner)* Carte £ 18/25

♦ Bright and buzzy modern room, where the informed Italian cooking is driven by the fresh ingredients, the prices are more than generous and the service is sweet and responsive. The appealing antipasti is great for sharing.

Blueprint Café

Design Museum, Shad Thames, Butlers Wharf ✉ SE1 2YD ⊖ London Bridge
– ℘ (020) 7378 7031 – www.blueprintcafe.co.uk – Closed Sunday dinner
Rest – Modern European – Menu £ 20/22 – Carte £ 24/38
34ASV**u**

♦ Champions British produce in dishes using simple, but informed, techniques. Bright, retro feel; located above the Design Museum, with retractable windows and binoculars on each table.

Village East

171-173 Bermondsey St. ✉ SE1 3UW ⊖ London Bridge – ℘ (020) 7357 6082
– www.villageeast.co.uk – Closed 25-27 December
20XZE**a**
Rest – Modern European – Carte £ 27/38

♦ In a glass-fronted block sandwiched by Georgian townhouses, this trendy restaurant has two loud, buzzy bars and dining areas serving ample portions of modern British fare.

SOUTHWARK

X **Cantina Del Ponte**
36c Shad Thames, Butlers Wharf ✉ SE1 2YE ⊖ London Bridge
– ☏ (020) 7403 5403 – www.cantina.co.uk – Closed 25-27 December
Rest – Italian – Menu £ 18 (lunch) – Carte £ 20/28   **34**ASV**c**

• This Italian stalwart offers an appealing mix of classic dishes and reliable favourites from a sensibly priced menu, in pleasant faux-rustic surroundings. Its pleasant terrace takes advantage of its riverside setting.

X **Butlers Wharf Chop House**
36e Shad Thames, Butlers Wharf ✉ SE1 2YE ⊖ London Bridge
– ☏ (020) 7403 3403 – www.chophouse.co.uk – Closed 1-2 January
Rest – British – Menu £ 27 (lunch) – Carte dinner £ 29/45   **34**ASV**n**

• Grab a table on the terrace in summer and dine in the shadow of Tower Bridge. Rustic feel to the interior; noisy and fun. The menu focuses on traditional English ingredients and dishes.

X **Champor-Champor**
62-64 Weston St. ✉ SE1 3QJ ⊖ London Bridge – ☏ (020) 7403 4600
– www.champor-champor.com – Closed 1 week Christmas, 1 week
Easter, Sunday and bank holidays   **34**ARV**a**
Rest – Asian – *(dinner only)* Carte £ 34/43

• Choice of two beguiling and colourful rooms: ask for the second as it has even more character, better lighting and a mezzanine. Food is rooted in Malay traditions with a hint of modernity.

X **Vivat Bacchus London Bridge**
4 Hays Ln ✉ SE1 2HB ⊖ London Bridge – ☏ (0207) 234 08 91
– www.vivatbacchus.co.uk – Closed 23 December-2 January, Saturday lunch,
Sunday and bank holidays   **34**ARV**n**
Rest – Traditional – Menu £ 17/18 – Carte £ 17/33

• South African element to both the menu and the very impressive wine list. International platters in ground floor wine bar; robust cooking in the basement restaurant, with its great cheese room.

X **José**
104 Bermondsey St ✉ SE1 3UB ⊖ London Bridge – ☏ (020) 7403 4902
– www.josepizarro.com – Closed 25-26 December and Sunday dinner
Rest – Spanish – *(bookings not accepted)* Carte approx. £ 25   **20**XZE**v**

• Standing up while eating tapas feels so right, especially at this small, fun bar that packs 'em in like boquerones. Five dishes each should suffice; go for the daily fish dishes from the blackboard. There's a great list of sherries too.

ID **Garrison**
99-101 Bermondsey St ✉ SE1 3XB ⊖ London Bridge. – ☏ (020) 7089 9355
– www.thegarrison.co.uk – Closed 25-27 December   **20**XZE**z**
Rest – *(booking essential at dinner)* Carte £ 23/30

• Known for its vintage look, booths and sweet-natured service, The Garrison boasts a warm, relaxed vibe. Open from breakfast until dinner where a Mediterranean-led menu pulls in the crowd.

SOUTHWARK

🛈 Level 2, Tate Modern, Bankside ☏ (020) 7401 52 66, www.visitlondon.com

XXX **Oxo Tower**
Oxo Tower Wharf (8th floor), Barge House St ✉ SE1 9PH ⊖ Southwark
– ☏ (020) 7803 3888 – www.harveynichols.com – Closed 25 December, dinner 24
December and lunch 26 December   **32**ANV**a**
Rest – Modern European – Menu £ 35 (lunch) – Carte £ 39/52
Rest Oxo Tower Brasserie – see restaurant listing

• Top of a converted iconic factory, providing stunning views of the Thames and beyond. Stylish, minimalist interior with huge windows. Expect quite ambitious, mostly European, cuisine.

SOUTHWARK

Roast
The Floral Hall, Borough Mkt. ✉ *SE1 1TL* ⊖ *London Bridge* – ☏ *(0845) 347 300*
– *www.roast-restaurant.com – Closed 25 December, 1 January and Sunday dinner*
33AQVe
Rest – British – *(booking essential)* Menu £ 28 (lunch and early dinner)
– Carte £ 37/60

• Set into the roof of Borough Market's Floral Hall. Extensive cocktail list in bar; split-level restaurant has views to St Paul's. Robust English cooking uses market produce.

Baltic
74 Blackfriars Rd ✉ *SE1 8HA* ⊖ *Southwark* – ☏ *(020) 7928 1111*
– *www.balticrestaurant.co.uk – Closed 24-25 December, 1 January and bank holidays*
33AOVe
Rest – Eastern European – *(booking advisable at dinner)* Menu £ 18 (weekday lunch) – Carte £ 27/37

• Enjoy big portions of authentic and hearty east European food, served in a Grade II listed 18C former coach house. The restaurant, which celebrated 10 years in 2011, also has some interesting vodkas; live jazz on Sundays.

Oxo Tower Brasserie
Oxo Tower Wharf (8th floor), Barge House St ✉ *SE1 9PH* ⊖ *Southwark*
– ☏ *(020) 7803 3888 – www.harveynichols.com – Closed 25 December, dinner 24 December and lunch 26 December*
32ANVa
Rest – Modern European – Menu £ 27 (weekday lunch) – Carte £ 33/49

• Less formal but more fun than the next-door restaurant. Open-plan kitchen produces modern, colourful and easy-to-eat dishes with influences from the Med. Great views too from the bar.

Cantina Vinopolis
No.1 Bank End ✉ *SE1 9BU* ⊖ *London Bridge* – ☏ *(020) 7940 8333*
– *www.cantinavinopolis.com – Closed bank holidays*
33AQVz
Rest – Mediterranean – Menu £ 30 – Carte £ 25/39

• Beneath vast Victorian arches and next to their wine museum sits this bustling restaurant, popular with larger parties. Impressive wine choice and carefully prepared food with a Mediterranean slant.

Tate Modern (Restaurant)
Tate Modern (7th floor), Bankside ✉ *SE1 9TG* ⊖ *Southwark*
– ☏ *(020) 7887 8888 – www.tate.org.uk/modern/eatanddrink – Closed 24-26 December*
33APVs
Rest – British – *(lunch only and dinner Friday-Saturday)* Carte £ 28/34

• 7th floor restaurant with floor to ceilings windows on two sides and large mural. Appealing mix of light and zesty dishes, with seasonal produce. Good choice of wines and non-alcoholic drinks.

Tapas Brindisa
18-20 Southwark St., Borough Market ✉ *SE1 1TJ* ⊖ *London Bridge*
– ☏ *(020) 7357 8880 – www.brindisa.com*
33AQVk
Rest – Spanish – *(bookings not accepted)* Carte £ 12/30

• Prime quality Spanish produce sold in owner's shops and this bustling eatery on edge of Borough Market. Freshly prepared, tasty tapas: waiters will assist with your choice.

Wright Brothers
11 Stoney St., Borough Market ✉ *SE1 9AD* ⊖ *London Bridge*
– ☏ *(020) 7403 9554 – www.wrightbrothers.co.uk – Closed bank holiday Mondays*
33AQVm
Rest – Seafood – *(booking advisable)* Carte £ 25/51

• Originally an oyster wholesaler; now offers a wide range of oysters along with porter, as well as fruits de mer, daily specials and assorted pies. It fills quickly and an air of contentment reigns.

SOUTHWARK

Brew Wharf
Brew Wharf Yard, Stoney St ⊠ SE1 9AD ⊖ London Bridge
– ℘ (020) 7378 6601 – www.brewwharf.com – Closed Sunday dinner and bank holidays
33AQV**h**
Rest – Traditional – Carte £ 23/35
♦ A busy bar, microbrewery and restaurant; come in a group to enjoy the sports screen and vast selection of beers and ales. The gutsy food and shared platters are the perfect match for the beer.

Anchor & Hope
36 The Cut ⊠ SE1 8LP ⊖ Southwark. – ℘ (020) 7928 9898
– Closed Christmas-New Year, Sunday dinner, Monday lunch and bank holidays
Rest – British – (bookings not accepted) Carte £ 23/32
32ANV**n**
♦ As popular as ever thanks to its congenial feel and lived-in looks but mostly because of the appealingly seasonal menu and the gutsy, bold cooking that delivers on flavour. No reservations so be prepared to wait at the bar.

SUTTON – Greater London   12 B3

SUTTON

Oak Sports Centre Carshalton Woodmansterne Rd, ℘ (020) 8643 83 63

Brasserie Vacherin
12 High St ⊠ SM1 1HN – ℘ (020) 8722 0180 – www.brasserievacherin.co.uk
– Closed 25 December
7EZ**x**
Rest – French – Menu £ 17 – Carte £ 25/34
♦ Relaxed, modern French brasserie with tiled walls, art nouveau posters and deep red banquettes. Good value midweek set price menu and à la carte of French classics. Diligent service.

WORCESTER PARK

Avventura
82-86 Central Rd ⊠ KT4 8HX – ℘ (020) 8335 3355
– www.avventura-restaurant.co.uk – Closed 2 weeks July-August, 1 week Easter, 24 December-3 January and bank holidays
6CZ**x**
Rest – Italian – (dinner only and lunch Saturday-Sunday) Menu £ 20
– Carte £ 28/33
♦ Keenly run, modern day trattoria in a busy suburban high street. Tiled floor, polished tables and informal atmosphere. Experienced owners offer homemade pasta and pizza cooked in a copper, wood-fired oven. Service is engaging and animated.

TOWER HAMLETS – Greater London   12 B3

BETHNAL GREEN

Town Hall
Patriot Sq ⊠ E2 9NF ⊖ Bethnal Green – ℘ (020) 7871 0460
– www.townhallhotel.com
14YZB**x**
97 rm – †£ 174/348 ††£ 207/414, ⊇ £ 15 – 1 suite
Rest *Viajante* ✿ – see restaurant listing
Rest *Corner Room* – (bookings not accepted) Carte £ 21/23
♦ Edwardian, former council offices converted into a hotel in 2010. Its period character is balanced with modernity, with individually decorated, understated bedrooms and frequently changing art. 'Corner Room' restaurant merely hints at the superlative cooking found in Viajante.

TOWER HAMLETS

Viajante – at Town Hall Hotel
Patriot Sq., (entrance on Cambridge Heath Rd) ✉ *E2 9NF* – Bethnal Green
– ℰ (020) 7871 0461 – www.viajante.co.uk – *Closed lunch Monday-Tuesday and bank holidays*

14YZBx

Rest – Innovative – *(booking essential)* Menu £ 28/65
Spec. Cod and potatoes with egg yolk and saffron. Pork secretos with artichokes and hot potato gel. White chocolate with grapefruit and lemon.
♦ Highly innovative and original cooking; you choose 6, 9 or 12 delicate courses. A converted Victorian town hall is the unlikely setting for this creative style of cooking; ask to sit in the front room if you want to watch the chefs at work.

Brawn
49 Columbia Rd. ✉ *E2 7RG* – Bethnal Green – ℰ (020) 7729 5692
– www.brawn.co – *Closed Sunday dinner and bank holidays*

20XZDz

Rest – Mediterranean – Carte £ 21/28
♦ Unpretentious and simply kitted out baby sister to Terroirs; the name captures the essence of the cooking perfectly: it is rustic, muscular and makes very good use of pig. Great local atmosphere and polite, helpful service.

BOW

Morgan Arms
43 Morgan St ✉ *E3 5AA* – Bow Road – ℰ (020) 8980 6389
– www.capitalpubcompany.com/The-Morgan-Arms – *Closed 25 December*

3GUc

Rest – Carte £ 24/34
♦ Characterful pub with mismatch of furniture and shabby-chic appeal. Constantly evolving menu offers robust cooking which occasionally uses some unfamiliar ingredients; simpler food is served in the lively bar.

CANARY WHARF

Four Seasons
Westferry Circus ✉ *E14 8RS* – Canary Wharf – ℰ (020) 7510 1999
– www.fourseasons.com/canarywharf

3GVa

128 rm – †£ 282/312 ††£ 282/312, ⌑ £ 26 – 14 suites
Rest *Quadrato* – see restaurant listing
♦ Professionally run international hotel geared primarily to the local corporate market; whose deluxe rooms boast impressive views across the river. Leisure facilities housed in an adjacent club.

Quadrato – at Four Seasons Hotel
Westferry Circus ✉ *E14 8RS* – Canary Wharf – ℰ (020) 7510 1999
– www.fourseasons.com/canarywharf

3GVa

Rest – Italian – Menu £ 39 – Carte £ 37/53
♦ Smart, spacious restaurant on the ground floor of the Four Seasons, with river-facing terrace. Luxury ingredients used in dishes that cover all parts of Italy. Knowledgeable service.

Dockmaster's House
1 Hertsmere Rd ✉ *E14 8JJ* – Canary Wharf – ℰ (020) 7345 0345
– www.dockmastershouse.com – *Closed Christmas, Sunday, Saturday lunch and bank holidays*

3GVr

Rest – Indian – *(booking advisable)* Menu £ 20 (lunch and early dinner)
– Carte £ 28/40
♦ A contemporary overhaul of a three storey Georgian house in the shadow of Canary Wharf's skyscrapers has created this slick operation. Elaborate Indian cooking, although sometimes a little pretentious.

TOWER HAMLETS

XX Plateau
Canada Place (4th floor), Canada Square ✉ E14 5ER ⊖ Canary Wharf – ℰ (020) 7715 7100 – www.plateaurestaurant.co.uk – Closed 25 December, 1 January and Sunday **3GVn**
Rest – Modern European – Menu £ 28 – Carte £ 39/55
◆ Impressive open-plan space with dramatic glass walls and ceilings and striking 1970s design. Rotisserie meats in the Grill; globally-influenced dishes in formal restaurant.

XX Roka Canary Wharf
4 Park Pavilion (1st Floor) ✉ E14 5FW ⊖ Canary Wharf – ℰ (020) 7636 5228 – www.rokarestaurant.com – Closed Christmas **3GVv**
Rest – Japanese – (booking essential) Carte £ 35/65
◆ You'll be hit by a wall of sound at this large and perennially busy operation in the shadow of Canary Wharf Tower. The meats cooked on the robata grill are highlights of the Japanese menu.

🍺 Gun
27 Coldharbour ✉ E14 9NS ⊖ Blackwall (DLR) – ℰ (020) 7515 5222 – www.thegundocklands.com – Closed 25-26 December **7GVx**
Rest – Menu £ 18 (lunch) – Carte £ 28/49
◆ Despite its 21C makeover, this 18C pub, with links to Lord Nelson, hasn't forgotten its roots. Smart dining room; menu a mix of classic and modern. Always busy, especially the large decked area.

LIMEHOUSE

🍺 Narrow
44 Narrow St ✉ E14 8DP ⊖ Limehouse (DLR). – ℰ (020) 7592 7950 – www.gordonramsay.com **3GVo**
Rest – (booking essential) Menu £ 22 (lunch) – Carte £ 24/36
◆ Grade II listed former dockmaster's house on the river; part of Gordon Ramsay's group. Menu specialises in British favourites, from shrimps to sardines, braised beef to trifle.

SPITALFIELDS

XXX Galvin La Chapelle
❀
35 Spital Sq. ✉ E1 6DY ⊖ Liverpool Street – ℰ (020) 7299 0400 – www.galvinrestaurants.com – Closed dinner 24-26 December and 1 January
Rest – French – Menu £ 26 (lunch)/30 (early dinner) **34ASTv**
– Carte £ 32/51
Spec. Lasagne of crab with velouté of girolles. Tagine of pigeon with aubergine purée and harissa sauce. Chilled Valhrona chocolate fondant, banana and yoghurt ice cream and fresh honeycomb.
◆ The Victorian splendour of St. Botolph's Hall, with its vaulted ceiling, arched windows and marble pillars, lends itself perfectly to its role as a glamorous restaurant. The food is bourgeois French with a sophisticated edge and is bound to satisfy.

XX Les Trois Garcons
1 Club Row ✉ E1 6JX ⊖ Shoreditch – ℰ (020) 7613 1924 – www.lestroisgarcons.com – Closed 23 December-3 January, Saturday lunch, Sunday dinner and bank holidays **20XZDr**
Rest – French – Menu £ 22/47
◆ Extraordinarily eccentric, with stuffed animals, twinkling beads, assorted chandeliers and ceiling handbags. The French food is more traditional and governed by the seasons.

X Hawksmoor
157 Commercial St. ✉ E1 6BJ ⊖ Shoreditch – ℰ (020) 7247 7392 – www.thehawksmoor.com – Closed 1 week Christmas and Sunday dinner
Rest – Beef specialities – (booking essential) Carte £ 40/60 **20XZDs**
◆ Unremarkable surroundings and ordinary starters and puds but no matter: this is all about great British beef, hung for 35 days, from Longhorn cattle in the heart of the Yorkshire Moors.

TOWER HAMLETS

Galvin Café a Vin
35 Spital Sq. (entrance on Bishops Sq.) ⊠ *E1 6DY* ⊖ *Liverpool Street*
– ℘ *(020) 7299 0404 – www.galvinrestaurants.com – Closed 25 December*
Rest – French – Carte £ 24/30
34AST**v**
♦ In the same building as La Chapelle is this simpler but equally worthy operation from the Galvin brothers. The room may not have the grandeur of next door but what it does offer is classic French bistro food at very appealing prices.

St John Bread and Wine
94-96 Commercial St ⊠ *E1 6LZ* ⊖ *Shoreditch* – ℘ *(020) 7251 0848*
– *www.stjohnbreadandwine.com – Closed Christmas-New Year and bank holidays*
34AST**x**
Rest – British – Carte £ 23/29
♦ Part-wine shop/bakery and local restaurant. Highly seasonal and appealing menu changes twice a day; cooking is British, uncomplicated and very satisfying. Try the less familiar dishes.

Owl & Pussycat
34 Redchurch St ⊠ *E2 7DP* ⊖ *Shoreditch.* – ℘ *(020) 3487 0088*
– *www.owlandpussycatshoreditch.com – Closed 25-26 December, 1 January and bank holidays*
20XZD**z**
Rest – British – Carte £ 25/43
♦ The former Crown now has a raggedly modish look with ironic touches of Victoriana to match the Edward Lear name. An appealingly stout British menu is offered in the upstairs dining room.

WAPPING

Smith's of Wapping
22 Wapping High St ⊠ *E1W 1NJ* ⊖ *Wapping* – ℘ *(020) 7488 3456*
– *www.smithsbrasserie.com – Closed Sunday dinner*
20XZE**c**
Rest – Seafood – *(booking advisable)* Menu £ 25 (lunch) – Carte £ 33/60
♦ Having provided seafood to the burghers of Essex for over 50 years, the Smiths opened this large riverside brasserie in 2011. The kitchen keeps it traditional; the best dishes are old favourites like dressed crab and Dover sole meunière.

Wapping Food
Wapping Wall ⊠ *E1W 3SG* ⊖ *Wapping* – ℘ *(020) 7680 2080*
– *www.thewappingproject.com – Closed 24 December-3 January, Sunday dinner and bank holidays*
20YZE**n**
Rest – Modern European – Carte £ 25/41
♦ This striking Victorian former hydraulic power station houses an atmospheric restaurant and art gallery. Sit among the old turbines and enjoy robust, straightforward dishes based on what's in season.

WHITECHAPEL

Cafe Spice Namaste
16 Prescot St. ⊠ *E1 8AZ* ⊖ *Tower Hill* – ℘ *(020) 7488 9242*
– *www.cafespice.co.uk – Closed 25 December-2 January, Saturday lunch, Sunday and bank holidays*
34ASU**z**
Rest – Indian – Carte £ 27/33
♦ Fresh, vibrant and fairly priced Indian cuisine from Cyrus Todiwala, served in a colourfully decorated room that was once a magistrate's court. Engaging service from an experienced team.

Whitechapel Gallery Dining Room
77-82 Whitechapel High St. ⊠ *E1 7QX* ⊖ *Aldgate East* – ℘ *(020) 7522 7896*
– *www.whitechapelgallery.org/dining-room – Closed Christmas-New Year, Monday and dinner Sunday and Tuesday*
34AST**x**
Rest – Italian influences – *(booking advisable)* Carte £ 24/30
♦ Founded in 1901 and best known for exhibiting Picasso's 'Guernica', the gallery underwent a major refit in 2009, which resulted in the creation of this sweet restaurant. Bright, European and Med influenced cooking from an accessible menu.

WANDSWORTH – Greater London

BALHAM

Brasserie James
47 Balham Hill ⊠ SW12 9DR ⊖ Clapham South – ℰ (020) 8772 0057
– www.brasseriejames.com – Closed 23-30 December
Rest – Modern European – Carte £ 28/36

6EX**x**

♦ Crisp and neat brasserie owned and run by former Conran/D&D chef. Something for everyone on the seasonal menu, from moules to pasta. Weekend brunches; good value set menus; wines by carafe.

Lamberts
2 Station Par. ⊠ SW12 9AZ ⊖ Balham – ℰ (020) 8675 2233
– www.lambertsrestaurant.com – Closed 24-26 December, 1 January, Sunday dinner and Monday

6EX**n**

Rest – Traditional – *(dinner only and lunch Saturday-Sunday)* Menu £ 20 (midweek) – Carte £ 27/34

♦ Locals come for the relaxed surroundings, hospitable service and tasty, seasonal food. Sunday lunch is very popular. The enthusiasm of the eponymous owner has rubbed off on his team.

Harrison's
15-19 Bedford Hill ⊠ SW12 9EX ⊖ Balham – ℰ (020) 8675 6900
– www.harrisonsbalham.co.uk – Closed 24-28 December
Rest – Mediterranean – Carte £ 30/39

6EX**a**

♦ Sister to Sam's Brasserie in Chiswick. Open all day, with an appealing list of favourites, from fishcakes to Cumberland sausages. Weekend brunches; kids' menu; good value weekday set menus.

Avalon
16 Balham Hill ⊠ SW12 9EB ⊖ Clapham South. – ℰ (020) 8675 8613
– www.theavalonlondon.com – Closed 25-26 December and 1 January
Rest – *(booking advisable)* Carte £ 25/30

6EX**r**

♦ Large, bustling and atmospheric pub with an appealing summer terrace. Snacks served in the busy, long bar and an appealingly broad menu offered in the tiled and characterful rear dining room.

BATTERSEA

Chada
208-210 Battersea Park Rd. ⊠ SW11 4ND – ℰ (020) 7622 2209
– www.chadathai.com – Closed Sunday and bank holidays
Rest – Thai – *(dinner only)* Carte £ 19/43

23QZH**x**

♦ Going strong after 20 years; its striking façade stands out in an otherwise unremarkable street. The welcome is warm, the service polite and the Thai food appealing and keenly priced.

Bennett
7-9 Battersea Sq. ⊠ SW11 3PA ⊖ Clapham Junction (rail) – ℰ (020) 7223 5545
– www.bennettsbrasserie.com – Closed Sunday dinner
Rest – British – Carte £ 29/36

23PZH**a**

♦ Smart, all-day brasserie with wine shop attached. The menu appeals to a broad constituency by offering everything from brasserie classics and a large seafood selection to traditional British staples and nursery favourites.

Ransome's Dock
35-37 Parkgate Rd. ⊠ SW11 4NP – ℰ (020) 7223 1611
– www.ransomesdock.co.uk – Closed Christmas, August bank holiday and Sunday dinner
Rest – British – Carte £ 24/37

23QZG**c**

♦ Husband and wife team run a brasserie-style operation in a converted warehouse, with a canal-side terrace. Careful sourcing underpins the cooking. Thoughtful, varied and sensibly priced wine list.

WANDSWORTH

✕ Tom Ilić
[AC] [VISA] [●●] [AE] [●]

123 Queenstown Rd. ⊠ SW8 3RH – ✆ (020) 7622 0555 – www.tomilic.com
– Closed Christmas, 1 week summer, Monday, Sunday dinner and Tuesday lunch
Rest – Traditional – *(booking essential)* Menu £ 20/22   **24**RZH**c**
– Carte £ 29/38

♦ Spacious, simply decorated neighbourhood restaurant offering an appealing offal-based menu, with plenty of pork. Skilled, intricate cooking with bold, gutsy flavours to the fore.

✕ Entrée
[AC] [VISA] [●●] [AE]

2 Battersea Rise ⊠ SW11 1ED ⊖ Clapham Junction (rail) – ✆ (020) 7223 5147
– www.entreebattersea.co.uk – Closed 24-28 December   **23**QZH**a**
Rest – Modern European – *(dinner only and lunch Saturday-Sunday)*
Carte £ 29/36

♦ They've gone for a casual bistro look which, along with a basement bar and weekend pianist, hits the right note with locals. Sensibly priced menu mixes French classic and modern European dishes.

✕ Lola Rojo
[🏠] [AC] [VISA] [●●] [●]

78 Northcote Rd ⊠ SW11 6QL ⊖ Clapham Junction (rail) – ✆ (020) 7350 2262
– www.lolarojo.net – Closed 25-26 December   **23**QZH**v**
Rest – Spanish – *(booking essential)* Menu £ 9 (weekday lunch) – Carte £ 22/31

♦ Few spots on Northcote Road are as fun as this lively, if cramped Spanish eatery. The owner-chef comes from Valencia so paella is a sure thing but other Catalan tapas specialities are also worth seeking out.

✕ Metrogusto
[AC] [VISA] [●●] [AE]

153 Battersea Park Rd. ⊠ SW8 4BX ⊖ Battersea Park (rail) – ✆ (020) 7720 0204
– www.metrogusto.co.uk – Closed 25-26 December, Easter and Sunday dinner
Rest – Italian – Carte £ 21/35   **24**RZG**a**

♦ Ambro Ianeselli, one of London's most affable restaurateurs, has moved from Islington back to his original Battersea base, along with his art collection. The Italian food is simple and as heart-warming as Ambro's never-ending hospitality.

🍺 Bolingbroke
[🏠] [AC] [VISA] [●●] [AE]

174 Northcote Rd ⊠ SW11 6RE ⊖ Clapham Junction (rail). – ✆ (020)
7228 4040 – www.thebolingbroke.com – Closed 25-28 December   **6**EX**z**
Rest – British – Carte £ 21/34

♦ Smart, locally popular pub whose more diminutive size adds extra charm. Glass-roofed dining room sees flavoursome dishes with a mostly British accent; more choice at dinner. Child friendly.

BATTERSEA HELIPORT

🏨 Verta
[various symbols] [AC] [VISA] [●●] [●]

Bridges Wharf ⊠ SW11 3BE – ✆ (020) 7801 3500 – www.hotelverta.co.uk
68 rm – ♦£ 124/285 ♦♦£ 314/475, ⊇ £ 19.50 – 2 suites   **23**PZH**v**
Rest *Patrisey* – Menu £ 20/25 – Carte £ 32/45

♦ Built in 2010, in a unique riverside location with a heliport. Well-equipped bedrooms; those without views are bigger than those with. Impressive spa facilities. Choose from a wide-ranging menu, while watching the helicopters land.

PUTNEY

✕✕ Enoteca Turi
[AC] [⇔] [VISA] [●●] [●]

28 Putney High St. ⊠ SW15 1SQ ⊖ Putney Bridge – ✆ (020) 8785 4449
– www.enotecaturi.com – Closed 25-26 December, 1 January, Sunday
and lunch bank holiday Mondays   **22**MZH**r**
Rest – Italian – Menu £ 20 (lunch) – Carte £ 32/40

♦ A long-standing owner-run Italian restaurant. Earthy cooking focuses on the northerly regions of Italy. Interesting wine list, with plenty by the glass and carafe

WANDSWORTH

Cantinetta
162-164 Lower Richmond Rd, (Entrance on Pentlow St) ✉ SW15 1LY
⊖ Putney Bridge – ☏ (020) 8780 3131 – www.cantinetta.co.uk
– Closed Sunday dinner and Monday lunch in winter
21LZHv
Rest – Italian – Menu £ 16/18 – Carte £ 21/32

♦ A bright and relaxed modern day trattoria, opening onto a popular terrace. Well-priced dishes deliver on flavour, whether that's deep-fried anchovies with carpione dressing or the Ligurian classic 'trofie al pesto'.

Prince of Wales
138 Upper Richmond Rd ✉ SW15 2SP ⊖ East Putney. – ☏ (020) 8788 1552
– www.princeofwalesputney.co.uk – Closed 23 December-1 January and Monday lunch except bank holidays
22MZHz
Rest – British – Carte £ 27/43

♦ Warmly run Victorian pub; eat in the busy bar or in lavishly decorated baronial style dining room. Seasonality to the fore, with game a speciality. Spit-roast chickens feature on Sunday lunchtimes.

SOUTHFIELDS
12 B3

Triphal
201 Replingham Rd ✉ SW18 5LY ⊖ Southfields – ☏ (020) 8870 0188 – Closed 25-26 December, 1 January and Monday
6DXe
Rest – Indian – Carte £ 15/19

♦ Created on a shoestring by three partners, two of whom are chefs, this is a sweet little place making efforts all round. Fish curries are the stand out dishes from a concise, good value menu of regional Indian cuisine.

WANDSWORTH

Chez Bruce (Bruce Poole)
2 Bellevue Rd ✉ SW17 7EG ⊖ Tooting Bec – ☏ (020) 8672 0114
– www.chezbruce.co.uk – Closed 24-26 December and 1 January
6EXe
Rest – French – (booking essential) Menu £ 28 (weekday lunch)/45
Spec. Rare grilled tuna à la Niçoise, fennel purée and anchovy beignet. Rump and shoulder of lamb with spring vegetables, creamed potato and rosemary. Hot chocolate pudding with praline parfait.

♦ Flavoursome, uncomplicated French cooking with hints of the Mediterranean prepared with innate skill; well-organised, personable service and an easy-going atmosphere - some of the reasons why Chez Bruce remains a favourite of so many.

WESTMINSTER (City of) – Greater London
12 B3

BAYSWATER AND MAIDA VALE

Lancaster London
Lancaster Ter. ✉ W2 2TY ⊖ Lancaster Gate – ☏ (020) 7262 6737
– www.lancasterlondon.com
28ADUe
394 rm – †£ 119/372 ††£ 119/372, ⊇ £ 15.50 – 22 suites
Rest *Island* **Rest** *Nipa* – see restaurant listing

♦ Still known to most people as The Royal Lancaster. Imposing 1960s purpose-built hotel overlooking Hyde Park. Extensive conference facilities. Well-equipped bedrooms are decorated in a traditional style.

The Hempel
31-35 Craven Hill Gdns. ✉ W2 3EA ⊖ Queensway – ☏ (020) 7298 9000
– www.the-hempel.co.uk – Closed 24-27 December
28ACUa
44 rm – †£ 214/310 ††£ 241/310, ⊇ £ 22.50 – 6 suites
Rest *No.35* – (closed Sunday) (dinner only) Carte £ 30/43

♦ A crisp, minimalist environment in a blizzard of white; room 110 has a suspended bed. Basement art gallery also used for private parties. Zen garden in the Square opposite. Bright, ground floor dining room has a British menu.

WESTMINSTER (City of)

Colonnade Town House *without rest*
2 Warrington Cres. ✉ W9 1ER ⊖ Warwick Avenue – ℰ (020) 7286 1052
– www.theetoncollection.co.uk
17OZD**e**
43 rm – †£ 125/234 ††£ 138/378, ⊡ £ 12.50

♦ Former hospital in quiet yet easily accessible location. Bedrooms range in size according to grade; all are comfortable and classically furnished with good amenities. Lower floor bar.

Royal Park *without rest*
3 Westbourne Terr ✉ W2 3UL ⊖ Lancaster Gate – ℰ (020) 7479 6600
– www.theroyalpark.com
28ADU**x**
45 rm – †£ 178/378 ††£ 202/390, ⊡ £ 17.95 – 3 suites

♦ Three attractive 19C townhouses set back from the road, in a pleasant location near Hyde Park. Quiet lounges with period furnishings. Breakfast served in the well-appointed bedrooms.

New Linden *without rest*
59 Leinster Sq. ✉ W2 4PS ⊖ Bayswater – ℰ (020) 7221 4321
– www.mayflower-group.co.uk
27ABU**e**
50 rm – †£ 99/140 ††£ 175/250

♦ Smart four storey white stucco façade. Basement breakfast room opens onto summer courtyard. Bedrooms are its strength: flat screen TVs and wooden floors; two split-level family rooms.

Le Café Anglais
8 Porchester Gdns ✉ W2 4BD ⊖ Bayswater – ℰ (020) 7221 1415
– www.lecafeanglais.co.uk – Closed 25-26 December and 1 January
Rest – Modern European – Menu £ 24 (weekday lunch)
– Carte £ 25/52
27ABU**r**

♦ Big, bustling and contemporary brasserie with art deco styling, within Whiteley's shopping centre. Large, appealing selection of classic brasserie food; the rotisserie is the centrepiece. More casual oyster bar by entrance.

Angelus
4 Bathurst St. ✉ W2 2SD ⊖ Lancaster Gate – ℰ (020) 7402 0083
– www.angelusrestaurant.co.uk – Closed 24 December-2 January
28ADU**c**
Rest – French – Menu £ 32 (lunch) – Carte £ 39/54

♦ Hospitable owner has created an attractive French brasserie within a 19C former pub, with a warm and inclusive feel. Satisfying and honest French cooking uses seasonal British ingredients.

Nipa – at Lancaster London Hotel
Lancaster Terr ✉ W2 2TY ⊖ Lancaster Gate – ℰ (020) 7551 6039
– www.niparestaurant.co.uk – Closed Christmas-NewYear, Saturday lunch and Sunday
28ADU**e**
Rest – Thai – Menu £ 29 – Carte £ 23/32

♦ On the 1st floor and overlooking Hyde Park. Authentic and ornately decorated restaurant offers subtly spiced Thai cuisine. Keen to please staff in traditional silk costumes.

Pearl Liang
8 Sheldon Sq., Paddington Central ✉ W2 6EZ ⊖ Paddington
– ℰ (020) 7289 7000 – www.pearlliang.co.uk – Closed 24 and 25 December
Rest – Chinese – Menu £ 25 – Carte £ 24/42
28ACT**b**

♦ Spacious, business-orientated Chinese restaurant within a corporate development. Extensive choice from a variety of set menus; try the more unusual dishes like jellyfish or pig's trotter.

Island – at Lancaster London Hotel
Lancaster Ter. ✉ W2 2TY ⊖ Lancaster Gate – ℰ (020) 7551 6070
– www.lancasterlondon.com
28ADU**e**
Rest – Modern European – Menu £ 13 (lunch) – Carte £ 17/32

♦ This split-level contemporary looking restaurant is a road-crossing away from Hyde Park. Menu includes jogging-adjourning items like pies and burgers alongside salads and grills.

WESTMINSTER (City of)

Hereford Road
3 Hereford Rd. ✉ W2 4AB ⊖ Bayswater – ☎ (020) 7727 1144
– www.herefordroad.org – Closed 24 December-3 January and 27-29 August
Rest – British – (booking essential) Menu £ 16 (weekday lunch) **27ABUs**
– Carte £ 22/27

♦ Converted butcher's shop specialising in tasty British dishes without frills, using first rate, seasonal ingredients; offal a highlight. Booths for six people are the prized seats. Friendly and relaxed feel.

Assaggi
39 Chepstow Pl, (above Chesterfield pub) ✉ W2 4TS ⊖ Bayswater – ☎ (020) 7792 5501 – Closed 2 weeks Christmas, Sunday and bank holidays **27AAUc**
Rest – Italian – (booking essential) Carte £ 37/50

♦ The pared-down simplicity to this room above a pub works well; regulars are given fulsome welcomes and the atmosphere is great. Cooking puts the focus on the quality of the ingredients and the wine list is exclusively Italian.

Casa Malevo
23 Connaught St ✉ W2 2AY ⊖ Marble Arch – ☎ (020) 7402 1988
– www.casamalevo.com – Closed Sunday dinner **29AFUa**
Rest – Argentinian – Menu £ 17 (lunch) – Carte £ 26/36

♦ Carnivores will be in clover at this friendly Argentinian restaurant, with its bare brick walls and intimate lighting. Most come for the grilled Argentine beef, accompanied by a bottle of Malbec.

El Pirata De Tapas
115 Westbourne Grove ✉ W2 4UP ⊖ Bayswater – ☎ (020) 7727 5000
– www.elpiratadetapas.co.uk – Closed 24-26 December, 2-3 September and 1 January **27ABUn**
Rest – Spanish – Menu £ 10/25 – Carte £ 16/18

♦ Contemporary yet warm Spanish restaurant with a genuine neighbourhood feel. Authentic flavours from a well-priced and appealing selection of tapas, ideal for sharing with friends.

Kateh
5 Warwick Pl ✉ W9 2PX ⊖ Warwick Avenue – ☎ (020) 7289 3393
– www.kateh.net **28ACTa**
Rest – Persian – (dinner only and lunch Friday-Sunday) (booking essential) Carte £ 17/30

♦ Booking is imperative if you want to join the locals who have already discovered what a little jewel they have in the form of this buzzy, busy Persian restaurant. Authentic stews, expert chargrilling and lovely pastries and teas.

Prince Alfred & Formosa Dining Room
5A Formosa St ✉ W9 1EE ⊖ Warwick Avenue. – ☎ (020) 7286 3287
– www.theprincealfred.com **17OZDn**
Rest – Modern European – Menu £ 16 (lunch) – Carte £ 25/39

♦ Characterful and classic Victorian pub, with a large, more modern dining room in side extension. Open kitchen and a mix of British specialities and European classics. Friendly service.

Warrington
93 Warrington Cres ✉ W9 1EH ⊖ Maida Vale. – ☎ (020) 7592 7960
– www.gordonramsay.com **17OZDa**
Rest – Modern European – Menu £ 22 (lunch and early dinner)
– Carte £ 27/36

♦ Wood panelling, mosaics and friezes add to the atmosphere in the ground floor of this Gordon Ramsay pub. Go upstairs to the restaurant if you want a more sophisticated menu of mostly British produce.

WESTMINSTER (City of)

Waterway
54 Formosa St ⊠ W9 2JU ⊖ Warwick Avenue. – ℰ (020) 7266 3557
– www.thewaterway.co.uk

17OZDp

Rest – Modern European – Carte £ 26/36

♦ Terrific decked terrace by the canal its most appealing feature. Contemporary interior with busy cocktail bar; menu in separate dining room mixes the classics with more ambitious dishes.

BELGRAVIA

Berkeley
Wilton Pl. ⊠ SW1X 7RL ⊖ Knightsbridge – ℰ (020) 7235 6000
– www.the-berkeley.co.uk

37AGXe

189 rm – †£ 588/708 ††£ 708, ⊆ £ 29 – 25 suites
Rest *Marcus Wareing at The Berkeley* ✿✿ **Rest** *Koffmann's* – see restaurant listing

♦ Discreet and rejuvenated hotel with rooftop pool and opulently decorated bedrooms. Relax in the gilded and panelled Caramel Room or have a drink in the cool Blue Bar.

Lanesborough
Hyde Park Corner ⊠ SW1X 7TA ⊖ Hyde Park Corner – ℰ (020) 7259 5599
– www.lanesborough.com

37AGXa

83 rm – †£ 630 ††£ 738, ⊆ £ 30 – 10 suites
Rest *Apsleys* ✿ – see restaurant listing

♦ Converted in the 1990s from 18C St George's Hospital. Butler service offered. Regency-era inspired decoration; lavishly appointed rooms with impressive technological extras.

Halkin
5 Halkin St ⊠ SW1X 7DJ ⊖ Hyde Park Corner – ℰ (020) 7333 1000
– www.halkin.como.bz

38AHXb

35 rm – †£ 312/540 ††£ 312/660, ⊆ £ 28.50 – 6 suites
Rest *Nahm* – see restaurant listing

♦ Opened in 1991 as London's first boutique hotel and still looking sharp today. Thoughtfully conceived bedrooms with silk walls and marbled bathrooms; everything at the touch of a button. Abundant Armani-clad staff. Small, discreet bar.

Jumeirah Lowndes
21 Lowndes St ⊠ SW1X 9ES ⊖ Knightsbridge – ℰ (020) 7823 1234
– www.jumeirah.com

37AGXh

87 rm – †£ 354 ††£ 636, ⊆ £ 30 – 14 suites
Rest *Mimosa* – Carte £ 25/44

♦ Compact yet friendly modern corporate hotel within this exclusive residential area. Good levels of personal service offered. Close to the famous shops of Knightsbridge. Modern restaurant opens onto street terrace.

Marcus Wareing at The Berkeley
✿✿
Wilton Pl. ⊠ SW1X 7RL ⊖ Knightsbridge – ℰ (020) 7235 1200
– www.marcus-wareing.com – Closed 1 January, Saturday lunch and Sunday
Rest – French – Menu £ 38/98

37AGXe

Spec. Layered foie gras with prune and Armagnac purée. Best end of lamb with pickled cucumber and pink peppercorn yoghurt. Warm chocolate moelleux with a salted caramel centre and banana ice cream.

♦ Marcus Wareing's cooking is creative, sophisticated and backed by sound classical techniques. The restaurant is sumptuously appointed; service is smooth and well-organised but has personality. The chef's table is one of the best in town.

WESTMINSTER (City of)

Apsleys – at Lanesborough Hotel
Hyde Park Corner ✉ *SW1X 7TA* – Hyde Park Corner – ℰ (020) 7333 7254
– www.apsleysrestaurant.com
37AGX**a**
Rest – Italian – Menu £ 35 (lunch) – Carte £ 59/81
Spec. Fish crudo. Carbonara fagottelli. Chocolate soufflé with vanilla and raspberry.
- Under the guidance of celebrated chef Heinz Beck from Rome's La Pergola. Exquisite and precise Italian cooking, in a grand, eye-catching but far from intimidating room, designed by Adam Tihany. The serving team are polished and the atmosphere reassuringly upbeat.

Pétrus
1 Kinnerton St ✉ *SW1X 8EA* – Knightsbridge – ℰ (020) 7592 1609
– www.gordonramsay.com/petrus – Closed 25 December and Sunday
Rest – Modern European – Menu £ 30/60
37AGX**v**
Spec. Langoustine tails with confit chicken leg, baby artichokes and buttered leeks. Best end of lamb with spring vegetables and a thyme jus. Chocolate sphere with milk ice cream and honeycomb.
- Elegant Gordon Ramsay restaurant, opened in 2010, in stylish tones of silver, oyster and – as a nod to the name – claret. Experienced team bring personality to the service. Elaborate French-based cooking uses top quality ingredients.

Amaya
Halkin Arcade, 19 Motcomb St ✉ *SW1X 8JT* – Knightsbridge – ℰ (020) 7823 1166 – www.realindianfood.com – Closed 25 December
37AGX**k**
Rest – Indian – Menu £ 29/42 – Carte £ 36/70
Spec. Tarragon and turmeric chicken tikka. Duck grilled wtih tamarind glaze. Mango brûlée.
- Order a selection of small dishes from the tawa griddle, tandoor or sigri grill and finish with a curry or biryani. Dishes are aromatic and satisfying and the cooking skilled and consistent. A stylish, colourful restaurant.

Zafferano
15 Lowndes St ✉ *SW1X 9EY* – Knightsbridge – ℰ (020) 7235 5800
– www.zafferanorestaurant.co.uk
37AGX**f**
Rest – Italian – (booking essential) Menu £ 26/45 – Carte £ 36/52
Spec. Octopus salad with potatoes and olives. Rib of beef with bone marrow. Tiramisu.
- Pasta is the star of the show at this perennially busy Italian restaurant. The cooking is reliable and assured and the menus balanced. The stylish surroundings are comfortable but also full of bustle; the bar is an appealing adjunct.

Koffmann's – at Berkeley Hotel
Wilton Pl. ✉ *SW1X 7RL* – Knightsbridge – ℰ (020) 7235 1010
– www.the-berkeley.co.uk
37AGX**u**
Rest – French – Menu £ 26 (lunch) – Carte £ 51/73
- Pierre Koffmann, one of London's most fêted chefs, was enticed out of retirement to open this smart, comfortable and spacious restaurant. Expect plenty of gutsy flavours true to his Gascon roots.

Nahm – at Halkin Hotel
5 Halkin St. ✉ *SW1X 7DJ* – Hyde Park Corner – ℰ (020) 7333 1234
– www.halkin.como.bz – Closed lunch Saturday and Sunday
38AHX**b**
Rest – Thai – (booking advisable) Menu £ 25/60 – Carte £ 45/60
- An appealing mix of copper tones, wood and candlelight, along with an understated hint of Asian design, gives the room a warm feel. The Thai cuisine served here is based on Royal Thai traditions.

Noura Brasserie
16 Hobart Pl. ✉ *SW1W 0HH* – Victoria – ℰ (020) 7235 9444
– www.noura.co.uk
38AHX**n**
Rest – Lebanese – Menu £ 18/45 – Carte £ 24/40
- Dine in either the bright bar or the comfortable, contemporary restaurant. Authentic, modern Lebanese cooking specialises in chargrilled meats and meze.

WESTMINSTER (City of)

Pantechnicon
10 Motcomb St ⊠ SW1X 8LA ⊖ Knightsbridge – ℘ (020) 7730 6074
– www.thepantechnicon.com – Closed 25 December-1 January
Rest – Carte £ 32/46

37AGXd

♦ Urbane, enthusiastically run pub with a busy ground floor and altogether more formal upstairs dining room. Traditional dishes are given a modern twist; oysters and Scottish steaks are perennials.

HYDE PARK AND KNIGHTSBRIDGE

Mandarin Oriental Hyde Park
66 Knightsbridge ⊠ SW1X 7LA ⊖ Knightsbridge
– ℘ (020) 7235 2000 – www.mandarinoriental.com/london
173 rm – †£810 ††£900, ⊑ £19.50 – 25 suites
Rest *Dinner by Heston Blumenthal* **Rest** *Bar Boulud* – see restaurant listing

37AGXx

♦ Built in 1889 this classic international hotel, with its striking façade, remains one of London's grandest. Many of the luxurious bedrooms, which have a charming English country feel, enjoy views of Hyde Park. Standards of service are extremely high.

Dinner by Heston Blumenthal – at Mandarin Oriental Hyde Park Hotel
66 Knightsbridge ⊠ SW1X 7LA ⊖ Knightsbridge
– ℘ (020) 7201 3833 – www.dinnerbyheston.com – Closed Christmas
Rest – British – Menu £ 28 (weekday lunch) – Carte £ 45/60
Spec. Mandarin meat fruit. Spiced pigeon with ale and artichokes. Tipsy cake with spit roast pineapple.

37AGXx

♦ Was the most eagerly anticipated restaurant opening in 2011. Expect no 'molecular' alchemy here; this is all about respect for, and an amazing renewal of, British food, with some occasional playfulness thrown in. Each meticulously crafted dish comes with a date relating to its historical provenance.

Zuma
5 Raphael St ⊠ SW7 1DL ⊖ Knightsbridge – ℘ (020) 7584 1010
– www.zumarestaurant.com – Closed Christmas
Rest – Japanese – Carte £ 50/70

37AFXm

♦ Eye-catching design that blends East with West. Bustling atmosphere; fashionable clientele; popular sushi bar. Varied and interesting contemporary Japanese food.

Bar Boulud – at Mandarin Oriental Hyde Park Hotel
66 Knightsbridge ⊠ SW1X 7LA ⊖ Knightsbridge
– ℘ (020) 7201 3899 – www.barboulud.com
Rest – French – Menu £ 20 (lunch and early dinner) – Carte £ 25/48

37AGXx

♦ Daniel Boulud's London outpost is fashionable, fun and frantic. His hometown is Lyon but he built his considerable reputation in New York, so charcuterie, sausages and burgers are the highlights.

Mr Chow
151 Knightsbridge ⊠ SW1X 7PA ⊖ Knightsbridge – ℘ (020) 7589 7347
– www.mrchow.com – Closed 1 January, 24-26 December, Easter Monday dinner and Monday lunch
Rest – Chinese – Carte £ 38/57

37AFXe

♦ Long-standing Chinese restaurant, opened in 1968. Smart clientele, stylish and comfortable surroundings and prompt service from Italian waiters. Carefully prepared and satisfying food.

Chabrot
9 Knightsbridge Grn ⊠ SW1X 7QL ⊖ Knightsbridge – ℘ (020) 7225 2238
– www.chabrot.co.uk
Rest – French – Carte £ 23/39

37AFXv

♦ In 2011 Thierry Laborde, formerly of Le Gavroche, got together with three friends to open this fervently French and atmospheric bistro. The kitchen looks to France's SW and Basque country for most of its influences.

Mayfair

Dorchester
Park Ln. ✉ *W1K 1QA* – *Hyde Park Corner* – ℰ *(020) 7629 8888*
– *www.thedorchester.com*
30AHVa
196 rm – ♦£ 378/798 ♦♦£ 510/798, ☕ £ 31.50 – 54 suites
Rest *Alain Ducasse at The Dorchester* ✤✤✤ **Rest** *China Tang* **Rest** *The Grill*
– see restaurant listing

♦ Luxury hotel on a grand scale offering every possible facility. Striking marbled and pillared promenade provides one of the best backdrops to afternoon tea. Impressive spa and bedrooms quintessentially English in style. Exemplary levels of service.

Claridge's
Brook St ✉ *W1K 4HR* – *Bond Street* – ℰ *(020) 7629 8860*
– *www.claridges.co.uk*
30AHUc
143 rm – ♦£ 792 ♦♦£ 792/936, ☕ £ 31.50 – 60 suites
Rest *Gordon Ramsay at Claridge's* – see restaurant listing

♦ Rightly celebrated for its art deco and one of London's finest hotels. Exceptionally well-appointed and sumptuous bedrooms, all with butler service. Magnificent Foyer for afternoon tea.

Four Seasons
Hamilton Pl, Park Ln ✉ *W1J 7DR* – *Hyde Park Corner* – ℰ *(020) 7499 0888*
– *www.fourseasons.com*
30AHVv
148 rm – ♦£ 690 ♦♦£ 714, ☕ £ 30 – 45 suites
Rest *Amaranto* – see restaurant listing

♦ Reopened in 2011 after a huge refurbishment project and has raised the bar for luxury hotels. Striking lobby sets the scene; sumptuous bedrooms have a rich, contemporary look and boast every conceivable comfort. Great views from the stunning roof-top spa.

Connaught
Carlos Pl. ✉ *W1K 2AL* – *Bond Street* – ℰ *(020) 7499 7070*
– *www.the-connaught.co.uk*
30AHUe
95 rm – ♦£ 660 ♦♦£ 780/1104, ☕ £ 30 – 26 suites
Rest *Hélène Darroze at The Connaught* ✤✤ – see restaurant listing
Rest *Espelette* – ℰ *(020) 3147 7100* – Carte £ 46/84

♦ One of London's most famous hotels; restored and renovated but still retaining an elegant British feel. All the luxurious bedrooms come with large marble bathrooms and butler service. There's a choice of two stylish bars and Espelette is an all-day venue for classic French and British dishes.

InterContinental
1 Hamilton Pl, Park Ln. ✉ *W1J 7QY* – *Hyde Park Corner* – ℰ *(020) 7409 3131*
– *www.london.intercontinental.com*
30AHVk
399 rm – ♦£ 287 ♦♦£ 671, ☕ £ 28 – 48 suites
Rest *Theo Randall* **Rest** *Cookbook Café* – see restaurant listing

♦ International hotel whose position facing the park is an impressive feature. Everything leads off from the large, open-plan lobby. English-style bedrooms with hi-tech equipment; luxurious suites.

London Hilton
22 Park Ln. ✉ *W1K 1BE* – *Hyde Park Corner* – ℰ *(020) 7493 8000*
– *www.hilton.co.uk/londonparklane*
30AHVe
397 rm – ♦£ 246/449 ♦♦£ 252/660, ☕ £ 26.50 – 56 suites
Rest *Galvin at Windows* ✤ – see restaurant listing
Rest *Podium* – ℰ *(020) 7208 4022* – Menu £ 23 – Carte £ 28/53

♦ This 28 storey tower may not be the city's most handsome building but it is certainly one of its tallest hotels, providing impressive views from the upper floors. On-going refurbishment; Club floor bedrooms are particularly comfortable.

WESTMINSTER (City of)

Grosvenor House
Park Ln ⊠ W1K 7TN – Marble Arch – ℰ (020) 7499 6363
– www.londongrosvenorhouse.co.uk

29AGUg

442 rm – ♦£ 263 ♦♦£ 395, ⊇ £ 29 – 52 suites
Rest *JW Steakhouse* – see restaurant listing

• A large, landmark property occupying a commanding position by Hyde Park. Uniform, comfortable but well proportioned bedrooms in classic Marriott styling. Busy banqueting department boasts the largest ballroom in Europe.

Westbury
Bond St ⊠ W1S 2YF – Bond Street – ℰ (020) 7629 7755
– www.westburymayfair.com

30AIUa

233 rm ⊇ – ♦£ 239/469 ♦♦£ 239/469 – 13 suites
Rest *Gallery* – Italian influences – Menu £ 23 – Carte £ 27/33
Rest *Tsukiji* – Japanese (Sushi) – *(booking advisable)* Menu £ 25 – Carte £ 25/32

• Caused a commotion with its New York styling when it opened in the 1950s. Designer brands all outside; inside you'll find smart, comfortable bedrooms with art deco inspired suites. Elegant, well-known Polo bar and a bright, fresh sushi bar.

Brown's
Albemarle St ⊠ W1S 4BP – Green Park – ℰ (020) 7493 6020
– www.roccofortehotels.com

30AIVd

105 rm – ♦£ 264/582 ♦♦£ 354/858, ⊇ £ 29.50 – 12 suites
Rest *HIX at The Albemarle* – see restaurant listing

• Opened in 1837 by James Brown, Lord Byron's butler. This urbane and very British hotel with an illustrious past offers a swish bar with Terence Donovan prints, bedrooms in neutral hues and a classic English sitting room for afternoon tea.

London Marriott H. Park Lane
140 Park Ln ⊠ W1K 7AA – Marble Arch
– ℰ (020) 7493 7000 – www.londonmarriott.parklane.co

29AGUb

144 rm – ♦£ 443 ♦♦£ 515, ⊇ £ 25 – 9 suites
Rest *140 Park Lane* – Menu £ 20 – Carte £ 26/72

• Usefully located international hotel, close to the park and shops of Oxford Street. Basement health club has Park Lane's only pool. Smart, generously sized bedrooms are well-equipped; the attractive restaurant overlooks Marble Arch.

Metropolitan
Old Park Ln ⊠ W1K 1LB – Hyde Park Corner – ℰ (020) 7447 1000
– www.metropolitan.como.bz

30AHVc

147 rm – ♦£ 251/468 ♦♦£ 287/504, ⊇ £ 28 – 3 suites
Rest *Nobu* ✻ – see restaurant listing

• Minimalist interior and a voguish reputation have made this hotel and its Met Bar the favoured choice of pop stars and celebrities. Sleek design and fashionably attired staff set it apart.

Athenaeum
116 Piccadilly ⊠ W1J 7BJ – Hyde Park Corner – ℰ (020) 7499 3464
– www.athenaeumhotel.com

30AHVg

153 rm – ♦£ 240 ♦♦£ 720, ⊇ £ 27.50 – 11 suites
Rest *Restaurant* – Menu £ 19/28 – Carte £ 42/62

• Refurbished 1920s building opposite the park; its stylish bedrooms come in cool pastel shades and have floor to ceiling windows. Bright restaurant and a bar offering over 270 different whiskies. The hotel also organises events for kids.

Chesterfield
35 Charles St ⊠ W1J 5EB – Green Park – ℰ (020) 7491 2622
– www.chesterfieldmayfair.com

30AHVf

103 rm – ♦£ 263/450 ♦♦£ 263/450, ⊇ £ 22.50 – 4 suites
Rest – Menu £ 23 (lunch) – Carte £ 32/57

• An assuredly English feel to this Georgian house. Discreet lobby leads to a clubby bar and wood panelled library. Individually decorated bedrooms, with some antique pieces. Intimate and pretty restaurant.

WESTMINSTER (City of)

London Marriott H. Grosvenor Square
Grosvenor Sq. ⌂ *W1K 6JP* – *Bond Street*
– ℱ *(020) 7493 1232* – *www.marriottgrosvenorsquare.com*
226 rm – †£ 251 ††£ 491, ⌑ £ 24 – 11 suites
30AHUs
Rest *Maze Grill* – see restaurant listing
♦ A well-appointed international group hotel that benefits from an excellent location in the heart of Mayfair. Many of the bedrooms specifically equipped for the business traveller.

Hilton London Green Park
Half Moon St ⌂ *W1J 7BN* – *Green Park* – ℱ *(020) 7629 7522*
– *www.hilton.co.uk/greenpark*
162 rm – †£ 191/407 ††£ 203/599, ⌑ £ 20.95
30AIVa
Rest – *(bar lunch Saturday and Sunday)* Carte £ 28/37
♦ A row of sympathetically adjoined townhouses in the heart of Mayfair, dating from the 1730s. Bedrooms vary in size and shape; those on the first and fifth floors have been refurbished in a bright, contemporary style. Modern menu served in airy restaurant.

Alain Ducasse at The Dorchester
Park Ln. ⌂ *W1K 1QA* – *Hyde Park Corner* – ℱ *(020) 7629 8866*
– *www.alainducasse-dorchester.com* – Closed Easter, 13 August-4 September, 1-10 January, 26-31 December, dinner 25 December, Saturday lunch, Sunday and Monday
30AHVa
Rest – French – Menu £ 50/78
Spec. Sauté of lobster, truffled chicken quenelles and homemade pasta. Fillet of beef Rossini with 'sacristain' potatoes. 'Baba like in Monte-Carlo'.
♦ Luxury and extravagance are the hallmarks of Alain Ducasse's London outpost. The dining room is elegant without being staid; food is modern and refined yet satisfying and balanced. Service is formal, thoughtful and well-organised.

Hélène Darroze at The Connaught
Carlos Pl. ⌂ *W1K 2AL* – *Bond Street* – ℱ *(020) 3147 7200*
– *www.the-connaught.co.uk* – Closed 2 weeks August, 2-9 January, Sunday and Monday
30AHUe
Rest – French – *(booking essential)* Menu £ 35/80
Spec. Line-caught calamari, ravioli with confit tomatoes. Black pork from Pays Basque, pan-roasted chop larded with black truffle. Manjari chocolate mousse and cumin ice cream.
♦ Landes and the SW of France inform Hélène Darroze's exquisite cooking, although international influences also play a part. The dining room is elegant and comfortable, with original mahogany wood panelling. Service is courteous and professional.

Le Gavroche (Michel Roux Jnr)
43 Upper Brook St. ⌂ *W1K 7QR* – *Marble Arch* – ℱ *(020) 7408 0881*
– *www.le-gavroche.co.uk* – Closed Christmas-New Year, Saturday lunch, Sunday and bank holidays
29AGUc
Rest – French – *(booking essential)* Menu £ 52 (lunch) – Carte £ 60/128
Spec. Soufflé Suissesse. Râble de lapin et galette au parmesan. Palet au chocolat amer et praliné croustillant.
♦ Classical, rich and indulgent French cuisine is the draw at Michel Roux's renowned London institution. The large, smart basement room has a clubby, masculine feel; service is formal and structured but also has charm.

Prices quoted after the symbol † refer to the lowest rate in low season followed by the highest rate in high season, for a single room.
The same principle applies to the symbol †† for a double room.

WESTMINSTER (City of)

XXXX Square (Philip Howard) 🅰🅒 ⇔ 💳 ⦿ 🅐🅔
❀❀ 6-10 Bruton St. ✉ W1J 6PU ⊖ Green Park – 𝒞 (020) 7495 7100
– www.squarerestaurant.com – Closed 25 December, 1 January and lunch
Saturday, Sunday and bank holidays
30AIU**v**
Rest – French – Menu £ 35/80
Spec. Langoustine with parmesan gnocchi and truffle. Loin of lamb, crushed broad beans, broccoli and mint. Brillat-Savarin cheesecake with pink grapefruit and champagne.
♦ Confident and accomplished kitchen which understands the importance of sound techniques, prime ingredients and clarity of flavour. The room is comfortable and the buoyant atmosphere prevents things becoming too formal. Good cheeseboard.

XXXX Sketch (The Lecture Room & Library) 🅰🅒 💳 ⦿ 🅐🅔
❀ 9 Conduit St (1st floor) ✉ W1S 2XG ⊖ Oxford Street – 𝒞 (020) 7659 4500
– www.sketch.uk.com – Closed last 2 weeks August, Saturday lunch, Sunday and Monday
30AIU**h**
Rest – French – (booking essential) Menu £ 35 (lunch) – Carte £ 70/129
Spec. Scallop, morel and braised veal sweetbreads 'osso buco'. Quercy lamb saddle, rack and sweetbreads. Pierre Gagnaire's 'grand dessert'.
♦ Pierre Gagnaire's London operation is within a striking 18C townhouse which is full of colour, energy and vitality. The sophisticated French cooking is ambitious and elaborate in conception and execution; dishes arrive artfully presented.

XXXX Galvin at Windows – at London Hilton Hotel ≤ 🅰🅒 💳 ⦿ 🅐🅔 ⦿
❀ 22 Park Ln (28th floor) ✉ W1K 1BE ⊖ Hyde Park Corner – 𝒞 (020) 7208 4021
– www.galvinatwindows.com – Closed Saturday lunch, Sunday dinner and bank holiday Mondays
30AHV**e**
Rest – French – Menu £ 29/65
Spec. Cured salmon, Cornish crab, avocado cream and fennel. Rack, shoulder and lamb's kidney with anchovy, capers and aubergine. Apple tarte Tatin, vanilla ice cream and caramel sauce.
♦ Spectacular views from the 28th floor of the Hilton are not the only draw. The room is contemporary and cleverly laid out; service is attentive and efficient; cooking is confident and detailed and dishes balanced and satisfying.

XXXX China Tang – at Dorchester Hotel 🅰🅒 ⇔ 💳 ⦿ 🅐🅔 ⦿
Park Ln ✉ W1A 2HJ ⊖ Hyde Park Corner – 𝒞 (020) 7629 9988
– www.thedorchester.com – Closed 25 December
30AHV**a**
Rest – Chinese – Menu £ 15 (lunch) – Carte £ 40/70
♦ Sir David Tang's atmospheric, art deco-inspired Chinese restaurant, downstairs at The Dorchester, is always abuzz with activity. Be sure to see the terrific bar, before sharing the traditional Cantonese specialities.

XXXX Gordon Ramsay at Claridge's 🅰🅒 💳 ⦿ 🅐🅔 ⦿
Brook St. ✉ W1K 4HR ⊖ Bond Street – 𝒞 (020) 7499 0099
– www.gordonramsay.com/claridges
30AHU
Rest – Modern European – (booking essential) Menu £ 30/70
♦ Grand and impressive room within the elegant surroundings of Claridge's hotel. Service is structured and ceremonial; the cooking is classically based, with modern touches. Popular chef's table in the kitchen.

XXX Cecconi's 🌀 🅰🅒 💳 ⦿ 🅐🅔 ⦿
5a Burlington Gdns ✉ W1S 3EP ⊖ Green Park – 𝒞 (020) 7434 1500
– www.cecconis.com
30AIU**c**
Rest – Italian – (booking essential) Carte £ 30/44
♦ Branches of this fashionable restaurant are now opening up around the world. Regulars pop in for a bite at the bar; the restaurant prepares the classic dishes with care. Open from breakfast onwards; popular for weekend brunches.

Hibiscus (Claude Bosi)

29 Maddox St ⊠ W1S 2PA ⊖ Oxford Circus – ℘ (020) 7629 2999
– www.hibiscusrestaurant.co.uk – Closed 23 December-3 January, Monday lunch, Sunday and bank holidays   **30**AIU**s**
Rest – Innovative – Menu £ 34/80
Spec. Ravioli of spring onion and lime, broad bean and mint purée. Smoked and roasted chicken, onion fondue and liquorice. Chocolate tart with basil ice cream.

♦ The genial Claude Bosi is a 'chef's chef' who brings his own style to the cooking at Hibiscus. That means elaborately constructed dishes with some deft and original touches. The oak walls and formal service create a somewhat sombre feel.

Benares (Atul Kochhar)

12a Berkeley Square House ⊠ W1J 6BS ⊖ Green Park
– ℘ (020) 7629 8886 – www.benaresrestaurant.com
– Closed 25- 26 December and 1 January   **30**AIU**q**
Rest – Indian – Menu £ 30 (lunch) – Carte £ 55/95
Spec. Fennel lamb chop, mustard chicken tikka and king prawn platter. Roasted fillet of roe deer, venison biryani and sesame peanut sauce. Lime mousse, lemon thyme jelly and basil sorbet.

♦ Modern techniques are used to add contemporary touches to the classical base; the inventive Indian food here continues to evolve. The smart first-floor surroundings match the food in their sophistication. Popular and smart Chef's Table.

Murano (Angela Hartnett)

20 Queen St ⊠ W1J 5PP ⊖ Green Park – ℘ (020) 7495 1127
– www.angela-hartnett.com – Closed Christmas and Sunday   **30**AHV**b**
Rest – Italian influences – Menu £ 30/65
Spec. Pumpkin tortellini with sage emulsion. Canon of lamb with courgettes and black olives. Apricot soufflé with biscotti.

♦ Now wholly owned by chef Angela Hartnett, this bright and stylishly decorated restaurant provides a luminous setting for her refined and balanced cooking. The Italian influences are particularly pronounced on the tasting menus.

Greenhouse

27a Hay's Mews ⊠ W1J 5NY ⊖ Hyde Park Corner
– ℘ (020) 7499 3331 – www.greenhouserestaurant.co.uk
– Closed Saturday lunch, Sunday and bank holidays   **30**AHV**m**
Rest – Innovative – Menu £ 29/75
Spec. Calves sweetbreads with black garlic and glazed cabbage. Roasted Anjou pigeon breast, pomegranate, turnip purée and a giblet and pancetta jus. "Snix" - chocolate, salted caramel and peanuts.

♦ Discreet and charming mews location for this smart and elegant restaurant. An extensive choice of elaborately presented dishes display plenty of inventive touches but are also underpinned with sound French culinary techniques.

Umu

14-16 Bruton Pl. ⊠ W1J 6LX ⊖ Bond Street
– ℘ (020) 7499 8881 – www.umurestaurant.com
– Closed Saturday lunch, Sunday and bank holidays   **30**AIU**k**
Rest – Japanese – Menu £ 26 (lunch) – Carte £ 35/151
Spec. Tuna tartare salad, Japanese pickles. Wild Scottish lobster, seven pepper shichimi. Japanese tiramisu with macha tea and sake.

♦ Stylish, discreet interior using natural materials, with central sushi bar. Extensive choice of Japanese dishes; choose one of the seasonal kaiseki menus for the full experience. Over 160 different labels of sake.

WESTMINSTER (City of)

XXX Tamarind
☸
20 Queen St. ✉ W1J 5PR ⊖ Green Park – ℰ (020) 7629 3561
– www.tamarindrestaurant.com – Closed 25-26 December, 1 January
and Saturday lunch
30AHV**h**
Rest – Indian – Menu £ 20/56 – Carte £ 45/68
Spec. Grilled scallops, oven roasted peppers and tomato chutney. Fillet of sea bass, mango and curry leaf sauce. Tandoor grilled pineapple, rose petal ice cream.
• Makes the best use of its basement location through smoked mirrors, gilded columns and a somewhat exclusive feel. The appealing and enjoyable Indian food is mostly traditionally based; kebabs and curries are the specialities, complemented by carefully judged vegetable dishes.

XXX Kai
☸
65 South Audley St. ✉ W1K 2QU ⊖ Hyde Park Corner – ℰ (020) 7493 8988
– www.kaimayfair.co.uk – Closed 25-26 December and 1 January
30AHV**n**
Rest – Chinese – (booking essential) Menu £ 27 (lunch) – Carte £ 36/84
Spec. Honey-roasted Duke of Berkshire char siew pork. Sea bass with chickpeas, shallots and ginger. Rice dumplings with honey ice ceam.
• Carefully prepared Chinese food, from a menu that mixes the classics with more innovative dishes; flavours are authentic and assured. Its smart surroundings are spread over two floors - ask for the ground floor; sweet natured service.

XXX The Grill – at Dorchester Hotel
Park Ln. ✉ W1K 1QA ⊖ Hyde Park Corner – ℰ (020) 7629 8888
– www.thedorchester.com
30AHV**a**
Rest – British – Menu £ 27 (weekday lunch) – Carte £ 47/75
• A bastion of Britishness, where timeless classics are served alongside more modern creations. The extravagantly kitted out room, bedecked in acres of tartans, is even more memorable.

XXX Theo Randall – at Intercontinental Hotel
1 Hamilton Pl, Park Ln. ✉ W1J 7QY ⊖ Hyde Park Corner – ℰ (020) 7318 8747
– www.theorandall.com – Closed 25-26 December, 1 January, Saturday lunch, Sunday and bank holidays
30AHV**k**
Rest – Italian – Menu £ 29 (lunch) – Carte £ 50/74
• Daily changing seasonal menu of comforting Italian dishes, served in the smart and spacious surroundings of an international hotel. Wood oven a feature; produce imported directly from Italy.

XXX HIX at The Albemarle – at Brown's Hotel
Albemarle St ✉ W1S 4BP ⊖ Green Park – ℰ (020) 7518 4004
– www.roccofortecollection.com
30AIV**d**
Rest – British – Menu £ 33 (lunch and early dinner) – Carte £ 29/67
• This wood-panelled dining room is lightened with the work of current British artists. Mark Hix's well-sourced menu of British classics will appeal to the hunter-gatherer in every man.

XXX Amaranto – at Four Seasons Hotel
Hamilton Pl, Park Ln ✉ W1J 7DR ⊖ Hyde Park Corner – ℰ (020) 7499 0888
– www.fourseasons.com
30AHV**v**
Rest – Italian – Menu £ 26 (lunch) – Carte £ 31/51
• It's all about flexibility as the Italian influenced menu is served in the stylish bar or comfortable lounge, on the great terrace or in the restaurant decorated in the vivid colours of the amaranth plant.

XXX Scott's
20 Mount St ✉ W1K 2HE ⊖ Bond Street – ℰ (020) 7495 7309
– www.scotts-restaurant.com – Closed 25-26 December
30AHU**d**
Rest – Seafood – Carte £ 36/56
• Stylish yet traditional and one of London's most fashionable addresses, so getting a table can be tricky. Oak panelling is juxtaposed with vibrant artwork from young British artists. Enticing choice of top quality fish and shellfish.

WESTMINSTER (City of)

XXX Corrigan's Mayfair 　AC VISA ◎ AE
28 Upper Grosvenor St. ✉ *W1K 7EH* ⊖ *Marble Arch* – ✆ *(020) 7499 9943*
– www.corrigansmayfair.com – Closed 25-26 December, 1 January and Saturday lunch   **29AGUa**
Rest – British – Menu £ 27 (lunch) – Carte £ 39/88

♦ Richard Corrigan's flagship celebrates British and Irish cooking, with game a speciality. The room is comfortable, clubby and quite glamorous and feels as though it has been around for years.

XXX Bentley's (Grill) 　AC VISA ◎ AE
11-15 Swallow St. ✉ *W1B 4DG* ⊖ *Piccadilly Circus* – ✆ *(020) 7734 4756*
– www.bentleys.org – Closed 25-26 December and 1 January   **30AJUc**
Rest – British – Carte £ 47/60

♦ Entrance into striking bar; panelled staircase to richly decorated restaurant. Carefully sourced seafood or meat dishes enhanced by clean, crisp cooking. Unruffled service.

XXX Sartoria 　AC 🕊 ⇔ VISA ◎ AE
20 Savile Row ✉ *W1S 3PR* ⊖ *Green Park* – ✆ *(020) 7534 7000*
– www.sartoriabar.com – Closed 25 December, Saturday lunch, Sunday and bank holidays   **30AIUb**
Rest – Italian – Menu £ 25 – Carte £ 30/53

♦ In the street renowned for English tailoring, a coolly sophisticated and stylish restaurant to suit those looking for classic Italian cooking with some modern touches thrown in. It also comes with confident service.

XXX Avista 　AC 🕊 ⇔ VISA ◎ AE ◐
Millennium Mayfair Hotel, 39 Grosvenor Sq ✉ *W1K 2HP* ⊖ *Bond Street*
– ✆ (020) 7596 3399 – www.avistarestaurant.com – Closed Saturday lunch and Sunday   **30AHUx**
Rest – Italian – Menu £ 26 (lunch) – Carte £ 30/66

♦ A large room, softened by neutral shades, within the Millennium Hotel. The menu traverses Italy and the cooking marries the rustic with the more refined. Pasta dishes are a highlight.

XX Wild Honey 　AC 🕊 VISA ◎ AE
☸
12 St George St. ✉ *W1S 2FB* ⊖ *Oxford Circus* – ✆ *(020) 7758 9160*
– www.wildhoneyrestaurant.co.uk – Closed 25-26 December and 1 January
Rest – Modern European – Menu £ 19 (weekday lunch)   **30AIUw**
– Carte £ 29/39
Spec. Belly pork with snails and onion purée. Short rib of Wagyu beef and a bone marrow gratin. Vanilla cheesecake scented with rosewater.

♦ Skilled kitchen uses seasonal ingredients at their peak to create dishes full of flavour and free from ostentation. Attractive oak-panelled room; ask for one of the booths. Personable and unobtrusive service adds to the relaxed feel.

XX Semplice (Marco Torri) 　AC ⇔ VISA ◎ AE
☸
9-10 Blenheim St ✉ *W1S 1LJ* ⊖ *Bond Street* – ✆ *(020) 7495 1509*
– www.ristorantesemplice.com – Closed 2 weeks Christmas, Easter, Saturday lunch, Sunday and bank holidays   **30AHUk**
Rest – Italian – *(booking essential at dinner)* Menu £ 30 (lunch)
– Carte £ 40/51 ❀
Spec. Fassone beef carpaccio. Milk-fed Piedmontese veal with courgettes, sweet potato sauce. Tiramisu with tiramisu ice cream.

♦ Plenty of regulars are always in evidence in this comfortable and stylish restaurant, decorated with ebony, leather and gold. The enthusiasm of the young owners is palpable; the kitchen uses small, specialist suppliers in unfussy, flavoursome dishes.

WESTMINSTER (City of)

XX Hakkasan Mayfair
17 Bruton St ⊠ W1J 6QB ⊖ Green Park – ☏ (020) 7907 1888
– www.hakkasan.com – Closed 25 December   **30AIUi**
Rest – Chinese – *(booking essential)* Carte £ 50/100 **s**
Spec. Salt and pepper squid. Stir-fried black pepper rib-eye of beef with Merlot. Chocolate soufflé with vanilla ice cream and raspberry sauce.
♦ Less a copy, more a sister to the original; a sister who's just as fun but lives in a nicer part of town. This one has a funky, more casual ground floor to go with the downstairs dining room. You can expect the same extensive choice of top quality, modern Cantonese cuisine; dim sum is a highlight.

XX Nobu Berkeley St
15 Berkeley St. ⊠ W1J 8DY ⊖ Green Park – ☏ (020) 7290 9222
– www.noburestaurants.com/berkeley – Closed 25-26 December, Saturday
and Sunday lunch and bank holiday Mondays   **30AIVb**
Rest – Japanese – *(booking essential)* Menu £ 32/90
Spec. King crab claw tempura with butter ponzu. Black cod with miso. Chocolate tart with sake kasu ice cream and chocolate sauce.
♦ Offers all the innovative Nobu favourites, along with specialities from the wood oven. Large, lively but smoothly run first floor operation with plenty of glamour; ground floor destination bar. Helpful, well-informed service.

XX Bellamy's
18 Bruton Pl. ⊠ W1J 6LY ⊖ Bond Street – ☏ (020) 7491 2727
– www.bellamysrestaurant.co.uk – Closed Saturday lunch, Sunday and bank holidays   **30AIUc**
Rest – French – Menu £ 29 – Carte £ 38/54
♦ French deli/brasserie tucked down a smart mews. Go past the caviar and cheeses into the restaurant proper for a very traditional, but well-executed, range of Gallic classics.

XX 5 Pollen St
5 Pollen St ⊠ W1S 1NE ⊖ Oxford Circus – ☏ (020) 7629 1555
– www.5pollenst.com – Closed Sunday   **30AIUz**
Rest – Italian – *(booking advisable)* Menu £ 36 (lunch) – Carte dinner £ 50/60
♦ Geared unashamedly to the glamorous Mayfair set untroubled by concepts such as value for money. Worth going for the Gary Hume artwork and wallpaper alone. Large menu features quality produce and covers all bases.

XX Nobu – at Metropolitan Hotel
19 Old Park Ln ⊠ W1Y 1LB ⊖ Hyde Park Corner – ☏ (020) 7447 4747
– www.noburestaurants.com – Closed 25-26 December   **30AHVc**
Rest – Japanese – *(booking essential)* Menu £ 60/95 – Carte £ 37/68
Spec. Yellowtail jalapeño. Black cod with miso. Chocolate bento box with green tea ice cream.
♦ Its celebrity clientele ensure this remains one of London's more glamorous spots. Staff are fully conversant in the innovative menu that adds South American influences to Japanese cooking. Has spawned many imitators around the world.

XX Maze
10-13 Grosvenor Sq ⊠ W1K 6JP ⊖ Bond Street – ☏ (020) 7107 0000
– www.gordonramsay.com   **30AHUz**
Rest – Innovative – Menu £ 25 (lunch) – Carte £ 29/46
Spec. Jasmine and miso cured salmon, ponzu dressing. Devon duck breast, beetroot and preserved lemon. Pistachio parfait, cherry sorbet.
♦ Choose a variety of small but expertly formed dishes at this sleek and stylish David Rockwell designed restaurant from the Gordon Ramsay stable. The cooking is contemporary and nicely balanced; four dishes per person should suffice.

WESTMINSTER (City of)

Pollen Street Social (Jason Atherton)
8-10 Pollen St ⊠ W1S 1NQ ⊖ Oxford Circus – ℰ (020) 7290 7606
– www.pollenstreetsocial.com – Closed Sunday and bank holidays **30**AIU**u**
Rest – Innovative – *(booking essential)* Menu £ 25 (lunch) – Carte £ 38/55
Spec. 'Full English breakfast'. Roasted Dingley Dell pork, beetroot, hops, seeds and grains. Peanut butter parfait, cherry jam and creamed rice puffs.
• Jason Atherton's cooking continues the style he displayed when at Maze; his restaurant is all about informality and flexibility. His food is exciting, innovative, delicate in looks but assured in flavour; it is also imaginative and playful.

Maze Grill – at London Marriott H. Grosvenor Square
10-13 Grosvenor Sq. ⊠ W1K 6JP ⊖ Bond Street – ℰ (020) 7495 2211
– www.gordonramsay.com **30**AHU**s**
Rest – Beef specialities – Menu £ 24 (lunch and early dinner) – Carte £ 27/52
• An addendum to Maze, with a menu specialising in steaks, from Hereford grass-fed to Wagyu 9th grade; all appealingly served on wooden boards, with a variety of sauces and side dishes.

Patterson's
4 Mill St ⊠ W1S 2AX ⊖ Oxford Street – ℰ (020) 7499 1308
– www.pattersonsrestaurant.com – Closed 25-26 December and Sunday
Rest – Modern European – Menu £ 25/47 – Carte £ 47/55 **30**AIU**p**
• Stylish modern interior in black and white. Elegant tables and attentive service. Modern British cooking with concise wine list and sensible prices.

Quince
Stratton St ⊠ W1J 8LT ⊖ Green Park – ℰ (020) 7915 3892
– www.quincelondon.com – Closed Saturday and Sunday lunch **30**AIV**s**
Rest – Turkish – Menu £ 24 (lunch) – Carte £ 37/53
• TV chef Silvena Rowe presents her inimitable Eastern Mediterranean cooking. Her personality is evident throughout, from personal references on the menu – "a homage to my grandfather Mehmed" – to the colourful, Ottoman-influenced decoration.

Alloro
19-20 Dover St ⊠ W1S 4LU ⊖ Green Park – ℰ (020) 7495 4768
– www.atozrestaurants.com/alloro – Closed 25 December, Saturday lunch and Sunday **30**AIV**r**
Rest – Italian – *(booking essential)* Menu £ 35/39
• Confidently run and smartly dressed Italian with an appealing menu of easy-to-eat dishes; breads and pasta are made in-house. Great atmosphere, especially at busy lunchtimes. Boisterous adjacent baretto.

Goodman
26 Maddox St. ⊠ W1S 1QH ⊖ Oxford Circus – ℰ (020) 7499 3776
– www.goodmanrestaurants.com – Closed Sunday and bank holidays
Rest – Beef specialities – *(booking essential)* Menu £ 20 (lunch) **30**AIU**u**
– Carte £ 42/54
• A worthy attempt at recreating a New York steakhouse; all leather and wood and macho swagger. Beef is dry or wet aged in-house and comes with a choice of four sauces; rib-eye the speciality.

Dolada
13 Albemarle St. ⊠ W1S 4HJ ⊖ Green Park – ℰ (020) 7409 1011
– www.dolada.co – Closed 24- December-4 January, Saturday lunch, Sunday and bank holidays **30**AIV**x**
Rest – Italian – Menu £ 30/35 – Carte £ 30/39
• Elegant and immaculately kept basement restaurant lightened by confident and thoughtful service. Expect cooking from across Italy; the deconstructed spaghetti carbonara is a speciality.

WESTMINSTER (City of)

XX Hush
8 Lancashire Ct., Brook St. ⊠ W1S 1EY ⊖ Bond Street
– ℰ (020) 7659 1500 – www.hush.co.uk – Closed Easter, 25-26 December,
1 January and Sunday
30AHUv
Rest – Modern European – *(booking essential)* Carte £ 27/44

♦ Accessible brasserie-style menu served in a large, busy room; smart destination bar upstairs and plenty of private dining. Tucked away in a charming courtyard, with a summer terrace.

XX Fakhreldine
85 Piccadilly ⊠ W1J 7NB ⊖ Green Park – ℰ (020) 7493 3424
– www.fakhreldine.co.uk
30AIVe
Rest – Lebanese – Menu £ 14/33 – Carte approx. £ 31

♦ Long-standing restaurant with great view of Green Park. Large selection of classic meze dishes and more modern European-style menu of original Lebanese dishes.

XX Tempo
54 Curzon St. ⊠ W1J 8PG ⊖ Green Park – ℰ (020) 7629 2742
– www.tempomayfair.co.uk – Closed 25-27 December, Saturday lunch, Sunday and bank holidays
30AIVm
Rest – Italian – Menu £ 23 (lunch) – Carte £ 29/52

♦ The hands-on presence is a reassuring presence in this cosy restaurant, which re-opened in 2010 after a full revamp. The menu covers all Italian regions and includes cicchetti, or small plates.

XX Sumosan
26 Albemarle St. ⊠ W1S 4HY ⊖ Green Park – ℰ (020) 7495 5999
– www.sumosan.com – Closed lunch Saturday-Sunday and bank holidays
Rest – Japanese – Carte £ 29/74
30AIUe

♦ Attracts a young and prosperous crowd with its cocktail list, modern interpretations of Japanese flavours and stylish surroundings. The skilled kitchen deftly executes a wide-ranging menu.

XX Mews of Mayfair
10-11 Lancashire Ct, Brook St, (1st floor) ⊠ W1S 1EY ⊖ Bond Street – ℰ (020) 7518 9388 – www.mewsofmayfair.com – Closed 25-26 December, Sunday dinner and bank holidays
30AHUa
Rest – Modern European – Carte £ 29/38

♦ This pretty restaurant, bright in summer and warm in winter, is on the first floor of a mews house, once used as storage rooms for Savile Row. Seasonal menus offer something for everyone.

XX Sketch (The Gallery)
9 Conduit St ⊠ W1S 2XG ⊖ Oxford Street – ℰ (020) 7659 4500
– www.sketch.uk.com – Closed 25-26 December, Sunday and bank holidays
Rest – International – *(dinner only) (booking essential)*
30AIUh
Carte £ 35/63

♦ Unlike anywhere else: an art gallery during the day that morphs into a noisy, bustling brasserie at night, when aphorisms are projected onto the white walls. Menu is international in its scope; the cocktail list is equally popular.

XX JW Steakhouse – at Lancaster London Hotel
Park Ln ⊠ W1K 7TN ⊖ Marble Arch – ℰ (020) 7399 8460
– www.londongrosvenorhouse.co.uk
29AGUg
Rest – Beef specialities – Carte £ 28/69

♦ With Aberdeen Angus or dry-aged American USDA steaks, as well as an impressive choice of bourbon in the bar, there's no guessing as to whom this smart hotel steakhouse is geared.

WESTMINSTER (City of)

Momo
25 Heddon St. ✉ *W1B 4BH* ⊖ *Oxford Circus* – ✆ *(020) 7434 4040*
– www.momoresto.com – *Closed Sunday lunch*
Rest – Moroccan – Menu £ 19/49 – Carte £ 35/40   **30**AIU**n**

♦ Lanterns, rugs, trinkets and music contribute to the authentic Moroccan atmosphere; come in a group to better appreciate it. The more traditional dishes are the kitchen's strength.

Cookbook Café – at InterContinental Hotel
1 Hamilton Pl, Park Ln. ✉ *W1J 7QY* ⊖ *Hyde Park Corner* – ✆ *(020) 7409 3131*
– www.london.intercontinental.com   **30**AHV**k**
Rest – Traditional – Menu £ 18 (lunch) – Carte £ 21/53

♦ Finding a casual spot for a light meal is not easy in Park Lane but the Cookbook Café is one option. Choose salads from the buffet or daily specials from the central cooking station.

Veeraswamy
Victory House, 99 Regent St, (entrance on Swallow St.) ✉ *W1B 4RS*
⊖ *Piccadilly Circus* – ✆ *(020) 7734 1401* – www.realindianfood.com
Rest – Indian – Menu £ 21 (lunch and early dinner)   **30**AIU**t**
– Carte £ 37/51

♦ May have opened back in 1926 but feels fresh and is awash with vibrant colours and always full of bustle. Skilled kitchen cleverly mixes the traditional with more contemporary creations.

Cafe at Sotheby's
34-35 New Bond St. ✉ *W1A 2AA* ⊖ *Bond Street* – ✆ *(020) 7293 5077*
– www.sothebys.com – *Closed 5-31 August, Saturday, Sunday and bank hoildays*
Rest – Modern European – *(lunch only) (booking essential)*   **30**AIU**y**
Carte £ 26/32 **s**

♦ Occupying a cosy space just off the foyer of the famous auction house. The appealing lunch menu changes weekly; the lobster sandwich is a perennial favourite. Service is discreet.

Kiku
17 Half Moon St. ✉ *W1J 7BE* ⊖ *Green Park* – ✆ *(020) 7499 4208*
– www.kikurestaurant.co.uk – *Closed 25-26 December, 1 January, Sunday and lunch on bank holidays*   **30**AIV**g**
Rest – Japanese – Menu £ 20/50 – Carte £ 25/56

♦ Bright and fresh feel thanks to minimalistic décor of stone and natural wood. A plethora of menus, a fierce adherence to seasonality and an authentic emphasis on presentation.

Bar Trattoria Semplice
22 Woodstock St. ✉ *W1C 2AR* ⊖ *Bond Street* – ✆ *(020) 7491 8638*
– www.bartrattoriasemplice.com   **30**AHU**m**
Rest – Italian – Menu £ 17 (lunch) – Carte £ 22/37

♦ Baby sister to Semplice a few yards away, offering simpler, well-priced cooking in a relaxed and fun room. Specialities from a different region of Italy are featured each month. All-day menu in bar.

Chisou
4 Princes St. ✉ *W1B 2LE* ⊖ *Oxford Circus* – ✆ *(020) 7629 3931*
– www.chisourestaurant.com – *Closed Christmas-New Year, Sunday and bank holidays*   **30**AIU**m**
Rest – Japanese – Menu £ 14 (lunch) – Carte £ 18/43

♦ In Mayfair's Japanese quarter; simple slate flooring and polished wood tables. Cosy sushi bar to rear. Elaborate menus of both modern and classic Japanese dishes. Gets very busy.

WESTMINSTER (City of)

Bentley's (Oyster Bar)
11-15 Swallow St. ✉ *W1B 4DG* ⊖ *Piccadilly Circus* – ✆ *(020) 7734 4756*
– *www.bentleys.org* – *Closed 25 December and 1 January*
Rest – Seafood – Menu £ 25 (lunch) – Carte £ 35/50

30AJUc

• Sit at the counter to watch white-jacketed staff open oysters by the bucket load. Interesting seafood menus feature tasty fish pies; lots of daily specials on blackboard.

Aubaine
4 Heddon St. ✉ *W1B 4BS* ⊖ *Oxford Circus* – ✆ *(020) 7440 2510*
– *www.aubaine.co.uk* – *Closed dinner Sunday and bank holidays*
Rest – French – Carte £ 22/52

30AIUo

• Sister to the Chelsea original but this time without the boulangerie. The look is of a farmhouse as imagined by a townie; the accessible menu wouldn't look out of place in a bistro.

Automat
33 Dover St. ✉ *W1S 4NF* ⊖ *Green Park* – ✆ *(020) 7499 3033*
– *www.automat-london.com* – *Closed 25 December and 1 January*
Rest – American – Carte £ 24/49

30AIVr

• In contrast to Mayfair's inherent Britishness is this buzzy NYC style brasserie. Stick to the classics – crab cakes, burgers and cheesecakes and don't get palmed off with a table in the first section.

Le Boudin Blanc
5 Trebeck St. ✉ *W1J 7LT* ⊖ *Green Park* – ✆ *(020) 7499 3292*
– *www.boudinblanc.co.uk* – *Closed 24-26 December*
Rest – French – Menu £ 15 (lunch and early dinner) – Carte £ 28/49

30AHVq

• Appealing, lively French bistro in Shepherd Market, spread over two floors. Satisfying French classics and country cooking is the draw, along with authentic Gallic service. Good value lunch menu.

Only Running Footman
5 Charles St ✉ *W1J 5DF* ⊖ *Green Park.* – ✆ *(020) 7499 2988*
– *www.therunningfootmanmayfair.com*
Rest – Traditional – Carte £ 21/37

30AHVx

• Busy ground floor bar with its appealing menu of pub classics doesn't take bookings. By contrast, upstairs is formal and its menu more European and ambitious but simpler dishes still the best.

REGENT'S PARK AND MARYLEBONE

The Landmark London
222 Marylebone Rd ✉ *NW1 6JQ* ⊖ *Edgware Rd* – ✆ *(020) 7631 8000*
– *www.landmarklondon.co.uk*
291 rm – †£ 239/660 ††£ 239/660, ⊇ £ 29 – 9 suites
Rest *Winter Garden* – see restaurant listing

29AFTa

• Imposing Victorian Gothic building with a vast glass-enclosed atrium, overlooked by many of the modern, well-equipped bedrooms. Choice of relaxed wood panelled cellar bar or more sophisticated Mirror bar.

Langham
1c Portland Pl., Regent St. ✉ *W1B 1JA* ⊖ *Oxford Circus* – ✆ *(020) 7636 1000*
– *www.langhamhotels.com*
357 rm – †£ 239/499 ††£ 239/499, ⊇ £ 30 – 21 suites
Rest *Roux at the Landau* – see restaurant listing

30AITn

• Was one of Europe's first purpose-built grand hotels when it opened in 1865. Now back to its best, with its famous Palm Court for afternoon tea, the stylish Artesian bar and bedrooms that are not without personality and elegance.

WESTMINSTER (City of)

Hyatt Regency London-The Churchill
30 Portman Sq ⊠ W1H 7BH ⊖ Marble Arch
– ℰ (020) 7486 5800 – www.london.churchill.hyatt.com
387 rm – †£ 240/552 ††£ 264/576, ⊆ £ 27.50 – 47 suites 29AGTx
Rest *The Montagu* – see restaurant listing
♦ Smart well-located property whose best bedrooms overlook the attractive square opposite. Elegant marbled lobby with plenty of staff. Well-appointed and refurbished bedrooms have the international traveller in mind.

Sanderson
50 Berners St ⊠ W1T 3NG ⊖ Oxford Circus – ℰ (020) 7300 1400
– www.morganshotelgroup.com
150 rm – †£ 270/654 ††£ 270/654, ⊆ £ 23 31AJTc
Rest *Suka* – see restaurant listing
♦ Designed by Philippe Starck and still attracting a suitably fashionable crowd. Purple Bar dark and moody; Long Bar bright and stylish. Pure white bedrooms with idiosyncratic design touches such as a framed picture...on the ceiling.

LONDON

Arch
50 Great Cumberland Pl ⊠ W1H 7FD ⊖ Marble Arch – ℰ (020) 7724 4700
– www.thearchlondon.com
80 rm – †£ 258/1020 ††£ 258/1020, ⊆ £ 19.50 – 2 suites 29AGTa
Rest *Hunter 486* – ℰ (020) 7725 4825 – Menu £ 20 (lunch) – Carte £ 35/60
♦ Fashioned out of a row of seven terrace houses and two mews cottages. Plenty of extras and thoughtful touches are found in the comfortable bedrooms. Interesting pieces of art throughout. Casual restaurant doubles as a bar.

Montcalm
34-40 Great Cumberland Pl. ⊠ W1H 7TW ⊖ Marble Arch – ℰ (020) 7402 4288
– www.montcalm.co.uk
126 rm – †£ 420 ††£ 420/1020, ⊆ £ 19.95 – 17 suites 29AGUm
Rest *Vetro* – Italian – Menu £ 24 (lunch) – Carte £ 27/41
♦ Named after an 18C French general, The Montcalm forms part of a crescent of townhouses with a Georgian façade. A top-to-toe refurbishment has created smart and contemporary bedrooms in lively colours. Classic Italian dishes in Vetro.

Durrants
26-32 George St ⊠ W1H 5BJ ⊖ Bond Street – ℰ (020) 7935 8131
– www.durrantshotel.co.uk
89 rm – †£ 156 ††£ 180, ⊆ £ 22.50 – 3 suites 29AGTe
Rest – *(closed dinner 25 December)* Carte £ 32/50
♦ Traditional, privately owned hotel with friendly, long-standing staff. Bedrooms are now brighter in style but still retain a certain English character. Clubby dining room for mix of British classics and lighter, European dishes.

Mandeville
Mandeville Pl. ⊠ W1U 2BE ⊖ Bond Street – ℰ (020) 7935 5599
– www.mandeville.co.uk
140 rm – †£ 383/407 ††£ 407, ⊆ £ 22.50 – 2 suites 30AHTx
Rest *de Ville* – *(closed Sunday dinner)* Menu £ 23 – Carte dinner £ 34/44
♦ Usefully located hotel with marbled reception leading into a very colourful and comfortable bar. Stylish rooms have flatscreen TVs and make good use of the space available. Modern British cuisine served in bright de Ville restaurant.

No. Ten Manchester Street
⊠ W1U 4DG ⊖ Baker Street – ℰ (020) 7317 5900
– www.tenmanchesterstreethotel.com 29AGTv
44 rm – †£ 179 ††£ 480, ⊆ £ 17.95 – 1 suite   **Rest** – *(room service only)*
♦ Converted Edwardian house in an appealing, central location. Discreet entrance leads into stylish little lounge; semi-enclosed cigar bar also a feature. Neat and well-kept bedrooms.

WESTMINSTER (City of)

Sumner without rest
54 Upper Berkeley St ⊠ W1H 7QR ⊖ Marble Arch – ℰ (020) 7723 2244
– www.thesumner.com **29AFUk**
19 rm – †£ 198/213 ††£ 222/237

♦ Two Georgian terrace houses in central location. Comfy, stylish sitting room; basement breakfast room. Largest bedrooms, 101 and 201, benefit from having full-length windows.

Marble Arch by Montcalm without rest
31 Great Cumberland Pl. ⊠ W1H 7TA ⊖ Marble Arch – ℰ (020) 7258 0777
– www.themarblearch.co.uk **29AGUs**
42 rm – †£ 290/350 ††£ 290/350, ⊇ £ 19.50

♦ Bedrooms at this 5-storey Georgian townhouse come with the same high standards of stylish, contemporary design as its parent hotel opposite, the Montcalm, but are just a little more compact.

Hart House without rest
51 Gloucester Pl ⊠ W1U 8JF ⊖ Marble Arch – ℰ (020) 7935 2288
– www.harthouse.co.uk **29AGTd**
15 rm – †£ 98/115 ††£ 150/175

♦ Within an attractive Georgian terrace and run by the same family for over 35 years. Warm and welcoming service; well-kept, competitively priced bedrooms over three floors.

Rhodes W1 (Restaurant)
Cumberland Hotel, Great Cumberland Pl. ⊠ W1H 7DL ⊖ Marble Arch – ℰ (020) 7616 5930 – www.rhodesw1.com – Closed 2 weeks January, 2 weeks August, Saturday lunch, Sunday, Monday and bank holidays **29AGUz**
Rest – French – *(booking advisable)* Menu £ 26/50
Spec. Fillet of mackerel, honey and sesame caramel and sea purslane. Pigeon with foie gras, chicory and pickled blackberries. Prune and Armagnac soufflé, vanilla bean ice cream.

♦ Just 12 tables in a formal but warm and textured room designed by Kelly Hoppen. Influences are more European and cooking more elaborate than usual for a Gary Rhodes restaurant, but you'll find the same emphasis on uncluttered flavours.

Locanda Locatelli
8 Seymour St. ⊠ W1H 7JZ ⊖ Marble Arch – ℰ (020) 7935 9088
– www.locandalocatelli.com **29AGUr**
Rest – Italian – Carte £ 32/62
Spec. Pan-fried scallops with celeriac purée and saffron vinaigrette. Homemade pasta ribbons with broad beans and rocket. Tasting of Amedei chocolate.

♦ Slick and dapper-looking Italian with a celebrity following and a sophisticated atmosphere. Plenty of interest on the extensive menu, with cooking that is confident, balanced and expertly rendered; pastas and desserts are the stand-out courses.

Roux at the Landau – at Langham Hotel
1c Portland Pl., Regent St. ⊠ W1B 1JA ⊖ Oxford Circus – ℰ (020) 7965 0165
– www.thelandau.com – Closed Saturday lunch and Sunday **30AITn**
Rest – French – Menu £ 48 (lunch and early dinner) – Carte £ 37/67

♦ Grand, oval-shaped hotel restaurant run under the aegis of the Roux organisation. Classical, French-influenced cooking is the order of the day, but a lighter style of cuisine using the occasional twist is also emerging.

Latium
21 Berners St. ⊠ W1T 3LP ⊖ Oxford Circus – ℰ (020) 7323 9123
– www.latiumrestaurant.com – Closed 25-26 December, 1 January, Saturday lunch, Sunday and bank holidays **31AJTn**
Rest – Italian – Menu £ 23/36

♦ Bright and contemporary surroundings but with warm and welcoming service. Owner-chef from Lazio but dishes come from across Italy, often using British produce. Ravioli is the house speciality.

WESTMINSTER (City of)

Orrery
55 Marylebone High St ✉ W1U 5RB ⊖ Regent's Park – ℰ (020) 7616 8000
– www.orrery-restaurant.co.uk **18RZDa**
Rest – Modern European – *(booking essential)* Menu £ 25 (lunch)
– Carte £ 37/48

• These are actually converted stables from the 19C but, such is the elegance and style of the building, you'd never know. Featured is elaborate, modern European cooking; dishes are strong on presentation and come with the occasional twist.

Texture (Agnar Sverrisson)
34 Portman St. ✉ W1H 7BY ⊖ Marble Arch – ℰ (020) 7224 0028
– www.texture-restaurant.co.uk – Closed Christmas-New Year, 2 weeks August,
Sunday and Monday **29AGUp**
Rest – Innovative – Menu £ 24 (lunch) – Carte £ 50/64
Spec. Organic Scottish salmon, horseradish and cucumber. Icelandic salted cod, barley risotto and prawns. Skyr ice cream, strawberry and muesli.

• Technically skilled but light and invigorating cooking from Icelandic chef-owner, who uses ingredients from home. Bright restaurant with high ceiling and popular adjoining champagne bar. Pleasant service from keen staff, ready with a smile.

L'Autre Pied
5-7 Blandford St. ✉ W1U 3DB ⊖ Bond Street – ℰ (020) 7486 9696
– www.lautrepied.co.uk – Closed 23 December-5 January and Sunday dinner
Rest – Modern European – Menu £ 23 (lunch and early dinner) **30AHTk**
– Carte £ 39/47
Spec. Cauliflower risotto, scallops and toasted almonds with lemongrass sauce. Pan-fried cod with carrot and star anise purée and tarragon sauce. Ginger mousse, vanilla poached apricots and honey ice cream.

• This more casual sibling to Pied à Terre is a lively, hospitable spot in the evening. The cooking may be slightly simpler but it's still carefully prepared and makes good use of classic combinations of ingredients.

Galvin Bistrot de Luxe
66 Baker St. ✉ W1U 7DJ ⊖ Baker Street – ℰ (020) 7935 4007
– www.galvinrestaurants.com – Closed 25-26 December, 1 January and dinner
24 December **29AGTb**
Rest – French – Menu £ 20 (lunch and early dinner) – Carte £ 35/41

• Firmly established modern Gallic bistro with ceiling fans, globe lights and wood panelled walls. Satisfying and precisely cooked classic French dishes from the Galvin brothers.

Zayna
25 New Quebec St. ✉ W1H 7SF ⊖ Marble Arch – ℰ (020) 7723 2229
– www.zaynarestaurant.co.uk **29AGUx**
Rest – Indian – Menu £ 15 (lunch) – Carte £ 30/39

• Enthusiastically run, elegant restaurant spread over two floors, with keen owner. Interesting north Indian and Pakistani delicacies; kitchen only uses halal meat and free-range chicken.

Ozer
5 Langham Pl., Regent St. ✉ W1B 3DG ⊖ Oxford Circus – ℰ (020) 7323 0505
– www.ozer.co.uk **30AITz**
Rest – Turkish – Menu £ 21/24

• The large front bar is always busy but go through to the equally popular but comfortable restaurant to enjoy authentic Turkish food. Wide range of appealing meze is the draw, along with succulent lamb dishes.

Rhodes W1 Brasserie
Cumberland Hotel, Great Cumberland Pl. ✉ W1H 7DL ⊖ Marble Arch
– ℰ (020) 7616 5930 – www.rhodesw1.com **29AGUz**
Rest – Modern European – Menu £ 21 (lunch) – Carte £ 24/43

• Large brasserie on the ground floor of the Cumberland hotel, with keen, helpful service and equally big bar. Expect Gary Rhodes' signature dishes, alongside others of a more European persuasion.

WESTMINSTER (City of)

XX Royal China
24-26 Baker St — W1U 7AB — Baker Street – ℰ (020) 7487 4688
– www.royalchinagroup.co.uk   **29**AGT**h**
Rest – Chinese – Menu £ 30 – Carte £ 31/42

♦ Barbeque meats, assorted soups and stir-fries attract plenty of large groups to this smart and always bustling Cantonese restaurant. Over 40 different types of dim sum served during the day.

XX Colony
8 Paddington St — W1U 5QH — Baker Street – ℰ (020) 7935 3353
– www.colonybarandgrill.com   **30**AHT**d**
Rest – Indian – Menu £ 17 (lunch) – Carte dinner £ 23/33

♦ Small tasting plates making good use of the grill and tandoor, lunchtime thalis and grazing menus with mostly Indian influences are served at this relaxed lounge bar, with chilled music and an extensive cocktail list.

XX Iberica
195 Great Portland St — W1W 5PS — Great Portland St – ℰ (020) 7636 8650
– www.ibericalondon.co.uk – Closed 1 January, Sunday dinner and bank
holidays   **18**RZD**x**
Rest – Spanish – (booking advisable at dinner) Carte £ 20/36

♦ These large premises pay homage to Spain's food and culture. Punchy flavoured tapas in the ground floor bar; more intimate upstairs. Wander through the deli to appreciate the quality of ingredients.

XX Verru
69 Marylebone Ln — W1U 2PH — Bond Street – ℰ (020) 7935 0858
– www.verru.co.uk   **30**AHT**a**
Rest – Modern European – Menu £ 17 (lunch) – Carte £ 35/42

♦ Chef-owner is Estonian so his cooking not only displays a Baltic boldness of flavour but also makes good use of northern European influences. The restaurant is tiny and tucked away but warmly run and smartly dressed.

XX Roganic
19 Blandford St — W1U 3DH — Baker Street – ℰ (020) 7486 0380
– www.roganic.co.uk – Closed Sunday and Monday   **29**AGT**r**
Rest – Innovative – (booking advisable) Menu £ 29 (lunch and early dinner)/80

♦ Simon Rogan of L'Enclume in the Lake District created this "extended pop-up restaurant" by taking on the last 2 years of an existing lease. From the tasting menus come dishes of invention and originality, using produce from their own farm.

XX The Providores
109 Marylebone High St. — W1U 4RX — Bond Street – ℰ (020) 7935 6175
– www.theprovidores.co.uk – Closed 24 December-4 January   **30**AHT**y**
Rest – Innovative – Menu £ 46 – Carte £ 34/49

♦ Packed ground floor for tapas; upstairs for innovative fusion cooking, with spices and ingredients from around the world, including Australasia. Starter-sized dishes at dinner allow for greater choice.

XX Cafe Luc
50 Marylebone High St — W1U 5HN — Regent's Park – ℰ (020) 7258 9878
– www.cafeluc.com – Closed 25 December   **30**AHT**b**
Rest – Modern European – Menu £ 16 (lunch) – Carte £ 29/41

♦ Spacious, grand and keenly run brasserie with smart leather banquette seating and clusters of lights. The menu offers a host of brasserie and continental classics to suit all tastes.

XX Levant
Jason Ct., 76 Wigmore St. — W1U 2SJ — Bond Street – ℰ (020) 7224 1111
– www.levant.co.uk – Closed 25-26 December   **30**AHT**c**
Rest – Lebanese – (dinner only and lunch Saturday-Sunday) Menu £ 22/28
– Carte £ 30/45

♦ Belly dancing, lanterns and a low-slung bar all add up to an exotic dining experience. The Lebanese food is satisfying and authentic, carefully prepared and ideal for sharing in groups.

WESTMINSTER (City of)

XX L'Aventure
3 Blenheim Terr ⊠ NW8 0EH ⊖ St John's Wood – ℘ (020) 7624 6232
– Closed first week January, Saturday lunch, Sunday and bank holidays
Rest – French – Menu £ 21/39   **11**PZB**b**

♦ Behind the pretty tree-lined entrance you'll find a charming neighbourhood restaurant. Relaxed atmosphere and service by personable owner. Authentic French cuisine.

XX The Montagu – at Hyatt Regency London-The Churchill
30 Portman Sq ⊠ W1H 7BH ⊖ Marble Arch – ℘ (020) 7299 2037
– www.london.churchill.hyatt.com   **29**AGT**x**
Rest – British – Menu £ 24/26 – Carte £ 37/57

♦ Offering sanctuary from Oxford Street, The Montagu is a light, spacious affair within the discreet Hyatt Regency hotel. Open all day; its afternoon teas are particularly popular.

XX Winter Garden – at The Landmark London Hotel
222 Marylebone Rd ⊠ NW1 6JQ ⊖ Edgware Rd – ℘ (020) 7631 8000
– www.landmarklondon.co.uk   **29**AFT**a**
Rest – Mediterranean – Menu £ 35 (lunch) – Carte £ 41/64

♦ Impressive glass atrium in an international hotel, of the sort more commonly found in Asia. Ideal for an informal lunch, when the Mediterranean dishes come into their own.

XX Suka – at Sanderson Hotel
50 Berners St ⊠ W1T 3NG ⊖ Oxford Circus – ℘ (020) 7300 1400
– www.morganshotelgroup.com   **31**AJT**c**
Rest – Asian influences – Carte £ 26/51

♦ Beyond the Sanderson hotel's trendy Long Bar is Suka, a casual eatery that extends into the garden terrace. Expect British ingredients and Asian influences, with Malaysia dominating.

XX Phoenix Palace
5 Glentworth St. ⊠ NW1 5PG ⊖ Baker Street – ℘ (020) 7486 3515
– www.phoenixpalace.co.uk – Closed 25 December   **17**QZD**x**
Rest – Chinese – (booking advisable at dinner) Menu £ 28 (dinner) – Carte approx. £ 24

♦ Huge restaurant offering a plethora of menus but the cooking is still good. Dim sum during the day and Cantonese dishes and rotisserie meats at night draw in the groups of families and friends.

X Trishna
15-17 Blandford St. ⊠ W1U 3DG ⊖ Baker Street – ℘ (020) 7935 5624
– www.trishnalondon.com – Closed 25-28 December and 1-3 January
Rest – Indian – Menu £ 18 (lunch) – Carte £ 24/37   **29**AGT**r**

♦ A franchise of the celebrated Mumbai restaurant. Specialises in fish and seafood dishes; the rich Cornish brown crab with butter garlic is certainly a highlight. Bright surroundings allow the focus to stay on the food.

X Riding House Café
43-51 Great Titchfield St ⊠ W1W 7PQ ⊖ Oxford Circus – ℘ (020) 7927 0840
– www.ridinghousecafe.co.uk – Closed 25-26 December   **30**AIT**k**
Rest – Modern European – Carte £ 24/42

♦ It's less a café, more a large, quirkily designed, all-day New York style brasserie and cocktail bar. The 'small plates' have more zing than the main courses. The unbookable side of the restaurant is the more fun part.

X The Wallace
Hertford House, Manchester Sq ⊠ W1U 3BN ⊖ Bond Street – ℘ (020) 7563 9505 – www.thewallacerestaurant.com – Closed 24-26 December
Rest – French – (lunch only and dinner Friday-Saturday)   **29**AGT**k**
Carte £ 30/39

♦ Large glass-roofed courtyard on the ground floor of Hertford House, home to the splendid Wallace Collection. French-influenced menu, with fruits de mer section; terrines are the house speciality.

WESTMINSTER (City of)

Hix (Selfridges)
Mezzanine Fl, Selfridges, 400 Oxford St ⊠ W1A 1AB ⊖ Bond St – ℰ (020) 7499 5400 – www.hixatselfridges.co.uk – Closed 25 December and Sunday dinner
Rest – Modern European – Menu £ 23 (lunch) – Carte £ 25/113   **30**AHU**p**
◆ On the mezzanine floor of the famous store; open from breakfast onwards, with a popular champagne bar to refuel shoppers. Menu is lighter and more European than at the other Hix restaurants.

Caffé Caldesi
118 Marylebone Ln. (1st floor) ⊠ W1U 2QF ⊖ Bond Street – ℰ (020) 7487 0754 – www.caldesi.com   **30**AHT**s**
Rest – Italian – Menu £ 20 (lunch) – Carte £ 28/44
◆ Head upstairs at this converted corner pub for generously proportioned, big flavoured classics from across Italy. Stay on the ground floor for a simpler and more accessibly priced menu.

Dinings
22 Harcourt St. ⊠ W1H 4HH ⊖ Marylebone – ℰ (020) 7723 0666 – www.dinings.co.uk – Closed Christmas, Saturday lunch and Sunday
Rest – Japanese – (booking essential) Carte £ 34/51   **29**AFT**c**
◆ Resembles an after-work Japanese izakaya, or pub, with chummy atmosphere and loud music. Food is a mix of small plates of delicate dishes, a blend of modern and the more traditional.

Il Baretto
43 Blandford St. ⊠ W1U 7HF ⊖ Baker Street – ℰ (020) 7486 7340 – www.ilbaretto.co.uk – Closed 25-26 December and lunch 1 January
Rest – Italian – Carte £ 40/53   **29**AGT**n**
◆ The wood-fired oven is the star of the show at this neighbourhood Italian. Extensive and variably priced menu has something for everyone. The basement room has a lively atmosphere, with frantic service to match.

Vinoteca
15 Seymour Pl. ⊠ W1H 5BD ⊖ Marble Arch – ℰ (020) 7724 7288 – www.vinoteca.co.uk – Closed 25-26 December, 1 January and Sunday dinner
Rest – Modern European – (booking advisable) Carte £ 24/30 ❀   **29**AFU**x**
◆ Follows the formula of the original: great fun, great wines, gutsy and wholesome food, enthusiastic staff and almost certainly a wait for a table. Influences from sunnier parts of Europe, along with some British dishes.

Yalla Yalla
12 Winsley St. ⊠ W1W 8HQ ⊖ Oxford Circus – ℰ (020) 7637 4748 – www.yalla-yalla.co.uk – Closed 27-29 August and Sunday   **30**ALT**v**
Rest – Lebanese – Carte £ 18/22
◆ Queues form for the Beirut street food which includes zesty mezze and succulent charcoal-grilled lamb dishes. Desserts come from the enticing pastry corner and wines from the Bekaa Valley. Takeaway also available.

Chada Chada
16-17 Picton Pl. ⊠ W1U 1BP ⊖ Bond Street – ℰ (020) 7935 8212 – www.chadathai.com – Closed 25 December and lunch Sunday-Monday
Rest – Thai – Carte £ 14/38   **30**AHU**b**
◆ Authentic and fragrant Thai cooking; the good value menu offers some interesting departures from the norm. Service is eager to please in the compact and cosy rooms.

Grazing Goat with rm
6 New Quebec St ⊠ W1H 7RQ ⊖ Marble Arch. – ℰ (020) 7724 7243 – www.thegrazinggoat.co.uk   **29**AGU**d**
8 rm – ♦£ 195/225 ♦♦£ 195/225, ⊇ £ 11
Rest – Traditional – (booking essential at dinner) Carte £ 30/45
◆ A smart city facsimile of a country pub; it's first-come-first-served in the bar but you can book in the upstairs dining room. Proper pub classics such as pies and Castle of Mey steaks are on offer. Bedrooms with Nordic style bathrooms.

WESTMINSTER (City of)

Larrik
32 Crawford Pl ⌧ W1H 5NN ⊖ Edgware Road. – ✆ (020) 7723 0066
– www.thelarrik.com – Closed 25 December   VISA ⦵ AE
Rest – Traditional – Menu £13 (dinner) – Carte £25/37   **29**AFT**x**
♦ The front section of this traditional looking pub is brighter and more fun. The kitchen is well-grounded in the basics and reliable, whether making a salad or burger. Regularly changing real ales.

Portman
51 Upper Berkeley St ⌧ W1H 7QW ⊖ Marble Arch. – ✆ (020) 7723 8996
– www.theportmanmarylebone.com   VISA ⦵ AE
Rest – Modern European – Carte £22/31   **29**AFU**n**
♦ The condemned on their way to Tyburn Tree gallows would take their last drink here. Now it's an urbane pub with a formal upstairs dining room. The ground floor is more fun for enjoying the down-to-earth menu.

ST JAMES'S

Ritz

150 Piccadilly ⌧ W1J 9BR ⊖ Green Park – ✆ (020) 7493 8181
– www.theritzlondon.com   **30**AIV**c**
116 rm – †£360/696 ††£426/822, ⌑ £35 – 20 suites
Rest *Ritz Restaurant* – see restaurant listing
♦ World famous hotel, opened 1906 as a fine example of Louis XVI architecture and decoration. Elegant Palm Court famed for its afternoon tea. Many of the lavishly appointed and luxurious rooms and suites overlook the park.

Haymarket
1 Suffolk Pl. ⌧ SW1Y 4HX ⊖ Piccadilly Circus – ✆ (020) 7470 4000
– www.haymarkethotel.com   **31**AKV**x**
47 rm – †£312 ††£564, ⌑ £20 – 3 suites
Rest *Brumus* – see restaurant listing
♦ Smart, spacious hotel in John Nash Regency building, with stylish blend of modern and antique furnishings. Large, comfortable bedrooms in soothing colours. Impressive basement pool often used in photo-shoots.

Dukes
35 St James's Pl. ⌧ SW1A 1NY ⊖ Green Park – ✆ (020) 7491 4840
– www.dukeshotel.com   **30**AIV**f**
84 rm – †£270 ††£420, ⌑ £24 – 6 suites
Rest *Thirty Six by Nigel Mendham* – 36 St James's Pl. – Menu £22 (lunch) – Carte £32/43
♦ The most recent redecoration retained the discreet, traditionally British feel of this hotel in a central but quiet location. Dukes bar famous for its martinis. Elegant bedrooms with country house feel. Calm, comfortable dining room offers seasonal British menu.

Stafford

16-18 St James's Pl. ⌧ SW1A 1NJ ⊖ Green Park – ✆ (020) 7493 0111
– www.kempinski.com/london   **30**AIV**u**
73 rm – †£330/492 ††£443/660, ⌑ £25 – 15 suites
Rest – Menu £28 (lunch) – Carte £34/55
♦ Currently being refurbished, the bedrooms of this 'country house in the city' are divided between the main house, converted 18C stables and more modern mews. Legendary American bar a feature; British food served in the restaurant.

St James's Hotel and Club

7-8 Park Pl. ⌧ SW1A 1LS ⊖ Green Park – ✆ (020) 7316 1600
– www.stjameshotelandclub.com   **30**AIV**k**
50 rm – †£282/414 ††£282/414, ⌑ £22 – 10 suites
Rest *Seven Park Place* – see restaurant listing
♦ 1890s hotel in cul-de-sac, formerly a private club, reopened as a hotel in 2008. Modern, boutique-style interior with over 200 mostly German works of art from the '30s and '40s. Fine finish to compact, but well-equipped bedrooms.

Cavendish

81 Jermyn St ⊠ SW1Y 6JF ⊖ Piccadilly Circus – ℰ (020) 7930 2111
– www.thecavendishlondon.com

30AIVp

228 rm – †£ 179/372, ††£ 179/372, ⌸ £ 21 – 2 suites
Rest – British – *(closed 25 December, lunch Saturday-Sunday and bank holidays)* Menu £ 21 (dinner) – Carte £ 30/45

• There's been a hotel on this site since the 18C; this one was built in the '60s but is smart and contemporary inside. Great location, bistro-style dining with British menu and good views across London from the top 5 floors; a parking space for every room too!

Ritz Restaurant – at The Ritz Hotel

150 Piccadilly ⊠ W1J 9BR ⊖ Green Park – ℰ (020) 7493 8181
– www.theritzlondon.com

30AIVc

Rest – Traditional – Menu £ 39/48 **s** – Carte £ 71/94 **s**

• Grand and lavish restaurant, with Louis XVI decoration, trompe l'oeil and ornate gilding. Delightful terrace over Green Park. Structured, formal service. Classic, traditional dishes are the highlight of the menu. Jacket and tie required.

Seven Park Place – at St James's Hotel and Club

7-8 Park Pl ⊠ SW1A 1LS ⊖ Green Park – ℰ (020) 7316 1614
– www.stjameshotelandclub.com – Closed Sunday and Monday

30AIVk

Rest – Modern European – *(booking essential)* Menu £ 30/55
Spec. Lobster tail with asparagus, pea shoots and truffle dressing. Saddle of lamb with peas, lettuce and onions. Piña colada bavarois with poached pineapple.

• Small restaurant concealed somewhat within St James's Hotel and divided between two rooms; ask for the gilded back room. The accomplished food has a French base, displays confidence and clarity and uses quality British ingredients.

The Wolseley

160 Piccadilly ⊠ W1J 9EB ⊖ Green Park – ℰ (020) 7499 6996
– www.thewolseley.com – Closed 25 December,
dinner 24 and 31 December and August bank holiday

30AIVq

Rest – Modern European – *(booking essential)* Carte £ 24/48

• Feels like a grand European coffee house, with pillars and high vaulted ceiling. Appealing menus range from caviar to a hot dog. Open from breakfast and boasts a celebrity following.

Sake No Hana

23 St James's St ⊠ SW1A 1HA ⊖ Green Park – ℰ (020) 7925 8988
– www.sakenohana.com – Closed Saturday lunch and Sunday

30AIVn

Rest – Japanese – Carte £ 38/50

• Ground floor sushi bar; first floor restaurant reached by elevator, where cedar wood goes some way to disguising an ugly, if iconic, '60s building. The Japanese menu has been simplified somewhat; service can also be a little lacklustre.

Le Caprice

Arlington House, Arlington St. ⊠ SW1A 1RJ ⊖ Green Park – ℰ (020) 7629 2239
– www.le-caprice.co.uk – Closed 25-26 December

30AIVh

Rest – Modern European – Carte £ 21/46

• Its clubby atmosphere, pianist, slick monochrome decoration and catch-all menu have been attracting a shiny, self assured clientele since 1981. Little wonder that a New York outpost opened in 2009.

Franco's

61 Jermyn St. ⊠ SW1Y 6LX ⊖ Green Park – ℰ (020) 7499 2211
– www.francoslondon.com – Closed Sunday and bank holidays

30AIVi

Rest – Italian – *(booking essential)* Menu £ 26 (lunch) – Carte £ 35/55

• Open from breakfast until late, with café at the front leading into smart, clubby restaurant. Menu covers all parts of Italy and includes popular grill section and plenty of classics.

Avenue

7-9 St James's St. ⊠ SW1A 1EE ⊖ Green Park – ℰ (020) 7321 2111
– www.avenue-restaurant.co.uk – Closed 25-26 December,
Saturday lunch and Sunday
30AIV**y**

Rest – Modern European – Menu £ 24 (lunch) – Carte £ 25/55

♦ Large, brash restaurant, with sheer white décor and a very popular bar. All-encompassing menu, with everything from caviar to burgers. Service comes with an urgency not always required.

Matsuri - St James's

15 Bury St. ⊠ SW1Y 6AL ⊖ Green Park – ℰ (020) 7839 1101
– www.matsuri-restaurant.com – Closed 25 December and 1 January
Rest – Japanese – Menu £ 35 (dinner) – Carte £ 28/39
30AIV**w**

♦ Sweet natured service at this traditional Japanese stalwart. Teppan-yaki is their speciality, with Scottish beef the highlight; sushi counter also available. Good value lunch menus.

Quaglino's

16 Bury St ⊠ SW1Y 6AJ ⊖ Green Park – ℰ (020) 7930 6767
– www.quaglinos.co.uk – Closed Sunday
Rest – Modern European – (booking essential) Menu £ 25 (lunch)
– Carte £ 43/59
30AIV**j**

♦ This big, bold restaurant achieved iconic status on reopening in the early '90s. No longer quite so glamorous but it still offers a good night out and a easy menu, with fruits de mer the highlight.

Mint Leaf

Suffolk Pl. ⊠ SW1Y 4HX ⊖ Piccadilly Circus – ℰ (020) 7930 9020
– www.mintleafrestaurant.com – Closed 25 December,
1 January, lunch Saturday and Sunday
31AKV**k**

Rest – Indian – Menu £ 18 (lunch and early dinner) – Carte £ 38/60

♦ Cavernous and moodily lit basement restaurant incorporating trendy bar with lounge music and extensive cocktail list. Contemporary Indian cooking with curries the highlight.

Brumus – at Haymarket Hotel

1 Suffolk Pl ⊠ SW1Y 4HX ⊖ Piccadilly Circus – ℰ (020) 7470 4000
– www.haymarkethotel.com
31AKV**x**
Rest – Modern European – Menu £ 19/23 – Carte £ 34/56

♦ Ideally positioned for pre or post theatre dining, when a good value menu is offered. Energetic room, with busy bar attached, and an unthreatening menu of Mediterranean favourites.

Al Duca

4-5 Duke of York St. ⊠ SW1Y 6LA ⊖ Piccadilly Circus – ℰ (020) 7839 3090
– www.alduca-restaurant.co.uk – Closed Easter, 25 December, Sunday and bank holidays
31AJV**r**

Rest – Italian – Menu £ 28

♦ Cooking which focuses on flavour continues to draw in the regulars at this warm and spirited Italian restaurant. Prices are keen when one considers the central location and service is brisk and confident.

Inn the Park

St James's Park ⊠ SW1A 2BJ ⊖ Charing Cross – ℰ (020) 7451 9999
– www.innthepark.com – Closed 26 December and 1 January
31AKV**n**
Rest – British – Carte £ 25/39

♦ Oliver Peyton's eco-friendly restaurant in the middle of the park, with a terrific terrace. British menu uses many small suppliers. Cooking is straightforward and wholesome.

WESTMINSTER (City of)

Portrait

National Portrait Gallery, (3rd floor), St Martin's Pl. ⊠ WC2H 0HE
⊖ Charing Cross – ℘ (020) 7312 2490 – www.searcys.co.uk
– Closed 24-26 December

31ALVn

Rest – Modern European – *(lunch only and dinner Thursday-Saturday) (booking essential)* Menu £ 25 – Carte £ 32/40

♦ On the top floor of National Portrait Gallery with rooftop local landmark views: a charming spot for lunch. Modern British/European dishes; weekend brunch.

The National Dining Rooms

Sainsbury Wing, The National Gallery, Trafalgar Sq ⊠ WC2N 5DN
⊖ Charing Cross – ℘ (020) 7747 2525 – www.peytonandbyrne.co.uk – Closed 24-26 December

31AKVb

Rest – British – *(lunch only)* Carte £ 27/37

♦ Set on the East Wing's first floor, you can tuck into cakes in the bakery or grab a prime corner table in the restaurant for great views and proudly seasonal British menus.

SOHO

Soho

4 Richmond Mews ⊠ W1D 3DH ⊖ Tottenham Court Road – ℘ (020) 7559 3000 – www.sohohotel.com

31AJUn

85 rm – †£ 354 ††£ 570, ⊇ £ 20 – 2 suites
Rest *Refuel* – see restaurant listing

♦ Stylish and very fashionable hotel that mirrors the vibrancy of the neighbourhood. Boasts two screening rooms, a comfortable drawing room and up-to-the-minute bedrooms, some vivid, others more muted but all boasting hi-tech extras.

W London

10 Wardour St ⊠ W1D 6QF ⊖ Leicester Square – ℘ (020) 7758 1000 – www.wlondon.co.uk

31AKUb

177 rm – †£ 503 ††£ 503, ⊇ £ 25 – 15 suites
Rest *Spice Market* – see restaurant listing

♦ Achingly trendy hotel, opened in 2011. A DJ in the lobby lounge, low slung tables in the bar and slick, über cool bedrooms in categories called 'Fantastic' or 'Spectacular'. Anyone over 40 will be lost.

Sanctum Soho

20 Warwick St. ⊠ W1B 5NF ⊖ Piccadilly Circus – ℘ (020) 7292 6100 – www.sanctumsoho.com

30AIUg

30 rm – †£ 240/276 ††£ 360/660, ⊇ £ 21
Rest *No. 20* – Modern – *(closed Sunday dinner)* Menu £ 18/21 – Carte £ 25/41

♦ Plenty of glitz and bling at this funky, self-styled rock 'n' roll hotel, with some innovative touches such as TVs behind mirrors. Rooftop lounge and hot tub. Relaxed and comfortable dining with plenty of classic dishes.

Dean Street Townhouse

69-71 Dean St. ⊠ W1D 3SE ⊖ Tottenham Court Road ~ ℘ (020) 7434 1775 – www.deanstreettownhouse.com

31AKUt

39 rm – †£ 90 ††£ 370, ⊇ £ 10
Rest *Dean Street Townhouse Restaurant* – see restaurant listing

♦ In the heart of Soho where bedrooms range from tiny to bigger; the latter have roll-top baths in the room. All are well designed and come with a good range of extras. Cosy ground floor lounge.

Hazlitt's

6 Frith St ⊠ W1D 3JA ⊖ Tottenham Court Road – ℘ (020) 7434 1771 – www.hazlittshotel.com

31AKUu

27 rm – †£ 222 ††£ 282 – 3 suites   **Rest** – *(room service only)*

♦ Three adjoining early 18C townhouses and former home of the eponymous essayist. Idiosyncratic bedrooms, many with antique furniture and Victorian baths; ask for one of the newer ones.

WESTMINSTER (City of)

Gauthier - Soho
21 Romilly St ⊠ W1D 5AF – ⊖ Leicester Square – ℰ (020) 7494 3111
– www.gauthiersoho.co.uk – Closed Saturday lunch, Sunday and bank holidays
Rest – French – Menu £ 25/35   **31**A**K**U**k**
Spec. Warm lobster salad with lemon balm and peach. Cuts of roe deer with truffle and celeriac. Orange blossom soufflé with warm madeleines.
- Professionally run restaurant with an intimate and somewhat secretive feel, spread over three floors of a bright 18C townhouse. The refined, elegant cooking emphasises the natural flavours and seasonal freshness of the quality ingredients.

Quo Vadis
26-29 Dean St. ⊠ W1D 3LL – ⊖ Tottenham Court Road – ℰ (020) 7437 9585
– www.quovadis.co.uk – Closed Christmas, Sunday and bank holidays
Rest – British – Menu £ 20 (lunch) – Carte £ 31/46   **31**A**K**U**v**
- Dating from the 1920s and renewed in 2008; a veritable Soho institution with an art deco feel. Instantly appealing menu of carefully prepared classics, from grilled Longhorn beef to assorted seafood.

Aqua Nueva
240 Regent St., (entrance on Argyll St.) ⊠ W1B 3BR – ⊖ Oxford Circus – ℰ (020) 7478 0540 – www.aqua-london.com – Closed 25 December and 1 January
Rest – Spanish – Carte £ 45/74   **30**A**I**U**x**
- Large operation on the 5th floor of a former department store. Choose between the elegant main dining room or the more buzzy but equally stylish tapas bar. Spanish food interpreted in a modern style.

Red Fort
77 Dean St. ⊠ W1D 3SH – ⊖ Tottenham Court Road – ℰ (020) 7437 2525
– www.redfort.co.uk – Closed 25 December, lunch Saturday, Sunday and bank holidays   **31**A**K**U**x**
Rest – Indian – *(booking advisable at dinner)* Menu £ 20/35 – Carte £ 35/41
- A feature in Soho since 1983 but the last makeover gave it a stylish, contemporary look. Balanced cooking uses much UK produce such as Herdwick lamb; look out for more unusual choices like rabbit.

Imperial China
White Bear Yard, 25a Lisle Street ⊠ WC2H 7BA – ⊖ Leicester Square – ℰ (020) 7734 3388 – www.imperial-china.co.uk – Closed 24-25 December   **31**A**K**U**l**
Rest – Chinese – *(booking advisable)* Menu £ 19 – Carte £ 30/50
- Sharp service and comfortable surroundings are not the only things that set this restaurant apart: the Cantonese cooking exudes freshness and vitality, whether that's the steamed dumplings or the XO minced pork with fine beans.

Dean Street Townhouse Restaurant
69-71 Dean St. ⊠ W1D 3SE – ⊖ Tottenham Court Road – ℰ (020) 7434 1775
– www.deanstreettownhouse.com   **31**A**K**U**t**
Rest – British – *(booking essential)* Menu £ 20 (lunch) – Carte £ 23/31
- Georgian house now home to a fashionable and very busy bar and restaurant; the Parlour is the less hectic area. Appealingly classic British food includes some retro dishes and satisfying puddings.

Yauatcha
15 Broadwick St ⊠ W1F 0DL – ⊖ Tottenham Court Road – ℰ (020) 7494 8888
– www.yauatcha.com – Closed 24-25 December and lunch 26 December and 1 January   **31**A**J**U**k**
Rest – Chinese – Carte £ 30/50
Spec. Scallop shui mai. Jasmine tea smoked ribs. Milk chocolate praline cake with kalamansi sorbet.
- Refined, delicate and delicious dim sum; ideal for sharing in a group. Stylish surroundings spread over two floors: the lighter, brighter ground floor or the darker, more atmospheric basement. Afternoon teas also a speciality.

WESTMINSTER (City of)

XX Aqua Kyoto
240 Regent St., (entrance on Argyll St.) ✉ W1F 7EB ⊖ Oxford Circus – ✆ (020) 7478 0540 – www.aqua-london.com – Closed 25 December and 1 January
Rest – Japanese – Carte £ 45/65 **s**   **30**AIU**x**

♦ The more boisterous of the two large restaurants on the 5th floor of Aqua London, along with a busy bar. Ideally suited to larger groups, as the contemporary Japanese food is designed for sharing.

XX Bob Bob Ricard
1 Upper James St ✉ W1F 9DF ⊖ Oxford Circus – ✆ (020) 3145 1000 – www.bobbobricard.com – Closed 25-26 December, 1 January, Sunday and Monday
Rest – Traditional – Menu £ 24 (lunch) – Carte £ 29/70   **31**AJU**a**

♦ Enigmatically decorated and flamboyant grand café, with a menu that offers everything from caviar and jelly, to beef Wellington or a bowl of cornflakes. Open from early to very late.

XX Spice Market – at W London Hotel
10 Wardour St ✉ W1D 6QF ⊖ Leicester Square – ✆ (020) 7758 1000 – www.spicemarketlondon.co.uk   **31**AKU**b**
Rest – Asian – Menu £ 18/24 – Carte £ 29/51

♦ Over two floors and as strikingly decorated and as fun as Jean-Georges Vongerichten's original in Manhattan's Meatpacking district. Influences from across Asia in dishes designed for sharing; curries a highlight.

XX Floridita
100 Wardour St. ✉ W1F 0TN ⊖ Tottenham Court Road – ✆ (020) 7314 4000 – www.floriditalondon.com – Closed Sunday, Monday and bank holidays
Rest – Latin American – (dinner only and lunch in December)   **31**AJU**z**
Menu £ 28 – Carte £ 24/56

♦ Mediterranean tapas on the ground floor; the huge downstairs for live music, dancing and Latin American specialities, from Cuban spice to Argentinean beef. Great cocktails and a party atmosphere.

XX Vasco and Piero's Pavilion
15 Poland St ✉ W1F 8QE ⊖ Oxford Circus – ✆ (020) 7437 8774 – www.vascosfood.com – Closed Saturday lunch, Sunday and bank holidays
Rest – Italian – (booking essential at lunch) Menu £ 20 (lunch and   **31**AJU**b**
early dinner) – Carte £ 30/38

♦ Celebrated forty years in 2011; its longevity down to its twice-daily changing menu and the simple but effective Umbrian-influenced cooking. The bright room attracts a high proportion of regulars.

XX Plum Valley
20 Gerrard St. ✉ W1D 6JQ ⊖ Leicester Square – ✆ (020) 7494 4366 – Closed 24-25 December   **31**AKU**i**
Rest – Chinese – Menu £ 38 – Carte £ 23/44

♦ Its striking black façade make this modern Chinese restaurant easy to spot in Chinatown. Mostly Cantonese cooking, with occasional forays into Vietnam and Thailand; dim sum is the strength.

XX Haozhan
8 Gerrard St ✉ W1D 5PJ ⊖ Leicester Square – ✆ (020) 7434 3838 – www.haozhan.co.uk – Closed 24-26 December   **31**AKU**n**
Rest – Chinese – Carte £ 21/41

♦ Interesting dishes in a fusion style, with mostly Cantonese but other Asian influences too. Specialities like jasmine ribs or wasabi prawns reveal a freshness that marks this restaurant out from the plethora of Chinatown mediocrity.

WESTMINSTER (City of)

Refuel – at Soho Hotel
4 Richmond Mews ⊠ W1D 3DH ⊖ Tottenham Court Road – ℰ (020) 7559 3007 – www.sohohotel.com
31AJUn
Rest – Modern European – Menu £ 25 – Carte £ 34/56

• At the heart of the cool Soho hotel is their aptly named bar and restaurant. With a menu to suit all moods and a cocktail list to lift all spirits, it's a fun and frantic spot.

Bistro du Vin
36 Dean St ⊠ W1D 4PS ⊖ Tottenham Court Road – ℰ (020) 7432 4800 – www.bistroduvin.co.uk – Closed 25 December
31AKUe
Rest – Modern European – Carte £ 25/48

• Followed hot on the heels of their first bistro in Clerkenwell; this one's slightly bigger but otherwise adopts the same formula, by offering an appealing selection of brasserie classics and a decent selection of well-priced wines.

Arbutus
63-64 Frith St. ⊠ W1D 3JW ⊖ Tottenham Court Road – ℰ (020) 7734 4545 – www.arbutusrestaurant.co.uk – Closed 25-26 December and 1 January
Rest – Modern European – *(booking advisable)* Menu £ 17 **31AKUh**
(lunch) – Carte £ 27/38

Spec. Squid and mackerel 'burger', razor clams and sea purslane. Saddle of rabbit, shoulder cottage pie. Cold chocolate fondant, salted caramel ice cream.

• It takes a lot of work and experience to make it all look so easy. Bubbly and enthusiastic service; relaxed, sociable surroundings and bistro-style dishes packed with flavour from a highly skilled kitchen. Terrific, affordable wine list.

Nopi
21-22 Warwick St. ⊠ W1B 5NE ⊖ Piccadilly Circus – ℰ (020) 7494 9584 – www.nopi-restaurant.com
30AIUg
Rest – International – Carte £ 32/40

• The bright, clean look of Yotam Ottolenghi's restaurant matches the fresh, invigorating food. The sharing plates take in the Mediterranean, Middle East and Asia and the veg dishes stand out.

St John with rm
1 Leicester St. ⊠ WC2H 7BL ⊖ Leicester Square – ℰ (020) 3301 8069 – www.stjohnhotellondon.com
31AKUs
15 rm – †£ 330 ††£ 330, ⊡ £ 15
Rest – British – *(booking advisable)* Carte £ 28/46

• There's a Nordic lucidity to the bedrooms but it is the restaurant that's the heart of the hotel. It follows the Clerkenwell original with its terse menu descriptions, fiercely seasonal, no-nonsense "nose to tail" cooking, municipal-white surroundings and clued-up staff. Dinner is served until 2am.

Bocca di Lupo
12 Archer St ⊠ W1D 7BB ⊖ Piccadilly Circus – ℰ (020) 7734 2223 – www.boccadilupo.com – Closed 24 December-4 January and Sunday dinner
Rest – Italian – *(booking essential)* Carte £ 24/35 **31AJUe**

• Atmosphere, food and service are all best when sitting at the marble counter, watching the chefs at work. Specialities from across Italy come in large or small sizes and are full of flavour and vitality. Try also their Gelato shop opposite.

Benja Bangkok Table
17 Beak St. ⊠ W1F 9RW ⊖ Oxford Circus – ℰ (020) 7287 0555 – www.benja-bankoktable.com
30AIUj
Rest – Thai – Menu £ 10/15 – Carte £ 18/22

• A recent makeover left this Thai restaurant on the edge of Soho with a simpler look that is more typical of a Bangkok eatery. The colourful mix of dishes is authentic and the set menus represent excellent value.

Polpo

41 Beak St. ✉ W1F 9SB ⊖ Oxford Circus – ☏ (0207) 734 44 79
– www.polpo.co.uk – Closed 25 December-1 January, Sunday dinner and bank holidays

30AJUd

Rest – Italian – (bookings not accepted at dinner) Carte £ 15/25

• A fun and lively Venetian bacaro, with a stripped-down, faux-industrial look. The small plates, from arancini and prosciutto to fritto misto and Cotechino sausage, are so well priced that waiting for a table is worth it.

Dehesa

25 Ganton St ✉ W1F 9BP ⊖ Oxford Circus – ☏ (020) 7494 4170
– www.dehesa.co.uk – Closed Sunday dinner

30AIUi

Rest – Mediterranean – Carte £ 20/29

• Repeats the success of its sister restaurant, Salt Yard, by offering tasty, good value Spanish and Italian tapas. Unhurried atmosphere in appealing corner location. Terrific drinks list too.

Wright Brothers Soho

13 Kingly St. ✉ W1B 5PW ⊖ Oxford Circus – ☏ (020) 7434 3611
– www.thewrightbrothers.co.uk – Closed 25-27 December and bank holidays

30AIUz

Rest – Seafood – Carte £ 24/35

• Bigger than the original in Borough Market, this branch is spread over three levels but the best spot is at the counter on the lower floor. Oysters a speciality but all seafood is handled deftly.

Hix

66-70 Brewer St. ✉ WIF 9UP ⊖ Piccadilly Circus – ☏ (020) 7292 3518
– www.hixsoho.co.uk – Closed 25-26 December

30AJUz

Rest – British – Menu £ 23 (lunch) – Carte £ 29/61

• The exterior hints at exclusivity but the enormous interior is fun and sociable and comes decorated with the works of eminent British artists. Expect classic British dishes and ingredients.

Tapas Brindisa

46 Broadwick St. ✉ W1F 7AF ⊖ Oxford Circus – ☏ (020) 7534 1690
– www.brindisa.com – Closed 25 December

31AJUf

Rest – Spanish – (bookings not accepted) Carte £ 18/44

• A few changes in 2011 to this sister of Tapas Brindisa in Borough Market. They moved the bar to the front, changed the name and no longer take bookings; but expect the same quality of tapas from these importers of Spanish produce.

Barrafina

54 Frith St. ✉ W1D 3SL ⊖ Tottenham Court Road – ☏ (020) 7813 8016
– www.barrafina.co.uk – Closed 24 December and 1 January

31AKUc

Rest – Spanish – (bookings not accepted) Carte £ 17/26

• Centred around a counter with seating for 20, come here if you want authentic Spanish tapas served in a buzzy atmosphere. Seafood is a speciality and the Jabugo ham a must.

Barshu

28 Frith St. ✉ W1D 5LF ⊖ Leicester Square – ☏ (020) 7287 8822
– www.bar-shu.co.uk – Closed 24-25 December

31AKUg

Rest – Chinese – (booking advisable) Carte £ 19/47

• The fiery and authentic flavours of China's Sichuan Province are the draw here; help is at hand as menu has pictures. It's decorated with carved wood and lanterns; downstairs is better for groups.

Polpetto

46 Dean St. (1st floor) ✉ W1D 5BG ⊖ Leicester Square – ☏ (020) 7734 1969
– www.polpetto.co.uk – Closed 24 December-2 January, Sunday and bank holidays

31AKUd

Rest – Italian – Carte £ 18/20

• Baby sister to Polpo is located, incongruously, above the iconic French House pub. It's just one small but thoughtfully designed room; order a number of the small, keenly priced plates.

WESTMINSTER (City of)

Spuntino
61 Rupert St. ✉ *W1D 7PW* ⊖ *Piccadilly Circus*
– www.spuntino.co.uk – Closed 25 December-2 January and dinner
24 December **31**AJU**j**
Rest – American – *(bookings not accepted)* Carte £ 12/22
• Influenced by Downtown New York, with its no-booking policy and industrial look. Sit at the counter and order classics like Mac 'n' cheese or mini burgers. The staff, who look like they could also fix your car, really add to the fun.

Ba Shan
24 Romilly St. ✉ *W1D 5AH* ⊖ *Leicester Square –* ℘ *(020) 7287 3266*
– Closed 24-25 December **31**AKU**f**
Rest – Chinese – *(booking advisable)* Carte £ 17/30
• 3-4 tables in each of the five rooms. Open all day, serving a mix of 'snack' and 'home-style' dishes, some with Sichuan leanings, others from northern areas and Henan province.

Imli
167-169 Wardour St ✉ *W1F 8WR* ⊖ *Tottenham Court Road*
– ℘ (020) 7287 4243 – www.imli.co.uk – Closed 25-26 December and 1 January
Rest – Indian – Menu £ 20 (dinner) – Carte £ 16/20 **31**AJU**w**
• Diffusion line from the people behind Tamarind restaurant, where good value, fresh and tasty Indian tapas-style dishes prove a popular currency. The long, spacious interior is a busy, buzzy place.

Cây Tre
42-43 Dean St ✉ *W1D 4PZ* ⊖ *Tottenham Court Road – ℘ (020) 7317 9118*
– www.caytreesoho.co.uk **31**AKU**m**
Rest – Vietnamese – *(booking advisable)* Menu £ 14/21 – Carte £ 20/40
• Bright, sleek and bustling surroundings where Vietnamese standouts include Cha La lot (spicy ground pork wrapped in betel leaves), slow-cooked Mekong catfish with a well-judged sweet and spicy sauce, and 6 versions of Pho (noodle soup).

Baozi Inn
25 Newport Court ✉ *WC2H 7JS* ⊖ *Leicester Square – ℘ (020) 7287 6877*
– Closed 24-25 December **31**AKU**o**
Rest – Chinese – Carte approx. £ 14
• Baozi, or steamed filled buns, are a good way to start, followed by some fiery Sichuan specialities. Simple, honest and friendly restaurant, just off the main strip of Chinatown.

Koya
49 Frith St ✉ *W1D 4SG* ⊖ *Tottenham Court Road – ℘ (020) 7434 4463*
– www.koya.co.uk – Closed Christmas **31**AKU**y**
Rest – Japanese – *(bookings not accepted)* Carte £ 14/18
• Come for authentic udon noodles, made with wheat kneaded by foot, at this sweetly run, simply adorned place. The dashi base stock is freshly made every day. Be respectful by slurping with abandon.

Beijing Dumpling
23 Lisle St. ✉ *WC2H 7BA* ⊖ *Leicester Square – ℘ (020) 7287 6888*
– Closed 24-25 December **31**AKU**l**
Rest – Chinese – Carte £ 15/25
• This relaxed little place serves freshly prepared dumplings of both Beijing and Shanghai styles. Although the range is not as comprehensive as the name suggests, they do stand out, especially varieties of the famed Siu Lung Bao.

WESTMINSTER (City of)

STRAND AND COVENT GARDEN

Savoy
Strand ✉ WC2R 0EU ⊖ Charing Cross – ℘ (020) 7836 4343
– www.fairmont.com/savoy
31ALU**s**
221 rm – †£ 678 ††£ 750, ⊇ £ 30 – 47 suites
Rest *Savoy Grill* **Rest** *River Room* – see restaurant listing
♦ The grande dame of London hotels dazzles once again! Reopened in 2010 following a 3 year restoration, its luxurious bedrooms and stunning suites come in an Edwardian or art deco style. Thames Foyer is the hotel's heart; choose the famous American Bar or new Beaufort Bar.

One Aldwych
1 Aldwych ✉ WC2B 4RH ⊖ Temple – ℘ (020) 7300 1000
– www.onealdwych.com
32AMU**r**
93 rm – †£ 288/415 ††£ 288/498, ⊇ £ 24 – 12 suites
Rest *Axis* – see restaurant listing
Rest *Indigo* – ℘ (020) 7300 0000 – Menu £ 20 (lunch) – Carte £ 39/52
♦ Former 19C bank, now a stylish hotel with lots of artwork; the lobby changes its look seasonally and doubles as a bar. Stylish, contemporary bedrooms with the latest mod cons; the deluxe rooms and suites are particularly desirable. Impressive leisure facilities. Light, accessible menu at Indigo.

St Martins Lane
45 St Martin's Ln ✉ WC2N 3HX ⊖ Charing Cross – ℘ (020) 7300 5500
– www.stmartinslane.com
31ALU**e**
202 rm – †£ 258/594 ††£ 258/594, ⊇ £ 25 – 2 suites
Rest *Asia de Cuba* – see restaurant listing
♦ The unmistakable hand of Philippe Starck evident at this most contemporary of hotels. Unique and stylish, from the starkly modern lobby to the state-of-the-art rooms. 350 varieties of rum and tasty Asian dishes at Asia de Cuba.

Savoy Grill – at Savoy Hotel
Strand ✉ WC2R 0EU ⊖ Charing Cross – ℘ (020) 7592 1600
– www.gordonramsay.com/thesavoygrill
31ALU**s**
Rest – British – Carte £ 30/56
♦ Archives were explored, designers briefed and much money spent, with the result that The Savoy Grill has returned to the traditions that made it famous. As befits the name, it is the charcoal grilling of meats that takes centre stage.

The Ivy
1-5 West St ✉ WC2H 9NQ ⊖ Leicester Square – ℘ (020) 7836 4751
– www.the-ivy.co.uk – Closed 25-26 December
31AKU**p**
Rest – International – Carte £ 38/50
♦ One of the original celebrity hang-out restaurants; still pulling them in. Appealing menu, from shepherd's pie to fishcakes and nursery puddings. Staff go about their business with alacrity.

Axis – at One Aldwych Hotel

1 Aldwych ✉ WC2B 4RH ⊖ Temple – ℘ (020) 7300 0300
– www.onealdwych.com – Closed Sunday and Monday
31AMU**r**
Rest – Modern European – Menu £ 20 (lunch and early dinner) – Carte £ 34/39
♦ A spiral marble staircase leading down to this impressively high-ceilinged restaurant adds to the expectation. The menu is a combination of British classics and lighter European choices.

River Room – at Savoy Hotel
Strand ✉ WC2R 0EU ⊖ Charing Cross – ℘ (020) 7836 4343
– www.fairmont.com/savoy
31ALU**s**
Rest – Modern European – Menu £ 35 (lunch) – Carte £ 24/67
♦ Few restaurants have boasted such an illustrious guest list. Its look has been rejuvenated and the menu updated but the formality, grandeur and river views are as impressive as ever.

WESTMINSTER (City of)

XX J. Sheekey
28-34 St Martin's Ct. ⊠ WC2 4AL ⊖ Leicester Square – ℰ (020) 7240 2565
– www.j-sheekey.co.uk – Closed 25-26 December   **31**ALU**v**
Rest – Seafood – *(booking essential)* Menu £ 28 (weekends) – Carte £ 30/72
♦ Festooned with photographs of actors and linked to the theatrical world since opening in 1890. Wood panels and alcove tables add famed intimacy. Accomplished seafood cooking.

XX Rules
35 Maiden Ln ⊠ WC2E 7LB ⊖ Leicester Square – ℰ (020) 7836 5314
– www.rules.co.uk – Closed Christmas   **31**ALU**n**
Rest – British – *(booking essential)* Carte £ 34/47
♦ London's oldest restaurant boasts a fine collection of antique cartoons, drawings and paintings. Tradition continues in the menu, specialising in game from its own estate.

XX Clos Maggiore
33 King St ⊠ WC2E 8JD ⊖ Leicester Square – ℰ (020) 7379 9696
– www.closmaggiore.com – Closed 25 December and 1 January   **31**ALU**z**
Rest – French – Menu £ 20 (lunch and early dinner) – Carte £ 32/36
♦ Well-dressed restaurant with poised service; ask for a table in the enchanting little rear conservatory, whose roof opens in summer. Sophisticated cooking from a largely French repertoire. Exceptional value lunch and pre-theatre menus.

XX Forge
14 Garrick St ⊠ WC2E 9BJ ⊖ Leicester Square – ℰ (020) 7379 1432
– www.theforgerestaurant.co.uk – Closed 2 days Easter and 24-26 December
Rest – Modern European – Menu £ 17/30 – Carte £ 29/38   **31**ALU**a**
♦ Décor mixes the old with the new; the front area is more intimate, the back more fun. Extensive menu offers something for everyone, from pasta to Dover sole, tournedos Rossini to a hamburger.

XX Le Deuxième
65a Long Acre ⊠ WC2E 9JH ⊖ Covent Garden – ℰ (020) 7379 0033
– www.ledeuxieme.com – Closed 24-25 December   **31**ALU**b**
Rest – Modern European – Menu £ 17 (lunch) – Carte £ 29/38
♦ Caters well for theatregoers: opens early, closes late. Buzzy eatery, simply decorated in white with subtle lighting. International menu but emphasis within Europe.

XX Les Deux Salons
40-42 William IV St ⊠ WC2N 4DD ⊖ Charing Cross – ℰ (020) 7420 2050
– www.lesdeuxsalons.co.uk – Closed 25-26 December and 1 January
Rest – French – Menu £ 16 (lunch) – Carte £ 28/40   **31**ALU**m**
♦ Authentic Parisian brasserie complete with smoked mirrors, globe lights and striking mosaic floor. Ground floor is the better salon for atmosphere. Appealing menu mixes French classics, chargrilled meats and the odd British interloper.

XX Opera Tavern
23 Catherine St. ⊠ WC2B 5JS ⊖ Covent Garden – ℰ (020) 7836 3680
– www.operatavern.co.uk – Closed 24 December-2 January and dinner
Sunday and bank holidays   **31**ALU**y**
Rest – Mediterranean – Carte £ 22/39
♦ Shares the same appealing concept of small plates of Spanish and Italian delicacies as its sisters, Salt Yard and Dehesa. All done in a smartly converted old boozer which dates from 1879; ground floor bar and upstairs dining room.

XX Kyashii
4a Upper St Martin's Lane ⊠ WC2H 9NY ⊖ Leicester Square – ℰ (020)
7836 5211 – www.kyashii.co.uk – Closed 25 December   **31**ALU**w**
Rest – Japanese – Carte £ 25/43
♦ Bright young things come for contemporary Japanese food at this eye-catching restaurant, with its mix of cream leather, mirrors, fish tanks and long marble sushi bar; trendy Shaker bar upstairs.

WESTMINSTER (City of)

Asia de Cuba – at St Martins Lane Hotel
45 St Martin's Ln ⊠ WC2N 3HX ⊖ Charing Cross – ℰ (020) 7300 5500
– www.morganshotelgroup.com
31ALUe
Rest – Asian – Carte £ 49/74
♦ The striking Philippe Starck designed room and the Asian and Cuban inspired cooking appeal to a young, hip crowd. Sharing is the key and that should also include the bill.

L'Atelier de Joël Robuchon
✧✧
13-15 West St. ⊠ WC2H 9NE ⊖ Leicester Square – ℰ (020) 7010 8600
– www.joelrobuchon.co.uk – Closed 25-26 December, 1 January, Sunday and bank holiday Mondays
31AKUa
Rest – French – Menu £ 29/125 – Carte £ 45/83
Spec. Chicken broth with foie gras ravioli and zesty whipped cream. Free-range quail stuffed with foie gras and truffled mashed potatoes. Warm yuzu soufflé with vanilla infused raspberry sorbet.
♦ Wonderfully precise, creative and occasionally playful cooking; dishes may look delicate but pack a punch. Ground floor Atelier with counter seating and chefs on view. More structured La Cuisine. Cool top floor bar.

J. Sheekey Oyster Bar
33-34 St Martin's Ct. ⊠ WC2 4AL ⊖ Leicester Square – ℰ (020) 7240 2565
– www.j-sheekey.co.uk – Closed 25-26 December
31ALUv
Rest – Seafood – Carte £ 24/57
♦ An addendum to J. Sheekey restaurant. Sit at the bar to watch the chefs prepare the same quality seafood as next door but at slightly lower prices; fish pie and fruits de mer are the popular choices. Open all day.

Terroirs
5 William IV St ⊠ WC2N 4DW ⊖ Charing Cross – ℰ (020) 7036 0660
– www.terroirswinebar.com – Closed 25-26 December, 1 January, Sunday and bank holidays
31ALUh
Rest – French – Carte £ 19/31
♦ Eat in the ground floor bistro/wine bar or two floors below at 'Downstairs at Terroirs' where the menu is a little more substantial. Flavoursome French cooking, with extra Italian and Spanish influences. Thoughtfully compiled wine list.

Hawksmoor
11 Langley St ⊠ WC2H 9GJ ⊖ Covent Garden – ℰ (020) 7856 2154
– www.thehawksmoor.com – Closed 2-4 January, 24-30 December and Sunday dinner
31ALUz
Rest – Beef specialities – Menu £ 23 (lunch and early dinner) – Carte £ 36/55
♦ Steaks from Longhorn cattle lovingly reared in North Yorkshire and dry-aged for at least 35 days are the stars of the show. Atmospheric, bustling basement restaurant in former brewery cellars.

da Polpo
6 Maiden Ln. ⊠ WC2E 7NA ⊖ Leicester Square – ℰ (020) 7836 8448
– www.dapolpo.co.uk – Closed dinner 24 December-1 January
31ALUp
Rest – Italian – (bookings not accepted at dinner) Carte £ 15/25
♦ First Soho, now Covent Garden gets a fun Venetian bacaro. The small plates are surprisingly filling, with delights such as pizzette of white anchovy vying with fennel and almond salad, fritto misto competing with spaghettini and meatballs.

Bedford & Strand
1a Bedford St ⊠ WC2E 9HH ⊖ Charing Cross – ℰ (020) 7836 3033
– www.bedford-strand.com – Closed 24 December-2 January, Sunday and bank holidays
31ALUc
Rest – British – (booking essential) Menu £ 18 (dinner) – Carte £ 26/35
♦ They call themselves a 'wine room and bistro' which neatly sums up both the philosophy and the style of the place – interesting wines, reassuringly familiar food and relaxed basement surroundings.

WESTMINSTER (City of)

VICTORIA

Corinthia
Whitehall Pl. ✉ *SW1A 2BD* — Embankment – ☎ *(020) 7930 8181*
– www.corinthia.com/london
31ALV**x**
271 rm – †£ 346/594 ††£ 370/900, ⊇ £ 33 – 23 suites
Rest *Northall* Rest *Massimo* – see restaurant listing
♦ London's latest grand hotel opened in 2011; its restored Victorian splendour cannot fail to impress. Tasteful, immaculately finished bedrooms are some of the largest in town; suites come with butlers. The stunning spa is over four floors.

Goring
15 Beeston Pl, Grosvenor Gdns ✉ *SW1W 0JW* — Victoria – ☎ *(020) 7396 9000*
– www.thegoring.com
38AIX**a**
62 rm – †£ 492/570 ††£ 550, ⊇ £ 25 – 7 suites
Rest *Goring* – see restaurant listing
♦ Celebrated its centenary in 2010; this very English hotel is still owned, invested in and run by the Goring family who built it – the fourth generation now at the helm. Many of the attractive rooms overlook a peaceful garden.

Crowne Plaza London - St James
45 Buckingham Gate ✉ *SW1E 6AF* — St James's Park
– ☎ *(020) 7834 6655* – www.london.crowneplaza.com
39AJX**e**
323 rm – †£ 142/546 ††£ 390/546, ⊇ £ 22.50 – 19 suites
Rest *Quilon* ✿ – see restaurant listing
♦ Built in 1897 as serviced accommodation for visiting aristocrats. Behind the impressive Edwardian façade lies an equally elegant interior. Quietest rooms overlook courtyard.

51 Buckingham Gate without rest
51 Buckingham Gate ✉ *SW1E 6AF* — St James's Park – ☎ *(020) 7769 7766*
– www.51-buckinghamgate.com
39AJX**s**
86 suites – ††£ 600, ⊇ £ 22.50
♦ In the courtyard of the Crowne Plaza but offering greater levels of comfort and service. Contemporary in style, suites range from one to nine bedrooms. Butler service available. Restaurants located in adjacent hotel.

St Ermin's
2 Caxton St. ✉ *SW1H 0QW* — St James's Park – ☎ *(020) 7222 7888*
– www.sterminshotel.co.uk
39AKX**a**
290 rm – †£ 412 ††£ 412, ⊇ £ 24 – 41 suites – ††£ 625/875
Rest *Caxton Grill* – Menu £ 25 (lunch) – Carte £ 35/50
♦ Built as an apartment block in 1897 but it has spent most of its life as a hotel and has been a favoured spot for many a politician. A comprehensive 2011 refurbishment restored many of its original features; the public areas are the strength. The restaurant specialises in meat cooked on the Josper grill.

41 without rest
41 Buckingham Palace Rd. ✉ *SW1W 0PS* — Victoria – ☎ *(020) 7300 0041*
– www.41hotel.com
38AIX**n**
29 rm – †£ 299 ††£ 443, ⊇ £ 25 – 1 suite
♦ Smart and discreet addendum to The Rubens hotel next door. Attractively decorated and quiet lounge where breakfast is served; comfortable bedrooms boast fireplaces and plenty of extras.

The Rubens at The Palace
39 Buckingham Palace Rd ✉ *SW1W 0PS* — Victoria – ☎ *(020) 7834 6600*
– www.rubenshotel.com
38AIX**n**
160 rm – †£ 167/311 ††£ 179/671, ⊇ £ 18.50 – 1 suite
Rest *Old Masters* – *(closed lunch Saturday and Sunday)* Menu £ 30
Rest *Library* – *(dinner only)* Menu £ 40 – Carte £ 45/58
Rest *bbar* – ☎ *(020) 7958 7000* *(closed Sunday)* Menu £ 21 – Carte £ 27/45
♦ Discreet, comfortable hotel in great location for visitors to London. Constant reinvestment ensures bright and contemporary bedrooms. Old Masters for grills., Fine dining in cosy Library. Casual dining in bbar.

463

WESTMINSTER (City of)

Tophams without rest
24-32 Ebury St ⊠ SW1W 0LU ⊖ Victoria – ℰ (020) 7730 3313
– www.tophamshotel.com
50 rm – †£ 180/225 ††£ 195/275, ⚌ £ 14.95

38AHYd

♦ A row of five pretty terraced houses, in a good spot for tourists and recently refurbished. Neat bedrooms with large bathrooms and good mod cons. Comfortable breakfast room.

B + B Belgravia without rest
64-66 Ebury St ⊠ SW1W 9QD ⊖ Victoria – ℰ (020) 7259 8570
– www.bb-belgravia.com
17 rm ⚌ – †£ 99 ††£ 150/275

38AHYx

♦ Two houses, three floors, and, considering the location, representing good value accommodation. Sleek, clean-lined bedrooms. Breakfast overlooking little garden terrace.

Lord Milner without rest
111 Ebury St ⊠ SW1W 9QU ⊖ Victoria – ℰ (020) 7881 9880
– www.lordmilner.com
10 rm – †£ 125/175 ††£ 155/175, ⚌ £ 14 – 1 suite

38AHYk

♦ A four storey terraced house, with individually decorated bedrooms, three with four-poster beds and all with marble bathrooms. Garden Suite the best room, with its own patio. No public areas.

Quilon – at Crowne Plaza London - St James Hotel
41 Buckingham Gate ⊠ SW1E 6AF ⊖ St James's Park – ℰ (020) 7821 1899
– www.quilon.co.uk – Closed 25 December and Saturday lunch
Rest – Indian – Menu £ 24/41 – Carte dinner £ 45/60

39AJXe

Spec. Crab cakes with curry leaves, ginger and green chillies. Seared fillet of monkfish in a shrimp, scallop and mustard sauce. Rice pudding with rose ice cream.

♦ Vibrant and well-balanced Indian dishes, many of which originate from the south west coast of India but are given a 'Western' twist. Skilled use of spices, appealing seafood specialities and well-organised service.

Roux at Parliament Square
RICS, Parliament Sq. ⊠ SW1P 3AD ⊖ Westminster – ℰ (020) 7334 3737
– www.rouxatparliamentsquare.co.uk – Closed 23 December-3 January, Saturday, Sunday and bank holidays
Rest – French – Menu £ 25 (lunch) – Carte £ 39/55

39ALXx

♦ Light floods through the Georgian windows of this comfortable Westminster restaurant, popular with MPs and surveyors. French base to the food, which is intricate but also light and contemporary.

Roussillon
16 St Barnabas St ⊠ SW1W 8PE ⊖ Sloane Square – ℰ (020) 7730 5550
– www.roussillon.co.uk – Closed 25 December, Saturday lunch
and Sunday, restricted opening on Bank Holidays
Rest – French – Menu £ 35/65

38AHZc

♦ A longstanding neighbourhood restaurant, with a comfortable, discreet and grown up feel. Expect quite formal service and a menu offering plenty of choice and a creative style of cooking.

The Cinnamon Club
30-32 Great Smith St ⊠ SW1P 3BU ⊖ St James's Park – ℰ (020) 7222 2555
– www.cinnamonclub.com – Closed 26 December, 1 January and Sunday
Rest – Indian – Menu £ 22 (lunch) – Carte £ 40/75

39AKXc

♦ Housed in former Westminster Library: exterior has ornate detail, interior is stylish and modern. Walls are lined with books. New Wave Indian cooking with plenty of choice.

WESTMINSTER (City of)

XXX Santini
*29 Ebury St ⊠ SW1W 0NZ ⊖ Victoria – ℰ (020) 7730 4094
– www.santini-restaurant.com – Closed Easter, 24-26 December, 1 January and
lunch Saturday-Sunday* **38**AHY**v**
Rest – Italian – Menu £ 25 (dinner) – Carte £ 32/54
♦ Smart, crisp and cool Italian restaurant, with a large, impressive terrace and old-school service. Menu has subtle Venetian accent but is not inexpensive; pastas and desserts are good.

XXX Shepherd's
*Marsham Ct., Marsham St. ⊠ SW1P 4LA ⊖ Pimlico – ℰ (020) 7834 9552
– www.langansrestaurants.co.uk – Closed Saturday, Sunday and bank holidays*
Rest – British – (booking essential) Carte £ 22/26 **39**AKY**z**
♦ A thoroughly British and enjoyably old-school restaurant where the menu reads like a UKIP manifesto; game and traditional puddings are a highlight. Popular with those from Westminster – the booths offer a degree of privacy.

XXX Goring – at Goring Hotel
*15 Beeston Pl, Grosvenor Gdns ⊠ SW1W 0JW ⊖ Victoria – ℰ (020) 7396 9000
– www.thegoring.com – Closed Saturday lunch* **38**AIX**a**
Rest – British – Menu £ 36/49 ❀
♦ Designed by David Linley, this is a refined and grown-up restaurant as befits a hotel as charming as The Goring. The menu celebrates British cooking; the roast from the trolley is always popular.

XXX Northall – at Corinthia Hotel
*Whitehall Pl. ⊠ SW1A 2BD ⊖ Embankment – ℰ (020) 7930 8181
– www.corinthia.com/london* **31**ALV**x**
Rest – British – Menu £ 28 – Carte £ 28/56
♦ The menu champions British produce and producers and you can get a choice of room, linked by a display of meats and cheeses: a modern bistro-style room or a more formal dining room set over two levels.

XXX Massimo – at Corinthia Hotel
*Whitehall Pl. ⊠ SW1A 2BD ⊖ Embankment – ℰ (020) 7930 8181
– www.corinthia.com/london* **31**ALV**x**
Rest – Italian – Menu £ 28 – Carte £ 35/75
♦ Opulent, visually impressive room with an oyster bar on one side. On offer are traditional dishes true to the regions; fish and seafood dishes stand out. Impressive private dining room comes with its own chef.

XX Il Convivio
*143 Ebury St ⊠ SW1W 9QN ⊖ Sloane Square – ℰ (020) 7730 4099
– www.ilconvivio.co.uk – Closed Christmas-New Year and Sunday* **38**AHY**a**
Rest – Italian – Carte £ 32/51
♦ Handsome Georgian house, with a retractable roof and Dante's poetry embossed on the walls. All pasta is made on the top floor of the house. Dishes are artfully presented and flavoursome.

XX Tinello
*87 Pimlico Rd ⊠ SW1W 8PH ⊖ Sloane Square – ℰ (020) 7730 3663
– www.tinello.co.uk – Closed Sunday and bank hoildays* **37**AGZ**s**
Rest – Italian – (booking essential at dinner) Carte £ 38/44
♦ Sleekly designed Italian restaurant run by two brothers, both alumni of Locanda Locatelli. Their native Tuscany informs the cooking; the antipasti or 'small eats' section is very appealing.

XX Boisdale
*15 Eccleston St ⊠ SW1W 9LX ⊖ Victoria – ℰ (020) 7730 6922
– www.boisdale.co.uk – Closed 1 week Christmas, Saturday lunch and Sunday*
Rest – Scottish – Carte £ 29/77 **38**AHY**c**
♦ A proudly Scottish restaurant with acres of tartan and a charmingly higgledy-piggledy layout. Stand-outs are the smoked salmon and the 28-day aged Aberdeenshire cuts of beef. Live nightly jazz.

WESTMINSTER (City of)

Bank – at Crowne Plaza London-St James Hotel
45 Buckingham Gate ⊠ SW1E 6BS ⊖ St James's Park – ℰ (020) 7630 6644
– www.bankrestaurants.com – Closed Sunday and bank holidays   **39**AJX**e**
Rest – Modern European – *(booking essential at lunch)* Menu £ 38 – Carte £ 35/80
♦ Behind the understated entrance lies a vibrant and busy interior. Pass through one of Europe's longest bars to reach the conservatory restaurant, where you'll find a varied, accessible menu.

Ebury Wine Bar
139 Ebury St. ⊠ SW1W 9QU ⊖ Victoria – ℰ (020) 7730 5447
– www.eburyrestaurant.co.uk – Closed 22 December-2 January   **38**AHY**n**
Rest – Modern European – Menu £ 22 (lunch and early dinner) – Carte £ 31/39
♦ Going strong for over 50 years and as likeable as ever. Some imaginative touches but generally quite classic cooking. Dairy and gluten free menus offered, along with a keenly-priced wine list.

Osteria Dell' Angolo
47 Marsham St. ⊠ SW1P 3DR ⊖ St. James's Park – ℰ (020) 3268 1077
– www.osteriadellangolo.co.uk – Closed Easter, 20 August-2 September,
24 December-3 January, Saturday lunch, Sunday and bank holidays
Rest – Italian – Menu £ 21 (lunch) – Carte £ 32/39   **39**AKY**n**
♦ Expert restaurateur Claudio Pulze opened this sunny Italian restaurant opposite the Home Office in 2009. Tuscan element to the cooking, along with some creativity; service is keen and friendly.

Olivo
21 Eccleston St ⊠ SW1W 9LX ⊖ Victoria – ℰ (020) 7730 2505
– www.olivorestaurant.com – Closed lunch Saturday-Sunday and bank holidays
Rest – Italian – Menu £ 28 (lunch) – Carte dinner £ 25/32   **38**AHY**z**
♦ Carefully prepared, authentic Sardinian specialities are the highlight at this popular Italian restaurant. Simply decorated in blues and yellows, with an atmosphere of bonhomie.

Olivomare
10 Lower Belgrave St ⊠ SW1W 0LJ ⊖ Victoria – ℰ (020) 7730 9022
– www.olivorestaurants.com – Closed bank holidays   **38**AHY**b**
Rest – Seafood – Carte £ 29/38
♦ Expect understated and stylish piscatorial decoration and seafood with a Sardinian base. Fortnightly changing menu, with high quality produce, much of which is available in shop next door.

Ebury
11 Pimlico Rd ⊠ SW1W 8NA ⊖ Sloane Square. – ℰ (020) 7730 6784
– www.theebury.co.uk   **38**AHZ**z**
Rest – Modern European – Carte £ 30/39
♦ Smart and stylish room, with an appealing menu ranging from burgers to black bream. Low-slung tables around popular central bar; efficient service. Upstairs is used for private parties.

Thomas Cubitt
44 Elizabeth St ⊠ SW1W 9PA ⊖ Sloane Square. – ℰ (020) 7730 6060
– www.thethomascubitt.co.uk – Closed Christmas and New Year   **38**AHY**e**
Rest – Modern European – *(booking essential)* Carte £ 29/49
♦ A pub of two halves: choose the busy ground floor bar with its accessible menu or upstairs for more ambitious, quite elaborate cooking with courteous service and a less frenetic environment.

Orange with rm
37 Pimlico Rd ⊠ SW1W 8NE ⊖ Sloane Square. – ℰ (020) 7881 9844
– www.theorange.co.uk   **38**AHZ**k**
4 rm – ♦£ 185/205 ♦♦£ 185/205, ⚃ £ 12
Rest – Modern European – Carte £ 24/41
♦ Family-friendly pub with laid-back atmosphere and slight colonial feel. Pizza from the wood-fired oven in the bar or rustic cooking in the upstairs dining room. Film nights on Monday. Bedrooms named after local streets.

LONDON HEATHROW AIRPORT – Greater London – **504** S29 – see Hillingdon (London)

LONG COMPTON – Warwickshire – pop. 705 – ✉ Shipston-On-Stour   **19** C3
▶ London 81 mi – Birmingham 53 mi – Liverpool 147 mi – Bristol 72 mi

Red Lion with rm
✉ CV36 5JS – ✆ (01608) 684 221 – www.redlion-longcompton.co.uk
5 rm ⊐ – †£ 55   ††£ 85/115
Rest – Menu £ 15 (lunch and early dinner) – Carte £ 26/36
♦ 18C former coaching inn with flag floors, log fires and a warm, modern feel. Seasonal menu of tasty, home-cooked pub classics, with more adventurous daily specials. Stylish, contemporary bedrooms.

LONG CRENDON – Buckinghamshire – **504** Q/R28 – pop. 2 383   **11** C2
– ✉ Aylesbury
▶ London 50 mi – Aylesbury 11 mi – Oxford 15 mi

Angel with rm
47 Bicester Rd ✉ HP18 9EE – ✆ (01844) 208 268 – www.angelrestaurant.co.uk
– Closed Sunday dinner
4 rm ⊐ – †£ 75   ††£ 100
Rest – Menu £ 15 (weekday lunch) – Carte £ 27/44
♦ Comfortable, characterful former pub with low ceilings, leather-furnished lounge/bar and airy conservatory. Wide-ranging menus offer tasty, globally influenced dishes. Well-chosen wine list. Stylish bedrooms, all individually decorated; Room 4 is the biggest.

LONG MELFORD – Suffolk – **504** W27 – pop. 2 734 ▮ Great Britain   **15** C3
▶ London 62 mi – Cambridge 34 mi – Colchester 18 mi – Ipswich 24 mi
◉ Melford Hall★ AC

Black Lion
Church Walk, The Green ✉ CO10 9DN – ✆ (01787) 312 356
– www.blacklionhotel.net
9 rm ⊐ – †£ 102/150   ††£ 150 – 1 suite   **Rest** – Menu £ 18/38
♦ 17C Georgian inn overlooking village green. Named after wines, bedrooms are smart, stylish and individually designed; good facilities and traditional bathrooms. Formal restaurant with enclosed rear terrace features extensive, popular menu.

Scutchers
Westgate St, on A 1092 ✉ CO10 9DP – ✆ (01787) 310 200 – www.scutchers.com
– Closed 2 weeks Christmas
Rest – Carte £ 27/47
♦ Former medieval hall house set in pleasant rural village: now a smart, split-level, personally run restaurant. Traditional dishes use quality ingredients and feature tried-and-tested combinations.

LONG SUTTON – Somerset – **503** L30 – ✉ Langport   **3** B3
▶ London 132 mi – Bridgwater 16 mi – Yeovil 10 mi

Devonshire Arms with rm
✉ TA10 9LP – ✆ (01458) 241 271 – www.thedevonshirearms.com – Closed 25-26 December and 1 January
9 rm ⊐ – †£ 78/130   ††£ 88/130   **Rest** – Carte £ 25/39
♦ Spacious Grade II listed hunting lodge set on village green; contemporary interior, with relaxing, open-plan bar and formal dining room. Locally sourced produce used in seasonal European dishes. Comfortable bedrooms boast excellent quality linen and toiletries.

LONGHORSLEY – Northumberland – **501** O18 – see Morpeth

LONGRIDGE – Lancashire – 502 M22 – pop. 7 491
20 A2
► London 241 mi – Blackburn 12 mi – Burnley 18 mi

※※ Longridge Restaurant
104-106 Higher Rd, Northeast : 0.5 mi by B 5269 following signs for Jeffrey Hill
✉ PR3 3SY – ℰ (01772) 784 969 – www.heathcotes.co.uk – *Closed January, Monday and Tuesday*
Rest – Carte £ 34/50
♦ Stylish, subtly hued restaurant with changing character: bright by day and intimate at night. Seasonal, regional cooking uses quality ingredients to create appealing, flavoursome dishes.

LONGSTOCK – Hampshire – 503 P30 – see Stockbridge

LONGTOWN – Cumbria – 502 L18
21 A1
► London 326 mi – Carlisle 9 mi – Newcastle upon Tyne 61 mi

⌂ Bessiestown Farm
Catlowdy, Northeast : 8 mi by Netherby St on B 6318 ✉ CA6 5QP
– ℰ (01228) 577 219 – www.bessiestown.co.uk – *Closed 25 December*
6 rm ⊇ – †£ 57 ††£ 89   **Rest** – Menu £ 20 s
♦ Immaculately kept converted farmhouse in rural location. Traditional, homely lounge with pleasant conservatory overlooking garden. Friendly owner. Spacious bedrooms; Dovecote is the largest. Bright, airy dining room; home-cooked meals available Monday-Saturday.

LOOE – Cornwall – 503 G32 – pop. 5 280
1 B2
► London 264 mi – Plymouth 23 mi – Truro 39 mi
🛈 Fore St ℰ (01503) 26 20 72, www.visit-southeastcornwall.co.uk
⛳ Bin Down, ℰ (01503) 24 02 39
⛳ Whitsand Bay Hotel Torpoint Portwrinkle, ℰ (01503) 23 02 76
◉ Town★ – Monkey Sanctuary★ **AC**

🏠 Barclay House
St Martins Rd, East Looe, East : 0.5 mi by A 387 on B 3253 ✉ PL13 1LP
– ℰ (01503) 262 929 – www.barclayhouse.co.uk
11 rm ⊇ – †£ 55/118 ††£ 150/200 – 1 suite
Rest *Restaurant* – see restaurant listing
♦ Imposing, whitewashed Victorian house in elevated position; most bedrooms come with a view. Room 7 is contemporary with superb estuary vista; 9 boasts a balcony and whirlpool bath.

※※ Restaurant – at Barclay House Hotel
St Martins Rd, East Looe, East : 0.5 mi by A 387 on B 3253 ✉ PL13 1LP
– ℰ (01503) 262 929 – www.barclayhouse.co.uk
Rest – *(closed Sunday dinner) (dinner only and Sunday lunch June-October)*
Menu £ 29
♦ Light, modern restaurant featuring abstract local art and with extensive views of the estuary. Dishes make use of local, seasonal produce, including seafood from the day boats.

※ Trawlers on the Quay
The Quay, East Looe ✉ PL13 1AH – ℰ (01503) 263 593
– www.trawlers-restaurant.co.uk – *Closed Monday in winter*
Rest – Seafood – Carte £ 20/31
♦ Bright, contemporary restaurant, perched on the edge of the quay; ask for a window table. The menu focuses on seafood and ranges from light lunches up to the full three courses.

LORTON – Cumbria – 502 K20 – see Cockermouth

LOUGHBOROUGH – Leicestershire – 502 Q25 – pop. 55 258   16 B2
▶ London 117 mi – Birmingham 41 mi – Leicester 11 mi – Nottingham 15 mi
🛈 Market Pl ℰ (01509) 23 19 14, www.loughboroughuk.co.uk
🏰 Lingdale Woodhouse Eaves Joe Moore's Lane, ℰ (01509) 89 07 03

at Woodhouse Eaves South : 4.5 mi by A 6 via Woodhouse – ✉ Loughborough

✕✕ **Woodhouse**   ⇔ P VISA ⦿ AE
43 Maplewell Rd ✉ LE12 8RG – ℰ (01509) 890 318 – www.thewoodhouse.co.uk
– Closed Sunday dinner and Monday
Rest – Menu £ 15 (lunch)/19 (midweek dinner) – Carte approx. £ 35
♦ Smart village restaurant with comfy lounge, bold modern colours and eye-catching art. Concise, understated menu relies on quality local produce: classical combinations have a personal twist.

LOUTH – Lincolnshire – 502 T/U23 – pop. 15 930   17 D1
▶ London 156 mi – Boston 34 mi – Great Grimsby 17 mi – Lincoln 26 mi
🛈 Cannon St. ℰ (01507) 60 11 11, www.louthuk.com

🏨 **Brackenborough**   🐾 ⓀK rest, ⚒ 📶 ♿ P VISA ⦿ AE
Cordeaux Corner, Brackenborough, North : 2 mi by A 16 ✉ LN11 0SZ
– ℰ (01507) 609 169 – www.oakridgehotels.co.uk
24 rm ⌑ – †£ 85/158 ††£ 100/158   **Rest** – Carte £ 19/38
♦ Contemporary, family-owned hotel with relaxed feel and warm, personal style. Spacious, individually designed bedrooms boast all mod cons; executive rooms include jacuzzi baths. Sexy cocktail bar. Lounge/bar and conservatory for all-day dining. Formal restaurant.

ENGLAND

LOVINGTON – Somerset – 503 M30 – see Castle Cary

LOW FELL – Tyne and Wear – see Gateshead

LOW ROW – North Yorkshire – 502 N20 – see Reeth

LOWER FROYLE – Hampshire – see Alton

LOWER HARDRES – Kent – 504 X30 – see Canterbury

LOWER ODDINGTON – Gloucestershire – see Stow-on-the-Wold

LOWER PEOVER – Cheshire East – see Knutsford

LOWER SHIPLAKE – Oxfordshire – 504 R29 – see Henley-on-Thames

LOWER SLAUGHTER – Gloucestershire – 503 – see Bourton-on-the-Water

LOWER SWELL – Gloucestershire – see Stow-on-the-Wold

LOWER VOBSTER – Somerset – pop. 2 222 – ✉ Radstock   4 C2
▶ London 119 mi – Bath 16 mi – Frome 5 mi

🍴 **Vobster Inn** with rm   🍃 ⚒ 📶 P VISA ⦿ ①
✉ BA3 5RJ – ℰ (01373) 812 920 – www.vobsterinn.co.uk – Closed Sunday dinner
and Monday
3 rm ⌑ – †£ 55/75 ††£ 68/95   **Rest** – Carte £ 19/31 **s**
♦ Solid stone pub with homely, traditional inner, featuring exposed beams and open fires. Seasonal, Mediterranean-inspired menu reflects owners' Spanish heritage. Popular theme evenings. Cosy, well-equipped bedrooms; the family room overlooks the garden.

LOWESTOFT – Suffolk – **504** Z26 – pop. 68 340 – Great Britain **15** D2

▶ London 116 mi – Ipswich 43 mi – Norwich 30 mi
- Royal Plain ✆ (01502) 53 36 00, www.visit-sunrisecoast.co.uk
- Rookery Park Carlton Colville, ✆ (01502) 50 91 90
- Norfolk Broads ★

Britten House *without rest*
21 Kirkley Cliff Rd ✉ NR33 0DB – ✆ (01502) 573 950 – www.brittenhouse.co.uk
8 rm ☐ – †£ 60/70 ††£ 75/95 – 1 suite
- Fine brick-built Victorian house overlooking the promenade; birthplace of Benjamin Britten in 1913. Classically furnished bedrooms named after composers; choose a front-facing room with sea view.

LUDFORD – Lincolnshire **17** C1

▶ London 174 mi – Sheffield 74 mi – Kingston upon Hull 43 mi – Nottingham 59 mi

Black Horse Inn
Magna Mile ✉ LN8 6AJ – ✆ (01507) 313 645 – www.blackhorseludford.co.uk
– Closed 2 weeks January, 25 December, Sunday dinner, Monday and bank holidays
Rest – Menu £ 14 (lunch) – Carte £ 20/28
- Slightly worn but well-loved pub with homely décor, simple furnishings and welcoming open fires. Concise menus feature good old-fashioned classics, including game, pies and stews in winter.

LUDLOW – Shropshire – **503** L26 – pop. 9 870 – Great Britain **18** B2

▶ London 162 mi – Birmingham 39 mi – Hereford 24 mi – Shrewsbury 29 mi
- Castle St ✆ (01584) 87 50 53, www.virtual-shropshire.co.uk
- Town ★ Z – Castle ★ **AC** – Feathers Hotel ★ – St Laurence's Parish Church ★ (Misericords ★) **S**
- Stokesay Castle ★ **AC**, NW : 6.5 mi by A 49

Overton Grange
Old Hereford Rd, South : 1.75 mi by B 4361 ✉ SY8 4AD – ✆ (01584) 873 500
– www.overtongrangehotel.com
14 rm ☐ – †£ 115/145 ††£ 145/245
Rest – (booking essential for non-residents) Menu £ 33/43
- Well-maintained Edwardian country house boasting subtle modern touches alongside original features. Bedrooms feature modern facilities and smart bathrooms. Superb pool. Dining rooms offer immaculately laid tables and countryside views; cooking has a French base.

Dinham Hall
Dinham ✉ SY8 1EJ – ✆ (01584) 876 464 – www.dinhamhall.com Z**b**
13 rm ☐ – †£ 110/145 ††£ 145/246 **Rest** – Menu £ 18/40
- 18C manor house, with pretty walled garden, situated by Ludlow Castle in the heart of charming medieval town. Period furnishings and individual rooms. Informal dining with crisp, bright décor.

Fishmore Hall
Fishmore Rd, North : 1.5 mi off A 4117 ✉ SY8 3DP – ✆ (01584) 875 148
– www.fishmorehall.co.uk
15 rm ☐ – †£ 75/100 ††£ 89/220 **Rest** – Menu £ 25/49
- Elegantly restored Georgian house – a former boys' school – set out of town in half an acre of land. Very modern, designer bedrooms, boasting bold wallpaper and flat screen TVs. Two smart dining rooms serve modern British menus.

LUDLOW

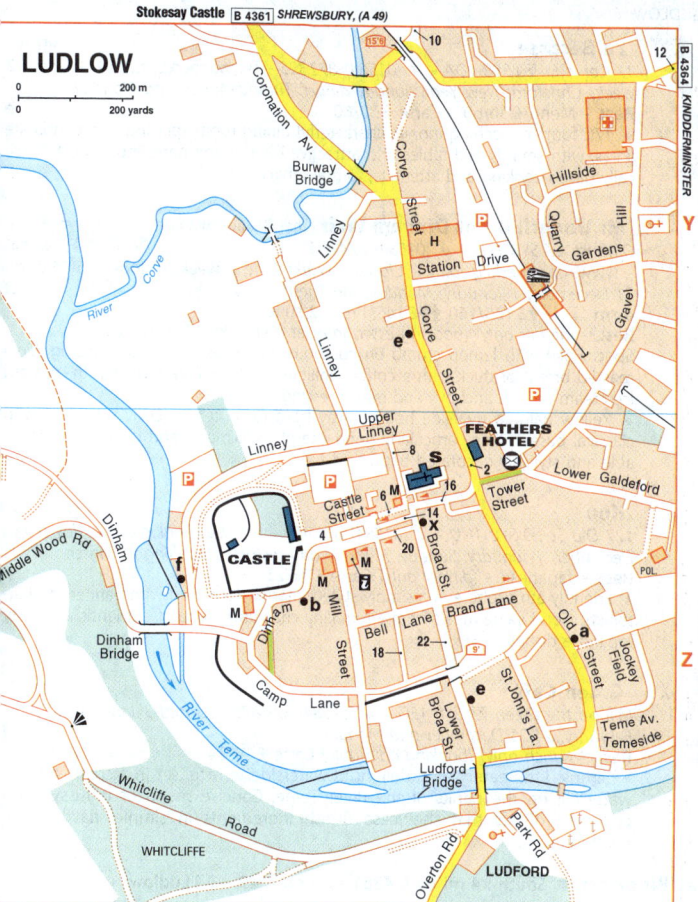

ll Ring	Z 2	Fishmore Rd	Y 10
stle Square	Z 4	Henley Rd	Y 12
urch St	Z 6	High St	Z 14
ollege St	Z 8	King St	Z 16

Lower Raven Lane	Z 18
Market St	Z 20
Silk Mill	Z 22

De Grey's Town House without rest
Broad St ⊠ *SY8 1NG* – ℰ *(01584) 872 764* – www.degreys.co.uk Zx
9 rm ⊇ – †£ 115 ††£ 145/165

♦ Dating back to 1570 this building retains all its good old English style and charm. Bedrooms are spacious, very individual and feature quality hand made oak furniture.

Bromley Court without rest
18-20 Lower Broad St ⊠ *SY8 1PQ* – ℰ *(01584) 876 996* – www.ludlowhotels.com
– *Closed January* Ze
3 rm – †£ 80/120 ††£ 100/120

♦ Delightful Tudor cottage with three self-contained units, traditionally furnished in keeping with the style of the house. Pleasant walled rear garden. Continental breakfasts.

LUDLOW

La Bécasse
17 Corve St ⊠ SY8 1DA – ℰ (01584) 872 325 – www.labecasse.co.uk – Closed 2 weeks Christmas-New Year, Sunday dinner, Tuesday lunch and Monday
Rest – Menu £ 30/60 – Carte £ 30/60

Ye

♦ 17C former coaching inn; its characterful dining room split into three intimate areas, with smartly laid tables and attractive listed wood panelling. Expect classically based cooking and attentive, formal service.

Mr Underhill's at Dinham Weir (Chris Bradley) with rm
Dinham ⊠ SY8 1EH – ℰ (01584) 874 431
– www.mr-underhills.co.uk – Closed 2 weeks June, 2 weeks October, 25-26 and 31 December, 1 January, Monday and Tuesday

Zf

4 rm – †£ 135/160 ††£ 145/175 – 2 suites
Rest – *(dinner only) (booking essential) (set menu only)* Menu £ 60

Spec. Hake with lemon crumb on couscous and a ras el hanout dressing. Slow roasted breast of duck with a coffee vinaigrette. Oakly Park rarebit with mustard ice cream and an anchovy and miso dressing.

♦ Yellow painted riverside house, away from town centre. Daily set menu with classical base makes particularly good use of local meats and cheeses. Comfortable and stylishly decorated bedrooms.

Koo
127 Old St ⊠ SY8 1NU – ℰ (01584) 878 462 – www.koo-ook.co.uk – Closed 25 December, 1 January, Sunday, Monday and restricted opening in winter
Rest – Japanese – *(dinner only)* Carte £ 18/23

Za

♦ Friendly atmosphere in a simply styled interior decorated with banners and artefacts. Good value meals from a regularly changing menu of authentic and tasty Japanese dishes.

Green Café
Mill on the Green ⊠ SY8 1EG – ℰ (01584) 879 872 – Closed 3 January-13 February, 24-25 December and Monday
Rest – *(lunch only) (booking advisable)* Carte £ 19/24

Zf

♦ Simple little eatery with delightful waterside terrace, set in a charming 14C watermill on the banks of the River Teme. Concise menu of unfussy, daily changing dishes that showcase British ingredients in simple, flavoursome combinations.

at Woofferton South : 4 mi by B 4361 - **Z** - on A 49 – ⊠ Ludlow

Ravenscourt Manor without rest
on A 49 ⊠ SY8 4AL – ℰ (01584) 711 905 – March-October
3 rm – †£ 55 ††£ 80/85

♦ Characterful black and white timbered 16C manor house in two and a half acres of lawned gardens. Friendly welcome; comfy lounge. Individually decorated, period style rooms.

at Bromfield Northwest : 2.5 mi on A 49 - **Y** – ⊠ Ludlow

Clive with rm
⊠ SY8 2JR – ℰ (01584) 856 565 – www.theclive.co.uk – Closed 25-26 December
15 rm – †£ 65/90 ††£ 90/115
Rest – *(booking essential at dinner)* Carte £ 23/33

♦ Large converted pub with modern décor in vivid colours. Restaurant, bar, café and bistro areas. Menu of internationally inspired traditional dishes. Very good modern bedrooms.

LUPTON – Cumbria – **502** L21 – see Kirkby Lonsdale

LUTON – Luton – **504** S28 – pop. 185 543 – Great Britain   12 A2

▶ London 35 mi – Cambridge 36 mi – Ipswich 93 mi – Oxford 45 mi
✈ Luton International Airport : ☎ (01582) 405100, E : 1.5 mi X
🛈 St George's Sq ☎ (01582) 40 15 79,
www.visitorinformationcentre.luton.towntalk.co.uk
⛳ Stockwood Park London Rd, ☎ (01582) 41 37 04
◉ Whipsnade Wild Animal Park★, West : 8 mi by B 489, signed from M 1 (junction 9) and M 25 (junction 21) X

Luton Hoo
The Mansion House, Southeast : 2.5 mi by A 505 on A 1081 ✉ *LU1 3TQ* – ☎ *(01582) 734 437 – www.lutonhoo.com*
135 rm ☐ – †£ 230 ††£ 230 – 9 suites
Rest *Wernher* – *(closed Monday and Tuesday)* Menu £ 30/43 – Carte £ 53/71
Rest *Adam's Brasserie* – *(closed Sunday dinner)* Carte £ 25/37
♦ Stunning 18C house set in over 1,000 acres of gardens, some designed by Capability Brown. Main mansion boasts numerous comfortable sitting rooms and characterful bedrooms. Formal, marble-filled Wernher restaurant offers sophisticated modern cuisine. Contemporary brasserie classics in more casual Adam's.

LUXBOROUGH – Somerset – **503** J30 – ✉ Watchet   3 A2

▶ London 205 mi – Exeter 42 mi – Minehead 9 mi – Taunton 25 mi

Royal Oak Inn of Luxborough with rm
Exmoor National Park ✉ *TA23 0SH* – ☎ *(01984) 640 319*
– *www.theroyaloakinnluxborough.co.uk – Closed 25 December*
11 rm ☐ – †£ 55/75 ††£ 100   **Rest** – Carte £ 18/32
♦ Red sandstone pub in an extremely beautiful location; well used by the community. Seasonal menu offers substantial dishes of classically prepared, boldly flavoured foods, with an international edge. Bedrooms are compact but charming; Room 14 has its own terrace.

LYDDINGTON – Rutland – see Uppingham

LYDFORD – Devon – **503** H32 – pop. 1 734 – ✉ Okehampton   2 C2

▶ London 234 mi – Exeter 33 mi – Plymouth 25 mi
◉ Village★★
◉ Dartmoor National Park★★

Dartmoor Inn with rm
Moorside, East : 1 mi on A 386 ✉ *EX20 4AY* – ☎ *(01822) 820 221*
– *www.dartmoorinn.com – Closed Sunday dinner and Monday lunch*
3 rm ☐ – †£ 80/95 ††£ 105/130   **Rest** – Menu £ 24 (lunch) – Carte £ 26/39
♦ Lovely pub on the edge of Dartmoor National Park, close to Lydford Gorge and the White Lady waterfall. Shabby-chic, French farmhouse styling. Set, easy dining and à la carte menus feature tasty modern dishes; the mixed grill of sea fish is popular. Spacious bedrooms and some unusual, yet appealing, breakfast choices.

LYME REGIS – Dorset – **503** L31 – pop. 4 406   3 B3

▶ London 160 mi – Dorchester 25 mi – Exeter 31 mi – Taunton 27 mi
🛈 Church St ☎ (01297) 44 21 38, www.lymeregis.org
⛳ Timber Hill, ☎ (01297) 44 29 63
◉ Town★ – The Cobb★

ENGLAND

LYME REGIS

Alexandra
Pound St ⊠ DT7 3HZ – ℰ (01297) 442 010 – www.hotelalexandra.co.uk – Closed Christmas-New Year
24 rm ⊊ – **†** £ 80/220 **††** £ 220   **Rest** – Menu £ 42 (dinner) – Carte £ 27/42
♦ Smart, extended 18C house in lawned gardens, superbly located with magnificent views out to sea. Family-run, the hotel features a comfortable lounge, a south-facing conservatory and modern bedrooms. Room 12 has a large bow window. Tasty, home-cooked menus.

Hix Oyster and Fish House
Lister Gdns, Cobb Rd ⊠ DT7 3JP – ℰ (01297) 446 910
– www.hixoysterandfishhouse.co.uk – Closed first 2 weeks January and Monday-Tuesday October-March
Rest – Seafood – *(booking essential)* Menu £ 21 (weekday lunch)
– Carte £ 28/66
♦ Small restaurant in a terrace by the new gardens; superb views over the bay and Cobb. Rustic, simple and understated. Daily seafood menu with a real understanding of less is more.

Mill Tea & Dining Room
The Town Mill ⊠ DT7 3PU – ℰ (01297) 445 757 – www.teaanddiningroom.co.uk – Closed January, Tuesday lunch and Monday
Rest – British – *(booking essential)* Carte £ 25/41
♦ Sweet little restaurant with quirky, vintage interior, in a listed mill building on the banks of the River Lym. Menus offer fresh, local, often foraged ingredients, in traditional, unadorned combinations. Even the soft drinks are homemade.

LYMINGTON – Hampshire – 504 P31 – pop. 14 227   6 A3
▶ London 103 mi – Bournemouth 18 mi – Southampton 19 mi – Winchester 32 mi
⛴ to the Isle of Wight (Yarmouth) (Wightlink Ltd) frequent services daily (30 mn)
🛈 New St ℰ (01590) 68 90 00, www.lymington.org

Stanwell House
14-15 High St ⊠ SO41 9AA – ℰ (01590) 677 123 – www.stanwellhouse.com
24 rm ⊊ – **†** £ 75/99 **††** £ 89/140 – 6 suites
Rest *Seafood at Stanwells* – see restaurant listing
Rest *Bistro* – *(dinner only)* Carte £ 31/41
♦ Neatly painted former coaching inn, set in the town centre and run by a friendly owner. Comfy, well-appointed bedrooms: those in the original house are more characterful, those in the extension, more contemporary. Trendy wine bar, smart restaurant and wood-furnished bistro with covered courtyard and terrace.

Mill at Gordleton
Silver St, Hordle, Northwest : 3.5 mi by A 337 off Sway Rd ⊠ SO41 6DJ
– ℰ (01590) 682 219 – www.themillatgordleton.co.uk – Closed 25 December
7 rm ⊊ – **†** £ 100/125 **††** £ 140 – 1 suite
Rest – Menu £ 18/28 – Carte £ 32/48
♦ Delightfully located part-17C water mill in well-kept gardens. Comfortable, traditional interior with a pubby bar and country house lounge. Homely, individually styled bedrooms. Formal restaurant offers classic British cooking, with terrace for alfresco dining.

Seafood at Stanwells – at Stanwell House Hotel
14-15 High St ⊠ SO41 9AA – ℰ (01590) 677 123 – www.stanwellhouse.com
Rest – Carte £ 31/42
♦ Smart hotel restaurant in a centrally located and keenly run former coaching inn. Trendy adjoining wine bar and wood-furnished bistro with terrace. Fresh seafood menu and attentive service.

LYMINGTON

at East End East : 3 mi by B3054

East End Arms with rm
Lymington Rd ✉ SO41 5SY – ✆ (01590) 626 223 – www.eastendarms.co.uk
– *Closed Sunday dinner*
5 rm – †£ 68 ††£ 95/115 **Rest** – Carte £ 19/27

♦ Traditional country pub owned by John Illsley of Dire Straits. Shabby locals bar and classical pine-furnished dining room; great display of music-based photos. Concise menus of satisfying British dishes. Modern, cottage-style bedrooms provide a smart contrast.

at Downton West : 3 mi on A 337 – ✉ Lymington

The Olde Barn without rest
Christchurch Rd, East : 0.5 mi on A 337 ✉ SO41 0LA – ✆ (01590) 644 939
– www.theoldebarn.co.uk
3 rm – †£ 50/70 ††£ 70/80

♦ Converted 17C barn with small, traditional lounge and communal breakfast room. Bedrooms in the barn annexe – a converted dairy – are spotlessly kept, with a homely, cottagey style.

LYMM – Warrington – 502 M23 – pop. 9 554   20 B3

London 190 mi – Liverpool 26 mi – Leeds 62 mi – Sheffield 68 mi

Church Green
Higher Ln, on A 56 ✉ WA13 0AP – ✆ (01925) 752 068
– www.thechurchgreen.co.uk
Rest – *(booking essential)* Menu £ 40 – Carte £ 24/40

♦ Double gable-fronted Victorian pub beside Lymm Dam. Smart, modern interior with conservatory, attractive terrace and kitchen garden. Simple pub-style bar dishes; more ambitious evening menu.

LYNDHURST – Hampshire – 503 – pop. 2 281 Great Britain   6 A2

London 95 mi – Bournemouth 20 mi – Southampton 10 mi – Winchester 23 mi

Main Car Park ✆ (023) 8028 22 69, www.new-forest-uk.co.uk
Dibden Golf Centre Main Rd, ✆ (023) 8020 75 08
New Forest Southampton Rd, ✆ (023) 8028 27 52
New Forest★★ (Bolderwood Ornamental Drive★★, Rhinefield Ornamental Drive★★)

Lime Wood
Beaulieu Rd, Southeast : 1 mi by A 35 on B 3056 ✉ SO43 7FZ – ✆ (023) 8028 7177 – www.limewoodhotel.co.uk
15 rm – †£ 445 ††£ 445, ⚂ £ 18 – 14 suites – ††£ 445/775
Rest Dining Room – ✆ (023) 8028 7167 *(closed Monday except lunch bank holidays)* Menu £ 23/50
Rest Scullery – ✆ (023) 8028 7168 – Carte £ 28/42

♦ Impressive extended Georgian mansion with stunning spa. Various stylish guest lounges with quality fabrics and furnishings; one set around a courtyard and boasting a retractable glass roof. Beautifully furnished bedrooms boast luxurious marble-tiled bathrooms; many have New Forest views. Refined restaurant or classic home favourites in relaxed, all-day Scullery.

LYNMOUTH – Devon – 503 I30 – see Lynton

LYNTON – Devon – 503 I30 – pop. 1 870   2 C1

London 206 mi – Exeter 59 mi – Taunton 44 mi

Lee Rd ✆ (01598) 75 22 25, www.lynton-lynmouth-tourism.co.uk
Town★ (≤★)
Valley of the Rocks★, W : 1 mi – Watersmeet★, E : 1.5 mi by A 39. Exmoor National Park★★ – Doone Valley★, SE : 7.5 mi by A 39 (access from Oare on foot)

LYNTON

🏠 Hewitt's - Villa Spaldi without rest
North Walk ✉ EX35 6HJ – ℰ (01598) 752 293 – www.hewittshotel.com
– April-September
7 rm ☕ – †£ 85/95 ††£ 130/190 – 1 suite
♦ Splendid 19C Arts and Crafts house in tranquil wooded cliffside setting. Stained glass window by Burne Jones and library filled with antiques. Stylish rooms with sea views.

🏠 Victoria Lodge without rest
30-31 Lee Rd ✉ EX35 6BS – ℰ (01598) 753 203 – www.victorialodge.co.uk
– 22 March-October
8 rm ☕ – †£ 119 ††£ 140
♦ Large 19C house decorated with period photographs, prints and Victoriana Traditional décor in communal areas and bedrooms which are comfortable and inviting.

🏠 St Vincent without rest
Market St, Castle Hill ✉ EX35 6JA – ℰ (01598) 752 244
– www.st-vincent-hotel.co.uk – Easter-October
5 rm ☕ – †£ 70/75 ††£ 80
♦ Grade II listed Georgian House with charming Belgian owners, set 200 metres from the coastal path. Lovely fire-lit lounge and fresh, uncluttered bedrooms with smart bathrooms.

at Lynmouth East : 1 mi

🏠 Shelley's without rest
8 Watersmeet Rd ✉ EX35 6EP – ℰ (01598) 753 219 – www.shelleyshotel.co.uk
– March-October
11 rm ☕ – †£ 75/95 ††£ 75/110
♦ Centrally located hotel named after eponymous poet who honeymooned here in 1812. Stylish public areas. Very comfortable bedrooms with good views of picturesque locale.

🏠 Heatherville
Tors Park, by Tors Rd ✉ EX35 6NB – ℰ (01598) 752 327 – www.heatherville.co.uk
– April-October
6 rm ☕ – †£ 110 ††£ 110 **Rest** – Menu £ 25
♦ Victorian house perched above the town. Well kept throughout with bright, warm décor. Rooms with bold fabrics and woodland views: room 6 has the best outlook. Home-cooked meals employ fresh, local produce.

at Martinhoe West : 4.25 mi via Coast rd (toll) – ✉ Barnstaple

🏠 Old Rectory
✉ EX31 4QT – ℰ (01598) 763 368 – www.oldrectoryhotel.co.uk – April-October
10 rm (dinner included) ☕ – †£ 165/180 ††£ 210/245
Rest – *(dinner only)* Menu £ 36
♦ Built in 19C for rector of Martinhoe's 11C church, this quiet country retreat is set in a charming spot, with a well-tended three acre garden and cascading brook. Fresh, bright bedrooms are modern, yet retain period touches: Heddon and Paddock are two of the best. Comfortable dining room; simple home-cooking.

LYTHAM – Lancashire – 502 L22 – see Lytham St Annes

LYTHAM ST ANNE'S – Lancashire – 502 L22 – pop. 41 327   20 A.

▶ London 237 mi – Blackpool 7 mi – Liverpool 44 mi – Preston 13 mi
🛈 St Annes Rd West ℰ (01253) 72 56 10, www.visitlythamstannes.co.uk
⛳ Fairhaven Ansdell, Oakwood Avenue, ℰ (01253) 73 67 41
⛳ St Annes Old Links Highbury Rd, ℰ (01253) 72 35 97

LYTHAM ST ANNE'S

at Lytham

Rooms without rest
35 Church Rd ✉ FY8 5LL – ℰ (01253) 736 000 – www.theroomslytham.com
5 rm ⊇ – †£ 105 ††£ 130

♦ Boutique-style guesthouse with striking, contemporary décor. Good-sized bedrooms boast modern facilities, including iPod docks and large flat screen TVs. Extensive breakfasts.

Hastings
26 Hastings Pl. ✉ FY8 5LZ – ℰ (01253) 732 400 – www.hastingslytham.com
– Closed Sunday dinner and Monday
Rest – Menu £ 14 (lunch)/18 (midweek dinner) – Carte £ 23/35

♦ Red-brick restaurant with modern bar, intimate ground floor dining room and brighter mezzanine, featuring exposed rafters and glass skylight. Wide-ranging menu with a regional slant.

at St Anne's

Grand
South Promenade ✉ FY8 1NB – ℰ (01253) 721 288 – www.the-grand.co.uk
– Closed 24-26 December
54 rm – †£ 111 ††£ 188, ⊇ £ 6.50
Rest *Café Grand* – ℰ (01253) 643 409 – Carte £ 29/47

♦ Impressive, turreted Victorian hotel on promenade. Stylish, contemporary guest areas. Variously sized bedrooms, most with good views; turret rooms are the most spacious, and have particularly good aspects. Laid-back, stylish Café Grand offers accessible menu.

MADINGLEY – Cambridgeshire – **504** U27 – see Cambridge

MAENPORTH – Cornwall – see Falmouth

MAIDEN BRADLEY – Wiltshire – **503** N30 – pop. 335   **4** C2

▶ London 114 mi – Bristol 36 mi – Cardiff 77 mi – Southampton 75 mi

Somerset Arms with rm
Church St ✉ BA12 7HW – ℰ (01985) 844 207 – www.thesomersetarms.org
5 rm ⊇ – †£ 70 ††£ 110   **Rest** – Carte £ 18/37

♦ Proudly run pub, with polite, well-paced service; popular with locals. Oft-changing menu uses local produce, including eggs from their own hens and veg from the garden. Flavourful, rustic cooking; steaks a speciality. Contemporary bedrooms; one with free-standing bath.

MAIDENCOMBE – Torbay – **503** J32 – see Torquay

MAIDENHEAD – Windsor and Maidenhead – **504** R29 – pop. 58 848   **11** C3

▶ London 33 mi – Oxford 32 mi – Reading 13 mi
⛴ to Marlow, Cookham and Windsor (Salter Bros. Ltd) (summer only) (3 h 45 mn)
🛈 St Ives Rd ℰ (01628) 79 65 02, www.windsor.gov.uk
⛳ Bird Hills Hawthorn Hill Drift Rd, ℰ (01628) 77 10 30
⛳ Shoppenhangers Rd, ℰ (01628) 62 46 93

Plan on next page

MAIDENHEAD

Street	Grid
Bad Godesberg Way	Y 2
Belmont Park Ave	Y 3
Blackamoor Lane	V 5
Boyn Hill Ave	Z 6
Braywick Rd	Z 7
Bridge St	Y 9
College Rd	V 13
Cookham Rd	Y 14
Crescent (The)	V 15
Ferry Rd	X 17
Frascati Way	YZ 18
Furze Platt Rd	V 20
Grenfell Pl	Z 21
Gringer Hill	V 22
Harrow Lane	V 24
High St	Y
High St BRAY-ON-THAMES	X 25
King's Grove	Z 27
Linden Ave	V 28
Lower Cookham Rd	V 29
Manor Lane	X 31
Market St	Y 32
Nicholson's Walk Shopping Centre	YZ
Norreys Drive	X 35
Oldfield Rd	X 36
Ray Mill Rd West	V 39
Ray St	V 38
St Ives Rd	Y 41
St Mark Rd	Y 42
Stafferton Way	Z 43
Upper Bray Rd	X 45

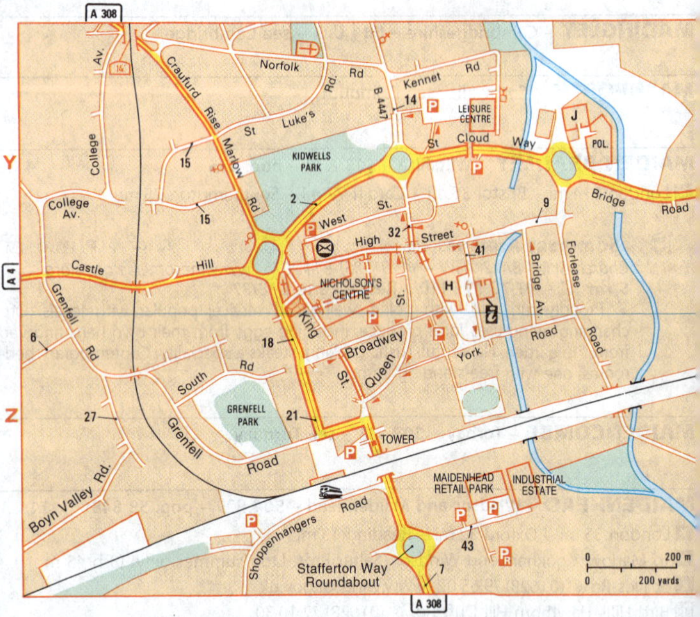

ENGLAND

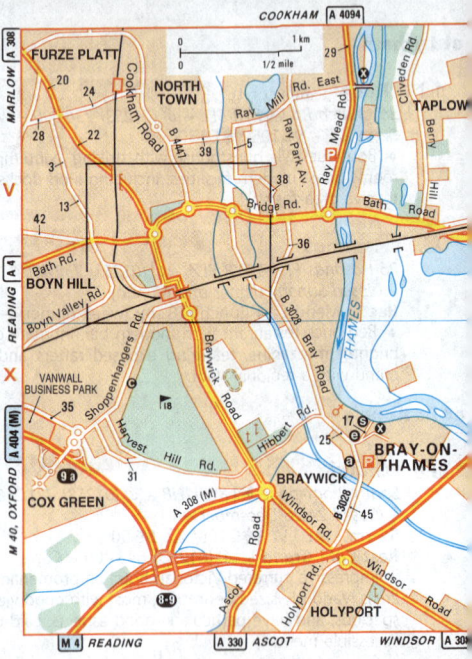

478

MAIDENHEAD

Fredrick's
*Shoppenhangers Rd ⊠ SL6 2PZ – ℰ (01628) 581 000 – www.fredricks-hotel.co.uk
– Closed 24-25 December*   Xc
36 rm – †£ 225/275 ††£ 275, ⊇ £ 23.50 – 1 suite
Rest *Fredrick's* – *(closed Saturday lunch)* Menu £ 25/40 – Carte £ 41/57
♦ Red-brick former inn with very stylish, well-equipped spa. Ornate, marble reception with smoked mirrors; wicker-furnished conservatory and comfortable, individually styled bedrooms. Large restaurant boasts chandeliers, full-length windows and elaborate British menus.

Boulters Riverside Brasserie
*Boulters Lock Island ⊠ SL6 8PE – ℰ (01628) 621 291
– www.boultersrestaurant.co.uk – Closed Sunday dinner and Monday*
Rest – Menu £ 20 (lunch) – Carte £ 25/46   Vx
♦ Stylish modern eatery beside a lock, on a small island in the Thames. Full-length windows open onto terrace; excellent river views. Hearty yet refined brasserie classics use quality produce.

MAIDENSGROVE – Oxfordshire – pop. 1 572 – ⊠ Henley-On-Thames   **11 C3**

▶ London 43 mi – Oxford 23 mi – Reading 15 mi

Five Horseshoes
⊠ RG9 6EX – ℰ (01491) 641 282 – www.thefivehorseshoes.co.uk
Rest – Carte approx. £ 25
♦ Walkers' paradise: a charming part-17C inn boasting characterful beamed bar and suntrap restaurant with countryside views. Doorstop sandwiches, comforting classics and homely desserts.

MAIDSTONE – Kent – **504** V30 – pop. 89 684 Great Britain   **8 B2**

▶ London 36 mi – Brighton 64 mi – Cambridge 84 mi – Colchester 72 mi
🛈 High St ℰ (01622) 60 21 69, www.visitmaidstone.com
⛳ Tudor Park Hotel Bearsted Ashford Rd, ℰ (01622) 73 43 34
⛳ Cobtree Manor Park Boxley Chatham Rd, ℰ (01622) 75 32 76
◉ Leeds Castle★ **AC**, SE : 4.5 mi by A 20 and B 2163

at Bearsted East : 3 mi by A 249 off A 20 – ⊠ Maidstone

Fish On The Green
*Church Ln, ⊠ ME14 4EJ – ℰ (01622) 738 300
– www.fishonthegreen.com – Closed 25 December-26 January, Sunday dinner and Monday*
Rest – Seafood – Menu £ 18 (lunch) – Carte £ 30/44
♦ Well-run, contemporary restaurant with pleasant terrace, tucked away in corner of the green. Focus on fresh fish, with a few local meat dishes. Good value lunch menu; friendly service.

MALMESBURY – Wiltshire – **503** N29 – pop. 5 094   **4 C2**

▶ London 108 mi – Bristol 28 mi – Gloucester 24 mi – Swindon 19 mi
🛈 Cross Hayes ℰ (01666) 82 37 48, www.malmesbury.gov.uk
◉ Town★ – Market Cross★★ – Abbey★

MALMESBURY

Whatley Manor
Easton Grey, West : 2.25 mi on B 4040 ✉ *SN16 0RB –* ✆ *(01666) 822 888*
– www.whatleymanor.com
15 rm – †£ 305/515 ††£ 305/515 – 8 suites
Rest *Le Mazot* – see restaurant listing
Rest *The Dining Room* – *(closed Monday and Tuesday) (dinner only) (booking essential for non-residents)* Menu £ 76/96 **s**
Spec. Poached and roasted squab pigeon with pan-fried foie gras, Pedro Ximenez reduction. Fillets of Dover sole with glazed shrimps, confit salt cod and onion cassonade. Prune and Armagnac soufflé, Ceylon tea granité.
• Cotswold stone buildings set in beautiful gardens. Chic, contemporary, luxurious bedrooms; sumptuous bathrooms. Stunning spa, top class business centre and cinema. The Dining Room offers comfortable surroundings in which to enjoy technically-skilled and innovative cooking, with charming service.

Old Bell
Abbey Row ✉ *SN16 0BW –* ✆ *(01666) 822 344*
– www.oldbellhotel.com
33 rm – †£ 90/99 ††£ 115/275
Rest *The Restaurant* – see restaurant listing
• Hugely characterful part-13C former abbots' hostel in pleasant gardens, set next to the abbey. Intimate bar. Mix of bedroom styles: bold and fashionable in main house, more classical in annexe.

Le Mazot – at Whatley Manor Hotel
Easton Grey, West : 2.25 mi on B 4040 ✉ *SN16 0RB –* ✆ *(01666) 822 888*
– www.whatleymanor.com
Rest – Menu £ 24 (lunch) **s** – Carte £ 33/37 **s**
• Unusual gold wood Swiss chalet restaurant within delightful country house, offering casual dining on comfy banquettes. Cooking is refined, light and skilled. Polite, careful service.

The Restaurant – at The Old Bell Hotel
Abbey Row ✉ *SN16 0BW –* ✆ *(01666) 822 344*
– www.oldbellhotel.com – Closed dinner Sunday and Monday
Rest – *(booking essential at dinner)* Menu £ 40 (dinner) – Carte £ 28/40
• Imposing, richly coloured dining room displaying old portraits and fine china. Skilled kitchen offers brasserie-style lunch and fine dining in evening. Refined, artful dishes; attentive service.

at Crudwell North : 4 mi on A 429 – ✉ Malmesbury

Rectory
✉ *SN16 9EP –* ✆ *(01666) 577 194*
– www.therectoryhotel.com
12 rm – †£ 105 ††£ 195 **Rest** – *(dinner only)* Menu £ 29
• 17C stone-built former Rectory with formal garden. A little quirky but personally run. Comfortable, individually-styled bedrooms with many modern extras, some with spa baths. Airy oak-panelled dining room; modern seasonal cooking.

Potting Shed
The Street ✉ *SN16 9EW –* ✆ *(01666) 577 833*
– www.thepottingshedpub.com
Rest – Carte £ 23/33
• Spacious, light-filled pub with contemporary décor, exposed beams and a relaxing feel. Monthly changing menus offer wholesome, satisfying dishes, with vegetables and herbs from their garden.

MALPAS – Cheshire West and Chester – **502** L24 – pop. 3 684   **20** A3

▶ London 177 mi – Birmingham 60 mi – Chester 15 mi – Shrewsbury 26 mi

at Tilston Northwest : 3 mi on Tilston Rd – ✉ Malpas

Tilston Lodge without rest
✉ SY14 7DR – ℰ (01829) 250 223
3 rm ⌂ – †£ 50 ††£ 100
♦ Large, red-brick former Victorian hunting lodge with neat gardens and mature grounds. Homely bedrooms boast good facilities and country views. Charming owner is Lord Mayor of Chester.

MALTBY – Stockton-on-Tees – **502** Q23   **24** B3

▶ London 251 mi – Liverpool 141 mi – Leeds 69 mi – Sheffield 101 mi

Chadwicks Inn
High Ln ✉ TS8 0B9 – ℰ (01642) 590 300 – www.chadwicksinnmaltby.co.uk
– Closed 25 December, 1 January and Monday
Rest – (booking advisable) Menu £ 16 (lunch) – Carte £ 26/40
♦ Dating back over 200 years and a favourite haunt of the Spitfire pilots before their missions. Open-fired bar and two smart dining rooms. Ambitious à la carte offers intricate dishes, supplemented by a set lunch and tapas in the afternoons.

MALVERN WELLS – Worcestershire – **503** N27 – see Great Malvern

---

MAN (Isle of) – I.O.M. – **502** G21 – pop. 80 058 Great Britain   **20** B1

⛴ from Douglas to Belfast (Isle of Man Steam Packet Co. Ltd) (summer only) (2 h 45 mn) – from Douglas to Republic of Ireland (Dublin) (Isle of Man Steam Packet Co. Ltd) (2 h 45 mn/4 h) – from Douglas to Heysham (Isle of Man Steam Packet Co.) (2 h/3 h 30 mn) – from Douglas to Liverpool (Isle of Man Steam Packet Co. Ltd) (2 h 30 mn/4 h)

◉ Laxey Wheel★★ - Snaefell★ (❅★★★) - Cregneash Folk Museum★

DOUGLAS – Douglas – pop. 26 218   **20** B1
✈ Ronaldsway Airport : ℰ (01624) 821600, SW : 7 mi
ℹ Sea Terminal Buildings ℰ (01624) 68 67 66, www.iomguide.com
⛳ Douglas Pulrose Park, ℰ (01624) 67 59 52
⛳ King Edward Bay Onchan Groudle Rd, ℰ (01624) 62 04 30

Sefton
Harris Promenade ✉ IM1 2RW – ℰ (01624) 645 500 – www.seftonhotel.co.im
90 rm ⌂ – ††£ 110/130 – 12 suites
Rest *The Gallery* – (closed Sunday in winter) (bar lunch) Menu £ 30
– Carte approx. £ 35 **s**
♦ Victorian-fronted promenade hotel, built around unique atrium water garden. Bedrooms may have balconies, look out to sea or have water garden views. Impressive apartment suites. The Gallery, with its boldly coloured Manx art, offers speciality flambé dishes.

Regency
Queens Promenade ✉ IM2 4NN – ℰ (01624) 680 680 – www.regency.im
34 rm ⌂ – †£ 80/145 ††£ 125/165 – 4 suites

Rest *Five Continents* – (dinner only) Menu £ 26 – Carte £ 26/43
♦ Perfect for business travellers: mobile phone loan, PCs with free internet in every bedroom and special office suites, combined with traditional seaside styling and Douglas Bay views. Oak panelled restaurant boasts original collection of Island pictures.

MAN (Isle of)

Penta without rest
Queens Promenade ✉ *IM9 4NE* – ℰ *(01624) 680 680 – www.regency.im*
22 rm – †£ 49/90 ††£ 59/100

♦ Set on the promenade, with views over Douglas Bay. Large, functional, well-equipped bedrooms feature computers with free internet access. Wine-themed, Mediterranean-style breakfast room.

JAR
Admirals House, 11-12 Loch Promenade ✉ *IM1 2LX* – ℰ *(01624) 663 553*
– www.jar.co.im – Closed 25 December
Rest – Menu £ 25 (lunch) – Carte £ 32/51

♦ Set on ground floor of hotel, with comfy, leather-furnished lounge and pleasant coastal outlook from front tables. Italian-influenced menus; clean, unfussy, flavoursome cooking.

Macfarlane's
24 Duke St ✉ *IM1 2AY* – ℰ *(01624) 624 777 – www.macfarlanes.im – Closed 1 week Spring, 2 weeks early August, 1 week Christmas-New Year, Sunday and Monday*
Rest – *(dinner only and lunch Thursday and Friday) (booking essential)*
Carte £ 27/47

♦ Small, simple restaurant in heart of town, with leather-topped tables and high-sided booths. Unfussy, regularly changing menu relies on fresh local produce, with fish to the fore.

PORT ERIN – Port Erin – pop. 3 575   20 B1

Rowany Cottier without rest
Spaldrick ✉ *IM9 6PE* – ℰ *(01624) 832 287 – www.rowanycottier.com*
5 rm – †£ 50/65 ††£ 80/96

♦ Large, purpose-built house set by Bradda Glen. Pleasant guest areas with views over Port Erin and Calf of Man. Simple, well-kept bedrooms. Locally sourced breakfast; homemade bread.

PORT ST MARY – Port Saint Mary – pop. 1 913   20 B1

Aaron House without rest
The Promenade ✉ *IM9 5DE* – ℰ *(01624) 835 702 – www.aaronhouse.co.uk*
– Closed Christmas-New Year
6 rm – †£ 98/108 ††£ 118/138

♦ Charming, antique-furnished guesthouse with bay/harbour views and strong Victorian feel. Comfy, traditional bedrooms. Afternoon tea on arrival. Interesting breakfast choices.

RAMSEY – Ramsey – pop. 7 309   20 B1

River House without rest
North : 0.25 mi by A 9 turning left immediately after bridge ✉ *IM8 3DA*
– ℰ *(01624) 816 412*
3 rm – †£ 70 ††£ 120

♦ Attractive Georgian country house with pleasant gardens. Tastefully furnished throughout, with comfy drawing room, antiques and objets d'art. Traditional, cottage-style bedrooms.

MANCHESTER

See city maps on following pages 20 B2

Greater Manchester – pop. 396 322 – 502 N23 – 503 N23 – 504 N23 – Great Britain
▶ London 202 – Birmingham 86 – Glasgow 221 – Leeds 43

Tourist Information

Manchester Visitor Centre, Town Hall Extension, Lloyd St ℰ(0871) 222 82 23, www.visitmanchester.com

Airport

✈ Manchester International Airport : ℰ (08712) 710 711, S : 10 m. by A 5103 - AX - and M 56

Golf Courses

⛳ Heaton Park Prestwich, ℰ(0161) 654 98 99
⛳ Houldsworth Park Stockport Houldsworth St, Reddish, ℰ(0161) 442 17 12

◎ SIGHTS

In the town : City★ • Castlefield Urban Heritage Park★ CZ • Town Hall★ CZ • Manchester Art Gallery★ CZM2 • Cathedral★ CY • Museum of Science and Industry★ CZM • Imperial War Museum North★, Trafford Park AXM
On the outskirts : Whitworth Art Gallery★, S : 1.5 m
In the surrounding area : Quarry Bank Mill★, S : 10 mi off B 5166, exit 5 from M 56

ENGLAND

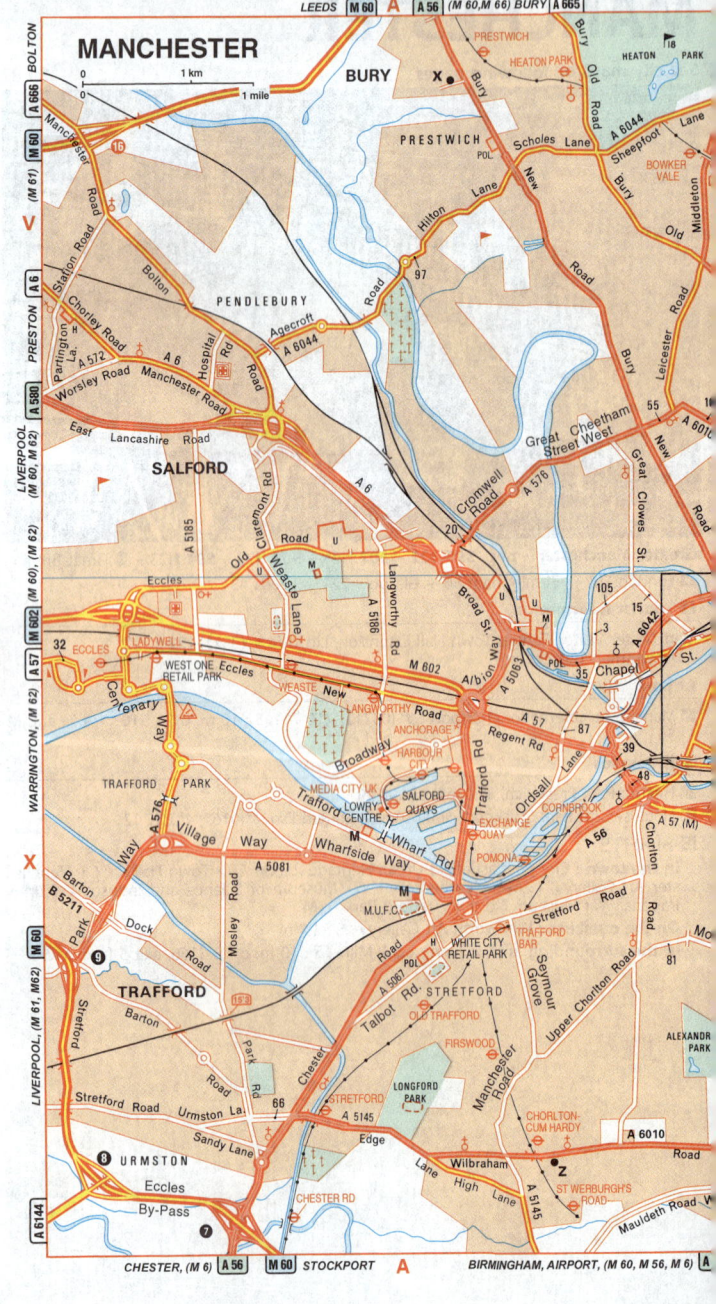

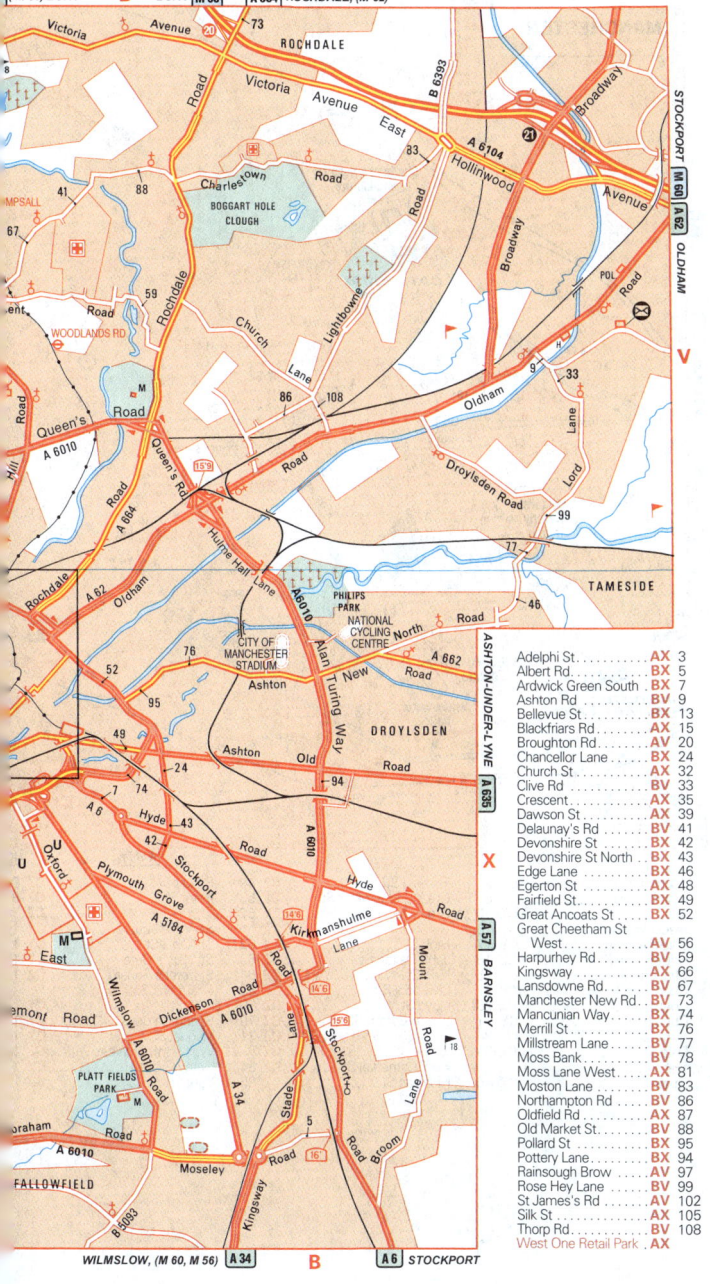

Adelphi St.	AX	3
Albert Rd.	BX	5
Ardwick Green South	BX	7
Ashton Rd	BV	9
Bellevue St.	BX	13
Blackfriars Rd	BX	15
Broughton Rd	AV	20
Chancellor Lane	BX	24
Church St.	BX	32
Clive Rd	BV	33
Crescent	AX	35
Dawson St	AX	39
Delaunay's Rd	BV	41
Devonshire St	BX	42
Devonshire St North	BX	43
Edge Lane	BX	46
Egerton St	AX	48
Fairfield St.	BX	49
Great Ancoats St	BX	52
Great Cheetham St West	AV	56
Harpurhey Rd	BV	59
Kingsway	AX	66
Lansdowne Rd.	BV	67
Manchester New Rd.	BV	73
Mancunian Way	BX	74
Merrill St	BX	76
Millstream Lane	BX	77
Moss Bank	BV	78
Moss Lane West	BX	81
Moston Lane	BV	83
Northampton Rd	BV	86
Oldfield Rd	AX	87
Old Market St.	AV	88
Pollard St	BX	95
Pottery Rd	BX	94
Rainsough Brow	AV	97
Rose Hey Lane	BX	99
St James's Rd	AV	102
Silk St	AX	105
Thorp Rd	BV	108
West One Retail Park	AX	

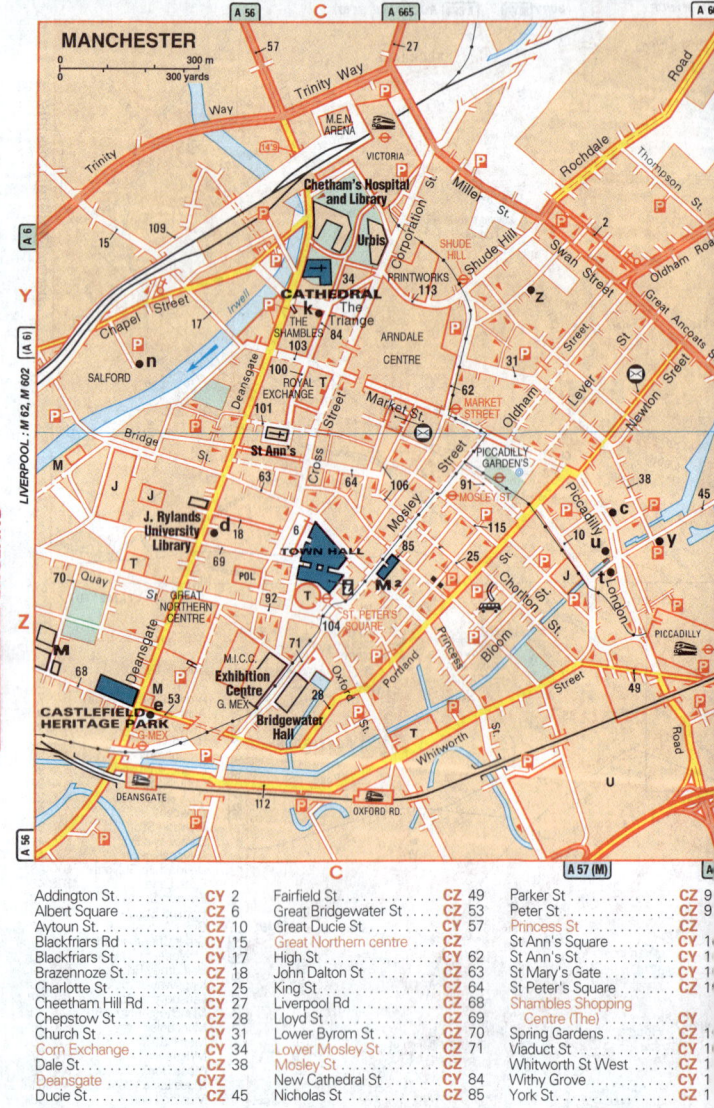

MANCHESTER

Addington St. . . . . CY 2	Fairfield St . . . . CZ 49	Parker St . . . . CZ 9
Albert Square . . . . CZ 6	Great Bridgewater St . . . . . CZ 53	Peter St . . . . CZ 9
Aytoun St. . . . . CZ 10	Great Ducie St . . . . CY 57	Princess St . . . . CZ
Blackfriars Rd . . . . CY 15	Great Northern centre . . . . CZ	St Ann's Square . . . . CY 1
Blackfriars St. . . . . CY 17	High St . . . . CY 62	St Ann's St . . . . CZ 1
Brazennoze St. . . . . CZ 18	John Dalton St . . . . CZ 63	St Mary's Gate . . . . CY 1
Charlotte St . . . . CZ 25	King St . . . . CZ 64	St Peter's Square . . . . CZ 1
Cheetham Hill Rd . . . . CY 27	Liverpool Rd . . . . CZ 68	Shambles Shopping
Chepstow St . . . . CZ 28	Lloyd St . . . . CZ 69	Centre (The) . . . . CY
Church St . . . . CY 31	Lower Byrom St . . . . CZ 70	Spring Gardens . . . . CZ 1
Corn Exchange . . . . CY 34	Lower Mosley St . . . . CZ 71	Viaduct St . . . . CY 1
Dale St . . . . CZ 38	Mosley St . . . . CZ	Whitworth St West . . . . CZ 1
Deansgate . . . . CYZ	New Cathedral St . . . . CY 84	Withy Grove . . . . CY 1
Ducie St. . . . . CZ 45	Nicholas St . . . . CZ 85	York St . . . . CZ 1

MANCHESTER

Lowry
50 Dearmans Pl, Chapel Wharf, Salford ⊠ M3 5LH – ℰ (0161) 827 40 00
– www.roccofortehotels.com CYn
158 rm – †£ 387 ††£ 453, ⊇ £ 18.50 – 7 suites
Rest *River* – see restaurant listing

♦ Modern and hugely spacious, with excellent facilities, impressive spa and minimalist feel: art displays and exhibitions feature throughout. Stylish bedrooms with oversized windows; some river views.

Hilton
303 Deansgate ⊠ M3 4LQ – ℰ (0161) 870 16 00
– www.hilton.co.uk/manchesterdeansgate CZe
275 rm – †£ 169/369 ††£ 169/369, ⊇ £ 17.95 – 5 suites
Rest *Podium* – Menu £ 20/27 – Carte £ 28/41

♦ 23 floors of a striking glass skyscraper. Smart atrium lobby with elevated walkways; glass bottomed pool above. Comfortable, contemporary bedrooms with views. Superb 360° outlook from Cloud bar. Stylish Podium restaurant offers modern brasserie menu of European dishes.

Malmaison

Piccadilly ⊠ M1 3AQ – ℰ (0161) 278 10 00 – www.malmaison-manchester.com
166 rm – †£ 99/170 ††£ 99/170, ⊇ £ 14.50 – 1 suite CZu
Rest *Brasserie* – see restaurant listing

♦ Old cotton warehouse and dolls hospital joined by a striking granite extension. Seductive red and black Moulin Rouge style décor and sensuous spa. Stylish bedrooms: uniquely designed suites include a Man Utd theme and mini cinema dark room.

ENGLAND

Abode
107 Piccadilly ⊠ M1 2DB – ℰ (0161) 247 77 44 – www.abodehotels.co.uk
61 rm – †£ 79/170 ††£ 79/170, ⊇ £ 14 CZc
Rest *Michael Caines* – see restaurant listing

♦ Late Victorian cotton merchant's former head office with iron columns and girders still in situ. Relaxed boutique ambience with modern, trendy open-plan rooms and stylish bathrooms.

Mint

One Piccadilly Place, 1 Auburn Street ⊠ M1 3DG – ℰ (0161) 242 10 00
– www.minthotel.com CZt
284 rm – †£ 245 ††£ 245, ⊇ £ 16 – 1 suite
Rest *Elements* – ℰ (0161) 242 10 20 – Menu £ 16/20 – Carte £ 24/34

♦ Contemporary glass building with spacious, airy interior and local art on display. Modern bedrooms boast pale hues, iMac computers and excellent entertainment facilities. Showers only. Smart, stylish restaurant with appealing, wide ranging menu.

River – at The Lowry Hotel
50 Dearmans Pl, Chapel Wharf, Salford ⊠ M3 5LH – ℰ (0161) 827 40 00
– www.roccofortehotels.com CYn
Rest – Menu £ 20 – Carte £ 44/50

♦ Airy first-floor restaurant with river views; vast mirrors, modern artwork and decorative plates fill the walls. Modern presentation of classic combinations with regional ingredients to the fore.

Wings
1 Lincoln Sq ⊠ M2 5LN – ℰ (0161) 834 90 00 – www.wingsrestaurant.co.uk
Rest – Chinese – Menu £ 33 – Carte £ 19/56 CZd

♦ Well-run restaurant off busy square. Narrow room with linen-clad tables, comfy booths, terracotta army replicas and Hong Kong skyline murals. Extensive menu of authentic Cantonese dim sum.

MANCHESTER

XX Second Floor - Restaurant – at Harvey Nichols
21 New Cathedral St ⊠ M1 1AD – ℰ (0161) 828 88 98 – www.harveynichols.com
– Closed 25-26 December, 1 January, Sunday and dinner Monday CYk
Rest – Menu £ 40

♦ Smart restaurant with stylish, colour-changing lighting and oversized windows offering big wheel and city views. Elaborate modern European menu with interesting twists; good presentation.

XX Michael Caines – at Abode Hotel
107 Piccadilly ⊠ M1 2DB – ℰ (0161) 247 77 44 – www.michaelcaines.co.uk
– Closed first 2 weeks January and Sunday CZc
Rest – Menu £ 14 (lunch) – Carte approx. £ 43

♦ Modern restaurant in hotel basement, featuring subdued lighting and a sophisticated style. Contemporary British cooking, with some Mediterranean influences. Tasting menu and matching wines.

XX Brasserie – at Malmaison Hotel
Piccadilly ⊠ M1 3AQ – ℰ (0161) 278 10 01 – www.malmaison-manchester.com
Rest – Menu £ 30 – Carte £ 25/30 CZu

♦ Richly decorated, two-roomed brasserie with intimate candlelit booths, set in a stylish hotel that was once an old cotton warehouse and dolls hospital. Menu offers unfussy British classics.

X Second Floor - Brasserie – at Harvey Nichols
21 New Cathedral St ⊠ M1 1AD – ℰ (0161) 828 88 98 – www.harveynichols.com
– Closed 25 December, 1 January and dinner Sunday-Monday CYk
Rest – Menu £ 20 (dinner) – Carte £ 21/31

♦ Relaxed, minimalist brasserie and bar, with colour-changing strip lighting and buzzy atmosphere. Extensive menu of modern British dishes, with some lighter meals available. Popular with shoppers.

X Northern Quarter
108 High St ⊠ M4 1HQ – ℰ (0161) 832 71 15 – www.tnq.co.uk – Closed 25 December, 1-2 January and Sunday dinner CYz
Rest – *(booking essential at dinner)* Menu £ 14 (lunch and early dinner) – Carte £ 24/37

♦ Friendly, modern restaurant with floor to ceiling windows. Keenly priced, seasonal menus offer classic dishes presented in a modern style. Popular, bi-monthly themed evenings.

at Didsbury South : 5.5 mi by 5103 - **AX** - on A 5145 – ⊠ Manchester

Didsbury House
Didsbury Pk, South : 1.5 mi on A 5145 ⊠ M20 5LJ – ℰ (0161) 448 22 00 – www.didsburyhouse.com
23 rm – †£ 143 ††£ 143, ⊇ £ 15.50 – 4 suites **Rest** – Carte £ 19/30 s

♦ Cream-washed Victorian villa – now a boutique townhouse; original features include an impressive stained glass window. Bedrooms are comfortable and stylish with a contemporary edge; some boast hot tubs. Small basement dining room; accessible, all-day menu.

Eleven Didsbury Park
11 Didsbury Pk, South : 1.5 mi by A 5145 ⊠ M20 5LH – ℰ (0161) 448 77 11 – www.elevendidsburypark.com
19 rm – †£ 143 ††£ 143, ⊇ £ 15.50 – 1 suite
Rest – *(room service only)* Carte £ 19/30 s

♦ Comfortable, boutique-style townhouse in pleasant residential setting, with simply furnished breakfast room overlooking delightful garden. Stylish, contemporary bedrooms with warm décor and good facilities; many have tubs in the rooms. Informal all-day menu.

MANCHESTER

✗ Jem&I VISA ⓪ AE
1c School Ln ✉ M20 6RD – ℰ (0161) 445 39 96 – jemandirestaurant.co.uk
Rest – Carte £ 20/34
♦ Simple, unpretentious cream-coloured building tucked away off the high street. Open-plan kitchen; homely, bistro feel. Good value, modern European menus. Polite, friendly service.

at West Didsbury South : 5.5 mi by A 5103 - **AX** - on A 5145 – ✉ Manchester

✗ Rhubarb 🌿 A/C VISA ⓪ AE
167 Burton Rd ✉ M20 2LN – ℰ (0161) 448 88 87 – www.rhubarbrestaurant.co.uk
– Closed 25 December and 1 January
Rest – (dinner only and Sunday lunch) – Carte £ 22/31
♦ Suburban eatery with small pavement terrace, where neutral hues are offset by large canvasses and a colourful feature wall. Large, seasonally changing menus display an eclectic mix of dishes.

at Chorlton-Cum-Hardy Southwest : 4 mi . by A 5103 - **AX** - on A 6010 – ✉ Manchester

⌂ Abbey Lodge without rest 🚗 📶 P VISA ⓪ AE
501 Wilbraham Rd ✉ M21 0UJ – ℰ (0161) 862 92 66 – www.abbey-lodge.co.uk
4 rm – ♦£ 50/60 ♦♦£ 70, ⌸ £ 7.50 **AXz**
♦ Attractive Edwardian house boasting many original features including stained glass windows. Owner provides charming hospitality and pine fitted rooms are immaculately kept.

at Prestwich Northwest : 5 mi on A 56

✗✗ Aumbry VISA ⓪
2 Church Ln ✉ M25 1AJ – ℰ (0161) 798 58 41 – www.aumbryrestaurant.co.uk
– Closed first 2 weeks January, 25 December, Sunday dinner, Monday and Tuesday **AVx**
Rest – (booking essential) Menu £ 22 (weekday lunch) – Carte £ 30/44
♦ Intimate neighbourhood restaurant offering small à la carte or 9 course tasting menu. Precise cooking with a good combination of flavours; local, seasonal produce well used.

MANSFIELD – Nottinghamshire – 502 Q24 – pop. 69 987 16 B1
▶ London 143 mi – Chesterfield 12 mi – Worksop 14 mi

✗✗ No.4 Wood Street A/C ⇔ P VISA ⓪ AE
4 Wood St ✉ NG18 1QA – ℰ (01623) 424 824 – www.4woodstreet.co.uk
– Closed 26 December, 1 January, Saturday lunch, Sunday dinner and Monday
Rest – Menu £ 18 (weekdays) – Carte £ 21/36
♦ Solid brick restaurant hidden away in town centre. Relax in lounge bar with comfy armchairs before enjoying well-executed, modern, seasonal dishes in rustic dining room.

✗✗ Lambs at the Market VISA ⓪
Cattle Market House, Nottingham Rd ✉ NG18 1BD – ℰ (01623) 424 880
– www.lambsatthemarket.co.uk – Closed first week January and Monday
Rest – (dinner only and Sunday lunch) Menu £ 18 (lunch) – Carte dinner £ 24/43
♦ Family-run restaurant in attractive Victorian building, with a more contemporary interior. Modern European cooking has a British bias; portions are generous and flavours, clear.

MARAZION – Cornwall – **503** D33 – pop. 1 381 – ✉ Penzance 1 A3

▶ London 318 mi – Penzance 3 mi – Truro 26 mi

🏌 Praa Sands Penzance, ✆ (01736) 76 34 45

◉ St Michael's Mount★★ (≤★★) – Ludgvan★ (Church★) N : 2 mi by A 30
– Chysauster Village★, N : 2 mi by A 30 – Gulval★ (Church★) W : 2.5 m – Prussia
Cove★, SE : 5.5 mi by A 30 and minor rd

Mount Haven
Turnpike Rd, East : 0.25 mi ✉ *TR17 0DQ* – ✆ *(01736) 710 249*
– *www.mounthaven.co.uk* – *Closed mid-December-early-February*
18 rm ☐ – †£ 90/120 ††£ 160/190
Rest – *(bar lunch Monday-Saturday)* Menu £ 30 – Carte £ 20/32
♦ Small hotel overlooking St Michael's Bay. Spacious bar and lounge featuring Indian crafts and fabrics. Contemporary rooms with modern amenities, most with balcony and view. Bright attractive dining room; menu mixes modern and traditional.

at Perranuthnoe Southeast : 1.75 mi by A 394 – ✉ Penzance

Ednovean Farm without rest
✉ *TR20 9LZ* – ✆ *(01736) 711 883* – *www.ednoveanfarm.co.uk* – *Closed Christmas*
3 rm ☐ – †£ 100/115 ††£ 105/120
♦ Very spacious, characterful converted 17C granite barn offering peace, tranquility and Mounts Bay views. Fine choice at breakfast on oak table. Charming, individual rooms.

Victoria Inn with rm
✉ *TR20 9NP* – ✆ *(01736) 710 309* – *www.victoriainn-penzance.co.uk* – *Closed 25-26 December, 1 January, Monday in winter and Sunday dinner*
2 rm ☐ – †£ 50/75 ††£ 75 **Rest** – Carte £ 27/34
♦ Characterful, pink-washed pub in the heart of the village, with a cosy, homely feel and a suntrap terrace. Short menu of wholesome dishes showcases local produce and is supplemented by blackboard of seafood specials. Simple, nautically themed bedrooms.

at St Hilary East : 2.5 mi by Turnpike Rd on B 3280 – ✉ Penzance

Ennys without rest
Trewhella Ln ✉ *TR20 9BZ* – ✆ *(01736) 740 262* – *www.ennys.co.uk*
– *April-October*
5 rm ☐ – †£ 85/135 ††£ 105/150
♦ A beautiful and delightfully remote guesthouse, its lovingly restored interior simply furnished in light colours, with Indian artefacts from the charming owner's travels. Grass tennis court and pool set in secluded part of the garden. Complimentary afternoon tea.

MARCHAM – Oxfordshire – **503** P29 – see Abingdon

MARGATE – Kent – **504** Y29 – pop. 58 465 9 D1

▶ London 74 mi – Canterbury 17 mi – Dover 21 mi – Maidstone 43 mi

🛈 12-13 The Parade ✆ (0872) 64 61 11, www.visitthanet.co.uk

Reading Rooms without rest
31 Hawley Sq ✉ *CT9 1PH* – ✆ *(01843) 225 166*
– *www.thereadingroomsmargate.co.uk*
3 rm ☐ – †£ 135/165 ††£ 170/180
♦ Passionately run guesthouse with stripped plaster, worn woodwork and unique shabby-chic style. Eclectic bedrooms – one per floor – boast distressed furniture, super comfy beds and huge bathrooms. Extensive breakfasts served in your room.

MARGATE

Ambrette
44 King St ⊠ CT9 1QE – ℰ (01843) 231 504 – www.theambrette.co.uk – Closed 25-26 December and Monday
Rest – Indian – Menu £ 20 (lunch) – Carte £ 17/31
♦ Quirky Indian restaurant in modest surroundings. Concise, seasonal menu showcases Kentish produce in an original style; freshly prepared dishes offer well-balanced flavours and subtle spicing.

MARKET DRAYTON – Shropshire – 502 M25 – pop. 10 407   18 B1

▶ London 159 mi – Nantwich 13 mi – Shrewsbury 21 mi

Goldstone Hall
Goldstone, South : 4.5 mi by A 529 ⊠ TF9 2NA – ℰ (01630) 661 202 – www.goldstonehall.com
12 rm ⊇ – †£ 82 ††£ 120   **Rest** – Menu £ 22 (lunch) **s** – Carte £ 31/49 **s**
♦ 16C red-brick country house that's been extensively added to over the ages. Five acres of formal garden: PG Wodehouse enjoyed its shade! Modern rooms with huge beds. Contemporary twists on daily changing menus.

MARLBOROUGH – Wiltshire – 503 O29 – pop. 7 713   4 D2

ENGLAND

▶ London 84 mi – Bristol 47 mi – Southampton 40 mi – Swindon 12 mi
🛈 High St ℰ (01225) 774 2 22, www.visitwiltshire.co.uk
🛈 The Common, ℰ (01672) 51 21 47
◉ Town ★
◉ Savernake Forest ★★ (Grand Avenue ★★★), SE : 2 mi by A 4 – Whitehorse (≤ ★), NW : 5 m – West Kennett Long Barrow ★, Silbury Hill ★, W : 6 mi by A 4. Ridgeway Path ★★ – Avebury ★★ (The Stones ★, Church ★), W : 7 mi by A 4 – Crofton Beam Engines ★ **AC**, SE : 9 mi by A 346 – Wilton Windmill ★ **AC**, SE : 9 mi by A 346, A 338 and minor rd

Coles
27 Kingsbury Hill ⊠ SN8 1JA – ℰ (01672) 515 004 – www.colesrestaurant.co.uk – Closed 25 December, Sunday and bank holidays, except Good Friday
Rest – Carte £ 25/32
♦ Shots of 70s film stars adorn a busy, bay-windowed former pub which retains its firelit bar. Friendly staff and elaborate but robust cuisine with an array of daily specials.

at Little Bedwyn East : 9.5 mi by A 4 – ⊠ Marlborough

Harrow at Little Bedwyn (Roger Jones)
⊠ SN8 3JP – ℰ (01672) 870 871 – www.theharrowatlittlebedwyn.co.uk – Closed 2 weeks August, 2 weeks Christmas, and Sunday-Tuesday
Rest – Menu £ 30/40 – Carte approx. £ 47
Spec. Lobster fish finger. Line caught turbot, chicken and morel broth. Chocolate, pistachio, golden raisin and praline torte.
♦ Former pub with smartly laid tables and an intimate atmosphere. Flavourful, seasonal cooking is presented in a modern style, whilst retaining its classical base. Top quality produce; fish plays an important role. Comprehensive wine list and regular wine evenings.

at East Kennett West : 5.25 mi by A4

Old Forge without rest
⊠ SN8 4EY – ℰ (01672) 861 686 – www.theoldforge-avebury.co.uk
4 rm ⊇ – †£ 70 ††£ 80
♦ Converted former smithy with a relaxing, homely feel. Comfortable bedrooms have classic country house style; the family room has pleasant countryside views. Communal breakfast.

MARLDON – Devon – **503** J32 – pop. 1 798
2 C2

▶ London 193 mi – Newton Abbott 7 mi – Paignton 3 mi

Church House Inn
Village Rd ⊠ TQ3 1SL – ℰ *(01803) 558 279* – www.churchhousemarldon.com
– *Closed 25 December and dinner 26 December*
Rest – Carte £ 22/35
♦ Charming inn of huge character displaying original Georgian windows. Fresh and simple décor. Menu leans towards the Mediterranean with some North African and Asian influences.

MARLOW – Buckinghamshire – **504** R29 – pop. 17 522
11 C3

▶ London 35 mi – Aylesbury 22 mi – Oxford 29 mi – Reading 14 mi
⛴ to Henley-on-Thames (Salter Bros. Ltd) (summer only) (2 h 15 mn) – to Maidenhead, Cookham and Windsor (Salter Bros. Ltd) (summer only)
🛈 31 High St ℰ (01628) 48 35 97, www.visitbuckinghamshire.org

Danesfield House
Henley Rd, Southwest : 2.5 mi on A 4155 ⊠ SL7 2EY
– ℰ *(01628) 891 010* – www.danesfieldhouse.co.uk
86 rm – ♦£ 134/249 ♦♦£ 249/299, ⊇ £ 10.50
Rest *Adam Simmonds at Danesfield House* ✿ – see restaurant listing
Rest *Orangery* – Menu £ 24 (lunch) – Carte £ 32/37
♦ Stunning house and gardens in Italian Renaissance style, with breathtaking views of the Thames. Grand lounge with country house feel, comfy bedrooms, cocktail bar and state-of-art health spa. Charming, informal terrace brasserie.

Compleat Angler
Marlow Bridge, Bisham Rd ⊠ SL7 1RG – ℰ *(0844) 879 91 28*
– www.macdonaldhotels.co.uk/compleatangler
61 rm ⊇ – ♦£ 125/205 ♦♦£ 125/215 – 3 suites
Rest *Aubergine at the Compleat Angler* – ℰ *(01628) 405 405 (closed Monday and Tuesday) (booking essential)* Menu £ 29/50
Rest *Bowaters* – ℰ *(01628) 405 406 (closed Sunday dinner)* Menu £ 23 (weekday lunch) – Carte £ 39/43
♦ Smart riverside hotel boasting superb views, in enviable location between the bridge and weir. Bedrooms mix classical furnishings with contemporary fabrics: some have waterfront balconies; feature rooms are the best. Ambitious French menu in Aubergine. More traditional British fare in contemporary Bowaters.

Adam Simmonds at Danesfield House
✿
Henley Rd, Southwest : 2.5 mi on A 4155 ⊠ SL7 2EY – ℰ *(01628) 891 010*
– www.danesfieldhouse.co.uk – *Closed Sunday and Monday*
Rest – *(dinner only and lunch Thursday-Saturday)* Menu £ 62
Spec. Crab salad, tartare of mackerel, cucumber and avocado purée. Slow cooked loin of lamb, lamb sweetbreads, carrot purée and cumin croquettes. Lemon parfait and mousse with fennel pollen ice cream and olive oil jelly.
♦ Elegant, very intimate fine dining restaurant with a huge fireplace, panelled walls, linen-laid tables and a relaxed air. Creative, flavourful, intricate cooking uses modern techniques, making skilful use of excellent quality, seasonal ingredients. Formal service.

Vanilla Pod
31 West St ⊠ SL7 2LS – ℰ *(01628) 898 101* – www.thevanillapod.co.uk
– *Closed 24 December-8 January, Sunday, Monday and bank holidays*
Rest – *(booking essential)* Menu £ 20 (lunch) **s** – Carte £ 20/40
♦ Discreet, well-established address with plush furnishings and just a few tables; formerly home to T. S. Elliot. Ambitious cooking boasts French foundations, original touches and artistic flair.

MARLOW

Hand and Flowers (Tom Kerridge) with rm
✿✿
126 West St. ⊠ SL7 2BP – ℰ (01628) 482 277 – www.thehandandflowers.co.uk
– Closed 24-26 December and Sunday dinner
4 rm ⌁ – †£ 140 ††£ 190
Rest – (booking essential) Menu £ 17 (weekday lunch) – Carte £ 37/48
Spec. Parsley soup with smoked eel, bacon and parmesan tortellini. Fillet of Cornish plaice with English asparagus, morels and razor clams. Vanilla crème brûlée.

• Softly lit pub with low beamed ceilings, flagstone floors and a characterful dining area. Friendly, young team serve refined, flavoursome dishes created using classical techniques. Ingredients marry perfectly and the simple is turned into the sublime. Charming cottage bedrooms; some boasting outdoor jacuzzis.

Royal Oak
Frieth Rd, Bovingdon Green, West : 1.25 mi by A 4155 ⊠ SL7 2JF – ℰ (01628) 488 611 – www.royaloakmarlow.co.uk – Closed 25-26 December
Rest – Carte £ 22/29

• Part-17C, country-chic pub with herb garden, petanque pitch and pleasant terrace. Set close to the M40 and M4: an ideal London getaway. Largely British menu with the odd Asian influence.

at Little Marlow East : 3 mi on A 4155

Queens Head
Pound Ln ⊠ SL7 3SR – ℰ (01628) 482 927 – www.marlowslittlesecret.co.uk
– Closed 25-26 December
Rest – Carte £ 20/25

• 16C pub popular with walkers. Lunch menu ranges from ploughman's and fish & chips to refined dishes from the à la carte, such as scallops with black pudding. Poised, friendly service.

MARPLE – Greater Manchester – **502** N23 – pop. 23 480   **20 B3**
▪ London 190 mi – Chesterfield 35 mi – Manchester 11 mi

Springfield without rest
99 Station Rd ⊠ SK6 6PA – ℰ (0161) 449 07 21
– www.springfieldhotelmarple.co.uk
8 rm ⌁ – †£ 60 ††£ 80

• Personally run, part-Victorian house with sympathetic extensions and pleasant rural views. Bright breakfast room; individually styled bedrooms. Useful for visits to the Peak District.

MARSDEN – West Yorkshire – **502** O23 – pop. 3 499 – ⊠ Huddersfield   **22 A3**
▪ London 195 mi – Leeds 22 mi – Manchester 18 mi – Sheffield 30 mi

Olive Branch with rm
⊠ HD7 6LU – ℰ (01484) 844 487 – www.olivebranch.uk.com – Closed first 2 weeks January
3 rm – †£ 65 ††£ 80, ⌁ £ 12.50
Rest – (dinner only and Sunday lunch) Carte £ 26/41

• Characterful drovers' inn with stone floors, rustic walls, secluded garden and pleasant views from terrace. Classical, French-influenced menu supplemented by fish specials. Good choice of wines by the glass. Bedrooms are modern, cosy and individually themed.

MARSTON MEYSEY – Wiltshire   **4 D1**
▪ London 91 mi – Birmingham 82 mi – Bristol 56 mi – Coventry 85 mi

Old Spotted Cow with rm
The Street ⊠ SN6 6LQ – ℰ (01285) 810 264 – www.theoldspottedcow.co.uk
– Closed Sunday dinner
1 rm ⌁ – †£ 45/55 ††£ 75/95   **Rest** – Carte £ 19/28

• Enthusiastically run country pub serving seasonal, rustic cooking, which combines hearty British classics with worldly spices. Sunday roasts, summer barbecues and monthly spice nights. One comfortable, contemporary bedroom.

MARTINHOE – Devon – see Lynton

MARTON – Shropshire – Great Britain   18 A1
▶ London 174 mi – Birmingham 57 mi – Shrewsbury 16 mi
◉ Powis Castle★★★, NW : 7 mi by B 4386 and A 490

Sun Inn
⊠ SY21 8JP – ℰ (01938) 561 211 – www.suninn.org.uk – *Closed lunch Monday-Tuesday and dinner Sunday*
Rest – Carte £ 22/30
• Welcoming, family-run country pub on the English-Welsh border. Pub snacks in the cosy fire-lit bar; regularly changing à la carte of classic dishes in the bright restaurant.

MASHAM – North Yorkshire – 502 P21 – pop. 1 171 – ⊠ Ripon   22 B1
▶ London 231 mi – Leeds 38 mi – Middlesbrough 37 mi – York 32 mi

Swinton Park
Swinton, Southwest : 1 mi ⊠ HG4 4JH – ℰ (01765) 680 900
– www.swintonpark.com
26 rm – †£ 105/180 ††£ 105/180 – 4 suites
Rest *Samuels* – Menu £ 25/48
• 17C castle with Georgian and Victorian additions, on a 20,000 acre estate and deer park. Luxurious, antique filled lounges. Very comfortable, individually styled bedrooms. Grand dining room with ornate gold leaf ceiling and garden views.

Bank Villa
on A 6108 ⊠ HG4 4DB – ℰ (01765) 689 605 – www.bankvilla.com
6 rm – †£ 50/60 ††£ 70/105   **Rest** – Menu £ 22 s
• Stone-built Georgian villa with Victorian additions. Two lounges and conservatory; delightful, sun-trap stepped garden. Cosy, cottagey rooms: some are in the eaves. Home-cooked menus in pastel dining room/tea room.

Vennell's
7 Silver St ⊠ HG4 4DX – ℰ (01765) 689 000 – www.vennellsrestaurant.co.uk
– *Closed first 2 weeks January, 1 week June, 1 week September, 26-30 December, Sunday dinner and Monday*
Rest – (dinner only and Sunday lunch) (booking essential) Menu £ 28 s
• Local art for sale at this personally run local eaterie with comfy basement bar. Bold, confident cooking executed with care and precision. Popular annual 'lobster week'.

MATFEN – Northumberland – 501 O18 – pop. 500   24 A2
▶ London 309 mi – Carlisle 42 mi – Newcastle upon Tyne 24 mi

Matfen Hall
⊠ NE20 0RH – ℰ (01661) 886 500 – www.matfenhall.com
53 rm – †£ 190 ††£ 190
Rest *Library and Print Room* – (dinner only) Menu £ 32 – Carte £ 45/60
• 19C country mansion built by Thomas Ruckman, master of Gothic design. Set in 500 acres with superb Grand Hall, fine paintings, plush drawing room and mix of bedroom styles. Characterful Library dining room has display of original books.

MAWGAN PORTH – Cornwall – 503 E32 – see Newquay

MEDBOURNE – Leicestershire – 504 R26   16 B2
▶ London 93 mi – Corby 9 mi – Leicester 16 mi

Homestead House *without rest*
Ashley Rd ⊠ LE16 8DL – ℰ (01858) 565 724 – www.homesteadhouse.co.uk
3 rm – †£ 36 ††£ 56
• Personally run, spotlessly kept guest house with comfortable, leather-furnished lounge and traditionally styled, homely bedrooms; two with a pleasant countryside outlook.

MELLOR – Lancashire – see Blackburn

MELTON MOWBRAY – Leicestershire – **502** R25 – pop. 25 554   **16** B2

▶ London 113 mi – Leicester 15 mi – Northampton 45 mi – Nottingham 18 mi
🛈 Nottingham Rd ✆ (01664) 48 09 92, www.goleicestershire.com
🏨 Thorpe Arnold Waltham Rd, ✆ (01664) 56 21 18

Stapleford Park
East : 5 mi by B 676 on Stapleford rd ✉ *LE14 2EF*
– ✆ (01572) 787 000 – www.staplefordpark.com
52 rm ⌂ – †£ 140/288 ††£ 140/288 – 3 suites
Rest *Grinling Gibbons Dining Room* – *(closed dinner Sunday-Tuesday)*
(booking essential) Menu £ 24/47
♦ Astoundingly beautiful stately home in 500 glorious acres, exuding a grandeur rarely surpassed. Extensive leisure facilities; uniquely designed rooms of sumptuous elegance. Ornate rococo dining room a superb example of master craftsman's work.

at Stathern North : 8 mi by A 607 – ✉ Melton Mowbray

Red Lion Inn
2 Red Lion St ✉ *LE14 4HS* – ✆ *(01949) 860 868 – www.theredlioninn.co.uk*
– Closed Sunday dinner
Rest – *(booking essential)* Menu £ 17 (lunch) – Carte £ 19/28
♦ Large, whitewashed village pub. Menus offer straightforward cooking and refined pub classics with the odd international twist. Produce is sourced from their allotment and local suppliers.

MEVAGISSEY – Cornwall – **503** F33 – pop. 2 221   **1** B3

▶ London 287 mi – Newquay 21 mi – Plymouth 44 mi – Truro 20 mi
◉ Town ★★
◉ NW : Lost Gardens of Heligan ★

Trevalsa Court
School Hill, East : 0.5 mi on B 3273 (St Austell rd) ✉ *PL26 6TH* – ✆ *(01726) 842 468 – www.trevalsa-hotel.co.uk – Closed January and December*
14 rm ⌂ – †£ 80/95 ††£ 215/235   **Rest** – *(dinner only)* Carte £ 25/36
♦ Charming Arts and Crafts style house combines dark wood panelling with bright modern art and bold soft furnishings. Well-appointed bedrooms; most with coastal views. Oak-panelled dining room looks onto terrace and garden; short, set price dinner menu.

MICKLETON – Gloucestershire – **503** O27 – see Chipping Campden

MIDDLEHAM – North Yorkshire – **502** O21 – pop. 754   **22** B1

▶ London 233 mi – Kendal 45 mi – Leeds 47 mi – Newcastle upon Tyne 63 mi

at Carlton-in-Coverdale Southwest : 4.5 mi by Coverham rd – ✉ Leyburn

Abbots Thorn without rest
✉ *DL8 4AY –* ✆ *(01969) 640 620 – www.abbotsthorn.co.uk*
– February-November
3 rm ⌂ – †£ 60 ††£ 75
♦ Well priced, comfortable, quiet guesthouse in attractive rural village. Handy for visits to Moors. Cosy sitting room. Sizeable bedrooms which are homely and well-kept.

MIDDLETON-IN-TEESDALE – Durham – **502** N20 – pop. 1 143   **24** A3

▶ London 447 mi – Carlisle 91 mi – Leeds 124 mi – Middlesbrough 70 mi
🛈 10 Market Pl ✆ (01833) 64 10 01, www.middletonplus.org.uk

Grove Lodge
Hude, Northwest : 0.5 mi on B 6277 ✉ *DL12 0QW* – ✆ *(01833) 640 798*
– www.grovelodgeteesdale.co.uk
6 rm ⌂ – †£ 52 ††£ 82   **Rest** – Carte £ 16/32
♦ Victorian former shooting lodge perched on a hill where the two front facing rooms have the best views. Neat and friendly house, traditionally decorated. Home-cooked dinners are proudly served.

MIDHURST – West Sussex – **504** R31 – pop. 6 120   7 C2
- London 57 mi – Brighton 38 mi – Chichester 12 mi – Southampton 41 mi
- North St ℰ (01730) 81 73 22, www.visitmidhurst.com

Spread Eagle
South St ⊠ GU29 9NH – ℰ (01730) 816 911 – www.hshotels.co.uk
37 rm ⊇ – †£ 95 ††£ 160 – 2 suites   **Rest** – Menu £ 22/44 **s**

♦ 15C hotel retaining plenty of character in the form of antiques, gleaming brass and inglenook fireplaces. Traditional bedrooms; good leisure facilities. Formally laid restaurant offers good value set price menus; classic dishes presented in a modern style.

at Henley North : 4.5 mi by A286

Duke of Cumberland
⊠ GU27 3HQ – ℰ (01428) 652 280 – www.dukeofcumberland.com – Closed Sunday and Monday dinner
Rest – Carte £ 31/41

♦ Hidden gem with delightful, low-beamed interior, huge fireplace and tiered gardens with babbling brooks. Appealing, daily changing menu of carefully prepared, seasonal dishes. Charming service.

at Bepton Southwest : 2.5 mi by A 286 on Bepton rd – ⊠ Midhurst

Park House
⊠ GU29 0JB – ℰ (01730) 819 000 – www.parkhousehotel.com – Closed 24-26 December
20 rm ⊇ – †£ 102/116 ††£ 208/224 – 1 suite
Rest – *(booking essential at lunch)* Menu £ 27/38

♦ Comfortable country house with light, modern style and smart spa and leisure facilities. Spacious bedrooms in neutral shades; most have views of well-tended gardens and golf course; some in separate two-storey house. Stylish restaurant/conservatory offers modern menus.

at Redford West : 3 mi by A272 then following signs for Redford

Redford Cottage without rest
⊠ GU29 0QF – ℰ (01428) 741 242 – Closed Christmas and New Year
3 rm ⊇ – †£ 65/125 ††£ 95/125

♦ Charming 15C cottage in delightful gardens. Uniquely styled, attractively furnished bedrooms; china, books and pictures abound. Hearty breakfast from the Aga can be taken on the terrace.

at Trotton West : 3.25 mi on A 272

Keepers Arms
⊠ GU31 5ER – ℰ (01730) 813 724 – www.keepersarms.co.uk – Closed 25 December, Monday in winter and Sunday dinner
Rest – Carte £ 21/32

♦ Cheery, welcoming neighbourhood inn with many regular diners and a family feel. Low ceilings, an open fire and a host of quirky tables. Good value, honest cooking and an oft-changing wine list.

MID LAVANT – West Sussex – **504** R31 – see Chichester

MIDSOMER NORTON – Bath and North East Somerset – **503** M30   4 C2
- London 125 mi – Bath 11 mi – Wells 12 mi

Moody Goose at the Old Priory with rm
Church Sq ⊠ BA3 2HX – ℰ (01761) 416 784 – www.theoldpriory.co.uk – Closed Christmas-New Year, Sunday and bank holiday Monday
6 rm ⊇ – †£ 75/85 ††£ 120/145   **Rest** – Menu £ 40

♦ 12C former priory, by a church, with an enviable walled garden. Impressive interior with open bar and smart dining room, featuring solid stone floors, beams and vast fireplaces. Classical French cooking utilises quality seasonal ingredients. Warm, comfy bedrooms.

MILFIELD – Northumberland 24 A1

▶ London 336 mi – Glasgow 118 mi – Edinburgh 72 mi – Aberdeen 204 mi

Red Lion Inn with rm
Main Rd ✉ *NE71 6JD* – ℘ *(01668) 216 224* – www.redlioninn-milfield.co.uk
2 rm – †£ 25 ††£ 50 **Rest** – *(booking advisable)* Carte £ 18/25

♦ Close to the border, a former coaching inn that plays a large part in the local community. Inside it has a traditional look matched by a classic menu which makes good use of the larders of both Scotland and England – you won't leave hungry. Simple, functional bedrooms.

MILFORD-ON-SEA – Hampshire – 503 P31 – pop. 4 229 6 A3
– ✉ Lymington

▶ London 109 mi – Bournemouth 15 mi – Southampton 24 mi – Winchester 37 mi

Westover Hall
Park Ln ✉ *SO41 0PT* – ℘ *(01590) 643 044* – www.westoverhallhotel.com
11 rm – †£ 99/135 ††£ 120/280 – 4 suites
Rest *Vista Bistro* – Menu £ 15/25 – Carte £ 29/38
Rest *One Park Lane* – *(closed Monday-Wednesday October-May) (dinner only)* Menu £ 42

♦ Characterful 19C mansion in delightful spot overlooking the coast. Impressive hall and minstrels gallery, comfortable sitting room and contemporary bedrooms. Informal Vista offers classic bistro menus. Wood-panelled One Park Lane has a formal, elegant feel.

MILLBROOK – Cornwall – 503 H32 2 C2

▶ London 235 mi – Liskeard 16 mi – Plymouth 23 mi

at Freathy West : 3 mi by B 3247, Whitsand Bay Rd on Treninnow Cliff Rd – ✉ Millbrook

View
East : 1 mi ✉ *PL10 1JY* – ℘ *(01752) 822 345* – www.theview-restaurant.co.uk
– *Closed February, Monday, Tuesday and restricted opening November-January*
Rest – Menu £ 15 *(lunch)* – Carte £ 26/33

♦ Charming and informal converted café perched on a cliff, with coastal views. Relaxed daytime vibe; more atmospheric in the evening. Assured, confident cooking and friendly service. Plenty of seafood; generous portions. Try the rustic homemade bread.

MILSTEAD – Kent – pop. 264 9 C1

▶ London 46 mi – Croydon 48 mi – Barnet 68 mi – Ealing 84 mi

Red Lion
Rawling St ✉ *ME9 0RT* – ℘ *(01795) 830 279* – www.theredlionmilstead.co.uk
– *Closed Sunday and Monday*
Rest – *(booking advisable at weekends)* Carte £ 24/32

♦ Simple, cosy country pub, personally run by an experienced couple. Ever-changing blackboard menu offers French-influenced country cooking. Dishes are honest, wholesome and richly flavoured.

MILTON ABBOT – Devon – 503 H32 – see Tavistock

MILTON KEYNES – Milton Keynes – 504 R27 – pop. 156 148 11 C1

▶ London 56 mi – Bedford 16 mi – Birmingham 72 mi – Northampton 18 mi

🛈 The Chapel, The Knoll, Newport Pagnell ℘ (01908) 614 6 38, www.destinationmiltonkeynes.co.uk

🏌 Abbey Hill Two Mile Ash Monks Way, ℘ (01908) 56 38 45

🏌 Tattenhoe Bletchley Tattenhoe Lane, ℘ (01908) 63 11 13

🏌 Wavendon Golf Centre Wavendon Lower End Rd, ℘ (01908) 28 18 11

Plans on following pages

HORIZONTAL ROADS

Bletcham Way (H10)	**CX**
Chaffron Way (H7)	**BX, CV**
Childs Way (H6)	**BX, CV**
Dansteed Way (H4)	**ABV**
Groveway (H9)	**CVX**
Millers Way (H2)	**AV**
Monks Way (H3)	**ABV**
Portway (H5)	**BCV**
Ridgeway (H1)	**AV**
Standing Way (H8)	**BX, CV**

MILTON KEYNES

Buckingham Rd	**BX**
London Rd	**CUV**
Manor Rd	**CX**
Marsh End Rd	**CU**
Newport Rd	**BV**
Northampton Rd	**AU**
Stoke Rd	**CX**
Stratford Rd	**AV**
Whaddon Way	**BX**
Wolverton Rd	**BU**

VERTICAL ROADS

Brickhill St (V10)	**BU, CX**
Fulmer St (V3)	**ABX**
Grafton St (V6)	**BVX**
Great Monks St (V5)	**AV**
Marlborough St (V8)	**BV, CX**
Overstreet (V9)	**BV**
Saxon St (V7)	**BVX**
Snelshall St (V1)	**BX**
Tattenhoe St (V2)	**ABX**
Tongwell St (V11)	**CVX**
Watling St (V4)	**AV, BX**

ENGLAND

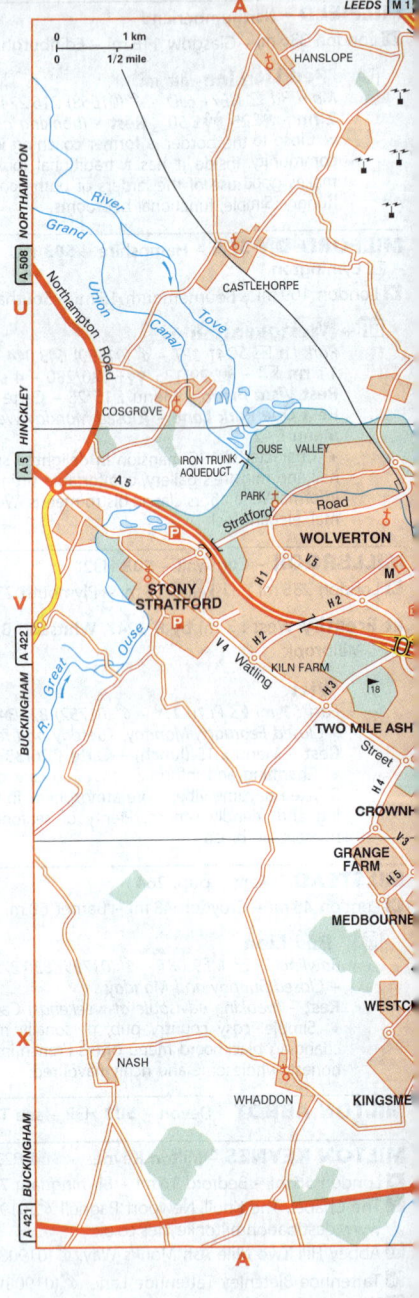

498

MILTON KEYNES

Avebury Boulevard	**EFY**
Boundary (The)	**FZ** 3
Boycott Ave	**EZ** 4
Bradwell Common Boulevard	**DEY**
Bradwell Rd	**DZ**
Brearley Ave	**EFZ**
Brill Pl.	**DY**
Burnham Drive	**DY**
Century Ave	**EFZ**
Chaffron Way (H7)	**FZ**
Childs Way (H6)	**EFZ**
Conniburrow Boulevard	**EY**
Dansteed Way (H4)	**DY**
Deltic Ave	**DY** 6
Dexter Ave	**FZ** 7
Elder Gate	**DZ** 9
Evans Gate	**EZ**
Fishermead Boulevard	**FZ**
Food Centre	**FY**
Fulwoods Drive	**FZ** 10
Gibsons Green	**DY**
Glovers Lane	**DY** 12
Grafton Gate	**DEZ**
Grafton St (V6)	**DY, EZ**
Ibstone Ave	**DEY** 13
Kirkstall Pl.	**EZ**
Leys Rd	**DZ**
Loughton Rd	**DY**
Mallow Gate	**EY** 15
Marlborough St (V8)	**FY**
Maydich Pl.	**FY**
Midsummer Boulevard	**EFY**
Oldbrook Boulevard	**EFZ**
Patriot Drive	**DY** 16
Pitcher Lane	**DZ**
Portway (H5)	**EFY**
Precedent Drive	**DY** 18
Quinton Drive	**DY**
Saxon Gate (V7)	**EY**
Saxon St (V7)	**EY, FZ**
Secklow Gate	**FY**
Silbury Boulevard	**EFY**
The Centre : MK.	**EFY**
Walgrave Drive	**DY** 19
Witan Gate	**EZ**

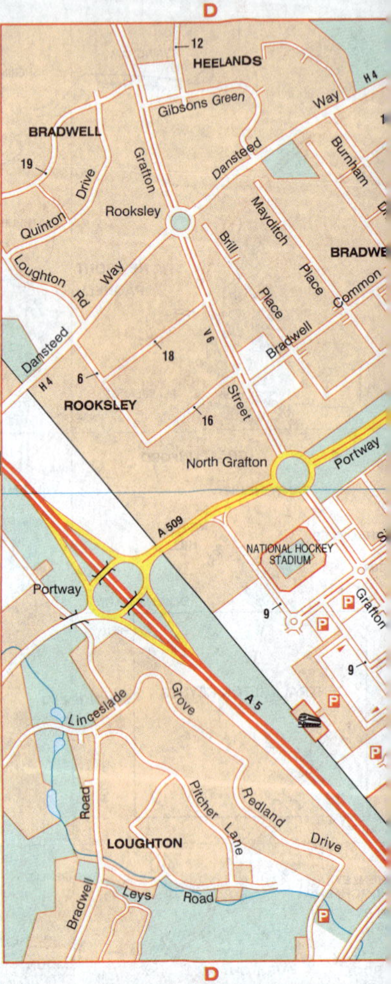

Brasserie Blanc

Chelsea House, 301 Avebury Blvd ✉ *MK9 2GA* – ✆ *(01908) 546 590*
– *www.brasserieblanc.com* **EZc**
Rest – French – *(booking essential)* Menu £ 14/16 – Carte £ 22/47
♦ Striking modern building with a bustling trade – part of the Raymond Blanc chain. Menu features refined French brasserie dishes, mainly classics, with some house specialities.

Don't confuse the couvert rating ✗ with the stars ✿!
Couverts defines comfort and service, while stars are awarded
for the best cuisine across all categories of comfort.

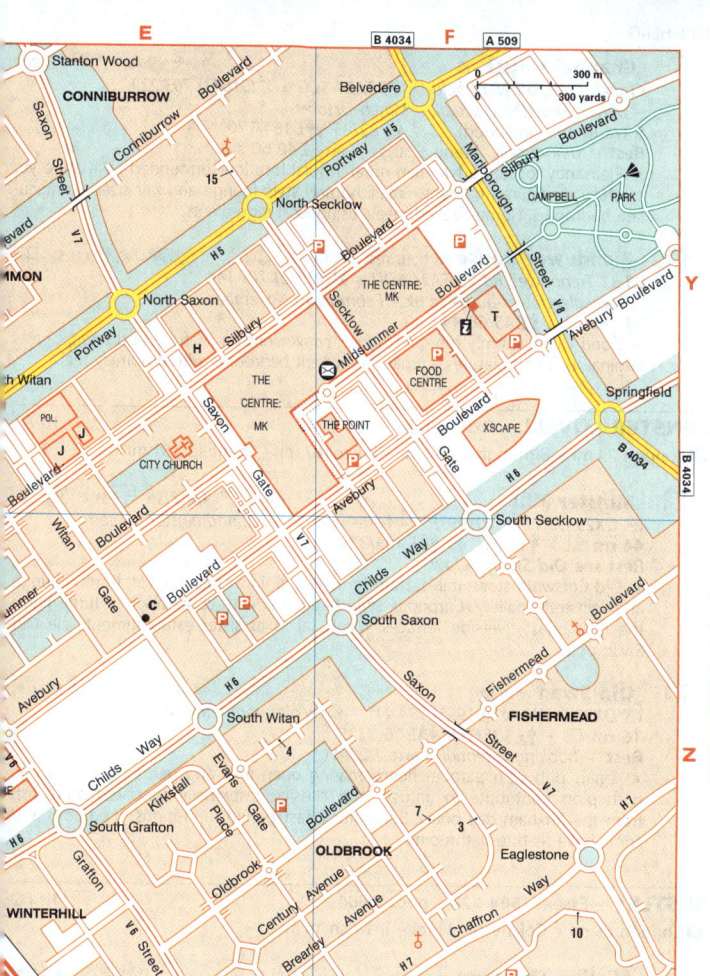

MINEHEAD – Somerset – 503 J30 – pop. 11 699 3 A2
- London 187 mi – Bristol 64 mi – Exeter 43 mi – Taunton 25 mi
- Warren Rd ℰ (01643) 70 26 24, www.visitsomerset.co.uk
- The Warren Warren Rd, ℰ (01643) 70 20 57
- Town★ – Higher Town (Church Steps★, St Michael's★)
- Dunster★★ – Castle★★ **AC** (upper rooms ≤★) Water Mill★ **AC**, St George's Church★, Dovecote★, SE : 2.5 mi by A 39
  – Selworthy★ (Church★, ≤★★) W : 4.5 mi by A 39. Exmoor National Park★★
  – Cleeve Abbey★★ **AC**, SE : 6.5 mi by A 39

MINEHEAD

Channel House
Church Path, off Northfield Dr ✉ *TA24 5QG* – ℰ *(01643) 703 229*
– *www.channelhouse.co.uk* – *March-October*
8 rm (dinner included) – ♦£ 82/85 ♦♦£ 164/170
Rest – *(dinner only)* Menu £ 30 **s** – Carte £ 40/60 **s**
♦ Pleasantly located Edwardian hotel in rural location surrounded by mature yet carefully manicured gardens. Small, homely style lounge and fair sized, immaculate bedrooms. Home-cooked meals using local ingredients.

Glendower House without rest
30-32 Tregonwell Rd ✉ *TA24 5DU* – ℰ *(01643) 707 144*
– *www.glendower-house.co.uk* – *February to November*
11 rm – ♦£ 45/60 ♦♦£ 80
♦ Good value, warmly run guesthouse, convenient for seafront and town; boasts original Victorian features. Immaculately kept bedrooms with a homely feel.

MINSTER LOVELL – Oxfordshire – 503 P28   10 A2
▶ London 74 mi – Birmingham 87 mi – Bristol 67 mi – Sheffield 151 mi

Minster Mill
✉ *OX29 0RN* – ℰ *(01993) 774 441* – *www.oldswanandminstermill.com*
44 rm – ♦£ 125/145 ♦♦£ 165/325
Rest *see Old Swan below* –
♦ Old Cotswold stone mill set on the riverbank in a small hamlet. Comfy lounge and minstrels' gallery. Corporate-style bedrooms with contemporary furnishings; the best boast riverside terraces. Meals taken at sister establishment, the Old Swan pub.

Old Swan with rm
✉ *OX29 0RN* – ℰ *(01993) 774 441* – *www.oldswanandminstermill.com*
16 rm – ♦£ 125/145 ♦♦£ 165/325
Rest – *(booking essential)* Carte £ 29/41
♦ Smart pub with parquet floors, roaring open fires and garden games. Large herb plots contribute to unfussy pub classics; tasty daily specials feature fish from the Brixham day boats. Bedrooms boast period furnishings, mod cons and some have feature bathrooms.

MISTLEY – Essex – 504 X28 – pop. 1 684   13 D2
▶ London 69 mi – Colchester 11 mi – Ipswich 14 mi

Mistley Thorn with rm
High St ✉ *CO11 1HE* – ℰ *(01206) 392 821* – *www.mistleythorn.com* – *Closed 25 December*
8 rm – ♦£ 75/85 ♦♦£ 90/130
Rest – Menu £ 15 (weekday lunch) – Carte £ 19/33
♦ Passionately run pub by the river in a small coastal village. Traditional, flavoursome cooking displays American and Italian influences – a reference to the owner's childhood; fish and game frequently feature on the tempting specials list. Spacious, wood-furnished bedrooms boast modern bathrooms; two have river views.

at Bradfield East : 2 mi by B 1352

Curlews without rest
Station Rd ✉ *CO11 2UP* – ℰ *(01255) 870 890*
– *www.curlewsaccommodation.co.uk*
5 rm – ♦£ 60 ♦♦£ 95
♦ Homely guest house where traditional bedrooms boast modern bathrooms; one is self contained disabled suite; others have balconies with splendid views over farmland and the Stour Estuary.

MITTON – Lancs. – 502 M22 – see Whalley

MOBBERLEY – Cheshire East – 502 N24 – see Knutsford

MONKS ELEIGH – Suffolk – 504 W27   15 C3

▶ London 72 mi – Cambridge 47 mi – Colchester 17 mi – Ipswich 16 mi

Swan
The Street ⊠ *IP7 7AU –* ✆ *(01449) 741 391 – www.monkseleigh.com – Closed 2 weeks July, 25-26 December, Sunday dinner and Monday*
Rest – *(booking essential in summer)* Menu £ 18 – Carte £ 21/35
♦ Thatched pub with fresh, bright interior. Frequently changing, seasonal menu of generous, flavoured dishes, with the occasional Italian influence; all homemade from local produce.

MONKTON COMBE – Bath and North East Somerset – see Bath

MORECAMBE – Lancashire – 502 L21 – pop. 49 569   20 A1

▶ London 247 mi – Preston 27 mi – Blackpool 39 mi – Blackburn 34 mi

Midland
Marine Road West ⊠ *LA4 4BU –* ✆ *(01524) 424 000 – www.englishlakes.co.uk*
43 rm – †£ 94 ††£ 128/348 – 1 suite   **Rest** – Carte £ 27/42
♦ Iconic 1933 hotel set in a stunning location, with views of Morecambe Bay and the mountains. Art deco styling; original features include a listed staircase. Variously sized, starkly decorated, contemporary bedrooms. Modern restaurant offers superb outlook.

MORETONHAMPSTEAD – Devon – 503 I32 – pop. 1 380   2 C2
– ⊠ Newton Abbot

▶ London 213 mi – Exeter 13 mi – Plymouth 30 mi
🏌 Bovey Castle North Bovey, ✆ (01647) 44 50 09
🌲 Dartmoor National Park★★

White Hart
The Square ⊠ *TQ13 8NF –* ✆ *(01647) 441 340 – www.whitehartdartmoor.co.uk*
28 rm – †£ 70/79 ††£ 99/109   **Rest** – Menu £ 23 – Carte £ 29/40
♦ 17C Grade II listed former coaching inn in the town; bright and comfortable; with a cosy lounge and pleasant locals bar. Simply furnished bedrooms have modern touches; the newer ones are in the annexe. Open-style, wood-floored dining room offers classic dishes.

Higher Westcott Farm
Westcott, East : 4 mi by B 3212 on Westcott rd ⊠ *TQ13 8SU –* ✆ *(01647) 441 205 – www.higherwestcottfarm.com*
3 rm – †£ 110/120 ††£ 110/120   **Rest** – Menu £ 30
♦ Part-thatched former longhouse, up a steep, leafy lane in a tiny hamlet. Modern, boutique interior with large lounge, honesty bar and communal dining room. Bedrooms offer good facilities, smart, natural stone bathrooms and country views. Home-cooked dinners feature local, organic produce and biodynamic wines.

White Horse Inn
7 George St ⊠ *TQ13 8PG –* ✆ *(01647) 440 267 – www.whitehorsedevon.co.uk*
– Closed Sunday except bank holidays and restricted opening in winter
Rest – Carte £ 18/30
♦ Pub with rustic, flag-floored rooms and a sunny, Mediterranean-style courtyard. Tasty, unfussy dishes offer more than a hint of Italy. Thin crust pizzas baked in a custom-built oven.

ENGLAND

MORETON-IN-MARSH – Gloucestershire – 503 O28 – pop. 3 198 4 D1
Great Britain

▶ London 86 mi – Birmingham 40 mi – Gloucester 31 mi – Oxford 29 mi
◉ Chastleton House★★, SE : 5 mi by A 44

Manor House
High St ✉ GL56 0LJ – ☏ (01608) 650 501
– www.cotswold-inns-hotels.co.uk/manor
34 rm ⌂ – †£ 120/160 ††£ 175/215 – 1 suite
Rest *Mulberry* – see restaurant listing
Rest *Brasserie* – Menu £ 16 (lunch) – Carte £ 29/35

♦ Part-16C manor house in an attractive town. Smart, modern interior features various lounge and bar areas; the latter being popular for cocktails. Chic, stylish bedrooms boast bold décor and feature walls; those in the main house are largest. Sophisticated restaurant or brasserie serving classical dishes.

Old School without rest
Little Compton, East : 4 mi on A 44 ✉ GL56 0SL – ☏ (01608) 674 588
– www.theoldschoolbedandbreakfast.com
4 rm ⌂ – †£ 96/120 ††£ 120/150

♦ Attractive stone-built former school with large monkey puzzle tree and chickens in the garden. Leather-furnished sitting room with communal dining table; upstairs lounge displays exposed beams and A-frame ceiling. Bright, modern bedrooms offer a high level of facilities. Homemade cakes served on arrival.

Mulberry – at Manor House Hotel
High St ✉ GL56 0LJ – ☏ (01608) 650 501
– www.cotswold-inns-hotels.co.uk/manor
Rest – (dinner only and Sunday lunch) Menu £ 39 – Carte £ 39/55

♦ Formal restaurant with enclosed walled garden, in a part-16C manor house. French-influenced 4 course set or 8 course tasting menus. Seasonal tasting menus offers some challenging combinations.

at Bourton-on-the-Hill West : 2 mi on A 44 – ✉ Moreton-In-Marsh

Horse & Groom with rm
✉ GL56 9AQ – ☏ (01386) 700 413 – www.horseandgroom.info – Closed 1 week early January, 25 December and Sunday dinner
5 rm ⌂ – †£ 80 ††£ 175 **Rest** – (booking essential) Carte £ 21/33

♦ Charcterful Grade II listed yellow-stone building with a friendly atmosphere, set in a remote Cotswold village. Menus feature classic pub dishes; cooking is hearty, unfussy and flavoursome. Modern bedrooms, each one individually styled.

MORPETH – Northumberland – 501 O18 – pop. 13 555 24 B2
▶ London 301 mi – Edinburgh 93 mi – Newcastle upon Tyne 15 mi
ℹ Bridge St ☏ (01670) 50 07 00, www.visitnorthumberland.com
⛳ The Clubhouse, ☏ (01670) 50 49 42

at Longhorsley Northwest : 6.5 mi by A 192 on A 697 – ✉ Morpeth

Thistleyhaugh Farm
Northwest : 3.75 mi by A 697 and Todburn rd taking first right turn ✉ NE65 8RG
– ☏ (01665) 570 629 – www.thistleyhaugh.co.uk – Closed 19 December-31 January
5 rm ⌂ – †£ 70/85 ††£ 90 **Rest** – Menu £ 25

♦ Attractive Georgian farmhouse set off the beaten track on an organic farm, with the River Coquet flowing through its grounds. Many of the bedrooms boast carved wood, sleigh or cast iron beds and most have luxurious bathrooms with feature baths. Charming, welcoming owner. Beef and lamb from the farm feature at dinner.

MORSTON – Norfolk – see Blakeney

MORTON – Nottinghamshire – 504 S25   16 B1
▶ London 149 mi – Birmingham 89 mi – Liverpool 117 mi – Leeds 51 mi

Full Moon
Main St ⊠ NG25 0UT – ℰ (01636) 830 251 – www.themoonatmorton.co.uk
– Closed Sunday dinner
Rest – Carte £ 20/30 s
♦ This modernised, child-friendly pub fashioned from 3 cottages is at the heart of village life; it even holds civil ceremonies. Cooking sticks to their motto of 'big flavours and no frills'. Open for breakfast and they even do takeaway.

MOULSFORD – Oxfordshire – pop. 491   10 B3
▶ London 53 mi – Newbury 16 mi – Reading 13 mi

Beetle & Wedge Boathouse with rm
Ferry Ln. ⊠ OX10 9JF – ℰ (01491) 651 381 – www.beetleandwedge.co.uk
– Closed 1 week January
3 rm ⊡ – †£ 75 ††£ 90
Rest – *(booking essential)* Menu £ 23 (weekdays) – Carte £ 27/38
♦ Busy Thameside restaurant with charming terrace; dine in the light conservatory or more rustic char grill. Classic menu with plenty of choice, including dishes from the grill. Comfortable bedrooms in Ferryman's Cottage; some boast roll-top baths.

MOULTON – North Yorkshire – 502 P20 – pop. 197 – ⊠ Richmond   22 B1
▶ London 243 mi – Leeds 53 mi – Middlesbrough 25 mi
– Newcastle upon Tyne 43 mi

Black Bull Inn
⊠ DL10 6QJ – ℰ (01325) 377 289 – www.blackbullmoulton.com – Closed Sunday dinner
Rest – Seafood – Carte £ 32/55
♦ Set in heart of rural village; dine in bar, conservatory, beamed dining room or Brighton Belle Pullman carriage from 1932. Seafood based menu and traditional desserts.

MOUSEHOLE – Cornwall – 503 D33 – ⊠ Penzance   1 A3
▶ London 321 mi – Penzance 3 mi – Truro 29 mi
◉ Village ★
◉ Penwith ★★ – Lamorna (The Merry Maidens and The Pipers Standing Stone ★) SW : 3 mi by B 3315. Land's End ★ (cliff scenery ★★★) W : 9 mi by B 3315

Old Coastguard
The Parade ⊠ TR19 6PR – ℰ (01736) 731 222 – www.oldcoastguardhotel.co.uk
– Closed 9 January-10 February and 24-26 December
14 rm ⊡ – †£ 150/165 ††£ 200/220 **Rest** – Carte £ 22/32 s
♦ Creamwash hotel in unspoilt village with good views of Mounts Bay. Spacious lounge has sun terrace overlooking water. Modern rooms: Premier variety are best for the vista. Gutsy, unfussy dishes of local produce served in modern, open-plan restaurant.

Cornish Range with rm
6 Chapel St ⊠ TR19 6SB – ℰ (01736) 731 488 – www.cornishrange.co.uk
– Closed 2 weeks January-February
3 rm ⊡ – ††£ 80/110 **Rest** – Seafood – *(booking essential)* Carte £ 23/35
♦ Converted 18C pilchard processing cottage hidden away in narrow street. Cottagey inner filled with Cornish artwork. Excellent local seafood dishes. Very comfortable bedrooms.

MOUSEHOLE

2 Fore Street

2 Fore St ⊠ TR19 6PF – ℰ (01736) 731 164 – www.2forestreet.co.uk – Closed Monday November-early December and restricted opening in winter
Rest – Seafood – *(booking essential at dinner)* Carte £ 24/28
♦ Cosy, bright bistro in pretty harbourside setting; popular with locals and tourists. Menu based on the best of the day's catch; simple, unfussy preparation. Casual, friendly service.

MUCH HADHAM – Hertfordshire   12 B2

▶ London 44 mi – Birmingham 130 mi – Bristol 152 mi – Croydon 64 mi

Hoops Inn

Perry Green, Southeast : 2.75 mi by B1004 and Perry Green rd ⊠ SG10 6EF – ℰ (01279) 843 568 – www.hoops-inn.co.uk – Closed Sunday dinner and Monday
Rest – Carte £ 18/27
♦ Smart 19C pub in a pretty hamlet, opposite the old home of Henry Moore. Compact interior is full of character. Fresh, tasty dishes from a concise, thoughtfully compiled menu; a tasting plate of all starters is offered and pudding is a must.

MUCH WENLOCK – Shropshire – 502 M26 – pop. 1 959   18 B2
Great Britain

▶ London 154 mi – Birmingham 34 mi – Shrewsbury 12 mi – Worcester 37 mi

🄸 High St ℰ (01952) 72 76 79, www.muchwenlockguide.info

◉ Priory★ **AC**

◉ Ironbridge Gorge Museum★★ **AC** (The Iron Bridge★★ - Coalport China Museum★★ - Blists Hill Open Air Museum★★ – Museum of the Gorge and Visitor Centre★) NE : 4.5 mi by A 4169 and B 4380

at Brockton Southwest : 5 mi on B 4378 – ⊠ Much Wenlock

Feathers at Brockton

⊠ TF13 6JR – ℰ (01746) 785 202 – www.feathersatbrockton.co.uk – Closed 26 December, 1 January, Monday and lunch Tuesday
Rest – Menu £ 13/15 – Carte £ 24/30
♦ Rustic 16C pub set in prime walking country, with a snug, characterful inner and relaxing atmosphere. Traditional dishes display some Mediterranean influences and are made using locally sourced produce.

MURCOTT – Oxfordshire – pop. 1 293 – ⊠ Kidlington   10 B2

▶ London 70 mi – Oxford 14 mi – Witney 20 mi

Nut Tree (Mike North)

Main St ⊠ OX5 2RE – ℰ (01865) 331 253 – www.nuttreeinn.co.uk – Closed Sunday dinner and Monday
Rest – Menu £ 22 (weekday lunch) – Carte £ 32/49
Spec. Pan-fried terrine of pig's head and black pudding. Olive oil poached fillet of halibut with green herb risotto. Sticky toffee pudding and praline ice cream.
♦ Traditional thatched village pub owned by a local and his wife; its unassuming interior a real contrast to the quality cuisine. Menus change constantly, relying on seasonal ingredients that arrive at the door: produce is organic, free range or wild where possible. Rare breed pigs and Dexter cattle are raised out back.

NAILSWORTH – Gloucestershire – 503 N28 – pop. 5 276   4 C1

▶ London 110 mi – Bristol 30 mi – Swindon 28 mi

✕✕ **Wild Garlic**
3 Cossack Sq ⊠ GL6 0DB – ℰ (01453) 832 615 – www.wild-garlic.co.uk – Closed first week January, Sunday dinner, Tuesday lunch and Monday
Rest – Carte £ 27/39
♦ Relaxed, friendly restaurant decorated with foodie photos. Produce sourced from within 30 miles where possible. Everything made in-house, including excellent garlic-infused bread.

NANTWICH – Cheshire East – 502 M24 – pop. 13 447   20 A3

▶ London 176 mi – Chester 20 mi – Liverpool 45 mi – Manchester 40 mi
🛈 Market St ℰ (01270) 61 09 83, www.nantwich.ivisitorguide.com
🛉 Alvaston Hall Middlewich Rd, ℰ (01270) 62 84 73

Rookery Hall
Worleston, North : 2.5 mi by A 51 on B 5074 ⊠ CW5 6DQ
– ℰ (01270) 610 016 – www.handpicked.co.uk
68 rm – †£ 99/140 ††£ 136/172 – 2 suites
Rest – (dinner only and Sunday lunch) (booking essential) Carte £ 30/50 **s**
♦ 19C property set in pleasant grounds, with considerable extensions. Main building offers characterful, country house bedrooms. More modern bedrooms in purpose-built rear wing. Smart impressive spa. Formal, two-roomed, wood-panelled dining room overlooking gardens.

NETHER BURROW – ⊠ Kirkby Lonsdale   20 B1

▶ London 257 mi – Liverpool 73 mi – Leeds 101 mi – Manchester 68 mi

🍺 **Highwayman**
⊠ LA6 2RJ – ℰ (01524) 273 338 – www.highwaymaninn.co.uk – Closed 25 December
Rest – Carte £ 19/38
♦ Sizeable 18C coaching inn with open-fired, stone-floored bar and lovely terrace. Extensive menu offers hearty, rustic cooking with a familiar, comforting feel. Very seasonal, local ethos.

NETHER WESTCOTE – Gloucestershire – see Stow-on-the-Wold

NETLEY MARSH – Hampshire – 503 P31 – see Southampton

NEW MILTON – Hampshire – 503 P31 – pop. 24 324   6 A3

▶ London 106 mi – Bournemouth 12 mi – Southampton 21 mi – Winchester 34 mi
🛉 Barton-on-Sea Milford Rd, ℰ (01425) 61 53 08

Chewton Glen
Christchurch Rd, West : 2 mi by A 337 and
Ringwood Rd on Chewton Farm Rd ⊠ BH25 6QS – ℰ (01425) 275 341
– www.chewtonglen.com
48 rm – †£ 299/625 ††£ 299/625, ⊇ £ 26 – 10 suites
Rest *Vetiver* – Menu £ 25 **s** – Carte £ 35/80 **s**
♦ 19C country house in 130 acres of New Forest parkland. Luxurious bedrooms and grand suites blend the classic with the contemporary; most have terraces or balconies. Impressive leisure facilities include croquet, archery and clay pigeon shooting. Restaurant offers a choice of rooms and accomplished cooking.

NEW ROMNEY – Kent – 504 W31　　　　　　　　　　　　　　9 C2

▶ London 71 mi – Brighton 60 mi – Folkestone 17 mi – Maidstone 36 mi

Romney Bay House
Coast Rd, Littlestone, East : 2.25 mi by B 2071 ✉ *TN28 8QY* – ✆ *(01797) 364 747*
– *www.romneybayhousehotel.co.uk – Closed 1 week Christmas*
10 rm – †£ 70/95　††£ 164
Rest – *(closed Sunday, Monday and Thursday) (dinner only) (booking essential for non-residents) (set menu only)* Menu £ 45
- Beach panorama for late actress Hedda Hopper's house, built by Portmeirion architect Clough Williams-Ellis. Individual rooms; sitting room with telescope and bookcases. Enjoy drinks on terrace before conservatory dining.

NEWARK-ON-TRENT – Nottinghamshire – 502 R24 – pop. 35 454　　17 C1
■ Great Britain

▶ London 127 mi – Lincoln 16 mi – Nottingham 20 mi – Sheffield 42 mi
🏌 Coddington, Newark, ✆ (01636) 62 62 82
◉ St Mary Magdalene ★

Grange
73 London Rd, South : 0.5 mi on Grantham rd (B 6326) ✉ *NG24 1RZ*
– ✆ *(01636) 703 399 – www.grangenewark.co.uk – Closed 23 December-4 January*
19 rm – †£ 85/110　††£ 125/170
Rest *Cutlers* – *(closed Sunday dinner) (dinner only and Sunday lunch)* Carte £ 25/30
- Small, personally run hotel with tranquil landscaped garden, set in residential area not far from the town. Traditional bedrooms vary in size but all are cosy and comfy; some have four-posters. Classical menu served in restaurant, amongst antique china and cutlery.

at Caunton Northwest : 7 mi by A 616 – ✉ Newark-On-Trent

Caunton Beck
Main St ✉ *NG23 6AB* – ✆ *(01636) 636 793 – www.wigandmitre.com*
Rest – Menu £ 16 – Carte £ 23/33
- Modern looking pub with tan coloured bricks, a wrought iron pergola and large front terrace. Menus offer gutsy masculine cooking, with the odd global influence. Open from 8am for breakfast.

NEWBIGGIN – Cumbria – 502 L19 – see Penrith

NEWBURY – West Berkshire – 503 Q29 – pop. 32 675　　　　　10 B3

▶ London 67 mi – Bristol 66 mi – Oxford 28 mi – Reading 17 mi
🏌 Newbury and Crookham Greenham Common Bury's Bank Rd, ✆ (01635) 4 00 35
🏌 Donnington Valley Donnington Snelsmore House, Snelsmore Common, ✆ (01635) 56 81 40

Plans on following pages

Vineyard at Stockcross
Stockcross, Northwest : 2 mi by A 4 on B 4000 ✉ *RG20 8JU* – ✆ *(01635) 528 770*
– *www.the-vineyard.co.uk*　　　　　　　　　　　　　　　　　　　　AV**b**
34 rm – ††£ 140/325, ⊆ £ 20.50 – 15 suites　**Rest** – Menu £ 29/72
- Extended, bay-windowed former hunting lodge with striking fire and water feature. Some bedrooms have a country house style; others are more contemporary – all boast marble bathrooms. Smart, split-level restaurant with immaculately dressed tables and professional service. French-rooted menus; intricate, detailed cooking.

NEWBURY

Almond Ave	BY	3
Andover Rd	BZ	4
Bartholomew St	BZ	6
Bone Lane	BZ	10
Carnegie Rd	BZ	13
Castle Grove	BY	15
Cheap St	BZ	16
Chesterfield Rd	BZ	18
Craven Rd	BZ	24
Dolman Rd	BY	25
Donnington Link	BY	27
Greenham Hill	BZ	31
Greenham Rd	BZ	33
Hambridge Rd	BZ	36
Kennett Shopping Centre	BZ	
Kiln Rd	BY	40
Kings Rd	BZ	
London Rd	BY	
Love Lane	BY	
Maple Crescent	BY	43
Market St	BZ	45
Mill Lane	BZ	
Newtown Rd	BZ	48
New Rd	BZ	46
Northbrook St	BYZ	
Northcroft Lane	BZ	
Old Bath Rd	BY	
Oxford Rd	BY	
Park Way	BYZ	50
Pound St	BZ	
Queens Rd	BZ	
Racecourse Rd	BZ	
Rockingham Rd	BZ	52
St Johns Rd	BZ	
Sandleford Link	BZ	54
Shaw Hill	BY	
Shaw Rd	BY	
Station Rd	BZ	
Strawberry Hill	BY	58
Western Ave	BY	
West St	BZ	66
Wharf St	BZ	67

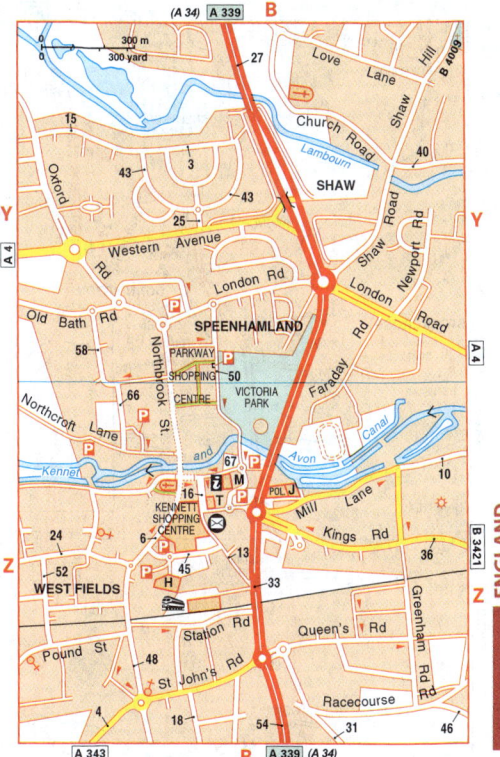

Donnington Valley H. & Spa
Old Oxford Rd, Donnington, North : 1.75 mi by A 4 off B 4494 ✉ *RG14 3AG* – ℘ *(01635) 551 199 – www.donningtonvalley.co.uk*
113 rm – †£ 99/200 ††£ 99/280, ⊇ £ 14.85
Rest *Winepress* – see restaurant listing   AVa
◆ Modern, business-orientated hotel with golf club and 18 hole course. Spacious, stylishly furnished guest areas and wine-themed bar. Smart bedrooms offer a high level of facilities; opt for 'Executive'. Excellent leisure and wellness centre.

Winepress – at Donnington Valley Hotel & Spa
Old Oxford Rd, Donnington, North : 1.75 mi by A 4 off B 4494 ✉ *RG14 3AG* – ℘ *(01635) 551 199 – www.donningtonvalley.co.uk*
Rest – Menu £ 23/28 **s** – Carte £ 33/45 **s**   AVa
◆ Intimate wine-themed restaurant in a business-led hotel. Local, seasonal produce features in both classically based and more modern dishes. Lighter 'Bar + Mezz' menu available during the day.

To make the most of your guide, look up the section 'How to use this guide' in the introduction: symbols, classification, abbreviations and other signs are explained to help you make an informed choice!

Andover Rd	**AX**	Fir Tree Lane	**AV** 30	Pinchington Lane	**AX** 51
Bath Rd	**AV** 7	Gravel Hill	**AV**	Sandleford Link	**AVX**
Benham Hill	**AV** 9	Greenham Rd	**AVX** 34	Skinners Green Lane	**AX** 55
Burys Bank Rd	**AX**	Grove Rd	**AV**	Station Rd	**AX** 57
Bussok Hill	**AV** 12	Hambridge Rd	**AV** 37	Stoney Lane	**AV**
Coombesbury Lane	**AV** 21	Lambourn Rd	**AV**	Tile Barn Row	**AX** 60
Cope Halle Lane	**AX** 22	London Rd	**AV**	Turnpike Rd	**AV** 61
Curridge Rd	**AV**	Long Lane	**AV**	Vanner's Lane	**AX** 63
Enborne Rd	**AX**	Lower Way	**AV** 42	Wantage Rd	**AV**
Enborne St	**AX**	Monks Lane	**AX**	Wash Water	**AX** 64
Ermin St	**AV**	Newtown Rd	**AVX**	Wheatlands Lane	**AX** 69
Essex St	**AX** 28	Oxford Rd	**AV** 49	Winterbourne Rd	**AV**

NEWBY BRIDGE – Cumbria – **502** L21 – ✉ Ulverston ▌ Great Britain **21** A3
► London 270 mi – Kendal 16 mi – Lancaster 27 mi
◉ Lake Windermere ★★

Lakeside
Lakeside, Northeast : 1 mi on Hawkshead rd ✉ LA12 8AT – ℘ (015395) 30 001
– www.lakesidehotel.co.uk – Closed 3-22 January
72 rm ⊇ – †£ 120/190 ††£ 280/380 – 3 suites
Rest *John Ruskins Brasserie* – see restaurant listing
Rest *Lakeview* – *(dinner only)* Menu £ 38
♦ Superbly situated on the water's edge, with great lake views from the conservatory. Very comfy, traditional guest areas. Smart, modern bedrooms; some with four-posters, feature walls or great views. Contemporary spa, leisure club and good-sized pool. Refined, formal dining room and stylish, modern brasserie.

Knoll
Lakeside, Northeast : 1.25 mi on Hawkshead rd ✉ LA12 8AU – ℘ (015395) 31 347 – www.theknoll-lakeside.co.uk – Closed 24-26 December, 31 December and 1 January
9 rm ⊇ – †£ 75/98 ††£ 90/140
Rest – *(closed Sunday and Monday)* *(dinner only)* *(booking essential for non-residents)* Menu £ 26 **s**
♦ Keenly run, late Victorian house opposite the lake, with smart interior that successfully blends classic and modern styles. Comfy, leather-furnished lounge. Good-sized bedrooms with bold décor and modern bathrooms. Simple dining room displays heart-themed art.

XX John Ruskins Brasserie – at Lakeside Hotel
Lakeside, Northeast : 1 mi on Hawkshead rd ✉ LA12 8AT – ℘ (015395) 30 001 – www.lakesidehotel.co.uk – Closed 3-22 January
Rest – *(dinner only)* Menu £ 38
♦ Stylish brasserie in a superbly situated hotel on the shore of Lake Windermere. Classical brasserie menu. Have a drink in the conservatory or on the terrace to fully appreciate the view.

ENGLAND

NEWCASTLE UPON TYNE

See city maps on following pages   24 B2

Tyne and Wear – pop. 168 075 – 501 O19 – 502 O19 – Great Britain
London 276 – Edinburgh 105 – Leeds 95

Tourist Information
8-9 Central Arcade ✆ (0191) 277 80 00, www.newcastlegateshead.com

Airport
Newcastle Airport : ✆ (0871) 882 1121, NW : 5 m. by A 696 AV

Ferries and Shipping Lines
to Norway (Bergen, Haugesund and Stavanger) (Fjord Line) (approx 26 h) – to The Netherlands (Amsterdam) (DFDS Seaways A/S) daily (15 h)

Tunnel
Tyne Tunnel (toll)

Golf Courses
Broadway East Gosforth, ✆ (0191) 285 05 53
City of Newcatle Gosforth Three Mill Bridge, ✆ (0191) 285 17 75

SIGHTS
In the town : City★ • Quayside★ CZ : Composition★, All Saints Church★ • Castle Keep★ AC CZ • Laing Art Gallery and Museum★ AC CYM1 • Great North Museum★ CYM2 • LIFE Interactive World★ CZ • Gateshead Millennium Bridge★ CZ
On the outskirts : Hadrian's Wall★★, W : by A 69 AV
In the surrounding area : Beamish : North of England Open-Air Museum★★ AC, SW : 7 mi by A 692 and A 6076 AX

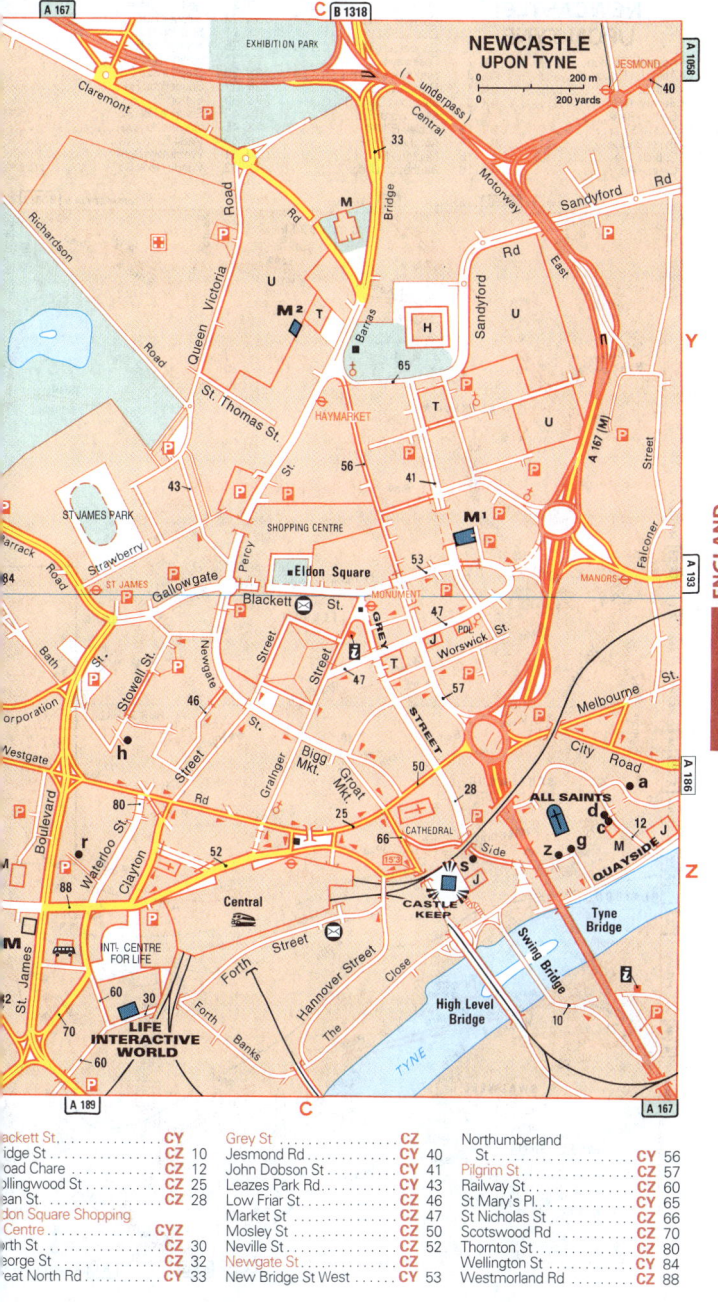

ackett St............**CY**	Grey St............**CZ**	Northumberland
idge St............**CZ** 10	Jesmond Rd............**CY** 40	St............**CY** 56
oad Chare............**CZ** 12	John Dobson St............**CY** 41	Pilgrim St............**CZ** 57
llingwood St............**CZ** 25	Leazes Park Rd............**CY** 43	Railway St............**CZ** 60
ean St............**CZ** 28	Low Friar St............**CZ** 46	St Mary's Pl............**CY** 65
don Square Shopping	Market St............**CZ** 47	St Nicholas St............**CZ** 66
Centre............**CYZ**	Mosley St............**CZ** 50	Scotswood Rd............**CZ** 70
rth St............**CZ** 30	Neville St............**CZ** 52	Thornton St............**CZ** 80
eorge St............**CZ** 32	Newgate St............**CZ**	Wellington St............**CY** 84
eat North Rd............**CY** 33	New Bridge St West............**CY** 53	Westmorland Rd............**CZ** 88

513

NEWCASTLE-UPON-TYNE

Adelaide Terrace	**AX** 2
Atkinson Rd	**AX** 3
Bath St	**BX** 4
Bensham Rd	**AX** 6
Benton Bank	**BV** 8
Buddle St	**BV** 13
Byker Bridge	**BV** 15
Church Ave	**AV** 16
Church Rd	**AV** 18
Clayton Rd	**BV** 21
Coldwell Lane	**BX** 22
Coldwell St	**BX** 24
Condercum Rd	**AX** 26
Fossway	**BV** 31
Haddrick's Mill Rd	**BV** 36
High St West	**BV** 37
Jesmond Dene Rd	**BV** 39
Killingworth Rd	**BV** 42
Lobley Hill Rd	**AX** 45
Matthew Bank	**BV** 49
Neptune Rd	**BV** 51
Redheugh Bridge	**AX** 62
Red Hall Drive	**BV**
Saltwell Rd	**BX**
Shipdon Rd	**AX**
Springfield Rd	**AV**
Station Rd	**BX**
Stephenson Rd	**BV**
Sunderland Rd	**BX**
Sutton St	**BV**
Swalwell Bank	**ABX**
Waverdale Ave	**BV**
West Farm Ave	**BV**
Whickham Bank	**AX**
Windy Nook Rd	**BX**

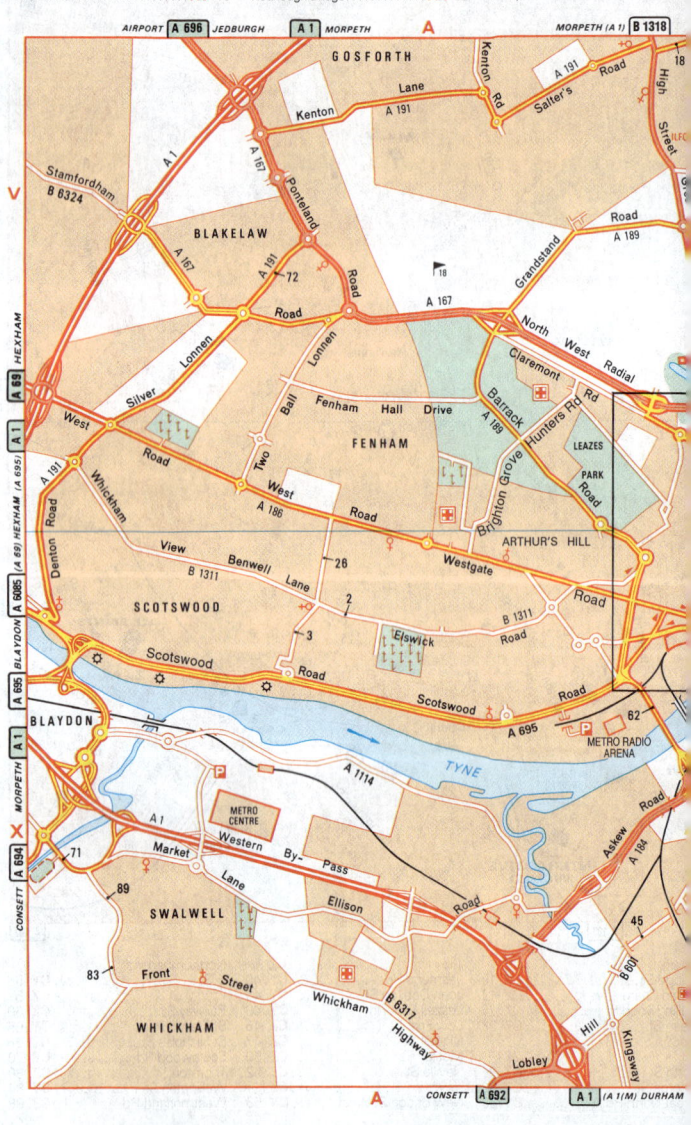

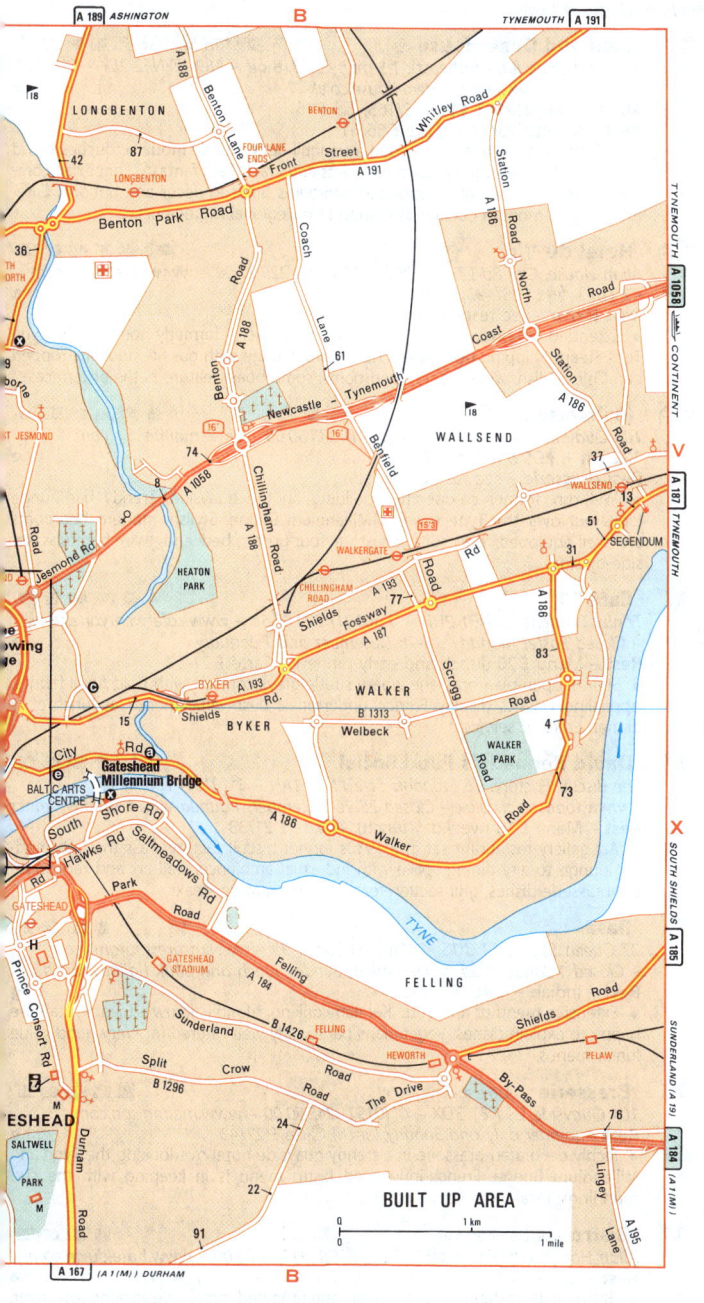

NEWCASTLE UPON TYNE

Jesmond Dene House
Jesmond Dene Rd, Northeast : 1.5 mi by B 1318 off A 189 – NE2 2EY – (0191) 212 30 00 – www.jesmonddenehouse.co.uk
BVx
40 rm – †£ 115/163 ††£ 115/163, ⊊ £ 16
Rest – Menu £ 23/27 – Carte £ 36/61

♦ 19C house attractively located in a tranquil dene. Subtle modern touches blend with period features to create a cosy, arts and crafts feel; fantastic inner hall complete with open fire. Well-appointed bedrooms differ in décor and outlook. Carefully judged modern cooking is crafted from regional ingredients.

Hotel du Vin
Allan House, City Rd – NE1 2BE – (0191) 229 22 00 – www.hotelduvin.com
42 rm – ††£ 105/495, ⊊ £ 15
BXa
Rest *Bistro* – see restaurant listing

♦ Extended red-brick building overlooking the river – formerly home to the Tyne Tees Steam Shipping Company. Characterful lounge with gas fire and zinc-topped bar. Chic, stylish, wine-themed bedrooms; some boast feature baths or terraces.

Malmaison
104 Quayside – NE1 3DX – (0191) 245 50 00 – www.malmaison.com
122 rm – †£ 99/160 ††£ 99/345, ⊊ £ 15
BXe
Rest *Brasserie* – see restaurant listing

♦ Well-run, former co-operative building on the quayside. Trendy bar-lounge looks out over the Tyne towards Millennium Bridge. Stylish, modern bedrooms are well-equipped; one suite boasts a four-poster bed and twin bathtubs set side-by-side.

Café 21
Trinity Gardens – NE1 2HH – (0191) 222 07 55 – www.cafetwentyone.co.uk
– *Closed Easter Monday, 25-26 December and 1 January*
CZa
Rest – Menu £ 20 (lunch and early dinner) – Carte £ 27/52

♦ Stylish, open-plan brasserie where subtle greys contrast with bold floral fabrics. Appealing classics display French undertones; best value menus at lunch/early dinner. Efficient service.

David Kennedy's Food Social
The Biscuit Factory, 16 Stoddart St – NE2 1AN – (0191) 260 54 11
– www.foodsocial.co.uk – *Closed 25-26 December, 1 January and Sunday dinner*
Rest – Menu £ 16 (weekday lunch) – Carte £ 21/33
BVc

♦ Art gallery restaurant set in a 1930s former biscuit factory. Pass through modish lounge to airy dining space with industrial ambience, wall art and recognisable brasserie dishes; grill section features tasty mature steaks.

Rasa
27 Queen St – NE1 3UG – (0191) 232 77 99 – www.rasarestaurants.com
– *Closed 1 January, 24-27 December, Sunday lunch and bank holiday lunch*
Rest – Indian – Carte £ 16/23
CZg

♦ Extensive menu of authentic Keralan cooking; friendly, knowledgeable staff are happy to explain dishes. Vegetarians particularly well catered for. Very good value lunch menus.

Brasserie – at Malmaison Hotel
104 Quayside – NE1 3DX – (0191) 245 50 00 – www.malmaison.com
Rest – (dinner only and Sunday lunch) Carte £ 27/43
BXe

♦ Richly decorated brasserie in a trendy quayside hotel overlooking the Tyne and Millennium Bridge. French-influenced bistro menu is in keeping with the surroundings; local ingredients feature.

Bistro – at Hotel du Vin
Allan House, City Rd – NE1 2BE – (0191) 229 22 00 – www.hotelduvin.com
Rest – Carte £ 21/35
BXa

♦ Bistro-style restaurant in a stylish wine-themed hotel overlooking the river. Classical brasserie menu name-checks suppliers on the rear. Impressive wine list and glass-fronted tasting room.

NEWCASTLE UPON TYNE

✕ Pan Haggerty   AC VISA ⓒ AE ①
21 Queen St ✉ NE1 3UG – ✆ (0191) 221 09 04 – www.panhaggerty.com
– Closed 25 December and Sunday dinner   CZ **z**
Rest – Menu £ 16 (lunch) – Carte £ 27/32
♦ Stylish, modern restaurant situated on the quayside, which appeals to both young and old alike. Mix of regional and British dishes made with locally sourced ingredients; well presented, with precise flavours.

✕ Caffé Vivo   AC ⓒ VISA AE
29 Broad Chare ✉ NE1 3DQ – ✆ (0191) 232 13 31 – www.caffevivo.co.uk
– Closed Sunday, Monday and bank holidays   CZ **d**
Rest – Italian – Menu £ 18 – Carte £ 20/36
♦ Housed within a quayside warehouse, along with a theatre. Much of the produce is imported from Italy and the Italian chefs ensure authenticity. Cooking is simple and satisfying, with dishes from Abbruzzi featuring heavily.

✕ Barn Asia   ⓒ VISA ⓒ AE
Waterloo Square, St James's Boulevard ✉ NE1 4DN – ✆ (0191) 221 10 00
– www.barnasia.com – Closed Sunday and Monday   CZ **r**
Rest – South-East Asian – *(dinner only and Friday lunch)* Carte £ 25/33
♦ Stark furnishings vibrantly decorated with interesting artwork and bright lanterns. Wide-ranging SE Asian menu offers dishes from Vietnamese classics to some Thai and Japanese.

✕ Blackfriars   ⓒ AC ⇔ VISA ⓒ AE ①
Friars St ✉ NE1 4XN – ✆ (0191) 261 59 45 – www.blackfriarsrestaurant.co.uk
– Closed Sunday dinner and bank holidays   CZ **h**
Rest – Menu £ 15 (lunch) – Carte dinner £ 22/30
♦ Late 13C stone-built monks' refectory; the split-level beamed restaurant overlooking the courtyard. Relaxed atmosphere with medieval feel and friendly service. Interesting, original menu of gutsy dishes that are firmly rooted in the region.

🍺 Broad Chare   AC ⓒ VISA ⓒ
25 Broad Chare ✉ NE1 3DQ – ✆ (0191) 211 2144 – www.thebroadchare.co.uk
– Closed 25 December and Sunday dinner   CZ **c**
Rest – *(booking advisable)* Carte £ 19/34
♦ Owned by Terry Laybourne and next to its sister, Caffé Vivo. Snug ground floor bar offers over 24 beers and a snack menu of 'Geordie Tapas'. Dine upstairs where the dish of the day is often the highlight, like steak and kidney pudding.

at Ponteland Northwest : 8.25 mi by A 167 on A 696 - **AV**
– ✉ Newcastle Upon Tyne

✕ Cafe Lowrey   AC VISA ⓒ AE
33-35 Broadway, Darras Hall Estate, Southwest : 1.5 mi by B 6323 off Darras Hall Estate rd ✉ NE20 9PW – ✆ (01661) 820 357 – www.cafelowrey.co.uk
– Closed Monday and bank holidays
Rest – *(dinner only and lunch Saturday and Sunday) (booking essential)*
Menu £ 19 (lunch) – Carte £ 26/36
♦ Small restaurant in shopping parade with wooden chairs and cloth-laid tables. Blackboard menus offering modern British cooking using local produce.

NEWICK – East Sussex – **504** U31 – pop. 2 129   **8** A2
▶ London 57 mi – Brighton 14 mi – Eastbourne 20 mi – Hastings 34 mi

🏠 Newick Park   ≤ 🚗 🐕 ③ ⌘ ✻ & rm, ⁽ᵗ⁾ ṡá P VISA ⓒ AE
Southeast : 1.5 mi following signs for Newick Park ✉ BN8 4SB – ✆ (01825) 723 633 – www.newickpark.co.uk – Closed 31 December-6 January
15 rm ☐ – †£ 125/215 ††£ 165/285 – 1 suite
Rest – *(booking essential for non-residents)* Carte £ 26/39
♦ Georgian manor in 200 acres; views of Longford river and South Downs. Stately hallway and lounge. Unique rooms, some with original fireplaces, all with Egyptian cotton sheets. Dine in relaxed formality on high-back crimson chairs.

NEWPORT PAGNELL – Milton Keynes – 504 R27 – pop. 14 739 11 C1
London 57 mi – Bedford 13 mi – Luton 21 mi – Northampton 15 mi

Plan : see Milton Keynes

Robinsons
18-20 St John St ⊠ MK16 8HJ – ✆ *(01908) 611 400*
– www.robinsonsrestaurant.co.uk – Closed 25 December, Easter, Saturday lunch, Sunday and bank holidays CUn
Rest – Menu £ 14/20 – Carte £ 35/40
♦ Smart restaurant combining exposed brick and wood floors with neutral hues and contemporary furnishings. Great value, seasonal menus display an interesting mix of British/European dishes.

NEWQUAY – Cornwall – 503 E32 – pop. 19 562 1 A2
London 291 mi – Exeter 83 mi – Penzance 34 mi – Plymouth 48 mi

Newquay Airport : ✆ (01637) 860600 Y
ℹ Marcus Hill ✆ (01637) 85 40 20, www.visitnewquay.org
Tower Rd, ✆ (01637) 87 20 91
Treloy, ✆ (01637) 87 85 54
Merlin Mawgan Porth, ✆ (01841) 54 02 22
Penhale Point and Kelsey Head★ (≤★★), SW : by A 3075 Y – Trerice★ **AC**, SE : 3.5 mi by A 392 - Y - and A 3058. St Agnes - St Agnes Beacon★★ (❋★★), SW : 12.5 mi by A 3075 - Y - and B 3285

at Watergate Bay Northeast : 3 mi by A 3059 on B 3276 – ⊠ Newquay

Fifteen Cornwall
On The Beach ⊠ TR8 4AA – ✆ *(01637) 861 000 – www.fifteencornwall.co.uk*
Rest – Italian – *(booking essential)* Menu £ 27/58 – Carte lunch £ 31/42
♦ Lively restaurant boasting fabulous bay views – a registered charity as well as Jamie Oliver's training academy. Unfussy Italian menus feature homemade bread and pasta, olives and oils imported from Italy and other ingredients sourced nearby. 5 course tasting menu offered at dinner; opens early for breakfast.

at Mawgan Porth Northeast : 6 mi by A 3059 on B 3276

Scarlet
Tredragon Rd ⊠ TR8 4DQ – ✆ *(01637) 861 800 – www.scarlethotel.co.uk*
– Closed 2 January-2 February
37 rm ⊇ – †£ 165/415 ††£ 180/430
Rest *Restaurant* – see restaurant listing
♦ Eco-centric hotel set high on the cliff and boasting stunning coastal views. Modern bar or lounges for relaxing and great spa offering extensive treatments. Bedrooms range from 'Just Right' to 'Indulgent' and have a cool, Scandic style and unusual open-plan bathrooms – every room has a terrace and sea view.

Restaurant – at Scarlet Hotel
Tredragon Rd ⊠ TR8 4DQ – ✆ *(01637) 861 800 – www.scarlethotel.co.uk*
– Closed 2 January-2 February
Rest – Menu £ 20/43
♦ Airy hotel restaurant with neutral hues, wood panelling and plush banquettes. Concise daily menu showcases local, seasonal ingredients and promotes small suppliers. Stunning coastal views.

NEWTON LONGVILLE – Buckinghamshire – 504 R28 – pop. 1 851 11 C1
London 52 mi – Birmingham 77 mi – Bristol 110 mi – Sheffield 126 mi

Crooked Billet
2 Westbrook End ⊠ MK17 0DF – ✆ *(01908) 373 936 – www.thebillet.co.uk*
– Closed 27-28 December, Sunday dinner and Monday lunch
Rest – *(booking advisable)* Menu £ 20/24 – Carte £ 24/41 ⁂
♦ Charming 17C thatched pub with smart yet informal interior. Modern, seasonal dishes are crafted from local produce and a 7 course tasting menu is available at dinner. Excellent wine list.

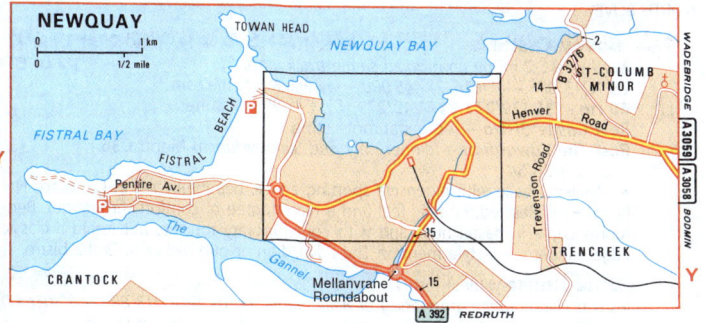

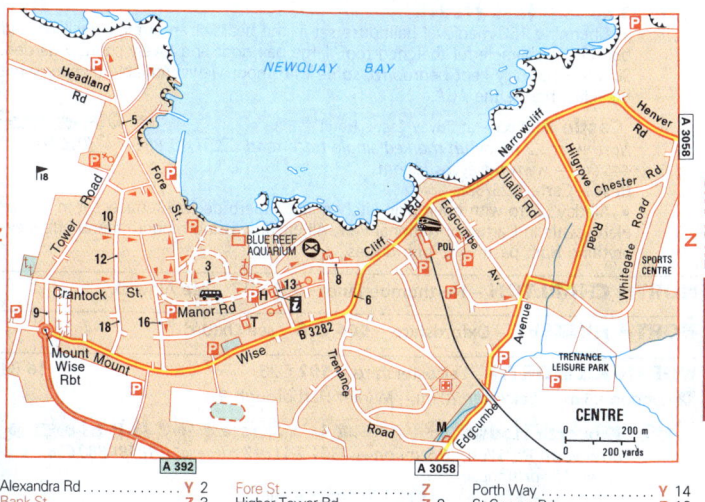

Alexandra Rd	Y 2	Fore St	Z	Porth Way	Y 14
Bank St	Z 3	Higher Tower Rd	Z 9	St George Rd	Z 16
Beacon Rd	Z 5	Hope Terrace	Z 10	St John's Rd	Z 18
Berry Rd	Z 6	Jubilee St	Z 12	Trevemper Rd	Y 15
East St	Z 8	Marcus Hill	Z 13		

NEWTON POPPLEFORD – Devon – **503** K31 – see Sidmouth

NEWTON-ON-OUSE – North Yorkshire – **502** Q22 – see York

NITON – Isle of Wight – **504** Q32 – see Wight (Isle of)

NOMANSLAND – Hampshire – **503** P31 **4 D3**

▶ London 96 mi – Bournemouth 26 mi – Salisbury 13 mi – Southampton 14 mi

Mirabelles
Forest Edge Rd ✉ SP5 2BN – ℰ (01794) 390 205 – www.lesmirabelles.co.uk
– Closed 1 week May, 22 December-13 January, Sunday and Monday
Rest – French – Menu £ 20 (except dinner Friday-Saturday) – Carte £ 28/43
♦ Bright, modern restaurant overlooking the common, enthusiastically run by a welcoming Frenchman. Well-balanced menu of classic Gallic dishes; superb wine list. Friendly atmosphere.

NORTH BOVEY – Devon – **503** I32 – pop. 254 – ✉ Newton Abbot **2 C2**

▶ London 214 mi – Exeter 13 mi – Plymouth 34 mi – Torquay 21 mi

Dartmoor National Park★★

NORTH BOVEY

Bovey Castle
Northwest : 2 mi by un-marked single track road.
✉ TQ13 8RE – ℰ (01647) 445 000 – www.boveycastle.com
60 rm – †£ 179/279 ††£ 249/279, ☑ £ 14.95 – 4 suites
Rest *Castle Bistro* – see restaurant listing
Rest *The Edwardian* – (dinner only and Sunday lunch) Menu £ 36 – Carte £ 38/54

♦ Opulent castle with extensive sporting estate, beautifully set in Dartmoor National Park. Relaxed, homely feel and a high degree of comfort throughout. Bedrooms come in pastel hues and with contemporary touches but retain a classic edge. Modern grill-style menu in The Edwardian or pub dishes in Castle bistro.

Gate House without rest
just off village green, past "Ring of Bells" public house ✉ TQ13 8RB – ℰ (01647) 440 479 – www.gatehouseondartmoor.com – Closed 24-26 December
3 rm ☑ – †£ 55 ††£ 84

♦ Charming 15C medieval hallhouse set in the heart of an attractive village and boasting a characterful thatched roof, large oak door and lovely country garden. Simple, spotlessly kept bedrooms; some with moor views. Amiable owners serve breakfast beside the AGA.

Castle Bistro – at Bovey Castle Hotel
Northwest : 2 mi by un-marked single track road. ✉ TQ13 8RE – ℰ (01647) 445 000 – www.boveycastle.com
Rest – Carte £ 25/33

♦ All-day bistro with open-plan kitchen and superb decked terrace, set in an opulent castle in Dartmoor National Park. All-encompassing modern menu offers everything from pastries to pub dishes.

NORTH CHARLTON – Northumberland – **501** O17 – see Alnwick

NORTH HINKSEY – Oxfordshire – **504** Q28 – see Oxford

NORTH KILWORTH – Leicestershire – **502** Q26   **16 B3**

▶ London 95 mi – Leicester 20 mi – Market Harborough 9 mi

Kilworth House
Lutterworth Rd, West : 0.5 mi on A 4304 ✉ LE17 6JE – ℰ (01858) 880 058 – www.kilworthhouse.co.uk
41 rm ☑ – †£ 110/150 ††£ 120/165 – 3 suites
Rest *Orangery* – see restaurant listing
Rest *Wordsworth* – (dinner only) Carte £ 35/46

♦ Impressively restored and extended Victorian mansion in 38 acres of tranquil grounds, with popular open-air theatre. Spacious, classical drawing rooms. Immaculately kept bedrooms boast luxurious bathrooms; the largest are in the main house. Traditional menus in ornate restaurant. Attractive bar and brasserie.

Orangery – at Kilworth House Hotel
Lutterworth Rd, West : 0.5 mi on A 4304 ✉ LE17 6JE – ℰ (01858) 880 058 – www.kilworthhouse.co.uk
Rest – Carte £ 26/39

♦ Charming orangery in an impressively restored Victorian mansion. Ornate wrought iron and plenty of glass make it light and airy by day and more intimate at night. Light, brasserie-style menu.

NORTH LOPHAM – Norfolk – **504** W26   **15 C2**

▶ London 98 mi – Norwich 34 mi – Ipswich 31 mi – Bury Saint Edmunds 20 mi

Church Farm House
Church Rd ✉ IP22 2LP – ℰ (01379) 687 270 – www.churchfarmhouse.org – Closed January
3 rm ☑ – †£ 50/60 ††£ 100   **Rest** – Menu £ 30

♦ Characterful thatched farmhouse with lovely garden, simple facilities, homely feel and personal touches. Individually styled bedrooms look to the church. Home cooked meals use local produce, with breakfast served outside in summer.

NORTH MOLTON – Devon – **503** I30

2 C1

▶ London 192 mi – Cardiff 118 mi – Plymouth 87 mi – Swansea 153 mi

Heasley House
Heasley Mill, Northwest : 1.25 mi by Heasley Mill rd. ✉ *EX36 3LE –* ✆ *(01598) 740 213 – www.heasley-house.co.uk – Closed February and Christmas-New Year*
7 rm – **†**£ 115 **††**£ 150/170
Rest – *(dinner only) (booking essential for non residents)* Menu £ 32

◆ Former Georgian Dower House in remote Devon village bordering Exmoor National Park. Clean, fresh style with whitewashed walls, rush matting and quirky modern artwork. Hands-on owners. Tea and cakes on arrival. Simple, wholesome cooking.

NORTH WALSHAM – Norfolk – **503** Y25 – pop. 11 845

15 D1

▌ Great Britain

▶ London 125 mi – Norwich 16 mi

◎ Blicking Hall★★ **AC**, W : 8.5 mi by B 1145, A 140 and B 1354

Beechwood
20 Cromer Rd ✉ *NR28 0HD –* ✆ *(01692) 403 231 – www.beechwood-hotel.co.uk*
17 rm – **†**£ 82 **††**£ 90/160
Rest – *(dinner only and Sunday lunch)* Menu £ 23/36

◆ Privately owned, peacefully set, part 19C hotel where Agatha Christie once stayed. Thoughtfully appointed bedrooms; newer ones are larger. Attentive service. Handsome dining room with flowers.

NORTHALLERTON – North Yorkshire – **502** P20 – pop. 15 517

22 B1

▶ London 238 mi – Leeds 48 mi – Middlesbrough 24 mi
– Newcastle upon Tyne 56 mi

🛈 Applegarth ✆ (01609) 77 68 64, www.visit-northallerton.com

at Staddlebridge Northeast : 7.5 mi by A 684 on A 19 at junction with A 172 – ✉ Northallerton

McCoys Bistro at The Tontine with rm
on southbound carriageway (A 19) ✉ *DL6 3JB –* ✆ *(01609) 882 671 – www.mccoystontine.co.uk – Closed 25-26 December and 1-2 January*
7 rm – **†**£ 100/115 **††**£ 130/140
Rest – *(booking essential)* Menu £ 20 (lunch) – Carte £ 33/53

◆ Established basement bistro with Parisian-themed décor, long wooden bar and conservatory bedecked with Indian-style parasols. Yorkshire meets France on the constantly evolving, classically based menus and steaks remain a firm favourite. Quirky modern bedrooms boast bold wallpapers and free-standing baths.

NORTHAMPTON – Northamptonshire – **504** R27 – pop. 185 255

16 B3

▌ Great Britain

▶ London 69 mi – Cambridge 53 mi – Coventry 34 mi – Leicester 42 mi

🛈 Guildhall Rd ✆ (01604) 62 26 77, www.explorenorthamptonshire.co.uk

⛳ Delapre Nene Valley Way, Eagle Drive, ✆ (01604) 76 40 36

⛳ Collingtree Park Windingbrook Lane, ✆ (01604) 70 00 00

◎ All Saints, Brixworth★, N : 7 mi on A 508 Y

Plan on next page

Dang's
205 Wellingborough Rd ✉ *NN1 4ED –* ✆ *(01604) 607 060 – www.dangs.ws – Closed 1 January, 25-26 December and Monday*

Z n

Rest – Vietnamese – *(dinner only)* Carte £ 15/40 **s**

◆ Immaculately furnished, contemporary Vietnamese restaurant. Passionately run, food is fresh, tasty, good value and mostly homemade. Noodle bowls are a speciality.

NORTHAMPTON

Street	Grid	No.
Abington Square	X	2
Abington St	X	
Bewick Rd	Y	4
Billing Rd	X	5
Bridge St	X	6
Campbell St	X	7
Castilian St	X	8
Charnwood Ave.	Y	10
Church Lane	X	12
Cliftonville Rd	Z	13
College St	X	14
Derngate	X	15
Drapery	X	18
Gold St	X	
Greyfriars	X	23
Grosvenor Centre	X	
Guildhall Rd	X	24
Hazelwood Rd	X	25
Horse Shoe St	X	28
Kettering Rd	X	30
Kingsthorpe Grove	Y	34
Lower Mounts	X	35
Oaklands Drive	Y	38
Overstone Rd	Y	39
Park Ave North	Y	40
Park Ave South	Z	43
Rushmere Rd	Z	44
St James Retail Park	X	
St Andrew's Rd	Y	45
St Edmund's Rd	X	48
St Edmund's St	Z	49
St James's Rd	Z	50
St John's St	X	51
St Leonard's Rd	Z	52
St Michael's Rd	X	53
St Peters Way Centre	X	
Sheep St	X	
Silver St	X	55
Spencer Bridge Rd	X, Z	
Towcester Rd	Z	
Upper Mounts	X, Y	
Waveney Way	Y	
Weston Favell Centre	Y	
West Bridge	X	6
Windrush Way	X	6

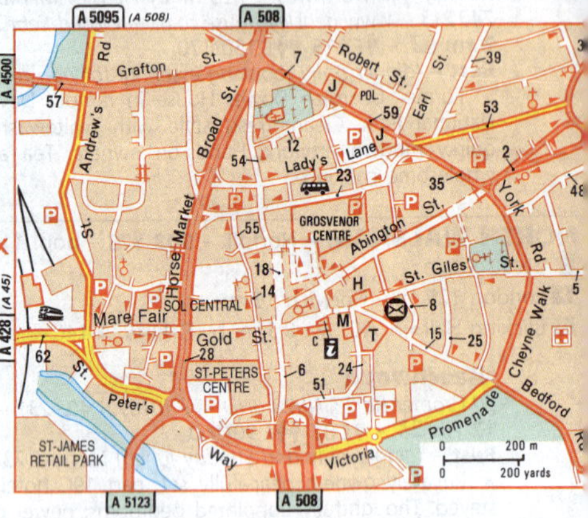

ENGLAND

NORTHAW – Hertfordshire – 504 T28

12 B2

▶ London 22 mi – Birmingham 110 mi – Bristol 134 mi – Croydon 57 mi

Sun at Northaw
1 Judges Hill ✉ *EN6 4NL* – ✆ *(01707) 655 507* – *www.thesunatnorthaw.co.uk*
– *Closed Sunday dinner and Monday*
Rest – Menu £ 18 (weekday lunch) – Carte £ 27/37
♦ Whitewashed 16C inn by village green; dine in the bar or either dining room. Hearty, traditional, flavoursome cooking uses East of England produce, and beers and ciders are equally local.

NORTHLEACH – Gloucestershire – pop. 1 923

4 D1

▶ London 87 mi – Birmingham 73 mi – Bristol 54 mi – Coventry 47 mi

Wheatsheaf Inn with rm
West End ✉ *GL50 3EZ* – ✆ *(01451) 860 244* – *www.cotswoldswheatsheaf.com*
14 rm – ♦£ 120 ♦♦£ 120/180, ⌑ £ 12
Rest – Menu £ 15 (lunch) – Carte £ 26/33
♦ Characterful 17C former coaching inn set in historic village, with stone-floored bar and open fires. Daily changing menus offer mostly pub classics; refined, flavoursome cooking.

NORTON ST PHILIP – Somerset – 503 N30 – pop. 820 – ✉ Bath

4 C2

▶ London 113 mi – Bristol 22 mi – Southampton 55 mi – Swindon 40 mi

Plaine without rest
✉ *BA2 7LT* – ✆ *(01373) 834 723* – *www.theplaine.com*
3 rm ⌑ – ♦£ 50/90 ♦♦£ 120/140
♦ Charming 16C stone cottages in a delightful village, on the site of the original market place. Snug, beamed interior with small lounge and airy breakfast room. Simple bedrooms feature fresh, colour-themed linens. Bubbly owner.

NORWICH – Norfolk – 504 Y26 – pop. 171 243 ▮ Great Britain

15 D2

▶ London 109 mi – Kingston-upon-Hull 148 mi – Leicester 117 mi – Nottingham 120 mi

✈ Norwich Airport : ✆ (0844) 748 0112, N : 3.5 mi by A 140 **V**
🛈 Millennium Plain ✆ (01603) 21 39 99, www.visitnorwich.co.uk
▮₁₈ Royal Norwich Hellesdon Drayton High Rd, ✆ (01603) 42 57 12
▮₁₈ Marriott Sprowston Manor Hotel Wroxham Rd, ✆ (0870) 4 00 72 29
▮₁₈ Costessy Park Costessey, ✆ (01603) 74 63 33
▮₁₈ Bawburgh Marlingford Rd, Glen Lodge, ✆ (01603) 74 04 04
◉ City★★ - Cathedral★★ **Y** – Castle (Museum and Art Gallery★ **AC**) **Z** – Market Place★ **Z**
◉ Sainsbury Centre for Visual Arts★ **AC**, W : 3 mi by B 1108 **X**. Blicking Hall★★ **AC**, N : 11 mi by A 140 - **V** - and B 1354 - NE : Norfolk Broads★

Plans on following pages

St Giles House
41-45 St Giles St ✉ *NR2 1JR* – ✆ *(01603) 275 180* – *www.stgileshousehotel.com*
23 rm ⌑ – ♦£ 120 ♦♦£ 130 – 1 suite   **Rest** – Carte £ 25/38   **YZo**
♦ Stylish, centrally located hotel with impressive façade, columns and wood panelling. Luxurious 'Deluxe' front suites. Rear bedrooms are quieter and more contemporary. Open-plan lounge/bar/dining room with pleasant terrace serves modern brasserie classics.

Catton Old Hall without rest
Lodge Ln., Old Catton, North : 3.5 mi by Catton Grove Rd. off St Faiths Rd.
✉ *NR6 7HG* – ✆ *(01603) 419 379* – *www.catton-hall.co.uk*
7 rm ⌑ – ♦♦£ 95/150
♦ Attractive 17C house with characterful interior. Individually designed bedrooms include 5 feature rooms; Anna Sewell, with exposed rafters and a vast four-poster, is the best.

ENGLAND

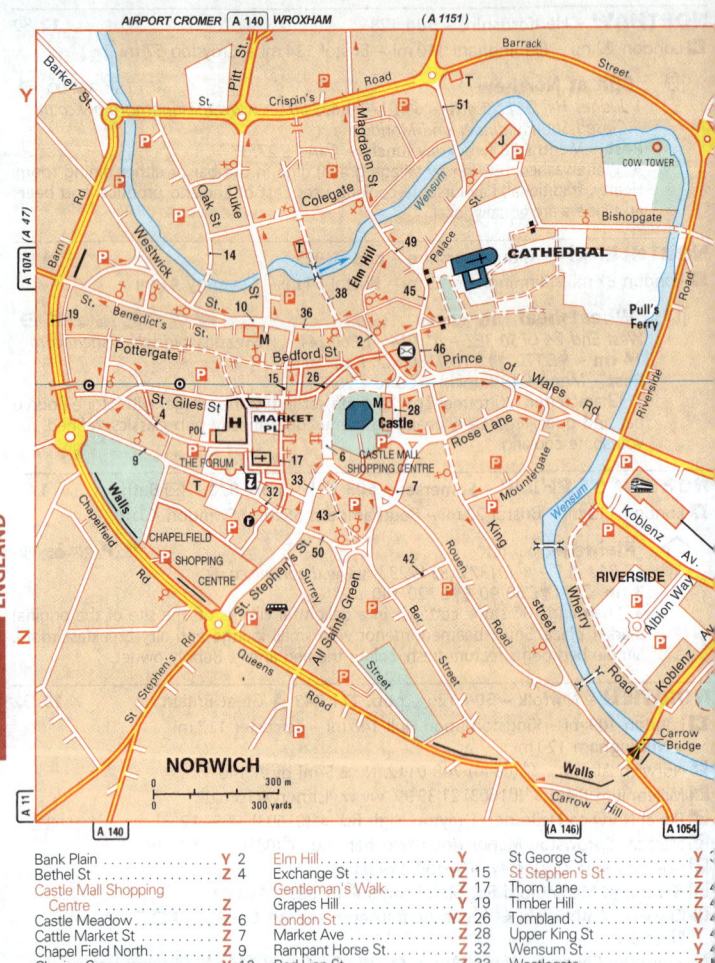

Bank Plain .... **Y** 2	Elm Hill .... **Y**	St George St .... **Y**
Bethel St .... **Z** 4	Exchange St .... **YZ** 15	St Stephen's St .... **Z**
Castle Mall Shopping	Gentleman's Walk ...... **Z** 17	Thorn Lane .... **Z**
Centre .... **Z**	Grapes Hill .... **Y** 19	Timber Hill .... **Z**
Castle Meadow .... **Z** 6	London St .... **YZ** 26	Tombland .... **Y**
Cattle Market St .... **Z** 7	Market Ave .... **Z** 28	Upper King St .... **Y**
Chapel Field North ..... **Z** 9	Rampant Horse St. .... **Z** 32	Wensum St .... **Y**
Charing Cross .... **Y** 10	Red Lion St .... **Z** 33	Westlegate .... **Z**
Coslany St .... **Y** 14	St Andrew's St .... **Y** 36	Whitefriars .... **Y**

※※ Roger Hickman's   AC VISA ⦿ AE

79 Upper St Giles St ✉ NR2 1AB – ☎ (01603) 633 522
– www.rogerhickmansrestaurant.com – Closed 1 week August, 1 week Christmas,
Sunday and Monday   **Zc**
Rest – Menu £ 20/39
♦ Traditionally styled restaurant with plenty of romantic corners. Classic combinations of ingredients presented in a distinctly contemporary style. Tasting menu available at dinner.

※ Mackintosh's Canteen   🈂 AC VISA ⦿ AE

Unit 410, Chapelfield Plain ✉ NR2 1SZ – ☎ (01603) 305 280
– www.mackintoshscanteen.co.uk   **Zr**
Rest – Menu £ 20 – Carte £ 25/33
♦ Smart modern brasserie boasting full length windows, combined with an all day terraced café: a shoppers' haven. Friendly, efficient team serve tasty, freshly prepared modern dishes.

arrack St . . . . V 3	Heigham St . . . . V 22	Mile End Rd . . . . X 29
owthorpe Rd. . . . . V 5	Ketts Hill . . . . V 23	Riverside Rd . . . . V 34
arrow Rd . . . . V 16	Lakenham Rd . . . . X 24	St Augustine's St . . . . V 37
uardian Rd. . . . . V 21	Long John Hill . . . . X 27	Waterloo Rd . . . . V 48

103

103 Unthank Rd ✉ NR2 2PE – ✆ (01603) 610 047 – www.103unthank.com
– Closed 25 December and Sunday dinner Xr
Rest – (bookings not accepted) Carte £ 28/30
♦ Popular deli/restaurant in the heart of the Golden Triangle, with open-plan kitchen, deli counter and heated pavement terrace. Daily changing menus; Mediterranean and Asian influences.

Mad Moose Arms

2 Warwick St., off Dover St. ✉ NR2 3LD – ✆ (01603) 627 687
– www.madmoose.co.uk – Closed 25 December Xn
Rest – Carte £ 21/30
♦ Attractive neighbourhood pub with busy, buzzy atmosphere and blackboard of pub favourites. More formal upstairs restaurant offers ambitious, classically based dishes with modern presentation.

at Stoke Holy Cross South : 5.75 mi by A 140 - **X** – ✉ Norwich

Wildebeest Arms

82-86 Norwich Rd ✉ NR14 8QJ – ✆ (01508) 492 497 – www.thewildebeest.co.uk
– Closed 25 December
Rest – (booking essential) Menu £ 17/22 – Carte £ 25/35
♦ Attractive pub with tree trunk tables, wild animal artefacts, a smartly furnished front terrace and a warm, friendly feel. Good value set menus and daily changing à la carte with a strong Mediterranean slant; accomplished, seasonal cooking. Well-organised service.

NOSS MAYO – Devon – **503** H33　　　　　　　　　　　　　　　　　　　　**2** C3

▶ London 242 mi – Plymouth 12 mi – Yealmpton 3 mi

◉ Saltram House★★, NW : 7 mi by B 3186 and A 379 – Plymouth★, NW : 9 mi by B 3186 and A 379

Ship Inn
✉ PL8 1EW – ☏ (01752) 872 387 – www.nossmayo.com
Rest – Carte £ 26/31

♦ Large, busy, well run pub with wonderful waterside views from its peaceful spot on the Yealm Estuary. Appealing menu of pub classics, with desserts from the tried-and-tested stable.

NOTTINGHAM – Nottingham – **502** Q25 – pop. 249 584　　　　　　　　**16** B2
Great Britain

▶ London 135 mi – Birmingham 50 mi – Leeds 74 mi – Leicester 27 mi

✈ Nottingham East Midlands Airport, Castle Donington : ☏ (0871) 9199000 SW : 15 mi by A 453 **AZ**

🛈 1-4 Smithy Row ☏ (08444) 77 56 78, www.visitnottingham.com

⛳ Bulwell Forest Hucknall Rd, ☏ (0115) 977 05 76
⛳ Wollaton Park, ☏ (0115) 978 75 74
⛳ Mapperley Central Ave, Plains Rd, ☏ (0115) 955 66 72
⛳ Nottingham City Bulwell Norwich Gardens, ☏ (0115) 927 27 67
⛳ Beeston Fields Beeston, ☏ (0115) 925 70 62
⛳ Ruddington Grange Ruddington Wilford Rd, ☏ (0115) 984 61 41
⛳ Edwalton Wellin Lane, ☏ (0115) 923 47 75
⛳ Cotgrave Place G. & C.C. Stragglethorpe Cotgrave, Nr Cotgrave Village, ☏ (0115) 933 33 44

◉ Castle Museum★ (alabasters★) **AC**, **CZ** **M**

◉ Wollaton Hall★ **AC**, W : 2.5 mi by Ilkeston Rd, A 609 **AZ** **M**. Southwell Minster★★, NE : 14 mi by A 612 **BZ** - Newstead Abbey★ **AC**, N : 11 mi by A 60, A 611 - **AY** - and B 683 – Mr Straw's House★, Worksop, N : 20 mi signed from B 6045 (past Bassetlaw Hospital) – St Mary Magdalene★, Newark-on-Trent, NE : 20 mi by A 612 **BZ**

Plans on following pages

Hart's
Standard Hill, Park Row ✉ NG1 6FN – ☏ (0115) 988 19 00
– www.hartsnottingham.co.uk　　　　　　　　　　　　　　　　　　　　**CZe**
30 rm – †£ 125 ††£ 175, ⚌ £ 14 – 2 suites
Rest *Hart's* – see restaurant listing

♦ Sophisticated, boutique-style hotel built on the ramparts of a medieval castle. Bedrooms boast superb linen and modern bathrooms; Garden Rooms come with a view. Small bar/lounge.

Lace Market
29-31 High Pavement ✉ NG1 1HE – ☏ (0115) 852 32 32
– www.thefinessecollection.com – Closed 1 week Christmas　　　　　　**DZa**
42 rm ⚌ – †£ 89/109 ††£ 119/249
Rest *Merchants* – (closed Sunday and Monday) Menu £ 15 (lunch)
– Carte dinner £ 32/41

♦ Boutique hotel situated in the old lacemaking quarter. Bedrooms are furnished in a contemporary style; those at the front, with their large windows, are the best. Minimalist, David Collins designed Merchants offers traditional dishes presented in a modern style.

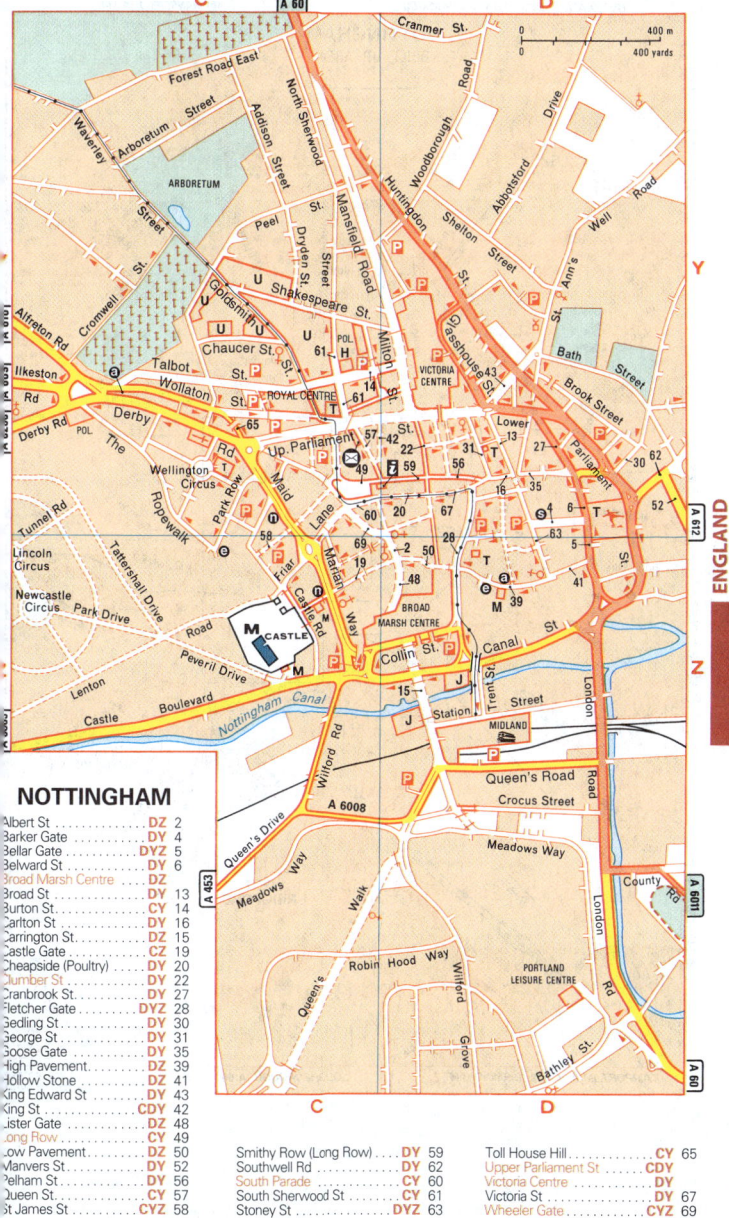

NOTTINGHAM

Street	Grid	No.
Albert St	DZ	2
Barker Gate	DY	4
Bellar Gate	DYZ	5
Belward St	DY	6
Broad Marsh Centre	DZ	
Broad St	DY	13
Burton St	CY	14
Carlton St	DY	16
Carrington St	DZ	15
Castle Gate	CZ	19
Cheapside (Poultry)	DY	20
Clumber St	DY	22
Cranbrook St	DY	27
Fletcher Gate	DYZ	28
Gedling St	DY	30
George St	DY	31
Goose Gate	DY	35
High Pavement	DZ	39
Hollow Stone	DZ	41
King Edward St	DY	43
King St	CDY	42
Lister Gate	DZ	48
Long Row	CY	49
Low Pavement	DZ	50
Manvers St	DY	52
Pelham St	DY	56
Queen St	CY	57
St James St	CYZ	58
Smithy Row (Long Row)	DY	59
Southwell Rd	DY	62
South Parade	CY	60
South Sherwood St	CY	61
Stoney St	DYZ	63
Toll House Hill	CY	65
Upper Parliament St	CDY	
Victoria Centre	DY	
Victoria St	DY	67
Wheeler Gate	CYZ	69

527

NOTTINGHAM

Restaurant Sat Bains with rm

Trentside, Old Lenton Ln ⊠ NG7 2SA – ℘ (0115) 986 65 66
– www.restaurantsatbains.com ~ Closed 3 weeks August, 2 weeks
December-January, Sunday and Monday AZn
5 rm ⊇ – †£ 114 ††£ 129/175 – 3 suites **Rest** – *(dinner only)* Menu £ 75/89
Spec. Pork belly with pearl barley, parsley and pickled turnip. Braised mutton with shallot textures, wild garlic and capers. Chocolate, yoghurt, cumin caramel and coriander.

♦ Restored farm buildings housing an intimate stone-floored dining room and conservatory. Formal atmosphere with smartly laid round tables and smooth, knowledgeable service. 7 and 10 course menus offer highly original, intricate and visually impressive dishes; bespoke lunches served for groups of 4 and more. Modern, individually furnished bedrooms.

Anoki

Barkergate ⊠ NG1 1JU – ℘ (0115) 948 38 88 – www.anoki.co.uk – Closed 25-26 December DYs
Rest – Indian – *(dinner only)* Menu £ 28 – Carte £ 24/34

♦ Elegant, modern Indian restaurant in city centre serving full flavoured, satisfying dishes cooked with vibrancy and skill. Smartly dressed staff delighted to give advice – or even a taster.

Hart's

Standard Ct., Park Row ⊠ NG1 6GN – ℘ (0115) 988 19 00
– www.hartsnottingham.co.uk – Closed dinner 25-26 December, lunch 31 December and 1 January CZe
Rest – Menu £ 18/26 (except Friday-Saturday) – Carte £ 24/50

♦ Light, contemporary restaurant in former A&E dept. of the old city hospital; sit in one of the central booths. Well-priced, flavourful, modern British dishes. Professional service.

World Service

Newdigate House, Castlegate ⊠ NG1 6AF – ℘ (0115) 847 55 87
– www.worldservicerestaurant.com – Closed 1-13 January and Sunday dinner
Rest – Menu £ 19 (lunch) – Carte £ 31/38 CZn

♦ Double-fronted Georgian property with modern extension; enter via Indonesian-inspired courtyard garden. Modern, visually appealing British dishes; excellent set price lunch. Formal service.

MemSaab

12-14 Maid Marian Way ⊠ NG1 6HS – ℘ (0115) 957 00 09
– www.mem-saab.co.uk – Closed 25 December CYn
Rest – Indian – *(dinner only)* Carte approx. £ 27

♦ Spacious restaurant dominated by a wooden copy of the Gateway of India, with some striking portraits on the walls. Authentic Indian cooking: dishes might include locally farmed ostrich.

1877

128 Derby Rd ⊠ NG1 5FB – ℘ (0115) 958 80 08 – www.restaurant1877.com
– Closed Sunday dinner and Monday CYa
Rest – *(dinner only and lunch Saturday-Sunday)* Carte £ 20/40

♦ Keenly run, contemporary restaurant set on corner site, with elegant private first floor dining room. Wholesome, tasty, modern English dishes made from seasonal, local produce.

Iberico World Tapas

High Pavement ⊠ NG1 1HN – ℘ (0115) 941 04 10 – www.ibericotapas.com
– Closed Sunday DZe
Rest – Menu £ 12 (lunch) **s** – Carte £ 25/38 **s**

♦ Lively restaurant in basement of former city jail and law courts, with vaulted ceiling and colourful Moorish tiles and fretwork. Tasty tapas menu with 'Spanish' and 'World' sections.

NOTTINGHAM

at Plumtree Southeast : 5.75 mi by A 60 - BZ - off A 606 – ✉ Nottingham

Perkins
Old Railway Station, Station Rd ✉ *NG12 5NA* – ☏ *(0115) 937 36 95*
– *www.perkinsrestaurant.co.uk* – *Closed Sunday dinner*
Rest – Menu £ 16 (lunch and early dinner) – Carte £ 28/34
♦ Former railway station; now a light, modern, airy restaurant; sit in the conservatory and watch the trains. Classically based menus include sharing boards and tureens; local produce features.

at Stapleford Southwest : 5.5 mi by A 52 - AZ - ✉ Nottingham

Crème
12 Toton Ln ✉ *NG9 7HA* – ☏ *(0115) 939 74 22* – *www.cremerestaurant.co.uk*
– *Closed 26 December-2 January, Saturday lunch, Sunday dinner and Monday*
Rest – Menu £ 15/18
♦ Smart, well run restaurant offering well-presented, modern British cooking served by friendly staff. Long lounge area with comfy sofas; airy, formally-laid dining room.

at Sherwood Business Park Northwest : 10 mi by A 611 - AY - off A 608 – ✉ Nottingham

Holiday Inn
Lake View Dr. ✉ *NG15 0DA* – ☏ *(01623) 727 670* – *www.holidayinn.com*
92 rm – †£ 129 ††£ 129, ⊑ £ 13.50
Rest *Grill* – Carte £ 25/43
♦ Situated close to the M1, in the heart of the business park. Spacious bedrooms feature exposed brickwork, king-sized beds and all mod cons; bathrooms have walk-in showers. Spacious restaurant with bar/lounge. Seasonal classics on grill-style menu.

NUNEATON – Warwickshire – 503 P26 – pop. 70 721   19 D2
▶ London 102 mi – Birmingham 25 mi – Coventry 17 mi

Leathermill Grange *without rest*
Leathermill Lane, Caldecote, Northwest : 3.5 mi by B 4114 on B 4111
✉ *CV10 0RX* – ☏ *(01827) 714 637* – *www.leathermillgrange.co.uk* – *Closed 2 weeks Christmas-New Year and 8-14 May*
5 rm ⊑ – †£ 70 ††£ 90
♦ Imposing Victorian farmhouse in peaceful rural spot. Spacious, spotless bedrooms - one four poster. Homebaking and tea on arrival. Guest lounge and conservatory with garden view.

OAKHAM – Rutland – 502 R25 – pop. 9 620 ▍ Great Britain   17 C2
▶ London 103 mi – Leicester 26 mi – Northampton 35 mi – Nottingham 28 mi
🛈 Catmose St ☏ (01572) 75 84 41, www.discover-rutland.co.uk
◉ Oakham Castle ★
◉ Rutland Water ★, E : by A 606 – Normanton Church ★ **AC**, SE : 5 mi by A 603 and minor road East

Barnsdale Lodge
The Avenue, Rutland Water, East : 2.5 mi on A 606 ✉ *LE15 8AH* – ☏ *(01572) 724 678* – *www.barnsdalelodge.co.uk*
45 rm ⊑ – †£ 90/105 ††£ 105/130
Rest *Restaurant* – see restaurant listing
♦ Collection of converted, interconnecting farm buildings set in neatly lawned gardens. Characterful guest areas with York stone flooring in lounge and bar. Individually designed bedrooms boast good facilities and a pleasant cottagey style.

OAKHAM

✗✗ **Restaurant** – at Barnsdale Lodge Hotel
The Avenue, Rutland Water, East : 2.5 mi on A 606 ✉ *LE15 8AH* – ℰ *(01572) 724 678 – www.barnsdalelodge.co.uk*
Rest – Menu £ 15 (lunch) – Carte £ 27/35
♦ Formal dining room with casual conservatory and large enclosed courtyard, set in a personally run hotel close to Rutland Water. Keen owners grow their own veg and raise their own chickens.

at Hambleton East : 3 mi by A 606 – ✉ Oakham

Hambleton Hall
✉ *LE15 8TH* – ℰ *(01572) 756 991 – www.hambletonhall.com*
16 rm – †£ 195/215 ††£ 360/420 – 1 suite
Rest – Menu £ 37/39 – Carte £ 63/80
Spec. Poached langoustine tails with asparagus. Whissendine veal with sweetbread raviolo and morel mushrooms. Pavé of chocolate and honeycomb.
♦ Beautiful red-brick Victorian manor house with mature grounds, in a peaceful location overlooking Rutland Water. Classical country house lounges and drawing rooms boast heavy drapes, open fires and antiques. Good-sized bedrooms are designed by the owner herself – who is part of the original founding family. Highly skilled cooking uses gutsy, seasonal ingredients in classic combinations.

Finch's Arms with rm
Oakham Rd ✉ *LE15 8TL* – ℰ *(01572) 756 575 – www.finchsarms.co.uk*
10 rm – †£ 75/95 ††£ 115/125   **Rest** – Menu £ 16/20 – Carte £ 21/27
♦ Attractive 17C sandstone inn boasting contemporary Mediterranean-style rooms and a large terrace with beautiful Rutland Water views. Menus feature both classic and modern British dishes. Smart, stylish bedrooms.

ENGLAND

OAKSEY – Wiltshire – **503** N29 — 4 C1
▶ London 98 mi – Cirencester 8 mi – Stroud 20 mi

Wheatsheaf at Oaksey
Wheatsheaf Ln ✉ *SN16 9TB* – ℰ *(01666) 577 348*
– *www.thewheatsheafatoaksey.co.uk – Closed Sunday dinner and Monday*
Rest – Carte £ 25/36
♦ Community pub with traditional fire-lit bar and more modern dining room. Blackboard menu of wholesome dishes with the occasional Thai influence. Appealing nursery puddings.

OARE – Kent – **504** W30 – see Faversham

OBORNE – Dorset – **503** M31 – see Sherborne

OCKLEY – Surrey – **504** S30 — 7 D2
▶ London 31 mi – Brighton 32 mi – Guildford 23 mi – Lewes 36 mi
☗ Gatton Manor Hotel G. & C.C. Standon Lane, ℰ (01306) 62 75 55

Bryce's
Old School House, Stane St, on A 29 ✉ *RH5 5TH* – ℰ *(01306) 627 430*
– *www.bryces.co.uk – Closed 25-26 December, 1 January and Sunday dinner January, February and November*
Rest – Seafood – Menu £ 16 (weekdays) – Carte £ 29/34
♦ Smart dining pub offering fresh seafood from the South Coast day boats. Choice of cheaper, simpler bar menu or more adventurous offerings and blackboard specials in the linen-laid dining room.

OFFCHURCH – Warwickshire – see Royal Leamington Spa

OLD BURGHCLERE – Hampshire – 504 Q29 – ✉ Newbury 6 B1
▶ London 77 mi – Bristol 76 mi – Newbury 10 mi – Reading 27 mi

Dew Pond
✉ RG20 9LH – ℰ (01635) 278 408 – www.dewpond.co.uk – Closed 2 weeks Christmas-New Year, Sunday and Monday
Rest – *(dinner only)* Menu £ 34
♦ Long-standing, personally run restaurant with attractive country views. Homely lounge; two dining rooms display local art for sale. Classical cooking with French influences. Friendly service.

OLD WARDEN – Central Bedfordshire – 504 S27 – pop. 275 12 A1
▶ London 51 mi – Birmingham 89 mi – Bristol 164 mi – Sheffield 134 mi

Hare & Hounds
The Village ✉ SG18 9HQ – ℰ (01767) 627 225
– www.hareandhoundsoldwarden.co.uk – Closed 26 December, 1 January, Sunday dinner and Monday except bank holidays
Rest – Carte £ 22/28
♦ Charming picture postcard pub in an idyllic village, boasting ornate barge-boards and manicured shrubs. Monthly changing à la carte offers hearty, flavoursome dishes; blackboard menu presents choices of a classic pub persuasion. Tasty homemade bread and pasta.

OLDHAM – Greater Manchester – 502 N23 – pop. 103 544 20 B2
▶ London 212 mi – Leeds 36 mi – Manchester 7 mi – Sheffield 38 mi
🏌 Crompton and Royton Royton High Barn, ℰ (0161) 624 21 54
🏌 Werneth Garden Suburb Green Lane, ℰ (0161) 624 11 90
🏌 Lees New Rd, ℰ (0161) 624 49 86

Plan : see Manchester

White Hart Inn with rm
51 Stockport Rd, Lydgate ✉ OL4 4JJ – ℰ (01457) 872 566
– www.thewhitehart.co.uk – Closed 26 December
12 rm – †£ 95 ††£ 128
Rest – Menu £ 20 (Sunday lunch) – Carte £ 26/35
♦ Stone-built inn overlooking Saddleworth Moor, boasting a large dark wood bar, exposed beams, open fires and photos of the owner's mountain travels. Good-sized menus display modern, brasserie-style dishes and a few pub classics – and at very reasonable prices. Individually styled bedrooms are furnished with antiques.

OLDSTEAD – North Yorkshire – 502 Q21 23 C2
▶ London 235 mi – Liverpool 125 mi – Leeds 54 mi – Sheffield 86 mi

Black Swan with rm
✉ YO61 4BL – ℰ (01347) 868 387 – www.blackswanoldstead.co.uk – Closed 2 weeks in January and lunch Monday-Wednesday
4 rm (dinner included) – †£ 165 ††£ 190/310
Rest – Menu £ 25 (lunch) – Carte £ 35/48
Spec. Scallops with cauliflower purée, raisins, curry and coriander. Lamb '4 ways' with Anna potatoes and baby gem lettuce. Set lemon custard with elderflower ice cream.
♦ Owned by a family who've lived and farmed here for generations. Top-rate bar meals in characterful beamed bar; more ambitious dishes in upstairs restaurant. Cooking is modern and highly skilled but satisfyingly unpretentious. Bedrooms boast modern fabrics, antiques, luxurious bathrooms and private patios.

OLTON – West Midlands – 502 O26 – see Solihull

OMBERSLEY – Worcestershire – **503** N27 – pop. 2 089 — 18 B3

▶ London 148 mi – Birmingham 42 mi – Leominster 33 mi
🏨 Bishopswood Rd, ✆ (01905) 62 07 47

✗✗ Venture In
Main St ✉ *WR9 0EW* – ✆ *(01905) 620 552 – Closed 2 weeks February, 2 weeks August, 1 week Christmas, Sunday dinner and Monday*
Rest – Menu £ 28/38
♦ Charming, restored Tudor inn, traditional from its broad inglenook to its fringed Victorian lights. Modern, flavourful menu, well judged and locally sourced. Friendly staff.

ORFORD – Suffolk – **504** Y27 – pop. 1 153 – ✉ Woodbridge — 15 D3

▶ London 103 mi – Ipswich 22 mi – Norwich 52 mi

🏨 Crown and Castle
✉ *IP12 2LJ* – ✆ *(01394) 450 205 – www.crownandcastle.co.uk*
18 rm – †£ 104 ††£ 220 – 1 suite
Rest *Trinity* – see restaurant listing
♦ Refreshingly well-run, mock-Tudor style house with relaxed yet professional service; set next to the 12C castle. Smart guest areas. Modern, individually designed bedrooms with good comforts and stylish bathrooms; some have terraces, others boast distant sea views.

✗✗ Trinity – at Crown and Castle Hotel
✉ *IP12 2LJ* – ✆ *(01394) 450 205 – www.crownandcastle.co.uk*
Rest – *(closed lunch 31 December) (booking essential at dinner)* Carte £ 27/39
♦ Relaxed dining room with red banquettes, eclectic art and chic, modern bar-lounge. Wide-ranging lunches and more sophisticated dinners; classical British puddings. Simple yet precise cooking relies on quality, seasonal ingredients. Friendly, efficient service.

ENGLAND

OSMOTHERLEY – North Yorkshire – **502** Q20 – pop. 1 217 — 22 B1
– ✉ Northallerton

▶ London 245 mi – Darlington 25 mi – Leeds 49 mi – Middlesbrough 20 mi

🍺 Golden Lion with rm
6 West End ✉ *DL6 3AA* – ✆ *(01609) 883 526*
– *www.goldenlionosmotherley.co.uk – Closed 25 December, lunch Monday and Tuesday except bank holidays*
5 rm – †£ 65/75 ††£ 90   **Rest** – Carte £ 24/33
♦ Set in a delightful village, with a warm, rustic, fire-lit interior. Staff make you feel instantly at ease; unpretentious, classic cooking leaves you relaxed, sated and satisfied. Modern bedrooms have good showers.

OSWESTRY – Shropshire – **502** K25 – pop. 16 660 — 18 A1

▶ London 182 mi – Chester 28 mi – Shrewsbury 18 mi
ℹ Mile End Services ✆ (01691) 66 24 88, www.oswestry-welshborders.org.uk
🏨 Aston Park, ✆ (01691) 61 05 35
🏨 Llanymynech Pant, ✆ (01691) 83 09 83

✗ Walls
Welsh Walls ✉ *SY11 1AW* – ✆ *(01691) 670 970 – www.the-walls.co.uk – Closed 26 December and 1 January*
Rest – Menu £ 15 – Carte £ 21/33
♦ Built in 1841 as a school; now a buzzy restaurant. High ceiling with wooden rafters; original wood flooring. Friendly atmosphere. Varied menu offers some adventurous options.

533

OSWESTRY

at Rhydycroesau West : 3.25 mi on B 4580 – ✉ Oswestry

Pen-Y-Dyffryn Country H.
✉ SY10 7JD – ℰ (01691) 653 700 – www.peny.co.uk
12 rm ⚏ – †£ 85/110 ††£ 136/164
Rest – (dinner only) (booking essential for non-residents) Menu £ 36
• Peaceful 19C listed rectory in five-acre informal gardens near Offa's Dyke. Cosy lounge, friendly ambience; good-sized, individually styled rooms, four in the coach house. Home-cooked dishes utilising organic ingredients.

OUNDLE – Northamptonshire – **504** S26 – pop. 5 219   **17** C3
– ✉ Peterborough

▶ London 89 mi – Leicester 37 mi – Northampton 30 mi
🛈 14 West St ℰ (01832) 27 43 33, www.northamptonshiretouristguide.com
⛳ Benefield Rd, ℰ (01832) 27 32 67

Oundle Mill with rm
Barnwell Rd, South : 1 mi by West St and Mill Rd ✉ PE8 5PB – ℰ (01832) 272 621 – www.oundlemill.co.uk
2 rm ⚏ – †£ 320 ††£ 320   **Rest** – Menu £ 17/21 – Carte £ 22/47
• 17C limestone watermill on the banks of the Nene. Interior fuses original features with strikingly modern new designs, including glass floors looking down to the water. Detailed modern British cooking; locally and ethically sourced produce. Well-appointed bedrooms boasts low beams and original mill workings.

at Fotheringhay North : 3.75 mi by A 427 off A 605 – ✉ Peterborough (cambs.)

Castle Farm without rest
✉ PE8 5HZ – ℰ (01832) 226 200 – www.castlefarm-guesthouse.co.uk
5 rm ⚏ – †£ 45/50 ††£ 80/90
• Large 19C wisteria-clad former farmhouse, with lawned gardens leading down to the river. Comfy open-fired lounge with country views and traditionally styled bedrooms; two are in the wing.

Falcon Inn
✉ PE8 5HZ – ℰ (01832) 226 254 – www.thefalcon-inn.co.uk
Rest – Menu £ 16 (lunch) – Carte £ 23/32
• Attractive ivy-clad inn with neat garden and terrace, set in a pretty village. Good-sized menus include unusual combinations and some interesting modern takes on traditional dishes.

OXFORD – Oxfordshire – **503** Q28 – pop. 146 692 🟢 Great Britain   **10** B2

▶ London 59 mi – Birmingham 63 mi – Brighton 105 mi – Bristol 73 mi
Access Swinford Bridge (toll)
🚢 to Abingdon Bridge (Salter Bros. Ltd) (summer only) daily (2 h)
🛈 15-16 Broad St ℰ (01865) 25 22 00, www.visitoxfordandoxfordshire.com

🔵 City★★★ - Christ Church★★ (Hall★★ **AC**, Tom Quad★, Tom Tower★, Cathedral★ **AC** - Choir Roof★) BZ – Merton College★★ **AC** BZ – Magdalen College★★ BZ – Ashmolean Museum★★ BY **M1** – Bodleian Library★★ (Ceiling★★, Lierne Vaulting★) **AC** BZ **A1** – St John's College★ BY – The Queen's College★ BZ – Lincoln College★ BZ – Trinity College (Chapel★) BY – New College (Chapel★) **AC**, BZ – Radcliffe Camera★ BZ **P1** – Sheldonian Theatre★ **AC**, BZ **T** – University Museum of National History★ BY **M4** – Pitt Rivers Museum★ BY **M3**

🟢 Iffley Church★ AZ **A**. Woodstock : Blenheim Palace★★★ (Park★★★) **AC**, NW : 8 mi by A 4144 and A 34 AY

Plans on following pages

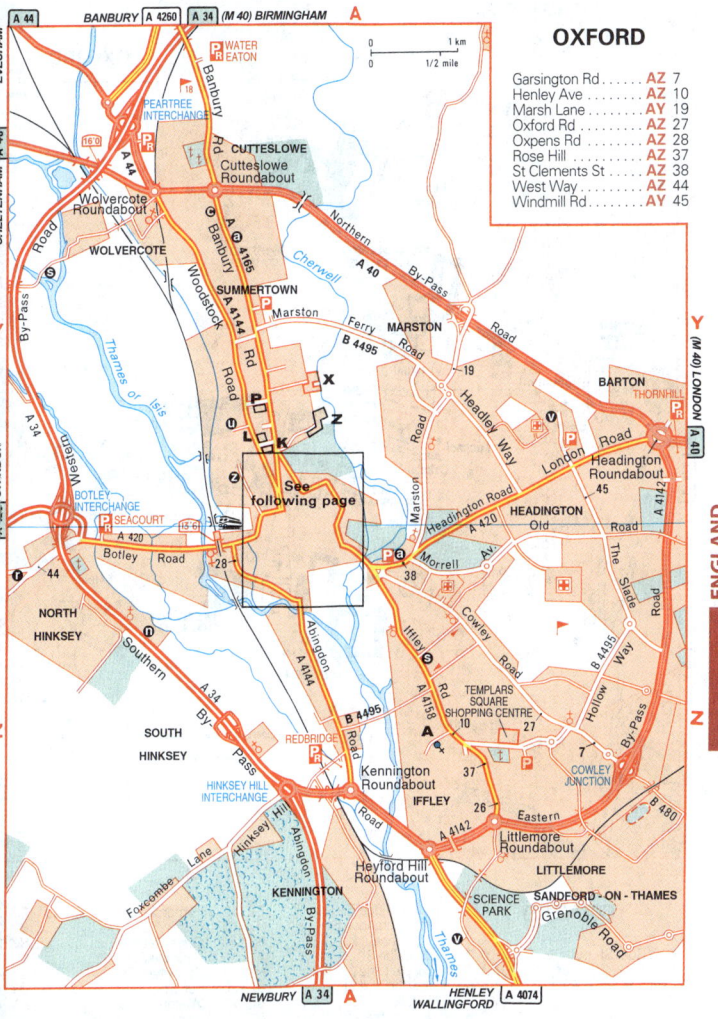

OXFORD

Garsington Rd	**AZ**	7
Henley Ave	**AZ**	10
Marsh Lane	**AY**	19
Oxford Rd	**AZ**	27
Oxpens Rd	**AZ**	28
Rose Hill	**AZ**	37
St Clements St	**AZ**	38
West Way	**AZ**	44
Windmill Rd	**AY**	45

Randolph
Beaumont St. ✉ OX1 2LN – ☎ (0844) 879 91 32
– www.macdonaldhotels.co.uk   BY**n**
142 rm – ♦£ 134/294 ♦♦£ 174/324, ☕ £ 17.50 – 9 suites
Rest *Restaurant at the Randolph* – ☎ (01865) 256 410 *(dinner only and lunch Saturday-Sunday)* Menu £ 30 – Carte £ 39/58
♦ Grand Victorian edifice. Lounge bar: deep burgundy, polished wood and chandeliers. Handsome rooms in a blend of rich fabrics; some, more spacious, have half-tester beds. Spacious, linen-clad Restaurant.

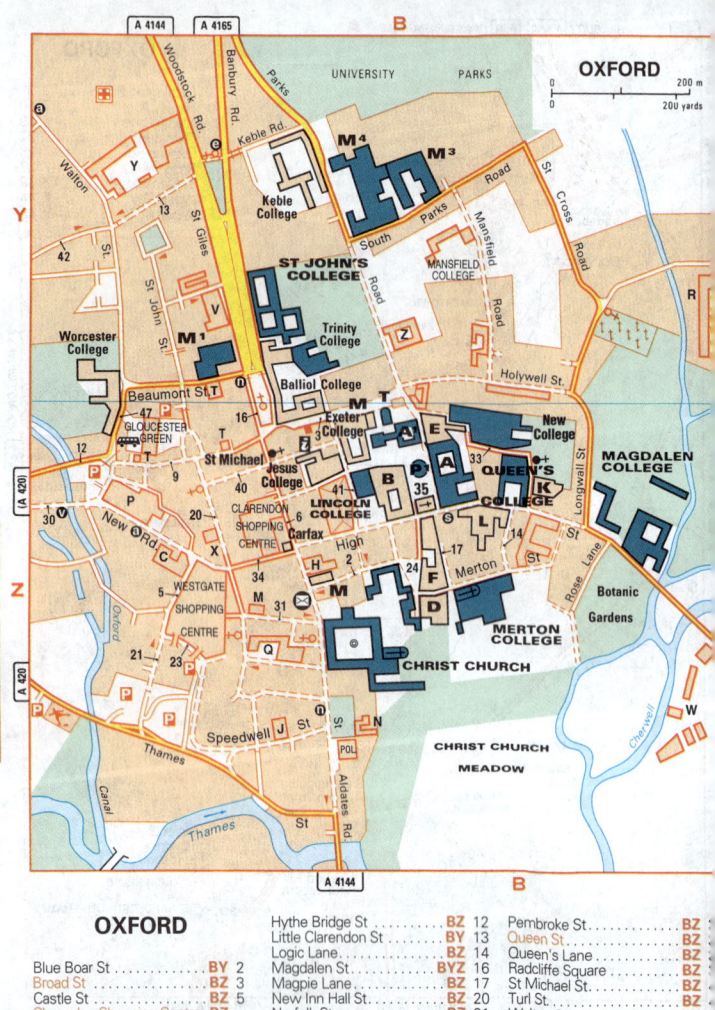

OXFORD

Blue Boar St	BY 2
Broad St	BZ 3
Castle St	BZ 5
Clarendon Shopping Centre	BZ
Cornmarket St	BZ 6
George St	BZ 9
High St	BZ
Hythe Bridge St	BZ 12
Little Clarendon St	BY 13
Logic Lane	BZ 14
Magdalen St	BYZ 16
Magpie Lane	BZ 17
New Inn Hall St	BZ 20
Norfolk St	BZ 21
Old Greyfriars St	BZ 23
Oriel Square	BZ 24
Park End St	BZ 30
Pembroke St	BZ
Queen St	BZ
Queen's Lane	BZ
Radcliffe Square	BZ
St Michael St	BZ
Turl St	BZ
Walton Crescent	BY
Westgate Shopping Centre	BZ
Worcester St	BZ

COLLEGES

All Souls	BZ A
Balliol	BY
Brasenose	BZ B
Christ Church	BZ
Corpus Christi	BZ D
Exeter	BZ
Hertford	BZ E
Jesus	BZ
Keble	BY
Lady Margaret Hall	AY Z
Linacre	BZ N
Lincoln	BZ
Magdalen	BZ
Mansfield	BY
Merton	BZ
New	BZ
Nuffield	BZ P
Oriel	BZ F
Pembroke	BZ Q
Queen's	BZ
St Anne's	AY K L
St Anthony's	AY
St Catherine's	BY R
St Cross	BY V
St Edmund Hall	BZ K
St Hilda's	BZ
St Hugh's	AY P
St John's	AY
St Peter's	BZ X Y
Sommerville	BY
Trinity	BZ
University	BZ L Z X
Wadham	BZ
Wolfson	AY X
Worcester	BY

OXFORD

Malmaison
3 Oxford Castle ⊠ *OX1 1AY* – ℰ *(01865) 268 400* – *www.malmaison.com*
92 rm – †£ 155/265 ††£ 155/265, ⊊ £ 15 – 3 suites BZ**a**
Rest *Brasserie* – see restaurant listing
♦ Unique hotel in an old 13C prison not far from the castle. Pleasant rooftop terrace contrasts with moody interior: the most characterful bedrooms are in the old A Wing Cells; feature rooms are in the Governors House and House of Correction.

Old Bank
92-94 High St. ⊠ *OX1 4BN* – ℰ *(01865) 799 599* – *www.oldbank-hotel.co.uk*
41 rm – †£ 132/255 ††£ 132/305, ⊊ £ 13.95 – 1 suite BZ**s**
Rest *Quod* – see restaurant listing
♦ Warm, welcoming hotel in the heart of the city, with smart neo-classical façade – formerly the area's first bank. Sleek, elegant bedrooms display modern furnishings and eclectic artwork; those higher up boast great views. Personable team.

Old Parsonage
1 Banbury Rd. ⊠ *OX2 6NN* – ℰ *(01865) 310 210*
– *www.oldparsonage-hotel.co.uk* BY**e**
30 rm – †£ 105/198 ††£ 133/295, ⊊ £ 14
Rest – Menu £ 18 (weekday lunch) – Carte £ 33/42
♦ Discreet address with airy, minimalist feel. Characterful guest areas include a library, richly coloured bar-lounge and terrace. Some of the bedrooms boast balconies or gardens. Afternoon tea is followed by contemporary Mediterranean dinner, with jazz on Fridays.

Remont without rest
367 Banbury Rd. ⊠ *OX2 7PL* – ℰ *(01865) 311 020* – *www.remont-oxford.co.uk*
– *Closed 17 December-5 January* AY**c**
25 rm ⊊ – †£ 75/139 ††£ 89/139
♦ Stylish hotel on outskirts of city. Crisp, contemporary bedrooms; superior rooms have sofas; rear room quietest. Light, airy breakfast room with buffet counter overlooks garden.

Burlington House without rest
374 Banbury Rd ⊠ *OX2 7PP* – ℰ *(01865) 513 513* – *www.burlington-house.co.uk*
– *Closed 20 December-6 January* AY**a**
12 rm ⊊ – †£ 66/96 ††£ 86/116
♦ Handsome former merchant's house dating from 1889, with smart lounge, Japanese courtyard and modern bedrooms (compact singles). Breakfast includes homemade bread and granola, served on blue china.

XX 4550 Miles from Delhi
40-41 Park End St ⊠ *OX1 1JD* – ℰ *(01865) 244 922*
– *www.milesfromdelhi.com/oxford* BZ**v**
Rest – Indian – Carte £ 18/30
♦ Capacious restaurant with open kitchen and friendly staff. Fantastic choice includes sizzling Tandoori specialities, Tawa dishes from the Punjab and good vegetarian selection.

XX Shanghai 30's
82 St Aldates ⊠ *OX1 1RA* – ℰ *(01865) 242 230* – *www.shanghai30s.com*
– *Closed 19 December-4 January and Monday lunch* BZ**n**
Rest – Chinese – Menu £ 11/23 – Carte £ 14/27
♦ Colonial-style restaurant in characterful 15C building; sit in more intimate wood panelled room. Menu focuses on fiery Sichuan and Shanghainese cooking. Friendly, eager staff.

XX Brasserie Blanc
71-72 Walton St. ⊠ *OX2 6AG* – ℰ *(01865) 510 999* – *www.brasserieblanc.com*
– *Closed 25 December* AY**z**
Rest – French – Menu £ 14/16 – Carte £ 21/42
♦ Busy, informal brasserie; striking interior and sharp service; French regional recipes with the new-wave touch: John Dory with coriander or ribeye steak in béarnaise.

OXFORD

XX Brasserie – at Malmaison Hotel
3 Oxford Castle ⊠ OX1 1AY – ℰ (01865) 268 400 – www.malmaison.com
Rest – Carte £ 24/45   BZa

• Basement brasserie in a unique hotel that was once a prison. Private dining rooms are in the old cells and original metal staircases remain. Modern British cooking displays French influences.

XX Quod – at Old Bank Hotel
92-94 High St. ⊠ OX1 4BN – ℰ (01865) 202 505 – www.oldbank-hotel.co.uk
Rest – Menu £ 15 (lunch) – Carte £ 20/33   BZs

• Lively Italian-influenced brasserie with busy, buzzy vibe, set within a city centre hotel and once the banking hall of the area's first bank. Accessible menu and twice-daily blackboard specials.

X Branca
111 Walton St. ⊠ OX2 6AJ – ℰ (01865) 556 111 – www.branca-restaurants.com
– Closed 25-26 December   BYa
Rest – Italian – Carte £ 19/31

• Modern restaurant with casual, friendly feel and minimalist décor. Vibrant, simple, fresh Italian influenced dishes: antipasti taster plates, pasta and pizza are specialities.

X Fishers
36-37 St Clements ⊠ OX4 1AB – ℰ (01865) 243 003
– www.fishers-restaurant.com – Closed 25-26 Decmber and 1 January
Rest – Seafood – Menu £ 20 (lunch) – Carte £ 26/33   AZa

• Well-established seafood restaurant on eastern side of city, with paper-topped tables, rustic décor and lively, informal atmosphere. Daily changing menus; friendly service.

🍺 Magdalen Arms
243 Iffley Rd ⊠ OX4 1SJ – ℰ (01865) 243 159 – Closed 2 weeks August, 24-26 December, 1 January, Sunday dinner, Tuesday lunch, Monday and bank holidays
Rest – Carte £ 26/38   AZs

• Battleship-grey pub that's a hit with the locals, boasting quirky standard lamps, eclectic 1920s posters, board games and a bar billiards table. Tasty, good value dishes rely on seasonal local produce. Delicious fresh juices and homemade lemonade.

🍺 Anchor
2 Hayfield Rd, Walton Manor ⊠ OX2 6TT – ℰ (01865) 510 282
– www.theanchoroxford.com – Closed 25-26 December   AYu
Rest – Carte £ 24/29

• Striking art deco pub with real community feel: host to a breakfast club and regular quiz nights. Chef promotes local, seasonal ingredients and creates tasty, gutsy, carefully presented dishes.

🍺 Black Boy
91 Old High St, Headington ⊠ OX3 9HT – ℰ (01865) 741 137
– www.theblackboy.uk.com   AYv
Rest – Carte £ 19/28

• Sizeable pub just off Headington village serving sensibly priced pub classics with a French edge. Homemade breads and pizzas; popular Sunday roasts. Thursday jazz night.

Symbols shown in red indicate particularly charming establishments 🏠 XxX.

at Sandford-on-Thames Southeast : 5 mi by A 4158 – ✉ Oxford

Oxford Thames Four Pillars
Henley Rd ✉ OX4 4GX – ℰ (01865) 334 444
– www.four-pillars.co.uk
AZv
62 rm – †£ 95/185 ††£ 120/240
Rest *River Room* – *(closed Saturday lunch)* Menu £ 18 (lunch) – Carte dinner £ 23/34
♦ Contemporary sandstone hotel set in 30 acres of peaceful parkland leading to the Thames. Bright Connoisseur rooms are the best; some have garden views and balconies. Lovely pool. Great outlook from The River Room, which has a formal air and serves old classics with a modern edge.

at Toot Baldon Southeast : 5.5 mi by B 480 - AZ – ✉ Oxford

Mole Inn
✉ OX44 9NG – ℰ (01865) 340 001 – www.themoleinn.com – Closed 25 December
Rest – *(booking advisable)* Carte £ 27/29
♦ Popular pub with pleasant terrace and beautiful landscaped gardens. Appealing menu suits all tastes and appetites. Sourcing is taken seriously, so when ingredients are gone, they're gone.

at Great Milton Southeast : 12 mi by A 40 off A 329 – AY – ✉ Oxford

Le Manoir aux Quat' Saisons (Raymond Blanc)
Church Rd ✉ OX44 7PD – ℰ (01844) 278 881
– www.manoir.com – Closed 3-13 January
25 rm – †£ 495/635 ††£ 635, ⊇ £ 16 – 7 suites   **Rest** – French – Carte £ 95/125
Spec. Warm salmon fillet with elderflower, garden radish and yuzu cream. Wild sea bass fillet, langoustine, smoked potato mash and star anis jus. 100% chocolate textures.
♦ Majestic property providing the ultimate guest experience: service levels are unparalleled. Sumptuous, open-fired lounges and lovely terrace. Luxurious bedrooms. Cosy restaurant and conservatory offer French-inspired cuisine using seasonal garden produce. Dishes are prepared with skill, clarity and a lightness of touch.

at North Hinksey Southwest : 3.5 mi by A 420 – ✉ Oxford

Gables without rest
6 Cumnor Hill ✉ OX2 9HA – ℰ (01865) 862 153 – www.gables-guesthouse.co.uk
– Closed 25-26 December
AZr
5 rm ⊇ – †£ 50/70 ††£ 75/90
♦ Proudly run guest house with welcoming owner and thoughtful touches in its immaculately kept rooms. Relaxing conservatory looks out onto pretty garden. Flexible arrival times.

Fishes
✉ OX2 0NA – ℰ (01865) 249 796 – www.fishesoxford.co.uk – Closed 25 December
Rest – Carte £ 20/40
AZn
♦ Lively, family-friendly pub with pretty riverside garden, perfect for picnics. Food is fresh, free range and available all day. Wednesday is steak night; Sunday means a roast.

at Fyfield Southwest : 9.5 mi by A 420 AZ – ✉ Abingdon

White Hart
Main Rd ✉ OX13 5LW – ℰ (01865) 390 585 – www.whitehart-fyfield.com
Rest – *(closed Monday except bank holidays)* Menu £ 19 (lunch) – Carte £ 25/35
♦ 15C former chantry house with cosy, open-fired bar and impressive flag-floored, vaulted dining room. Honest British cooking relies on produce from the vegetable plot; excellent desserts.

at Kingston Bagpuize Southwest : 7 mi by A 420 AZ – ✉ Oxford

Fallowfields Country House
Faringdon Rd. ✉ OX13 5BH – ℰ (01865) 820 416 – www.fallowfields.com
10 rm ⊇ – †£ 108 ††£ 175   **Rest** – Menu £ 18/49
♦ 19C manor house with lawned garden and fire-lit lounge. Spacious, individually styled bedrooms boast lovely views; most have spa baths. The elephant emblem appears throughout. Modern menus feature locally sourced produce; much is home-grown.

OXFORD

at Wolvercote Northwest : 2.5 mi by A 4144 (Woodstock Rd) on Godstow Rd

Trout Inn
195 Godstow Rd ⊠ OX2 8PN – ℰ (01865) 510 930 – www.thetroutoxford.co.uk
Rest – *(booking advisable)* Carte £ 22/30   AYs
- Idyllically set Cotswold stone inn with delightful riverside terrace. Menus display strong Italian influences, as well as more international dishes. Popular in summer, when booking is a must.

OXHILL – Warwickshire – **503** P27 – pop. 303   **19** C3
▶ London 90 mi – Banbury 11 mi – Birmingham 37 mi

Oxbourne House
⊠ CV35 0RA – ℰ (01295) 688 202 – www.oxbournehouse.com
3 rm – †£ 65 ††£ 90   **Rest** – Menu £ 30
- Large brick house in a quiet village, with lovely mature garden and tennis court to the rear. Elegant, antique-furnished lounge features a wood burning stove. Comfy, immaculately kept bedrooms offer good facilities and extras; one room is split-level. Traditionally styled communal dining room offers tasty home-cooking.

PADSTOW – Cornwall – **503** F32 – pop. 2 449   **1** B2
▶ London 288 mi – Exeter 78 mi – Plymouth 45 mi – Truro 23 mi
🛈 North Quay ℰ (01841) 53 34 49, www.padstowlive.com
⛳ Trevose Constantine Bay, ℰ (01841) 52 02 08
◉ Town★ - Prideaux Place★
◎ Trevone (Cornwall Coast Path★★) W : 3 mi by B 3276 – Trevose Head★ (≤★★) W : 6 mi by B 3276. Bedruthan Steps★, SW : 7 mi by B 3276 – Pencarrow★, SE : 11 mi by A 389

Metropole
Station Rd ⊠ PL28 8DB – ℰ (01841) 532 486 – www.the-metropole.co.uk
58 rm – †£ 118/203 ††£ 152/236   BYa
Rest – *(bar lunch Monday-Saturday)* Menu £ 16/30
- Grand 19C hotel perched on a cliff above the old railway station, just a short walk from town. Characterful, well-appointed guest areas. Smart, contemporary bedrooms; No.6 boasts great harbour and estuary views. Simply prepared lunches; more elaborate dinners.

Old Custom House Inn
South Quay ⊠ PL28 8BL – ℰ (01841) 532 359 – oldcustomhousepadstow.co.uk
21 rm – †£ 105/125 ††£ 120/180   BYc
Rest *Pescadou* – Seafood – *(booking essential)* Carte £ 18/31 **s**
- Well-run, slate hotel; formerly a grain store and exciseman's house. Smart beauty studio and ice cream parlour. Nautically themed bedrooms feature good mod cons – some have roll-top baths or harbour/estuary views. Traditional bar and open-plan seafood restaurant.

Treverbyn House without rest
Station Rd ⊠ PL28 8DA – ℰ (01841) 532 855 – www.treverbynhouse.com
– Closed 25 December-13 February   BYe
5 rm – †£ 108 ††£ 120
- Charming Edwardian house built for a wine merchant. Comfortable bedrooms boast polished floors and interesting furniture from local sale rooms – one has a huge roll-top bath; some have harbour views. Breakfast in the garden or lovely dining room. Delightful owner.

Woodlands Country House without rest
Treator, West : 1.25 mi on B 3276 ⊠ PL28 8RU
– ℰ (01841) 532 426 – www.woodlands-padstow.co.uk
– Closed 20 December-1 February
8 rm – †£ 88/94 ††£ 126/138
- Characterful Victorian house with great coastal outlook to rear. Tastefully furnished lounge, breakfast room and honesty bar; pictures, books and objets d'art abound. Comfy, homely bedrooms; Beach is the largest and best. Homemade muesli and hot specials at breakfast.

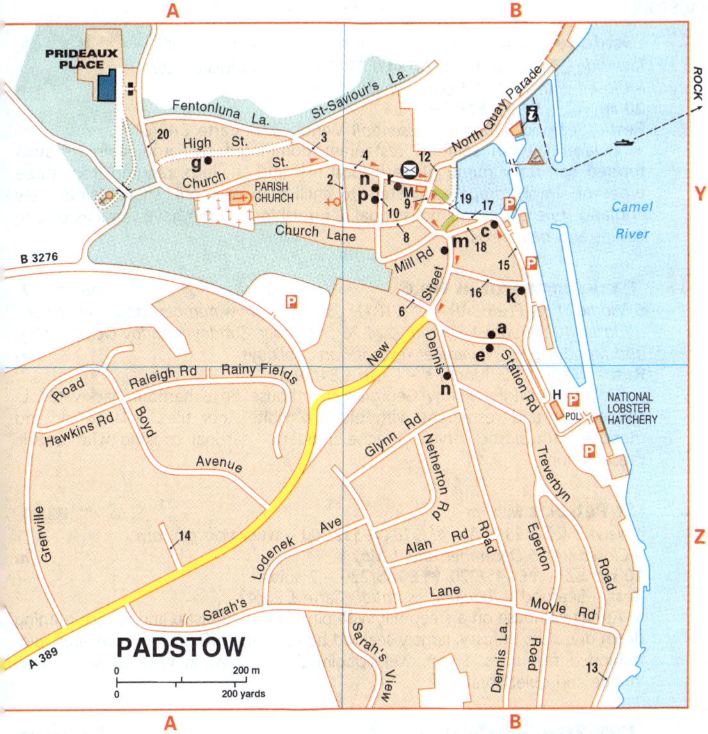

Barry's Lane.........**ABY** 2	Middle St.............**BY** 10	St Edmund's	
Cross St..............**AY** 3	Mill Square...........**BY** 12	Lane..............**BY** 16	
Duke St...............**BY** 4	Porthilly	South Quay........**BY** 17	
Hill St.................**BY** 6	View...............**BZ** 13	Strand St...........**BY** 18	
Lanadwell St........**BY** 8	Raleigh Close......**AZ** 14	The Strand.........**BY** 19	
Market Pl............**BY** 9	Riverside............**BY** 15	Tregirls Lane.......**AY** 20	

🏠 **Treann** without rest ⟵ 🚭 🛜 **P** **VISA** 🔵
24 Dennis Rd ✉ *PL28 8DE* – 📞 *(01841) 533 855* – *www.treannhouse.com*
– Closed Christmas-February **BZn**
3 rm 🛏 – ☝£ 85/95 ☝☝£ 125

♦ Edwardian house set in an elevated position, with first floor views over the Camel Estuary. Chic breakfast room, cool lounge and superb bedrooms which mix antiques with contemporary furnishings to create an understated, elegant style.

🏠 **Althea Library** without rest 🛜 **P** **VISA** 🔵
27 High St, (access via Church St.) ✉ *PL28 8BB* – 📞 *(01841) 532 717*
– www.althealibrary.co.uk – Closed 30 April-1 May and 22-26 December
3 rm 🛏 – ☝£ 80/96 ☝☝£ 96 **AYg**

♦ Grade II listed former school library, just 5min from the harbour. Homely lounge and breakfast room. Beamed bedrooms boast sitting areas and smart bathrooms. Lovely terraced garden with pond.

Guesthouses 🏠 don't provide the same level of service as hotels. They are often characterised by a warm welcome and a décor which reflects the owner's personality. Those shown in red 🏠 are particularly pleasant.

PADSTOW

Seafood with rm
Riverside ⊠ PL28 8BY – ℰ (01841) 532 700 – www.rickstein.com
– Closed dinner 24-26 December and 1 May
20 rm – †£ 97 ††£ 280
BYk

Rest – Seafood – *(booking essential)* Menu £ 37 – Carte £ 40/81

♦ Relaxed, stylish seafood restaurant dominated by large stainless steel topped bar. Daily menu of fresh local fish and shellfish, ranging from three types of simply prepared oysters to chilli crab or monkfish vindaloo. New England style bedrooms boast quality furnishings; some have terraces or balconies and bay views.

Paul Ainsworth at No.6
6 Middle St ⊠ PL28 8AP – ℰ (01841) 532 093 – www.number6inpadstow.co.uk
– Closed 10 January-1 February, 24-26 December, Sunday-Monday October-May and Monday June-November (except bank holidays)
BYn

Rest – Menu £ 20 (lunch) **s** – Carte £ 34/39 **s**

♦ Delightful bright yellow Georgian townhouse on a harbour backwater. L-shaped bar and restaurant with black & white floor tiles. Relaxed air and friendly, enthusiastic service. Precise, modern, seasonal cooking with artistic presentation.

St Petroc's with rm
4 New St ⊠ PL28 8EA – ℰ (01841) 532 700 – www.rickstein.com
– Closed 24-26 December and 1 May
10 rm – †£ 145/220 ††£ 145/220 – 2 suites
BYm

Rest – Seafood – *(booking essential)* Carte £ 26/42

♦ Attractive house on a steep hill, with pine-furnished bistro and terrace running down one side. Unfussy, largely seafood-based menu offers simply prepared, old-fashioned favourites. Smart, well-appointed bedrooms in house/annexe; small lounge and quiet library.

Rick Stein's Café with rm
10 Middle St ⊠ PL28 8AP – ℰ (01841) 532 700 – www.rickstein.com
– Closed dinner 25-26 December and 2 May
3 rm – †£ 97/105 ††£ 105/145
BYp

Rest – *(booking essential at dinner)* Menu £ 22 – Carte £ 23/29

♦ Deceptively large café hidden behind a tiny shop front on a small side street. Concise, seasonally changing menu of tasty, unfussy cooking with influences from Thailand, Morocco and the Med. Homemade bread to start; great value set menus. Comfy, simply furnished bedrooms. Breakfast in café or small courtyard garden.

Margot's
11 Duke St ⊠ PL28 8AB – ℰ (01841) 533 441 – Closed January, 24-31 December, Sunday and Monday
BYr

Rest – *(booking essential at dinner)* Menu £ 23/30

♦ Small yellow and blue bistro with relaxed atmosphere and loyal local following. Daily menu features the latest seasonal produce. Dinner also offers a good value set selection and tasting menu.

at Little Petherick South : 3 mi on A 389 – ⊠ Wadebridge

Molesworth Manor without rest
⊠ PL27 7QT – ℰ (01841) 540 292 – www.molesworth.co.uk
– February-October
9 rm – †£ 75/80 ††£ 115

♦ Part 17C and 19C former rectory. Charming individual establishment with inviting country house atmosphere amid antique furniture and curios. Rooms furnished in period style.

PADSTOW

at St Merryn West : 2.5 mi by A 389 on B 3276 – **503** F32 – ✉ Padstow

Rosel & Co.   VISA ⦿ AE
The Dog House ✉ *PL28 8NF* – ⌀ *(01841) 521 289* – *www.roselandco.co.uk*
– *Closed November-March, Sunday and Monday*
Rest – *(dinner only)* Menu £ 35
♦ Simply styled restaurant with chunky wooden tables, open kitchen and warm, relaxed ambience. Concise menu of precise, flavourful cooking: well-sourced ingredients used to create classic combinations with interesting modern twists.

Cornish Arms
Churchtown ✉ *PL28 8ND* – ⌀ *(01841) 532 700* – *www.rickstein.com*
Rest – Carte £ 18/27
♦ A real locals pub, surprisingly leased by Rick Stein. Sound, sensibly priced cooking offer typical pub dishes and a few fish specials; and doesn't exclude the regulars. Smart terrace.

at Constantine Bay West : 4 mi by B 3276 – ✉ Padstow

Treglos
✉ *PL28 8JH* – ⌀ *(01841) 520 727* – *www.tregloshotel.com* – *March-November*
38 rm ⚏ – ♦£ 70/177 ♦♦£ 140/236 – 4 suites
Rest – *(bar lunch Monday-Saturday)* Menu £ 30 – Carte £ 30/50
♦ An extensive, family run building surrounded by garden. Facilities include games rooms, children's play area and a lounge bar. Consistently decorated, bright, neat bedrooms. Smart attire the code in very comfortable dining room.

ENGLAND

at St Issey South : 3.5 mi on A 389 – ✉ Wadebridge

Higher Trevorrick Country House
Northwest : 0.75 mi by Burgois rd on Sea Mills and Trevorrick rd. ✉ *PL27 7QH* – ⌀ *(01841) 540 943* – *www.higher-trevorrick.co.uk* – *Closed January*
3 rm ⚏ – ♦£ 156/201 ♦♦£ 108/138 **Rest** – *(closed Tuesday)* Menu £ 28
♦ Restored property with spectacular first floor views out over Camel Estuary and towards Rock. Spacious, well-kept bedrooms. Experienced, personable owners. No children policy. Daily changing menu served in pleasant conservatory overlooking garden.

PAINSWICK – Gloucestershire – **503** N28 – pop. 1 666 ▌Great Britain   4 C1

▶ London 107 mi – Bristol 35 mi – Cheltenham 10 mi – Gloucester 7 mi
◉ Town ★

Cotswolds 88
Kemps Ln ✉ *GL6 6YB* – ⌀ *(01452) 813 688* – *www.cotswolds88hotel.com*
17 rm ⚏ – ♦£ 88/95 ♦♦£ 95/395 **Rest** – Menu £ 18/45 – Carte £ 22/33
♦ Stone-built, Regency-style house with attractive garden and terrace. Bold stylish colours, quirky furnishings and striking fixtures abound. Eclectic bedrooms and modern bathrooms. Restaurant offers modern menu of organic produce.

PATELEY BRIDGE – North Yorkshire – **502** O21 – pop. 2 504   22 B2
– ✉ Harrogate ▌Great Britain

▶ London 225 mi – Leeds 28 mi – Middlesbrough 46 mi – York 32 mi
🛈 18 High St ⌀ (01423) 71 11 47, www.aboutbritain.com
◉ Fountains Abbey ★★★ **AC** - Studley Royal **AC** (≤ ★ from Anne Boleyn's Seat)
 - Fountains Hall (Fa 0.5ade ★), NE : 8.5 mi by B 6265

543

PATELEY BRIDGE

at Ramsgill-in-Nidderdale Northwest : 5 mi by Low Wath Rd – ✉ Harrogate

XXX **Yorke Arms** (Frances Atkins) with rm
✉ HG3 5RL – ✆ (01423) 755 243 – www.yorke-arms.co.uk
15 rm (dinner included) – †£ 150/250 ††£ 340/399 – 1 suite
Rest – (closed Sunday dinner to non-residents) Menu £ 35 (lunch)
– Carte (dinner) £ 51/63
Spec. Stuffed oxtail pastry, celery and truffle cream. Grouse with bilberries, roots and a heather scented jus. Tarragon parfait, pistachio brûlée, lemon and roasted fig.
♦ Charming, part-17C former shooting lodge overlooking a small village green and run in a friendly, professional manner. Traditional, antique-furnished restaurant with beamed ceiling and open fires. Measured and accomplished classical cooking demonstrates a good understanding for flavours; modern presentation. Bedrooms have a subtle modern style and offer good comforts.

PATRICK BROMPTON – North Yorkshire – **502** P21 – ✉ Bedale   22 B1

▶ London 242 mi – Newcastle upon Tyne 58 mi – York 43 mi

⌂ **Elmfield House**
Arrathorne, Northwest : 2.25 mi by A 684 on Richmond rd ✉ DL8 1NE
– ✆ (01677) 450 558 – www.elmfieldhouse.co.uk
4 rm – †£ 65/70 ††£ 86   **Rest** – Menu £ 15
♦ Spacious, uncluttered guest house set in peaceful farmland, with nearby fishing lake and 14 acre forest. Neat, classically styled bedrooms with modern touches; some four-posters.

⌂ **Mill Close Farm** without rest
Patrick Brompton ✉ DL8 1JY – ✆ (01677) 450 257 – www.millclose.co.uk
– *Closed January and December*
3 rm – †£ 50/65 ††£ 80/100
♦ Modernised farmhouse with walled garden and summerhouse. Bedrooms blend contemporary furnishings with traditional features and have an uncluttered, homely feel; two boast whirlpool baths.

PATTISWICK – Essex – see Coggeshall

PAULERSPURY – Northamptonshire – **503** R27 – see Towcester

PAXFORD – Gloucestershire – **504** O27 – see Chipping Camden

PENN – Buckinghamshire – **504** R/S29 – pop. 3 779   11 D2

▶ London 31 mi – High Wycombe 4 mi – Oxford 36 mi

⌑ **Old Queens Head**
Hammersley Ln ✉ HP10 8EY – ✆ (01494) 813 371
– *www.oldqueensheadpenn.co.uk – Closed 25-26 December*
Rest – Carte £ 22/29
♦ Lively pub with characterful rustic feel, part-dating back to 1666; head for the old barn. Menus offer generous, hearty dishes and some appealing sides. Homemade puddings are a must.

PENRITH – Cumbria – **501** L19 – pop. 14 471   21 B2

▶ London 290 mi – Carlisle 24 mi – Kendal 31 mi – Lancaster 48 mi
ℹ Middlegate ✆ (01768) 86 74 66, www.penrithtown.co.uk
⛳ Salkeld Rd, ✆ (01768) 89 19 19

PENRITH

Brooklands without rest
2 Portland Pl ✉ *CA11 7QN* – ℰ *(01768) 863 395*
– *www.brooklandsguesthouse.com* – *Closed Christmas and New Year*
6 rm ⊇ – †£ 40/60 ††£ 85
♦ Victorian terraced house located close to the town centre; run by warm, welcoming owners. Traditional, antique-furnished hall and smart breakfast room with marble-topped tables. Homely, pine-furnished bedrooms boast good modern facilities; one has a four-poster.

at Temple Sowerby East : 6.75 mi by A 66 – ✉ Penrith

Temple Sowerby House
✉ *CA10 1RZ* – ℰ *(01768) 361 578* – *www.templesowerby.com* – *Closed Christmas-New Year*
12 rm ⊇ – †£ 90/110 ††£ 125/160
Rest – *(dinner only) (booking essential to non residents)* Menu £ 40
♦ Attractive, red-brick Georgian mansion with spacious, classically styled guest areas. Traditional country house bedrooms boast antique furnishings and contemporary facilities. Modern menus of local, seasonal produce served overlooking enclosed, lawned gardens.

at Clifton Southeast : 3 mi on A 6

George and Dragon with rm
✉ *CA10 2ER* – ℰ *(01768) 865 381* – *www.georgeanddragonclifton.co.uk* – *closed 26 December*
10 rm ⊇ – †£ 75 ††£ 145   **Rest** – Carte £ 22/39
♦ 18C coaching inn belonging to local landowners, the Lowther family. Simple, effective cooking; organic meats, seasonal game and vegetables come fresh from the surrounding estate. Comfortable, modern bedrooms are decorated in bold colours.

at Newbiggin West : 3.5 mi by A 66 – ✉ Penrith

Old School
✉ *CA11 0HT* – ℰ *(01768) 483 709* – *www.theold-school.com* – *Closed 23 December-1 January*
3 rm ⊇ – †£ 38/55 ††£ 75/80   **Rest** – Carte approx. £ 20
♦ Grey-stone Victorian schoolhouse in a small village. Compact, traditionally styled guest areas. Classical bedrooms are named after the colour of their décor – red, green and blue – the latter is the largest and has the best outlook. Home-cooked meals.

PENZANCE – Cornwall – 503 D33 – pop. 20 255   1 A3

▶ London 319 mi – Exeter 113 mi – Plymouth 77 mi – Taunton 155 mi

Access Access to the Isles of Scilly by helicopter, British International Heliport (01736) 364296, Fax (01736) 363871

▬ to the Isles of Scilly (Hugh Town) (Isles of Scilly Steamship Co. Ltd) (summer only) (approx. 2 h 40 mn)

🛈 Station Rd ℰ (01736) 362 2 07, www.purelypenzance.co.uk

◉ Town★ - Outlook★★★ – Western Promenade (≤★★★) YZ – National Lighthouse Centre★ **AC** Y – Chapel St★ Y – Maritime Museum★ **AC** Y M1 – Penlee House Gallery and Museum★, **AC**

🟢 St Buryan★★ (church tower★★), SW : 5 mi by A 30 and B 3283 - Penwith★★ – Trengwainton Garden★★, NW : 2 mi – Sancreed - Church★★ (Celtic Crosses★★) - Carn Euny★, W : 3.5 mi by A 30 Z – St Michael's Mount★★ (≤★★), E : 4 mi by B 3311 - Y - and A 30 – Gulval★ (Church★), NE : 1 mi – Ludgvan★ (Church★), NE : 3.5 mi by A 30 – Chysauster Village★, N : 3.5 mi by A 30, B 3311 and minor rd – Newlyn★ - Pilchard Works★, SW : 1.5 mi by B 3315 Z - Lanyon Quoit★, NW : 3.5 mi by St Clare Street – Men-an-Tol★, NW : 5 mi by B 3312 - Madron Church★, NW : 1.5 mi by St Clare Street Y. Morvah (≤★★), NW : 6.5 mi by St Clare Street Y – Zennor (Church★), NW : 6 mi by B 3311 Y – Prussia Cove★, E : 8 mi by B 3311 - Y - and A 394 – Land's End★ (cliff scenery★★★), SW : 10 mi by A 30 Z – Porthcurno★, SW : 8.5 mi by A 30, B 3283 and minor rd

Plan on next page

545

PENZANCE

Street	Ref
Adelaide St	Y 2
Alexandra Pl	Z 3
Alverton Rd	Y 4
Battery Rd	Y 6
Causeway Head	Y 8
Clarence St	Y 10
Fore St	Z 12
Jennings St	Y 13
Market Jew St	Y 15
Market Pl	Y 14
Mount St	Y 16
Penalverne Drive	Y 17
Quay St	Y 18
Rosevean Rd	Z 20
St Peters Hill	Z
Taroveor Rd	Y 21
Tolver Pl	Y 22
Tolver Rd	Y 23
Wharfside Shopping Centre	Y

Hotel Penzance

Britons Hill ⊠ TR18 3AE – ℰ (01736) 363 117 – www.hotelpenzance.com
– Closed first 2 weeks January
25 rm ⊇ – †£ 85/125 ††£ 190/195   Yc
Rest *Bay* – see restaurant listing

♦ Adjoining Edwardian merchants' houses, overlooking the bay and St Michael's Mount. Several lounges, pleasant garden terrace and outdoor pool. Mix of classic and contemporary bedrooms.

Abbey

Abbey St ⊠ TR18 4AR – ℰ (01736) 366 906 – www.theabbeyonline.co.uk
– Closed January-February and December except 20 December-4 January
6 rm ⊇ – †£ 75/90 ††£ 150/200 – 2 suites   Yu
Rest *Untitled by Robert Wright* – see restaurant listing

♦ 17C country house in powder blue, with tranquil walled gardens. Relaxed, slightly quirky atmosphere with shabby-chic charm. Lovely antique-filled sitting room and bright, well-kept bedrooms.

PENZANCE

Beachfield
The Promenade ⊠ *TR18 4NW –* ℰ *(01736) 362 067 – www.beachfield.co.uk*
– Closed 2 weeks Christmas-New Year Za
18 rm – †£ 58/93 ††£ 125/160 **Rest** *– (dinner only)* Carte £ 20/33
♦ Classic seaside hotel with good views. Well-kept public areas include traditional lounge. Comfy bedrooms are well maintained and have a neat, bright feel. Traditional, varied menus, featuring fish specials.

Chy-An-Mor without rest
15 Regent Terr ⊠ *TR18 4DW –* ℰ *(01736) 363 441 – www.chyanmor.co.uk – 16 March-14 November* Ye
9 rm – †£ 40/70 ††£ 80/90
♦ Terraced guesthouse overlooking the promenade. Lounge displays various artefacts from the charming owners' travels. Bedrooms boast lovely soft furnishings; some have 6ft iron beds.

Summer House
Cornwall Ter ⊠ *TR18 4HL –* ℰ *(01736) 363 744*
– www.summerhouse-cornwall.com – Closed 1 April to 30 September
5 rm – †£ 95/120 ††£ 120/150 **Rest** – Menu £ 39 Zs
♦ There's a friendly atmosphere to this listed Regency House in bright blues and yellows. Pleasant patio garden. Residents can enjoy Mediterranean influenced cooking.

Untitled by Robert Wright – at Abbey Hotel
Abbey St ⊠ *TR18 4AR –* ℰ *(01736) 448 022 – www.untitledbyrobertwright.com*
– Closed Sunday-Monday Yc
Rest *– (booking essential at dinner)* Carte £ 26/28
♦ The chef credits Alistair Little for instilling in him the philosophy of simplicity and keeping flavours honest. A slight French edge runs through the menu, where the focus is on fish. Alternatively, you can order tapas on the ground floor.

Bay – at Hotel Penzance
Britons Hill ⊠ *TR18 3AE –* ℰ *(01736) 366 890 – www.bay-penzance.co.uk*
– Closed first 2 weeks January Yc
Rest *– (closed Saturday lunch) (booking essential for non-residents)*
Menu £ 16/30 – Carte £ 20/45
♦ Large, contemporary hotel restaurant with lovely terrace boasting harbour views. Adventurous modern menus showcase local produce. Every third Sunday, lunch comes from within a 25 mile radius.

Harris's
46 New St ⊠ *TR18 2LZ –* ℰ *(01736) 364 408 – www.harrissrestaurant.co.uk*
– Closed 3 weeks winter, 25-26 December, Sunday and Monday except Monday dinner June-September Ya
Rest – Carte £ 27/46
♦ Long-standing, split-level restaurant with spiral staircase and unusual metal ceiling; run by keen husband and wife. Classical cooking uses seasonal Cornish produce – everything is homemade.

at Gulval Northeast : 1.25 mi by A 30

Coldstreamer with rm
⊠ *TR18 3BB –* ℰ *(01736) 362 072 – www.coldstreamer-penzance.co.uk – Closed 25 December*
3 rm – †£ 60/75 ††£ 70/85
Rest – Menu £ 17 (weekday lunch) – Carte £ 20/28
♦ Handsome pub in the heart of Gulval with large bar and bright dining room. Concise menus feature local, seasonal produce; cooking is clean, generous and modern, with more elaborate dishes in the evening. Popular wine dinners. Fresh, well-appointed bedrooms.

PERRANUTHNOE – Cornwall – **503** D33 – see Marazion

PERSHORE – Worcestershire – 503 N27 – pop. 7 104   19 C3

▶ London 106 mi – Birmingham 33 mi – Worcester 8 mi

Barn without rest
Pensham Hill House, Pensham, Southeast : 1 mi by B 4084 ✉ *WR10 3HA*
– ℰ *(01386) 555 270 – www.pensham-barn.co.uk*
3 rm ⌂ – †£ 55 ††£ 90

♦ Stylish barn renovation in enviable hillside location. Attractive open-plan lounge and breakfast area with exposed roof timbers. Rooms individually styled to a high standard.

Belle House
Bridge St ✉ *WR10 1AJ* – ℰ *(01386) 555 055 – www.belle-house.co.uk*
– *Closed first 2 weeks January, 24-25 December, Sunday and Monday*
Rest – Menu £ 21/32 **s**

♦ 16C and 18C high street building with some very characterful parts, including heavily beamed bar. Accomplished cooking on modern menus using carefully sourced ingredients.

at Eckington South : 4 mi by A 4104 on B 4080

Eckington Manor
Manor Farm, Hammock Rd, (by Drakesbridge Rd.) ✉ *WR10 3BH*
– ℰ *(01386) 751 600 – www.eckingtonmanor.co.uk*
14 rm ⌂ – †£ 65/150 ††£ 110/275   **Rest** – Menu £ 32

♦ Characterful converted 13C manor house with popular cookery school, set on a 260 acre working farm. Comfortable, contemporary bedrooms and stylish bathrooms with underfloor heating. Dinner served Friday and Saturday in the cookery school.

PETERBOROUGH – Peterborough – 502 T26 – pop. 136 292   14 A2
 Great Britain

▶ London 85 mi – Cambridge 35 mi – Leicester 41 mi – Lincoln 51 mi
🛈 Bridge St ℰ (01733) 45 23 36, www.visitpeterborough.com
🏌 Thorpe Wood Nene Parkway, ℰ (01733) 26 77 01
🏌 Peterborough Milton Milton Ferry, ℰ (01733) 38 04 89
🏌 Orton Meadows Ham Lane, ℰ (01733) 23 74 78
◉ Cathedral★★ **AC** Y

Jim's Bistro
52 Broadway ✉ *PE1 1SB* – ℰ *(01733) 341 122 – www.jimsyard.biz*
– *Closed 24 December-6 January, last week July, first week August, Sunday and Monday*   **Ya**
Rest – Carte £ 20/37 **s**

♦ Bright room with quirky mural, bar and open-plan kitchen; choose banquette seating under the mirror. Daily changing menu of tasty, wholesome, seasonal dishes. Friendly service.

Beehive
62 Albert Pl. ✉ *PE1 1DD* – ℰ *(01733) 310 600 – www.jimsyard.biz – Closed 1 January and Sunday dinner*   **Zx**
Rest – Carte £ 20/29

♦ Just off the city centre ring road, with smart, modern interior, stripped floorboards, zinc-topped bar and range of seating options. Light lunches and well-presented, satisfying dinner menu.

PETERBOROUGH

Bridge St	Z
Cattle Market Rd	Y 2
Church St	YZ
City Rd	Y 3
Cowgate	Y 5
Cross St	Z 6
Dogsthorpe Rd	BV 8
Edgerley Drain Rd	BV 9
Embankment Rd	Y 12
Exchange St	Y 13
Fletton Ave	BX 15
Geneva St	Y 16
Guntons Rd	BV 17
High St	Y 18
Hurn Rd	Y 19
Longthorpe Parkway	BX 26
Long Causeway	Y 25
Market Way	Y 28
Midgate	Y 29
New Rd	BX 35
Park Rd	Y 36
Paston Parkway	BV 37
Peterborough Rd	BX 38
Phorpres Way	BX 40
Queensgate Shopping Centre	Y
Rivergate	Z 42
Rivergate Shopping Centre	Z
St Paul's Rd	BV 43
Thorpe Rd	Y 45
Velland Rd	BV 46
Wentworth St	Z 48
Werrington Parkway	BV 50
Wheelyard	Y 52
Whittlesey Rd	BX 53
Woodcroft Rd	BV 55

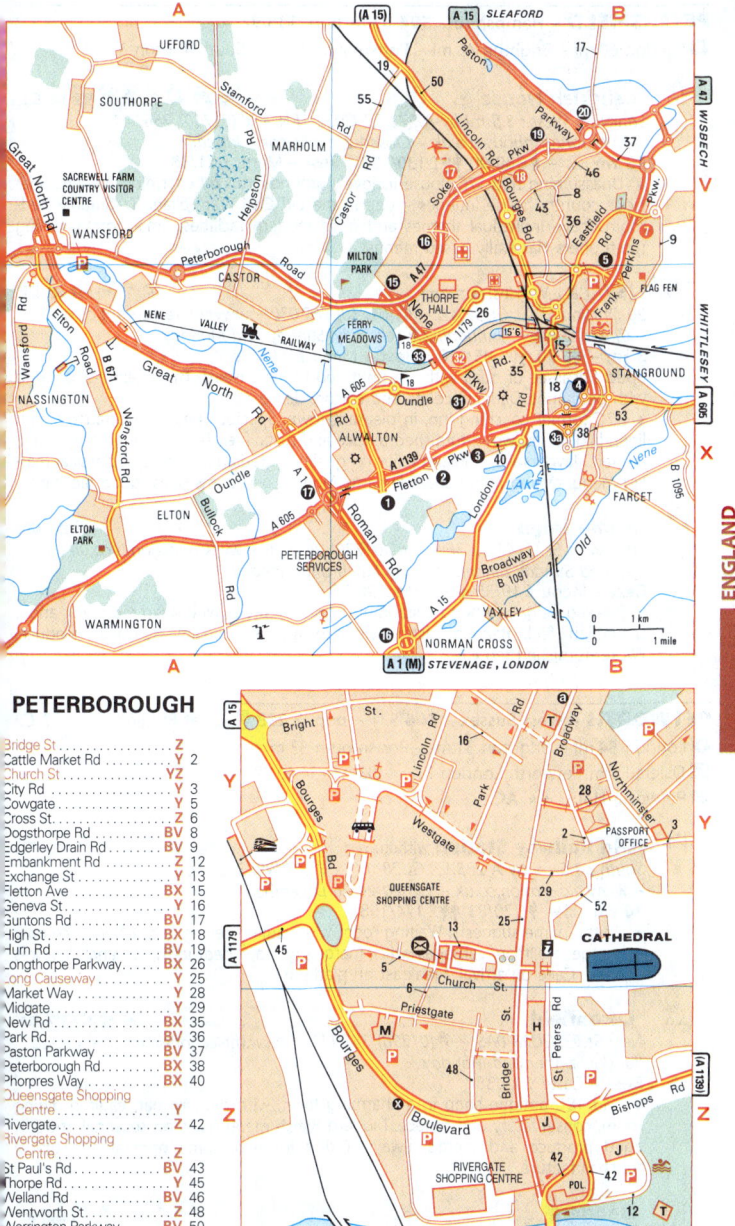

ENGLAND

PETERSFIELD – Hampshire – 504 R30 – pop. 13 092   7 C2
▶ London 60 mi – Brighton 45 mi – Portsmouth 21 mi – Southampton 34 mi

Langrish House
Langrish, West : 3.5 mi by A 272 ⊠ GU32 1RN – ℰ (01730) 266 941
– www.langrishhouse.co.uk – Closed 2 weeks early January
13 rm – †£ 80/90 ††£ 130/170   **Rest** – Menu £ 21/38

◆ Unassuming mid-17C house in lovely grounds; run by charming owners. Spacious country house lounges – one in the old Civil War cellars. Traditional bedrooms have individual themes and good modern facilities. Small formal dining room offers classically based menus.

JSW (Jake Watkins) with rm
20 Dragon St ⊠ GU31 4JJ – ℰ (01730) 262 030 – www.jswrestaurant.com
– Closed 2 weeks January, 2 weeks July, Sunday and Monday
3 rm – †£ 70 ††£ 85/110   **Rest** – Menu £ 28/48 s

Spec. Fricassee of quail with chestnut and truffle custard. Three textures of lamb with bergamot. Dark chocolate and chicory délice.

◆ 17C former coaching inn, in pleasant town. Spacious beamed restaurant with linen-laid tables, wood-furnished terrace and rustic feel. Technically accomplished, refined, flavoursome cooking relies on quality ingredients. Choice of classical market menu, tasting menu and à la carte. Modern bedrooms boast good facilities.

Annie Jones
10 Lavant St ⊠ GU32 3EW – ℰ (01730) 262 728 – www.anniejones.co.uk
– Closed Sunday dinner, Tuesday lunch and Monday
Rest – Menu £ 19/35 **s** – Carte £ 28/36 **s**

◆ Relaxed neighbourhood restaurant on a busy street, with deep red décor and a bohemian feel. Refined bistro-style cooking uses quality seasonal produce. Wicker-furnished terrace.

PETWORTH – West Sussex – 504 S31 – pop. 2 298 ▌Great Britain   7 C2
▶ London 54 mi – Brighton 31 mi – Portsmouth 33 mi
Osiers Farm Petworth London Rd, ℰ (01798) 34 40 97
◉ Petworth House★★ **AC**

Old Railway Station without rest
South : 1.5 mi by A 285 ⊠ GU28 0JF – ℰ (01798) 342 346
– www.old-station.co.uk – Closed 24-26 December
10 rm ⊇ – †£ 70/83 ††£ 174/198

◆ As the name suggests. Waiting room with vaulted ceiling and ticket office now a lounge, Pullman carriages with marquetry now bedrooms; original features abound. Cake on arrival; breakfast on platform.

Leconfield
New St ⊠ GU28 0AS – ℰ (01798) 345 111 – www.theleconfield.co.uk – Closed Sunday dinner and Monday
Rest – Carte £ 28/38

◆ Old 18C antique shop in a charming town, with modern bar, vaulted dining room, conservatory and terrace. Modern British menu relies on seasonal and foraged produce and there's always a dish for two; some original and global touches feature.

Badgers
Coultershaw Bridge, South : 1.5 mi on A 285 ⊠ GU28 0JF – ℰ (01798) 342 651
– www.badgerspetworth.co.uk – Closed Sunday dinner in winter
Rest – Carte £ 25/36

◆ Homely pub close to the river, boasting log fires, fresh flowers and candles. Eclectic menus offer robust, flavoursome cooking with international influences. In summer, lobster is a speciality.

PETWORTH

at Halfway Bridge West : 3 mi on A 272 – ✉ Petworth

Halfway Bridge Inn with rm
✉ GU28 9BP – ✆ (01798) 861 281 – www.halfwaybridge.co.uk – Closed 25 December
6 rm – †£ 75/95 ††£ 100/130 **Rest** – Carte £ 25/31

♦ 17C pub with several cosy, fire-lit rooms, set on the edge of Cowdray Park. Lunchtime baguettes, traditional pub dishes and nursery puddings. Bedrooms are set in converted stables and, like the pub, blend rustic charm with modern fittings and facilities.

at Tillington West : 1 mi on A272 – **504** S31

Horse Guards Inn with rm
Upperton Rd ✉ GU28 9AF – ✆ (01798) 342 332 – www.thehorseguardsinn.co.uk
3 rm – †£ 80/105 ††£ 80/105 **Rest** – Carte £ 22/36

♦ In an elevated spot in the heart of a quiet village sits this pretty mid-17C inn; which is equally charming on the inside as it is out. Local seafood stands out and some of the vegetables come from their own patch. Young, friendly service. Simple, rustic bedrooms, with a family room in the cottage opposite.

PICKERING – North Yorkshire – **502** R21 – pop. 6 616 — 23 C1

▶ London 237 mi – Middlesbrough 43 mi – Scarborough 19 mi – York 25 mi

White Swan Inn
Market Pl ✉ YO18 7AA – ✆ (01751) 472 288 – www.white-swan.co.uk
20 rm – †£ 115/135 ††£ 150/180 – 1 suite **Rest** – Carte £ 26/46

♦ Well-run former coaching inn, with bar and lounges in modern hues. Appealing bedrooms boast good mod cons and smart bathrooms: those in the outbuildings have heated stone floors; one has a bath in the lounge. Brasserie-style restaurant offers classical menus.

17 Burgate without rest
17 Burgate ✉ YO18 7AU – ✆ (01751) 473 463 – www.17burgate.co.uk
– Restricted opening in winter
5 rm – †£ 70/100 ††£ 110

♦ Restored 17C townhouse with colourful gardens; run by charming, experienced couple. Lounge boasts honesty bar and large inglenook; breakfast room has Mackintosh-style chairs. Spacious bedrooms furnished in comfy, modern style: two have a subtle oriental theme.

Bramwood without rest
19 Hall Garth ✉ YO18 7AW – ✆ (01751) 474 066
– www.bramwoodguesthouse.co.uk
8 rm – †£ 50/70 ††£ 80/90

♦ Georgian townhouse with pretty gardens, set close to town. Cosy, homely interior with fire-lit lounge and tea on arrival. Breakfast in large kitchen, beside china-filled dressers, or in more formal dining room. Comfy, cottagey bedrooms. Owners go the extra mile.

at Levisham Northeast : 6.5 mi by A 169 – ✉ Pickering

Moorlands Country House
✉ YO18 7NL – ✆ (01751) 460 229 – www.moorlandslevisham.co.uk – March-19 November, minimum 2 night stay
4 rm – †£ 70/90 ††£ 130/150 **Rest** – Menu £ 25

♦ 19C restored vicarage in the heart of the national park, boasting superb views down the valley. Spacious, well-maintained interior with a classically decorated lounge and flowery wallpapers. Comfortable bedrooms boast rich colour schemes; one has a four-poster bed. Traditional three course dinners. Menu changes daily.

PICKERING

at Sinnington Northwest : 4 mi by A 170 – ⊠ York

Fox and Hounds with rm
Main St ⊠ *YO62 6SQ* – ℰ *(01751) 431 577* – *www.thefoxandhoundsinn.co.uk*
– *Closed 25-26 December*
10 rm ⊒ – †£ 59/89 ††£ 100/130 **Rest** – Carte £ 22/37
♦ Handsome and sturdy 18C coaching inn in pretty village; substantial interior has plenty of charm. Flexible menus, with local specialities the popular choice. Comfortable, cottagey bedrooms are popular at weekends.

PICKHILL – North Yorkshire – **502** P21 – pop. 412 – ⊠ Thirsk   **22** B1
▶ London 229 mi – Leeds 41 mi – Middlesbrough 30 mi – York 34 mi

Nags Head Country Inn
⊠ *YO7 4JG* – ℰ *(01845) 567 391* – *www.nagsheadpickhill.co.uk* – *Closed 25 December*
14 rm ⊒ – †£ 50/67 ††£ 80/95 **Rest** – Carte £ 20/29
♦ Atmospheric 300 year old inn in an ancient hamlet, an easy drive to Thirsk and Ripon races. Neat rooms in soft floral fabrics. Over 800 ties on display in the rustic bar. Rural restaurant adorned with bookshelves and patterned rugs.

PILLERTON PRIORS – Warwickshire – **503** P27 – pop. 123   **19** C3
– ⊠ Stratford-Upon-Avon
▶ London 93 mi – Birmingham 43 mi – Liverpool 137 mi – Leeds 141 mi

Fulready Manor without rest
South : 0.75 mi on Halford rd ⊠ *CV37 7PE* – ℰ *(01789) 740 152*
– *www.fulreadymanor.co.uk*
3 rm ⊒ – †£ 100 ††£ 125/140
♦ Delightfully run manor house next to a lake, in 125 acres of peaceful arable farmland. Spacious lounge. Elegant bedrooms with feature beds, smart bathrooms and extras. Excellent views.

PLUMTREE – Nottinghamshire – see Nottingham

PLYMOUTH – Plymouth – **503** H32 – pop. 253 188   **2** C2
▶ London 242 mi – Bristol 124 mi – Southampton 161 mi
Access Tamar Bridge (toll) AY
✈ Plymouth City (Roborough) Airport : ℰ (01752) 204090, N : 3.5 mi by A 386 ABY
⛴ to France (Roscoff) (Brittany Ferries) 1-3 daily (6 h) – to Spain (Santander) (Brittany Ferries) 2 weekly (approx 24 h)
🛈 3-5 The Barbican ℰ (01752) 30 63 30, www.visitplymouth.co.uk
🏌 Plymouth Mayflower
🏌 Staddon Heights Plymstock, ℰ (01752) 40 24 75
🏌 Elfordleigh Hotel G. & C.C. Plympton Colebrook, ℰ (01752) 34 84 25
◉ Town ★ - Smeaton's Tower (≤★★) **AC** BZ **T1** – Royal Citadel (ramparts ≤★★) **AC** BZ – City Museum and Art Gallery ★ BZ **M1**
◉ Saltram House ★★ **AC**, E : 3.5 mi BY **A** - Tamar River ★★ – Anthony House ★ **AC**, W : 5 mi by A 374 – Mount Edgcumbe (≤★) **AC**, SW : 2 mi by passenger ferry from Stonehouse AZ. NE : Dartmoor National Park ★★ – Buckland Abbey ★★ **AC**, N : 7.5 mi by A 386 ABY

Plans on following pages

Bowling Green without rest
9-10 Osborne Pl, Lockyer St, The Hoe ⊠ *PL1 2PU* – ℰ *(01752) 209 090*
– *www.thebowlinggreenplymouth.com*   BZ**r**
12 rm ⊒ – †£ 50/60 ††£ 75
♦ Georgian house, half overlooking Hoe, near site of Drake's legendary game. High-ceilinged rooms in pine and modern fabrics; some have power showers. Stroll to promenade.

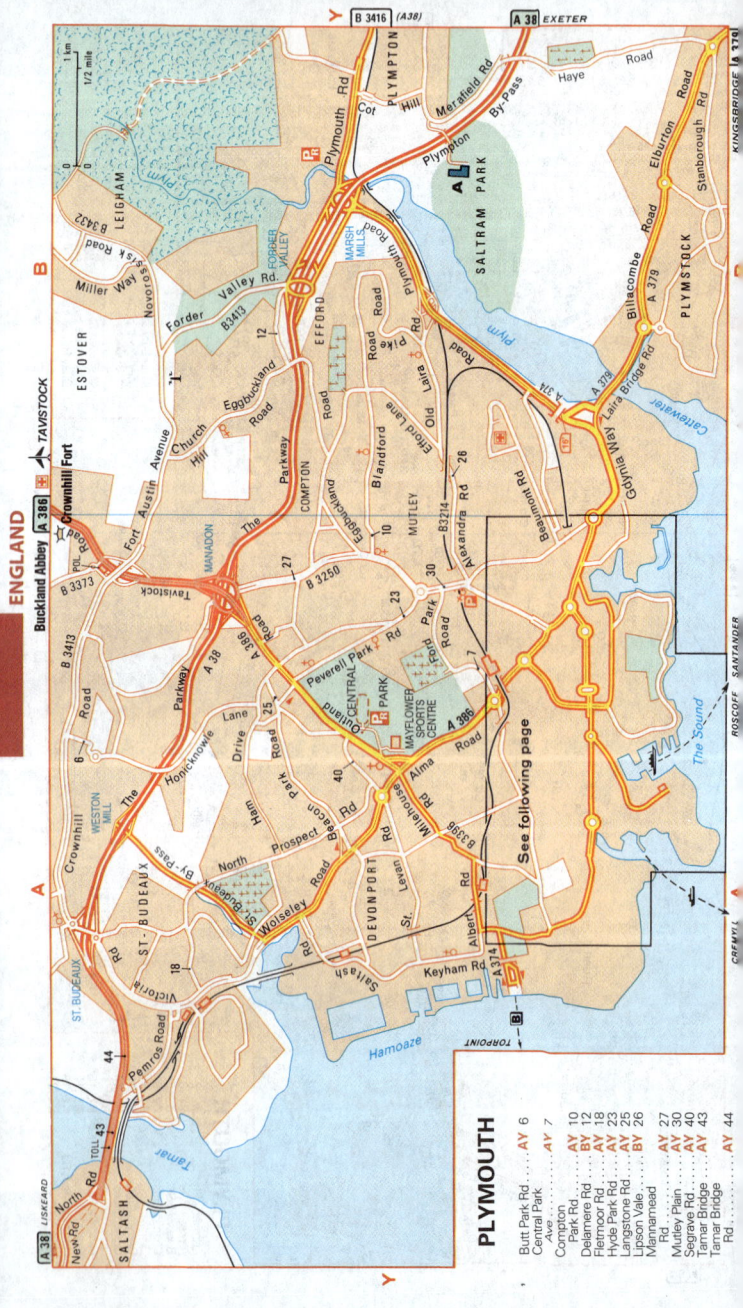

PLYMOUTH

XXX **Tanners** VISA ⊚ AE ⊕
Prysten House, Finewell St ✉ PL1 2AE – ℰ (01752) 252 001
– www.tannersrestaurant.com – Closed 24 December-10 January, Sunday and
Monday BZ**n**
Rest – *(booking essential)* Menu £ 20 (lunch) **s** – Carte £ 39/45 **s**

♦ Characterful 15C house, reputedly Plymouth's oldest building: mullioned windows, tapestries, exposed stone and an illuminated water well. Modern, interesting cooking.

XX **Artillery Tower** VISA ⊚
Firestone Bay ✉ PL1 3QR – ℰ (01752) 257 610 – www.artillerytower.co.uk
– Closed Saturday lunch, Sunday and Monday AZ**a**
Rest – *(booking essential at lunch)* Menu £ 37

♦ Uniquely located in 500 year-old circular tower, built to defend the city. Courteous service of mostly well executed local dishes: blackboard fish specialities.

XX **Barbican Kitchen** VISA ⊚ AE ⊕
Black Friars Distillery, 60 Southside St ✉ PL1 2LQ – ℰ (01752) 604 448
– www.barbicankitchen.com – Closed 25-26 December and dinner 31 December
Rest – *(booking advisable)* Carte £ 21/33 **s** BZ**u**

♦ Fun, informal eatery set in the Plymouth Gin Distillery. Two long, industrial style rooms decorated in vibrant fuschia and lime. Brasserie menus offer a good selection of simply cooked dishes.

XX **Chloe's** VISA ⊚ AE
Gill Akaster House, Princess St ✉ PL1 2EX – ℰ (01752) 201 523 – www.
chloesrestaurant .co.uk – Closed 3-5 January, 25-31 December, Sunday and
Monday BZ**a**
Rest – Menu £ 19/40

♦ Airy, open plan restaurant with simple neighbourhood feel, neutral décor and hanging Hessian lights. Tasty dishes display a classical French base. Live pianist every night.

ENGLAND

at Plympton St Maurice East : 6 mi by A 374 on B 3416 - **BY** – ✉ Plymouth

St Elizabeth's House VISA ⊚
Longbrook St ✉ PL7 1NJ – ℰ (01752) 344 840 – www.stelizabeths.co.uk – Closed
25-26 December
13 rm ⌑ – †£ 139 ††£ 159 – 1 suite
Rest – Menu £ 11 (lunch) – Carte £ 21/36

♦ Immaculate cream-washed former convent, now a stylish boutique hotel; lounge is dressed in period décor while light bedrooms are contemporary, with up-to-date facilities. Formal dining room offers classically based cooking with a modern twist.

PLYMPTON SAINT MAURICE Devon – Plymouth – **503** H32 – see Plymouth

POLPERRO – Cornwall – **503** G33 – ✉ Looe **1** B2
▶ London 271 mi – Plymouth 28 mi
◉ Village ★

⌂ **Trenderway Farm** without rest VISA ⊚
Northeast : 2 mi by A 387 ✉ PL13 2LY – ℰ (01503) 272 214
– www.trenderwayfarm.co.uk
8 rm ⌑ – †£ 125/175 ††£ 125/175

♦ 16C farmhouse and outbuildings in 206 acres of working farmland. Well-appointed bedrooms in mix of styles; some with seating areas and kitchenettes. Cream tea on arrival; Aga-cooked breakfasts.

PONTELAND – Northumberland - **501** O19 – see Newcastle upon Tyne

POOLE – Poole – 503 O31 – pop. 144 800   4 C3

▶ London 116 mi – Bournemouth 4 mi – Dorchester 23 mi – Southampton 36 mi

🚢 to France (Cherbourg) (Brittany Ferries) 1-2 daily May-October (4 h 15 mn) day (5 h 45 mn) night – to France (St Malo) (Brittany Ferries) daily (8 h) – to France (St Malo) (Condor Ferries Ltd)

🛈 Poole Quay ☏ (01202) 25 32 53, www.pooletourism.com

⛳ Parkstone Links Rd, ☏ (01202) 70 71 38

⛳ Bulbury Woods Lytchett Minster Bulbury Lane, ☏ (01929) 45 95 74

◉ Town★ (Waterfront **M1**, Scaplen's Court **M2**)

◉ Compton Acres★★, (English Garden ⇐★★★) **AC**, SE : 3 mi by B 3369 **BX** (on Bournemouth town plan) – Brownsea Island★ (Baden-Powell Stone ⇐★★) **AC**, by boat from Poole Quay or Sandbanks **BX** (on Bournemouth town plan)

Plan of Built up Area : see Bournemouth BX

Hotel du Vin   AK 📶 ♿ P VISA ◎ AE

7-11 Thames St. ✉ BH15 1JN – ☏ (01202) 785 570 – www.hotelduvin.com
38 rm ⌒ – † £ 170/190 †† £ 245/400   **a**
Rest *Bistro* – see restaurant listing

♦ Strikingly extended Queen Anne property in the heart of the old town. Smart guest areas with eye-catching, wine-themed murals. Stylish, modern bedrooms are named after wine or champagne houses; one boasts an 8ft bed and twin roll-top baths.

ENGLAND

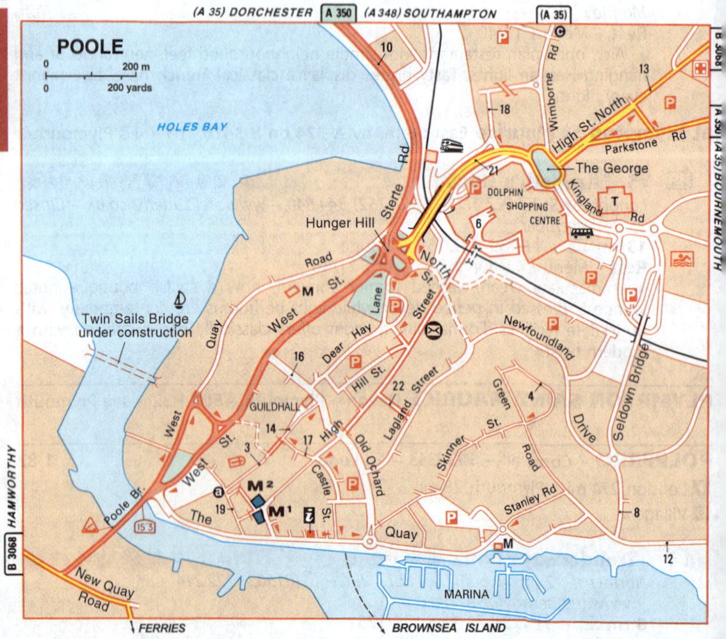

Church St 3	Furnell Rd 8	New Orchard 16
Dolphin Quay Shopping Centre	High St	New St 17
Emerson Rd 4	Holes Bay Rd 10	Serpentine Rd 18
Falkland Square 6	Labrador Drive 12	Thames St 19
Fishermans Rd 7	Longfleet Rd 13	Towngate Bridge 21
	Market St 14	Westons Lane 22

POOLE

Harbour Heights
Haven Rd, Sandbanks, Southeast : 3 mi by B 3369 ✉ BH13 7LW – ℰ (01202) 707 272 – www.harbourheights.com BXn
38 rm ☐ – ♦£ 135/230 ♦♦£ 200/390
Rest *Habar Bistro* – Menu £ 27/30 – Carte £ 32/45
♦ Refurbished 1920s whitewashed hotel perched on the hillside; overlooking the bay and Brownsea Island. Modern lounge-bar boasts superb three-tiered terrace. Contemporary bedrooms come with good mod cons and smart bathrooms. Open-plan restaurant serves modern menu.

Cranborne House *without rest*
45 Shaftesbury Rd ✉ BH15 2LU – ℰ (01202) 685 200
– www.cranborne-house.co.uk c
5 rm ☐ – ♦£ 49/69 ♦♦£ 69/89
♦ Victorian house on the main road; run by friendly owners. Small, homely lounge-cum-breakfast room. Bedrooms – in modern extension – boast quality handmade furniture and good modern facilities.

Bistro – at Hotel du Vin
7-11 Thames St. ✉ BH15 1JN – ℰ (01202) 785 570 – www.hotelduvin.com
Rest – Carte £ 30/45 a
♦ Large hotel bistro in a striking Queen Anne property set in the heart of the old town. Local produce appears in dishes with a classical French base. 300 bin wine list and superb tasting room.

Cow
58 Station Rd, Ashley Cross ✉ BH14 8UD – ℰ (01202) 749 569
– www.thecowpub.co.uk – Closed 25 December and Sunday dinner
Rest – Menu £ 25 – Carte £ 27/40 BXa
♦ Smart, modern pub next to the railway station. Light lunch menu of pub favourites. Evening à la carte steps things up a gear, but is only available in the French-style bistro.

POOLEY BRIDGE – Cumbria – **501** L20 – *see* Ullswater

PORLOCK – Somerset – **503** J30 – pop. 1 395 – ✉ Minehead **3** A2
▶ London 190 mi – Bristol 67 mi – Exeter 46 mi – Taunton 28 mi
◉ Village★ - Porlock Hill (≤★★) - St Dubricius Church★
◉ Dunkery Beacon★★★ (≤★★★), S : 5.5 mi – Exmoor National Park★★
 - Selworthy★ (≤★★, Church★), E : 2 mi by A 39 and minor rd
 - Luccombe★ (Church★), E : 3 mi by A 39 – Culbone★ (St Beuno), W : 3.5 mi by B 3225, 1.5 mi on foot – Doone Valley★, W : 6 mi by A 39, access from Oare on foot

Oaks

✉ TA24 8ES – ℰ (01643) 862 265 – www.oakshotel.co.uk – April-October
7 rm (dinner included) ☐ – ♦£ 145 ♦♦£ 210/220
Rest – *(dinner only) (booking essential for non-residents)* Menu £ 38 **s**
♦ Imposing Edwardian house boasting great views over the weir and Porlock Bay. Antique-filled entrance hall with beautiful parquet floor. Cake on arrival in snug lounge. Large, comfy bedrooms come with fresh fruit bowls, good mod cons and smart bathrooms. Dining room offers classical daily menu and views from every table.

PORT ERIN – Port Erin – **502** F21 – *see* Man (Isle of)

PORT ST MARY – Port Saint Mary – **502** F/G21 – *see* Man (Isle of)

PORT SUNLIGHT – Merseyside – 502 L23 20 A3

► London 206 mi – Liverpool 6 mi – Bolton 42 mi – St Helens 20 mi

Leverhulme H. & Spa
Lodge Ln, Central Rd ✉ CH62 5EZ – ✆ (0151) 644 55 55
– www.leverhulmehotel.co.uk
15 rm ⌷ – †£ 160 ††£ 395
Rest *Richard Fox at Leverhulme* – ✆ (0151) 644 66 55 – Menu £ 15 (lunch)
– Carte £ 29/40
 • Originally the cottage hospital for a Victorian conservation village. Now a hotel with personality, whose bright interior mixes contemporary design with art deco. Retro restaurant with vivid purple carpet, glass-topped tables and classic British menu.

PORTGATE – Devon – pop. 1 453 2 C2

► London 211 mi – Launceston 8 mi – Plymouth 34 mi

Harris Arms
✉ EX20 4PZ – ✆ (01566) 783 331 – www.theharrisarms.co.uk – Closed Sunday dinner and Monday
Rest – Carte £ 20/33 ✿
 • Simple exterior hides classical rooms, a large terrace and lovely rear views. Concise menus offer fresh, tried-and-tested dishes, supplemented by tasty daily specials. Excellent wine list.

PORTHLEVEN – Cornwall – pop. 3 190 1 A3

► London 284 mi – Helston 3 mi – Penzance 12 mi

Kota with rm
Harbour Head ✉ TR13 9JA – ✆ (01326) 562 407 – www.kotarestaurant.co.uk
– Closed 1 January-12 February, 25-26 December, Monday in low season and Sunday except bank holiday weekends
2 rm ⌷ – †£ 50/80 ††£ 80/95
Rest – *(dinner only and lunch Friday-Saturday)* Menu £ 15 (lunch and early dinner) – Carte £ 23/34
 • Cottagey converted 18C harbourside granary. Characterful restaurant - thick walls, tiled floors - serves modern Asian inspired dishes with local fish specials. Simple rooms.

PORTINSCALE – Cumbria – see Keswick

PORTSCATHO – Cornwall – 503 F33 – ✉ Truro 1 B3

► London 298 mi – Plymouth 55 mi – Truro 16 mi

◉ St Just-in-Roseland Church★★, W : 4 mi by A 3078 – St Anthony-in-Roseland (≤★★) S : 3.5 m

Driftwood ✿
Rosevine, North : 2 mi by A 3078 ✉ TR2 5EW – ✆ (01872) 580 644
– www.driftwoodhotel.co.uk – Closed 10 December-4 February
14 rm (dinner included) ⌷ – †£ 210/251 ††£ 270/357
Rest – *(dinner only) (booking essential)* Menu £ 46
Spec. Spider crab and dill risotto with seaweed and samphire. Crisp shoulder of spring lamb, broad beans and onion purée. Strawberries with toasted marshmallow and clotted cream jelly.
 • Charming and delightfully run house whose stylish décor and contemporary feel make it a lovely spot to lay one's head. Terrific sea views, mature gardens and smart powder-blue bedrooms; some have their own terrace. Seasonally pertinent food displays excellent combinations of flavours and textures.

Rosevine

Rosevine, North : 2 mi by A 3078 ✉ *TR2 5EW* – ✆ *(01872) 580 206*
– www.rosevine.co.uk – Closed January
15 suites – ♦♦ £ 155/250, ⌴ £ 7
Rest – *(closed Sunday dinner) (bar lunch)* Carte £ 27/35

♦ Dramatically refurbished and extended country house overlooking the sea. Cool, contemporary, neutrally hued inner. Stylish, modern bedrooms boast kitchenettes. Strongly family orientated services; kids have their own lounge. All-day brasserie uses local produce.

PORTSMOUTH and SOUTHSEA – Portsmouth – **503** Q31   **6** B3

– pop. 203 646 Great Britain

▶ London 78 mi – Brighton 48 mi – Salisbury 44 mi – Southampton 21 mi

⛴ to the Isle of Wight (Ryde) (Wightlink Ltd) frequent services daily (15 mn) – from Southsea to the Isle of Wight (Ryde) (Hovertravel Ltd) frequent services daily (10 mn)

⛴ to France (St Malo) (Brittany Ferries) daily (8 h 45 mn) day (10 h 45 mn) night – to France (Caen) (Brittany Ferries) 2-4 daily (6 h) day (6 h 45 mn) night – to France (Cherbourg) (Brittany Ferries) 2 daily (5 h) day, (7 h) night – to France (Le Havre) (LD Lines) daily (5 h 30 mn/7 h 30 mn) – to France (Cherbourg) (Brittany Ferries) 1-2 daily (2 h 45 mn) – to France (Caen) (Brittany Ferries) 2-4 daily (3 h 45 mn) – to Spain (Bilbao) (P & O European Ferries Ltd) 1-2 weekly (35 h) – to Guernsey (St Peter Port) and Jersey (St Helier) (Condor Ferries) daily except Sunday (10 hrs) – to the Isle of Wight (Fishbourne) (Wightlink Ltd) frequent services daily (35 mn)

🛈 Southsea ✆ (023) 9282 67 22, www.visitportsmouth.co.uk
⛳ Southsea Burrfields Rd, ✆ (023) 9266 86 67
⛳ Crookhorn Lane Waterlooville Widley, ✆ (023) 9237 22 10
⛳ Southwick Park Southwick Pinsley Drive, ✆ (023) 9238 01 31

◉ City★ – Naval Portsmouth BY : H.M.S. Victory★★★ **AC**, The Mary Rose★★, National Museum of the Royal Navy★★ **AC** – Old Portsmouth★ BYZ : The Point (⩽★★) - St Thomas Cathedral★ – Southsea (Castle★ **AC**) AZ – Royal Marines Museum, Eastney★ **AC**, AZ **M1**

◉ Portchester Castle★ **AC**, NW : 5.5 mi by A 3 and A 27 AY

Plans pages 560, 561

Clarence without rest

Clarence Rd. ✉ *PO5 2LQ* – ✆ *(023) 9287 6348* – www.theclarencehotel.co.uk
– Closed 24 December-2 January   AZc
8 rm ⌴ – ♦£ 95/135 ♦♦£ 99/225

♦ Red-brick, bay windowed house a short walk from the sea. Variously sized bedrooms feature contemporary décor, a good level of facilities, superb modern bathrooms and pleasing extra touches.

Retreat without rest

35 Grove Rd South, Southsea ✉ *PO5 3QS* – ✆ *(023) 9235 3701*
– www.theretreatguesthouse.co.uk   CZe
4 rm ⌴ – ♦£ 80 ♦♦£ 105

♦ Grade II listed Arts and Crafts house; originally built for the mayor. Original terrazzo floors and stained glass. Relaxed, spacious inner with stylish, understated décor. One four-poster room.

Restaurant 27

27a South Par, Southsea ✉ *PO5 2JF* – ✆ *(023) 9287 6272*
– www.restaurant27.com – Closed 25-31 December, Sunday dinner, Monday and Tuesday   AZx
Rest – *(dinner only and Sunday lunch) (booking advisable)* Menu £ 40

♦ Keenly run, open-plan restaurant with lounge area for aperitifs and canapés. Cooking is skilful with creative touches. Attentive, knowledgeable service from smart young team.

PORTSMOUTH AND SOUTHSEA

CENTRE

ec Rose Lane	CY	2
undel St	CY	5
ellevue Terrace	CZ	6
ambridge Junction	BY	7
ascade Centre	CY	
ommercial Rd	CY	
omwell Rd	AZ	9
don St	CY	10
wcett Rd	AZ	13
adys Ave	AY	14
eat Southsea St	CZ	15
uildhall Walk	CY	17
unwharf Quay Shopping Centre	BY	
ampshire Terrace	CY	18
ard (The)	BY	20
gh St	BYZ	21

Isambard Brunel Rd	CY	22
Kingston Crescent	AY	24
Kings Road Roundabout	CY	23
Landport Terrace	CY	25
Lawrence Rd	AZ	27
Lennox Rd South	AZ	28
Lombard St	BYZ	29
Main Rd	BY	31
Norfolk St	CYZ	32
Ocean Retail Park	AY	
Ordnance Row	BY	34
Palmerston Rd	CZ	
Paradise St	CY	35
Penny St	BZ	36
Pier Road Roundabout	CZ	37
Pompey Centre	AZ	

St George's Rd	AZ	38
St George's Square	BY	39
St Helen's Parade	AZ	40
St Michael's Rd	CY	41
Southsea Terrace	CZ	43
South Parade	AZ	42
Spring St	CY	45
Stamshaw Rd	AZ	46
Stanhope Rd	CY	48
Unicorn Rd	CY	49
Victoria Rd North	AZ	50
Victoria Rd South	AZ	52
Warblington St	BY	53
Waverley Rd	AZ	56
White Hart Rd	BYZ	57
Wiltshire St	CY	59

561

PORTSMOUTH and SOUTHSEA

XX Montparnasse
*103 Palmerston Rd, Southsea ⊠ PO5 3PS – ℰ (023) 9281 6754
– www.bistromontparnasse.co.uk – Closed 25-26 December, 1 January, Sunday and Monday*
CZa
Rest – Menu £ 37
◆ Keenly run, suburban restaurant with shabby-chic styling. Set lunch and dinner menus. Ambitious cooking features original, sometimes unusual, combinations. Refined appearance but hearty to eat.

XX Brasserie Blanc
1 Gunwharf Quays ⊠ PO1 3FR – ℰ (023) 9289 1320 – www.brasserieblanc.com
Rest – French – Menu £ 14/16 – Carte £ 21/45
BYx
◆ Bustling brasserie on ground floor of 'The Lipstick', serving well-priced, tasty classics prepared with care. Comfy seating, well-spaced tables, open kitchen and super terrace.

POSTBRIDGE – Devon – 503 I32
2 C2
▶ London 207 mi – Exeter 21 mi – Plymouth 21 mi

Lydgate House
⊠ PL20 6TJ – ℰ (01822) 880 209 – www.lydgatehouse.co.uk
7 rm ⊡ – †£ 55/80 ††£ 120
Rest – *(closed Sunday and Monday) (dinner only)* Menu £ 30
◆ In an idyllic secluded location high up on the moors within woodland and overlooking the East Dart River. Comfortable sitting room with log fires and neat, snug bedrooms. Candlelit conservatory dining room.

POTTERNE – Wiltshire – 503 O29 – see Devizes

POWERSTOCK – Dorset
3 B3
▶ London 144 mi – Bristol 92 mi – Cardiff 113 mi – Plymouth 87 mi

Three Horseshoes with rm
⊠ DT6 3TF – ℰ (01308) 485 328 – Closed dinner 25 December, Monday in winter and Sunday dinner
3 rm ⊡ – †£ 45/70 ††£ 50/70   **Rest** – Carte £ 21/36
◆ Looks-wise, it's nothing special, despite the lovely setting – it's simply all about the food at the 'Shoes. They make their own breads, ice creams, chutneys and pickles; try the wild boar Scotch egg or veal and bone marrow burger.

PRESTBURY – Cheshire East – 502 N24 – pop. 3 269
20 B3
▶ London 184 mi – Liverpool 43 mi – Manchester 17 mi – Stoke-on-Trent 25 mi
☷ Mottram Hall Hotel Mottram St Andrews Wilmslow Rd, ℰ (01625) 82 00 64

White House Manor without rest
New Road ⊠ SK10 4HP – ℰ (01625) 829 376 – www.thewhitehousemanor.co.uk – Closed 25-26 December
12 rm – †£ 60/115 ††£ 130/150, ⊡ £ 11.95
◆ Attractive Georgian house with mature lawned garden and sheltered terrace. Nicely furnished lounge boasts an honesty bar. Beautifully appointed bedrooms display quality furnishings and extras.

PRESTON – Lancashire – 502 L22
20 A2
▶ London 226 mi – Blackpool 18 mi – Burnley 22 mi – Liverpool 30 mi
🛈 Lancaster Rd ℰ (01772) 25 37 31, www.visitpreston.com
☷ Fulwood Fulwood Hall Lane, ℰ (01772) 70 00 11
☷ Ingol Tanterton Hall Rd, ℰ (01772) 73 45 56
☷ Ashton & Lea Lea Tudor Ave, Blackpool Rd, ℰ (01772) 73 52 82
☷ Penwortham Blundell Lane, ℰ (01772) 74 46 30

PRESTON

XX **Inside Out**
100 Higher Walton Rd, Walton-le-Dale, Southeast : 1.75 mi by A 6 on A 675
✉ *PR5 4HR* – ℰ *(01772) 251 366* – *www.insideoutrestaurant.co.uk* – *Closed first week January and Monday*
Rest – Menu £ 16/18 **s** – Carte £ 28/33 **s**
♦ Inside - a chic and stylish restaurant; 'out' - a lovely decked terrace with heaters overlooking a garden. Well sourced, quality ingredients assembled with love and flair.

PRESTON CANDOVER – Hampshire – **504** Q30

6 B2

▶ London 59 mi – Croydon 67 mi – Barnet 72 mi – Ealing 54 mi

🏠 **Purefoy Arms**

✉ *RG25 2EJ* – ℰ *(01256) 389 777* – *www.thepurefoyarms.co.uk* – *Closed 1 January*
Rest – *(closed Sunday dinner and Monday except bank holidays)* Carte £ 20/35
♦ Dating from the 1860s, this once crumbling pub was thoughtfully restored and is run by a charming, young but experienced couple. There are hints of Spain on the menu, especially in the bar nibbles; prices are very competitive and the focus is on flavour.

PRESTWICH – Greater Manchester – **503** N23 – see Manchester

PULHAM MARKET – Norfolk – **504** X26 – pop. 919 – ✉ Diss

15 C2

▶ London 106 mi – Cambridge 58 mi – Ipswich 29 mi – Norwich 16 mi

⌂ **Old Bakery** without rest
Church Walk ✉ *IP21 4SL* – ℰ *(01379) 676 492* – *www.theoldbakery.net* – *Closed Christmas-New Year*
4 rm ⌑ – †£ 80 ††£ 95
♦ Pretty 16C former bakery just off the village green. Characterful interior features exposed beams and inglenooks: homely lounge and breakfast room; good-sized bedrooms with modern facilities.

PURTON – Wiltshire – **503** O29 – pop. 3 328 – ✉ Swindon

4 D2

▶ London 94 mi – Bristol 41 mi – Gloucester 31 mi – Oxford 38 mi

🏨 **Pear Tree at Purton**
Church End, South : 0.5 mi by Church St on Lydiard Millicent rd ✉ *SN5 4ED* – ℰ *(01793) 772 100* – *www.peartreepurton.co.uk* – *Closed 26 December*
15 rm ⌑ – †£ 114 ††£ 144 – 2 suites **Rest** – Menu £ 21/36 **s**
♦ Personally run, extended 16C sandstone vicarage in mature seven-acre garden. Spacious flower-filled lounge. Rooms with traditional comforts and thoughtful extras. Conservatory restaurant overlooks wild flower borders.

RADNAGE – Buckinghamshire – see Stokenchurch

RAINHAM – Medway – **504** U29

9 C1

▶ London 14 mi – Basildon 16 mi – Dartford 9 mi

XX **Barn**
507 Lower Rainham Rd, North : 1.75 mi by Station Rd ✉ *ME8 7TN* – ℰ *(01634) 361 363* – *www.thebarnrestaurantrainham.co.uk* – *Closed 2 weeks January, 25 December, Saturday lunch, Sunday dinner and Monday*
Rest – Menu £ 18/24 **s** – Carte £ 24/43 **s**
♦ Black and white timbered, 18C Essex barn, reconstructed on this site. Heavily beamed, rustic dining room and upstairs lounge. Good choice of menus. Elaborate cooking comes in generous portions.

RAMSBOTTOM – Greater Manchester – 502 N23 – pop. 17 352 20 B2
▶ London 223 mi – Blackpool 39 mi – Burnley 12 mi – Leeds 46 mi

※※ ramsons VISA ⦿
18 Market Pl ⊠ *BL0 9HT –* ℘ *(01706) 825 070 – www.ramsons-restaurant.com – Closed 26 December, 1 January, Sunday dinner, Monday and Tuesday lunch*
Rest – Italian influences – *(booking essential)* Menu £ 18/23 – Carte £ 30/39 ⊛
♦ Intimate, two-roomed restaurant run by passionate owner. Array of menus includes 6/10 course tasting options. Clean, refined, Italian-influenced cooking mixes quality local/imported produce.

※※ Sanmini's VISA ⦿
7 Carrbank Lodge, Ramsbottom Ln. ⊠ *BL0 9DJ –* ℘ *(01706) 821 831 – www.sanminis.com – Closed Monday*
Rest – Indian – *(booking essential)* Menu £ 10 (lunch) – Carte £ 19/30
♦ Charming little restaurant in Victorian gatehouse. Neatly presented, authentic south Indian dishes with gentle spicing; every one is made from scratch. Family are doctors, so it's healthy too.

RAMSEY – Ramsey – 502 G21 – see Man (Isle of)

RAMSGATE – Kent – 504 Y30 – pop. 37 967 9 D1
▶ London 77 mi – Southend-on-Sea 89 mi – Ipswich 128 mi

※※ Age & Sons 🌳 VISA ⦿ AE
Charlotte Ct ⊠ *CT11 8HE –* ℘ *(01843) 851 515 – www.ageandsons.co.uk – Closed 1-24 January, Sunday dinner and Monday*
Rest – Menu £ 13/16 (weekdays) – Carte £ 20/28
♦ Attractive converted wine warehouse in centre of town. Sexy basement bar; rustic ground floor café; more formal 1st floor restaurant and lovely terrace. Interesting modern menu of gutsy, flavoured cooking. Charming service.

※ Eddie Gilberts VISA ⦿ AE ①
32 King St. ⊠ *CT11 8NT –* ℘ *(01843) 852 123 – www.eddiegilberts.com – Closed Sunday dinner*
Rest – Seafood – Carte £ 19/31
♦ High street fish shop; head upstairs to light, airy restaurant, with fishing nets and piscatorial pictures. Extensive array of fresh fish; well presented in generous portions.

RAMSGILL-IN-NIDDERDALE – North Yorkshire – 502 O21 – see Pateley Bridge

RAVENSTONEDALE – Cumbria – 502 M20 – see Kirkby Stephen

RAYLEIGH – Essex – 504 V29 – pop. 30 629 13 C3
▶ London 35 mi – Chelmsford 13 mi – Southend-on-Sea 6 mi

at Thundersley South : 1.25 mi on A 129 – ⊠ Rayleigh

🍺 Woodmans Arms 🌳 P VISA ⦿ AE ①
Rayleigh Rd ⊠ *SS7 3TA –* ℘ *(01268) 775 799 – www.thewoodmans.co.uk*
Rest – Carte £ 25/35
♦ Comfy sofas for drinkers; neatly laid tables for diners. Seasonal cooking is hearty and flavourful; traditional in the main with lighter choices at lunch. Service from a cheerful young team.

READING – Reading – 503 Q29 – pop. 232 662 11 C3
▶ London 43 mi – Brighton 79 mi – Bristol 78 mi – Croydon 47 mi
Access Whitchurch Bridge (toll)
🚢 to Henley-on-Thames (Salter Bros. Ltd) (summer only)
🏌 Calcot Park Calcot Bath Rd, ℘ (0118) 942 71 24

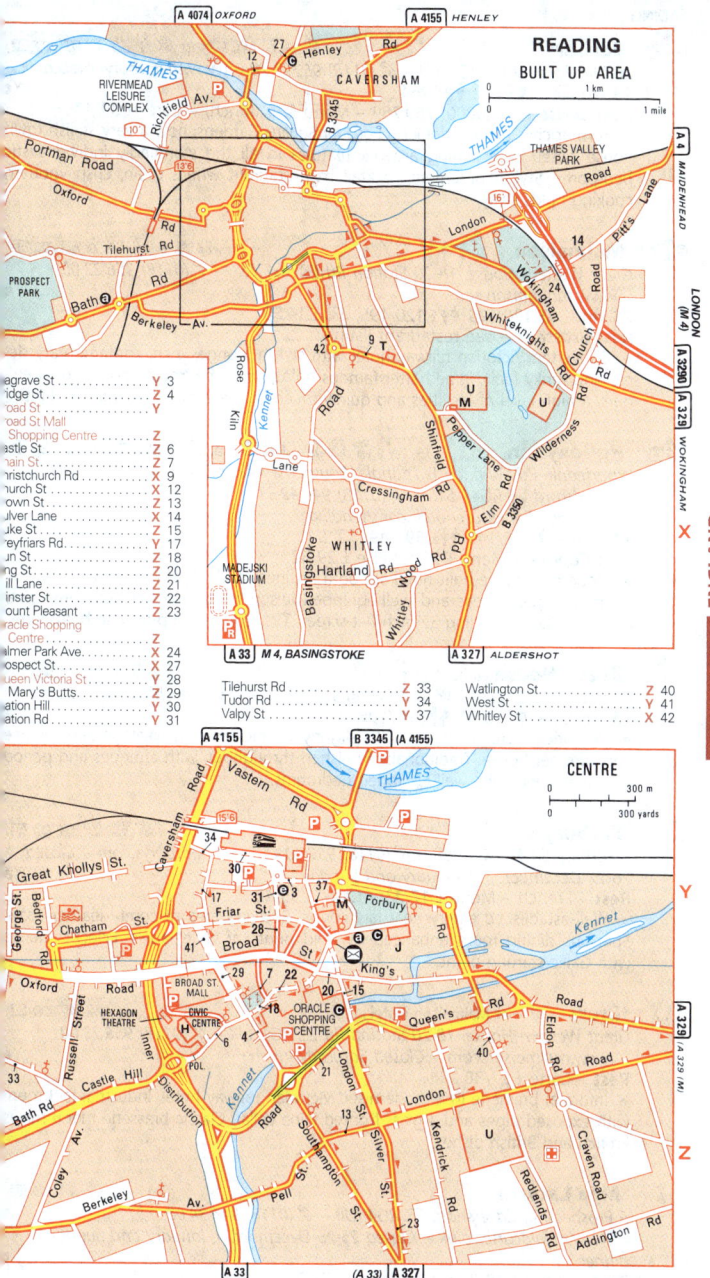

agrave St	Y	3
idge St	Z	4
oad St	Y	
oad St Mall		
Shopping Centre	Z	
astle St	Z	6
ain St	Z	7
hristchurch Rd	X	9
hurch St	X	12
rown St	Z	13
ulver Lane	X	14
uke St	Z	15
reyfriars Rd	Y	17
n St	Z	18
g St	Z	20
ll Lane	Z	21
nster St	Z	22
ount Pleasant	Z	23
racle Shopping Centre	Z	
lmer Park Ave.	X	24
ospect St	X	27
ueen Victoria St	Y	28
Mary's Butts	Y	29
ation Hill	Z	30
ation Rd	Y	31
Tilehurst Rd	Z	33
Tudor Rd	Y	34
Valpy St	Y	37
Watlington St	Z	40
West St	Y	41
Whitley St	X	42

565

READING

Forbury
26 The Forbury ✉ *RG1 3EJ* – ☏ *(0118) 952 77 70* – *www.theforburyhotel.co.uk*
23 rm ⊇ – †£ 252 ††£ 264
Rest *Cerise* – ☏ *(0800) 789 789* – Menu £ 20 (lunch) – Carte £ 30/47
• Former civic hall overlooking Forbury Square Gardens; now a very stylish town house hotel. Eye-catching artwork features in all the stunningly individualistic bedrooms. Stylish basement cocktail bar/restaurant where clean, crisp, modern cooking holds sway.

Malmaison
Great Western House, 18-20 Station Rd ✉ *RG1 1JX* – ☏ *(0118) 956 23 00*
– *www.malmaison.com*
75 rm – †£ 120/195 ††£ 120/195, ⊇ £ 14.50
Rest *Brasserie* – see restaurant listing
• Converted Victorian railway hotel with stylish lounges, rich, contemporary décor and funky feel. Named after famous trains, smart bedrooms display bold colours, a high level of facilities and quirky touches; one even has a train set in it.

Holiday Inn
Wharfedale Rd., Winnersh Triangle, Southeast : 4.5 mi by A 4, A 3290 off Winnersh rd ✉ *RG41 5TS* – ☏ *(0118) 944 42 33*
– *www.meridianleisurehotels.com/reading*
174 rm – †£ 59/149 ††£ 59/149, ⊇ £ 10
Rest *Caprice* – Menu £ 21 – Carte £ 29/32
• Modern, purpose-built hotel set on a business park close to the M4. Spacious, open-plan guest areas and well-equipped leisure club. Uniform bedrooms offer good facilities, including 32 inch flat-screen TVs. Compact, up-to-date bathrooms.

Beech House without rest
60 Bath Rd ✉ *RG30 2AY* – ☏ *(0118) 959 19 01* – *www.beechhousehotel.com*
15 rm ⊇ – †£ 75/95 ††£ 95/105
• Red-brick Victorian house with slightly Gothic exterior. Neat garden, terrace and summer house. Traditionally furnished throughout, with antiques and period ornaments. Pleasant, well-equipped bedrooms.

Forbury's
1 Forbury Sq ✉ *RG1 3BB* – ☏ *(0118) 957 40 44* – *www.forburys.com* – Closed 26-27 December, 1-2 January and Sunday
Rest – French – Menu £ 17/23 – Carte £ 36/42
• Well-established eatery near law courts. Relaxing area of comfy leather seats. Spacious dining room enhanced by bold prints of wine labels. Eclectic menus with Gallic starting point.

Brasserie – at Malmaison Hotel
Great Western House, 18-20 Station Rd ✉ *RG1 1JX* – ☏ *(0118) 956 23 00*
– *www.malmaison.com* – Closed Saturday lunch
Rest – Carte £ 27/38
• Informal brasserie in a modernised Victorian railway hotel. Industrial-feel room with exposed pipes and a glass-fronted wine cellar. Classic brasserie menu mixes French and British dishes.

Mya Lacarte
5 Prospect St, Caversham ✉ *RG4 8JB* – ☏ *(0118) 946 34 00*
– *www.myalacarte.co.uk* – Closed 25-26 December, 1 January and Sunday dinner
Rest – Menu £ 18 (lunch) – Carte £ 27/37
• Buzzy, well-run neighbourhood restaurant. Friendly team serve modern British cooking with a twist. Produce is from nearby farms and allotments; 10kg of produce from local growers = a free meal.

READING

London Street Brasserie
2-4 London St ✉ RG1 4PN – ℰ (0118) 950 50 36 – www.londonstbrasserie.co.uk – Closed 25 December   Zc
Rest – *(booking essential)* Menu £ 20 (lunch) – Carte £ 30/37
♦ Lively and modern: a polite, friendly team serve appetising British classics and international dishes. Deck terrace and first-floor window tables overlook the river Kennett.

at Shinfield South : 4.25 mi on A 327 - ✗ – ✉ Reading

L'Ortolan
Church Lane ✉ RG2 9BY – ℰ (0118) 988 85 00 – www.lortolan.com – Closed 25 December-6 January, Sunday and Monday
Rest – Menu £ 30/67
Spec. Marinated terrine and pan-fried foie gras with rhubarb chutney and sloe gin jelly. Shoulder, loin and lamb sweetbreads with peas, anchovies and capers. Raspberry soufflé, peach salad and vanilla cheesecake.
♦ Red brick former vicarage with lawned gardens and stylish lounge and conservatory. Bright, comfortable dining room; classically based cooking with some original touches and pretty presentation. Smart, busy private dining rooms.

at Sonning-on-Thames Northeast : 4.25 mi by A 4 on B 4446

French Horn with rm
✉ RG4 6TN – ℰ (0118) 969 22 04 – www.thefrenchhorn.co.uk – Closed 25-30 December
17 rm ⊇ – ♰£ 135 ♰♰£ 170 – 4 suites
Rest – *(booking essential)* Menu £ 26 (lunch) – Carte £ 36/72 s
♦ Long-standing, family-owned restaurant in pretty riverside setting. Bay windowed dining room overlooks lovely garden and offers French-influenced menus crafted from seasonal ingredients. Comfy, traditional bedrooms; some in an annexe, some with views.

REDDITCH – Worcestershire – **503** O27 – pop. 74 803   **19** C2
▶ London 111 mi – Birmingham 15 mi – Cheltenham 33 mi
  – Stratford-upon-Avon 15 mi
🛈 Alcester St ℰ (01527) 6 08 06, www.ukinformationcentre.com
🏌 Abbey Hotel G. & C.C. Dagnell End Rd, ℰ (01527) 40 66 00
🏌 Lower Grinsty Callow Hill Green Lane, ℰ (01527) 54 30 79
🏌 Pitcheroak Plymouth Rd, ℰ (01527) 54 10 54

Old Rectory
Ipsley Lane, Ipsley ✉ B98 0AP – ℰ (01527) 523 000
– www.theoldrectory-hotel.co.uk – Closed 25-31 December
10 rm ⊇ – ♰£ 168 ♰♰£ 175
Rest – *(closed Friday-Sunday) (booking essential for non-residents)*
Menu £ 20/25 – Carte £ 25/33
♦ Converted early Georgian rectory surrounded by pleasant mature gardens creating a quiet and secluded haven. Smart, traditional interior décor and individually styled rooms. Charming Georgian style conservatory restaurant.

REDFORD – West Sussex – see Midhurst

REED – Hertfordshire – pop. 273   **12** B2
▶ London 51 mi – Birmingham 115 mi – Sheffield 148 mi – Croydon 75 mi

Cabinet at Reed
High St ✉ SG8 8AH – ℰ (01763) 848 366 – www.thecabinetatreed.co.uk – Closed 25 December, 1 January and Monday lunch
Rest – Menu £ 16/26 – Carte £ 23/35
♦ White clapperboard pub with pleasant restaurant and delightful snug. Cooking is flavoursome but not always what it seems, as traditional dishes are given a more modern twist.

REETH – North Yorkshire – 502 O20 – pop. 939 – ✉ Richmond 22 B1

▶ London 253 mi – Leeds 53 mi – Middlesbrough 36 mi
– Newcastle upon Tyne 61 mi

🛈 The Green ℰ (01748) 88 40 59, www.reeth.org

Burgoyne
On The Green ✉ *DL11 6SN –* ℰ *(01748) 884 292 – www.theburgoyne.co.uk*
– Closed 2 January-10 February
8 rm ⊒ – †£ 111/121 ††£ 151/161 – 1 suite
Rest – *(dinner only) (booking essential for non-residents)* Menu £ 36
♦ Late Georgian hotel overlooking the green with views of the Dales. A charming, personally run, traditionally furnished house with well-appointed, individually styled rooms. Deep green dining room complements surrounding fells.

at Low Row West : 4 mi on B 6270

Punch Bowl Inn with rm
✉ *DL11 6PF –* ℰ *(01748) 886 233 – www.pbinn.co.uk – Closed 25 December*
11 rm ⊒ – †£ 102/105 ††£ 123/129 **Rest** – Carte £ 22/32
♦ Popular with walkers, this traditional 17C stone-built inn has a modernised, shabby-chic interior. Classic dishes are listed on mirrors above the fireplace. Supremely comfortable bedrooms, decorated in a fresh, modern style; all with views over Swaledale.

at Langthwaite Northwest : 3.25 mi on Langthwaite rd – ✉ Reeth

Charles Bathurst Inn with rm
✉ *DL11 6EN –* ℰ *(01748) 884 567 – www.cbinn.co.uk*
19 rm ⊒ – †£ 77/105 ††£ 131/137 **Rest** – Carte £ 20/27
♦ Characterful 18C hostelry set in a peaceful hillside village, boasting commanding rural views. The daily menu, inscribed on a mirror, offers refined yet hearty classical British dishes. Bedrooms are spacious and extremely comfy.

REIGATE – Surrey – 504 T30 – pop. 47 602 7 D2

▶ London 26 mi – Brighton 33 mi – Guildford 20 mi – Maidstone 38 mi

Tony Tobin @ The Dining Room
59a High St ✉ *RH2 9AE –* ℰ *(01737) 226 650 – www.tonytobinrestaurants.co.uk*
– Closed 23 December-3 January, Saturday lunch, Sunday dinner and bank holidays
Rest – Menu £ 21 (lunch) – Carte £ 40/50
♦ Contemporary first floor restaurant with pale hues and comfy lounge/bar above. Classical set lunch, more modern à la carte and 5 course tasting menu; the latter with wine recommendations.

Westerly
✉ *RH2 9AN –* ℰ *(01737) 222 733 – www.thewesterly.co.uk – Closed 24 December-6 January, 1 week August, Sunday, Monday and lunch Tuesday and Saturday*
Rest – *(booking essential at dinner)* Menu £ 22 (lunch) – Carte dinner £ 29/37
♦ Popular, two-roomed restaurant on the corner of a busy road. Concise menus follow the seasons; well-executed dishes are a mix of traditional preparations and modern interpretations of classics.

Barbe
71 Bell St ✉ *RH2 7AN –* ℰ *(01737) 241 966 – www.labarbe.co.uk – Closed 2-3 January, 26-28 December, Saturday lunch, Sunday dinner and bank holiday Mondays*
Rest – French – Menu £ 25/35
♦ Long-standing French bistro with cheery owner and huge local following. Two main dining areas strewn with Gallic memorabilia. Simply laid, tightly packed tables. Classical, bi-monthly menu.

RETFORD – Nottinghamshire – **502** R24 – pop. 20 679   16 B1

▶ London 148 mi – Lincoln 23 mi – Nottingham 31 mi – Sheffield 27 mi
ℹ 40 Grove St ℰ (01777) 86 07 80, www.visitnottingham.com

Barns without rest
Morton Farm, Babworth, Southwest : 2.25 mi by A 6420 ✉ DN22 8HA
– ℰ (01777) 706 336 – www.thebarns.co.uk – Closed Christmas-New Year
6 rm ☐ – †£ 42/68 ††£ 75

♦ Privately owned and run converted part 18C farmhouse on a quiet country road. Informal, old-fashioned, cottage décor throughout. Beams within and lawned gardens without.

RHYDYCROESAU – Shropshire – **502** K25 – see Oswestry

RICHMOND – North Yorkshire – **502** O20 – pop. 8 178   Great Britain   22 B1

▶ London 243 mi – Leeds 53 mi – Middlesbrough 26 mi
– Newcastle upon Tyne 44 mi
ℹ Victoria Rd ℰ (01748) 828 7 42, www.guide2richmond.com
ᛟ Bend Hagg, ℰ (01748) 82 53 19
ᛟ Catterick Leyburn Rd, ℰ (01748) 83 32 68
◉ Town★ - Castle★ **AC** – Georgian Theatre Royal and Museum★
◉ The Bowes Museum★, Barnard Castle, NW : 15 mi by B 6274, A 66 and minor rd (right) – Raby Castle★, NE : 6 mi of Barnard Castle by A 688

Millgate House without rest
3 Millgate ✉ DL10 4JN – ℰ (01748) 823 571 – www.millgatehouse.com
4 rm ☐ – †£ 95/145 ††£ 145

♦ Georgian townhouse with fine elevated views of river Swale and Richmond Castle. Award winning terraced garden. Antique furnished interior. Bedrooms are tastefully restrained.

RINGWOOD – Hampshire – **503** O31 – pop. 13 387   6 A2

▶ London 102 mi – Bournemouth 11 mi – Salisbury 17 mi – Southampton 20 mi
ℹ Visitor Information Point ℰ (01425) 47 08 96, www.ringwood.inuklocal.co.uk

Moortown Lodge without rest
244 Christchurch Rd, South : 1 mi on B 3347 ✉ BH24 3AS – ℰ (01425) 471 404
– www.moortownlodge.co.uk
7 rm ☐ – †£ 73 ††£ 96

♦ Welcoming Georgian hunting lodge, on a busy road at the edge of the forest. Large room with soft seating and neatly laid breakfast tables. Comfy bedrooms; some larger, with feature beds.

RIPLEY – North Yorkshire – **502** P21 – pop. 193 – ✉ Harrogate   22 B2

▶ London 213 mi – Bradford 21 mi – Leeds 18 mi – Newcastle upon Tyne 79 mi

Boar's Head
✉ HG3 3AY – ℰ (01423) 771 888 – www.boarsheadripley.co.uk
25 rm ☐ – †£ 85 ††£ 150
Rest *Restaurant* – Carte £ 20/32
Rest *Bistro* – Carte £ 20/32

♦ 18C coaching inn within estate village of Ripley Castle, reputedly furnished from castle's attics. Comfy, stylish, unique rooms are individually furnished; some in courtyard or adjacent house. Classically based, seasonal dishes in The Restaurant. More informal dining in The Bistro.

RIPLEY – Surrey – 504 S30 – pop. 2 041
7 C1

▶ London 28 mi – Guildford 6 mi

Talbot Inn
High St ⊠ GU23 6BB – ℰ (01483) 225 188 – www.thetalbotinn.com
39 rm – †£ 90/125 ††£ 110/125, ⊆ £ 7.95
Rest – (closed Sunday dinner) Carte £ 26/37
◆ Historic coaching inn dating back to the 15C. Characterful bedrooms in the main house; more uniform rooms in the courtyard. Charming lounge and bar with low beams and open fires. Brasserie-style dining room offers a mix of classic pub and more modern dishes.

Drake's (Steve Drake)
The Clock House, High St ⊠ GU23 6AQ – ℰ (01483) 224 777
– www.drakesrestaurant.co.uk – Closed 2 weeks August, 10 days January, 2 days Christmas, Tuesday lunch, Sunday and Monday
Rest – Menu £ 28/55
Spec. Grilled mackerel, burnt aubergine and cucumber ceviche. Lamb, anchovy, pickled rhubarb and ceps. Raspberry and pineapple ravioli with white pepper.
◆ Georgian restaurant's red brick façade dominated by large clock. Intimate lounges and relaxing, open plan dining room with local gallery art on walls. Simple, seasonal menu; kitchen makes use of modern techniques and interesting combinations. Well-established team provide formal service.

ENGLAND

RIPON – North Yorkshire – 502 P21 – pop. 17 557 ▌Great Britain
22 B2

▶ London 222 mi – Leeds 26 mi – Middlesbrough 35 mi – York 23 mi
🛈 Minster Rd ℰ (01765) 60 46 25, www.visitripon.org
Ripon City Palace Rd, ℰ (01765) 60 36 40
◉ Town★ - Cathedral★ (Saxon Crypt) **AC**
◉ Fountains Abbey★★★ **AC** :- Studley Royal **AC** (≤★ from Anne Boleyn's Seat) - Fountains Hall (Fa 0.5ade★), SW : 2.5 mi by B 6265 – Newby Hall (Tapestries★) **AC**, SE : 3.5 mi by B 6265

Old Deanery
Minster Rd ⊠ HG4 1QS – ℰ (01765) 600 003 – www.theolddeanery.co.uk
– Closed first week January
11 rm ⊆ – †£ 80/105 ††£ 130/155
Rest – (closed Sunday dinner) Menu £ 17 (lunch) – Carte dinner £ 26/38
◆ Eponymously named hotel opposite cathedral. Stylish interior blends seamlessly with older charms. Afternoon tea in secluded garden. 18C oak staircase leads to modern rooms. Appealing seasonal cooking in spacious dining room.

Sharow Cross House
Dishforth Rd, Sharow, Northeast : 1.75 mi by A 61 on Sharow rd ⊠ HG4 5BQ – ℰ (01765) 609 866 – www.sharowcrosshouse.co.uk – Closed Christmas-New Year
3 rm ⊆ – †£ 60/70 ††£ 90/100 **Rest** – Menu £ 25
◆ Late Victorian villa, originally a country residence for a soap manufacturer. Characterful interior with spacious, light-filled rooms; tea served in comfy lounge on arrival. Tastefully furnished bedrooms with thoughtful extras; master room offers cathedral views. Set dinners – choose in advance from a series of seven.

at Aldfield Southwest : 3.75 mi by B 6265 – ⊠ Ripon

Bay Tree Farm
⊠ HG4 3BE – ℰ (01765) 620 394 – www.baytreefarm.co.uk
6 rm ⊆ – †£ 50/60 ††£ 85 **Rest** – (closed Sunday dinner) Menu £ 18
◆ 18C sandstone barn with rural views, set on a working farm. Lounge with wood burning stove and French windows opening into garden; bright, spacious bedrooms with modern bathrooms. Homely food could include beef from the farm.

RISHWORTH – West Yorkshire – see Sowerby Bridge

ROADE – Northamptonshire – **504** R27 – pop. 2 254   **16** B3
▶ London 66 mi – Coventry 36 mi – Leicester 42 mi – Northampton 5 mi

XX **Roade House** with rm   AC rest, ⏻ P VISA ◐ AE
16 High St ✉ *NN7 2NW – ℘ (01604) 863 372 – www.roadehousehotel.co.uk
– Closed 26-30 December, Sunday dinner and bank holiday Mondays*
10 rm ⌑ – †£ 85/150 ††£ 90/150
Rest – Menu £ 25 (lunch) – Carte dinner £ 26/38
♦ Personally run, former village pub and schoolhouse, with open-fired lounge and simple linen-laid dining room. Crafted from local produce, set lunch and à la carte dinner menus offer classical cooking with modern touches. Pleasant bedrooms are furnished in pine.

ROCHDALE – Greater Manchester – **502** N23 – pop. 95 796   **20** B2
▶ London 224 mi – Blackpool 40 mi – Burnley 11 mi – Leeds 45 mi
🛈 The Esplanade ℘ (01706) 92 49 28, www.manchesterscountryside.com
⛳ Bagslate Edenfield Rd, ℘ (01706) 64 38 18
⛳ Marland Bolton Rd, Springfield Park, ℘ (01706) 64 98 01
⛳ Castle Hawk Castleton Chadwick Lane, ℘ (01706) 64 08 41

XX **Peacock Room at The Crimble**   🚗 AC P VISA ◐ AE ①
Crimble Ln, Bamford , West : 2 mi on B 6222 ✉ *OL11 4AD – ℘ (01706) 368 591
– www.thedeackersgroup.com – Closed Saturday lunch, Sunday dinner, Monday and Tuesday*
Rest – Menu £ 16 (lunch and early dinner)/19 – Carte £ 30/41
♦ Large, mirror-ceilinged dining room with vast chandeliers, candelabras, crisp linen and an elegant lounge, set in a landmark Victorian house. Constantly evolving menus and modern presentation.

XX **Nutters**   ≤ AC ⇔ P VISA ◐ AE
Edenfield Rd, Norden, West : 3.5 mi on A 680 ✉ *OL12 7TT – ℘ (01706) 650 167
– www.nuttersrestaurant.com – Closed 27-28 December, 2-3 January and Monday*
Rest – Menu £ 17/40 – Carte £ 26/40
♦ Views of the lyrical gardens contrast with a menu of often complex modern British dishes with international twists and influences. Best views at either end of the room.

ROCK – Cornwall – **503** F32 – pop. 4 593 – ✉ Wadebridge   **1** B2
▶ London 266 mi – Newquay 24 mi – Tintagel 14 mi – Truro 32 mi
◉ Pencarrow★, SE : 8.5 mi by B 3314 and A 389

 **St Enodoc**   ≤ 🚗 ⅃ 🕭 ※ ⏻ P VISA ◐ AE ①
✉ *PL27 6LA – ℘ (01208) 863 394 – www.enodoc-hotel.co.uk – Closed 10 December-10 February*
16 rm ⌑ – †£ 115/185 ††£ 170/235 – 4 suites
Rest *Restaurant Nathan Outlaw* ✿✿ **Rest** *Seafood and Grill* – see restaurant listing
♦ Beautifully located hotel boasting stunning bay views. Strong New England theme throughout with pastel painted woodwork and stripy sofas. Comfy guest areas and modern, well-appointed bedrooms.

XXX **Restaurant Nathan Outlaw** – at the St Enodoc Hotel   ≤ P
✿✿ ✉ *PL27 6LA – ℘ (01208) 863 394 – www.nathan-outlaw.com*   VISA ◐ ①
– Closed 18 December-1February, Sunday and Monday
Rest – Seafood – *(dinner only) (booking essential) (set menu only)* Menu £ 75
Spec. John Dory with parsley dumpling, bacon and hazelnut dressing and asparagus. Roasted turbot with slow cooked lamb belly, beetroot and rosemary. Rhubarb jelly with vanilla cream, rhubarb compote and ginger sorbet.
♦ Intimate fine dining restaurant consisting of just 9 tables, featuring pale colours and modern art. Clean, precise cooking uses the finest quality, seasonal ingredients. Frequently changing set menu showcases fresh, locally caught seafood.

ROCK

✕✕ Dining Room

*Pavilion Buildings, Rock Rd ⊠ PL27 6JS – ✆ (01208) 862 622
– www.thediningroomrock.co.uk – Closed 2 weeks January-February, 2 weeks November, Monday and Tuesday*
Rest – Menu £ 20 (lunch) – Carte dinner £ 30/36
♦ Immaculately kept restaurant with small terrace and friendly team. Flavoursome, classically based cooking features local, seasonal produce: good value set lunches; dinner is more of an event. Everything is homemade, including the butter.

✕ Seafood and Grill – at the St Enodoc Hotel

⊠ *PL27 6LA – ✆ (01208) 863 394 – www.nathan-outlaw.com – Closed 10 December-10 February*
Rest – Carte £ 23/38
♦ All day, split-level restaurant and bar overlooking the Camel Estuary and opening out onto a lovely rear terrace. Menus feature light offerings and simply executed steak and seafood dishes.

at Trebetherick North : 1 mi by Trewint Lane

St Moritz

⊠ *PL27 6SD – ✆ (01208) 862 242 – www.stmoritzhotel.co.uk*
30 rm ⊇ – ♦£ 85/150 ♦♦£ 140/230 – 15 suites
Rest – *(dinner only)* Carte £ 31/43
♦ Art deco style hotel with leisure club, indoor and outdoor swimming pools and a 6 room spa. Smartly furnished bedrooms; spacious bathrooms. Suites have a lounge, kitchen and estuary views. Restaurant displays a simple, flavoursome menu of unfussy dishes.

ROCKBEARE – Devon – see Exeter

ROECLIFFE – North Yorkshire – see Boroughbridge

ROGATE – West Sussex – **504** R30 – pop. 1 785 – ⊠ Petersfield (hants.)   7 C2

▶ London 63 mi – Brighton 42 mi – Guildford 29 mi – Portsmouth 23 mi

⌂ Mizzards Farm without rest

Southwest : 1 mi by Harting rd ⊠ GU31 5HS – ✆ (01730) 821 656 – Closed Christmas and New Year
3 rm ⊇ – ♦£ 55/60 ♦♦£ 90
♦ 17C farmhouse with delightful landscaped gardens, which include a lake, bordered by river Rother. Views of woods and farmland. Fine fabrics and antiques in appealing rooms.

ROMALDKIRK – Durham – **502** N20 – see Barnard Castle

ROMSEY – Hampshire – **503** P31 – pop. 17 386 ▮ Great Britain   6 A2

▶ London 82 mi – Bournemouth 28 mi – Salisbury 16 mi – Southampton 8 mi
🛈 13 Church St ✆ (01794) 51 29 87, www.manchesterscountryside.com
▫ Dunwood Manor Awbridge Danes Rd, ✆ (01794) 34 05 49
▫ Nursling, ✆ (023) 8073 46 37
▫ Wellow East Wellow Ryedown Lane, ✆ (01794) 32 28 72
◉ Abbey★ (interior★★)
◉ Broadlands★ **AC**, S : 1 m

⌂ Ranvilles Farm House without rest

Ower, Southwest : 2 mi on A 3090 (southbound carriageway) ⊠ SO51 6AA – ✆ (023) 8081 4481 – www.ranvilles.com – Closed 25 December
5 rm ⊇ – ♦£ 30/40 ♦♦£ 60/90
♦ Attractive part-16C former farmhouse in mature grounds. Spacious beamed interior has a cottagey, country house feel. Comfy lounge with antique breakfast table and good-sized, homely bedrooms.

ROMSEY

Three Tuns
58 Middlebridge St ⊠ SO51 8HL – ℰ (01794) 512 639
– www.the3tunsromsey.co.uk – Closed Sunday dinner in winter
Rest – Carte £ 15/26
♦ This delightful pub, dating back to the 1720s, now has the tenants it deserves. It oozes charm, with a beamed bar for great nibbles. Expect a proper pub menu with steak and kidney pie, honey-glazed ham and Hampshire rhubarb crumble.

ROSS-ON-WYE – Herefordshire – 503 M28 – pop. 10 085   18 B3
Great Britain

▶ London 118 mi – Gloucester 15 mi – Hereford 15 mi – Newport 35 mi
🛈 Edde Cross St ℰ (01989) 56 27 68, www.wyenot.com
◉ Market House★ – Yat Rock (≤★)
◉ SW : Wye Valley★ – Goodrich Castle★ AC, SW : 3.5 mi by A 40

Wilton Court
Wilton Ln, Wilton, West : 0.75 mi by B 4260 (A 49 Hereford) ⊠ HR9 6AQ
– ℰ (01989) 562 569 – www.wiltoncourthotel.com – Closed 2-15 January
10 rm ⊑ – †£ 100/155 ††£ 125/175
Rest *Mulberry* – Menu £ 18/33 – Carte £ 32/39
♦ Attractive, part-Elizabethan house on the banks of the river Wye. 16C wood panelling in situ in bar and two of the bedrooms: others have a distinctly William Morris influence. Light, airy conservatory restaurant boasts Lloyd Loom furniture and garden views.

Orles Barn with rm
Wilton ⊠ HR9 6AE – ℰ (01989) 562 155 – www.orles-barn.co.uk
6 rm ⊑ – †£ 75/135 ††£ 145/175   **Rest** – (booking essential) Menu £ 22/35
♦ Lovely period house with parts dating from the 14C, 16C and 18C. Spacious dining room and cosy open-fired bar with sage green panelling; cooking is flavoursome and seasonal. Chatty owner provides the service. Smart, comfortable bedrooms boast designer fabrics.

at Kerne Bridge South : 3.75 mi on B 4234 – ⊠ Ross-On-Wye

Lumleys without rest
⊠ HR9 5QT – ℰ (01600) 890 040 – www.thelumleys.co.uk
3 rm ⊑ – †£ 65 ††£ 65/75
♦ Double-fronted brick house with colourful gardens; formerly the village pub, now a cosy, characterful guesthouse run with love and care. Cluttered, homely bedrooms, comfy lounge, and drying room for walkers. Well-located for the Wye Valley and Forest of Dean.

at Walford South: 3.75 mi on B 4234

Mill Race
⊠ HR9 5QS – ℰ (01989) 562 891 – www.millrace.info
Rest – Carte £ 21/34
♦ Surprisingly modern-looking pub in a small country village. Regulars gather at the bar and families are welcome. Cooking is simple and lets the locally sourced ingredients speak for themselves.

ROTHBURY – Northumberland – 501 O18 – pop. 1 963 – ⊠ Morpeth   24 A2
Great Britain

▶ London 311 mi – Edinburgh 84 mi – Newcastle upon Tyne 29 mi
🛈 Church St ℰ (01669) 62 08 87, www.visitnorthumberland.com
◉ Cragside House★ (interior★) AC

ROTHBURY

Farm Cottage without rest
Thropton, West : 2.25 mi on B 6341 ⊠ NE65 7NA – ℰ (01669) 620 831
– www.farmcottageguesthouse.co.uk – Closed 1 week Christmas
5 rm ⊡ – †£ 55/65 ††£ 75/100
♦ 18C stone cottage and gardens; the owner was actually born here. Two comfy lounges filled with family prints and curios. Individually styled rbedooms with plenty of extra touches; the Garden Room is located outside and is the most modern.

Thropton Demesne Farmhouse without rest
Thropton, West : 2.25 mi on B 6341 ⊠ NE65 7LT – ℰ (01669) 620 196
– www.throptondemesne.co.uk – March-October
4 rm ⊡ – †£ 50 ††£ 75
♦ Early 19C stone-built former farmhouse; unbroken Coquet Valley views. Lounge defined by quality décor. Artwork on walls by owner. Individually styled rooms with lovely vistas.

ROWDE – Wiltshire – **503** N29 – see Devizes

ROWHOOK – West Sussex – see Horsham

ROWSLEY – Derbyshire – **502** P24 – pop. 451 – ⊠ Matlock   **16** A1
■ Great Britain

▶ London 157 mi – Derby 23 mi – Manchester 40 mi – Nottingham 30 mi
◉ Chatsworth★★★ (Park and Garden★★★) **AC**, N : by B 6012

East Lodge
⊠ DE4 2EF – ℰ (01629) 734 474 – www.eastlodge.com
12 rm ⊡ – †£ 80/150 ††£ 80/150
Rest – Menu £ 40 (dinner) – Carte £ 27/39
♦ 17C hunting lodge in 10 acres of landscaped gardens. Elegant, well-appointed guest areas. Smart bedrooms – several with four-posters – have good views and state-of-the-art bathrooms, some with TVs. Fresh cooking: everything made in-house; simpler dishes at lunch.

Peacock
Bakewell Rd ⊠ DE4 2EB – ℰ (01629) 733 518 – www.thepeacockatrowsley.com
– Closed 24-26 December
16 rm – †£ 105/215 ††£ 190/250, ⊡ £ 7.25
Rest – *(closed dinner 24-26 December and Sunday)* Menu £ 26 (lunch)
– Carte £ 41/55
♦ Characterful 17C house with gardens leading down to the river. Bold modern colours sit alongside fine art and period furnishings in both the guest areas and bedrooms. Charming bar boasts stone walls, large fireplace and snack menu. Restaurant offers modern dishes.

ROYAL LEAMINGTON SPA – Warwickshire – **503** P27   **19** D3
– pop. 61 595

▶ London 99 mi – Birmingham 23 mi – Coventry 9 mi – Leicester 33 mi
🛈 The Parade ℰ (01926) 74 27 62, www.royal-leamington-spa.co.uk
⛳ Leamington and County Whitnash Golf Lane, ℰ (01926) 42 59 61

ROYAL LEAMINGTON SPA

elaide Rd	V
enue Rd	V 2
h St	V 3
auchamp Ave	U
auchamp Hill	U 4
swood St	U 6
ndon Parade	U 10
rch Hill	UV 16
rendon Ave	U
rendon Pl	U 18
e St	UV
milton Terrace	V 21
h St	V 22
ly Walk	U
nilworth Rd	V
m Terrace	V
cester St	U
ngton Ave	U
ngton Rd	U
ver Ave	V 28
wbold Terrace	V 30
thumberland Rd	U 33
Warwick Rd	U
ade	UV
ory Terrace	V 37
dford Rd	UV
gent Grove	UV 40
gent St	U
al Priors Shopping Centre	U
gby Rd	U
ssell Terrace	V 44
encer St	V
hbrook Rd	V 47
toria Terrace	V 49
rwick St	U
les Rd	UV

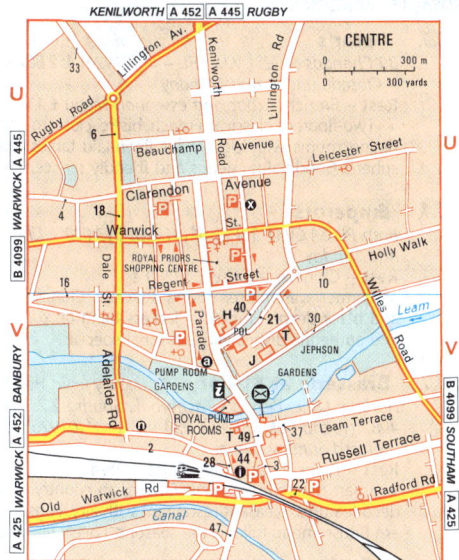

 Mallory Court
Harbury Lane, Bishop's Tachbrook, South : 2.25 mi by B 4087 (Tachbrook Rd) ⊠ CV33 9QB – ℘ (01926) 453 939 – www.mallory.co.uk
30 rm – †£ 105/395 ††£ 159/495
Rest *Brasserie at Mallory* – see restaurant listing
Rest *The Dining Room* – *(closed Saturday lunch) (booking essential)*
Menu £ 33/60
Spec. Salad of blue lobster, compressed melon and Parma ham. Chump of lamb, tagine style spring roll and tahini. 'K' lime pie with chocolate ice cream and meringues.
♦ Charming part-Edwardian country house in Lutyens style, with delightful gardens. Classical lounges display fine antiques and quality furnishings; more modern extension houses the function room. Smart bedrooms are in keeping with the age of the building and come with fresh flowers and fruit. Excellent service. Smart brasserie or elegant, wood-panelled dining room offering daily set menu and elaborate à la carte.

 Adams without rest
22 Avenue Rd ⊠ CV31 3PQ – ℘ (01926) 450 742 – www.adams-hotel.co.uk
– Closed 23 December-2 January   **Vn**
12 rm – †£ 68/88 ††£ 88/115
♦ Delightful house of the Regency period with plenty of charm and character: original features include ceiling mouldings. Immaculate and similarly attractive bedrooms.

Restaurant 23
23 Dormer Pl. ⊠ CV32 5AA – ℘ (01926) 422 422 – www.restaurant23.co.uk
– Closed 1-14 January, last 2 weeks August, 25-26 December, Sunday and Monday   **Va**
Rest – Menu £ 20/25 – Carte £ 38/55
♦ Intimate restaurant with open kitchen and elegantly appointed surroundings. Classically based, seasonal, modern dishes are created by the owner. Interesting wine list features some rarely seen 'esoteric' wines.

ROYAL LEAMINGTON SPA

Oscar's
39 Chandos St ⊠ CV32 4RL – ℰ (01926) 452 807 – www.oscarsfrenchbistro.co.uk – Closed Sunday and Monday Ux
Rest – French – *(booking essential)* Menu £ 11/28
- Two-floored, classical French bistro close to the main shopping street. Three dining rooms with closely set linen-laid tables, busy walls and plenty of atmosphere. Good value menus and friendly service.

Emperors
Bath Pl. ⊠ CV31 3BP – ℰ (01926) 313 030 – Closed 1 January, 25-26 December and Sunday Vi
Rest – Chinese – Carte £ 21/30 **s**
- Former warehouse, now a spacious Chinese restaurant with smart red, gold and black décor. Emperors' jackets hang on the walls. Large menus mix popular and authentic dishes with seasonal specials.

Brasserie at Mallory – at Mallory Court Hotel
Harbury Lane, Bishop's Tachbrook, South : 2.25 mi by B 4087 (Tachbrook Rd) ⊠ CV33 9QB – ℰ (01926) 453 939 – www.mallory.co.uk – Closed Sunday dinner
Rest – *(booking essential)* Carte £ 25/42
- Smart brasserie in a part-Edwardian country house. Striking bar with black art deco features; pleasant restaurant with airy, conservatory style. Wide-ranging modern British menu follows the seasons. Lovely views of the pretty walled garden.

ENGLAND

at Weston under Wetherley Northeast : 4.5 mi by A 445 on B 4453
– ⊠ Royal Leamington Spa

Wethele Manor without rest
⊠ CV33 9BZ – ℰ (01926) 831 772 – www.wethelemanor.com
9 rm ⊡ – †£ 70 ††£ 70/95
- 16C farmhouse with large garden, patio and water feature, set in 250 acres of working farm. Comfy lounge in old dairy; wood-furnished breakfast room complete with well. Classical bedrooms.

at Offchurch East : 3.5 mi by A 425

Stag
Welsh Rd ⊠ CV33 9AQ – ℰ (01926) 425 801 – www.thestagatoffchurch.com
Rest – Carte £ 22/40
- 16C thatched pub with boldly coloured bar and 2 modern dining rooms. Extensive menu changes with the seasons, offering generous, classically based dishes and sharing plates. Efficient service.

ROYAL TUNBRIDGE WELLS – Kent – **504** U30 – pop. 59 371   8 B2
Great Britain

▶ London 36 mi – Brighton 33 mi – Folkestone 46 mi – Hastings 27 mi
▮ The Pantiles ℰ (01892) 51 56 75, www.visittunbridgewells.com
◉ Langton Rd, ℰ (01892) 52 30 34
◉ The Pantiles★ B **26** – Calverley Park★ B

Hotel du Vin
Crescent Rd ⊠ TN1 2LY – ℰ (01892) 526 455 – www.hotelduvin.com
34 rm ⊡ – †£ 130/290 ††£ 130/290 Bc
Rest *Bistro* – see restaurant listing
- Attractive 18C property in the town centre, boasting southerly views over the park. Wine-themed throughout, with comfy lounge, clubby bar and even its own vineyard. Contemporary bedrooms; some have baths in the room and emperor-sized beds.

ROYAL TUNBRIDGE WELLS

Benhall Mill Rd	**A** 3	Hall's Hole Rd	**A** 13	Pantiles (The)	**B** 26
Bishop's Down	**A** 4	High Rocks Lane	**A** 16	Prospect Rd	**A** 27
Calverley Rd	**B**	High St	**B** 14	Royal Victoria Pl. Shopping Centre	**B**
Crescent Rd	**B** 9	Hungershall Park Rd	**A** 17	Rusthall Rd	**A** 28
Fir Tree Rd	**A** 10	Lansdowne Rd	**B** 18	St John's Rd	**B** 29
Grosvenor Rd	**B** 12	Lower Green Rd	**A** 20	Tea Garden Lane	**A** 30
		Major York's Rd	**A** 21	Vale Rd	**B** 33
		Monson Rd	**B** 22	Victoria Rd	**B** 34
		Mount Ephraim	**A, B** 23	Warwick Park	**B** 35
		Mount Ephraim Rd	**B** 24		
		Mount Pleasant Rd	**B** 25		

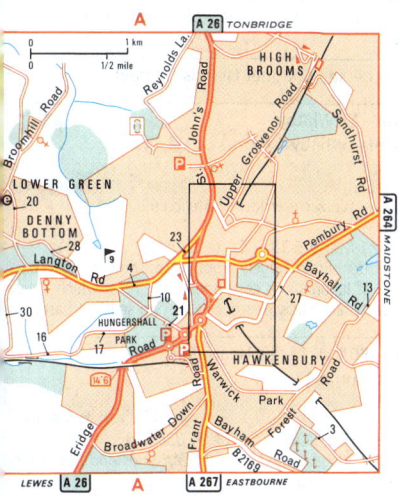
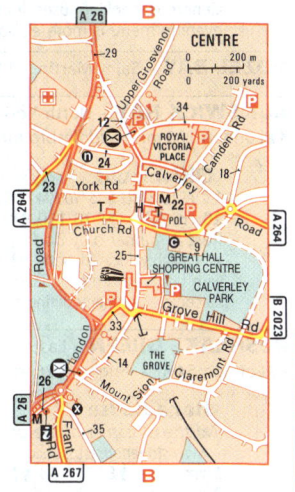

Brew House
1 Warwick Pk. ✉ *TN2 5TA –* ℡ *(01892) 520 587 – www.brewhousehotel.com*
15 rm – †£ 155 ††£ 199   **B**x
Rest *One* – Carte £ 18/37
♦ Former brewhouse and Subbuteo factory; now a boutique hotel. Bedrooms - 3 of which have balconies - boast a clean, minimalist style; bathrooms have glass walls which turn opaque at the touch of a button. Stylish restaurant decorated in vivid pinks and stark whites.

Danehurst without rest
41 Lower Green Rd, Rusthall, West : 1.75 mi by A 264 ✉ *TN4 8TW –* ℡ *(01892) 527 739 – www.danehurst.net – Closed Christmas and New Year*   **A**e
4 rm ⊡ – †£ 70/95 ††£ 99/139
♦ Quiet Victorian house with terrace and koi carp pond. Quality furnishings and good attention to detail in bedrooms. Comfy lounge, library and conservatory breakfast room with homemade bread/jam.

Thackeray's
85 London Rd ✉ *TN1 1EA –* ℡ *(01892) 511 921*
– www.thackerays-restaurant.co.uk – Closed Sunday dinner and Monday
Rest – Menu £ 19/27 – Carte £ 42/53   **B**n
♦ Attractive clapperboard house; former residence of the author Thackeray. Lovely terrace, lounge and two dining rooms with bold art. Classical cooking uses good ingredients; modern presentation.

Bistro – at Hotel du Vin
Crescent Rd ✉ *TN1 2LY –* ℡ *(01892) 526 455 – www.hotelduvin.com*
Rest – (booking essential) Carte £ 25/36   **B**c
♦ Popular bistro in an attractive 18C town centre hotel. Walls are covered with wine-themed pictures and hops hang from the ceiling. Concise menu offers classic British and international dishes.

ROYAL TUNBRIDGE WELLS

at Speldhurst Northwest : 3.5 mi by A 26 - **A**

George & Dragon
Speldhurst Hill ⊠ TN3 0NN – ℰ (01892) 863 125 – www.speldhurst.com – Closed 1 January, Sunday dinner and bank holiday Monday dinner
Rest – Carte £ 23/31
♦ Impressive and hugely characterful Wealden Hall house dating back to 1212. Generous cooking uses local, organic produce. Lunch offers pub classics; the evening menu is more elaborate.

ROZEL BAY – Saint Martin – **503** P33 – see Channel Islands (Jersey)

RUNSWICK BAY – North Yorkshire – ⊠ Whitby   **23** C1
▶ London 285 mi – Middlesbrough 24 mi – Whitby 9 mi

Cliffemount
⊠ TS13 5HU – ℰ (01947) 840 103 – www.cliffemounthotel.co.uk
20 rm ⊑ – †£ 70/110 ††£ 175
Rest – (dinner only and light lunch) Menu £ 33 – Carte £ 28/43
♦ Enviably located hotel which has benefitted hugely from refurbishment. Cosy bar with blackboard menu. Balanced mix of luxurious or cosy bedrooms, 10 of which have balconies. Light, airy dining room boasts fantastic views of bay. Strong seafood base.

RUSHLAKE GREEN – East Sussex – **504** U31 – ⊠ Heathfield   **8** B2
▶ London 54 mi – Brighton 26 mi – Eastbourne 13 mi

Stone House
(Northeast corner of the green.) ⊠ TN21 9QJ – ℰ (01435) 830 553
– www.stonehousesussex.co.uk – Closed 20 February-16 March, Christmas and New Year
5 rm ⊑ – †£ 102/138 ††£ 204/275 – 2 suites
Rest – (dinner only and lunch May-August) (residents only) Menu £ 29 (dinner) **s** – Carte lunch approx. £ 19 **s**
♦ Impressive gates and beautiful gardens lead to charming, part-15C house; personally run and still in the same family. Country house interior with original staircases, wood-panelling and antiques. Individually decorated bedrooms feature period furnishings and some four-posters. Classical menus use kitchen garden produce.

RYE – East Sussex – **504** W31 – pop. 3 708 ▮ Great Britain   **9** C2
▶ London 61 mi – Brighton 49 mi – Folkestone 27 mi – Maidstone 33 mi
ℹ 4/5 Lion St ℰ (01797) 22 90 49, www.visitrye.co.uk
◉ Old Town★★ : Mermaid Street★, St Mary's Church (≼★)

George in Rye
98 High St. ⊠ TN31 7JT – ℰ (01797) 222 114 – www.thegeorgeinrye.com
24 rm ⊑ – ††£ 195   **Rest** – Carte £ 16/34
♦ Part 16C coaching inn; appealing mix of contemporary design and original features. Variously-sized bedrooms have state-of-the-art TVs and quality linen. Pleasant courtyard. Trendy restaurant offers Mediterranean dishes made with locally sourced produce and good choice of wines by glass.

Mermaid Inn
Mermaid St. ⊠ TN31 7EY – ℰ (01797) 223 065 – www.mermaidinn.com
31 rm ⊑ – †£ 90/260 ††£ 220/260   **Rest** – Menu £ 25/38 – Carte £ 27/61
♦ Historic inn dating from 15C. Immense character from the timbered exterior on a cobbled street to the heavily beamed, antique furnished interior warmed by roaring log fires. Two dining options: both exude age and character.

Jeake's House without rest
Mermaid St. ⊠ TN31 7ET – ℰ (01797) 222 828 – www.jeakeshouse.com
11 rm ⊑ – †£ 69/79 ††£ 138
♦ Down a cobbled lane, a part 17C house, once a wool store and a Quaker meet- ing place. Welcoming atmosphere amid antiques, sloping floors and beams. Pretty, traditional rooms.

RYE

Oaklands without rest
Udimore Rd, Southwest : 1.25 mi on B 2089 – TN31 6AB – ℰ (01797) 229 734
– www.oaklands-rye.co.uk
3 rm – †£ 70/80 ††£ 100/120
♦ Friendly Edwardian house with town/coast/white cliff views. Guest areas feature souvenirs from owner's time abroad – breakfast table is an Omani front door. Well-kept bedrooms; 2 four-posters.

Willow Tree House without rest
113 Winchelsea Rd., South : 0.5 mi on A 259 – TN31 7EL – ℰ (01797) 227 820
– www.willow-tree-house.com
6 rm – †£ 75/95 ††£ 90/130
♦ Lovingly restored 18C house close to harbour. Light colours and modern fabrics sit beside exposed brickwork and original fireplaces. Bedrooms boast excellent bathrooms with power showers. Good breakfasts.

Webbe's at The Fish Café
17 Tower St. – TN31 7AT – ℰ (01797) 222 226 – www.webbesrestaurants.co.uk
– Closed 24 December-2 January
Rest – Seafood – Carte £ 21/42
♦ Relaxed café in former antiques warehouse, with terracotta-coloured brick walls, open-plan kitchen and small counter. Extensive menu of simply prepared seafood from Rye/Hastings day boats.

Ship Inn with rm
The Strand – TN31 7DB – ℰ (01797) 222 233 – www.theshipinnrye.co.uk
10 rm – †£ 80 ††£ 100   **Rest** – Carte £ 23/28
♦ 16C former warehouse with shabby, slightly wacky styling and extremely laid-back feel. Carefully prepared, rustic dishes arrive in generous, flavoursome portions and ingredients are well-sourced. Compact bedrooms boast unusual feature walls and bold styling.

at Camber Southeast : 4.25 mi by A 259 – ⊠ Rye

Gallivant
New Lydd Rd. – TN31 7RB – ℰ (01797) 225 057 – www.thegallivanthotel.com
18 rm – †£ 85/125 ††£ 95/135
Rest *Beach Bistro* – see restaurant listing
♦ Laid-back hotel opposite Camber Sands, run by a keen, friendly team. Small lounge and terrace with slightly bohemian feel. Bedrooms come in blues and whites, with distressed wood furniture and good modern facilities; four are studio-style.

Beach Bistro – at Gallivant Hotel
New Lydd Rd. – TN31 7RB – ℰ (01797) 225 057 – www.thegallivanthotel.com
Rest – Carte £ 23/36
♦ Informal hotel restaurant displaying distressed wood furniture and white and blue hues, set opposite Camber Sands. All-day menus have local seafood to the fore. Pleasant covered terrace.

SAFFRON WALDEN – Essex – 504 U27 – pop. 14 313   12 B1
▶ London 43 mi – Bishop's Stortford 12 mi – Cambridge 18 mi

the restaurant
Victoria House, 2 Church St – CB10 1JW – ℰ (01799) 526 444 – www.trocs.co.uk
– Closed 2 weeks summer, 26 December-2 January, Easter, Sunday and Monday
Rest – (dinner only) Menu £ 18 (weekdays) – Carte £ 24/35 **s**
♦ Cosy basement restaurant in town centre, displaying stone floors, exposed brick and modern art. Stylishly presented dishes boast well-defined flavours and some interesting Mediterranean touches.

SAFFRON WALDEN

Dish
13a King St ⊠ CB10 1HE – ℰ (01799) 513 300 – www.dishrestaurant.co.uk
– Closed 25-26 December, 1 January, Sunday dinner and bank holiday Mondays
Rest – Menu £ 20/25
♦ First floor restaurant within characterful beamed house in town centre. Modern oil paintings exude jazzy theme. Classically based dishes take on adventurous note at dinner.

ST ALBANS – Hertfordshire – 504 T28 – pop. 80 664 ▍Great Britain   12 A2

▶ London 27 mi – Cambridge 41 mi – Luton 10 mi
🛈 Market Pl ℰ (01727) 86 45 11, www.allaboutstalbans.com
🇷18 Batchwood Hall Batchwood Drive, ℰ (01727) 83 33 49
🇷27 Redbourn Kinsbourne Green Lane, ℰ (01582) 79 34 93
◎ City★ - Cathedral★ **BZ** – Verulamium★ (Museum★ **AC AY**)
◎ Hatfield House★★ **AC**, E : 6 mi by A 1057

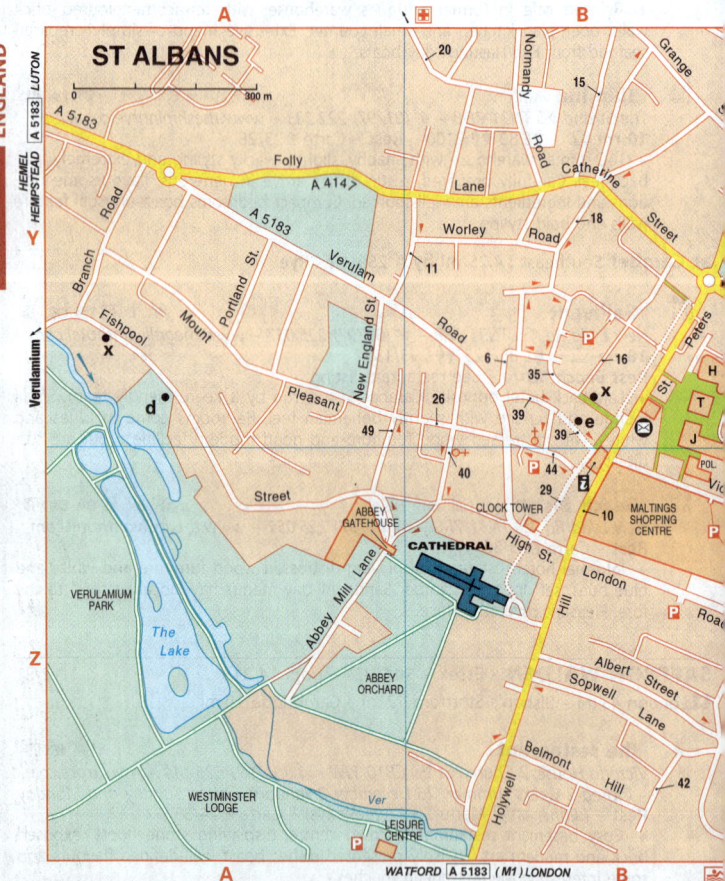

ST ALBANS

St Michael's Manor
St Michael's Village, Fishpool St ⊠ AL3 4RY – ℰ (01727) 864 444
– www.stmichaelsmanor.com   AYd
29 rm – †£ 125/180 ††£ 260 – 1 suite
Rest *The Lake* – see restaurant listing
♦ Part-16C William and Mary manor house boasting well-tended gardens and lake views. Characterful guest areas display contemporary touches. Well-appointed, traditionally styled bedrooms; annexe rooms are more modern and some have terraces.

Cibo DiVino
4-5 Waddington Rd ⊠ AL3 5FX – ℰ (01727) 899 189 – www.cibodivino.co.uk
– Closed Sunday dinner and Monday   BYx
Rest – Italian – Menu £ 14 (lunch) – Carte £ 28/37
♦ Keenly run restaurant hidden down a side street; a partnership between an Italian and an experienced English chef. Authentic Italian cooking displays fresh, clear flavours. Pasta is homemade and many ingredients are imported from Italy.

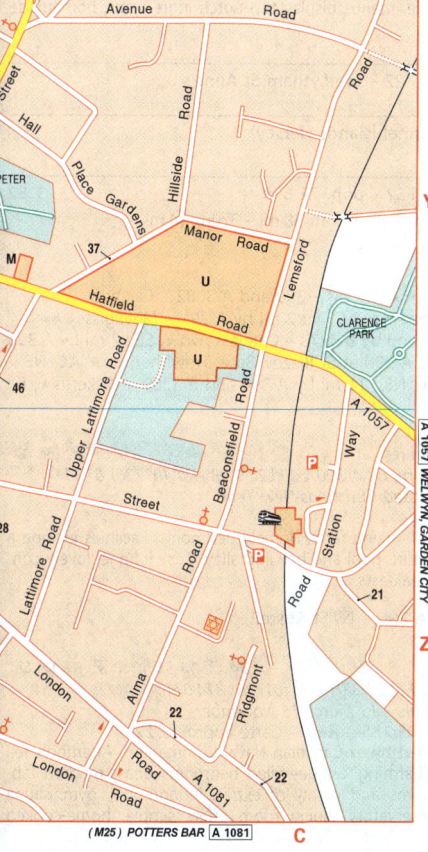

Abbey Mill Lane	AZ
Albert St.	BZ
Alma Rd.	CZ
Avenue Rd	CY
Beaconsfield Rd.	CYZ
Belmont Hill	BZ
Branch Rd	AY
Bricket Rd	BCYZ 5
Britton Ave	BY 6
Carlisle Ave.	BCY
Catherine St	BY
Chequer St	BZ 10
Church Crescent	ABY 11
Cottonmill Lane	BCZ 13
Dalton St	BY 15
Drovers Way	BY 16
Etna Rd	BY 18
Fishpool St	AYZ
Folly Ave	BY 20
Folly Lane	ABY
Grange St	BY
Grimston Rd	CZ 21
Grosvenor Rd	CZ 22
Hall Pl. Gardens	CY
Hatfield Rd	CY
High St.	BZ
Hillside Rd	CY
Holywell Hill	BZ
Lattimore Rd	CZ
Lemsford Rd	CY
London Rd	BCZ
Lower Dagnall St	BYZ 26
Maltings Shopping Centre	BZ
Manor Rd	CY
Market Pl.	BZ 29
Marlborough Rd	CZ 28
Mount Pleasant	AY
New England St	AY
Normandy Rd	BY
Old London Rd	CZ
Portland St.	AY
Ridgemont Rd	CZ
Russell Ave	BY 35
St Peter's Rd.	CY 37
St Peter's St	BCY
Sopwell Lane	BZ
Spencer St	BY 39
Spicer St College	BYZ 40
Station Way	CZ
Thorpe Rd	BZ 42
Upper Dagnall St	BYZ 44
Upper Lattimore Rd	CYZ
Upper Marlborough Rd	CYZ 46
Verulam Rd	ABY
Victoria St	BCZ
Watson's Walk	CZ 48
Welclose St	AYZ 49
Worley Rd	BY

ST ALBANS

The Lake – at St Michael's Manor Hotel
St Michael's Village, Fishpool St ✉ AL3 4RY – ℰ (01727) 864 444
– www.stmichaelsmanor.com   AYd
Rest – *(closed dinner 25 December)* Menu £ 17/21 (weekday dinner)
– Carte £ 34/43
♦ Light, airy conservatory restaurant in a family owned, part-16C William and Mary manor house; set to the rear, it looks out over well-tended gardens. Modern menu has a largely classical base.

Sukiyaki
6 Spencer St ✉ AL3 5EG – ℰ (01727) 865 009 – Closed 2 weeks in summer, 1
week Christmas, Sunday, Monday and Tuesday lunch   BYe
Rest – Japanese – Menu £ 9/22 – Carte £ 17/20
♦ A pared-down style, minimally decorated restaurant with simple, precise helpings of Japanese food. No noodles or sushi, expect instead sukiyaki (a beef dish), and tempura.

Blue Anchor
145 Fishpool St ✉ AL3 4RY – ℰ (01727) 855 038
– www.theblueanchorstalbans.co.uk – Closed Sunday dinner   AYx
Rest – Menu £ 17 (lunch) – Carte £ 22/30
♦ Smart pub with bistro-style interior and riverside garden. The chef is passionate about local, seasonal produce; menus display top notch ingredients, homemade and home-smoked products.

ST ANNE'S – Lancashire – **502** K22 – see Lytham St Anne's

ST AUBIN – **503** P33 – see Channel Islands (Jersey)

ST AUSTELL – Cornwall – **503** F32 – pop. 22 658   **1** B2

▶ London 281 mi – Newquay 16 mi – Plymouth 38 mi – Truro 14 mi
🛈 Carlyon Bay, ℰ (01726) 81 42 50
◉ Holy Trinity Church★
◉ St Austell Bay★★ (Gribbin Head★★) E : by A 390 and A 3082 – Carthew : Wheal Martyn China Clay Heritage Centre★★ **AC**, N : 2 mi by A 391 – Mevagissey★★ - Lost Gardens of Heligan★, S : 5 mi by B 3273 – Charlestown★, SE : 2 mi by A 390 – Eden Project★★, NE : 3 mi by A 390 at St Blazey Gate. Trewithen★★★ **AC**, NE : 7 mi by A 390 – Lanhydrock★★, NE : 11 mi by A 390 and B 3269 – Polkerris★, E : 7 mi by A 390 and A 3082

Poltarrow Farm without rest
St Mewan, Southwest : 1.75 mi by A 390 ✉ PL26 7DR – ℰ (01726) 67 111
– www.poltarrow.co.uk – Closed Christmas-New Year
5 rm 🖃 – †£ 60 ††£ 80
♦ Appealing 19C house on working farm. Homely bedrooms. Facilities include a snooker table, badminton court, pool and bowling alley. Cosy lounge; lovely conservatory for Aga-cooked breakfasts.

at Tregrehan East : 2.5 mi by A 390 – ✉ St Austell

Anchorage House
Nettles Corner, Boscundle ✉ PL25 3RH – ℰ (01726) 814 071
– www.anchoragehouse.co.uk – 15 March-15 November
5 rm 🖃 – †£ 70/75 ††£ 105/135   **Rest** – Carte approx. £ 22
♦ Modern guesthouse owned by ex-Canadian Naval Commander. Afternoon tea served in comfy lounge. Charming, antique-filled bedrooms boast modern fabrics, state-of-the-art bathrooms and plenty of extras. Indoor pool, gym, sauna and chill out lounge. Conservatory dining room offers simple, home-cooked dishes. Lovely owners.

ST AUSTELL

at Carlyon Bay East : 2.5 mi by A 3601 – ✉ St Austell

Carlyon Bay
✉ PL25 3RD – ℰ (01726) 812 312 – www.carlyonbay.com
86 rm (dinner included) ☑ – ♦£ 95/300 ♦♦£ 280/400
Rest *Bay View* – Menu £ 22/38 – Carte £ 38/53
Rest *Taste* – (dinner only) Carte £ 33/59

♦ Imposing 1920s hotel boasting original art deco features and superb bay views. Large, traditionally furnished guest areas. Modern bedrooms feature lightly hued fabrics: rear rooms are bright; front rooms have views. Bay View serves unfussy classics. Taste offers modern brasserie fare.

Austell's
10 Beach Rd. ✉ PL25 3PH – ℰ (01726) 813 888 – www.austells.net – Closed 1-14 January, 25-26 December and Monday
Rest – (dinner only) Menu £ 20/33

♦ Keenly run restaurant with relaxed, stylish interior. Small bar and open-plan kitchen. Modern, seasonal menu showcases local produce and features original touches. More casual weekend lunches.

ST BLAZEY – Cornwall – 503 F32 – pop. 8 837   1 B2
▶ London 276 mi – Newquay 21 mi – Plymouth 33 mi – Truro 19 mi
◉ Eden Project★★, NW; 1.5 mi by A 390 and minor roads

Penarwyn House without rest
West : 0.75 mi by A 390 turning left at Doubletree School ✉ PL24 2DS
– ℰ (01726) 814 224 – www.penarwyn.co.uk – Closed 1 week Christmas
3 rm ☑ – ♦£ 65/85 ♦♦£ 80/150

♦ Whitewashed former gentleman's residence, surrounded by mature gardens and run by welcoming owners. Spacious lounge, clubby snooker room and formal breakfast room. Bedrooms boast bold features walls, antique furniture and modern facilities.

ST BRELADE'S BAY – 503 P33 – see Channel Islands (Jersey)

ST HELIER – 503 P33 – see Channel Islands (Jersey)

ST HILARY – Cornwall – see Marazion

ST ISSEY – Cornwall – 503 F32 – see Padstow

ST IVES – Cornwall – 503 D33 – pop. 9 866   1 A3
▶ London 319 mi – Penzance 10 mi – Truro 25 mi
🛈 Street-an-Pol ℰ (01736) 79 62 97, www.stives-cornwall.co.uk
🏌 Tregenna Castle H., ℰ (01736) 79 52 54
🏌 West Cornwall Lelant, ℰ (01736) 75 34 01
◉ Town★★ - Barbara Hepworth Museum★★ **AC** Y **M1** – Tate St Ives★★ (≤★★) - St Nicholas Chapel (≤★★) Y – Parish Church★ Y **A**
◉ S : Penwith★★ Y. St Michael's Mount★★ (≤★★) S : 10 mi by B 3306 - Y - B 3311, B 3309 and A 30

Plan on next page

Blue Hayes without rest
Trelyon Ave ✉ TR26 2AD – ℰ (01736) 797 129 – www.bluehayes.co.uk
– March-October   Y**u**
6 rm ☑ – ♦£ 100/140 ♦♦£ 210/230

♦ 19C house with super view from terrace over the harbour; access to coast path from garden. Hi-tech interior. Single course supper available. Well-appointed bedrooms.

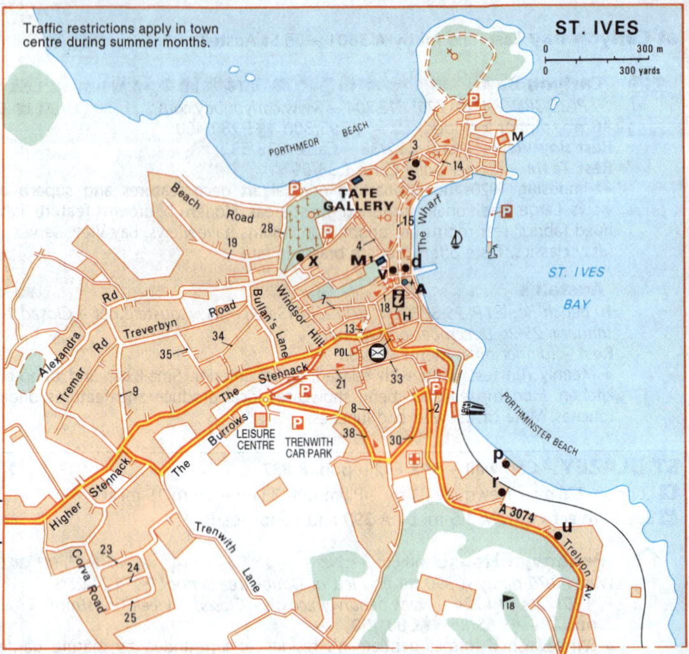

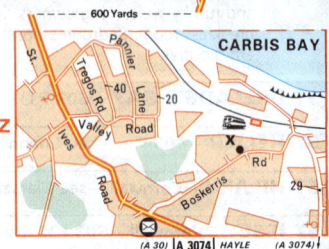

Albert Rd	Y 2	Porthia Crescent	Y 24
Back Rd West	Y 3	Porthia Rd	Y 25
Barnoon Hill	Y 4	Porthmeor Hill	Y 28
Bedford Rd	Y 7	Porthrepta Rd	Z 29
Bishop's Rd	Y 8	Talland Rd	Y 30
Carnellis Rd	Y 9	Tregenna Terrace	Y 33
Chapel Rd	Y 13	Trelawney Rd	Y 34
Fish St	Y 14	Trerice Rd	Y 35
Fore St	Y 15	Trewidden Rd	Y 38
High St	Y 18	Wheal Whidden	Z 40
Orange Lane	Y 19		
Parc Owles	Z 20		
Park Ave	Y 21		
Penwith Rd	Y 23		

Primrose Valley without rest

Porthminster Beach ✉ TR26 2ED – ✆ (01736) 794 939
– www.primroseonline.co.uk – Closed 21-26 December and 3-31 January
9 rm ⊑ – †£ 130/160 ††£ 140/240 – 1 suite   Yr
♦ Edwardian villa with unrivalled proximity to beach. Stylish café bar and lounge; relaxing front patio. Local suppliers ensure good breakfast choice. Individually styled rooms.

abode st ives without rest

1 Fern Glen ✉ TR26 1QP – ✆ (01736) 799 047 – www.abodestives.co.uk
4 rm ⊑ – †£ 100/120 ††£ 110/130   Yx
♦ Chic, contemporary guesthouse offering stylish, immaculately kept bedrooms; two with sea views. Cosy minimal sitting room. Open-plan kitchen/breakfast room. Laid-back owners.

ST IVES

Alba ✂✂
Old Lifeboat House, The Wharf ✉ TR26 1LF – ✆ (01736) 797 222
– www.thealbarestaurant.com – closed 25-26 December   Y**d**
Rest – Menu £ 19 (lunch and early dinner) – Carte £ 26/33
♦ Ideally situated in centre of town, on both floors of Old Lifeboat House; good harbour views. Modern feel; artwork on walls. Tasty, extensive menus with a modern slant.

Porthminster Beach Cafe ✂
Porthminster Beach ✉ TR26 2EB – ✆ (01736) 935 352
– www.porthminstercafe.co.uk – Closed January and December 25   Y**p**
Rest – Seafood – (booking advisable) Carte £ 24/36
♦ 1930s beach house on Porthminster sands. Super views: large terrace for al fresco dining. Colourful local artwork on walls. Seafood oriented dishes plus eclectic dinner menus.

Loft ✂
Norway Ln ✉ TR26 1LZ – ✆ (01736) 794 204
– www.theloftrestaurantandterrace.co.uk – March-November, closed Sunday and Monday during November   Y**s**
Rest – Menu £ 16 (lunch and early dinner) – Carte £ 24/48
♦ Long, narrow first floor restaurant; choose a table on the roof terrace with views out towards the harbour and beaches. Generous portions; plenty of local seafood. Relaxed, friendly service.

Black Rock ✂
Market Pl ✉ TR26 1RZ – ✆ (01736) 791 911 – www.theblackrockstives.co.uk
– Closed January, November, Sunday and restricted opening in winter
Rest – (dinner only) (booking advisable) Carte £ 23/30   Y**v**
♦ Relaxed, modern bistro, featuring contemporary artworks and a minimalist style; well run, with attentive, friendly service. Menu of fresh local produce with the emphasis on seafood.

at Carbis Bay South : 1.75 mi on A 3074 – ✉ St Ives

Boskerris
Boskerris Rd ✉ TR26 2NQ – ✆ (01736) 795 295 – www.boskerrishotel.co.uk
– mid-February-mid-November   Z**x**
15 rm ⌑ – †£ 128/154 ††£ 170/240
Rest – (closed Sunday) (dinner only) Carte £ 24/31
♦ Ever-improving, contemporary hotel with panoramic views of Carbis Bay and coastline. Tastefully appointed bedrooms; relaxing lounge. Enthusiastic young owners. Good, honest home-cooking.

ST KEVERNE – Cornwall – 503 E33 – pop. 1 843   1 A3
▶ London 302 mi – Penzance 26 mi – Truro 28 mi

Old Temperance House without rest
The Square ✉ TR12 6NA – ✆ (01326) 280 986 – www.oldtemperancehouse.co.uk
4 rm ⌑ – †£ 55 ††£ 84
♦ Pretty pink-washed cottage framed by olive trees. Immaculately kept, contemporary interior; bright bedrooms display thoughtful touches. Fresh fruit and produce from local butcher for breakfast.

Greenhouse ✂
6 High St. ✉ TR12 6NN – ✆ (01326) 280 800 – www.tgor.co.uk – Closed last 2 weeks January, Sunday lunch at bank holidays and Mother's Day
Rest – (dinner only and Sunday lunch) Carte £ 20/34
♦ Simply furnished eatery with open kitchen, set in a sleepy little village. Daily blackboard menu is centred around local, organic and gluten free produce. Cooking is unfussy and flavoursome.

ST KEW – Cornwall – see Wadebridge

ST LAWRENCE – Saint Lawrence – 503 P33 – see Channel Islands (Jersey)

ST MARGARET'S AT CLIFFE – Kent – **504** Y30 – see Dover

ST MARTIN – **503** P33 – see Channel Islands (Guernsey)

ST MARTIN'S – **503** B34 – see Scilly (Isles of)

ST MARY'S – **503** B34 – see Scilly (Isles of)

ST MAWES – Cornwall – **503** E33 – ✉ Truro 1 B3
▶ London 299 mi – Plymouth 56 mi – Truro 18 mi
◉ Town★ - Castle★ **AC** (≤★)
◉ St Just-in-Roseland Church★★, N : 2.5 mi by A 3078

Hotel Tresanton
27 Lower Castle Rd ✉ *TR2 5DR* – ✆ *(01326) 270 055* – *www.tresanton.com*
– *Closed 2 weeks January*
30 rm ☐ – †£ 230/365 ††£ 230/365 – 1 suite
Rest *Restaurant Tresanton* – see restaurant listing
♦ Collection of old fishermen's cottages, a yacht club and cinema. Elegant, nautically themed guest areas include an intimate bar and a movie room. Understated bedrooms, some in cottages, have a high level of facilities and afford superb sea views. Lovely split-level terrace shares the outlook. Delightful team.

Nearwater without rest
Polvarth Rd., East : 0.5 mi on A 3078 ✉ *TR2 5AY* – ✆ *(01326) 279 278*
– *www.nearwaterstmawes.co.uk*
3 rm ☐ – †£ 85/90 ††£ 90/100
♦ Modern, purpose-built guesthouse with small lawned garden, set on the main road of a popular coastal town. Open-plan lounge and breakfast room with real fires and subtle nautical theme. Smart, New England style bedrooms offer good mod cons.

Restaurant Tresanton – at Hotel Tresanton
27 Lower Castle Rd ✉ *TR2 5DR* – ✆ *(01326) 270 055* – *www.tresanton.com*
– *Closed 2 weeks January*
Rest – *(booking essential)* Menu £ 35/44
♦ Appealing hotel restaurant boasting a large terrace and superb bay views; popular for its Sunday BBQs and live jazz band. Bright interior with nautical theme and attractive mosaic flooring. Daily menus offer unfussy dishes crafted from quality local produce; seafood is a feature. Polite, efficient service.

ST MERRYN – Cornwall – **503** F32 – see Padstow

ST OSYTH – Essex – **504** X28 – pop. 4 119 13 D2
▶ London 83 mi – Croydon 88 mi – Barnet 81 mi – Ealing 94 mi

Park Hall without rest
Park Hall, East : 1.5 mi on B 1027 ✉ *CO16 8HG* – ✆ *(01255) 820 922*
– *www.parkhall.info* – *Closed first two weeks January*
3 rm ☐ – †£ 75/110 ††£ 130/190
♦ 14C antique-filled former monastery in 600 acres of arable farmland, with 5 acres of grounds, where peacocks roam free. Traditionally styled rooms come with many thoughtful extras.

ST PETER PORT – **503** P33 – see Channel Islands (Guernsey)

ST SAVIOUR – **503** P33 – see Channel Islands (Jersey)

ST SAVIOUR – **503** P33 – see Channel Islands (Guernsey)

SALCOMBE – Devon – 503 I33 – pop. 1 893 — 2 C3

▶ London 243 mi – Exeter 43 mi – Plymouth 27 mi – Torquay 28 mi
🛈 Market St ✆ (01548) 84 39 27, www.salcombeinformation.co.uk
◉ Sharpitor (Overbecks Museum and Garden★) (≤★★), **AC**, S : 2 mi by South Sands
Z. Prawle Point (≤★★★) E : 16 mi around coast by A 381 - Y - and A 379

South Sands   ≤ 🏠 & rm, 🛜 **P** VISA ●●
Bolt Head ✉ TQ8 8LL – ✆ (01548) 859 000 – www.southsands.com
22 rm ☕ – †£ 135/190 ††£ 250/350 – 5 suites   Zx
Rest – Carte £ 28/42
♦ Stylish hotel by the water's edge, with subtle New England theme and stunning spiral staircase. Subtle, tasteful bedrooms; go for one at the front with a balcony. Large, airy restaurant with delightful decked terrace; menus place their emphasis on fresh seafood.

at Soar Mill Cove Southwest : 4.25 mi by A 381 - Y - via Malborough village – ✉ Salcombe

Soar Mill Cove 🛎   ≤ 🏞 🏠 🏊 🛌 🛎 🍴 **P** VISA ●●
✉ TQ7 3DS – ✆ (01548) 561 566 – www.soarmillcove.co.uk – mid February-October
22 rm ☕ – †£ 115/215 ††£ 190/240   **Rest** – Menu £ 29
♦ Family-run hotel built from local slate and stone; delightfully set by the water's edge in a secluded cove. Good range of leisure facilities. Spacious bedrooms in bright, contemporary styles; half have sea views. Smart champagne bar. Classically based modern menu.

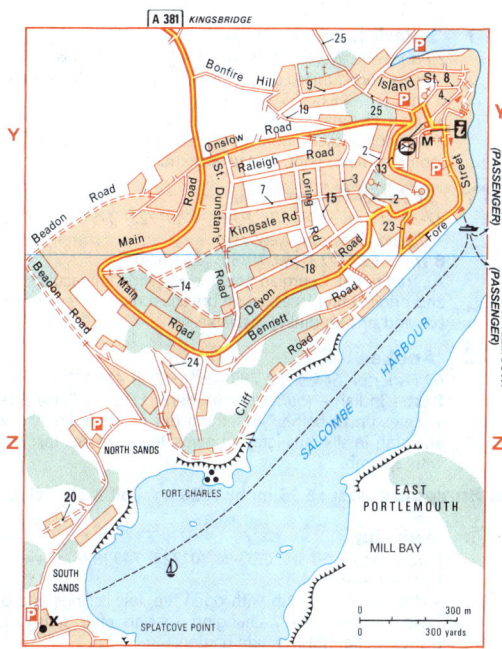

SALCOMBE

Allenhayes Rd .... Y 2
Bonaventure Rd ...... Y 3
Buckley St .... Y 4
Camperdown Rd ..... Y 7
Church St .... Y 8
Coronation Rd .... Y 9
Devon Rd .... Y 13
Fore St .... Y
Fortescue Rd .... Z 14
Grenville Rd .... Y 15
Herbert Rd .... Z 18
Knowle Rd .... Y 19
Moult Rd .... Z 20
Newton Rd .... Y 23
Sandhills Rd .... Z 24
Shadycombe Rd ..... Y 25

SALE – Greater Manchester – **502** N23 – pop. 55 234 – ✉ **Manchester** **20** B3
▶ London 212 mi – Liverpool 36 mi – Manchester 6 mi – Sheffield 43 mi
🏌 Sale Lodge Golf Rd, ℰ (0161) 973 16 38

Cornerstones without rest
*230 Washway Rd, (on A 56) ✉ M33 4RA – ℰ (0161) 283 69 09
– www.cornerstonesguesthouse.com – Closed 25 December-1 January*
9 rm – †£ 30/55 ††£ 60/68, ⊡ £ 6.50
♦ Substantial red-brick Victorian house with neat garden, in leafy suburban location. Slightly wacky interior with bohemian-style lounge and breakfast room. Bedrooms range from retro to modern.

SALISBURY – Wiltshire – **503** O30 – pop. 42 940 **4** D3
▶ London 91 mi – Bournemouth 28 mi – Bristol 53 mi – Southampton 23 mi
🛈 Fish Row ℰ (01722) 33 49 56, www.visitwiltshire.co.uk
Salisbury & South Wilts. Netherhampton, ℰ (01722) 74 26 45
🏌 High Post Great Durnford, ℰ (01722) 78 23 56
◉ City★★ - Cathedral★★★ **AC** Z – Salisbury and South Wiltshire Museum★ **AC** Z **M2** – Close★ Z : Mompesson House★ **AC** Z **A** – Sarum St Thomas Church★ Y **B** – Redcoats in the Wardrobe★ Z **M1**
◉ Wilton Village★ (Wilton House★★ **AC**, Wilton Carpet Factory★ **AC**), W : 3 mi by A 30 Y – Old Sarum★ **AC**, N : 2 mi by A 345 Y – Woodford (Heale House Garden★) **AC**, NW : 4.5 mi by Stratford Rd Y. Stonehenge★★★ **AC**, NW : 10 mi by A 345 - Y - and A 303 – Wardour Castle★ **AC**, W : 15 mi by A 30 Y

Cricket Field House without rest
*Wilton Rd, West : 1.25 mi on A 36 ✉ SP2 9NS – ℰ (01722) 322 595
– www.cricketfieldhouse.co.uk*
14 rm ⊡ – †£ 50/85 ††£ 65/105
♦ Personally run extended house overlooking the County Cricket Ground. Bedrooms are prettily decorated with pictures and floral touches; majority of rooms are in the annex.

2 Park Lane without rest
*2 Park Lane, North : 1.25 mi by A 345 ✉ SP1 3NP – ℰ (01722) 321 001
– www.2parklane.co.uk – Closed 25-26 December and 1 January*
6 rm ⊡ – †£ 60/65 ††£ 70/80
♦ Fine Victorian house hidden away on a private road. Pleasant entranceway with original tiled floor; smart period breakfast room. Comfortable, modern bedrooms come in light, understated hues.

St Anns House without rest
*32-34 St Ann St ✉ SP1 2DP – ℰ (01722) 335 657 – www.stannshouse.co.uk
– Closed Christmas-New Year* Z**e**
8 rm – †£ 54/79 ††£ 79/89, ⊡ £ 8.50
♦ Traditional Georgian townhouse with immaculate bedrooms, sash windows and original fireplaces. Large breakfast menu offers well sourced options. Honesty bar and private dining available.

Anokaa
60 Fisherton St ✉ SP2 7RB – ℰ (01722) 414 142 – www.anokaa.com
Rest – Indian – *(buffet lunch)* Menu £ 9/24 – Carte £ 19/24 Y**e**
♦ Lives up to being "something out of the ordinary", with eye-catching interior and staff in silky full-length gowns. Indian dishes mix modern and classical styles with aplomb.

at Burcombe West : 5.25 mi by A 36 - Y - off A 30 – ✉ Salisbury

Ship Inn
Burcombe Ln ✉ SP2 0EJ – ℰ (01722) 743 182 – www.theshipburcombe.co.uk
Rest – Carte £ 24/35
♦ Charming 17C pub with open fire, low ceilings and oak beams. Seasonal à la carte and twice-daily changing specials offer satisfying portions of traditional dishes. Delightful riverside garden.

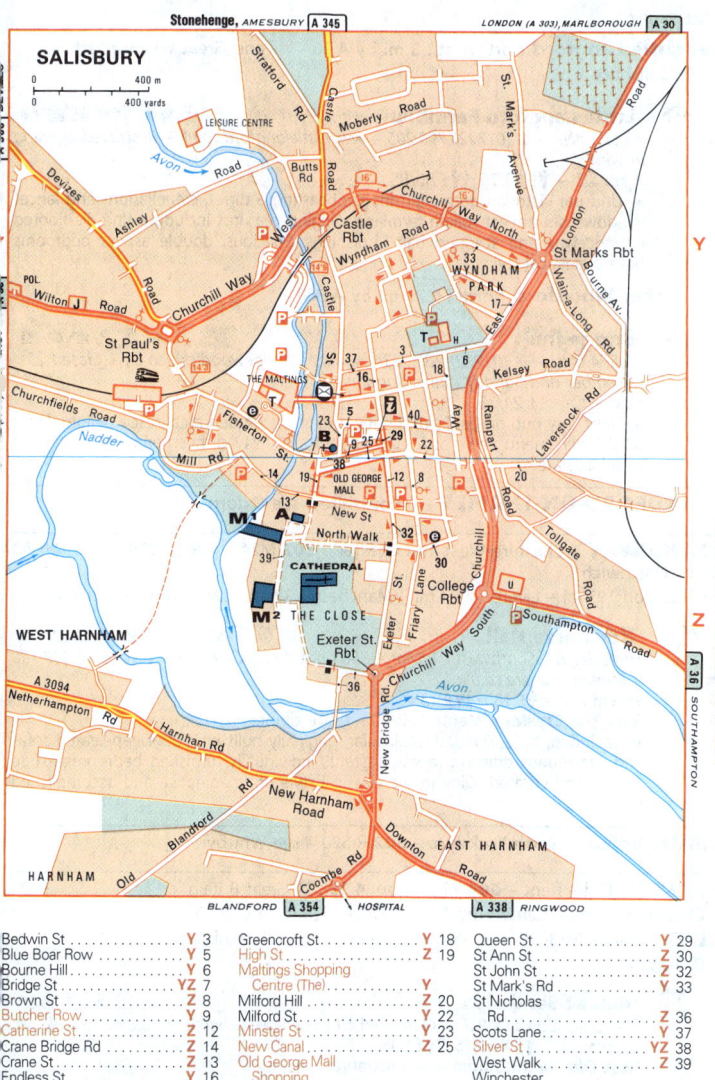

Bedwin St . . . . Y 3	Greencroft St. . . . . Y 18	Queen St . . . . Y 29
Blue Boar Row . . . . Y 5	High St . . . . Z 19	St Ann St . . . . Z 30
Bourne Hill . . . . Y 6	Maltings Shopping	St John St . . . . Z 32
Bridge St . . . . YZ 7	Centre (The). . . . . Y	St Mark's Rd . . . . Y 33
Brown St . . . . Z 8	Milford Hill . . . . Y 20	St Nicholas
Butcher Row . . . . Y 9	Milford St. . . . . Y 22	Rd. . . . . Z 36
Catherine St. . . . . Y 12	Minster St . . . . Y 23	Scots Lane . . . . Y 37
Crane Bridge Rd . . . . Z 14	New Canal . . . . Z 25	Silver St. . . . . YZ 38
Crane St. . . . . Z 13	Old George Mall	West Walk . . . . Z 39
Endless St . . . . Y 16	Shopping	Winchester
Estcourt Rd . . . . Y 17	Centre . . . . Z	St . . . . Y 40

at Teffont West : 10.25 mi by A 36 - **Y** - and A 30 on B 3089 – ✉ Salisbury

Howard's House 🍴

Teffont Evias ✉ SP3 5RJ – 📞 (01722) 716 392 – www.howardshousehotel.co.uk
– Closed 1 week Christmas

9 rm 🍽 – †£ 120 ††£ 210   **Rest** – Menu £ 20 (lunch) – Carte £ 30/45

◆ Personally run, part 17C dower house boasting fine gardens in a quaint, quiet village. Comfortable lounge and pleasant bedrooms with village or garden vistas. Garden herbs and vegetables grace accomplished cooking.

SALISBURY

at Little Langford Northwest : 8 mi by A 36 - Y - and Great Wishford rd
– ✉ Salisbury

Little Langford Farmhouse without rest
✉ SP3 4NP – ✆ (01722) 790 205 – www.littlelangford.co.uk – Restricted opening in winter
3 rm – †£ 60/75 ††£ 80/85
♦ Unusual Victorian gothic farmhouse boasting a turret, crenellations and lancet windows; set amidst rolling farmland. Original features include a fine tile-floored entranceway and stripped oak furnishings. Spacious, double aspect bedrooms have a classical style.

at Upper Woodford North : 6.75 mi by A 360

Bridge Inn
✉ SP4 6NU – ✆ (01722) 782 323 – www.thebridgewoodford.co.uk – Closed 25 December and Sunday dinner January-February
Rest – Carte £ 24/35
♦ Light, airy pub on banks of the River Avon, its garden an alfresco delight. Light bites lunch menu and classic à la carte; fresh, tasty dishes neatly presented on wood or slate.

SANDFORD-ON-THAMES – Oxfordshire – see Oxford

SANDIWAY – Cheshire West and Chester – 502 M24 – pop. 4 299 — 20 A3
– ✉ Northwich

🚆 London 191 mi – Liverpool 34 mi – Manchester 22 mi – Stoke-on-Trent 26 mi

Nunsmere Hall
Tarporley Rd, Southwest : 1.5 mi A 556 on A 49 ✉ CW8 2ES – ✆ (01606) 889 100 – www.nunsmere.co.uk
36 rm – †£ 135 ††£ 135
Rest *The Crystal* – Menu £ 22/30 – Carte dinner £ 41/51
♦ Secluded, on a wooded peninsular, originally built in 1900. Deep-seated sofas and sumptuous drawing rooms. Tasteful, individually furnished bedrooms exude quality and comfort. Dine in the classical style on imaginative and accomplished cuisine.

SANDSEND – North Yorkshire – 502 R/S20 – see Whitby

SANDWICH – Kent – 504 Y30 – pop. 4 398 ▌Great Britain — 9 D2
🚆 London 72 mi – Canterbury 13 mi – Dover 12 mi
ℹ Guildhall ✆ (01304) 61 35 65, www.discoversandwich.co.uk
◉ Town ★

Bell at Sandwich
The Quay ✉ CT13 9EF – ✆ (01304) 613 388 – www.bellhotelsandwich.co.uk
37 rm – †£ 80/115 ††£ 105/115
Rest *Old Dining Room* – see restaurant listing
♦ Substantial Victorian property with a cool modern interior, located next to the River Stour. Clubby, intimate bar; airy conservatory for coffee and light meals. Stylish, modern bedrooms come in cool pastel shades; some overlook the river.

Old Dining Room – at Bell Hotel at Sandwich
The Quay ✉ CT13 9EF – ✆ (01304) 626 992 – www.bellhotelsandwich.co.uk
Rest – Menu £ 16 (lunch) – Carte £ 25/34
♦ Hotel dining room of grand proportions, set within a coolly modernised Victorian property overlooking the River Stour. Modern menu relies on seasonal ingredients sourced from local suppliers.

SANDYPARK – Devon – 503 I31 – see Chagford

SAPPERTON – Gloucestershire – see Cirencester

SARK – Sark – **503** P33 – see Channel Islands

SAWDON – North Yorkshire – see Scarborough

SCARBOROUGH – North Yorkshire – **502** S21 – pop. 38 364   **23** D1
▌Great Britain
▶ London 253 mi – Kingston-upon-Hull 47 mi – Leeds 67 mi – Middlesbrough 52 mi
🛈 Brunswick, Westborough- Harbourside, Sandside ✆ (01723) 38 36 36,
www.discoveryorkshirecoast.co.uk
▤ Scarborough North Cliff North Cliff Ave, Burniston Rd, NW : 2 mi. by A 165,
✆ (01723) 35 53 97
▤ Scarborough South Cliff Deepdale Ave, S : 1 mi. by A 165, off Filey Rd,
✆ (01723) 37 47 37
◉ Robin Hood's Bay★, N : 16 mi on A 171 and minor rd to the right (signposted)
– Whitby Abbey★, N : 21 mi on A 171 – Sledmere House★, S : 21 mi on A 645, B
1249 and B 1253 (right)

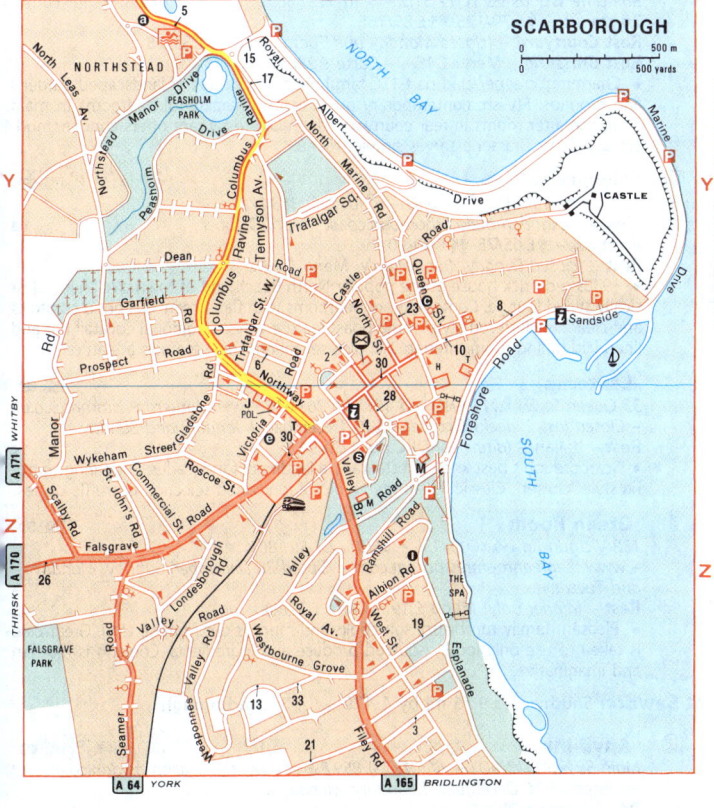

Aberdeen Walk .... Y 2	Falsgrave Rd .... Z	St Thomas St .... Y 23
Avenue Victoria .... Z 3	Newborough .... Y 10	Stepney Rd .... Y 26
Brunswick Pavilion	Oriel Crescent .... Z 13	Vernon Rd .... Z 28
Shopping Centre .... Z 4	Peasholm Gap .... Y 15	Victoria Rd .... YZ
Burniston Rd .... Y 5	Peasholm Rd .... Y 17	Westborough .... YZ 30
Cambridge St .... Y 6	Prince of Wales Terrace ..... Z 19	Westbourne
Eastborough .... Y 8	Queen Margaret's Rd .... Z 21	Rd .... Z 33

SCARBOROUGH

Crown Spa
8-10 Esplanade ⊠ YO11 2AG – ℘ (01723) 357 400 – www.crownspahotel.com
114 rm ⊡ – †£ 104/154 ††£ 178/248 – 1 suite   Zi
Rest *Taste* – ℘ (01723) 357 439 – Menu £ 30 **s** – Carte £ 27/36 **s**
◆ Refurbished 19C landmark hotel, in a prime position on the headland. Contemporary guest areas and good leisure facilities. Smart bedrooms with bespoke furnishings and latest mod cons. Four-roomed restaurant: 2 in bistro style, 2 more informal with a TV and bar.

Beiderbecke's
1-3 The Cres ⊠ YO11 2PW – ℘ (01723) 365 766 – www.beiderbeckes.com
26 rm ⊡ – †£ 85/90 ††£ 120/130 – 1 suite   Zs
Rest *Marmalade's* – ℘ (01723) 350 349 – Menu £ 22 (dinner) – Carte £ 27/35
◆ Named after the jazz musician. Although housed in a restored Georgian building, the rooms' décor is balanced between period style and contemporary feel with bright colours. Colourful, contemporary brasserie.

Ox Pasture Hall
Lady Edith's Dr., Raincliffe Woods, West : 3.25 mi by A 171 following signs for Raincliffe Woods ⊠ YO12 5TD – ℘ (01723) 365 295 – www.oxpasturehall.com
20 rm ⊡ – †£ 79/125 ††£ 89/165
Rest *Courtyard* – (closed Monday and Tuesday) Carte £ 31/38 **s**
Rest *Brasserie* – Menu £ 18 **s** – Carte £ 22/30 **s**
◆ Charming, creeper-clad part-17C farmhouse, in 17 acres of landscaped gardens and grounds. Stylish, contemporary guest areas. Characterful bedrooms in main house; smarter rooms in rear courtyard. Linen-laid restaurant offers concise, modern à la carte. Brasserie serves simpler menu.

Alexander
33 Burniston Rd ⊠ YO12 6PG – ℘ (01723) 363 178
– www.alexanderhotelsscarborough.co.uk – April-October
8 rm ⊡ – †£ 65/75 ††£ 80/90   Ya
Rest – (closed Sunday) (dinner only) Menu £ 19 **s**
◆ 1930s red-brick house at the popular North Beach end of town. Well-kept, classically styled lounge. Contemporary bedrooms with flat-screen TVs, good comforts and clean, uncluttered style; some have feature walls. Traditional cocktail bar and linen-laid dining room offering 3 choice set menu. Local seafood a feature.

Lanterna
33 Queen St ⊠ YO11 1HQ – ℘ (01723) 363 616 – www.lanterna-ristorante.co.uk
– Closed last 2 weeks October, 25-26 December, 1 January and Sunday
Rest – Italian – (dinner only) Carte £ 30/94   Yc
◆ Scarborough's best known restaurant: a landmark for decades. Endearing trattoria style "clutter". Classic Italian menu, plus a renowned selection of truffle dishes.

Green Room
138 Victoria Rd ⊠ YO11 1SL – ℘ (01723) 501 801
– www.thegreenroomrestaurant.com – Closed 26 December, Sunday, Monday and Tuesday   Ze
Rest – (dinner only) Menu £ 19 – Carte £ 32/41
◆ Pleasant family run bistro; son cooks and mum is out front serving. Great care is taken to use only locally sourced produce and ingredients. Cooking is modern and imaginative.

at Sawdon Southwest : 9.75 mi by A 170 - Z – ⊠ Scarborough

Anvil Inn
Main St ⊠ YO13 9DY – ℘ (01723) 859 896 – www.theanvilinnsawdon.co.uk
– Closed 25-26 December, 1 January, Monday and Tuesday
Rest – Carte £ 21/30
◆ Formerly a smithy, with bellows, tools, forge and anvil still in situ. Classical cooking features locally sourced produce and the odd international influence. Intimate restaurant.

SCAWTON – North Yorkshire – **502** Q21 – see Helmsley

SCILLY (Isles of) – Cornwall – 503 A/B34 1 A3

▶ London 295 mi – Camborne 23 mi – Saint Austell 52 mi – Falmouth 36 mi
Access Helicopter service from St Mary's and Tresco to Penzance : ℘ (01736) 363871
✈ St Mary's Airport : ℘ (01720) 422677, E : 1.5 mi from Hugh Town
⛴ from Hugh Town to Penzance (Isles of Scilly Steamship Co. Ltd) (summer only) (2 h 40 mn)
🛈 St Mary's ℘ (01720) 42 40 31, www.simplyscilly.co.uk
◉ Islands★ – The Archipelago (≤★★★)
⛳ St Agnes : Horsepoint★

BRYHER – Cornwall – pop. 78 – ✉ New Grimsby 1 A3
🛈 St Mary's ℘ (01720) 42 40 31, www.simplyscilly.co.uk
◉ Watch Hill (≤★) – Hell Bay★

🏨 Hell Bay
✉ TR23 0PR – ℘ (01720) 422 947 – www.hellbay.co.uk – 17 March-October
11 rm (dinner included) – †£ 169/600 ††£ 169/300 – 14 suites – ††£ 270/600
Rest – *(booking essential for non-residents)* Menu £ 35 – Carte approx. £ 30
♦ Several charming New England style buildings set around a central courtyard. Fabulous coastal location with far-reaching views. Contemporary inner has nautical edge and impressive modern art collection. Immaculately kept bedrooms come with good extras. Informal lunches in bar/courtyard/terrace; elaborate daily dinners.

🏠 Bank Cottage without rest
✉ TR23 0PR – ℘ (01720) 422 612 – www.bank-cottage.com – May-October
4 rm – †£ 54 ††£ 110
♦ Friendly guesthouse with bright sub-tropical garden, koi carp pond and rowing boat. Breakfast room, lounge and honesty bar; free use of kitchen. Simple, compact bedrooms; one with roof terrace.

ENGLAND

ST MARTIN'S – Cornwall – pop. 113 1 A3
🛈 St Mary's ℘ (01720) 42 40 31, www.simplyscilly.co.uk
◉ St Martin's Head (≤★★)

🏨 St Martin's on the Isle
✉ TR25 0QW – ℘ (01720) 422 092 – www.stmartinshotel.co.uk – April-September
27 rm (dinner included) – †£ 125/150 ††£ 250/350 – 3 suites
Rest *Teän* – see restaurant listing
Rest *Bistro* – Menu £ 40
♦ Contemporary hotel in stunning location, with unrivalled views of white beaches and blue sea. Comfortable bedrooms: most overlook the water; some look onto the garden. The best is 'Volunteer'; a large first floor suite with views to the lighthouse. Lively ground floor bistro with terrace; simple dishes, ideal for lunch.

🍴 Teän – St Martin's on the Isle
✉ TR25 0QW – ℘ (01720) 422 092 – www.stmartinshotel.co.uk – April-September
Rest – *(Closed Monday evenings) (booking essential)* Carte £ 28/35 **s**
♦ First floor restaurant with fantastic views. Short menu of classically based dishes; cooking is precise, with hearty portions making the best of local produce. Professional service.

ST MARY'S – Cornwall – pop. 1 607 1 A3
🛈 St Mary's ℘ (01720) 42 40 31, www.simplyscilly.co.uk
⛳ Carn Morval, ℘ (01720) 42 26 92
◉ Gig racing★★ – Garrison Walk★ (≤★★) – Peninnis Head★ – Hugh Town – Museum★

SCILLY (Isles of)

Star Castle
The Garrison ⊠ TR21 0JA – ℰ (01720) 422 317 – www.star-castle.co.uk
– Closed 2 January-10 February
34 rm (dinner included) – †£ 96/250 ††£ 190/324 – 4 suites
Rest *Castle Dining Room* – *(dinner only)* Menu £ 33
Rest *Conservatory* – Seafood – *(closed November-March) (dinner only)* Menu £ 33

♦ Elizabethan castle in the shape of an 8-pointed star. Well-appointed, classical bedrooms; brighter garden suites – some harbour/island views. 17C staircase leads from stone ramparts to charming Dungeon bar. Fabulous fireplace and kitchen garden produce in dining room. Seafood menus in Conservatory.

Atlantic
Hugh St, Hugh Town ⊠ TR21 0PL – ℰ (01720) 422 417
– www.atlantichotelscilly.co.uk – 7 February-19 November
25 rm (dinner included) – †£ 89/135 ††£ 170/270
Rest – *(bar lunch)* Menu £ 25 – Carte £ 26/31

♦ Former Customs Office in a charming bay setting, affording lovely views across the harbour. Bedrooms – accessed through twisty passages – are well-equipped; many share the view. Comfortable lounge and small bar. Wicker-furnished restaurant offers accessible menu.

Evergreen Cottage without rest
Parade, Hugh Town ⊠ TR21 0LP – ℰ (01720) 422 711
– www.evergreencottageguesthouse.co.uk – Closed 1 week February and Christmas-New Year
5 rm – †£ 38/60 ††£ 76/82

♦ 300 year old captain's cottage in the heart of town. Welcoming window boxes. Cosy inner with small, low-ceilinged lounge and breakfast room. Compact, spotlessly kept, pine-furnished bedrooms.

TRESCO – Cornwall – pop. 167 – ⊠ New Grimsby   1 A3

St Mary's ℰ (01720) 42 40 31, www.simplyscilly.co.uk
Island★ - Abbey Gardens★★ **AC** (Lighthouse Way ≤★★)

New Inn
New Grimsby ⊠ TR24 0QQ – ℰ (01720) 423 006 – www.tresco.co.uk
16 rm – †£ 75/180 ††£ 150/240
Rest – *(booking essential for non-residents)* Carte £ 21/34

♦ Stone-built inn boasting a large terrace, an appealing outdoor pool and pleasant coastal views. Bedrooms are bright, fresh and very comfy. Regular live music events attract guests from near and far. Hugely characterful bar and restaurant offer accessible menu.

SCUNTHORPE – North Lincolnshire – 502 S23 – pop. 72 660   23 C3

London 167 mi – Leeds 54 mi – Lincoln 30 mi – Sheffield 45 mi
Humberside Airport : ℰ (01652) 688456, E : 15 mi by A 18
Ashby Decoy Burringham Rd, ℰ (01724) 84 29 13
Kingsway, ℰ (01724) 84 09 45
Grange Park Messingham Butterwick Rd, ℰ (01724) 76 29 45

San Pietro
11 High St East ⊠ DN15 6UH – ℰ (01724) 277 774 – www.sanpietro.uk.com
– Closed first week January, 25-26 December, Monday lunch, Sunday and bank holiday Mondays
Rest – Menu £ 17/23 – Carte £ 29/53

♦ Characterful former pub with private dining room, housed in 19C listed windmill. Seasonal menus offer skilfully cooked Mediterranean dishes. Professional service from smartly attired staff.

SEAHAM – Durham – **501** P/Q19 – pop. 21 153 — 24 B2

▶ London 284 mi – Carlisle 77 mi – Leeds 84 mi – Middlesbrough 24 mi

Seaham Hall
Lord Byron's Walk, North : 1.25 mi by B 1287 ✉ SR7 7AG
– ℰ (0191) 516 14 00 – www.seaham-hall.co.uk
18 rm – †£ 175/375 ††£ 225/425 – 2 suites
Rest *White Room* – (dinner only and Sunday lunch) (booking essential for non-residents) Menu £ 32/55
Rest *Ozone* – Menu £ 23

◆ Impressive extended coastal mansion with portico entrance, modern styling, spacious sitting room and superb oriental spa, complete with impressive indoor pool and outdoor hot-tubs. Large bedrooms boast luxury bathrooms and impressive technology. Well-presented, modern dishes in the White Room. A blend of Asian and European food in Ozone.

SEAHOUSES – Northumberland – **501** P17 — Great Britain — 24 B1

▶ London 328 mi – Edinburgh 80 mi – Newcastle upon Tyne 46 mi
🛈 Seafield Rd ℰ (01665) 72 08 84, www.seahouses.org
⛳ Beadnell Rd, ℰ (01665) 72 07 94
◎ Farne Islands★ (by boat from harbour)

Olde Ship
9 Main St ✉ NE68 7RD – ℰ (01665) 720 200 – www.seahouses.co.uk
– February-November
13 rm – †£ 51/118 ††£ 102/130 – 5 suites
Rest – (bar lunch Monday-Saturday) Menu £ 10 (weekday dinner)
– Carte £ 17/31 **s**

◆ Cosy, part-18C, family-run inn, close to the thriving harbour – boasting old ships' decking floors, nautical bric-a-brac and great harbour views from the wardroom. Comfortable, individually designed bedrooms. Characterful bar and classical dining room.

SEASALTER – Kent – **504** X29 – see Whitstable

SEAVIEW – Isle of Wight – **503** Q31 – see Wight (Isle of)

SEER GREEN – Buckinghamshire – see Beaconsfield

SETTLE – North Yorkshire – **502** N21 – pop. 3 621 — 22 A2

▶ London 238 mi – Bradford 34 mi – Kendal 30 mi – Leeds 41 mi
🛈 Cheapside ℰ (01729) 82 51 92, www.settle.org.uk
⛳ Giggleswick, ℰ (01729) 82 52 88

Little House
17 Duke St ✉ BD24 9DJ – ℰ (01729) 823 963 – www.littlehouserestaurant.co.uk
– Closed 2 weeks January, 1 week spring, 1 week September, Monday, Tuesday and Sunday in winter
Rest – (dinner only) (booking essential) Carte £ 23/30

◆ Former 19C gate house, a 'little house' of stone that was once a cobblers. Well-kept, rustic style within a compact space. Traditional and classic styles of cooking prevail.

SHAFTESBURY – Dorset – **503** N30 – pop. 6 665 — 4 C3

▶ London 115 mi – Bournemouth 31 mi – Bristol 47 mi – Dorchester 29 mi
🛈 8 Bell St ℰ (01747) 85 35 14, www.shaftesburydorset.com
◎ Gold Hill★ (≤★) – Local History Museum★ **AC**
◎ Wardour Castle★ **AC**, NE : 5 m

SHAFTESBURY

Hotel Grosvenor
The Commons ✉ SP7 8JA – ☏ (01747) 850 580 – www.hotelgrosvenor.com
16 rm ⌂ – †£ 175 ††£ 175
Rest *Greenhouse* – see restaurant listing
• Stylish former coaching inn with Georgian-style façade and spacious, trendy bar. Bedrooms feature stark décor and modern facilities including flat screen TVs and espresso machines.

Fleur de Lys
Bleke St ✉ SP7 8AW – ☏ (01747) 853 717 – www.lafleurdelys.co.uk – *Closed 2 weeks January*
7 rm ⌂ – †£ 80/100 ††£ 135/175
Rest – *(closed lunch Monday-Tuesday and Sunday dinner)* Menu £ 33 – Carte approx. £ 32
• Keenly run, ivy-clad stone house in lovely market town. Comfortable, well-kept bedrooms named after grape varieties; each comes with its own laptop. Cosy lounge with mahogany bar. Dine from traditional menus in L-shaped restaurant or on wood-furnished terrace.

Retreat without rest
47 Bell St ✉ SP7 8AE – ☏ (01747) 850 372 – www.the-retreat.co.uk – *Closed 25 December and 1 January*
10 rm ⌂ – †£ 55/70 ††£ 85/90
• Pretty Georgian house on narrow street in delightful market town – once a school for poor boys. Wood-furnished breakfast room; immaculately kept bedrooms with good facilities. Charming owner.

Greenhouse – at Hotel Grosvenor
The Commons ✉ SP7 8JA – ☏ (01747) 850 580 – www.hotelgrosvenor.com
Rest – Menu £ 25 – Carte £ 27/44
• Ground floor restaurant enlivened by boldly coloured abstract art. Enjoy aperitifs in the enclosed courtyard. Refined brasserie cooking; good value set menus. Excellent service.

SHALDON – Devon – 503 J32 – pop. 1 628   2 D2
▶ London 188 mi – Exeter 16 mi – Torquay 7 mi – Paignton 13 mi

ODE
21 Fore St ✉ TQ14 0DE – ☏ (01626) 873 977 – www.odetruefood.co.uk
– *Closed 2 weeks February, 2 weeks October, 25-26 December, Sunday-Tuesday and bank holidays*
Rest – Organic – *(dinner only and lunch Thursday-Friday) (booking essential)* Menu £ 22 (lunch) – Carte dinner £ 30/40
• Intimate neighbourhood restaurant in glass-fronted Georgian house – leave time to park. Cooking has a strong seafaring base and often involves water baths. Produce is local and 100% organic.

SHANKLIN – Isle of Wight – 503 Q32 – see Wight (Isle of)

SHEDFIELD – Hampshire – 503 Q31 – pop. 3 558 – ✉ Southampton   6 B2
▶ London 75 mi – Portsmouth 13 mi – Southampton 10 mi
⛳ Meon Valley Shedfield Sandy Lane, off A 334, ☏ (01329) 83 34 55

Vatika
Botley Rd, Wickham Vineyard, on A334 ✉ SO32 2HL – ☏ (01329) 830 405
– www.vatikarestaurant.co.uk – *Closed November-February, Monday, Tuesday, Sunday dinner and lunch Wednesday and Thursday*
Rest – *(dinner only and lunch Friday-Sunday) (booking advisable at dinner)* Menu £ 40
• Sleek, contemporary restaurant overlooking delightful vineyard. Refined fusion cooking uses modern techniques to create unusual, highly artistic British and Indian combinations.

SHEFFIELD – South Yorkshire – 502 P23 – pop. 415 175 — 22 B3
Great Britain

- London 174 mi – Leeds 36 mi – Liverpool 80 mi – Manchester 41 mi
- 14 Norfolk Row ℘ (0114) 221 19 00, www.spinsheffield.com
- Tinsley Park Darnall High Hazel Park, ℘ (0114) 203 74 35
- Beauchief Abbey Lane, ℘ (0114) 236 72 74
- Birley Wood Birley Lane, ℘ (0114) 264 72 62
- Concord Park Shiregreen Lane, ℘ (0114) 257 73 78
- Abbeydale Dore Twentywell Lane, ℘ (0114) 236 07 63
- Lees Hall Norton Hemsworth Rd, ℘ (0114) 255 44 02
- Cutlers' Hall★ CZ **A** – Cathedral Church of SS. Peter and Paul CZ **B** : Shrewsbury Chapel (Tomb★)
- Magna★ **AC**, NE : 3 mi by A 6178 - BY - and Bessemer Way

Plans pages 598, 599

Leopold
Leopold Sq ⌧ S1 1GZ – ℘ (0114) 252 40 00 – www.leopoldhotelssheffield.com – Closed 23 December-2 January — CZ**a**
76 rm – ✝£ 120/140 – 14 suites **Rest** – (bar meals) Carte approx. £ 34

♦ Former Boys Grammar School, now an elegant boutique townhouse with stylish, contemporary bedrooms, state-of-the-art facilities and old school photos on the walls. Light meals served in the bar.

Westbourne House *without rest*
25 Westbourne Rd ⌧ S10 2QQ – ℘ (0114) 266 01 09 – www.westbournehousehotel.com — AZ**c**
8 rm – ✝£ 49/65 ✝✝£ 75/80

♦ Red brick Victorian house in residential area; lovely breakfast room and rear bedrooms overlook mature gardens. Individually styled bedrooms boast original features and good facilities.

Old Vicarage (Tessa Bramley)
Ridgeway Moor, Southeast : 6.75 mi by A 6135 (signed Hyde Park) and B 6054 turning right at Ridgeway Arms ⌧ S12 3XW – ℘ (0114) 247 58 14 – www.theoldvicarage.co.uk – Closed 26 December-6 January, first two weeks August, Saturday lunch, Sunday, Monday and Tuesday after bank holidays
Rest – (lunch by arrangement) Menu £ 40/65

Spec. Langoustine tails on wild garlic risotto. Roast fillet of local beef with truffles and thyme-roasted beetroot. Strawberry and vanilla millefeuille, violet ice cream.

♦ Long-standing, family-run restaurant in an old Victorian vicarage just outside the city. Traditional, homely lounge. Two dining rooms – one a wood-floored, bay-windowed room, the other, an airy conservatory. Refined, classical cooking uses sophisticated techniques and top quality ingredients. Formal service.

Rafters
220 Oakbrook Rd, Nether Green, Southwest : 2.5 mi by A 625 and Fulwood rd, turning left at mini roundabout, on right at traffic lights ⌧ S11 7ED – ℘ (0114) 230 48 19 – www.raftersrestaurant.co.uk – Closed first week January, 2 weeks August, 25-26 December, Sunday and Tuesday
Rest – (dinner only) Menu £ 36

♦ Small first floor restaurant above residential parade of shops, displaying exposed brickwork and vibrant decor. Classical menu with some Asian influences; produce sourced from within 100 miles.

Artisan
32-34 Sandygate Rd, West : 2.25 mi by A 57, turning left at Crosspool Tavern ⌧ S10 5RY – ℘ (0114) 266 60 96 – www.relaxeatanddrink.co.uk – Closed 26 December and bank holidays
Rest – Menu £ 16/27 **s** – Carte £ 22/39 **s**

♦ Smart brasserie with roomy bar and dark, clubby dining room. Careful, honest cooking is fiercely British and very seasonal. Choice of menus to suit all tastes, including a daily ladies' menu, good value set selections and largely fish-based blackboard specials.

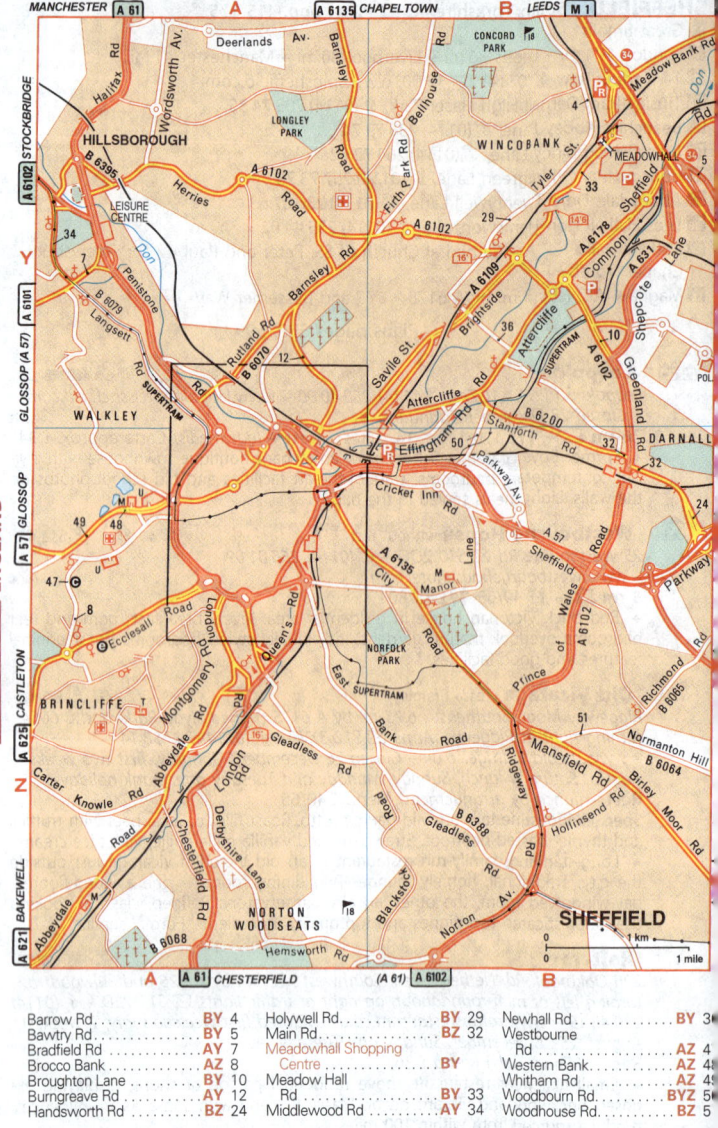

Barrow Rd.	BY 4	Holywell Rd.	BY 29	Newhall Rd.	BY 3
Bawtry Rd.	BY 5	Main Rd.	BZ 32	Westbourne	
Bradfield Rd.	AY 7	Meadowhall Shopping		Rd.	AZ 4
Brocco Bank	AZ 8	Centre	BY	Western Bank	AZ 4
Broughton Lane	BY 10	Meadow Hall		Whitham Rd.	AZ 4
Burngreave Rd.	AY 12	Rd.	BY 33	Woodbourn Rd.	BYZ 5
Handsworth Rd.	BZ 24	Middlewood Rd.	AY 34	Woodhouse Rd.	BZ 5

Nonnas

535-541 Ecclesall Rd ⊠ S11 8PR – ✆ (0114) 268 61 66 – www.nonnas.co.uk
– Closed 25 December and 1 January

AZe

Rest – Italian – Menu £ 13/24 – Carte £ 19/29

♦ Long-standing Italian restaurant with rustic, bistro-style; run by friendly family team. Coffee and cakes in bar. Classical menu of generous, full-flavoured dishes; lighter options available.

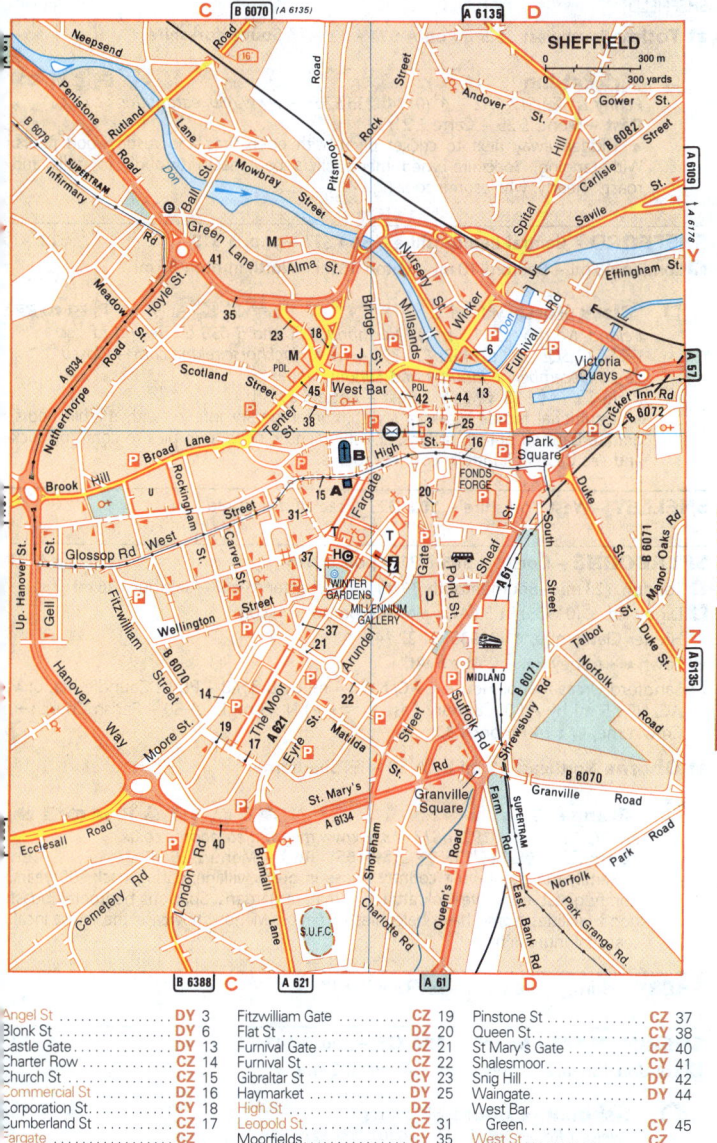

Angel St . . . . DY 3	Fitzwilliam Gate . . . . CZ 19	Pinstone St . . . . CZ 37	
Blonk St . . . . DY 6	Flat St . . . . DZ 20	Queen St. . . . . CY 38	
Castle Gate . . . . DY 13	Furnival Gate . . . . CZ 21	St Mary's Gate . . . . CZ 40	
Charter Row . . . . CZ 14	Furnival St . . . . CZ 22	Shalesmoor . . . . CY 41	
Church St . . . . CZ 15	Gibraltar St . . . . CY 23	Snig Hill . . . . DY 42	
Commercial St . . . . DZ 16	Haymarket . . . . DY 25	Waingate . . . . DY 44	
Corporation St . . . . CY 18	High St . . . . DZ	West Bar	
Cumberland St . . . . CZ 17	Leopold St . . . . CZ 31	Green . . . . CY 45	
Fargate . . . . CZ	Moorfields . . . . CY 35	West St . . . . CZ	

Milestone CYe

84 Green Ln ✉ S3 8SE – ℰ (0114) 272 83 27 – www.the-milestone.co.uk – Closed 25-26 December and 1 January

Rest – Carte £ 26/30

♦ Spacious 18C pub in industrial area of the city. Emphasis firmly on seasonal, organic, locally sourced produce. Hearty gastro menu downstairs; more formal first floor dining.

SHEFFIELD

at Totley Southwest : 5.5 mi on A 621 – **AZ** – ✉ South Yorkshire

Cricket Inn
Penny Ln ✉ S17 3AZ – ℰ (0114) 236 52 56 – www.relaxeatanddrink.co.uk
Rest – Menu £ 25 – Carte £ 21/39
♦ Hidden away next to cricket pitch, with open fires and rustic wood floors. Wide-ranging, Yorkshire-based menu offers bar snacks through to grills and roasts. Hearty, wholesome cooking.

SHEFFORD – Central Bedfordshire – **504** S27 – pop. 3 319   **12 A1**

▶ London 48 mi – Bedford 10 mi – Luton 16 mi – Northampton 37 mi

Black Horse with rm
Ireland, Northwest : 1.5 mi by Northbridge St and B 658 on Ireland rd
✉ SG17 5QL – ℰ (01462) 811 398 – www.blackhorseireland.com – Closed 25-26 December, 1 January and Sunday dinner
2 rm – †£ 55 ††£ 55 **Rest** – Carte £ 23/38
♦ Traditional façade masks a stylish, contemporary interior with marble floors, granite bar and hi-tech fittings. Eclectic menu ranges from pies to confit of duck and sea bass. Delightfully cosy bedrooms.

SHELLEY – West Yorkshire – **502** O23 – see Huddersfield

SHERBORNE – Dorset – **503** M31 – pop. 9 835   **4 C3**

▶ London 128 mi – Bournemouth 39 mi – Dorchester 19 mi – Salisbury 36 mi
🛈 Digby Rd ℰ (01935) 81 53 41, www.sherbornetown.com
🏌 Higher Clatcombe, ℰ (01935) 81 22 74
◉ Town★ - Abbey★★ – Castle★ **AC**
◎ Sandford Orcas Manor House★ **AC**, NW : 4 mi by B 3148 – Purse Caundle Manor★ **AC**, NE : 5 mi by A 30. Cadbury Castle (≤★★) N : 8 mi by A 30 – Parish Church★, Crewkerne, W : 14 mi on A 30

at Oborne Northeast : 2 mi by A 30 – ✉ Sherborne

Grange
✉ DT9 4LA – ℰ (01935) 813 463 – www.thegrangeatoborne.co.uk
18 rm – †£ 125/135 ††£ 159/165 **Rest** – Menu £ 26/35
♦ Family-run, stone-built country house in pretty village; dating back 200 years. Comfy guest areas overlook attractive mature gardens. Spacious bedrooms boast good facilities; some have balconies or patios. Menus showcase the latest local, seasonal ingredients.

SHERE – Surrey – **504** S30 – see Guildford

SHERINGHAM – Norfolk – **504** X25 – pop. 7 143   **15 C1**

▶ London 136 mi – Cromer 5 mi – Norwich 27 mi

Ashbourne House without rest
1 Nelson Rd ✉ NR26 8BT – ℰ (01263) 821 555
– www.ashbournehousesheringham.co.uk
3 rm – †£ 45/50 ††£ 65/75
♦ Well-appointed guesthouse in elevated position, with large, landscaped garden. Comfortable bedrooms: two with coastal views. Impressive fireplace in wood-panelled breakfast room.

SHERWOOD BUSINESS PARK – Nottinghamshire – see Nottingham

SHILTON – Warwickshire – **503** P26 – see Coventry

SHINFIELD – Wokingham – **504** R29 – see Reading

SHIPLAKE ROW – Oxfordshire – see Henley-on-Thames

SHIPLEY – West Yorkshire – **502** O22 – pop. 28 162   22 B2
▶ London 216 mi – Bradford 4 mi – Leeds 12 mi
▪ Northcliffe High Bank Lane, ☏ (01274) 58 40 85
▪ Bingley Beckfoot Lane, Cottingley Bridge, ☏ (01274) 56 86 52

Zaara's
34-38 Bradford Rd ⌧ BD18 3NT – ☏ (01274) 588 114 – www.zaaras.com
Rest – Indian – *(dinner only)* Carte £ 15/22   AT**a**
♦ Funky, modern restaurant with bright décor and lots of neon. Tasty, authentic Indian cooking, with an emphasis on Punjabi dishes. Efficient service from smartly dressed team.

SHOTTLE – Derbyshire – see Belper

SHREWSBURY – Shropshire – **502** L25 – pop. 65 326 – Great Britain   18 B2
▶ London 164 mi – Birmingham 48 mi – Chester 43 mi – Derby 67 mi
ℹ Barker St ☏ (01743) 28 12 00, www.visitshrewsbury.com
▪ Condover, ☏ (01743) 87 29 77
▪ Meole Brace, ☏ (01743) 36 40 50
◉ Abbey★ **D**
◉ Ironbridge Gorge Museum★★ **AC** (The Iron Bridge★★ - Coalport China Museum★★ - Blists Hill Open Air Museum★★ – Museum of the Gorge and Visitor Centre★) SE : 12 mi by A 5 and B 4380

ENGLAND

Plan on next page

Lion and Pheasant
49-50 Wyle Cop ⌧ SY1 1XJ – ☏ (01743) 770 345 – www.lionandpheasant.co.uk – Closed 25 December   s
22 rm ⌑ – †£ 75/95 ††£ 130/175   **Rest** – Carte £ 29/38
♦ Collection of adjoining 16C and 18C townhouses, located on a famous medieval street towards the edge of town. Modern, minimalist décor throughout: bedrooms, designed by the owners daughter, vary in shape and size and have a Scandic feel. Bistro-style menu offered at wooden tables in a choice of dining rooms.

Pinewood House *without rest*
Shelton Park, The Mount, Northwest : 1.5 mi on A 458 ⌧ SY3 8BL – ☏ (01743) 364 200 – Closed 1 week Christmas
3 rm ⌑ – †£ 45/48 ††£ 58/60
♦ Lovely Edwardian property on the edge of town, converted from three coach houses. Fresh, uncluttered feel throughout, with large, light-filled drawing room and flowers all around. One split-level bedroom with bathroom in the old dovecote. Communal breakfasts.

Hayward
The Lion Hotel, Wyle Cop ⌧ SY1 1UY – ☏ (01743) 353 107
– www.thelionhotelshrewsbury.co.uk – Closed Monday   x
Rest – Menu £ 20/38
♦ Spacious, modern restaurant set within the historic Lion hotel, boasting elegant furnishings and formally laid tables. Ambitious, modern cooking and refined presentation; huge polished carving trolley is a feature. Simpler dishes at lunch.

Barker St	2	Coleham Head	13	Pride Hill	26
Beeches Lane	3	Darwin Centre	15	Princess St	27
Belmont	4	Dogpole	16	St Chad's Terrace	29
Bridge St	6	High St	18	St John's Hill	30
Castle Foregate	7	Kingsland Bridge	19	St Mary's St	31
Castle Gates	8	Mardol	20	Shoplatch	33
Castle St	9	Mardol Quay	22	Smithfield	
Chester St	10	Moreton Crescent	23	Rd	34
Claremont Bank	12	Murivance	24	Wyle Cop	38

Mad Jack's with rm

15 St. Mary's St — SY1 1EQ — ℰ (01743) 358 870 — www.madjacks.uk.com
– Closed 25 December

4 rm — ♦ £ 70/100 ♦♦ £ 80/145 **Rest** – Carte £ 21/33

♦ Centrally located in the heart of a busy market town. Spacious main dining area, snug and hidden courtyard, with plain décor and marble tables. Good service, slightly eclectic menu. Modern, comfy bedrooms.

at Grinshill North : 7.5 mi by A 49 – ✉ Shrewsbury

Inn at Grinshill with rm

The High St — SY4 3BL — ℰ (01939) 220 410 — www.theinnatgrinshill.co.uk
– Closed Sunday dinner and Monday

6 rm — ♦ £ 60/90 ♦♦ £ 120 **Rest** – Menu £ 33 (dinner) **s** – Carte £ 25/32 **s**

♦ 18C former stable block in small village. Rustic bar and light, airy restaurant boasting an open kitchen, grand piano and wine bar. À la carte offers mix of old classics and more modern tasting boards; simpler bar menu. Up-to-date bedrooms provide good comforts.

at Atcham Southeast : 3 mi by A 5064 on B 4380

Mytton and Mermaid
✉ SY5 6QG – ✆ (01743) 761 220 – www.myttonandmermaid.co.uk – Closed 25 December
16 rm – ♦£85/110 ♦♦£110/185
Rest *Restaurant* – see restaurant listing
♦ Impressive Georgian riverside house with neat lawned gardens. Characterful, traditionally styled bedrooms in main house, some with views; smaller, more contemporary rooms in old stables.

Restaurant – at The Mytton and Mermaid Hotel
✉ SY5 6QG – ✆ (01743) 761 220 – www.myttonandmermaid.co.uk – Closed 25 December
Rest – Carte £ 24/28
♦ Choice of three dining areas: casual bar, more formal dining room or pleasant outside terraces. Same menu served throughout, offering tasty classically based dishes and daily specials.

SHREWTON – Wiltshire – **503** O30 – pop. 1 648   4 D2

▶ London 91 mi – Bristol 53 mi – Southampton 52 mi – Reading 69 mi

Manor
Southeast : 0.5 mi on A 360 ✉ SP3 4HF – ✆ (01980) 620 216
– www.rollestonemanor.com
7 rm – ♦£80 ♦♦£130
Rest – *(dinner only and Sunday lunch)* Carte £ 24/32
♦ Grade II listed former farmhouse set on main road, just out of the village. Good-sized, antique-furnished bedrooms offer modern facilities. Traditional lounge. Two-roomed restaurant for classic dishes at linen-laid tables.

SHURDINGTON – Gloucestershire – **503** N28 – see Cheltenham

SIBFORD GOWER – Oxfordshire – see Banbury

SIDFORD – Devon – **503** K31 – see Sidmouth

SIDLESHAM – West Sussex – see Chicester

SIDMOUTH – Devon – **503** K31 – pop. 12 066   2 D2

▶ London 176 mi – Exeter 14 mi – Taunton 27 mi – Weymouth 45 mi
🛈 Ham Lane ✆ (01395) 51 64 41, www.visitsidmouth.co.uk
⛳ Cotmaton Rd, ✆ (01395) 51 34 51
◉ Bicton ★ (Gardens ★) **AC**, SW : 5 m

Riviera
The Esplanade ✉ EX10 8AY – ✆ (01395) 515 201 – www.hotelriviera.co.uk
26 rm (dinner included) – ♦£132/194 ♦♦£264/368
Rest – Menu £ 30/42 – Carte £ 42/50
♦ Long-standing, family-run hotel with characterful Regency façade. Superbly kept classical guest areas; fresh flowers and friendly staff abound. Smart bedrooms in rich blues and gold, some with a view. Traditional menus have a modern edge. Cream teas a speciality.

SIDMOUTH

at Sidford North : 2 mi – ✉ Sidmouth

XX **Salty Monk** with rm
Church St, on A 3052 – ✉ EX10 9QP – ✆ (01395) 513 174 – www.saltymonk.co.uk
– Closed January, 2 weeks November and lunch Monday-Wednesday
6 rm – †£ 70/75 ††£ 120/180
Rest – (booking essential) Menu £ 43 (dinner) – Carte lunch £ 24/34
♦ Former 16C salt house, where monks stayed en route to Exeter Cathedral. Characterful beamed lounge and conservatory dining room. Extensive modern menus feature fresh fish and local produce; tasting option available weekends. Smart bedrooms and mini spa facility.

at Newton Poppleford Northwest : 4 mi by B 3176 on A 3052 – ✉ Sidmouth

XX **Moores'**
6 Greenbank, High St ✉ EX10 0EB – ✆ (01395) 568 100
– www.mooresrestaurant.co.uk – Closed first two weeks January, Sunday dinner and Monday
Rest – Menu £ 21/29 **s**
♦ Two pretty 18C cottages set back from the main road are the setting for this busy, personally run restaurant with conservatory extension. Modern, locally sourced dishes.

ENGLAND

SINNINGTON – North Yorkshire – **502** R21 – see Pickering

SISSINGHURST – Kent – **504** V30 – see Cranbrook

SITTINGBOURNE – Kent – **504** W29 – pop. 39 974 **9** C1
▶ London 44 mi – Canterbury 18 mi – Maidstone 15 mi – Sheerness 9 mi

🏠 **Hempstead House**
London Rd, Bapchild, East : 2 mi on A 2 ✉ ME9 9PP – ✆ (01795) 428 020
– www.hempsteadhouse.co.uk
27 rm – †£ 85 ††£ 160
Rest Lakes – see restaurant listing
♦ Privately run, red-brick Victorian house with extensions, set in pleasant landscaped gardens. Cosy, wood-panelled lounges. Classical bedrooms in the main house; more contemporary rooms boasting the latest mod cons above the luxurious spa.

XX **Lakes** – at Hempstead House Hotel
London Rd, Bapchild, East : 2 mi on A 2 ✉ ME9 9PP – ✆ (01795) 428 020
– www.hempsteadhouse.co.uk
Rest – (residents only Sunday dinner) Menu £ 19/28 – Carte £ 28/40
♦ Formal conservatory restaurant featuring Georgian columns, crystal chandeliers and linen-laid tables, set within a red-brick Victorian house in pleasant landscaped gardens. Classical menus.

SIZERGH – Cumbria – see Kendal

SKIPTON – North Yorkshire – **502** N22 – pop. 14 313 ┃ Great Britain **22** A2
▶ London 217 mi – Kendal 45 mi – Leeds 26 mi – Preston 36 mi
🛈 35 Coach St ✆ (01756) 79 28 09, www.skiptonweb.co.uk
⛳ Short Lee Lane, off NW Bypass, ✆ (01756) 79 39 22
◉ Castle ★ AC

🍴 **Bull**
West : 3 mi on A 59 ✉ BD23 3AE – ✆ (01756) 792 065
– www.thebullatbroughton.co.uk – Closed 25 December
Rest – Carte £ 19/33
♦ Part of Ribble Valley Inns, a burgeoning pub company which proudly promotes local and very British ingredients and dishes. This solid, sizeable pub boasts log fires, beams and stone floors.

SKIPTON

at Hetton North : 5.75 mi by B 6265 – ✉ Skipton

XXX **Angel Inn and Barn Lodgings** with rm
✉ BD23 6LT – ℰ (01756) 730 263 – www.angelhetton.co.uk – Closed 4 days January
9 rm ⌘ – †£ 140 ††£ 190
Rest *Angel Inn* – see restaurant listing
Rest – *(booking essential)* Carte £ 22/36
♦ Well regarded restaurant with stone walls, beams and roaring log fire. Fine quality, locally sourced produce. Bedrooms with antique furniture and modern appointments.

Angel Inn
✉ BD23 6LT – ℰ (01756) 730 263 – www.angelhetton.co.uk – Closed 4 days January
Rest – *(booking essential)* Menu £ 15 (lunch and weekday dinner) – Carte £ 19/34
♦ Remotely set 18C stone inn that's become a Yorkshire institution: the wine cave is worth a visit. Menus offer something for everyone, featuring local produce in tasty, satisfying dishes.

SLALEY – Northumberland – see Hexham

SLAPTON – Devon – **503** J33 — **2** C3

◨ London 223 mi – Dartmouth 7 mi – Plymouth 29 mi
☉ Dartmouth★★, N : 7 mi by A 379 – Kingsbridge★, W : 7 mi by A 379

Tower Inn with rm
Church Rd ✉ TQ7 2PN – ℰ (01548) 580 216 – www.thetowerinn.com – Closed first 2 weeks January and Sunday in winter
3 rm ⌘ – †£ 65 ††£ 85 **Rest** – Carte £ 24/33
♦ Charming pub overlooked by the ruins of a chantry tower. Menus differ between services and offer pub food with a twist: maybe venison sausages with sauerkraut or fish and chips in vodka batter. Simple bedrooms await.

SNAINTON – North Yorkshire – **502** S21 — **23** C2

◨ London 241 mi – Pickering 8 mi – Scarborough 10 mi

Coachman Inn with rm
Pickering Rd West, West : 0.5 mi by A 170 on B 1258 ✉ YO13 9PL – ℰ (01723) 859 231 – www.coachmaninn.co.uk
5 rm ⌘ – †£ 60 ††£ 85 **Rest** – Carte £ 19/30
♦ Grade II listed coaching inn with a rustic bar and spacious linen-laid restaurant – which is run with some formality. Cooking is classical but presentation is modern and refined. Simpler pub favourites offered at lunch. Bedrooms are smart and spacious.

SNAPE – Suffolk – **504** Y27 – pop. 1 509 — **15** D3

◨ London 113 mi – Ipswich 19 mi – Norwich 50 mi

Crown Inn
Bridge Rd ✉ IP17 1SL – ℰ (01728) 688 324 – www.snape-crown.co.uk
Rest – Carte £ 19/29
♦ Charming 15C former smugglers' inn on village outskirts. Constantly evolving menu offers highly seasonal dishes, light bites and appealing specials. Produce is local, home-grown or home-reared.

ENGLAND

SNETTISHAM – Norfolk – **504** V25 – pop. 2 145

14 B1

▶ London 113 mi – King's Lynn 13 mi – Norwich 44 mi

Rose and Crown with rm
Old Church Rd ✉ *PE31 7LX* – ℰ *(01485) 541 382*
– www.roseandcrownsnettisham.co.uk
16 rm ⊡ – †£ 70/85 ††£ 90/110 **Rest** – Carte £ 21/29

♦ A warren of rooms with uneven floors and low beamed ceilings. Gutsy cooking uses locally sourced produce, with globally influenced dishes alongside trusty pub classics. Modern bedrooms are decorated in sunny colours, with a good level of facilities.

SOAR MILL COVE – Devon – **503** i33 – see Salcombe

SOLIHULL – West Midlands – **503** O26 – pop. 94 753

19 C2

▶ London 109 mi – Birmingham 7 mi – Coventry 13 mi – Warwick 13 mi
🛈 Homer Rd ℰ (0121) 704 61 30, www.solihull.gov.uk

Town House
727 Warwick Rd ✉ *B91 3DA* – ℰ *(0121) 704 15 67* – www.thetown-house.com
– *Closed Monday from 1 April-30 August and Sunday*
Rest – Menu £ 17 (lunch) – Carte £ 26/41

♦ Smart, keenly run eatery with bright interior and spacious bar-lounge for cocktails. Keenly priced, international menu ranges from small plates and mini desserts to a 5 course tasting selection.

at Olton Northwest : 2.5 mi on A 41 – ✉ Solihull

Rajnagar
256 Lyndon Rd., Northeast : 1 mi by Richmond rd. ✉ *B92 7QW* – ℰ *(0121) 742 81 40* – www.rajnagar.com
Rest – Indian – *(dinner only)* Menu £ 16 – Carte £ 22/33

♦ A busy, modern neighbourhood favourite, privately owned, offering authentic regional specialities of Indian cuisine. Service is flexible and friendly.

SOMERTON – Somerset – **503** L30 – pop. 4 133

3 B2

▶ London 138 mi – Bristol 32 mi – Taunton 17 mi
◉ Town★ - Market Place★ (cross★) – St Michael's Church★
◉ Long Sutton★ (Church★★) SW : 2.5 mi by B 3165 – Huish Episcopi (St Mary's Church Tower★★) SW : 4.5 mi by B 3153 – Lytes Cary★, SE : 3.5 mi by B 3151 – Street - The Shoe Museum★, N : 5 mi by B 3151. Muchelney★★ (Parish Church★★) SW : 6.5 mi by B 3153 and A 372 – High Ham (≤★★, St Andrew's Church★), NW : 9 mi by B 3153, A 372 and minor rd – Midelney Manor★ **AC**, SW 9 mi by B 3153 and A 378

Lynch Country House without rest
4 Behind Berry ✉ *TA11 7PD* – ℰ *(01458) 272 316*
– www.thelynchcountryhouse.co.uk
9 rm ⊡ – †£ 65/80 ††£ 80/115

♦ Stands on a crest overlooking the Cary Valley. The grounds of this Regency house are equally rich with unusual shrubs, trees and lake. Coach house rooms more modern.

SONNING-ON-THAMES – Wokingham – **504** R29 – see Reading

SOUTH BRENT – 503 I32 – pop. 2 847 – ✉ Devon   2 C2
▶ London 201 – Plymouth 17 – Torbay 15 – Exeter 29

🍺 **Oak Inn** with rm   ⛔ 🅰🅺 rest, 𝑽𝑰𝑺𝑨 ⓒⓞ
Station Rd ✉ TQ10 9BE – ☏ (01364) 72 133 – www.oakonline.net
5 rm ⌂ – †£ 65/95 ††£ 90/130   **Rest** – Carte £ 15/29
♦ This pub boasts a traditional bar and a more modern restaurant with an attractive courtyard. Lunch offers a simple bar menu and a fish and a dish 'of the day', while dinner is more complex. The cheesecakes are worth saving room for. Modern, spacious bedrooms.

SOUTH DALTON – East Riding of Yorkshire – see Beverley

SOUTH MOLTON – Devon – 503 I30 – pop. 4 093   2 C1
▶ London 197 mi – Barnstaple 11 mi – Bristol 81 mi

at Knowstone Southeast : 9.5 mi by A 361 – ✉ South Molton

🍺 **Masons Arms** (Mark Dodson)   🚗 ⛔ 🅿 𝑽𝑰𝑺𝑨 ⓒⓞ 🅐🅔
✿ ✉ EX36 4RY – ☏ (01398) 341 231 – www.masonsarmsdevon.co.uk – Closed first 2 weeks January, 1 week spring and August, Sunday dinner and Monday
Rest – (booking essential) Carte £ 34/46
Spec. Salted cod with crushed potatoes and chorizo, tomato and thyme vinaigrette. Beef fillet and oxtail, parsnip purée and red wine jus. Mango parfait with coconut sorbet.
♦ Pretty 13C thatched inn set in Exmoor's foothills, with cosy bar and bright dining room featuring celestial ceiling mural. Sophisticated cooking of French and British classics using local produce. Pronounced, assured flavours.

SOUTH RAUCEBY – Lincolnshire – 502 S24/2 – pop. 335   17 C2
▶ London 131 – Sheffield 68 – Leicester 54 – Kingston upon Hull 69

🍺 **Bustard Inn**   ⛔ 🅿 𝑽𝑰𝑺𝑨 ⓒⓞ 🅐🅔
44 Main St ✉ NG34 8QG – ☏ (01529) 488 250 – www.thebustardinn.co.uk
– Closed 1 January, Sunday dinner and Monday
Rest – Menu £ 19 (lunch) – Carte £ 24/43
♦ Grade II listed inn set in a peaceful hamlet. Traditional pub favourites served in flag-floored bar. Modern-style English dishes and old-fashioned puddings in the spacious beamed restaurant.

SOUTHAMPTON – Southampton – 503 P31 – pop. 236 895   6 B2
📗 Great Britain
▶ London 87 mi – Bristol 79 mi – Plymouth 161 mi
Access Itchen Bridge (toll) AZ
✈ Southampton/Eastleigh Airport : ☏ (0844) 481 7777, N : 4 mi BY
⛴ to Hythe (White Horse Ferries Ltd) frequent services daily (12 mn) – to the Isle of Wight (Cowes) (Red Funnel Ferries) frequent services daily (approx. 22 mn)
⛴ to the Isle of Wight (East Cowes) (Red Funnel Ferries) frequent services daily (55 mn)
🛈 9 Civic Centre Rd ☏ (023) 8083 33 33, www.visit-southampton.co.uk
⛳ Southampton Municipal Bassett Golf Course Rd, ☏ (023) 8076 05 46
⛳ Stoneham Bassett Monks Wood Close, ☏ (023) 8076 92 72
⛳ Chilworth Main Rd, ☏ (023) 8074 05 44
◉ Old Southampton AZ : Bargate★ **B** - Tudor House Museum★ **M1**

Plans on following pages

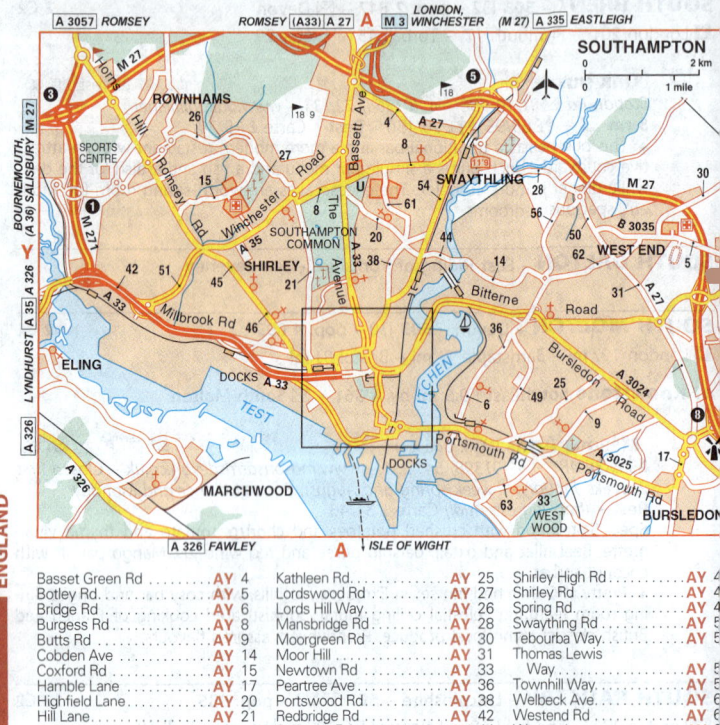

Basset Green Rd	AY 4	Kathleen Rd	AY 25	Shirley High Rd	AY
Botley Rd	AY 5	Lordswood Rd	AY 27	Shirley Rd	AY
Bridge Rd	AY 6	Lords Hill Way	AY 26	Spring Rd	AY
Burgess Rd	AY 8	Mansbridge Rd	AY 28	Swaythling Rd	AY
Butts Rd	AY 9	Moorgreen Rd	AY 30	Tebourba Way	AY
Cobden Ave	AY 14	Moor Hill	AY 31	Thomas Lewis	
Coxford Rd	AY 15	Newtown Rd	AY 33	Way	AY
Hamble Lane	AY 17	Peartree Ave	AY 36	Townhill Way	AY
Highfield Lane	AY 20	Portswood Rd	AY 38	Welbeck Ave	AY
Hill Lane	AY 21	Redbridge Rd	AY 42	Westend Rd	AY
Kane's Hill	AY 24	St Denys Rd	AY 44	Weston Lane	AY

✕ Oxfords

35-36 Oxford St ✉ SO14 3DS – ✆ (023) 8022 4444
– www.oxfordsrestaurant.com   AZ**x**
Rest – Menu £ 16/18 (except Saturday dinner) – Carte £ 26/30
♦ Double-fronted restaurant in lively area. Wood-furnished bar and semi open-plan dining room with brushed velvet banquettes. Good choice of classic brasserie dishes with an international edge.

🍺 White Star Tavern, Dining and Rooms with rm

28 Oxford Street ✉ SO14 3DJ – ✆ (023) 8082 1990
– www.whitestartavern.co.uk – Closed 25-26 December   AZ**x**
13 rm – ♦£ 79/99 ♦♦£ 129/149, ⊇ £ 8   **Rest** – Carte £ 21/34
♦ Eye-catching black pub with vast windows and smart pavement terrace, set in the lively maritime district. Choice of all day tapas-style small plates or modern British à la carte of meaty dishes. Smart, modern bedrooms boast good facilities and extra touches.

at Hamble-le-Rice Southeast : 5 mi by A 3025 - **A** - on B 3397
– ✉ Southampton

🍺 Bugle

High St ✉ SO31 4HA – ✆ (023) 8045 3000 – www.buglehamble.co.uk
Rest – (booking essential) Carte £ 20/28 **s**
♦ Attractive pub down a cobbled street, its terrace overlooking the marina. Bar menu offers sandwiches, small plates and pub classics. More ambitious à la carte available in the dining room.

Above Bar St.	**AZ**	High St	**AZ**	Pound Tree Rd	**AZ** 39
Avenue (The)	**AZ** 2	Houndwell Pl.	**AZ** 22	Queen's Terrace	**AZ** 40
Bargate St	**AZ** 3	Inner Ave	**AZ** 23	Queen's Way	**AZ** 41
Brunswick Pl.	**AZ** 7	Marlands Shopping		St Andrew's Rd	**AZ** 43
Central Bridge	**AZ** 10	Centre	**AZ** 29	South Front	**AZ** 48
Central Station Bridge	**AZ** 12	Marsh Lane	**AZ** 30	Terminus Terrace	**AZ** 52
Civic Centre Rd	**AZ** 13	Mountbatten Way	**AZ** 32	Threefield Lane	**AZ** 55
Cumberland Pl.	**AZ** 16	Orchard St	**AZ** 34	Town Quay	**AZ** 57
Hanover Buildings	**AZ** 18	Oxford Ave	**AZ** 35	West Quay Shopping	
Havelock Rd	**AZ** 19	Portland Terrace	**AZ** 37	Centre	**AZ**

at **Netley Marsh** West : 6.5 mi by A 33 off A 336

Hotel TerraVina

174 Woodlands Rd ⊠ SO40 7GL – ℰ (023) 8029 3784
– www.hotelterravina.co.uk

11 rm – ♦ £ 160 ♦♦ £ 265, ⌑ £ 14.50
Rest – Menu £ 29 (lunch) – Carte dinner £ 33/48

♦ Neat Victorian red-brick house with wood-clad extensions, set in a peaceful New Forest location. Comfy lounge and good-sized bar. Brown and orange hues create a relaxed Mediterranean atmosphere. Bedrooms boast good facilities and extras; some have roof terraces. Menus mix modern British and Mediterranean influences.

Good food and accommodation at moderate prices? Look for the Bib symbols: red Bib Gourmand for food, blue Bib Hotel for accommodation.

SOUTHEND-ON-SEA – Southend-on-Sea – **504** W29 – pop. 160 257   **13** C3

- London 39 mi – Cambridge 69 mi – Croydon 46 mi – Dover 85 mi
- Southend-on-Sea Airport : ℰ (01702) 608100, N : 2 m
- Western Esplanade ℰ (01702) 21 51 20, www.visitsouthend.co.uk
- Belfairs Leigh-on-Sea Eastwood Road North, ℰ (01702) 52 53 45
- Ballards Gore G. & C.C. Gore Rd, Canewdon, ℰ (01702) 25 89 17
- Garon Park Golf Complex Garon Park, Eastern Ave, ℰ (01702) 60 17 01

Beaches without rest
192 Eastern Esplanade, Thorpe Bay ⊠ SS1 3AA – ℰ (01702) 586 124
– www.beachesguesthouse.co.uk
7 rm – ♦£ 40/70 ♦♦£ 80

◆ Attractive terraced guesthouse on the promenade, boasting fine views over Thorpe Bay and the Thames Estuary. Individually decorated bedrooms are comfortable and well-furnished; those to the front have balconies and afford the best views. Good buffet breakfasts.

Pier View without rest
5 Royal Terr. ⊠ SS1 1DY – ℰ (01702) 437 900
– www.pierviewguesthouse.co.uk
8 rm – ♦£ 60/100 ♦♦£ 130

◆ Set in Georgian terrace close to centre of town, with superb views of cliffs, pier and estuary. Bedrooms decorated in pastel shades, with flat screen TVs and Egyptian bedding.

SOUTHPORT – Merseyside – **502** K23 – pop. 91 404   **20** A2

- London 221 mi – Liverpool 25 mi – Manchester 38 mi – Preston 19 mi
- 112 Lord St ℰ (01704) 53 33 33, www.visitsouthport.com
- Southport Golf Links Park Road West, ℰ (01704) 53 52 86

Vincent
98 Lord St. ⊠ PR8 1JR – ℰ (01704) 883 800
– www.thevincenthotel.com
59 rm ⊇ – ♦£ 140 ♦♦£ 180 – 3 suites
Rest *V-Cafe* – see restaurant listing

◆ Striking glass, steel and stone hotel beside the gardens and bandstand. Stylish, boutique interior with chic bar, fitness room and spa. Sleek, modern bedrooms come in dark colours, boasting Nespresso machines and deep Japanese soaking tubs.

Bistrot Vérité
7 Liverpool Rd, Birkdale, South : 1.5 mi by A 565 ⊠ PR8 4AR
– ℰ (01704) 564 199 – www.bistrotverite.co.uk
– Closed 1 week summer, 1 week winter, 25-26 December, 1 January, Sunday and Monday
Rest – French – *(booking essential)* Carte £ 21/35

◆ Simple bistro with tiled floor and panelled walls; sit on the red banquette which runs down one side. Rustic, hearty French cooking; desserts a speciality. Friendly, efficient service.

V-Cafe – at Vincent Hotel
98 Lord St. ⊠ PR8 1JR – ℰ (01704) 883 800
– www.thevincenthotel.com
Rest – Carte £ 24/34

◆ Relaxed café in a striking modern hotel, its glass façade overlooking the street. Open all-day and offering everything from sushi at the counter to 3 courses of globally influenced dishes.

SOUTHROP – Gloucestershire – 503 O28 4 D1

▶ London 87 mi – Birmingham 77 mi – Bristol 60 mi – Sheffield 146 mi

Swan VISA ◉◎ AE
✉ GL7 3NU – ☏ (01367) 850 205 – www.theswanatsouthrop.co.uk – Closed 25 December and Sunday dinner
Rest – Menu £ 19 (weekdays) – Carte £ 30/37

♦ Ex-London restaurateur combines Italian-influenced cooking with pub classics at this delightful creeper-clad inn, set in a picture perfect Cotswold village. Charming service.

SOUTHWOLD – Suffolk – 504 Z27 – pop. 3 858 15 D2

▶ London 108 mi – Great Yarmouth 24 mi – Ipswich 35 mi – Norwich 34 mi
🛈 69 High St ☏ (01502) 72 47 29, www.exploresouthwold.co.uk
 The Common, ☏ (01502) 72 32 34

Swan
Market Pl. ✉ IP18 6EG – ☏ (01502) 722 186 – www.adnams.co.uk
40 rm – †£ 95/137 ††£ 170/284 – 2 suites
Rest – Menu £ 22/39 – Carte £ 25/41

♦ Attractive 18C coaching inn set in the town centre. Subtle modernisations and stylish touches in cosy lounge and bar. Mix of bedrooms: some traditional, some boldly coloured, some charming. Grand dining room with portraits and chandeliers; modern European menu.

Crown with rm
90 High St ✉ IP18 6DP – ☏ (01502) 722 275 – www.adnams.co.uk
14 rm – †£ 100/118 ††£ 184/195 – 1 suite **Rest** – Carte £ 22/37

♦ 17C Georgian-fronted former coaching inn with appealing, relaxed style, buzzing atmosphere and nautically themed locals bar. Modern, seasonal menu served in all areas. Contemporary, individually styled bedrooms; those at the rear are the quietest.

ENGLAND

SOWERBY BRIDGE – West Yorkshire – 502 O22 – pop. 9 901 22 A2
– ✉ Halifax

▶ London 211 mi – Bradford 10 mi – Burnley 35 mi – Manchester 32 mi

El Gato Negro
Oldham Rd ✉ HX6 4DN – ☏ (01422) 823 070 – www.elgatonegrotapas.co.uk – Closed first 2 weeks June, 24 December-7 January, Monday and Tuesday
Rest – Spanish – (dinner only and lunch Friday-Sunday) (booking advisable) Carte £ 25/36

♦ Fun, relaxed former pub with solid stone walls and open fires, serving tasty, authentic tapas. Menus printed on placemats: choose 5 or 6 dishes between 2 people. Staff give sound advice.

at Rishworth Southwest : 4 mi by A 58 on A 672 – ✉ Sowerby Bridge

Old Bore
Oldham Rd, South : 0.5 mi on A 672 ✉ HX6 4QU – ☏ (01422) 822 291 – www.oldbore.co.uk – Closed 2 weeks January, Monday and Tuesday
Rest – Carte £ 30/38

♦ 19C stone coaching inn hidden away in a charming rural area. Cosy, characterful interior crammed with knick-knacks and memorabilia. Appealingly robust cooking often features local game.

SPARSHOLT – Hampshire – 503 P30 – see Winchester

SPEEN – Buckinghamshire – 504 R28 – ⊠ Princes Risborough — 11 C2
▶ London 41 mi – Aylesbury 15 mi – Oxford 33 mi – Reading 25 mi

✕✕ Old Plow
Flowers Bottom, West : 0.5 mi by Chapel Hill and Highwood Bottom
⊠ HP27 0PZ – ℰ (01494) 488 300 – www.yeoldplough.co.uk – Closed August, 1 week late May, Christmas, Sunday and Monday
Rest – Carte £ 29/42

◆ Characterful 17C building with beams and log fires, in a peaceful hamlet. Restaurant has extensive set menu of traditional French dishes. Cosy bistro offers several different menus, including a blackboard selection and tapas Saturday lunch.

SPELDHURST – Kent – 504 U30 – see Royal Tunbridge Wells

SPRIGG'S ALLEY – Oxfordshire – see Chinnor

STADDLE BRIDGE – North Yorkshire – see Northallerton

STADHAMPTON – Oxfordshire – 503 Q28 – pop. 718 — 10 B2
▶ London 53 mi – Aylesbury 18 mi – Oxford 10 mi

✕✕ Crazy Bear with rm
Bear Ln., off Wallingford rd ⊠ OX44 7UR – ℰ (01865) 890 714
– www.crazybeargroup.co.uk
17 rm – †£ 90 ††£ 340, ⊇ £ 19
Rest – Menu £ 19 (lunch) – Carte £ 29/46
Rest *Thai Thai* – Thai – (booking essential) Menu £ 30 (dinner)/40
– Carte £ 20/42

◆ Wacky eatery with red London bus reception, smart glasshouse and huge toy bear in trendy bar. Flamboyant English restaurant serves British and French brasserie dishes. More intimate room offers authentic Thai cuisine. Glamorous, individually styled bedrooms boast chic designer furnishings; some have infinity baths.

STAFFORD – Staffordshire – 502 N25 – pop. 63 681 — 19 C1
▶ London 142 mi – Birmingham 26 mi – Derby 32 mi – Shrewsbury 31 mi
🛈 Eastgate St ℰ (0871) 7 16 19 32, www.enjoystaffordshire.com
🏛 Stafford Castle Newport Rd, ℰ (01785) 22 38 21

🏨 Moat House
Lower Penkridge Rd, Acton Trussell, South : 3.75 mi by A 449 ⊠ ST17 0RJ
– ℰ (01785) 712 217 – www.moathouse.co.uk – Closed 25 December
40 rm ⊇ – †£ 135 ††£ 155/195 – 1 suite
Rest *The Conservatory* – Menu £ 20/30 – Carte dinner £ 23/38

◆ Timbered 15C moated manor house with modern extensions and lawned gardens, within sight of the M6. Characterful rustic bar. Colourful rooms with individual style. Bright, airy conservatory restaurant overlooks canal.

STAINES – Surrey – 504 S29 – pop. 50 538 — 7 C1
▶ London 26 mi – Reading 25 mi

🍴 Three Horseshoes
25 Shepperton Rd, South : 2 mi on B 376 ⊠ TW18 1SE – ℰ (01784) 455 014
– www.3horseshoeslaleham.co.uk
Rest – Carte £ 21/35

◆ A sturdy 17C inn which has had a sympathetic makeover. Pretty enclosed garden and inviting interior divided into three dining areas with charm and character. Traditional food, done well.

STAMFORD – Lincolnshire – **502** S26 – **pop. 22 009** ▌Great Britain **17** C2

▶ London 92 mi – Leicester 31 mi – Lincoln 50 mi – Nottingham 45 mi

🅘 27 St Mary's St ✆ (01780) 75 56 11, www.stamford.co.uk

◉ Town★★ - St Martin's Church★ – Lord Burghley's Hospital★ – Browne's Hospital★ **AC**

◎ Burghley House★★ **AC**, SE : 1.5 mi by B 1443

George of Stamford
71 St Martin's ✉ *PE9 2LB* – ✆ *(01780) 750 750*
– *www.georgehotelofstamford.com*
46 rm ⬜ – †£ 95/115 ††£ 280 – 1 suite
Rest *Garden Room* – see restaurant listing
Rest – Carte £ 43/65
♦ Historic coaching inn dating back over 900 years and still offering good, old-fashioned hospitality. Plenty of seating options in various bars, lounges, the courtyard and walled garden. Bedrooms have a surprisingly contemporary feel. Formal oak-panelled restaurant requires smart dress; menu has a modern edge.

Crown
All Saints Pl. ✉ *PE9 2AG* – ✆ *(01780) 763 136*
– *www.thecrownhotelstamford.co.uk*
28 rm ⬜ – †£ 160/180 ††£ 180/210 **Rest** – Carte £ 21/34
♦ Former coaching inn set in historic market town. Main house bedrooms have a funky, boutique style; those in the Town House are larger with a more classical feel. Dine in the modern cocktail bar, in one of the cosy lounges or in the quieter rear dining room.

Rock Lodge without rest
1 Empingham Rd ✉ *PE9 2RH* – ✆ *(01780) 481 758* – *www.rock-lodge.co.uk*
– *Closed 25 December-5 January*
7 rm ⬜ – †£ 72/82 ††£ 110/115
♦ Victorian house built in 1900 by the town's mayor. Displays a mix of influences, with mullioned windows, mock-Tudor gables, gargoyles and stones from old churches in the garden walls. Comfy lounge and breakfast room; well-equipped bedrooms.

Jim's Yard

3 Ironmonger St, off Broad St ✉ *PE9 1PL* – ✆ *(01780) 756 080*
– *www.jimsyard.biz* – *Closed last week July, first week August, 25 December-10 January, Sunday and Monday*
Rest – Menu £ 17 (lunch) – Carte £ 22/33
♦ Two 18C houses in a courtyard: conservatory or first-floor dining options. Smart tableware enhances enjoyment of great value menus employing well-executed, classic cooking.

Garden Room – at George of Stamford
71 St Martin's ✉ *PE9 2LB* – ✆ *(01780) 750 750*
– *www.georgehotelofstamford.com*
Rest – Carte £ 28/48
♦ Relaxed all-day restaurant within a 900 year old coaching inn. Extensive menu is accompanied by a steak counter in winter and salad bar in summer. The enclosed courtyard is a popular spot.

Bull & Swan with rm
St Martins ✉ *PE9 2LJ* – ✆ *(01780) 766 412* – *www.thebullandswan.co.uk*
7 rm ⬜ – †£ 90 ††£ 110 **Rest** – Carte £ 22/34
♦ Stone-built former hall house converted to an inn during the 1600s and still the only pub south of the river. Characterful beamed bar and smarter dining room. Menu ranges from sharing slates to regional classics and locally sourced steaks. Stylish, individually designed bedrooms boast Egyptian cotton sheets.

STANDISH – Greater Manchester – **502** M23 – pop. 14 350 – ✉ Wigan **20** A2
▶ London 210 mi – Liverpool 25 mi – Manchester 21 mi – Preston 15 mi

at Wrightington Bar Northwest : 3.5 mi by A 5209 on B 5250 – ✉ Wigan

Mulberry Tree
9 Wood Ln ✉ WN6 9SE – ☏ (01257) 451 400 – www.themulberrytree.info
Rest – Carte £ 27/40
◆ Spacious 19C pub with laid-back bar and more formal, linen-laid dining room. Wide-ranging menus of good value, generously proportioned dishes, with plenty of pub favourites.

STANSTED MOUNTFITCHET – Essex – **504** U28 – pop. 5 311 **12** B2
▶ London 38 mi – Birmingham 125 mi – Croydon 59 mi – Barnet 37 mi

Chimneys without rest
44 Lower St, on B 1351 ✉ CM24 8LR – ☏ (01279) 813 388
– www.chimneysguesthouse.co.uk
4 rm ⌁ – ♦£ 58/62 ♦♦£ 80
◆ Charming 17C house with low-beamed ceilings, a cosy lounge and snug breakfast room. Bedrooms have a modern, cottagey style, displaying pine furnishings and homely touches. Tasty breakfast offerings might include Manx kippers or smoked haddock with poached eggs.

STANTON – Suffolk – **504** W27 – pop. 2 073 **15** C2
▶ London 88 mi – Cambridge 38 mi – Ipswich 40 mi – King's Lynn 38 mi

Leaping Hare
Wyken Vineyards, South : 1.25 mi by Wyken Rd ✉ IP31 2DW – ☏ (01359) 250 287 – www.wykenvineyards.co.uk – Closed 25 December-5 January
Rest – (lunch only and dinner Friday-Saturday) (booking essential) Menu £ 19 (lunch) – Carte £ 26/29
◆ Beautiful 17C barn with lovely terrace; at the centre of a vineyard. Interesting all-day light bites or accomplished weekly menu. Well-sourced, seasonal ingredients; many from their own farm. Carefully judged cooking relies on quality produce and natural flavours.

STANTON ST QUINTIN – Wiltshire – **503** N29 – see Chippenham

---

STAPLEFORD – Nottinghamshire – **504** Q25 – see Nottingham

STATHERN – Leicestershire – see Melton Mowbray

STAVERTON – Northants. – **504** Q27 – see Daventry

STAVERTON – Northamptonshire – **503** I32 – pop. 468 – ✉ Daventry **16** B3
▶ London 220 mi – Exeter 20 mi – Torquay 33 mi

Kingston House
Northwest : 1 mi on Kingston rd ✉ TQ9 6AR – ☏ (01803) 762 235
– www.kingston-estate.com – Closed Christmas-New Year
3 rm ⌁ – ♦£ 110/120 ♦♦£ 180/200
Rest – (dinner only) (residents only, set menu only) Menu £ 38 **s**
◆ Attractive Georgian mansion in a stunning location. Original features and antiques abound. Spacious bedrooms boast feature beds and good views over the parterre garden; some have original baths. Vaulted basement dining room serves classical, home-cooked dishes.

STILTON – Cambridgeshire – 504 T26 – pop. 2 500 – ✉ Peterborough — 14 A2

▶ London 76 mi – Cambridge 30 mi – Northampton 43 mi – Peterborough 6 mi

Bell Inn
Great North Rd ✉ *PE7 3RA* – ℰ *(01733) 241 066* – *www.thebellstilton.co.uk*
– *Closed 25 December*
22 rm ⌑ – ♦£ 76 ♦♦£ 115
Rest *Village Bar* – see restaurant listing
Rest *Galleried Restaurant* – *(dinner only and Sunday lunch)* Menu £ 25

♦ Historic coaching inn with hospitable, hands-on owner. Comfortable bedrooms have traditional feel: some have four-posters; the three newest are in the former smithy, overlooking the garden. First floor restaurant offers seasonal menu with strong classical base.

Village Bar – at Bell Inn
Great North Rd ✉ *PE7 3RA* – ℰ *(01733) 241 066* – *www.thebellstilton.co.uk*
– *Closed 25 December*
Rest – Carte £ 20/30 s

♦ 17C coaching inn where Stilton cheese was born. Choose from a characterful bar or more modern bistro area. Served throughout, the classical menu is a step above your usual pub fare.

STOCKBRIDGE – Hampshire – 503 P30 – pop. 570 — 6 B2

▶ London 75 mi – Salisbury 14 mi – Southampton 19 mi – Winchester 9 mi

Greyhound with rm
31 High St ✉ *SO20 6EY* – ℰ *(01264) 810 833* – *www.thegreyhound.info* – *Closed 24-26 December and Sunday dinner*
7 rm ⌑ – ♦£ 70 ♦♦£ 95/125 **Rest** – Carte £ 23/35

♦ Unassuming pub with low-beamed bar and comfy lounge. Lunch mainly aimed at one course; concise evening à la carte features pub dishes with restaurant-style touches and refined presentation. Picnic by the river in the garden. Spacious bedrooms with huge showers.

at Longstock North : 1.5 mi on A 3057 – ✉ Stockbridge

Peat Spade Inn with rm
Village St ✉ *SO20 6DR* – ℰ *(01264) 810 612* – *www.peatspadeinn.co.uk*
6 rm ⌑ – ♦£ 145 ♦♦£ 145 **Rest** – *(booking essential)* Carte £ 20/30

♦ Charming 19C inn with country pursuits theme, period furnishings and welcoming candlelight. Menus offer classically based dishes that have been brought up-to-date. Stylish bedrooms are split between the inn and annexe. Shooting/fishing trips can be arranged.

STOCKPORT – Greater Manchester – 502 N23 – pop. 136 082 — 20 B3

▶ London 201 mi – Liverpool 42 mi – Leeds 50 mi – Sheffield 52 mi

Damson
113 Heaton Moor Rd, Northwest : 2.25 mi by A 6, Heaton Rd, A 5145 and Bank Hall Rd ✉ *SK4 4HY* – ℰ *(0161) 432 46 66* – *www.damsonrestaurant.co.uk*
– *Closed 25-26 December and 1 January*
Rest – Menu £ 17 (lunch) – Carte £ 28/45

♦ Smart, modern, glass-fronted restaurant with damson walls, velvet chairs and rustic tables. Appealing menu of traditional dishes with modern touches. Attentive, formal service.

STOKE BY NAYLAND – Suffolk – 504 W28   15 C3

▶ London 70 mi – Bury St Edmunds 24 mi – Cambridge 54 mi – Colchester 11 mi

Crown with rm
✉ CO6 4SE – ℰ (01206) 262 001 – www.crowninn.net – *Closed 25-26 December*
11 rm ⌧ – ♦£ 80 ♦♦£ 135/200   **Rest** – Carte £ 23/38

- Spacious 16C pub with smart wood-furnished patio; set in a hillside village overlooking the valley. Menus feature locally sourced, seasonal produce, a daily catch and seafood specials. Spacious bedrooms boast country views; some have French windows and a terrace.

STOKE HOLY CROSS – Norfolk – 504 X26 – see Norwich

STOKE-ON-TRENT – Stoke-on-Trent – 502 N24 – pop. 259 252   19 C1
▌Great Britain

▶ London 162 – Birmingham 46 – Leicester 59 – Liverpool 58

🛈 City Centre ℰ (01782) 23 60 00, www.visitstoke.co.uk

⛳ Greenway Hall Stockton Brook, ℰ (01782) 50 31 58

⛳ Parkhall Weston Coyney Hulme Rd, ℰ (01782) 59 95 84

◉ The Potteries Museum and Art Gallery★ Y **M** – Gladstone Pottery Museum★ **AC** V

◉ The Wedgwood Story★ **AC**, S : 7 mi on A 500, A 34 and minor rd V. Little Moreton Hall★★ **AC**, N : 10 mi by A 500 on A 34 U – Biddulph Grange Garden★, N : 7 mi by A 52, A 50 and A 527 U

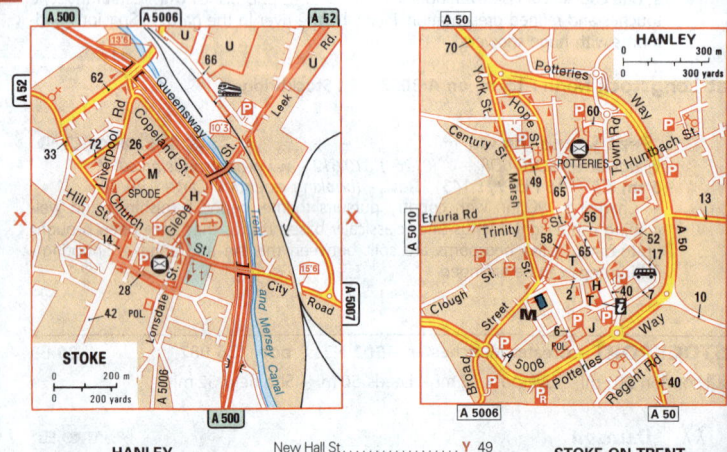

HANLEY

Albion St	Y 2
Bethesda St	Y 6
Birch Terrace	Y 7
Botteslow St	Y 10
Bucknall New Rd	Y 13
Charles St	Y 17
Lichfield St	Y 40
New Hall St	Y 49
Old Hall St	Y 52
Parliament Row	Y 55
Percy St	Y 56
Piccadilly	Y 58
Potteries Shopping Centre	Y
Quadrant Rd	Y 60
Stafford St	Y 65
Vale Pl.	Y 70

STOKE-ON-TRENT

Campbell Pl.	X 14
Church St	X
Elenora St	X 26
Fleming Rd	X 28
Hartshill Rd	X 33
London Rd	X 42
Shelton Old Rd	X 62
Station Rd	X 66
Vale St	X 72

STOKE-ON-TRENT NEWCASTLE-UNDER-LYME

Alexandra Rd	U 3
Bedford Rd	U 4
Brownhills Rd	U 12
Church Lane	U 19
Cobridge Rd	U 21
Davenport St	U 23
Elder Rd	U 24
Etruria Vale Rd	U 27
Grove Rd	V 30
Hanley Rd	U 31
Heron St	V 34
Higherland	U 37
High St	U 35
Manor St	V 44
Mayne St	V 45
Moorland Rd	U 48
Porthill Rd	U 59
Snow Hill	U 63
Stoke Rd	U 68
Strand (The)	V 69
Victoria Park Rd	U 75
Victoria Pl. Link	U 76
Watlands View	U 77
Williamson St	U 78
Wolstanton Link Rd	U 80

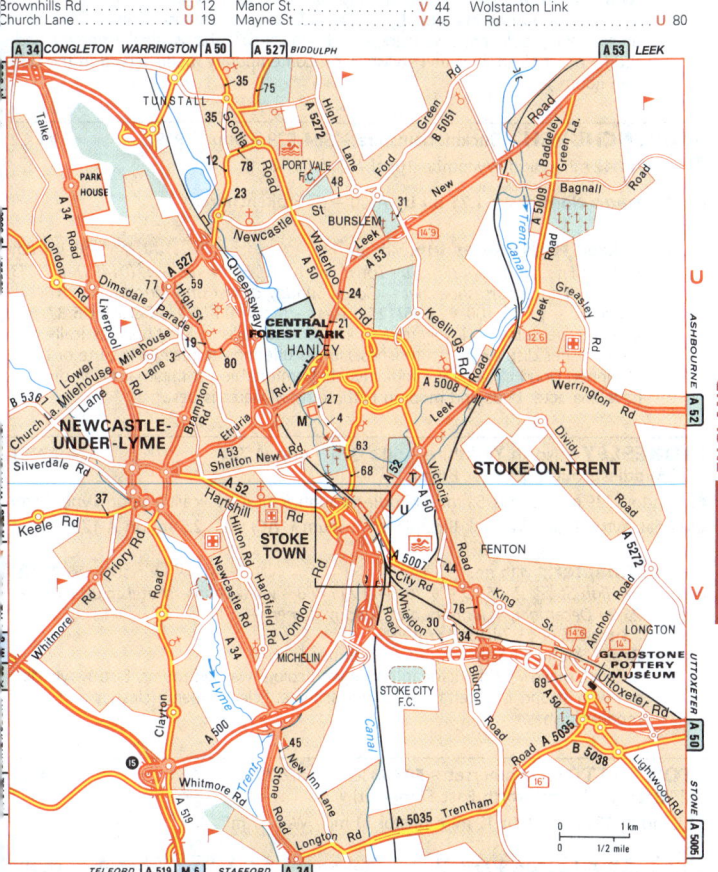

STOKE POGES – Buckinghamshire – 504 S29 – pop. 4 112 — 11 D3

▶ London 30 mi – Aylesbury 28 mi – Oxford 44 mi
🅿 Stoke Park Park Rd, ℰ (01753) 71 71 71

Stoke Park

Park Rd ✉ SL2 4PG – ℰ (01753) 717 171
– www.stokepark.com – Closed 25-26 December
49 rm – †£ 265/675 ††£ 495/675, ⌑ £ 22
Rest *Dining Room* – Menu £ 30/48 – Carte lunch £ 43/59

♦ Grand, palatial hotel in huge grounds, with golf course, extensive sporting activities and impressive spa. Choice of smart classical or stunning contemporary bedrooms. Lounge offers all day brasserie menu. Stylish restaurant displays classical à la carte.

STOKE POGES

Stoke Place
Stoke Green, South : 0.5 mi by B 416 – ✉ SL2 4HT – ✆ (01753) 534 790
– www.stokeplace.co.uk – *Closed 24 December-8 January*
39 rm ⊒ – †£ 130/225 ††£ 155/285
Rest *Garden Room* – *(closed Sunday lunch)* Menu £ 25/40
♦ 17C Queen Anne mansion, by a lake, in 22 acres of grounds. Chic, quirky guest areas display bold print wallpapers and original furnishings; sleek, modern bedrooms boast clean lines and stylish beds. Contemporary menu served in the Garden Room.

STOKENCHURCH – Buckinghamshire – 504 R29 – pop. 3 949   11 C2
▶ London 42 mi – High Wycombe 10 mi – Oxford 18 mi

at Radnage Northeast : 1.75 mi by A 40 – ✉ Stokenchurch

Three Horseshoes Inn with rm
Bennett End, North : 1.25 mi by Town End rd. ✉ HP14 4EB – ✆ (01494) 483 273
– www.thethreehorseshoes.net – *Closed Sunday dinner and Monday lunch*
6 rm ⊒ – †£ 85/100 ††£ 95/125   **Rest** – Menu £ 17/20 – Carte £ 26/37
♦ Attractive pub with lovely terrace, in a fantastic hillside location. Classically prepared dishes display French touches. Lighter offerings at lunch; à la carte or tapas at dinner. Good choice for Sunday lunch. Comfortable yet minimalistic bedrooms have character beds and modern bathrooms; Molières is best.

STOKESLEY – North Yorkshire – 502 Q20 – pop. 4 725   23 C1
– ✉ Middlesbrough ▮ Great Britain
▶ London 239 mi – Leeds 59 mi – Middlesbrough 8 mi – Newcastle upon Tyne 49 mi
◉ Great Ayton (Captain Cook Birthplace Museum ★ **AC**), NE : 2.5 mi on A 173

Chapter's with rm
27 High St ✉ TS9 5AD – ✆ (01642) 711 888 – www.chaptershotel.co.uk – *Closed 25-26 December, 1 January and Sunday dinner*
13 rm ⊒ – †£ 74/89 ††£ 89/99
Rest – Menu £ 15 (lunch) – Carte dinner £ 29/42
♦ Solid, mellow brick Victorian house with colour washed rooms. Bistro style dining with strong Mediterranean colour scheme. Eclectic menu: classics and more modern dishes.

STON EASTON – Somerset – 503 M30 – pop. 579   4 C2
– ✉ Bath (bath And North East Somerset)
▶ London 131 mi – Bath 12 mi – Bristol 11 mi – Wells 7 mi

Ston Easton Park
✉ BA3 4DF – ✆ (01761) 241 631 – www.stoneaston.co.uk
20 rm ⊒ – †£ 150/210 ††£ 170/230 – 2 suites
Rest *Sorrel* – see restaurant listing
♦ Striking aristocratic Palladian mansion, in 36 acres of attractive grounds designed by Humphrey Repton. Fine rooms of epic proportions are filled with antiques, curios and impressive floral arrangements. Stylish, individually designed bedrooms – many with coronet or four-poster beds – one is set in a cottage.

Sorrel – at Ston Easton Park Hotel
✉ BA3 4DF – ✆ (01761) 241 631 – www.stoneaston.co.uk
Rest – *(booking essential for non-residents)* Menu £ 23 (lunch) – Carte £ 40/51
♦ Formal country house dining room in a striking Palladian mansion, surrounded by 36 acres of parkland. Classical menus offer luxurious ingredients and produce from the Victorian kitchen garden.

STONEHALL COMMON – Worcestershire – see Worcester

STORRINGTON – West Sussex – **504** S31 – pop. 7 727 7 C2
▶ London 54 mi – Brighton 20 mi – Portsmouth 36 mi

Old Forge
6 Church St ✉ RH20 4LA – ℘ (01903) 743 402 – www.oldforge.co.uk – Closed 2 weeks spring, 1 week autumn, Christmas-New Year, Saturday lunch, Sunday and Wednesday dinner, Monday and Tuesday
Rest – Menu £ 19/35
♦ Appealing whitewashed and brick cottages with three dining rooms bearing all hallmarks of flavoursome traditional cuisine. Array of cheeses; fine wine from small producers.

STOWMARKET – Suffolk – **504** W27 – pop. 15 059 15 C3
▶ London 95 mi – Ipswich 14 mi – Colchester 35 mi – Clacton-on-Sea 40 mi

at Buxhall West : 3.75 mi by B 115 – ✉ Stowmarket

Buxhall Crown
Mill Rd ✉ IP14 3DW – ℘ (01449) 736 521 – www.thebuxhallcrown.co.uk – Closed 25 December and Sunday dinner
Rest – Menu £ 16 (lunch) – Carte £ 19/31
♦ Part-16C country pub set off the beaten track, with bright dining room and cosy, low-beamed bar. Classic dishes offered on seasonal menu. Good value set 2 course menu and fun retro puds.

STOW-ON-THE-WOLD – Gloucestershire – **503** O28 – pop. 2 074 4 D1
🟦 Great Britain
▶ London 86 mi – Birmingham 44 mi – Gloucester 27 mi – Oxford 30 mi
🛈 12 Talbot Court ℘ (01451) 87 01 50, www.stowonthewold.info
◉ Chastleton House ★★, NE : 6.5 mi by A 436 and A 44

Number Four at Stow
Fosseway, South : 1.25 mi by A 429 on A 424 ✉ GL54 1JX – ℘ (01451) 830 297 – www.hotelnumberfour.co.uk – Closed 24-29 December
14 rm ⌑ – †£ 100/120 ††£ 130/145 – 4 suites
Rest *Cutlers at Number Four* – (closed Sunday dinner except bank holiday weekends) Carte £ 25/36
♦ Contemporary, open-plan hotel with small bar and comfy lounge boasting bold brushed velvet and white leather seating. Bright, compact bedrooms feature smart leather headboards, cream furniture and modern facilities. Informal brasserie offers modern British menu.

Grapevine
Sheep St ✉ GL54 1AU – ℘ (01451) 830 344 – www.thegrapevinehotel.com
22 rm ⌑ – †£ 72/88 ††£ 113/164
Rest *La Vigna* – see restaurant listing
Rest *Conservatory* – Menu £ 35
♦ Two extended 17C houses, nestled in amongst the local antique shops. The bar, guest areas and bedrooms that are set in the main house have a traditional feel; bedrooms in the annexe are boldly coloured, more modern in style and quieter. Classical dishes served in conservatory; Mediterranean menu in La Vigna.

Royalist
Digbeth St ✉ GL56 1BN – ℘ (01451) 830 670 – www.theroyalisthotel.com
14 rm ⌑ – †£ 68/120 ††£ 103/185
Rest *Eagle & Child* – Carte £ 19/25
Rest *947 AD* – Menu £ 37 (dinner) – Carte lunch £ 24/29
♦ Historic high street inn - reputedly England's oldest. Comfortable, stylish rooms, individual in shape and décor and quieter at the rear. Two-room bar in exposed stone. Robust cooking in the attached stone pub. Fine dining in the intimate, beamed restaurant with inglenook fireplace.

STOW-ON-THE-WOLD

Number Nine without rest
9 Park St ⊠ GL54 1AQ – ℘ (01451) 870 333 – www.number-nine.info
3 rm – †£ 45/65 ††£ 65/89

♦ Ivy-clad, 18C Cotswold stone house set on the high street of a historic market town, close to the square. Comfy lounge and breakfast room boast exposed stone, open fires and dark beams. Winding staircase leads to simple, neutrally-hued, wood-furnished bedrooms.

Old Butchers
Park St ⊠ GL54 1AQ – ℘ (01451) 831 700 – www.theoldbutchers.com – Closed 1 week May and 1 week October
Rest – Carte £ 24/30

♦ Former butcher's, now a smart, modern restaurant with welcoming ambience and flower-filled terrace. Brightly painted bar with food-themed prints, church candles, cushions and display of fresh bread. Well-priced menus evolve from service to service, featuring hearty, flavoursome dishes and comforting desserts.

La Vigna – at Grapevine Hotel
Sheep St ⊠ GL54 1AU – ℘ (01451) 830 344 – www.thegrapevinehotel.com
Rest – Carte £ 18/23

♦ Informal, brasserie-style, hotel restaurant in a traditional 17C extended house. Menu offers plenty of choice and displays Mediterranean-influences; most produce is sourced from within 20 miles.

White Hart Inn with rm
The Square ⊠ GL54 1AF – ℘ (01451) 830 674 – www.whitehartstow.com – Closed 1 week October and 1 week May
5 rm – †£ 70 ††£ 80/100 **Rest** – Carte £ 21/28

♦ 13C former coaching inn with contemporary, individual style. Small, open-fired bar, leather-furnished lounge and slightly kitsch dining room. Light dishes or soup and sandwich combos at lunch; classic British offerings at dinner. Antique-furnished bedrooms.

at Upper Oddington East : 2 mi by A 436 – ⊠ Stow-On-The-Wold

Horse & Groom Village Inn with rm
⊠ GL56 0XH – ℘ (01451) 830 584 – www.horseandgroom.uk.com
7 rm – †£ 65/79 ††£ 89/110 **Rest** – Carte £ 21/33

♦ Part-16C mellow-stone inn in a village designated an AONB. Seasonal menus feature strictly homemade and local produce, with consideration given to ethical production and sustainable sourcing. Cosy bedrooms; serious breakfasts include local eggs and sausages.

at Lower Oddington East : 3 mi by A 436 – ⊠ Stow-On-The-Wold

Fox Inn with rm
⊠ GL56 0UR – ℘ (01451) 870 555 – www.foxinn.net
3 rm – †£ 75/95 ††£ 75/95 **Rest** – (booking essential) Carte £ 24/32

♦ Quintessentially English, creeper-clad inn with cosy, characterful bar, charming garden and heated terrace. Cooking is hearty and satisfying; produce is sourced from local markets. Uniquely designed bedrooms display lovely antiques; some boast feature beds.

at Daylesford East : 3.5 mi by A 436 – ⊠ Stow-On-The-Wold

Café at Daylesford Organic
⊠ GL56 0YG – ℘ (01608) 731 700 – www.daylesfordorganic.com – Closed 25-26 December and 1 January
Rest – Organic – (lunch only) (bookings not accepted) Carte £ 23/32

♦ Stylish café attached to the rear of a farm shop, its rustic interior boasting an open charcoal grill and wood-fired oven. Menus showcase an interesting array of home-cooked dishes. Everything is organic, with much of the produce coming from the farm itself.

STOW-ON-THE-WOLD

at Bledington Southeast : 4 mi by A 436 on B 4450 – ✉ Kingham

Kings Head Inn with rm
The Green ✉ *OX7 6XQ –* ✆ *(01608) 658 365 – www.kingsheadinn.net – Closed 25-26 December*
12 rm – †£ 50/70 ††£ 100/125 **Rest** – Carte £ 21/35
♦ 15C stone inn with low-ceilinged, beamed bar and comfortable dining room. Traditional dishes with odd international influence; robust, rustic cooking. Smart bedrooms; those in pub more characterful; those in annex more stylish.

at Nether Westcote Southeast : 4.75 mi by A 429 and A 424

Feathered Nest with rm
✉ *OX7 6SD –* ✆ *(01993) 833 030 – www.thefeatherednestinn.co.uk – Closed 25 December*
4 rm – †£ 110 ††£ 185
Rest – *(closed Monday except bank holidays) (booking advisable)*
Carte £ 25/34
♦ With its laid-back bar, rustic snug, casual conservatory and formal dining room, this pub offers something for everyone. Sit on quirky stools made from horse saddles and choose from the simple bar menu or try more complex dishes while sitting at elegant antique tables. Wine list features over 200 bins. Comfy bedrooms boasts antiques, quality linens and roll-top baths.

at Lower Swell West : 1.25 mi on B 4068 – ✉ Stow-On-The-Wold

Rectory Farmhouse without rest
by Rectory Barns Rd ✉ *GL54 1LH –* ✆ *(01451) 832 351 – Closed Christmas-New Year*
3 rm – †£ 60/70 ††£ 93/100
♦ 17C former farmhouse of Cotswold stone. Bedrooms are very comfortable and decorated in distinctive cottage style. Breakfast in kitchen, conservatory or, in summer, on the terrace.

STRATFORD-UPON-AVON – Warwickshire – **503** P27   **19** C3
– pop. 23 085 – Great Britain

▶ London 96 mi – Birmingham 23 mi – Coventry 18 mi – Leicester 44 mi
🛈 Bridgefoot ✆ (0870) 160 79 30, www.shakespeare-country.co.uk
⛳ Tiddington Rd, ✆ (01789) 20 57 49
⛳ Menzies Welcombe Hotel & GC Warwick Rd, ✆ (01789) 41 38 00
⛳ Stratford Oaks Snitterfield Bearley Rd, ✆ (01789) 73 19 80
◉ Town ★★ - Shakespeare's Birthplace ★ **AC**, AB
◉ Mary Arden's House ★ **AC**, NW : 4 mi by A 3400 A. Ragley Hall ★ **AC**, W : 9 mi by A 422 A

Plan on next page

Ettington Park
Alderminster, Southeast : 6.5 mi on A 3400 ✉ *CV37 8BU –* ✆ *(0845) 072 74 54 – www.handpicked.co.uk*
48 rm – †£ 105/205 ††£ 145/225
Rest *Oak Room* – see restaurant listing
♦ Impressive Gothic mansion surrounded by lovely gardens. Characterful guest areas display ornate plasterwork, marble fireplaces and vast portraits. Feature bedrooms boast original fires and grand beds; others bedrooms are more contemporary.

STRATFORD-UPON-AVON

Banbury Rd	**B**	2
Bell Court Shopping Centre	**A**	39
Benson Rd.	**B**	3
Bridge Foot	**B**	6
Bridge St	**A**	8
Chapel Lane	**A**	13
Chapel St	**A**	14
Church St	**A**	16
Clopton Bridge	**B**	18
College Lane	**A**	19
Ely St	**A**	22
Evesham Pl.	**A**	24
Great William St	**A**	25
Greenhill St	**A**	27
Guild St	**A**	28
Henley St.	**A**	29
High St	**A**	31
Rother St	**A**	32
Scholars Lane	**A**	33
Sheep St.	**AB**	35
Tiddington Rd	**B**	38
Trinity St.	**A**	40
Warwick Rd.	**B**	42
Waterside	**B**	43
Windsor St	**A**	45
Wood St	**A**	47

Welcombe H. Spa and Golf Club
Warwick Rd, Northeast : 1.5 mi on A 439
✉ CV37 0NR – ✆ (01789) 295 252 – www.menzieshotels.co.uk
73 rm – †£ 92/205 ††£ 112/215 – 5 suites
Rest *Trevelyan* – Menu £ 25/30 **s** – Carte £ 29/50 **s**
◆ Imposing Jacobean-style house built in 1866, with attractive grounds, superb spa/leisure club and classical guest areas. Choose from corporate, or traditional, antique-filled bedrooms. Formal dining room overlooks the gardens and water features.

Arden
Waterside ✉ CV37 6BA – ✆ (01789) 298 682 – www.theardenhotelstratford.com
45 rm – †£ 213/228 ††£ 325/355   **Bx**
Rest *Waterside Brasserie* – see restaurant listing
◆ Great location opposite the RSC Theatre. Plush interior with smart, modern sitting rooms. Twisty corridors lead to stylish, sage green bedrooms. Large terrace and gardens overlook the Avon.

Cherry Trees without rest
Swan's Nest Ln ✉ CV37 7LS – ✆ (01789) 292 989
– www.cherrytrees-stratford.co.uk   **Be**
3 rm – †£ 75 ††£ 120
◆ Smart, proudly run guesthouse with town just a short stroll away over the River Avon. Spacious bedrooms boast quality furnishings, state-of-the-art showers, conservatory seating areas and thoughtful extras. Cake served on arrival.

White Sails without rest
85 Evesham Rd, Southwest : 1 mi on B 439 ✉ CV37 9BE – ✆ (01789) 550 469
– www.white-sails.co.uk
5 rm – †£ 125 ††£ 125/132
◆ Friendly guest house boasting excellent bedrooms; all individually furnished and with a high level of facilities, including superb bathrooms. Leather furnished lounge with local info.

STRATFORD-UPON-AVON

XXX Oak Room – at Ettington Park Hotel
Alderminster, Southeast : 6.5 mi on A 3400 – CV37 8BU – ℰ (0845) 727 454
– www.handpicked.co.uk
Rest – Menu £ 35 **s** – Carte £ 33/45 **s**
♦ Named after its smart wood panelling, an intimate hotel dining room in an impressive Gothic mansion with beautiful façade. Modern menu has classical undertones. Private room in the old chapel.

XX Waterside Brasserie – at Arden Hotel
Waterside – CV37 6BA – ℰ (01789) 298 682 – www.theardenhotelstratford.com
Rest – Menu £ 19 (lunch) – Carte £ 36/44   **Bx**
♦ Large, contemporary hotel brasserie with lovely outlook courtesy of multi-paned, Georgian-style doors. Appealing modern British menu; tasty, well-prepared dishes follow the seasons closely.

XX Church Street Town House with rm
16 Church St – CV37 6HB – ℰ (01789) 262 222
– www.churchstreettownhouse.com   **An**
12 rm – †£ 100 ††£ 160   **Rest** – Carte £ 22/32
♦ Handsome, part-17C property run by an experienced local team. Series of charming dining rooms display rich fabrics and a mix of furniture. Contemporary menu offers an extensive choice of globally influenced dishes and sharing platters. Beautiful bedrooms display bold colours, smart bathrooms and great extras.

XX Rooftop
Royal Shakespeare Theatre, Waterside – CV37 6BB – ℰ (01789) 403 449
– www.rsc.org.uk/eat – Closed Sunday dinner   **Ba**
Rest – Menu £ 19 (lunch) – Carte dinner £ 26/38
♦ Modern, open-plan restaurant with lovely terrace, set on top of the Royal Shakespeare Theatre and boasting views over the canal basin, river and gardens. Interesting modern menu with classical British undertones; attractive presentation.

XX No 9 Church St.
9 Church St – CV37 6HB – ℰ (01789) 415 522 – www.no9churchst.com – Closed 25 December-3 January, Sunday dinner and Monday   **Aa**
Rest – Menu £ 16 (lunch) – Carte £ 24/33 **s**
♦ Cosy little restaurant set within a 400 year old townhouse, a little off the main streets. Experienced chef-owner has returned home to offer honest, flavoursome British cooking with a modern twist. Classical puddings and friendly service.

X Lambs
12 Sheep St – CV37 6EF – ℰ (01789) 292 554 – www.lambsrestaurant.co.uk
– Closed 25-26 December and Monday lunch   **Bc**
Rest – Menu £ 12/15 – Carte £ 22/38
♦ Attractive 16C timbered house, with characterful beams, original features and split-level dining rooms. Concise menu offers refined modern dishes and fish specials, with good value pre-theatre options.

at Alveston East : 2 mi by B 4086 - B – Stratford-Upon-Avon

X Baraset Barn
1 Pimlico Ln, on B 4086 – CV37 7RJ – ℰ (01789) 295 510
– www.barasetbarn.co.uk – Closed 1 January and Sunday dinner
Rest – Menu £ 16 (lunch and early dinner) – Carte £ 21/38
♦ Modernised barn offering something for everyone: original features, contemporary furnishings and large terraces. Good-sized menu caters for all and includes daily fish specials and tasty rotisserie selection.

STRETE – Devon – see Dartmouth

STRETTON – Staffordshire – **502** P25 – see Burton-upon-Trent

---

STUCKTON – Hampshire – see Fordingbridge

STUDLAND – Dorset – 503 O32 – pop. 471   4 C3
▶ London 135 mi – Bournemouth 25 mi – Southampton 53 mi – Weymouth 29 mi

✗ Shell Bay
Ferry Rd, North : 3 mi or via car ferry from Sandbanks ✉ *BH19 3BA* – ✆ *(01929) 450 363* – *www.shellbay.net* – *March-October*
Rest – Seafood – *(booking essential)* Carte £ 24/32
♦ Airy, simply furnished seafood restaurant with decked terrace; superbly set on the waterfront and boasting views over the harbour to Brownsea Island – all tables have a view. Choose between an informal lunch/early evening menu or classically based daily menu.

SUMMERCOURT – Cornwall – 503 F32 – ✉ Newquay   1 B2
▶ London 263 mi – Newquay 9 mi – Plymouth 45 mi

✗ Viners
Carvynick, 1.5 mi Northwest off the junction of A 30 and A 3058. ✉ *TR8 5AF* – ✆ *(01872) 510 544* – *www.vinersrestaurant.co.uk* – *Closed 2 weeks early January, and Sunday dinner and Monday out of season*
Rest – Menu £ 14 (lunch)/19 – Carte £ 24/39 **s**
♦ Rustic, stone-built former farmhouse. Snacks available amongst roaring log fires and low slung beams in the bar. Relaxed first floor restaurant offers seasonal menu of old classics, a few more ambitious dishes and tasty daily specials. Keen, friendly service.

SUMMERHOUSE – Darlington – see Darlington

SUNBURY ON THAMES – Surrey – 504 S29 – pop. 27 415   7 C1
▶ London 16 mi – Croydon 38 mi – Barnet 44 mi – Ealing 10 mi

✗✗ Indian Zest
21 Thames St ✉ *TW16 5QF* – ✆ *(01932) 765 000* – *www.indianzest.co.uk*
Rest – Indian – Carte £ 21/25
♦ Original in its decoration and food. 450 year old building; a series of small rooms set around a bar; subtle colonial feel. Interesting mix of modern Indian and traditional regional cuisine.

SUNNINGDALE – Windsor and Maidenhead – 504 S29   11 D3
▶ London 33 mi – Croydon 39 mi – Barnet 46 mi – Ealing 22 mi

✗✗✗ Bluebells
Shrubbs Hill, London Rd, Northeast : 0.75 mi on A 30 ✉ *SL5 0LE* – ✆ *(01344) 622 722* – *www.bluebells-restaurant.com* – *Closed 1-12 January, 25-26 December, Sunday dinner and Monday*
Rest – Menu £ 17/25 – Carte dinner £ 33/59
♦ Smart, well-manicured façade matched by sophisticated interior of deep green. Large rear terrace, deck and garden. Modern British cooking with original starting point.

SUNNISIDE – Tyne and Wear   24 B2
▶ London 283 mi – Newcastle upon Tyne 6 mi – Sunderland 16 mi
  – Middlesbrough 41 mi

⌂ Hedley Hall *without rest*
Hedley Lane, South : 2 mi by A 6076 ✉ *NE16 5EH* – ✆ *(01207) 231 835* – *www.hedleyhall.com* – *Closed Christmas-New Year*
4 rm ⊡ – †£ 55/65 ††£ 86
♦ Pleasant former farmhouse in quiet rural location close to Beamish, with spacious conservatory and sitting room. Rooms are large, with good levels of comfort and country views.

SUTTON COLDFIELD – West Midlands – **503** O26 – pop. 105 452   **19** C2
► London 124 mi – Birmingham 8 mi – Coventry 29 mi – Nottingham 47 mi
🏌 Pype Hayes Walmley Eachelhurst Rd, ℰ (0121) 351 10 14
🏌 Boldmere Monmouth Dr., ℰ (0121) 354 33 79
🏌 110 Thornhill Rd, ℰ (0121) 580 78 78
🏌 The Belfry Wishaw Lichfield Rd, ℰ (01675) 47 03 01

Plan : see Birmingham pp. 2 and 3

XX **Mint**   🛜 AC VISA ⓞ
52 Thornhill Rd, Little Aston, Northwest : 3.5 mi by A 5127, A 454 and B 4151 on B 4138. ✉ *B74 3EN –* ℰ *(0121) 353 04 88 – www.mint-restaurant.com – Closed first week January, one week Easter, last week August, Monday and Tuesday*
Rest – Menu £ 19/37   DT**x**
♦ Bright, modern, brasserie-style restaurant set in a smart residential area. Short menu of flavoursome, visually appealing British dishes. Good value lunch menu. Hands-on owner.

SUTTON COURTENAY – Oxfordshire – **504** Q29 – pop. 2 413   **10** B2
► London 72 mi – Bristol 77 mi – Coventry 70 mi

🍴 **Fish**   🚗 P VISA AE
4 Appleford Rd ✉ *OX14 4NQ –* ℰ *(01235) 848 242*
– www.thefishatsuttoncourtenay.co.uk – Closed Monday except bank holidays and Sunday dinner
Rest – Menu £ 17 (lunch) – Carte £ 24/34
♦ Robust, seasonal country cooking: escargots and crème brûlée meet steak and kidney pie and profiteroles on Franco-Anglo menu. Neat garden and bright conservatory. Charming service.

SUTTON GAULT – Cambridgeshire – **504** U26 – see Ely

SUTTON-ON-THE-FOREST – North Yorkshire – **502** P21 – pop. 281   **23** C2
► London 230 mi – Kingston-upon-Hull 50 mi – Leeds 52 mi – Scarborough 40 mi

🍴 **Rose & Crown**   🚗 P VISA ⓞ AE
😊 *Main St* ✉ *YO61 1DP –* ℰ *(01347) 811 333 – www.rosecrown.co.uk – Closed Sunday dinner and Monday*
Rest – *(booking essential)* Menu £ 18 (lunch) **s** – Carte £ 26/30 **s**
♦ Always a welcoming atmosphere at this village pub, with its cosy bar and busy dining room. Variety of menus ensures something for everyone; good food and local specialities. Large terrace and gazebo.

🍴 **Blackwell Ox Inn** with rm   🛜 ⬚ ⚒ rest, P VISA ⓞ
Huby Rd ✉ *YO61 1DT –* ℰ *(01347) 810 328 – www.blackwellox inn.co.uk*
7 rm ⌑ – †£ 65 ††£ 110
Rest – *(closed Sunday dinner)* Menu £ 15 (lunch) **s** – Carte £ 20/30 **s**
♦ Smart, contemporary inn with homely bar/lounge and formal, linen-clad dining room. Blackboard snacks and daily changing à la carte; dishes range from the down-to-earth to more ambitious. Spacious, stylish bedrooms; some boast four-posters and Room 2 has a roll-top bath.

SWETTENHAM – Cheshire East – pop. 248   **20** B3
► London 177 mi – Birmingham 63 mi – Liverpool 43 mi – Leeds 79 mi

🍴 **Swettenham Arms**   🚗 🛜 P VISA ⓞ AE
✉ *CW12 2LF –* ℰ *(01477) 571 284 – www.swettenhamarms.co.uk*
Rest – Carte £ 17/40
♦ Traditional pub with beaten copper bar, open fires, horse brasses and lavender meadow. Seasonal menu provides plenty of choice, ranging from sharing platters and pub classics to carefully prepared, well-presented restaurant-style dishes.

SWINBROOK – Oxfordshire – **503** P28 – see Burford

SWINDON – Swindon – **503** O29 – pop. 155 432   **4** D2

▶ London 83 mi – Bournemouth 69 mi – Bristol 40 mi – Coventry 66 mi
ℹ 37 Regent St ⌕ (01793) 53 03 28, www.visitwiltshire.co.uk
Broome Manor Pipers Way, ⌕ (01793) 53 24 03
Shrivenham Park Shrivenham Penny Hooks, ⌕ (01793) 78 38 53
The Wiltshire G & CC Wootton Bassett Vastern, ⌕ (01793) 84 99 99
Wrag Barn G & C.C. Highworth Shrivenham Rd, ⌕ (01793) 86 13 27
◉ Great Western Railway Museum★ **AC** – Railway Village Museum★ **AC** Y M
◉ Lydiard Park (St Mary's★) W : 4 mi U. Ridgeway Path★★, S : 8.5 mi by A 4361
– Whitehorse (≤★)E : 7.5 mi by A 4312, A 420 and B 400 off B 4057

at Bishopstone East : 5.5 mi by A 4312 off A 420

🍺 **Royal Oak**   🚗 **P** VISA ◉ ①
Cues Ln ✉ SN6 8PP – ⌕ (01793) 790 481 – www.royaloakbishopstone.co.uk
Rest – Carte £ 24/35
 ♦ Relaxing country pub with open fires and rustic décor. Menu changes according to what's fresh, local and seasonal, with much of the produce coming from the owner's organic farm.

TADCASTER – North Yorkshire – **502** Q22 – pop. 6 548   **22** B2

▶ London 206 mi – Harrogate 16 mi – Leeds 14 mi – York 11 mi

at Wighill North : 3 mi by A 659 – ✉

🍺 **White Swan**   🚗 🍴 **P** VISA ◉
Main St ✉ LS24 8BQ – ⌕ (01937) 832 217 – www.whiteswanwighill.co.uk
Rest – Carte £ 19/24
 ♦ Warm, welcoming pub with a cosy snug, several comfy dining rooms and a small shop. Blackboard specials supplement the main monthly menu, which features pub classics, some more ambitious dishes and a popular selection of 'Yorkshire Tapas'.

at Colton Northeast : 3 mi by A 659 off A 64 – ✉ Tadcaster

🍺 **Ye Old Sun Inn** with rm   🚗 🍴 ⁽⁾ **P** VISA ◉ AE
Main St ✉ LS24 8EP – ⌕ (01904) 744 261 – www.yeoldsuninn.co.uk – Closed 26 December
3 rm ⌸ – †£ 75 ††£ 100   **Rest** – Carte £ 23/30
 ♦ Rustic, family-run pub with warming open fires and a small deli. Owners are great ambassadors of local suppliers and seasonal produce, and give regular cookery demonstrations. Smart bedrooms are located in the house next door.

TANGMERE – West Sussex – **504** R31 – see Chichester

TAPLOW – Buckinghamshire – **504** R29   **11** C3

▶ London 33 mi – Maidenhead 2 mi – Oxford 36 mi – Reading 12 mi

🏛 **Cliveden** ⚘   ← 🚗 🐕 ⛳ ♨ 🏊 🎾 🎣 👥 ⁽⁾ 🧖 **P** VISA ◉ AE ①
North : 2 mi by Berry Hill ✉ SL6 0JF – ⌕ (01628) 668 561
– www.clivedenhouse.co.uk
31 rm ⌸ – †£ 210/590 ††£ 210/590 – 8 suites
Rest *Waldo's* – Modern – (dinner only) (booking essential) Menu £ 79
Rest *Terrace* – Modern – Menu £ 39/60
 ♦ Stunning 19C stately home in a superb location, boasting views over the parterre and National Trust gardens to the Thames. Opulent interior with sumptuous, antique-filled lounges and luxuriously appointed bedrooms; choose one in the main house. Journey in style in their classic cars, vintage launches or helicopters. Modern classics in Waldo's; simpler menu in Terrace.

TAPLOW

Taplow House
Berry Hill ⊠ SL6 ODA – ℰ (01628) 670 056 – www.taplowhouse.com
32 rm ⊑ – †£ 95/205 ††£ 95/205
Rest *Berry's* – Menu £ 18/30 – Carte £ 29/35
♦ Georgian house built in 1751, its expansive gardens boasting Europe's tallest tulip tree, which was reputedly planted by Elizabeth I. Characterful guest areas; mix of modern furnishings and period furniture in the well-equipped bedrooms. Formal restaurant overlooks the grounds – menu offers modern classics.

TARPORLEY – Cheshire West and Chester – 502 L/M24 – pop. 2 634   20 A3
▶ London 186 mi – Chester 11 mi – Liverpool 27 mi – Shrewsbury 36 mi
🏌 Portal G & C.C. Cobblers Cross Lane, ℰ (01829) 73 39 33
🏌 Portal Premier Forest Rd, ℰ (01829) 73 38 84

at Cotebrook Northeast : 2.5 mi on A 49 – ⊠ Tarporley

Fox and Barrel
Foxbank ⊠ CW6 9DZ – ℰ (01829) 760 529 – www.foxandbarrel.co.uk – Closed dinner 25-26 December and 1 January
Rest – Carte £ 23/30
♦ Well-run pub with wood-panelled walls, heaving bookshelves and smart terrace. Constantly evolving menu offers originality and interest. Sensibly priced dishes are generous and neatly presented.

at Little Budworth Northeast : 3.5 mi on A 49 – ⊠ Tarporley

Cabbage Hall
Forest Rd. ⊠ CW6 9ES – ℰ (01829) 760 292 – www.cabbagehallrestaurant.com – Closed 2-16 January, 24-25 December, Tuesday and dinner Sunday
Rest – Menu £ 22 – Carte £ 32/38
♦ Unassuming former pub in 11 acres; run by experienced chef. Bold, modern inner with comfy lounge, laminated tables and low-backed dining chairs. Several classical menus from which to choose.

TARR STEPS – Somerset – 503 J30   3 A2
▶ London 191 mi – Taunton 31 mi – Tiverton 20 mi
◉ Tarr Steps★★ (Clapper Bridge★★)

Tarr Farm Inn with rm
⊠ TA22 9PY – ℰ (01643) 851 507 – www.tarrfarm.co.uk – Closed 1-13 February
9 rm ⊑ – †£ 95/120 ††£ 150   **Rest** – Carte £ 18/36
♦ Beside a river, in idyllic countryside, this is a true destination pub. Food ranges from cream teas and sandwiches to three courses at lunch, with more ambitious dishes at dinner. Bedrooms are elegant, luxurious and extremely well-equipped.

TATTENHALL – Cheshire West and Chester – 502 L24 – pop. 1 860   20 A3
▶ London 200 mi – Birmingham 71 mi – Chester 10 mi – Liverpool 29 mi

Higher Huxley Hall without rest
North : 2.25 mi on Huxley rd ⊠ CH3 9BZ – ℰ (01829) 781 484
– www.huxleyhall.co.uk – Closed Christmas
4 rm ⊑ – †£ 55/75 ††£ 90/95
♦ Attractive part-13C farmhouse boasting field and castle views. Classical, open-fired lounge and linen-laid breakfast room. Original Elizabethan staircase. Homely bedrooms have good facilities.

ENGLAND

627

TATTENHALL

at Higher Burwardsley Southeast : 1 mi – ✉ Tattenhall

Pheasant Inn with rm
✉ CH3 9PF – ☏ (01829) 770 434 – www.thepheasantinn.co.uk
12 rm – †£ 75/95 ††£ 95/150 **Rest** – Carte £ 17/30

♦ Characteristic stone pub boasting reclaimed beams, stone columns and great views over the Cheshire Plains. Extensive daily menus offer refined pub dishes and Mediterranean influences. Bedrooms are compact, stylish and comfortable; most have views.

TAUNTON – Somerset – 503 K30 – pop. 58 241 3 B3

▶ London 168 mi – Bournemouth 69 mi – Bristol 50 mi – Exeter 37 mi
🛈 Paul St ☏ (01823) 33 63 44, www.visitsomerset.co.uk
🏌 Taunton Vale Creech Heathfield, ☏ (01823) 41 22 20
🏌 Vivary Vivary Park, ☏ (01823) 28 92 74
🏌 Taunton and Pickeridge Corfe, ☏ (01823) 42 15 37
◉ Town★ - St Mary Magdalene★ **V** – Somerset County Museum★ **AC V M** – St James'★ **U** – Hammett St★ **V 25** – The Crescent★ **V** – Bath Place★ **V 3**
◉ Trull (Church★), S : 2.5 mi by A 38 – Hestercombe Gardens★, N : 5 mi by A 3259 **BY** and minor roads to Cheddon Fitzpaine. Bishops Lydeard★ (Church★), NW : 6 mi – Wellington : Church★, Wellington Monument (≤★★), SW : 7.5 mi by A 38 – Combe Florey★, NW : 8 mi – Gaulden Manor★ **AC**, NW : 10 mi by A 358 and B 3227

Castle
Castle Green ✉ TA1 1NF – ☏ (01823) 272 671 – www.the-castle-hotel.com
44 rm ⊇ – †£ 145/175 ††£ 225/325   **V**a
Rest *Brazz* – see restaurant listing

♦ Part-12C Norman castle boasting impressive gardens, a keep and two wells. Traditional furnished throughout and run by the same family for three generations. Well-kept, individually decorated bedrooms; great views from the penthouse suite.

Meryan House
Bishop's Hull Rd, West : 0.75 mi by A 38 ✉ TA1 5EG – ☏ (01823) 337 445
– www.meryanhouse.co.uk   **AZ**c
12 rm ⊇ – †£ 65/70 ††£ 75/90
Rest – *(dinner only) (booking essential for non-residents)* Menu £ 22/26 **s**

♦ Spacious house; well-run run by charming owner. Open sitting room features fantastic juke box. Highly individual bedrooms boast quality wallpapers and beautiful feature beds – many are antiques. Cosy bar. Traditional, open-fired dining room with classical menu.

Willow Tree
3 Tower Ln ✉ TA1 4AR – ☏ (01823) 352 835
– www.thewillowtreerestaurant.com – *Closed January, August, Sunday, Monday and Thursday*   **V**c
Rest – *(dinner only) (booking essential)* Menu £ 28/34

♦ Converted 17C townhouse with intimate dining rooms, exposed beams and large inglenook. Bi-monthly menu blends a classical base with artful, innovative ideas. Friendly, efficient service.

Augustus
3 The Courtyard, St James St. ✉ TA1 1JR – ☏ (01823) 324 354
– www.augustustaunton.co.uk – *Closed 23 December-2 January, Sunday and Monday*   **V**x
Rest – Menu £ 18 – Carte £ 26/34

♦ Simple little bistro set in a small courtyard and run by an experienced chef. Good-sized menu of hearty, unfussy dishes which mix French, British and some Asian influences. Good value 3 course blackboard menu. Bright and breezy service.

TAUNTON

Bath Pl.	V 3
Billetfield	V 6
Billet St.	V 4
Birch Grove	U 7
Bishop's Hull Rd	AZ 9
Bridge St	U 12
Bridge (The)	U 10
Burton Pl.	V 13
Cann St	V 15
Chritchard Parkway	BYZ 45
Cleveland St	V 16
Comeytrowe Lane	AZ 18
Corporation St	V 19
County Walk Shopping Centre	V
Duke St	V 21
East St.	V
Fore St.	V 22
Hamilton Rd	BZ 24
Hammet St	V 25
High St.	V
Hurdle Way	V 27
Ilminster Rd.	BZ 28
Magdalene St	V 30
Middleway	AZ 31
North St	V 33
Obridge Viaduct	BY 34
Old Market Shopping Centre	V
Portland St.	V 36
Priory Ave	U 37
Shoreditch Rd	BZ 39
Shuttern	V 40
Silver St South	V, Z 42
Upper High St	V 43
Upper Wood St.	U 44
Wellington New Rd	AZ 46
Wilton St	V 48
Winchester St	V 49
Wood St	U 51

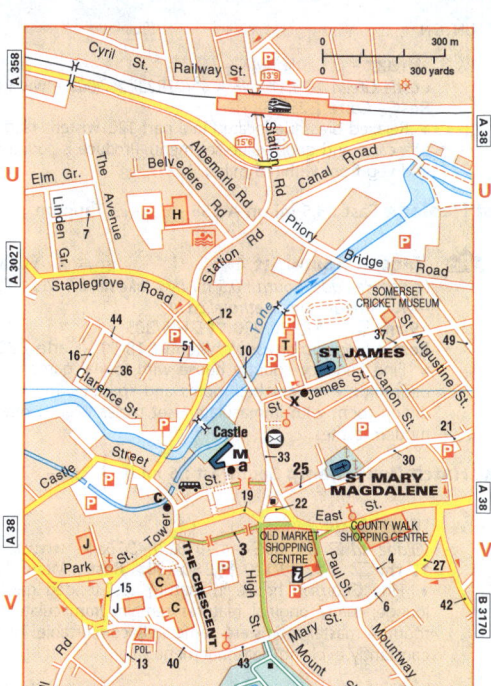

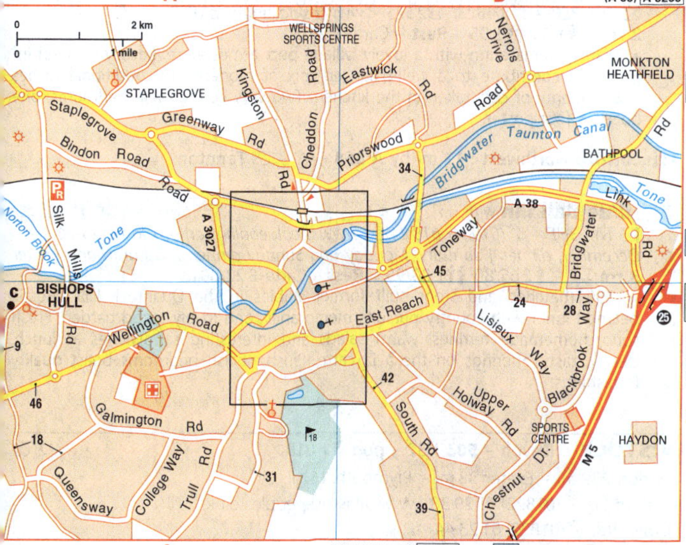

629

TAUNTON

Brazz – at Castle Hotel
Castle Green – TA1 1NF – ℰ (01823) 252 000 – www.the-castle-hotel.com
Rest – Carte £ 25/35
Va
♦ Relaxed brasserie located in a part-12C, wisteria-clad Norman castle. Accessible à la carte and good value set menu. Produce is sourced locally, with fruits, herbs and veg from within 5 miles.

at Henlade East : 3.5 mi on A 358 - BZ – ⊠ Taunton

Mount Somerset
Lower Henlade, South : 0.5 mi by Stoke Rd – TA3 5NB – ℰ (01823) 442 500
– www.mountsomersethotel.co.uk
19 rm – †£ 130/230 ††£ 145/305
Rest – (booking advisable) Menu £ 18/50 – Carte £ 35/50 **s**
♦ Fine Regency country house with formal gardens, set in four acres. Elegant bedrooms, excellent bathrooms and spacious, modern sitting rooms. Capacious dining room with immaculately set tables. Menus offer a mix of traditional and modern dishes.

at Hatch Beauchamp Southeast : 6 mi by A 358 - BZ – ⊠ Taunton

Farthings
Village Rd – TA3 6SG – ℰ (01823) 480 664 – www.farthingshotel.co.uk
12 rm – †£ 70/120 ††£ 80/130 **Rest** – Menu £ 24/29 **s** – Carte £ 32/41 **s**
♦ Fine Georgian house in mature, well-tended gardens. Small bar and open lounge; many original features remain. Immaculately kept, antique-filled bedrooms – master rooms are particularly comfortable. Two-roomed restaurant offers constantly evolving, seasonal menu.

at West Bagborough Northwest : 10.5 mi by A 358 - AY – ⊠ Taunton

Rising Sun Inn with rm
– TA4 3EF – ℰ (01823) 432 575 – www.risingsuninn.info
2 rm – †£ 65 ††£ 95 **Rest** – Carte £ 24/34
♦ Warm, intimate inn with a lovely 'village pub' atmosphere. Locally sourced ingredients contribute to a well-balanced mix of modern and traditional dishes – with plenty of care taken in the kitchen. Two very comfortable bedrooms; one boasts a four-poster.

at Triscombe Northwest : 11 mi by A 358 - AY – ⊠ Taunton

Blue Ball Inn with rm
– TA4 3HE – ℰ (01984) 618 242 – www.theblueballinn.com – Closed 25-26 December, dinner 1 January, Monday and Sunday dinner in autumn and winter
3 rm – †£ 65/80 ††£ 80/95 **Rest** – Carte £ 22/30
♦ 15C thatched and stone-built former stables in the Quantock Hills. Rustic beamed inner with country pursuits memorabilia and lovely tiered garden. Fresh soup, homemade terrines, warm salads and interesting sandwiches at lunch. Hearty, tasty offerings on the à la carte. Plush, stylish bedrooms boast quality furnishings.

TAVISTOCK – Devon – 503 H32 – pop. 11 018
2 C2

▶ London 239 mi – Exeter 38 mi – Plymouth 16 mi

🛈 Bedford Sq ℰ (01822) 61 29 38, www.tavistockpeople.co.uk

🏌 Down Rd, ℰ (01822) 61 23 44

🏌 Hurdwick Tavistock Hamlets, ℰ (01822) 61 27 46

◎ Morwellham ★ **AC**, SW : 4.5 m. E : Dartmoor National Park★★ – Buckland Abbey★★ **AC**, S : 7 mi by A 386 – Lydford★★, N : 8.5 mi by A 386

TAVISTOCK

Horn of Plenty
Gulworthy, West : 4 mi by A 390 off B 3362 ⊠ *PL19 8JD* – ℰ *(01822) 832 528*
– *www.thehornofplenty.co.uk*
10 rm ⊊ – †£ 185/215 ††£ 195/225   **Rest** – Menu £ 20/50
♦ Attractive creeper-clad house in a peaceful countryside location, boasting lovely Tamar Valley and Bodmin Moor views. Comfy, contemporary guest areas. Well-equipped, modern bedrooms in the house and annexe; some with balconies or terraces. Linen-laid dining room offers classical menu and impressive outlook.

Browns
80 West St ⊠ *PL19 8AQ* – ℰ *(01822) 618 686* – *www.brownsdevon.co.uk*
20 rm – †£ 55/99 ††£ 119/209, ⊊ £ 9   **Rest** – Menu £ 24/40 – Carte £ 27/54
♦ Smart hotel in former coaching inn – the oldest licensed premises in town. Bedrooms take on a modern style while still retaining original features; those in the old coach house are best. Open-plan bar and lounge. Simple, all-day brasserie offering modern menu.

at Milton Abbot Northwest : 6 mi on B 3362 – ⊠ Tavistock

Hotel Endsleigh
Southwest : 1 mi ⊠ *PL19 0PQ* – ℰ *(01822) 870 000* – *www.hotelendsleigh.com*
– *Closed 2 weeks January*
14 rm ⊊ – †£ 162/198 ††£ 220/260 – 2 suites   **Rest** – Menu £ 25/40
♦ Painstakingly restored Regency lodge in magnificent Devonian gardens and grounds. Stylish lounge and refined bedrooms are imbued with an engaging, understated elegance. Interesting, classically based dishes served in two minimalist dining rooms.

at Chillaton Northwest : 6.25 mi by Chillaton rd – ⊠ Tavistock

Tor Cottage *without rest*
Southwest : 0.75 mi by Tavistock rd, turning right at bridle path sign, down unmarked track for 0.5 mi ⊠ *PL16 0JE* – ℰ *(01822) 860 248*
– *www.torcottage.co.uk* – *Closed mid-December-1 February*
5 rm ⊊ – †£ 98 ††£ 140
♦ Remotely set cottage set in 28 hillside acres, with peaceful gardens and lovely outdoor pool. Bedrooms, most in converted outhouses, boast small kitchenettes and wood burning stoves. Breakfast is taken on the terrace or in the conservatory. Charming owner.

TEFFONT – Wiltshire – see Salisbury

TEIGNMOUTH – Devon – **503** J32 – pop. 14 799   **2** D2
▶ London 216 mi – Exeter 16 mi – Torquay 8 mi
🛈 Sea Front ℰ (01626) 21 56 66, www.visitsouthdevon.co.uk

Thomas Luny House *without rest*
Teign St, follow signs for the Quays, off the A 381 ⊠ *TQ14 8EG* – ℰ *(01626) 772 976* – *www.thomas-luny-house.co.uk* – *Closed January-mid-February*
4 rm ⊊ – †£ 68/75 ††£ 90/102
♦ Georgian merchant's house with attractive walled garden. Classical lounge and antique-filled breakfast room; tea and cake on arrival. One bedroom with hand-painted oriental furniture, another with a four-poster. Quality breakfasts and home-grown figs in season.

TEMPLE SOWERBY – Cumbria – **502** M20 – see Penrith

TENTERDEN – Kent – **504** W30 – pop. 6 977   **9** C2
▶ London 57 mi – Folkestone 26 mi – Hastings 21 mi – Maidstone 19 mi
🛈 High St ℰ (01580) 76 35 72, www.tententown.co.uk

TENTERDEN

Richard Phillips at Chapel Down
Tenterden Vineyard, Small Hythe, South: 2.5 mi on B 2082 ✉ *TN30 7NG*
– ℘ *(01580) 761 616 – www.richardphillipsatchapeldown.co.uk – Closed Monday*
Rest – *(lunch only and dinner Thursday-Saturday)* Menu £ 16 (lunch)
– Carte £ 28/50

♦ Spacious modern restaurant and casual bar on 1st floor of a barn conversion; terrace has countryside views. Good value lunch menu and more elaborate à la carte showcase seasonal produce.

TETBURY – Gloucestershire – 503 N29 – pop. 5 250 — Great Britain   4 C1

▶ London 113 mi – Bristol 27 mi – Gloucester 19 mi – Swindon 24 mi
🛈 33 Church St ℘ (01666) 50 35 52, www.visittetbury.co.uk
⛳ Westonbirt, ℘ (01666) 88 02 42
◉ Westonbirt Arboretum★ **AC**, SW : 2.5 mi by A 433

Calcot Manor
Calcot, West : 3.5 mi on A 4135 ✉ *GL8 8YJ – ℘ (01666) 890 391 – www.calcotmanor.co.uk*
34 rm – †£ 234 ††£ 460 – 1 suite
Rest *Gumstool Inn* – see restaurant listing
Rest *Conservatory* – *(booking essential)* Menu £ 27 (lunch) – Carte £ 39/52

♦ Impressive Cotswold farmhouse, gardens and meadows with converted ancient barns and stables. Superb spa. Variety of luxuriously appointed rooms with contemporary flourishes. Stylish Conservatory serves interesting modern dishes.

Chef's Table
49 Long St ✉ *GL8 8AA – ℘ (01666) 504 466 – www.thechefstable.co.uk – Closed 25-26 December, 1 January, Sunday, bank holidays and dinner Monday-Tuesday*
Rest – Carte £ 30/37

♦ Glass-fronted deli shop with busy, informal restaurant to the rear; mix of tables and high stools. Daily blackboard menu displays rustic, generous dishes of local, organic produce.

Gumstool Inn – at Calcot Manor Hotel
West : 3.5 mi on A 4135 ✉ *GL8 8YJ – ℘ (01666) 890 391*
– www.calcotmanor.co.uk
Rest – *(booking essential)* Carte £ 24/32

♦ Converted farm out-building on the Calcot Estate, which dates back to the 14C. Cooking is seasonal, rustic and hearty, with a wide-ranging menu and extensive daily specials.

Trouble House
Cirencester Rd, Northeast : 2 mi on A 433 ✉ *GL8 8SG – ℘ (01666) 502 206 – www.troublehousetetbury.co.uk – Closed 2 weeks January, 25 December, Sunday dinner and Monday except bank holidays*
Rest – Menu £ 15 (weekday lunch) – Carte £ 23/36

♦ Unassuming roadside pub with shabby, homely style, where you'll discover a warm welcome and tasty food. Dishes range from sardines on toast to rib of beef for two. Daily specials usually feature fish.

TEWKESBURY – Gloucestershire – 503 N28 – pop. 9 978   4 C1
— Great Britain

▶ London 108 mi – Birmingham 39 mi – Gloucester 11 mi
🛈 100 Church St ℘ (01684) 85 50 40, www.visitcotswoldsandsevernvale.gov.uk
⛳ Tewkesbury Park Hotel Lincoln Green Lane, ℘ (01684) 29 54 05
◉ Town★ – Abbey★★ (Nave★★, vault★)
◉ St Mary's, Deerhurst★, SW : 4 mi by A 38 and B 4213

TEWKESBURY

Owens
73 Church St ⊠ GL20 5RX – ℰ (01684) 292 703 – www.eatatowens.co.uk
– Closed Monday lunch
Rest – Menu £ 15 (lunch and early dinner) – Carte £ 19/35
♦ Simple restaurant set behind the Cathedral, with characterful beamed interior and just 10 tables. Concise, good value menu of French and British dishes. Clean, unfussy, flavoursome cooking.

at Corse Lawn Southwest : 6 mi by A 38 and A 438 on B 4211 – ⊠ Gloucester

Corse Lawn House
⊠ GL19 4LZ – ℰ (01452) 780 771 – www.corselawn.com – Closed 24-26 December
15 rm – †£ 100 ††£ 160 – 3 suites
Rest *Restaurant* – see restaurant listing
Rest *Bistro* – Menu £ 20 **s** – Carte £ 25/34 **s**
♦ Elegant Grade II listed Queen Anne house, with a pond in front, just off the village green. Traditionally appointed lounges boast open fires and antiques; spacious bedrooms have a cottagey style. Large pool in glass-enclosed outbuilding. Formal restaurant and characterful bistro-cum-bar with simpler menu.

Restaurant – at Corse Lawn House Hotel
⊠ GL19 4LZ – ℰ (01452) 780 771 – www.corselawn.com – Closed 24-26 December
Rest – Menu £ 26/34 **s** – Carte £ 27/41 **s**
♦ Formally laid restaurant set within an elegant Grade II listed Queen Anne house, affording pleasant views over the rear gardens. Good-sized menus offer classically based dishes. Helpful team.

ENGLAND

THIRSK – North Yorkshire – **502** P21 – pop. 9 099   **22** B1
🅱 London 227 mi – Leeds 37 mi – Middlesbrough 24 mi – York 24 mi
🅸 49 Market Pl ℰ (01845) 52 27 55, www.visit-thirsk.com
🅶 Thirsk & Northallerton Thornton-Le-Street, ℰ (01845) 52 51 15

at Felixkirk Northeast : 3 mi by A 170

Carpenter's Arms
⊠ YO7 2DP – ℰ (01845) 537 369 – www.thecarpentersarmsfelixkirk.com
Rest – Carte £ 21/29
♦ Proper village pub with one long, open-fired room and 18C origins, set in a village mentioned in the Domesday Book. Choose from blackboard specials or a wide-ranging menu of seasonal dishes that offers everything from gammon to sea bass.

at Asenby Southwest : 5.25 mi by A 168 – ⊠ Thirsk

Crab Manor
Dishforth Rd ⊠ YO7 3QL – ℰ (01845) 577 286 – www.crabandlobster.co.uk
14 rm – †£ 120 ††£ 240
Rest *Crab and Lobster* – see restaurant listing
♦ Split between an 18C Georgian Manor and individual Scandinavian log cabins, the stylish bedrooms are themed around famous hotels of the world. All have sharing or private hot tubs.

Crab and Lobster – at Crab Manor Hotel
Dishforth Rd ⊠ YO7 3QL – ℰ (01845) 577 286 – www.crabandlobster.com
Rest – Seafood – Carte £ 20/42
♦ Charming thatched pub with characterful, quirky interior. Extensive menu features plenty of seafood – from fish soup to whole lobster – as well as traditional British dishes.

THORNBURY – South Gloucestershire – **503** M29 – pop. 11 969   **4** C1
– ⊠ Bristol
🅱 London 128 mi – Bristol 12 mi – Gloucester 22 mi – Swindon 43 mi

633

THORNBURY

Thornbury Castle
Castle St ⊠ BS35 1HH – ℰ (01454) 281 182 – www.thornburycastle.co.uk
24 rm – †£ 120/180 ††£ 175/535 – 3 suites **Rest** – Menu £ 30/50
♦ 16C castle built by Henry VIII with gardens and vineyard. Two lounges boast plenty of antiques. Rooms of stately comfort; several bathrooms resplendent in marble. Restaurant exudes formal aura.

THORNHAM – Norfolk – **504** V25 – see Hunstanton

THORNTON – Lancashire – **502** K22 – see Blackpool

THUNDER BRIDGE – West Yorkshire – see Huddersfield

THUNDERSLEY – Essex – **504** V29 – see Rayleigh

THURSFORD GREEN – Norfolk   15 C1
▶ London 120 mi – Fakenham 7 mi – Norwich 29 mi

Holly Lodge
The Street ⊠ NR21 0AS – ℰ (01328) 878 465 – www.hollylodgeguesthouse.co.uk
3 rm – †£ 90 ††£ 120 **Rest** – Menu £ 20
♦ Remotely set 18C house with delightful gardens and nice pond. Individually themed bedrooms are located in the old stable block and boast exposed beams, feature beds and numerous extra touches. Communal breakfasts, in smart conservatory, use local and homemade produce. Home-cooked dinners from daily changing set menu.

TICKTON – East Riding of Yorkshire – **502** S22 – see Beverley

---

TILLINGTON – West Sussex – **504** S31 – see Petworth

TILSTON – Cheshire West and Chester – **502** L24 – see Malpas

---

TINTINHULL – Somerset – **503** L31 – pop. 956   3 B3
▶ London 131 mi – Bristol 39 mi – Cardiff 97 mi – Southampton 92 mi

Crown and Victoria Inn with rm
*14 Farm St ⊠ BA22 8PZ – ℰ (01935) 823 341 – www.thecrownandvictoria.co.uk
– Closed Sunday dinner*
5 rm – †£ 75/85 ††£ 95 **Rest** – Carte £ 19/32
♦ Enthusiastically run, solid stone pub boasting mature grounds – set next to award winning National Trust gardens. Flavoursome cooking has an honest, homemade, classical base and produce is local, organic and ethically sourced. Bedrooms are cosy and welcoming.

TITCHWELL – Norfolk – **504** V25 – pop. 99   15 C1
▶ London 128 mi – King's Lynn 25 mi – Boston 56 mi – Wisbech 36 mi

Titchwell Manor
⊠ PE31 8BB – ℰ (01485) 210 221 – www.titchwellmanor.com
27 rm – †£ 65/125 ††£ 110/250 **Rest** – Carte £ 26/35 s
♦ Attractive red-brick former farmhouse. Stylish inner with bare floorboards, leather sofas and seaside photos. Classical bedrooms in main house; stylish rooms in grounds. Informal bar and terrace. Smart, conservatory restaurant with modern 7 course tasting menu.

TITLEY – Herefordshire – **503** L27 – see Kington

TOLLARD ROYAL – Wiltshire   4 C3
▶ London 118 mi – Bristol 63 mi – Southampton 40 mi – Portsmouth 59 mi

King John Inn with rm
✉ SP5 5PS – ℰ (01725) 516 207 – www.kingjohninn.co.uk – Closed 25 December
8 rm ⊇ – †£ 145 ††£ 195   **Rest** – Carte £ 29/41

• Red-brick Victorian pub in pretty village; smart, spacious and open-plan. Daily changing, classically based menus, with game a speciality. Comfortable, contemporary bedrooms mix modern facilities with antique furniture; some are in the coach house opposite.

TOOT BALDON – Oxfordshire – see Oxford

TOPSHAM – Devon – 503 J31 – pop. 3 545 – ✉ Exeter   2 D2
▶ London 175 mi – Torbay 26 mi – Exeter 4 mi – Torquay 24 mi

Petite Maison
35 Fore St ✉ EX3 OHR – ℰ (01392) 873 660 – www.lapetitemaison.co.uk
– Closed 2 weeks autumn, 1 week April, 26-30 December, Sunday and Monday
Rest – (booking essential at lunch) Menu £ 37

• Cosy two-roomed restaurant in charming village by River Clyst. Flavourful, classic dishes are presented in a modern style and come in generous portions. Friendly, welcoming owners.

TORQUAY – Torbay – 503 J32 – pop. 62 968   2 C-D2
▶ London 223 mi – Exeter 23 mi – Plymouth 32 mi
🛈 5 Vaughan Parade ℰ (01803) 21 12 11, www.torquay.com
St Marychurch Petitor Rd, ℰ (01803) 32 74 71
◉ Torbay★ – Kent's Cavern★ **AC** CX **A**
◎ Paignton Zoo★★ **AC**, SE : 3 mi by A 3022 - Cockington★, W : 1 mi **AX**

Plans on following pages

Osborne
Hesketh Cres, Meadfoot ✉ TQ1 2LL – ℰ (01803) 213 311
– www.osborne-torquay.co.uk   CX**n**
32 rm ⊇ – †£ 65/125 ††£ 69/230
Rest *Langtry's* – (dinner only) Menu £ 19/23 **s**
Rest *Brasserie* – (closed Sunday dinner, Monday and Tuesday October-April)
Carte £ 19/30 **s**

• Smart hotel in stunning Regency crescent, with lovely gardens and Torbay views. Modern lounge. Stylish bedrooms with light wood furniture, dark leather chairs and good mod cons; some have balconies. Traditional Langtry's offers British classics. Informal dining in split-level Brasserie.

Marstan without rest
Meadfoot Sea Rd ✉ TQ1 2LQ – ℰ (01803) 292 837 – www.marstanhotel.co.uk
– Closed 1 November-23 December and 4 January-28 February   CX**a**
9 rm ⊇ – †£ 55/120 ††£ 120/148

• Substantial 19C house in quiet area; given a 21C edge with hot tub, sun deck and pool. Opulent interior with gold coloured furniture and antiques. Room décor of high standard.

Somerville without rest
515 Babbacombe Rd. ✉ TQ1 1HJ – ℰ (01803) 294 755
– www.somervillehotel.co.uk   CX**u**
9 rm ⊇ – †£ 70/98 ††£ 105/125

• Comfortable hotel, an easy walk down the hill into town. Modern, opulently decorated bedrooms boast all mod cons. One has a small private courtyard; Room 4 is the largest.

TORQUAY
CENTRE
400 m
400 yards
UPTON
TORRE
CHELSTON
UPTON PARK
UNION SQUARE
PRINCESS GARDENS
ABBEY GARDENS
RIVIERA CENTRE
LIVING COASTS
BRIXHAM
A 379
A 3022
A 379 Torbay
Newton
Avenue
Road
Lymington
Union
Belgrave
Mill
Lane
Rd
Old
Walnut Road
Seaway
Rathmore
Falkland
The King's Drive
Croft
Abbey
Warren
St.Luke's Rd North
Market St.
Fleet
Street
St. Marychurch
Rd
Ellacombe
Church
Windsor
Princes
Hoxton
Torbay
TORQUAY
TORRE
Y
Z
B
C

A 3022
A 379
A 380
A 385
PLYMOUTH
BRIXHAM
DARTMOUTH
TWEENAWAYS
CROSS
ZOO
STEAM
RAILWAY
Dartmouth
Road
Torquay
Avenue
Southfield
Road
End
Colley
Ash
Totnes
Penwill
Way
Brixham
Long
Goodrington
Rd
Y
Z
A

ENGLAND

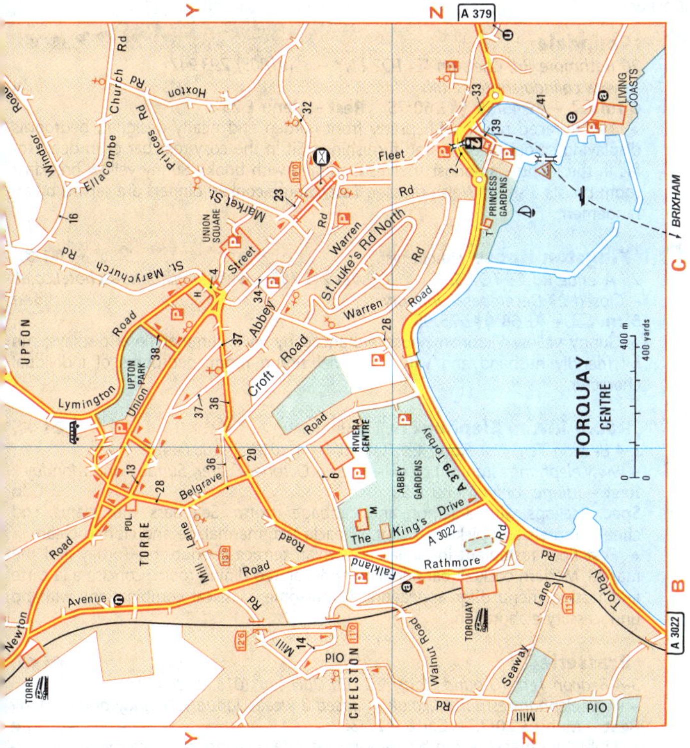

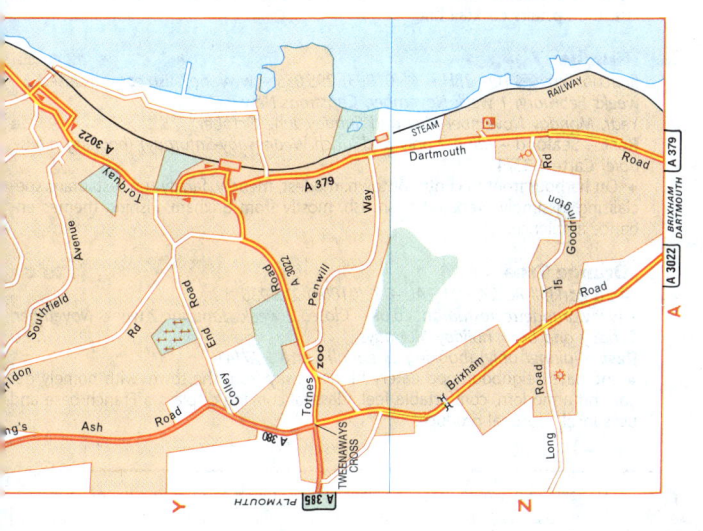

TORQUAY

↑ Colindale
20 Rathmore Rd, Chelston ✉ TQ2 6NY – ℰ (01803) 293 947
– www.colindalehotel.co.uk
BZa
6 rm ⊇ – †£45/55 ††£60/75 **Rest** – Menu £25 s

◆ 19C terraced house with pretty front garden and neatly designed bedrooms displaying colour co-ordinated furnishings. Sit in the cosy rear bar or in deep sofas in the lounge, amongst shelves crammed with books. Sunny yellow breakfast room boasts a smart Welsh dresser. Tasty, home-cooked dinners are served by arrangement.

↑ Kingston House without rest
75 Avenue Rd ✉ TQ2 5LL – ℰ (01803) 212 760 – www.kingstonhousehotel.co.uk
– Closed 23 December-2 January
BYn
5 rm ⊇ – †£68 ††£75/95

◆ Sunny yellow Victorian house enhanced by vivid summer floral displays; run by friendly husband and wife. Convivial sitting room; bedrooms of individual character.

XX Room in the Elephant (Simon Hulstone)
3-4 Beacon Terr, (1st Floor) ✉ TQ1 2BH – ℰ (01803) 200 044
– www.elephantrestaurant.co.uk – Closed October-Easter, Sunday and Monday
Rest – (dinner only) Menu £50
CZe
Spec. Scallops with a lemon and cabbage risotto. Sea bass with clams, cod cheeks, morels and pickled shallots. Treacle tart, marmalade and clotted cream.

◆ First floor restaurant in elegant Georgian terrace overlooking Torbay and the marina. Modern cocktail bar and simply decorated dining room. Concise à la carte and tasting menu offer appealing, flavoursome, classical combinations with no unnecessary elaboration.

X Brasserie
3-4 Beacon Terr, (Ground Floor) ✉ TQ1 2BH – ℰ (01803) 200 044
– www.elephantrestaurant.co.uk – Closed 3 weeks January, Sunday and Monday
Rest – Menu £20/25 – Carte £27/38
CZe

◆ Light, airy brasserie run by pleasant team. Appealing, set price menus revolve around the seasons; cooking is fresh and simple. Good value wine selection – or visit the upstairs cocktail bar.

X Number 7
Beacon Terr. ✉ TQ1 2BH – ℰ (01803) 295 055 – www.no7-fish.com – Closed 2 weeks February, 1 week November, Christmas-New Year, Monday November-May and Sunday June-October
CZe
Rest – Seafood – (dinner only and lunch Wednesday-Saturday) (booking advisable) Carte £33/41

◆ On harbour front in centre of town: modest, friendly, family run restaurant specialising in simply prepared fresh fish, mostly from Brixham. Fishing themes enhance ambience.

X Orange Tree
14-16 Parkhill Rd ✉ TQ1 2AL – ℰ (01803) 213 936
– www.orangetreerestaurant.co.uk – Closed 2 weeks January, 2 weeks November, Sunday and bank holiday Mondays
CZu
Rest – (dinner only) (booking essential) Carte £27/41

◆ Intimate neighbourhood eatery hidden away from the town, with homely décor and a modern, comfortable feel. Classical cooking displays a French base and uses local, seasonal produce.

Undecided between two equivalent establishments in the same town? Within each category, establishments are classified in our order of preference: the best first.

at Babbacombe Northeast : 2 mi on A 379

Cary Arms with rm
Babbacombe Beach, East : 0.25 mi by Beach Rd. ✉ TQ1 3LX – ℰ (01803) 327 110 – www.caryarms.co.uk
8 rm ☑ – †£ 105/210 ††£ 205/260 **Rest** – Carte £ 24/31
• Idyllic location built into the rocks, with terraces down to the shore. Stone/slate-floored bar serving traditional pub dishes. Nautically styled residents lounge and modern, boutique-chic bedrooms in New England style, with roll-top baths looking out to sea.

at Maidencombe North : 3.5 mi by A 379 - BX – ✉ Torquay

Orestone Manor
Rockhouse Ln ✉ TQ1 4SX – ℰ (01803) 328 098 – www.orestonemanor.com
– Closed 3-30 January
12 rm ☑ – †£ 99 ††£ 150/225 **Rest** – Menu £ 32 – Carte £ 17/32
• Characterful house set among thick shrubbery and mature trees. Colonial feel throughout with dark wood furniture, Oriental/African artefacts and recurring elephant motif. Individually designed bedrooms – some with feature beds; most have sea/country views. Classical menus; dine in restaurant, conservatory or on terrace.

TOTFORD – Hampshire   6 B2
London 104 mi – Birmingham 210 mi – Bristol 149 mi – Cardiff 202 mi

Woolpack Inn with rm
✉ SO24 9TJ – ℰ (0845) 293 8066 – www.thewoolpackinn.co.uk – Closed dinner 25 December and bank holiday Mondays
7 rm ☑ – †£ 85/100 ††£ 85/100 **Rest** – Carte £ 22/32
• Grade II listed pub, popular with walkers and shooters. Two menus for the rustic bar and dining room – one of pub classics, the other more ambitious – and two wine lists; one for quaffing, one for sipping. They smoke their own salmon and game is a highlight. Bedrooms are housed in the former skittle alley.

TOTLEY – South Yorkshire – 502 P24 – see Sheffield

TOTNES – Devon – 503 I32 – pop. 7 929   2 C2
London 224 mi – Exeter 24 mi – Plymouth 23 mi – Torquay 9 mi
ℹ Coronation Rd ℰ (01803) 86 31 68, www.totnesinformation.co.uk
Dartmouth G & C.C. Blackawton, ℰ (01803) 71 26 86
◉ Town★ – Elizabethan Museum★ – St Mary's★ – Butterwalk★ – Castle (≤★★★) **AC**
Paignton Zoo★★ **AC**, E : 4.5 mi by A 385 and A 3022 – British Photographic Museum, Bowden House★ **AC**, S : 1 mi by A 381 – Dartington Hall (High Cross House★), NW : 2 mi on A 385 and A 384. Dartmouth★★ (Castle ≤★★★), SE : 12 mi by A 381 and A 3122

Royal Seven Stars
The Plains ✉ TQ9 5DD – ℰ (01803) 862 125 – www.royalsevenstars.co.uk
21 rm ☑ – †£ 85/95 ††£ 149
Rest *TQ9* – (dinner only and Sunday lunch and Sunday lunch) Carte £ 20/29
• 17C former coaching inn in centre of town. Lounge with smart colonial edge, contemporary, light and fresh bedrooms; some have jacuzzi baths, Agatha Christie has a four poster. TQ9 a dining room in converted stables.

Steam Packet Inn with rm
St Peter's Quay ✉ TQ9 5EW – ℰ (01803) 863 880 – www.steampacketinn.co.uk
4 rm ☑ – †£ 60 ††£ 80 **Rest** – Carte £ 21/26
• Deservedly popular pub with vast terrace; set on the River Dart, in a slightly bohemian market town. Traditional bar and light, airy conservatory. Eclectic, wide-ranging menu, with fresh fish a speciality. Bedrooms are comfortable, cosy and have a modern feel.

TOTNES

at Ashprington South : 3.5mi by A 381 – ✉ Devon

Vineyard Café
Sharpham Estate ✉ TQ9 7UT – ℰ (01803) 732 178 – www.thevineyardcafe.co.uk
– Easter-September
Rest *– (lunch only)* Carte £ 15/25
◆ Simple, teak-furnished café on an estate famed for its wines and cheeses; located in a lovely chocolate box village and offering far-reaching country views. Fresh, unfussy dishes are packed with flavour and feature local, organic produce.

TOWCESTER – Northamptonshire – 503 R27 – pop. 8 073   16 B3
▶ London 70 mi – Birmingham 50 mi – Northampton 9 mi – Oxford 36 mi
▣ Whittlebury Park G. & C.C. Whittlebury, ℰ (01327) 85 00 00
▣ Farthingstone Hotel Farthingstone, ℰ (01327) 36 12 91

at Paulerspury Southeast : 3.25 mi by A 5 – ✉ Towcester

Vine House with rm
100 High St ✉ NN12 7NA – ℰ (01327) 811 267 – www.vinehousehotel.com
– Closed 1 week Christmas, Monday lunch and Sunday
6 rm – †£ 69/85 ††£ 95   **Rest** – Menu £ 31
◆ Keenly run 17C stone cottage with lovely garden, traditional lounges and split-level dining room. Concise set menus feature refined, flavoursome dishes with a classical base and modern edge. Individually styled, period bedrooms are named after grape vines.

TREBETHERICK – Cornwall – see Rock

TREGREHAN – Cornwall – 503 F32 – see St Austell

TRELOWARREN – Cornwall – see Helston

TRESCO – 503 B34 – see Scilly (Isles of)

TRISCOMBE – Somerset – 503 K30 – see Taunton

TROTTON – West Sussex – see Midhurst

TROUTBECK – Cumbria – 502 L20 – see Windermere

TROWBRIDGE – Wiltshire – 503 N30 – pop. 34 401   4 C2
▶ London 115 mi – Bristol 27 mi – Southampton 55 mi – Swindon 32 mi
▣ St Stephen's Pl ℰ (01225) 71 05 35, www.visitwiltshire.co.uk
◉ Westwood Manor★, NW : 3 mi by A 363 – Farleigh Hungerford★ (St Leonard's Chapel★) **AC**, W : 4 m. Longleat House★★★ **AC**, SW : 12 mi by A 363, A 350 and A 362 – Bratton Castle (≤★★) SE : 7.5 mi by A 363 and B 3098 – Steeple Ashton★ (The Green★) E : 6 mi – Edington (St Mary, St Katherine and All Saints★) SE : 7.5 m

Old Manor
Trowle, Northwest : 1 mi on A 363 ✉ BA14 9BL – ℰ (01225) 777 393
– www.oldmanorhotel.com
21 rm – †£ 99/130 ††£ 99/175
Rest *– (dinner only)* Menu £ 26 – Carte £ 20/26
◆ Attractive Grade II listed Queen Anne house with 15C origins, French château styling and lovely gardens; run by an eccentric owner. Quirky interior filled with antiques and curios. Uniquely designed bedrooms, some with feature beds or wet rooms. Traditional menu served in the open-fired dining room.

TROWBRIDGE

XX Red or White

Evolution House, 46 Castle St ⊠ BA14 8AY – ℰ (01225) 781 666
– www.redorwhite.biz – Closed 15 August-1 September, 25-26 December, Sunday and bank holidays
Rest – Italian – Menu £ 16/23 – Carte £ 27/31
♦ Spacious restaurant whose names indicates its owners' passion for wine. Frequently changing Sicilian-based menu and regular theme nights. Impressive coloured-glass dome and small food shop.

TRUMPET – Herefordshire – see Ledbury

TRURO – Cornwall – **503** E33 – pop. 20 920 **1** B3

▶ London 295 mi – Exeter 87 mi – Penzance 26 mi – Plymouth 52 mi
🛈 Boscawen St ℰ(01872) 27 45 55, www.tourism.truro.gov.uk
🏌 Treliske, ℰ (01872) 27 26 40
🏌 Killiow Kea Killiow, ℰ (01872) 27 02 46
◉ Royal Cornwall Museum★★ **AC**
◉ Trelissick Garden★★ (≤★★) **AC**, S : 4 mi by A 39 – Feock (Church★) S : 5 mi by A 39 and B 3289. Trewithen★★★, NE : 7.5 mi by A 39 and A 390 – Probus★ (tower★ - garden★) NE : 9 mi by A 39 and A 390

ENGLAND

🏨 Mannings

Lemon St ⊠ TR1 2QB – ℰ (01872) 270 345 – www.manningshotels.co.uk
– Closed 1 week Christmas
34 rm – ♦£ 79/99 ♦♦£ 99/129, ⊆ £ 7.50
Rest *Mannings* – see restaurant listing
♦ Imposing hotel located in the city centre, close to the cathedral. Boutique bedrooms are bright, modern and stylish; spacious apartment-style rooms in the neighbouring mews boast over-sized beds and galley kitchens. Chic cocktail bar.

XX Tabb's

85 Kenwyn St ⊠ TR1 3BZ – ℰ (01872) 262 110 – www.tabbs.co.uk – Closed 1 week January, 1 week October, Saturday lunch, Sunday and Monday
Rest – Menu £ 25 (lunch) – Carte £ 29/37
♦ Series of pleasant slate-floored rooms in a small cottage conversion. Appealing menu of refined dishes, where quality produce shines through. Chef is a passionate chocolatier and duck is a speciality.

X Saffron

5 Quay St ⊠ TR1 2HB – ℰ (01872) 263 771 – www.saffronrestauranttruro.co.uk
– Closed 25-26 December, Monday dinner January-June, Sunday and bank holidays
Rest – Menu £ 20 – Carte £ 26/34
♦ Keenly run restaurant in the heart of town, close to the cathedral. Simply appointed, rustic inner with hearty, flavoursome cooking to match. Extensive menus showcase seasonal Cornish produce.

X Mannings – at Mannings Hotel

Lemon St ⊠ TR1 2QB – ℰ (01872) 247 900 – www.manningshotels.co.uk
– Closed 1 week Christmas
Rest – *(closed Sunday lunch)* Carte £ 21/40
♦ Stylish restaurant in an imposing boutique hotel, close to the cathedral. Extensive, all-day menu follows the seasons, relying on locally sourced produce and displaying some Asian influences.

TUDDENHAM – Suffolk – 504 V27 – pop. 400   14 B2
▶ London 76 mi – Birmingham 120 mi – Sheffield 152 mi – Croydon 96 mi

Tuddenham Mill with rm
High St ⊠ IP28 6SQ – ℰ (01638) 713 552 – www.tuddenhammill.co.uk
15 rm – †£ 275 ††£ 395   **Rest** – Carte £ 31/42
• Delightful 18C watermill overlooking the millpond. Stylish bar with mill workings in situ; beamed restaurant with black furnishings above. Cooking uses innovative techniques and showcases quality seasonal produce in unusual combinations. Trendy bedrooms are located in attractive, timber-faced outbuildings.

TURNERS HILL – West Sussex – 504 T30 – pop. 1 534   7 D2
▶ London 33 mi – Brighton 24 mi – Crawley 7 mi

Alexander House
East St, East : 1 mi on B 2110 ⊠ RH10 4QD – ℰ (01342) 714 914
– www.alexanderhouse.co.uk
36 rm ⊇ – †£ 185/225 ††£ 220/410 – 2 suites
Rest *Reflections Brasserie* – Menu £ 16 (weekday lunch) – Carte £ 42/58
Rest *AG's Grill Room* – (booking essential) Carte £ 32/54
• Stunning country house in extensive grounds; once owned by Percy Shelley's family. Comfy guest areas; superb spa with 25 treatment rooms. Spacious, well-equipped bedrooms – some with four-posters, claw-foot baths or double showers. Light, seasonal dishes in brasserie. Grill menu in AG's.

ENGLAND

TWO BRIDGES – Devon – 503 I32 – ⊠ Yelverton   2 C2
▶ London 226 mi – Exeter 25 mi – Plymouth 17 mi
◉ Dartmoor National Park★★

Prince Hall
East : 1 mi on B 3357 ⊠ PL20 6SA – ℰ (01822) 890 403 – www.princehall.co.uk
8 rm ⊇ – †£ 70/170 ††£ 120/190
Rest – (booking essential for non-residents) Menu £ 15/40 s
• Remotely set hotel with welcoming interior. Cosy lounges boast real fires and eclectic art. Comfy, homely bedrooms display subtle modern touches and smart bathrooms; some overlook the moor. Small bar. Bright restaurant with wood burning stove and classical menus.

TYNEMOUTH – Tyne and Wear – 501 P18 – pop. 17 056   24 B2
▶ London 290 mi – Newcastle upon Tyne 8 mi – Sunderland 7 mi

Grand
Grand Par ⊠ NE30 4ER – ℰ (0191) 293 66 66 – www.grandhotel-uk.com
45 rm – †£ 85/95 ††£ 119/125
Rest *Victoria* – (closed Sunday dinner) Menu £ 22 (dinner) – Carte lunch £ 21/34
• Victorian hotel with superb sea views, once the Duchess of Northumberland's holiday home. Impressive carved staircase and sizeable guest areas boasting ornate coving and pillars. Mix of simply furnished and more comfortable bedrooms; 222 has a four-poster and jacuzzi. Classical dining room with menu to match.

Martineau without rest
57 Front St ⊠ NE30 4BX – ℰ (0191) 257 90 38 – www.martineau-house.co.uk
4 rm ⊇ – †£ 60/80 ††£ 85/95
• Attractive 18C stone guesthouse located down a narrow alleyway and named after Harriet Martineau. Cosy, individually furnished bedrooms come with thoughtful extras; two boast pleasant Tyne views. Communal breakfasts feature award-winning sausages and are also accompanied by a river and South Shields outlook.

UCKFIELD – East Sussex – **504** U31 – pop. 15 374   8 A2
▶ London 45 mi – Brighton 17 mi – Eastbourne 20 mi – Maidstone 34 mi

Horsted Place
Little Horsted, South : 2.5 mi by B 2102 and A 22 on A 26 ✉ *TN22 5TS*
– ℰ *(01825) 750 581 – www.horstedplace.co.uk – Closed first week January*
15 rm – †£ 145/180 ††£ 145/180 – 3 suites
Rest – *(closed Saturday lunch)* Menu £ 21 (lunch) – Carte approx. £ 38
♦ Imposing country house from the height of the Victorian Gothic revival; handsome Pugin-inspired drawing rooms and luxurious bedrooms overlook formal gardens and parkland. Pristine restaurant with tall 19C archways and windows.

UFFORD – Peterborough – pop. 163   14 A2
▶ London 90 mi – Leicester 38 mi – Coventry 69 mi – Nottingham 50 mi

White Hart with rm
Main St ✉ *PE9 3BH* – ℰ *(01780) 740 250 – www.whitehartufford.co.uk – Closed Sunday dinner*
6 rm – †£ 70/90 ††£ 80/110   **Rest** – Carte £ 21/38
♦ Delightful 17C inn with superb sun-trap of a terrace and garden. Eat in the cosy bar, rustic restaurant or conservatory. Menus offer a broad range of dishes, with much of the meat coming from their own farm. They have a brewery on-site and the sweet, individually styled bedrooms are named after their beers.

ULLSWATER – Cumbria – **502** L20 – pop. 1 199 – ✉ Penrith   21 B2
▶ London 296 mi – Carlisle 25 mi – Kendal 31 mi – Penrith 6 mi
🛈 Beckside Car Park, Glenridding, Penrith ℰ (017684) 8 24 14, www.ullswater.co.uk

at Pooley Bridge on B 5320 – ✉ Penrith

Sharrow Bay Country House
South : 2 mi on Howtown rd ✉ *CA10 2LZ* – ℰ *(017684)*
86 301 – www.sharrowbay.co.uk
21 rm (dinner included) – †£ 160/340 ††£ 280/600 – 3 suites
Rest – *(booking essential)* Menu £ 25/75
Spec. Suissesse soufflé of spinach and stilton. Fillet of beef, fricassee of wild mushrooms and roasted shallots. Francis Coulson's icky sticky toffee pudding with cream.
♦ Celebrated Victorian villa in mature gardens, beautifully located on the shores of Ullswater. Traditional country house style throughout, with very charming drawing rooms. Bedrooms come with a cottagey feel. Expect classical cooking in the delightful dining rooms; dinner is particularly special.

at Watermillock on A 592 – ✉ Penrith

Rampsbeck Country House
✉ *CA11 0LP* – ℰ *(017684) 86 442 – www.rampsbeck.co.uk*
18 rm – †£ 98/200 ††£ 145/300 – 1 suite
Rest *Restaurant* – see restaurant listing
♦ Immaculately whitewashed country house in mature grounds, affording lovely views over Ullswater and the fells. Spacious guest areas boast heavy fabrics and antique furniture. Contemporary country house bedrooms display up-to-date facilities and marble bathrooms.

Restaurant – at Rampsbeck Country House Hotel
✉ *CA11 0LP* – ℰ *(017684) 86 442 – www.rampsbeck.co.uk*
Rest – *(booking essential)* Menu £ 32/50 **s**
♦ Elegant restaurant with good-sized tables, high-backed chairs and beautiful lake/fell views. Oft-changing set menu of well-prepared, refined, classical dishes. Canapés and coffee in the lounge.

ULVERSTON – Cumbria – **502** K21 – pop. 11 210   21 A3
▶ London 278 mi – Kendal 25 mi – Lancaster 36 mi
🛈 County Sq ℰ (01229) 58 71 40, www.cumbria-the-lake-district.co.uk

ULVERSTON

Eden Lodge

Coast Rd, Bardsea, South : 2 mi on A 5087 ✉ *LA12 9QZ* – ℰ *(01229) 587 067*
– *www.eden-lodge.com*
11 rm (dinner included) – †£ 80/99 ††£ 105/210
Rest – Menu £ 12/20 – Carte £ 28/49

♦ Large, bay-windowed Victorian house with pleasant gardens. Variously sized, modern bedrooms boast excellent bathrooms; superior rooms are larger, with a view out to Morecambe Bay. Therapies and treatments available. Good value weekend rates. Traditional menus.

UPPER ODDINGTON – Gloucestershire – **503** O28 – see Stow-on-the-Wold

UPPER SLAUGHTER – Gloucestershire – **503** O28 – see Bourton-on-the-Water

UPPER WOODFORD – Wiltshire – **503** O30 – see Salisbury

UPPINGHAM – Rutland – **504** R26 – pop. 3 947   **17** C2

▶ London 101 mi – Leicester 19 mi – Northampton 28 mi – Nottingham 35 mi

Lake Isle with rm

16 High St East ✉ *LE15 9PZ* – ℰ *(01572) 822 951* – *www.lakeisle.co.uk* – *Closed 26 December-2 January, Sunday dinner and Monday lunch*
12 rm – †£ 58/80 ††£ 110
Rest – (light lunch) Menu £ 19 (weekdays) – Carte £ 27/35

♦ Pleasant town centre property accessed via a narrow passageway, with small, characterful lounge and heavy wood furnishings. Light lunches and much more elaborate dinners with modern influences and the odd Asian touch. Bedrooms boast good facilities and extras: superior are the largest, with whirlpool baths.

at Lyddington South : 2 mi by A 6003 – ✉ Uppingham

Marquess of Exeter with rm

52 Main St ✉ *LE15 9LT* – ℰ *(01572) 822 477* – *www.marquessexeter.co.uk*
17 rm – †£ 70/80 ††£ 90/115   **Rest** – Menu £ 15 (lunch) – Carte £ 26/31

♦ Attractive 16C thatched pub with cosy bar, characterful exposed beams, inglenook fireplaces and a rustic dining room. Daily menu offers tasty, classical combinations of local, home-grown and home-reared produce. Comfy bedrooms located across the car park.

Old White Hart with rm

51 Main St ✉ *LE15 9LR* – ℰ *(01572) 821 703* – *www.oldwhitehart.co.uk*
– *Closed 25 December*
10 rm – †£ 60/70 ††£ 85/95
Rest – (closed Sunday dinner in winter) Menu £ 14 (lunch and early dinner)
– Carte £ 20/31

♦ Traditional coaching inn with neat garden and canopy covered terrace. Monthly changing menus display simple, unfussy pub classics. Regular petanque evenings offer game play and dinner. Stylish, modern bedrooms boast smart bathrooms.

UPTON SCUDAMORE – Wiltshire – **503** N30 – see Warminster

URMSTON – Greater Manchester – **502** M23 – pop. 40 964   **20** B2

▶ London 204 mi – Manchester 9 mi – Sale 4 mi

Isinglass

46 Flixton Rd ✉ *M41 5AB* – ℰ *(0161) 749 84 00* – *www.isinglassrestaurant.com*
Rest – English – (dinner only and lunch Friday-Sunday) Menu £ 20
– Carte £ 24/37

♦ Rustic neighbourhood eatery with simple, almost bohemian atmosphere. Hearty, flavourful cooking features generously proportioned, homemade British dishes. Only seasonal English produce used.

UTTOXETER – Staffordshire – 503 O25 – pop. 12 023   19 C1
▶ London 150 mi – Birmingham 41 mi – Stafford 16 mi

at Beamhurst Northwest : 3 mi on A 522 – ✉ Uttoxeter

XX **Gilmore at Strine's Farm**
✉ ST14 5DZ – ℰ (01889) 507 100 – www.restaurantgilmore.com – Closed 1 week January, 1 week Easter, 1 week July-August, 1 week October-November, Monday, Tuesday, and dinner Sunday.
Rest – (dinner only and lunch Thursday, Friday and Sunday) (booking essential) Menu £ 30/43
♦ Personally run converted farmhouse in classic rural setting. Three separate, beamed, cottage style dining rooms. New approach to classic dishes: fine local ingredients used.

VENTNOR – Isle of Wight – 503 Q32 – see Wight (Isle of)

VERYAN – Cornwall – 503 F33 – pop. 877 – ✉ Truro   1 B3
▶ London 291 mi – St Austell 13 mi – Truro 13 mi
◉ Village ★

Nare
Carne Beach, Southwest : 1.25 mi ✉ TR2 5PF – ℰ (01872) 501 111
– www.narehotel.co.uk
30 rm – †£ 136/325 ††£ 396/488 – 7 suites
Rest *Quarterdeck* – see restaurant listing
Rest *The Dining Room* – (dinner only and Sunday lunch) (booking essential to non-residents) Menu £ 50 – Carte £ 25/38
♦ Personally run country house hotel boasting a stunning bay outlook. Classical bedrooms: some with patios/balconies; most with a view. Have afternoon tea in the drawing room and canapés in the bar in the evening. Outdoor pool and hot tub. Classical daily menu in dining room or lighter dishes in Quarterdeck.

X **Quarterdeck** – at Nare Hotel
Carne Beach, Southwest : 1.25 mi ✉ TR2 5PF – ℰ (01872) 500 000
– www.narehotel.co.uk
Rest – (booking essential to non-residents) Carte £ 25/38
♦ Informal restaurant in a personally run country house, with large black and white prints on the walls and a nautical theme. The fish platter and roast rib of beef to share are specialities.

VIRGINSTOW – Devon – 503 H31   2 C2
▶ London 227 mi – Bideford 25 mi – Exeter 41 mi – Launceston 11 mi

Percy's
Coombeshead Estate, Southwest : 1.75 mi on Tower Hill rd ✉ EX21 5EA
– ℰ (01409) 211 236 – www.percys.co.uk
7 rm – †£ 110/150 ††£ 150/250
Rest – (dinner only) (booking essential for non residents) (set menu only) Menu £ 40
♦ Stone hotel in 130 acres of fields and woodland; where the owners grow veg, rear pigs and sheep, breed racehorses and sell wool, skins and produce. Spacious, comfy bedrooms in the former barn; one has a jacuzzi bath. Set menu uses ingredients from the estate.

WADDESDON – Buckinghamshire – 504 R28 – pop. 1 865   11 C2
– ✉ Aylesbury ■ Great Britain
▶ London 51 mi – Aylesbury 5 mi – Northampton 32 mi – Oxford 31 mi
◉ Chiltern Hills ★
◉ Waddesdon Manor ★★, S : 0.5 mi by a 41 and minor rd – Claydon House ★, N : by minor rd

ENGLAND

WADDESDON

✕✕ Five Arrows with rm
High St ✉ *HP18 0JE* – ✆ *(01296) 651 727* – www.thefivearrows.com
10 rm – †£ 69/99 ††£ 129 – 1 suite
Rest – Menu £ 18 (lunch) – Carte £ 26/39
◆ Beautiful 19C inn on the Rothschild estate, an influence apparent in the pub crest and wine cellar. Striking architecture, stylish dining, relaxed ambience and classical menu. Individually decorated bedrooms – some four posters – divided between main house and courtyard; the latter being smaller but quieter.

WADEBRIDGE – Cornwall – **503** F32 – pop. 6 222 — 1 B2
London 245 mi – Plymouth 41 mi – Torbay 68 mi – Torquay 88 mi

at St Kew Northeast : 4.5 mi by A 39

⌂ St Kew Inn
✉ *PL30 3HB* – ✆ *(01208) 841 259* – www.stkewinn.co.uk
Rest – Carte £ 23/34
◆ Characterful country pub in quintessentially English location. Wide-ranging menu of fresh, tasty dishes and St Austell beer in wooden casks. Attractive garden with picnic tables and heaters.

WALBERSWICK – Suffolk – **504** Y27 – pop. 1 648 — 15 D2
London 115 mi – Norwich 31 mi – Ipswich 31 mi – Lowestoft 16 mi

⌂ Anchor with rm
Main St ✉ *IP18 6UA* – ✆ *(01502) 722 112* – www.anchoratwalberswick.com
8 rm – †£ 95/115 ††£ 110/150
Rest – (closed 25 December) Carte £ 23/33
◆ An Arts and Crafts building with a sizeable garden and seaward views. Global flavours alongside British classics on interesting menu; careful cooking uses local, seasonal produce. Excellent beers and wines. Simple chalet bedrooms; impressive breakfasts.

WALFORD – Herefordshire – see Ross-on-Wye

WALLINGFORD – Oxfordshire – **503** Q29 – pop. 8 019 ▍ Great Britain — 10 B3
London 54 mi – Oxford 12 mi – Reading 16 mi
🛈 Market Pl ✆ (01491) 82 69 72, www.wallingford.co.uk
Ridgeway Path ★★

⌂ North Moreton House without rest
North Moreton, West : 4 mi by A 4130 ✉ *OX11 9AT* – ✆ *(01235) 813 283*
– www.northmoretonhouse.co.uk
3 rm – †£ 50/60 ††£ 70/80
◆ Grade II listed former rectory and 17C barn, set in a picture postcard village. Two spacious, classical drawing rooms and traditional bedrooms. Have breakfast on a vast antique oak table beside an inglenook fireplace or in the conservatory; try the daily special.

✕✕ Partridge
32 St Mary's St ✉ *OX10 0ET* – ✆ *(01491) 825 005* – www.partridge-inn.com
– Closed Sunday dinner
Rest – Menu £ 16/20 **s** – Carte £ 24/37 **s**
◆ Former pub, now a stylish, contemporary restaurant, with separate lounge, garden and raised rear terrace. Well-priced market menu offered alongside interesting à la carte of European dishes: cooking is flavourful, confident and accomplished. Efficient service.

WANTAGE – Oxfordshire – **504** P29 – pop. 9 452 — 10 B3
London 71 mi – Oxford 16 mi – Reading 24 mi – Swindon 21 mi
🛈 19 Church St ✆ (01235) 76 01 76, www.wantage.com

at East Hendred West : 4.5 mi by A 417 – ✉ Oxfordshire

Eyston Arms
High St. ✉ OX12 8JY – ☏ (01235) 833 320 – www.eystonarms.co.uk – Closed 25 December and Sunday dinner
Rest – Carte £ 21/32
♦ Set in a characterful, modern estate-owned village, a modern dining pub with scrubbed tables, original tiled floors and exposed brick. Tasty, unfussy dishes include popular antipasti boards and desserts with a twist. Warm, welcoming team.

at Letcombe Regis South : 1.5 mi by B 4507

Brook Barn
✉ OX12 9JD – ☏ (01235) 766 502 – www.brookbarn.com
– Closed Christmas-New Year
5 rm ⬜ – †£ 85/225 ††£ 180/225
Rest – Carte £ 27/39
♦ Converted barns with welcoming beamed lounge – complete with inglenook – and small library on mezzanine. Spacious, stylish bedrooms boast modern comforts; some have terraces out to the garden, croquet lawn and chalk stream. Afternoon tea and set dinners offered.

WAREHAM – Dorset – 503 N31 – pop. 2 568   4 C3
▶ London 123 mi – Bournemouth 13 mi – Weymouth 19 mi
ℹ South St ☏ (01929) 55 27 40, www.visit-dorset.com
◉ Town★ – St Martin's★★
◉ Blue Pool★ **AC**, S : 3.5 mi by A 351 – Bovington Tank Museum★ **AC**, Woolbridge Manor★, W : 5 mi by A 352. Moreton Church★★, W : 9.5 mi by A 352 – Corfe Castle★ (⩽★★) **AC**, SE : 6 mi by A 351 – Lulworth Cove★, SW : 10 mi by A 352 and B 3070 – Bere Regis★ (St John the Baptist Church★), NW : 6.5 mi by minor rd

 Priory
Church Green ✉ BH20 4ND – ☏ (01929) 551 666 – www.thepriory hotel.co.uk
16 rm ⬜ – †£ 164/236 ††£ 205/295 – 2 suites
Rest – Menu £ 43 (dinner) – Carte lunch £ 32/40
♦ Charming, privately run part 16C priory, friendly and discreetly cosy. Well-equipped rooms. Manicured four-acre gardens lead down to River Frome: luxury suites in boathouse. Charming restaurant beneath stone vaults of undercroft.

Gold Court House without rest
St John's Hill ✉ BH20 4LZ – ☏ (01929) 553 320 – www.goldcourthouse.co.uk
3 rm ⬜ – †£ 55 ††£ 80
♦ Attractive Georgian house in small square off the high street. Built in 1762 it was once a goldsmith's and next to the mint. Antique-furnished lounge and traditionally styled bedrooms with private bathrooms. Communal breakfasts. Cellar dates from Saxon times.

WAREN MILL – Northumberland – 501 O17 – see Bamburgh

WARKWORTH – Northumberland – 502 P17   24 B2
▶ London 316 mi – Alnwick 7 mi – Morpeth 24 mi

 Roxbro House without rest
5 Castle Terr ✉ NE65 0UP – ☏ (01665) 711 416 – www.roxbrohouse.co.uk
– Closed 24-28 December
6 rm ⬜ – †£ 60 ††£ 150/180
♦ A discreet style enhances this 19C stone house in the shadow of Warkworth Castle. Well-appointed lounge. Very smart boutique bedrooms with elegant wallpapers and opulent styling; two face the castle.

WARMINSTER – Wiltshire – **503** N30 – pop. 17 486   4 C2

▶ London 111 mi – Bristol 29 mi – Exeter 74 mi – Southampton 47 mi

🛈 Central Car Park ✆ (01985) 21 85 48, www.visitwiltshire.co.uk

◉ Longleat House★★★ **AC**, SW : 3 m. Stonehenge★★★ **AC**, E : 18 mi by A 36 and A 303 – Bratton Castle (≤★★) NE : 6 mi by A 350 and B 3098

at Upton Scudamore North : 2.5 mi by A 350 – ✉ Warminster

Angel Inn with rm
✉ BA12 0AG – ✆ (01985) 213 225 – www.theangelinn.co.uk
10 rm ⌑ – †£ 80 ††£ 80/98   **Rest** – Carte £ 18/28

♦ Dependable village local with cottagey dining room and lovely terrace. Menus are fairly formal and classical, offering the likes of home-cured gravadlax, roast duck, venison steak and old-fashioned puddings. Individually themed bedrooms are cosy and well-kept.

at Heytesbury Southeast : 3.75 mi by B 3414 – ✉ Warminster

Resting Post without rest
67 High St ✉ BA12 0ED – ✆ (01985) 840 204 – www.therestingpost.co.uk
3 rm ⌑ – †£ 50/60 ††£ 75

♦ Immaculately kept Grade II listed building dating back to 17C – originally a post office and general store run by the same couple. Individually styled bedrooms, one with a 6ft bed.

Angel Inn
High St ✉ BA12 0ED – ✆ (01985) 840 330 – www.theangelheytesbury.co.uk
Rest – Carte £ 20/35

♦ Pretty 16C pub with open fires and wooden beams; boasts a typically English feel emphasized by the locals and their dogs. Dishes make good use of fresh, local produce; steaks are a speciality.

at Crockerton South : 2 mi by A 350

Bath Arms with rm
Clay St, on Shearwater rd ✉ BA12 8AJ – ✆ (01985) 212 262
– www.batharmscrockerton.co.uk
2 rm ⌑ – †£ 80/110 ††£ 80/110   **Rest** – Carte £ 21/31

♦ Down-to-earth pub with big ambitions, situated on Longleat Estate. Daily changing menu features classic pub dishes, snacks and grills alongside more modern fare. Two ultra-spacious, contemporary bedrooms.

at Horningsham Southwest : 5 mi by A 362 – ✉ Wiltshire

Bath Arms with rm
Longleat ✉ BA12 7LY – ✆ (01985) 844 308 – www.batharms.co.uk
15 rm ⌑ – †£ 95/135 ††£ 155/175
Rest – Menu £ 30 (dinner) – Carte £ 25/30

♦ Charming pub within the Longleat estate, with open fire in bar, grand dining room and delightful terrace. Appealing menus offer something for everyone; produce is locally sourced, much of it from the estate. Quirky, comfortable, individually themed bedrooms.

WARTLING – East Sussex – **504** V31 – see Herstmonceux

WARWICK – Warwickshire – **503** P27 – pop. 23 350 🟢 Great Britain   19 C3

▶ London 96 mi – Birmingham 20 mi – Coventry 11 mi – Leicester 34 mi

🛈 Jury St ✆ (01926) 49 22 12, www.visitwarwick.co.uk

🛈 Warwick Racecourse, ✆ (01926) 49 43 16

◉ Town★ - Castle★★ **AC** Y – Leycester Hospital★ **AC** Y **B** – Collegiate Church of St Mary★ (Tomb★) Y **A**

648

WARWICK-ROYAL LEAMINGTON SPA

Birmingham Rd	Z	7
Bowling Green St	Y	9
Brook St.	Y	12
Butts (The)	Y	13
Castle Hill	Y	15
Church St.	Y	17
High St.	Y	23
Jury St.	Y	
Lakin Rd.	Y	25
Linen St	Y	26
Market Pl.	Y	29
Old Square	Y	35
Old Warwick Rd	Z	36
Radford Rd.	Z	39
Rock	Y	32
St John's Rd	Y	42
St Nicholas Church St.	Y	43
Shires Retail Park	Z	
Smith St.	Y	
Swan St.	Y	46
Theatre St	Y	48
West St	Y	50

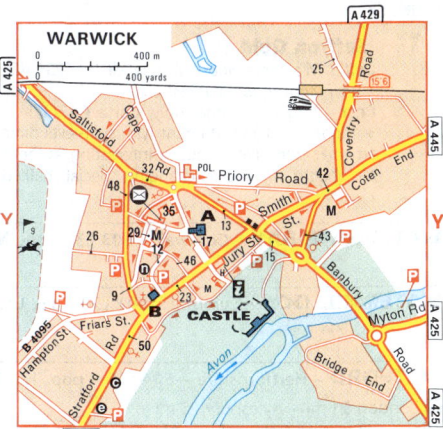

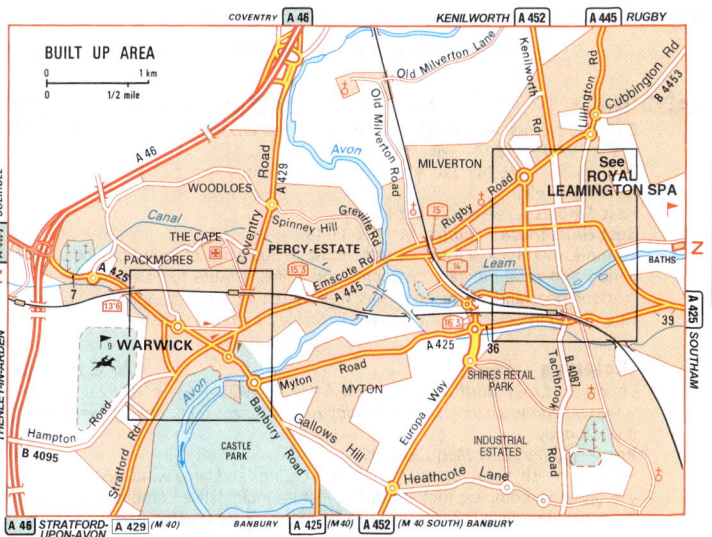

Charter House without rest
87 West St ⊠ CV34 6AH – ℰ (01926) 496 965 – Closed 1 week Christmas
3 rm – †£ 65/69 ††£ 85/95 Yc

♦ Timbered 15C house not far from the castle. Comfortable, delicately ordered rooms with a personal touch: pretty counterpanes and posies of dried flowers. Tasty breakfasts.

Park Cottage without rest
113 West St ⊠ CV34 6AH – ℰ (01926) 410 319 – www.parkcottagewarwick.co.uk
– Closed 23-30 December Ye
7 rm – †£ 55/65 ††£ 70/85

♦ 15C cross wing house with wattle and daub walls, originally belonging to the Earl and sited within the grounds of Warwick Castle; the 300 year old yew tree behind was used to make longbows. Small lounge, cottagey breakfast room and spacious bedrooms with lots of extras.

WARWICK

✗✗ Saffron Gold AC VISA ☉ AE ①
Unit 1, Westgate House, Market St ✉ CV34 4DE – ℰ (01926) 402 061
– www.saffrongoldwarwick.co.uk Yn
Rest – Indian – *(dinner only)* Carte £ 17/32
◆ Modern Indian restaurant with split-level dining room hung with contemporary artwork. Extensive menus of interesting, authentic cooking, with Goan fish dishes a highlight and a daily changing special chalked on the board. Friendly owner.

WATERGATE BAY – Cornwall – 503 E32 – see Newquay

WATERMILLOCK – Cumbria – 502 L20 – see Ullswater

WATFORD – Hertfordshire – 504 S29 – pop. 120 960 12 A2
▶ London 21 mi – Aylesbury 23 mi
🏌 West Herts. Cassiobury Park, ℰ (01923) 23 64 84
🏌 Oxhey Park South Oxhey Prestwick Rd, ℰ (01923) 24 82 13

Plan : see Greater London (North-West) 2

ENGLAND

🏨🏨🏨🏨🏨 Grove
Chandler's Cross, Northwest : 2 mi on A 411 ✉ WD3 4TG VISA ☉ AE ①
– ℰ (01923) 807 807 – www.thegrove.co.uk
215 rm ⌕ – †£ 285/390 ††£ 310/776 – 12 suites
Rest *Colette's*
Rest *Stables* – see restaurant listing
Rest *Glasshouse* – *(buffet)* Menu £ 33/49
◆ Impressive Grade II listed country house in 300 acres of pretty grounds. Mix of period and contemporary bedrooms and suites. Leisure facilities include a spa, outdoor pool and urban beach; as well as tennis, croquet, golf and volleyball. Fine dining in Colette's; casual meals in Stables; buffet in Glasshouse.

✗✗✗ Colette's – at Grove Hotel AC P VISA ☉ AE
Chandler's Cross, Northwest : 2 mi on A 411 ✉ WD3 4TG – ℰ (01923) 296 010
– www.thegrove.co.uk – Closed Sunday dinner except bank holiday weekends and Monday
Rest – *(dinner only)* Menu £ 45/65
◆ Sleek, stylish, hotel restaurant with high ceilings and large windows overlooking the grounds. Complex, modern dishes feature imaginative combinations; choose from an extensive à la carte, 7 course tasting menu or simpler market selection.

✗✗ Clarendon AC P VISA ☉ AE
Redhall Ln, Chandlers Cross, West : 5 mi by A 412, Baldwins Lane and Sarratt Rd ✉ WD3 4LU – ℰ (01923) 270 009 – www.theclarendon.co.uk – Closed 25 December
Rest – Menu £ 16 (lunch) – Carte £ 22/45
◆ Former pub deep in country lanes; now a vibrantly decorated, modern restaurant with bar and open kitchen. Tasty British classics and good old-fashioned puds. Attentive service.

✗✗ Stables – at Grove Hotel AC P VISA ☉ AE ①
Chandler's Cross, Northwest : 2 mi on A 411 ✉ WD3 4TG – ℰ (01923) 296 015
– www.thegrove.co.uk
Rest – Carte £ 35/50
◆ Informal, New England style restaurant in the clubhouse of an impressive Grade II listed country house. It boasts its own sports bar and pleasant views over the course, and offers a grill menu.

WATTON – Norfolk – **504** W26 – pop. 7 435   **15** C2
▶ London 95 mi – Norwich 22 mi – Swaffham 10 mi

Café at Brovey Lair with rm
Carbrooke Rd., Ovington, Northeast : 1.75 mi by A 1075 ✉ IP25 6SD – ℰ (01953) 882 706 – www.broveylair.com
3 rm ⌷ – †£ 120 ††£ 135
Rest – Seafood – *(booking essential 2 days in advance) (set menu only)*
Menu £ 48/53
♦ Keenly run restaurant with integral kitchen. Unique dinner party style dining from single-choice seafood menu, where ambitious dishes display largely Asian and Mediterranean influences. Well-appointed bedrooms sit beside a pool and terrace in lovely gardens.

WELLINGHAM – Norfolk – **504** W25   **15** C1
▶ London 120 mi – King's Lynn 29 mi – Norwich 28 mi

Manor House Farm without rest
✉ PE32 2TH – ℰ (01328) 838 227 – www.manor-house-farm.co.uk
3 rm ⌷ – †£ 65/75 ††£ 90/100
♦ Attractive, wisteria-clad farmhouse with large gardens, set by a church in a beautifully peaceful spot. Spacious, airy bedrooms in former stables. Home-grown/home-reared produce at breakfast.

WELLINGTON – Herefordshire – **503** L27   **18** B3
▶ London 161 mi – Gloucester 38 mi – Worcester 31 mi – Hereford 6 mi

Wellington
✉ HR4 8AT – ℰ (01432) 830 367 – www.wellingtonpub.co.uk – *Closed 25 December, Sunday dinner and Monday*
Rest – Carte £ 25/30
♦ Bright and airy neighbourhood pub where locals gather fireside in the spacious bar. Enjoy flavourful dishes from the daily changing menu in the more formal conservatory dining room.

ENGLAND

WELLS – Somerset – **503** M30 – pop. 11 148   **4** C2
▶ London 132 mi – Bristol 20 mi – Southampton 68 mi – Taunton 28 mi
🛈 Market Pl ℰ (01749) 67 25 52, www.wellssomerset.com
⛳ East Horrington Rd, ℰ (01749) 67 50 05
◉ City★★ – Cathedral★★★ – Bishop's Palace★ (≤★★) **AC** – St Cuthbert★
◎ Glastonbury★★ - Abbey★★ (Abbot's Kitchen★) **AC**, St John the Baptist★★, Somerset Rural Life Museum★ **AC**, Glastonbury Tor★ (≤★★★), SW : 5.5 mi by A 39 – Wookey Hole★ (Caves★ **AC**, Papermill★), NW : 2 m. Cheddar Gorge★★ (Gorge★★, Caves★, Jacob's Ladder ⁂★) - St Andrew's Church★, NW : 7 mi by A 371 – Axbridge★★ (King John's Hunting Lodge★, St John the Baptist Church★), NW : 8.5 mi by A 371

Swan
11 Sadler St ✉ BA5 2RX – ℰ (01749) 836 300 – www.swanhotelwells.co.uk
48 rm ⌷ – †£ 98/118 ††£ 120/198 – 1 suite   **Rest** – Carte £ 27/40
♦ Refurbished to a very good standard, this friendly former posting inn faces the Cathedral's west front. Two firelit lounges; stylish, individually decorated rooms. Stunning Cathedral suite. Restaurant boasts framed antique clothing and oak panelling.

Beryl without rest
East : 1.25 mi by B 3139 off Hawkers Lane ✉ BA5 3JP – ℰ (01749) 678 738 – www.beryl-wells.co.uk – Closed 23-26 December
10 rm ⌷ – †£ 75/95 ††£ 95/140
♦ Neo-gothic former hunting lodge in formal gardens run in idiosyncratic style. Impeccable antique-filled drawing room. Traditional rooms, larger on first floor. Charming hosts.

WELLS

Old Spot
12 Sadler St ⊠ BA5 2SE – ℰ (01749) 689 099 – www.theoldspot.co.uk – Closed 1 week Christmas, Monday, Sunday dinner and Tuesday lunch
Rest – Menu £ 16 (lunch) – Carte dinner £ 28/31
♦ Simple, understated, city centre restaurant run by a husband and wife team; its plain walls hung with framed menus and opening out to boast stunning cathedral views at the rear. Well-executed, classical dishes rely on flavoursome English produce. Preparation is kept simple.

at Easton Northwest : 3 mi on A 371 – ⊠ Wells

Beaconsfield Farm without rest
on A 371 ⊠ BA5 1DU – ℰ (01749) 870 308 – www.beaconsfieldfarm.co.uk – Closed 23 December-2 January
3 rm – †£ 70/80 ††£ 70/90
♦ Former farmhouse hidden away in the foothills of the Mendips and run by a personable owner. Snug, homely interior with comfy lounge and pleasant breakfast room overlooking the grounds. Well-kept, cottage-style bedrooms; ask for the one with the four-poster bed.

WELLS-NEXT-THE-SEA – Norfolk – 504 W25 – pop. 2 451   15 C1
▶ London 122 mi – Cromer 22 mi – Norwich 38 mi

Crown
The Buttlands ⊠ NR23 1EX – ℰ (01328) 710 209 – www.flyingkiwisiinns.co.uk
12 rm – †£ 70/155 ††£ 90/175
Rest *Crown* – Carte £ 21/37
♦ Characterful 16C former coaching inn located in the centre of town, overlooking the green. Individually styled bedrooms blend classical furniture with more modern décor and facilities. Dine from an accessible menu in the charming bar, orangery or dining room.

Machrimore without rest
Burnt St., on A 149 ⊠ NR23 1HS – ℰ (01328) 711 653 – www.machrimore.co.uk
4 rm – †£ 70 ††£ 84
♦ Converted farm buildings with delightful gardens and illuminated water features. Accessed via the garden, bedrooms have quality furniture, good facilities, their own patio and seating.

at Wighton Southeast : 2.5 mi by A 149

Meadowview without rest
53 High St ⊠ NR23 1PF – ℰ (01328) 821 527 – www.meadow-view.net
5 rm – †£ 65 ††£ 90/105
♦ Set in peaceful village, with neat garden, hot tub, comfy furniture and gazebo overlooking meadow. Smart, modern interior with comfy furnishings; good facilities. Breakfast cooked on Aga.

WELWYN – Hertfordshire – 504 T28 – pop. 10 512   12 B2
▶ London 31 mi – Bedford 31 mi – Cambridge 31 mi

Tewin Bury Farm
Southeast : 3.5 mi by A 1000 on B 1000 ⊠ AL6 0JB – ℰ (01438) 717 793 – www.tewinbury.co.uk
29 rm – †£ 123 ††£ 138
Rest *Tewin Bury Farm* – see restaurant listing
♦ Collection of converted farm buildings on a 400 acre working farm, next to a nature reserve. Rustic interior with comfortable, oak-furnished bedrooms in various wings. Function room is in an impressive tithe barn beside the old mill race.

Tewin Bury Farm – at Tewin Bury Farm Hotel
Southeast : 3.5 mi by A 1000 on B 1000 ✉ *AL6 0JB* – ✆ *(01438) 717 793*
– www.tewinbury.co.uk
Rest – Carte approx. £ 25
♦ Hotel restaurant in an old timber granary, set among converted farm buildings on a 400 acre farm. Contemporary interior with open kitchen and smart bar. Classical menu displays modern touches.

at Ayot St Lawrence West : 2.75 mi by B 656

Brocket Arms with rm
✉ *AL6 9BT* – ✆ *(01438) 820 250 – www.brocketarms.com – Closed Sunday dinner*
6 rm – †£ 95/125 ††£ 95/125 **Rest** – Menu £ 25 – Carte lunch £ 23/28
♦ Characterful 14C inn boasting leaded windows, a wood-furnished restaurant and a cosy beamed bar with huge inglenook and monk's hole. Good value bar menu and more ambitious 'menu du jour' offering original, flavoursome combinations; regular BBQs in summer. Simple, comfortable bedrooms, some in the courtyard.

WELWYN GARDEN CITY – Hertfordshire – 504 T28 – pop. 43 512   12 B2

▶ London 22 mi – Luton 21 mi

🏌 Panshanger Golf Complex Old Herns Lane, ✆ (01707) 33 33 12

Auberge du Lac
Brocket Hall, West : 3 mi by A 6129 on B 653 ✉ *AL8 7XG* – ✆ *(01707) 368 888*
– www.brocket-hall.co.uk – Closed 27 December-14 January, Sunday and Monday
Rest – Menu £ 33/55
Spec. Sandalwood-smoked sea trout, pickled winkles, honeycomb and watercress. Rump of lamb, salt-baked goat's cheese, pomme dauphine and rosemary. Rhubarb and custard soufflé, crisp gingerbread and rose petal.
♦ You get buzzed in at the gates to reach this part-18C former hunting lodge in the grounds of Brocket Hall; a charming setting with its lakeside terrace. Cooking is technically adept, elaborate and complicated, with ambitious flavour combinations. Excellent cheeseboard.

WENTBRIDGE – West Yorkshire – 502 Q23 – ✉ Pontefract   22 B3

▶ London 183 mi – Leeds 19 mi – Nottingham 55 mi – Sheffield 28 mi

Wentbridge House
Old Great North Rd. ✉ *WF8 3JJ* – ✆ *(01977) 620 444*
– www.wentbridgehouse.co.uk
41 rm – †£ 110 ††£ 170/220
Rest *Fleur de Lys* – see restaurant listing
Rest *Wentbridge Brasserie* – Carte £ 24/37
♦ Personally run, bay-windowed house, dating back to 18C and surrounded by 20 acres of immaculately kept gardens. Bedrooms are a mix of characterful, wood-panelled, period styles and spacious, modern designs boasting up-to-date facilities. Modern restaurant or smart brasserie offering classics and newer dishes.

Fleur de Lys – at Wentbridge House Hotel
Old Great North Rd. ✉ *WF8 3JJ* – ✆ *(01977) 620 444*
– www.wentbridgehouse.co.uk – Closed Sunday dinner
Rest – *(dinner only and Sunday lunch)* Carte £ 34/54
♦ Formal hotel dining room boasting contemporary fabrics, etched fleur mirrors and Italian chandeliers; set in a personally run, Victorian house. Appealing menu offers creative modern dishes.

WEST BAGBOROUGH – Somerset – 503 K30 – see Taunton

WEST DIDSBURY – Greater Manchester – see Manchester

WEST END – Surrey – 504 S29 – pop. 4 135 – ✉ Guildford   7 C1

▶ London 37 mi – Bracknell 7 mi – Camberley 5 mi – Guildford 8 mi

The Inn @ West End
42 Guildford Rd, on A 322 ✉ *GU24 9PP* – ✆ *(01276) 858 652*
– *www.the-inn.co.uk*
Rest – Carte £ 28/40
♦ A snug and friendly village pub with a roaring fire and a country feel. An array of menus offer something for everyone. Interesting selection of wines and a pleasant garden/terrace.

WEST HOATHLY – West Sussex – pop. 2 121   7 D2

▶ London 36 mi

Cat Inn with rm
Queen's Sq ✉ *RH19 4PP* – ✆ *(01342) 810 369* – *www.catinn.co.uk*
– *Closed Sunday dinner*
4 rm – ♦£ 80 ♦♦£ 100/140 **Rest** – *(closed 25 December)* Carte £ 25/32
♦ Charming 17C pub in a pleasant hamlet, run by experienced owners and a bubbly team. A myriad of rooms range from rustic and intimate, to larger and more formally laid. Menus feature satisfying country classics. Bedrooms are modern and extremely comfortable.

WEST KIRBY – Merseyside – 502 K23 ▌Great Britain   20 A3

▶ London 219 mi – Chester 19 mi – Liverpool 12 mi

◉ Liverpool★ - Cathedrals★★, The Walker★★, Merseyside Maritime Museum★ and Albert Dock★, E : 13.5 mi by A 553

Peel Hey without rest
Frankby Rd, Frankby, East : 2.25 mi by A 540 on B 5139 ✉ *CH48 1PP* – ✆ *(0151) 677 90 77* – *www.peelhey.com*
10 rm – ♦£ 75/95 ♦♦£ 95/120
♦ Personally run, 19C house with attractive bedrooms; those to the rear are quieter, with countryside views. Comfortable conservatory and pleasant lawned garden. Pubs for dinner close by.

Collingwood
19 Black Horse Hill, East : 0.5 mi by A 540 on B 5139 ✉ *CH48 6DS* – ✆ *(0151) 625 45 25* – *www.thecollingwood.co.uk* – *Closed 25 December*
Rest – Menu £ 15/35
♦ Contemporary restaurant in an old pub, boasting a huge central bar and tables and sofas scattered about. Tasty pub classics at lunch; accomplished, modern, restaurant-style dishes at dinner.

WEST MALLING – Kent – 504 V30 – pop. 2 144   8 B1

▶ London 35 mi – Maidstone 7 mi – Royal Tunbridge Wells 14 mi
🛈 Addington Maidstone, ✆ (01732) 84 47 85

Swan
35 Swan St. ✉ *ME19 6JU* – ✆ *(01732) 521 910* – *www.theswanwestmalling.co.uk*
Rest – *(booking essential)* Carte £ 26/37
♦ Informal 15C former coaching inn where original beams blend with stylish, contemporary furnishings. Nicely appointed bar and comfy lounge are located upstairs. Modern European menus offer cleanly presented, flavoursome combinations; side dishes are required.

WEST MEON – Hampshire – **504** Q30 — 6 B2
▶ London 74 mi – Southampton 27 mi – Portsmouth 21 mi – Basingstoke 32 mi

Thomas Lord
High St ✉ GU32 1LN – ✆ (01730) 829 244 – www.thethomaslord.co.uk – Closed 1 January, 25 December and Monday
Rest – Menu £ 20 (weekdays) – Carte £ 26/36
♦ Named after the founder of Lord's Cricket Ground; memorabilia abounds among the shabby-chic styling. Locally sourced produce informs oft-changing menu of tasty British dishes.

WEST OVERTON – Wiltshire – **503** O29 — 4 D2
▶ London 82 mi – Bristol 54 mi – Cardiff 87 mi – Southampton 62 mi

Bell at West Overton
Bath Rd ✉ SN8 1QD – ✆ (01672) 861 099 – www.thebellwestoverton.co.uk
Rest – *(closed dinner Sunday and Monday)* Menu £ 21 – Carte £ 23/43
♦ A simple, friendly pub, rescued from oblivion by a local couple who were sensible enough to hire an experienced pair to run it. Menu mixes pub classics with Med-influenced dishes; fish from Cornish day boats a highlight.

WEST TANFIELD – North Yorkshire – **502** P21 – pop. 551 – ✉ Ripon — 22 B2
▶ London 237 mi – Darlington 29 mi – Leeds 32 mi – Middlesbrough 39 mi

Old Coach House *without rest*
2 Stable Cottage, Southeast : 1 mi on A 6108 ✉ HG4 3HT – ✆ (01765) 634 900 – www.oldcoachhouse.info
8 rm – †£ 55/75 ††£ 99
♦ Smart 18C former coach house, nestled between the dales and moors. Bedrooms – in two main buildings – differ in size, but all have a bright, modern style and are furnished by local craftsmen. Breakfast room overlooks the pleasant courtyard garden and fountain.

WEST WITTON – North Yorkshire – **502** O21 – ✉ Leyburn — 22 B1
▶ London 241 mi – Kendal 39 mi – Leeds 60 mi – Newcastle upon Tyne 65 mi

Wensleydale Heifer
✉ DL8 4LS – ✆ (01969) 622 322 – www.wensleydaleheifer.co.uk
13 rm – †£ 110/130 ††£ 130/210
Rest – Seafood – Menu £ 18/20 – Carte £ 30/41
♦ Pretty whitewashed former pub on main street of village. Quirky, themed bedrooms boast quality linen and all mod cons. Characterful lounge with roaring fire. Dine in the fish bar or at clothed tables in the beamed restaurant; cooking has strong seafood base.

WESTFIELD – East Sussex – **504** V31 – pop. 1 509 — 8 B3
▶ London 66 mi – Brighton 38 mi – Folkestone 45 mi – Maidstone 30 mi

Wild Mushroom
Woodgate House, Westfield Ln., Southwest : 0.5 mi on A 28 ✉ TN35 4SB – ✆ (01424) 751 137 – www.webbesrestaurants.co.uk – Closed Sunday dinner and Monday
Rest – *(booking essential)* Menu £ 20 (weekday lunch) – Carte £ 25/34
♦ Rural roadside house with classical dining room and intimate conservatory bar. Good value French/European menus feature well-presented, tried-and-tested combinations. Tasting menu available.

WESTLETON – Suffolk – **504** Y27 – pop. 1 317 – ✉ Saxmundham — 15 D2
▶ London 97 mi – Cambridge 72 mi – Ipswich 28 mi – Norwich 31 mi

Westleton Crown *with rm*
The Street ✉ IP17 3AD – ✆ (01728) 648 777 – www.westletoncrown.co.uk
34 rm – †£ 80/110 ††£ 105/120   **Rest** – Carte £ 28/38
♦ Good-looking, red-brick 17C former coaching inn, set in a pretty little village. Welcoming beamed bar with open fires – venture further in for the more modern conservatory. The same appealing menu is served throughout. Uncluttered bedrooms boast smart bathrooms.

WESTON SUBEDGE – Gloucestershire – see Chipping Campden

WESTON-SUPER-MARE – North Somerset – 503 K29 – pop. 78 044   3 B2

- ▶ London 147 mi – Bristol 24 mi – Taunton 32 mi
- 🛈 Beach Lawns, ☏ (01934) 88 88 00, www.visitsomerset.co.uk
- 📍18 Worlebury Monks Hill, ☏ (01934) 62 57 89
- ◉ Seafront (≤★★) BZ
- ⊙ Axbridge★★ (King John's Hunting Lodge★, St John the Baptist Church★) SE : 9 mi by A 371 - BY - and A 38 – Cheddar Gorge★★ (Gorge★★, Caves★, Jacob's Ladder ✻★) – Clevedon★ (≤★★, Clevedon Court★), NE : 10 mi by A 370 and M 5 – St Andrew's Church★, SE : 10.5 mi by A 371

Albert Quadrant	BZ 2	Royal Parade	BZ 11
Flowerdown Bridge	BY 4	Sovereign Centre	BZ
High St.	BZ 7	Upper Bristol Rd.	BY 12
Meadow St.	BZ 8	Upper Church Rd.	AY 13
Oxford St.	BZ 9	Walliscote Rd	BZ 14
Regent St.	BZ 10	Waterloo St.	BZ 15
		Windwhistle Rd	AZ 16

WESTON-SUPER-MARE

Duets
103 Upper Bristol Rd. ✉ *BS22 8ND –* ℘ *(01934) 413 428 – www.duets.co.uk – Closed 1 week spring, 1 week summer, 1 week winter, Sunday dinner, Monday and Tuesday* BY**a**

Rest – Menu £ 17/30 – Carte £ 32/36

♦ Diligent and unfussy service sets the tone in this traditionally styled restaurant, deservedly a neighbourhood favourite. Ably judged cooking on a tasty classical base.

Cove
Birnbeck Rd ✉ *BS23 2BX –* ℘ *(01934) 418 217 – www.the-cove.co.uk – Closed 25 December, Sunday dinner and Monday except bank holidays* AY**e**

Rest – Menu £ 17 (lunch) – Carte £ 22/32

♦ Seafront eatery with striking lines, contemporary styling and bay views. Modern, seasonal menu displays European flair and seafood slant; most produce from within 20 miles. Tapas 3-9pm.

WESTON UNDER WETHERLEY – Warwickshire – **503** P27 – see Royal Leamington Spa

---

WEYBRIDGE – Surrey – **504** S29 – pop. 19 463 7 C1

▶ London 23 mi – Crawley 27 mi – Guildford 17 mi – Reading 33 mi

Brooklands
Brooklands Dr, Southwest : 1.5 mi by B 374 and A 318 ✉ *KT13 0SL –* ℘ *(01937) 355 700 – www.brooklandshotelsurrey.com*

105 rm – †£ 120/240 ††£ 120/240, ⊒ £ 15.95 – 15 suites

Rest *Brasserie* – see restaurant listing

♦ Contemporary hotel with art deco feel, situated next to Mercedes Benz World on what was Brooklands racetrack. Buzzy bar; great spa. Stylish, comfortable, good-sized bedrooms.

Brasserie – at Brooklands Hotel
Brooklands Dr, Southwest : 1.5 mi by B 374 and A 318 ✉ *KT13 0SL –* ℘ *(01932) 355 700 – www.brooklandshotelsurrey.com*

Rest – Italian influences – Carte £ 23/48

♦ Bright, modern dining room, with black décor and a funky feel. Choose a traditional 3 course meal or a number of tasting plates. Tasty, authentic Italian cooking; effective service.

Queen's Head
1 Bridge Rd ✉ *KT13 8XS –* ℘ *(01932) 839 820 – www.whitebrasserie.com – Closed 25 December*

Rest – Menu £ 14/16 – Carte £ 22/30

♦ Lovingly restored 18C coach house with a series of snug little rooms, warming open fires and a pewter bar, that can't fail to impress. Menus mix British pub dishes with French brasserie classics. Spacious restaurant boasts an open-kitchen.

WEYMOUTH – Dorset – **503** M32 – pop. 48 279 4 C3

▶ London 142 mi – Bournemouth 35 mi – Bristol 68 mi – Exeter 59 mi

⛴ to Guernsey (St Peter Port) and Jersey (St Helier) (Condor Ferries Ltd)

ℹ The Esplanade ℘ (01305) 78 57 47, www.visitweymouth.co.uk

▣ Links Rd, ℘ (0844) 980 99 09

◉ Town★ – Timewalk★ **AC** – Nothe Fort (≤★) **AC** – Boat Trip★ (Weymouth Bay and Portland Harbour) **AC**

◉ Chesil Beach★★ – Portland★ - Portland Bill (✻★★) S : 2.5 mi by A 354. Maiden Castle★★ (≤★) N : 6.5 mi by A 354 – Sub-Tropical Gardens★ **AC**, St Catherine's Chapel★) NW : 9 mi by B 3157

WEYMOUTH

Chandlers without rest
4 Westerhall Rd ⌂ DT4 7SZ – ℰ (01305) 771 341 – www.chandlershotel.com
– Closed Christmas and New Year
10 rm – †£ 62/125 ††£ 155
♦ Substantial Victorian house near the promenade, run by friendly owners. Stylish, modern interior with comfy lounge and airy breakfast room. Bedrooms have plain walls and colour-themed fabrics.

WHALLEY – Lancashire – 502 M22 – pop. 3 230 – ⌂ Blackburn   20 B2
▶ London 233 mi – Blackpool 32 mi – Burnley 12 mi – Manchester 28 mi
🛈 Long Leese Barn Clerkhill, ℰ (01254) 82 22 36

Food by Breda Murphy
Abbots Ct, 41 Station Rd ⌂ BB7 9RH – ℰ (01254) 823 446
– www.foodbybredamurphy.com – Closed 24 December-4 January, Sunday and Monday
Rest – *(lunch only)* Carte £ 22/29
♦ Bright, modern restaurant with popular deli. Extensive menu of tasty, traditional, home-cooked dishes – from salads and sandwiches to the full three courses. Charming service.

at Mitton Northwest : 2.5 mi on B 6246 – ⌂ Whalley

Three Fishes
Mitton Rd ⌂ BB7 9PQ – ℰ (01254) 826 888 – www.thethreefishes.com – Closed 25 December
Rest – *(bookings not accepted)* Carte £ 21/33
♦ Spacious, modern country inn offering extensive, seasonally changing menu which celebrates Lancastrian produce. Family-friendly, with a children's menu and popular Sunday roast.

WHEPSTEAD – Suffolk – 504 W27 – see Bury St Edmunds

WHITBY – North Yorkshire – 502 S20 – pop. 13 594 ▌Great Britain   23 C1
▶ London 257 mi – Middlesbrough 31 mi – Scarborough 21 mi – York 45 mi
🛈 Langborne Rd ℰ (01723) 38 36 37, www.visitwhitby.com
🛈 Low Straggleton Sandsend Rd, ℰ (01947) 60 06 60
◉ Abbey★

Bagdale Hall
1 Bagdale ⌂ YO21 1QL – ℰ (01947) 602 958 – www.bagdale.co.uk
14 rm – †£ 60/130 ††£ 80/220
Rest – *(dinner only)* Menu £ 15 – Carte £ 20/29
♦ Tudor manor with fine fireplaces in carved wood and 19C Delft tiles; panelled rooms with mullioned windows; four-posters in period style bedrooms. Annexe for more modern rooms. Dining room boasts timbered ceiling and massive wooden fireplace.

Green's
13 Bridge St ⌂ YO22 4BG – ℰ (01947) 600 284 – www.greensofwhitby.com
– Closed 25-26 December and 1 January
Rest – Seafood – *(booking essential)* Menu £ 43 (dinner) – Carte £ 27/43
♦ Established eatery near the quay. Formal dining room offers 3 course menu. Lively bistro serves concise à la carte and daily specials – mainly market fish. Influences range from Italian to Thai.

Red Chard Lounge and Grill
22-23 Flowergate ⌂ YO21 3BA – ℰ (01947) 606 660 – www.redchard.com
– Closed first week January, Sunday lunch and dinner Monday-Tuesday
Rest – Beef specialities – Carte £ 28/35
♦ Modern town centre bar/lounge/dining room in one; funky and relaxing, with art-covered walls. Wide ranging menu with local produce to the fore; quality 21 day hung beef.

at Briggswath Southwest : 3.5 mi by A 171 (Teesdale Rd), A 169 on B 1410 – ✉ Whitby

Lawns without rest ⇐ 🚗 🐾 📶 **P**
73 Carr Hill Ln. ✉ *YO21 1RS –* 𝒞 *(01947) 810 310*
– www.thelawnsbedandbreakfastwhitby.co.uk – Closed 22 December-1 January
3 rm 🛏 – 👤£ 38 👥£ 76
♦ Large converted house with south-facing garden, set in an elevated position 3 miles from the coast. Comfortable lounge and well-kept bedrooms with understated décor. Delightful views over the Esk Valley to the North York Moors. Tea and cake served on arrival.

at Sandsend Northwest : 3 mi on A 174 – ✉ Whitby

Woodlands 🌿 ⇐ 🚗 🐾 📶 **P** VISA ⊕
The Valley ✉ *YO21 3TE –* 𝒞 *(01947) 893 438*
– www.thewoodlands-sandsend.com – Closed January and restricted opening in winter
5 rm 🛏 – 👤£ 125 👥£ 135
Rest – *(booking essential) Carte approx. £ 22* **s**
♦ Laid-back country house in a peaceful valley, set back from the sea. Small lounge with honesty bar; individually designed bedrooms in colourful, contemporary style. Breakfast on the terrace in summer or in your room from a hamper in winter. All-day café offers cakes and home-cooked local produce at dinner.

XX Estbek House with rm 📶 VISA ⊕
East Row ✉ *YO21 3SU –* 𝒞 *(01947) 893 424 – www.estbekhouse.co.uk – Closed January-10 February*
4 rm 🛏 – 👤£ 80/125 👥£ 100/190
Rest – Seafood – *(dinner only) Carte £ 36/50*
♦ This personally run Regency house, adjacent to beach, boasts delightful terrace, basement bar, smart restaurant serving local, wild seafood, and utterly charming rooms.

at Goldsborough Northwest : 6 mi by A 174

X Fox & Hounds ⇔ **P** VISA ⊕ ①
✉ *YO21 3RX –* 𝒞 *(01947) 893 372 – www.foxandhoundsgoldsborough.co.uk – Closed Christmas and Sunday-Tuesday*
Rest – *(dinner only) Carte £ 29/40*
♦ Former village pub with homely, cottagey style, set in tiny coastal hamlet. Constantly evolving menu features local produce and unfussy cooking, with emphasis on fresh fish and seafood.

WHITEHAVEN – Cumbria – 502 J20 – pop. 24 978   21 A2

▶ London 332 mi – Carlisle 39 mi – Keswick 28 mi – Penrith 47 mi

XX Zest **P** VISA ⊕ ①
Low Rd, South : 0.5 mi on B 5345 (St Bees) ✉ *CA28 9HS –* 𝒞 *(01946) 692 848*
– www.zestwhitehaven.com – Closed 25 December, 1 January and Sunday-Tuesday
Rest – *(dinner only) Carte £ 21/41*
♦ Unassuming exterior conceals stylish, red-hued room with brushed velvet chairs and leather banquettes. Large, modern menu with Asian edge and blackboard specials. Unfussy, flavoursome cooking.

WHITEWELL – Lancashire – **502** M22 – pop. 5 617 – ✉ Clitheroe   20 B2
▶ London 281 mi – Lancaster 31 mi – Leeds 55 mi – Manchester 41 mi

Inn at Whitewell with rm
Forest of Bowland ✉ BB7 3AT – ℰ (01200) 448 222 – www.innatwhitewell.com
23 rm ⌷ – †£ 88/158 ††£ 120/200 – 1 suite   **Rest** – Carte £ 16/43
◆ 14C creeper-clad inn, high on the banks of the River Hodder, with panoramic valley views. Atmospheric bar and more formal restaurant. Classic menus of regionally inspired dishes. Spacious bedrooms; some traditional in style, with four-posters and antique baths.

WHITSTABLE – Kent – **504** X29 – pop. 30 195   9 C1
▶ London 68 mi – Dover 24 mi – Maidstone 37 mi – Margate 12 mi
ℹ 7 Oxford St ℰ (0871) 7 16 24 49, www.canterbury.co.uk

Whitstable Oyster Fishery Co.
Royal Native Oyster Stores, The Horsebridge ✉ CT5 1BU – ℰ (01227) 276 856
– www.whitstableoystercompany.com – Closed 25-26 December and Monday dinner
Rest – Seafood – (booking essential) Carte £ 35/50
◆ Former oyster warehouse right by the sea. Large, rough, wood-furnished interior with great informal atmosphere. Blackboard displays simply prepared seafood dishes. Fresh oysters at the counter.

Pearson's Arms
The Horsebridge, Sea Wall ✉ CT5 1BT – ℰ (01227) 773 133
– www.pearsonsarmsbyrichardphillips.co.uk – Closed Sunday-Tuesday dinner
Rest – Menu £ 13 (lunch) – Carte £ 23/37
◆ Characterful refurbished pub in a great spot, with the Thames Estuary stretched out in front. Busy ground floor bar for nibbles like jellied eels; top floor dining room serves reassuringly familiar dishes, with Kentish produce to the fore.

at Seasalter Southwest : 2 mi by B 2205 – ✉ Whitstable

The Sportsman (Steve Harris)
Faversham Rd, Southwest : 2 mi following coast rd ✉ CT5 4BP – ℰ (01227)
273 370 – www.thesportsmanseasalter.co.uk – Closed 25-26 December, Sunday dinner and Monday
Rest – (booking advisable) Carte £ 32/41
Spec. Slip sole grilled in seaweed butter. Roast pork belly, crackling and apple sauce. Warm chocolate mousse, salted caramel and milk sorbet.
◆ Unassuming pub set by the sea wall, with a modest, open-plan interior. Concise daily blackboard menu offers simple-sounding dishes, which are rarely as straightforward as they seem. Preparation is precise; flavours, well-judged; and presentation, original.

WICKHAM – Hampshire – **503** – pop. 1 915   6 B2
▶ London 74 mi – Portsmouth 12 mi – Southampton 11 mi – Winchester 16 mi

Old House
The Square ✉ PO17 5JG – ℰ (01329) 833 049 – www.oldhousehotel.co.uk
– Closed 19-20 May
12 rm ⌷ – †£ 110 ††£ 110/150
Rest – (closed Sunday dinner) Menu £ 18/25 – Carte £ 35/46
◆ Lovely, creeper-clad, Queen Anne townhouse built in 1707. Characterful bedrooms; some with original fireplaces, all with modern furnishings. Those in the garden have a slightly Mediterranean feel, boasting tiled floors and large bathrooms. Small restaurant and airy conservatory offer modern takes on classics.

WIGHILL – North Yorkshire – **502** Q22 – see Tadcaster

WIGHT (Isle of) – Isle of Wight – **503** P/Q31 – pop. 138 500   **6** A/B 3
Great Britain

🚢 from Ryde to Portsmouth (Hovertravel Ltd) frequent services daily (10 mn) – from Ryde to Portsmouth (Wightlink Ltd) frequent services daily (15 mn) – from East Cowes to Southampton (Red Funnel Ferries) frequent services daily (22 mn)

🚢 from East Cowes to Southampton (Red Funnel Ferries) frequent services daily (1 h) – from Yarmouth to Lymington (Wightlink Ltd) frequent services daily (30 mn) – from Fishbourne to Portsmouth (Wightlink Ltd) frequent services daily (35 mn)

◉ Island ★★

⊙ Osborne House, East Cowes ★★ **AC** – Carisbrooke Castle, Newport ★★ **AC** (Keep ⩽ ★) – Brading ★ (Roman Villa ★ **AC**, St Mary's Church ★, Nunwell House ★ **AC**) – Shorwell : St Peter's Church ★ (wall paintings ★)

BONCHURCH – Isle of Wight   **6** B3

🍴 Pond Café
PO38 1RG – ℰ (01983) 855 666 – www.robert-thompson.com – Closed 1-26 January
Rest – Menu £ 18 (lunch) – Carte £ 23/36
◆ Intimate neighbourhood restaurant with candlelit, bistro-style interior. Attractive terrace with fairy lights overlooks duck pond. Generously proportioned, flavoursome dishes use island produce.

GODSHILL – Isle of Wight   **6** B3

🍺 Taverners
High St ⊠ PO38 3HZ – ℰ (01983) 840 707 – www.thetavernersgodshill.co.uk – Closed first 3 weeks January
Rest – Carte £ 21/24
◆ Whitewashed pub with cosy bar and two large dining rooms. Cooking is fresh and tasty, mixing traditional pub classics with more ambitious daily specials. Local island produce is a feature.

NITON – Isle of Wight   **6** B3

🏠 Hermitage
North : 3 mi by Newport rd (A 3020) ⊠ PO38 2PD – ℰ (01983) 730 010 – www.hermitage-iow.co.uk – Closed 22 December-9 January
10 rm ⊇ – †£ 100/120 ††£ 125/145   **Rest** – (dinner only) Carte £ 19/31
◆ Large 19C country house with 12 acres of gardens/woodland; set in pleasant rural location. Traditionally styled drawing room and peaceful lounge. Individually designed, well-equipped bedrooms. Elegant dining room displays a contemporary edge; classical menus.

SEAVIEW – Isle of Wight – pop. 2 286   **6** B3

🏨 Priory Bay
Priory Dr., Southeast : 1.5 mi by B 3330 ⊠ PO34 5BU – ℰ (01983) 613 146 – www.priorybay.co.uk
18 rm ⊇ – †£ 105/225 ††£ 200/300 – 2 suites
Rest *The Restaurant* – Menu £ 20/35 – Carte £ 25/49
◆ Peacefully located medieval priory overlooking the water. Romantic shabby-chic interior, spacious guest areas and relaxed vibe. Bedrooms range in style from classical country house to nautical, boasting good facilities and modern bathrooms.

🏨 Seaview
High St ⊠ PO34 5EX – ℰ (01983) 612 711 – www.seaviewhotel.co.uk – Closed 1 week Christmas
25 rm ⊇ – †£ 115/210 ††£ 170/210 – 3 suites
Rest *The Restaurant and Sunshine Room* – (dinner only and lunch during summer) (booking essential) Carte £ 27/31
◆ Long-standing, bay-windowed hotel covered in foliage. Interesting nautical-themed décor with paintings/model ships throughout. Smart, modern bedrooms in various styles; some in outbuildings. One bright and one more intimate room in restaurant; classical cooking.

WIGHT (Isle of)

SHANKLIN – Isle of Wight – pop. 8 055   6 B3
▶ Newport 9 mi
🛈 67 High St , ☏ (01983) 81 38 13, www.visitshanklin.co.uk
⛳ The Fairway Lake Sandown, ☏ (01983) 40 32 17

Rylstone Manor
Rylstone Gdns ✉ PO37 6RG – ☏ (01983) 862 806 – www.rylstone-manor.co.uk
– Closed 28 November-10 February
9 rm ⌑ – †£ 70/75 ††£ 170/180 **Rest** – *(dinner only)* Menu £ 32
◆ Originally a gift from the Queen to one of her physicians: an attractive part-Victorian house close to the historic gardens. Classical interior boasts heavy fabrics and warm, cosy feel. Bedrooms combine antique furniture and modern facilities. Formal dining room.

Foxhills without rest
30 Victoria Ave ✉ PO37 6LS – ☏ (01983) 862 329 – www.foxhillsofshanklin.co.uk
8 rm ⌑ – †£ 59/96 ††£ 96/106
◆ Large, stone-built house in leafy residential avenue. Spacious, Victorian-styled lounge and modern breakfast room; comfy bedrooms in pastel hues. Jacuzzi, spa and beauty treatments available.

VENTNOR – Isle of Wight – pop. 6 257   6 B3
▶ Newport 10 mi
⛳ Steephill Down Rd, ☏ (01983) 85 33 26

Royal
Belgrave Rd ✉ PO38 1JJ – ☏ (01983) 852 186 – www.royalhoteliow.co.uk
– Closed 2 weeks January
53 rm ⌑ – †£ 125/190 ††£ 235/275
Rest – *(closed Sunday lunch July and August) (dinner only and Sunday lunch)*
Menu £ 20/40
◆ Large Victorian building with mature lawned gardens and heated outdoor pool. Modern touches in lounge and bar. Traditionally styled bedrooms with good facilities: premier rooms are larger; some have lovely sea views. Classical menu served in formal dining room.

Hambrough with rm
Hambrough Rd ✉ PO38 1SQ – ☏ (01983) 856 333 – www.robert-thompson.com
– Closed January, November, 10 days April, Sunday and Monday
7 rm ⌑ – †£ 210 ††£ 300
Rest – *(booking essential)* Menu £ 28/55
Spec. Lemon sole with clam and cockle risotto. Rose veal with bone marrow sauce and white asparagus. Chocolate delice with Earl Grey tea and walnut.
◆ Eye-catching clifftop villa with leather-furnished lounge and two warm, stylish dining rooms boasting excellent sea views. Skilful, confident chef uses top quality ingredients to create refined, modern dishes. Service is polite and knowledgeable. Smart, comfortable bedrooms feature quality linens and espresso machines.

WOOTTON BRIDGE – IOW – pop. 3 618   6 B3

Lakeside Park
High St. ✉ PO33 4LJ – ☏ (01983) 882 266 – www.lakesideparkhotel.com
44 rm ⌑ – †£ 120/175 ††£ 120/175
Rest *Oyster Room* – *(closed Sunday, Monday and Tuesday) (booking essential)*
Menu £ 25/59
Rest *Brasserie* – Menu £ 15 (lunch) – Carte £ 21/30
◆ Purpose-built hotel with lawned gardens. Stylish, comfortable, modern bedrooms offer a high level of facilities. Smart, fine dining restaurant with lounge and private terrace. Open-plan split-level bar, lounge and brassiere with large decked terrace and view over lake.

WIGHT (Isle of)

YARMOUTH – Isle of Wight – pop. 855   6 A3
▶ Newport 10 mi

George
Quay St ⊠ PO41 0PE – ℰ (01983) 760 331 – www.thegeorge.co.uk
19 rm – †£ 99/140 ††£ 290
Rest *Brasserie* – see restaurant listing
♦ Smart 17C townhouse that blends subtle modern touches with characterful period features. Bedrooms boast up-to-date facilities: one has a large wet room and opens onto the garden; another boasts a sizeable balcony and excellent Solent views.

Brasserie – at George Hotel
Quay St ⊠ PO41 0PE – ℰ (01983) 760 331 – www.thegeorge.co.uk
Rest – Carte £ 35/48
♦ Contemporary hotel restaurant with pewter bar and small heated terrace. Modern menu offers some interesting combinations, with a tasting option in the evening. Tasty homemade bread and daily fish specials, with local game dishes in season.

WIGHTON – Norfolk – 504 W25 – see Wells-Next-The-Sea

WILLIAN – Hertfordshire – 504 T28 – pop. 326   12 B2
▶ London 39 mi – Birmingham 107 mi

Fox
⊠ SG6 2AE – ℰ (01462) 480 233 – www.foxatwillian.co.uk – Closed Sunday dinner
Rest – Carte £ 21/33
♦ Bright, airy pub that's always bustling. Lunch served throughout; dinner in the dining room only. Menu offers modern dishes with game in season and plenty of seafood; some Asian influences.

WIMBORNE MINSTER – Dorset – 503 O31 – pop. 14 844   4 C3
▶ London 112 mi – Bournemouth 10 mi – Dorchester 23 mi – Salisbury 27 mi
🛈 29 High St ℰ (01202) 88 61 16, www.visit-dorset.org.uk
◉ Town★ – Minster★ – Priest's House Museum★ **AC**
◉ Kingston Lacy★★ **AC**, NW : 3 mi by B 3082

Les Bouviers with rm
Arrowsmith Rd, Canford Magna, Southeast : 2.25 mi by A 349 on A 341
⊠ BH21 3BD – ℰ (01202) 889 555 – www.lesbouviers.co.uk
6 rm – ††£ 175/225, ⊡ £ 5   **Rest** – *(closed Sunday dinner)* Menu £ 20/34
♦ Formerly a private residence, now a two-roomed restaurant overlooking a terrace and large lawned grounds. Small leather-furnished lounge; large rear function room. Formal team serve complex dishes from traditional menus. Smart, comfy, slightly kitsch bedrooms.

WIMBORNE ST GILES – Dorset – 504 O31 – pop. 366   4 C3
▶ London 107 mi – Bristol 72 mi – Southampton 32 mi – Reading 75 mi

Bull Inn with rm
Coach Rd ⊠ BH21 5NF – ℰ (01725) 517 300 – www.bullwsg.com
5 rm ⊡ – †£ 65/100 ††£ 110/130
Rest – Carte £ 25/34
♦ Smart, modern, olive green pub with neutrally hued interior. Menus change daily and sometimes between services. Produce is sourced from their farm and within the county. Refined dishes use interesting ingredients and unusual cuts. Smart, stylish bedrooms.

WINCHCOMBE – Gloucestershire – **503** O28 – pop. 3 682   **4** D1

▶ London 100 mi – Birmingham 43 mi – Gloucester 26 mi – Oxford 43 mi
ℹ️ High St ✆ (01242) 60 29 25, www.winchcombewelcomeswalkers.com

⌂ Westward without rest
Sudeley Lodge, East : 1.5 mi by Castle St on Sudeley Lodge rd ⊠ GL54 5JB
– ✆ (01242) 604 372 – www.westward-sudeley.co.uk – Closed December-January
3 rm ☐ – †£ 65/95 ††£ 100/110

◆ Secluded, personally run, 18C former hunting lodge to nearby Studeley Castle. Elegant wood-floored drawing room and charming sitting room; bedrooms share fine views of the 550 acre estate and mature gardens.

XX 5 North St (Marcus Ashenford)
5 North St ⊠ GL54 5LH – ✆ (01242) 604 566
– www.5northstreetrestaurant.co.uk – Closed 2 weeks January, 1 week August, Monday, Tuesday lunch and Sunday dinner
Rest – Menu £ 26/48

Spec. Lobster and crab terrine with shellfish dressing. Belly pork and roasted scallop, artichoke purée and sage jus. Presentation of British desserts

◆ Long-standing neighbourhood restaurant that's very personally run by a husband and wife team. Characterful low-beamed ceilings and burgundy walls create an intimate feel. Menus change with the seasons and feature British ingredients in tried-and-tested combinations. Dishes are precise, well-crafted and full of flavour.

XX Wesley House with rm
High St ⊠ GL54 5LJ – ✆ (01242) 602 366 – www.wesleyhouse.co.uk
5 rm ☐ – †£ 65 ††£ 75/110
Rest – *(closed Sunday dinner)* Menu £ 16/25 – Carte £ 24/46

◆ Hugely characterful part 15C house: dine amongst the beams or in the stylish glass-roofed extension. Tasty modern British cooking with original twists. Smilingly quaint rooms.

WINCHELSEA – East Sussex – **504** W31 – Great Britain   **9** C3

▶ London 64 mi – Brighton 46 mi – Folkestone 30 mi
◉ Town★ – St Thomas Church (effigies★)

⌂ Strand House
Tanyard's Ln., East : 0.25 mi on A 259 ⊠ TN36 4JT – ✆ (01797) 226 276
– www.thestrandhouse.co.uk
10 rm ☐ – †£ 95/140 ††£ 115/165
Rest – *(closed Monday and Tuesday)* Menu £ 30 **s**

◆ 14C and 15C half-timbered house of low beams and inglenook fireplaces: carefully tended rear garden shaded by tall trees, snug lounge; well-kept rooms in traditional style. Simple homecooking.

WINCHESTER – Hampshire – **503** P30 – pop. 44 144 – Great Britain   **6** B2

▶ London 72 mi – Bristol 76 mi – Oxford 52 mi – Southampton 12 mi
ℹ️ High Street ✆ (01962) 84 05 00, www.visitwinchester.co.uk
◉ City★★ - Cathedral★★★ **AC** B – Winchester College★ **AC** B **B** – Castle Great Hall★ B **D** – God Begot House★ B **A**
◉ St Cross Hospital★★ **AC** A

🏨 Hotel du Vin
14 Southgate St ⊠ SO23 9EF – ✆ (01962) 841 414 – www.hotelduvin.com
24 rm – †£ 125/165 ††£ 140/295, ☐ £ 14.50   B**i**
Rest *Bistro* – see restaurant listing

◆ Attractive Georgian house dating from 1715; the first ever Hotel du Vin. Shabby-chic lounge and characterful champagne bar. Split between the house and garden, stylish, minimalist bedrooms are well-equipped; some have baths in the room.

664

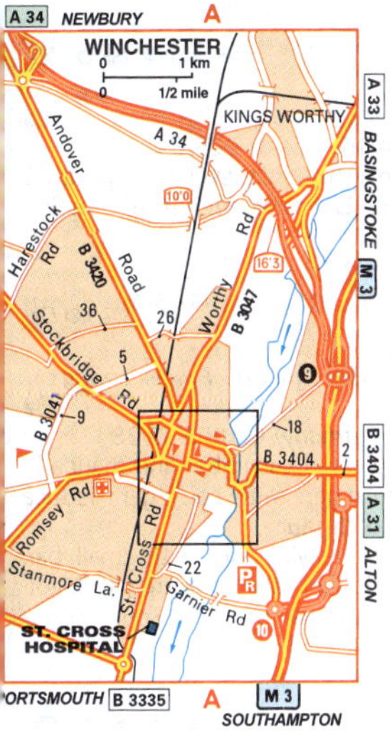

Street	Ref	Street	Ref	Street	Ref
Alresford Rd	A 2	Eastgate St	B 16	St George's St	B 32
Andover Rd	B 3	Easton Lane	A 18	St Paul's Hill	B 33
Bereweeke Rd	A 5	East Hill	B 15	St Peter's St	B 34
Bridge St	B 6	Friarsgate	B 19	Southgate St	B 35
Broadway (The)	B 7	High St	B	Stockbridge Rd	B 37
Brooks Shopping Centre	B 8	Kingsgate Rd	A 22	Stoney Lane	A 36
Chilbolton Ave	A 9	Magdalen Hill	B 23	Sussex St	B 38
City Rd	B 10	Middle Brook St	B 24	Union St	B 39
Clifton Terrace	B 12	Park Rd	A 26	Upper High St	B 40

 Giffard House without rest

50 Christchurch Rd ⊠ SO23 9SU – ℰ (01962) 852 628
– www.giffardhotel.co.uk – Closed 24 December-2 January
13 rm ⌑ – †£71/85 ††£91/128   B**s**

♦ Imposing red-brick house. Spacious, classically styled guest areas with comfy drawing room and formal breakfast room. Individually styled bedrooms boast quality furnishings and good facilities.

29 Christchurch Road without rest

29 Christchurch Rd. ⊠ SO23 9SU – ℰ (01962) 868 661
– www.fetherstondilke.com   B**v**
3 rm ⌑ – †£55/100 ††£85/100

♦ Modern, Regency style guesthouse in attractive residential area close to town. Comfortable lounge and communal, linen-laid breakfast room. Simple bedrooms with plain walls and floral drapes.

XX **Chesil Rectory**

Chesil St. ⊠ SO23 0HU – ℰ (01962) 851 555
– www.chesilrectory.co.uk – Closed 25-26 December and bank holidays except Good Friday   B**r**
Rest – Menu £20 (lunch and early dinner Monday-Friday) – Carte £28/33

♦ Timbered 15C house on edge of the town centre; its characterful interior taking in beamed ceilings and a large inglenook fireplace. Appealing menu of classically based dishes.

 A red **Rest** mention denotes an establishment with an award for culinary excellence, ✤ (star) or ⓐ (Bib Gourmand).

665

WINCHESTER

Brasserie Blanc
19-20 Jewry St ⊠ SO23 8RZ – ℰ *(01962) 810 870*
– www.brasserieblanc.com – Closed 25 December Bx
Rest – French – *(booking advisable)* Menu £ 14/16 – Carte £ 25/34
♦ Bustling informal brasserie in city centre. Spacious, split-level dining with 2 small terraces; open-plan kitchen on first-floor. Extensive menus of classical French dishes and local specials.

The Black Rat
88 Chesil St. ⊠ SO23 0HX – ℰ *(01962) 844 465*
– www.theblackrat.co.uk – Closed 2 weeks December-January, 1 week spring and 1 week autumn Ba
Rest – British – *(dinner only and lunch Saturday-Sunday)* Carte £ 32/38
Spec. Octopus carpaccio, wasabi whitebait, compressed cucumber and mandarin dressing. Lamb rump, tongue and shoulder boulangère with baby gem lettuce and peas. Honey baked madeleines and butterscotch sauce.
♦ Unassuming exterior conceals quirky, bohemian-style inner with small bar, lounge and two-roomed restaurant. Refined, classically based cooking with Mediterranean influences and modern twists; local, seasonal produce. Four wicker-roofed booths on rear terrace.

Bistro – at Hotel du Vin
14 Southgate St ⊠ SO23 9EF – ℰ *(01962) 841 414*
– www.hotelduvin.com Bi
Rest – *(booking essential)* Carte £ 28/42
♦ Characterful hotel bistro set within the original Hotel du Vin, in an attractive Georgian house dating from 1715. Wine-related pictures and memorabilia adorn the walls. French-inspired menu.

Wykeham Arms with rm
75 Kingsgate St ⊠ SO23 9PE – ℰ *(01962) 853 834*
– www.wykehamarmswinchester.co.uk Bu
14 rm – †£ 72/112 ††£ 145
Rest – *(booking essential)* Menu £ 15/21 – Carte £ 29/44
♦ Appealingly shabby, 18C red-brick inn tucked away on a cobbled street and packed with memorabilia. Dishes range from simple soups, pies and pastas to more elaborate lobster. Bedrooms have good facilities: those upstairs are characterful; those opposite, quieter.

at Sparsholt Northwest : 3.5 mi by B 3049 - **A** – ⊠ Winchester

Lainston House
Woodman Lane ⊠ SO21 2LT – ℰ *(01962) 776 088*
– www.exclusivehotels.co.uk
49 rm – †£ 150/245 ††£ 170/245, ⊇ £ 21 – 1 suite
Rest *Avenue* – see restaurant listing
♦ Impressive 17C William and Mary manor house with attractive gardens and a striking Avenue of lime trees in the grounds. Guest areas include a clubby, wood-panelled drawing room, a modern country house lounge and a small gym. Spacious bedrooms vary from classical to contemporary; all boast good facilities.

Avenue – at Lainston House Hotel
Woodman Lane ⊠ SO21 2LT – ℰ *(01962) 776 088*
– www.exclusivehotels.co.uk
Rest – Menu £ 33/55
♦ Hotel restaurant in an impressive 17C manor house, named after the striking Avenue of lime trees it overlooks. One traditional and one contemporary room. Modern menus include a tasting option.

WINDERMERE – Cumbria – 502 L20 – pop. 7 941 Great Britain 21 A2

▶ London 274 mi – Blackpool 55 mi – Carlisle 46 mi – Kendal 10 mi
🛈 Victoria St ☏ (015394) 4 64 99, www.golakes.co.uk
◉ Lake Windermere ★★ – Brockhole National Park Centre ★ **AC**,
NW : 2 mi by A 591

Plan on next page

Holbeck Ghyll
Holbeck Ln., Northwest : 3.25 mi by A 591 ⌧ LA23 1LU
– ☏ *(015394) 32 375*
– *www.holbeckghyll.com*
20 rm (dinner included) – ♦£ 263 ♦♦£ 301/450
– 3 suites
Rest – *(booking advisable at lunch)* Menu £ 30/60
Spec. Honey glazed pork belly with spiced carrot. Best end of lamb, confit peppers, aubergine and black olive gnocchi. Vanilla poached pineapple, coconut sorbet and banana beignets
♦ Victorian hunting lodge in mature grounds, boasting excellent lake/country views. Traditional guest areas display antiques and heavy fabrics. Similarly styled bedrooms, some in annexes, have good facilities. Two-roomed restaurant; one room with a view. Precise, confident, classical cooking employs quality local produce.

Miller Howe
Rayrigg Rd ⌧ LA23 1EY – ☏ (015394) 42 536 – www.millerhowe.com – Closed 2 weeks January **Ys**
13 rm (dinner included) – ♦£ 120/160 ♦♦£ 240
– 2 suites
Rest – *(booking essential)* Menu £ 25/45
– Carte £ 29/48
♦ Superbly situated Victorian villa in mature gardens, looking down the lake to the mountains. Spacious, comfortable bedrooms display a classical style and contemporary edge. Fabulous views from conservatory. Split-level dining room offers traditional cooking.

Windermere Suites *without rest*
New Rd ⌧ LA23 2LA – ☏ (01539) 444 739
– *www.windermeresuites.co.uk* **Yo**
7 rm – ♦♦£ 146/180 – 1 suite
♦ Spacious Victorian house with seductive interior. Luxurious bedrooms boast bold modern décor, designer furniture and walk-in wardrobes. Huge bathrooms feature TVs and colour-changing lights. Breakfast served in your room.

Cedar Manor
Ambleside Rd ⌧ LA23 1AX – ☏ (015394) 43 192 – www.cedarmanor.co.uk
– *Closed 3-23 January and 14-26 December* **Yi**
10 rm – ♦£ 100/120 ♦♦£ 160/180 – 1 suite
Rest – *(dinner only)* Menu £ 40
♦ Attractive slate house complete with cedar tree. Modern guest areas boast smart furnishings. Contemporary country house bedrooms display locally made furniture, feature walls and up-to-date facilities; some have lovely views. Appealing menus of local produce.

Howbeck *without rest*
New Rd ⌧ LA23 2LA – ☏ (015394) 44 739
– *www.howbeck.co.uk* **Yo**
11 rm – ♦♦£ 78/135
♦ Smart slate house 5min from town. Comfy leather-furnished lounge with honesty bar; black-themed breakfast room with interesting menu. Plain, modern décor in bedrooms; some feature four-posters.

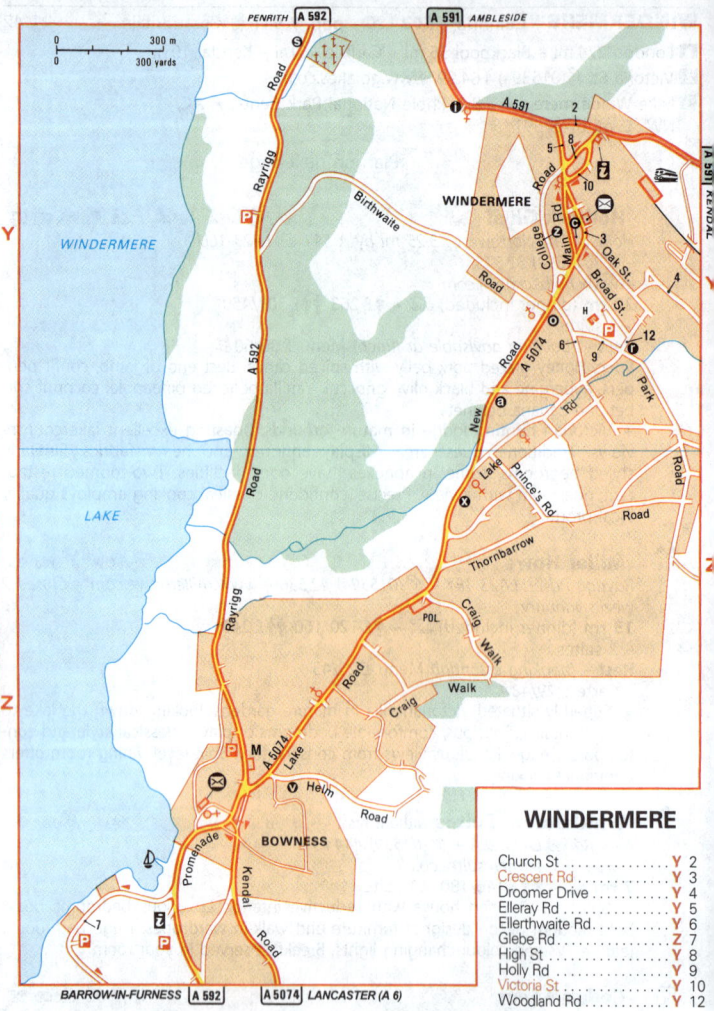

WINDERMERE

Church St	Y 2
Crescent Rd	Y 3
Droomer Drive	Y 4
Elleray Rd	Y 5
Ellerthwaite Rd	Y 6
Glebe Rd	Z 7
High St	Y 8
Holly Rd	Y 9
Victoria St	Y 10
Woodland Rd	Y 12

↑ **Newstead** without rest 〒 🕾 📶 P VISA ①③
New Rd ✉ *LA23 2EE –* 𝒞 *(015394) 44 485 – www.newstead-guesthouse.co.uk*
– Closed 1-28 December   Ya
9 rm ⊡ – †£ 60/85 ††£ 70/95
♦ Imposing Victorian house with spacious, classical interior; original features include servants' bells and ornate coving. Traditional bedrooms have sinks in the rooms; some boast four-posters.

↑ **Fir Trees** without rest 🚗 〒 🕾 📶 P VISA ①③ AE ①
Lake Rd ✉ *LA23 2EQ –* 𝒞 *(015394) 42 272 – www.fir-trees.co.uk*   Zx
9 rm ⊡ – †£ 55/60 ††£ 64/72
♦ Welcoming guesthouse boasting original Victorian staircase and lovely tile-floored hallway. Surprisingly spacious interior includes simple, comfy bedrooms and wood-furnished breakfast room.

WINDERMERE

1 Park Rd
1 Park Rd ⊠ LA23 2AW – ℰ (015394) 42 107 – www.1parkroad.com
6 rm ⊇ – †£ 56/64 ††£ 96/104 **Rest** – Menu £ 25   Yr

♦ Larger corner property in residential part of town; run by friendly owners. Comfy lounge complete with piano. Good-sized, homely bedrooms with modern facilities and locally made toiletries. Simple, linen-laid dining room serving home-cooked meals by arrangement.

Jerichos with rm
College Rd ⊠ LA23 1BX – ℰ (015394) 42 522 – www.jerichos.co.uk – Closed last 3 weeks January, last 2 weeks November, first week December, 24-26 December, 1 January and Thursday   Yz
10 rm ⊇ – †£ 40/85 ††£ 85/125 **Rest** – *(dinner only)* Carte £ 27/45

♦ Traditional Victorian house in town centre. Two-roomed restaurant with modern, understated styling. Concise, constantly evolving menus of ambitious dishes crafted from quality produce. Smart, contemporary bedrooms boast bold feature walls and good facilities.

Francine's
27 Main Rd ⊠ LA23 1DX – ℰ (015394) 44 088
– www.francinesrestaurantwindermere.co.uk – Closed last 2 weeks January, first week December, 25-26 December, 1 January, Monday and dinner Sunday and Tuesday   Yc
Rest – *(booking essential at dinner)* Menu £ 16/20 – Carte £ 19/30

♦ Intimate neighbourhood restaurant decorated in red and cream. Simple, homely feel and friendly service. Straightforward classical cooking has French influences; chef is passionate about game.

ENGLAND

at Bowness-on-Windermere South : 1 mi - Z - ⊠ Windermere

Gilpin H. & Lake House
Crook Rd, Southeast : 2.5 mi by A 5074 on B 5284
⊠ LA23 3NE – ℰ (015394) 88 818 – www.gilpinlodge.co.uk
26 rm (dinner included) ⊇ – †£ 200 ††£ 380/400
Rest – *(booking essential for non-residents)* Menu £ 30/58 – Carte £ 31/34

♦ Family-run, country house hotel in appealing rural location, with comfy lounge, retro bar and landscaped terrace. Individually themed bedrooms, most in contemporary styles: vast Garden Suites boast hot-tubs; Lake House Suites are the most peaceful and luxurious. Slick service. Four differently styled dining rooms, where classical cooking displays modern touches.

Linthwaite House
Crook Rd, South : 0.75 mi by A 5074 on B 5284 ⊠ LA23 3JA – ℰ (015394) 88 600
– www.linthwaite.com
31 rm (dinner included) ⊇ – †£ 172/204 ††£ 274/564
Rest – Menu £ 20/52

♦ Traditional country house in peaceful setting, overlooking the lake/fells. Stylish, modern lounges; funky bar with fish tank in wall. Smart bedrooms boast feature walls, mood lighting, double showers and views from the front. Contemporary, three-roomed restaurant.

Lindeth Howe
Lindeth Dr., Longtail Hill, South : 1.25 mi by A 5074 on B 5284 ⊠ LA23 3JF
– ℰ (015394) 45 759 – www.lindeth-howe.co.uk – Closed 3-12 January
33 rm ⊇ – †£ 95/160 ††£ 360 – 1 suite
Rest *The Dining Room* – Menu £ 18/43 – Carte dinner £ 32/44

♦ Attractive country house once owned by Beatrix Potter. Homely, clubby bar and lounge; pleasant views from drawing room. Traditional bedrooms – top floor boasts the best views; suites are more contemporary. Large, classically styled restaurant has menus to match.

WINDERMERE

Storrs Hall
LA23 3LG – ✆ (015394) 47 111 – www.englishlakes.co.uk
29 rm – †£ 129/149 ††£ 286 – 1 suite
Rest *The Terrace* – Menu £ 20/44 – Carte £ 42/57

• Part-Georgian mansion in 17 acres, with gardens leading to the lakeside. Variety of spacious, country house guest areas. Comfy, well-equipped bedrooms range from classical to bold, modern styles; some have lake views. Formal restaurant offers traditional menus.

Fayrer Garden House
Lyth Valley Rd, South : 1 mi on A 5074 – LA23 3JP – ✆ (015394) 88 195
– www.fayrergarden.com
28 rm (dinner included) – †£ 72/150 ††£ 144/300
Rest *The Terrace* – (dinner only) (booking essential for non-residents)
Menu £ 43

• Edwardian slate house on the hillside, affording lovely views over the lake and mountains. Comfy lounges with quality, cottagey furniture. Cosy, classical bedrooms with floral themes; some have whirlpool baths. Two-roomed restaurant offers traditional menus.

Angel Inn
Helm Rd – LA23 3BU – ✆ (015394) 44 080 – www.the-angelinn.com – Closed 24-25 December
13 rm – †£ 75/90 ††£ 170/180 **Rest** – Carte £ 21/33
Zv

• Cream-washed pub off the main street, boasting smart, contemporary bedrooms with iPod docks, flat screen TVs and modern bathrooms; the largest in an annexed 18C cottage. Large, semi-open-plan bar and wood-furnished, terraced garden offer classic pub-style dishes.

Fair Rigg without rest
Ferry View, South : 0.5 mi on A 5074 – LA23 3JB – ✆ (015394) 43 941
– www.fairrigg.co.uk – April to late December
6 rm – †£ 50/55 ††£ 72/90

• Late 19C detached house affording distant lake and hill views; run by friendly owners. Neat, linen-laid breakfast room. Immaculately kept bedrooms with quality furniture and good facilities.

Prices quoted after the symbol † refer to the lowest rate in low season followed by the highest rate in high season, for a single room.
The same principle applies to the symbol †† for a double room.

at Troutbeck North : 4 mi by A 592 - Y – ✉ Windermere

Queen's Head with rm
North : 0.75 mi on A 592 – LA23 1PW – ✆ (01539) 432 174
– www.queensheadtroutbeck.co.uk
15 rm – †£ 75 ††£ 150 **Rest** – Menu £ 20 – Carte £ 24/42

• Amazingly characterful, memorabilia-filled pub in delightful Lakeland setting, with several interlinking rooms and unique four-poster bar counter. Extensive menu offers something for everyone. Smart bedrooms with strong comforts; 10 and 11 have the best views.

at Winster South : 4 mi on A 5074 – ✉ Windermere

Brown Horse Inn with rm
on A 5074 – LA23 3NR – ✆ (01539) 443 443 – www.thebrownhorseinn.co.uk
9 rm – †£ 50/75 ††£ 65/100 **Rest** – Carte £ 22/33

• Shabby-chic coaching inn with lovely split-level terrace. Seasonal menus feature unfussy, generous dishes and more adventurous specials. Much of the produce is from their fields out the back. Bedrooms are a mix of classic and boutique styles; some have terraces.

WINDLESHAM – Surrey – **504** S29 – pop. 4 103   7 C1
▶ London 40 mi – Reading 18 mi – Southampton 53 mi

The Bee
School Rd ⊠ *GU20 6PD* – ℰ *(01276) 479 244* – *www.thebeepub.co.uk* – *Closed Sunday dinner*
Rest – Menu £ 16 (lunch) – Carte £ 26/38

♦ Stylish, modern pub with buzzing atmosphere. Daily changing menus showcase seasonal, local produce in precisely cooked dishes. Good value two course lunch. Summer barbecues.

Brickmakers
Chertsey Rd, East : 1 mi on B 386 ⊠ *GU20 6HT* – ℰ *(01276) 472 267* – *www.thebrickmakerswindlesham.co.uk*
Rest – Menu £ 24 – Carte £ 23/30

♦ Red-brick pub in pretty location; its immaculately kept garden is quite a feature in summer. Simple bar menu and more interesting à la carte; dishes are good value and full of flavour.

WINDSOR – Windsor and Maidenhead – **504** S29 – pop. 31 954   11 D3
🟩 Great Britain
▶ London 28 mi – Reading 19 mi – Southampton 59 mi
⛴ to Marlow, Maidenhead and Cookham (Salter Bros. Ltd) (summer only)
🛈 The Old Booking Hall, Central Station, Thames St ℰ *(01753) 74 39 00, www.windsor.gov.uk*
◉ Town★ – Castle★★★ : St George's Chapel★★★ **AC** (stalls★★★), State Apartments★★ **AC**, North Terrace (≤★★) Z – Eton College★★ **AC** (College Chapel★★, Wall paintings★) Z
◉ Windsor Park★ **AC** Y

ENGLAND

Plan on next page

Macdonald Windsor
23 High St. ⊠ *SL4 1LH* – ℰ *(0844) 879 91 01* – *www.macdonaldhotels.co.uk/windsor*   **Zr**
118 rm – †£ 195/245 ††£ 295/345, ⊐ £ 15.50 – 2 suites
Rest *Caleys* – Menu £ 20/25 – Carte £ 20/38

♦ Opened in 2010 in a former department store. Attractive open-plan guest areas in striking grey, cream and silver; small but state-of-the-art meeting rooms. Contemporary bedrooms with warm hues and high level of facilities. Modern brasserie with menus to match.

Sir Christopher Wren's House
Thames St ⊠ *SL4 1PX* – ℰ *(01753) 442 400* – *www.sirchristopherwren.co.uk*
94 rm ⊐ – †£ 100/235 ††£ 140/245 – 1 suite   **Ze**
Rest *Strok's* – see restaurant listing

♦ Built by Wren in 1676 as his family home, this characterful house sits on the riverbank by Windsor bridge. Traditional guest areas; smart gym. Bedrooms, some in annexes, range from classical to modern – some boast balconies and river views.

Royal Adelaide
46 Kings Rd ⊠ *SL4 2AG* – ℰ *(01753) 863 916* – *www.theroyaladelaide.com*
42 rm ⊐ – †£ 99/220 ††£ 145/220 **Rest** – Carte £ 20/40   **Zv**

♦ Three adjoining Georgian houses with light blue painted façade, built for Queen Adelaide. Bedooms vary in shape and size, and all are decorated in an individual, traditional style. Dining room offers international, brasserie-style menu.

Christopher
110 High St, Eton ⊠ *SL4 6AN* – ℰ *(01753) 852 359* – *www.thechristopher.co.uk*
34 rm – †£ 127/146 ††£ 186, ⊐ £ 12.50 **Rest** – Carte £ 22/31   **Za**

♦ 17C former coaching inn close to Eton College and perfect for walking to the castle. Contemporary bedrooms are split between main building and a mews annexe. International menus display North African influences.

WINDSOR

- Bexley St .... Z 2
- Bolton Rd .... Y 3
- Castle Hill .... Z 4
- Charles St .... Z 5
- Claremont Rd .... Z 6
- Clarence Crescent .. Z 7
- Clewer Crescent Rd . Z 8
- Datchet Rd .... Z 9
- Goswell Rd .... Z 10
- Grove Rd .... Z 12
- High St .... Z 13
- High St DATCHET ... Y 14
- Horton Rd .... Y 16
- Keats Lane .... Z 17
- King Edward Court Centre .... Z
- Peascod St .... Z 19
- Ragstone Rd .... Y 20
- River St .... Z 21
- Sheet St Rd .... Z 22
- Stovell Rd .... Z 23
- Thames Ave .... Z 24
- Thames St .... Z 25
- Trinity Pl .... Z 27
- Windsor Bridge ..... Z 28
- Windsor Rd .... Y 29

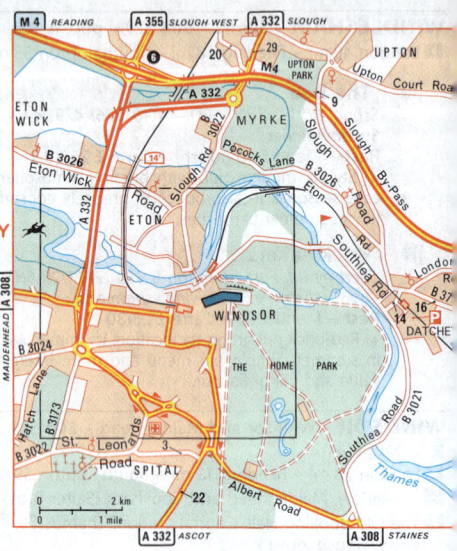

WINDSOR

XX Windsor Grill
65 St Leonards Rd ⊠ SL4 3BX – ℰ (01753) 859 658 – www.awtrestaurants.com
– Closed 25-26 December and Sunday   Zx
Rest – Beef specialities – *(dinner only)* Carte £ 32/46

♦ Rustic Victorian property owned by Antony Worrall Thompson. Wide menu displays classic comfort dishes, including well flavoured hung beef and pork/chicken from his farm.

XX Strok's – at Sir Christopher Wren's House Hotel
Thames St ⊠ SL4 1PX – ℰ (01753) 442 400 – www.sarova.com   Ze
Rest – Menu £ 28 **s** – Carte £ 30/46 **s**

♦ Classical hotel restaurant in a characterful 17C house, built by Wren as his family home. Wood-furnished terrace and lovely Thames views. Accessible menu displays international influences.

🏠 Greene Oak
Oakley Grn, West : 3 mi by A 308 on B 3024 ⊠ SL4 5UW – ℰ (01753) 864 294
– www.thegreeneoak.co.uk – Closed Sunday dinner
Rest – *(booking advisable)* Menu £ 15 (lunch except Friday and Sunday)
– Carte £ 25/36

♦ Set on the west side of Windsor, with appealing green-hued décor and contemporary soft furnishings. Seasonal menu of tasty European dishes. Popular terrace for alfresco dining.

WINEHAM – West Sussex – **504** T31 – see Henfield

WINFORTON – Herefordshire – **503** L27 – see Hereford

WINSFORD – Somerset – **503** J30 – pop. 270 – ⊠ Minehead   **3** A2

▶ London 194 mi – Exeter 31 mi – Minehead 10 mi – Taunton 32 mi
◉ Village ★
◉ Exmoor National Park ★★

🏠 Royal Oak Inn with rm
Exmoor National Park ⊠ TA24 7JE – ℰ (01643) 851 455
– www.royaloakexmoor.co.uk
8 rm ⊇ – †£ 55 ††£ 100/120
Rest – Carte £ 20/27

♦ Delightful 12C thatched pub set by a ford in a picturesque Exmoor village. Arriving exactly as described, British dishes use homemade, local and seasonal produce. Smart, individually styled bedrooms; private in-room therapy treatments available.

WINSTER – Cumbria – **502** L20 – see Windermere

WINSTON – Durham   **24** A3

▶ London 252 mi – Leeds 71 mi

🏠 Bridgewater Arms
⊠ DL2 3RN – ℰ (01325) 730 302 – www.thebridgewaterarms.com
– Closed 25-26 December, Sunday and Monday
Rest – Carte £ 22/36

♦ Originally located by the bridge but moved into the old school in the 1950s; look for the copperplate alphabet and old school programme. Seafood is the highlight here, from Dover Sole to langoustines, but the steaks are also good.

WINTERBOURNE STEEPLETON – Dorset – **503** M31 – see Dorchester

---

WINTERINGHAM – North Lincolnshire – **502** S22 – pop. 4 714   **23** C3
– ⊠ Scunthorpe

▶ London 176 mi – Kingston-upon-Hull 16 mi – Sheffield 67 mi

WINTERINGHAM

XXX Winteringham Fields with rm   P VISA ⦾ AE
1 Silver St ✉ DN15 9ND – ☏ (01724) 733 096 – www.winteringhamfields.co.uk
– Closed first week January and 25 December
10 rm – ♦£ 145 ♦♦£ 180/220, ⌸ £ 20 – 1 suite
Rest – *(closed Sunday-Monday) (booking essential for non-residents)*
Menu £ 40/75

♦ Characterful 16C house with pleasant garden, elegant dining room and several antique-filled private rooms. Self-taught chef adopts a complex, modern approach to cooking, offering a concise à la carte and daily 6 course 'Menu Surprise'. Comfortable, antique-furnished bedrooms, with breakfast in spacious rear dining room.

The symbol ☾ guarantees a good night's sleep. In red ☾ ? The very essence of peace: only the sound of birdsong in the early morning…

WISWELL – Lancashire – 502 M22 – see Clitheroe

WITHERSLACK – Cumbria – 502 L21   21 A3
▶ London 266 mi – Liverpool 83 mi – Manchester 78 mi

Derby Arms with rm   📶 📡 P VISA ⦾ ①
✉ LA11 6RH – ☏ (015395) 52 207 – www.thederbyarms.co.uk
6 rm – ♦£ 50/65 ♦♦£ 55/85
Rest – Menu £ 10 (lunch and early dinner)/16
– Carte £ 22/32

♦ Substantial 19C coaching inn with characterful shabby-chic interior, beams, open fires and a small community shop. Cooking is rustic yet refined and puddings are suitably old-fashioned. Classical bedrooms display antiques; some boast views or roll-top baths.

WIVETON – Norfolk – see Blakeney

WOBURN – 504 S28 – pop. 1 534 – ✉ Milton Keynes ▮ Great Britain   12 A2
▶ London 49 mi – Bedford 13 mi – Luton 13 mi
– Northampton 24 mi
👁 Woburn Abbey★★

Inn at Woburn   ♿ rm, AC rest, ※ 📡 ☆ P VISA ⦾ AE
George St ✉ MK17 9PX – ☏ (01525) 290 441 – www.woburn.co.uk/inn
51 rm – ♦£ 90/140 ♦♦£ 90/140, ⌸ £ 12.25 – 4 suites
Rest *Olivier's* – Menu £ 16 (lunch) – Carte dinner £ 26/36

♦ 18C coaching inn, part of Woburn Estate with its abbey and 3000 acre park. Pleasant modern furnishings and interior décor. Tastefully decorated rooms: book a Cottage suite. Classic dishes in contemporary Olivier's.

XXX Paris House   🚗 ♢ 🍴 ⇔ P VISA ⦾ AE
ॐ
Woburn Park, Southeast : 2.25 mi on A 4012 ✉ MK17 9QP – ☏ (01525) 290 692
– www.parishouse.co.uk – Closed dinner 24 December-7 January, Sunday dinner, Tuesday lunch and Monday
Rest – *(booking essential)* Menu £ 30/67
Spec. Confit sea trout, pickled cucumber, guacamole and wasabi mayonnaise. Rabbit saddle stuffed with chorizo and prawn, saffron braised rice and Gewürztraminer sauce. Jaffa orange soufflé, orange sponge and chocolate sorbet.

♦ Striking black and white timbered house, originally built in Paris and reassembled in this charming location, where deer wander freely. Classic dishes are given an imaginative modern makeover, with confident flavours and artistic presentation. Polished, unobtrusive service.

WOBURN

✕ **Birch**
20 Newport Rd, North : 0.5 mi on A 5130 ✉ *MK17 9HX*
– ✆ *(01525) 290 295* – *www.birchwoburn.com*
– *Closed 25-26 December, 1 January and Sunday dinner*
Rest – *(booking essential)* Carte £ 22/33

♦ Smart, well-run former pub, whose traditional façade masks a bright, modern interior with contemporary furnishings. Menu offers old favourites, daily specials and grills by the ounce.

WOKING – Surrey – **504** S30   **7** C1
▶ London 34 mi · Farnborough 14 mi – Guildford 7 mi

🍴 **Red Lion**
High St, Horsell, Northwest : 1.5 mi by A 324 ✉ *GU21 4SS*
– ✆ *(01483) 768 497* – *www.redlionhorsell.co.uk*
Rest – *(booking advisable)* Carte £ 23/36

♦ A modern take on the traditional pub, with all-day dining, plenty of outside seating and occasional live music. Traditional pub food, with sharing plates and fish dishes the highlights.

WOLD NEWTON – East Riding of Yorkshire   **23** D2
▶ London 229 mi – Bridlington 25 mi – Scarborough 13 mi

ENGLAND

🏠 **Wold Cottage**
South : 0.5 mi on Thwing rd ✉ *YO25 3HL*
– ✆ *(01262) 470 696* – *www.woldcottage.com*
5 rm ⌑ – †£ 65/75 ††£ 110/150
Rest – Menu 25

♦ Fine Georgian house and extensive collection of outbuildings, at the centre of 300 acres of rolling farmland. Welcoming owner. Homely interior where personal items abound; snug lounge displays large oils. Sizeable bedrooms boast quality soft furnishings and antiques; the two in the courtyard are more simply furnished. Formal dining room offers hearty British dishes.

WOLVERCOTE – Oxfordshire – **504** Q28 – see Oxford

WOLVERHAMPTON – Staffordshire – **502** N26 – pop. 251 462   **19** C2
▶ London 132 mi – Birmingham 15 mi – Liverpool 89 mi – Shrewsbury 30 mi
ℹ 18 Queen Sq ✆ *(01902) 31 20 51, www.wolverhampton.co.uk*

Plan of Enlarged Area : see Birmingham pp. 4 and 5

Plan on next page

✕✕ **Bilash**
No 2 Cheapside ✉ *WV1 1TU* – ✆ *(01902) 427 762*
– *www.thebilash@co.uk* – *Closed 25-26 December and Sunday*   B**c**
Rest – Indian – Menu £ 16/19
– Carte £ 28/55

♦ Long-standing, personally-run restaurant with several family generations involved. Appealing menu of freshly cooked Indian dishes and tempting specials. Strictly local and homemade produce.

WOOBURN COMMON – Bucks. – **504** S29 – see Beaconsfield

675

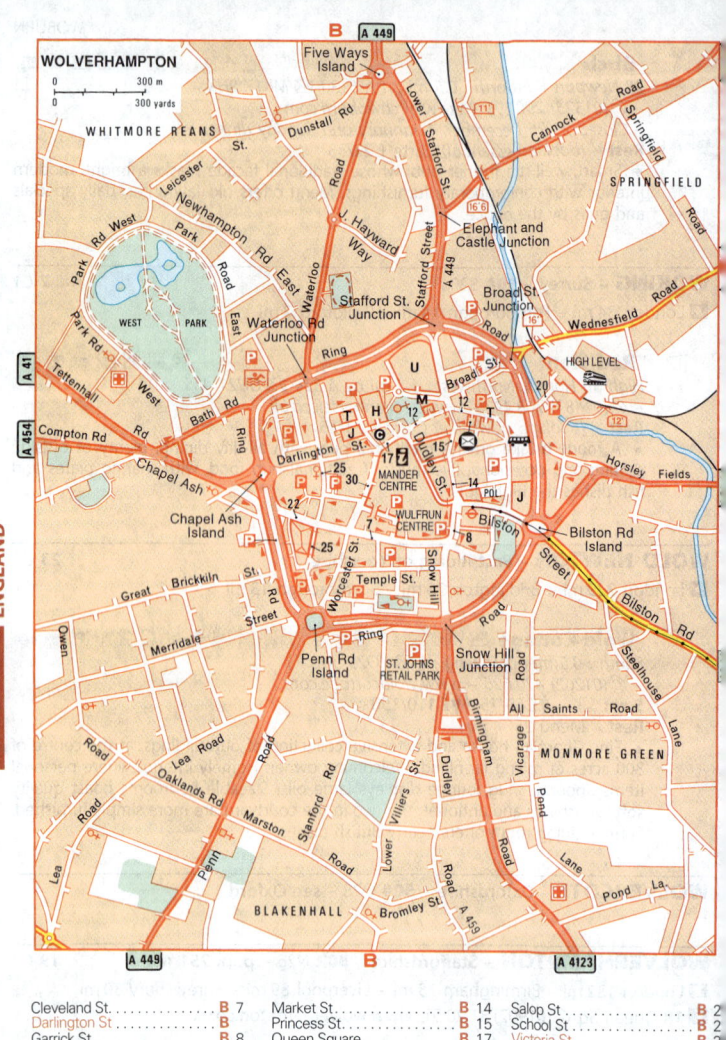

Cleveland St.	B 7	Market St.	B 14	Salop St.	B 2
Darlington St	B	Princess St.	B 15	School St.	B 2
Garrick St.	B 8	Queen Square	B 17	Victoria St.	B 3
Lichfield St.	B 12	Railway Drive	B 20	Wulfrun	
Mander Centre	B	St Johns Retail Park	B	Centre	B

WOODBRIDGE – Suffolk – 504 X27 – pop. 10 956 15 D3

▶ London 81 mi – Great Yarmouth 45 mi – Ipswich 8 mi – Norwich 47 mi

🏠 Cretingham Grove Farm, ☎ (01728) 68 52 75

🏠 Seckford Great Bealings Seckford Hall Rd, ☎ (01394) 38 80 00

WOODBRIDGE

Seckford Hall
Southwest : 1.25 mi by A 12 — IP13 6NU — ℰ (01394)
385 678 – www.seckford.co.uk – Closed 25 December
25 rm – †£ 85/150 ††£ 150/230, ⊇ £ 13.95 – 7 suites
Rest – (closed lunch Monday) Menu £ 17 (weekday lunch)/33 **s**
♦ Reputedly once visited by Elizabeth I, a part Tudor country house set in attractive gardens. Charming traditionally panelled public areas. Comfortable bedrooms. Local lobster proudly served in smart dining room.

Riverside
Quayside — IP12 1BH – ℰ (01394) 382 587 – www.theriverside.co.uk – Closed 25-26 December, 1 January and Sunday dinner
Rest – (booking essential) Menu £ 30 (dinner) – Carte £ 25/36
♦ Not just a restaurant, but a cinema too! Floor to ceiling windows and busy terrace. Appealing menus offer modern, well-presented cooking. Set menu includes ticket for film.

Crown with rm
Thoroughfare — IP12 1AD – ℰ (01394) 384 242
– www.thecrownatwoodbridge.co.uk
10 rm – †£ 110/180 ††£ 125/180 **Rest** – Menu £ 20 – Carte £ 24/32
♦ Modern dining pub in town centre, with smart granite-floored bar and four different dining areas. Extensive menu makes good use of local produce. Well presented, rustic cooking and polite, friendly service. Stylish, contemporary bedrooms boast good facilities.

at Bromeswell Northeast : 2.5 mi by B 1438 off A 1152 – ⊠

British Larder
Orford Rd, on A 1152 — IP12 2PU – ℰ (01394) 460 310
– www.britishlardersuffolk.co.uk – Closed Sunday dinner and Monday in winter except December
Rest – Carte £ 28/40
♦ Once down-at-heel, this 17C pub has been modernised in looks and transformed into a beacon for local Suffolk produce. Skilled cooking uses ingredients thoughtfully; wine events and cookery classes held regularly.

WOODHOUSE EAVES – Leicestershire – **503** Q25 – see Loughborough

WOODSTOCK – Oxfordshire – **503** P28 – pop. 2 389 ▌Great Britain   **10** B2

▶ London 65 mi – Gloucester 47 mi – Oxford 8 mi
▌Park St ℰ (01993) 81 32 76, www.woodstock-oxfordshire.co.uk
◉ Blenheim Palace★★★ (Park★★★) **AC**

Bear
Park St. — OX20 1SZ – ℰ (0844) 879 91 43 – www.macdonald-hotels.co.uk/bear
47 rm ⊇ – †£ 120 ††£ 120/250 – 7 suites
Rest – Menu £ 32
♦ Characterful part 16C inn. Original personality and charm; oak beams, open fires and stone walls. Particularly comfortable contemporarily furnished rooms. Dining room exudes an elegant air.

Feathers
Market St — OX20 1SX – ℰ (01993) 812 291 – www.feathers.co.uk
17 rm ⊇ – †£ 104/194 ††£ 229/459 – 4 suites
Rest – (booking essential) Carte £ 40/50
♦ Stylish 17C house boasting individually styled bedrooms with boutique twists: some have feature walls; others, modern art and bold fabrics. Bar-lounge and terrace offer casual menu. Formal dining room serves classically based dishes with a creative, original edge.

WOODSTOCK

Kings Arms
19 Market St. ✉ *OX20 1SU* – ✆ *(01993) 813 636*
– *www.kings-hotel-woodstock.co.uk*
15 rm – †£ 75 ††£ 140
Rest *Atrium* – Menu £ 25 (dinner) – Carte £ 22/29
♦ Keenly run, contemporary hotel in heart of a busy market town. Immaculately kept, with sleek bedrooms – named after Kings – displaying golden wood, starched linen and plump cushions. Informal bar-restaurant offers local, seasonal British dishes.

WOOFFERTON – Shropshire – 503 L26 – see Ludlow

WOOLACOMBE – Devon – 503 H30   2 C1

▶ London 237 mi – Barnstaple 15 mi – Exeter 55 mi

 Exmoor National Park★★ - Mortehoe★★ (St Mary's Church★, Morte Point - vantage point★) N : 0.5 mi – Ilfracombe : Hillsborough (≤★★) **AC**, Capstone Hill★ (≤★), St Nicholas' Chapel (≤★) **AC**, NE : 5.5 mi by B 3343 and A 361. Braunton★ (St Brannock's Church★, Braunton Burrows★), S : 8 mi by B 3343 and A 361

Cleeve House
North Morte Rd, Mortehoe, North : 0.5 mi ✉ *EX34 7ED* – ✆ *(01271) 870 719*
– *www.cleevehouse.co.uk* – *April-September*
6 rm – †£ 59/62 ††£ 90/94
Rest – *(closed 21 July-31 August and Wednesday) (dinner only)* Menu £ 29
– Carte £ 26/31
♦ Bright and welcoming feel in décor and atmosphere. Very comfortable lounge and individually styled bedrooms with co-ordinated fabrics. Rear rooms with great country views. Neat dining room; walls hung with local artwork.

WOOLER – Northumberland – 502 N17 – pop. 1 857   24 A1

▶ London 330 mi – Alnwick 17 mi – Berwick-on-Tweed 17 mi

Firwood *without rest*
Middleton Hall, South : 1.75 mi by Earle rd on Middleton Hall rd ✉ *NE71 6RD*
– ✆ *(01668) 283 699* – *www.firwoodhouse.co.uk* – *February-November*
3 rm – †£ 60 ††£ 90
♦ 19C former hunting lodge with beautiful original tiled hall, set in tranquil spot overlooking the Cheviots. Comfy bay-windowed guest areas great for sighting red squirrels/wild birds. Spacious bedrooms.

WOOLHOPE – Herefordshire   18 B3

▶ London 138 mi – Birmingham 70 mi

Butchers Arms
✉ *HR1 4RF* – ✆ *(01432) 860 281* – *www.butchersarmswoolhope.co.uk* – *Closed 25 December, Sunday dinner and Monday except bank holidays*
Rest – Menu £ 22 (Sunday lunch) – Carte £ 21/28
♦ Stephen Bull's third pub is an attractive, half-timbered 16C inn, with a pretty garden by a babbling brook and charming bars with low-slung beams and open fires. Daily changing menu of honest, well-priced, regional dishes; local lamb and cheese the highlights.

WOOLSTHORPE BY BELVOIR – Lincolnshire – 502 R25 – see Grantham

WOOTTON BRIDGE – 503 P31 – see WIGHT (Isle of)

WORCESTER – Worcestershire – 503 N27 – pop. 96 613

Great Britain

- London 124 mi – Birmingham 26 mi – Bristol 61 mi – Cardiff 74 mi
- High St ☎ (01905) 72 63 11, www.visitworcestershire.org
- Perdiswell Park Bilford Rd, ☎ (01905) 75 46 68
- City★ – Cathedral★★ – Royal Worcester Porcelain Works★ (Museum of Worcester Porcelain★) **M**
- The Elgar Trail★

Glasshouse

Sidbury ✉ WR1 2HU – ☎ (01905) 611 120 – www.theglasshouse.co.uk
– Closed 25-26 December, Sunday and bank holidays

Rest – Menu £ 20 (lunch)
– Carte £ 27/39

c

♦ Leather furnished lounge. Stylish chocolate and blue hued dining areas; the first floor has glass wall and views of city. Brasserie style menu offers modern British dishes.

Brown's

24 Quay St ✉ WR1 2JJ – ☎ (01905) 26 263 – www.brownsrestaurant.co.uk
Rest – Carte £ 23/33

x

♦ Converted riverside corn mill. Spacious, open interior as befits the building's origins. Impressive collection of modern artwork. Mainly British dishes are renowned locally.

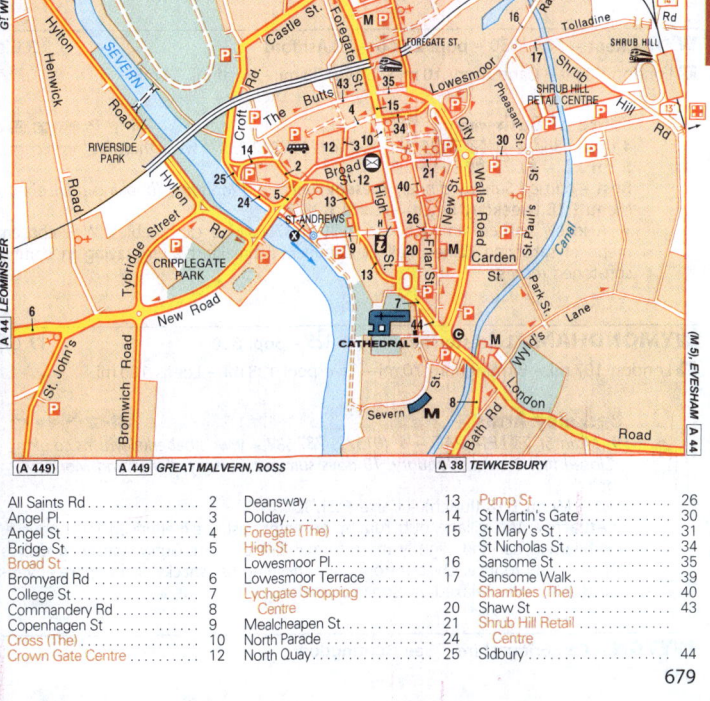

All Saints Rd 2	Deansway 13	Pump St 26
Angel Pl 3	Dolday 14	St Martin's Gate 30
Angel St 4	Foregate (The) 15	St Mary's St 31
Bridge St 5	High St	St Nicholas St 34
Broad St	Lowesmoor Pl 16	Sansome St 35
Bromyard Rd 6	Lowesmoor Terrace ... 17	Sansome Walk 39
College St 7	Lychgate Shopping	Shambles (The) 40
Commandery Rd 8	Centre 20	Shaw St 43
Copenhagen St 9	Mealcheapen St 21	Shrub Hill Retail
Cross (The) 10	North Parade 24	Centre
Crown Gate Centre 12	North Quay 25	Sidbury 44

WORCESTER

at Stonehall Common Southeast : 5.75 mi by A 38 and Norton rd.

Inn at Stonehall

✉ WR5 3QG – ℘ (01905) 820 462 – www.theinnatstonehall.com – Closed first week January, Sunday dinner and Monday
Rest – Carte £ 22/29

♦ Smart, modern dining pub in a peaceful hamlet, with comfy lounge, airy dining room and lovely views. Concise menus feature well-prepared, flavoursome, seasonal dishes; desserts a speciality.

WORFIELD – Shropshire – see Bridgnorth

WORKSOP – Nottinghamshire – **502** Q24 – pop. 39 072   **16** B1

▶ London 160 mi – Sheffield 20 mi – Nottingham 37 mi – Rotherham 17 mi

Browns without rest

The Old Orchard Cottage, Holbeck, Southwest : 4.5 mi by A 60 ✉ S80 3NF – ℘ (01909) 720 659 – www.brownsholbeck.co.uk – Closed 24-26 December
3 rm – †£ 59/68 ††£ 79/89

♦ Cosy, comfortable, individually-decorated bedrooms in cottage dating from 1730 and named after the owners. Mature orchard and tranquil garden. Comprehensive breakfast.

ENGLAND

WORTH – Kent – **504** Y30 – see Deal

WRIGHTINGTON BAR – Lancashire – **502** L23 – see Standish

WYE – Kent – **504** W30 – pop. 2 066 – ✉ Ashford   **9** C2

▶ London 60 mi – Canterbury 10 mi – Dover 28 mi – Hastings 34 mi

Wife of Bath with rm

4 Upper Bridge St ✉ TN25 5AF – ℘ (01233) 812 232 – www.thewifeofbath.com
5 rm – †£ 75 ††£ 115
Rest – (closed Sunday dinner, Tuesday lunch and Monday) (booking advisable) Menu £ 18 (weekday lunch) – Carte £ 28/35

♦ A lovely timber-framed house built in 1760. Fine cloth tables. Well chosen menu of satisfying dishes. Full or Continental breakfast after staying in comfy, soft-toned rooms.

WYMONDHAM – Leicestershire – **504** R25 – pop. 600   **17** C2

▶ London 107 mi – Birmingham 70 mi – Liverpool 138 mi – Leeds 100 mi

Berkeley Arms

59 Main St ✉ LE14 2AG – ℘ (01572) 787 587 – www.theberkeleyarms.co.uk – Closed first 2 weeks January, 10 days summer, Sunday dinner and Monday lunch
Rest – Menu £ 18 (lunch) – Carte £ 21/32

♦ Attractive 16C village pub run by an enthusiastic, experienced local couple. Low-beamed bar and slightly more formal dining room. Gutsy, satisfying dishes rely on local produce. Choose from daily changing bar snacks or the more adventurous à la carte. Relaxed, personable service.

WYTON – Cambridgeshire – See Huntingdon

YARM – Stockton-on-Tees – **502** P20 – pop. 8 929   **24** B3

▶ London 242 mi – Middlesbrough 8 mi – Newcastle upon Tyne 47 mi

Judges Country House
Kirklevington Hall, Kirklevington, South : 1.5 mi on A 67 – ⊠ TS15 9LW
– ℰ (01642) 789 000 – www.judgeshotel.co.uk
21 rm – †£ 90/180 ††£ 130/210, ⊇ £ 15
Rest – Menu £ 28 (lunch) – Carte £ 49/68

♦ Former Victorian judge's residence surrounded by gardens. Welcoming panelled bar and spacious lounge filled with antiques and curios. Attractive rooms with a host of extras. Conservatory dining room overlooks the gardens.

YARMOUTH – Isle of Wight – **503** P31 – see Wight (Isle of)

YATTENDON – West Berkshire – **503** Q29 – pop. 288 – ⊠ Newbury   **10** B3

▶ London 61 mi – Oxford 23 mi – Reading 12 mi

Royal Oak with rm
The Square ⊠ RG18 0UF – ℰ (01635) 201 325 – www.royaloakyattendon.com
5 rm ⊇ – †£ 85 ††£ 85
Rest – *(booking advisable)* Menu £ 15 (lunch) – Carte £ 27/34

♦ Eye-catching red-brick pub with attractive gardens, in picture postcard village close to the M4; a beamed bar with roaring fire at its hub. Honest British dishes and traditional puddings; Sunday roast of 28-day aged rib of beef. Comfy bedrooms in country house style.

at Frilsham South : 1 mi by Frilsham rd on Bucklebury rd – ⊠ Yattendon

Pot Kiln
⊠ RG18 0XX – ℰ (01635) 201 366 – www.potkiln.org – Closed 25 December and Tuesday
Rest – Menu £ 16 (weekday lunch) – Carte £ 28/33

♦ Pleasant pub in prime game country. Flavoursome British dishes arrive in unashamedly gutsy portions. Chef-owner stalks or gathers much of the produce himself. Fish is from Looe or local rivers.

YEOVIL – Somerset – **503** M31 – pop. 41 871   **3** B3

▶ London 136 mi – Exeter 48 mi – Southampton 72 mi – Taunton 26 mi
🛈 Hendford ℰ (01935) 84 59 46, www.yeoviltown.com
Sherborne Rd, ℰ (01935) 42 29 65
◉ St John the Baptist★
Monacute House★★ **AC**, W : 4 mi on A 3088 – Fleet Air Arm Museum, Yeovilton★★ **AC**, NW : 5 mi by A 37 – Tintinhull House Garden★ **AC**, NW: 5.5 mi – Ham Hill (≤★★) W : 5.5 mi by A 3088 – Stoke sub Hamdon (parish church★) W : 5.25 mi by A 3088. Muchelney★★ (parish church★★) NW : 14 mi by A 3088, A 303 and B 3165 – Lytes Cary★, N : 7.5 mi by A 37, B 3151 and A 372 – Sandford Orcas Manor House★, NW : 8 mi by A 359 – Cadbury Castle (≤★★) NE : 10.5 mi by A 359 – East Lambrook Manor★ **AC**, W : 12 mi by A 3088 and A 303

Lanes
West Coker, Southwest : 3 mi on A 30 ⊠ BA22 9AJ – ℰ (01935) 862 555
– www.laneshotel.net
29 rm ⊇ – †£ 90 ††£ 130   **Rest** – Menu £ 17 (lunch) – Carte £ 19/30

♦ 18C former rectory in pleasant walled grounds. Airy interior boasts modern meeting rooms, laid-back lounge and large bar. Relax in smart leisure suite or on croquet lawn. Stylish bedrooms with up-to-date bathrooms. Modern bistro dishes in striking dining room.

YEOVIL

at Barwick South : 2 mi by A 30 off A 37 – ⊠ Yeovil

XX **Little Barwick House** with rm
⊠ BA22 9TD – ℰ (01935) 423 902 – www.littlebarwickhouse.co.uk – Closed 3 weeks Christmas, 1 week August, Sunday dinner, Monday and lunch Tuesday
6 rm – †£ 85/100 ††£ 230/260
Rest – (booking essential) Menu £ 28/44
♦ Charming Georgian dower house in a secluded spot, run by a delightful and hospitable couple. The cooking is robust, gutsy and visually bold but without gimmicks. Comfortable, stylish and immaculately kept bedrooms.

YORK – York – **502** Q22 – pop. 198 900 ▮ Great Britain   23 C2
▶ London 203 mi – Kingston-upon-Hull 38 mi – Leeds 26 mi – Middlesbrough 51 mi
▮ Museum St ℰ (01904) 55 00 99, www.visityork.org
▮ Strensall Lords Moor Lane, ℰ (01904) 49 18 40
▮ Heworth Muncastergate Muncaster House, ℰ (01904) 42 46 18
◉ City★★★ – Minster★★★ (Stained Glass★★★, Chapter House★★, Choir Screen★★) CDY – National Railway Museum★★★ CY – The Walls★★ CDXYZ – Castle Museum★ AC DZ M2 – Jorvik Viking Centre★ AC DY M1 – Fairfax House★ AC DY A – The Shambles★ DY 54

Cedar Court Grand H. & Spa
Station Rise ⊠ YO1 6HT – ℰ (01904) 380 038
– www.cedarcourtgrand.co.uk   CYv
94 rm – †£ 125/295 ††£ 125/295, ⊇ £ 20 – 13 suites
Rest *HQ* – ℰ (01904) 655 554 – Menu £ 25 (lunch) – Carte £ 35/48
♦ Early 20C building – the former offices of the North Eastern Railway Co. – where original features blend with contemporary décor. Impressive spa and leisure facilities in cellar. Spacious bedrooms. Modern menu served in HQ, with views of the castle walls.

Middlethorpe Hall
Bishopthorpe Rd, South : 1.75 mi ⊠ YO23 2GB – ℰ (01904) 641 241
– www.middlethorpe.com
20 rm – †£ 99/189 ††£ 199/269, ⊇ £ 7 – 9 suites
Rest – (booking essential for non-residents) Menu £ 24 (lunch) **s**
– Carte £ 35/54 **s**
♦ Impressive William and Mary country house dating from 1699. Elegantly and carefully restored; abundantly furnished with antiques. Most characterful rooms in main house. Wood-panelled, three-roomed restaurant with period feel.

Grange
1 Clifton ⊠ YO30 6AA – ℰ (01904) 644 744 – www.grangehotel.co.uk
35 rm ⊇ – †£ 123/180 ††£ 168/208 – 1 suite   CXu
Rest *Ivy Brasserie* – see restaurant listing
Rest *New York Grill* – (closed Sunday lunch) Carte £ 26/38
♦ Well-run, classical Grade II listed hotel: floral decorations (by the owner) and horse racing memorabilia abound. Choose between traditionally styled bedrooms – some with four-posters – or more contemporary rooms with TVs in the bathrooms. Modern brasserie or informal grill with classical American à la carte.

Hotel du Vin
89 The Mount ⊠ YO24 1AX – ℰ (01904) 557 350 – www.hotelduvin.com
44 rm – †£ 210 ††£ 210, ⊇ £ 14.50   CZa
Rest *Bistro* – see restaurant listing
♦ Georgian house close to Knavesmire racecourse and just outside of city centre. As part of a 'wine-orientated' group, the contemporary bedrooms boast smart, wine-coloured themes.

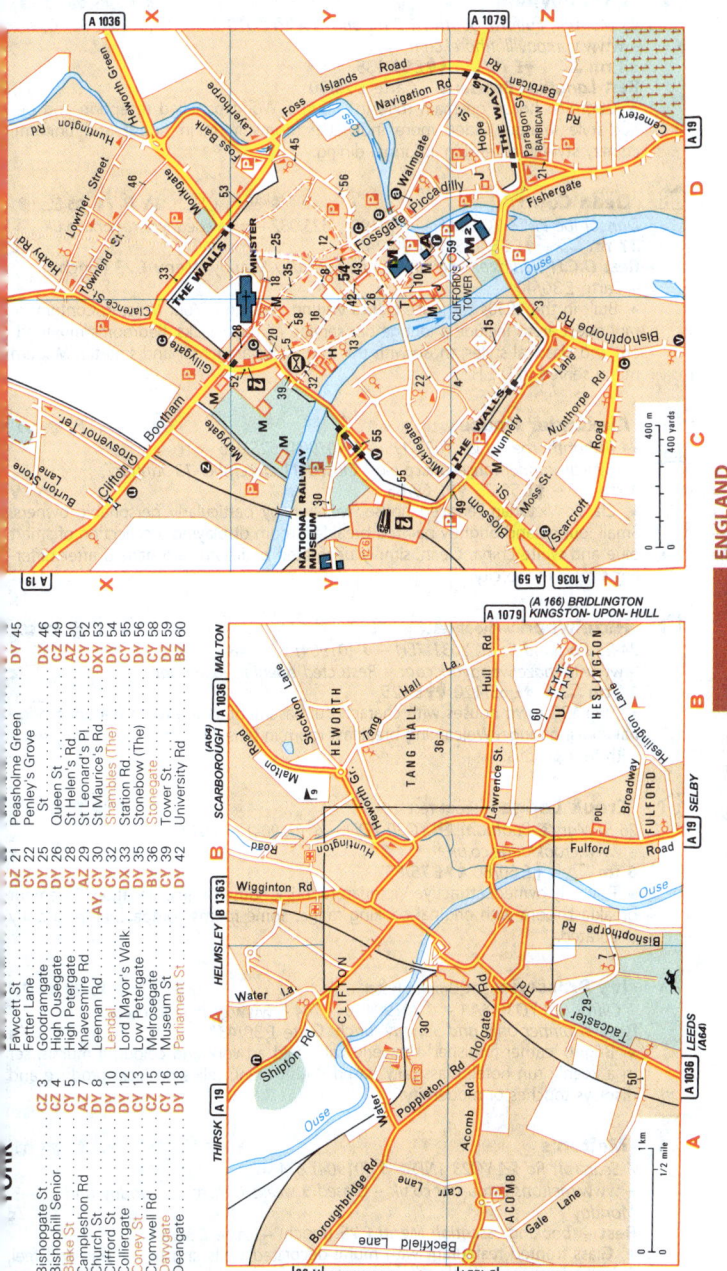

YORK

York Pavilion
45 Main St, Fulford, South : 1.5 mi on A 19 ✉ *YO10 4PJ* – ℰ *(01904) 622 099*
– *www.yorkpavilionhotel.com*
63 rm – †£79/135 ††£99/135
Rest *Langtons Brasserie* – Carte £24/30

♦ Georgian house on main road in suburbs. Wood panelled reception and period-style lounge. Older, more individual rooms in main house and uniform, chintzy style in extension. Informal dining.

Dean Court
Duncombe Pl ✉ *YO1 7EF* – ℰ *(01904) 625 082* – *www.deancourt-york.co.uk*
37 rm – †£75/145 ††£99/240   CYc
Rest *D.C.H* – *(dinner only and lunch Saturday-Sunday)* Menu £23 (lunch)
– Carte £30/40

♦ Built in the 1950s to house clerics visiting next door York Minster. Contemporary guest areas include a lounge-bar serving all day snacks. Bedrooms mix modern and classical styles; those with the best views are larger and smarter. Modern menu served in D.C.H.

Alexander House without rest
94 Bishopthorpe Rd ✉ *YO23 1JS* – ℰ *(01904) 625 016*
– *www.alexanderhouseyork.co.uk* – *Closed 11 December-13 January*
4 rm – †£59/75 ††£69/85   CZv

♦ Classic Victorian terraced house, well run by particularly personable owners. Small lounge and brightly painted breakfast room displaying a collection of smart blue and white china. Clean, simply decorated bedrooms are named after different streets in the city.

Hazelwood without rest
24-25 Portland St ✉ *Y031 7EH* – ℰ *(01904) 626 548*
– *www.thehazelwoodyork.com* – *Restricted opening in January*   CXc
14 rm – †£65/120 ††£125

♦ Two 19C town houses with characterful basement sitting room featuring original cooking range. Welcoming breakfast room in blue. Individual bedrooms, some with four posters.

Crook Lodge without rest
26 St Mary's, Bootham ✉ *YO30 7DD* – ℰ *(01904) 655 614*
– *www.crooklodge.co.uk*   CXz
6 rm – †£60/80 ††£75/85

♦ Privately owned, attractive Victorian redbrick house in quiet location. Basement breakfast room with original cooking range. Some rooms compact, all pleasantly decorated.

Ivy Brasserie – at Grange Hotel
1 Clifton ✉ *YO30 6AA* – ℰ *(01904) 644 744* – *www.grangehotel.co.uk*
Rest – *(dinner only and Sunday lunch)* Carte £30/43   CXu

♦ Bright, leather-furnished brasserie with bold artwork and colourful murals, set in a keenly run hotel. Classically based British menu relies on local produce and displays touches of modernity.

Melton's
7 Scarcroft Rd ✉ *YO23 1ND* – ℰ *(01904) 634 341*
– *www.meltonsrestaurant.co.uk* – *Closed 3 weeks Christmas, Sunday and Monday*   CZc
Rest – *(booking essential)* Menu £25 (lunch) – Carte £30/35

♦ Glass fronted restaurant with mural decorated walls and neighbourhood feel. Smart, crisp tone in both service and table cover. Good modern British food with some originality.

YORK

J. Baker's
7 Fossgate ✉ YO1 9TA – ℰ (01904) 622 688 – www.jbakers.co.uk
– Closed first week January, Sunday and Monday
Rest – Menu £ 12/30 – Carte lunch £ 20/40

DYc

♦ Lively, double-fronted bistro on cobbled street, with simple, up-to-date interior. Interesting modern dishes on the à la carte and grazing menus. Chocolate dessert menu also served in the bar.

Bistro – at Hotel du Vin
89 The Mount ✉ YO24 1AX – ℰ (01904) 567 350 – www.hotelduvin.com
Rest – French – Carte £ 27/41

CZa

♦ Typical bustling Bistro offering modern French dishes as well as all the old favourites. Set in Hotel du Vin, it offers a good selection of wines by the glass.

Blue Bicycle with rm
34 Fossgate ✉ YO1 9TA – ℰ (01904) 673 990 – www.thebluebicycle.com
– Closed 1-8 January, 24-26 December and lunch 27 and 31 December
6 rm – †£ 175 ††£ 175

DYe

Rest – (dinner only and lunch Thursday-Sunday and December) (booking essential) Carte £ 31/48

♦ Split-level restaurant with Mediterranean-style dining room and cosy bar. Menus offer modern classics: some simple, some more elaborate in style. Smart, studio style bedrooms in rear mews, each with a kitchen; create your own breakfast from ingredients provided.

31 Castlegate
31 Castlegate ✉ YO1 9RN – ℰ (01904) 621 404 – www.31castlegate.co.uk
– Closed 25-26 December, 1 January and Monday
Rest – Menu £ 16 – Carte £ 27/31

DYr

♦ Former Georgian architect's house boasting original fireplaces and plasterwork. Café atmosphere by day; more intimate restaurant by night. Classical cooking is presented in a modern manner.

Melton's Too
25 Walmgate ✉ YO1 9TX – ℰ (01904) 629 222 – www.meltonstoo.co.uk
– Closed dinner 24 December-26 December and dinner 31 December-2 January
Rest – Carte £ 20/24

DYa

♦ Café-bistro 'descendant' of Melton's restaurant. Located in former saddlers shop with oak beams and exposed brick walls. Good value eclectic dishes, with tapas a speciality.

at Newton-on-Ouse Northwest : 8 mi by A 19

Dawnay Arms
✉ YO30 2BR – ℰ (01347) 848 345 – www.thedawnayatnewton.co.uk
– Closed 1 January, Sunday dinner and Monday except bank holidays
Rest – Menu £ 15 (lunch) – Carte £ 23/34

♦ Spacious 18C inn boasting handsome rustic style, with beamed ceilings and roaring fires. Tasty, good value dishes on seasonal menus. Dining room looks out over River Ouse.

ZENNOR – Cornwall – 503 D33

1 A3

▶ London 305 mi – Penzance 11 mi – St Ives 5 mi

Gurnard's Head with rm
Treen, West : 1.5 mi on B 3306 ✉ TR26 3DE – ℰ (01736) 796 928
– www.gurnardshead.co.uk – Closed 24 and 25 December
7 rm – †£ 70/85 ††£ 90/110
Rest – Menu £ 17 (lunch) – Carte £ 25/29

♦ Remotely located and dog-friendly, with stone floors, shabby-chic décor, blazing fires and a relaxed, cosy feel. Simple menu relies on regional produce. Traditional puddings; interesting wine list. Comfy beds feature good quality linen; communal breakfasts.

685

ABERDEEN – Aberdeen City – 501 N12 – pop. 184 788 ▐ Scotland   28 D1

▶ Edinburgh 130 mi – Dundee 67 mi
✈ Aberdeen Airport, Dyce : ✆ (0844) 481 6666, NW : 7 mi by A 96 X
⛴ to Shetland Islands (Lerwick) and via Orkney Islands (Stromness) (P and O Scottish Ferries) 1-2 daily
🛈 23 Union St ✆ (01224) 28 88 28, www.aberdeen-grampian.com
🏌 Hazelhead Hazelhead Park, ✆ (01224) 32 18 30
🏌 Royal Aberdeen Bridge of Don Links Rd, ✆ (01224) 70 25 71
🏌 Balnagask St Fitticks Rd, ✆ (01224) 87 12 86
🏌 King's Links Golf Rd, ✆ (01224) 63 22 69
🏌 Portlethen Badentoy Rd, ✆ (01224) 78 10 90
🏌 Murcar Links Bridge of Don, ✆ (01224) 70 43 54
🏌 Auchmill West Heatheryfold Bonnyview Rd, ✆ (01224) 71 52 14

◉ City★★ - Old Aberdeen★★ X – St Machar's Cathedral★★ (West Front★★★, Heraldic Ceiling★★★) X **A** – Art Gallery★★ (Macdonald Collection★★) Y **M** – Mercat Cross★★ Y **B** – King's College Chapel★ (Crown Spire★★★, medieval fittings★★★) X **D** – Provost Skene's House★ (painted ceilings★★) Y **E** – Maritime Museum★ Z **M1** – Marischal College★ Y **U**

◉ Brig o' Balgownie★, by Don St X. SW : Deeside★★ - Crathes Castle★★ (Gardens★★★) **AC**, SW : 16 mi by A 93 X – Dunnottar Castle★★ **AC** (site★★★), S : 18 mi by A 90 X – Pitmedden Garden★★, N : 14 mi by A 90 on B 999 X – Castle Fraser★ (exterior★★) **AC**, W : 16 mi by A 944 X – Fyvie Castle★, NW : 26.5 mi on A 947

Marcliffe H. and Spa
North Deeside Rd ⊠ *AB15 9YA* – ✆ *(01224) 861 000* – *www.marcliffe.com*
40 rm ⊇ – ♦£ 165/229 ♦♦£ 185/249 – 2 suites   X**r**
Rest *Conservatory* – see restaurant listing
♦ Spacious, professionally run, modern country house; popular with business travellers. Eleven acres of pleasant grounds. Individually decorated rooms with antique furniture. Small spa and hairdressing salon.

Malmaison
49-53 Queens Rd ⊠ *AB15 4YP* – ✆ *(01224) 327 370* – *www.malmaison.com*
79 rm – ♦£ 195 ♦♦£ 215, ⊇ £ 14.50   X**v**
Rest *Brasserie* – see restaurant listing
♦ Located in a smart city suburb and built around a period property; now the height of urban chic. Black slate floored reception adorned with bagpipes and kilts; stylish bar with whisky cellar. Luxurious tartan bedrooms boast smart bathrooms.

bauhaus
52-60 Langstane Pl. ⊠ *AB11 6EN* – ✆ *(01224) 212 122* – *www.thebauhaus.co.uk*
38 rm ⊇ – ♦£ 90/115 ♦♦£ 70/115 – 1 suite   Z**r**
Rest – Menu £ 28 – Carte £ 20/38
♦ Modern hotel just off the main street; its functional, minimalist style in keeping with the Bauhaus school of design. Trendy lounge. Stylish, colour-coded bedrooms with sharp, clean lines and uncluttered feel; Gropius and Kandinsky are the best. First-floor restaurant offers accessible menu of modern classics.

Atholl
54 King's Gate ⊠ *AB15 4YN* – ✆ *(01224) 323 505* – *www.atholl-aberdeen.com*
– Closed 1 January   X**s**
34 rm ⊇ – ♦£ 95/110 ♦♦£ 145   **Rest** – Carte £ 18/32
♦ Baronial style hotel set in leafy suburbs; well run by friendly staff. Traditional lounge bar; well-priced, up-to-date rooms. A useful address for visitors to the city. Dining room specialises in tried-and-tested Scottish cooking.

XXX Conservatory – at Marcliffe Hotel and Spa
North Deeside Rd ⊠ *AB15 9YA* – ✆ *(01224) 861 000* – *www.marcliffe.com*
Rest – Carte £ 37/50 **s**   X**r**
♦ Spacious conservatory dining room with large open kitchen. Good-sized classical menu offers hearty tasty dishes, including superbly flavoured steaks; king crab is a speciality. Warm service and a relaxing atmosphere.

Fusion ✕✕

10 North Silver St ✉ AB10 1RL – ✆ (01224) 652 959 – www.fusionbarbistro.com
– Closed 2 weeks January, 2 weeks July, 25 December, Sunday and Monday
Rest – (dinner only) Menu £ 28   Zc

♦ Very stylish, modernised townhouse with cavernous, stark white room, neatly laid tables and designer touches. Concise monthly menu offers creative modern dishes in well-presented, interesting combinations. The bar is the place to be seen.

Silver Darling ✕✕

Pocra Quay, North Pier ✉ AB11 5DQ – ✆ (01224) 576 229
– www.thesilverdarlingrestaurant.co.uk – Closed 2 weeks Christmas-New Year, Saturday lunch, Sunday dinner and Sunday lunch in winter   Xa
Rest – Seafood – Menu £ 22 (lunch) – Carte £ 33/50

♦ Former customs house attractively set at port entrance; panoramic views across harbour and coastline. Attentive service of superb quality seafood prepared in imaginative ways.

Brasserie – at Malmaison Hotel ✕✕

49-53 Queens Rd ✉ AB15 4YP – ✆ (01224) 327 370 – www.malmaison.com
Rest – Beef specialities – Menu £ 20 (early dinner Friday & Saturday)   Xv
– Carte £ 22/54

♦ Vast hotel brasserie with high ceiling, tartan and red leather banquettes and huge photos of foodstuffs on the walls. Accessible menu of classics; speciality steaks can be viewed in the meat room and are then cooked on the Josper grill.

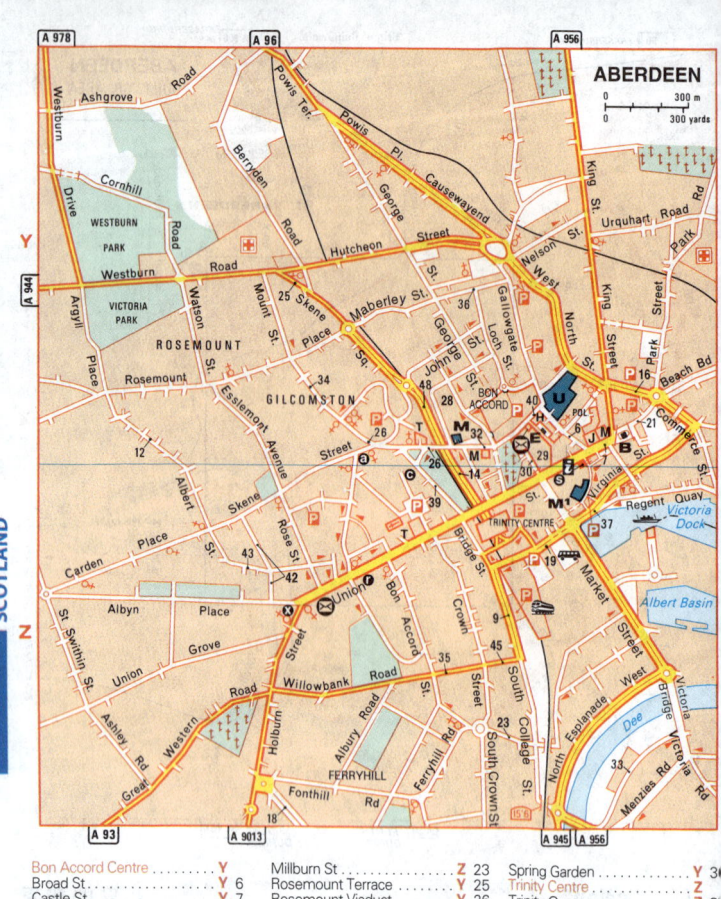

Bon Accord Centre ...... Y	Millburn St .... Z 23	Spring Garden .... Y 3
Broad St .... Y 6	Rosemount Terrace ...... Y 25	Trinity Centre .... Z
Castle St .... Y 7	Rosemount Viaduct ...... Y 26	Trinity Quay .... Z 3
College St. .... Z 9	St Andrew St .... Y 28	Union St. .... Z
Craigie Loanings .... Y 12	St Nicholas Centre .... Y 29	Union Terrace............ Y 3
Denburn Rd. .... YZ 14	St Nicholas St. .... YZ 30	Upperkirkgate .... Y 4
East North St............ Y 16	School Hill .... YZ 32	Victoria St............... Z 4
George St .... Y	South Esplanade	Waverley Pl. .... Z 4
Great Southern Rd .... Y 18	West. .... Z 33	Wellington
Guild St. .... Z 19	South Mount St........... Y 34	Pl. .... Z 4
Justice St .... Y 21	Springbank Terrace .... Z 35	Woolmanhill. .... Y 4

Courtyard

1 Alford Pl — AB10 1YD — ℰ (01224) 589 109 — www.thecourtyardaberdeen.co.uk
– Closed first week January and Sunday
Rest – Menu £ 16/37
♦ Contemporary restaurant with modern bar, linen-clad tables and efficient service. Menus feature up-to-date classics: lunch offers simple dishes and a set menu; dinner is more elaborate and includes a blackboard of local seafood specials.

Stella

28 Adelphi — AB11 5BL — ℰ (01224) 211 414 — www.lastella.co.uk – Closed Sunday
Rest – Menu £ 16/37
♦ Snug bistro hidden away down a side street, with simple, bright décor and a neighbourhood feel. Seasonally changing menus focus on quality ingredients, with fish a speciality.

ABERDEEN

XX Nargile

77-79 Skene St ⊠ AB10 1QD – ℰ (01224) 636 093 – closed 25-26 December, 1 January, Monday lunch and Sunday
Rest – Turkish – Menu £ 25 – Carte £ 20/34

Ya

♦ Traditionally decorated Turkish restaurant with subdued lighting from Turkish lamps. Open-plan kitchen allows the diner to watch the chefs prepare the authentic dishes.

X Rendezvous at Nargile

106-108 Forest Ave ⊠ AB15 4UP – ℰ (01224) 323 700
– www.rendezvousatnargile.co.uk – Closed 1-2 January and 25-26 December
Rest – Turkish – Menu £ 19 – Carte £ 23/28

Xi

♦ Bright, refreshing neighbourhood restaurant set opposite the Rendezvous Gallery. All day menus offer plenty of choice, with cooking influenced by the Mediterranean, and in particular, Turkey.

ABERFELDY – Perth and Kinross – **501** I14 – pop. 1 895   **28** C2

▶ Edinburgh 75 mi – Dunkeld 17 mi – Pitlochry 14 mi

at Fortingall West : 8 mi by B 846 on Fortingall rd

Fortingall

⊠ PH15 2NQ – ℰ (01887) 830 367 – www.fortingall.com
10 rm ⊇ – ♦♦ £ 150/250
Rest – Carte £ 20/46

♦ Arts and Crafts style house on tranquil private estate, boasting lovely country views. Stylish interior with contemporary country fabrics. Modern bedrooms remain in keeping with the building's age. Light snacks in cosy bar; contemporary cooking in restaurant.

ABRIACHAN – Highland – **501** G11 – pop. 120   **30** C2

▶ London 573 mi – Edinburgh 168 mi – Inverness 11 mi – Elgin 50 mi

Loch Ness Lodge

Brachla, on A 82 ⊠ IV3 8LA – ℰ (01456) 459 469 – www.loch-ness-lodge.com
– Closed first 3 weeks January and 23-27 December
7 rm (dinner included) ⊇ – ♦ £ 224/269 ♦♦ £ 334/379
Rest – (dinner only) (booking essential to non residents) Carte approx. £ 55

♦ Comfortable, modern country house overlooking Loch Ness; warmly decorated, spacious bedrooms boast a high level of facilities. Sauna and hot tub for guests. Daily changing 5 course menu uses Scottish produce; cooking is flavourful and classically based. Linen laid dining room with excellent views; attentive service.

ACHILTIBUIE – Highland – **501** D9   **30** C1

▶ Edinburgh 243 mi – Inverness 84 mi – Ullapool 25 mi

Summer Isles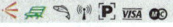

⊠ IV26 2YG – ℰ (01854) 622 282 – www.summerisleshotel.com – April to October
10 rm ⊇ – ♦ £ 115/155 ♦♦ £ 155/190 – 3 suites
Rest *Summer Isles (Bar)* – see restaurant listing
Rest – (booking essential) (set menu only at dinner, light seafood lunch) Menu £ 58

♦ Remotely located hotel, with magnificent views over the eponymous islands. Individually styled, comfortable bedrooms split between main house and various converted outbuildings. Pleasant restaurant, with polished, well-set tables. Daily set menu of traditional dishes, with emphasis on seafood.

ACHILTIBUIE

Summer Isles (Bar) – at Summer Isles Hotel
✉ IV26 2YG – ☏ (01854) 622 282 – www.summerisleshotel.com
– April-October
Rest – Seafood – *(bookings not accepted)* Carte £ 14/30
• 19C former crofters' bar boasting two snug rooms, a large garden and a small terrace with glorious views. Daily changing menus feature local ingredients and have a strong seafood base.

ALYTH – Perth and Kinross – 501 J14 – pop. 2 301 28 C2
▶ Edinburgh 63 mi – Aberdeen 69 mi – Dundee 16 mi – Perth 21 mi
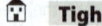 Pitcrocknie, ☏ (01828) 63 22 68

Tigh Na Leigh
22-24 Airlie St ✉ PH11 8AJ – ☏ (01828) 632 372 – www.tighnaleigh.co.uk
– Closed 24 December-4 February
5 rm ⊡ – †£ 43/75 ††£ 107/125 **Rest** – *(residents only)* Menu £ 28
• Imposing Victorian house, once owned by a doctor, run in a professional yet relaxed manner. Surprisingly modern interior with spacious, inviting guest areas. Contemporary bedrooms boast feature beds and great bathrooms; some have spa baths. Superb kitchen garden informs unfussy modern menu; great garden view.

ANNBANK – South Ayrshire – 501 G17 – pop. 854 25 B2
▶ Edinburgh 84 mi – Ayr 6 mi – Dumfries 54 mi – Paisley 34 mi

Enterkine
Southeast : 0.5 mi on B 742 (Coylton rd) ✉ KA6 5AL – ☏ (01292) 520 580
– www.enterkine.com
13 rm ⊡ – †£ 60/85 ††£ 100/150 – 1 suite
Rest – *(booking essential)* Menu £ 19 (lunch) – Carte £ 29/47
• 1930s country house surrounded by extensive gardens and woodlands. Spacious, comfortable lounges. Luxurious bedrooms; one with large roof terrace. Charming library. Formal restaurant with views over River Ayr serves modern cooking; popular with non-residents.

ANSTRUTHER – Fife – 501 L15 – pop. 3 442 – Scotland 28 D2
▶ Edinburgh 46 mi – Dundee 23 mi – Dunfermline 34 mi
🛈 Harbourhead ☏ (01333) 31 10 73, www.visitscotland.com
⛳ Marsfield Shore Rd, ☏ (01333) 31 09 56
◉ Scottish Fisheries Museum★★ **AC**
◉ The East Neuk★★ – Crail★★ (Old Centre★★, Upper Crail★) NE : 4 mi by A 917. Kellie Castle★ **AC**, NW : 7 mi by B 9171, B 942 and A 917

Spindrift
Pittenweem Rd ✉ KY10 3DT – ☏ (01333) 310 573 – www.thespindrift.co.uk
– Closed January and 24-26 December
8 rm ⊡ – †£ 45/65 ††£ 60/80 **Rest** – Menu £ 23
• Detached Victorian house on the edge of the village, originally owned by a tea clipper captain. Comfortable lounge with honesty bar. Cosy, individually furnished bedrooms, some with distant sea views – opt for the top floor Captain's Cabin. Homely cooking relies on local produce, with seafood from East Neuk to the fore.

Cellar
24 East Green ✉ KY10 3AA – ☏ (01333) 310 378 – www.cellaranstruther.co.uk
– Closed 24-26 December, Monday in winter and Sunday
Rest – Seafood – *(booking essential)* Menu £ 25/40
• Long-standing restaurant hidden behind the Fisheries Museum. Atmospheric beamed room with flickering candlelight and open fire. Simply prepared, fresh, quality seafood from Scottish waters.

APPLECROSS – Highland – 501 C11   29 B2
► London 639 mi – Edinburgh 234 mi – Gairloch 56 mi – Portree 76 mi

Applecross Walled Garden
*Northeast : 0.5 mi ⌂ IV54 8ND – ℘ (01520) 744 440
– www.applecrossgarden.co.uk – February-October*
Rest – Menu £ 22 (dinner) – Carte £ 17/29
♦ Lovely 17C walled kitchen garden whose restaurant has grown from a tearoom. Its simple structure belies its tasty dishes, fresh from owner's fishing boat or the garden itself.

Applecross Inn with rm
Shore St ⌂ IV54 8LR – ℘ (01520) 744 262 www.applecross.uk.com – Closed 25 December and 1 January
7 rm ⌂ – †£ 70/80 ††£ 100/120 **Rest** – *(booking essential)* Carte £ 18/27
♦ Charming Highland inn set in an extremely remote location, boasting stunning water and hill views. Menus feature local, seasonal produce from the nearby estate and bay; seafood a speciality. Set in old fishermen's cottages, smart, comfy bedrooms boast sea views.

ARBROATH – Angus – 501 M14 – pop. 22 785   28 D2
► Edinburgh 72 mi – Dundee 17 mi – Montrose 12 mi

Old Vicarage without rest
*2 Seaton Rd, Northeast : 0.75 mi by A 92 and Hayshead Rd ⌂ DD11 5DX
– ℘ (01241) 430 475 – www.theoldvicaragebandb.co.uk*
3 rm ⌂ – ††£ 80/90
♦ Detached 19C house, of large proportions, clothed in Victorian style throughout. Antique furnished bedrooms: ask for view of Arbroath Abbey.

ARCHIESTOWN – Moray – 501 K11 – ⌂ Aberlour (aberdeenshire)   28 C1
► Edinburgh 194 mi – Aberdeen 62 mi – Inverness 49 mi

Archiestown
*The Square ⌂ AB38 7QL – ℘ (01340) 810 218 – www.archiestownhotel.co.uk
– Closed 2 January-10 February and 22-29 December*
11 rm ⌂ – †£ 60/100 ††£ 130/160
Rest *Bistro* – Menu £ 17/30
♦ Welcoming hotel hidden away in a small hamlet; ideally located for shooters/-fishermen. Spacious, comfy sitting rooms with warming open fires. Cosy bedrooms, many boasting country views. Daily changing dishes in laid-back bistro.

ARDHASAIG – Western Isles – 501 Z10 – see Lewis and Harris (Isle of)

ARDUAINE – Argyll and Bute – 501 D15 – ⌂ Oban ▌Scotland   27 B2
► Edinburgh 142 mi – Oban 20 mi
◉ Loch Awe★★, E : 12 mi by A 816 and B 840

Loch Melfort
*⌂ PA34 4XG – ℘ (01852) 200 233 – www.lochmelfort.co.uk
– Closed 2 weeks January*
25 rm (dinner included) ⌂ – †£ 128 ††£ 196/306
Rest *Asknish Bay* – see restaurant listing
Rest *Chartroom II* – Carte £ 20/35
♦ Large hotel next to the beautiful Arduaine Gardens, affording superb views out over the bay and Sound of Jura. Modern lounges with tartan/nautical themes. Bigger bedrooms in the main house; great outlook from private terraces in the wing. Simple, largely seafood menu in Chartroom II; more formal Asknish Bay.

ARDUAINE

Asknish Bay – at Loch Melfort Hotel
PA34 4XG – ✆ (01852) 200 233 – www.lochmelfort.co.uk – Closed 2 weeks January
Rest – Seafood – *(dinner only)* Menu £ 37 – Carte £ 26/38
♦ Formal hotel restaurant boasting fantastic bay views. Daily 5 course menu and à la carte showcase local produce; everything from bread to ice cream is homemade. Sunday seafood buffet in July/Aug.

ARRAN (Isle of) – North Ayrshire – 501 E17 – pop. 5 058 – Scotland   25 A2

London 449 mi – Edinburgh 95 mi – Glasgow 45 mi – Paisley 31 mi
from Brodick to Ardrossan (Caledonian MacBrayne Ltd) 4-6 daily (55 mn) – from Lochranza to Kintyre Peninsula (Claonaig) (Caledonian MacBrayne Ltd) frequent services daily (30 mn) – from Brodick to Isle of Bute (Rothesay) (Caledonian MacBrayne Ltd) 3 weekly (2 h 5 mn)
◉ Island★★ - Brodick Castle★★ AC

BRODICK – North Ayrshire – pop. 621   25 A2
🛈 Welcome Centre ✆ (01770) 30 37 76, www.visitscotland.com
Brodick, ✆ (01770) 30 23 49
Machrie Bay, ✆ (01770) 85 02 32

Auchrannie
Northwest : 0.75 mi by Shore Rd. ✉ KA27 8BZ – ✆ (01770) 302 234 – www.auchrannie.co.uk
64 rm – †£ 80/115 ††£ 109/204, ⌑ £ 12.95
Rest *Eighteen69* – *(closed November-March except Christmas, Sunday and Monday) (dinner only)* Menu £ 33 – Carte £ 32/48
Rest *Brambles* – Carte £ 26/45
Rest *Cruize* – Carte £ 21/33
♦ Mini resort hotel set in 96 acres and offering a good range of family orientated leisure facilities. Built in 1869, the old dower house boasts well-equipped, classical and contemporary bedrooms; family rooms are located in the spa house. Smart conservatory restaurant offers fine dining menu; Brambles serves seafood and grills; all-day Cruize is ideal for families.

Kilmichael Country House
Glen Cloy, West : 1 mi by Shore Rd, taking left turn opposite Golf Club ✉ KA27 8BY – ✆ (01770) 302 219 – www.kilmichael.com – *Easter-October*
5 rm ⌑ – †£ 78/98 ††£ 130/163 – 3 suites
Rest – *(Closed Monday and Tuesday) (dinner only) (booking essential)* Menu £ 45
♦ Reputedly the oldest house on the Isle of Arran, in peaceful location with immaculate lawned grounds. Comfortable country house style and individually decorated bedrooms. Welcoming owners. Restaurant housed in extension. Daily-changing menus.

Douglas
✉ KA27 8AW – ✆ (01770) 302 968 – www.thedouglashotel.co.uk
21 rm ⌑ – †£ 90/135 ††£ 90/250
Rest *Bistro* – Carte £ 25/34
♦ Set just past the ferry terminal and thought to have been built in 1830 by the occupants of the nearby castle to accommodate their guests. Spacious, light-filled bedrooms are decorated in a contemporary style; one has a large roof terrace. Large bistro offers classical French dishes with slight modern twists.

Alltan without rest
Knowe Rd, West : 0.5 mi by Shore Rd taking left at Golf Club ✉ KA27 8BY – ✆ (01770) 302 937 – www.alltanarran.co.uk – *March-October*
3 rm ⌑ – †£ 72 ††£ 80
♦ Friendly, modern guesthouse built into the hillside, not far from the ferry terminal; an ideal base for exploring the island. Communal breakfast room, decked balcony and comfy lounge overlooking the garden and river. Bright, fresh bedrooms.

ARRAN (Isle of)

LAMLASH – North Ayrshire – pop. 1 010 – ⊠ Brodick

🖼 Lamlash, ✆ (01770) 60 02 96

 Glenisle   ← 🛏 🐾 ♵ ⁽¹⁾ **P** VISA ⊛

Shore Rd. ⊠ KA27 8LY – ✆ (01770) 600 559 – www.glenislehotel.com
13 rm ⊇ – †£ 75/100 ††£ 168/184
Rest – Carte £ 19/31

♦ Attractive whitewashed Victorian property, formerly an inn, boasting views over the bay to Holy Island. Open-plan bar-lounge and small snug. Bright, airy bedrooms come in natural hues; one covers the whole top floor and has a roll-top bath. Rustic dining room with terrace offers fresh, simple, homely cooking.

LOCHRANZA

 Apple Lodge   ← 🛏 ♵ **P**

⊠ KA27 8HJ – ✆ (01770) 830 229 – Closed 15 December-15 January, minimum 3 night stay in high season
4 rm ⊇ – †£ 54 ††£ 78   **Rest** – (closed July-August and Tuesday) Menu £ 25

♦ Extended period house with small garden and pleasing views, in centre of quiet village. Homely cottage-style decor with antique furniture and a welcoming atmosphere. Food is home-cooked and uses island and home produce in good, hearty, varied dishes.

ASCOG – Argyll and Bute – **501** E16 – see Bute (Isle of)

AUCHENCAIRN – Dumfries and Galloway – **501** I19 – **25** B3
– ⊠ Castle Douglas

▶ Edinburgh 94 mi – Dumfries 21 mi – Stranraer 60 mi

 Balcary Mews without rest 🍃   ← 🛏 ♵ ⁽¹⁾ **P**

Balcary Bay, Southeast : 2 mi on Balcary rd ⊠ DG7 1QZ – ✆ (01556) 640 270
– www.balcarymews.co.uk – Closed mid December to mid January
3 rm ⊇ – †£ 55 ††£ 80

♦ Former mews for the neighbouring country house, boasting superb views over Balcary Bay and the Solway Firth. Lovely garden with a gate down to the shore. Neat sun lounge and traditional bedrooms; all have views. Homemade bread and jam feature at breakfast.

AUCHTERARDER – Perth and Kinross – **501** I15 – pop. 3 945   **28** C2
▌Scotland

▶ Edinburgh 55 mi – Glasgow 45 mi – Perth 14 mi
🖼 Ochil Rd, ✆ (01764) 66 28 04
⛳ Dunning Rollo Park, ✆ (01764) 68 47 47
◉ Tullibardine Chapel★, NW : 2 m

🏨🏨🏨 **Gleneagles**   ← 🛏 🍴 🐾 🏊 ♨ 🎾 ⛳ 🎳 🏇 🎯 🎿 & rm, ⚒ ⁽¹⁾ 🍸 **P**
Southwest : 2 mi by A 824 on A 823 ⊠ PH3 1NF   VISA ⊛ AE ①
– ✆ (01764) 662 231 – www.gleneagles.com
216 rm ⊇ – ††£ 315/435 – 16 suites
Rest *Andrew Fairlie at Gleneagles* ✿✿ – see restaurant listing
Rest *Strathearn* – ✆ (01764) 694 270 (dinner only and Sunday lunch)
Menu £ 58
Rest *Deseo* – ✆ (01764) 694 270 – Carte £ 25/58

♦ World-famous resort hotel with renowned championship golf course. Excellent leisure facilities include state-of-the-art spa, popular equestrian centre and gun-dog school. Majestic, art deco styling, elegant interior and luxurious bedrooms. Strathearn offers classical menu and superb estate views. All-day Deseo serves Mediterranean-influenced dishes, including tapas.

AUCHTERARDER

XXXX Andrew Fairlie at Gleneagles 🏵🏵
Southwest : 2 mi by A 824 on A 823 – PH3 1NF – ℰ (01764) 694 267 – www.andrewfairlie.co.uk – Closed 3 weeks January, 24-25 December and Sunday

Rest – *(dinner only)* Menu £ 85/95

Spec. Home smoked lobster, lime and herb butter. Slow cooked rump and shoulder of beef, soy and balsamic. Hot mango soufflé, piña colada sorbet and exotic fruit sauce.

♦ Elegant, understated restaurant where reserved yet passionate chef creates precise, balanced, flavourful dishes with a refined French style and Scottish edge. Concise à la carte includes signature smoked lobster. Dégustation menu showcases dishes 'en miniature'. Menu du Marché offers latest seasonal produce.

AVIEMORE – Highland – **501** I12 – pop. 2 397 🟢 Scotland 30 D3

▶ Edinburgh 129 mi – Inverness 29 mi – Perth 85 mi

ℹ Grampian Rd ℰ (08452) 25 51 21, www.visitcairngorms.com

◉ Town★

🟢 The Cairngorms★★ (≤★★★) - ✱★★★ from Cairn Gorm, SE : 11 mi by B 970 – Landmark Visitor Centre (The Highlander★) **AC**, N : 7 mi by A 9 – Highland Wildlife Park★ **AC**, SW : 7 mi by A 9

⌂ Old Minister's Guest House *without rest*
Rothiemurchus, Southeast : 1 mi on B 970 – PH22 1QH – ℰ (01479) 812 181 – www.theoldministershouse.co.uk
4 rm – †£ 45/65 ††£ 90/96

♦ Early 20C house on outskirts of town, with a river at the bottom of its pretty garden. Nicely-laid breakfast room. Spacious bedrooms, finished to high standard.

AYR – South Ayrshire – **501** G17 – pop. 46 431 🟢 Scotland 25 A2

▶ Edinburgh 81 mi – Glasgow 35 mi

ℹ 22 Sandgate ℰ (01292) 29 03 00, www.visitscotland.com

⛳ Seafield Doonfoot Rd, Belleisle Park, ℰ (01292) 44 12 58
⛳ Dalmilling Westwood Ave, ℰ (01292) 26 38 93
⛳ Doon Valley Patna Hillside, ℰ (01292) 53 16 07

🟢 Alloway★ (Burns Cottage and Museum★ **AC**) S : 3 mi by B 7024 BZ. Culzean Castle★ **AC** (setting★★★, Oval Staircase★★) SW : 13 mi by A 719 BZ

⌂ No.26 The Crescent *without rest*
26 Bellevue Cres – KA7 2DR – ℰ (01292) 287 329 – www.26crescent.co.uk
5 rm – †£ 45/70 ††£ 70/80   BZ**c**

♦ Well-run Georgian terraced guesthouse, displaying a pleasing mix of traditional features – such as original fireplaces – and smart, modern décor. Comfortable throughout, boasting cosy, individually furnished bedrooms; the best one, at the front, has a four-poster.

⌂ Coila *without rest*
10 Holmston Rd – KA7 3BB – ℰ (01292) 262 642 – www.coila.co.uk
4 rm – †£ 35/50 ††£ 55/80   AY**u**

♦ Spotlessly kept Georgian guesthouse on the edge of town, proudly decorated with the owners' personal ornaments and family photos. Warm, homely lounge and small breakfast room. Well-kept bedrooms with king-sized beds and modern facilities. Very warm welcome.

AYR AND PRESTWICK

Street	Grid
...ison St	BZ 2
...oway St	AY 3
...ran Mall	AY
...resford Terrace	AY 6
...swell Park	AY 7
...rns' Statue Square	AY 9
...rrick Rd	BZ 10
...rrick St	AY 12
...llarton St	AY 13
...athfield Retail Park	BY
...gh Rd	BYZ 14
...gh St	AY
...lmston Rd	AY 15
...ac Call's Ave	BZ 20
...wmarket St	AY 25
...w Bridge St	AY 24
Germain-en-Laye (Pl. de)	AY 26
...Leonard's Rd	BZ 27
...Quivox Rd	BY 28
...ndgate	AY 30
...toria Bridge	AY 31
...aggon Rd	BZ 33
...alker Rd	BZ 34
...ellington Square	AY 36

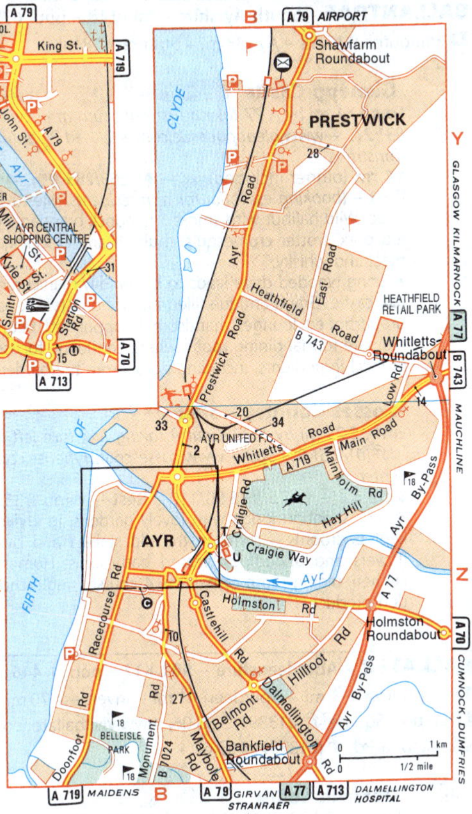

BALLACHULISH – Highland – 501 E13 – pop. 615 ⁣ Scotland   30 C3

▶ Edinburgh 117 mi – Inverness 80 mi – Kyle of Lochalsh 90 mi
  – Oban 38 mi
☐ Loan sern ☏ (01855) 81 18 66, www.glencoetourism.co.uk
◉ Glen Coe ★★, E : 6 mi by A 82

↑ **Ardno House** without rest

Lettermore, Glencoe, West : 3.5 mi by A 82 on A 828 ✉ PH49 4JD
– ☏ (01855) 811 830 – www.ardnohouse.co.uk
– February-October
4 rm 🖃 – †£ 48/56 ††£ 76/86
♦ Purpose-built guesthouse with fine view of Loch Linnhe and the Morven Hills. Personally run and providing good value, comfortable accommodation. Spacious bedrooms.

Guesthouses ↑ don't provide the same level of service as hotels. They are often characterised by a warm welcome and a décor which reflects the owner's personality. Those shown in red ↑ are particularly pleasant.

BALLANTRAE – South Ayrshire – 501 E18 – pop. 672 – ✉ Girvan — 25 A2
▶ Edinburgh 115 mi – Ayr 33 mi – Stranraer 18 mi

Glenapp Castle
South : 1 mi by A 77 taking first right turn after bridge ✉ KA26 0NZ – ℰ (01465) 831 211 – www.glenappcastle.com – Closed 2 January to mid-March and 1 week Christmas
14 rm (dinner included) – ₤ 265/285 ₤ 415/620 – 3 suites
Rest – (booking essential for non-residents) Menu £ 38/60
Spec. Wild halibut with smoked haddock brandade, garlic and lemon purée. Milk-fed pork, trotter cromesquis, rhubarb and crackling. Cranachan soufflé with oatmeal and whisky.
♦ Long wooded drive leads to beautifully manicured gardens and stunning baronial castle. Grand antique-filled interior boasts oak-panelled hallways, impressively proportioned lounges, handsomely appointed bedrooms and Ailsa Craig views. Intimate formal dining room, where confident, focused cooking employs a wealth of local ingredients, including herbs from the garden.

Cosses Country House
East : 2.25 mi by A 77 (South) taking first turn left after bridge ✉ KA26 0LR – ℰ (01465) 831 363 – www.cossescountryhouse.com – Restricted opening in winter
3 rm – ₤ 75 ₤ 90/110 **Rest** – Menu £ 35
♦ 17C shooting lodge with lovely gardens, in idyllic rural location. Immaculately kept bedrooms – some in the old stables and byre – boast iPod docks, fresh flowers and underfloor heated bathrooms. Homemade cake on arrival in the kitchen, dining room or garden. 4 course, single-choice set dinner uses local/garden produce.

BALLATER – Aberdeenshire – 501 K12 – pop. 1 446 — 28 C1
▶ Edinburgh 111 mi – Aberdeen 41 mi – Inverness 70 mi – Perth 67 mi
🛈 Station Square ℰ (013397) 5 53 06, www.visitballater.com
⛳ Victoria Rd, ℰ (013397) 5 55 67

Darroch Learg
Braemar Rd ✉ AB35 5UX – ℰ (013397) 55 443 – www.darrochlearg.co.uk – Closed last 3 weeks January and Christmas
12 rm (dinner included) – ₤ 130/195 ₤ 210/330
Rest *Conservatory* – see restaurant listing
♦ Late Victorian country house affording superb views over the Dee Valley and Grampians. Personally run by the second family generation, it boasts comfy, open-fired, antique-furnished lounges and traditional, individually designed bedrooms.

Moorside House *without rest*
26 Braemar Rd ✉ AB35 5RL – ℰ (013397) 55 492 – www.moorsidehouse.co.uk – April-October
9 rm – ₤ 45 ₤ 65
♦ 19C former manse with large garden, simple, homely bedrooms and comfy lounge filled with books about the local area. Original Victorian features include ornate cornicing and an attractive pine staircase. Hearty breakfasts feature homemade bread and preserves.

Conservatory – at Darroch Learg Hotel
Braemar Rd ✉ AB35 5UX – ℰ (013397) 55 443 – www.darrochlearg.co.uk – Closed last 3 weeks January and Christmas
Rest – (dinner only and Sunday lunch) Menu £ 45
♦ Conservatory dining room in a Victorian country house, boasting attractive mountain views from majority of its smartly laid tables. Concise menu with quality seasonal ingredients to the fore; carefully judged, well-crafted modern cooking.

BALLATER

Green Inn with rm
9 Victoria Rd ⊠ AB35 5QQ – ℰ (013397) 55 701 – www.green-inn.com – Closed December, Sunday in winter and Tuesday
2 rm – †£ 80 ††£ 80, ⊋ £ 12.50
Rest – *(dinner only) (booking essential)* Menu £ 45
♦ Former temperance hall, opposite the green, boasting comfy lounges and pleasant conservatory. Interesting, well sourced and accomplished modern British cooking. Cosy rooms.

Auld Kirk with rm
Braemar Rd ⊠ AB35 5RQ – ℰ (013397) 55 762 – www.theauldkirk.com – Closed January, 25-26 December and Monday
6 rm ⊋ – †£ 65/73 ††£ 110/140
Rest – *(dinner only and Sunday lunch)* Menu £ 38
♦ Built in 1870 and operating as a church until 1938. The stylish modern bar and lounge contrast with original windows and a pine panelled ceiling in the elegant dining room. Concise menu offers elaborate dishes in well-matched combinations. Pleasant, comfortable bedrooms come with smart, fully tiled bathrooms.

BALLOCH – West Dunbartonshire – **501** G15 – ⊠ Alexandria — 25 B1
Scotland

▶ Edinburgh 72 mi – Glasgow 20 mi – Stirling 30 mi
🛈 Balloch Rd ℰ (08707) 20 06 07, www.explore-callander.com
◉ N : Loch Lomond ★★

Cameron House
Loch Lomond, Northwest : 1.5 mi by A 811 on A 82 ⊠ G83 8QZ – ℰ (01389) 755 565 – www.cameronhouse.co.uk
121 rm ⊋ – †£ 145/355 ††£ 145/355 – 7 suites
Rest *Martin Wishart at Loch Lomond* ❀ **Rest** *Camerons Grill* **Rest** *Boat House* – see restaurant listing
♦ Extensive Victorian house and timeshare lodges, set in 250 acres on the shore of Loch Lomond. Excellent leisure facilities include a health club, spa, golf course and use of a launch and seaplane. Moody, modern bedrooms; traditional suites.

Martin Wishart at Loch Lomond – at Cameron House Hotel
Loch Lomond, Northwest : 1.5 mi by A 811 on A 82 ⊠ G83 8QZ – ℰ (01389) 722 504 – www.martinwishartlochlomond.co.uk – Closed 1-18 January, Monday and Tuesday
Rest – *(dinner only and Saturday-Sunday lunch) (booking essential)* Menu £ 25/65
Spec. Tortellini of roe deer, cauliflower cream and grand veneur sauce. Fillets of Dover sole, baby artichoke, parsley and lemon. Valrhona chocolate mousse with hazelnuts and exotic fruits.
♦ Formal restaurant within the grounds of a resort hotel, superbly situated on the banks of Loch Lomond and boasting water and mountain views. Seasonal, modern menus showcase Scottish ingredients in complementary combinations. Haggis bon bons have become a signature dish. Professional yet personable service.

Camerons Grill – at Cameron House Hotel
Loch Lomond, Northwest : 1.5 mi by A 811 on A 82 ⊠ G83 8QZ – ℰ (01389) 755 565 – www.cameronhouseco.uk
Rest – *(dinner only)* Carte £ 42/54
♦ Contemporary, leather-furnished grill restaurant located within an extensive Victorian house, where 250 acres of grounds lead down to Loch Lomond. Concise menu of dishes from the Josper grill.

Boat House – at Cameron House Hotel
Loch Lomond, Northwest : 1.5 mi by A 811 on A 82 ⊠ G83 8QZ – ℰ (01389) 755 565 – www.cameronhouse.co.uk
Rest – Carte £ 26/36
♦ Set in the grounds of Cameron House, on the loch shore, this casual restaurant has a true New England feel. The Mediterranean menu offers unfussy dishes, including pizzas from the wood-oven.

BALLYGRANT – Argyll and Bute – **501** B16 – see Islay (Isle of)

BALMACARA – ✉ Highland 29 B2
▶ London 582 mi – Edinburgh 198 mi – Inverness 75 mi

Balmacara Mains without rest
Glaick, West : 0.75 mi by A 87 ✉ IV40 8DN – ☏ (01599) 566 240
– www.ontheloch.com
8 rm ⌧ – †£ 60/75 ††£ 105/120
• Superb lochside location, between Eilean Donan Castle and Skye Bridge. Stylish bedrooms vary in size, some cosy, some huge; most have loch views. Large lounge with open fire.

BALMEDIE – Aberdeenshire – **501** N12 – pop. 1 653 28 D1
▶ Edinburgh 137 mi – Aberdeen 7 mi – Peterhead 24 mi

Cock and Bull with rm
Ellon Rd, Blairton, North : 1 mi on A 90 ✉ AB23 8XY – ☏ (01358) 743 249
– www.thecockandbull.co.uk
3 rm ⌧ – †£ 85 ††£ 85   **Rest** – Carte £ 26/48
• Quirky pub with a profusion of knick-knacks; dine in the cosy, open-fired lounge, formal dining room or airy conservatory. Menu offers classic pub fare and well-presented, restaurant style dishes. Bedrooms boast striking modern black and white designs.

BALQUHIDDER – Stirling – **501** G14 – see Lochearnhead

BANCHORY – Aberdeenshire – **501** M12 – pop. 6 034 Scotland 28 D2
▶ Edinburgh 118 mi – Aberdeen 17 mi – Dundee 55 mi – Inverness 94 mi
🛈 Bridge St ☏ (01330) 82 20 00, www.aberdeen-grampian.com
🏌 Kinneskie Kinneskie Rd, ☏ (01330) 82 23 65
🏌 Torphins Bog Rd, ☏ (013398) 8 21 15
🌿 Crathes Castle★★ (Gardens★★★) **AC**, E : 3 mi by A 93 – Cairn o'Mount Road★ (≤★★), S : by B 974. Dunnottar Castle★★ (site★★★) **AC**, SW : 15.5 mi by A 93 and A 957 – Aberdeen★★, NE : 17 mi by A 93

Raemoir House
North : 2.5 mi by A 980 ✉ AB31 4ED – ☏ (01330) 824 884 – www.raemoir.com
20 rm – †£ 120 ††£ 160/200
Rest *Raemoir House* – see restaurant listing
• One of the best-known Scottish estate country houses, in an idyllic rural spot and surrounded by mature grounds. Original features include an intricately carved bar and charming drawing room with flock wallpaper. Subtly modernised bedrooms.

Banchory Lodge
Dee St ✉ AB31 5HS – ☏ (01330) 822 625 – www.banchorylodge.co.uk
22 rm ⌧ – †£ 70/95 ††£ 130/160
Rest – Menu £ 23/30 **s** – Carte £ 17/44 **s**
• Part 16C former coaching inn delightfully situated on River Dee. Country house style accentuated by antiques and china. Individually decorated bedrooms. Dee views and floral displays enhance the attraction of the dining room.

XX Raemoir House
North : 2.5 mi by A 980 ✉ AB31 4ED – ☏ (01330) 824 884 – www.raemoir.com
Rest – (bar lunch Monday-Saturday) Menu £ 40
• Formal dining room in a well-known Georgian country house, boasting grand dimensions and pitch pine panelling on both the walls and ceiling. Set dinner menu offers classically based dishes.

BARCALDINE – Argyll and Bute – **501** D14   **27** B2
▶ London 504 mi – Edinburgh 150 mi – Glasgow 100 mi – Dundee 122 mi

Barcaldine House
✉ PA37 1SG – ☏ (01631) 720 219 – www.barcaldinehouse.co.uk
10 rm – †£ 135 ††£ 195 – 1 suite
Rest – *(light lunch) (booking advisable)* Menu £ 50 (dinner)
• Charming grey-stone country house built in 1709 by 'Red Patrick'. Lovely guest areas include a comfy lounge, well-stocked bar and baronial-style billiard room. Well-appointed bedrooms with heavy drapes, quality beds and antique furnishings. Delightful dining room serves precise, well-crafted 6 course dinners.

BARRA (Isle of) – Western Isles – **501** X12/1 – ✉ Castlebay   **29** A3
▶ London 506 mi – Edinburgh 132 mi

CASTLEBAY – Western Isles   **29** A3

Castlebay
✉ HS9 5XD – ☏ (01871) 810 223 – www.castlebayhotel.com – *Closed 22 December-6 January*
15 rm – †£ 49/105 ††£ 95/160   **Rest** – *(bar lunch)* Carte £ 20/32
• Homely hotel boasting excellent castle and island views – the hub of the island community. Bedrooms mix styles: newer rooms feature subtle tartan fabrics; MacNeil has harbour views. Cosy lounge and busy locals bar. Linen-clad dining room serves seafood specials.

Grianamul *without rest*
✉ HS9 5XD – ☏ (01871) 810 416 – www.isleofbarraaccommodation.com – *April-September*
3 rm – ††£ 70
• Set at the heart of a small hamlet; a homely guesthouse run by caring owners. Bright, clean, spacious bedrooms. Comfortable lounge and sunny breakfast room, where huge breakfasts are served.

NORTH BAY – Western Isles   **29** A3

Heathbank
✉ HS9 5YQ – ☏ (01871) 890 266 – www.barrahotel.co.uk – *Easter-October*
5 rm – †£ 60/80 ††£ 90
Rest – *(bar lunch) (booking essential)* Carte £ 18/31
• Former Presbyterian Church, now a smart, modern hotel that's popular with locals and visitors alike. Fresh, up-to-date bedrooms. Bright, airy bar that forms the hotel's hub and, along with the dining room, serves straightforward, local seafood orientated menus.

BENDERLOCH – Argyll and Bute – **501** D14 – see Connel

BERNISDALE – Highland – **501** A/B11 – see Skye (Isle of)

BISHOPTON – Renfrewshire – **501** G16   **25** B1
▶ Edinburgh 59 mi – Dumbarton 9 mi – Glasgow 13 mi

Mar Hall
Earl of Mar Dr., Northeast : 1 mi on B 815 ✉ PA7 5NW – ☏ (0141) 812 99 99 – www.marhall.com
50 rm – †£ 129/219 ††£ 245/295 – 3 suites
Rest *Cristal* – *(closed Sunday-Monday) (dinner only)* Carte £ 30/65
• Stunning Gothic mansion with period charm, well-equipped gym, impressive spa and championship golf course. Great Hall displays ornate plaster ceiling. Spacious bedrooms; those by the spa have golf course views. 250 acres of parkland stretch to the Clyde. High-ceilinged Cristal offers accessible menu.

BLAIRGOWRIE – Perth and Kinross – 501 J14 – pop. 7 965 ▮ Scotland 28 C2
▶ Edinburgh 60 mi – Dundee 19 mi – Perth 16 mi
🛈 26 Wellmeadow ℰ (01250) 87 29 60, www.perthshire.co.uk
◉ Scone Palace★★ **AC**, S : 12 mi by A 93

Kinloch House
West : 3 mi on A 923 ⌧ PH10 6SG – ℰ (01250) 884 237
– www.kinlochhouse.com – Closed 14-29 December
16 rm ⌸ – †£ 110/225 ††£ 215/305 – 1 suite   **Rest** – Menu £ 28/55
◆ Imposing ivy-clad country house in a tranquil, elevated setting, with beautiful walled gardens to the rear and 25 acres of grounds. Smart oak-panelled hall and vast array of welcoming guest areas complete with log fires and antiques. Classical bedrooms are individually styled and well-appointed. Formal restaurant offers concise daily menu of traditional dishes.

Heathpark House without rest
Coupar Angus Rd, Rosemount, Southeast : 0.75 mi on A 923 ⌧ PH10 6JT
– ℰ (01250) 870 700 – www.heathparkhouse.com – Closed 24-26 December and 1 January
3 rm ⌸ – †£ 45/50 ††£ 75
◆ Substantial Victorian guesthouse in a quiet residential spot with mature gardens. Spacious lounge; breakfasts taken in welcoming dining room. Large, individually styled rooms.

Gilmore House without rest
Perth Rd, Southwest : 0.5 mi on A 93 ⌧ PH10 6EJ – ℰ (01250) 872 791
– www.gilmorehouse.co.uk
3 rm ⌸ – †£ 70/80 ††£ 70/80
◆ Traditional stone-built house with flower-filled entrance, only a few minutes' walk from town. Quaint, comfortable lounge complete with bottles of whisky and sherry. Cosy, up-to-date bedrooms with little extras. Extensive buffet and cooked options at breakfast.

BOWMORE – Argyll and Bute – 501 B16 – see Islay (Isle of)

BRAEMAR – Aberdeenshire – 501 J12 – pop. 500 ▮ Scotland 28 C2
▶ Edinburgh 85 mi – Aberdeen 58 mi – Dundee 51 mi – Perth 51 mi
🛈 Mar Rd ℰ (013397) 4 16 00, www.braemarscotland.co.uk
⛳ Cluniebank Rd, ℰ (013397) 4 16 18
◉ Lin O'Dee★, W : 5 m

Callater Lodge without rest
9 Glenshee Rd ⌧ AB35 5YQ – ℰ (013397) 41 275 – www.callaterlodge.co.uk
– Closed 1 week Christmas
6 rm ⌸ – †£ 40/65 ††£ 80
◆ Victorian granite house on the village outskirts. Classically furnished interior with tartan carpets and stag's heads. Bright breakfast room and comfy lounge with local info. Fresh, individually styled bedrooms; some with valley views.

BREASCLETE – Western Isles – 501 Z9 – see Lewis and Harris (Isle of)

BROADFORD – Highland – 501 C12 – see Skye (Isle of)

BRODICK – North Ayrshire – 501 E17 – see Arran (Isle of)

BRORA – Highland – 501 I9 – pop. 1 140 30 D2
▶ Edinburgh 234 mi – Inverness 78 mi – Wick 49 mi
⛳ Golf Rd, ℰ (01408) 62 14 17

Royal Marine
Golf Rd ⊠ *KW9 6QS* – ℰ *(01408) 621 252* – *www.royalmarinebrora.com*
21 rm ⊑ – †£ 95/135 ††£ 140/200
Rest – Carte £ 17/40
• Cream-washed former laird's house set next to a top golf course. Leather-furnished lounges and wood-floored bar. Smart, modern, country house bedrooms with warm fabrics and good level of facilities. Formal linen-laid restaurant offers traditional Scottish menus.

BROUGHTY FERRY – Dundee City – **501** L14 – see Dundee

BUNCHREW – Highland – see Inverness

BURRAY – **501** L7 – see Orkney Islands (Mainland)

BUTE (Isle of) – Argyll and Bute – **501** E16 – pop. 7 354 — **27** B3

from Rothesay to Wemyss Bay (Mainland) (Caledonian MacBrayne Ltd) frequent services daily (35 mn) – from Rhubodach to Colintraive (Mainland) (Caledonian MacBrayne Ltd) frequent services daily (5 mn)

ASCOG – Argyll and Bute — **27** B3

Balmory Hall without rest
Balmory Rd ⊠ *PA20 9LL* – ℰ *(01700) 500 669* – *www.balmoryhall.com* – Closed 25 December and 1 January
4 rm ⊑ – †£ 170 ††£ 170/200
• 19C Italianate mansion with boules pitch and croquet lawn. Impressive original features include ornate plaster ceilings, gilt cornicing, Doric columns and a grand cantilevered staircase. Dramatic photos and family artwork abound. Homemade bread/jam at breakfast.

CADBOLL – Highland – see Tain

CALLANDER – Stirling – **501** H15 – pop. 2 754 ▮ Scotland — **28** C2

▶ Edinburgh 52 mi – Glasgow 43 mi – Oban 71 mi – Perth 41 mi
🛈 Ancaster Sq ℰ *(08707) 20 06 28, www.explore-callander.com*
Aveland Rd, ℰ *(01877) 33 00 90*
◎ Town★
The Trossachs★★★ (Loch Katrine★★) – Hilltop Viewpoint★★★ (✵★★★)
W : 10 mi by A 821

Roman Camp
Main St ⊠ *FK17 8BG* – ℰ *(01877) 330 003* – *www.romancamphotel.co.uk*
12 rm ⊑ – †£ 95/150 ††£ 195/200 – 3 suites
Rest *Restaurant* – see restaurant listing
• Attractive 17C former hunting lodge next to a Roman settlement. Characterful interior with beautiful drawing room, antique-filled library and chapel. Classical bedrooms have a subtle contemporary edge.

Lubnaig without rest
Leny Feus ⊠ *FK17 8AS* – ℰ *(01877) 330 376* – *www.lubnaighouse.co.uk* – Mid April to October
8 rm ⊑ – †£ 45/55 ††£ 65/80
• Built in 1864, a characterful Victorian house on the outskirts of town. Well-kept mature gardens visible from communal rooms. Homely bedrooms, two in converted stables.

Restaurant – at Roman Camp Hotel
Main St ⊠ *FK17 8BG* – ℰ *(01877) 330 003* – *www.romancamphotel.co.uk*
Rest – Menu £ 27/50 – Carte dinner £ 47/71
• Spacious country house restaurant with unique ceiling and impressive flower displays. Daily changing set menu and concise à la carte offer ambitious modern dishes of local, seasonal produce.

CALLANDER

✗ Mhor Fish   VISA ◉◉
75-77 Main St ⊠ FK17 8DX – ℰ (01877) 330 213 – www.mhor.net – Closed 1 January, 25-26 December and Monday except bank holidays
Rest – Seafood – Menu £ 25 – Carte £ 18/30
♦ Simple, busy, well-run eatery on main street; popular with locals. Great variety of fish, homemade pies and chips cooked in beef dripping. All-day menu and more ambitious specials.

CARINISH – Western Isles – **501** Y11 – see Uist (Isles of)

CARNOUSTIE – Angus – **501** L14 – pop. 10 561   28 D2
▶ Edinburgh 68 mi – Aberdeen 59 mi – Dundee 12 mi
🛈 21 High St ℰ (01241) 85 96 20, www.angusanddundee.co.uk
⛳ Monifieth Golf Links Princes St, Medal Starter's Box, ℰ (01382) 53 27 67
⛳ Burnside Links Par, ℰ (01241) 80 22 90
⛳ Panmure Barry, ℰ (01241) 85 51 20
⛳ Buddon Links Links Par, ℰ (01241) 80 22 80

⌂ Old Manor *without rest*   VISA ◉◉
Panbride, Northeast : 1.25 mi by A 930 on Panbride Rd ⊠ DD7 6JP – ℰ (01241) 854 804 – www.oldmanorcarnoustie.com – Closed 2 weeks October and Christmas-New Year
5 rm ⌑ – †£ 55/60 ††£ 70/80
♦ Sizeable house built in 1765, commanding great views over patchwork fields to the sea beyond. Comfy lounge and good-sized breakfast room. Spotlessly kept bedrooms come with quality bedding, chocolates and biscuits; Balmoral and Dunotter boast superb outlooks.

CARRADALE – Argyll and Bute – **501** D17 – see Kintyre (Peninsula)

CASTLEBAY – Western Isles – **501** X12/1 – see Barra (Isle of)

CASTLE DOUGLAS – Dumfries and Galloway – **501** I19 – pop. 3 671   25 B3
▮ Scotland
▶ Edinburgh 98 mi – Ayr 49 mi – Dumfries 18 mi – Stranraer 57 mi
🛈 Market Hill ℰ (01556) 50 26 11, www.visitscotland.com
⛳ Abercromby Rd, ℰ (01556) 50 28 01
◉ Threave Garden★★ AC, SW : 2.5 mi by A 75 – Threave Castle★ AC, W : 1 m

⌂ Douglas House *without rest*   VISA ◉◉
63 Queen St ⊠ DG7 1HS – ℰ (01556) 503 262 – www.douglas-house.com – Closed Christmas
4 rm ⌑ – †£ 36/65 ††£ 74/90
♦ Attractive 19C stone-built house, set close to the high street. Open-plan lounge and breakfast room. Comfy, individually decorated bedrooms with contemporary feel. Extensive breakfast menu.

CAWDOR – Highland – **501** I11 – pop. 812 – ⊠ Inverness   30 D2
▶ Edinburgh 170 mi – Aberdeen 100 mi – Inverness 14 mi

⅋ Cawdor Tavern   P VISA ◉◉ AE
The Lane ⊠ IV12 5XP – ℰ (01667) 404 777 – www.cawdortavern.co.uk – Closed 2 weeks January, 25 December and 1 January
Rest – (booking essential) Carte £ 18/27
♦ Charming, personally run whitewashed pub – formerly the joiners' workshop of Cawdor Castle. Wide-ranging menu offers a good selection of frequently changing, classically based dishes.

CHIRNSIDE – The Scottish Borders – **501** N16 – pop. 1 204 – ⊠ Duns   26 D1
▶ Edinburgh 52 mi – Berwick-upon-Tweed 8 mi – Glasgow 95 mi – Newcastle upon Tyne 70 mi

CHIRNSIDE

🏠 Chirnside Hall
East : 1.75 mi on A 6105 ✉ *TD11 3LD* – 📞 *(01890) 818 219*
– *www.chirnsidehallhotel.com* – *Closed March*
10 rm – †£ 90/160 ††£ 160/175
Rest – *(dinner only) (booking essential for non-residents)* Menu £ 35
◆ Sizeable 1834 country house with lovely revolving door; boasting beautiful views over the Cheviots. Grand lounges with original cornicing and huge fireplaces. Cosy, classical bedrooms, some have four-posters. Local, seasonal dishes in traditional dining room.

CLEAT – **501** K/L6 – see Orkney Islands (Island of Westray)

COLONSAY (Isle of) – Argyll and Bute – **501** B15 – pop. 106   **27** A2

▶ London 502 mi – Edinburgh 129 mi – Greenock 98 mi

🚢 from Scalasaig to Oban (Caledonian MacBrayne Ltd) 3 weekly (2 h) – from Scalasaig to Kintyre Peninsula (Kennacraig) via Isle of Islay (Port Askaig) (Caledonian MacBrayne Ltd) weekly

ℹ Colonsay, 📞 (01951) 20 02 90

SCALASAIG – Argyll and Bute – ✉ Colonsay   **27** A2

🏠 Colonsay
✉ *PA61 7YP* – 📞 *(01951) 200 316* – *www.colonsayestate.co.uk* – *March-October, Christmas and New Year*
9 rm – †£ 70 ††£ 90/145, ⊇ £ 6.50   **Rest** – *(bar lunch)* Carte £ 21/29
◆ Listed building from mid-18C; a thoroughly rural, remote setting. Public areas include excellent photos of local scenes and the only bar on the island. Bright, modern rooms. Welcoming, informal dining room.

COMRIE – Perth and Kinross – **501** I14 – pop. 1 926   **28** C2

▶ Edinburgh 66 mi – Glasgow 56 mi – Oban 70 mi – Perth 24 mi

ℹ Comrie Laggan Braes, 📞 (01764) 67 00 55

🏠 Royal
Melville Sq ✉ *PH6 2DN* – 📞 *(01764) 679 200* – *www.royalhotel.co.uk* – *Closed 25-26 December*
11 rm ⊇ – †£ 85 ††£ 140/180
Rest *Royal* – see restaurant listing
◆ Charming coaching inn dating back to the 18C and set at the heart of a riverside town. Cosy bar and lovely open-fired library with squashy sofas. Well-appointed bedrooms; some with four-posters and antiques. Relaxed, personable service.

XX Royal – at Royal Hotel
Melville Sq ✉ *PH6 2DN* – 📞 *(01764) 679 200* – *www.royalhotel.co.uk* – *Closed 25-26 December*
Rest – Menu £ 30 – Carte £ 21/28
◆ Intimate dining room and bright conservatory, set within a stylishly decorated coaching inn. Concise menu of locally sourced, seasonal produce; classically based dishes display modern touches.

CONNEL – Argyll and Bute – **501** D14 – ✉ Oban   **27** B2

▶ Edinburgh 118 mi – Glasgow 88 mi – Inverness 113 mi – Oban 5 mi

🏠 Ards House *without rest*
on A 85 ✉ *PA37 1PT* – 📞 *(01631) 710 255* – *www.ardshouse.com* – *Closed mid December-mid January*
4 rm ⊇ – †£ 50/65 ††£ 80/100
◆ Attractive house with equally welcoming, hospitable owner. Large, homely, open-fired lounge packed with books and antiques. Cosy, personally decorated bedrooms show good attention to detail; small bathrooms boast locally made toiletries. Excellent breakfasts.

SCOTLAND

CONNEL

Oyster Inn with rm
PA37 1PJ – ℰ (01631) 710 666 – www.oysterinn.co.uk – Closed 25-26 December
11 rm – †£ 55/75 ††£ 100/130
Rest – Seafood – (dinner only) Carte £ 27/57

• Cosy 18C pub looking over the Falls or Lora and the bay. Rustic bar serves pub classics. Smarter, nautically themed restaurant offers a regularly changing seafood menu and views of the sunset. Bedrooms are modern and colourful; budget bunk rooms are available.

CRIEFF – Perth and Kinross – **501** I14 – **pop. 6 579** – Scotland — **28** C2

▶ Edinburgh 60 mi – Glasgow 50 mi – Oban 76 mi – Perth 18 mi
🛈 High St ℰ (01764) 65 25 78, www.crieffandstrathearn.co.uk
Perth Rd, ℰ (01764) 65 29 09
Muthill Peat Rd, ℰ (01764) 68 15 23
◉ Town ★
◉ Drummond Castle Gardens★ **AC**, S : 2 mi by A 822. Scone Palace★★ **AC**, E : 16 mi by A 85 and A 93

Merlindale without rest
Perth Rd, on A 85 ⊠ PH7 3EQ – ℰ (01764) 655 205 – www.merlindale.co.uk
– Closed mid December-mid January
3 rm – †£ 50/80 ††£ 70/90

• Spacious manor house with comfy lounge, well-stocked library and dark wood furnished dining room. Immaculate bedrooms have classical furnishings, heavy floral drapes and large bathrooms; some boast roll-top baths. Family style breakfasts.

Yann's at Glenearn House with rm
Perth Rd, on A 85 ⊠ PH7 3EQ – ℰ (01764) 650 111
– www.yannsatglenearnhouse.com
5 rm – †£ 55 ††£ 80
Rest – French – (closed Monday and Tuesday) (dinner only and lunch Saturday & Sunday) Carte £ 25/30

• Busy, keenly run, bistro-style restaurant with informal lounge. Well-priced, French cooking makes good use of Scottish produce; Savoyard sharing dishes a speciality. Polite, swift service. Comfortable bedrooms with good facilities and a relaxed, bohemian style.

at Muthill South : 3mi. by A 822

Barley Bree with rm
6 Willoughby St ⊠ PH5 2AB – ℰ (01764) 681 451 – www.barleybree.com
– Closed 2 weeks February, 2 weeks October, Christmas, Monday and Tuesday
6 rm – †£ 70 ††£ 130/140 **Rest** – (booking advisable) Carte £ 19/37 **s**

• Converted coaching inn, in the centre of a busy village, with spacious, fire-lit sitting room and dining room hung with angling memorabilia. Generous portions of rustic, classical cooking; dishes utilise local ingredients. Friendly service. Comfortable, well-thought-out bedrooms.

CRINAN – Argyll and Bute – **501** D15 – ⊠ Lochgilphead – Scotland — **27** B2

▶ Edinburgh 137 mi – Glasgow 91 mi – Oban 36 mi
◉ Hamlet★
◉ Kilmory Knap (Macmillan's Cross★) SW : 14 m

Crinan
⊠ PA31 8SR – ℰ (01546) 830 261 – www.crinanhotel.com – Closed Christmas
20 rm (dinner included) – †£ 130/155 ††£ 290/360
Rest *Westward* – see restaurant listing
Rest *Seafood Bar* – Carte £ 19/33

• Built in the 19C to accommodate the Laird of Jura's business associates and boasting lovely Sound views. Simply furnished bedrooms – some with balconies and views. Small coffee shop sells homemade cakes; superb 3rd floor bar with terrace. Larger, wood-panelled bar offers an appealing menu of seafood dishes.

CRINAN

Westward – at Crinan Hotel
✉ PA31 8SR – ℰ (01546) 830 261 – www.crinanhotel.com – Closed Christmas
Rest – (dinner only) Menu £ 45
• Set within a welcoming, family-run hotel and boasting lovely views over the loch and Sound of Jura. Concise seafood-based menus rely on local and island produce. Homemade chocolates to finish.

CULLODEN – Highland – **501** H11 – see Inverness

CUPAR – Fife – **501** K15 – pop. 8 506 **28** C2
▶ Edinburgh 45 mi – Dundee 15 mi – Perth 23 mi

Ostler's Close
25 Bonnygate ✉ KY15 4BU – ℰ (01334) 655 574 – www.ostlerclose.co.uk – Closed 1-2 January, 2 weeks April, 2 weeks October, 25-26 December, Sunday and Monday
Rest – (dinner only and Saturday lunch) Carte £ 25/44
• Long-standing, personally run restaurant down a narrow alley just off the main street. Three cosy rooms decorated in warm reds; friendly, chatty service. Concise, traditional menus with beef and seafood to the fore and a Mediterranean edge.

CURRIE – City of Edinburgh – **501** K16 – see Edinburgh

DALKEITH – Midlothian – **501** K16 – pop. 11 566 **26** C1
▶ London 402 mi – Edinburgh 7 mi – Glasgow 52 mi – Aberdeen 138 mi

Sun Inn with rm
Lothian Bridge, Southwest : 2 mi by A 6094, B 6392 on A 7 ✉ EH22 4TR – ℰ (0131) 663 24 56 – www.thesuninnedinburgh.co.uk
5 rm ⊇ – †£ 70/125 ††£ 90/175
Rest – Menu £ 14 (lunch and early dinner) – Carte £ 13/28
• Former 17C blacksmith's with two large, open-fired rooms, wood and stone-faced walls and modern black and white photos. Extensive menus feature good quality local produce; dinner is more ambitious. Smart bedrooms boast hand-made furniture and Egyptian cotton.

DALRY – North Ayrshire – **501** F16 **25** A1
▶ Edinburgh 70 mi – Ayr 21 mi – Glasgow 25 mi

Lochwood Farm Steading without rest
Southwest : 5 mi by A 737 and Saltcoats rd ✉ KA21 6NG – ℰ (01294) 552 529 – www.lochwoodfarm.co.uk – Closed Christmas and New Year
3 rm ⊇ – †£ 55 ††£ 75
• Remote farmhouse on a 100 acre working dairy farm. Bedrooms are split between a converted barn and Scandinavian-style wood house complete with hot tub; the best are luxuriously appointed suites with fine linens and Isle of Arran toiletries.

Braidwoods (Keith Braidwood)
Drumastle Mill Cottage, Southwest : 1.5 mi by A 737 on Saltcoats rd ✉ KA24 4LN – ℰ (01294) 833 544 – www.braidwoods.co.uk – Closed 25 December-23 January, 2 weeks September, Sunday dinner, Monday, Tuesday lunch and Sunday from May-mid September
Rest – (booking essential) Menu £ 28/48
Spec. Timbale of Arbroath smokies with leeks and horseradish hollandaise. West coast turbot with braised fennel and langoustine jus. Valrhona chocolate truffle cake with salted caramel ice cream.
• Well-established crofter's cottage in remote location; very personally run by husband and wife team. Two-part dining room with homely feel. Seasonal, regional produce is the cornerstone of the flavoursome classical dishes. Smooth service.

DINGWALL – Highland – **501** G11 – pop. 5 026   30 C2
▶ Edinburgh 172 mi – Inverness 14 mi

✕✕ Cafe India Brasserie   AC VISA ⦿ AE
Lockhart House, Tulloch St ✉ *IV15 9JZ* – ✆ *(01349) 862 552*
– *www.cafeindiadingwall.co.uk*
– *Closed 25 December*
Rest – Indian – Carte £ 24/38
♦ Bustling, locally regarded Indian restaurant, handily located in town centre. Updated décor is fresh and modern. Authentically prepared, tasty regional Indian food.

DORNOCH – Highland – **501** H10 – pop. 1 206 Scotland   30 D2
▶ Edinburgh 219 mi – Inverness 63 mi – Wick 65 mi
🛈 Castle St ✆ (08452) 25 51 21, www.visitdornoch.com
⛳ Royal Dornoch Golf Rd, ✆ (01862) 81 02 19
◉ Town ★

⌂ Highfield House *without rest*   ⇐ 🚗 ⌀ ⁽ᵗ⁾ P
Evelix Rd ✉ *IV25 3HR* – ✆ *(01862) 810 909*
– *www.highfieldhouse.co.uk*
4 rm ⌁ – ♦£ 55 ♦♦£ 85
♦ Welcoming guesthouse with immaculately kept gardens and pleasant summer house. Spacious interior boasts conservatory style lounge and smart breakfast room. Comfy bedrooms have good facilities.

DOUNBY – **501** K16 – see Orkney Islands (Mainland)

DRUMBEG – Highland – **501** E9 – ✉ Highland   30 C1
▶ Edinburgh 262 mi – Inverness 105 mi – Ullapool 48 mi

⌂ Blar na Leisg at Drumbeg House ⌘   ⇐ 🚗 ⌀ ⁽ᵗ⁾ P VISA
take first right on entering village from Kylesku direction ✉ *IV27 4NW*
– ✆ *(01571) 833 325* – *www.blarnaleisg.com*
4 rm ⌁ – ♦£ 100/160 ♦♦£ 160
Rest – Menu £ 50
♦ Remotely set Edwardian house, affording lovely loch views. Large, open-fired sitting room filled with a vast array of books; spacious, luxuriously appointed bedrooms. Impressive modern art collection includes lots of Bauhaus works. Smart, contemporary dining room; fresh, local fish and shellfish are a speciality.

DRUMNADROCHIT – Highland – **501** G11 – pop. 813 – ✉ Milton   30 C2
 Scotland
▶ Edinburgh 172 mi – Inverness 16 mi – Kyle of Lochalsh 66 mi
◉ Loch Ness ★★ – Loch Ness Monster Exhibition ★ **AC** – The Great Glen ★

⌂ Drumbuie Farm *without rest*   ⇐ 🐄 ⌀ P VISA
Drumbuie, East : 0.75 mi by A 82 ✉ *IV63 6XP* – ✆ *(01456) 450 634*
– *www.loch-ness-farm.co.uk* – *February-November*
3 rm ⌁ – ♦£ 45/48 ♦♦£ 66/70
♦ Immaculate purpose-built guesthouse on working farm with Highland cattle. Pleasant breakfast room has Loch Ness views. Good collection of malt whiskies. Spacious bedrooms.

DUISDALEMORE – Highland – see Skye (Isle of)

DUMFRIES – Dumfries and Galloway – **501** J18 – pop. 31 146   26 C3
Scotland

▶ Edinburgh 80 mi – Ayr 59 mi – Carlisle 34 mi – Glasgow 79 mi

🛈 64 Whitesands ℘ (01387) 25 38 62, www.visitdumfriesandgalloway.co.uk

🏌 Dumfries & Galloway Maxwelltown 2 Laurieston Ave,
℘ (01387) 25 35 82

🏌 Dumfries & County Edinburgh Rd, Nunfield, ℘ (01387) 25 35 85

🏌 Crichton Bankend Rd, ℘ (01387) 24 78 94

⊙ Town★ – Midsteeple★ **A A**

◉ Lincluden College (Tomb★) **AC**, N : 1.5 mi by College St **A**.
Drumlanrig Castle★★ (cabinets★) **AC**, NW : 16.5 mi by A 76 **A** – Shambellie House Museum of Costume (Costume Collection★) S : 7.25 mi by A 710 **A** – Sweetheart Abbey★ **AC**, S : 8 mi by A 710 **A** – Caerlaverock Castle★ (Renaissance fa 0.5ade★★) **AC**, SE : 9 mi by B 725 **B** – Glenkiln (Sculptures★) W : 9 mi by A 780 - **A** - and A 75

DUMFRIES

Aldermanhill Rd.	B 2
Bank St.	A 3
Buccleuch St.	A 4
Cardoness St.	B 5
Cassalands	A 6
Castle Douglas Rd	A 8
Castle St	A 7
Catherine St.	B 9
Corberry Ave	A 10
Cornwall Mount Rd.	B 12
Cuckoo Bridge Retail Park	A
Friars Vennel	A 13
Galloway St.	A 14
Glebe St.	B 15
Great King St.	A 16
Hermitage Drive	A 17
High St.	A 18
Loreburn Centre	A 20
Loreburn St.	A 21
Nith St.	AB 22
Queensberry St.	A 24
Queen St.	B 23
Rae St.	B 26
St Mary's St.	B 27
St Michael St.	B 28
St Michael's Bridge Rd.	A 30
Shakespeare St.	B 31
Union St.	A 32
Whitesands	A 34

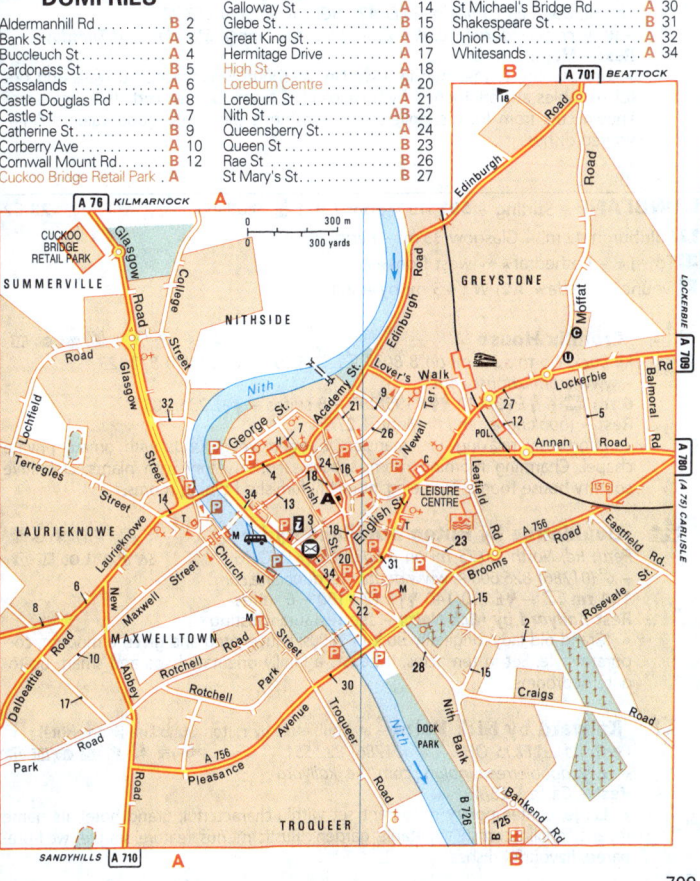

709

DUMFRIES

Hazeldean House without rest
4 Moffat Rd ✉ *DG1 1NJ* – ✆ *(01387) 266 178* – www.hazeldeanhouse.com
6 rm ⊑ – †£ 35/45 ††£ 60 **Bu**
• Victorian villa built in 1898. Lovely garden; curio-filled lounge and conservatory breakfast room. Victorian-themed bedrooms, 3 with four-posters; basement room has a nautical cabin style.

Hamilton House without rest
12 Moffat Rd ✉ *DG1 1NJ* – ✆ *(01387) 266 606*
– www.hamiltonhousedumfries.co.uk – Closed 24 December-3 January
7 rm ⊑ – †£ 35/45 ††£ 58/65 **Bc**
• Converted Victorian townhouse next to the bowls club. Large conservatory lounge; neat breakfast tables overlook the tennis courts. Large bedrooms combine the classical and the contemporary.

DUNBAR – East Lothian – 501 M15 – pop. 6 354 26 D1
▶ London 377 mi – Edinburgh 31 mi – Glasgow 77 mi – Aberdeen 162 mi

Creel
The Harbour, 25 Lamer St ✉ *EH42 1HG* – ✆ *(01368) 863 279*
– www.creelrestaurant.co.uk – Closed Sunday dinner, Monday and Tuesday
Rest – Menu £ 18/25
• Unassuming former pub in a working harbour. Wood panelled walls and polished tables are brightened by a welcoming team. Experienced chef uses lesser known cuts from local suppliers and transforms them into good value, full-flavoured dishes.

DUNBLANE – Stirling – 501 I15 – pop. 7 911 Scotland 28 C2
▶ Edinburgh 42 mi – Glasgow 33 mi – Perth 29 mi
 Town ★ – Cathedral ★★ (west front ★★)
Doune ★ (castle ★ AC) W : 4.5 mi by A 820

Cromlix House
Kinbuck, North : 3.5 mi on B 8033 ✉ *FK15 9JT* – ✆ *(01786) 822 125*
– www.cromlixhouse.com
6 rm ⊑ – †£ 95/140 ††£ 195/285 – 8 suites – ††£ 235/285
Rest – (booking essential) Menu £ 27/54
• Effortlessly relaxing 19C mansion in extensive grounds with ornate private chapel. Charming morning room; spacious conservatory with plants. Definitive country house rooms. Two elegant, richly furnished dining rooms.

Doubletree by Hilton Dunblane Hydro
Perth Rd, North : .0.75 mi on B 8033 ✉ *FK15 OHG*
– ✆ *(01786) 826 600* – www.doubletreedunblane.com
194 rm ⊑ – †£ 110/140 ††£ 120/150 – 6 suites
Rest *Kailyard by Nick Nairn* – see restaurant listing
• 'Grand old lady' originally built in 1800s; rejuvenated and given a modern, corporate style. Set in ten acres, it boasts a family orientated spa and smart, up-to-date bedrooms.

Kailyard by Nick Nairn – at Doubletree by Hilton Dunblane Hydro Hotel
Perth Rd ✉ *FK15 OHG* – ✆ *(01786) 822 551*
– www.doubletreedunblane.com/the_kailyard
Rest – Carte £ 28/45
• Large, contemporary restaurant set within characterful, grand hotel; its name means 'small Scottish vegetable garden'. Rustic menus feature simple, well-prepared, flavourful dishes.

DUNDEE – Dundee City – **501** L14 – pop. 154 674   **28** C2
Scotland

- Edinburgh 63 mi – Aberdeen 67 mi – Glasgow 83 mi

Access Tay Road Bridge (toll) Y

- Dundee Airport : ☏ (01382) 662200, SW : 1.5 mi Z
- Discovery Quay ☏ (01382) 52 75 27, www.angusanddundee.co.uk
- Caird Park Mains Loan, ☏ (01382) 45 36 06
- Camperdown Camperdown Park, ☏ (01382) 62 33 98
- Downfield Turnberry Ave, ☏ (01382) 82 55 95
- Town ★ - The Frigate Unicorn ★ **AC** Y **A** – Discovery Point ★ **AC** Y **B** – Verdant Works ★ Z **D** – McManus Galleries ★ Y **M**

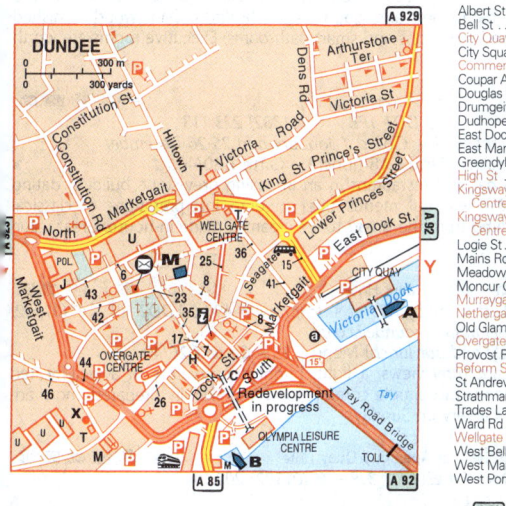

Albert St	Z 2
Bell St	Y 6
City Quay	Y
City Square	Y 7
Commercial St	Y 8
Coupar Angus Rd	Z 9
Douglas Rd	Z 10
Drumgeith Rd	Z 12
Dudhope Terrace	Z 13
East Dock St	Z 14
East Marketgait	Y 15
Greendykes Rd	Z 16
High St	Y 17
Kingsway East Shopping Centre	Z
Kingsway West Shopping Centre	Z
Logie St	Z 18
Mains Rd	Z 21
Meadowside	Y 23
Moncur Crescent	Y 24
Murraygate	Y 25
Nethergate	Y 26
Old Glamis Rd	Z 32
Overgate Centre	Y
Provost Rd	Z 34
Reform St	Y 35
St Andrews St	Y 36
Strathmartine Rd	Z 40
Trades Lane	Y 41
Ward Rd	Y 42
Wellgate Centre	Y
West Bell St	Y 43
West Marketgait	Y 44
West Port	Y 46

DUNDEE

Apex City Quay
1 West Victoria Dock Rd ⊠ DD1 3JP – ⌀ (01382) 202 404
– www.apexhotels.co.uk   Ya
150 rm – †£ 80/230 ††£ 80/230, ⌑ £ 13.50 – 2 suites
Rest *Metro Brasserie* – see restaurant listing

♦ Modern waterfront hotel in an up-and-coming area. Vast bar-lounge and good business facilities. Spacious, contemporary bedrooms boast king-sized beds and large windows looking over the city or marina. Atmospheric spa and treatment rooms.

Landmark
Kingsway West, West 4.5mi by A85 at junction with A90 ⊠ DD2 5JT – ⌀ (01382) 641 122 – www.thelandmarkdundee.co.uk
95 rm – †£ 59/129 ††£ 79/139, ⌑ £ 13.95
Rest *Garden Room* – see restaurant listing

♦ Imposing granite country house – formerly a private residence – dating back to 1870. Welcoming bar-lounge and good leisure facilities. Dark wood furnished bedrooms with good mod cons and smart bathrooms; Executive rooms are worth the extra.

Playwright
11 Tay Sq, South Tay St. ⊠ DD1 1PB – ⌀ (01382) 223 113
– www.theplaywright.co.uk – Closed 1 January and 25-26 December
Rest – *(closed Sunday)* Menu £ 18 (lunch) – Carte £ 30/46   Yx

♦ Smart, modern bar and restaurant in an imposing grey-stone building dating back to the 1800s. Seasonal menus offer modern interpretations of classical dishes and everything from the bread to ice cream is made in-house. Great value lunch.

Garden Room – at Landmark Hotel
Kingsway West, West 4.5mi by A85 at junction with A90 ⊠ DD2 5JT – ⌀ (01382) 641 122 – www.thelandmarkdundee.co.uk
Rest – *(dinner only and bar lunch)* Menu £ 25 – Carte £ 26/40

♦ Boasting pleasant rural views, a light, bright conservatory in a well-located country house. Menus mix simple comfort food and skilfully prepared, more adventurous dishes. Carvery on Sundays.

Metro Brasserie – at Apex City Quay Hotel
1 West Victoria Dock Rd ⊠ DD1 3JP – ⌀ (01382) 202 404
– www.apexhotels.co.uk   Ya
Rest – Menu £ 14/22 – Carte £ 24/35

♦ Popular brasserie set in a contemporary waterfront hotel, boasting comfy banquette booths and pleasant views across the quay. Long-standing chef offers a modern, seasonal, grill-based menu.

at Broughty Ferry East : 4.5 mi by A 930 - Z – ⊠ Dundee

Broughty Ferry
16 West Queen St ⊠ DD5 1AR – ⌀ (01382) 480 027
– www.hotelbroughtyferry.co.uk
15 rm ⌑ – †£ 70/82 ††£ 90   **Rest** – Indian – Carte £ 16/29 **s**

♦ Friendly, family-run hotel, located on the roadside in a small village outside Dundee. Traditionally decorated interior and spacious, individually decorated bedrooms with complimentary mini bottles of wine. High tea features homemade cakes. Restaurant offers classic European dishes and extensive Indian menu.

DUNKELD – Perth and Kinross – **501** J14 – pop. 1 005 ▌Scotland   **28** C2

▶ Edinburgh 58 mi – Aberdeen 88 mi – Inverness 98 mi – Perth 14 mi
ℹ The Cross ⌀ (01350) 72 76 88, www.dunkeldandbirnam.co.uk
⛳ Dunkeld & Birnam Fungarth, ⌀ (01350) 72 75 24
◉ Village★ - Cathedral Street★

DUNKELD

Letter Farm without rest
Loch of the Lowes, Northeast : 3 mi by A 923 on Loch of Lowes rd ✉ PH8 0HH
– ℰ (01350) 724 224 – www.letterfarm.co.uk – May-November
3 rm – †£ 50 ††£ 80

♦ Traditional farmhouse on a family-run stock farm, nestled between Butterstone Loch and the Loch of the Lowes Nature Reserve. Open-fired lounge with TV/DVD player; homely communal breakfast room. Comfortable, simply furnished bedrooms boast king-sized beds; no TVs.

DUNOON – Argyll and Bute – 501 F16 – pop. 8 251 – Scotland — 27 B3

▶ Edinburgh 73 mi – Glasgow 27 mi – Oban 77 mi

🚢 from Dunoon Pier to Gourock Railway Pier (Caledonian MacBrayne Ltd) frequent services daily (20 mn) – from Hunters Quay to McInroy's Point, Gourock (Western Ferries (Clyde) Ltd) frequent services daily (20 mn)

🛈 7 Alexandra Parade ℰ (08707) 20 06 29, www.visitcowal.co.uk

⛳ Cowal Ardenslate Rd, ℰ (01369) 70 56 73
⛳ Innellan Knockamillie Rd, ℰ (01369) 83 02 42
◉ The Clyde Estuary ★

Dhailling Lodge
155 Alexandra Par, North : 0.75 mi on A 815 ✉ PA23 8AW – ℰ (01369) 701 253
– www.dhaillinglodge.com
7 rm – †£ 40/76 ††£ 81
Rest – (dinner only) (booking essential) Menu £ 20

♦ Proudly run Victorian villa on main seafront, with pleasant gardens and nice bay views. Snug, homely lounge; cosy, individually decorated bedrooms with good extras. Smart dining room with period fireplace; classical daily menu of unfussy pies, roasts and fish.

DUNVEGAN – Highland – 501 A11 – see Skye (Isle of)

DURNESS – Highland – 501 F8 – ✉ Highland — 30 C1

▶ Edinburgh 266 mi – Thurso 78 mi – Ullapool 71 mi
🛈 Durine ℰ (0845) 2 25 51 21, www.durness.org
⛳ Durness Balnakeil, ℰ (01971) 51 13 64

Mackay's
✉ IV27 4PN – ℰ (01971) 511 202 – www.visitmackays.com – May-October
7 rm – †£ 110/125 ††£ 125
Rest – Carte £ 23/38

♦ Smart grey house at most north westerly point of mainland – the family own a number of places in the village. Two nicely furnished, oak-clad lounges. Lovely bedrooms with exposed wood floors, plasma screens and iPod docks. Formal dining room offers ambitious menu.

DUROR – Highland – 501 E14 — 29 B3

▶ Edinburgh 131 mi – Ballachulish 7 mi – Oban 26 mi

Bealach House
Salachan Glen, Southeast : 4.5 mi by A 828 ✉ PA38 4BW – ℰ (01631) 740 298
– www.bealach-house.co.uk – March-October
3 rm – †£ 70/80 ††£ 100/120   **Rest** – Menu £ 30

♦ Superbly set, former crofter's house with impressive 1.5 mile driveway lined with mature, deer-filled forest: the scenery is breathtaking. Snug conservatory and cosy bedrooms; homely guest areas are hung with Lowry tapestries. Classical, daily changing menu.

DYKE – Moray – 501 J11 – see Forres

EDDLESTON – The Scottish Borders – 501 K16 – see Peebles

EDINBANE – Highland – 501 A11 – see Skye (Isle of)

EDINBURGH

See city maps on following pages 26 C1

SCOTLAND

City of Edinburgh – pop. 430 082 – 501 K16 – Scotland

▶ Glasgow 46 – Newcastle upon Tyne 105

Tourist Information

3 Princes St ✆ (08452) 255 1 21, www.edinburgh.org

Airport

Edinburgh Airport : ✆ (0844) 481 8989, W : 6 m. by A 8 AV

Golf Courses

- Braid Hills Braid Hills Rd, ✆ (0131) 447 66 66
- Carrick Knowe Glendevon Park, ✆ (0131) 3 37 10 96
- Duddingston Duddingston Road West, ✆ (0131) 661 76 88
- Silverknowes Parkway, ✆ (0131) 336 38 43

◉ SIGHTS

In the town : City★★★ • Edinburgh International Festival★★★ (August) • Royal Museum of Scotland★★★ EZ**M2** • National Gallery of Scotland★★ DY**M4** • Royal Botanic Garden★★★ AV • The Castle★★★ AC DY**Z** • Abbey and Palace of Holyroodhouse★★ AC BV • New Town★★ CY**14** • The Georgian House★ AC CY**D** • Scottish National Portrait Gallery★ EY**M6** • Dundas House★ EY**E**) • Scottish National Gallery of Modern Art★ AV**M1** • Scott Monument★ ≤AC EY**F** • Craigmillar Castle★ AC, SE : 3 mi by A 7 BX • Dean Gallery★ AV opposite M1 • Royal Yacht Britannia★ BV

On the outskirts : Edinburgh Zoo★★ AC AV • The Royal Observatory ≤★ AC BX

In the surrounding area : Rosslyn Chapel★★ AC S : 7.5 mi by A 701 - BX - and B 7006 • Forth Bridges★★, NW : 9.5 mi by A 90 AV • Hopetoun House★★ AC, NW : 11.5 mi by A 90 - AV - and A 904

EDINBURGH

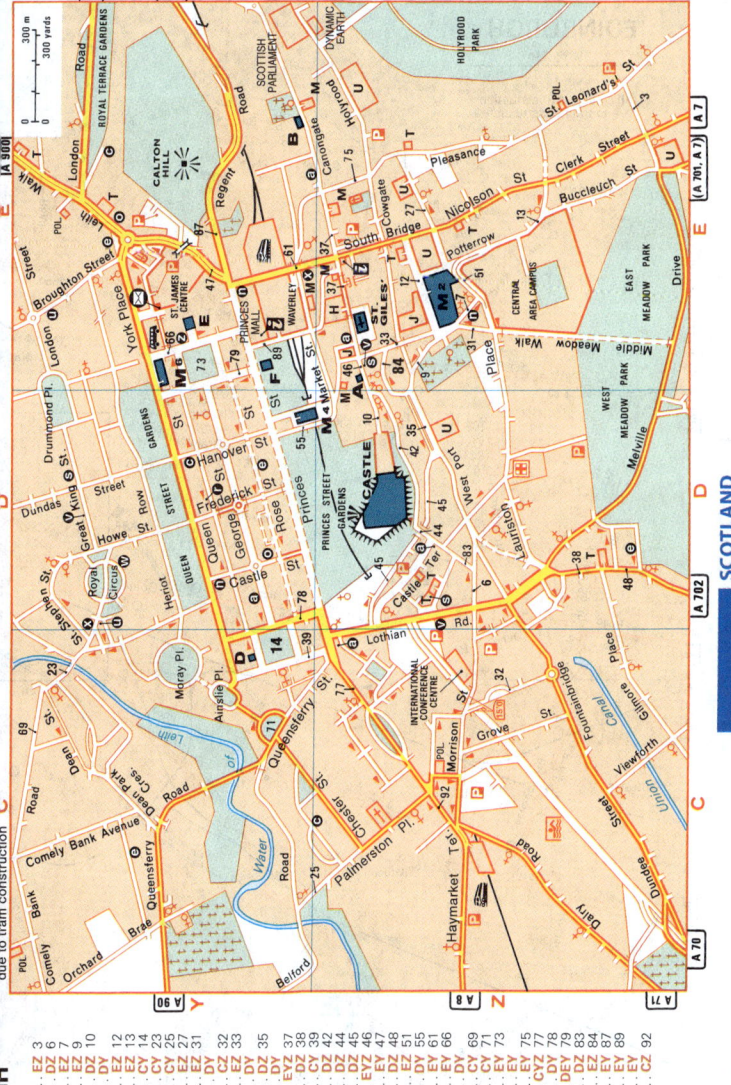

Street	Grid
Bernard Terrace	EZ 3
Bread St.	DZ 6
Bristo Pl.	EZ 7
Candlemaker Row	EZ 9
Castlehill	DZ 10
Castle St.	DY
Chambers St.	EZ 12
Chapel St.	EZ 13
Charlotte Square	CY 14
Deanhaugh St.	CY 23
Douglas Gardens	CY 25
Drummond St.	EZ 27
Forrest Rd.	EZ 31
Frederick St.	DY
Gardner's Crescent	CZ 32
George IV Bridge	EZ 33
George St.	DY
Grassmarket	DZ 35
Hanover St.	DY
High St.	EY 37
Home St.	DZ 38
Hope St.	CY 39
Johnston Terrace	DZ 42
King's Bridge	DZ 44
King's Stables Rd.	DZ 45
Lawnmarket	EYZ 46
Leith St.	EY 47
Leven St.	DZ 48
Lothian St.	EZ 51
Mound (The)	DY 55
North Bridge	EY 61
North St. Andrew St.	EY 66
Princes St.	DY
Raeburn Pl.	CY 69
Randolph Crescent	CY 71
St. Andrew Square	EY 73
St. James Centre	EY
St. Mary's St.	EY 75
Shandwick Pl.	CYZ 77
South Charlotte St.	DY 78
South St. David St.	DEY 79
Spittal St.	DZ 83
Victoria St.	EZ 84
Waterloo Pl.	EY 87
Waverley Bridge	EY 89
West Maitland St.	CZ 92

715

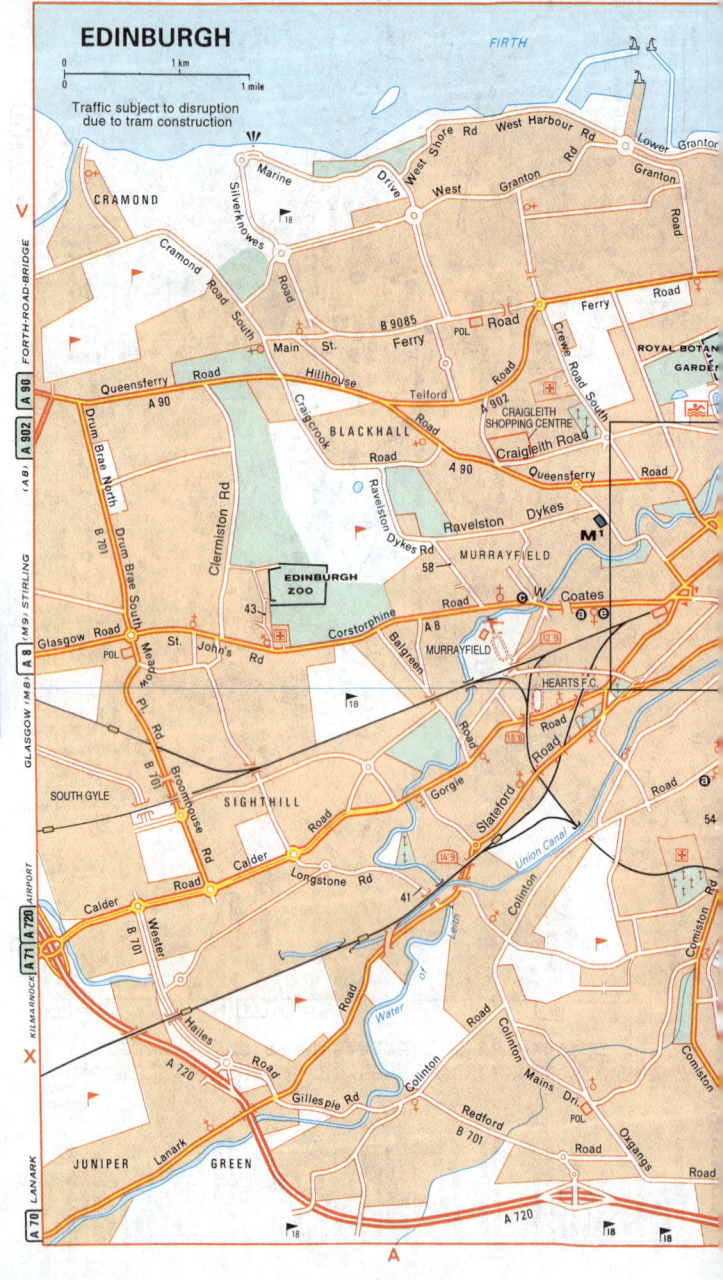

Bruntsfield Pl.	**BX** 8
Cameron Toll Centre	**BX**
Commercial St	**BV** 15
Constitution St	**BV** 17
Craigleith Shopping Centre	**AV**
Craigmillar Park	**BX** 20
Duddingston Park	**BX** 28
Gilmerton Dykes St	**BX** 34
Great Junction St	**BV** 36
Howden Hall Rd	**BX** 40
Inglis Green Rd	**AX** 41
Kaimes Rd	**AV** 43
Morningside Rd	**AX** 54
Murrayfield Rd	**AV** 58
Newtoft St	**BX** 60
North Junction St	**BV** 62
Ocean Terminal Shopping Centre	**BV**
Portobello High St	**BV** 67
Salamander St	**BV** 76

717

EDINBURGH

Balmoral
1 Princes St ⊠ EH2 2EQ – ℰ (0131) 556 24 14 – www.roccofortehotels.com
168 rm – †£ 165/415 ††£ 165/415, ⊇ £ 21 – 20 suites EYn
Rest *Number One* ✿ **Rest** *Hadrian's* – see restaurant listing
• Deluxe Edwardian hotel boasting classically styled bedrooms with rich fabrics and a subtle contemporary edge. Have traditional afternoon tea to the accompaniment of live harp music or try out the cocktails in the bar. Highly detailed service.

Sheraton Grand H. & Spa
1 Festival Sq ⊠ EH3 9SR – ℰ (0131) 229 91 31
– www.sheratonedinburgh.co.uk CDZv
258 rm – †£ 265/305 ††£ 285/325, ⊇ £ 20 – 11 suites
Rest *Santini* – see restaurant listing
• Spacious, modern hotel with two entrances. Sleek, stylish bedrooms boast strong comforts, the latest mod cons and smart bathrooms complete with mood lighting. Impressive four-storey glass cube houses a stunning spa.

Prestonfield
Priestfield Rd ⊠ EH16 5UT – ℰ (0131) 225 78 00 – www.prestonfield.com
18 rm ⊇ – †£ 295 ††£ 295 – 5 suites BXr
Rest *Rhubarb* – see restaurant listing
• 17C country house in a pleasant rural spot, with dimly lit, opulent interior displaying warm colours, fine furnishings and old tapestries – one of the most romantic hotels around. Various elegant lounges and a whisky room. Unique, luxurious bedrooms boast a high level of modern facilities. Excellent service.

Howard
34 Great King St ⊠ EH3 6QH – ℰ (0131) 557 35 00 – www.thehoward.com
17 rm ⊇ – †£ 115/210 ††£ 210/260 – 1 suite DYs
Rest *Atholl* – (booking essential for non-residents) Menu £ 32
• Series of 3 Georgian townhouses displaying characterful original features and plenty of charm. Comfy period lounges. Spacious, luxurious bedrooms with classic furnishings and a contemporary edge; each room is assigned a butler. Fine dining in elegant restaurant.

Scotsman
20 North Bridge ⊠ EH3 1TR – ℰ (0131) 556 55 65
– www.thescotsmanhotel.co.uk EYx
67 rm – †£ 320/350 ††£ 320/350, ⊇ £ 16.95 – 2 suites
Rest *North Bridge Brasserie* – see restaurant listing
• Characterful Victorian hotel set within the old 'Scotsman' newspaper offices. Lovely period guest areas with wood panelling, stained glass and marble staircase. Good business facilities and large leisure club. Traditionally styled bedrooms.

Hotel Missoni
1 George IV Bridge ⊠ EH1 1AD – ℰ (0131) 220 66 66 – www.hotelmissoni.com
134 rm – †£ 190/400 ††£ 205/415, ⊇ £ 18.50 – 2 suites EZv
Rest *Cucina* – see restaurant listing
• Striking, modern hotel; the first from this Milan fashion house, whose trademark stripes feature throughout. Funky bar; boldly coloured bedrooms with clever design features, complimentary mini bar and smart, black mosaic floored bathrooms.

Channings
15 South Learmonth Gdns ⊠ EH4 1EZ – ℰ (0131) 274 74 01
– www.channings.co.uk CYe
38 rm ⊇ – †£ 95/250 ††£ 125/250 – 3 suites **Rest** – Carte £ 14/30 s
• Cosy Edwardian townhouse, tastefully furnished and run by a friendly team. Individually appointed bedrooms: the newer rooms are spacious, contemporary and themed after Shackleton, who lived in one of the four houses that now make up the hotel. Formal basement restaurant serves Gallic dishes.

EDINBURGH

Hotel du Vin
11 Bristo Pl ⊠ EH1 1EZ – ℰ (0131) 247 49 00 – www.hotelduvin.com/edinburgh
47 rm – †£ 195/250, ††£ 195/250, ☐ £ 14.95   EZ**n**
Rest *Bistro* – see restaurant listing
♦ Boutique hotel boasting unique modern murals, not far from the Royal Mile. Guest areas include a whisky snug offering 300 spirits and mezzanine bar with wine tasting room and glass-fronted cellars. Dark wood furnished, wine-themed bedrooms.

Tigerlily
125 George St ⊠ EH2 4JN – ℰ (0131) 225 50 05 – www.tigerlilyedinburgh.co.uk
– Closed 25 December   DY**a**
33 rm ☐ – †£ 165/195 ††£ 165/195   **Rest** – Carte £ 25/50
♦ Classic Georgian townhouse concealing a funky, boutique interior. Large, individually designed bedrooms are luxurious, boasting seductive lighting, quality furnishings and superb wet rooms. Busy open-plan bar and dining room have similarly stylish, modern décor.

Glasshouse without rest
2 Greenside Pl ⊠ EH1 3AA – ℰ (0131) 525 82 00 – www.theetoncollection.com
– Closed 24-26 December   EY**o**
65 rm – †£ 150/325 ††£ 190/325, ☐ £ 18.50
♦ Contemporary glass hotel with 150 year old church façade. Stylish bedrooms have floor to ceiling windows and some balconies. Impressive two acre roof garden; honesty bar and 3 course room service.

SCOTLAND

Number Ten
6-10 Gloucester Pl ⊠ EH3 6EF – ℰ (0131) 225 27 20
– www.numbertenedinburgh.com   DY**u**
28 rm – †£ 99/190 ††£ 135/250, ☐ £ 12.50
Rest – *(closed Saturday) (dinner only)* Carte £ 23/34
♦ Luxurious adjoining townhouses with romantic interiors and stunningly restored staircases. Decorated in gold, black and silver colour schemes, bedrooms boast top class furnishings and jacuzzis. Sleek, modern dining room – set in the original house – offers simple, Scottish-based menu.

Rutland
1-3 Rutland St. ⊠ EH1 2AE – ℰ (0131) 229 34 02 – www.therutland.com
– Closed 25 December   CZ**a**
12 rm – †£ 135/250 ††£ 135/250, ☐ £ 7.95
Rest – Menu £ 13 – Carte £ 26/44
♦ Boutique hotel with commanding position at top of Princes Street. Stylish, modern bedrooms have bold décor, flat screen TVs and large, slate-floored shower rooms; ask for one with a castle view. Contemporary restaurant uses plenty of Scottish produce in its classic dishes.

Chester Residence without rest
9 Rothesay Pl ⊠ EH3 7SL – ℰ (0131) 226 2075 – www.chester-residence.com
25 suites – ††£ 165/275, ☐ £ 9   CZ**c**
♦ Collection of townhouses boasting one or two bedrooms suites. State-of-the-art facilities include video entry and sounds systems wired throughout. Fully equipped kitchens: the owners provide breakfast items or deliver a continental option. Concise selection of pre-prepared dishes available at dinner.

Dunstane City without rest
5 Hampton Terr, Haymarket ⊠ EH12 5JD – ℰ (0131) 337 61 69
– www.dunstanehotels.co.uk   AV**e**
16 rm – †£ 79/169 ††£ 89/179 – 1 suite
♦ Victorian house with modern feature wallpapers, black granite tiled floors and large chandeliers in guest areas. Stylish, wood-furnished bedrooms offer good facilities; some boast jacuzzis.

719

EDINBURGH

Kingsburgh House without rest
2 Corstorphine Rd ⊠ EH12 6HN – ℰ (0131) 313 16 79
– www.thekingsburgh.co.uk
6 rm ⊡ – ♦£ 120/145

AVc

♦ Attractive Victorian villa with hands-on owners. Comfy lounge and formally laid breakfast room; ornate coving features throughout. Warm, classically styled bedrooms feature antiques, modern facilities and good extras; some are four-posters.

Kildonan Lodge
27 Craigmillar Pk. ⊠ EH16 5PE – ℰ (0131) 667 27 93
– www.kildonanlodgehotel.co.uk – Closed 25-26 December
12 rm ⊡ – ♦£ 69/129 ♦♦£ 89/159

BXa

Rest – (closed Sunday) (dinner only, booking essential) Carte £ 18/24
♦ Well-managed detached Victorian house on main road into city. Spacious and traditionally furnished, with cosy fire-lit drawing room and comfy bedrooms; some with four-posters and jacuzzis. Mathew's offers classical dining and plenty of Scottish produce.

One Royal Circus without rest
1 Royal Circus ⊠ EH3 6SU – ℰ (0131) 625 6669 – www.oneroyalcircus.com
5 rm ⊡ – ♦£ 139/199 ♦♦£ 178/258

DYw

♦ Stunning Georgian house at the end of a crescent; designed by William Playfair in 1823. Spacious interior with billiard room and 2 lounges boasting ornate plasterwork, a grand piano and bar. Stylish, understated bedrooms; marble bathrooms.

94 DR without rest
94 Dalkeith Rd ⊠ EH16 5AF – ℰ (0131) 662 92 65 – www.94dr.com – Closed 5-26 January and 25-26 December
6 rm ⊡ – ♦£ 80/120 ♦♦£ 95/125

BXn

♦ Victorian terraced house on the main road into the city. Brightly tiled hallway leads to retro-style lounge with honesty bar. Lovely breakfast conservatory opens onto a decked terrace. Stylish, well-equipped bedrooms boast Scottish touches.

Millers64 without rest
64 Pilrig St ⊠ EH6 5AS – ℰ (0131) 454 3666 – www.millers64.co.uk
3 rm ⊡ – ♦£ 80/90 ♦♦£ 90/140

BVe

♦ Modernised Victorian house in a renovated terrace, in an up and coming part of town. Smart, spacious bedrooms are all suites and boast good quality linen and extras. Communal breakfasts include a hot special and homemade pastries and jams.

Kew House without rest
1 Kew Terr, Murrayfield ⊠ EH12 5JE – ℰ (0131) 313 07 00 – www.kewhouse.com
– Closed January and 25-26 December
7 rm ⊡ – ♦£ 79/130 ♦♦£ 99/195

AVa

♦ Personally run stone-built house, close to Murrayfield Stadium. Larger than it looks from the outside. Neat lounge and wood furnished breakfast room. Immaculately kept bedrooms are up-to-date, of a decent size and come with good extras.

Ardmor House without rest
74 Pilrig St ⊠ EH6 5AS – ℰ (0131) 554 4944 – www.ardmorhouse.com
5 rm ⊡ – ♦£ 55/90 ♦♦£ 85/145

BVn

♦ Comfortable, laid-back guesthouse on a quiet residential street. Bedrooms range in size and boast bright, fresh décor, original plaster ceilings and granite fireplaces. Homemade bread, preserves and cakes at breakfast. Good local knowledge.

Davenport House without rest
58 Great King St ⊠ EH3 6QY – ℰ (0131) 558 84 95 – www.davenport-house.com
– Closed 1 week Christmas
6 rm ⊡ – ♦£ 65/110 ♦♦£ 75/110

DYv

♦ Traditional Georgian townhouse restored to its former glory; set on an attractive cobbled street. Cosy sitting room and spacious breakfast room. Bedrooms are at the top of the house and furnished in individual styles.

EDINBURGH

Elmview without rest
15 Glengyle Terr ⊠ EH3 9LN – ℰ (0131) 228 19 73 – www.elmview.co.uk
– April-November
5 rm – †£ 75/115 ††£ 90/140

DZ**e**

♦ Occupies the basement of a Victorian house in pretty terrace overlooking The Meadows. Bedrooms are spotlessly kept and are very large, with modern bathrooms. Owners are very welcoming.

Number One – at Balmoral Hotel
1 Princes St ⊠ EH2 2EQ – ℰ (0131) 557 67 27 – www.restaurantnumberone.com
Rest – Modern – *(dinner only)* Menu £ 62

EY**n**

Spec. Scallops with apple purée, Iberico ham and chorizo crumb. Fillet of beef with Anna potato, sweetbreads and Madeira jus. Slow-cooked cherries, goat's cheese sorbet and honey and fennel mousse.

♦ Stylish restaurant in a grand hotel, displaying bold red walls hung with fine art, well-spaced tables and deep corner banquettes. Ambitious cooking uses quality Scottish produce to create elaborate, precisely executed dishes. Assured, attentive service.

21212 (Paul Kitching) with rm
3 Royal Terr ⊠ EH7 5AB – ℰ (0845) 222 12 12 – www.21212restaurant.co.uk
– Closed 10 days January and 10 days summer
4 rm – †£ 325 ††£ 325

EY**c**

Rest – Inventive – *(closed Sunday and Monday)* Menu £ 26/67 **s**
Spec. Nugget of smoked salmon with chickpeas, pimento, aubergine, yoghurt, kidney bean and thyme cream sauce. Baby halibut with golden beetroot, smoked chicken wafers, sweet ginger butter sauce and piccalilli mayonnaise. Layered trifle of Granny Smith, Williams pear and Victoria plum purée, crushed 'Weetabix' crumble.

♦ Smart Georgian townhouse with high-ceilinged dining room, contemporary décor and an open kitchen. The restaurant's name reflects the number of dishes per course; skilful and innovative cooking offers some quirky combinations. Opulent 1st floor sitting room and luxurious bedrooms.

Castle Terrace (Dominic Jack)
33-35 Castle Terr ⊠ EH1 2EL – ℰ (0131) 229 12 22
– www.castleterracerestaurant.com – Closed Christmas, New Year, Sunday and Monday

DZ**a**

Rest – Modern European – Menu £ 20 (lunch) – Carte £ 34/53
Spec. Spelt risotto with crispy ox tongue and veal heart confit. Seared hampe of beef with potato millefeuille and beef jus. Ravioli of lemongrass with poached rhubarb.

♦ Set in the shadows of the castle, an understatedly stylish restaurant with gilded ceiling and attractive bar-lounge. Refined cooking showcases seasonal, local produce in an assured, unfussy manner, following a 'nature to plate' philosophy.

Hadrian's – at Balmoral Hotel
2 North Bridge ⊠ EH1 1TR – ℰ (0131) 557 50 00 – www.roccofortehotels.com
Rest – Brasserie – Menu £ 23/27 – Carte £ 31/50

EY**n**

♦ Delightful restaurant where a light, bright interior offsets dark floors and brown leather chairs. Brasserie classics display plenty of Scottish produce; excellent value 3 course set menu.

Oloroso
33 Castle St ⊠ EH2 3DN – ℰ (0131) 226 76 14 – www.oloroso.co.uk – Closed 25-26 December

DY**o**

Rest – Modern European – Menu £ 25/40 **s** – Carte £ 31/43 **s**

♦ Contemporary rooftop restaurant with buzzy atmosphere and good service. Huge glass windows and superb terrace boast city, river and castle views. Bar and grill menus display modern cooking.

EDINBURGH

XX Rhubarb – at Prestonfield Hotel
Priestfield Rd ⊠ EH16 5UT – ℰ (0131) 225 13 33 – www.prestonfield.com
Rest – Modern – Menu £ 30 – Carte £ 37/59   BXr

• Richly decorated dining room set within a romantic 17C country house; so named, as this was the first place in Scotland where rhubarb was grown. Concise menu of both classic and modern dishes.

XX The Honours
58A North Castle St. ⊠ EH2 3LU – ℰ (0131) 220 2513 – www.thehonours.co.uk
– Closed first 2 weeks January, Sunday dinner and Monday   DYn
Rest – Modern European – Menu £ 18 (weekday lunch)/20 (early dinner)
– Carte £ 26/38

• Owned by a well-established chef, a bustling brasserie with a smart, stylish interior and pleasingly informal atmosphere. Menus take their influences from throughout Europe but have a French leaning and always offer some Scottish dishes.

XX Santini – at Sheraton Grand Hotel & Spa.
8 Conference Sq ⊠ EH3 8AN – ℰ (0131) 221 77 88
– www.santiniedinburgh.co.uk   CDZv
Rest – Italian – *(Closed Saturday lunch and all day Sunday)* Menu 19
– Carte £ 22/49

• Smart hotel restaurant; the more relaxed sister to Santini in London. Dining room split in two: the right side is more relaxed with a pleasant terrace. Wide-ranging menu of Italian classics; good value set selection.

XX Ondine
2 George IV Bridge (first floor) ⊠ EH1 1AD – ℰ (0131) 226 18 88
– www.ondinerestaurant.co.uk – Closed 1 week early January and
24-26 December   EZs
Rest – Seafood – Menu £ 20 (lunch and early dinner) – Carte £ 32/61

• Smart, lively restaurant dominated by granite-topped bar and crustacean counter. Classic menus showcase prime Scottish seafood. Straightforward, tasty cooking. Well-structured service.

XX Mark Greenaway
12 Picardy Pl. ⊠ EH1 3JT – ℰ (0131) 557 09 52 – www.no12picardyplace.com
– Closed 25 December, 1 January, Sunday and Monday   EYe
Rest – Modern – Menu £ 20 (lunch and early dinner) – Carte £ 29/45

• Modern restaurant set within a Georgian house in the heart of the city. Cooking is original, innovative and very visual, with Scottish produce arriving in unusual flavour and texture combinations. Good value set lunch and pre-theatre menus.

XX Angels with Bagpipes
343 High St., Royal Mile ⊠ EH1 1PW – ℰ (0131) 220 1111
– www.angelswithbagpipes.co.uk – Closed 24-26 December   EZa
Rest – Modern – Menu £ 20 (lunch) – Carte £ 26/42

• Small, split-level restaurant, just across from St Giles Cathedral on the Royal Mile. Simple interior; some tables overlook a rear courtyard. Seasonal menus change every six weeks, offering a mix of unfussy classics and more modern dishes.

XX Forth Floor - Restaurant (at Harvey Nichols)
30-34 St Andrew Sq ⊠ EH2 2AD – ℰ (0131) 524 83 50
– www.harveynichols.com – Closed 1 January, 25 December, Sunday and
Monday dinner   EYz
Rest – Modern European – Menu £ 28/35 – Carte £ 33/44

• Wonderful skyline views from huge room-length window; great sunsets. Bar divides it into formal area with pricier modern European menu, and more casual brasserie; good Scottish ingredients.

EDINBURGH

XX Cucina – at Hotel Missoni AC VISA ⓞ AE ①
1 George IV Bridge ✉ *EH1 1AD –* ☏ *(0131) 220 66 66 – www.hotelmissoni.com*
Rest – Italian – *(closed dinner 25 December, and lunch 31 December and 1 January)* Menu £20 (lunch) – Carte £32/58   EZ**v**

♦ Stylish mezzanine restaurant with buzzy atmosphere, set amongst the trademark stripes of this fashion house hotel. Classic Italian dishes served on boldly patterned china; some sharing plates.

XX North Bridge Brasserie – at Scotsman Hotel VISA ⓞ AE ①
20 North Bridge ✉ *EH1 1TR –* ☏ *(0131) 622 29 00*
– www.northbridgebrasserie.com   EY**x**
Rest – Scottish – Carte £25/48

♦ Stylish brasserie in a characterful Victorian hotel; once home to 'The Scotsman' newspaper. Beautiful room with ornate ceiling, dark wood panelling and minstrels gallery. Scottish cuisine.

XX Bistro – at Hotel du Vin AC VISA ⓞ AE
11 Bristo Pl ✉ *EH1 1EZ –* ☏ *(0131) 247 49 00 – www.hotelduvin.com/edinburgh*
Rest – French – Carte £21/29 ⌘   EZ**n**

♦ Located within a boutique hotel, a classical French bistro which plays host to regular themed lunches. Main menu offers traditional European choices and is accompanied by a superb wine list.

X Café St Honoré VISA ⓞ AE
34 North West Thistle Street Ln. ✉ *EH2 1EA –* ☏ *(0131) 226 22 11*
– www.cafesthonore.com – Closed 1 January and 24-26 December
Rest – French – *(booking essential)* Menu £20/23 – Carte £26/41   DY**r**

♦ Long-standing classical French bistro, hidden away down a side street. Simple interior crammed full of mirrors and bric-a-brac. Affordable daily menu with Gallic touch. Friendly service.

X Cafe Fish VISA ⓞ AE
15 North West Circus Pl. ✉ *EH3 6SX –* ☏ *(0131) 538 61 31 – www.cafefish.net*
– Closed 25 December   DY**x**
Rest – Seafood – Menu £25 (dinner) – Carte £19/29

♦ Well-established, family-run restaurant, previously located in Leith. Set in the city centre in a converted 1930s bank, it boasts characterful original features and excellent quality seafood. Menus are classically based with modern hints.

X L'Escargot Bleu VISA ⓞ AE ①
56-56a Broughton St ✉ *EH1 3SA –* ☏ *(0131) 557 16 00*
– www.lescargotbleu.co.uk – Closed 25 December, 1 January and Sundays
Rest – French – Carte £15/30   EY**u**

♦ Authentic French bistro with basement épicerie; sit in the front room, with its large windows, gingham tablecloths and buzzy atmosphere. Keenly priced menus offer classic French dishes.

X Zucca ☂ AC 🅥 VISA ⓞ AE
15-17 Grindlay St ✉ *EH3 9AX –* ☏ *(0131) 221 93 23*
– www.zuccarestaurant.co.uk – Closed 1 January, 25-26 December, Sunday and Monday   DZ**s**
Rest – Italian – *(booking essential)* Menu £12/18 – Carte £18/29

♦ Friendly, well-run restaurant adjacent to Lyceum Theatre. Head upstairs for classic Italian dishes and all-Italian wine list, with great value pre-theatre menus. Book or come after 8pm.

X Bia Bistrot 🅥 VISA ⓞ AE ①
19 Colinton Rd ✉ *EH10 5DP –* ☏ *(0131) 452 84 53 – www.biabistrot.co.uk*
– Closed first week January, second week July, Sunday and Monday
Rest – Bistro – Menu £11 (lunch and early dinner)   AX**a**
– Carte £20/31

♦ Good value neighbourhood bistro with buzzy vibe and shabby chic style. Unfussy, flavoursome dishes range in influence due to the friendly owners' Irish-Scottish and French-Spanish heritages.

EDINBURGH

Wedgwood
267 Canongate ⊠ EH8 8BQ – ℰ (0131) 558 87 37
– www.wedgwoodtherestaurant.co.uk – Closed 3-20 January and
25-26 December   EYa
Rest – Bistro – Menu £ 14 (lunch) – Carte £ 28/42
♦ Popular, atmospheric, split-level bistro with bold white and crimson décor, hidden away at bottom of Royal Mile. Personally run, with friendly staff. Well-presented, seasonal dishes.

Seadogs
43 Rose St ⊠ EH2 2NH – ℰ (0131) 225 80 28 – www.seadogsonline.co.uk
– Closed 1 January and 25 December   DYe
Rest – Seafood – Carte £ 18/21
♦ Lively seafood restaurant with canine motif, funky wallpaper and fast, friendly service. Well-priced menus offer sustainable fish and chips, plus a choice of tasty lighter dishes.

Amore Dogs
104 Hanover St ⊠ EH2 1DR – ℰ (0131) 220 51 55 – www.amoredogs.co.uk
– Closed 25 December and 1 January   DYc
Rest – Italian – Carte £ 14/24
♦ Sister to 'The Dogs' next door, with similar canine-themed décor. Simple, spacious and open-plan, with a buzzy atmosphere and friendly service. Good value, rustic Italian dishes.

Dogs
110 Hanover St ⊠ EH2 1DR – ℰ (0131) 220 12 08 – www.thedogsonline.co.uk
– Closed 1 January and 25 December   DYc
Rest – British – Carte £ 12/23
♦ Simple eatery set on the first floor of a classic Georgian mid-terraced property; the original opening in the 'Dogs' group. Two high-ceilinged, shabby chic dining rooms and appealing bar area. Robust, good value comfort food is crafted from fresh, local, seasonal produce.

at Leith

Malmaison
1 Tower Pl ⊠ EH6 7DB – ℰ (0131) 468 50 00 – www.malmaison-edinburgh.com
100 rm – †£ 100/205 ††£ 100/205, ⊇ £ 14.50   BVi
Rest *Brasserie* – see restaurant listing
♦ Impressive former seamen's mission, set on the quayside; the first of the Malmaison hotels. Mix of bold stripes and black and white décor. Imitate bar and comfortable, well-equipped bedrooms; one with a four-poster and tartan roll-top bath.

Martin Wishart
54 The Shore ⊠ EH6 6RA – ℰ (0131) 553 35 57 – www.martin-wishart.co.uk
– Closed 25-26 December, 1-19 January, Sunday and Monday   BVu
Rest – Innovative – *(booking essential)* Menu £ 29/65
Spec. Roasted Kilbrannan langoustines with parsnip and white chocolate purée. Loin of Borders roe deer with goat's cheese gnocchi. Jivara dark chocolate, milk chocolate mousse and Earl Grey ice cream.
♦ Discrete façade leads to tastefully decorated room with bold, modern designs. Underpinned by a classical base, well presented dishes display carefully judged modern touches and excellent ingredients. Two tasting menus available.

Kitchin (Tom Kitchin)
78 Commercial Quay ⊠ EH6 6LX – ℰ (0131) 555 17 55 – www.thekitchin.com
– Closed Christmas, New Year, Sunday and Monday   BVz
Rest – Modern European – *(booking essential)* Menu £ 25 (lunch)
– Carte £ 53/64
Spec. Razor clams with chorizo and lemon confit. Saddle of Highland lamb, cooked on local hay. Rhubarb and crème fraîche tart with rhubarb sorbet.
♦ Converted dockside warehouse overlooking the quay. Expect refreshingly honest, very flavoursome and unfussy cooking from menus offering considerable choice. Seasonality, freshness and provenance are at the heart of the chef's philosophy.

Plumed Horse

50-54 Henderson St ✉ EH6 6DE – ☎ (0131) 554 55 56 – www.plumedhorse.co.uk
– Closed 2 weeks summer, 1 week Easter, autumn and Christmas, Sunday and Monday
Rest – Modern – Menu £ 26/55   BV**a**

• Personally run restaurant with ornate ceiling, vivid paintings, an intimate feel and formal service. Well-crafted, classical cooking with strong, bold flavours and good use of Scottish ingredients.

Vintners Rooms

The Vaults, 87 Giles St ✉ EH6 6BZ – ☎ (0131) 554 67 67
– www.vintersrooms.com – Closed Sunday and Monday   BV**r**
Rest – Mediterranean – Menu £ 24 (lunch) – Carte £ 38/51

• Hugely atmospheric former wine merchants. Characterful, flag-floored room displays over 1,300 whiskies. More intimate, candlelit room with superb 1739 stucco ceiling is used for dining. Wide-ranging Mediterranean menu.

Brasserie – at Malmaison Hotel

1 Tower Pl ✉ EH6 7DB – ☎ (0131) 468 50 00 – www.malmaison-edinburgh.com
Rest – French – Carte £ 28/50   BV**i**

• Popular French brasserie in what was the first of the Malmaison hotels. Menus offers a choice of classically based Gallic dishes. Dine outside in the summer, overlooking the Port of Leith.

Ship on the Shore

24-26 The Shore ✉ EH6 6QN – ☎ (0131) 555 04 09
– www.theshipontheshore.co.uk – Closed 24-26 December   BV**x**
Rest – Seafood – Menu £ 17 – Carte £ 29/41

• Smart period building on the quayside, modelled on the Royal Yacht Britannia and filled with nautical memorabilia. Seafood menu offers fresh, simply prepared, classical dishes.

at Currie Southwest : 5 m on A 70

Violet Bank House *without rest*

167 Lanark Rd West ✉ EH14 5NZ – ☎ (0131) 451 51 03 – www.violetbankhouse.co.uk
3 rm ⊒ – †£ 65/85 ††£ 136

• Comfortable, well-run cottage with charming, individually decorated bedrooms and attractive garden running down to river. Impressive Scottish breakfast features lots of choice.

at Kirknewton Southwest : 7 mi on A 71 - AX – ✉ Edinburgh

Dalmahoy H. & Country Club

✉ EH27 8EB – ☎ (0131) 333 18 45
– www.marriottdalmahoy.co.uk
213 rm ⊒ – †£ 90/120 ††£ 100/130 – 2 suites
Rest *Pentland* – (dinner only) Carte £ 32/40
Rest *Long Weekend* – Carte £ 21/30

• Extended Georgian mansion boasting 2 championship golf courses and extensive leisure facilities. Country house style guest areas and well-equipped, uniformly styled bedrooms. Fine dining and good views over the 1,000 acre grounds in Pentland. Laid-back dining in The Long Weekend.

at Ingliston 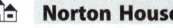 West : 7 mi on A 8 – ✉ EH28 8

Norton House

West : 6 mi on A 89 ✉ EH28 8LX – ☎ (0131) 333 12 75
– www.handpicked.co.uk/nortonhouse
79 rm ⊒ – †£ 120/220 ††£ 122/230 – 4 suites
Rest *Ushers* – (closed Sunday-Tuesday) (dinner only) Carte £ 37/45
Rest *Brasserie* – Carte £ 21/38

• 19C country house in mature grounds, with impressive oak staircase and superb spa. Classic bedrooms in original house. Large, luxurious junior suites in extension; most have balconies. Classic cooking with seasonal Scottish produce in intimate Ushers. Stylish, modern Brasserie.

EDNAM – The Scottish Borders – see Kelso

ELGIN – Moray – **501** K11 – pop. 20 829 28 C1
Scotland

▶ Edinburgh 198 mi – Aberdeen 68 mi – Fraserburgh 61 mi – Inverness 39 mi
🛈 Cooper Park ✆ (01343) 562 6 08, www.visitscotland.com
Moray Lossiemouth Stotfield Rd, ✆ (01343) 81 20 18
Hardhillock Birnie Rd, ✆ (01343) 54 23 38
Hopeman Moray, ✆ (01343) 83 05 78
Town★ - Cathedral★ (Chapter house★★)**AC**
Glenfiddich Distillery★, SE : 10 mi by A 941

Mansion House
The Haugh, via Haugh Rd ✉ IV30 1AW
– ✆ (01343) 548 811 – www.mansionhousehotel.co.uk
– Closed 25 December
23 rm – †£ 102/120 ††£ 161/192
Rest *Mansion House* – see restaurant listing
♦ Sizeable Victorian country house in attractive gardens. Grand inner with beautiful Georgian-style drawing room featuring a grand piano; snooker table in the 'wee bar'. Luxurious bedrooms – some with sleigh beds, four-posters or river views.

Pines without rest
East Rd, East : 0.5 mi on A 96 ✉ IV30 1XG
– ✆ (01343) 552 495 – www.thepinesguesthouse.com
6 rm – †£ 45/55 ††£ 60/74
♦ Charming Victorian house featuring original tiled floors and stained glass windows. Homely lounge and comfortable bedrooms; one with an antique four poster bed. Highland products at breakfast.

Mansion House – at Mansion House Hotel
The Haugh, via Haugh Rd ✉ IV30 1AW
– ✆ (01343) 548 811 – www.mansionhousehotel.co.uk
– Closed 25 December
Rest – Menu £ 24/35 – Carte £ 28/40
♦ Classically furnished formal dining room with linen-laid tables, set within a substantial 19C baronial mansion. À la carte offers traditional dishes and relies on locally sourced ingredients.

ELIE – Fife – **501** L15 – pop. 942 28 D2
▶ Edinburgh 44 mi – Dundee 24 mi – St Andrews 13 mi

Sangster's (Bruce Sangster)
51 High St ✉ KY9 1BZ
– ✆ (01333) 331 001 – www.sangsters.co.uk
– Closed January-mid February, 1 week November,
25-26 December, Sunday dinner, Monday and Tuesday
November-March
Rest – *(dinner only and Sunday lunch)* *(booking essential)*
Menu £ 40
Spec. Scallop tempura on gingered lentils and wasabi dressing. Fillet of turbot shallots, mushrooms and red wine sauce. Lemon and raspberry tart, lemon posset and lemon and poppy seed sorbet.
♦ This sweet little restaurant is run by a husband and wife team. The understated decoration includes a collection of local artwork on the walls. The cooking is detailed, finely tuned and informed by the seasons.

ERISKA (Isle of) – Argyll and Bute – **501** D14 – ✉ Oban 27 B2
▶ Edinburgh 127 mi – Glasgow 104 mi – Oban 12 mi

Isle of Eriska
Benderloch ✉ *PA37 1SD* – ℰ *(01631) 720 371*
– www.eriska-hotel.co.uk – Closed 3-20 January
23 rm ☑ – ✝£ 170/250 ✝✝£ 340/400 – 7 suites
Rest – *(light lunch residents only) (booking essential)* Menu £ 44 (dinner)
♦ 19C baronial mansion on private island, boasting fantastic views over Lismore and the mountains. Classically styled, open-fired guest areas display modern touches. Comfy bedrooms feature bright fabrics and hi-tech equipment. Superb spa and leisure facilities. Contemporary dining room offers daily menu of local produce.

EUROCENTRAL – Glasgow – see Glasgow

FAIRLIE – North Ayrshire – **501** F16 – pop. 1 510 25 A1
▶ Edinburgh 75 mi – Ayr 50 mi – Glasgow 36 mi

Fins
Fencebay Fisheries, Fencefoot Farm, South : 1.5 mi on A 78 ✉ *KA29 0EG*
– ℰ *(01475) 568 989 – www.fencebay.co.uk – Closed 1-2 January, 25-26 December, Sunday dinner and Monday*
Rest – Seafood – *(booking essential)* Carte £ 30/49
♦ Sweet, simply furnished little restaurant and conservatory, set on a trout and oyster farm, complete with smokery and farm shop. Menus offer straightforward dishes of fresh fish and shellfish, alongside their own beech-smoked products.

FIONNPHORT – Argyll and Bute – **501** A15 – see MULL (Isle of)

FLODIGARRY – Highland – **501** B11 – see Skye (Isle of)

FORGANDENNY – Perth and Kinross – **501** J14 – see Perth

FORRES – Moray – **501** J11 – pop. 8 967 28 C1
▮ Scotland
▶ Edinburgh 165 mi – Aberdeen 80 mi – Inverness 27 mi
🛈 116 High St ℰ (01309) 67 29 38, www.forresweb.net
▦ Muiryshade, ℰ (01309) 67 29 49
◉ Sueno's Stone★★, N : 0.5 mi by A 940 on A 96 – Brodie Castle★ **AC**, W : 3 mi by A 96. Elgin★ (Cathedral★, chapter house★★ **AC**), E : 10.25 mi by A 96

Knockomie
Grantown Rd., South : 1.5 mi on A 940 ✉ *IV36 2SG* – ℰ *(01309) 673 146*
– www.knockomie.co.uk – Closed 2 weeks January and 24-27 December
15 rm ☑ – ✝£ 100/145 ✝✝£ 120/180
Rest *Grill Room* – see restaurant listing
♦ Personally run, extended Arts and Crafts house, which resembles an old hunting lodge. Relaxed lounge and pubby bar. Individually styled bedrooms: those in the original house are classical; those in the extension are more modern in style.

Grill Room – at Knockomie Hotel
Grantown Rd., South : 1.5 mi on A 940 ✉ *IV36 2SG* – ℰ *(01309) 673 146*
– www.knockomie.co.uk – Closed 23-28 December
Rest – Carte £ 26/39
♦ Contemporary hotel restaurant with formal atmosphere, located in a charming, rurally set Arts and Crafts house. Seasonally changing Scottish-based menu showcases locally sourced produce.

FORRES

at Dyke West : 3.75 mi by A 96 – ✉ Forres

Old Kirk without rest
Northeast : 0.5 mi ✉ IV36 2TL – ⌀ (01309) 641 414 – www.oldkirk.co.uk
3 rm ⊡ – †£ 50/53 ††£ 70/76
♦ Peacefully set, converted 1856 church, surrounded by grain fields. Airy inner, with open-fired lounge displaying an original stained glass window. Charming bedrooms boast original stonework and arched windows; one has a carved four-poster.

FORT AUGUSTUS – Highland – **501** F12 – pop. 508 – ✉ PH32 — 30 C3
▶ London 543 mi – Edinburgh 159 mi – Inverness 34 mi – Fort William 32 mi

The Lovat
✉ PH32 4DU – ⌀ (01456) 459 250 – www.thelovat.com
28 rm ⊡ – †£ 85/185 ††£ 180/280
Rest – Carte £ 22/39
♦ Professionally run Victorian house with traditional lounge and lawned gardens, set in pleasant village at southern end of Loch Ness. Variously sized bedrooms have a contemporary feel and good facilities. Smart, modern brasserie offers classic cooking.

FORT WILLIAM – Highland – **501** E13 – pop. 9 908 ▌Scotland — 30 C3
▶ Edinburgh 133 mi – Glasgow 104 mi – Inverness 68 mi – Oban 50 mi
🛈 15 High St ⌀ (0845) 2 25 51 21, www.visit-fortwilliam.co.uk
🖂 North Rd, ⌀ (01397) 70 44 64
◉ Town ★
◉ The Road to the Isles ★★ (Neptune's Staircase (≤★★), Glenfinnan★ ≤★, Arisaig★, Silver Sands of Morar★, Mallaig★), NW : 46 mi by A 830 – Ardnamurchan Peninsula★★ – Ardnamurchan Point (≤★★), NW : 65 mi by A 830, A 861 and B 8007 - SE : Ben Nevis★★ (≤★★) - Glen Nevis★

Inverlochy Castle
Torlundy, Northeast : 3 mi on A 82 ✉ PH33 6SN – ⌀ (01397) 702 177
– www.inverlochycastlehotel.com
17 rm ⊡ – †£ 265/525 ††£ 420/525 – 1 suite
Rest – *(booking essential for non-residents)* Menu £ 38/67 ❀
Spec. Blue lobster with melon, sesame biscuit and herb salad. Smoked pigeon with roasted foie gras, dandelion salad and morels. Pineapple tarte Tatin with pineapple sorbet and spiced syrup.
♦ Striking castellated house in beautiful grounds, boasting stunning loch/mountain views. Classical country house interior with sumptuous open-fired lounges. Elegant bedrooms offer the height of luxury Choice of smart dining rooms serving traditional dishes executed with care and precision. Top quality Scottish produce.

Distillery Guesthouse without rest
North Rd. ✉ PH33 6LR – ⌀ (01397) 700 103 – www.stayinfortwilliam.co.uk
– Closed 1 week Christmas
10 rm ⊡ – †£ 55/75 ††£ 76/89
♦ Smart hotel – formerly 3 distillery workers' cottages – at the foot of Ben Nevis. Comfy lounge with shortbread, whisky and books about the area. Landscaped gardens; terrace boasts lovely views.

Grange without rest
Grange Rd., South : 0.75 mi by A 82 and Ashburn Lane ✉ PH33 6JF – ⌀ (01397) 705 516 – www.thegrange-scotland.co.uk – April-October
4 rm ⊡ – †£ 108 ††£ 120
♦ Delightful Victorian house with attractive garden and immaculate interior, set in a quiet residential area. Beautiful lounge displays fine fabrics; lovely breakfast room boasts Queen Anne style chairs. Bedrooms are extremely well appointed, with smart bathrooms.

FORT WILLIAM

Ashburn House without rest
18 Achintore Rd., South : 0.5 mi on A 82 ✉ *PH33 6RQ* – ℰ *(01397) 706 000*
– www.highland5star.co.uk
7 rm ⊔ – ♦£ 45/55 ♦♦£ 90/120
• Attractive Victorian house with comfy lounge and conservatory breakfast room. Bright, modern pine-furnished bedrooms; Room 2 is largest and has the best view. Homemade shortbread on arrival.

The Gantocks without rest
Achintore Rd., South : 1 mi on A 82 ✉ *PE33 6RN* – ℰ *(01397) 702 050*
– www.fortwilliam5star.co.uk – March-October
3 rm ⊔ – ♦£ 70/90 ♦♦£ 100/120
• Whitewashed bungalow with loch views; run by experienced owners. Spacious, modern bedrooms boast king-sized beds, large baths and nice toiletries. Unusual offerings and water views at breakfast.

Crannog
Town Pier ✉ *PH33 6DB* – ℰ *(01397) 705 589 – www.crannog.net – Closed 25 December, 1 January and dinner 24 and 31 December*
Rest – Seafood – *(booking essential)* Menu £ 16 (lunch) – Carte £ 31/38
• Brightly painted eatery set on the pier over Loch Eil. Good value set lunch. À la carte and daily blackboard menu of local fish and shellfish; try the mussels. Owners also have a seafood shop.

FORTINGALL – Perth and Kinross – **501** H14 – see Aberfeldy

FORTROSE – Highland – **501** H11 – pop. 1 174   30 C2

▶ London 574 mi – Edinburgh 168 mi – Inverness 14 mi – Nairn 27 mi

Water's Edge without rest
Canonbury Ter., on A 832 ✉ *IV10 8TT* – ℰ *(01381) 621 202*
– www.watersedge.uk.com – April-October
3 rm ⊔ – ♦£ 80 ♦♦£ 120
• Personally run guest house with attractive gardens and superb views over the Moray Firth. Immaculately kept guest areas. Three 1st floor rooms have French windows onto terrace.

GALSON – Western Isles – **501** A8 – see Lewis and Harris (Isle of)

GATTONSIDE – The Scottish Borders – see Melrose

GLASGOW

See city maps on following pages　　　　　　　　　　　　　　　　　**25** B1

Glasgow City – pop. 629 501 – 501 H16 – **502** H16 – Scotland
▶ Edinburgh 46 – Manchester 221

🛈 Tourist Information

11 George Sq ℰ (0141) 204 44 00, www.visitscotland.com

Airports

✈ Glasgow Airport : ℰ (0844) 481 5555, W : 8 m. by M 8, AV
Access to Oban by helicopter

Golf courses

⛳ Littlehill Auchinairn Rd, ℰ (0141) 2 76 07 04
⛳ Rouken Glen Thornlibank Stewarton Rd, ℰ (0141) 638 70 44
⛳ Linn Park Simshill Rd, ℰ (0141) 633 03 77

◉ SIGHTS

In the town : City★★★ • Cathedral★★★ ≤ DZ • The Burrell Collection★★★ AXM1 • Hunterian Art Gallery★★ AC CYM4 • Museum of Transport★★ AVM6 • Art Gallery and Museum Kelvingrove★★ CY • Pollok House★ AXD • Tolbooth Steeple★ DZ • Hunterian Museum★ CYM5 • City Chambers★ DZC • Glasgow School of Art★ AC CYM3 • Necropolis ≤ ★ DYZ • Gallery of Modern Art★

On the outskirts : Paisley Museum and Art Gallery★, W : 4 mi by M 8 AV

In the surrounding area : The Trossachs★★★, N : 31 mi by A 879 - BV -, A 81 and A 821 • Loch Lomond★★, NW : 19 mi by A 82 AV

INDEX OF STREET NAMES IN GLASGOW

Street	Ref	No
Admiral St	CZ	
Aikenhead Rd	BX	3
Albert Bridge	DZ	2
Alexandra Parade	BV	4
Allison St	BX	
Anderston Quay	CZ	
Anniesland Rd	AV	
Argyle St	CZ	
Bain St	DZ	
Baird St	DY	
Balgrayhill	BV	5
Ballater St	BX	6
Balmore Rd	BV	
Balornock Rd	BV	8
Balshagray Ave	AV	9
Bank St	CY	
Barrack St	DZ	
Barrhead Rd	AX	
Bath St	CY	
Battlefield Rd	BX	12
Belmont St	CY	
Berkeley St	CY	
Berryknowes Rd	AX	15
Bilsland Drive	BV	16
Blackfriars Street	DZ	7
Blairbeth Rd	BX	18
Borron St	DY	
Boydstone Rd	AX	
Braidcraft Rd	AX	20
Brand St	CZ	22
Bridgegate	DZ	24
Bridge St	DZ	25
Brockburn Rd	AX	
Broomfield Rd	BV	
Broomielaw	CZ	
Broomloan Rd	AV	26
Brownside Rd	BX	
Buchanan Galleries	DY	
Buchanan St	DZ	
Burnhill Chapel St	BX	28
Byres Rd	AV	29
Caldarvan St	DY	
Calder St	BX	
Caledonia Rd	BX	30
Cambridge St	DY	32
Cambuslang Rd	BX	
Cardowan Rd	BV	
Carmunnock Rd	BX	33
Carntynehall Rd	BV	
Carntyne Rd	BV	
Castle St	DY	
Cathcart Rd	BX	
Cathedral St	DY	
Claremont Ter	CY	34
Clarkston Rd	BX	
Clydeside Expressway	AV	
Clyde Pl	CZ	35
Clyde St	DZ	
Clyde Tunnel	AV	
Cochrane St	DZ	36
Commerce St	DZ	37
Cook St	BV	38
Corkerhill Rd	AX	
Cornwald St	CZ	39
Cowcaddens St	DY	
Craighall Rd	DY	
Croftfoot Rd	BX	
Crookston Rd	AX	
Crow Rd	AV	
Cumbernauld Rd	BV	40
Dalmarnock Rd	BX	
Derby St	CY	42
Dobbie's Loan	DY	
Douglas St	CZ	
Duke St	DZ	
Duke's Rd	BX	
Dumbarton Rd	CY	47
Dumbreck Rd	AX	
East Kilbride Rd	BX	
Edinburgh Rd	BV	
Edmiston Drive	AV	48
Eglinton Rd	BX	
Eglinton St	BX	
Elderslie St	CY	
Eldon St	CY	50
Elmbank St	CY	
Farmeloan Rd	BX	53
Fenwick Rd	AX	55
Finnieston St	CZ	
Gallowgate	DZ	
Garscube Rd	DY	
George Square	DZ	
George St	DZ	
Gibson St	CY	
Glasgow Bridge	DZ	60
Glasgow Rd PAISLEY	AX	62
Glasgow Rd RENFREW	AV	
Glasgow Rd RUTHERGLEN	BX	
Glassford St	DZ	
Gorbals St	BX	63
Gordon St	DZ	65
Govan Rd	CZ	
Grange Rd	BX	67
Great Western Rd	CY	
Greendyke St	DZ	
Haggs Rd	AX	68
Hamiltonhill Rd	DY	
Hardgate Rd	AV	
Harriet St	AX	70
Helen St	AV	72
High St	DZ	
Hillington Rd	AV	
Holmfauld Rd	AV	73
Holmlea Rd	BX	74
Hopehill Rd	CY	
Hope St	DZ	
Hospital St	BX	75
Howard St	DZ	
Hydepark St	CZ	
Ingram St	DZ	
Jamaica St	DZ	77
James St	BX	79
John Knox St	DZ	80
Kelvinhaugh St	CY	
Kelvin Way	CY	
Kennedy St	DY	
Kennishead Rd	AX	
Kent Rd	CY	
Kent St	DZ	
Keppoch Hill Rd	DY	
Killermont St	DY	
Kilmarnock Rd	AX	
Kingston Bridge	CZ	85
Kingston St	CZ	
Kingsway	AV	
Kings Park Rd	BX	84
King's Drive	BX	83
King's Park Ave	BX	
Kyle St	DY	86
Lamont Rd	BV	88
Lancefield Quay	CZ	
Lancefield St	CZ	
Langlands Rd	AV	
Langside Ave	AX	89
Langside Drive	AX	
Langside Rd	BX	90
Lincoln Ave	AV	91
Linthaugh Rd	AV	
London Rd	BX	
Lorne St	CZ	93
Lymburn St	CY	95
Lyoncross Rd	AX	97
Main St	BX	
Maryhill Rd	CY	
Meiklerig Crescent	AX	98
Merrylee Rd	AX	
Middlesex St	CZ	100
Miller St	DZ	
Mill St	BX	
Milnpark St	CZ	
Milton St	DY	
Minard Rd	AX	101
Moir St	DZ	102
Morrison St	CZ	
Mosspark Blvd	AX	
Moss Rd	AV	103
Napiershall St	CY	
Nelson St	CZ	
Nether Auldhouse Rd	AX	104
Newlands Rd	AX	
Newton St	CYZ	
Nitshill Rd	AX	
Norfolk St	DZ	
North Canalbank St	DY	
North Hanover St	DY	
North St	CY	
North Woodsitde Rd	CY	
Oswald St	DZ	
Otago St	CY	105
Oxford St	CZ	106
Paisley Rd	AV	
Paisley Rd West	AX	
Parkhead Forge Shopping Centre	BX	
Park Gdns	CY	107
Park Quadrant	CY	
Park Ter	CY	108
Peat Rd	AX	
Petershill Rd	BV	
Pinkston Rd	BV	
Pitt St	CZ	
Pollokshaws Rd	AX	
Port Dundas Rd	DY	110
Possil Rd	DY	
Prospecthill Rd	BX	112
Provan Rd	BV	114
Queen Margaret Drive	CY	116
Queen St	DZ	
Raeberry St	CY	
Red Rd	BV	118
Renfield St	CY	
Renfrew Rd	AV	
Renfrew St	DY	
Ring Rd	BV	
Riverford Rd	AX	119
Robertson St	CZ	120
Rotten Row	DZ	
Royal Ter	CY	
Royston Rd	BV	
Rutherglen Rd	BX	
St Andrew's Drive	AX	
St Enoch Shopping Centre	DZ	
St George's Rd	CY	
St James Rd	DY	
St Mungo Ave	DY	
St Vincent St	DZ	
Saltmarket	DZ	
Sandwood Rd	AV	123
Saracen St	DY	
Sauchiehall St	DY	
Scott St	CY	
Seaward St	CZ	
Shettleston Rd	BX	
Shieldhall Rd	AV	
Shields Rd	AX	124
Southbrae Drive	AV	
Springburn Rd	BV	
Springfield Rd	BX	
Stirling Rd	DY	126
Stobcross Rd	CZ	
Stockwell St	DZ	127
Stonelaw Rd	BX	
Striven Gdns	CY	128
Thornliebank Rd	AX	
Todd St	BV	131
Tollcross Rd	BX	
Trongate	DZ	
Union St	DZ	
Victoria Bridge	DZ	132
Victoria Rd	BX	
Wallacewell Rd	BV	
Waterloo St	CZ	
Westmuir Pl	BX	136
Westmuir St	BX	138
West Campbell St	CZ	
West George St	DZ	
West Graham St	CY	135
West Nile St	DYZ	139
West Paisley Rd	CZ	
West Prince's St	CY	
West Regent St	DY	
West St	CZ	
Wilson St	DZ	
Wilton St	CY	
Wishart St	DZ	
Woodlands Drive	CY	140
Woodlands Rd	CY	
Woodside Crescent	CY	141
Woodside Pl	CY	
Woodside Ter	CY	143
York St	CZ	

SCOTLAND

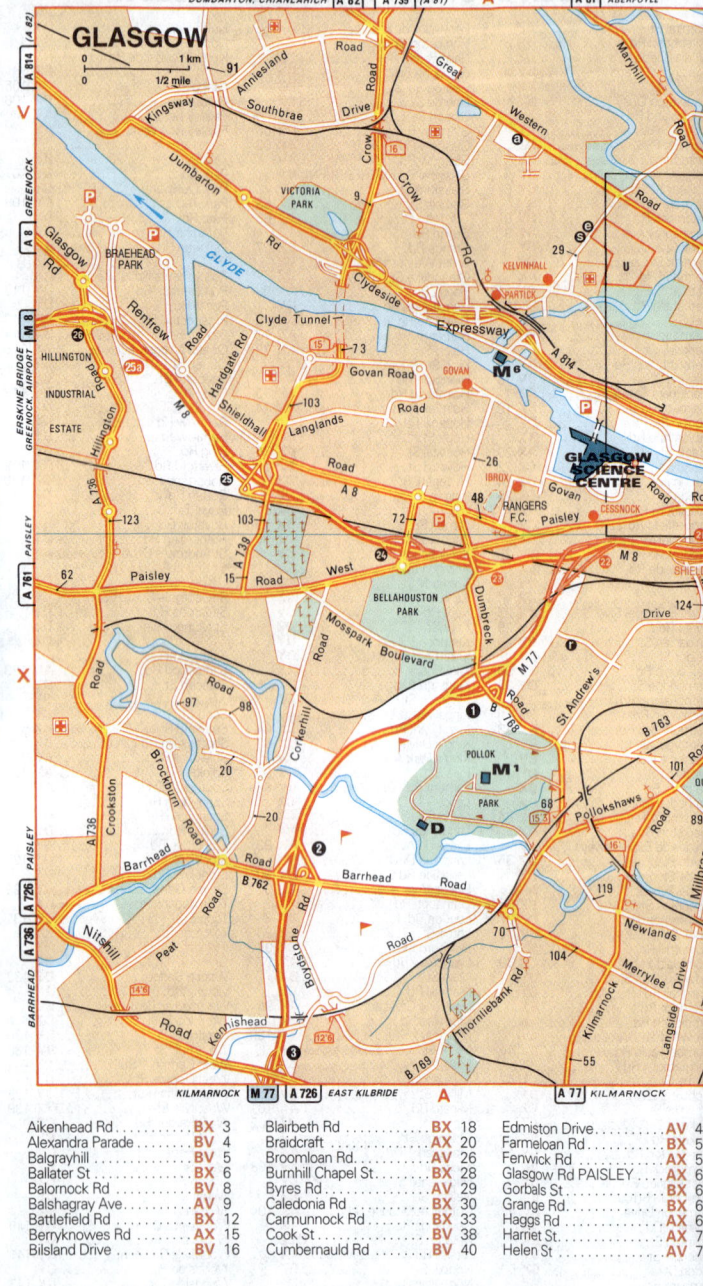

Aikenhead Rd .... BX 3	Blairbeth Rd .... BX 18	Edmiston Drive .... AV 48
Alexandra Parade .... BV 4	Braidcraft .... AX 20	Farmeloan Rd .... BX 53
Balgrayhill .... BV 5	Broomloan Rd .... AV 26	Fenwick Rd .... AX 55
Ballater St .... BX 6	Burnhill Chapel St .... BX 28	Glasgow Rd PAISLEY .... AX 62
Balornock Rd .... BV 8	Byres Rd .... AV 29	Gorbals St .... BX 63
Balshagray Ave .... AV 9	Caledonia Rd .... BX 30	Grange Rd .... BX 67
Battlefield Rd .... BX 12	Carmunnock Rd .... BX 33	Haggs Rd .... AX 68
Berryknowes Rd .... AX 15	Cook St .... BV 38	Harriet St. .... AX 70
Bilsland Drive .... BV 16	Cumbernauld Rd .... BV 40	Helen St .... AV 72

Holmfauld Rd	**AV**	73
Holmlea Rd	**BX**	74
Hospital St	**BX**	75
James St	**BX**	79
King's Drive	**BX**	83
King's Park Rd	**BX**	84
Lamont Rd	**BV**	88
Langside Ave	**AX**	89
Langside Rd	**BX**	90
Lincoln Ave	**AV**	91
Lyoncross Rd	**AX**	97
Meiklerig Crescent	**AX**	98
Minard Rd	**AX**	101
Moss Rd	**AX**	103
Nether Auldhouse Rd	**AX**	104
Parkhead Forge Shopping Centre	**BX**	
Prospecthill Rd	**BX**	112
Provan Rd	**BV**	114
Red Rd	**BV**	118
Riverford Rd	**AX**	119
Sandwood Rd	**AV**	123
Shields Rd	**AX**	124
Todd St	**BV**	131
Westmuir Pl	**BX**	136
Westmuir St	**BX**	138

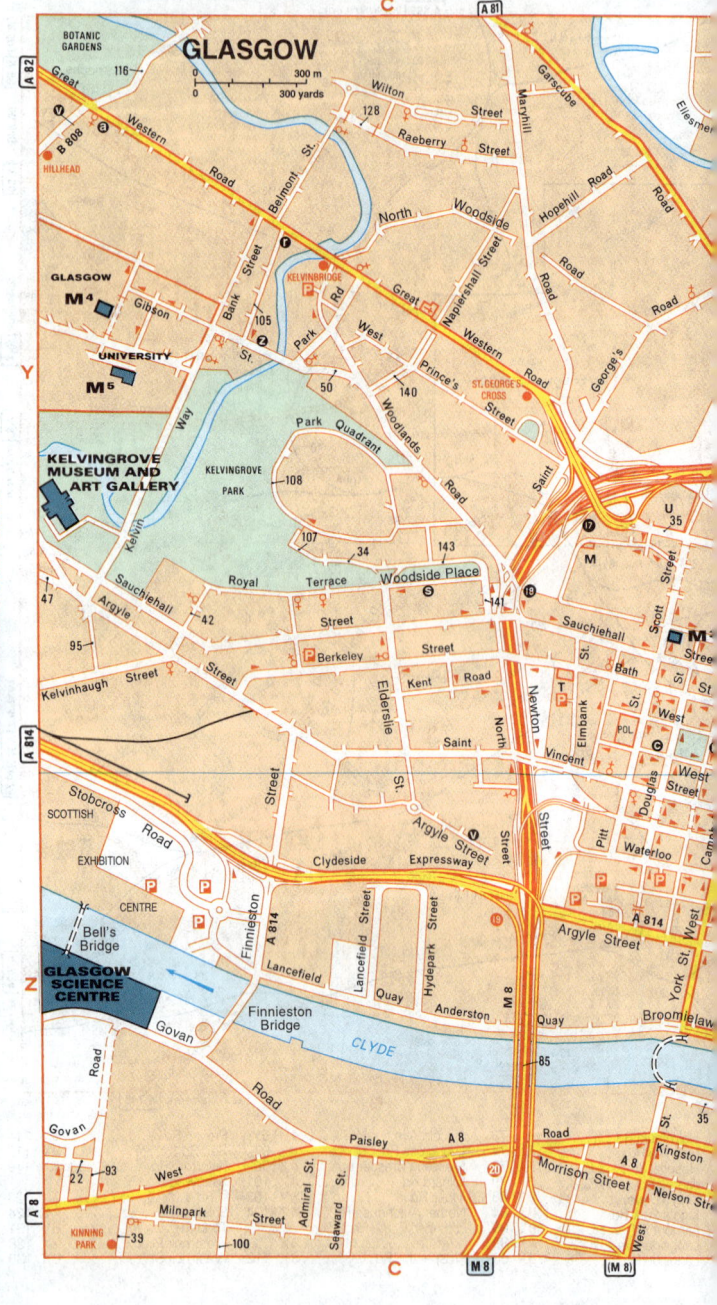

GLASGOW

Blythswood Square
11 Blythswood Sq ⊠ G2 4AD – ℰ (0141) 248 88 88
– www.blythswoodsquare.com
CYn
99 rm ⊇ – †£ 195/245 ††£ 245 – 1 suite
Rest *Restaurant* – see restaurant listing
• Stunning property on delightful Georgian square; formerly the Scottish RAC HQ. Modern décor contrasts with original fittings. Dark, moody bedrooms and marble bathrooms; Penthouse Suite displays a bed adapted from a snooker table. Smart spa.

Hotel du Vin at One Devonshire Gardens
1 Devonshire Gdns ⊠ G12 0UX – ℰ (0141) 339 20 01
– www.hotelduvin.com
AVa
45 rm ⊇ – †£ 125/165 ††£ 125/165 – 4 suites
Rest *Bistro* – see restaurant listing
• Collection of adjoining 19C townhouses boasting original stained glass, wood panelling and a labyrinth of corridors. Furnished in dark, moody shades but with a modern, country house air. Stylish bedrooms; one with a small gym and sauna.

Radisson Blu Glasgow
301 Argyle St. ⊠ G2 8DL – ℰ (0141) 204 33 33
– www.radissonblu.co.uk/hotel-glasgow
DZo
246 rm – †£ 99/205 ††£ 99/205, ⊇ £ 16 – 1 suite
Rest *Collage* – Modern – *(closed Sunday lunch)* Menu £ 20 – Carte £ 27/43
• Stylish, modern, commercial hotel with impressive open-plan interior; set in central location close to the station. Three styles of bedroom – all offering good levels of comfort. Spacious dining room with central buffet area and all-encompassing menu.

Malmaison
278 West George St ⊠ G2 4LL – ℰ (0141) 572 10 00 – www.malmaison.com
68 rm – ††£ 160, ⊇ £ 14.50 – 4 suites
CYc
Rest *Brasserie* – see restaurant listing
• Impressive-looking, former Masonic chapel with moody, masculine décor. Stylish, boldly coloured bedrooms offer good facilities. Named after Billy Connolly, the Big Yin Suite has a roll-top bath in the room. Chic, glass-roofed champagne bar.

Abode Glasgow
129 Bath St. ⊠ G2 2SZ – ℰ (0141) 221 67 89 – www.abodehotels.co.uk
59 rm – †£ 99/175 ††£ 99/175, ⊇ £ 14
DYv
Rest *Bar MC & Grill* – *(Closed Sunday lunch and Monday)* Menu £ 14 (lunch) – Carte approx. £ 35
• 20C former offices for the education authority. Original brass lift runs up the centre of a spiral staircase. Small art exhibition; pictures of city landmarks on every headboard – the best room boasts wood panelling and a feature fireplace. Sizeable bar and restaurant with buzzy atmosphere and grill menu.

Grand Central
99 Gordon St ⊠ G1 3SF – ℰ (0141) 240 37 00
– www.principal-hayley.com/grandcentralhotel
DZa
183 rm – †£ 79/199 ††£ 89/199, ⊇ £ 17 – 3 suites
Rest *Tempus* – Modern – *(dinner only)* Carte £ 28/45
• Renowned hotel built into the main station; the first TV signal broadcast from London was to this hotel. Smart bedrooms aimed at corporate market. Original plasterwork in ballroom; marble floors in champagne bar. Contemporary restaurant boasts Murano chandeliers.

Sherbrooke Castle
11 Sherbrooke Ave, Pollokshields ⊠ G41 4PG – ℰ (0141) 427 42 27
– www.sherbrooke.co.uk
AXr
16 rm ⊇ – †£ 90/150 ††£ 95/175 – 1 suite
Rest *Morrisons* – Menu £ 14 – Carte £ 23/39
• Late 19C baronial Romanticism given free rein inside and out. The hall is richly furnished and imposing; rooms in the old castle have a comfortable country house refinement. Panelled Victorian dining room with open fire.

GLASGOW

15 Glasgow without rest
15 Woodside Pl. ✉ *G3 7QL –* ℰ *(0141) 332 12 63 – www.15glasgow.com*
– Closed 25 December and 1 January CYs
5 rm ☐ – †£ 110/120 ††£ 120/150

♦ Charming Georgian townhouse on quiet square. Extremely spacious bedrooms with quality furnishings and some original mosaic and parquet floors. Cooked breakfast trays delivered to your door.

Brian Maule at Chardon d'Or
176 West Regent St. ✉ *G2 4RL –* ℰ *(0141) 248 38 01 – www.brianmaule.com*
– Closed 1 January, 25 December, Sunday and bank holidays CYi
Rest – Modern – Menu £ 21 (lunch) – Carte £ 42/53

♦ Georgian house in the heart of the city, boasting original pillars, ornate carved ceiling and modern art. Well-spaced, linen-clad tables; friendly, formal service from well-versed team. Classically based cooking presented in a modern style.

Rogano
11 Exchange Pl. ✉ *G1 3AN –* ℰ *(0141) 248 40 55 – www.roganoglasgow.com*
– Closed 1 January DZc
Rest – Seafood – Menu £ 17 (lunch) – Carte £ 34/61

♦ City institution established over 75 years ago. Charming art deco interior with marquetry reputedly from the craftsmen who fitted the Queen Mary. Formal service and largely seafood-based menu. More keenly priced dishes in basement bistro.

Two Fat Ladies at The Buttery
652 Argyle St ✉ *G3 8UF –* ℰ *(0141) 221 81 88*
– www.twofatladiesrestaurant.com – Closed 26 December and 1 January
Rest – Traditional – Menu £ 19 (lunch) – Carte £ 29/45 CZv

♦ Wood-panelled restaurant with banquette seating and tartan furnishings; an old classic revived. Tasty, seasonal cooking; charming, attentive service and a great range of whiskies.

Bistro – at Hotel du Vin at One Devonshire Gardens
1 Devonshire Gdns ✉ *G12 0UX –* ℰ *(0141) 339 20 01 – www.hotelduvin.com*
Rest – Modern – *(Closed Saturday lunch)* Menu £ 18 (weekday AVa
lunch) – Carte £ 35/53

♦ Elegant oak-panelled hotel restaurant in a terraced Georgian townhouse. Dark, moody feel, with modern wine-themed canvases on the walls. Menu offers classically based Gallic dishes and steaks.

La Vallée Blanche
360 Byres Rd., (1st floor) ✉ *G12 8AY –* ℰ *(0141) 334 33 33*
– www.lavalleeblanche.com – Closed 1 January, 25 December and Monday
Rest – French – Menu £ 17 (lunch) – Carte dinner £ 28/39 CYv

♦ First floor restaurant-cum-ski-lodge, with wood-clad walls, stag antler lights and myriad candles. Classical cooking with a seasonal French base. Formal service from a jolly team.

Grill Room at The Square
29 Royal Exchange Sq (2nd Floor) ✉ *G1 3AJ –* ℰ *(0141) 225 56 15*
– www.grillroomglasgow.com DZr
Rest – Steakhouse – *(booking advisable)* Menu £ 21 (lunch) – Carte £ 24/55

♦ Second floor of impressive Georgian building on Royal Exchange Square. Appealing menu focuses on seafood and 28-day hung Scottish steak, with choice of sauce and chunky chips.

Urban
23-25 St Vincent Pl. ✉ *G1 2DT –* ℰ *(0141) 248 56 36 – www.urbanbrasserie.co.uk*
– Closed 1-2 January and 25-26 December DZi
Rest – Modern – Menu £ 20 – Carte £ 26/46

♦ Imposing 19C building in heart of city centre. Stylish, modern interior with individual booths and illuminated glass ceiling. Modern English cooking. Live piano at weekends.

SCOTLAND

GLASGOW

XX Gamba
225a West George St. ✉ *G2 2ND* – 📞 *(0141) 572 08 99* – *www.gamba.co.uk*
– *Closed 1January, 25-26 December and Sunday lunch*   DZ**x**
Rest – Seafood – Menu £ 20 (lunch) – Carte £ 27/69

• Extensive and appealing seafood menu; simple and effective cooking from chef-owner, with lemon sole a speciality. Comfortable dining room with good service from well-versed team.

XX Parmigiana
447 Great Western Rd, Kelvinbridge ✉ *G12 8HH* – 📞 *(0141) 334 06 86*
– *www.laparmigiana.co.uk* – *Closed 1 January, 25-26 December and Sunday dinner*   CY**r**
Rest – Italian – *(booking essential)* Menu £ 16 (lunch and early dinner)/19
– Carte £ 28/43

• Compact, pleasantly decorated traditional eatery with a lively atmosphere and good local reputation. Obliging, professional service and a sound, authentic Italian repertoire.

XX Ubiquitous Chip
12 Ashton Ln ✉ *G12 8SJ* – 📞 *(0141) 334 5007* – *www.ubiquitouschip.co.uk*
– *Closed 1 January and 25 December*   AV**e**
Rest – Modern European – *(booking advisable at dinner)* Menu £ 30/40

• Iconic Glaswegian restaurant on a cobbled street close to Byres Road. Brasserie on the mezzanine level serves traditional Scottish dishes, while the restaurant – in a glass-roofed former courtyard – offers set selections of modern classics.

XX Brasserie – at Malmaison Hotel
278 West George St ✉ *G2 4LL* – 📞 *(0141) 572 10 00* – *www.malmaison.com*
Rest – French – Menu £ 17 (weekday lunch) – Carte £ 20/36   CY**c**

• Characterful hotel brasserie set in the vaults of a former Masonic chapel, with informal, intimate atmosphere, booth seating and adjoining champagne bar. Classical menus have a French edge.

XX Restaurant – at Blythswood Square Hotel
11 Blythswood Sq ✉ *G2 4AD* – 📞 *(0141) 248 88 88*
– *www.blythswoodsquare.com*   CY**n**
Rest – Modern – Menu £ 20 (lunch) – Carte £ 31/61

• Stylish hotel restaurant in the old ballroom of the stunning former RAC building. Menus divide each course into 'classic' and 'contemporary' dishes, and there's a dedicated steak selection.

X Balthassar
33 Ingham St ✉ *G1 1HA* – 📞 *(0141) 552 57 36* – *www.balthassar.co.uk* – *Closed 1 January, 25 December and Monday*   DZ**s**
Rest – French – Menu £ 12/20 – Carte £ 19/43

• Former fire station in merchant city area. Brasserie styling with range of seating options, floor-to-ceiling windows and buzzy atmosphere. Offers snacks, brunch and unfussy French classics.

X Dhabba
44 Candleriggs ✉ *G1 1LE* – 📞 *(0141) 553 12 49* – *www.thedhabba.com*
Rest – Indian – Menu £ 10 (lunch) – Carte £ 20/35   DZ**u**

• In the heart of the Merchant City, this large, modern restaurant boasts bold colours and huge wall photos. Concentrates on authentic, accomplished North Indian cooking.

X Stravaigin
28 Gibson St ✉ *G12 8NX* – 📞 *(0141) 334 26 65* – *www.stravaigin.com*
– *Closed 25 December and 1 January*   CY**z**
Rest – Modern – Menu £ 15 (lunch) – Carte £ 23/38

• Well-run, long-standing restaurant with shabby-chic style and relaxed feel. Bustling bar and choice of dining areas on 3 levels. Their motto is 'think global, eat local', with interesting menus ranging from old favourites to Asian-inspired dishes. Cooking is careful and full flavoured. Monthly 'thali' nights.

GLASGOW

Stravaigin 2
8 Ruthven Ln., off Byres Rd ⊠ G12 9BG – ℰ (0141) 334 71 65
– www.stravaigin.com – Closed 1 January and 25 December   AVs
Rest – Modern – Menu £ 13 (lunch) – Carte £ 18/37

• Simple neighbourhood eatery set back from the main road. Cosy split-level interior and warm, friendly service. Eclectic menu offers old favourites alongside Asian and fusion dishes. Clean, fresh flavours and well-thought-out combinations.

Cail Bruich West
725 Great Western Rd. ⊠ G12 8QX – ℰ (0141) 334 62 65 – www.cailbruich.co.uk
– Closed 1 January, 26 December, 1 week spring, 1 week winter and Monday
Rest – Modern – Menu £ 17 (lunch) – Carte £ 25/43   CYa

• Friendly, brasserie-style eatery – a real family-run affair – set opposite the botanic gardens. Extensive menu of tasty dishes that respect their ingredients. It's name means 'to eat well'.

Dakhin
89 Candleriggs, (1st Floor) ⊠ G1 1NP – ℰ (0141) 553 25 85 – www.dakhin.com
Rest – South Indian – Menu £ 10 (lunch) – Carte £ 18/35   DZn

• Large open-plan first floor restaurant in redeveloped area of city, serving authentic, flavoursome south Indian cooking. Friendly, informal atmosphere; knowledgeable service.

Shandon Belles
652 Argyle St ⊠ G3 8UF – ℰ (0141) 221 81 88
– www.twofatladiesrestaurant.com – Closed 25-26 December and 1-2 January
Rest – Traditional – (booking advisable) Menu £ 15   CZv

• Rustic restaurant in the basement of The Buttery, with exposed brick walls, church pews and formally laid tables. Tasty, unfussy dishes with a hearty base. Friendly service.

Babbity Bowster
16-18 Blackfriars St ⊠ G1 1PE – ℰ (0141) 552 50 55 – www.babbitybowster.com
– Closed 25 December and 1 January   DZe
Rest – Traditional – (closed Sunday) Carte £ 25/34

• Double-fronted Georgian pub with fiercely Scottish interior; close to the Merchant City. Honest, seasonal cooking features traditional Scottish favourites; restaurant menu is more elaborate.

at Eurocentral East : 12 mi by M 8 off A 8 – ⊠ Glasgow

Dakota
⊠ ML1 4WJ – ℰ (01698) 835 444 – www.dakotahotels.co.uk
92 rm – †£ 99 ††£ 99, ⊇ £ 11.95
Rest *Grill* – Menu £ 17/30 – Carte £ 16/37

• Stylish, modern hotel with sleek, masculine feel. Well-thought out bedrooms have king-sized beds and plasma TVs. Comfortable lounge popular for afternoon tea. Open plan bar and grill offers good selection of modern cooking.

GLENDEVON – Perth and Kinross – 501 I/J15   28 C2
▶ Edinburgh 37 mi – Perth 26 mi – Stirling 19 mi

Tormaukin Inn with rm
⊠ FK14 7JY – ℰ (01259) 781 252 – www.tormaukinhotel.co.uk
13 rm ⊇ – †£ 55 ††£ 80   **Rest** – Carte £ 18/35

• Characterful inn run by truly welcoming team. Huge granite fireplace, dark, beamed bar and spacious, traditional dining room. Carefully executed dishes are largely traditional, with the odd contemporary offering; tasty homemade bread and ice cream. Tartan-floored bedrooms spread between the inn, stable block and chalet.

GLENKINDIE – Aberdeenshire – 501 L12 — 28 D1

▶ London 537 mi – Edinburgh 125 mi – Aberdeen 41 mi – Dundee 85 mi

Glenkindie Arms with rm
✉ AB33 8SX – ☎ (01975) 641 288 – www.theglenkindiearms.co.uk – Closed 25-26 December, restricted opening in winter
3 rm ☑ – †£ 40/57 ††£ 75/90
Rest – (booking essential) Menu £ 28 – Carte £ 24/44

♦ Remotely set, 400 year old, rustic Highland inn. Charming bar with an open fire and a huge collection of malt whiskies. Concise, daily changing blackboard menu of unfussy, seasonal dishes crafted from local produce. Simple bedrooms complete the picture.

GLENROTHES – Fife – 501 K15 – pop. 38 679 ▮ Scotland — 28 C2

▶ Edinburgh 33 mi – Dundee 25 mi – Stirling 36 mi

▮ Thornton Station Rd, ☎ (01592) 77 11 73
▮ Golf Course Rd, ☎ (01592) 75 86 86
▮ Balbirnie Park Markinch, ☎ (01592) 61 20 95
▮ Auchterderran Cardenden Woodend Rd, ☎ (01592) 72 15 79
▮ Leslie Balsillie Laws, ☎ (01592) 62 00 40

◉ Falkland ★ (Palace of Falkland ★ AC, Gardens ★ AC) N : 5.5 mi by A 92 and A 912

Balbirnie House
Balbirnie Park, Markinch, Northeast : 1.75 mi by A 911 and A 92 on B 9130
✉ KY7 6NE – ☎ (01592) 610 066 – www.balbirnie.co.uk
30 rm ☑ – †£ 95/125 ††£ 210
Rest *Orangery* – (closed Monday and Tuesday) Menu £ 18 (lunch)/35 – Carte lunch £ 26/32
Rest *Bistro* – Menu £ 13 – Carte £ 17/31

♦ Stunning Palladian mansion with formal gardens and extensive parkland. Large, well-furnished drawing rooms in country house style; period features abound. Luxurious, comfortable bedrooms come in varying sizes. Elegant glass-roofed Orangery serves classics with a twist. Basement Bistro offers French favourites.

GRANTOWN-ON-SPEY – Highland – 501 J12 – pop. 2 166 — 30 D2

▶ Edinburgh 143 mi – Inverness 34 mi – Perth 99 mi

ℹ 54 High St ☎ (01479) 87 27 73, www.visitgrantown.co.uk
▮ Golf Course Rd, ☎ (01479) 87 20 79
▮ Abernethy Nethy Bridge, ☎ (01479) 82 13 05

Culdearn House
Woodlands Terrace ✉ PH26 3JU – ☎ (01479) 872 106 – www.culdearn.com
6 rm (dinner included) ☑ – †£ 92/110 ††£ 220/260
Rest – (booking essential for non-residents) Menu £ 37

♦ Personally run Victorian granite stone hotel offering a high degree of luxury, including beautifully furnished drawing room and very tastefully furnished bedrooms. Formally attired dining room; good Scottish home cooking.

Dulaig without rest
Seafield Ave ✉ PH26 3JF – ☎ (01479) 872 065 – www.thedulaig.com – Closed 20 December-7 January
3 rm ☑ – †£ 100/110 ††£ 140/150

♦ Small, detached, personally run guest house, built in 1910 and tastefully furnished with original Arts and Crafts pieces. Modern fabrics and uncluttered feel in comfortable bedrooms. Tea on arrival. Communal breakfast includes homemade muffins and bread.

GRULINE – Argyll and Bute – see Mull (Isle of)

GUILDTOWN – Perth and Kinross – 501 J14 – see Perth

GULLANE – East Lothian – **501** L15 – pop. 2 172 🟩 Scotland 26 C1
▶ Edinburgh 19 mi – North Berwick 5 mi
◉ Dirleton★ (Castle★) NE : 2 mi by A 198

Greywalls
Duncur Rd, Muirfield, Northeast : 0.75 mi by A 198 ✉ EH31 2EG – ☏ (01620) 842 144 – www.greywalls.co.uk
23 rm ☐ – †£ 80/105 ††£ 260/320
Rest *Chez Roux* – see restaurant listing
♦ Classic Edwardian country house by Lutyens, in superb location adjoining the famous Muirfield golf course. Spacious, antique-furnished bedrooms. Delightful formal gardens by Jekyll.

XX La Potinière
Main St ✉ EH31 2AA – ☏ (01620) 843 214 – www.la-potiniere.co.uk – Closed January, 25-26 December, Sunday dinner October-May, Monday, Tuesday and bank holidays
Rest – *(booking essential)* Menu £ 23/42
♦ Intimate restaurant dressed in pink and white, serving fresh, seasonal cooking. Regularly changing menus of traditional dishes, with ingredients from the owner's vegetable plot and herb greenhouse, as well as local suppliers. Good value lunch.

XX Chez Roux – at Greywalls Hotel
Duncur Rd, Muirfield, Northeast : 0.75 mi by A 198 ✉ EH31 2EG – ☏ (01620) 842 144 – www.greywalls.co.uk
Rest – French – *(booking essential for non-residents)* Menu £ 25/28 – Carte £ 31/42
♦ Country house style dining room with a modern edge; sit on high-backed chairs at well-spaced tables, overlooking the golf course. Classical French menus with a Roux signature style.

HARRAY – **501** K6 – see Orkney Islands (Mainland)

HARRIS – Highland – **501** Z10 – see Lewis and Harris (Isle of)

INGLISTON – City of Edinburgh – **501** J16 – see Edinburgh

INNERLEITHEN – The Scottish Borders – **501** K17 – pop. 2 586 26 C2
– ✉ Scottish Borders
▶ Edinburgh 31 mi – Dumfries 57 mi – Glasgow 60 mi

Caddon View
14 Pirn Rd. ✉ EH44 6HH – ☏ (01896) 830 208 – www.caddonview.co.uk
8 rm ☐ – †£ 55/95 ††£ 94/115
Rest – *(closed Sunday and Monday) (dinner only)* Carte £ 18/27 **s**
♦ Substantial Victorian house run by hospitable couple. Individually decorated bedrooms with modern touches; spacious Yarrow, and Moorfoot with its view, are the best. Bright, airy dining room; regularly changing menu of local produce from the Tweed Valley.

INVERGARRY – Highland – **501** F12 – ✉ Inverness 🟩 Scotland 30 C3
▶ Edinburgh 159 mi – Fort William 25 mi – Inverness 43 mi – Kyle of Lochalsh 50 mi
◉ The Great Glen★

Glengarry Castle
on A 82 ✉ PH35 4HW – ☏ (01809) 501 254 – www.glengarry.net
– 23 March-4 November
26 rm ☐ – †£ 67/97 ††£ 160/180
Rest – *(light lunch Monday-Saturday)* Menu £ 29 **s**
♦ Family-run Victorian house, named after the ruined castle in its 60 acre grounds. 2 large, open-fired sitting rooms; stuffed wild animals abound. Classical, individually styled bedrooms, some with original art deco baths. Formal dining from 4 course Scottish menu.

INVERGARRY

Invergarry
on A 87 – ℰ *(01809) 501 206 – www.invergarryhotel.co.uk – Closed 2 January to mid-February*
12 rm – †£ 55/90 ††£ 80/150 **Rest** – Carte £ 25/37
♦ Welcoming hotel in the style of a traditional inn. Smaller, quirky bedrooms in the eaves; first floor superior rooms offer more space and luxury. Comfy lounge featuring shotguns, open fires and tartan carpets. Simple cooking focuses on fresh Highland produce.

INVERKEILOR – Angus – 501 M14 – pop. 902 – ✉ Arbroath 28 D2
▶ Edinburgh 85 mi – Aberdeen 32 mi – Dundee 22 mi

Gordon's with rm
32 Main St ✉ DD11 5RN – ℰ *(01241) 830 364 – www.gordonsrestaurant.co.uk – Closed 2 weeks January*
5 rm – †£ 50/80 ††£ 100/130
Rest – *(closed Tuesday and Saturday lunch) (booking essential)* Menu £ 28/48
♦ Long-standing, passionately run restaurant; wife oversees service, husband and son are in the kitchen. Charming interior with stone walls, open fires and exposed beams. Concise menu of classical dishes, well-crafted from local, seasonal produce. Well-kept bedrooms; the courtyard suite is the biggest and best.

INVERMORISTON – Highland – 501 G12 30 C2
▶ London 550 mi – Edinburgh 166 mi – Inverness 28 mi – Dingwall 42 mi

Tigh na Bruach without rest
Southwest : 0.5 mi on A 82 ✉ IV63 7YE – ℰ *(01320) 351 349 – www.tighnabruach.com – Restricted opening in winter*
3 rm – †£ 87/96 ††£ 116/128
♦ Name means 'house on the bank'. Located by Loch Ness, it boasts splendid loch/mountain views and beautiful gardens. Very comfy bedrooms have pleasant terraces which overlook the lake.

INVERNESS – Highland – 501 H11 – pop. 40 949 ▌Scotland 30 C2
▶ Edinburgh 156 mi – Aberdeen 107 mi – Dundee 134 mi
✈ Inverness Airport, Dalcross : ℰ (01667) 464000, NE : 8 mi by A 96 Y
🛈 Castle Wynd ℰ (01463) 23 43 53, www.visithighlands.com
⛳ Culcabock Rd, ℰ (01463) 23 98 82
⛳ Torvean Glenurquhart Rd, ℰ (01463) 22 56 51
◉ Town★ – Museum and Art Gallery★ Y M
◉ Loch Ness★★, SW : by A 82 Z – Clava Cairns★, E : 9 mi by Culcabock Rd, B 9006 and B 851 Z – Cawdor Castle★ **AC**, NE : 14 mi by A 96 and B 9090 Y

Rocpool Reserve
14 Culduthel Rd ✉ IV2 4AG – ℰ *(01463) 240 089 – www.rocpool.com*
11 rm – †£ 150/175 ††£ 320/395 Z r
Rest *Chez Roux* – see restaurant listing
♦ Ultra-stylish boutique hotel with elegant, modern furnishings and sexy bar. Chic, comfortable bedrooms; some with their own terrace and hot tub. Attentive, professional service.

Glenmoriston Town House
20 Ness Bank ✉ IV2 4SF – ℰ *(01463) 223 777 – www.glenmoristontownhouse.com – Closed 8-9 January*
30 rm – †£ 100/170 ††£ 140/170 Z x
Rest *Abstract* – see restaurant listing
Rest *Contrast* – Menu £ 12/15 – Carte £ 24/35
♦ Chic, stylish town house. Modern cocktail bar a trendy meeting point. Bedrooms are individualistic, those on the front enjoying river views; those at the rear are quieter. Locally sourced cooking at Contrast.

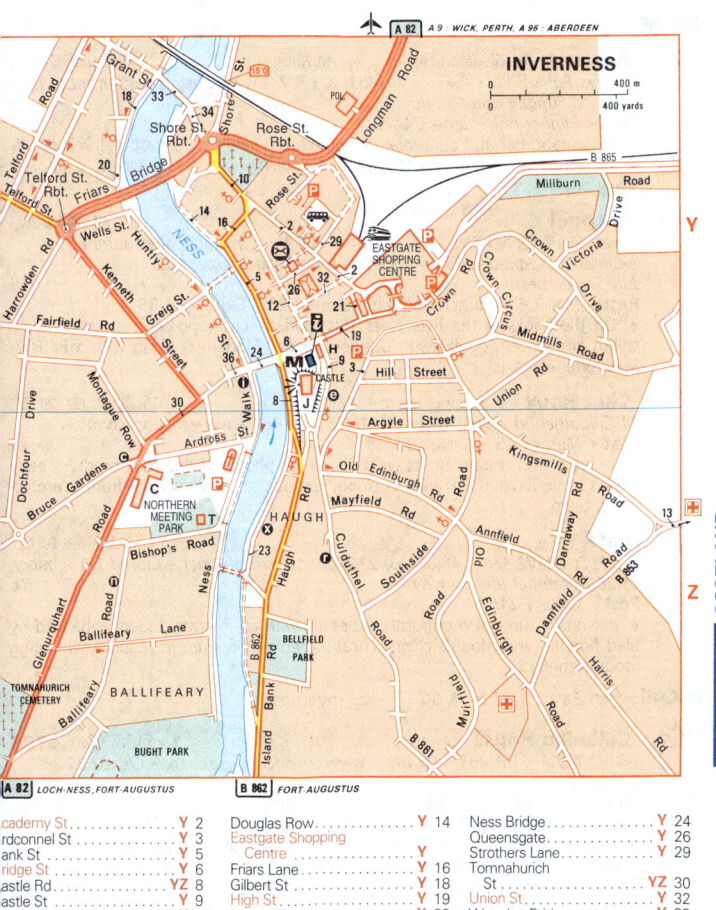

cademy St	Y	2	Douglas Row	Y	14	Ness Bridge	Y	24
rdconnel St	Y	3	Eastgate Shopping Centre	Y		Queensgate	Y	26
ank St	Y	5				Strothers Lane	Y	29
ridge St	Y	6	Friars Lane	Y	16	Tomnahurich St	YZ	30
astle Rd	YZ	8	Gilbert St	Y	18			
astle St	Y	9	High St	Y	19	Union St	Y	32
hapel St	Y	10	Huntly Pl	Y	20	Waterloo Bridge	Y	33
hurch St	Y	12	Inglis St	Y	21	Waterloo Pl	Y	34
ulcabock Rd	Z	13	Ness Bank	Z	23	Young St	Y	36

↑ **Ballifeary Guest House** without rest   📶 🅿 VISA ⦾

10 Ballifeary Rd ✉ *IV3 5PJ –* 📞 *(01463) 235 572*
– www.ballifearyguesthouse.co.uk
– Closed 24-28 December   **Z n**
7 rm 🛏 – †£ 40/70 ††£ 70/85

♦ Pleasant house set away from town centre, with homely sitting room and comfortable, immaculately kept bedrooms. Smart breakfast room with crisp linen and polished glassware.

↑ **Moyness House** without rest   📶 🅿 VISA ⦾

6 Bruce Gdns ✉ *IV3 5EN –* 📞 *(01463) 233 836 – www.moyness.co.uk*
– Closed 24-26 December   **Z c**
6 rm 🛏 – †£ 65/85 ††£ 94/110

♦ Immaculately clipped hedges frame this attractive Victorian villa. Bedrooms vary in shape and size but all are comfortable, individually decorated and fully en suite.

INVERNESS

Abstract – at Glenmoriston Town House Hotel
20 Ness Bank ⊠ IV2 4SF – ℰ (01463) 223 777 – www.abstractrestaurant.com
– Closed Sunday and Monday
Rest – (dinner only) Carte £ 44/52

♦ Restaurant, bar and conservatory with considerable style. Vast wall mirror off-sets abstract ink pictures. Accomplished cooking with Gallic accent is impressively original.

Rocpool
1 Ness Walk ⊠ IV3 5NE – ℰ (01463) 717 274 – www.rocpoolrestaurant.com
– Closed 1-3 January, 25-26 December and Sunday except dinner July-September
Rest – Menu £ 18 (lunch and early dinner)/20 – Carte £ 22/38

♦ On the banks of the river Ness, this modern, cosmopolitan restaurant has a stylish ambience, popular with business diners. Modern cooking with a British/Mediterranean axis.

Chez Roux – at Rocpool Reserve Hotel
14 Culduthel Rd ⊠ IV2 4AG – ℰ (01463) 240 089 – www.rocpool.com
Rest – Menu £ 25 – Carte £ 28/39

♦ Smart, stylish restaurant; its walls filled with photos of the Roux brothers' early days. Classic flavourful French cooking; smooth, attentive service from a professional team.

Café 1
Castle St ⊠ IV2 3EA – ℰ (01463) 226 200 – www.cafe1.net – Closed 1-2 January, 25-26 December and Sunday
Rest – Carte £ 24/33

♦ Personally run bistro opposite the castle with an informal touch, enhanced by tiled flooring and modish chairs. Local ingredients feature in regularly changing modern menus.

at Culloden East : 3 mi by A 96 - Y – ⊠ Inverness

Culloden House
⊠ IV2 7BZ – ℰ (01463) 790 461 – www.cullodenhouse.co.uk – Closed 25-26 December
25 rm ⊇ – †£ 95/270 ††£ 135/270 – 3 suites
Rest *Adams Dining Room* – Menu £ 45 (dinner) – Carte £ 33/54

♦ Imposing Georgian country house in 40 acres, requisitioned by Bonnie Prince Charlie in 1746. Drawing rooms boast ornate wall-hung plaster friezes. Antique-furnished rooms. Adam's plaster reliefs adorn walls and ceiling of grand dining room; traditional menu.

at Bunchrew West : 3 mi on A 862 - Y – ⊠ Inverness

Bunchrew House
⊠ IV3 8TA – ℰ (01463) 234 917 – www.bunchrewhousehotel.com
16 rm ⊇ – †£ 170/185 ††£ 178/270 **Rest** – Menu £ 24/40

♦ Unhurried relaxation is assured at this 17C Scottish mansion nestling in a tranquil spot on the shores of Bealy Firth. Drawing room is wood panelled; bedrooms restful. Gardens seen through the windows provide a pleasant backdrop to spacious dining room.

ISLAY (Isle of) – Argyll and Bute – 501 B16   27 A3

✈ Port Ellen Airport : ℰ (01496) 302361

⛴ from Port Askaig to Isle of Jura (Feolin) (Caledonian MacBrayne Ltd) frequent services daily (approx. 4 mn) – from Port Ellen or Port Askaig to Kintyre Peninsula (Kennacraig) (Caledonian MacBrayne Ltd) 1-2 daily – from Port Askaig to Oban via Isle of Colonsay (Scalasaig) (Caledonian MacBrayne Ltd) weekly – from Port Askaig to Isle of Colonsay (Scalasaig) and Kintyre Peninsula (Kennacraig) (Caledonian MacBrayne Ltd) weekly

🛈 The Square, Main St, Bowmore ℰ (01496) 81 02 54, www.islayinfo.com
 Port Ellen 25 Charlotte St, ℰ (01496) 30 00 94

ISLAY (Isle of)

BALLYGRANT – Argyll and Bute   27 A3

Kilmeny
Southwest : 0.5 mi on A 846 – PA45 7QW – ⌀ (01496) 840 668
– www.kilmeny.co.uk – Closed Christmas and New Year
5 rm – †£ 90/95 ††£ 130/150   **Rest** – Menu £ 38 **s**

• Delightful house in over 350 acres of working farmland. Large lounge with mock open fire and fine array of books about Islay. Superb bedrooms with beautiful feature beds, lovely tartans/tweeds/woollens woven on the island and thoughtful extras. Spacious dining room serves garden/island produce. Truly welcoming owner.

BOWMORE – Argyll and Bute   27 A3

Harbour Inn with rm
The Square – PA43 7JR – ⌀ (01496) 810 330 – www.harbour-inn.com
7 rm – †£ 135 ††£ 160   **Rest** – Carte £ 25/40

• Traditional restaurant with pleasant bar and chunky wooden tea tables covered in deep blue cloths. Classical cooking uses fresh local seafood and island meats. Bedrooms are brightly decorated. Two cosy residents' lounges afford fantastic bay and island views.

PORT CHARLOTTE – Argyll and Bute   27 A3

Port Charlotte
Main St – PA48 7TU – ⌀ (01496) 850 360 – www.portcharlottehotel.co.uk
– Closed 24-26 December
10 rm – †£ 95 ††£ 170   **Rest** – (bar lunch) Carte £ 21/33

• Waterside hotel packed full of modern art. Large lounge with wood burning stove; cosy bar hung with old island photos. Bedrooms display traditional furniture and modern colour schemes; most have a sea view. Good mix of meat and fish dishes in the restaurant.

PORT ELLEN – Argyll and Bute   27 A3

Glenegedale House
Northwest : 4.75 mi on A 846 – PA42 7AS – ⌀ (01496) 300 400
– www.glenegedalehouse.co.uk – March-October
8 rm – †£ 90 ††£ 115   **Rest** – Menu £ 35

• Well-run hotel opposite the airport. Immaculately kept bedrooms feature designer fabrics. Choice of two sitting rooms, both displaying leather sofas, coffee tables and an array of curios. Traditional menu of island produce served in smartly laid dining rooms.

Glenmachrie Farmhouse without rest
Northwest : 4.5 mi on A 846 – PA42 7AQ – ⌀ (01496) 302 560
– www.glenmachrie.com – Closed Christmas and New Year
5 rm – †£ 90 ††£ 100

• Homely tartan-themed guesthouse where antiques and curious abound. Exclusive access to private loch; catch a fish and they will prepare and even smoke it for you. Breakfast at Glenegedale House.

JEDBURGH – The Scottish Borders – 501 M17 – pop. 4 090   Scotland   26 D2

▶ Edinburgh 48 mi – Carlisle 54 mi – Newcastle upon Tyne 57 mi
▯ Murray's Green ⌀ (01835) 86 31 70, www.visitscotland.com
▯ Jedburgh Dunion Rd, ⌀ (01835) 86 35 87
◉ Town★ - Abbey★★ **AC** – Mary Queen of Scots House Visitor Centre★ **AC** – The Canongate Bridge★
◉ Waterloo Monument (★★) N : 4 mi by A 68 and B 6400

JEDBURGH

Willow Court without rest

The Friars ✉ TD8 6BN – ⌕ (01835) 863 702 – www.willowcourtjedburgh.co.uk
3 rm ⌑ – †£70/75 ††£75/85

♦ Contemporary guesthouse looking out over the town's rooftops. Comfortable ground floor bedrooms offer a light, stylish space, with flat screen TVs, iPod docks and DVD players, as well as smart, modern bathrooms. Communal breakfasts, with eggs from their own hens.

KELSO – The Scottish Borders – **501** M17 – pop. 5 116   Scotland   **26** D2

▶ Edinburgh 44 mi – Hawick 21 mi – Newcastle upon Tyne 68 mi
ℹ The Square ⌕ (01835) 86 31 70, www.kelso.bordernet.co.uk
⛳ Golf Course Rd, ⌕ (01573) 22 30 09
◉ Town★ - The Square★★ – ≤★ from Kelso Bridge
◉ Tweed Valley★★ – Floors Castle★ **AC**, NW : 1.5 mi by A 6089.
Mellerstain★★ (Ceilings★★★, Library★★★) **AC**, NW : 6 mi by A 6089 – Waterloo Monument (⁂★★), SW : 7 mi by A 698 and B 6400 – Jedburgh Abbey★★ **AC**, SW : 8.5 mi by A 698 - Dryburgh Abbey★★ **AC** (setting★★★), SW : 10.5 mi by A 6089, A 6397 and B 6404 – Scott's View★★, W : 11 mi by A 6089, B 6397, B 6404 and B 6356 – Smailholm Tower★ (⁂★★), NW : 6 mi by A 6089 and B 6397 - Lady Kirk (Kirk o'Steil★), NE : 16 mi by A 698, A 697, A 6112 and B 6437

Roxburghe

Heiton, Southwest : 3.5 mi by A 698 ✉ TD5 8JZ – ⌕ (01573) 450 331
– www.roxburghe-hotel.com
20 rm ⌑ – †£99/190 ††£159/250 – 2 suites
Rest – Carte £23/41 s

♦ Characterful Jacobean style mansion in extensive parkland, owned by the Duke of Roxburghe. Plush lounge and cosy library bar boating antiques/heirlooms. Feature bedrooms the most luxurious; courtyard rooms, more modern. Formal dining – local produce to the fore.

Ednam House

Bridge St. ✉ TD5 7HT – ⌕ (01573) 224 168 – www.ednamhouse.com
– Closed 24 December-9 January
32 rm ⌑ – †£91/138 ††£119/167
Rest – Menu £14/33

♦ Longstanding sports hotel on the Tweed; in the family since 1928. Original features, grand drawing rooms and classically styled bedrooms boasting a timeless elegance. Fishing-themed bar displays mural of the Tweed. 4 course classical dinner overlooking the river.

at Ednam North : 2.25 mi on B 6461 – ✉ Kelso

Edenwater House

off Stichill rd ✉ TD5 7QL – ⌕ (01573) 224 070 – www.edenwaterhouse.co.uk
– March-November
5 rm ⌑ – †£85 ††£120
Rest – (Closed Sunday-Monday) (dinner only) Menu £38

♦ Delightful house run by charming couple, boasting a lovely garden and stream. Antique-filled lounges and comfy, classical bedrooms with tasteful décor and antique furniture. Pleasant dining room overlooks a meadow and offers a traditional, daily changing set menu.

KENMORE – Perth and Kinross – **501** I14 – pop. 596   Scotland   **28** C2

▶ Edinburgh 82 mi – Dundee 60 mi – Oban 71 mi – Perth 38 mi
⛳ Taymouth Castle Aberfeldy, ⌕ (01887) 83 02 28
⛳ Mains of Taymouth, ⌕ (01887) 83 02 26
◉ Village★
◉ Loch Tay★★. Ben Lawers★★, SW : 8 mi by A 827

Kenmore

 Kenmore
The Square ✉ *PH15 2NU* – ✆ *(01887) 830 205* – *www.kenmorehotel.com*
40 rm (dinner included) – ₤100/110 ₤167/230
Rest – Carte £ 21/35
♦ Scotland's oldest inn. Standing on the Tay, it is now a smart, white-fronted hotel with Poet's Parlour featuring original pencilled verse by Burns. Cosy, well-kept rooms. Restaurant with panoramic river views.

KILBERRY – Argyll and Bute – **501** D16 – see Kintyre (Peninsula)

KILCHRENAN – Argyll and Bute – **501** E14 – ✉ Taynuilt ▌Scotland 27 B2

▶ Edinburgh 117 mi – Glasgow 87 mi – Oban 18 mi
◉ Loch Awe★★, E : 1.25 m

 Ardanaiseig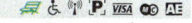
Northeast : 4 mi ✉ *PA35 1HE* – ✆ *(01866) 833 333* – *www.ardanaiseig.com*
– *Closed 2 January-1 February*
17 rm – ₤69/108 ₤138/218 – 1 suite
Rest – *(booking essential for non-residents)* Menu £ 30/50
♦ Stunningly located, laid-back country house boasting a vast azalea-filled estate and lovely views down the loch. Large sitting room with impressive columns; bedrooms mix styles – the Lake Suite is best. Elegant formal dining room; daily set menu of local produce.

⌂ **Roineabhal** without rest
✉ *PA35 1HD* – ✆ *(01866) 833 207* – *www.roineabhal.com* – *Easter-October*
3 rm – ₤70/90 ₤100
♦ Purpose-built, log cabin style guesthouse; jolly owner serves tea and homemade biscuits on arrival. Cosy bedrooms reached via spiral staircase: all have showers; roll-top bath is shared. Bluebell-lined walk in garden.

KILDRUMMY – Aberdeenshire – **501** L12 – ✉ Alford ▌Scotland 28 D1

▶ Edinburgh 137 mi – Aberdeen 35 mi
◉ Castle★ AC
◉ Huntly Castle (Heraldic carvings★★★) N : 15 mi by A 97 – Craigievar Castle★, SE : 13 mi by A 97, A 944 and A 980

 Kildrummy Castle
South : 1.5 mi on A 97 ✉ *AB33 8RA* – ✆ *(019755) 71 288*
– *www.kildrummycastlehotel.co.uk* – *Closed January*
16 rm – ₤98/120 ₤175/217
Rest *Dining Room* – see restaurant listing
♦ Imposing stone mansion in beautiful grounds, overlooking a 13C castle. Impressive gallery corridor hung with tapestries; lovely lounge, library and drawing room with attractive Georgian plasterwork. Traditional bedrooms; one with a terrace.

✕✕✕ **Dining Room** – at Kildrummy Castle Hotel
South : 1.5 mi on A 97 ✉ *AB33 8RA* – ✆ *(019755) 71 288*
– *www.kildrummycastlehotel.co.uk* – *Closed January and lunch Monday*
Rest – Menu £ 21/37
♦ Grand dining room with linen-laid tables, imposing wooden ceiling and original fireplace, set in a stone-built baronial mansion dating back to 1900. Classical dishes display some modern twists.

KILLIECRANKIE – Perth and Kinross – **501** I13 – see Pitlochry

KINCLAVEN – Perth and Kinross – **501** J14 – pop. 394 – ✉ Stanley   28 C2

▶ Edinburgh 56 mi – Perth 12 mi

Ballathie House
Stanley ✉ *PH1 4QN* – ℰ *(01250) 883 268* – *www.ballathiehousehotel.com*
39 rm (dinner included) – †£ 105/165 ††£ 290/370 – 3 suites
Rest – Menu £ 27/44 **s**

♦ Well-established, mid-19C former shooting lodge, set on a peaceful estate of several hundred acres, on the banks of the River Tay. Comfortable guest areas and individually furnished bedrooms: some with floral themes, some more contemporary. Concise country house menu showcases seasonal, regional produce.

KINGAIRLOCH – HLD Highland – **501** D14   29 B3

▶ London 521 mi – Edinburgh 147 mi – Greenock 116 mi

Boathouse and Steadings with rm
Ardgour ✉ *PH33 7AE* – ℰ *(01967) 411 232* – *www.kingairloch.co.uk*
– *23 March-27 October*
5 rm – †£ 80 ††£ 80
Rest – *(closed Monday-Wednesday and Sunday dinner) (booking advisable)*
Carte £ 17/31

♦ A converted Victorian boathouse on the shore of Loch a'Choire in the heart of the Kingairloch Estate. Appealing dishes use estate produce, including full-flavoured venison, and seasonal herbs and vegetables from the kitchen garden. Spacious, immaculately maintained bedrooms in The Steadings. Dramatic mountain views.

KINGUSSIE – Highland – **501** H12 – pop. 1 410 ▮ Scotland   30 C3

▶ Edinburgh 117 mi – Inverness 41 mi – Perth 73 mi

🛈 Gynack Rd, ℰ (01540) 66 16 00

◉ Highland Wildlife Park★ **AC**, NE : 4 mi by A 9. Aviemore★, NE : 11 mi by A 9 – The Cairngorms★★ (≤★★★) - ❋★★★ from Cairn Gorm, NE : 18 mi by B 970

Hermitage
Spey St ✉ *PH21 1HN* – ℰ *(01540) 662 137* – *www.thehermitage-scotland.com*
– *Closed 20 December-4 January*
5 rm – †£ 32/55 ††£ 60/100
Rest – Menu £ 24 **s**

♦ Traditional Victorian house built from stone and slate; formerly a doctor's surgery. Spacious garden affords great views of the Cairngorm Mountains and Ruthven Barracks. Warm, cosy lounge and comfy bedrooms; one has a super-king-sized bed and wet room. Simple dining room offers daily menu of home-cooked local produce.

Cross at Kingussie with rm
Tweed Mill Brae, Ardbroilach Rd ✉ *PH21 1LB* – ℰ *(01540) 661 166*
– *www.thecross.co.uk* – *Closed 3 January-9 January, 25 December, Sunday and Monday*
8 rm (dinner included) – †£ 150/185 ††£ 230/250
Rest – *(dinner only) (booking essential)* Menu £ 50 **s**

♦ Personally run converted tweed mill restaurant in four acres of waterside grounds with beamed ceilings and modern artwork. Modish Scottish cuisine. Comfortable rooms.

KINTILLO – Perth and Kinross – see Perth

KINTYRE (Peninsula) – Argyll and Bute – 501 D16 Scotland   27 B3

✈ Campbeltown Airport : ℰ (01586) 553797

⛴ from Claonaig to Isle of Arran (Lochranza) (Caledonian MacBrayne Ltd) frequent services daily (30 mn) – from Kennacraig to Isle of Islay (Port Ellen or Port Askaig) (Caledonian MacBrayne Ltd) 1-3 daily – from Kennacraig to Oban via Isle of Colonsay (Scalasaig) and Isle of Islay (Port Askaig) 3 weekly

🏌 Machrihanish Campbeltown, ℰ (01586) 81 02 13

🏌 Dunaverty Campbeltown Southend, ℰ (01586) 83 06 77

🏌 Gigha Isle of Gigha, ℰ (01583) 50 52 42

◉ Carradale★ – Saddell (Collection of grave slabs★)

CARRADALE – Argyll and Bute   27 B3

Dunvalanree

Port Righ Bay ✉ *PA28 6SE* – ℰ *(01583) 431 226* – *www.dunvalanree.com*
5 rm (dinner included) – †£ 95 ††£ 175
Rest – *(dinner only)* Menu £ 23/28

♦ 1930s house in its own bay, with gardens and terrace overlooking the beach and Sound. Charming interior with many original Arts and Crafts features. Individually furnished bedrooms – one in Mackintosh style; some with views. Homely cooking with a seafood base.

KILBERRY – Argyll and Bute   27 A3

SCOTLAND

Kilberry Inn with rm

✉ *PA29 6YD* – ℰ *(01880) 770 223* – *www.kilberryinn.com* – *Closed January-February and Christmas*
5 rm (dinner included) – †£ 110 ††£ 195
Rest – *(closed Monday and lunch November to mid-March) (booking essential at dinner)* Carte £ 25/36

♦ Remotely set, rustic country inn with wooden beams, stone walls, open fires and mix of bare and linen-laid tables. Classical dishes are crafted from carefully sourced local produce; meat and fish are smoked in-house. Well-stocked bar. Comfy, modern bedrooms are named after nearby islands; one has an outdoor hot tub.

KIRKBEAN – Dumfries and Galloway – 501 J19 Scotland   26 C3

▶ Edinburgh 92 mi – Dumfries 13 mi – Kirkcudbright 29 mi

◉ Sweetheart Abbey★, N : 5 mi by A 710. Threave Garden★★ and Threave Castle★, W : 20 mi by A 710 and A 745

Cavens

✉ *DG2 8AA* – ℰ *(01387) 880 234* – *www.cavens.com* – *Closed January-February and 25 December*
8 rm – ††£ 150/190
Rest – *(dinner only)* Menu £ 35

♦ Attractive 18C country house in mature grounds. Elegant drawing room with grand piano and cosy, book-filled 'Green Room'. Luxurious 'Estate' bedrooms boast views over the Solway Firth; comfy 'Country' rooms are simpler. Linen-clad dining room offers unfussy 3 course menu of local produce. Complimentary afternoon tea.

KIRKCUDBRIGHT – Dumfries and Galloway – 501 H19 – pop. 3 447   25 B3
Scotland

▶ Edinburgh 108 mi – Dumfries 28 mi – Stranraer 50 mi

🛈 Harbour Sq ℰ (01557) 33 04 94, www.kirkcudbright.co.uk

🏌 Stirling Crescent, ℰ (01557) 33 03 14

◉ Town★

◉ Dundrennan Abbey★ **AC**, SE : 5 mi by A 711

KIRKCUDBRIGHT

Selkirk Arms
High St ⊠ DG6 4JG – ℰ (01557) 330 402 – www.selkirkarmshotel.co.uk
17 rm ⌕ – †£ 70/150 ††£ 90/116 – 2 suites
Rest *Artistas* – see restaurant listing
♦ Well-run 18C former coaching inn where Robert Burns reputedly wrote the Selkirk Grace. Spacious, comfortable bedrooms; some recently refurbished. Light lunches in the cosy sports bar, which displays caricatures of famous sporting figures.

Gladstone House
48 High St ⊠ DG6 4JX – ℰ (01557) 331 734 – www.kirkcudbrightgladstone.com
– Closed 2 weeks January-February and Christmas
3 rm ⌕ – †£ 55 ††£ 75
Rest – Menu £ 26
♦ Attractive 18C former merchant's house with friendly owners. Comfy, antique-furnished lounge. Simple, pastel-hued bedrooms with seating areas by the windows and views over the rooftops. 3 course dinner of local produce, tailored around guests' preferences.

Artistas – at Selkirk Arms Hotel
High St ⊠ DG6 4JG – ℰ (01557) 330 402 – www.selkirkarmshotel.co.uk
Rest – Menu £ 29 – Carte £ 24/38
♦ Formal hotel restaurant in an 18C former coaching inn. Extensive set menu offers traditional dishes crafted from regional ingredients. Galloway Beef and Kirkcudbright scallops are a feature.

KIRKMICHAEL – Perth and Kinross – 501 J13 28 C2
▶ Edinburgh 73 mi – Aberdeen 85 mi – Inverness 102 mi – Perth 29 mi

Strathardle Inn with rm
on A 924 ⊠ PH10 7NS – ℰ (01250) 881 224 – www.strathardleinn.co.uk
– Closed Monday lunch and Tuesday-Friday lunch November-March
8 rm ⌕ – †£ 45/50 ††£ 70/80
Rest – *(dinner only and lunch Saturday-Sunday)* Carte £ 21/31
♦ 18C drover's inn serving robust cooking with a Scottish twist. Concise lunch menu of pub favourites. Dinner menu might feature smoked salmon or local venison. Simple, modern bedrooms.

KIRKNEWTON – West Lothian – 501 J16 – see Edinburgh

KIRKWALL – 501 L7 – see Orkney Islands (Mainland)

KIRK YETHOLM – The Scottish Borders 26 D2
▶ London 346 mi – Edinburgh 57 mi – Hawick 26 mi – Galashiels 27 mi

Mill House without rest
Main St ⊠ TD5 8PE – ℰ (01573) 420 604 – www.millhouseyetholm.co.uk
3 rm ⌕ – †£ 50/60 ††£ 90
♦ Charming former grain mill set on the edge of the village, looking down the valley. Spacious interior with vast lounge. Comfy bedrooms are simply furnished, with modern bathrooms. Indoor hot tub. Extensive offerings at breakfast.

KYLESKU – Highland – 501 E9 Scotland 30 C1
▶ Edinburgh 256 mi – Inverness 100 mi – Ullapool 34 mi
ⓖ Loch Assynt★★, S : 6 mi by A 894

KYLESKU

Kylesku
✉ IV27 4HW – ✆ (01971) 502 231 – www.kyleskuhotel.co.uk – March-October
8 rm ⌑ – †£ 69 ††£ 99/104
Rest *Kylesku (Bar)* – see restaurant listing
Rest – *(dinner only)* Menu £ 33 – Carte £ 20/35

♦ Delightfully located 17C coaching inn, set beside 2 sea-lochs in a peaceful village. Spectacular panoramic views from cosy lounge, restaurant and most of the homely bedrooms. Cooking centres around fresh Highland game and locally landed seafood.

Kylesku (Bar) – at Kylesku Hotel
✉ IV27 4HW – ✆ (01971) 502 231 – www.kyleskuhotel.co.uk – March-October
Rest – Carte £ 22/38

♦ Friendly staff and relaxed atmopshere, with breathtaking views of Loch Glendhu and the spectacular surrounding scenery. Menu focuses on fresh seafood landed daily in front of the inn.

LAIRG – Highland – **501** G9 – pop. 857   30 C2
▶ Edinburgh 218 mi – Inverness 61 mi – Wick 72 mi
ℹ Sutherland ✆ (01549) 40 21 60, www.visitscotland.com

Park House
✉ IV27 4AU – ✆ (01549) 402 208 – www.parkhousesporting.com – Closed 20 December-2 January
4 rm ⌑ – †£ 50/60 ††£ 80/90
Rest – Menu £ 25

♦ Victorian sporting lodge offering fishing and field sports, its walls fittingly hung with rods and hunting prints. Cosy, open-fired sitting room and good-sized, homely bedrooms. Dining room offers loch views and a classical menu. Game and seafood feature highly.

LANGASS – Western Isles – see Uist (Isles of)

LEITH – City of Edinburgh – **501** K16 – see Edinburgh

LERWICK – **501** Q3 – see Shetland Islands (Mainland)

LEWIS and HARRIS (Isle of) – **501** A9 Scotland

🚢 from Stornoway to Ullapool (Mainland) (Caledonian MacBrayne Ltd) 2/3 daily (2 h 40 mn) – from Kyles Scalpay to the Isle of Scalpay (Caledonian MacBrayne Ltd) (10 mn) – from Tarbert to Isle of Skye (Uig) (Caledonian MacBrayne Ltd) 1-2 daily (1 h 45 mn) – from Tarbert to Portavadie (Caledonian MacBrayne Ltd) (summer only) frequent services daily (25 mn) – from Leverburgh to North Uist (Otternish) (Caledonian MacBrayne Ltd) (3-4 daily) (1 h 10 mn)

👁 Callanish Standing Stones★★ – Carloway Broch★ – St Clement's Church, Rodel (tomb★)

LEWIS – Western Isles   29 A1
▶ London 618 mi – Edinburgh 212 mi

BREASCLETE – Western Isles   29 B1

Eshcol
21 Breasclete ✉ HS2 9ED – ✆ (01851) 621 357 – www.eshcol.com
– March-October
3 rm ⌑ – †£ 55 ††£ 80/90
Rest – Menu £ 22 (dinner)

♦ Immaculately kept guesthouse set on a small croft, in a former weaving village. Lovely loch and island views from the lounge and conservatory. Simple, homely bedrooms also share the view. Breakfast and dinner served in next door sister guesthouse 'Loch Roag'.

LEWIS AND HARRIS (ISLE OF) - Lewis

⌂ **Loch Roag**
22A Breasclete ✉ *HS2 9EF* – ☏ *(01851) 621 771 – www.lochroag.com*
– April-September
4 rm – †£ 40/55 ††£ 80/90
Rest – ☏ (01851) 621 357 *(by arrangement)* Menu £ 22
♦ Run in conjunction with sister guesthouse 'Eshcol'. Simple, well-maintained bedrooms are a little larger than next door. Comfy lounge and dining room; big windows take in the view. Local specialities to start the day – home-cooked regional produce to finish it.

GALSON – Western Isles   29 B1

⌂ **Galson Farm**
South Galson ✉ *HS2 0SH* – ☏ *(01851) 850 492 – www.galsonfarm.co.uk*
4 rm – †£ 48 ††£ 96
Rest – Menu £ 25
♦ Welcoming guesthouse in a wonderfully remote location, boasting views out across the Atlantic. Traditional, homely guest areas and cosy bedrooms. The owner also operates the village post office from just inside the porch. Freshly prepared, home-cooked meals.

STORNOWAY – Western Isles   29 B1

🛈 26 Cromwell St ☏ (01851) 70 30 88, www.visitscotland.com
⛳ Lady Lever Park, ☏ (01851) 70 22 40

⌂ **Braighe House** without rest
20 Braighe Rd, Southeast : 3 mi on A 866 ✉ *HS2 0BQ*
– ☏ (01851) 705 287 – www.braighehouse.co.uk
– March-November
5 rm – †£ 75/105 ††£ 95/125
♦ Smart dormer bungalow with relaxed, modern interior. Deluxe rooms have sleigh beds and sea outlooks. Complimentary port and use of fishing rods. Car-/golf club hire arranged. Diverse breakfasts.

HARRIS – Western Isles   29 A1

▶ London 638 mi – Edinburgh 254 mi

ARDHASAIG – Western Isles   29 A1

✕✕ **Ardhasaig House** with rm
✉ *HS3 3AJ* – ☏ *(01859) 502 500 – www.ardhasaig.co.uk*
6 rm – †£ 45/120 ††£ 120/200
Rest – *(dinner only)* Menu £ 35
♦ Purpose-built house that's been in the family for over 100 years. Modern, airy bar-lounge; flag-floored dining room with antique tables and dramatic bay/mountain views. Set menu offers local meats and seafood. Cosy bedrooms; the one in the stone lodge is the best.

SCALPAY – Western Isles   29 B2

Hirta House without rest
✉ *HS4 3XZ* – ☏ *(01859) 540 394*
– www.hirtahouse.co.uk
3 rm – †£ 60/65 ††£ 70
♦ Simple, characterful guesthouse in a small fishing village. Harbour views from lounge and conservatory. One traditional four-poster bedroom; two more modern rooms, one with a queen-sized bed.

LEWIS AND HARRIS (ISLE OF) - Harris

SCARISTA – Western Isles 29 A2

Scarista House
HS3 3HX – ℰ *(01859) 550 238* – www.scaristahouse.com
– Closed 18 December-29 February
6 rm – †£ 155 ††£ 200/220
Rest – *(dinner only) (booking essential for non-residents) (set menu only)*
Menu £ 45
♦ Simple whitewashed house boasting amazing bay and mountain views. Caring owners; cosy, homely interior with open-fired library and drawing room. Traditional bedrooms, those at the rear are best. Set dinners use garden produce and offer the choice of meat or fish.

TARBERT – Western Isles – pop. 1 338 – ✉ Harris 29 A2

Hotel Hebrides
Pier Rd ✉ *HS3 3DG* – ℰ *(01859) 502 364* – www.hotel-hebrides.com
21 rm – †£ 50/150 ††£ 120/180
Rest *Pier House* – see restaurant listing
♦ Keenly run boutique hotel situated on the harbourside, next to the ferry terminal. Bedrooms are stylish, well-thought-out and come in bold designs; good facilities, they even have hair straighteners available to borrow. Smart, friendly bar.

Ceol na Mara without rest
7 Direcleit, South : 1 mi by A 859 ✉ *HS3 3DP* – ℰ *(01859) 502 464*
– www.ceolnamara.com
3 rm – †£ 90/100 ††£ 90/100
♦ Former crofter's cottage – one of only three on the island with three storeys. Spacious, homely interior. Various well-kept lounges and good-sized, comfy bedrooms. Stunning lochside location.

Pier House – at Hotel Hebrides
Pier Rd ✉ *HS3 3DG* – ℰ *(01859) 502 364* – www.hotel-hebrides.com
Rest – Carte £ 21/41 **s**
♦ Well-run restaurant in a stylish harbourside hotel close to the ferry terminal. Modern à la carte menu showcases local island produce, which appears in some original, unexpected combinations.

LEWISTON – Highland – **501** G12 – Scotland 30 C2

▶ Edinburgh 173 mi – Inverness 17 mi
◉ Loch Ness★★ – The Great Glen★

Woodlands without rest
East Lewiston ✉ *IV63 6UJ* – ℰ *(01456) 450 356*
– www.woodlands-lochness.co.uk – April-October
3 rm – †£ 43 ††£ 65
♦ Spacious, purpose-built guesthouse with large garden and decked terrace; situated just away from the village centre. Bedrooms are airy, comfortable and immaculately kept.

Loch Ness Inn with rm
✉ *IV63 6UW* – ℰ *(01456) 450 991* – www.staylochness.co.uk
12 rm – †£ 69/89 ††£ 89/112
Rest – Carte £ 19/32
♦ Honest local pub with traditional bar, contemporary dining room and smart wood-furnished rear terrace. Pub classics on the blackboard at lunch, more restaurant-style dishes at dinner. Individually styled bedrooms have a country feel.

LINLITHGOW – West Lothian – **501** J16 – pop. 13 370 ■ Scotland   **26** C1

▶ Edinburgh 19 mi – Falkirk 9 mi – Glasgow 35 mi

🛈 High St ✆ (01506) 77 53 20, www.visitscotland.com

⛳ Braehead, ✆ (01506) 84 25 85

⛳ West Lothian Airngath Hill, ✆ (01506) 82 60 30

👁 Town★★ – Palace★★ **AC** : Courtyard (fountain★★), Great Hall (Hooded Fireplace★★), Gateway★ – Old Town★ – St Michaels★

🟢 Cairnpapple Hill★ **AC**, SW : 5 mi by A 706 – House of the Binns (plasterwork ceilings★) **AC**, NE : 4.5 mi by A 803 and A 904. Hopetoun House★★ **AC**, E : 7 mi by A 706 and A 904 – Abercorn Parish Church (Hopetoun Loft★★) NE : 7 mi by A 803 and A 904

⌂ **Arden House** without rest
Belsyde, Southwest : 2.25 mi on A 706 ✉ *EH49 6QE* – ✆ *(01506) 670 172*
– *www.ardencountryhouse.com* – *Closed 25 December*
3 rm ⎕ – ♦£ 58/100 ♦♦£ 86/104
♦ Purpose built guesthouse set in 105 acres of sheep farming land. Spacious, tastefully styled bedrooms boast modern, slate-floored bathrooms and plenty of extras. Tasty, wide-ranging breakfasts are a highlight. Welcoming owner pays great attention to detail.

✕✕✕ **Champany Inn** with rm
Northeast : 2 mi on A 803 at junction with A 904 ✉ *EH49 7LU*
– ✆ *(01506) 834 532* – *www.champany.com*
– *Closed 1-2 January, 25-26 December, Saturday lunch and Sunday*
16 rm ⎕ – ♦£ 99/110 ♦♦£ 125/140
Rest *Chop and Ale House* – see restaurant listing
Rest – Beef specialities – Menu £ 29/43 – Carte £ 58/73
♦ Collection of buildings that create a 'mini-village'. Polished tables, smart silverware and formal service in restaurant. Classically based dishes, with top quality 21-day aged Aberdeen Angus beef their speciality. Excellent wine list with extensive South African selection. Smart, spacious, tartan-themed bedrooms.

✕✕ **Livingston's**
52 High St ✉ *EH49 7AE* – ✆ *(01506) 846 565* – *www.livingstons-restaurant.co.uk*
– *Closed 2 weeks January, 1 week June, 1 week October, Sunday and Monday*
Rest – Menu £ 20/39
♦ Long-standing, family-run restaurant. Conservatory-like dining room with large garden and terrace; friendly, efficient service. Set menus feature Scottish produce and Mediterranean touches.

✕ **Chop and Ale House** – at Champany Inn
Northeast : 2 mi on A 803 at junction with A 904 ✉ *EH49 7LU*
– ✆ *(01506) 834 532* – *www.champany.com*
– *Closed 1 January and 25-26 December*
Rest – Carte £ 24/40
♦ Cosy restaurant with stone walls and beamed ceilings hung with animal traps and hunting prints. Menu offers quality steaks, speciality burgers, South African Boerewors and seafood classics.

LOANS – South Ayrshire – **501** G17 – see Troon

LOCHALINE – Highland – **501** C14   **29** B3

▶ Edinburgh 162 mi – Craignure 6 mi – Oban 7 mi

✕ **Whitehouse**
✉ *PA34 5XT* – ✆ *(01967) 421 777* – *www.thewhitehouserestaurant.co.uk*
– *Closed November-Easter, Monday and Sunday*
Rest – Menu £ 25/30 – Carte £ 28/38
♦ Understated, wood-panelled restaurant in remote headland village. Constantly evolving blackboard menu of local seafood, game and garden produce. Unfussy, flavoursome cooking. Hands-on owners.

LOCHEARNHEAD – Stirling – 501 H14 🏴 Scotland — 28 C2

▶ Edinburgh 65 mi – Glasgow 56 mi – Oban 57 mi – Perth 36 mi

at Balquhidder Southwest : 5 mi by A84 – ✉ Stirling

Monachyle Mhor
West : 4 mi ✉ *FK19 8PQ –* ✆ *(01877) 384 622 – www.mhor.net – Closed 3-31 January*
16 rm (dinner included) – **†**£ 235/303 **††**£ 235/359
Rest *– (booking essential for non residents)* Menu £ 47 (dinner)
– Carte lunch £ 28/32

◆ Eye-catching pink former farmhouse, located in a beautiful, very remote valley. Contemporary furnishings blend with original features in the reception, lounge and bar. Smart, modern bedrooms boast slate-tiled bathrooms; those in the main house are smaller but afford great views over the Braes of Balquhidder.

LOCHINVER – Highland – 501 E9 – pop. 470 – ✉ Lairg 🏴 Scotland — 30 C1

▶ Edinburgh 251 mi – Inverness 95 mi – Wick 105 mi

ℹ Kirk Lane ✆ (01506) 832 2 22, www.visitscotland.com

◉ Village ★

◉ Loch Assynt ★★, E : 6 mi by A 837

Inver Lodge
Iolaire Rd ✉ *IV27 4LU –* ✆ *(01571) 844 496 – www.inverlodge.com – April-October*
20 rm – **†**£ 115 **††**£ 215/220
Rest *Chez Roux* – see restaurant listing

◆ Well-run hotel on the hillside, overlooking a quiet fishing village. Spacious open-fired lounge, elegant bar and billiard room. Smart bedrooms with good mod cons and great bay/island views.

Ruddyglow Park Country House
Loch Assynt, Northeast : 6.75 mi on A 837 ✉ *IV27 4HB*
– ✆ *(01571) 822 216 – www.ruddyglowpark.com – March-November*
3 rm – **†**£ 120/140 **††**£ 120/200 **Rest** – Menu £ 30/45 **s**

◆ Yellow-washed house in superb location, boasting fantastic loch and mountain views. Spacious guest areas filled with antiques, paintings and silverware. High level of facilities and extras in classically styled bedrooms; modern log cabin room offers extra privacy. Communal, home dining; local seafood and game feature.

Albannach (Colin Craig and Lesley Crosfield) with rm
Baddidarroch, West : 1 mi by Baddidarroch rd ✉ *IV27 4LP*
– ✆ *(01571) 844 407 – www.thealbannach.co.uk – Closed 12 December- 22 March and Monday to Wednesday November to 14 December*
5 rm (dinner included) – **†**£ 180/210 **††**£ 257/365
Rest *– (Closed Monday to non residents) (dinner only) (booking essential for non-residents) (set menu only)* Menu £ 58
Spec. Seared monkfish with Parma ham and red pepper essence. Roast wild turbot, black potatoes and red wine sauce. Lime soufflé, chocolate ice cream and brambles.

◆ Substantial 19C Scottish house in remote location, boasting exceptional bay/mountain views from the conservatory, terrace and garden. Strong focus on the food. Traditional daily 5 course set menu of local, seasonal produce. Well-appointed bedrooms are spread about the building; one boasts a private terrace and hot tub.

Chez Roux – at Inver Lodge Hotel
Iolaire Rd ✉ *IV27 4LU –* ✆ *(01571) 844 496 – www.inverlodge.com – April-October*
Rest – Menu £ 44

◆ Romantic restaurant hung with photos of the eponymous brothers and boasting well-spaced tables that take in fantastic bay and mountain views. Regularly changing, classical French menus.

LOCHMADDY – Western Isles – **501** Y11 – see Uist (Isles of)

LOCHRANZA – North Ayrshire – **501** E16 – see Arran (Isle of)

MELROSE – The Scottish Borders – **501** L17 – pop. 1 656 Scotland 26 D2

▶ Edinburgh 38 mi – Hawick 19 mi – Newcastle upon Tyne 70 mi
ℹ Abbey St ℰ (01835) 86 31 70, www.visitscotland.com
⛳ Melrose Dingleton Dingleton Rd, ℰ (01896) 82 28 55
✦ Town★ - Abbey★ (decorative sculpture★★★) **AC**
✦ Eildon Hills (❄★★★) – Scott's View★★ – Abbotsford★★ **AC**, W : 4.5 mi by A 6091 and B 6360 – Dryburgh Abbey★★ **AC** (setting★★★), SE : 4 mi by A 6091 – Tweed Valley★★. Bowhill★★ **AC**, SW : 11.5 mi by A 6091, A 7 and A 708 – Thirlestane Castle (plasterwork ceilings★★) **AC**, NE : 21 mi by A 6091 and A 68

Burts

Market Sq. ✉ *TD6 9PL* – ℰ *(01896) 822 285* – *www.burtshotel.co.uk* – *Closed 2-9 January and 26 December*
20 rm ☕ – †£ 70/130 ††£ 100/133
Rest – Menu £ 28/36

♦ Characterful coaching inn on the main square; run by the same family for two generations. Appealing bedrooms blend contemporary furnishings with original features. Cosy bar serves old classics; formal dining room offers a mix of modern and traditional dishes.

Townhouse

Market Sq. ✉ *TD6 9PQ* – ℰ *(01896) 822 645* – *www.thetownhousemelrose.co.uk* – *Closed 2-9 January and 26 December*
11 rm ☕ – †£ 90/136 ††£ 124/136
Rest – Menu £ 26/34 – Carte £ 20/35

♦ Former home of Catherine Spence and contemporary sister to nearby Burts. Stylish bedrooms are decorated in black and purple and display bold feature walls; standards are shower only. Trendy all day café-cum-bar; dining room offers the best Border ingredients.

at Gattonside North : 2 mi by B 6374 on B 6360 – ✉ Melrose

Fauhope House without rest

East : 0.25 mi by B 6360 taking unmarked lane to the right of Monkswood Rd at edge of village ✉ *TD6 9LU* – ℰ *(01896) 823 184* – *www.fauhopehouse.com*
3 rm ☕ – †£ 70/100 ††£ 100/110

♦ Charming 19C house by the Tweed, overlooking Melrose. Quirky interior displays an eclectic mix of art and antiques. Bedrooms are all very different; some boast stylish bold colour schemes.

MEMUS – Angus 28 D2

▶ London 497 mi – Edinburgh 86 mi – Aberdeen 52 mi – Dundee 25 mi

Drovers Inn

✉ *DD8 3TY* – ℰ *(01307) 860 322* – *www.the-drovers.com*
Rest – Carte £ 15/26

♦ Attractive Highland inn with immaculately kept lawned garden, set in an extremely remote spot. Wide-ranging menu represents good value for money and showcases local, seasonal produce, with game and vegetables coming from the estate.

MOFFAT – Dumfries and Galloway – **501** J17 – pop. 2 135 Scotland 26 C2

▶ Edinburgh 61 mi – Carlisle 43 mi – Dumfries 22 mi – Glasgow 60 mi
ℹ Churchgate ℰ (01683) 22 06 20, www.visitmoffat.co.uk
⛳ Coatshill, ℰ (01683) 22 00 20
✦ Grey Mare's Tail★★, NE : 9 mi by A 708

MOFFAT

🏠 Hartfell House
Hartfell Cres. ✉ *DG10 9AL –* ℰ *(01683) 220 153 – www.hartfellhouse.co.uk*
– Closed 1 week January, spring, autumn and Christmas
7 rm ⌑ – †£ 35/50 ††£ 60/70
Rest *Lime Tree* – see restaurant listing
♦ Keenly run Victorian house in quiet crescent. Original features include parquet floors and ornate cornicing. Comfy lounge boasts nice southerly aspect. Large, traditionally decorated bedrooms.

🏠 Bridge House
Well Rd., East : 0.75 mi by Selkirk rd (A 708) taking left hand turn before bridge
✉ *DG10 9JT –* ℰ *(01683) 220 558 – www.bridgehousemoffat.co.uk – Closed 25 December-February*
7 rm ⌑ – †£ 55 ††£ 70 **Rest** – Menu £ 24
♦ Large Victorian house on quiet residential road, run by experienced owners. Comfy lounge with deep sofas. Individually decorated bedrooms – those to the front are biggest. Beautiful valley views. Lovely cornicing in dining room; extensive menu has Asian twists.

🏠 Well View
Ballplay Rd., East : 0.75 mi by Selkirk rd (A 708) ✉ *DG10 9JU –* ℰ *(01683) 220 184 – www.wellview.co.uk*
3 rm ⌑ – †£ 60/75 ††£ 90/110 **Rest** – Menu £ 22/35
♦ Substantial 19C house located in a peaceful suburb, boasting spacious, traditionally styled bedrooms and good comforts. Formerly a restaurant, dinner is still a key focus here. The daily changing 4 course set menu is taken at a communal table; wine is included.

XX Lime Tree – at Hartfell House Hotel
Hartfell Cres. ✉ *DG10 9AL –* ℰ *(01683) 220 153 – www.hartfellhouse.co.uk*
– Closed 1 week January, spring, autumn and Christmas, Sunday dinner and Monday
Rest – *(dinner only and Sunday lunch) (booking essential)* Menu £ 20/28
♦ Small hotel restaurant with smartly laid tables, open fire and attractive marquetry. Large bay window looks down the valley. Good value weekly menu features tasty, well-presented classics.

MONTROSE – Angus – **501** M13 – **pop. 10 845** ▮ Scotland   **28** D2

▶ Edinburgh 92 mi – Aberdeen 39 mi – Dundee 29 mi
🛈 Panmure Place ℰ (01674) 67 32 32, www.visitmontrose.co.uk
₃₆ Traill Drive, ℰ (01674) 67 29 32
◉ Edzell Castle★ (The Pleasance★★★) **AC**, NW : 17 mi by A 935 and B 966 – Cairn O'Mount Road★ (≤★★) N : 17 mi by B 966 and B 974 – Brechin (Round Tower★) W : 7 mi by A 935 – Aberlemno (Aberlemno Stones★, Pictish sculptured stones★) W : 13 mi by A 935 and B 9134

🏠 36 The Mall *without rest*
36 The Mall, North : 0.5 mi by A 92 at junction with North Esk Road
✉ *DD10 8SS –* ℰ *(01674) 673 646 – www.36themall.co.uk*
3 rm ⌑ – †£ 48/65 ††£ 60/80
♦ Lovely bay-windowed, 19C former manse with pleasant conservatory lounge overlooking the garden. Immaculately kept, high-ceilinged bedrooms with tasteful styling and handy extras. Impressive plate collection is the talking point of the communal breakfast room.

XX Quay
1-4 Wharf St ✉ *DD10 8BD –* ℰ *(01674) 672 821 – www.thequaymontrose.co.uk*
– Closed 1-18 January, 25-26 December and Monday
Rest – Menu £ 29 (dinner) – Carte lunch £ 17/21
♦ Set on the quayside and run by a bubbly local couple. Large bar and smart columned dining room with bold wallpaper. Accessible lunch menu is stepped up at dinner; local, seasonal dishes are precisely executed, tasty and full of flavour.

MUIR OF ORD – Highland – **501** G11 – pop. 1 812 — **30** C2

▶ Edinburgh 173 mi – Inverness 10 mi – Wick 121 mi
🛈 Great North Rd, ✆ (01463) 87 08 25

Dower House
Highfield, North : 1 mi on A 862 ✉ *IV6 7XN* – ✆ *(01463) 870 090*
– www.thedowerhouse.co.uk – Closed 1 week November and 25 December
3 rm ⌑ – ♦£ 75/95 ♦♦£ 120/175
Rest – *(dinner only) (residents only)* Menu £ 22/42
♦ Personally run, part 17C house in mature garden. Stacked bookshelves, soft fireside armchairs, cosy bedrooms and fresh flowers: a relaxed but well-ordered country home. Dining room offers careful cooking of fine fresh ingredients.

MULL (Isle of) – Argyll and Bute – **501** B/C14 – pop. 1 841 ▮ Scotland — **27** A2

⛴ from Fionnphort to Isle of Iona (Caledonian MacBrayne Ltd) frequent services daily (10 mn) – from Pierowall to Papa Westray (Orkney Ferries Ltd) (summer only) (25 mn)
⛴ from Craignure to Oban (Caledonian MacBrayne Ltd) frequent services daily (45 mn) – from Fishnish to Lochaline (Mainland) (Caledonian MacBrayne Ltd) frequent services daily (15 mn) – from Tobermory to Isle of Tiree (Scarinish) via Isle of Coll (Arinagour) (Caledonian MacBrayne Ltd) 3 weekly (2 h 30 mn) – from Tobermory to Kilchoan (Caledonian MacBrayne Ltd) 4 daily (summer only) (35 mn)
🛈 Craignure ✆ (08707) 20 06 10, www.holidaymull.co.uk
🛈 Craignure Scallastle, ✆ (01688) 30 25 17
◉ Island★ - Calgary Bay★★ – Torosay Castle **AC** (Gardens★ ≼★)
◉ Isle of Iona★ (Maclean's Cross★, St Oran's Chapel★, St Martin's High Cross★, Infirmary Museum★ **AC** (Cross of St John★))

FIONNPHORT – Argyll and Bute

Ninth Wave
Bruach Mhor, East : 0.75 mi by A 849 ✉ *PA66 6BL* – ✆ *(01681) 700 757*
– www.ninthwaverestaurant.co.uk – Restricted opening in winter
Rest – Seafood – *(dinner only) (booking essential)* Menu £ 40
♦ Converted farm building featuring stylish, modern décor, with trinkets from the owner's travels. Daily changing menu focuses on local seafood, with strong Asian flavours. Try the lobster.

GRULINE – Argyll and Bute — **27** A2

Gruline Home Farm
✉ *PA71 6HR* – ✆ *(01680) 300 581 – www.gruline.com – Closed Christmas-New Year*
3 rm (dinner included) ⌑ – ♦£ 148 ♦♦£ 200
Rest – Menu £ 40
♦ Very rurally set, in 3 acres of land, with colourful gardens and lovely mountain views. Relax in the large lounges or spot sea eagles from the telescope in the spacious conservatory. Good-sized, antique-furnished bedrooms. Mousey Thompson pieces in the traditionally styled dining room. Classical, daily changing menu.

TIRORAN – Argyll and Bute — **27** A2

Tiroran House
✉ *PA69 6ES* – ✆ *(01681) 705 232 – www.tiroran.com – mid-March to mid-November*
9 rm ⌑ – ♦£ 100/120 ♦♦£ 195/210
Rest – *(dinner only)* Menu £ 48
♦ Stunning 19C whitewashed house, set in 17 acres of parkland that run down to the water's edge. Charming, antique-filled interior with two open-fired lounges and immaculate, highly individual bedrooms. Welcoming owner. Dining room split into conservatory area and darker, more clubby area. Concise, daily changing menus.

MULL (Isle of)

TOBERMORY – Argyll and Bute – pop. 980 27 A2

Erray Rd, ℰ (01688) 30 23 87

Tobermory
53 Main St ⊠ PA75 6NT – ℰ (01688) 302 091 – www.thetobermoryhotel.com
– Closed 7 January-7 February and 1 week Christmas
16 rm ⊡ – †£ 40/70 ††£ 78/132
Rest *Waters Edge* – (dinner only) Menu £ 32
♦ Converted fishermen's cottages right on the quayside, close to the local distillery. Bedrooms vary in size but most have a pleasant harbour view. Small lounge; popular dining room with seafaring feel. Concise, classical menu of island produce. Plenty of seafood.

Sonas House without rest
The Fairways, North : 0.5 mi by Black Brae and Erray Rd following signs for the golf club ⊠ PA75 6PS – ℰ (01688) 302 304 – www.sonashouse.co.uk
– March-October
3 rm ⊡ – †£ 50/80 ††£ 90/125
♦ In elevated position above Tobermory, with views over the Sound of Mull. Choose a room in the house or the annexe studio; all come with a host of extras and superb views. Luxury swimming pool.

Brockville without rest
Raeric Rd, by Back Brae ⊠ PA75 6RS – ℰ (01688) 302 741
– www.brockville-tobermory.co.uk
3 rm ⊡ – †£ 40/65 ††£ 70/80
♦ Welcoming guesthouse with warm, homely feel. Good-sized bedrooms offer everything you could want. Communal breakfast room boasts nice sea views. Friendly owner has plenty of local knowledge.

SCOTLAND

Highland Cottage with rm
Breadalbane St, via B 8073 ⊠ PA75 6PD – ℰ (01688) 302 030
– www.highlandcottage.co.uk – March-October
6 rm ⊡ – †£ 125/140 ††£ 150/190
Rest – (dinner only) (booking essential for non-residents) Menu £ 48
♦ Long-standing, personally run restaurant in intimate cottage; family antiques and knick-knacks abound. Classical linen-laid dining room and homely lounge. Traditional daily menu with a seafood base and plenty of local produce. Snug, individually styled bedrooms.

MUTHILL – Perth and Kinross – 501 I15 – pop. 675 – see Crieff

NAIRN – Highland – 501 I11 – pop. 8 418 ▌Scotland 30 D2

Edinburgh 172 mi – Aberdeen 91 mi – Inverness 16 mi
Seabank Rd, ℰ (01667) 45 32 08
Nairn Dunbar Lochloy Rd, ℰ (01667) 45 27 41
 Forres (Sueno's Stone★★) E : 11 mi by A 96 and B 9011 - Cawdor Castle★ **AC**, S : 5.5 mi by B 9090 – Brodie Castle★ **AC**, E : 6 mi by A 96. Fort George★, W : 8 mi by A 96, B 9092 and B 9006

Golf View
The Seafront ⊠ IV12 4HD – ℰ (01667) 452 301 – www.golfviewhotel.com
41 rm ⊡ – †£ 95/190 ††£ 130/250 – 1 suite
Rest *Restaurant* – (dinner only and Sunday lunch) Menu £ 34 – Carte £ 20/39
Rest *Conservatory* – Carte £ 23/33
♦ Non-golfers may prefer the vista of the Moray Firth from one of the sea-view rooms or a poolside lounger. Smart, traditional accommodation, up-to-date gym and beauty salon. Half-panelled dining room. Stylish, spacious conservatory restaurant.

759

NAIRN

Boath House
Auldearn, East : 2 mi on A 96 ⊠ IV12 5TE – ℰ *(01667) 454 896*
– www.boath-house.com
8 rm (dinner included) – †£ 260 ††£ 450
Rest – *(booking essential)* Menu £ 30/70 s
Spec. Mackerel, cauliflower, capers and sorrel. Lamb shoulder, onions and asparagus. Rhubarb, parkin parfait and ginger jelly.
♦ 1820s neo-classical mansion, owned by a charming couple, hosts modern Highland art collections. Intimate, elegant bedrooms; some have half-tester beds/views of the trout lake. Smart, contemporary bathrooms. Formally laid dining room has garden views; accomplished cooking, with vivid presentation and subtle flavours.

Bracadale House *without rest*
Albert St ⊠ IV12 4HF – ℰ *(01667) 452 547 – www.bracadalehouse.com*
– Closed Christmas-New Year
3 rm – †£ 40/50 ††£ 60
♦ Elegant Victorian guesthouse close to a championship golf course and the beach, and run by a friendly, enthusiastic owner. Enjoy complimentary sherry beside the open fire in the cosy, intimate first floor lounge. Traditionally styled bedrooms boast huge windows.

Cawdor House
7 Cawdor St ⊠ IV12 4QD – ℰ *(01667) 455 855 – www.cawdorhousenairn.co.uk*
– Closed 21 December-14 January
5 rm – †£ 50/90 ††£ 70/90
Rest – Menu £ 28
♦ Comfortable house whose original features blend with contemporary styling; friendly owners are a font of local knowledge. Variously sized bedrooms are clean and uncluttered. Cosy lounge with log fire. Simple dining room; set menu dinner by arrangement.

NEWTON STEWART – Dumfries and Galloway – **501** G19
– pop. 3 573 Scotland   25 B3

▶ Edinburgh 131 mi – Dumfries 51 mi – Glasgow 87 mi – Stranraer 24 mi
🛈 Dashwood Sq ℰ (01671) 40 24 31, www.newtonstewart.org
▣ Minnigaff Kirroughtree Ave, ℰ (01671) 40 21 72
▣ Wigtownshire County Glenluce Mains of Park, ℰ (01581) 30 04 20
◉ Galloway Forest Park★, Queen's Way★ (Newton Stewart to New Galloway)
N : 19 mi by A 712

Kirroughtree House
Northeast : 1.5 mi by A 75 on A 712 ⊠ DG8 6AN – ℰ *(01671) 402 141*
– www.kirroughtreehouse.co.uk – Closed 2 January-mid February
15 rm – †£ 115/150 ††£ 230/250 – 2 suites
Rest – *(booking essential for non-residents)* Menu £ 18/35 **s** – Carte lunch Monday-Saturday £ 24/35 **s**
♦ Impressive 1719 mansion in landscaped gardens, overlooking the woods and bay. Grand interior with vast open-fired hall and impressive staircase. Traditionally styled bedrooms with plenty of extras. Concise 4 course menu of quality produce in classic combinations.

NIGG – **501** H10 – see Tain

NORTH BAY – Western Isles – see Barra (Isle of)

NORTH BERWICK – East Lothian – **501** L15 – pop. 6 223 – Scotland   26 D1

▶ Edinburgh 24 mi – Newcastle upon Tyne 102 mi

🛈 1 Quality St ℰ (01620) 89 21 97, www.northberwickuk.com

⛳ North Berwick Beach Rd, West Links, ℰ (01620) 89 03 12

⛳ Glen East Links, Tantallon Terrace, ℰ (01620) 89 27 26

◉ North Berwick Law (✵★★★) S : 1 mi - Tantallon Castle★★ (clifftop site★★★) **AC**, E : 3.5 mi by A 198 – Dirleton★ (Castle★ **AC**) SW : 2.5 mi by A 198. Museum of Flight★, S : 6 mi by B 1347 – Preston Mill★, S : 8.5 mi by A 198 and B 1047 – Tyninghame★, S : 7 mi by A 198 – Coastal road from North Berwick to Portseton★, SW : 13 mi by A 198 and B 1348

🏠 Glebe House without rest

Law Rd ✉ *EH39 4PL* – ℰ *(01620) 892 608* – *www.glebehouse-nb.co.uk*
– *Closed Christmas*

3 rm ⌑ – †£ 75 ††£ 100/110

♦ Spacious, welcoming Georgian house with walled gardens and views over the town and sea. Classical, country house drawing room and antique communal breakfast table. Comfortable, well-furnished bedrooms.

NORTH QUEENSFERRY – Fife – **501** J15 – pop. 1 102   28 C3

▶ Edinburgh 13 mi – Dunfermline 6 mi – Glasgow 45 mi

✕ Wee Restaurant

17 Main St ✉ *KY11 1JT* – ℰ *(01383) 616 263* – *www.theweerestaurant.co.uk*
– *Closed 25-26 December*

Rest – Menu £ 20/32 **s**

♦ Simple, quarry-floored restaurant in the shadow of the Forth Rail Bridge. Fresh Scottish ingredients are served in neatly presented, classical combinations. Lunch represents the best value.

NORTH UIST – Western Isles – **501** X/Y10 – see Uist (Isles of)

OBAN – Argyll and Bute – **501** D14 – pop. 8 120 – Scotland   27 B2

▶ Edinburgh 123 mi – Dundee 116 mi – Glasgow 93 mi – Inverness 118 mi

Access Access to Glasgow by helicopter

⛴ to Isle of Mull (Craignure) (Caledonian MacBrayne Ltd) (45 mn) – to Isle of Tiree (Scarinish) via Isle of Mull (Tobermory) and Isle of Coll (Arinagour) (Caledonian MacBrayne Ltd) – to Isle of Islay (Port Askaig) and Kintyre Peninsula (Kennacraig) via Isle of Colonsay (Scalasaig) (Caledonian MacBrayne Ltd) (summer only) – to Isle of Lismore (Achnacroish) (Caledonian MacBrayne Ltd) 2-3 daily (except Sunday) (55 mn) – to Isle of Colonsay (Scalasaig) (Caledonian MacBrayne Ltd) 3 weekly (2 h)

🛈 Argyll Sq ℰ (08707) 20 06 30, www.oban.org.uk

⛳ Glencruitten Glencruitten Rd, ℰ (01631) 56 28 68

◉ Loch Awe★★, SE : 17 mi by A 85 – Bonawe Furnace★, E : 12 mi by A 85 – Cruachan Power Station★ **AC**, E : 16 mi by A 85 – Seal and Marine Centre★ **AC**, N : 14 mi by A 828

🏛 Manor House

Gallanach Rd. ✉ *PA34 4LS* – ℰ *(01631) 562 087* – *www.manorhouseoban.com*
– *Closed 25-26 December*

11 rm ⌑ – †£ 99/199 ††£ 120/210

Rest – (lunch by arrangement) Menu £ 24/38

♦ 18C dower house, formerly part of the Argyll Estate. Country house style interior offers traditional comforts; spacious lounge and rustic bar boast delightful bay and harbour views. Individually styled bedrooms. Classical daily menu served in formal dining room.

OBAN

Glenburnie House without rest
Corran Esplanade ✉ PA34 5AQ – ℰ (01631) 562 089 – www.glenburnie.co.uk
– April-November
12 rm ⊇ – †£ 50/100 ††£ 80/110
♦ Bay-windowed house on main esplanade, affording great bay and island views. Period features include a delightful staircase and etched glass widows; antiques abound. Comfy, good-sized bedrooms.

Alltavona without rest
Corran Esplanade ✉ PA34 5AQ – ℰ (01631) 565 067 – www.alltavona.co.uk
– March-November
10 rm ⊇ – †£ 35/85 ††£ 70/95
♦ Commanding bay and island views from this charming 19C villa on the main esplanade. Fresh, tasty breakfasts in stylish black, white and red room. Striking modern bedrooms boast feature beds.

Coast
104 George St ✉ PA34 5NT – ℰ (01631) 569 900 – www.coastoban.com
– Closed 25-26 December, Sunday lunch and Sunday October-March
Rest – Menu £ 16 (lunch) – Carte £ 25/39
♦ Busy high street restaurant with wooden floor and khaki fabric strips on the walls. Unfussy, modern cooking with good seasoning; local produce is key. Plenty of shellfish and steaks on offer.

Waterfront
No 1, The Pier ✉ PA34 4LW – ℰ (01631) 563 110 – www.waterfrontoban.co.uk
– Closed 25 December
Rest – Seafood – Carte £ 24/33
♦ Former seaman's mission boasting harbour/bay views. Extensive menu features local produce and mixes modern and classical cooking. Lots of daily specials; fish a strength. Relaxed bistro feel.

Ee-usk
The North Pier ✉ PA34 5QD – ℰ (01631) 565 666 – www.eeusk.com
– Closed 1 January, 25-26 December and restricted opening in January
Rest – Seafood – Carte £ 26/38
♦ Long-standing local seafood restaurant on the harbour, run by experienced owners. Stylish modern building with brasserie feel and great bay views. Large, in-depth menu with good value specials.

> Undecided between two equivalent establishments in the same town? Within each category, establishments are classified in our order of preference: the best first.

ONICH – Highland – **501** E13 – ✉ Fort William
◨ Edinburgh 123 mi – Glasgow 93 mi – Inverness 79 mi – Oban 39 mi

Lochleven Seafood Café
Lochleven, Southeast : 6.5 mi by A 82 on B 863 ✉ PH33 6SA – ℰ (01855) 821 048 – www.lochlevenseafoodcafe.co.uk – Restricted opening in winter
Rest – Seafood – (booking advisable at dinner) Carte £ 19/50 **s**
♦ Stunning Lochside location looking toward Glencoe Mountains. Extremely fresh, simply prepared seafood; shellfish platter and razor clams a speciality. Themed evenings in winter.

ORKNEY ISLANDS – 501 K/L7 – pop. 19 800 🟢 Scotland

✈ see Kirkwall

🚢 from Burwick (South Ronaldsay) to John O'Groats (John O'Groats Ferries) 2-4 daily (40 mn) (summer only)

🚢 service between Isle of Hoy (Longhope), Isle of Hoy (Lyness), Isle of Flotta and Houton (Orkney Ferries Ltd) – from Stromness to Scrabster (P & O Scottish Ferries) (1-3 daily) (2 h) – from Stromness to Shetland Islands (Lerwick) and Aberdeen (Northlink Ferries) 1-2 daily – from Kirkwall to Westray, Stronsay via Eday and Sanday (Orkney Ferries Ltd) – from Tingwall to Wyre via Egilsay and Rousay (Orkney Ferries Ltd) – from Kirkwall to Shapinsay (Orkney Ferries Ltd) (25 mn) – from Stromness to Isle of Hoy (Moness) and Graemsay (Orkney Ferries Ltd) – from Kirkwall to North Ronaldsay (Orkney Ferries Ltd) weekly (2 h 40 mn) - from Kirkwall to Invergordon (Orcargo Ltd) daily (8 h 30 mn) – from Houton to Isle of Hoy (Lyness), Flotta and Longhope (Orkney Ferries Ltd)

👁 Old Man of Hoy★★★ – Islands★★ – Maes Howe★★ **AC** – Skara Brae★★ **AC** – Kirkbuster Museum and Corrigal Farm Museum★ **AC** – Brough of Birsay★ **AC** – Birsay (≼★) – Ring of Brodgar★ – Unstan Cairn★

MAINLAND – Orkney Islands   31 A3

▶ London 683 mi – Edinburgh 278 mi

BURRAY – Orkney Islands   31 A3

🏠 Sands   ≼ ⌘ ⁽⁾ 🅿 VISA ⦿ AE ⓞ
✉ KW17 2SS – ☏ (01856) 731 298 – www.thesandshotel.co.uk
– Closed 1-3 January and 25-26 December
6 rm ⌒ – ♦£ 60/90 ♦♦£ 95/115 – 2 suites
Rest – Carte £ 17/28

♦ Converted 19C herring packing store in small hamlet overlooking Scapa Flow. Pleasant bedrooms boast smart bathrooms. Bar with pool table and dartboard offers traditional menu. Dining room serves more refined dishes, featuring island produce and lots of shellfish.

DOUNBY – Orkney Islands   31 A3

🏠 Ashleigh without rest ⌘   ≼ 🚗 ⌘ ⁽⁾ 🅿
Howaback Rd, South : 0.75 mi by A986 ✉ KW17 2JA – ☏ (01856) 771 378
– www.ashleigh-orkney.com – Closed 20 December-10 January
4 rm ⌒ – ♦£ 38/40 ♦♦£ 80

♦ Purpose-built house in the heart of the island's countryside, boasting loch/mountain views. Large breakfast room and lounge filled with guidebooks. Good-sized bedrooms with modern facilities.

HARRAY – Orkney Islands   31 A3

🏠🏠 Merkister ⌘   ≼ 🚗 ⌘ ⅋ rm, ⁽⁾ 🅿 VISA ⦿ AE ⓞ
off A 986 ✉ KW17 2LF – ☏ (01856) 771 366 – www.merkister.com – Closed 23 December-4 January
16 rm ⌒ – ♦£ 55/95 ♦♦£ 75/175
Rest – (bar lunch) Menu £ 24 **s**
– Carte £ 19/40 **s**

♦ Family-run, lochside hotel affording wonderful water and mountain views. Comfortable, well-kept bedrooms; those outside have their own terraces and gardens. Snug, open-fired bar serves snacks. Dining room offers strictly Orkney-based produce and a scenic backdrop.

ORKNEY ISLANDS - Mainland

Holland House without rest
on St Michael's Church rd ✉ *KW17 2LQ –* ✆ *(01856) 771 400*
– www.hollandhouseorkney.co.uk – Closed 7 December-12 January and restricted opening in winter
3 rm ⊇ – †£ 48/60 ††£ 96

◆ Converted manse run by a welcoming owner, with commanding views throughout. Open-fired lounge – packed with local art and handmade furniture – stone-floored breakfast room and conservatory. Spotless bedrooms with a host of extras and great attention to detail.

KIRKWALL – Orkney Islands ▌Scotland   31 A3

✈ Kirkwall Airport : ✆ (01856) 886210, S : 3.5 mi
🛈 West Castle St ✆ (01856) 87 28 56, www.visitorkney.com
⛳ Grainbank, ✆ (01856) 87 24 57

◉ Kirkwall★★ - St Magnus Cathedral★★ – Western Mainland★★, Eastern Mainland (Italian Chapel★) - Earl's Palace★ **AC** – Tankerness House Museum★ **AC** – Orkney Farm and Folk Museum★

Ayre
Ayre Rd. ✉ *KW15 1QX –* ✆ *(01856) 873 001 – www.ayrehotel.co.uk – Closed 25 December and 1 January*
51 rm ⊇ – †£ 70/90 ††£ 113/130   **Rest** – *(bar lunch)* Carte £ 20/37

◆ Well-run hotel close to the harbour. Formerly 3 Victorian houses, now a traditionally styled hotel with comfortable bedrooms – the newer extension rooms are biggest and best. Spacious bar filled with locals. Dining room offers sizeable menu of Orcadian produce.

Lynnfield
Holm Rd ✉ *KW15 1SU –* ✆ *(01856) 872 505 – www.lynnfieldhotel.com – Closed 1-7 January and 25-26 December*
7 rm ⊇ – †£ 70/95 ††£ 110/135 – 3 suites   **Rest** – Carte £ 20/37

◆ Spacious hotel with cosy sitting rooms, Orcadian furniture and a fine range of Scotch whiskies. Supremely comfortable bedrooms; two with four-posters. Formal dining room with large conservatory affording great views of the countryside. Seasonal menus.

Avalon House without rest
Carness Rd, Northeast : 1.5 mi by Shore St. ✉ *KW15 1UE –* ✆ *(01856) 876 665 – www.avalon-house.co.uk – Closed 2 weeks Christmas*
5 rm – †£ 50/55 ††£ 60/70

◆ Modern, purpose-built guesthouse in a pleasant residential area. Lounge filled with maps and books about the islands. Good-sized bedrooms with simple, homely feel. Nice coastal outlook.

XX Foveran with rm
St Ola, Southwest : 3 mi on A 964 ✉ *KW15 1SF –* ✆ *(01856) 872 389 – www.foveranhotel.co.uk – Restricted opening October-April*
8 rm ⊇ – †£ 78/95 ††£ 116   **Rest** – *(dinner only)* Carte £ 26/36

◆ Spacious restaurant boasting superb panoramic views over Scapa Flow and the south islands. Traditional menu features local, seasonal produce, including Orcadian lamb/beef and plenty of fresh seafood. Homely, well-kept bedrooms display simple colour schemes.

ST MARGARET'S HOPE – Orkney Islands   31 A3

XX Creel with rm
Front Rd ✉ *KW17 2SL –* ✆ *(01856) 831 311 – www.thecreel.co.uk – May-September*
3 rm ⊇ – †£ 75 ††£ 110   **Rest** – Seafood – *(dinner only)* Menu £ 38

◆ Long-standing, family-run restaurant in seafront village. Spacious dining room is hung with local oils and prints. Daily changing menu displays a fresh, traditional seafood base. Comfortable, cosy bedrooms boast modern, co-ordinated furnishings and bay views.

ORKNEY ISLANDS - Mainland

STROMNESS – Orkney Islands Scotland 31 A3
Town★ - Pier Gallery (collection of abstract art★)

Hamnavoe VISA ⦿ ⦿
35 Graham Pl, off Victoria St ✉ KW16 3BY – ℰ *(01856) 850 606 – restricted opening in winter*
Rest – *(closed Monday) (dinner only)* Carte £ 28/35
- Homely restaurant in a sleepy harbourside town. Plain walls are dotted with local oils and open fires. Unfussy home cooking uses fresh market produce; local, where possible. Booking essential.

ISLE OF WESTRAY – Orkney Islands 31 A2
London 696 mi – Edinburgh 290 mi

CLEAT – ✉ Orkney Islands 31 A3

Cleaton House
✉ KW17 2DB – ℰ *(01857) 677 508 – www.cleatonhouse.com*
6 rm – ✝£ 65 ✝✝£ 95/120
Rest – *(bar lunch) (booking essential for non-residents)* Menu £ 35
- Victorian former laird's mansion, set on a peninsula and boasting panoramic views over the bay and Papa Westray. Original tiled floors, antique-filled lounge and rear bar. Spacious, classically styled bedrooms. Formal set menu relies on local island produce.

PIEROWALL – Orkney Islands 31 A2

No 1 Broughton without rest
✉ KW17 2DA – ℰ *(01857) 677 726 – www.no1broughton.co.uk – Closed 24-25 December*
3 rm – ✝£ 35/60 ✝✝£ 60
- 19C pink-washed house boasting views over Pierowall Bay and out to Papa Westray. Comfy lounge and conservatory. Simple, homely bedrooms with modern bathrooms. Sauna on request. Home-cooked meals showcase local meats/seafood; homemade bread and shortcake feature.

PEAT INN – Fife 28 D2
London 462 mi – Edinburgh 45 mi – Dundee 17 mi – Kirkcaldy 19 mi

Peat Inn (Geoffrey Smeddle) with rm
✉ KY15 5LH – ℰ *(01334) 840 206 – www.thepeatinn.co.uk – Closed 2 weeks January, Christmas, Sunday and Monday*
8 rm – ✝£ 120/150 ✝✝£ 180/195
Rest – *(booking essential)* Menu £ 18/35 – Carte £ 27/54
Spec. Poached langoustines, braised squid and asparagus. Roast loin and confit flank of lamb with wild garlic. Amedei chocolate ganache with caramel ice cream and macadamia nut brownie.
- Passionately run, former inn found in the heart of the Fife countryside. Roaring fire in the lounge; three cosy dining rooms with beams. The accomplished, classically based cooking – with just a hint of the modern – uses fine Scottish produce. Stylish, split-level bedrooms with good facilities, set in an annexe and overlooking the lovely back garden and surrounding countryside.

PEEBLES – The Scottish Borders – 501 K17 – pop. 8 065 Scotland 26 C2
Edinburgh 24 mi – Glasgow 53 mi – Hawick 31 mi
High St ℰ (01835) 86 31 70, www.peebles.info
Kirkland St, ℰ (01721) 72 01 97
Tweed Valley★★. Traquair House★★ **AC**, SE : 7 mi by B 7062 – Rosslyn Chapel★★ **AC**, N : 16.5 mi by A 703, A 6094, B 7026 and B 7003

PEEBLES

Cringletie House
Edinburgh Rd., North : 3 mi on A 703 – EH45 8PL – ℰ (01721) 725 750
– www.cringletie.com – Closed 8-27 January
12 rm ⊡ – †£ 110/160 ††£ 140/190 – 1 suite
Rest *Sutherland Room* – Menu £ 15/33 **s** – Carte £ 33/45 **s**

♦ Handsome Victorian house boasting far-reaching Tweed Valley views. Luxurious interior with library, drawing room and cosy bar. Tastefully furnished bedrooms have subtle contemporary style. Formal restaurant offers elaborate dining beneath stunning 1902 mural.

Rowanbrae without rest
103 Northgate – EH45 8BU – ℰ (01721) 721 630 – February-November
3 rm ⊡ – †£ 40/50 ††£ 60/65

♦ Tiny cottage close to the town, with pretty front terrace and surprisingly spacious interior. Long-standing owners provide a warm welcome and a cosy, homely atmosphere reigns. Pleasant, well-kept bedrooms have a modern edge courtesy of their soft furnishings.

Osso
Innerleithen Rd – EH45 8BA – ℰ (01721) 724 477 – www.ossorestaurant.com
– Closed 1 January, 25 December, dinner Sunday and Monday
Rest – Menu £ 24 (dinner) – Carte £ 17/33

♦ By day, a coffee shop serving light snacks, tapas and daily specials. By night, much more sophisticated restaurant offering a regularly changing, great value menu of tasty, well-presented dishes, with the occasional Asian influence. Friendly, attentive service.

at Eddleston North : 4.5 mi on A 703

Horseshoe Inn with rm
Edinburgh Rd. – EH45 8QP – ℰ (01721) 730 225 – www.horseshoeinn.co.uk
– Closed 2 weeks January and Monday except bank holidays
8 rm ⊡ – †£ 70 ††£ 100
Rest – (closed Sunday) Menu £ 20/40
Rest *Bistro* – Carte £ 19/33

♦ Former roadside inn; now a smart, columned restaurant with elegant tableware and formal, white-gloved service. Sophisticated à la carte and tasting menu offer ambitious, well-presented, European-influenced dishes. Old classics served in the bistro. Chic, modern bedrooms are in the annexe.

PERTH – Perth and Kinross – **501** J14 – pop. 43 450 ┃ Scotland — 28 C

▶ Edinburgh 44 mi – Aberdeen 86 mi – Dundee 22 mi – Dunfermline 29 mi
ℹ West Mill St ℰ (01738) 45 06 00, www.perthshire.co.uk
⛳ Craigie Hill Cherrybank, ℰ (01738) 62 08 29
⛳ King James VI Moncreiffe Island, ℰ (01738) 62 51 70
⛳ Murrayshall New Scone, ℰ (01738) 55 48 04
⛳ North Inch, c/o Perth & Kinross Council 35 Kinncoll St, ℰ (01738) 63 64 81
◉ City ★ – Black Watch Regimental Museum ★ Y **M1** – Georgian Terraces ★ Y
– Museum and Art Gallery ★ Y **M2**
◎ Scone Palace ★★ **AC**, N : 2 mi by A 93 Y – Branklyn Garden ★ **AC**, SE : 1 mi by A 8 Z – Kinnoull Hill (≤ ★) SE : 1.25 mi by A 85 Z – Huntingtower Castle ★ **AC**, NW : 3 mi by A 85 Y – Elcho Castle ★ **AC**, SE : 4 mi by A 912 - Z - and Rhynd rd. Abernethy (11C Round Tower ★), SE : 8 mi by A 912 - Z - and A 913

Parklands
2 St Leonard's Bank – PH2 8EB – ℰ (01738) 622 451
– www.theparklandshotel.com – Closed 25 December-5 January
15 rm ⊡ – †£ 93/129 ††£ 129/169
Rest *No.1 The Bank* **Rest** *63@Parklands* – see restaurant listing

♦ Personally run, extended Georgian house by the railway station, with contemporary interior. Spacious, modern bedrooms boast good facilities and sizeable bathrooms; those to the front are quietest and afford pleasant views over the park

PERTH

Taythorpe without rest
Isla Rd, North : 1 mi on A 93 – PH2 7HQ – ℰ (01738) 447 994
– www.taythorpe.co.uk   **Ya**
3 rm – ✝£ 40/50 ✝✝£ 70/80
♦ Modern, stone-built house close to Scone Palace, run by a bubbly owner. Immaculately kept interior with fresh flower displays. Homely lounge and cosy breakfast room – order in advance from a vast menu. Warm, well-kept bedrooms display good attention to detail.

63 Tay Street
63 Tay St – PH2 8NN – ℰ (01738) 441 451 – www.63taystreet.co.uk
– Closed 1-9 January, 2-8 July, 26-31 December, Sunday and Monday
Rest – Menu £ 35 (dinner)   **Zr**
– Carte £ 33/44
♦ Well-established riverside restaurant with fresh décor, bold modern artwork and attentive team. Good value lunches and choice of grill or gourmet dinners, the latter where the cooking really comes into its own. Wine list of over 250 bins.

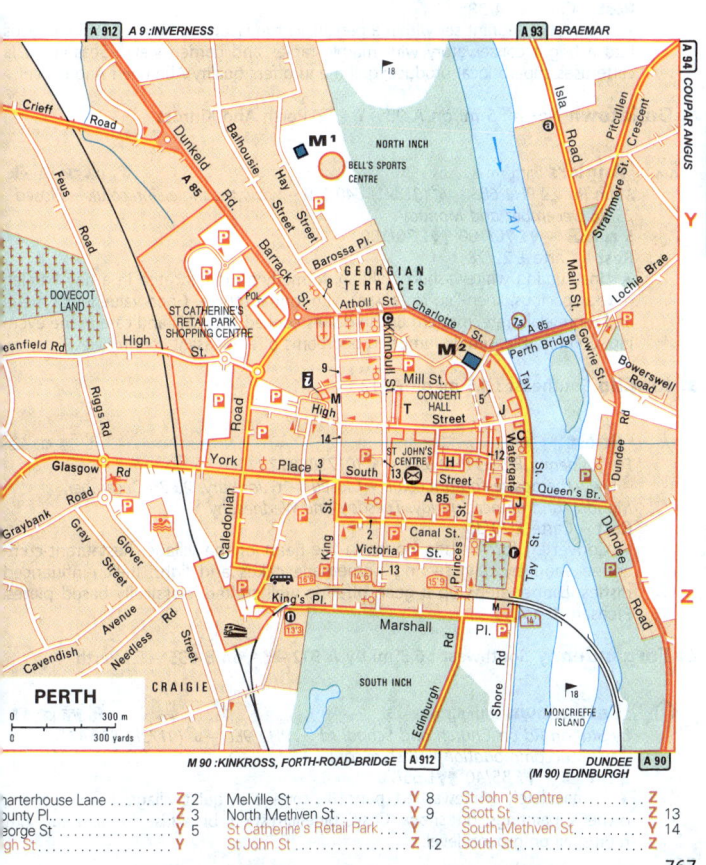

PERTH

Charterhouse Lane	Z 2	Melville St	Y 8	St John's Centre	Z
County Pl.	Z 3	North Methven St	Y 9	Scott St	Z 13
George St	Y 5	St Catherine's Retail Park	Y	South-Methven St	Y 14
High St	Y	St John St	Z 12	South St	Z

767

PERTH

Deans @ Let's Eat
77-79 Kinnoull St — PH1 5EZ – ℰ (01738) 643 377 – www.letseatperth.co.uk
– Closed 2 weeks January, Sunday and Monday
Rest – Menu £ 18/20 – Carte £ 24/38

Yc

• Bottle-green corner restaurant close to the theatre and concert hall. Comfy lounge and friendly, chatty team. All-encompassing menus feature seasonal deals and special events. Passionate, classically based cooking with an ambitious edge.

63@Parklands – at Parklands Hotel
2 St Leonard's Bank — PH2 8EB – ℰ (01738) 622 451 – www.63atparklands.com
– Closed 25 December-6 January
Rest – (dinner only Thursday-Monday) Menu £ 35

Zn

• Located within a privately run hotel, an intimate conservatory restaurant and relaxed lounge. Gourmet-style 5 course menu offers one or two choices per course and changes weekly. Cooking is modern and features some interesting combinations.

No.1 The Bank – at Parklands Hotel
2 St Leonard's Bank — PH2 8EB – ℰ (01738) 622 451
– www.theparklandshotel.com – Closed 26 December-5 January
Rest – Carte £ 24/38

Zn

• Informal restaurant set within a personally run Georgian house. Small bar leads into a bright conservatory with marble tables and garden views. Seasonal à la carte uses superb local produce; grill menu offers quality Aberdeen Angus beef.

at Guildtown North : 5 mi on A 93 - Y – ⊠ Perth And Kinross

Anglers with rm
Main Rd — PH2 6BS – ℰ (01821) 640 329 – www.theanglersinn.co.uk – Closed 25-26 December and Monday
5 rm – †£ 70/100 ††£ 70/100
Rest – Carte £ 22/28

• Unassuming whitewashed building, formerly an inn, located in a tiny hamlet; now a spacious, linen-laid restaurant with formal service. Good value lunch menu and more elaborate, modern British dishes cooked with skill and care in the evening. Comfortable, simply furnished bedrooms offer pleasant country views.

at Kintillo Southeast : 4.5 mi off A912

Roost
Forgandenny Rd — PH2 9AZ – ℰ (01738) 812 111
– www.theroostrestaurant.co.uk – Closed 1-16 January, 25-26 December, Monday and dinner Sunday, Tuesday and Wednesday
Rest – Carte £ 20/36

• Converted former hen house in the heart of the village. Restaurant-cum-coffee shop by day, serving homemade cakes and light, Italian-influenced dishes. Dinner steps up a gear, offering well-crafted, classically based plates. Pleasant team.

at Forgandenny Southwest : 6.5 mi by A 912 - Z - on B 935 – ⊠ Perth

Battledown without rest
by Station Rd on Church and School rd — PH2 9EL – ℰ (01738) 812 471
– www.accommodationperthshire.com
3 rm – †£ 35/40 ††£ 65/70

• Immaculately whitewashed, part 18C cottage in quiet village. Lovely garden; owner's paintings on show. Cosy, pine-furnished breakfast room. Neat, tidy rooms, all on ground level.

at Stanley North : 7 mi off A9 (Inverness)

✂ **Apron Stage** VISA ⊚ AE
5 King St ✉ PH1 4ND – ℘ (01738) 828 888 – www.apronstagerestaurant.co.uk
– Closed one week May, one week September, and Sunday-Tuesday
Rest – *(dinner only and Friday lunch)* Menu £ 16 (lunch) – Carte £ 22/33
♦ Lovely little restaurant in a small village, consisting of a cosy room with formally laid tables and an open-kitchen to the rear. Appealing, weekly menu mixes Scottish, French and Asian influences in generous, flavoursome portions.

PIEROWALL – **501** K6 – see Orkney Islands (Isle of Westray)

PITLOCHRY – Perth and Kinross – **501** I13 – pop. 2 564 Scotland   **28** C2
▶ Edinburgh 71 mi – Inverness 85 mi – Perth 27 mi
🛈 22 Atholl Rd ℘ (01796) 47 22 15, www.pitlochry.org
  Pitlochry Estate Office, ℘ (01796) 47 27 92
◉ Town★
⊙ Blair Castle★★ **AC**, NW : 7 mi by A 9 A – Queen's View★★, W : 7 mi by B 8019 A
– Falls of Bruar★, NW : 11 mi by A 9 A

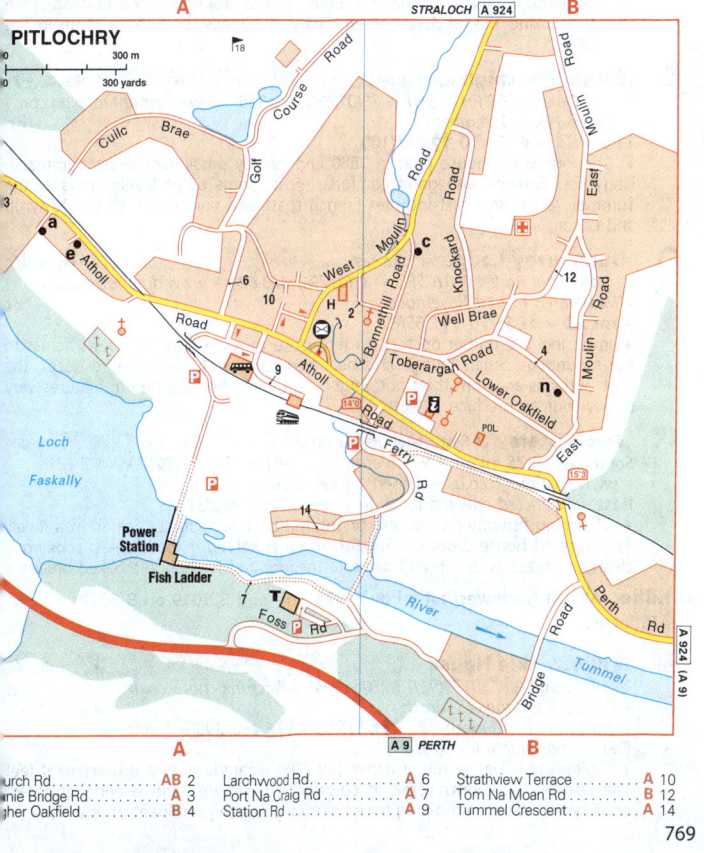

urch Rd..............AB 2   Larchwood Rd..............A 6   Strathview Terrace..........A 10
nie Bridge Rd..........A 3   Port Na Craig Rd..........A 7   Tom Na Moan Rd..........B 12
her Oakfield............B 4   Station Rd..................A 9   Tummel Crescent..........A 14

PITLOCHRY

Green Park
Clunie Bridge Rd ⊠ PH16 5JY – ℰ (01796) 473 248 – www.thegreenpark.co.uk
– Closed 25 December Aa
51 rm (dinner included) ⊋ – †£ 73/103 ††£ 146/206
Rest – (light lunch residents only) (booking essential at dinner for non-residents) Menu £ 16/21 – Carte £ 21/29

♦ Family run 1860s summer retreat on Loch Faskally. Rooms in the old house are decorated in floral patterns; impressive up-to-date wing has good, contemporary facilities. Unhurried dinners at lochside setting.

East Haugh House
Southeast : 1.75 mi off A 924 (Perth Rd) ⊠ PH16 5TE – ℰ (01796) 473 121
– www.easthaugh.co.uk – Closed 1 week Christmas
14 rm ⊋ – †£ 118/178 ††£ 118/258 – 1 suite
Rest *Two Sisters* – see restaurant listing

♦ 17C turreted stone house in 2 acres of gardens; originally part of the Atholl Estate. Traditionally appointed bedrooms, named after fishing flies, are split between the house and two lodges. They also own fishing rights to Dalmarnock Beat.

Craigatin House and Courtyard without rest
165 Atholl Rd ⊠ PH16 5QL – ℰ (01796) 472 478
– www.craigatinhouse.co.uk – Closed Christmas Ae
12 rm ⊋ – †£ 65/75 ††£ 75/95 – 1 suite

♦ Built in 1822 as a doctor's house, now a stylish boutique hotel. Stunning modern open-plan lounge and breakfast room centred around a wood burning stove and overlooking the garden. Contemporary, minimalist bedrooms; some in the old stables.

Beinn Bhracaigh without rest
Higher Oakfield ⊠ PH16 5HT – ℰ (01796) 470 355 – www.beinnbhracaigh.co.uk
– Closed 22-28 December Bn
11 rm ⊋ – †£ 50/90 ††£ 77/100

♦ Spacious stone house built in 1880 and run by passionate owners. Immaculately kept interior with good comforts; most rooms boast lovely views of the Tummel Valley. Breakfast includes French toast and pancakes with maple syrup and bacon.

Dunmurray Lodge without rest
72 Bonnethill Rd ⊠ PH16 5ED – ℰ (01796) 473 624 – www.dunmurray.co.uk
– Mid-March to mid-November Bc
4 rm ⊋ – †£ 55/70 ††£ 65/80

♦ Imposing 19C former doctors surgery, close to town, boasting views across to the mountains. Smart lounge and neat bedrooms with co-ordinated décor; the best outlooks are from the front. Bright, neatly laid breakfast room features very locally sourced produce.

✕✕ Two Sisters – at East Haugh House Hotel
Southeast : 1.75 mi off A 924 (Perth Rd) ⊠ PH16 5TE – ℰ (01796) 473 121
– www.easthaugh.co.uk – Closed 1 week Christmas
Rest – (restricted opening lunch in winter) Carte £ 22/31

♦ Charming fishermens bar and bright, laid-back restaurant, located in a lovely 17C turreted house. Seasonal Scottish menu is served in both areas; cooking is clean and exact, with fish and game to the fore and fresh, home-baked breads.

at Killiecrankie Northwest : 4 mi by A 924 - A - and B 8019 **on B 8079**
– ⊠ Pitlochry

Killiecrankie House
⊠ PH16 5LG – ℰ (01796) 473 220 – www.killiecrankiehotel.co.uk
– Closed 3 January-15 March
9 rm (dinner included) ⊋ – †£ 115/195 ††£ 250/290 – 1 suite
Rest – (bar lunch) Menu £ 38

♦ Quiet and privately run, a converted 1840 vicarage with a distinct rural feel. The sizeable bedrooms come in co-ordinated patterns and overlook pleasant countryside. Warm, red dining room; garden produce prominent on menus.

PLOCKTON – Highland – **501** D11 – Scotland   29 B2

▶ Edinburgh 210 mi – Inverness 88 mi
◉ Village ★
◉ Wester Ross ★★★

Plockton Hotel with rm
41 Harbour St ✉ IV52 8TN – ℰ (01599) 544 274 – www.plocktonhotel.co.uk
15 rm ☐ – †£ 40/90 ††£ 100/130 **Rest** – Carte £ 16/38
♦ Formerly two cottages on the lochside, now a family-run pub with small terrace and restaurant. Cooking uses local Highland or Scottish produce, with fresh seafood dishes a speciality. Bedrooms, in the pub and annexe, boast bay views to the front.

PORT APPIN – Argyll and Bute – **501** D14 – ✉ Appin   27 B2

▶ Edinburgh 136 mi – Ballachulish 20 mi – Oban 24 mi

Airds
✉ PA38 4DF – ℰ (01631) 730 236 – www.airds-hotel.com – Closed Monday-Tuesday November, December and January
11 rm (dinner included) ☐ – †£ 194/235 ††£ 317/460
Rest – (booking essential for non-residents) Menu £ 53 (dinner) – Carte £ 27/33
♦ Former ferry inn boasting loch/mountain views and warm, welcoming interior. Two sumptuously furnished, open-fired sitting rooms display antiques. Intimate, floral-themed bedrooms provide good comforts. Excellent views from well-laid dining room. Classical cooking with a modern edge; 7 course tasting menu available.

PORT CHARLOTTE – Argyll and Bute – **501** A16 – see Islay (Isle of)

PORT ELLEN – Argyll and Bute – **501** B17 – see Islay (Isle of)

PORTMAHOMACK – Highland – **501** I10   30 D2

▶ Edinburgh 194 mi – Dornoch 21 mi – Tain 12 mi

Oystercatcher with rm
Main St ✉ IV20 1YB – ℰ (01862) 871 560 – www.the-oystercatcher.co.uk
– restricted opening in winter
3 rm ☐ – †£ 45/78 ††£ 108
Rest – Seafood – *(closed Sunday dinner, Wednesday lunch, Monday and Tuesday) (booking essential)* Menu £ 33 (dinner) **s** – Carte £ 37/79 **s**
♦ Personally run bistro and piscatorially themed main dining room in a lovely setting. Numerous seafood menus, offering a vast choice and some unusual combinations. Simple bedrooms.

PORTPATRICK – Dumfries and Galloway – **501** E19 – pop. 585   25 A3
– ✉ Stranraer

▶ Edinburgh 141 mi – Ayr 60 mi – Dumfries 80 mi – Stranraer 9 mi
⛳ Golf Course Rd, ℰ (01776) 81 02 73

Knockinaam Lodge
Southeast : 5 mi by A 77 off B 7042 ✉ DG9 9AD – ℰ (01776) 810 471
– www.knockinaamlodge.com
10 rm (dinner included) ☐ – †£ 165/215 ††£ 340/440
Rest – (booking essential for non-residents) (set menu only) Menu £ 40/58
Spec. Steamed fillet of sea bass with gazpacho emulsion. Fillet of beef with truffle pomme purée, trio of shallots and a tarragon reduction. Raspberry panna cotta with a strawberry doughnut.
♦ Charming country house in a private cove. Classical guest areas include open-fired sitting rooms and a wood-panelled bar; a relaxed atmosphere pervades. Traditionally furnished bedrooms boast antiques. Gold-hued dining room offers sea views and a carefully judged, 5 course daily menu of top quality, seasonal produce.

RANNOCH STATION – Perth and Kinross – **501** G13 — **27** B2

▶ Edinburgh 108 mi – Kinloch Rannoch 17 mi – Pitlochry 36 mi

Moor of Rannoch
✉ PH17 2QA – ☏ (01882) 633 238 – www.moorofrannoch.co.uk – 23 March-October
5 rm – †£ 62/92 ††£ 92
Rest – (dinner only) Carte £ 21/32 **s**

♦ Immaculately whitewashed 19C property "in the middle of nowhere", next to railway station with link to London! Comfy, sofa-strewn lounges. Rustic rooms with antiques. Home-cooked menus in characterful dining room with conservatory.

RATAGAN – Highland — **29** B2

▶ London 572 mi – Edinburgh 187 mi – Inverness 65 mi

Grants at Craigellachie
✉ IV40 8HP – ☏ (01599) 511 331 – www.housebytheloch.co.uk – restricted opening November-Easter
4 rm (dinner included) – †£ 95/103 ††£ 160/175
Rest – (closed Sunday) (dinner only) (booking essential for non residents) Carte £ 31/39

♦ Set in an idyllic spot beside Loch Duich; compact modern bedrooms are divided between the main house and a building in the rear garden. Local produce and Mediterranean influences inform the menu. Interesting wine list and a good selection of malt whiskies.

ST ANDREWS – Fife – **501** L14 – pop. 14 209 – Scotland — **28** D2

▶ Edinburgh 51 mi – Dundee 14 mi – Stirling 51 mi

🛈 70 Market St ☏ (01334) 47 20 21, www.standrews.co.uk

⛳ Duke's Craigtoun Park, ☏ (01334) 47 43 71

◉ City★★ • Cathedral★ (※★★) **AC**B• British Golf Museum **AC**AM1• St Andrews Preservation Trust BM2 • St Andrews Aquarium **AC**AM3 • MUSA University of St Andrews Museum BM4 • West Port★A

◎ Leuchars (parish church★), NW : 6 mi by A 91 and A 919. The East Neuk★★, SE : 9 mi by A 917 and B 9131 B – Crail★★ (Old Centre★★, Upper Crail★) SE : 9 mi by A 917 B – Kellie Castle★ **AC**, S : 9 mi by B 9131 and B 9171 B – Ceres★, SW : 9 mi by B 939 – E : Inland Fife★ A

Old Course H. Golf Resort and Spa
Old Station Rd ✉ KY16 9SP – ☏ (01334) 474 371 – www.oldcoursehotel.co.uk
Ab
123 rm – †£ 220/390 ††£ 250/420 – 21 suites
Rest *Road Hole* **Rest** *Sands Grill* – see restaurant listing

♦ Vast resort hotel on a world-famous championship golf course, overlooking the bay. Spacious guest areas with stylish Scottish theme; superb spa, leisure and meeting facilities. Chic, comfortable bedrooms: some sumptuous, some contemporary.

Fairmont St Andrews
Southeast : 3 mi on A 917 ✉ KY16 8PN – ☏ (01334) 837 000 – www.fairmont.com/standrews
203 rm – †£ 90/150 – 6 suites
Rest *Squire* – ☏ (01334) 837 441 (dinner only) Menu £ 25 – Carte £ 24/37
Rest *Esperante* – ☏ (01334) 837 271 (closed Monday-Tuesday) (dinner only) Menu £ 50

♦ Modern, purpose-built property set in 520 acres. Spacious guest areas display a subtle Scottish theme. Extensive conference and leisure facilities; two golf courses; superb spa and wellness centre. Well-appointed bedrooms with smart bathrooms. Informal Squires in vast atrium. Mediterranean menu in Esperante.

ST ANDREWS

Abbey St. . . . . **B** 2	Church St. . . . . **AB** 13	Murray Park . . . . **A** 28
Abbey Walk . . . . **B** 3	Ellice Pl. . . . . **A** 15	Murray Pl. . . . . **A** 29
Alexandra Pl. . . . . **A** 5	Gibson Pl. . . . . **A** 17	Pilmour Links . . . . **A** 31
Alfred Pl. . . . . **A** 6	Gillespie Terrace . . . . **B** 18	Pilmour Pl. . . . . **A** 32
Bridge St. . . . . **A** 7	Greenside Pl. . . . . **B** 20	Playfair Terrace . . . . **A** 34
Butts Wynd . . . . **B** 9	Gregory Lane . . . . **B** 21	Queen's Gardens . . . . **A** 35
Castle St. . . . . **B** 10	Gregory Pl. . . . . **B** 22	Queen's Terrace . . . . **B** 36
	Greyfriars Garden . . . . **A** 24	St Mary's
	Hepburn Gardens . . . . **A** 25	Pl. . . . . **A** 37
	Link Crescent . . . . **A** 27	Union St . . . . **B** 38

Rufflets Country House

Strathkinness Low Rd, West : 1.5 mi on B 939 ✉ *KY16 9TX*
– ☎ *(01334) 472 594 – www.rufflets.co.uk*
22 rm ⌑ – †£ 125/225 ††£ 200/260 – 2 suites
Rest *Terrace* – Menu £ 13/35 – Carte £ 27/53

♦ Handsome 1920s house set in ornamental gardens. Traditional drawing room with cosy fireside sofas. Thoughtfully appointed bedrooms that mix classic and contemporary styles. Terrace restaurant offers fine vantage point to view the lawns.

Fairways without rest

8a Golf Pl. ✉ *KY16 9JA – ☎ (01334) 473 319 – www.fairwaysofstandrews.co.uk*
3 rm ⌑ – †£ 60/80 ††£ 80/95   **A**z

♦ Run by the same friendly owners as older sister 6 Murray Park and the closest guesthouse in town to the famous 'Old Course'. Bedrooms are contemporary and offer good modern facilities; the suite boasts a balcony and overlooks the 18th hole.

Six Murray Park without rest

6 Murray Pk. ✉ *KY16 9AW – ☎ (01334) 473 319 – www.sixmurraypark.co.uk*
8 rm ⌑ – †£ 40/80 ††£ 80/95   **A**n

♦ Victorian terraced property with smart window boxes. Modern bedrooms boast bold feature walls and good facilities, including flat screen TVs and iPod docks. Hot daily specials are taken in the linen-laid, leather-furnished breakfast room.

Five Pilmour Place without rest

5 Pilmour Pl. ✉ *KY16 9HZ – ☎ (01334) 478 665 – www.5pilmourplace.com*
– February-November   **A**x
6 rm ⌑ – †£ 58/75 ††£ 105/160

♦ Terraced Victorian house with neatly lawned rear garden. Flag-floored hall leads to clubby lounge and communal breakfast room. Bedrooms range in size and come with boldly coloured feature walls and good facilities; one has a clawfoot bath.

ST ANDREWS

Aslar House without rest
120 North St ✉ *KY16 9AF* – ☏ *(01334) 473 460* – *www.aslar.com* – *Closed 2-20 January and 20-28 December*
Ar
6 rm ⌂ – †£ 47/90 ††£ 94/100
♦ Victorian terraced house in the town centre, run by a friendly, enthusiastic couple. Open-plan lounge and breakfast room. Neat, tidy bedrooms offer good modern facilities. Largest rooms are at the top; one has a lounge inside the turret.

Seafood
The Scores ✉ *KY16 9AB* – ☏ *(01334) 479 475* – *www.theseafoodrestaurant.com*
Rest – Seafood – *(booking essential)* Carte £ 22/45
Ac
♦ Overhanging the town's beach, with super views, as all four sides are made of glass. A very pleasant attitude and attention to detail accompanies agreeable, top quality, regularly changing seafood menus.

Road Hole – at Old Course Hotel Golf Resort and Spa
Old Station Rd ✉ *KY16 9SP* – ☏ *(01334) 474 371*
– *www.oldcoursehotel.co.uk*
Ab
Rest – *(Closed January, February, Sunday and Monday) (dinner only)* Carte approx. £ 42
♦ Fine dining restaurant within a smart golf resort and spa, boasting views out across St Andrews golf course and the bay. Menus are largely classically based but display some modern touches.

Sands Grill – at Old Course Hotel Golf Resort and Spa
Old Station Rd ✉ *KY16 9SP* – ☏ *(01334) 474 371*
– *www.oldcoursehotel.co.uk*
Ab
Rest – *(dinner only)* Carte approx. £ 27
♦ Informal grill restaurant located in a stylish golf resort and spa next to St Andrews golf course. Menus comprise mainly of seafood and steak dishes, with all meats cooked in the Josper oven.

ST BOSWELLS – The Scottish Borders – 501 L17 – pop. 1 199
26 D2
– ✉ Melrose ▮ Scotland

▶ Edinburgh 39 mi – Glasgow 79 mi – Hawick 17 mi – Newcastle upon Tyne 66 mi

St Boswells, ☏ (01835) 82 35 27

Dryburgh Abbey★★ **AC** (setting★★★), NW : 4 mi by B 6404 and B 6356 – Tweed Valley★★. Bowhill★★ **AC**, SW : 11.5 mi by A 699 and A 708

Whitehouse
Northeast : 3 mi on B 6404 ✉ *TD6 0ED* – ☏ *(01573) 460 343*
– *www.whitehousecountryhouse.com*
3 rm ⌂ – †£ 60/75 ††£ 90/110
Rest – Menu £ 29
♦ Former dower house built in 1872 by the Duke of Sutherland, boasting excellent views across the estate. Traditionally furnished bedrooms; cosy, country house feel. Many people come for the on-site shooting/fishing. Local game and wild salmon feature at dinner.

Clint Lodge
North : 2.25 mi by B 6404 on B 6356 ✉ *TD6 0DZ* – ☏ *(01835) 822 027*
– *www.clintlodge.co.uk* – *Closed 1 week Christmas*
5 rm ⌂ – †£ 50 ††£ 75/110
Rest – Menu £ 33
♦ Former shooting lodge with superb river and hill views. Characterful interior boasts antiques and fishing memorabilia. Traditionally decorated bedrooms; luxurious No. 4 and south facing rooms are the best. Daily changing 5 course dinner served at beautiful table.

ST FILLANS – Perth and Kinross – 501 H14   28 C2
▶ Edinburgh 65 mi – Lochearnhead 8 mi – Perth 29 mi

Achray House
✉ PH6 2NF – ✆ (01764) 685 231 – www.achrayhouse.com – Closed January and first 2 weeks December
8 rm ⌑ – ✝£ 89/109 ✝✝£ 176/200
Rest – *(closed Monday-Tuesday November-March)* Menu £ 9/27
♦ Superbly located Edwardian villa affording stunning views over Loch Earn. Bright breakfast room and inviting lounge with open fires and Douglas Fir polished wood floor. Modern bedrooms have bespoke pine furniture and contemporary bathrooms. Simple restaurant offers classical dishes crafted from local produce.

ST MARGARET'S HOPE – 501 L7 – see Orkney Islands (Mainland)

ST MONANS – Fife – 501 L15 – pop. 3 965   28 D2
▶ Edinburgh 47 mi – Dundee 26 mi – Perth 40 mi – Stirling 56 mi

Craig Millar @ 16 West End
16 West End ✉ *KY10 2BX – ✆ (01333) 730 327 – www.16westend.com – Closed Monday-Tuesday March-September and restricted opening October-March*
Rest – Seafood – *(booking essential)* Menu £ 26/40
♦ Unassuming former pub with attractive interior and charming team. Characterful lounge and smart, linen-laid restaurant with small terrace and great views over the harbour and sea. Experienced chef offers clean, refined, flavoursome dishes.

SANQUHAR – Dumfries and Galloway – 501 I17 – pop. 2 028   25 B2
▶ London 368 mi – Edinburgh 58 mi – East Kilbride 51 mi – Hamilton 43 mi

Blackaddie House with rm
Blackaddie Rd ✉ *DG4 6JJ – ✆ (01659) 50 270 – www.blackaddiehotel.co.uk*
9 rm ⌑ – ✝£ 65/80 ✝✝£ 120
Rest – Menu £ 27 (lunch) – Carte £ 35/51
♦ 16C stone house by the river. Lunch offers good value classics. Dinner is more elaborate and features complex, original cooking. Ingredients are luxurious and dishes, well presented. Simpler bar menu also available. Bedrooms are named after whisky distilleries.

SCALASAIG – Argyll and Bute – 501 B15 – see Colonsay (Isle of)

SCALPAY – Western Isles – 501 A10 – see Lewis and Harris (Isle of)

SCARISTA – Western Isles – 501 Y10 – see Lewis and Harris (Isle of)

SCOURIE – Highland – 501 E8 – ✉ Lairg ▮ Scotland   30 C1
▶ Edinburgh 263 mi – Inverness 107 mi
◉ Cape Wrath★★★ (≤★★) **AC**, N : 31 mi (including ferry crossing) by A 894 and A 838 – Loch Assynt★★, S : 17 mi by A 894

Eddrachilles ⌑
Badcall Bay, South : 2.5 mi on A 894 ✉ *IV27 4TH – ✆ (01971) 502 080 – www.eddrachilles.com – April-September*
11 rm ⌑ – ✝£ 77/80 ✝✝£ 104/110
Rest – *(bar lunch)* Menu £ 30
♦ Remotely set, converted 18C manse with views of the countryside, Badcall Bay and its islands. Cosy, well-kept bedrooms. Snug bar and flag-floored dining room; delightful outlook from conservatory lounge. Daily menu with strong French slant. Meats cured on-site.

SCRABSTER – Highland – 501 J8 – see Thurso

SHETLAND ISLANDS – 501 P/Q3 – pop. 21 988 🏴 Scotland

✈ Sumburgh Airport : ℰ (01950) 460905, S : 25 mi of Lerwick by A 970 - Tingwall Airport: 01595) 840246, NW: 6m. of Lerwick by A971

⛴ from Foula to Walls (Shetland Islands Council) 1-2 weekly (2 h 30 mn) – from Fair Isle to Sumburgh (Shetland Islands Council) 1-2 weekly (2 h 40 mn)

⛴ from Lerwick (Mainland) to Aberdeen and via Orkney Islands (Stromness) (P and O Scottish Ferries) – from Vidlin to Skerries (Shetland Islands Council) booking essential 3-4 weekly (1 h 30 mn) – from Lerwick (Mainland) to Skerries (Shetland Islands Council) 2 weekly (booking essential) (2 h 30 mn) – from Lerwick (Mainland) to Bressay (Shetland Islands Council) frequent services daily (7 mn) – from Laxo (Mainland) to Isle of Whalsay (Symbister) (Shetland Islands Council) frequent services daily (30 mn) – from Toft (Mainland) to Isle of Yell (Ulsta) (Shetland Islands Council) frequent services daily (20 mn) – from Isle of Yell (Gutcher) to Isle of Fetlar (Oddsta) and via Isle of Unst (Belmont) (Shetland Islands Council) – from Fair Isle to Sumburgh (Mainland) (Shetland Islands Council) 3 weekly (2 h 40 mn)

◉ Islands★ - Up Helly Aa (last Tuesday in January) – Mousa Broch★★★ **AC** (Mousa Island) – Jarlshof★★ - Lerwick to Jarlshof★ (≤★) – Shetland Croft House Museum★ **AC**

MAINLAND – Shetland Islands 31 B2
▶ London 559 mi – Edinburgh 148 mi

LERWICK – Shetland Islands – pop. 6 830 🏴 Scotland 31 B2
🛈 Lerwick ℰ (08452) 255 1 21, www.visitscotland.com
⛳ Shetland Gott Dale, ℰ (01595) 84 03 69
◉ Clickhimin Broch★
◉ Gulber Wick (≤★), S : 2 mi by A 970

Kveldsro House
Greenfield Pl ✉ *ZE1 0AQ* – ℰ *(01595) 692 195 – www.shetlandhotels.com*
– *Closed 1-2 January and 25-26 December*
17 rm ☐ – †£ 105 ††£ 130
Rest – *(bar lunch Monday-Saturday, carvery lunch Sunday)* Carte £ 21/34 **s**
♦ Spacious Georgian house hidden in the town centre; its name means 'evening peace'. Cosy sitting room with original ceiling mouldings, comfy bar with views of the islands and traditionally styled bedrooms. Menus offer mainly island produce; portions are hearty.

Glen Orchy House
20 Knab Rd ✉ *ZE1 0AX* – ℰ *(01595) 692 031 – www.guesthouselerwick.com*
24 rm ☐ – †£ 65/90 ††£ 90
Rest – Thai – *(booking essential) (residents only)* Carte £ 18/23
♦ Family-run hotel set in a 1904 former convent. Neat, well-kept guest areas include an honesty bar and spacious, comfortable lounge. Simple, cosy bedrooms – those in the wing boast underfloor heating. Homely dining room; unusually, cooking is totally Thai-based.

VEENSGARTH – Shetland Islands 31 B2

Herrislea House
✉ *ZE2 9SB* – ℰ *(01595) 840 208 – www.herrisleahouse.co.uk*
– *Closed 12 December-8 January*
9 rm ☐ – †£ 85/110 ††£ 120/130
Rest – *(dinner only) (booking essential for non-residents)* Carte £ 19/32
♦ Large, family-run hotel set just out of town. Unusual African hunting theme with mounted antlers, animal heads and skins on display. Cosy, individually designed bedrooms; some with valley views. Fresh cooking uses local produce and meats from the family crofts.

SHIELDAIG – Highland – **501** D11 – ✉ Strathcarron ▌Scotland   29 B2

▶ Edinburgh 226 mi – Inverness 70 mi – Kyle of Lochalsh 36 mi
◉ Wester Ross★★★

Tigh An Eilean
✉ IV54 8XN – ☏ (01520) 755 251 – www.tighaneilean.co.uk – *Restricted opening in winter*
11 rm ⌑ – †£70/110 ††£140
Rest – *(booking essential for non-residents) (bar lunch)* Menu £45 (dinner) – Carte £15/25
◆ In a sleepy lochside village, an attractive, personally run 19C inn with fine views of the Shieldaig Islands. Cosy, well-kept bedrooms and a comfy lounge with a homely feel. Linen-clad dining room showing eclectic variety of art; Scottish produce to the fore.

SKIRLING – The Scottish Borders – **501** J17 – ✉ Biggar ▌Scotland   26 C2

▶ Edinburgh 29 mi – Glasgow 45 mi – Peebles 16 mi
◉ Biggar★ - Gladstone Court Museum★, Greenhill Covenanting Museum★,
S : 3 mi by A 72 and A 702. New Lanark★★, NW : 16 mi by A 72 and A 73

Skirling House
✉ ML12 6HD – ☏ (01899) 860 274 – www.skirlinghouse.com – *Closed January, February and 1 week November-December*
5 rm ⌑ – †£60/85 ††£140 **Rest** – Menu £32
◆ On the green in an attractive hamlet; a personally run, Scots Pine, Arts and Crafts house. Beautiful Florentine carved ceiling and eclectic range of memorabilia in drawing room. Simple, characterful bedrooms with extras. Accomplished cooking uses home-grown produce; daily 4 course menu can be taken in the conservatory.

SKYE (Isle of) – Highland – **501** B11 – pop. 9 232 ▌Scotland   29 B2

🚢 from Mallaig to Isles of Eigg, Muck, Rhum and Canna (Caledonian MacBrayne Ltd) (summer only) – from Mallaig to Armadale (Caledonian MacBrayne Ltd) (summer only) 1-2 weekly (30 mn)
🚢 from Mallaig to Armadale (Caledonian MacBrayne Ltd) 1-5 daily (30 mn) – from Uig to North Uist (Lochmaddy) or Isle of Harris (Tarbert) (Caledonian MacBrayne Ltd) 1-3 daily (1 h 50 mn) – from Sconser to Isle of Raasay (Caledonian MacBrayne Ltd) 9-10 daily (except Sunday) (15 mn)
◉ Island★★ - The Cuillins★★★ – Skye Museum of Island Life★ **AC**
◉ N : Trotternish Peninsula★★ – W : Duirinish Peninsula★ – Portree★

BERNISDALE – Highland

Spoons *without rest*
75 Aird Bernisdale ✉ IV51 9NU – ☏ (01470) 532 217
– www.thespoonsonskye.com – *Closed 1 week February, 1 week October and 20-27 December*
3 rm ⌑ – †£105/125 ††£135/155
◆ Luxurious, purpose-built guest house in unspoilt hamlet, with airy, wood-floored lounge and breakfast room overlooking the loch. Bedrooms are individually decorated in a crisp, modern style and provide every conceivable extra. Superb 3 course breakfasts, with eggs from the charming owners' chickens.

BROADFORD – Highland   29 B2

Tigh an Dochais
13 Harrapool, on A 87 ✉ IV49 9AQ – ☏ (01471) 820 022
– www.skyebedbreakfast.co.uk – *April-November*
3 rm ⌑ – †£80 ††£90 **Rest** – Menu £25
◆ Striking house with award-winning architecture, overlooking Broadford Bay and the Applecross Peninsula. Comfortable lounge has well-stocked bookshelves. Modern, minimalist bedrooms boast superb views and good facilities, including underfloor heating and plenty of extras. Communal, home-cooked meals by arrangement.

SKYE (Isle of)

DUISDALEMORE – Highland   29 B2

Duisdale House
Sleat, on A 851. ✉ IV43 8QW – ✆ (01471) 833 202 – www.duisdale.com
18 rm – †£ 85/190 ††£ 160/280 – 1 suite
Rest – Menu £ 22/42 – Carte £ 13/45

• Stylish, up-to-date hotel with lawned gardens, hot tub and coastal views. Comfortable bedrooms boast bold décor, excellent bathrooms and a pleasing blend of contemporary and antique furniture. Modern cooking makes good use of local produce. Smart uniformed staff.

DUNVEGAN – Highland   29 B2

Roskhill House without rest
Roskhill, Southeast : 2.5 mi by A 863 ✉ IV55 8ZD – ✆ (01470) 521 317
– www.roskhillhouse.co.uk – Closed 15 December-16 February
5 rm – †£ 52/60 ††£ 76/86

• Welcoming 19C croft house with small garden, set in peaceful location close to the water. Formerly the old post office, the lounge boasts exposed stone, wooden beams and an open fire. Fresh, bright bedrooms have a contemporary edge and smart, modern bathrooms.

Three Chimneys & The House Over-By with rm
Colbost ✉ IV55 8ZT – ✆ (01470) 511 258
– www.threechimneys.co.uk – Closed 6-21 January
6 rm – †£ 196/295 ††£ 196/295
Rest – Seafood – (closed Sunday lunch November-March) (booking essential)
Menu £ 37/60

• Immaculately kept crofter's cottage in stunning lochside setting. Three characterful low-beamed dining rooms display modern artwork. Choose from accomplished, classical seafood-orientated dishes or 7 course tasting menu. Split-level bedrooms are spacious and stylishly understated; great outlook from residents' lounge.

EDINBANE – Highland   29 B2

Greshornish House
North : 3.75 mi by A 850 in direction of Dunvegan ✉ IV51 9PN
– ✆ (01470) 582 266 – www.greshornishhouse.com – Restricted opening in winter
6 rm – †£ 125/155 ††£ 150/185
Rest – (Closed Monday, and Tuesday in winter) (booking essential)
Menu £ 23/40 – Carte £ 25/48

• Early 18C lochside house in 10 acres. Comfy panelled drawing room; old billiard room with snooker table, piano, books and games. Country house style bedrooms; some four-posters/loch views. Breakfast in conservatory; seasonal, island dinners in candlelit dining room.

FLODIGARRY – Highland – ✉ Staffin   29 B2

Flodigarry Country House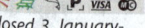
✉ IV51 9HZ – ✆ (01470) 552 203 – www.flodigarry.co.uk – Closed 3 January-8 February and 5 November-21 December
18 rm – †£ 105/135 ††£ 150/210
Rest – (dinner only and Sunday lunch) Carte £ 40/60 **s**

• Victorian house and cottage annexe which was once Flora MacDonald's home. Comfy, antique-filled interior with excellent island views over gardens that run down to the coast. Cosy, homely bedrooms. Characterful bar and part-panelled dining room; classical menu.

SKYE (Isle of)

PORTREE – Highland – pop. 1 917   29 B2
i Bayfield Rd ✆ (08452) 25 51 21, www.visitscotland.com

Cuillin Hills
Northeast : 0.75 mi by A 855 ⊠ IV51 9QU – ✆ (01478) 612 003
– www.cuillinhills-hotel-skye.co.uk
26 rm ⊇ – †£ 210 ††£ 310
Rest – (bar lunch Monday-Saturday, buffet lunch Sunday) Menu £ 35
– Carte £ 18/34 **s**

♦ Yellow-washed 19C hunting lodge in 15 acres of gardens and grounds; overlooking the bay and hills. Comfy lounge and stylish open-plan bar. Bedrooms offer good facilities; the best are to the front. Bright dining room offers good outlook and traditional menus.

Bosville
Bosville Ter ⊠ IV51 9DG – ✆ (01478) 612 846
– www.macleodhotels.co.uk/bosville
19 rm ⊇ – †£ 69/120 ††£ 88/260
Rest *Chandlery* – see restaurant listing
Rest *Bistro* – Carte £ 17/33

♦ Boldly painted, purpose-built hotel in town centre. Wood-furnished bar – formerly the village bank – and small, traditionally decorated, first floor lounge. Modern bedrooms with co-ordinating fabrics and good facilities. Accessible menu served in popular bistro.

Almondbank without rest
Viewfield Rd, Southwest : 0.75 mi on A 87 ⊠ IV51 9EU – ✆ (01478) 612 696
4 rm ⊇ – †£ 60 ††£ 76

♦ Friendly guesthouse with large lawned gardens, set on a sloping bank and boasting lovely views across the bay. Spacious lounge and linen-laid breakfast room. Immaculately kept bedrooms.

Chandlery – at Bosville Hotel

Bosville Ter ⊠ IV51 9DG – ✆ (01478) 612 846 – www.macleodhotels.co.uk
Rest – (dinner only) Menu £ 44

♦ Hotel restaurant displaying deep red walls, linen-laid tables and high-backed chairs. Concise 3 course set menu offers classically based meat and seafood dishes. Friendly service.

SLEAT – Highland   30 C1

Kinloch Lodge
⊠ IV43 8QY – ✆ (01471) 833 214 – www.kinloch-lodge.co.uk
14 rm (dinner included) ⊇ – †£ 149/199 ††£ 280/440 – 1 suite
Rest – (booking essential for non-residents) Menu £ 35/60 **s**

Spec. Home-cured and steamed organic salmon with beetroot, crème fraîche and dill dressing. Rabbit stuffed with venison and prunes, Kinloch croquette and brandy sauce. Orange crème, warm dark chocolate sauce and apricot fudge.

♦ 17C lochside hunting lodge surrounded by heather-strewn moorland. Antique-filled country house interior with comfy lounges. Individually styled bedrooms boast good facilities/extras. Menus offer 2 choices per course and showcase local island produce. Classical cooking displays some clever modern touches. Good service.

STRUAN – Highland   29 B2

Ullinish Country Lodge

West : 1.5 mi by A 863 ⊠ IV56 8FD – ✆ (01470) 572 214
– www.theisleofskye.co.uk – Closed January and 1 week November
6 rm ⊇ – †£ 120 ††£ 170   **Rest** – (dinner only) Menu £ 49

♦ Personally run, 17C whitewashed house in windswept location, affording lovely loch/hill views. Comfy lounge filled with ornaments and books about the area. Warmly decorated bedrooms boast good facilities and extras. Formal dining room offers complex 5 course menu.

SKYE (Isle of)

TEANGUE – Highland 29 A2

Toravaig House
Knock Bay, on A 851 ⊠ IV44 8RE – ℰ (01471) 820 200 – www.skyehotel.co.uk
9 rm – †£ 80/150 ††£ 130/230
Rest – *(booking essential for non-residents)* Menu £ 28/49

• Stylish whitewashed house with neat gardens, set on the road to the Mallaig ferry. Cosy, open-fired lounge with baby grand piano and heavy fabrics. Individually designed bedrooms boast quality materials and furnishings. Good service with extras. Two-roomed restaurant offers concise, classical menu of island produce.

WATERNISH – Highland 29 A2

Loch Bay Seafood
1 MacLeod Terr, Stein ⊠ IV55 8GA – ℰ (01470) 592 235
– www.lochbay-seafood-restaurant.co.uk – Easter-October
Rest – Seafood – *(closed Sunday and Monday) (booking essential)*
Carte £ 23/32

• Whitewashed cottage in a tiny hamlet overlooking the loch. Small room with low-backed chairs and benches. Concise menu of simply prepared seafood and blackboard specials. Friendly service.

Stein Inn with rm
MacLeod Ter, Stein ⊠ IV55 8GA – ℰ (01470) 592 362 – www.stein-inn.co.uk
– Closed 1 January and 25 December
5 rm – †£ 46/58 ††£ 110
Rest – Seafood – *(residents only Monday dinner except Bank Holidays)*
Carte £ 15/22

• Set in a tiny fishing village, this characterful inn is the oldest on Skye. Menus are formed around the latest local produce available, with lighter toasties and salads on offer at lunchtime. Bedrooms are simple, well-kept and boast lovely bay outlooks.

SLEAT – Highland – see Skye (Isle of)

SORN – East Ayrshire – 501 H17 25 B2

▶ Edinburgh 67 mi – Ayr 15 mi – Glasgow 35 mi

Sorn Inn with rm
35 Main St ⊠ KA5 6HU – ℰ (01290) 551 305 – www.sorninn.com – Closed 10 days January and Monday
4 rm – †£ 40/50 ††£ 50/70 **Rest** – Menu £ 14 (lunch) – Carte £ 19/27

• Unassuming whitewashed inn set in a small backwater village. Very much a family affair – the father checks you in and the son cooks. Choose either the smart bar or larger dining room. Extensive menu includes a variety of British dishes plus a choice of more elaborate international offerings. Neat, simple bedrooms represent good value.

SPEAN BRIDGE – Highland – 501 F13 30 C3

▶ Edinburgh 143 mi – Fort William 10 mi – Glasgow 94 mi – Inverness 58 mi

🛈 The Kingdom of Scotland, by Fort William, Inverness-shirev ℰ (0845) 2 25 51 21, www.visitscotland.com

🏌 Spean Bridge GC Station Rd, ℰ 077 471 4 70 90

Corriegour Lodge
Loch Lochy, North : 8.75 mi on A 82 ⊠ PH34 4EA – ℰ (01397) 712 685
– www.corriegour-lodge-hotel.com – Easter-November
12 rm 🖂 – †£ 90 ††£ 90 **Rest** – *(dinner only)* Menu £ 50

• 19C hunting lodge with pretty gardens, in great lochside location; owner's father is the local gamekeeper. Homely, curio-filled sitting room; high quality beds, linens and fabrics. Every dining table has a loch view; classical 4 course menu features local meats.

SPEAN BRIDGE

⌂ Distant Hills without rest
Roy Bridge Rd, East : 0.5 mi on A86 ⊠ PH34 4EU – ℰ (01397) 712 452
– www.distanthills.com – March-October
7 rm ⊇ – †£ 43/73 ††£ 72/85
♦ Welcoming guesthouse with friendly owners, who suggest walks and provide packed lunches. French windows in large lounge lead to stream-side seating. Modern bedrooms. Wide-ranging breakfasts.

⌂ Corriechoille Lodge
East : 2.75 mi on Corriechoille rd ⊠ PH34 4EY – ℰ (01397) 712 002
– www.corriechoille.com – Closed November-March, Sunday and Monday
4 rm ⊇ – †£ 48 ††£ 76   **Rest** – Menu £ 27
♦ Charming, part-18C house in remote location, boasting large gardens and views over the Grey Corries and Aonach Mor. Comfy lounge and spacious, pine-furnished bedrooms; two wooden bothy lodges provide more intimacy. Homely cooking; the fish is smoked on site.

ⅩⅩ Russell's at Smiddy House with rm
Roybridge Rd ⊠ PH34 4EU – ℰ (01397) 712 335 – www.smiddyhouse.co.uk
– Restricted opening in winter
4 rm ⊇ – †£ 70/95 ††£ 90/115
Rest – *(dinner only) (booking essential)* Menu £ 35
♦ Passionately run restaurant in an appealing Highland village. Snug lounge and two intimate, candlelit dining rooms. Classical menus of tried-and-tested combinations which rely on natural flavours. Cosy, well-equipped bedrooms boast comfy beds and fine linens.

Ⅹ Old Pines with rm
Northwest : 1.5 mi by A 82 on B 8004 ⊠ PH34 4EG – ℰ (01397) 712 324
– www.oldpines.co.uk – February-October
7 rm ⊇ – †£ 70/80 ††£ 90/120
Rest – *(booking essential for non-residents)* Carte £ 21/35
♦ Log cabin style building that blends well with the Highland scenery. Comfy lounge; simple dining room with tables arranged around the windows. Classical menus offer lots of local seafood and beef. Up-to-date, pine-furnished bedrooms feature traditional quilts.

SCOTLAND

SPITTAL OF GLENSHEE – Perth and Kinross – **501** J13   28 C2
– ⊠ Blairgowrie ▮ Scotland
▶ Edinburgh 69 mi – Aberdeen 74 mi – Dundee 35 mi
❄ Glenshee (❄★★) (chairlift **AC**)

🏨 Dalmunzie Castle
⊠ PH10 7QG – ℰ (01250) 885 224 – www.dalmunzie.com
– Closed 1 week Christmas
17 rm (dinner included) ⊇ – †£ 105/180 ††£ 170/295
Rest – *(bar lunch)* Menu £ 16/45
♦ Edwardian hunting lodge in a magnificent spot, encircled by mountains. Traditional rooms mix antique and pine furniture. Bar with cosy panelled alcove and leather chairs. Modern dining room with views down the valley.

STANLEY – Perth and Kinross – **501** J14 – see PERTH

STEVENSTON – North Ayrshire – **501** F17 – pop. 9 129   25 A2
▶ Edinburgh 82 mi – Ayr 19 mi – Glasgow 36 mi

⌂ Ardeer Farm Steading without rest
Ardeer Mains Farm, East : 0.75 mi by A 738 and B 752, on no through rd
⊠ KA20 3DD – ℰ (01294) 465 438 – www.ardeersteading.co.uk
8 rm ⊇ – †£ 35 ††£ 48/52
♦ Smart, family-owned farmhouse on the edge of a 100 acre working farm. Large, cream leather furnished lounge and breakfast room boast pleasant country views. Immaculately kept contemporary bedrooms display sleek, modern lines. Complimentary pick-up from station.

STIRLING – Stirling – **501** I15 – pop. 32 673

28 C2

Scotland

▶ Edinburgh 37 mi – Dunfermline 23 mi – Falkirk 14 mi – Glasgow 28 mi

🛈 41 Dumbarton Rd ✆ (08707) 20 06 20, www.visitstirling.org

◉ Town★★ – Castle★★ **AC** (Site★★★, external elevations★★★, Stirling Heads★★, Argyll and Sutherland Highlanders Regimental Museum★) **B** – Argyll's Lodging★ (Renaissance decoration★) **B A** – Church of the Holy Rude★ **B B**

◉ Wallace Monument (❊★★) NE : 2.5 mi by A 9 - **A** - and B 998.
Dunblane★ (Cathedral★★, West Front★★), N : 6.5 mi by A 9 **A**

Park Lodge

32 Park Ter ✉ FK8 2JS – ✆ (01786) 474 862 – www.parklodge.net
– Closed Christmas and New Year

B a

9 rm ⌁ – ♦ £ 60/75 ♦♦ £ 75/85

Rest – Menu £ 17/26 **s** – Carte £ 18/26

♦ Lovely part-Georgian, part-Victorian, creeper-clad house, with mature garden and fruit trees to the rear. Warm, intimate bar and sitting room. Traditional, individually designed bedrooms; the four-poster room being particularly popular. Formal dining room has a beautiful ornate ceiling and traditional menu.

STIRLING

Barnton St.	**B** 2
Borestone Crescent	**A** 3
Causewayhead Rd.	**A, B** 4
Cornton Rd.	**A** 7
Corn Exchange Rd	**B** 5
Coxithill Rd	**A** 8
Drummond Pl.	**B** 9
Dumbarton Rd	**B** 10
Goosecroft Rd	**B** 12
King St	**B** 13
Leisure Centre	**B**
Murray Pl.	**B** 15
Newhouse	**A** 16
Park Pl.	**B** 18
Port St.	**B**
Queen St	**B** 20
Randolph Terrace	**A** 22
St John St	**B** 23
St Mary's Wynd	**B** 24
Seaforth Pl.	**B** 25
Shirra's Brae Rd	**A** 26
Spittal St	**B** 27
Thistle Centre	**B**
Union St	**B** 28
Upper Craigs	**B** 29
Weaver Row	**B** 31

STIRLING

Number 10 without rest
Gladstone Pl ⊠ FK8 2NN – ℰ (01786) 472 681 – www.cameron-10.co.uk
3 rm ⊑ – †£ 40/50 ††£ 60/65   **Bv**
- Light-stone Victorian townhouse with attractive rear garden and surprisingly spacious interior; set in a quiet street. Linen-laid breakfast room displays ornate coving. Individually furnished bedrooms have good facilities and tartan themes.

West Plean House without rest
*South : 3.5 mi on A 872 (Denny rd) ⊠ FK7 8HA – ℰ (01786) 812 208
– www.westpleanhouse.com – Closed 15 December-15 January*
3 rm ⊑ – †£ 48/80 ††£ 78/80
- Attractive house with long history – its latest extensions added in 1803 – on a working farm in a peaceful, rural location. Beautiful tiled hall, classic country house lounge and communal breakfast room. Warm, traditionally styled bedrooms.

STONEHAVEN – Aberdeenshire – 501 N13 – pop. 9 577 – Scotland   28 D2

▶ Edinburgh 109 mi – Aberdeen 16 mi – Montrose 22 mi
◉ Dunnottar Castle ★★, S : 1.5 mi by A 92

Beachgate House without rest
Beachgate Ln ⊠ AB39 2BD – ℰ (01569) 763 155 – www.beachgate.co.uk
3 rm ⊑ – †£ 60/80 ††£ 85
- Well-run guesthouse located on the seashore and looking out over Stonehaven Bay. Super views from well-appointed, first floor lounge. Comfortable bedrooms are furnished in a luxurious, modern style. Breakfast, taken at linen-laid tables, includes fresh poached fish or a full Scottish with hen or duck eggs.

Tolbooth
*Old Pier, Harbour ⊠ AB39 2JU – ℰ (01569) 762 287
– www.tolbooth-restaurant.co.uk – Closed first 3 weeks January, 25 December, Sunday October-April and Monday*
Rest – Seafood – Menu £ 15 (lunch) – Carte £ 33/44
- Stonehaven's oldest building, delightfully located by the harbour. Rustic interior with lovely picture window table. Various menus available, with the emphasis on local seafood.

STORNOWAY – Western Isles – 501 A9 – see Lewis and Harris (Isle of)

STRACHUR – Argyll and Bute – 501 E15 – pop. 628   27 B2

▶ Edinburgh 112 mi – Glasgow 66 mi – Inverness 162 mi – Perth 101 mi

Creggans Inn
⊠ PA27 8BX – ℰ (01369) 860 279 – www.creggans-inn.co.uk
13 rm ⊑ – †£ 75/85 ††£ 120/140 – 1 suite
Rest *Loch Fyne Dining Room* – see restaurant listing
Rest *Mac Phunn's Bar* – Carte £ 22/37
- Well-established inn located on the shores of Lock Fyne and boasting enviable views. Spacious, well-kept bedrooms; traditional décor is in keeping with the building's age. Conservatory popular for afternoon teas while taking in the view. Pubby bar with pool tables and accessible menu of local ingredients.

Loch Fyne Dining Room – at Creggans Inn Hotel
⊠ PA27 8BX – ℰ (01369) 860 279 – www.creggans-inn.co.uk
Rest – (dinner only) Menu £ 37
- Vast restaurant in a long-standing inn on the shore of Loch Fyne. Warm décor, linen-clad tables and great watery views. Formal 4 course menu changes daily and offers traditionally based dishes.

STRACHUR

Inver Cottage
Strathlaclan, Southwest : 6.5 mi by A 886 on B 8000 ⊠ PA27 8BU – ℰ (01369) 860 537 – www.invercottage.com – Closed late December-March, Monday and Tuesday except July-August
Rest – Carte £ 19/33

♦ Lochside former crofter's cottage boasting water/mountain views. Small bar and casual tables for drinks/afternoon tea; simple, airy restaurant. Constantly evolving menu uses only local produce.

STRATHPEFFER – Highland – 501 G11 – pop. 918 30 C2
▶ Edinburgh 174 mi – Inverness 18 mi
🛈 Pump Room Museum ℰ (01997) 42 14 15, www.visitscotland.com
⛳ Strathpeffer Spa Golf Course Rd, ℰ (01997) 42 12 19

Craigvar without rest
The Square ⊠ IV14 9DL – ℰ (01997) 421 622 – www.craigvar.com – Closed 8-21 October and 23 December-12 January
3 rm ⊠ – †£ 45/70 ††£ 80/84

♦ Attractive Georgian house overlooking the main square of a delightful spa village. Traditional guest areas include a comfy lounge and linen-laid breakfast room. Spacious bedrooms have a modern edge and plenty of personal touches. Proudly run by a charming owner.

STRATHYRE – Stirling – 501 H15 – ⊠ Callander – Scotland 27 B2
▶ Edinburgh 62 mi – Glasgow 53 mi – Perth 42 mi
◎ The Trossachs★★★ (Loch Katrine★★) SW : 14 mi by A 84 and A 821 – Hilltop viewpoint★★★ (※★★★) SW : 16.5 mi by A 84 and A 821

Creagan House with rm
on A 84 ⊠ FK18 8ND – ℰ (01877) 384 638 – www.creaganhouse.co.uk – Closed 18 January-8 March, 7-22 November and 24-26 December
5 rm ⊠ – †£ 75 ††£ 130
Rest – *(Closed Wednesday and Thursday) (dinner only)* Menu £ 32

♦ Personally run baronial dining room in 17C former farmhouse. Concise fixed price menu of fine seasonal Scottish produce; classical dishes prepared with care. 'Smokie in a Pokie,' a speciality. Watch red squirrels in the garden from the cosy bedrooms.

STROMNESS – 501 K7 – see Orkney Islands (Mainland)

STRONTIAN – Highland – 501 D13 29 B3
▶ Edinburgh 139 mi – Fort William 23 mi – Oban 66 mi
🛈 Acharacle ℰ (08452) 25 51 21, www.visitscotland.com

Kilcamb Lodge
⊠ PH36 4HY – ℰ (01967) 402 257 – www.kilcamblodge.co.uk – Closed January
10 rm (dinner included) ⊠ – †£ 145/208 ††£ 229/309
Rest – Menu £ 18/50

♦ Charming lochside hunting lodge, with 19 acres of gardens and woodland running down to a private shore. Traditional interior boasts rich fabrics, log fires and up-to-date bedrooms. Formal restaurant offers a traditional menu; seafood and game feature highly.

STRUAN – Highland – see Skye (Isle of)

SWINTON – The Scottish Borders – 501 N16 – pop. 472 – ⊠ Duns 26 D2
▶ Edinburgh 49 mi – Berwick-upon-Tweed 13 mi – Glasgow 93 mi
– Newcastle upon Tyne 66 mi

Wheatsheaf with rm

*Main St ⌧ TD11 3JJ – ℰ (01890) 860 257 – www.wheatsheaf-swinton.co.uk
– Closed 24-26 December*
10 rm ⌱ – †£ 75 ††£ 112
Rest – *(closed lunch Monday-Thursday)* Carte £ 22/40
♦ Substantial stone inn overlooking the village green. Lunch menu offers pub classics; concise evening à la carte is more adventurous. Both feature local produce, including meat from nearby farms and fish from Eyemouth. Bedrooms are spacious, cosy and well-equipped.

TAIN – Highland – 501 H10 – pop. 4 540   30 D2

▶ Edinburgh 191 mi – Inverness 35 mi – Wick 91 mi

🏌 Tain Chapel Rd, ℰ (01862) 89 23 14

🏌 Tarbat Portmahomack, ℰ (01862) 87 12 78

Golf View House without rest

*13 Knockbreck Rd ⌧ IV19 1BN – ℰ (01862) 892 856
– www.tainbedandbreakfast.co.uk – mid-March to October*
5 rm ⌱ – †£ 45/55 ††£ 65/75
♦ 19C former manse near the golf course. Neat lawned garden with comfy seating in wooden bothy hut. Leather-furnished lounge and bright, modern bedrooms; front rooms have water/mountain views.

at Nigg Southeast : 7 mi by A 9, B 9175 and Pitcalnie Rd.

Wemyss House

*Bayfield, South : 1 mi past church ⌧ IV19 1QW – ℰ (01862) 851 212
– www.wemysshouse.com*
3 rm ⌱ – †£ 90/95 ††£ 90/95
Rest – Menu £ 35
♦ Remote, rurally set guesthouse with charming owners, well-maintained gardens and pleasant views. Cosy sitting room with grand piano. Spacious, immaculately kept bedrooms. Freshly prepared dishes use local ingredients. Excellent quality breakfasts.

at Cadboll Southeast : 8.5 mi by A 9 and B 9165 (Portmahomack rd) off Hilton rd
– ⌧ Tain

Glenmorangie House

Fearn ⌧ IV20 1XP – ℰ (01862) 871 671 – www.theglenmorangiehouse.com
9 rm (dinner included) ⌱ – †£ 220 ††£ 400 – 3 suites
Rest – *(dinner only)* Menu £ 55
♦ Charming 17C house owned by the famous distillery. Antiques, hand-crafted local furnishings and open peat fires feature; there's even a small whisky tasting room. Luxuriously appointed bedrooms show good attention to detail; those in the courtyard cottages are suites. Communal dining from classical Scottish-based menu.

TALMINE – Highland – 501 G8 – ⌧ Lairg   30 C1

▶ Edinburgh 245 mi – Inverness 86 mi – Thurso 48 mi

Cloisters without rest

*Church Holme ⌧ IV27 4YP – ℰ (01847) 601 286 – www.cloistertal.demon.co.uk
– Closed 25 December and 1 January*
3 rm ⌱ – †£ 35 ††£ 60
♦ Converted church boasting great views over Tongue Bay and the Rabbit Islands. Homely interior packed with memorabilia. Leather-furnished lounge, snug breakfast area and simple, well-kept bedrooms.

TARBERT – Western Isles – 501 Z10 – see Lewis and Harris (Isle of)

TARBET – Argyll and Bute – 501 F15 – ✉ Arrochar 27 B2
▶ Edinburgh 88 mi – Glasgow 42 mi – Inverness 138 mi – Perth 78 mi

Lomond View Country House without rest
on A 82 ✉ G83 7DG – ℰ (01301) 702 477
– www.lomondview.co.uk
3 rm ⌑ – †£ 65/75 ††£ 80/90

♦ Purpose-built guesthouse which lives up to its name: there are stunning loch views. Spacious sitting room. Light and airy breakfast room. Sizeable, modern bedrooms.

TAYVALLICH – Argyll and Bute – 501 D15 – ✉ Lochgilphead 27 B2
▶ Edinburgh 148 mi – Glasgow 103 mi – Inverness 157 mi

Tayvallich Inn
✉ PA31 8PL – ℰ (01546) 870 282 – www.tayvallichinn.co.uk – Closed Monday November-March
Rest – Carte £ 19/32

♦ Dine in bar, more formal dining room or on decked terrace, with views over the bay. Menu focuses on locally caught fish and shellfish, but also lists classic pub dishes like steak and chips.

TEANGUE – Highland – see Skye (Isle of)

THORNHILL – Dumfries and Galloway – 501 I18 – pop. 1 633 25 B2
▮ Scotland
▶ Edinburgh 64 mi – Ayr 44 mi – Dumfries 15 mi – Glasgow 63 mi
◉ Drumlanrig Castle★★ (cabinets★) **AC**, NW : 4 mi by A 76

Gillbank House without rest
8 East Morton St ✉ DG3 5LZ – ℰ (01848) 330 597 – www.gillbank.co.uk
6 rm ⌑ – †£ 50 ††£ 75

♦ Red stone house built in 1895; originally the Jenner family holiday home. Lovely stained glass front door, spacious, light-filled interior and airy breakfast room with distant hill views. Large, simply furnished bedrooms: two with feature beds; all with wet rooms.

THURSO – Highland – 501 J8 – pop. 7 737 ▮ Scotland 30 D1
▶ Edinburgh 289 mi – Inverness 133 mi – Wick 21 mi
⛴ from Scrabster to Stromness (Orkney Islands) (P and O Scottish Ferries) (2 h)
🛈 Riverside ℰ (0845) 2 25 51 21, www.visitscotland.com
⛳ Newlands of Geise, ℰ (01847) 89 38 07
◉ Strathy Point★ (≤★★★) W : 22 mi by A 836

Forss House
Forss, West : 5.5 mi on A 836 ✉ KW14 7XY – ℰ (01847) 861 201
– www.forsshousehotel.co.uk – Closed 24 December-2 January
14 rm ⌑ – †£ 115 ††£ 165   **Rest** – (dinner only) Carte £ 32/39 **s**

♦ Traditional Scottish hotel centred around fishing and offering timeshares on the river. Rods and mounted fish sit beside deer heads and open fires. Good-sized bedrooms – annexe rooms are most modern. Elegant dining room serves classic menu; seafood a speciality.

Murray House
1 Campbell St ✉ KW14 7HD – ℰ (01847) 895 759 – www.murrayhousebb.com
– Closed Christmas-New Year
5 rm ⌑ – †£ 30/60 ††£ 60/70   **Rest** – (by arrangement) Menu £ 15

♦ A centrally located and family owned Victorian town house. Pine furnished bedrooms are colourfully decorated and carefully maintained. Modern dining room with home-cooked evening meals.

at Scrabster Northwest : 2.25 mi on A 9

Captain's Galley
The Harbour ⊠ *KW14 7UJ* – ℰ *(01847) 894 999* – *www.captainsgalley.co.uk*
– Closed 1-2 January, 25-26 December, Sunday and Monday
Rest – Seafood – *(dinner only) (booking essential)* Carte £ 47/57
• Rustic seafood restaurant on the pier, with vaulted stone dining room, cosy lounge and old chimney from its former smokery days. Owner was once a fisherman, so has excellent local contacts; he keeps some produce in creels in the harbour. Classical daily menu.

TIGHNABRUAICH – Argyll and Bute – 501 E16   27 B3
▶ Edinburgh 113 mi – Glasgow 63 mi – Oban 66 mi

Royal An Lochan
⊠ *PA21 2BE* – ℰ *(01700) 811 239* – *www.theroyalanlochan.co.uk*
11 rm – †£ 75/125 ††£ 125/150
Rest – Carte £ 15/30 **s**
• Spacious 19C hotel located in a peaceful village, overlooking the Kyles of Bute. Comfortable bedrooms; some with excellent outlooks. Charming bar with nautical theme serves snack menu. Formal conservatory restaurant offers water views and mainly seafood dishes.

TIRORAN – Argyll and Bute – 501 B14 – see Mull (Isle of)

TOBERMORY – Argyll and Bute – 501 B14 – see Mull (Isle of)

TONGUE – Highland – 501 G8 – pop. 552 – ⊠ Lairg ▮ Scotland   30 C1
▶ Edinburgh 257 mi – Inverness 101 mi – Thurso 43 mi
◉ Cape Wrath★★★ (≼★★) W : 44 mi (including ferry crossing) by A 838 – Ben Loyal★★, S : 8 mi by A 836 – Ben Hope★ (≼★★★) SW : 15 mi by A 838 – Strathy Point★ (≼★★★) E : 22 mi by A 836 – Torrisdale Bay★ (≼★★) NE : 8 mi by A 836

Tongue
Main St ⊠ *IV27 4XD* – ℰ *(01847) 611 206* – *www.tonguehotel.co.uk* – *Closed 1 December-28 February*
18 rm – †£ 45/75 ††£ 90/110
Rest – *(bar lunch)* Menu £ 28 – Carte £ 18/34
• Fiercely Scottish former hunting lodge overlooking the Kyle of Tongue; Highland shooting and fishing memorabilia abounds. Snug, open-fired lounge and contemporary bedrooms. Snacks served in linen-laid bars; classical menus of local ingredients in dining room.

TORRIDON – Highland – 501 D11 – ⊠ Achnasheen ▮ Scotland   29 B2
▶ Edinburgh 234 mi – Inverness 62 mi – Kyle of Lochalsh 44 mi
◉ Wester Ross★★★

Torridon
South : 1.5 mi on A 896 ⊠ *IV22 2EY* – ℰ *(01445) 791 242*
– www.thetorridon.com – Closed January and Monday-Tuesday November-March
18 rm – †£ 130/225 ††£ 195/430 – 1 suite
Rest – *(bar lunch) (booking essential)* Menu £ 50 **s**
• Family-owned and run former hunting lodge; remotely set, with wonderful views of Loch Torridon and mountains. Ornate ceilings, peat fires and Highland curios. Some very contemporary bedrooms; others more classic in style. Traditional wood-panelled restaurant uses fine local produce, some from the grounds.

TORRIDON

Torridon Inn
South : 1.5 mi on A 896 ✉ *IV22 2EY* – ✆ *(01445) 791 242*
– *www.thetorridon.com* – *Closed mid-December-February and Monday-Thursday November-March*
12 rm – †£ 99 ††£ 99, ⊇ £ 6.50   **Rest** – Carte £ 16/32 **s**
♦ Peaceful, rural location in grounds of Torridon House. Spacious, functional bedrooms in annexe; the larger ones ideal for families. Characterful, rustic restaurant serving classic pub dishes.

TROON – South Ayrshire – **501** G17 – pop. 14 766   25 A2

▶ Edinburgh 77 mi – Ayr 7 mi – Glasgow 31 mi
⛴ to Northern Ireland (Larne) (P and O Irish Sea) 2 daily
⛳ Troon Municipal Harling Drive, ✆ (01292) 31 24 64

Lochgreen House
Monktonhill Rd, Southwood, Southeast : 2 mi on B 749 ✉ *KA10 7EN* – ✆ *(01292) 313 343* – *www.costley-hotels.co.uk*
37 rm ⊇ – †£ 113/154 ††£ 215/241 – 1 suite
Rest *Tapestry* – see restaurant listing
♦ Attractive, coastal Edwardian house in mature grounds. Lounges exude luxurious country house feel. Large rooms, modern or traditional, have a good eye for welcoming detail.

XXX **Tapestry** – at Lochgreen House Hotel
Monktonhill Rd, Southwood, Southeast : 2 mi on B 749 ✉ *KA10 7EN* – ✆ *(01292) 313 343* – *www.costley-hotels.co.uk*
Rest – Menu £ 18/30 – Carte £ 35/55
♦ Spacious dining room with baronial feel. Elegant chandeliers; large pottery cockerels. Classical, modern cooking, with a strong Scottish base.

at Loans East : 2 mi on A 759 – ✉ Troon

Highgrove House
Old Loans Rd, East : 0.25 mi on Dundonald rd ✉ *KA10 7HL* – ✆ *(01292) 312 511*
– *www.costleyhotels.co.uk*
9 rm ⊇ – †£ 69/85 ††£ 85/110
Rest – Menu £ 12 – Carte £ 18/38
♦ Immaculate whitewashed hotel in elevated position, offering superb coastal panorama. Comfy floral bedrooms; 1 and 2 have the best views. Tartan carpets remind you where you are. Large restaurant with floor to ceiling windows and granite columns.

TURNBERRY – South Ayrshire – **501** F18 – ✉ Girvan ▮ Scotland   25 A2

▶ Edinburgh 97 mi – Ayr 15 mi – Glasgow 51 mi – Stranraer 36 mi
◎ Culzean Castle★ **AC** (setting★★★, Oval Staircase★★) NE : 5 mi by A 719

Turnberry
on A 719 ✉ *KA26 9LT* – ✆ *(01655) 331 000*
– *www.luxurycollection.com/turnberry* – *Closed 4-12 January*
194 rm ⊇ – †£ 160/300 ††£ 180/400 – 4 suites
Rest *1906* – see restaurant listing
Rest *Tappie Toorie* – (lunch only) Menu £ 15 (Sunday) – Carte £ 24/35
Rest *James Miller* – (booking essential) Menu £ 65 – Carte £ 27/58
♦ Resort-style, Edwardian railway hotel boasting a smart spa and 3 championship golf courses. Spacious inner with some areas in a light, contemporary style. Luxurious bedrooms; suites have stunning coast and course views. Cocktails and snacks in Ailsa; French classics in 1906; pub favourites in simpler Tappie Toorie; ambitious, modern offerings in intimate James Miller.

XXX **1906** – at Turnberry Hotel
on A 719 ✉ *KA26 9LT* – ✆ *(01655) 331 000*
– *www.luxurycollection.com/turnberry* – *Closed 4-12 January*
Rest – *(dinner only)* Carte £ 34/49
♦ Named after the year that the Turnberry opened, this smart hotel restaurant boasts lovely views across the sea. Classical French menus feature dishes true to the spirit of Auguste Escoffier.

UDNY GREEN – Aberdeenshire — 28 D1
London - 554 mi – Edinburgh 143 mi – Aberdeen 15 mi – Arbroath 67 mi

XX **Eat on the Green**
✉ *AB41 7RS* – ✆ *(01651) 842 337* – *www.eatonthegreen.co.uk* – *Closed Monday, Tuesday and Saturday lunch*
Rest – Menu £ 25 (lunch) – Carte dinner £ 32/44
♦ Converted pub by the village green, with snug seating area and two smart dining rooms. Accomplished, flavourful dishes make good use of seasonal, local produce. Polished service.

UIST (Isles of) – 501 X/Y11 – pop. 3 510
from Lochmaddy to Isle of Skye (Uig) (Caledonian MacBrayne Ltd) 1-3 daily (1 h 50 mn) – from Otternish to Isle of Harris (Leverburgh) (Caledonian MacBrayne Ltd) (1 h 10 mn)

NORTH UIST – Western Isles — 29 A2
London 639 mi – Edinburgh 254 mi

CARINISH – Western Isles — 29 A2

Temple View
✉ *HS6 5EJ* – ✆ *(01876) 580 676* – *www.templeviewhotel.co.uk*
10 rm ⊑ – †£ 55/75 ††£ 95/105
Rest – *(bar lunch)* Menu £ 24 **s** – Carte £ 18/24 **s**
♦ Victorian house with uncluttered interior and modern yet homely style. Small bar, sitting room and sun lounge. Simple, comfortable bedrooms with moor views to rear and sea/13C ruins of Trinity Temple to front. Cosy dining room offers popular seafood specials.

LANGASS – Western Isles

Langass Lodge
✉ *HS6 5HA* – ✆ *(01876) 580 285* – *www.langasslodge.co.uk* – *Closed 1 January, 24-25 and 31 December*
12 rm ⊑ – †£ 60/90 ††£ 95/140
Rest – *(dinner only)* Menu £ 48
♦ Former Victorian shooting lodge nestled in heather-strewn hills and boasting distant loch views. Characterful bedrooms in main house; more modern, spacious rooms with good views in wing. Eat in comfy bar or linen-clad dining room from simple, seafood based menu.

LOCHMADDY – Western Isles — 29 A2

Tigh Dearg
✉ *HS6 5AE* – ✆ *(01876) 500 700* – *www.tighdearghotel.co.uk*
9 rm ⊑ – †£ 79/129 ††£ 80/169
Rest – *(October-March closed Sunday and dinner only)* Carte £ 19/34
♦ Stylish hotel with sleek, boutique style. Well-equipped gym, sauna and steam room. Chic, modern bedrooms offer good facilities. Forward-thinking owner continually reinvests. Smart bar and dining room; menus display plenty of seafood. Bikes available for hire.

ULLAPOOL – Highland – **501** E10 – pop. 1 308 🟢 Scotland   30 C2

▶ Edinburgh 215 mi – Inverness 59 mi

🚢 to Isle of Lewis (Stornoway) (Caledonian MacBrayne Ltd) (2 h 40 mn)

ℹ️ 20 Argyle St ☎ (0845) 2 25 51 21, www.ullapool.com

👁 Town ★

🟢 Wester Ross ★★★ - Loch Broom ★★. Falls of Measach ★★, S : 11 mi by A 835 and A 832 - Corrieshalloch Gorge ★, SE : 10 mi by A 835 – Northwards to Lochinver ★★, Morefield (≼★★ of Ullapool), ≼★ Loch Broom

Point Cottage without rest
22 West Shore St ✉ IV26 2UR – ☎ (01854) 613 702
– www.ullapoolbedandbreakfast.co.uk – closed Christmas-New Year
3 rm ☕ – ♦£ 50/60 ♦♦£ 60/70

♦ 18C converted fisherman's cottage on the shores on Loch Broom, not far from the ferry terminal. Simple, homely interior; cosy, floral bedrooms boast lovely views. Snug sitting room is filled with oil paintings, locals maps and guides. Friendly, chatty owner.

Ardvreck without rest
Morefield Brae, Northwest : 2 mi by A 835 ✉ IV26 2TH – ☎ (01854) 612 028
– www.smoothhound.co.uk/hotels/ardvreck – March-November
10 rm ☕ – ♦£ 37/70 ♦♦£ 75/80

♦ Modern house set away from the town centre, affording amazing views over the loch and mountains. Bedrooms are fresh and up-to-date; local watercolours feature. Friendly, accommodating owner.

VEENSGARTH – see Shetland Islands (Mainland)

WALKERBURN – The Scottish Borders – pop. 647   26 C2
▶ Edinburgh 30 mi – Galashiels 23 mi – Peebles 8 mi

🏠 Windlestraw Lodge
on A 72 ✉ EH43 6AA – ☎ (01896) 870 636 – www.windlestraw.co.uk
– Closed 1 week February, 25 December and 1 January
6 rm (dinner included) ☕ – ♦£ 140 ♦♦£ 300   **Rest** – (dinner only) Menu £ 46

♦ Attractive Arts and Crafts property built in 1906, boasting original fireplaces, old plaster ceilings and great valley views. Stylish, tastefully modernised bedrooms. Comfy bar, plush lounge and attractive, wood-panelled dining room offering daily changing menu.

WATERNISH – Highland – **501** A11 – see Skye (Isle of)

WESTRAY (Isle of) – **501** K/L6 – see Orkney Islands

WICK – Highland – **501** K8 – pop. 9 713 🟢 Scotland   30 D1
▶ Edinburgh 282 mi – Inverness 126 mi

✈ Wick Airport : ☎ (01955) 602215, N : 1 m

ℹ️ Whitechapel Rd ☎ (0845) 2 25 51 21, www.visitscotland.com

🚉 Reiss, ☎ (01955) 60 27 26

🟢 Duncansby Head ★ (Stacks of Duncansby ★★) N : 14 mi by A 9 – Grey Cairns of Camster ★ (Long Cairn ★★) S : 17 mi by A 9 – The Hill O'Many Stanes ★, S : 10 mi by A 9

Clachan without rest
13 Randolph Pl, South Rd, South : 0.75 mi on A 99 ✉ KW1 5NJ – ☎ (01955) 605 384 – www.theclachan.co.uk – Closed 2 weeks Christmas-New Year
3 rm ☕ – ♦£ 55 ♦♦£ 70

♦ Detached house on edge of town, in an area formerly housing herring workers during the 1930s. Rebuilt and having undergone a contemporary makeover, it now boasts stylish, modern bedrooms and a smart breakfast room hung with period photos. Accommodating owner.

WICK

※ **Bord De L'Eau** VISA ◉◉
2 Market St (Riverside) ✉ *KW1 4AR –* ✆ *(01955) 604 400 – Closed first 2 weeks January, 25-26 December, Sunday lunch and Monday*
Rest – French – Carte £ 22/35
♦ Long-standing riverside bistro with simple dining room and conservatory. Framed Eiffel Tower prints and French posters on the walls. Authentic, classic Gallic dishes; plenty of local seafood.

WORMIT – Fife – **501** L14 – ✉ Fife   28 C2
▶ Edinburgh 53 mi – Dundee 6 mi – St Andrews 12 mi
⛳ Scotscraig Tayport Golf Rd, ✆ (01382) 55 25 15

※ **View** ≤ 🍽 **P** VISA ◉◉
Naughton Rd ✉ *DD6 8NE –* ✆ *(01382) 542 287 – www.view-restaurant.co.uk – Closed 2 weeks November, 25-26 December, 1-2 January, Sunday dinner, Monday and lunch Tuesday*
Rest – Carte £ 29/45
♦ Unassuming former pub in a small village, boasting superb views over the Tay railway bridge to Dundee. Extensive menu and daily specials board offer homemade small plates that can be served in succession or all at once; quality ingredients.

SCOTLAND

Wales

ABERAERON (Aber Aeron) – Ceredigion – 503 H27 – pop. 1 520   33 B3

▶ Cardiff 90 mi – Aberystwyth 16 mi – Fishguard 41 mi

Ty Mawr Mansion Country House
Cilcennin, East : 4.5 mi by A 482 ✉ *SA48 8DB* – ℰ *(01570) 470 033 – www.tymawrmansion.co.uk – Closed 27 December-16 January*
8 rm – †£ 130/240 ††£ 240/320 – 1 suite
Rest – *(closed Sunday dinner) (dinner only and Sunday lunch)* Menu £ 27 – Carte £ 34/48

♦ Grade II listed Georgian stone mansion in 12 acres of delightful grounds. Several well-appointed lounges with high ceilings. Spacious bedrooms boast marble bathrooms and a good level of facilities. Small basement cinema offers dining packages. Smart restaurant has a concise menu of bold, wide-ranging dishes.

3 Pen Cei without rest
3 Quay Par ✉ *SA46 OBT* – ℰ *(01545) 571 147 – www.pencei.co.uk – Closed 25-26 December*
5 rm – †£ 90 ††£ 140

♦ Brightly painted, modern-style guest house on the harbourfront, formerly the headquarters of the Packet Steam Company. Spacious bedrooms are named after nearby rivers; Aeron has a bathroom with a free-standing bath and large walk-in shower.

Llys Aeron without rest

Lampeter Rd, on A 482 ✉ *SA46 0ED* – ℰ *(01545) 570 276 – www.llysaeron.co.uk – Closed 25-26 December*
3 rm – †£ 50/70 ††£ 75/105

♦ Charmingly run Georgian guesthouse with conservatory lounge. Modern bedrooms come in warm pastel shades and boast large bathrooms. Breakfast room overlooks the walled garden; choose from extensive Aga-cooked options, alongside local honey and homemade preserves.

Harbourmaster with rm
Quay Par ✉ *SA46 0BA* – ℰ *(01545) 570 755 – www.harbour-master.com – Closed 25 December*
13 rm – †£ 65/185 ††£ 170/195   **Rest** – Carte £ 32/41

♦ Vibrant blue pub with modern bar-lounge, traditional dining room and lovely harbour views. Choice of bar menu or more substantial evening à la carte, supplemented by daily specials. Comfortable, brightly decorated bedrooms; some boast huge windows or terraces.

ABERDOVEY (Aberdyfi) – Gwynedd – 503 H26 – pop. 869   32 B2

▶ London 230 mi – Dolgellau 25 mi – Shrewsbury 66 mi
◉ Snowdonia National Park★★★

Llety Bodfor without rest
Bodfor Terr ✉ *LL35 0EA* – ℰ *(01654) 767 475 – www.lletybodfor.co.uk – Closed 1-29 December*
8 rm – †£ 40/110 ††£ 100/120, ⚏ £ 10

♦ Two 19C seafront houses, now a guest house with a difference: a relaxed atmosphere prevails but the design is stylish and contemporary. Spacious New England themed bedrooms boast bay views. Breakfast is served three doors down.

ABERGAVENNY (Y-Fenni) – Monmouthshire – 503 L28 – pop. 14 055   33 C4

▶ London 163 mi – Cardiff 31 mi – Gloucester 43 mi – Newport 19 mi
ℹ Monmouth Rd ℰ (01873) 85 32 54, www.abergavenny.org.uk
⛳ Monmouthshire Llanfoist, ℰ (01873) 85 26 06
◉ Town★ - St Mary's Church★ (Monuments★★)
◉ Brecon Beacons National Park★★ – Blaenavon Ironworks★, SW : 5 mi by A 465 and B 4246. Raglan Castle★ **AC**, SE : 9 mi by A 40

ABERGAVENNY

Llansantffraed Court
Llanvihangel Gobion, Southeast : 6.5 mi by A 40 and B 4598 off old Raglan rd – NP7 9BA – ℰ (01873) 840 678 – www.llch.co.uk
21 rm – †£ 85/115 ††£ 125/145 **Rest** – Menu £ 20/33 – Carte £ 31/38
♦ Historic country house beside ornamental pond and fountain, in 19 acres of grounds. Large lounges and bar. Dark-hued bedrooms with smart bathrooms: room 19 has double aspect mountain/valley views. Classical menus showcase local ingredients.

Angel
15 Cross St – NP7 5EN – ℰ (01873) 857 121 – www.angelabergavenny.com – *Closed 25 December*
33 rm – †£ 74/80 ††£ 96, ⚏ £ 5 – 2 suites
Rest – *(closed dinner 24-31 December)* Carte £ 22/36
♦ Georgian former coaching inn run by friendly, attentive team. Smart exterior and very modern guest areas: traditionally styled bedrooms undergoing refurbishment. Contemporary bar and restaurant with courtyard offer extensive bistro menu and popular afternoon teas.

Hardwick with rm
Old Raglan Rd, Southeast : 2 mi by A 40 on B 4598 – NP7 9AA – ℰ (01873) 854 220 – www.thehardwick.co.uk – *Closed 1 week January and 25 December*
8 rm ⚏ – †£ 100 ††£ 170
Rest – *(booking essential)* Menu £ 27 (lunch) – Carte £ 31/50
♦ Whitewashed former pub overlooking the mountains. Rustic bar and three dining rooms – one cosy and open-fired with wood beams, another with a glass-fronted wine cellar and the third, with large windows and an airy feel. Extensive menus of robust, flavoursome dishes with Italian influences. Spacious, modern bedrooms boast light oak furnishings and excellent bathrooms.

Charthouse
Llanvihangel Gobion, Southeast : 5 mi by A 40 on B 4598 – NP7 9AY – ℰ (01873) 840 414 – www.thecharthouse-abergavenny.co.uk – *Closed 25-26 December, 1 January, Sunday dinner and Monday*
Rest – Carte £ 30/37
♦ Former pub with beamed ceilings, wood burning stove, stylish tongue and groove panelling and pleasant terrace. Daily à la carte offers refreshingly unfussy, modern dishes that let ingredients speak for themselves. Relaxed, friendly service.

at Llanddewi Skirrid Northeast : 3.25 mi on B 4521

Walnut Tree (Shaun Hill)
– NP7 8AW – ℰ (01873) 852 797 – www.thewalnuttreeinn.com – *Closed 1 week Christmas, Sunday and Monday*
Rest – *(booking essential)* Menu £ 24 (lunch) – Carte £ 37/42
Spec. Chicken consommé with scallops and herb pasta. Turbot in spiced mussel and clam broth. Orange and almond cake.
♦ A reinvigorated, long-standing Welsh institution set in a valley. Welcoming staff and always bustling with regulars. It takes skill to make cooking look this simple; it's seasonal and each dish bursts with flavour.

at Cross Ash Northeast : 8.25 mi on B 4521

1861
– NP7 8PB – ℰ (01873) 821 297 – www.18-61.co.uk – *Closed first 2 weeks January, Sunday dinner and Monday*
Rest – Menu £ 24/32 – Carte £ 32/43
♦ Victorian former pub; now a cosy restaurant, with contemporary furnishings and exposed brick fireplace. Classically based menus make use of good quality local produce. Personable service.

ABERGAVENNY

at Nant-Y-Derry Southeast : 6.5 mi by A 40 off A 4042 – ✉ Abergavenny

Foxhunter

✉ NP7 9DD – ☏ (01873) 881 101 – www.thefoxhunter.com – Closed 25-26 December, 1 January, Sunday dinner and Monday
Rest – Menu £ 24 (lunch) – Carte £ 31/37

♦ Former station master's house with fresh, bright feel, flagstone floors and wood burning stoves. Dishes range in style from classic British to fusion and come in large, hearty portions.

at Llanover South : 5.5 mi by A 40 off A 4042

Llansabbath Country House without rest

✉ NP7 9BY – ☏ (01873) 840 068 – www.llansabbathcountryhouse.co.uk – Closed Christmas and New Year
5 rm ⌑ – †£ 70 ††£ 90/105

♦ Former farmhouse renovated in a modern style. Large lounge with wood burning stove; conservatory breakfast with eggs from hens who roam the garden. Comfortable bedrooms have all mod cons.

ABERGELE – Conwy – 503 J24 – pop. 17 574 — 32 C1

▶ London 229 mi – Cardiff 182 mi – Liverpool 51 mi – Manchester 75 mi

at Betws-yn-Rhos Southwest : 4.25 mi by A 548 on B 5381

Ffarm Country House without rest

✉ LL22 8AR – ☏ (01492) 680 448 – www.ffarmcountryhouse.co.uk – Closed 1 week Christmas
8 rm ⌑ – †£ 79/90 ††£ 98/188

♦ Gothic-style country house; stylish, comfortable and personally run. Beautiful tiled hall with vaulted wood ceiling. Tastefully furnished bedrooms are named after wine regions.

ABERSOCH – Gwynedd – 502 G25 – pop. 805 – ✉ Pwllheli — 32 B2

▶ London 265 mi – Caernarfon 28 mi – Shrewsbury 101 mi

🔞 Golf Rd, ☏ (01758) 71 26 36

🅖 Lleyn Peninsula★★ – Plas-yn-Rhiw★ **AC**, W : 6 mi by minor roads. Bardsey Island★, SW : 15 mi by A 499 and B 4413 – Mynydd Mawr★, SW : 17 mi by A 499, B 4413 and minor roads

Venetia with rm

Lon Sarn Bach ✉ LL53 7EB – ☏ (01758) 713 354 – www.venetiawales.com – Closed 1 January-10 February and 25-26 December
5 rm ⌑ – †£ 103/133 ††£ 118/148
Rest – Italian – (dinner only) Carte £ 25/33

♦ Smart, modernised detached house boasts minimalist bar/lounge and stark white dining room. Classic Italian dishes, well presented in a distinctly modern style, with fish a speciality. Friendly, efficient service. Comfortable, well-equipped bedrooms.

at Bwlchtocyn South : 2 mi – ✉ Pwllheli

Porth Tocyn

✉ LL53 7BU – ☏ (01758) 713 303 – www.porthtocyn-hotel.co.uk – April-October
17 rm – †£ 72/176 ††£ 99/176, ⌑ £ 6.75
Rest – (bar lunch Monday-Saturday, buffet lunch Sunday) Menu £ 42

♦ Set high on the headland overlooking Cardigan Bay, a traditional hotel that's been in the family for 3 generations. Comfy lounges. Mix of classical and more modern bedrooms; some with balconies or sea views. Great leisure and children's facilities. Modern menus display interesting, soundly executed dishes.

ABERYSTWYTH (Aberestuuth) – Ceredigion – 503 H26　　32 B2
– pop. 21 877

▶ London 238 mi – Chester 98 mi – Fishguard 58 mi – Shrewsbury 74 mi
🛈 Terrace Rd ✆ (01970) 61 21 25, www.aberystwyth-online.co.uk
⛳ Bryn-y-Mor, ✆ (01970) 61 51 04
◉ Town★★ – The Seafront★ – National Library of Wales (Permanent Exhibition★)
◉ Vale of Rheidol★★ (Railway★★ **AC**) – St Padarn's Church★, SE : 1 mi by A 44. Devil's Bridge (Pontarfynach)★, E : 12 mi by A 4120 – Strata Florida Abbey★ **AC** (West Door★), SE : 15 mi by B 4340 and minor rd

Gwesty Cymru
19 Marine Terr ✉ *SY23 2AZ* – ✆ *(01970) 612 252* – *www.gwestycymru.com*
– *Closed 23 December-5 January*
8 rm ⌂ – †£ 65/133 – ††£ 87/183
Rest – *(closed Tuesday lunch) (booking essential)* Carte £ 28/33
♦ Georgian Grade II listed building on the promenade, with a nice front terrace and sea views. Thoughtfully designed, contemporary bedrooms are colour-themed in décor and furnishings; impressive bathrooms. Small basement dining room serves dishes using Welsh produce, with some international influences.

ANGLESEY (Isle of) (Sir Ynys Môn) – Isle of Anglesey – 503 G/H24　　32 B1
– pop. 68 900

▶ London 270 mi – Cardiff 205 mi – Liverpool 92 mi – Birkenhead 86 mi

WALES

BEAUMARIS – Isle of Anglesey – ✉ Isle Of Anglesey　　32 B1

▶ London 253 mi – Birkenhead 74 mi – Holyhead 25 mi
⛳ Baron Hill, ✆ (01248) 81 02 31
◉ Town★★ – Castle★ **AC**
◉ Anglesey★★ – Penmon Priory★, NE : 4 mi by B 5109 and minor roads. Plas Newydd★ **AC**, SW : 7 mi by A 545 and A 4080

Ye Olde Bull's Head Inn
Castle St ✉ *LL58 8AP* – ✆ *(01248) 810 329* – *www.bullsheadinn.co.uk*
– *Closed 24-25 December*
13 rm ⌂ – †£ 85/110 ††£ 100/120
Rest *Brasserie* **Rest** *Loft* – see restaurant listing
♦ Characterful 1670s coaching inn. Bedrooms are split between the main house and adjacent block; the former, traditional and named after Dickens' characters; the latter, more colourful and contemporary. Vast inglenook fireplace in the lounge.

Cleifiog *without rest*
Townsend ✉ *LL58 8BH* – ✆ *(01248) 811 507* – *www.cleifiogbandb.co.uk*
– *Closed Christmas-New Year*
3 rm ⌂ – †£ 65 ††£ 95
♦ Delightful seafront guesthouse overlooking the mountains and Menai Strait. Cosy, antique-furnished lounge with watercolours hung on wood-panelled walls. Comfy bedrooms with fine linens, large bathrooms and local toiletries. Excellent breakfasts. Welcoming owner.

Loft – at Ye Olde Bull's Head Inn
Castle St ✉ *LL58 8AP* – ✆ *(01248) 810 329* – *www.bullsheadinn.co.uk*
– *Closed 25-26 December, 1 January, Sunday and Monday*
Rest – *(dinner only)* Menu £ 41
♦ Formal restaurant set in an old coaching inn, with plush, open-fired lounge and dining room in the old loft above. Elegant décor, exposed beams and immaculately laid, candlelit tables. Ambitious dishes feature lots of different ingredients.

ANGLESEY (Isle of)

🍴 Brasserie – at Ye Olde Bull's Head Inn VISA ⓒ AE
Castle St ✉ LL58 8AP – ☏ (01248) 810 329 – www.bullsheadinn.co.uk
– Closed 24-25 December
Rest – (bookings not accepted) Carte £ 20/31
♦ Large brasserie set in the rear of a charming 17C coaching inn. Relaxed, contemporary feel with a Welsh slate floor, local stone fireplace and light wood tables. Extensive international menu.

BENLLECH – Isle of Anglesey – ✉ Isle Of Anglesey   32 B1

⌂ Hafod *without rest*
Amlwch Rd ✉ LL74 8SR – ☏ (01248) 853 092 – Closed 24-26 December
4 rm ☐ – †£ 50/55 ††£ 70/72
♦ 19C house with large lawned garden and view out over the bays. Cosy lounge and traditional breakfast room; fantastic parquet floor and original staircase. Good-sized bedrooms have open fires.

CEMAES (Cemais) – Isle of Anglesey – ✉ Isle Of Anglesey   32 B1

⌂ Hafod Country House *without rest*
South : 0.5 mi on Llanfechell rd ✉ LL67 0DS – ☏ (01407) 711 645
– www.anglesey-countryhouse.co.uk – April-September
3 rm ☐ – †£ 40/50 ††£ 65/75
♦ Charming Edwardian house on outskirts of a fishing village, on far side of the island. Lovely garden with pair of majestic oaks. Spacious interior with original tiled floors, delightful staircase, antique-filled lounge and homely bedrooms.

LLANERCHYMEDD – Isle of Anglesey – ✉ Isle Of Anglesey   32 B1

⌂ Llwydiarth Fawr *without rest*
North : 1 mi on B 5111 ✉ LL71 8DF – ☏ (01248) 470 321
– www.llwydiarthfawr.com
4 rm ☐ – †£ 60 ††£ 85/100
♦ Sizeable Georgian house in 1,000 acres of farmland. Country house feel with impressive hallway/landing, plush drawing room and fine views. Individually decorated bedrooms boast extras.

MENAI BRIDGE – Isle of Anglesey – ✉ Isle Of Anglesey   32 B1

⌂ Neuadd Lwyd
Penmynydd, Northwest : 4.75 mi by B 5420 on Eglwys St Gredifael Church rd
✉ LL61 5BX – ☏ (01248) 715 005 – www.neuaddlwyd.co.uk – Closed 28 November-20 January
4 rm (dinner included) ☐ – †£ 155/215 ††£ 205/265 **Rest** – Menu £ 45
♦ This fine 19C rectory, set in a beautiful rural location, has had a sleek and stylish refit, lending it a luxurious air. Elegant interiors are matched by stunning bedrooms. Freshest Welsh ingredients incorporated into tasty evening meals.

RHOSCOLYN – Isle of Anglesey – ✉ Isle Of Anglesey

🍺 White Eagle
✉ LL65 2NJ – ☏ (01407) 860 267 – www.white-eagle.co.uk
Rest – Carte £ 22/33
♦ Spacious pub with cosy bar, modern dining room, decked terrace and stunning sea views. Monthly menu offers everything from sandwiches and salads to pub classics and more sophisticated fare.

VALLEY – Isle of Anglesey – ✉ Isle Of Anglesey

🏠 Cleifiog Uchaf
off Spencer Rd ✉ LL65 3AB – ☏ (01407) 741 888 – www.cleifioguchaf.co.uk
6 rm ☐ – †£ 69/79 ††£ 95/145 – 2 suites
Rest – (closed Sunday and Monday) (dinner only) Carte £ 23/45
♦ Restored 16C longhouse, simply and stylishly furnished. Bedrooms boast character beds and every mod con including flat screens, DVDs and Roberts radios. Slate-floored, bistro-style dining room for classical combinations of locally sourced, seasonal ingredients.

BALA – Gwynedd – **503** J25 – pop. 1 980 – ✉ Gwynedd   **32** B2
▶ London - 213 mi – Cardiff 160 mi – Liverpool 75 mi – Stoke-on-Trent 84 mi

Abercelyn Country House *without rest*
Llanycil, Southwest : 1 mi on A 494 ✉ *LL23 7YF* – ℰ *(01678) 521 109*
– www.abercelyn.co.uk – *February-October*
3 rm ⊇ – †£ 53/60 ††£ 72/90

◆ Attractive former rectory, with pleasant garden and brook. Warmly decorated bedrooms, named after surrounding mountains. Eggs from owners' hens, plus homemade jams and breads.

BEAUMARIS – **504** H24 – see Anglesey (Isle of)

BEDDGELERT (Bedkelerd) – Gwynedd – **502** H24 – pop. 535   **32** B1
▶ London 249 mi – Caernarfon 13 mi – Chester 73 mi
◉ Snowdonia National Park★★★ - Aberglaslyn Pass★, S : 1.5 mi on A 498

Sygun Fawr Country House
Northeast : 0.75 mi by A 498 ✉ *LL55 4NE* – ℰ *(01766) 890 258*
– www.sygunfawr.co.uk – *Closed 3 January-10 February and 16-27 December*
12 rm ⊇ – †£ 41 ††£ 107
Rest – *(closed Monday-Tuesday to non-residents) (dinner only) (booking essential)* Carte £ 18/26

◆ Part-16C stone-built house, located halfway up a mountain and boasting views over the Gwynant Valley towards Snowdon. Charming open-fired interior with snug sitting room and spacious conservatory. Good-sized bedrooms with a cosy, homely feel. Traditional dining room offers a range of hearty, regional dishes.

BENLLECH – **502** H24 – see Anglesey (Isle of)

BETWS GARMON – Gwynedd   **32** B1
▶ Cardiff 194 mi – Betws-y-Coed 25 mi – Caernarfon 5 mi

Betws Inn
Northwest : 1 mi on A 4085 ✉ *LL54 7YY* – ℰ *(01286) 650 324*
– www.betws-inn.co.uk
3 rm ⊇ – †£ 60/80 ††£ 70/90   **Rest** – Menu £ 25 **s**

◆ Rustic former coaching inn surrounded by the towering mountains of Snowdonia. Superb inglenook fireplace on display in the cosy lounge; exposed stone walls and pine dresser in the breakfast room. Warm, beamed bedrooms boast half-tester or four-poster beds and modern bathrooms. Home-cooked meals feature local produce.

BETWS-Y-COED – Conwy – **502** I24 – pop. 848   **32** B1
▶ London 226 mi – Holyhead 44 mi – Shrewsbury 62 mi
ℹ Royal Oak Stables ℰ (01690) 71 04 26, www.betws-y-coed.co.uk
⛳ Clubhouse, ℰ (01690) 71 05 56
◉ Town★
◉ Snowdonia National Park★★★. Blaenau Ffestiniog★ (Llechwedd Slate Caverns★ **AC**), SW : 10.5 mi by A 470 – The Glyders and Nant Ffrancon (Cwm Idwal★), W : 14 mi by A 5

Tan-y-Foel Country House
East : 2.5 mi by A 5, A 470 and Capel Garmon rd on Llanwrst rd ✉ *LL26 0RE*
– ℰ *(01690) 710 507 – www.tyfhotel.co.uk – Closed December and restricted opening January*
6 rm ⊇ – †£ 90/145 ††£ 125/245
Rest – *(closed Monday) (dinner only)* Menu £ 49

◆ Personally run, part-16C country house in 4 acres of grounds, affording stunning views over the Vale of Conwy and Snowdonia. Individually designed modern bedrooms with smart bathrooms. Snug lounge and contemporary breakfast room. Much of the produce used at dinner is grown in the owners' greenhouse.

799

BETWS-Y-COED

Bryn without rest
Lôn Muriau, Llanrwst Rd, Northeast : 1 mi by A 5 on A 470 ⊠ LL24 0HD
– ℰ (01690) 710 627 – www.bryn-bella.co.uk
5 rm ⊇ – †£ 80/85 ††£ 80/85
♦ Comfy, well-kept guesthouse with pleasant garden, valley views and every conceivable extra in the bedrooms. Keen owners provide reliable local info. Fresh, tasty eggs from their rescued hens.

Pengwern without rest
Allt Dinas, Southeast : 1.5 mi on A 5 ⊠ LL24 0HF – ℰ (01690) 710 480
– www.snowdoniaaccommodation.co.uk – Closed 24 December-2 January
3 rm ⊇ – †£ 62/68 ††£ 77/83
♦ Former Victorian artist 'colony' with a comfy, homely and stylish lounge, warmly decorated breakfast room and individually appointed bedrooms, two with superb valley vistas.

at Penmachno Southwest : 4.75 mi by A 5 on B 4406 – ⊠ Betws-Y-Coed

Penmachno Hall
on Ty Mawr rd ⊠ LL24 0PU – ℰ (01690) 760 410 – www.penmachnohall.co.uk
– Closed Christmas-New Year
3 rm ⊇ – †£ 100 ††£ 100 **Rest** – Carte £ 18/38
♦ Former rectory built in 1862, set in a pleasant rural location and boasting delightful views. Breakfast-cum-sitting room is filled with books and portraits; boldly coloured bedrooms are personally decorated by the friendly owners. Lovely mature gardens. Snug dining room offers traditional menus, serving 2 courses on weekdays and 5 on Saturdays.

BETWS-YN-RHOS – Conwy – **502** J24 – see Abergele

BODUAN – Gwynedd – see Pwllheli

BRECHFA – Carmarthenshire – **503** H28   33 B3
▶ London 216 mi – Cardiff 71 mi – Birmingham 183 mi – Liverpool 164 mi

Ty Mawr
⊠ SA32 7RA – ℰ (01267) 202 332 – www.wales-country-hotel.co.uk
6 rm ⊇ – †£ 70 ††£ 128
Rest – (dinner only) (booking essential) Menu £ 29
♦ 16C stone-built farmhouse set in the centre of the village, next to the river. Personally run, it boasts charm and character aplenty, with exposed brick, wooden beams, open fires, a comfortable lounge and spacious, pine-furnished bedrooms. Modern menu has a Welsh twist; produce is homemade or from the valley.

BRECON – Powys – **503** J28 – pop. 7 901   33 C3
▶ London 171 mi – Cardiff 40 mi – Carmarthen 31 mi – Gloucester 65 mi
🛈 Cattle Market Car Park ℰ (01874) 62 24 85, www.breconbeacons.org
⛳ Cradoc, Penoyre Park, ℰ (01874) 62 36 58
⛳ Newton Park Llanfaes, ℰ (01874) 62 20 04
◉ Town★ - Cathedral★ **AC** – Penyclawdd Court★
◉ Brecon Beacons National Park★★. Llanthony Priory★★, S : 8 mi of Hay-on-Wye by B 4423 - Dan-yr-Ogof Showcaves★ **AC**, SW : 20 mi by A 40 and A 4067 – Pen-y-Fan★★, SW : by A 470

Canal Bank without rest
Southeast : 0.5 mi by B 4601 turning right over bridge onto unmarked road after petrol station ⊠ LD3 7HG – ℰ (01874) 623 464
– www.accommodation-breconbeacons.co.uk
3 rm ⊇ – †£ 60/90 ††£ 98
♦ Delightfully stylish and peaceful 18C canalside cottage. Charming garden with pergola and access to River Usk. Organic breakfasts. Immaculate rooms with extra attention to detail.

BRECON

⌂ **Cantre Selyf** without rest
5 Lion St ✉ LD3 7AU – ℰ (01874) 622 904 – www.cantreselyf.co.uk – Closed Christmas and New Year
3 rm ⌑ – †£ 60 ††£ 90
♦ Charming, centrally located 17C townhouse with peaceful garden, period bedrooms and modern shower rooms. Contemporary colours blend with original Georgian features and antiques throughout.

⌂ **Felin Glais** ⌘
Aberyscir, West : 4 mi by Upper Chapel rd off Cradoc Golf Course rd turning right immediately after bridge ✉ LD3 9NP – ℰ (01874) 623 107 – www.felinglais.co.uk – Closed 25 December
4 rm ⌑ – †£ 85 ††£ 95 **Rest** – Menu £ 40 **s**
♦ 17C house and barn in tranquil hamlet. Spacious interior with pleasant 'lived in' feel; rooms filled with books and knick-knacks. Homely bedrooms; good toiletries; towels and bedding from Harrods. Owners interest in cooking is evident in the lengthy menu: order dinner two days ahead.

at Pwllgloyw Northwest : 4 mi on B 4520 (Upper Chapel rd) – ✉ Powys

🅟 **Felin Fach Griffin** with rm
Felin Fach, Northeast : 4.75 mi by B 4602 off A 470 ✉ LD3 0UB – ℰ (01874) 620 111 – www.felinfachgriffin.co.uk – Closed 25 December
7 rm ⌑ – †£ 75/85 ††£ 115 **Rest** – Menu £ 19/27 – Carte £ 25/33 ❀
♦ Rather unique pub with extremely laid back atmosphere. Following the motto "simple things, done well", dishes are straightforward, tasty and arrive in refined, well presented portions. Bedrooms boast super-comfy beds and excellent bedding.

WALES

BRIDGEND (Pen-y-Bont) – Bridgend – **503** J29 – pop. 39 429   **33** B4

▶ London 177 mi – Cardiff 20 mi – Swansea 23 mi
ℹ Bridgend Designer Outlet Village ℰ (01656) 65 49 06, www.bridgend.gov.uk

at Laleston West : 2 mi on A 473 – ✉ Bridgend

🏨 **Great House**
High St ✉ CF32 0HP – ℰ (01656) 657 644 – www.great-house-laleston.co.uk
12 rm ⌑ – †£ 85 ††£ 140
Rest *Leicester's* – (closed Sunday dinner and bank holidays) Menu £ 15/22 – Carte £ 22/50
♦ Welcoming 15C, Grade II listed property; the home of the Lordship of Laleston and reputedly a gift from Elizabeth I to the Earl of Leicester. Characterful bar and lounge. Individually styled bedrooms with extras; those in the coach house are most modern. Restaurant offers a seasonal menu of regional produce.

BWLCHTOCYN – Gwynedd – **502** G25 – see Abersoch

CAERNARFON – Gwynedd – **502** H24 – pop. 10 066   **32** B1

▶ London 249 mi – Birkenhead 76 mi – Chester 68 mi – Holyhead 30 mi
ℹ Castle St. ℰ (01286) 67 22 32, www.caernarfononline.co.uk
⛳ Aberforeshore Llanfaglan, ℰ (01286) 67 37 83
◉ Town★★ - Castle★★★ **AC**
◉ Snowdonia National Park★★★

Plas Dinas ⌘
South : 2 mi on A 487 ✉ LL54 7YF – ℰ (01286) 830 214 – www.plasdinas.co.uk – Closed Christmas and New Year
10 rm ⌑ – †£ 79/199 ††£ 89/250
Rest – (closed Sunday and Monday) (dinner only) (residents only) Menu £ 30
♦ Former family home of Lord Snowdon, set in large gardens and full of antiques, oils and family portraits. Spacious lounge with piano. Smart bedrooms boast designer touches and immaculate bathrooms. Café-style dining from concise menu of unfussy, hearty dishes.

CAERNARFON

at Seion Northeast : 5.5 mi by A 4086 and B 4366 on Seion rd – ✉ Gwynedd

XX **Ty'n Rhos Country House** with rm
Southwest : 0.25 mi ✉ LL55 3AE – ✆ (01248) 670 489 – www.tynrhos.co.uk
14 rm – †£ 65/120 ††£ 90/150
Rest – *(booking essential at lunch)* Menu £ 23/38 – Carte £ 25/38
♦ Formal restaurant with contemporary furnishings, French windows and views over Anglesey. Classic country house cooking uses local, seasonal produce to create hearty old favourites. Modern bedrooms, some with views/terraces.

at Groeslon South : 3 mi by A 487

⌂ **Y Goeden Eirin**
Dolydd, North : 0.5 mi ✉ LL54 7EF – ✆ (01286) 830 942
– www.ygoedeneirin.co.uk – Closed Christmas-New Year
3 rm – †£ 70 ††£ 90
Rest – Menu £ 28
♦ Attractive stone house between mountains and sea. Picture windows in lounge; interesting artwork and furniture. Charming bedrooms – those in annexe have stable doors and slate-floored bathrooms. Dining room boasts original oils, grand piano and fresh, seasonal dishes.

at Llandwrog South : 4.25 mi by A 487 on A 499

XX **Rhiwafallen** with rm
North : 1 mi on A 499 ✉ LL54 5SW – ✆ (01286) 830 172
– www.rhiwafallen.co.uk – Closed 25-26 December, 1 January, Sunday dinner and Monday
5 rm – †£ 80 ††£ 150
Rest – *(dinner only and Sunday lunch)* Menu £ 35
♦ 19C farmhouse run by enthusiastic young couple; dine in slate-floored conservatory with pleasant view. Seasonal, monthly changing menu; well presented, modern-style dishes based on classic combinations. Stylish, contemporary bedrooms, with bathrooms to match.

CAERSWS – Powys – **502** J26   **32** C2
▶ London 194 mi – Aberystwyth 39 mi – Chester 63 mi – Shrewsbury 42 mi

at Pontdolgoch Northwest : 1.5 mi on A 470 – ✉ Newtown

🛏 **Talkhouse** with rm
Newtown ✉ SY17 5JE – ✆ (01686) 688 919 – www.talkhouse.co.uk – Closed 2 weeks January, Monday and Tuesday
3 rm – †£ 70 ††£ 125
Rest – *(booking essential)* Carte £ 25/35
♦ 17C coaching inn with comfy lounge and cosy bar; dining room overlooks garden. Daily changing menu offers hearty portions and bold flavours. Cottage-style bedrooms with antique furniture; Myfanwy is the best.

CARDIFF

See city maps on following pages

Cardiff – pop. 316 793 – 503 K29 – Wales
▶ London 155 – Birmingham 110 – Bristol 46 – Coventry 124

Tourist Information

The Old Library, The Hayes, Working St ℰ(0870) 1 21 12 58, www.visitcardiff.com

Airport

Cardiff (Wales) Airport : ℰ (01446) 711111, SW : 8 m. by A 48 AX

Golf Courses

Dinas Powis Old Highwalls, ℰ(029) 2051 27 27

SIGHTS

In the town : City★★★ • National Museum and Gallery★★★ **AC** BY • Castle★ **AC** BZ • Llandaff Cathedral★ AV**B** • Cardiff Bay★ (Techniquest★ **AC**) AX
On the outskirts : Museum of Welsh Life★★ **AC**, St Fagan's, W : 5 mi by A 4161 AV • Castell Coch★★ **AC**, NW : 5 mi by A 470 AV
In the surrounding area : Caerphilly Castle★★ **AC**, N : 7 mi by A 469 AV • Dyffryn Gardens★ **AC**, W : 8 mi by A 48 AX

St David's H. & Spa
Havannah St, Cardiff Bay ⊠ CF10 5SD – ℰ (029) 2045 4045 – www.principal-hayley.com/thestdavids
CUa
120 rm – †£ 85/325 ††£ 114/600, ⊇ £ 18.50 – 12 suites
Rest *Tempus at Tides* – see restaurant listing
♦ Modern, purpose-built hotel set on the waterfront, affording lovely 360° views. Good-sized, minimalist bedrooms have a slightly funky feel; all boast balconies and bay outlooks. Smart spa features seawater pools and a dry floatation tank.

Hilton Cardiff
Kingsway ⊠ CF10 3HH – ℰ (029) 2064 6300 – www.hilton.co.uk/cardiff
193 rm – †£ 99/170 ††£ 120/170, ⊇ £ 18 – 4 suites
BZx
Rest *Razzi* – Menu £ 19/28
♦ Imposing former tax office in the city centre, with excellent views of the castle, law courts and city hall. Large atrium; well-equipped function rooms and leisure club. Spacious bedrooms offer good comforts – some have fabulous outlooks. Choice of bars. Conservatory style restaurant with international menu.

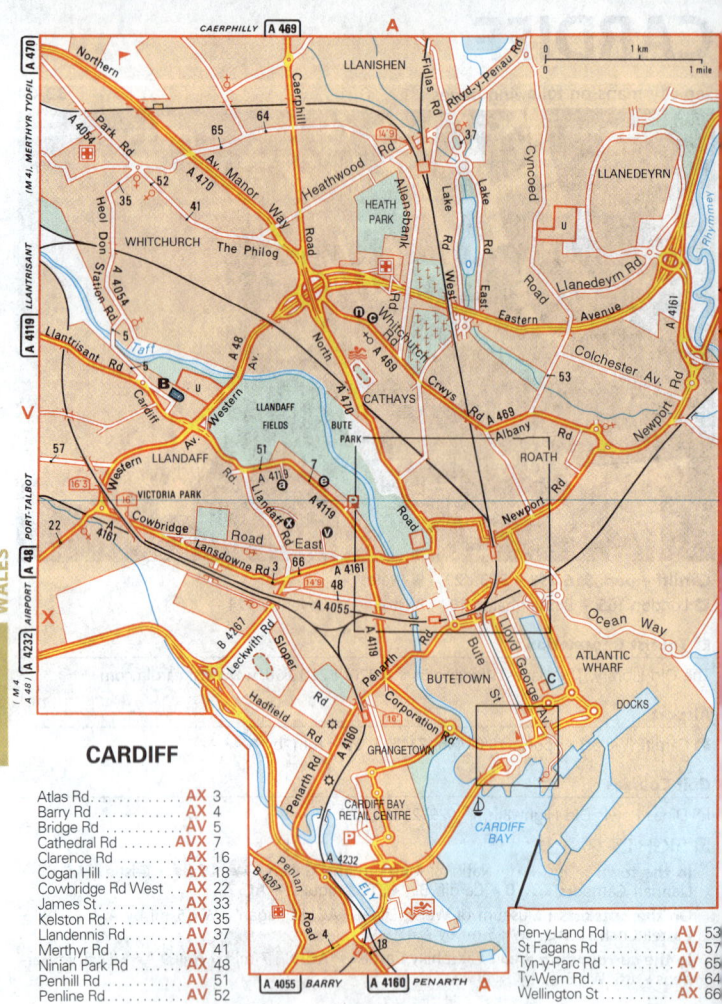

CARDIFF

Atlas Rd.	AX 3
Barry Rd	AX 4
Bridge Rd	AV 5
Cathedral Rd	AVX 7
Clarence Rd	AX 16
Cogan Hill	AX 18
Cowbridge Rd West	AX 22
James St.	AX 33
Kelston Rd.	AV 35
Llandennis Rd	AV 37
Merthyr Rd	AV 41
Ninian Park Rd	AX 48
Penhill Rd	AV 51
Penline Rd.	AV 52
Pen-y-Land Rd	AV 53
St Fagans Rd	AV 57
Tyn-y-Parc Rd	AV 65
Ty-Wern Rd.	AV 64
Wellington St	AX 66

Park Plaza

Greyfriars Rd ⊠ CF10 3AL – ℰ (029) 2011 1111
– www.parkplazacardiff.com
BYs
129 rm – ♦£89/280 ♦♦£99/290,
☐ £12.95

Rest *Laguna Kitchen and Bar* – ℰ (029) 2011 1103 – Menu £19 (lunch)
– Carte £17/36

♦ Formerly municipal offices, now a light, airy hotel with stylish lounge, extensive conference facilities and vast leisure centre boasting 8 treatment rooms. Modern bedrooms have international power sockets, laptop safes and slate bathrooms.

Street	Ref		Street	Ref		Street	Ref
pitol Centre	BZ		Greyfriars Rd	BY 29		Queen St	BZ
stle St	BZ 9		Guilford St	BZ 30		St Andrews	
hays Terrace	BY 10		Hayes (The)	BZ 32		Pl.	BY 56
ntral Square	BZ 12		High St	BZ		St-David's 2.	BZ
irch St	BZ 14		King Edward VII			St David's Centre	BZ
y Hall Rd	BY 15		Ave	BY 36		St John St	BZ 58
lege Rd	BY 20		Lloyd George Ave	BZ 38		St Mary St	BZ
bett Rd	BY 21		Mary Ann St	BZ 39		Station Terrace	BZ 61
stomhouse St	BZ 23		Moira Terrace	BZ 42		Stuttgarter	
vid St	BZ 25		Nantes (Boulevard de)	BY 44		Strasse	BY 62
ke St	BZ 26		Queens Arcade Shopping			Tresillian Way	BZ 63
mfries Pl.	BY 28		Centre	BZ 54		Working St	BZ 67

Radisson Blu Cardiff ⇐ 🛁 📶 ♿ rm, AC ✻ 🛜 🐾 🚭 VISA ⓪ AE ①

Meridian Gate, Bute Terr. ✉ *CF10 2FL*
– ☎ *(029) 2045 4777*
– *www. radissonblu.co.uk/hotel-cardiff*   BZ**a**

215 rm 🛏 – †£ 99/150 ††£ 120/240

Rest *Filini* – Italian – *(closed Sunday) (dinner only)*
Carte £ 19/46

♦ Large glass building in great central location. Spacious, modern guest areas, excellent meeting facilities and smart bar. Modern, slightly minimalist bedrooms in three styles – Fresh, Fashion and Chic – all boast slate-tiled bathrooms and city views. Simply furnished restaurant offers accessible Italian menu.

CARDIFF BAY

Britannia Quay .... **CU** 2	Clarence Embankment ... **CT** 8
Bute Crescent .... **CT** 4	Dudley St .... **CU** 9
	Hemingway Rd .... **CT** 12
	Lloyd George Ave ...... **CT** 14
Mermaid Quay Shopping Centre .... **CU**	Mount Stuart Square .... **CT**
	Pomeroy St. .... **CT**
	Windsor Esplanade ..... **CU**

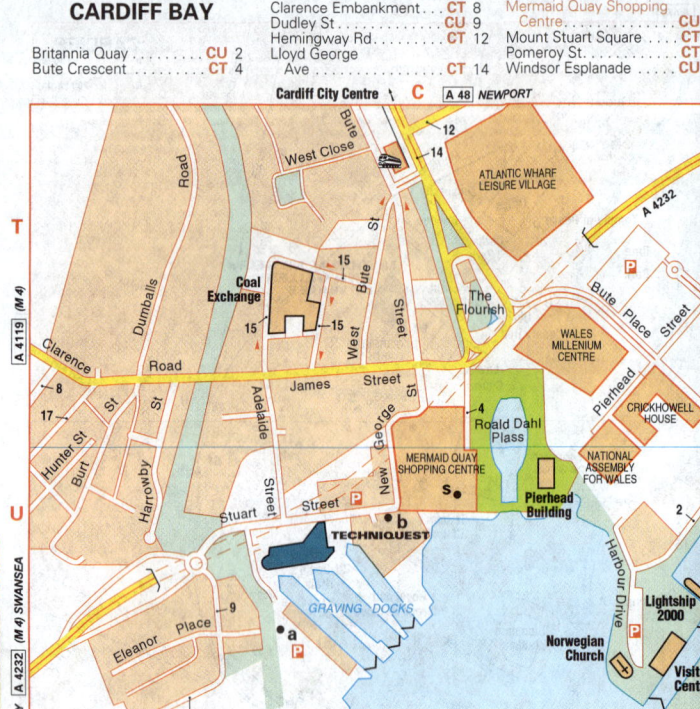

Parc
Park Pl ⊠ CF10 3UD – ℰ (0871) 376 9011 – www.thistle.com/theparchotel
139 rm – †£ 250/340 ††£ 350, ⌑ £ 15.95 – 1 suite   BZ**n**
Rest *Crown Social* – see restaurant listing
◆ Centrally located, commercial hotel hidden behind a Victorian façade. Marble-tiled lobby, fashionable bar and contemporary bedrooms with dark wood furnishings – modern art hangs on the walls. 3 large functions rooms; each has its own bar.

Lincoln House without rest
118-120 Cathedral Rd ⊠ CF11 9LQ – ℰ (029) 2039 5558
– www.lincolnhotel.co.uk
23 rm ⌑ – †£ 70/85 ††£ 90/110 – 1 suite   AV**e**
◆ Two lovingly restored houses with original features still in situ. Comfy bedrooms boast contemporary fabrics and wallpapers; some have period furniture/four-posters. Ultra-modern attic penthouse.

Tempus at Tides – at St David's Hotel & Spa
Havannah St, Cardiff Bay ⊠ CF10 5SD – ℰ (029) 2045 4045
– www.principal-hayley.com/thestdavids
Rest – Menu £ 26 – Carte £ 34/59   CU**a**
◆ Stylish hotel restaurant whose dining terrace affords stunning views out over the bay. Contemporary cooking displays international influences. Live entertainment towards the end of the week.

Crown Social – at Parc Hotel
Park Pl ⊠ CF10 3UD – ℰ (029) 2078 5593 – www.crownsocial.co.uk
Rest – Carte £ 20/34   BZ**n**

◆ Smart hotel restaurant with two dark-wood furnished dining areas and small private room showing live kitchen footage. Precise, well-presented and flavoursome dishes range from nibbles and sharing plates to 6 or 8 course on the tasting menu.

Woods Brasserie
The Pilotage Building, Stuart St, Cardiff Bay ⊠ CF10 5BW – ℰ (029) 2049 2400 – www.woods-brasserie.com – Closed 25-26 December, dinner Sunday October-June and bank holidays   CU**b**
Rest – *(booking essential at dinner)* Menu £ 18 (lunch) – Carte £ 29/38

◆ Modern brasserie dishes and European influences from an open kitchen. Bay view from the first floor terrace. Popular for business lunches and bay visitors in the evening.

Mint & Mustard
134 Whitchurch Rd ⊠ CF14 3LZ – ℰ (029) 2062 0333 – www.mintandmustard.com – Closed 25-26 December and Sunday
Rest – Indian – *(dinner only)* Carte £ 24/30   AV**n**

◆ Warm, welcoming Indian restaurant with modern, laid-back feel; a real hit with the locals. The keen chef-owner's training in Kerala is reflected in the extensive menu of original, authentic dishes. Spicing is subtle yet effective and combinations work well. Desserts are tasty and attractively presented.

Garçon
9 Upper Mermaid Quay ⊠ CF10 5BZ – ℰ (029) 2049 0990 – www.garcon-resto.co.uk – Closed first week January, 24-26 December, dinner Sunday and bank holiday Mondays   CU**s**
Rest – French – Menu £ 16 (lunch) – Carte £ 27/48

◆ Traditional French brasserie with a large marble-topped bar, mirrored panelling, powder blue banquettes and a pleasant terrace – set on the top floor of a quayside complex. Classical Gallic dishes with gutsy flavours; good value set menu.

Patagonia
11 Kings Rd ⊠ CF11 9BZ – ℰ (029) 2019 0265 – www.patagonia-restaurant.co.uk – Closed 24 December-18 January, Sunday and Monday   AX**v**
Rest – *(dinner only)* Menu £ 31

◆ Friendly neighbourhood restaurant set over two floors, with brightly coloured walls and eclectic artwork. Short menu offers wholesome and tasty modern European cooking.

'Bully's
5 Romilly Cres. ⊠ CF11 9NP – ℰ (029) 2022 1905 – www.bullysrestaurant.co.uk – Closed 1-10 January, 1-10 April, 27 August-4 September, 24-26 December, Sunday dinner, Monday and Tuesday   AX**x**
Rest – French – Menu £ 18 (weekday lunch) – Carte £ 24/51

◆ Welcoming neighbourhood bistro run by a passionate, hands-on owner. Simply furnished interior boasts a fascinating array of memorabilia. Classical cooking displays a strong Gallic edge; carefully prepared dishes feature quality ingredients.

chai st
132 Whitchurch Rd ⊠ CF14 3LZ – ℰ (029) 2062 0333 – www.chaistreet.com – Closed 25-26 December and Monday   AV**c**
Rest – Indian – *(lunch only)* Carte £ 13/16

◆ Trendy, vibrant sister to Mint & Mustard, with modern Bollywood pop art and bold printed canvases on the walls. Keen, helpful team serve excellent value Indian street food. Highlights are the large, daily changing 'Thali' platters: tapas-style portions served in small stainless steel dishes on a large tray.

CARDIFF

New Conway
53 Conway Rd ⊠ CF11 9NW – ℰ (029) 2022 4373 – www.theconway.co.uk
Rest – Carte £ 25/34
AVa
♦ Neighbourhood pub with pleasingly simple approach to food which sees fresh, seasonal, local produce used to create tasty pub classics like toad in the hole or apple and raisin crumble.

at Penarth South : 3 mi by A 4160 - AX – ⊠ Cardiff

Holm House
Marine Par ⊠ CF64 3BG – ℰ (029) 2070 1572 – www.holmhouse.com
12 rm ⊆ – †£ 120 ††£ 425
Rest *Neale's* – *(dinner only and lunch Friday-Sunday)* Menu £ 20 (lunch)
– Carte £ 35/44
♦ Built in 1920s for son of local shipbuilder. Part art deco, part modern styling, displaying flock wallpapers and bold colours; some bedrooms boast feature baths and oversized windows. Restaurant with views to distant Holm Islands; weekly menus of simple, wholesome combinations.

Olive Tree
21 Glebe St ⊠ CF64 1EE – ℰ (029) 2070 7077 – www.the-olive-tree.net
– Closed 25-27 December, Sunday dinner and Monday
Rest – *(dinner only and Sunday lunch)* Menu £ 23 (weekday dinner)
– Carte £ 27/38
♦ Rewarding discovery tucked away in the centre of town. Relaxing feel augmented by vivid artwork. Warm, friendly service of good value, seasonal, frequently changing dishes.

WALES

CARMARTHEN – Carmarthenshire – 503 H28 – pop. 14 648   33 B3
▶ London 219 mi – Fishguard 47 mi – Haverfordwest 32 mi – Swansea 27 mi
🛈 113 Lammas St ℰ (01267) 23 15 57, www.visitcarmarthenshire.co.uk
◉ Kidwelly Castle ★ – National Botanic Garden ★

at Felingwm Uchaf Northeast : 8 mi by A 40 on B 4310 – ⊠ Carmarthen

Allt y Golau Uchaf without rest
North : 0.5 mi on B 4310 ⊠ SA32 7BB – ℰ (01267) 290 455
– www.alltygolau.com – Closed 20 December-2 January
3 rm ⊆ – †£ 45 ††£ 68
♦ Georgian farmhouse rebuilt in Victorian times, up a steep slope on a 2 acre smallholding. Well-kept, rustic interior. Neat, pine-furnished bedrooms with homely feel. Extensive breakfast features local meats and eggs from the hens out back.

at Llanllawddog Northeast : 8 mi by A485

Glangwili Mansion without rest
⊠ SA32 7JE – ℰ (01267) 253 735 – www.glangwilimansion.co.uk – Closed 24-25, 31 December and 1 January
3 rm – †£ 90/100 ††£ 125/135
♦ Part-16C mansion rebuilt in Georgian style, in a great location on the edge of the forest. Spacious, modern interior with sleek tiled floors and modern art. Airy lounge and breakfast room; bright, bold bedrooms with modern oak furnishings.

at Nantgaredig East : 5 mi on A 40 – ⊠ Carmarthen

Y Polyn
South : 1 mi on B 4310 ⊠ SA32 7LH – ℰ (01267) 290 000
– www.ypolynrestaurant.co.uk – Closed Sunday dinner and Monday
Rest – Menu £ 15/30 – Carte £ 21/30
♦ Welcoming dining pub in a great rural location by a stream. Hearty, wholesome dishes are classically based with modern touches. À la carte or 'express' lunch and fixed price dinners.

CEMAES – 502 G23 – see Anglesey (Isle of)

CLYNNOG-FAWR – Gwynedd – pop. 100   32 B1
▶ London 273 mi – Cardiff 179 mi – Dublin 47 mi – Birmingham 148 mi

Y Beuno with rm   rest, P VISA ⦿ ⓓ
✉ LL54 5PB – ☎ (01286) 660 785 – www.ybeuno.com – *Restricted opening in winter*
7 rm ⊡ – †£75/85 ††£105/135
Rest – *(closed lunch Monday-Thursday in low season)* Carte £ 23/34
♦ Sizeable pub set close to the coast, with delightfully rustic bar and series of snug, homely rooms. Experienced French chef – choose a classic Gallic daily special or in summer, a fresh, unfussy seafood dish. Bedrooms are comfy and modern; some boast bay views.

COLWYN BAY (Bae Colwyn) – Conwy – 502 I24 – pop. 30 269   32 B1
▶ London 237 mi – Birkenhead 50 mi – Chester 42 mi – Holyhead 41 mi
🛈 Information Point, Cayley Promenade, Rhos-on-Sea ☎ (01492) 54 87 78, www.ukinformationcentre.com/north-wales
🏌 Abergele Tan-y-Goppa Rd, ☎ (01745) 82 40 34
🏌 Old Colwyn Woodland Ave, ☎ (01492) 51 55 81
◉ Welsh Mountain Zoo★ **AC** (≤★)
◉ Bodnant Garden★★ **AC**, SW : 6 mi by A 55 and A 470

Rathlin Country House without rest   🛏 ⊠ 🐾 ⌘ 🍽 P VISA ⦿
48 Kings Rd, Southwest : 0.25 mi on B 5113 ✉ LL29 7YH – ☎ (01492) 532 173 – www.rathlincountryhouse.co.uk – *Closed 24-25 December*
3 rm ⊡ – †£69/75 ††£85/95
♦ Large Arts and Crafts house set in mature gardens, boasting ornate ceilings, leaded windows, oak panelling and parquet floors. Outdoor pool and sauna. Individually furnished bedrooms display modern touches; one even has a steam shower. Extensive breakfast menu.

Pen-y-Bryn   🛏 🍽 P VISA ⦿ AE
Pen-y-Bryn Rd, Upper Colwyn Bay., Southwest : 1 mi by B 5113 ✉ LL29 6DD – ☎ (01492) 533 360 – www.penybryn-colwynbay.co.uk – *Closed 25 December*
Rest – Carte £ 17/24
♦ Modern, laid-back pub set on a residential street; its unassuming façade concealing impressive bay views. Extensive all-day menu ranges from pub classics to more adventurous fare.

at Rhos-on-Sea Northwest : 1 mi – ✉ Colwyn Bay

Plas Rhos without rest   ≤ ⌘ 🍽 P VISA ⦿ AE
Cayley Promenade ✉ LL28 4EP – ☎ (01492) 543 698 – www.plasrhos.co.uk – *February-mid-December*
7 rm ⊡ – †£50/75 ††£90/100
♦ 19C house on first promenade from Colwyn Bay. Homely front lounge with bay view. Breakfasts feature local butcher's produce. Immaculately kept rooms: superior ones to front.

CONWY – Conwy – 502 I24 – pop. 3 847   32 B1
▶ London 241 mi – Caernarfon 22 mi – Chester 46 mi – Holyhead 37 mi
🛈 Conwy Castle Visitor Centre ☎ (01492) 59 22 48, www.touristnetuk.com/wa/northwales
🏌 Penmaenmawr Conway Old Rd, ☎ (01492) 62 33 30
◉ Town★★ - Castle★★ **AC** – Town Walls★★ - Plas Mawr★★
◉ Snowdonia National Park★★★ – Bodnant Garden★★ **AC**, S : 8 mi by A 55 and A 470 – Conwy Crossing (suspension bridge★)

809

CONWY

Castle
High St ⊠ LL32 8DB – ℰ (01492) 582 800 – www.castlewales.co.uk
– Closed 2-10 January
27 rm ⊇ – †£ 89/166 ††£ 160/166 – 1 suite
Rest *Dawson's* – (closed to non-residents dinner 25 December) Carte £ 27/41
♦ Adjoining brick and flint coaching inns within walled town, on site of former Cistercian abbey. Comfy firelit country house sitting room; mix of classic/modern bedrooms. Some castle views. Contemporary dining room offers extensive menu of brasserie classics.

Signatures
Northwest 1 mi by A 55 ⊠ LL32 8GA – ℰ (01492) 583 513
– www.signaturesrestaurant.co.uk – Closed Monday and Tuesday
Rest – (dinner only) (booking advisable) Menu £ 24 (weekdays) – Carte £ 30/40
♦ Unusually set on an upmarket static caravan site. Smart dining room boasts flocked wallpapers and elegantly laid, polished tables. All-encompassing menu offers a daily set selection and signature dishes are marked out. Well-versed team.

Groes Inn with rm
South : 3 mi on B 5106 ⊠ LL32 8TN – ℰ (01492) 650 545 – www.groesinn.com
– Closed 25 December
14 rm ⊇ – †£ 95/105 ††£ 160/190 **Rest** – Carte £ 18/42
♦ Characterful inn, beautifully set overlooking the estuary, in the foothills of Snowdonia. Local Welsh and British dishes arrive in neat, generous portions; more adventurous restaurant menu. Tastefully styled bedrooms boasts views; some have terraces and balconies.

at Llansanffraid Glan Conwy Southeast : 2.5 mi by A 547 on A 470
– ⊠ Conwy

Old Rectory Country House without rest
Llanrwst Rd ⊠ LL28 5LF – ℰ (01492) 580 611
– www.oldrectorycountryhouse.co.uk – Closed 24-25 and 31 December
5 rm ⊇ – †£ 99/119 ††£ 99/159
♦ Personally run country house with attractive gardens and estuary views. Beautifully furnished Georgian-style sitting room displays china and antiques. Bedrooms, split between the house and annexe, boast comfy feature beds and luxury bathrooms. Good breakfasts.

at Rowen South : 3.5 mi by B 5106

Tir Y Coed
⊠ LL32 8TP – ℰ (01492) 650 219 – www.tirycoed.com
7 rm ⊇ – †£ 110 ††£ 125/175 **Rest** – (dinner only) Menu £ 37
♦ In secluded valley at foothills of Snowdonia, with balcony terrace overlooking mature garden. Tastefully furnished bedrooms. Intimate, candlelit dining room features fine collection of Victorian lithographs. Daily changing menu reflects the best of local produce.

COWBRIDGE (Y Bont Faen) – The Vale of Glamorgan – 503 J29   33 B4
– pop. 3 616
London 170 mi – Cardiff 15 mi – Swansea 30 mi

Huddarts
69 High St ⊠ CF71 7AF – ℰ (01446) 774 645 – www.huddartsrestaurant.co.uk
– Closed 26 December-9 January, 1 week spring, 1 week autumn, Sunday dinner and Monday
Rest – Menu £ 26 (lunch) – Carte dinner £ 28/32
♦ Honest restaurant on high street of an ancient market town; husband cooks and wife looks after the friendly service. Traditional décor with a stone fireplace and Welsh tapestries. Carefully executed, classical dishes and good presentation.

CRICCIETH – Gwynedd – **502** H25 – pop. 1 826 — 32 B2

▶ London 249 mi – Caernarfon 17 mi – Shrewsbury 85 mi
🏨 Ednyfed Hill, ☏ (01766) 52 21 54
◉ Lleyn Peninsula★★ – Ffestiniog Railway★★

🏠 Mynydd Ednyfed Country House
Caernarfon Rd, Northwest : 0.75 mi on B 4411 ✉ *LL52 0PH* – ☏ *(01766) 523 269*
– *www.cricceith.net* – *Closed 22 December-5 January*
8 rm 🛏 – †£ 70/75 ††£ 98/120 **Rest** – *(dinner only)* Carte £ 20/29

♦ Cosy, personally run 17C country house in eight acres of gardens and woodland. Traditional bedrooms – some with four-posters and fine bay views; all with stylish modern bathrooms. Dinner served in conservatory, which also boasts great outlook.

CRICKHOWELL (Crucywel) – Powys – **503** K28 – pop. 2 166 — 33 C4

▶ London 169 mi – Abergavenny 6 mi – Brecon 14 mi – Cardiff 40 mi
🏨 Beaufort St ☏ (01873) 81 19 70, www.crickhowellinfo.org.uk
◉ Brecon Beacons National Park★★. Llanthony Priory★★, NE : 10 mi by minor roads

🏠🏠🏠 Gliffaes Country House
West : 3.75 mi by A 40 ✉ *NP8 1RH* – ☏ *(01874) 730 371*
– *www.gliffaeshotel.com* – *Closed 2 January-1 February*
23 rm 🛏 – †£ 93/115 ††£ 248
Rest – *(light lunch Monday-Saturday)* Menu £ 39 **s**

♦ Impressive country house built in 1886 in semi-Italianate style, set in 32 acres of delightful grounds that lead down to the river. Spacious, well-appointed lounges and great views from terrace. Smart, individually styled bedrooms; some with balconies. Victorian-style restaurant; menus showcase Welsh produce.

WALES

🏠🏠 Bear

High St ✉ *NP8 1BW* – ☏ *(01873) 810 408* – *www.bearhotel.co.uk* – *Closed 25 December*
34 rm (dinner included) 🛏 – †£ 75/126 ††£ 92/163 – 1 suite
Rest *Bear* – see restaurant listing

♦ Well-maintained 15C coaching inn full of nooks and crannies. Comfortable bedrooms, some with jacuzzis; most characterful are in main house and feature beams, four-posters and fireplaces.

🏠 Glangrwyney Court
Southeast : 2 mi on A 40 ✉ *NP8 1ES* – ☏ *(01873) 811 288*
– *www.glancourt.co.uk*
5 rm 🛏 – †£ 65/95 ††£ 130/145 **Rest** – Carte £ 31/35

♦ Passionately run guesthouse with large lounge and high-ceilinged breakfast room. Fresh flowers and objets d'art cover every surface. Bedrooms boasts rich fabrics, good facilities and country views. Dinner by arrangement or transport to the local pub arranged.

🏠 Ty Gwyn *without rest*

Brecon Rd ✉ *NP8 1DG* – ☏ *(01873) 811 625* – *www.tygwyn.com*
– *February-November*
3 rm 🛏 – †£ 45/50 ††£ 75

♦ A homely place boasting spotlessly kept, simply furnished bedrooms, with comfort and character. Well-tended garden with stream. Enthusiastic owner has vast local knowledge.

🍴 Bear
High St ✉ *NP8 1BW* – ☏ *(01873) 810 408* – *www.bearhotel.co.uk* – *Closed 25 December*
Rest – Carte £ 22/35

♦ Keenly run coaching inn serving classical, tried-and-tested menu available both in characterful bar and more formal restaurant. Swift, assured service from young, cheery team.

CROSS ASH – Monmouthshire – see Abergavenny

CROSSGATES – Powys – 503 J27 – see Llandrindod Wells

DEGANWY – Conwy – 502 I24 – see Llandudno

DOLFOR – Powys – 503 K26
32 C2
▶ London 199 – Cardiff 93 – Oswestry 34 – Ludlow 39

Old Vicarage
North : 1.5 mi by A 483 ✉ *SY16 4BN* – ✆ *(01686) 629 051*
– www.theoldvicaragedolfor.co.uk
4 rm – †£ 65/75 ††£ 95/110   **Rest** – Menu £ 25/30
◆ Characterful 19C detached house with large gardens; formerly a vicarage. Cosy bedrooms, named after nearby rivers, mix period furniture with modern colours. Concise menu of home-cooked dishes features local produce and veg from garden. Preserves/chutneys for sale.

DOLGELLAU – Gwynedd – 502 I25 – pop. 2 407
32 B2
▶ London 221 mi – Birkenhead 72 mi – Chester 64 mi – Shrewsbury 57 mi
🛈 Eldon Sq ✆ (01341) 42 28 88, www.dolgellau-snowdonia.co.uk
⛳ Hengwrt Estate Pencefn Rd, ✆ (01341) 42 26 03
◉ Town★
Snowdonia National Park★★★ - Cadair Idris★★★ - Precipice Walk★, NE : 3 mi on minor roads

Penmaenuchaf Hall
Penmaenpool, West : 1.75 mi on A 493 (Tywyn Rd) ✉ *LL40 1YB* – ✆ *(01341) 422 129 – www.penhall.co.uk – Closed 12-22 December and 4-19 January*
14 rm – †£ 100/150 ††£ 250   **Rest** – Menu £ 19/43 – Carte £ 43/49
◆ Personally run Victorian house with wood panelling, ornate ceilings and original stained glass. Country house style bedrooms; some with balconies. Beautiful grounds and superb mountain and estuary views. Friendly staff and family feel. Formal conservatory dining room with garden outlook.

Ffynnon without rest
Love Ln, (off Cader Rd) ✉ *LL40 1RR* – ✆ *(01341) 421 774*
– www.ffynnontownhouse.com
6 rm – †£ 130 ††£ 175
◆ A haven of luxury; lovingly restored and modernised, yet retaining many original features. Stylish sitting room and spacious, tastefully decorated suites, boasting every mod con.

Tyddyn Mawr without rest
Islawdref, Cader Rd, Southwest : 2.5 mi by Tywyn rd on Cader Idris rd
✉ *LL40 1TL* – ✆ *(01341) 422 331 – www.wales-guesthouse.co.uk*
– February-November
3 rm – †£ 55 ††£ 78
◆ Set on secluded working sheep farm, stunningly situated beneath Cader Idris mountain. Immaculate bedrooms boast superb views and plenty of extras; one has a balcony, another, a terrace. Five course breakfast taken beside impressive inglenook. Great hospitality.

at Llanelltyd Northwest : 2.25 mi by A 470 on A 496

Mawddach
✉ *LL40 2TA* – ✆ *(01341) 424 020 – www.mawddach.com – Closed 2 weeks November, 1 week January, 1 week spring, Sunday dinner, Monday and Tuesday*
Rest – Carte £ 26/32
◆ Stylish barn conversion on family farm. First floor dining room with huge glass wall and superb view. Straightforward cooking uses beef and lamb from the farm; more adventurous dinner menu.

EAST ABERTHAW (Aberddawan) – The Vale of Glamorgan – 503 J29 – ✉ Barry 33 B-C4
▶ London 180 mi – Cardiff 20 mi – Swansea 33 mi

Blue Anchor Inn P VISA ⦿
✉ CF62 3DD – ☏ (01446) 750 329 – www.blueanchoraberthaw.com
– Closed Sunday dinner
Rest – Carte £ 17/28
♦ Thatched stone-built pub dating back to 1380, with characterful bar and vast upstairs restaurant. Traditional, wholesome dishes boast straightforward presentation and plenty of flavour.

FELINGWM UCHAF – Carmarthenshire – see Carmarthen

FISHGUARD – Pembrokeshire – 503 F28 – pop. 3 193 33 A3
▶ London 265 mi – Cardiff 114 mi – Gloucester 176 mi – Holyhead 169 mi
⛴ to Republic of Ireland (Rosslare) (Stena Line) 2-4 daily (1 h 50 mn/3 h 30 mn)
ℹ The Square ☏ (01437) 77 66 36, www.visitpembrokeshire.com
⊚ Pembrokeshire Coast National Park★★

Manor Town House without rest
11 Main St ✉ SA65 9HG – ☏ (01348) 873 260 – www.manortownhouse.com
– Closed 24-26 December
6 rm ⊐ – †£ 60/75 ††£ 105/165
♦ Well-run, listed Georgian townhouse, boasting fabulous harbour views from its garden. Cosy lounges and personally styled, antique-furnished bedrooms; some art deco, some Victorian. Tasty breakfast includes a waffle menu. Charming owners.

WALES

GRESFORD = Groes-ffordd – Wrexham – 502 L24 – see Wrexham

GROESLON – Gwynedd – see Caernarfon

HARLECH – Gwynedd – 502 H25 – pop. 1 233 32 B2
▶ London 241 mi – Chester 72 mi – Dolgellau 21 mi
ℹ High St ☏ (01766) 78 06 58, www.harlech-snowdonia.co.uk
⛳ Royal St David's, ☏ (01766) 78 02 03
⊚ Castle★★ **AC**
⊚ Snowdonia National Park★★★

Castle Cottage with rm VISA ⦿
Pen Llech, by B 4573 ✉ LL46 2YL – ☏ (01766) 780 479
– www.castlecottageharlech.co.uk – Closed 2 weeks November
7 rm ⊐ – †£ 85 ††£ 170
Rest – (dinner only) (booking essential) Menu £ 39
♦ Attractive cottage behind Harlech Castle, with cosy yet surprisingly contemporary interior. Classical, daily changing menus display passionately sourced local produce and modern touches. Bedrooms are spacious and comfy; some boast stunning castle/mountain views.

HAVERFORDWEST (Hwlffordd) – Pembrokeshire – 503 F28 33 A3
– pop. 13 367
▶ London 250 mi – Fishguard 15 mi – Swansea 57 mi
ℹ Old Bridge ☏ (01437) 76 31 10, www.visitpembrokeshire.com
⛳ Arnolds Down, ☏ (01437) 76 35 65
⊚ Scolton Museum and Country Park★
⊚ Pembrokeshire Coast National Park★★. Skomer Island and Skokholm Island★, SW : 14 mi by B 4327 and minor roads

HAVERFORDWEST

Lower Haythog Farm
Spittal, Northeast : 5 mi on B 4329 ✉ *SA62 5QL –* ☎ *(01437) 731 279*
– www.lowerhaythogfarm.co.uk
5 rm – †£ 45/65 ††£ 75/85 **Rest** – Menu £ 25
♦ Friendly atmosphere, traditional comforts and a warm welcome at this 250 acre working dairy farm with accessible woodland walks. Well-kept and comfortable throughout. Dining room in homely, country style reflected in hearty, home-cooked food.

Paddock
Northeast : 5 mi on B 4329 ✉ *SA62 5QL –* ☎ *(01437) 731 531*
– www.thepaddockwales.co.uk
3 rm – †£ 55/70 ††£ 75/90 **Rest** – Menu £ 28
♦ Very modern new build guesthouse set on working farm; minimalist ground floor bedrooms feature chunky furniture and Egyptian cotton bedding. Comfy lounge with books, magazines and board games. Set 2 or 3 course dinner makes good use of local produce.

HAY-ON-WYE (Y Gelli) – Powys – 503 K27 – pop. 1 846   33 C3

▶ London 154 mi – Brecon 16 mi – Cardiff 59 mi – Hereford 21 mi
🛈 Oxford Rd ☎ (01497) 82 01 44, www.hay-on-wye.co.uk
 Rhosgoch Builth Wells, ☎ (01497) 85 12 51
◉ Town ★
◉ Brecon Beacons National Park ★★. Llanthony Priory ★★, SE : 12 mi by minor roads

Old Black Lion with rm
26 Lion St ✉ *HR3 5AD –* ☎ *(01497) 820 841 – www.oldblacklion.co.uk – Closed 24-26 December*
10 rm – †£ 53/70 ††£ 90 **Rest** – Carte £ 23/34
♦ Characterful part-13C inn with lots of old world charm. Traditional menu offers tasty, honest dishes, hearty portions and plenty of choice, with more favourites on the board. Bedrooms boast either antique furnishings or rich colours and modern bathrooms.

Three Tuns
4 Broad St ✉ *HR3 5DB –* ☎ *(01497) 821 855 – www.three-tuns.com*
Rest – *(closed 25 December)* Carte £ 22/32
♦ Grade II listed 16C pub, reputedly the oldest building in town. Wide-ranging menus: bar and terrace offer blackboard classics; formal upstairs dining room comes into its own in the evening.

HOWEY – Powys – see Llandrindod Wells

KNIGHTON (Trefyclawdd) – Powys – 503 K26 – pop. 2 851   33 C3

▶ London 162 mi – Birmingham 59 mi – Hereford 31 mi – Shrewsbury 35 mi
🛈 West St ☎ (01547) 52 87 53, www.visitknighton.co.uk
Ffrydd Wood, ☎ (01547) 52 86 46
◉ Town ★
◉ Offa's Dyke ★, NW : 9.5 m

Milebrook House
Ludlow Rd, Milebrook, East : 2 mi on A 4113 ✉ *LD7 1LT –* ☎ *(01547) 528 632*
– www.milebrookhouse.co.uk – Closed December-February
10 rm (dinner included) – †£ 114 ††£ 194
Rest – *(closed Sunday dinner and Monday lunch)* Menu £ 19/34 – Carte £ 31/35
♦ Part-Georgian dower house located in the Teme Valley; once home to explorer Wilfred Thesiger. Several well-appointed lounges; spacious, comfortable bedrooms furnished in country house style. Superb formal gardens boast lovely exotic plants. Traditional restaurant with menu showcasing kitchen garden produce.

LAKE VYRNWY – Powys – 502 J25 – ✉ Llanwddyn 32 C2

▶ London 204 mi – Chester 52 mi – Llanfyllin 10 mi – Shrewsbury 40 mi
🛈 The Shop in the Corner, Vyrnwy Craft Workshops ✆ (01691) 87 03 46, www.lake-vyrnwy.com
◉ Lake★

Lake Vyrnwy
✉ SY10 0LY – ✆ (01691) 870 692 – www.lakevyrnwyhotel.com
51 rm – †£ 116/126 ††£ 213/225 – 1 suite
Rest – Menu £ 40 (dinner) **s** – Carte lunch £ 19/26 **s**
Rest *Tavern* – Carte £ 19/26 **s**
♦ Victorian country house, stunningly located overlooking Lake Vyrnwy and a sporting estate. Bedrooms range in style – most are traditionally furnished and some have balconies; one even has a roll-top bath looking down the lake. Restaurant opens out onto a terrace and offers classical menus, while the Tavern serves informal pub favourites.

LALESTON – Bridgend – 503 J29 – see Bridgend

LAMPHEY = Llandyfai – Pembrokeshire – 503 F28 – see Pembroke

LLANARMON DYFFRYN CEIRIOG – Wrexham – 502 K25 32 C2
– ✉ Llangollen (denbighshire)

▶ London 196 mi – Chester 33 mi – Shrewsbury 32 mi

Hand at Llanarmon with rm
✉ LL20 7LD – ✆ (01691) 600 666 – www.thehandhotel.co.uk
13 rm ⌑ – †£ 50/70 ††£ 108/128 **Rest** – Menu £ 20 – Carte £ 21/33
♦ Rustic, personally run inn providing a warm welcome and wholesome meals to travellers through the lush Ceiriog Valley. Generous portions of fresh, flavoursome cooking. Cosy bedrooms with hill views and modernised bathrooms.

LLANDDERFEL – Gwynedd – pop. 4 500 32 C2

▶ London 210 mi – Cardiff 157 mi – Birmingham 97 mi – Liverpool 72 mi

Palé Hall
Palé Estate – ✆ (01678) 530 285 – www.palehall.co.uk – *Closed January*
15 rm ⌑ – †£ 90/155 ††£ 125/210 – 2 suites **Rest** – Menu £ 25/38
♦ Mid-Victorian house boasting fine oil paintings and Scottish hunting lodge feel, set in 17 acres of parkland. Beautiful wood-panelled hall and traditional lounges. Bedrooms boast period fireplaces and antique furniture. Elegant dining room offers classical menu.

LLANDDEWI SKIRRID – Monmouthshire – see Abergavenny

LLANDEILO – Carmarthenshire – 503 I28 – pop. 1 731 33 B3

▶ London 218 mi – Brecon 34 mi – Carmarthen 15 mi – Swansea 25 mi
◉ Town★ - Dinefwr Park★ **AC**
ⓖ Brecon Beacons National Park★★ – Black Mountain★, SE : by minor roads – Carreg Cennen Castle★ **AC**, SE : 4 mi by A 483 and minor roads

Plough Inn
Rhosmaen, Northeast : 1 mi on A 40 ✉ SA19 6NP – ✆ (01558) 823 431
– www.ploughrhosmaen.com – *Closed 26 December*
14 rm ⌑ – †£ 70 ††£ 90 **Rest** – Menu £ 16/19 – Carte £ 17/25
♦ Powder blue building boasting contemporary interior and pleasant country views to the rear. Modern bedrooms are spacious, comfy and well-equipped: deluxe rooms have whirlpool baths. Snacks and light lunches in the conservatory; more substantial dinners served in the vaulted restaurant.

WALES

LLANDEILO

Fronlas without rest
7 Thomas St. ✉ *SA19 6LB* – ☏ *(01558) 824 733* – www.fronlas.com
4 rm ⌑ – †£ 80/100 ††£ 100/120
• Old Edwardian house furnished in a very contemporary, minimalist style. Smart bedrooms display funky wallpapers, bold fabrics and stylish bathrooms. They operates a sustainable ethos with solar panels, recycling bins and organic breakfasts.

LLANDENNY – Monmouthshire – 503 L28 – see Usk

LLANDOVERY – Carmarthenshire – 503 I28 – pop. 2 235 — 33 B3
▶ London 207 mi – Cardiff 61 mi – Swansea 37 mi – Merthyr Tydfil 34 mi

New White Lion
43 Stone St ✉ *SA20 0BZ* – ☏ *(01550) 720 685* – www.newwhitelion.co.uk
– *Closed 25-27 December*
6 rm ⌑ – †£ 80 ††£ 120
Rest – *(dinner only) (booking essential residents only)* Menu £ 28
• Laid-back, Grade II listed former pub set in a small town; now a stylish hotel. Comfortable lounge with honesty bar. Smart, individually designed bedrooms are named after folklore characters and boast contemporary fabrics and furnishings. Cosy, designer dining room where menus feature local, seasonal produce.

LLANDRILLO – Denbighshire – 502 J25 – pop. 1 048 – ✉ Corwen — 32 C2
▶ London 210 mi – Chester 40 mi – Dolgellau 26 mi – Shrewsbury 46 mi

Tyddyn Llan (Bryan Webb) with rm
✉ *LL21 0ST* – ☏ *(01490) 440 264* – www.tyddynllan.co.uk – *Closed last 2 weeks January*
13 rm (dinner included) ⌑ – †£ 150 ††£ 300
Rest – *(dinner only and lunch Friday-Sunday) (booking essential)*
Menu £ 35/50
Spec. Dressed crab with fennel and pea shoot salad. Local pork 4 ways with shallot and thyme purée. Panna cotta with blood orange and Grappa.
• Personally run country house with pretty gardens. Dine in one of two spacious rooms. Menu offers considerable choice; cooking is classical in style and dishes are expertly balanced, using sensible combinations. Tidy, well-equipped bedrooms.

LLANDRINDOD WELLS – Powys – 503 J27 – pop. 5 024 — 33 C3
▶ London 204 mi – Brecon 29 mi – Carmarthen 60 mi – Shrewsbury 58 mi
🛈 Memorial Gardens ☏(01597) 82 26 00, www.llandrindod.co.uk
🛈 Llandrindod Wells The Clubhouse, ☏(01597) 82 38 73
◉ Elan Valley★★ (Dol-y-Mynach and Claerwen Dam and Reservoir★★, Caban Coch Dam and Reservoir★, Garreg-ddu Viaduct★, Pen-y-Garreg Reservoir and Dam★, Craig Goch Dam and Reservoir★), NW : 12 mi by A 4081, A 470 and B 4518

Metropole
Temple St ✉ *LD1 5DY* – ☏ *(01597) 823 700* – www.metropole.co.uk
112 rm ⌑ – †£ 82/111 ††£ 105/125 – 2 suites
Rest *Radnor* – *(dinner only)* Menu £ 24 s – Carte £ 25/32 s
Rest *Spencer's* – Carte £ 23/28 s
• Brightly painted hotel run for many years by the Baird-Murray family. Some modern bedrooms, others more traditional; the tower rooms are particularly popular. Swimming pool is in the Victorian-style conservatory. Dishes in formal Radnor showcase local produce. Contemporary bar and brasserie offers an all-day menu.

at Crossgates Northeast : 3.5 mi on A 483 – ✉ Llandrindod Wells

Guidfa House without rest
✉ *LD1 6RF* – ☏ *(01597) 851 241* – www.guidfahouse.co.uk
6 rm ⌑ – †£ 65/90 ††£ 85/95
• Georgian gentlemen's residence with pleasant garden, smart breakfast room and period lounge displaying an original cast iron rose on the ceiling. Bright, airy bedrooms; the best is in the coach house. Friendly owners serve tea on arrival.

LLANDRINDOD WELLS

at Howey South : 1.5 mi by A 483 – ✉ Llandrindod Wells

Acorn Court Country House without rest
Chapel Rd, Northeast : 0.5 mi ✉ *LD1 5PB* – ✆ *(01597) 823 543*
– www.acorncourt.co.uk – Closed 25-26 December
3 rm ⌑ – †£ 38/60 ††£ 70/78
• Chalet-style house in 35 acres, with views over rolling countryside towards the river and lake. Welcoming owner and real family feel. Simple lounge and breakfast room; spacious, well-kept bedrooms with extras. Try the Welsh whisky porridge.

LLANDUDNO – Conwy – **502** I24 – pop. 15 250   32 B1

▶ London 243 mi – Birkenhead 55 mi – Chester 47 mi – Holyhead 43 mi
🛈 Mostyn St ✆ (01492) 57 75 77, www.visitllandudno.org.uk
🏌 Rhos-on-Sea Penrhyn Bay, ✆ (01492) 54 96 41
🏌 72 Bryniau Rd West Shore, ✆ (01492) 87 53 25
🏌 Hospital Rd, ✆ (01492) 87 64 50
◉ Town★ - Pier★ B – The Great Orme★ (panorama★★, Tramway★, Ancient Copper Mines★ **AC**) AB
🌿 Bodnant Garden★★ **AC**, S : 7 mi by A 470 B

Plan on next page

Bodysgallen Hall
Southeast : 2 mi on A 470 ✉ *LL30 1RS* – ✆ *(01492) 584 466*
– www.bodysgallen.com
13 rm – †£ 149/349 ††£ 169/425, ⌑ £ 7.50 – 18 suites – ††£ 220/425
Rest *Dining Room* – see restaurant listing
Rest *1620* – *(closed Sunday lunch)* Carte £ 26/32 **s**
• Stunning country house with 13C tower, surrounded by 200 acres of delightful gardens and parkland, and boasting a superb outlook to the mountains beyond. Welcoming, open-fired hall and characterful wood-panelled lounge. Antique-furnished bedrooms: some set in cottages; some affording splendid Snowdon views.

Empire
73 Church Walks ✉ *LL30 2HE* – ✆ *(01492) 860 555 – www.empirehotel.co.uk*
– Closed 16-30 December   A**e**
50 rm ⌑ – †£ 70/95 ††£ 130 – 1 suite
Rest *Watkins and Co.* – see restaurant listing
• Family-run, Victorian hotel with grand columned façade, its interior hung with chandeliers and Russell Flint prints. Well-equipped gym and good-sized pool. Antique-furnished bedrooms feature brass or cast iron beds and have good facilities.

Osborne House
17 North Par ✉ *LL30 2LP* – ✆ *(01492) 860 330 – www.osbornehouse.co.uk*
– Closed 16-30 December   A**c**
8 rm – †£ 150/210 ††£ 150/210
Rest *Osborne's Cafe Grill* – see restaurant listing
• Smart townhouse overlooking the bay. All of the bedrooms are large, luxurious suites and have stunning, almost whimsical styles; they boast canopied beds, spacious sitting rooms with Victorian fireplaces and marble bathrooms with double-ended, roll-top baths.

St Tudno
North Par ✉ *LL30 2LP* – ✆ *(01492) 874 411 – www.st-tudno.co.uk*   A**c**
17 rm ⌑ – †£ 75/95 ††£ 98/104 – 1 suite
Rest *Terrace* – see restaurant listing
• Long-standing, personally run seaside hotel, set opposite the old Victorian pier. Classical sitting room and warm bar-lounge afford bay views. Simply furnished bedrooms with mini-bars and Molton Brown toiletries; some have whirlpool baths.

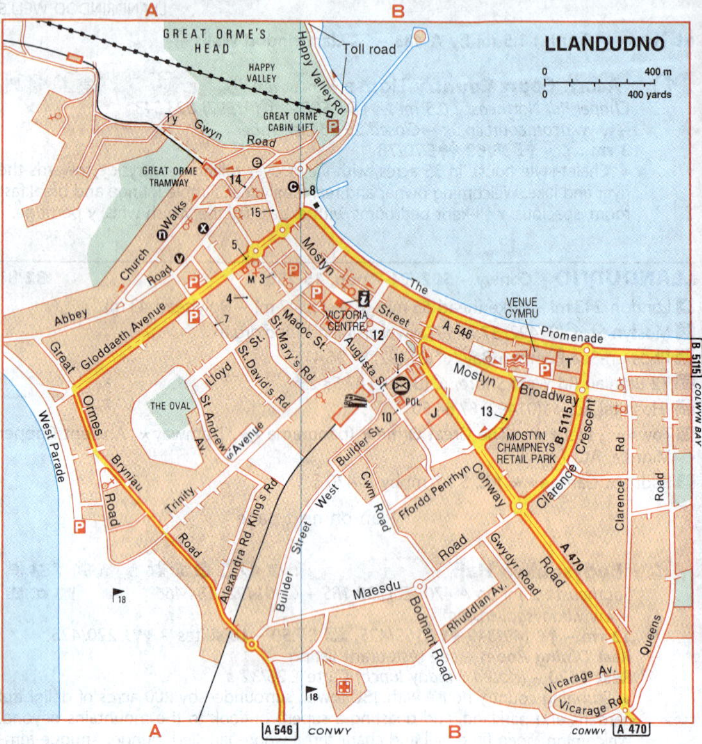

LLANDUDNO

Chapel St. .... A 3	Mostyn	Tudor Crescent .... B 13
Deganwy Ave .... A 4	St. .... B	Upper Mostyn
Gloddaeth St .... A 5	North Parade .... AB 8	St. .... A 15
Maelgwyn Rd .... A 7	Oxford Rd .... B 10	Vaughan
Mostyn Champneys	Trinity Square .... B 12	St. .... B 16
Retail Park .... B	Tudno St. .... A 14	Victoria Centre .... B

🏠 Escape Boutique B&B without rest
48 Church Walks ✉ LL30 2HL – ☏ (01492) 877 776 – www.escapebandb.co.uk
– Closed 1 week Christmas
An
9 rm ⌂ – †£73/123 ††£88/136
◆ Attractive Arts and Crafts house with stained glass windows, parquet floors and a chic, modern interior that sets it apart. Spacious, contemporary bedrooms; the lounge is suitably stylish.

🏠 Bryn Derwen without rest
34 Abbey Rd ✉ LL30 2EE – ☏ (01492) 876 804 – www.bryn-derwen.co.uk
– February-October
Av
9 rm ⌂ – †£55 ††£92
◆ Well-run, welcoming house built in 1878 for a wealthy family. Original features remain, including an ornate pitch pine staircase. Well-appointed lounge and spacious, individually designed bedrooms. Beauty salon offers a range of treatments.

Take note of the classification: you should not expect the same level of service in a 🍴 or 🏠 as in a 🍴🍴🍴🍴 or 🏨🏨🏨.

LLANDUDNO

Lympley Lodge without rest
Colwyn Rd, East : 2.5 mi on B 5115 ✉ *LL30 3AL*
– ℰ *(01492) 549 304 – www.lympleylodge.co.uk*
– *Closed mid-December-February*
3 rm ⊐ – †£ 55 ††£ 85

♦ Detached Victorian house close to the Little Orme headland; built in 1870 as a summer residence for a local family. Antique-filled lounge with promenade views. Individually themed bedrooms come with good extras and sea outlooks. Hearty breakfasts of local produce taken at antique tables.

Abbey Lodge without rest
14 Abbey Rd ✉ *LL30 2EA* – ℰ *(01492) 878 042*
– *www.abbeylodgeuk.com – March-October* Ax
4 rm ⊐ – †£ 40 ††£ 70/75

♦ Welcoming terraced property – built in the early 1850s as a gentleman's residence. Individually decorated, pine-furnished bedrooms; all with baths. Cosy lounge and communal breakfasts from extensive menu. Pleasant rear garden boasts views up to the Great Orme.

Sefton Court without rest
49 Church Walks ✉ *LL30 2HL* – ℰ *(01492) 875 235*
– *www.seftoncourt-hotel.co.uk – Closed December-January* An
10 rm ⊐ – †£ 50/55 ††£ 72/80

♦ Substantial Victorian house in an elevated position, affording good town views. Original features include pretty stained glass windows and interesting friezes. Contemporary bedrooms provide a pleasant contrast with their stylish wallpapers.

Dining Room – at Bodysgallen Hall Hotel
Southeast : 2 mi on A 470 ✉ *LL30 1RS* – ℰ *(01492) 584 466*
– *www.bodysgallen.com – Closed Sunday dinner and Monday*
Rest – *(booking essential)* Menu £ 23/44

♦ Delightful, two-roomed dining room overlooking stunning gardens, located within a beautiful country house which part-dates from the 13C. Formal, classically based dishes. Smart dress required.

Watkins and Co. – at Empire Hotel
73 Church Walks ✉ *LL30 2HE* – ℰ *(01492) 860 555*
– *www.empirehotel.co.uk – Closed 16-30 December* Ae
Rest – *(dinner only and Sunday lunch)* Menu £ 22

♦ Smart dining room with wooden floor and linen-covered chairs, set on the site of a former wine merchants, in a grand, column-fronted hotel. Appealing set menu supplemented by daily specials.

Terrace – at St Tudno Hotel
North Par ✉ *LL30 2LP* – ℰ *(01492) 874 411*
– *www.st-tudno.co.uk* Ac
Rest – Menu £ 27/38 **s**

♦ Unique restaurant with murals of Lake Como running the length of the wall and chandeliers adorned with flowers. Set within a personally run seaside hotel and offering a modern, seasonal menu.

Osborne's Cafe Grill – at Osborne House Hotel
17 North Par ✉ *LL30 2LP* – ℰ *(01492) 860 330*
– *www.osbornehouse.co.uk – Closed 16-30 December* Ac
Rest – Menu £ 19 – Carte £ 20/45

♦ All-day hotel restaurant with opulent lounge and ornate dining room boasting Corinthian columns and gilded mirrors. All-encompassing menu ranges from tasty afternoon tea to British classics.

LLANDUDNO

at Deganwy South : 2.75 mi on A 546 - A - ✉ Llandudno

Quay H. & Spa
Deganwy Quay ✉ LL31 9DJ – ✆ (01492) 564 100 – www.quayhotel.com
55 rm – †£ 95/145 ††£ 115/215 – 19 suites
Rest *Grill Room* – see restaurant listing

◆ Smart hotel by the Conwy Estuary, in a modern marina development. Large guest areas have superb outlook over the harbour and castle. Extensive meeting facilities, great pool and well-run spa. Contemporary bedrooms include 3 private towers.

Grill Room – at Quay Hotel & Spa
Deganwy Quay ✉ LL31 9DJ – ✆ (01492) 564 100 – www.quayhotel.com
Rest – Carte £ 11/30

◆ Stylish, nautically-themed, first-floor hotel restaurant, boasting stunning views over the harbour, castle and mountains. Extensive menu offers locally sourced meat, fish and grill dishes.

Nikki Ip's
57 Station Rd ✉ LL31 9DF – ✆ (01492) 596 611 – www.nikkiips.com – Closed 25 December and 1 January
Rest – Chinese – (booking essential) Menu £ 12/29 – Carte £ 21/35

◆ Choice of casual eatery/bar or friendly restaurant with estuary views. Dim sum and concise set menu at lunch; extensive à la carte and specials at dinner. Fresh, tasty ingredients; good flavours.

WALES

LLANDWROG – Gwynedd – 503 H24 – see Caernarfon

LLANDYRNOG – Denbighshire – 503 J/K24   32 C1

▶ Cardiff 158 mi – Denbigh 7 mi – Ruthin 6 mi

Pentre Mawr
North : 1.25 mi by B 5429 taking left hand fork after 0.75 mi ✉ LL16 4LA
– ✆ (01824) 790 732 – www.pentremawrcountryhouse.co.uk – Closed Christmas
7 rm – †£ 100/110 ††£ 130/190
Rest – Menu £ 35

◆ Set in 200 acres. Choice of 17C farmhouse with cosy open-fired lounges, country house atmosphere and antique-furnished bedrooms; or luxury African-themed canvas lodges with private terraces and hot tubs. Dinner served in wood-floored conservatory; local ingredients a feature.

LLANELLTYD – Gwynedd – 503 I25 – see Dolgellau

LLANERCHYMEDD – 502 G24 – see Anglesey (Isle of)

LLAN FFESTINIOG – Gwynedd   32 B2

▶ London 234 mi – Bangor 35 mi – Wrexham 52 mi
◉ Llechwedd Slate Caverns★ **AC** N : 4 mi by A 470

Cae'r Blaidd Country House
North : 0.75 mi by A 470 on Blaenau Rd ✉ LL41 4PH – ✆ (01766) 762 765
– www.caerblaidd.fsnet.co.uk – Closed January
3 rm – †£ 49 ††£ 79   **Rest** – (dinner only) Menu £ 20 **s**

◆ Sizeable Victorian house in remote setting, boasting panoramic mountain views. Spacious guest areas; light, airy bedrooms – two with superb outlooks. Welcoming owners are mountain guides. Daily changing dishes of local produce served at large communal table.

LLANFIHANGEL – Powys – see Llanfyllin

LLANFIHANGEL-Y-CREUDDYN – Ceredigion – **503** I26   33 B3

▶ London 235 mi – Cardiff 109 mi – Birmingham 121 mi – Liverpool 123 mi

Y Ffarmers
✉ SY23 4LA – ✆ (01974) 261 275 – www.yffarmers.co.uk – Closed first week January, Monday except bank holidays and Sunday dinner
Rest – (dinner only and lunch Thursday-Sunday) Carte £ 17/29
♦ Life in the remote, picturesque valley revolves around this passionately run village pub, with its locals bar and homely restaurant opening onto the garden. Concise, monthly menu of satisfying, original dishes; regional and valley produce.

LLANFYLLIN – Powys – **502** K25 – pop. 1 267   32 C2

▶ London 188 mi – Chester 42 mi – Shrewsbury 24 mi – Welshpool 11 mi
Pistyll Rhaeadr★, NW : 8 mi by A 490, B 4391, B 4580 and minor roads

Seeds
5 Penybryn Cottages, High St ✉ SY22 5AP – ✆ (01691) 648 604 – Closed Monday
Rest – (restricted opening in winter) Menu £ 28 (dinner) – Carte lunch £ 20/33
♦ Converted 16C red-brick cottages in sleepy town, run by hands-on husband and wife team. Simple, rustic interior featuring old kitchen range; matched by unfussy, flavoursome, classical dishes.

at Llanfihangel Southwest : 5 mi by A 490 and B 4393 on B 4382 – ✉ Llanfyllin

Cyfie Farm
South : 1.5 mi by B 4382 ✉ SY22 5JE – ✆ (01691) 648 451
– www.cyfiefarm.co.uk – March-October
4 rm ⌆ – ♦£ 90 ♦♦£ 130   **Rest** – Menu £ 28
♦ 17C longhouse and barn conversions, set in a great spot and boasting far-reaching views across the Meifod Valley. Mix of bedrooms and self-catering cottages; some with beams and wood-burning stoves. Spacious lounges and communal dining room, with porridge cooked overnight on the Aga and cordon bleu dinners.

LLANGAMMARCH WELLS – Powys – **503** J27   33 B3

▶ London 200 mi – Brecon 17 mi – Builth Wells 8 mi – Cardiff 58 mi

Lake Country House and Spa
East : 0.75 mi ✉ LD4 4BS – ✆ (01591)
620 202 – www.lakecountryhouse.co.uk
22 rm ⌆ – ♦£ 220 ♦♦£ 270 – 8 suites
Rest – (booking essential) Menu £ 24/39
♦ Extended, part-timbered 19C country house, in 50 acres of mature gardens and parkland, with a pond, lake and river. Comfy lounges and well-appointed bedrooms with antiques and extras; some set in the lodge. Impressive spa overlooks the river. Personally run, with excellent service. Breakfasts in the orangery; elegant restaurant for classical, candlelit dinners.

LLANGOLLEN – Denbighshire – **502** K25 – pop. 3 093   32 C2

▶ London 194 mi – Chester 23 mi – Holyhead 76 mi – Shrewsbury 30 mi
ℹ Castle St ✆ (01978) 86 08 28, www.llangollen.org
Vale of Llangollen Holyhead Rd, ✆ (01978) 86 09 06
◉ Town★ - Railway★ **AC** - Plas Newydd★ **AC**
Pontcysyllte Aqueduct★★, E : 4 mi by A 539 - Castell Dinas Bran★, N : by footpath – Valle Crucis Abbey★ **AC**, N : 2 mi by A 542. Chirk Castle★★ **AC** (wrought iron gates★), SE : 7.5 mi by A 5 - Rug Chapel★ **AC**, W : 11 mi by A 5 and A 494

821

LLANGOLLEN

Gales
18 Bridge St ⊠ *LL20 8PF* – ℰ *(01978) 860 089* – www.galesofllangollen.co.uk
– *Closed 24 December-2 January*
15 rm – ✝£ 60 ✝✝£ 80, ⊇ £ 5
Rest – *(closed Sunday dinner)* Carte £ 17/29
♦ Pair of family-run, brick-built townhouses with characterful wine theme throughout. Spacious beamed bedrooms boast modern bathrooms and complimentary port. Below are a wine/kitchenware shop and atmospheric wood-panelled wine bar with wide-ranging blackboard menu.

LLANGRANNOG – Ceredigion – 503 G27   33 B3

▶ London 241 mi – Caerdydd / Cardiff 96 mi – Aberystwyth / Aberyswyth 30 mi
– Caerfyrddin / Carmarthen 28 mi

Grange without rest
Pentregat, Southeast : 3 mi by B 4321 on A 487 ⊠ *SA44 6HW* – ℰ *(01239) 654 121* – www.grangecountryhouse.co.uk
4 rm ⊇ – ✝£ 45/55 ✝✝£ 75/85
♦ Originally the manor house of the adjacent estate. Traditionally furnished guest areas; afternoon tea from real silver teapot on arrival. Well-maintained bedrooms boast roll-top baths.

LLANGYBI – Monmouthshire – 503 L29 – see Usk

LLANLLAWDDOG – Carmarthenshire – see Carmarthen

LLANOVER – Monmouthshire – see Abergavenny

LLANRHIDIAN – Swansea – 503 H29 – see Swansea

LLANSANFFRAID GLAN CONWY – Conwy – 502 I24 – see Conwy

LLANUWCHLLYN – Gwynedd – 503 I/J25   32 B2

▶ Cardiff 147 mi – Dolgellau 13 mi – Llangollen 27 mi

Eifionydd without rest
⊠ *LL23 7UB* – ℰ *(01678) 540 622* – www.visitbala.com – *March-October*
4 rm ⊇ – ✝£ 40/70 ✝✝£ 70/100
♦ Comfortable guesthouse located in a small hamlet and boasting beautiful rear views across a stream to the mountains beyond. Pleasant sun lounge, conservatory and breakfast room. Immaculately kept, individually decorated bedrooms with compact, modern bathrooms.

LLANWRTYD WELLS – Powys – 503 J27 – pop. 649   33 B3

▶ London 214 mi – Brecon 32 mi – Cardiff 68 mi – Carmarthen 39 mi
🛈 The Square ℰ (01591) 61 06 66, www.llanwrtyd.com
◉ Abergwesyn-Tregaron Mountain Road★, NW : 19 mi on minor roads

Lasswade Country House
Station Rd ⊠ *LD5 4RW* – ℰ *(01591) 610 515* – www.lasswadehotel.co.uk
8 rm ⊇ – ✝£ 65/80 ✝✝£ 80/120
Rest – *(dinner only)* Menu £ 35
♦ Keenly run, detached Edwardian house, close to town, with book-filled lounge and conservatory breakfast room. Comfortable, uncluttered bedrooms come in light hues and boast pleasant countryside views. Concise menu features their own hot-smoked salmon, Elan Valley mutton and sustainable local produce.

LLANWRTYD WELLS

✕✕ **Carlton Riverside** with rm
Irfon Cres ✉ LD5 4SP – ℘ (01591) 610 248 – www.carltonriverside.com
– Closed 22-30 December and Sunday
5 rm ⌒ – †£ 50/75 ††£ 100
Rest – *(dinner only)* Menu £ 25 – Carte approx. £ 40
♦ Traditional stone building in the centre of the village, overlooking the River Irfon. Two comfy lounges and small bar filled with books and modern art; well-spaced tables in the dining room. Two set menus and elaborate à la carte utilise local produce. Courteous service. Simple, well-priced bedrooms.

LLYSWEN – Powys – 503 K27 – ✉ Brecon   33 C3
▶ London 188 mi – Brecon 8 mi – Cardiff 48 mi – Worcester 53 mi
◉ Brecon Beacons National Park★★

Llangoed Hall
Northwest : 1.25 mi on A 470 ✉ LD3 0YP – ℘ (01874) 754 525
– www.llangoedhall.com
23 rm ⌒ – †£ 175/205 ††£ 195/225
Rest – *(booking essential for non-residents)* Menu £ 25/45 **s**
♦ Homely country house by the River Wye, built by Sir Clough Williams-Ellis and restored by the late Sir Bernard and Laura Ashley. Spacious rooms mix period and modern furnishings. Impressive art collection includes Whistler. Restaurant serves classical dishes with a modern edge.

MACHYNLLETH – Powys – 503 I26 – pop. 2 147   32 B2
▶ London 220 mi – Shrewsbury 56 mi – Welshpool 37 mi
ℹ Penrallt St ℘ (01654) 70 24 01, www.ukinformationcentre.com/central-wales
⛳ Felingerrig, ℘ (01654) 70 20 00
◉ Town★ - Celtica★ **AC**
◉ Snowdonia National Park★★★ - Centre for Alternative Technology★★ **AC**,
N : 3 mi by A 487

Ynyshir Hall
Eglwysfach, Southwest : 6 mi on A 487 ✉ SY20 8TA – ℘ (01654) 781 209
– www.ynyshir-hall.co.uk
6 rm ⌒ – †£ 205/335 ††£ 295/345 – 3 suites
Rest – *(closed lunch Monday and Tuesday) (booking essential)* Menu £ 25/73
♦ Part-Georgian house set within 1,000 acre RSPB reserve. Bright, individually appointed bedrooms, cosy drawing room with art, antiques and Welsh pottery. Charming and very attentive service. Intimate and comfortable dining room.

WALES

MENAI BRIDGE – 502 H24 – see Anglesey (Isle of)

MOLD (Yr Wyddgrug) – Flintshire – 502 K24 – pop. 9 568   32 C1
▶ London 211 mi – Chester 12 mi – Liverpool 22 mi – Shrewsbury 45 mi
ℹ Earl Rd ℘ (01352) 75 93 31, www.visitmold.com
⛳ Pantymwyn Clicain Rd, ℘ (01352) 74 03 18
⛳ Old Padeswood Station Rd, Old Padeswood, ℘ (01244) 54 77 01
⛳ Padeswood & Buckley Station Lane, The Caia, ℘ (01244) 55 05 37
⛳ Caerwys, ℘ (01352) 72 12 22
◉ St Mary's Church★

Tower without rest
Nercwys, South : 1 mi by B 5444, Nercwys rd on Treuddyn rd ✉ CH7 4EW
– ℘ (01352) 700 220 – www.towerwales.co.uk – March-November
3 rm ⌒ – †£ 90 ††£ 120
♦ Impressive fortified house with pond and extensive grounds, dating from 1465 and in family almost as long. Huge high-ceilinged bedrooms boast character beds, antiques and vast modern showers.

MOLD

56 High Street
VISA
56 High St. ⊠ CH7 1BD – ℰ (01352) 759 225 – www.56highst.co.uk – Closed 1 January, Sunday and Monday
Rest – Menu £ 15/18 – Carte £ 28/40
♦ Intimate neighbourhood restaurant in busy market town, run by brother and sister. Extensive menus evolve over time. Dishes range from classical to modern, with a focus on sustainable seafood.

Glasfryn
Raikes Ln, Sychdyn, North : 1 mi by A 5119 on Civic Centre rd (Theatr Clwyd) ⊠ CH7 6LR – ℰ (01352) 750 500 – www.glasfryn-mold.co.uk – Closed 25 December
Rest – Carte £ 22/33
♦ Sizeable red-brick pub with Arts and Crafts styling and pleasant town outlook. Menu offers plenty of choice from pub to culinary classics. Portions are generous and service is swift.

MONMOUTH (Trefynwy) – Monmouthshire – 503 L28 – pop. 8 547   33 C4
▶ London 135 mi – Abergavenny 19 mi – Cardiff 40 mi
◉ Town ★

at Whitebrook South : 8.25 mi by A 466 – ⊠ Monmouth

Crown at Whitebrook with rm
⊠ NP25 4TX – ℰ (01600) 860 254 – www.crownatwhitebrook.co.uk – Closed 2 weeks Christmas
8 rm – †£ 90/120 ††£ 135/170   **Rest** – (booking essential) Menu £ 30/50
Spec. Grey mullet, smoked eel, avocado and shiso. Loin of wild rabbit, almond, gingerbread and pear. Banana bread with walnuts and condensed milk.
♦ Attentively run by smart, personable staff. Lounge bar with deep leather sofas and immaculately laid dining room. The kitchen effectively employs modern techniques to produce original, flavoursome dishes. Smart bedrooms in contemporary colours.

at Rockfield Northwest : 2.5 mi on B 4233 – ⊠ Monmouth

Stonemill
West : 1 mi on B 4233 ⊠ NP25 5SW – ℰ (01600) 716 273
– www.thestonemill.co.uk – Closed 2 weeks January, 25-26 December, Sunday dinner and Monday
Rest – Menu £ 16/20 – Carte £ 21/33
♦ Converted 16C stone cider mill with exposed timbers, and leather sofa in sitting area/bar. Attentive service. Well-sourced modern seasonal dishes feature produce from small local suppliers.

MONTGOMERY (Trefaldwyn) – Powys – 503 K26 – pop. 1 059   32 C2
▶ London 194 mi – Birmingham 71 mi – Chester 53 mi – Shrewsbury 30 mi
◉ Town ★

The Checkers (Stéphane Borie) with rm
Broad St ⊠ SY15 6PN – ℰ (01686) 669 822
– www.thecheckersmontgomery.co.uk – Closed 2 weeks January, 1 week autumn, 25 December, Sunday and Monday
3 rm – †£ 85/110 ††£ 95/150   **Rest** – Carte £ 28/40 s
Spec. Cheddar cheese soufflé with roasted red peppers. Pork belly with roasted pear, creamed potato and braising jus. Lemon crème brûlée with candied ginger ice cream.
♦ Charming 18C former coaching inn, set in the main square of a hilltop town. Spacious panelled bar and lounge; stylish restaurant opens onto a terrace. Monthly changing menus of classical dishes that are executed with a deft touch; flavours are sharply defined. Elegant, antique-furnished bedrooms.

NANTGAREDIG – Carmarthenshire – **503** H28 – see Carmarthen

NANT-Y-DERRY – Monmouthshire – see Abergavenny

Guesthouses ⇑ don't provide the same level of service as hotels. They are often characterised by a warm welcome and a décor which reflects the owner's personality. Those shown in red ⇑ are particularly pleasant.

NARBERTH – Pembrokeshire – **503** F28 – pop. 1 869 — 33 A4

▶ London 234 mi – Cardiff 88 mi – Swansea 51 mi – Rhondda 79 mi

Grove
Molleston, South : 2 mi by A 478 on Herons Brook rd ✉ *SA67 8BX* – ✆ *(01834) 860 915* – *www.thegrove-narberth.co.uk*
9 rm ☐ – †£ 200/260 ††£ 210/270 – 3 suites
Rest – *(booking essential at lunch)* Menu £ 23/40 **s**
♦ Part-Stuart, part-Victorian house and adjacent 15C longhouse, set in a charming rural location. Bedrooms blend boldly coloured walls and fabrics with traditional furnishings; spacious bathrooms boast every modern amenity. Seasonal menus offer creative, modern dishes with a classical base.

⇑ **Canaston Oaks** *without rest*
Canaston Bridge, West : 3 mi by B 4314 and A 40 on A 4075 ✉ *SA67 8DE* – ✆ *(01437) 541 254* – *www.canastonoaks.co.uk*
7 rm ☐ – †£ 90 ††£ 125
♦ Converted longhouse and outbuildings set in 35 acres of gardens and grasslands leading down to the river. Set around a courtyard water feature, wood-furnished bedrooms boast fridges and DVD players; some have jacuzzis, others, patio areas.

NEWPORT – Newport – **503** L29 – pop. 116 143 — 33 C4

▶ London 145 mi – Bristol 31 mi – Cardiff 12 mi – Gloucester 48 mi
🛈 John Frost Sq ✆ (01633) 84 29 62, www.newport.gov.uk
🐦 Caerleon Broadway, ✆ (01633) 42 03 42
🐦 Parc Coedkernew Church Lane, ✆ (01633) 68 09 33
◉ Museum and Art Gallery★ AX **M** - Transporter Bridge★ **AC** AY - Civic Centre (murals★) AX
🜲 Caerleon Roman Fortress★★ **AC** (Fortress Baths★ - Legionary Museum★ - Amphitheatre★), NE : 2.5 mi by B 4596 AX – Tredegar House★★ (Grounds★ - Stables★), SW : 2.5 mi by A 48 AY. Penhow Castle★, E : 8 mi by A 48 AX

Celtic Manor Resort
Coldra Woods, East : 3 mi on A 48 ✉ *NP18 1HQ*
– ✆ *(01633) 413 000* – *www.celtic-manor.com*
315 rm – †£ 268/1500 ††£ 268/1500, ☐ £ 17.95 – 19 suites
Rest *Crown at Celtic Manor*
Rest *Rafters* – see restaurant listing
Rest *Olive Tree* – Buffet – *(dinner only and Sunday lunch)* Menu £ 33 **s**
Rest *Patio* – French – *(dinner only)* Carte £ 24/56 **s**
♦ Vast resort hotel in 1,400 acres, boasting 3 golf courses, an impressive pool and spa, two floors of function rooms and even a shopping arcade. Classical bedrooms range from standard to presidential suites and boast smart marble bathrooms. Modern fine dining in The Crown, grills in Rafters, buffet and carvery in main restaurant Olive Tree, French bistro menu in Patio.

825

NEWPORT

Crown at Celtic Manor – at Celtic Manor Resort Hotel
Coldra Woods, East : 3 mi on A 48 ✉ *NP18 1HQ*
– ✆ *(01633) 413 000* – *www.celtic-manor.com*
– *Closed Sunday and Monday*
Rest – Menu £ 50 **s**
♦ Set within a huge resort hotel, a contemporary fine dining restaurant with dedicated bar. Modern cooking; express lunch contrasts with more elaborate and pricier tasting and à la carte menus.

Chandlery
77-78 Lower Dock St ✉ *NP20 1EH*
– ✆ *(01633) 256 622* – *www.thechandleryrestaurant.com*
– *Closed Sunday dinner and Monday*   AY**a**
Rest – Menu £ 18 (lunch)
– Carte £ 28/41
♦ 18C former chandlery near the river, with cosy bar, lounge and dining room downstairs, and airy, antique-furnished restaurant above. Good value set lunch and daily offers; adventurous à la carte and 6 course tasting menu. Regular events.

Rafters – at Celtic Manor Resort Hotel
Coldra Woods, East : 3 mi on A 48 ✉ *NP18 1HQ*
– ✆ *(01633) 413 000* – *www.celtic-manor.com*
Rest – Carte £ 27/51 **s**
♦ Modern restaurant with solid cedar wood beams, set in the clubhouse of a sizeable resort hotel. Serves breakfast, lunch, snacks and wide selection of steaks at dinner. Smart-casual dress code.

WALES

NEWPORT (Trefdraeth) – Pembrokeshire – 503 F27 – pop. 1 162   33 A3

▶ London 258 mi – Fishguard 7 mi
🛈 Long St ✆ (01239) 82 09 12, www.newport-pembs.co.uk
⛳ Newport Links, ✆ (01239) 82 02 44
◉ Pembrokeshire Coast National Park★★

Cnapan
East St, on A 487 ✉ *SA42 0SY*
– ✆ *(01239) 820 575* – *www.cnapan.co.uk*
– *Closed 25-26 December and January-mid-March*
5 rm ⊆ – †£ 54 ††£ 88
Rest – *(closed Tuesday) (dinner only) (booking essential)* Menu £ 34
♦ Keenly run, well-maintained, part-Georgian house with traditionally furnished lounge and bar. Fresh, compact bedrooms with white walls, coloured throws and slightly old-fashioned feel. Candlelit restaurant opens onto spacious garden and offers extensive home-cooked menu.

Llys Meddyg with rm
East St ✉ *SA42 0SY* – ✆ *(01239) 820 008* – *www.llysmeddyg.com*
– *Closed 1 week January, 1 week November, Sunday except bank holiday weekends and Monday*
8 rm ⊆ – †£ 70/85 ††£ 100/180
Rest – *(booking essential at lunch)* Menu £ 33
♦ Centrally located restaurant with kitchen garden behind. Eat in the formal dining room or characterful, laid-back cellar bar; the owner's father's art is displayed throughout. Simple, classical lunches and more innovative, modern dinners. Contemporary, Scandinavian-style bedrooms are located in the annexe.

NEWTOWN – Powys – 503 K26 – pop. 10 358 – ✉ Blaenau Gwent 32 C2
▶ London 194 mi – Cardiff 98 mi – Birmingham 81 mi – Wolverhampton 69 mi

Highgate without rest
Bettws Cedewain, Northeast : 2.5 mi by B 4568 off B 4389 ✉ *SY16 3LF*
– ✆ *(01686) 623 763 – www.highgatebandb.co.uk. – Closed Christmas-New Year*
4 rm ⌑ – †£ 45/55 ††£ 90
◆ Timbered farmhouse built in 1631, with colourful gardens, stables for your horse and superb views across rolling fields. Tastefully furnished, it boasts good-sized bedrooms and a warm, welcoming feel. Homemade breads and preserves feature at breakfast.

OLD RADNOR (Pencraig) – Powys – 503 J27 – pop. 400 33 C3
▶ London 180 mi – Cardiff 81 mi – Birmingham 86 mi – Liverpool 121 mi

Harp Inn with rm
✉ *LD8 2RH* – ✆ *(01544) 350 655 – www.harpinnradnor.co.uk – Closed Monday except bank holidays and restricted opening in winter*
5 rm ⌑ – †£ 50/55 ††£ 80/85
Rest – *(dinner only and lunch Saturday-Sunday)* Carte £ 22/28
◆ 15C stone inn that welcomes its drinkers and diners alike. Charming, flag-floored, open-fired inner, its beams hung with hop bines; glorious views from the terrace. 'Seasonality' and 'sustainability' are key; menus are concise but original.

PARKMILL – Swansea – 503 H29 – see Swansea

PEMBROKE (Penfro) – Pembrokeshire – 503 F28 – pop. 7 214 33 A4
▶ London 252 mi – Carmarthen 32 mi – Fishguard 26 mi
Access Cleddau Bridge (toll)
⛴ to Republic of Ireland (Rosslare) (Irish Ferries) 2 daily (4 h) – to Republic of Ireland (Cork) (Swansea Cork Ferries) daily (8 h 30 mn)
ℹ Commons Rd ✆ (01646) 62 23 88, www.pembrokeshire.gov.uk
Pembroke Dock Military Rd, ✆ (01646) 62 14 53
◉ Town★★ - Castle★★ AC
◉ Pembrokeshire Coast National Park★★ - Carew Castle★ AC, NE : 4 mi by A 4075. Bosherston (St Govan's Chapel★), S : 7 mi by B 4319 and minor roads – Stack Rocks★, SW : 9 mi by B 4319 and minor roads

Poyerston Farm without rest
Cosheston, Northeast : 2.75 mi by A 4075 on A 477 ✉ *SA72 4SJ*
– ✆ *(01646) 651 347 – www.poyerstonfarm.co.uk – February-October*
3 rm ⌑ – †£ 45/55 ††£ 70/80
◆ Victorian farmhouse with well-tended gardens, on a working dairy farm in 220 acres. Intimate breakfast room, airy conservatory and cosy lounge. Immaculate bedrooms with light oak furnishings and extras. Warm welcome from experienced owner.

at Lamphey East : 1.75 mi on A 4139 – ✉ Pembroke

Lamphey Court
✉ *SA71 5NT* – ✆ *(01646) 672 273 – www.lampheycourt.co.uk*
39 rm ⌑ – †£ 88/100 ††£ 110/160
Rest – Menu £ 28
◆ Large Georgian mansion surrounded by parkland, built by Charles Mathias in an idyllic location. Well-furnished throughout with fine mahogany in the coordinated bedrooms. Formal restaurant with a good country house style menu.

PENARTH – The Vale of Glamorgan – 503 K29 – see Cardiff

PENMACHNO – Conwy – 502 I24 – see Betws-y-Coed

PONTDOLGOCH – Powys – see Caersws

PORTHCAWL – Bridgend – 503 I29 – pop. 15 640   33 B4
▶ London 183 mi – Cardiff 28 mi – Swansea 18 mi
🛈 John St ✆ (01656) 78 66 39, www.bridgend.gov.uk
◉ Glamorgan Heritage Coast ★

⌂ **Foam Edge** without rest
9 West Dr ✉ CF36 3LS – ✆ (01656) 782 866 – www.foam-edge.co.uk
– Closed 25 December
3 rm ☕ – †£ 40/70 ††£ 90

♦ Unassuming house by the promenade masks stylish, modern interior with superb Bristol Channel views. A family home in essence, with comfy lounge and communal breakfast. Bedrooms in pastel hues.

PORTMEIRION – Gwynedd – 502 H25   32 B2
▶ London 245 mi – Caernarfon 23 mi – Colwyn Bay 40 mi – Dolgellau 24 mi
◉ Village ★★★ **AC**
◉ Snowdonia National Park ★★★ - Lleyn Peninsula ★★ – Ffestiniog Railway ★★ **AC**

🏨 **Portmeirion**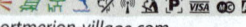
✉ LL48 6ET – ✆ (01766) 770 000 – www.portmeirion-village.com
28 rm (dinner included) ☕ – †£ 100/216 ††£ 145/279 – 14 suites
Rest *– (booking essential for non-residents)* Menu £ 40
– Carte £ 24/38

♦ Unique Italianate village built on a private peninsula and boasting wonderful estuary views: the life work of Sir Clough Williams-Ellis. Appealing 1930s hotel and snug, well-appointed bedrooms spread about the village. Dining room features lovely parquet floor.

🏨 **Castell Deudraeth**
✉ LL48 6EN – ✆ (01766) 772 400 – www.portmeirion-village.com
9 rm ☕ – †£ 180/250 ††£ 215/285 – 2 suites
Rest *Grill* – Carte £ 27/58

♦ Impressive crenellated manor house displaying original stone fireplace. Relaxed, informal atmosphere; fine Snowdonia views. Huge bedrooms boast chic, contemporary décor and kitchen areas. Choose from brasserie classics in conservatory or pleasant walled garden.

  Large towns and cities include detailed plans locating hotels and restaurants. Use the given coordinates (ex.: **12**B**M**e) to find them easily.

PWLLGLOYW – Powys – see Brecon

PWLLHELI – Gwynedd – 502 G25 – pop. 3 861   32 B2
▶ London 261 mi – Aberystwyth 73 mi – Caernarfon 21 mi
🛈 Station Sq ✆ (01758) 61 30 00, www.ukinformationcentre.com/north-wales
⛳ Golf Rd, ✆ (01758) 70 16 44
◉ Lleyn Peninsula ★★

PWLLHELI

✗✗ Plas Bodegroes with rm
Northwest : 1.75 mi on A 497 – ✉ *LL53 5TH* – ✆ *(01758) 612 363*
– www.bodegroes.co.uk – March-November
10 rm ⌑ – ♦£ 110 ♦♦£ 180
Rest – *(closed Monday except bank holidays) (dinner only and Sunday lunch)
(booking essential)* Menu £ 20/45
♦ Delightful Grade II listed Georgian house in secluded gardens. Local art decorates the pale green dining room. Classically based cooking, using good quality local ingredients. Contemporary, Scandinavian-style bedrooms.

at Boduan *Northwest : 3.75 mi on A 497* – ✉ Pwllheli

🏠 Old Rectory without rest
✉ *LL53 6DT* – ✆ *(01758) 721 519* – *www.theoldrectory.net* – *Closed Christmas*
3 rm ⌑ – ♦£ 75/95 ♦♦£ 85/110
♦ Lovely part-Georgian family home with paddock, run by charming owner. Comfy lounge with carved wooden fireplace; cakes on arrival. Tasteful bedrooms boast period furnishings and garden views.

RHOSCOLYN – **503** G24 – see Anglesey (Isle of)

RHOS-ON-SEA = **Llandrillo-yn-Rhos** – Conwy – **502** I24 – see Colwyn Bay

---

RHYL – Denbighshire – **502** J24 – pop. 24 889   **32** C1

▶ Cardiff 182 mi – Chester 34 mi – Llandudno 18 mi

▣ Rhuddlan Castle★★, S : 3 mi by A 525 – Bodelwyddan★★, S : 5 mi by A 525 and minor rd – St Asaph Cathedral★, S : 5 mi by A 525. Llandudno★, W : 16 mi by A 548, A 55 and B 5115

✗✗ Barratt's at Ty'n Rhyl with rm
167 Vale Rd., South : 0.5 mi on A 525 ✉ *LL18 2PH* – ✆ *(01745) 344 138*
– www.barrattsoftynrhyl.co.uk
3 rm ⌑ – ♦£ 70 ♦♦£ 95
Rest – *(dinner only and Sunday lunch) (booking essential)* Carte approx. £ 39
♦ Rhyl's oldest house boasts comfortable lounges with rich oak panelling. Dine in either the conservatory or original house. Ambitious cooking displays a classic base. Bedrooms are individually designed.

ROCKFIELD – Monmouthshire – **503** L28 – see Monmouth

ROWEN – Conwy – see Conwy

RUTHIN (Rhuthun) – Denbighshire – **502** K24 – pop. 5 218   **32** C1

▶ London 210 mi – Birkenhead 31 mi – Chester 23 mi – Liverpool 34 mi

▣ Ruthin-Pwllglas, ✆ (01824) 70 22 96

▣ Llandyrnog (St Dyfnog's Church★), Llanrhaeder-yng-Nghinmeirch (Jesse Window★★), N : 5.5 mi by A 494 and B 5429. Denbigh★, NW : 7 mi on A 525

🏠 Firgrove
Llanfwrog, West : 1.25 mi by A 494 on B 5105 ✉ *LL15 2LL* – ✆ *(01824) 702 677*
– www.firgrovecountryhouse.co.uk – February-November
3 rm ⌑ – ♦£ 60 ♦♦£ 90   **Rest** – Menu £ 35
♦ Attractive stone-built house set in stunning gardens. Sit in the snug by the cosy inglenook fireplace in winter or in the delightful glasshouse in summer. Two comfortable four-poster bedrooms and a self-contained cottage offer valley pleasant views. Communal, home-cooked dinners showcase locally sourced farm produce.

RUTHIN

Eyarth Station without rest
Llanfair Dyffryn Clwyd, South : 1.75 mi by A 525 ⊠ LL15 2EE
– ℰ (01824) 703 643 – www.eyarthstation.co.uk – February-December
6 rm ⊆ – †£ 50/80 ††£ 75/80

♦ Former railway station: platform at heart of house, tracks under conservatory. Simple pine-furnished bedrooms feature railway memorabilia. Panoramic windows in lounge afford great rural views.

Manorhaus with rm
Well St ⊠ LL15 1AH – ℰ (01824) 704 830 – www.manorhaus.com
8 rm ⊆ – †£ 68/98 ††£ 90/145
Rest – (dinner only and lunch Saturday-Sunday) Menu £ 35

♦ Boutique restaurant and gallery in 17C townhouse, displaying frequently changing Bauhaus art. Chic lounge and modern conservatory dining room laid with designer tableware. Seasonal, country-style menu and modern presentation. Snug bedrooms boast good facilities.

On the Hill
1 Upper Clwyd St ⊠ LL15 1HY – ℰ (01824) 707 736
– www.onthehillrestaurant.co.uk – Closed last 2 weeks January, last 2 weeks September, 1 week May, Sunday, Monday and lunch Tuesday
Rest – (booking essential) Menu £ 15 (lunch) – Carte dinner £ 21/31

♦ Immensely charming 16C house located in a busy market town, and boasting characterful sloping floors, exposed beams and buzzy, bistro atmosphere. Accessible menu of keenly priced, internationally influenced classics. A real family business.

ST ASAPH – Denbighshire – 503 J24 – pop. 3 491   32 C1
▶ London 223 mi – Cardiff 176 mi – Liverpool 46 mi – Manchester 69 mi

Tan-yr-Onnen
Waen, East : 1.5 mi by A 55 and B 5429 on Tremeirchion rd ⊠ LL17 0DU
– ℰ (01745) 583 821 – www.northwalesbreaks.co.uk – Closed 25-26 December
6 rm ⊆ – †£ 69 ††£ 125   **Rest** – Menu £ 29

♦ Spacious house with large rear garden filled with trees and shrubs. Immaculately kept bedrooms are of a good size and well-equipped; three of them have their own sitting rooms. Large conservatory and lounge also offer plenty of seating. Full Welsh breakfasts and homely dinners served in pleasant dining room.

ST CLEARS – Carmarthenshire – 503 G28 – pop. 1 587   33 B3
▶ London 221 mi – Cardiff 76 mi – Swansea 37 mi – Llanelli 33 mi

Coedllys Country House without rest
Llangynin, Northwest : 3.5 mi by A 40 turning first left after 30 mph sign on entering village. ⊠ SA33 4JY – ℰ (01994) 231 455
– www.coedllyscountryhouse.co.uk – Closed 23-27 December
4 rm ⊆ – †£ 50/65 ††£ 90/100

♦ Idyllic country house and animal sanctuary with picture perfect façade. Delightful owner keeps everything immaculate. Superb breakfasts. Bedrooms with an unerring eye for detail.

ST DAVIDS (Tyddewi) – Pembrokeshire – 503 E28 – pop. 1 959   33 A3
– ⊠ Haverfordwest
▶ London 266 mi – Carmarthen 46 mi – Fishguard 16 mi
🛈 Oriel Y Parc ℰ (01437) 72 03 92, www.stdavids.co.uk
⛳ St Davids City Whitesands Bay, ℰ (01437) 72 17 51
◉ Town ★ – Cathedral ★★ – Bishop's Palace ★ **AC**
◉ Pembrokeshire Coast National Park ★★

ST DAVIDS

Warpool Court
Southwest : 0.5 mi by Porth Clais rd ✉ SA62 6BN – ℰ (01437) 720 300
– www.warpoolcourthotel.com – Closed November and first 2 weeks December
22 rm – †£ 110 ††£ 330
Rest *Warpool Court* – see restaurant listing
• Characterful clifftop property built in 1860 to house the cathedral choir. Traditional bar and light, airy lounges. Over 3,000 hand-painted Celtic and heraldic tiles feature. Bedrooms range in style; one boasts nice sea views from its bath.

Ramsey House
Lower Moor, Southwest : 0.5 mi on Porth Clais rd ✉ SA62 6RP – ℰ (01437) 720 321 – www.ramseyhouse.co.uk – Closed January, December and restricted opening November and February
6 rm – †£ 60/110 ††£ 100/110
Rest – Menu £ 35
• Unassuming bungalow hiding stylish, contemporary interior with superb comforts, small lounge and bar. Bedrooms display modern colour schemes and state-of-the-art shower rooms. Traditional menus offer tasty three course dinners.

XX **Warpool Court** – at Warpool Court Hotel
Southwest : 0.5 mi by Porth Clais rd ✉ SA62 6BN – ℰ (01437) 720 300
– www.warpoolcourthotel.com – Closed November and first 2 weeks December
Rest – (light lunch/dinner) Menu £ 40
• Smart restaurant boasting sea views, set in a 19C house originally built to accommodate the cathedral choir. Daily changing menus are classically based and feature plenty of local produce.

X **Cwtch**
22 High St ✉ SA62 6SD – ℰ (01437) 720 491 – www.cwtchrestaurant.co.uk
– Closed 25 December and Sunday-Monday November-March
Rest – (dinner only) (booking advisable) Menu £ 30
• Popular, friendly restaurant; its name meaning 'hug' in Welsh. Rustic dining room boasts stone walls, crammed bookshelves and log-filled alcoves. Classical British dishes arrive in generous portions; each comes with a wine recommendation.

ST GEORGE (Llan Sain Siôr) – Conwy   32 C1

▶ London 227 mi – Cardiff 180 mi – Dublin 62 mi – Birmingham 113 mi

Kinmel Arms with rm
The Village ✉ LL22 9BP – ℰ (01745) 832 207 – www.thekinmelarms.co.uk
– Closed 1 January, 25 December, Sunday, Monday and bank holidays
4 rm – †£ 115 ††£ 115/175
Rest – Carte £ 23/41
• Early 17C stone inn hidden away in a hamlet by the entrance to Kinmel Hall. Delightful open-fired bar and two spacious dining areas; the latter offering much more formal service and food.

SAUNDERSFOOT – Pembrokeshire – 503 F28 – pop. 2 946   33 A4

▶ London 241 mi – Cardiff 90 mi – Pembroke 12 mi

St Brides Spa
St Brides Hill ✉ SA69 9NH – ℰ (01834) 812 304 – www.stbridesspahotel.com
40 rm – †£ 110/125 ††£ 230/280 – 6 suites
Rest *Cliff* – see restaurant listing
• Nautically styled hotel overlooking the harbour and bay, displaying wood panelling and pastel shades. Impressive spa boasts marine and outdoor infinity pools. Well-appointed bedrooms and apartments feature mosaic and limestone bathrooms.

SAUNDERSFOOT

Cliff – at St Brides Spa Hotel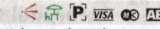
St Brides Hill ⊠ *SA69 9NH* – ℰ *(01834) 812 304* – www.stbridesspahotel.com
Rest – Carte £ 23/38

• Smart yet casual fine dining restaurant within a New England style hotel, boasting a beautiful terrace and stunning views over Carmarthen Bay. Good range of appealing modern European dishes.

SEION – Gwynedd – see Caernarfon

SENNYBRIDGE (Pontsenni) – Powys   33 B3
▶ London 189 mi – Cardiff 43 mi – Birmingham 127 mi – Liverpool 147 mi

Blaencar Farm without rest
South : 1 mi off A 4067 ⊠ *LD3 8HA* – ℰ *(01874) 636 610* – www.blaencar.co.uk
– *Closed 25 December*
3 rm ⊑ – †£ 45 ††£ 70

• Set on a 450 acre working farm; its name meaning 'Mouth of the Brook'. Superb welcome from hands-on owner, who is a fountain of local knowledge. Dark-wood furnished breakfast room, lounge with log burner and simple, comfortable bedrooms.

WALES

SKENFRITH – Monmouthshire – 503 L28   33 C4
▶ London 135 mi – Hereford 16 mi – Ross-on-Wye 11 mi

Bell at Skenfrith with rm
⊠ *NP7 8UH* – ℰ *(01600) 750 235* – www.skenfrith.co.uk
– *Closed last week January and first week February*
11 rm ⊑ – †£ 120 ††£ 220
Rest – *(closed Tuesday November-Easter)* *(booking essential)* Menu £ 20 (lunch)
– Carte £ 26/36

• Well-run pub in verdant valley offering clean, fresh cooking with an innovative, modern twist and using ingredients from the organic kitchen garden. Excellent choice of champagnes and cognacs; warm and unobtrusive service. Understated elegance in super-comfy bedrooms.

SWANSEA – Swansea – 503 I29 – pop. 173 868   33 B4
▶ London 191 mi – Birmingham 136 mi – Bristol 82 mi – Cardiff 40 mi
🛈 Plymouth St ℰ(01792) 46 83 21, www.swansea.info
⛳ Morriston 160 Clasemont Rd, ℰ(01792) 79 65 28
⛳ Clyne Mayals 120 Owls Lodge Lane, ℰ(01792) 40 19 89
⛳ Langland Bay, ℰ(01792) 36 17 21
◉ Town★ - Maritime Quarter★ B – Maritime and Industrial Museum★ B
– Glynn Vivian Art Gallery★ B – Guildhall (British Empire Panels★ A **H**)
◉ Gower Peninsula★★ (Rhossili★★), W : by A 4067 A. The Wildfowl and Wetlands Trust★, Llanelli, NW : 6.5 mi by A 483 and A 484 A

Plans pages 833, 834

Morgans
Somerset Pl ⊠ *SA1 1RR* – ℰ *(01792) 484 848* – www.morganshotel.co.uk
42 rm ⊑ – †£ 250 ††£ 250   **Bb**
Rest – *(closed Monday-Wednesday)* Menu £ 14/22

• Impressive Edwardian building by the docks; once the harbour offices. Beautiful façade and charming interior with original plasterwork, stained glass and soaring cupola. Sizeable modern bedrooms in main house; Town House rooms more compact. Restaurant boasts original hand-painted mural and a modern menu.

SWANSEA

Clase Rd. . . . . A 12
Martin St . . . . A 24
Pen-y-Graig Rd. . . . . . . A 30
Plasmarl By-Pass. . . . . . A 32
Ravenhill Rd. . . . . A 35
St Helen's Rd. . . . . A 40
Station Rd . . . . A 37
Terrace Rd . . . . A 45
Uplands Crescent . . . . . A 49
Walter Rd. . . . . A 52
Woodfield St . . . . A 60

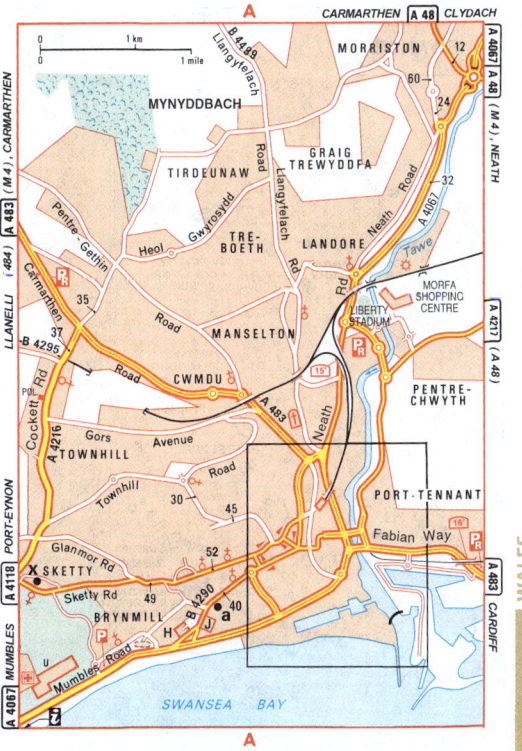

XX Didier & Stephanie's

56 St Helens Rd ✉ SA1 4BE – ℰ (01792) 655 603 – Closed Sunday and Monday
Rest – *(booking essential)* Menu £ 18 (lunch) – Carte £ 29/32   A**a**
♦ Well-run neighbourhood restaurant in a pleasant Victorian building, with light, airy interior, smart wood panelling, original plaster ceiling and small bar to the rear. French owners offer interesting menus of flavoursome Gallic classics.

X Slice

73-75 Eversley Rd, Sketty, West : 2 mi by A 4118 ✉ SA2 9DE
– ℰ (01792) 290 929 – www.sliceswansea.co.uk
– *Closed 3 weeks January, 2 weeks summer, 2 weeks autumn, 1 week spring, Christmas-New Year and Monday-Wednesday*   A**x**
Rest – *(booking essential)* Menu £ 22/34
♦ Former haberdashery in a residential suburb; the name reflecting its tapered shape. Simple polished tables and unfussy, honest cooking. Concise set menus feature homemade bread and ice cream, home-grown veg and home-smoked fish and meat.

at Parkmill West : 8.5 mi on A 4118

XX Maes-Yr-Haf with rm

✉ SA3 2EH – ℰ (01792) 371 000 – www.maes-yr-haf.com
– *Closed Monday in low season*
5 rm ☐ – †£ 80/100 ††£ 130/140   **Rest** – Menu £ 20 (lunch) – Carte £ 27/36
♦ Minimalist restaurant within an old farmhouse in a wooded valley, set by a small stream leading down to the sea. Contemporary interior is matched by adventurous modern cooking that showcases seasonal produce from the Gower Peninsular. Well-kept bedrooms boast stylish furnishings and smart bathrooms.

SWANSEA

Alexandra Rd	B 2	East Bank Way	C 18	Princess Way	B
Belle Vue Way	B 4	Grove Pl.	B 22	Quadrant Centre	B
Carmarthen Rd	B 7	Kingsway (The)	B	St David's Square	B
Castle St	B 8	Nearth Rd	B 25	St Mary's Square	B 4
Christina St	B 9	Nelson St	B 26	Tawe Bridge.	C 4
Clarence Terrace	B 10	New Cut Bridge	C 27	Union St	B 4
College St	B 13	Oxford St	B	Wellington St	B 5
De la Beche St	B 15	Parc Tawe Shopping		West Way	B 5
Dillwyn St	B 17	Centre	B		

at Llanrhidian West : 10.5 mi by A 4118 - **A** - on B 4271 – ✉ Reynoldston

Fairyhill
Reynoldston, West : 2.5 mi by Llangennith Rd ✉ SA3 1BS
– ☏ (01792) 390 139 – www.fairyhill.net
– Closed 2-27 January and 25-26 December
8 rm – †£ 160 ††£ 280
Rest – Menu £ 25/45

♦ Georgian country house in 24 acres of grounds, with a lake and well-manicured gardens. Charming guest areas include a cosy bar and contemporary lounge complete with piano. Eclectic, individually styled bedrooms offer good extras and holistic treatments are popular. Dining room and terrace serve a modern, seasonal menu of Gower produce. Friendly, accommodating service.

SWANSEA

✕✕ Welcome To Town   🅿 VISA ◉◉
✉ SA3 1EH – ✆ (01792) 390 015 – www.thewelcometotown.co.uk
– *Closed last week October, Christmas-New Year, Tuesday November-April, Sunday dinner and Monday*
Rest – *(booking essential)* Carte £ 34/48
◆ 17C whitewashed building – formerly a pub, gaol and courthouse – located on a picturesque peninsula. Traditional interior with well-spaced tables. Appealing, classically based dishes display modern touches and champion local Gower produce.

TALSARNAU – Gwynedd – **502** H25 – pop. 647 – ✉ Harlech   **32** B2
▶ London 236 mi – Caernafon 33 mi – Chester 67 mi – Dolgellau 25 mi
 Snowdonia National Park ★★★

🏨 Maes-y-Neuadd   ⇐ 🚗 🅿 VISA ◉◉
South : 1.5 mi by A 496 off B 4573 ✉ LL47 6YA – ✆ (01766) 780 200
– www.neuadd.com
14 rm ⊇ – †£ 133/145 ††£ 276/296 – 1 suite
Rest – Menu £ 18/40 – Carte lunch £ 19/32
◆ Part-14C country house with pleasant gardens in delightful rural seclusion. Furnished throughout with antiques and curios. Charming service. Individually styled bedrooms. Traditional dining room with linen-clad tables.

TREMEIRCHION – Denbighshire – **502** J24 – ✉ St Asaph   **32** C1
▶ London 225 mi – Chester 29 mi – Shrewsbury 59 mi

🏠 Bach-Y-Graig *without rest*   🚗 🐕 ⚙ ⚛ 🅿 VISA ◉◉
Southwest : 2 mi by B 5429 off Denbigh rd ✉ LL17 0UH – ✆ (01745) 730 627
– www.bachygraig.co.uk
3 rm ⊇ – †£ 50/55 ††£ 75/84
◆ Attractive brick-built farmhouse dating from the 16C, set on a working farm, in a quiet spot, with woodland trails nearby. Large open fires and wood-furnished bedrooms with cast iron beds.

USK – Monmouthshire – **503** L28 – pop. 2 318   **33** C4
▶ London 144 mi – Bristol 30 mi – Cardiff 26 mi – Gloucester 39 mi
🏌 Alice Springs Usk Kemeys Commander, ✆ (01873) 88 07 08
◎ Raglan Castle ★ **AC**, NE : 7 mi by A 472, A 449 and A 40

🏨 Glen-Yr-Afon House   🚗 📶 ♿ ⚛ ♨ 🅿 VISA ◉◉ AE
Pontypool Rd ✉ NP15 1SY – ✆ (01291) 672 302 – www.glen-yr-afon.co.uk
27 rm ⊇ – †£ 99 ††£ 159
Rest *Clarkes* – see restaurant listing
◆ Extended Victorian villa with well-tended gardens, set just across the bridge from town. Comfortable, traditionally styled guest areas and well-booked function rooms. Mix of country house and more contemporary bedrooms; one is four-poster.

✕✕ Clarkes – *at Glen-Yr-Afon House Hotel*   🚗 AC 🅿 VISA ◉◉ AE ①
Pontypool Rd ✉ NP15 1SY – ✆ (01291) 672 302 – www.glen-yr-afon.co.uk
Rest – Carte £ 22/36
◆ Stylish, formal dining room in an extended Victorian villa. Monthly changing à la carte has a distinct Welsh edge, and offers a few modern dishes alongside a largely traditional selection.

at Llandenny *Northeast : 4.25 mi by A 472 off B 4235* – ✉ Usk

🍴 Raglan Arms   🌿 ⚛ 🅿 VISA ◉◉ AE
✉ NP15 1DL – ✆ (01291) 690 800 – www.raglanarms.com – *Closed 25-26 December*
Rest – *(closed Sunday dinner and Monday)* Carte £ 29/36
◆ Cosy village pub with fireside sofas and simply laid tables. Local produce employed in a range of cooking styles; lunchtime main courses offer particularly good value.

USK

at Llangybi South : 2.5 mi on Llangybi rd – ✉ Ceredigion

White Hart
✉ NP15 1NP – ✆ (01633) 450 258 – www.thewhitehartvillageinn.com
– Closed Monday except bank holidays
Rest – (closed Sunday dinner) Carte £ 29/38
♦ Characterful 16C pub with interesting history, 11 fireplaces and priest's hole. Blackboard lunch and more ambitious evening à la carte offer well-prepared, precisely presented, restaurant-style dishes; most produce is from within 10 miles.

VALLEY – 503 G24 – see Anglesey (Isle of)

WHITEBROOK – Monmouthshire – see Monmouth

WHITTON – Powys – 503 J27 – pop. 300   33 C3

▶ London 185 mi – Cardiff 84 mi – Birmingham 84 mi – Liverpool 108 mi

Pilleth Oaks
Northwest : 1.25 mi on B 4356 ✉ LD7 1NP – ✆ (01457) 560 272
– www.pillethoaks.co.uk
3 rm – †£ 40 ††£ 70 **Rest** – Carte £ 15/22
♦ Smart, double-gabled country house in 100 acres, overlooking two lakes and the surrounding hills. Traditional, antique-filled interior with elegant lounge; comfortable bedrooms – one with a balcony. Welcoming owner offers tea on arrival. Communal dining at a smart oak table; desserts are worth investigating.

WOLF'S CASTLE (Cas-Blaidd) – Pembrokeshire – 503 F28 – pop. 616   33 A3
– ✉ Haverfordwest

▶ London 258 mi – Fishguard 7 mi – Haverfordwest 8 mi
◉ Pembrokeshire Coast National Park★★

Wolfscastle Country H.
✉ SA62 5LZ – ✆ (01437) 741 225 – www.wolfscastle.com
– Closed 24-26 December
20 rm – †£ 82 ††£ 150 **Rest** – Menu £ 17/18 – Carte £ 21/34
♦ Former manor house that's been greatly expanded over the years and is popular for weddings and conferences. Tidy, well-equipped bedrooms – some with four-posters; some recenlty refurbished. Traditional bar. Contemporary restaurant offers everything from snacks to the full 3 courses.

WREXHAM (Wrecsam) – Wrexham – 502 L24 – pop. 42 576   32 C1

▶ London 192 mi – Chester 12 mi – Liverpool 35 mi – Shrewsbury 28 mi
🛈 Lambpit St ✆ (01978) 29 20 15, www.wrexham.gov.uk
⛳ Chirk, ✆ (01691) 77 44 07
⛳ Clays Golf Centre Bryn Estyn Rd, ✆ (01978) 66 14 06
⛳ Moss Valley Moss Rd, ✆ (01978) 72 05 18
⛳ Pen-y-Cae Ruabon Rd, ✆ (01978) 81 01 08
⛳ Plassey Oaks Golf Complex Eyton, ✆ (01978) 78 00 20
◉ St Giles Church★
◉ Erddig★★ **AC** (Gardens★★), SW : 2 m – Gresford (All Saints Church★), N : 4 mi by A 5152 and B 5445

at Gresford Northeast : 3 mi by A 483 on B 5445

Pant-yr-Ochain
Old Wrexham Rd, South : 1 mi ⊠ LL12 8TY – ℰ *(01978) 853 525*
– www.pantyrochain-gresford.co.uk – Closed 25 December
Rest – Carte £ 20/31

♦ Classic country manor house with mature, manicured gardens leading down to a lake. Daily changing menu offers hearty, wholesome, all-day dishes, ranging from pub classics to more modern fare.

Ireland

Northern Ireland

ANNAHILT = Eanach Eilte – Lisburn – **712** N/O4 – see Hillsborough

BALLINTOY – Moyle – **712** M2 35 C1
▶ Belfast 59 mi – Ballycastle 8 mi – Londonderry 48 mi – Lisburn 67 mi

Whitepark House without rest
150 Whitepark Rd, West : 1.5 mi on A 2 ⊠ BT54 6NH – ℰ (028) 2073 1482 – www.whiteparkhouse.com
3 rm – †£75 ††£100
♦ Charming 18C house with lovely wall hangings, framed silks and other Asian artefacts from the personable owner's travels. Comfy, open-fired lounge and individually decorated, antique-furnished bedrooms. Breakfast around communal table.

BALLYCLARE (Bealach Cláir) – Newtownabbey – **712** N/O3 35 D2
– pop. 8 770
▶ Belfast 14 mi – Newtownabbey 6 mi – Lisburn 23 mi

Oregano
29 Ballyrobert Rd, South : 3.25 mi by A 57 on B 56 ⊠ BT39 9RY – ℰ (028) 9084 0099 – www.oreganorestaurant.co.uk – Closed 11-13 July, 24-27 December, Saturday lunch and Monday
Rest – Menu £ 15/18 – Carte £ 24/34
♦ Very remotely set, unassuming Victorian house concealing a spacious, modern bar and lounge, and a stylish restaurant hung with contemporary art. Good value modern British cooking uses local produce and displays some European influences. Flavours are honest, clean and clear.

BALLYMENA (An Baile Meánach) – Ballymena – **712** N3 35 C2
– pop. 28 717 ▌Ireland
▶ Belfast 27 mi – Dundalk 78 mi – Larne 21 mi – Londonderry 51 mi
🛈 1-29 Bridge St ℰ (028) 2563 59 00, www.ballymena.gov.uk
🏌 128 Raceview Rd, ℰ (028) 2586 12 07
◉ Antrim Glens★★★ - Murlough Bay★★★ (Fair Head ≤★★★), NE : 32 mi by A 26, A 44, A 2 and minor road - Glengariff Forest Park★★ **AC** (Waterfall★★), NW : 13 mi by A 43 – Glengariff★, NE : 18 mi by A 43 – Glendun★, NE : 19 mi by A 43, B 14 and A2 – Antrim (Round Tower★) S : 9.5 mi by A 26

at Galgorm West : 3 mi on A 42

Galgorm Resort and Spa
136 Fenaghy Rd, West : 1.5 mi on Cullybacky rd ⊠ BT42 1EA – ℰ (028) 2588 1001 – www.galgorm.com
75 rm – †£105/155 ††£105/245
Rest *River Room* **Rest** *Gillies* – see restaurant listing
♦ Victorian manor house with newer extensions, set in large grounds. Stylish interior with plenty of lounge space, huge function capacity and excellent spa/leisure club. Modern bedrooms boast state-of-the-art facilities; some have balconies.

River Room – at Galgorm Resort and Spa
136 Fenaghy Rd, West : 1.5 mi on Cullybacky rd ⊠ BT42 1EA – ℰ (028) 2588 1001 – www.galgorm.com
Rest – (closed Monday-Tuesday) (dinner only and Sunday lunch) Menu £ 25 (lunch) – Carte £ 33/40
♦ Formal fine dining room set in a stylishly furnished, whitewashed Victorian manor house. Floor to ceiling windows provide panoramic views across the River Mein. Menus are classically based.

Gillies – at Galgorm Resort and Spa
136 Fenaghy Rd, West : 1.5 mi on Cullybacky rd ⊠ BT42 1EA – ℰ (028) 2588 1001 – www.galgorm.com
Rest – Carte £ 19/36
♦ Laid-back, split-level steakhouse with large outside dining area; set within a smartly appointed, whitewashed Victorian manor house. Extensive all-day menu. Live music in the bar at weekends.

BANGOR (Beannchar) – North Down – **712** O/P4 – pop. 58 388

Ireland

▶ Belfast 15 mi – Newtownards 5 mi

ℹ 34 Quay St ℘ (028) 9127 00 69, www.bangor-local.com

👁 North Down Heritage Centre★

🄶 Ulster Folk and Transport Museum★★ **AC**, W : 8 mi by A 2. Newtownards : Movilla Priory (Cross Slabs★) S : 4 mi by A 21 - Mount Stewart★★★ **AC**, SE : 90 mi by A 21 and A 20 – Scrabo Tower (≤★★) S : 6.5 mi by A 21 – Ballycopeland Windmill★, SE : 10 mi by B 21 and A 2, turning right at Millisle – Strangford Lough★ (Castle Espie Centre★ **AC** - Nendrum Monastery★) - Grey Abbey★ **AC**, SE : 20 mi by A 2, A 21 and A 20

Clandeboye Lodge

10 Estate Rd, Clandeboye, Southwest : 3 mi by A 2 and Dundonald rd following signs for Blackwood Golf Centre ✉ BT19 1UR
– ℘ (028) 9185 2500 – www.clandeboyelodge.com
– Closed 24-26 December
43 rm ⌑ – †£ 70/85 ††£ 85/130
Rest *Clanbrasserie* – see restaurant listing

♦ Well-run property on the site of a former estate school house, surrounded by 4 acres of woodland and well-placed for country and coast. Airy, open-plan guest areas and contemporary bedrooms. Huge array of function rooms in separate block.

Cairn Bay Lodge without rest

278 Seacliffe Rd, East : 1.25 mi by Quay St ✉ BT20 5HS
– ℘ (028) 9146 7636 – www.cairnbaylodge.com
– Closed 6-27 February
5 rm ⌑ – †£ 45/70 ††£ 70/90

♦ Large, whitewashed Edwardian house overlooking the bay. Comfy guest areas feature unusual objets d'art and ornaments; spacious, individually styled bedrooms boast plenty of extras. Friendly owners leave homemade cake on the landing. Small beauty/therapy facility.

Shelleven House without rest

59-61 Princetown Rd ✉ BT20 3TA – ℘ (028) 9127 1777
– www.shellevenhouse.com
11 rm ⌑ – †£ 37/60 ††£ 70/80

♦ Double-fronted, three-storey, Victorian end terrace, in a smart residential area close to the marina. Open-plan lounge and breakfast room; excellent breakfasts. Well-kept bedrooms vary in shape and size; front rooms boast great coast views.

Boat House

Seacliff Rd ✉ BT20 5HA – ℘ (028) 9146 9253 – www.theboathouseni.co.uk
– Closed 1 week October, 1 January, Monday and Tuesday
Rest – Menu £ 22 (lunch and early dinner)/25 – Carte £ 28/40

♦ Delightful former lifeboat station with harbourside terrace. Experienced brothers source quality local produce. Inventive tasting menu and classical, seasonal à la carte with Dutch twists.

Jeffers at Blackwood

Blackwood Golf Centre, Southwest: 3 mi by A 2 and Dundonald Rd ✉ BT19 1GB
– ℘ (028) 9185 3818 – www.jeffersbythemarina.com
– Closed 25-26 December, 1 January, 12 July, Sunday and Monday
Rest – (booking advisable) Menu £ 25 – Carte £ 20/37

♦ Set within Blackwood Golf Centre, this is a restaurant of two halves: upstairs is an all-day affair serving breakfast and light snacks; downstairs is a formal dining room with red banquettes, a semi-open kitchen and traditional grill menu.

BANGOR

✕✕ Clanbrasserie – at Clandeboye Lodge Hotel
10 Estate Rd, Clandeboye, Southwest : 3 mi by A 2 and Dundonald rd following signs for Blackwood Golf Centre ✉ *BT19 1UR –* ✆ *(028) 9185 2500 – www.clandeboyelodge.com – Closed 24-26 December*
Rest – *(bar lunch Monday-Saturday)* Menu £ 20 – Carte £ 20/30
• Airy, high-ceilinged dining room in a well-run hotel that's surrounded by 4 acres of woodland. Stylish, minimalist décor: dine beside the fire in winter or alfresco in summer. Modish menus.

✕ Jeffers by the Marina
7 Grays Hill ✉ *BT20 3BB –* ✆ *(028) 9185 9555 – www.jeffersbythemarina.com – Closed second week July, 25-26 December and Monday except bank holidays*
Rest – Menu £ 23 – Carte £ 22/33
• Smart restaurant with granite-topped tables and white tiles and newspaper clippings on the walls. Extensive menu has a strong seafood base and good value specials evolve throughout the day.

🍺 Coyle's
44 High St ✉ *BT20 5AZ –* ✆ *(028) 9127 0362 – www.coylesbistro.co.uk – Closed 25 December*
Rest – *(closed Monday)* Carte £ 19/30
• Friendly, laid-back, typically Irish pub; a great place for a quiet drink and a good meal. Bar menu offers classics and some international influences; bistro menu steps things up a gear.

🍺 Salty Dog with rm
✉ *BT20 5EY –* ✆ *(028) 9127 0696 – www.thesaltydogbistro.com – Closed 25-26 December*
15 rm – †£ 50/70 ††£ 80/95
Rest – *(booking advisable)* Menu £ 19 (lunch) – Carte £ 19/28
• Large Victorian pub at the head of the harbour, affording pleasant sea views. Smart, modern interior, polished tables and glass-fronted terrace. Unfussy cooking of local produce - set menu evolves throughout the day. Good-sized bedrooms come with period charm.

BELFAST

See city maps on following pages   **35** D2

NORTHERN IRELAND

Belfast – pop. 276 459 – 712 O4 – Ireland
▶ Dublin 103 – Londonderry 70

Tourist Information

47 Donegal Pl ✆(028) 9024 66 09, www.gotobelfast.com

Airports

✈ Belfast International Airport, Aldergrove : ✆ (028) 9448 4848, W : 15 ½ m. by A 52 AY
✈ George Best Belfast City Airport : ✆ (028) 9093 9093

Ferries and Shipping Lines

⛴ to Isle of Man (Douglas) (Isle of Man Steam Packet Co. Ltd) (summer only) (2 h 45 mn) – to Stranraer (Stena Line) 4-5 daily (1 h 30 mn/3 h 15 mn), (Seacat Scotland) March-January (90 mn) – to Liverpool (Norfolkline Irish Sea) daily (8 h 30 mn)

Golf Courses

⛳ Balmoral 518 Lisburn Rd, ✆(028) 9038 15 14
⛳ Belvoir Park Newtonbreda 73 Church Rd, ✆(028) 90 49 16 93
⛳ Fortwilliam Downview Ave, ✆(028) 9037 07 70

⊙ SIGHTS

In the town : City★ • Ulster Museum★ AZ**M1** • City Hall★ BY • Donegall Square★ BY**20** • Botanic Gardens★ AZ • St Anne's Cathedral★ BX • Crown Liquor Saloon★ BY • Sinclair Seamens Church★ BX • St Malachy's Church★ BY
In the surrounding area : Carrickfergus Castle★★ **AC** NE : 9.5 mi by A 2
On the outskirts : Belfast Zoological Gardens★★ AC, N : 5 mi by A 6 AY

846

BELFAST

INDEX OF STREET NAMES IN BELFAST

Street	Ref
Adelaïde St	BY
Airport Rd	AY
Albert Bridge	AZ 2
Albert Bridge Rd	AZ
Albert Square	BX 3
Alexandre Park Ave	AY
Alfred St	BY
Annadale Ave	AZ
Annadale Embankment	AZ 4
Ann St	BY 5
Antrim Rd	AY
Ardenlee Rd	AZ
Balmoral Ave	AZ
Bedford St	BY
Beersbridge Rd	AZ
Belmont Rd	BZ 7
Botanic Ave	BZ
Bradbury Pl	BZ 9
Bridge End	AZ 10
Bridge St	BY 12
Castlecourt Shopping Centre	BXY
Castlereagh Rd	AZ
Castlereagh St	AZ 14
Castle Pl	BY
Castle St	BY
Cavehill Rd	AY
Chichester St	BX
City Hospital St	BZ
Cliftonville Rd	AY
Clifton St	BX 15
College Square	BY
Corporation Square	BX 16
Corporation St	BX
Cranmore Park	AZ
Cregagh Rd	AZ
Cromac St	BY
Crumlin Rd	AY, BX
Dargan Rd	AY
Divis St	BY
Donegall Park Ave	AY
Donegall Pass	BZ
Donegall Pl	BY
Donegall Quay	BXY 19
Donegall Rd	AZ, BZ
Donegall Square	BY 20
Donegall St	BX
Dublin Rd	BZ
Durham St	BY
East Bridge St	AZ 23
Falls Rd	AZ
Forestside Shopping Centre	AZ
Frederic St	BX
Galwally Rd	AZ
Garmoyle St	AY 24
Grand Parade	AZ 25
Gray's Lane	AY
Great George's St	BX
Great Victoria St	BY, BZ
Grosvenor Rd	AZ, BY
High St	BXY 28
Holywood Rd	AZ
Howard St	BY 29
James Street South	BY 30
Ladas Drive	BY 31
Lagan Bridge	BX 32
Lansdowne Rd	AY
Lisburn Rd	AZ, BZ
Malone Rd	AZ
May St	BX
Middlepath St	AZ 34
Millfield Carrick Hill	BXY
Mountpottinger Rd	AZ 36
Mount Merrion Ave	AZ 35
Nelson St	BX
Newtownards Rd	AZ 38
North Circular Rd	AY
North Queen St	AY
North St	BX
Oldpark Rd	AY
Ormeau Ave	BZ
Ormeau Embankment	AZ
Ormeau Rd	AZ, BZ
Oxford St	BY
Peters Hill	BX
Queens Rd	AY
Queen Elizabeth Bridge	BY 40
Queen's Bridge	BY 41
Queen's Square	BX 42
Ravenhill	AZ
Rosemary St	BY 44
Rosetta Park	AZ 45
Royal Ave	BXY
Saintfield Rd	AZ 47
Sandy Row	BZ
Shankill Rd	AZ
Shore Rd	AY
Short Strand	AZ 48
Springfield Rd	AZ
Stranmillis Rd	AZ
Sydenham Rd	AZ 49
Townsend St	BX
University Rd	BZ
University Square	AZ 52
University St	BZ
Upper Knockbreda Rd	AZ
Victoria St	BY
Waring St	BX 54
Wellington Pl	BY 55
Westlink	BY
Woodstock Rd	AZ
Woodvale Rd	AY
York Rd	AY
York St	BX

 Merchant

16 Skipper St ✉ *BT1 2DZ* – ℰ *(028) 9023 4888*
– *www.themerchanthotel.com*   BXx
60 rm – †£ 150/240 ††£ 150/350 – 2 suites
Rest *Great Room* – see restaurant listing
Rest *Berts* – *(dinner only and lunch Saturday and Sunday)* Menu £ 20
– Carte £ 25/35
♦ Former Ulster Bank HQ with an impressive Victorian façade. Plush, intimately styled bedrooms; those in the annexe are more contemporary. Rooftop gym comes with an outdoor hot tub and skyline view; afterwards relax in the swish cocktail bar. Choice of fine dining or brasserie classics accompanied by live jazz.

 Fitzwilliam

Great Victoria St ✉ *BT2 7BQ* – ℰ *(028) 9044 2080*
– *www.fitzwilliamhotelbelfast.com*   BYe
129 rm – †£ 190 ††£ 200, ⍰ £ 19 – 1 suite
Rest *Menu by Kevin Thornton* – see restaurant listing
♦ Stylish, contemporary hotel next to Grand Opera House, boasting striking bold colours and comfy bedrooms with good facilities; the higher you go, the better the view. Afternoon teas in snug lobby and comfort food in brightly coloured bar.

 Malmaison

34-38 Victoria St ✉ *BT1 3GH* – ℰ *(028) 9022 0200* – *www.malmaison.com*
62 rm – †£ 160 ††£ 160, ⍰ £ 14.50 – 2 suites   BYv
Rest *Brasserie* – see restaurant listing
♦ Converted Victorian seed warehouse with ornate exterior. Original features blends with modern furnishings throughout. Dark-hued reception leads to a snug bar; stylish bedrooms offer good facilities – one boasts a 9' bed and snooker table.

BELFAST

Radisson Blu

3 Cromac Pl, Cromac Wood ⊠ BT7 2JB – ℰ (028) 9043 4065
– www.radissonblu.co.uk/hotelbelfast   BYz
119 rm – †£ 95/184 ††£ 170/196 – 1 suite
Rest *Filini* – Italian influences – *(closed Sunday)* Menu £ 20 (lunch)
– Carte £ 25/40

♦ Stylish, modern hotel on the site of former gasworks. Smart, up-to-date facilities. Two room styles – Urban or Nordic; both boast fine views over city and waterfront. Restaurant/bar with floor-to-ceiling windows and part-open kitchen.

Ten Square

10 Donegall Sq South ⊠ BT1 5JD – ℰ (028) 9024 1001 – www.tensquare.co.uk
– Closed 25 December   BYx
22 rm – †£ 155 ††£ 175, ⊇ £ 12
Rest *Grill Room* – see restaurant listing

♦ Sizeable Victorian property in the town centre, hidden behind city hall. Stylish, modern bedrooms display bold feature walls and offer a good level of facilities. Large first floor function room is popular for both meetings and weddings.

Malone Lodge

60 Eglantine Ave ⊠ BT9 6DY – ℰ (028) 9038 8000
– www.malonelodgehotelbelfast.com   AZn
90 rm ⊇ – †£ 70/140 ††£ 70/140 – 3 suites
Rest *The Green Door* – *(closed Sunday dinner)* Carte £ 20/25

♦ Well-run, privately owned hotel in peaceful 19C terrace. Bedrooms display good facilities, with smart corporate bedrooms in main house and executive rooms/apartments in various annexes. Wood-furnished bar; simple restaurant offering classical menus.

Crescent Townhouse

13 Lower Cres ⊠ BT7 1NR – ℰ (028) 9032 3349 – www.crescenttownhouse.com
– Closed 24-26 December, 1 January and 11-12 July   BZx
17 rm ⊇ – †£ 75 ††£ 85/100
Rest *Metro Brasserie* – see restaurant listing

♦ Centrally located Regency-style townhouse run by a welcoming team. Snug first floor lounge hung with oils. Well-equipped, spacious bedrooms are split between the old house and newer extension; some boast four-poster beds and huge bathrooms.

Ravenhill House without rest

690 Ravenhill Rd ⊠ BT6 0BZ – ℰ (028) 9020 7444 – www.ravenhillhouse.com
– Closed 20-31 December, 1-7 January, 1-15 July and 27 August-2 September
5 rm ⊇ – †£ 50/55 ††£ 75   AZs

♦ Friendly, red-brick Victorian house with bay windows, set in the city suburbs. Bright, homely lounge and wood-furnished breakfast room. Colourful bedrooms boast good facilities. Organic breakfasts feature homemade muesli and wheat for the bread is home-milled.

Roseleigh House without rest

19 Rosetta Park, South : 1.5 mi by A 24 (Ormeau Rd) ⊠ BT6 0DL – ℰ (028)
9064 4414 – www.roseleighhouse.co.uk – Closed Christmas-New Year
6 rm ⊇ – †£ 45 ††£ 65   AZr

♦ Imposing Victorian house close to the Belvoir Park golf course and in a fairly quiet residential suburb. Brightly decorated and well-kept bedrooms with modern amenities.

Great Room – at Merchant Hotel

16 Skipper St ⊠ BT1 2DZ – ℰ (028) 9023 4888 – www.themerchanthotel.com
– Closed Saturday lunch   BXx
Rest – Menu £ 23/27 – Carte dinner £ 30/50

♦ Grand old banking hall, set behind the impressive Victorian façade of the former Ulster Bank HQ. Impressive ornate plasterwork and original stained glass windows. Ambitious French-based menu.

BELFAST

XX Menu by Kevin Thornton – at Fitzwilliam Hotel
Great Victoria St ⊠ *BT2 7BQ* – ℰ *(028) 9044 2080*
– *www.fitzwilliamhotelbelfast.com*
BYr
Rest – *(dinner only) (booking essential)* Carte £ 30/42

◆ Three-roomed restaurant on 1st floor of stylish hotel; large centre table seats one large party or several smaller; if you're a couple, choose a booth. Classic dishes cooked in modern Irish style.

XX James Street South
21 James St South ⊠ *BT2 7GA* – ℰ *(028) 9043 4310*
– *www.jamesstreetsouth.co.uk* – *Closed 25-26 December, 1 and 12 January, Easter Sunday and Monday, 12 July and Sunday lunch*
BYo
Rest – Menu £ 17 (lunch) – Carte £ 28/42

◆ Smart backstreet restaurant with Victorian façade, slate-floored bar and bright, modern dining room. Good-sized menus offer tasty dishes of simply cooked local produce. Efficient service.

XX Cayenne
7 Ascot House, Shaftesbury Sq ⊠ *BT2 7DB* – ℰ *(028) 9033 1532*
– *www.cayenne-restaurant.co.uk* – *Closed 25-26 December, 1 January, 12-13 July and Tuesday*
BZr
Rest – Asian influences – *(dinner only and lunch Thursday, Friday and Sunday) (booking essential)* Menu £ 16/28 – Carte £ 28/44

◆ Stylish restaurant with leather-furnished lounge and large dining room displaying Asian/Oriental touches. Choice of good value set or more adventurous à la carte menus, offering unfussy, flavoursome cooking with an Asian base. Service is friendly and efficient.

XX Shu
253 Lisburn Rd ⊠ *BT9 7EN* – ℰ *(028) 9038 1655* – *www.shu-restaurant.com*
– *Closed 24-26 December, 1 January, 11-13 July and Sunday*
AZz
Rest – Menu £ 28 – Carte £ 26/35

◆ Modern L-shaped restaurant in affluent residential district, with cream/dark wood décor and lively, vibrant atmosphere. Modern British cooking is guided by seasonality and availability of local produce.

XX Deanes
36 Howard St ⊠ *BT1 6PF* – ℰ *(028) 9033 1134* – *www.michaeldeane.co.uk*
– *Closed Sunday and bank holidays*
BYn
Rest – Menu £ 18 (lunch and early dinner) – Carte £ 31/43

◆ Three places in one. Stylish brasserie serves interesting, classically based dishes with original modern style. Smaller eatery offers more casual seafood dining. Limited opening in upstairs restaurant, which has elaborate, inventive, 5 or 7 course tasting menus.

XX Grill Room – at Ten Square Hotel
10 Donegall Sq South ⊠ *BT1 5JD* – ℰ *(028) 9024 1001* – *www.tensquare.co.uk*
– *Closed 25 December*
BYx
Rest – Carte £ 18/35

◆ Set within an attractive building, in a great central location. Menus feature fresh fish, seafood and locally reared, prime-aged, grain-fed beef. Entertainment in the vibrant bar at weekends.

XX Brasserie – at Malmaison Hotel
34-38 Victoria St ⊠ *BT1 3GH* – ℰ *(028) 9022 0200* – *www.malmaison.com*
Rest – Menu £ 18 – Carte £ 27/30
BYv

◆ Located within a fine old warehouse, with high beamed ceilings, richly coloured décor and intimate booths. Choice of à la carte or daily changing set menu; ingredients are strictly regional.

No 27

27 Talbot St ⊠ BT1 2LD – ℘ (028) 9031 2884 – www.no27.co.uk – Closed 24-26 December, 1 January, 12-13 July, Sunday and Monday   BXa
Rest – Carte £ 27/41
• Bustling restaurant opposite the cathedral; sleekly styled with wooden floor, modern lighting and open kitchen. Simple lunch choices; daily changing dinner menu of modern, globally influenced dishes. Fresh market produce.

Deanes Deli

42-44 Bedford St ⊠ BT2 7FF – ℘ (028) 9024 8800 – www.michaeldeane.co.uk – Closed 25-26 December, 1 January, Easter, 1 week July and Sunday
Rest – Menu £ 28 – Carte £ 25/33   BYa
• Spacious, glass-fronted city centre restaurant serving a mix of comfort food and globally influenced dishes, with a good choice of daily specials. Bustling, chatty atmosphere. Small coffee shop serves homemade cakes.

Ginger Bistro

7-8 Hope St ⊠ BT2 5EE – ℘ (028) 9024 4421 – www.gingerbistro.com – Closed Christmas, New Year, Easter, 3 days mid-July, lunch Monday, Sunday and bank holidays   BYZi
Rest – Carte £ 26/32
• Keenly run neighbourhood eatery with modern artwork for sale and bespoke fish-themed paintings. Eclectic menus display worldwide influences; good value lunch/pre-theatre. Owner is passionate about using only Irish ingredients.

Molly's Yard

1 College Green Mews, Botanic Ave ⊠ BT7 1LW – ℘ (028) 9032 2600 – www.mollysyard.co.uk – Closed 24-26 December, 1 January and Sunday
Rest – (booking essential) Carte £ 19/31   BZs
• Friendly split-level bistro in former coach house and stables, with exposed brickwork and pleasant courtyard. Menus display fresh, unfussy, modern bistro fare; simpler dishes at lunch. Fine locally brewed ales and stouts.

Mourne Seafood Bar

34-36 Bank St ⊠ BT1 1HL – ℘ (028) 9024 8544 – www.mourneseafood.com – Closed 24-26 December, 1 January, 17 March, Easter Sunday and Monday, and dinner Sunday-Monday   BYc
Rest – Seafood – (booking essential at dinner) (lunch bookings not accepted) Carte £ 17/26
• Popular, split-level seafood restaurant with small shop and cookery school. Blackboard menus offer a huge array of fresh dishes; go for the specials or the Carlingford oysters and a pint of stout. Large rear bar serves tapas-style dishes.

Metro Brasserie – at Crescent Townhouse Hotel

13 Lower Cres ⊠ BT7 1NR – ℘ (028) 9032 3349 – www.crescenttownhouse.com – Closed 24-26 December, 1 January and 12-13 July   BZx
Rest – (dinner only) Carte £ 18/28
• Large, modern brasserie on the ground floor of a Regency-style townhouse hotel. Accessible modern dishes and dedicated vegetarian menu. Pub quiz on Thursdays and DJ on Saturdays in the bar.

Each starred restaurant lists three specialities that are typical of its style of cuisine. These may not always be on the menu but in their place expect delicious seasonal dishes. Be sure to try them.

BENBURB – Dungannon – **712** L4 – see Dungannon

BUSHMILLS (Muileann na Buaise) – Moyle – 712 M2 – pop. 1 319 — 35 C1
– ✉ Bushmills ▌Ireland

▶ Belfast 57 mi – Ballycastle 12 mi – Coleraine 10 mi

🏌 Bushfoot Portballintrae 50 Bushfoot Rd, ℰ (028) 2073 13 17

🅖 Giant's Causeway★★★ (Hamilton's Seat ≤★★) N : 2 mi by A 2 and minor road
- Dunluce Castle★★ **AC** W : 3 mi by A 2 – Carrick-a-rede Rope Bridge★★★ **AC**, E :
8 mi by A 2 – Magilligan Strand★★, W : 18 mi by A 2, A 29 and A 2 – Gortmore
Viewpoint★★, SW : 23 mi by A 2, A 29, A 23 and minor road from Downhill
– Downhill★ (Mussenden Temple★), W : 15 mi by A 2, A 29 and A 2

🏨 Bushmills Inn
9 Dunluce Rd ✉ BT57 8QG – ℰ (028) 2073 3000 – www.bushmillsinn.com
– Closed 25 December
41 rm ⌑ – †£ 98/158 ††£ 138/298
Rest *Restaurant* – see restaurant listing

♦ Proudly run, part-17C whitewashed inn that successfully blends the old with the
new. Lovely cinema, state-of-the-art function rooms and spacious, modern bedrooms boasting up-to-date facilities. Old whiskey bar features an open peat fire.

✂✂ Restaurant – at Bushmills Inn
9 Dunluce Rd ✉ BT57 8QG – ℰ (028) 2073 3000 – www.bushmillsinn.com
– Closed 25 December
Rest – (carvery lunch Sunday) Carte £ 22/38

♦ Three-roomed restaurant and old whiskey bar complete with peat fire, set in a
proudly run, smartly refurbished 17C inn. Choose from main room, garden room
or charming booths. Traditional menu.

COLERAINE (Cúil Raithin) – Coleraine – 712 L2 – pop. 24 089 — 35 C1
▌Ireland

▶ Belfast 53 mi – Ballymena 25 mi – Londonderry 31 mi – Omagh 65 mi

🅘 Railway Rd ℰ (028) 7034 47 23, www.causewaycoastandglens.com

🏌 Castlerock 65 Circular Rd, ℰ (028) 7084 83 14

🏌 Brown Trout 209 Agivey Rd, Aghadowey, ℰ (028) 7086 82 09

🅖 Giant's Causeway★★★ (Hamilton's Seat ≤★★), NE : 14 mi by A 29 and A2
- Dunluce Castle★★ **AC**, NE : 8 mi by A 29 and A 2 – Carrick-a-rede-Rope
Bridge★★★ **AC**, NE : 18 mi by A 29 and A2 – Benvarden★ **AC** E : 5 mi by B 67
– Magilligan Strand★★, NW : 8 mi by A 2 - Gortmore Viewpoint★★, NW : 12 mi by
A 2 and minor road from Downhill - Downhill★**AC** (Mussenden Temple★), NE :
7 mi by A 2

🏠 Greenhill House without rest
24 Greenhill Rd, Aghadowey, South : 9 mi by A 29 on B 66 ✉ BT51 4EU
– ℰ (028) 7086 8241 – www.greenhill-house.co.uk – Closed 1 November-31
December
6 rm ⌑ – †£ 45 ††£ 70

♦ An agreeably clean-lined Georgian house with large windows overlooking
fields. Game and course fishing available locally. Neat bedrooms replete with extra touches.

COMBER (An Comar) – Ards – 712 O4 – pop. 8 933 — 35 D2
▶ Belfast 10 mi – Newtownards 5 mi – Lisburn 17 mi

🏠 Anna's House without rest
Tullynagee, 35 Lisbarnett Rd., Southeast : 3.5 mi by A 22 ✉ BT23 6AW – ℰ (028)
9754 1566 – www.annashouse.com – Closed Christmas-New Year
4 rm ⌑ – †£ 60/65 ††£ 110

♦ Farmhouse with cosy lounge and comfy bedrooms with lovely vistas. Glass-
walled extension has geo-thermal heating and lake views. Organic breakfasts utilise produce from garden.

CRUMLIN (Cromghlinn) – Antrim – 712 N4 – pop. 4 259   35 C2

▶ Belfast 14 mi – Ballymena 20 mi

Ballyrobin
144-146 Ballyrobin Rd, North : 7 mi by A 26 ⊠ BT29 4EG – ℰ (028) 9422 2211
– www.ballyrobincountrylodge.com – Closed 25 December
21 rm – ♦£ 45/83 ♦♦£ 72/86, ⊆ £ 8.95   **Rest** – Carte £ 17/29

♦ Smart, country style lodge, just a stone's throw from the airport and offering a week's free parking. Stylish, modern bedrooms are luxuriously appointed. Eat in one of the cosy rooms in the original pub building or the conservatory-style extension. Menus offer hearty portions of good old Irish dishes.

Caldhame Lodge without rest
102 Moira Rd, Nutts Corner, Southeast : 1.25 mi on A 26 ⊠ BT29 4HG – ℰ (028) 9442 3099 – www.caldhamelodge.co.uk
8 rm ⊆ – ♦£ 40/45 ♦♦£ 60/70

♦ Purpose-built guesthouse near the airport, with pleasant mix of lawns and paved terracing. Comfy, slightly kitsch guest areas include a leather-furnished lounge filled with family photos and a conservatory breakfast room. Good-sized bedrooms boast warm fabrics.

DERRY/LONDONDERRY = Doire – Sligo – 712 K2/3 – see Londonderry

DONAGHADEE (Domhnach Daoi) – Ards – 712 P4 – pop. 6 470   35 D2
🔹 Ireland

▶ Belfast 18 mi – Ballymena 44 mi

🏌 Warren Rd, ℰ (028) 9188 36 24

◉ Ballycopeland Windmill★ **AC** S : 4 mi by A 2 and B 172. Mount Stewart★★★ **AC**, SW : 10 mi by A 2 and minor road SW – Movilla (cross slabs★), Newtownards, SW : 7 mi by B 172

Grace Neill's
33 High St ⊠ BT21 0AH – ℰ (02891) 884 595 – www.graceneills.com
Rest – Menu £ 18 (lunch) – Carte £ 18/38

♦ Characterful beamed pub – the oldest in Ireland – decorated with antiques and old pictures. Extensive, largely classical menu, with express lunches and daily fish and seafood specials.

Pier 36 with rm
36 The Parade ⊠ BT21 0HE – ℰ (028) 9188 4466 – www.pier36.co.uk – Closed 25 December
7 rm ⊆ – ♦£ 50 ♦♦£ 99   **Rest** – Carte £ 18/38

♦ Spacious harbourside pub, set opposite a lighthouse. Extensive menus feature a mix of classic, modern and international influences, and plenty of fresh, local seafood. Good weekday deals. Simple, comfy bedrooms boast sea views.

DOWNPATRICK (Dún Pádraig) – Down – 712 O4/5 – pop. 10 316   35 D3
🔹 Ireland

▶ Belfast 23 mi – Newry 31 mi – Newtownards 22 mi

◉ Cathedral★ **AC** - Down County Museum★ **AC**

◉ Struell Wells★ **AC**, SE : 2 mi by B 1 - Ardglass★ (Jordan's Castle**AC**), SE : 7 mi by B 1 – Inch Abbey★ **AC**, NW : 2 mi by A 7 – Quoile Countryside Centre★ **AC**, E : 2 mi by A 25 – Castle Ward★★ **AC** (Audley's Castle★), E : 8 mi by A 25

DOWNPATRICK

⌂ Pheasants' Hill Farm without rest 🐾 🐕 📶 🅿 VISA ⊙⊙
37 Killyleagh Rd, North : 3 mi on A 22 ✉ *BT30 9BL* – ✆ *(028) 4461 7246*
– www.pheasantshill.com – Closed 10 December-3 January
3 rm ⊇ – ♦£ 75 ♦♦£ 85
♦ Simple guesthouse surrounded by a 20 acre organic smallholding, complete with rare breeds livestock and a small shop selling their meats. Cosy, homely bedrooms come with pine furnishings and compact shower rooms. Hearty breakfasts.

DUNDRUM (Dún Droma) – Down – 712 O5 – pop. 1 065 🟢 Ireland   35 D3

▶ Belfast 29 mi – Downpatrick 9 mi – Newcastle 4 mi
◉ Castle★ **AC**
⬢ Castlewellan Forest Park★★ **AC**, W : 4 mi by B 180 and A 50 - Tollymore Forest Park★ **AC**, W : 3 mi by B 180 - Drumena Cashel and Souterrain★, W : 4 mi by B 180

⌂ Carriage House without rest 🐾 🛜 📶 🅿
71 Main St ✉ *BT33 0LU* – ✆ *(028) 4375 1635*
– www.carriagehousedundrum.com
3 rm ⊇ – ♦£ 45/50 ♦♦£ 75/80
♦ Welcoming, lilac-washed terraced house with colourful window boxes and attractive rear garden. Comfy, traditionally styled guest areas. Simple bedrooms with plain décor and antique furniture.

✕ Buck's Head Inn 🐾 🍴 VISA ⊙⊙ AE
77-79 Main St ✉ *BT33 0LU* – ✆ *(028) 4375 1868*
– www.bucksheadrestaurant.com
Rest – Seafood – Menu £ 30 (dinner) – Carte £ 20/29
♦ Informal restaurant with attractive terrace and garden. Have drinks in the lounge then choose a dining room; the front bar is a good spot to dine. Good-sized menus of unfussy, traditional cooking with a local seafood base.

✕ Mourne Seafood Bar 🍴 VISA ⊙⊙ AE
10 Main St ✉ *BT33 0LU* – ✆ *(028) 4375 1377* – *www.mourneseafood.com*
– Closed dinner 24 December, 25 December and Monday-Tuesday in winter
Rest – Seafood – *(booking essential in summer)* Carte £ 25/29
♦ Informal, rustic restaurant, set on main street; wood-furnished interior with coastal oil paintings. Classical seafood cooking, with oysters and mussels from owners' beds a speciality.

DUNGANNON (Dún Geanainn) – Dungannon – 712 L4   35 C2
– pop. 11 139 🟢 Ireland

▶ Belfast 42 mi – Ballymena 37 mi – Dundalk 47 mi – Londonderry 60 mi
⬢ The Argory★, S : 5 mi by A 29 and east by minor rd. Ardboe Cross★, NW : 17 mi by A 45, B 161 and B 73 – Springhill★ **AC**, NE : 24 mi by A 29 – Sperrin Mountains★ : Wellbrook Beetling Mill★ **AC**, NW : 22 mi by A 29 and A 505 - Beaghmore Stone Circles★, NW : 24 mi by A 29 and A 505

⌂ Grange Lodge ⌘ 🐾 🛜 📶 🅿 VISA ⊙⊙
7 Grange Rd, Moy, Southeast : 3.5 mi by A 29 ✉ *BT71 7EJ* – ✆ *(028) 8778 4212*
– www.grangelodgecountryhouse.com – Closed 20 December-1 February
5 rm ⊇ – ♦£ 60/69 ♦♦£ 85/89   **Rest** – *(closed Sunday)* Menu £ 36
♦ Attractive Georgian country house set in a peaceful area and surrounded by mature, well-kept gardens, where guests can have afternoon tea. Antique-furnished guest areas display fine sketches and lithographs. Snug, well-appointed bedrooms are immaculately kept and come with good extras. Flower-filled dining room serves traditional menu of unfussy Irish dishes.

DUNGANNON

at Benburb South : 8 mi by B 45 and B 130

Priory House — VISA ⦾ AE
14 Main Street – ⌀ *(028) 3754 7767* – *www.prioryhouserestaurant.com*
– Closed 1 January, Good Friday, 2 weeks spring, 25-26 December, Monday and Tuesday
Rest – Menu £ 25 – Carte £ 22/32
♦ Laid-back, almost bohemian-style bistro and restaurant set within a 200 year old priory that's attached to an art school. Interesting antiques, clocks and pottery abound. Simple, rustic Irish cooking; dinner is of a more ambitious nature.

ENNISKILLEN (Inis Ceithleann) – Fermanagh – 712 J4 – pop. 13 599 — 34 A2

Ireland

▶ Belfast 87 mi – Londonderry 59 mi
🛈 Wellington Rd ⌀ (028) 6632 31 10, www.enniskillen.com
▦ Castlecoole, ⌀ (028) 6632 52 50
◉ Castle Coole★★★ **AC**, SE : 1 m – Florence Court★★ **AC**, SW : 8 mi by A 4 and A 32 – Marble Arch Caves and Forest Nature Reserve★ **AC**, SW : 10 mi by A 4 and A 32. NW by A 26 : Lough Erne★★ : Cliffs of Magho Viewpoint★★★ **AC** - Tully Castle★ **AC** – N by A 32, B 72, A 35 and A 47 : Devenish Island★ **AC** - Castle Archdale Forest Park★ **AC** - White Island★ - Janus Figure★

Lough Erne Resort
Belleek Rd, Northwest : 4 mi on A 46 ✉ *BT93 7ED* — VISA ⦾ AE ①
– ⌀ *(028) 6632 3230* – *www.locherngolfresort.com*
89 rm ☐ – †£ 130/202 ††£ 150/402 – 31 suites – ††£ 280/340
Rest *Catalina* – see restaurant listing
Rest *Lochside* – (dinner only) Carte £ 19/45
♦ Vast, luxurious golf and leisure resort, set between two loughs. Bedrooms have a glitzy feel and are extremely well-appointed; suites and lodges are dotted about the place. Beautiful Thai spa and huge pool boasting a stunning mosaic wall. Fine dining or steaks and tapas-style small plates in the clubhouse.

Manor House
Killadeas, North : 7.5 mi by A 32 on B 82 ✉ *BT94 1NY* – ⌀ *(028) 6862 2200*
– *www.manorhouseresorthotel.com*
79 rm ☐ – †£ 73/125 ††£ 81/140 – 2 suites
Rest *Belleek* – Menu £ 18/28
Rest *Cellar Door* – Carte approx. £ 28
♦ Impressive manor house overlooking Lough Erne. Characterful guest areas and well-equipped leisure and meeting facilities. Traditional bedrooms in main house, more modern rooms in extensions. Formal dining room boasts ornate plasterwork and offers classical menus; more casual all-day dining in the old vaults.

Cedars
301 Killadeas Rd., Irvinestown, North : 10 mi by A 32 on B 82 ✉ *BT94 1PG*
– ⌀ *(028) 6862 1493* – *www.cedarsguesthouse.com*
– Closed 1 week Christmas
10 rm ☐ – †£ 45/55 ††£ 100/110
Rest *Rectory Bistro* – (closed Monday-Tuesday) (dinner only and Sunday lunch) Carte £ 23/31
♦ Good value, converted 19C former rectory with pleasant gardens. Exudes impression of spaciousness; country-style décor. Individually designed bedrooms: ask for numbers 2 or 5. Rustic bistro serves hearty cuisine.

ENNISKILLEN

Catalina – at Lough Erne Resort
Belleek Rd, Northwest : 4 mi on A 46 ✉ *BT93 7ED* – ✆ *(028) 6632 3230*
– *www.lochernegolfresort.com*
Rest – *(dinner only and Sunday lunch)* Menu £ 40 – Carte £ 45/55
♦ Fine dining restaurant boasting great views over Lough Erne, set within a large, luxurious, resort hotel. Contemporary menu showcases top quality ingredients from local and artisan producers.

GALGORM Antrim – Ballymena – 712 N3 – see Ballymena

HILLSBOROUGH (Cromghlinn) – Lisburn – 712 N4 – pop. 3 400   35 C2
📗 Ireland
▶ Belfast 12 mi
🛈 The Square ✆ (028) 9268 97 17, www.discovernorthernireland.com
⊙ Town★ – Fort★
🅶 Rowallane Gardens★ **AC**, Saintfield, E : 10 mi by B 178 and B 6. The Argory★, W : 25 mi by A 1 and M 1

Plough Inn
3 The Square ✉ *BT26 6AG* – ✆ *(028) 9268 2985* – *www.bar-retro.com* – *Closed 25 December*
Rest – Menu £ 12/20 – Carte £ 15/25
♦ Family-run 18C coaching inn that's three establishments in one: a bar with adjoining dining room, café and bistro. Dishes range from light snacks and pub classics to modern, international fare.

Parson's Nose
48 Lisburn St. ✉ *BT26 6AB* – ✆ *(028) 9268 3009* – *www.theparsonsnose.co.uk*
– Closed 25 December
Rest – *(booking advisable)* Menu £ 17/22 – Carte £ 21/34
♦ Characteristical Georgian property built by the first Marquis of Downshire. Rustic, open-fired bar; restaurant above overlooks a lake in the castle grounds. Unashamedly traditional menus and generous portions; the daily fish specials are a hit.

at Annahilt Southeast : 4 mi on B 177 – ✉ Hillsborough

Fortwilliam without rest
210 Ballynahinch Rd, Northwest : 0.25 mi on B 177 ✉ *BT26 6BH* – ✆ *(028) 9268 2255* – *www.fortwilliamcountryhouse.com*
4 rm ⊇ – ♦£ 45 ♦♦£ 70
♦ Attractive bay-windowed farmhouse with neat gardens, set in 80 acres of land. Keenly run and comfortable throughout. Individually designed bedrooms boast pleasant outlooks and extras; two have private bathrooms.

Pheasant
410 Upper Ballynahinch Rd, North : 1 mi on Lisburn rd ✉ *BT26 6NR* – ✆ *(028) 9263 8056* – *www.thepheasantrestaurant.co.uk* – *Closed 12 July and 25-26 December*
Rest – Menu £ 10/12 – Carte £ 15/30
♦ Sizeable yellow-washed pub with gothic styling and typical Irish feel. Menus offer local, seasonal produce, with seafood a speciality in summer and game featuring highly in the winter.

HOLYWOOD (Ard Mhic Nasca) – North Down – 712 O4   35 D2
– pop. 12 037 📗 Ireland
▶ Belfast 7 mi – Bangor 6 mi
🏌 Holywood Demesne Rd, Nuns Walk, ✆ (028) 9042 21 38
🅶 Cultra : Ulster Folk and Transport Museum★★ **AC**, NE : 1 mi by A 2

HOLYWOOD

Culloden
142 Bangor Rd, East : 1.5 mi on A 2 – BT18 0EX – ℘ (028) 9042 1066
– www.hastingshotels.com
102 rm ⊇ – †£ 190 ††£ 240 – 3 suites
Rest *Cultra Inn* – see restaurant listing
Rest *Mitre* – *(dinner only and Sunday lunch)* Menu £ 30/45 – Carte Monday-Friday £ 31/38

◆ Gothic mansion with well-maintained, sculpture-filled gardens and lough views. Charming, antique-filled interior boasts open fires and fine frescoes. Mix of characterful bedrooms with pleasant views or more contemporary rooms. Smart spa. Classical menus and good views in Mitre; informal dining in Cultra Inn.

Rayanne House
60 Demesne Rd, by My Lady's Mile Rd – BT18 9EX – ℘ (028) 9042 5859
– www.rayannehouse.com – Closed 24 December-15 January and August
11 rm ⊇ – †£ 70/95 ††£ 110/130
Rest – *(dinner only) (residents only)* Menu £ 35/48 – Carte £ 25/45

◆ Victorian red-brick house in peaceful residential area. Homely, antique-filled guest areas. Stylish, contemporary bedrooms with country house feel, good facilities, smart bathrooms and extras. Formal dining room with seasonal menu; interesting breakfasts.

Beech Hill without rest
23 Ballymoney Rd, Craigantlet, Southeast : 4.5 mi by A 2 on Craigantlet rd
– BT23 4TG – ℘ (028) 9042 5892 – www.beech-hill.net
3 rm ⊇ – †£ 55/60 ††£ 90/100

◆ Country house in rural location. Pleasant clutter of trinkets and antiques in guest areas which include a conservatory. Neat, traditionally styled bedrooms: a very fine home.

Fontana
61A High St – BT18 9AE – ℘ (028) 9080 9908 – Closed 25-26 December, 1-2 January, Saturday lunch, Sunday dinner and Monday
Rest – Menu £ 18 (lunch) – Carte £ 17/32

◆ Smart, first floor restaurant, accessed via a narrow, town centre passageway. Modern British cooking displays Mediterranean influences; specials include local fish, in unfussy, flavoursome combinations. Good value set lunch and midweek dinner.

Cultra Inn – at Culloden Hotel
142 Bangor Rd, East : 1.5 mi on A 2 – BT18 0EX – ℘ (028) 9042 5840
– www.hastingshotels.com
Rest – Carte approx. £ 25

◆ Informal restaurant located within the grounds of a famous, antique-filled Gothic mansion overlooking Belfast Loch. Picnic benches for alfresco dining. Choose between light bites and grills.

KILLINCHY – Ards – 712 O4   35 D2
▶ Belfast 16 mi – Newtownards 11 mi – Lisburn 17 mi – Bangor 16 mi

Balloo House - Restaurant
1 Comber Rd, (1st floor), West : 0.75 mi on A 22 – BT23 6PA – ℘ (028) 9754 1210 – www.balloohouse.com – Closed 25 December
Rest – *(closed Sunday and Monday) (dinner only) (booking essential)* Menu £ 27 – Carte £ 29/38

◆ Intimate, first floor restaurant with high beamed ceilings and linen-laid tables. Flavourful classic cooking has modern touches; hearty yet refined dishes feature local produce.

LARNE (Latharna) – Larne – **712** O3 – pop. 18 228 — Ireland — 35 D2

▶ Belfast 23 mi – Ballymena 20 mi

🚢 to Fleetwood (Stena Line) daily (8 h) – to Cairnryan (P & O Irish Sea) 3-5 daily (1 h/2 h 15 mn)

🛈 Narrow Gauge Rd ℰ (028) 2826 00 88, www.larne.gov.uk

⛳ Cairndhu Ballygally 192 Coast Rd, ℰ (028) 2858 39 54

👁 SE : Island Magee (Ballylumford Dolmen★), by ferry and 2 mi by B 90 or 18 mi by A 2 and B 90. NW : Antrim Glens★★★ - Murlough Bay★★★ (Fair Head ≼★★★), N : 46 m by A 2 and minor road – Glenariff Forest Park★★ **AC** (Waterfall★★), N : 30 mi by A 2 and A 43 - Glenariff★, N : 25 mi by A 2 - Glendun★, N : 30 mi by A 2 – Carrickfergus (Castle★★ - St Nicholas' Church★), SW : 15 mi by A 2

⌂ Manor House without rest
23 Olderfleet Rd, Harbour Highway ✉ BT40 1AS
– ℰ (028) 2827 3305 – www.themanorguesthouse.com
– Closed 25-26 December
8 rm ☐ – †£ 30/35 ††£ 55/60

♦ Large Victorian house filled with antiques; the owner has been here nearly 50 years. Lounge boasts immense Chinese vase and gilded art; snug dining room has flocked walls. Cosy, immaculate bedrooms reached via original carved staircase.

LIMAVADY (Léim an Mhadaidh) – Limavady – **712** L2 – pop. 12 135 — 34 B1
Ireland

▶ Belfast 62 mi – Ballymena 39 mi – Coleraine 13 mi – Londonderry 17 mi

🛈 7 Connell St ℰ (028) 7776 03 07, www.limavady.gov.uk

⛳ Benone Par Three Benone 53 Benone Ave, ℰ (028) 7775 05 55

👁 Sperrin Mountains★ : Roe Valley Country Park★ **AC**, S : 2 mi by B 68 - Glenshane Pass★, S : 15 mi by B 68 and A 6

✕ Lime Tree
60 Catherine St ✉ BT49 9DB – ℰ (028) 7776 4300
– www.limetreerest.com – Closed Sunday and Monday
Rest – *(dinner only)* Menu £ 18 (early dinner weekdays)/26 – Carte £ 28/38

♦ Keenly run neighbourhood restaurant, where a traditional exterior hides smart modern hues. Good-sized menus of unfussy classical dishes, with seafood a speciality. Meats and veg are from the village. Friendly, detailed service.

LISNASKEA – Fermanagh – **712** J5 – pop. 2 739 — 34 B3

▶ London 388 mi – Belfast 83 mi – Enniskillen 17 mi – Dublin 91 mi

✕✕✕ Watermill with rm
Kilmore Quay, Southwest: 3 mi by B 127 ✉ BT92 ODT
– ℰ (028) 6772 4369 – www.watermillrestaurant.org
– Closed 2-17 January
7 rm ☐ – †£ 59/79 ††£ 79
Rest – French – *(closed Monday and Tuesday)* *(dinner only)* *(booking advisable)* Menu £ 20 (early dinner) – Carte £ 28/43

♦ Charming brick new-build with thatched roof, delightful terrace and superb water gardens flowing down to Lough Erne. Rustic inner boasts immaculately laid tables and a 25,000 litre aquarium. Classical Gallic menu is served by white-gloved waiters. Comfortable, airy bedrooms; some look out across the water.

LONDONDERRY/DERRY (Doire) – Derry – **712** K2/3 – pop. 83 699   **34** B1
Ireland

▶ Belfast 70 mi – Dublin 146 mi
✈ City of Derry Airport : ℰ (028) 7181 0784, E : 6 mi by A 2
🛈 44 Foyle St ℰ (028) 7126 72 84, www.derryvisitor.com
🛈 City of Derry 49 Victoria Rd, ℰ (028) 7134 63 69
◉ Town★ - City Walls and Gates★★ – Guildhall★ **AC** – Long Tower Church★ – St Columb's Cathedral★ **AC** – Tower Museum★ **AC**
◉ Grianan of Aileach★★ (≤★★) (Republic of Ireland) NW : 5 mi by A 2 and N 13. Ulster-American Folk Park★★, S : 33 mi by A 5 - Ulster History Park★ **AC**, S : 32 mi by A 5 and minor road – Sperrin Mountains★ : Glenshane Pass★ (≤★★), SE : 24 mi by A 6 - Sawel Mountain Drive★ (≤★★), S : 22 mi by A 5 and minor roads via Park – Roe Valley Country Park★ **AC**, E : 15 mi by A 2 and B 68 – Beaghmore Stone Circles★, S : 52 mi by A 5, A 505 and minor road

---

City   ≤ 🖼 ⌂ ᖘ ☰ ♿ **AC** rest, ✕ ⟟ ⚐ **P** VISA ⦵ AE
Queens Quay ⊠ *BT48 7AS* – ℰ *(028) 7136 5800* – *www.cityhotelderry.com*
– *Closed 24-26 December*
145 rm ⚏ – †£ 79/109 ††£ 86/129 – 1 suite
Rest *Thompson's on the River* – *(bar lunch Monday-Saturday)* Menu £ 21 **s** – Carte dinner £ 24/30 **s**

♦ Large, centrally located hotel with underground car park, next to the river and looking towards the bridge. Modern interior with vast lobby, plenty of seating areas and well-equipped leisure centre. Smart bedrooms; those on the upper floors have great outlooks. Formal dining room affords pleasant water views.

Beech Hill Country House ⚐   🌿 🐕 🐎 ✕ ☰ ♿ ⟟ ⚐ **P**   VISA ⦵ AE
32 Ardmore Rd, Southeast : 3.5 mi by A 6 ⊠ *BT47 3QP*
– ℰ *(028) 7134 9279* – *www.beech-hill.com*
– *Closed 24-25 December*
25 rm ⚏ – †£ 105 ††£ 140 – 2 suites
Rest *Ardmore* – Menu £ 20/30 **s** – Carte £ 32/43 **s**

♦ 18C country house, now personally run but once a US marine camp; one lounge is filled with memorabilia. Accommodation varies from vast rooms to more traditional, rural ones. Restaurant housed within conservatory and old billiard room. Fine garden.

Ramada H. Da Vinci's   ☰ ♿ **AC** rest, ✕ ⟟ ⚐ **P** VISA ⦵ AE ⦿
15 Culmore Rd, North : 1 mi following signs for Foyle Bridge ⊠ *BT48 8JB*
– ℰ *(028) 7127 9111* – *www.davincishotel.com*
– *Closed 24-25 December*
70 rm – †£ 50/90 ††£ 50/90, ⚏ £ 8.95
Rest *Grill Room* – *(dinner only and Sunday lunch)* Carte £ 17/25

♦ Set beside a characterful Irish pub – now the trendy hotel bar – at the northern edge of the city. Photos of stars who've stayed here fill one wall. Well-equipped, uniform bedrooms improve with grade. Charming brasserie displays rustic beams and exposed brickwork.

✕✕ **Browns**   **AC** VISA ⦵
1 Bonds Hill ⊠ *BT47 6DW* – ℰ *(028) 7134 5180*
– *www.brownsrestaurant.com* – *Closed Monday, Saturday lunch and Sunday dinner*
Rest – *(booking advisable)* Menu £ 18 – Carte £ 25/35

♦ Long-standing neighbourhood restaurant. Plush lounge and intimate dining room with black and white photos and some banquette seating. Cooking is surprisingly modern and technical, and relies on local produce, home-baking and home-smoking.

MAGHERA (Machaire Rátha) – Magherafelt – 712 L3 – pop. 3 711 35 C2

▶ Belfast 40 mi – Ballymena 19 mi – Coleraine 21 mi – Londonderry 32 mi

Ardtara Country House
8 Gorteade Rd, Upperlands, North : 3.25 mi by A 29 off B 75 ✉ BT46 5SA
– ✆ (028) 7964 4490 – www.ardtara.com
– Closed 25-26 December
9 rm ⊐ – †£ 60/65 ††£ 100/130
Rest – (closed Sunday lunch) (booking essential for non-residents) Menu £ 20/32
♦ 19C house with a charming atmosphere. The interior features 'objets trouvés' collected from owner's travels; original fireplaces set off the individually styled bedrooms. Restaurant set in former billiard room with hunting mural and panelled walls.

NEWCASTLE (An Caisleán Nua) – Down – 712 O5 – pop. 7 444 35 D3
Ireland

▶ Belfast 32 mi – Londonderry 101 mi
🛈 10-14 Central Promenade ✆ (028) 4372 22 22, www.newcastle.gov.uk
Castlewellan Forest Park★★ **AC**, NW : 4 mi by A 50 – Tolymore Forest Park★ **AC**, W : 3 mi by B 180 – Dundrum Castle★ **AC**, NE : 4 mi by A 2. Silent Valley Reservoir★ (≤★) – Spelga Pass and Dam★ – Kilbroney ForestPark (viewpoint★) – Annalong Marine Park and Cornmill★ **AC**, S : 8 mi by A 2 – Downpatrick : Cathedral★ **AC**, Down Country Museum★ **AC**, NE : 20 mi by A 2 and A 25

Slieve Donard
Downs Rd ✉ BT33 0AH – ✆ (028) 4372 1066 – www.hastingshotels.com
172 rm ⊐ – †£ 130/190 ††£ 170/200 – 6 suites
Rest *Oak* – (dinner only and lunch July-August) Carte £ 30/40
Rest *Percy French* – Carte £ 20/27
♦ Grand railway hotel right beside the beach, boasting marble-floored lobby, interesting museum, superb leisure facilities and excellent sea and mountain views. Spacious bedrooms in classic or contemporary styles; good mod cons. Formal Oak offers classical menu. More accessible fare in casual bar-restaurant Percy French.

Burrendale H. & Country Club
51 Castlewellan Rd, North : 1 mi on A 50
✉ BT33 0JY – ✆ (028) 4372 2599 – www.burrendale.com
67 rm ⊐ – †£ 80 ††£ 140 – 1 suite
Rest *Vine* – (dinner only and Sunday lunch) Carte £ 24/27 **s**
Rest *Cottage Kitchen* – Carte £ 18/32 **s**
♦ Privately owned hotel between the Mourne Mountains and Irish Sea, close to the Royal County Down Golf Course. Well-equipped, contemporary bedrooms. Excellent leisure facilities and vast spa offering a comprehensive range of treatments. Large, open-plan bar and lounge, traditional linen-laid restaurant or all-day dining in Cottage Kitchen.

NEWTOWNARDS (Baile Nua na hArda) – Ards – 712 O4 35 D2
– pop. 27 821

▶ Belfast 10 mi – Bangor 144 mi – Downpatrick 22 mi

Edenvale House without rest
130 Portaferry Rd, Southeast : 2.75 mi on A 20 ✉ BT22 2AH
– ✆ (028) 9181 4881 – www.edenvalehouse.com
– Closed Christmas and New Year
3 rm ⊐ – †£ 50 ††£ 90
♦ Attractive Georgian farmhouse with pleasant mountain views. Traditionally decorated, with comfy drawing room and wicker-furnished sun room. Spacious, homely bedrooms boast good facilities.

PORTRUSH (Port Rois) – Coleraine – **712** L2 – **pop. 6 372** ▌Ireland　　**35** C1

▶ Belfast 58 mi – Coleraine 4 mi – Londonderry 35 mi

🛈 Sandhill Drive ℰ (028) 7082 33 33, www.portrush.org.uk

⛳ Royal Portrush Dunluce Rd, ℰ (028) 7082 23 11

◉ Giant's Causeway★★★ (Hamilton's Seat ≤★★, E: 9 m by A 2) - Carrick-a-rede Rope Bridge★★★, E: 14 mi by A 2 and B 15 - Dunluce Castle★★ **AC**, E: 3 mi by A 2 – Gortmore Viewpoint★★, E: 14 mi by A 29, A 2 and minor road - Magilligan Strand★★, E: 13 mi by A 29 and A 2 – Downhill★ (Mussenden Temple★), E: 12 mi by A 29 and A 2

⌂　**Beulah** without rest　　　　　　　　　　　　　　　　🀫 ⁽ⁱ⁾ **P** VISA ◎ ①
16 Causeway St ✉ BT56 8AB – ℰ (028) 7082 2413
– www.beulahguesthouse.com
9 rm ⌑ – †£ 40/50　††£ 60/70

♦ Terraced Victorian house in perfect central location. Sound Irish breakfasts. Homely guest lounge. Colourful, co-ordinated and immaculately kept modern bedrooms.

PORTSTEWART (Port Stióbhaird) – Coleraine – **712** L2　　**35** C1

▶ Belfast 60 mi – Ballymena 32 mi – Coleraine 6 mi

🏠　**York**　　　　　　　　　　　　　　　　🀫 |≡| 🀫 ⁽ⁱ⁾ **P** VISA ◎
2 Station Rd, on A2 ✉ BT55 7DA – ℰ (028) 7083 3594
– www.theyorkportstewart.co.uk
8 rm ⌑ – †£ 59/79　††£ 99/115　**Rest** – Menu £ 9 (lunch) – Carte £ 19/30

♦ Smart, contemporary hotel overlooking the North Coast. Stylish bedrooms offer good mod cons; the two front rooms are the largest, with terraces and excellent views. Trendy, marble-floored bar with vivid red stools. Ground floor restaurant offers extensive menus and has a large terrace.

WARRENPOINT (An Pointe) – Newry and Mourne – **712** N5　　**35** C3
– **pop. 7 000**

▶ Belfast 44 mi – Newry 7 mi – Lisburn 37 mi

✕✕　**Restaurant 23**　　　　　　　　　　　　　　　　≤ AC VISA ◎
😊　Balmoral Hotel (1st floor), 13 Seaview ✉ BT34 3NJ – ℰ (028) 4175 3222
– www.restaurant23.com – Closed 25 December
Rest – Menu £ 15 (weekday dinner) **s** – Carte £ 29/31 **s**

♦ Long-standing restaurant that moved from the high street to the first floor of a seafront hotel. Trendy bar and lounge; dining room with boldly patterned wallpapers, red banquettes and fantastic lough views. Neatly presented, unfussy classics at lunchtime; carefully executed, enticing modern dishes at dinner.

Republic of Ireland

ACHILL ISLAND (Acaill) – Mayo – 712 B5/6 – Ireland 36 A2

- Dublin 288 km – Castlebar 54 km – Galway 144 km
- Achill Sound ℰ (098) 4 53 84, www.achilltourism.com
- Achill Island Keel, ℰ (098) 4 34 56
- Island★

DOOGORT (Dumha Goirt) – Mayo – ✉ Achill Island

Gray's
- ℰ (098) 43 244 – www.grays-guesthouse.ie – April-September
- **14 rm** ☑ – † € 40/56 †† € 80/100 **Rest** – (dinner only) Menu € 26/32
- ♦ A row of tranquil whitewashed cottages with a homely atmosphere; popular with artists. Cosy sitting rooms with fireplaces and simple but spotless bedrooms. Local scene paintings adorn dining room walls.

KEEL – Mayo – ✉ Achill Island

Achill Cliff House
- ℰ (098) 43 400 – www.achillcliff.com – Closed 10 January-12 February and 23-26 December
- **10 rm** ☑ – † € 60/90 †† € 80/100
- **Rest** – (dinner only and Sunday lunch) Menu € 27 – Carte € 36/47
- ♦ Whitewashed modern building against a backdrop of countryside and ocean. Within walking distance of Keel beach. Well-kept, spacious bedrooms with modern furnishings. Spacious restaurant with sea views.

ADARE (Áth Dara) – Limerick – 712 F10 – pop. 982 – Ireland 38 B2

- Dublin 210 km – Killarney 95 km – Limerick 16 km
- Mains St ℰ (061) 39 62 55, www.ireland-travel-guide.com
- Town★ – Adare Friary★ - Adare Parish Church★
- Rathkeale (Castle Matrix★ **AC** - Irish Palatine Heritage Centre★) W : 12 km by N 21 – Newcastle West★, W : 26 km by N 21 – Glin Castle★ **AC**, W : 46.5 km by N 21, R 518 and N 69

Adare Manor H. and Golf Resort
- ℰ (061) 396 566 – www.adaremanor.com
- closed 24-26 December
- **60 rm** ☑ – † € 290/493 †† € 290/493
- **Rest** *Oakroom* – see restaurant listing
- **Rest** *The Carriagehouse* – Carte € 30/46 **s**
- ♦ Part-19C Gothic mansion in 750 acres of riverside parkland; home to the Irish Open. Spacious, elaborately decorated guest areas. Most characterful bedrooms are in the main house and boast fireplaces, wood-panelling and ornate plasterwork. Choose between formal Oakroom or more casual Carriagehouse for dinner.

Dunraven Arms
- Main St – ℰ (061) 605 900 – www.dunravenhotel.com
- **86 rm** ☑ – † € 100/155 †† € 195
- **Rest** *Maigue Restaurant* – see restaurant listing
- ♦ Greatly extended Irish coaching inn dating back to 1792. Various small lounges and good-sized, classical bedrooms – some with four-posters and colourful garden outlooks – are dotted about the place. Busy bar and annexed conference suite.

Oakroom – at Adare Manor Hotel and Golf Resort
- ℰ (061) 396 566 – www.adaremanor.com – closed 24-26 December
- **Rest** – (dinner only) Carte € 51/70 **s**
- ♦ Formal dining room and intimate conservatory boasting pleasant water views, located in a part-19C Gothic mansion on the banks of the River Maigue. Classically based menus follow the seasons.

ADARE

✕✕ Wild Geese VISA ⓒⓞ AE ⓘ
Rose Cottage – ℰ (061) 396 451 – www.thewild-geese.com – Closed 24-26 December, 2 weeks January, Sunday dinner and Monday
Rest – *(dinner only and Sunday lunch) (booking essential)* Menu € 25/35 (early dinner) – Carte € 35/48

♦ Traditional 18C cottage on main street. Friendly service and cosy welcoming atmosphere. Varied menu with classic and international influences uses much fresh local produce.

✕✕ Maigue Restaurant – at Dunraven Arms Hotel 🛌 P VISA ⓒⓞ AE ⓘ
Main St – ℰ (061) 396 633 – www.dunravenhotel.com
Rest – *(dinner only and Sunday lunch)* Menu € 30 – Carte € 31/44

♦ Linen-clad restaurant with crystal chandeliers, set in a greatly extended 18C Irish coaching inn. Menus are firmly rooted in tradition and a beef trolley is wheeled around at every service.

✕ White Sage 🌿 VISA ⓒⓞ AE ⓘ
Main St – ℰ (061) 396 004 – www.whitesagerestaurant.com – Closed last 2 weeks January, 24-26 December, Good Friday, Sunday and Monday (except bank holidays)
Rest – *(dinner only) (booking advisable)* Menu € 32 (weekday dinner) – Carte € 35/45

♦ Set in a row of 300 year old thatched cottages, with a spacious, candlelit inner, a small rear terrace and a pleasant alfresco seating area in front. The experienced chef creates tasty European-based dishes using regionally sourced produce. Service is charming.

REPUBLIC OF IRELAND

ARAN ISLANDS (Oileáin Árann) – Galway – 712 C/D8 – pop. 1 280 38 B1
▮ Ireland

▶ Dublin 260 km – Galway 43 km – Limerick 145 km – Ennis 111 km

Access Access by boat or aeroplane from Galway city or by boat from Kilkieran, Rossaveel or Fisherstreet (Clare) and by aeroplane from Inverin

🛈 Inis Mor ℰ (099) 6 12 63, www.aranislands.ie

◉ Islands★ – Inishmore (Dún Aonghasa★★★)

INISHMORE – Galway

🏨 Óstán Árann ≤ 🛌 🌿 📶 ♿ rm, ✕ P VISA ⓒⓞ
Kilronan – ℰ (099) 61 104 – www.aranislandshotel.com – mid-February to October
22 rm 🛏 – ♦ € 59/79 ♦♦ € 78/118
Rest – *(bar lunch)* Menu € 20 **s** – Carte € 26/40 **s**

♦ Comfortable, family-owned hotel with great view of harbour. Bustling bar with live music most nights in high season. Spacious, up-to-date bedrooms are decorated in bright colours. Traditional dishes served in wood-floored restaurant.

🏠 Pier House ≤ 🛌 ✕ P VISA ⓒⓞ
Kilronan – ℰ (099) 61 417 – www.pierhousearan.com – March-October
12 rm 🛏 – ♦ € 50/80 ♦♦ € 80/100
Rest *The Restaurant* – see restaurant listing

♦ Smart hotel in a great location overlooking Kilronan pier, not far from the ferry point and village centre; take advantage of the wonderful outlook from the comfortable lounge. Cosy bedrooms come with good mod cons and some share the view.

⌂ Ard Einne Guesthouse ♲ ≤ 🛌 ✕ rm, P VISA ⓒⓞ
Killeany – ℰ (099) 61 126 – www.ardeinne.com – Closed December-January
8 rm 🛏 – ♦ € 55/90 ♦♦ € 80/120 **Rest** – Menu € 27

♦ Close to the airport, an attractive chalet-style guesthouse set back on a hill and boasting superb views of Killeany Bay; relax in the comfy lounge while taking it all in. Uniformly decorated bedrooms have pine furnishings and afford great outlooks. Homely cooking with a menu featuring lots of island fish.

ARAN ISLANDS

The Restaurant – at Pier House Hotel
Kilronan – ℰ (099) 61 417 – www.pierhouserestaurant.com – March-October
Rest – (light lunch) Menu € 25 – Carte € 30/44
♦ Well-regarded hotel restaurant with cosy, intimate interior; popular for celebrating occasions. Light lunches and more substantial dinners where they offer homely country cooking with a modern edge. Try the blackboard seafood specials.

INISHMAAN – Galway   38 B1

Inis Meáin Restaurant & Suites with rm
– ℰ (086) 826 60 26 – www.inismeain.com – March-September, 2 night minimum stay
4 rm – †† € 250/400 – 1 suite
Rest – (closed Sunday-Tuesday) (dinner only) (booking essential) Carte € 30/60
♦ Striking stone building in futuristic design, owned and run by charming native of this unspoilt island and his wife. Unpretentious modern cooking exploits finest local ingredients, including seafood caught in currachs and delicious home-grown potatoes. Minimalist bedrooms feature natural furnishings. Breakfast is delivered to your room.

ARDMORE (Aird Mhór) – Waterford – 712 I12 – pop. 412   39 C3

▶ Dublin 240 km – Waterford 71 km – Cork 60 km – Kilkenny 123 km

 Cliff House
– ℰ (024) 87 800 – www.thecliffhousehotel.com – Closed 24-26 December
36 rm – † € 175/200 †† € 200/225 – 3 suites
Rest *House* – see restaurant listing
Rest *Bar* – Menu € 32/40 – Carte € 33/49
♦ Stylish hotel on the cliffside, overlooking the bay. Slate walls, Irish fabrics and bold colours feature throughout; lower floor houses a relaxing spa. Modern bedrooms boast backlit glass artwork: some have balconies; all have smart bathrooms and a view. Comfy bar and slate-floored terrace offer an extensive menu.

House – at Cliff House Hotel
– ℰ (024) 87 800 – www.thecliffhousehotel.com – Closed 24-26 December
Rest – (Restricted opening in low season) (dinner only) Menu € 65
Spec. Organic Bantry Bay salmon with beetroot textures. Skeaghanore duck with Earl Grey raisins. Dark chocolate mousse with olive oil crumbs.
♦ Smart hotel restaurant, where full length windows provide every table with an impressive coastal view. Irish/garden produce features in concise menus; cooking is technically strong and complex. Creative, original dishes combine good flavours and textures.

ARTHURSTOWN (Colmán) – Wexford – 712 L11 – pop. 159   39 D2

▶ Dublin 166 km – Cork 159 km – Limerick 162 km – Waterford 42 km

Dunbrody Country House
– ℰ (051) 389 600 – www.dunbrodyhouse.com
– Closed 19-27 December and Monday-Tuesday except July-August
16 rm – † € 145/165 †† € 245/325 – 6 suites
Rest – (closed Sunday and Monday) (dinner only and Sunday lunch) (booking essential for non-residents) Menu € 35/65 – Carte € 40/65
♦ Part-Georgian former hunting lodge that once belonged to the Marquis of Donegal. Comfortable lounge and large bar with marble-topped counter. Spacious bedrooms are furnished in a period style. Classical restaurant offers modern menu with some Mediterranean influences; dishes feature top quality Irish produce.

ASHFORD (Áth na Fuinseog) – Wicklow – **712** N8 – pop. 1 349 — 39 D2

▶ Dublin 43 km – Rathdrum 17 km – Wicklow 6 km

Ballyknocken House
Glenealy, South : 4.75 km on L 1096 – ✆ *(0404) 44 627* – *www.ballyknocken.com*
– *February-November*
7 rm – ♦ € 90/94 ♦♦ € 110/118
Rest – *(dinner only Friday-Saturday)* Menu € 45
♦ Part-Victorian house with neat gardens and adjoining cookery school, located next to the family farm. Traditional lounge and good-sized bedrooms with antique furnishings, modern feature walls and bright fabrics; some have claw-foot baths. Traditional dishes of local produce taken at gingham-clothed tables.

ATHLONE (Baile Átha Luain) – Westmeath – **712** I7 – pop. 17 544 — 37 C3
 Ireland

▶ Dublin 120 km – Galway 92 km – Limerick 120 km – Roscommon 32 km
St Peter's Sq ✆ (090) 647 21 07, www.athlonechamber.ie
Hodson Bay, ✆ (090) 6 49 20 73
Clonmacnois ★★★ (Grave Slabs★, Cross of the Scriptures★) S : 21 km by N 6 and N 62 – N : Lough Ree (Ballykeeran Viewpoint★)

Sheraton Athlone
Gleeson St – ✆ *(090) 645 1000* – *www.sheratonathlone.com* – *Closed 25 December*
166 rm – ♦ € 155 ♦♦ € 230 – 1 suite
Rest – Menu € 25/40 – Carte € 36/43
♦ 12 storey glass tower beside the shopping centre. Bedroom grades increase with floor number: all have excellent mod cons; some boast super lough and river views. Very smart leisure, spa and aquatics area. Eat in laid-back café, chic bar or elegant restaurant.

Shelmalier House *without rest*
Retreat Rd., Cartrontroy, East : 2.5 km by Dublin rd (N 6) – ✆ *(090) 647 22 45*
– *www.shelmalierhouse.com* – *March-November*
7 rm – ♦ € 40 ♦♦ € 70
♦ Well-run guesthouse with homely décor, sauna and hot tub. Clean, comfortable bedrooms, most with polished wood floors – Room 3 is best. Extensive breakfast menu includes a daily special.

Left Bank Bistro
Fry Pl – ✆ *(090) 649 44 46* – *www.leftbankbistro.com* – *Closed 1 week Christmas, Sunday and Monday*
Rest – Menu € 25 (early dinner) – Carte € 24/40
♦ Keenly run bistro with airy interior, rough floorboards, brick walls and open-plan kitchen. Extensive menus offer an eclectic mix, from Irish beef and local fish specials through to Asian fare.

Kin Khao
Abbey Lane – ✆ *(090) 649 88 05* – *www.kinkhaothai.ie* – *Closed 24-26 December*
Rest – Thai – *(dinner only and lunch Wednesday-Friday and Sunday)*
Menu € 10/20 – Carte € 22/36
♦ Vivid yellow building with red window frames, hidden down a side street, close to the castle. Small downstairs bar; tapestries hang in main room. Good choice of authentic Thai dishes and daily specials – try the owner's recommendations.

ATHLONE

at Glasson Northeast : 8 km on N 55 – ✉ Athlone

Glasson Golf H. & Country Club
West : 2.75 km – ☎ (090) 648 51 20
– www.glassongolfhotel.ie
65 rm – † €100/160 †† €190/240
Rest – *(bar lunch)* Menu €38 **s** – Carte €21/43 **s**
◆ Greatly extended period house with views over the golf course and Lough Ree. The owner was born here and several family generations are now involved. Many visitors are golfers and golfing memorabilia fills the walls. Spacious, modern bedrooms; some with huge balconies. Classical menu served in dining room.

Wineport Lodge
Southwest : 1.5 km – ☎ (090) 643 90 10 – www.wineport.ie – Closed 24-26 December
28 rm – † €125/155 †† €210/240 – 1 suite
Rest – *(dinner only and Sunday lunch)* Carte €30/59
◆ Superbly set, with the bedroom wing following the line of the lough shore and each room boasting a waterside terrace or balcony. Luxurious bedrooms range in size; it's worth paying the extra for the Captain's Suite. 2 treatment rooms and a rooftop hot tub for relaxation. Extensive menus of seasonal produce.

Glasson Stone Lodge without rest
– ☎ (090) 648 50 04 – www.glassonstonelodge.com – May-October
6 rm – † €50 †† €70
◆ Smart guesthouse built from Irish limestone. Pine features strongly; bedrooms boast thoughtful extras and locally made furniture. Breakfast includes homemade bread and fruit from the garden.

Fatted Calf
– ☎ (09064) 85 208 – www.thefattedcalf.ie – Closed 25 December, Good Friday and Monday except bank holidays
Rest – Carte €22/44
◆ Well-run pub with attractive wood-panelled bar hung original Guinness and Gilbeys signs and a locals snug complete with pool table. Dishes range from handmade sausages to local rabbit terrine; tasty specials are a feature in the evening.

AUGHRIM (Eachroim) – Wicklow – **712** N9 – pop. 1 145 — **39** D2
▶ Dublin 74 km – Waterford 124 km – Wexford 96 km
ℹ Ballinasloe ☎ (090) 9 76 39 39, www.wicklowtourism.ie

Brooklodge H & Wells Spa
Macreddin Village, North : 3.25 km – ☎ (0402) 36 444
– www.brooklodge.com
89 rm – † €140/160 †† €200/240 – 1 suite
Rest *Strawberry Tree* **Rest** *Armento* – see restaurant listing
◆ Sprawling hotel in 180 peaceful acres in the Wicklow Valley. Flag-floored reception, comfy lounge, informal café and bar. Smart, modern bedrooms with large bathrooms; some in an annexe, along with the conference rooms. State-of-the-art spa.

Strawberry Tree – at Brooklodge Hotel & Wells Spa
Macreddin Village, North : 3.25 km – ☎ (0402) 36 444
– www.brooklodge.com
Rest – *(dinner only)* Menu €65
◆ Formal restaurant with intimate, atmospheric feel, set on a village-style estate. Menus feature wild and organic ingredients sourced form local artisan suppliers. Communal 'Feasts' available.

AUGHRIM

✕ **Armento** – at Brooklodge Hotel & Wells Spa
*Macreddin Village, North : 3.25 km – ℰ (0402) 36 444 – www.brooklodge.com
– closed Monday except March-August, Tuesday October-February and Wednesday November-March)*
Rest – Italian – *(dinner only)* Menu € 30
♦ Informal Italian restaurant set in a smart hotel on a secluded 180 acre estate. Southern Italian menus feature artisan produce imported from Armento and pizzas cooked in the wood-fired oven.

AVOCA (Abhóca) – Wicklow – 712 N9 – pop. 734 ▮ Ireland   39 D2

▶ Dublin 75 km – Waterford 116 km – Wexford 88 km
◉ Avondale★, N : by R 752 – Meeting of the Waters★, N : by R 752

⌂ **Keppel's Farmhouse** without rest
*Ballanagh, South : 3.25 km by unmarked rd – ℰ (0402) 35 168
– www.keppelsfarmhouse.ie – mid-May to mid-October*
5 rm – ♦ € 45/50 ♦♦ € 70/80
♦ Small farmhouse with colourful garden and friendly owners. Neat, brightly decorated bedrooms with compact shower rooms and lovely views over the vale. Large home-cooked and buffet breakfasts feature duck and hen eggs from their own flock.

BAGENALSTOWN (Muine Bheag) – Carlow – 712 L9 – pop. 2 532   39 D2

▶ Dublin 101 km – Carlow 16 km – Kilkenny 21 km – Wexford 59 km

🏠 **Kilgraney Country House**
*South : 6.5 km by R 705 (Borris Rd) – ℰ (059) 977 52 83
– www.kilgraneyhouse.com – March-October*
7 rm – ♦ € 135 ♦♦ € 240 – 2 suites
Rest – *(closed Monday-Wednesday March-June and September-October, and Tuesday-Wednesday July and August) (dinner only) (booking essential)* Menu € 52
♦ Georgian country house adopting a truly holistic approach. Period features blend with modern, minimalist furnishings; the mood is calm and peaceful. Small tea room, craft gallery and spa with relaxation room; pleasant herb, veg, zodiac and monastic gardens. Modern menus of clean, fresh cooking with European influences.

BALLINA (Béal an Átha) – Mayo – 712 E5 – pop. 10 490 ▮ Ireland   36 B2

▶ Dublin 241 km – Galway 117 km – Roscommon 103 km – Sligo 59 km
ℹ Cathedral Rd ℰ (096) 7 08 48, www.towns.mayo-ireland.ie
▦ Mossgrove Shanaghy, ℰ (096) 2 10 50
◉ Rosserk Abbey★, N : 6.5 km by R 314. Moyne Abbey★, N : 11.25 km by R 314 – Pontoon Bridge View (≤★), S : 19.25 km by N 26 and R 310 – Downpatrick Head★, N : 32 km by R 314

🏨 **Ice House**
*The Quay Village, Northeast : 2.5 km by N 59 – ℰ (096) 23 500
– www.theicehouse.ie – closed 24-26 December*
32 rm – ♦ € 110/220 ♦♦ € 150/250 – 6 suites
Rest – *(dinner only and Sunday lunch)* Menu € 29/39 – Carte € 34/49
♦ A former ice vault for local fishermen with two modern extensions. Terrific river views. The bedrooms a quirky mix of the old and the new; some with full-length windows. Modern menus in restaurant.

🍴 **Crockets on the Quay** with rm
*The Quay, Northeast : 2.5 km by N 59 – ℰ (096) 75 930
– www.crocketsonthequay.ie – Closed 25 December and Good Friday*
8 rm – ♦ € 30 ♦♦ € 50, ⌑ € 10
Rest – *(dinner only and lunch Saturday and Sunday)* Carte € 26/36
♦ Vibrant orange pub with a lively atmosphere, which hosts regular poker, quiz and music nights. Tasty, generously proportioned dishes include local Irish steaks. Serves dinner only. Modest, well-kept bedrooms; those over the restaurant are the quietest.

BALLINADEE (Baile na Daidhche) - Cork – **712** G12 – pop. 425   38 B3
▶ Dublin 185 km – Cork 25 km – Limerick 86 km – Galway 148 km

Glebe Country House
– ℰ *(021) 477 82 94* – www.glebecountryhouse.com – *Closed Christmas*
4 rm ⌑ – ∱ €45/50 ∱∱ €90/100   **Rest** – Menu €35 **s**

♦ Creeper-clad rectory dating back to 1854. Handsomely furnished drawing room; well-chosen fabrics and fine wooden beds in pretty bedrooms, one with French windows opening into the garden. Classical county house cooking with veg from the garden and fish from the local boats.

BALLINASLOE (Béal Átha na Sluaighe) – Galway – **712** H8   36 B3
– pop. 6 303   Ireland

▶ Dublin 146 km – Galway 66 km – Limerick 106 km – Roscommon 58 km
🛈 Bridge St ℰ *(0909) 64 26 04*, www.ballinasloe.com
⛳ Rossgloss, ℰ *(0905) 4 21 26*
⛳ Mountbellew, ℰ *(090) 9 67 92 59*

◉ Clonfert Cathedral★ (west doorway★★), SW: by R 355 and minor roads. Turoe Stone, Bullaun★, SW: 29 km by R 348 and R 350 – Loughrea (St Brendan's Cathedral★), SW: 29 km by N 6 – Clonmacnoise★★★ (grave slabs★, Cross of the Scriptures★) E: 21 km by R 357 and R 444

Melodys at Moycarn
Shannonbridge Rd, Southeast : 2.5 km by N 6 off R 357 – ℰ *(090) 964 50 50*
– www.moycarnlodge.ie – *Closed 25-26 December*
15 rm ⌑ – ∱ €39/49 ∱∱ €78/99   **Rest** – Carte €19/32

♦ Purpose-built hotel run by friendly, experienced owners, with pleasant gardens and terrace overlooking the river – where there's free berthing for guests. Light, airy bedrooms; five open onto a large shared balcony boasting river views. Rustic bar and restaurant offer accessible menu of traditional dishes.

BALLINGARRY (Baile an Gharraí) – Limerick – **712** F10 – pop. 348   38 B2
Ireland

▶ Dublin 227 km – Killarney 90 km – Limerick 29 km

◉ Kilmallock★ (Kilmallock Abbey★, Collegiate Church★), SE: 24 km by R 518 – Lough Gur Interpretive Centre★ **AC**, NE: 29 km by R 519, minor road to Croom, R 516 and R 512 – Monasteranenagh Abbey★, NE: 24 km by R 519 and minor road to Croom

Mustard Seed at Echo Lodge
– ℰ *(069) 68 508* – www.mustardseed.ie – *Closed late January-mid February and 24-26 December*
14 rm ⌑ – ∱ €130 ∱∱ €240 – 2 suites   **Rest** – *(dinner only)* Menu €63

♦ Converted convent with very neat gardens and peaceful appeal. Cosy lounge with fireplace and beautiful fresh flowers. Individually furnished rooms with mix of antiques. Meals enlivened by home-grown herbs and organic farm produce.

BALLINROBE (Baile an Róba) – Mayo – **712** E7 – pop. 2 098   36 B3
▶ Dublin 163 km – Castlebar 18 km – Galway 31 km – Westport 20 km

JJ Gannons with rm
Main St – ℰ *(094) 954 10 08* – www.jjgannons.com – *Closed 25 December*
10 rm ⌑ – ∱ €65/70 ∱∱ €135/150
Rest – Menu €25 (dinner) – Carte €21/40

♦ Run by the third generation of the Gannon family, with an atmospheric front bar and a smart, spacious restaurant. Satisfyingly traditional dishes, fish specials and eager service. Spacious, comfortable bedrooms have a bright, minimalist style.

BALLSBRIDGE = Droichead na Dothra – Dublin – **712** N8 – see Dublin

---

BALLYBOFEY (Bealach Féich) – Donegal – **712** I3 – pop. 4 176   **37** C1

▶ Dublin 238 km – Londonderry 48 km – Sligo 93 km
🏌 Ballybofey & Stranorlar The Glebe, ℰ (074) 3 10 93

🏨 Kee's
Main St, Stranorlar, Northeast : 0.75 km on N 15 – ℰ *(074) 913 10 18*
– www.keeshotel.ie
53 rm ⌑ – 🛏 € 96/106 🛏🛏 € 158/178   **Rest** – Carte € 25/50 **s**

♦ Long-standing, family-run hotel in town centre. Bedrooms in newer building are more spacious and modern. Atmospheric bar and raised lounge area. Popular favourites served in informal, wood-furnished restaurant.

BALLYBUNION (Baile an Bhuinneánaigh) – Kerry – **712** D10   **38** A2
– pop. 1 365   Ireland

▶ Dublin 283 km – Limerick 90 km – Tralee 42 km
🏌 Ballybunnion Sandhill Rd, ℰ (068) 2 71 46

◉ Rattoo Round Tower★, S : 10 km by R 551. Ardfert★, S : 29 km by R 551, R 556 and minor road W – Banna Strand★, S : 28 km by R 551 – Carrigafoyle Castle★, NE : 21 km by R 551 – Glin Castle★ **AC**, E : 30.5 km by R 551 and N 69

🏠 Teach de Broc Country House
Link Rd, South : 2.5 km on Golf Club Rd – ℰ *(068) 27 581*
– www.ballybuniongolf.com – March-October
14 rm ⌑ – 🛏 € 80/100 🛏🛏 € 120/150
Rest *Strollers* – *(light lunch)* Menu € 25 (Sunday lunch) – Carte € 24/40

♦ Stylish house by the Ballybunion golf course. Spacious, modern interior boasts a nicely furnished bar-lounge with outdoor seating. Bedrooms are extremely comfortable and have smart bathrooms. Elegant dining room with smartly laid tables offers wide-ranging menu.

⛺ 19th Lodge without rest
– ℰ *(068) 27 592 – www.ballybuniongolflodge.com – Closed Christmas, restricted opening in winter*
14 rm ⌑ – 🛏 € 70/130 🛏🛏 € 100/180

♦ Comfortable house overlooking the fairways of the famed course and filled with golfing memorabilia. Comfy first floor lounge; pleasant, classical décor throughout. Executive bedrooms boast both showers and spa baths. Substantial breakfasts.

BALLYCASTLE (Baile an Chaisil) – Mayo – **712** D5 – pop. 215   **36** B2
Ireland

▶ Dublin 267 km – Galway 140 km – Sligo 88 km
◉ Cáide Fields★, **AC**, NE : 8 km by R 314

🏨 Stella Maris
Northwest : 3 km by R 314 – ℰ *(096) 43 322 – www.stellamarisireland.com – 24 April-September*
12 rm ⌑ – 🛏 € 170 🛏🛏 € 250
Rest – *(dinner only) (booking essential)* Carte € 35/55

♦ Former coastguard station and fort in a great spot overlooking the bay. Public areas include a long conservatory. Attractive rooms with antique and contemporary furnishings. Modern menus in stylish dining room.

BALLYCONNELL (Báal Atha Conaill) – Cavan – **712** J5 – pop. 747   **37** C2

▶ Dublin 143 km – Drogheda 122 km – Enniskillen 37 km
🏌 Slieve Russell, ℰ (049) 952 64 58

BALLYCONNELL

Slieve Russell
Southeast : 2.75 km on N 87 – ℰ (049) 952 64 44
– www.slieverussell.ie
220 rm – †€ 109 ††€ 158 – 2 suites
Rest *Conall Cearnach* – *(Sunday lunch and open dinner Friday-Saturday during off-peak season)* Menu € 27/50 **s** – Carte € 34/56 **s**
Rest *Setanta* – ℰ (049) 952 50 14 *(closed Sunday lunch) (dinner only and lunch Saturday and Monday)* Menu € 19 (lunch) **s** – Carte € 29/53 **s**
• Impressive façade in mock-Georgian style, with neo-classical lobby. Bedrooms overlooking grounds are large and luxurious with every modern convenience. Restaurants named after Irish folk heroes. Classical dishes in formal Conall Cearnach. Relaxed, stylish Setanta offers eclectic Mediterranean menu.

BALLYCOTTON (Baile Choitín) – Cork – 712 H12 – pop. 412   39 C3
Ireland

▶ Dublin 265 km – Cork 43 km – Waterford 106 km
◉ Cloyne Cathedral★, NW : by R 629

Bayview
– ℰ (021) 464 67 46 – www.thebayviewhotel.com – May-October
33 rm – †€ 70/149 ††€ 70/149, ⊒ € 15 – 2 suites
Rest – *(bar lunch Monday-Saturday)* Carte € 41/57
• A series of cottages in an elevated position with fine views of bay, harbour and island. Bar and lounge in library style with sofas. Spacious, comfy rooms with ocean views. Warm, inviting dining room.

BALLYFARNAN (Béal Átha Fearnáin) – Roscommon – 712 H5   37 C2
– pop. 182

▶ Dublin 111 km – Roscommon 42 km – Sligo 21 km – Longford 38 km

Kilronan Castle
South East : 3.5 km on Keadew rd – ℰ (071) 961 80 00
– www.kilronancastle.ie
84 rm – †€ 145/165 ††€ 165/185
Rest *Douglas Hyde* – *(dinner only and Sunday lunch)* Menu € 45
– Carte € 40/50
• Imposing restored castle, with wood panelling, antiques, portraits and a suit of armour. Opulent red and gold bedrooms offer a high level of comfort. Impressive hydrotherapy centre. Grand dining room; traditional menu uses local produce.

BALLYFIN – Laois – 712 J8   39 C1
▶ Dublin 69 km – Portlaoise 11 km – Cork 114 km – Limerick 67 km

Ballyfin
– ℰ (057) 875 58 66 – www.ballyfin.com – March-December
13 rm (dinner included) ⊒ – †€ 600/950 ††€ 1150/1400 – 2 suites
Rest – *(residents only)*
• Immaculate Regency mansion built in 1820 and set in 600 acres. Stunning interior with gold leaf decorated drawing room and library featuring 7,000 antique books. Elegant, antique-furnished bedrooms boast marble bathrooms. Excellent service. 5 course tasting menu of classical dishes with contemporary touches.

BALLYLICKEY (Béal Átha Leice) – Cork – 712 D12 – ✉ Bantry 38 A3
Ireland

▶ Dublin 347 km – Cork 88 km – Killarney 72 km

🛈 Bantry Bay Donemark, ✆ (027) 5 05 79

◉ Bantry Bay★ – Bantry House★ **AC**, S : 5 km by R 584. Glengarriff★ (Ilnacullin★★, access by boat) NW : 13 km by N 71 – Healy Pass★★ (≤★★) W : 37 km by N 71, R 572 and R 574 – Slieve Miskish Mountains (≤★★) W : 46.75 km by N 71 and R 572 – Lauragh (Derreen Gardens★ **AC**) NW : 44 km by N 71, R 572 and R 574 – Allihies (copper mines★) W : 66.75 km by N 71, R 572 and R 575 – Garnish Island (≤★) W : 70.75 km by N 71 and R 572

Seaview House
– ✆ (027) 50 462 – www.seaviewhousehotel.com – Mid March-mid November
25 rm ⌂ – † € 75/95 †† € 140/200
Rest – (dinner only and Sunday lunch) Menu € 35/45

◆ Well-run, whitewashed Victorian house that upholds tradition in both its décor and service. Pleasant drawing room and cosy bar. Bedrooms feature antique furnishings; some boast sea views. Attractive gardens lead down to the bay shore. Classical menu served at elegant polished tables laid with silver tableware.

Ballylickey House without rest
– ✆ (027) 50 071 – www.ballylickeymanorhouse.com – May-September
6 rm ⌂ – † € 90/100 †† € 110/180

◆ Attractive country house with beautiful gardens reaching down to the sea. Spacious, individually furnished bedrooms are split between the house and 'chalets'. Smart, period-style breakfast room displays pleasant art. Heated outdoor pool.

BALLYLIFFIN (Baile Lifín) – Donegal – 712 J2 – pop. 357 37 C1

▶ Dublin 174 km – Lifford 46 km – Letterkenny 39 km

Ballyliffin Lodge
Shore Rd – ✆ (074) 937 82 00 – www.ballyliffinlodge.com
– Restricted opening in winter
40 rm ⌂ – † € 105/124 †† € 160/198
Rest – Menu € 25 – Carte approx. € 32

◆ Remote hotel with well-kept gardens, affording superb outlook over the countryside to the beach. Cosy bedrooms – ask for one facing the front – and great spa with lovely pool. Relax in the snug bar or have afternoon tea and take in the view from the lounge. Large dining room offers an all-encompassing menu.

BALLYMACARBRY (Baile Mhac Cairbre) – Waterford – 712 I11 39 C2
– pop. 436 – ✉ Clonmel Ireland

▶ Dublin 190 km – Cork 79 km – Waterford 63 km

◉ Clonmel★ (St Mary's Church★, County Museum★ **AC**), N : 16 km by R 671 – Lismore★ (Castle Gardens★ **AC**, St Carthage's Cathedral★), SW : 26 km by R 671 and N 72 – W : Nier Valley Scenic Route★★

Hanora's Cottage
Nire Valley, East : 6.5 km by Nire Drive rd on Nire Valley Lakes rd – ✆ (052) 613 61 31 – www.hanorascottage.com – Closed 1 week Christmas
10 rm ⌂ – † € 80 †† € 160
Rest – (closed Sunday and bank holiday Mondays) (dinner only and Sunday lunch) (booking essential for non-residents) Menu € 40

◆ Dating back to 1891 and named after the owner's grandmother, who it once belonged to; a great base for exploring the Comeragh Mountains. Spacious, brightly painted bedrooms with characterful furnishings and spa baths, No.11 overlooks the river. Comfy dining room offers a menu of classically inspired dishes.

Glasha Farmhouse

Northwest : 4 km by R 671 – ℰ (052) 613 61 08 – www.glashafarmhouse.com – January-November

6 rm – † € 50/60 †† € 90/100 **Rest** – Menu € 40

♦ Large farmhouse set between the Knockmealdown and Comeragh Mountains. Guest areas include a spacious lounge, airy conservatory and patio. Comfy bedrooms; some with jacuzzis. Welcoming owners have good local knowledge. Home-cooked meals; picnic lunches available.

BALLYMORE EUSTACE (An Baile Mór) – Kildare – 712 J2 — 39 D1
– pop. 725

▶ Dublin 48 km – Naas 12 km – Drogheda 99 km

Ballymore Inn

– ℰ (045) 864 585 – www.ballymoreinn.com
Rest – Menu € 22/35 – Carte € 28/39

♦ Remote village pub with spacious bar and Parisian brasserie style dining area. Generous portions include tasty homemade bread, pizzas, tarts and pastries. Small artisan producers favoured.

BALLYNAHINCH (Baile na hInse) – Galway – 712 C7 – ✉ Recess — 36 A3
Ireland

▶ Dublin 225 km – Galway 66 km – Westport 79 km

◉ Connemara★★★ – Roundstone★, S : by R 341 – Cashel★, SE : by R 341 and R 340

Ballynahinch Castle

– ℰ (095) 31 006 – www.ballynahinch-castle.com – Closed February and 1 week at Christmas

37 rm – † € 240/300 †† € 300/420 – 3 suites
Rest – *(dinner only) (booking essential for non-residents)* Menu € 48 **s**

♦ Part-17C, grey-stone castle within extensive grounds, set in an unrivalled location by the river. Log-fired entrance and well-appointed sitting rooms. Modern country house style bedrooms with up-to-date facilities. Pub attracts the locals. Restaurant offers classical 4 course dinners overlooking the river.

BALLYVAUGHAN (Baile Uí Bheacháin) – Clare – 712 E8 – pop. 224 — 38 B1
Ireland

▶ Dublin 240 km – Ennis 55 km – Galway 46 km

◉ The Burren★★ (Scenic Route★★, Aillwee Cave★ **AC** (Waterfall★★), Corcomroe Abbey★, Poulnabrone Portal Tomb★) – Kilfenora (Crosses★, Burren Centre★ **AC**), S : 25 km N 67 and R 476. Cliffs of Moher★★★, S : 32 km by N 67 and R 478

Gregans Castle

Southwest : 6 km on N 67 – ℰ (065) 707 70 05 – www.gregans.ie – 11 February-27 November

16 rm – † € 152/195 †† € 195/245 – 4 suites
Rest – *(bar lunch) (booking advisable)* Menu € 60/90 **s**

♦ Part-18C country house with superb views of The Burren and Galway Bay. Open-fired hall, rustic bar-lounge and elegant sitting room. Antique-furnished bedrooms: one in the old kitchen with panelled ceiling and four-poster; two opening onto the garden. Good service, with tea on arrival. Conservatory dining room offers elaborate modern menu with a Scandinavian edge.

Drumcreehy House without rest

Northeast : 2 km on N 67 – ℰ (065) 707 73 77 – www.drumcreehyhouse.com – Closed 25-26 December, restricted opening in winter

10 rm – † € 58/100 †† € 84/100

♦ Well-run, pristine house overlooking Galway Bay. Stylish lounge with honesty bar. Named and colour themed after flowers, bedrooms are excellent value: spacious, comfortable and furnished in German stripped oak. Pleasant terrace. Excellent choice at breakfast.

BALLYVAUGHAN

⌂ **Ballyvaughan Lodge** without rest
– ℘ (065) 707 72 92 – www.ballyvaughanlodge.com – Closed 25-26 December
11 rm – † € 35/45 †† € 75/85
• Welcoming guesthouse with colourful flower display and decking. Comfy, light-filled lounge. Bedrooms boast co-ordinating fabrics and furnishings. Quality farmers' market produce at breakfast.

⌂ **Cappabhaile House** without rest
Southwest : 1.5 km on N 67 – ℘ (065) 707 72 60 – www.cappabhaile.com
– April-September
10 rm – † € 55/75 †† € 84/90
• Proudly run, grey-stone house with nice gardens, offering great views over The Burren. Spacious lounge-cum-breakfast room; comfy, good-sized bedrooms. Pool table and regular live music sessions.

BALTIMORE (Dún na Séad) – Cork – **712** D13 – pop. 377 ▮ Ireland — 38 A3

▶ Dublin 344 km – Cork 95 km – Killarney 124 km
◉ Sherkin Island★ (by ferry) – Castletownshend★, E : 20 km by R 595 and R 596 – Glandore★, E : 26 km by R 595, N 71 and R 597

🏠 **Casey's of Baltimore**
East : 0.75 km on R 595 – ℘ (028) 20 197 – www.caseysofbaltimore.com – Closed 20-27 December
14 rm – † € 70/120 †† € 120/180 **Rest** – Menu € 24 – Carte € 25/49 s
• Popular hotel near seashore. Cosy bar with open fires and traditional music at weekends, with beer garden overlooking bay. Large, well-decorated rooms with pine furniture. Great sea views from dining room.

⌂ **Baltimore Townhouse** without rest
– ℘ (028) 20 197 – www.baltimoretownhouse.com – Closed 20-27 December
6 rm – † € 100/160 †† € 100/160
• Six open plan suites comprising of a bedroom, living area, small kitchen and bathroom. Check in at Casey's on your way into the village; where your breakfast is also served.

⌂ **Slipway** without rest
The Cove, East : 0.75 km – ℘ (028) 20 134 – www.theslipway.com
– May-September
4 rm – † € 60/72 †† € 72/80
• Relaxed, informal guesthouse with yellow façade and lovely views of local harbour, particularly from veranda outside breakfast room. Simple, individualistic, well-kept rooms.

BANDON (Droichead na Bandan) – Cork – **712** F12 – pop. 5 822 — 38 B3

▶ Dublin 181 km – Cork 20 km – Carrigaline 28 km – Cobh 33 km

⌂ **Kilbrogan House** without rest
Kilbrogan Hill, North : 1 km on Macroom rd (R 589) – ℘ (023) 884 49 35
– www.kilbrogan.com – March-October
4 rm – † € 50 †† € 80
• Georgian townhouse set above the town and boasting a stunning original staircase, fine cornicing in the lounge and a turn-of-the-century conservatory overlooking pleasant gardens. Simple, antique-furnished bedrooms. Breakfast from the Aga.

🍺 **Poacher's Inn**
Clonakilty Rd, Southwest : 1.5 km on N 71 – ℘ (023) 884 1159
– www.poachersinnbandon.com
Rest – Menu € 25 – Carte € 25/40
• Cosy neighbourhood pub that's popular with the locals. Light snack menu in the bar and snug; hearty, classical seafood dishes in the upstairs restaurant, which opens later in the week.

BANSHA – South Tipperary – **712** H10 – pop. 288   39 C2

▶ Dublin 121 km – Clonmel 21 km – Cork 59 km – Limerick 31 km

Rathellen House
Southeast : 3.5 km. by N 24 on Coopers Cottage rd – ℰ (062) 54 376
– www.rathellenhouse.com
6 rm ⊐ – † €60/65 †† €90/110
Rest – *(dinner only) (residents only set menu)* Menu €40

♦ Very comfortable, Georgian-style house with classic country house feel, set in peaceful location. Variously-sized bedrooms feature antique furniture and pleasant countryside/mountain outlooks; bathrooms boast heated flooring. Formal dining room with antique tables; home-cooked meals utilise local, often organic produce.

BARNA (Bearna) – Galway – **712** E8 – pop. 12 795   36 B3

▶ Dublin 227 km – Galway 9 km

Twelve
Barna Crossroads – ℰ (091) 597 000 – www.thetwelvehotel.ie
38 rm ⊐ – † €100/145 †† €110/155 – 10 suites
Rest *West* – see restaurant listing
Rest *The Pins* – Menu €25 – Carte €25/35 **s**

♦ Unassuming exterior hides a keenly run boutique hotel. On-site bakery in the pubby bar. Stylish, modern bedrooms with large gilt mirrors, mood lighting and designer 'seaweed' toiletries in the bathrooms; some boast bars or giant spa baths. Ambitious fusion menu in West; modern European dishes in The Pins.

West – at Twelve Hotel
Barna Crossroads – ℰ (091) 597 000 – www.thetwelvehotel.ie
Rest – *(closed Monday and Tuesday) (dinner only)* Menu €25 **s**
– Carte €35/45 **s**

♦ Stylish restaurant with booth seating, set in a smart boutique hotel. Fusion menu offers ambitious, innovative dishes and features plenty of locally landed seafood. Chef's table in the kitchen.

O'Grady's on the Pier
– ℰ (091) 592 223 – www.ogradysonthepier.com – *Closed 24-26 December*
Rest – Seafood – *(booking essential)* Carte €31/47

♦ Converted quayside pub on two floors with great views of Galway Bay. Cheerful, attentive staff and daily menus of simple, flavourful seafood have earned good local reputation.

BARRELLS CROSS – Cork – **712** G12 – see Kinsale

BEAUFORT = Lios an Phúca – Kerry – **712** D11 – see Killarney

BIRR (Biorra) – Offaly – **712** I8 – pop. 5 081 – Ireland   39 C1

▶ Dublin 140 km – Athlone 45 km – Kilkenny 79 km – Limerick 79 km
🛈 Wilmer Rd ℰ (057) 912 09 23, www.heritagetowns.com
🏌 The Glenns, ℰ (057) 9 12 00 82

◉ Town★ – Birr Castle Demesne★★ **AC** (Telescope★★)

◉ Clonfert Cathedral★ (West doorway★★), NW : 24 km by R 439, R 356 and minor roads – Portumna★ (Castle★ **AC**), W : 24 km by R 489 – Roscrea★ (Damer House★ **AC**) S : 19.25 km by N 62 – Slieve Bloom Mountinas★, E : 21 km by R 440

Maltings without rest
Castle St – ℰ (057) 912 13 45
10 rm ⊐ – † €40/80 †† €70/80

♦ Characterful stone-built house once used to store malt in the production of Guinness. Set on the riverside, its breakfast-room-cum-lounge overlooks the castle grounds. Simple, pine furnished bedrooms. Homemade soda bread, scones and jams.

BLACKLION (An Blaic) – Cavan – 712 I5 – pop. 174   34 A3

▶ Dublin 194 km – Drogheda 170 km – Enniskillen 19 km
🖪 Blacklion Toam, ℰ (071) 9 85 30 24

XXX **MacNean House** with rm   AC rest, VISA ◉◉
Main St – ℰ (071) 985 30 22 – www.macneanrestaurant.com – Closed January
19 rm ⌑ – ♦ €80/100 ♦♦ €85/100
Rest – *(closed Monday-Tuesday and Sunday dinner) (dinner only and Sunday lunch) (booking essential)* Carte approx. €70
♦ Stylish, modern restaurant in a smart townhouse, with plush seating, linen-clad tables and subtle cream décor. Choice of three menus; refined, complex dishes use good quality ingredients and skilled techniques. Keenly run, with friendly local team. Comfortable, contemporary bedrooms.

BLARNEY (An Bhlarna) – Cork – 712 G12 – pop. 2 400 – ✉ Cork   38 B3
▌Ireland

▶ Dublin 268 km – Cork 9 km
◉ Blarney Castle★★ **AC** – Blarney Castle House★ **AC**

⌂ **Killarney House** without rest
Station Rd, Northeast : 1.5 km on Carrignavar rd. – ℰ (021) 438 18 41
– www.killarneyhouseblarney.com
6 rm ⌑ – ♦ €38/50 ♦♦ €60/68
♦ Spacious, modern guesthouse set above attractive village. Very comfortable lounge. Breakfast room equipped to high standard. Sizeable, immaculately kept rooms.

at Tower West : 3.25 km on R 617 – ✉ Cork

⌂ **Ashlee Lodge**
– ℰ (021) 438 53 46 – www.ashleelodge.com – closed 20 December-20 January
10 rm ⌑ – ♦ €65/95 ♦♦ €70/240
Rest – *(closed Sunday and Monday) (dinner only)* Carte approx. €39 **s**
♦ Smart hotel with open-fired lounge complete with board games and honesty bar. Comfy bedrooms offer all you could want; some have whirlpool baths. Outdoor Canadian hot tub, sauna and in-room treatments. Dining room offers freshly prepared, home-cooked dishes.

BORRIS – Carlow – 712 L10 – pop. 582   39 D2

▶ Dublin 121 km – Carlow 36 km – Waterford 66 km

⌂ **Step House**
– ℰ (059) 977 32 09 – www.stephousehotel.ie – Closed 9-26 January and 25 December
19 rm ⌑ – ♦ €90/110 ♦♦ €190/220 – 1 suite
Rest *Reubens* – see restaurant listing
♦ Welcoming, family-run, Georgian townhouse, located in a small heritage village. Spacious, modern bedrooms with gilt furniture and a slightly kitsch feel; the penthouse boasts a terrace and lovely mountain views. Red leather furnished bar.

XX **Reubens** – at Step House Hotel
– ℰ (059) 977 32 09 – www.stephousehotel.ie – Closed 9-26 January and 25 December
Rest – *(dinner only Friday-Saturday and Sunday lunch)* Carte €33/49
♦ Atmospheric hotel restaurant with vaulted ceilings and archways; set in the kitchens of the old McMurrough Kavanagh Estate dower house. Interesting modern menu of local and artisan ingredients.

BOYLE (Mainistir na Búille) – Roscommon – 712 H6 – pop. 2 522 36 B2
Ireland

▶ Dublin 175 km – Longford 53 km – Sligo 45 km

🛈 King House ☏ (071) 966 21 45, www.visitboyle.net

◉ King House★ **AC**

◉ Boyle Abbey★ **AC**, E : 2 km by N 4 – Lough Key Forest Park★ **AC**, E : 3.25 km by N 4. Arigna Scenic Drive★ (≤★), NE : 20 km by N 4, R 280 and R 207 – Curlew Mountains (≤★), NW : 3.5 km by N 4

⌂ Rosdarrig House without rest
*Carrick Rd, (East : 1.5 km) – ☏ (071) 966 20 40 – www.rosdarrig.com
– April-October*
5 rm ⌑ – ♦ €40/45 ♦♦ €70

♦ Neat house on the edge of town, close to the abbey, where friendly owners offer genuine Irish hospitality. Comfy lounge and linen-laid breakfast room. Pleasant bedrooms overlook the garden.

BRIDGE END – Donegal – 712 J2 – pop. 298 37 C1

▶ Dublin 158 km – Lifford 25 km – Belfast 78 km – Londonderry 5 km

✕✕ Harrys
– ☏ (074) 936 85 44 – www.harrys.ie
Rest – Menu €20 (dinner) – Carte €30/38

♦ Long-standing, passionately run restaurant with large, open-plan interior and modern bistro feel. Menus evolve with the seasons, offering flavoursome, classically prepared dishes. Traceability is key: they hang and mature their own steaks.

BUNDORAN (Bun Dobhráin) – Donegal – 712 H4 – pop. 1 964 37 C2
Ireland

▶ Dublin 259 km – Donegal 27 km – Sligo 37 km

🛈 Main St ☏ (071) 9 84 25 39, www.discoverbundoran.com

◉ Creevykeel Court Cairn★, S : 5 km by N 15 – Rossnowlagh Strand★★, N : 8.5 km by N 15 and R 231

🏨 Fitzgerald's
– ☏ (071) 984 13 36 – www.fitzgeraldshotel.com – Restricted opening in winter
16 rm ⌑ – ♦ €55/80 ♦♦ €80/120
Rest *The Bistro* – *(closed Monday-Tuesday) (dinner only)* Carte €25/38 **s**

♦ Family owned hotel in centre of popular seaside town overlooking Donegal Bay. Reception rooms warmed by wood-burning stove. Sumptuous sofas abound. Seafacing front bedrooms. Linen-clad, informal Bistro with carefully compiled menu.

BUNRATTY (Bun Raite) – Clare – 712 F9 **Ireland** 38 B2

▶ Dublin 207 km – Ennis 24 km – Limerick 13 km

◉ Town★★ – Bunratty Castle★★

🏠 Bunratty Manor
– ☏ (061) 707 984 – www.bunrattymanor.net – Closed 1 week Christmas
20 rm ⌑ – ♦ €79/99 ♦♦ €99/120
Rest – *(closed Monday) (dinner only and Sunday lunch)* Carte €30/45

♦ Smart hotel not far from the castle and folk park, in a busy tourist town. Good-sized, brightly decorated bedrooms display colourful fabrics; most bathrooms have showers only. Comfy lounge. Traditional bar with courtyard offers both pub and restaurant-style menus.

⌂ Bunratty Grove without rest
*Castle Rd., North : 3 km on Buratty Castle rd – ☏ (061) 369 579
– www.bunrattygrove.com*
6 rm ⌑ – ♦ €35/50 ♦♦ €50/65

♦ Purpose-built guesthouse with mature gardens, set in a peaceful area out of town. Tidy, well-kept lounge and pine-furnished breakfast room. Good-sized bedrooms with polished wood floors.

CAHERLISTRANE (Cathair Loistreáin) – Galway – 712 E7 36 B3

▶ Dublin 256 km – Ballina 74 km – Galway 42 km

Lisdonagh House
Northwest : 4 km by R 333 off Shrule rd – ℰ (093) 31 163 – www.lisdonagh.com
– May-October
9 rm – † € 80/98 †† € 140/180   **Rest** – (dinner only) Menu € 45
♦ Ivy-clad Georgian house with lough views. Traditional country house interior boasts eye-catching mural and open-fired lounges. Antique-furnished bedrooms have marble bathrooms; first floor rooms are larger and brighter. Formal dining room offers home-cooked meals.

CAHERSIVEEN (Cathair Saidhbhín) – Kerry – 712 B12 – pop. 1 294 38 A2
▌Ireland

▶ Dublin 355 km – Killarney 64 km

◉ Ring of Kerry★★

QC's with rm
3 Main St – ℰ (066) 947 22 44 – www.qcbar.com – Closed Monday-Wednesday in winter and Sunday lunch
5 rm – † € 60/70 †† € 90/110
Rest – Seafood – (dinner only and lunch in summer) Menu € 20 (dinner) – Carte € 31/46
♦ Cosy little pub with characterful flagged floors, exposed stone walls and a strong nautical theme. Seafood-orientated menus offer fresh, unfussy classics and some more unusual daily specials; the family also own a local fish wholesalers. Spacious, well-equipped bedrooms are located just around the corner.

O'Neill's (The Point) Seafood Bar
Renard Point, Southwest : 2.75 km by N 70 – ℰ (066) 947 21 65 – Closed November-February
Rest – (bookings not accepted) Carte € 28/38
♦ Striking blue pub beside the Valentia Island ferry terminal; run by the O'Neill family for over 150 years. Traditional Irish cooking; generous dishes with a strong seafood base. Unusually, no chips or desserts and no credit card payments.

CAMPILE (Ceann Poill) – Wexford – 712 L11 – pop. 347 ▌Ireland 39 D2

▶ Dublin 154 km – Waterford 35 km – Wexford 37 km

◉ Dunbrody Abbey★, S : 3.25 km by R 733 – J F Kennedy Arboretum★, N : 3.25 km by R 733. Tintern Abbey★, SE : 12.75 km by R 733 – Duncannon Fort★, S : 12.75 km by R 733

Kilmokea Country Manor
West : 8 km by R 733 and Great Island rd – ℰ (051) 388 109
– www.kilmokea.com – February-4 November
6 rm – † € 75/150 †† € 180/300
Rest – (booking essential for non-residents) Menu € 50 (dinner) – Carte lunch approx. € 28
♦ Georgian rectory set in 20 acres, 7 of which are formal gardens open to the public. Small antique-furnished drawing room with oils and piano. Bedrooms, some in the old coach house, are more contemporary. Conservatory tea rooms and smart restaurant with daily changing classical menu of organic garden produce.

CAPPOQUIN (Ceapach Choinn) – Waterford – 712 I11 – pop. 740 39 C2
▌Ireland

▶ Dublin 219 km – Cork 56 km – Waterford 64 km

◉ Lismore★ (Lismore Castle Gardens★ **AC**, St Carthage's Cathedral★), W : 6.5 km by N 72. The Gap★ (≤★) NW : 14.5 km by R 669

CAPPOQUIN

XX Richmond House with rm
Southeast : 0.75 km on N 72 – ℰ (058) 54 278 – www.richmondhouse.net
– *Closed 2 weeks Christmas-New Year, Sunday and Monday*
9 rm ☐ – †€ 70/100 ††€ 130/190
Rest – *(dinner only)* Menu €33/55 – Carte approx. €33 **s**
♦ Built for Earl of Cork and Burlington in 1704; retains Georgian style with stately, cove-ceilinged dining room: local produce to the fore. Individually decorated period rooms.

at Millstreet East : 11.25 km by N 72 on R 671 – ✉ Cappoquin

↑ Castle Country House without rest
– ℰ (058) 68 049 – www.castlecountryhouse.com – *mid-March-October*
5 rm ☐ – †€ 50/65 ††€ 90/100
♦ Extended farmhouse on working dairy and beef farm with 15C origins. Rural location and lovely gardens. Individual bedrooms with cottage style decor.

CARAGH LAKE (Loch Cárthaí) – Kerry – 712 C11 ▌Ireland 38 A2

▶ Dublin 341 km – Killarney 35 km – Tralee 40 km
🏌 Dooks Glenbeigh, ℰ (066) 9 76 82 05
◉ Lough Caragh ★
◉ Iveragh Peninsula ★★ (Ring of Kerry ★★)

Ard-Na-Sidhe
– ℰ (066) 976 91 05 – www.ardnasidhe.com – *May-October*
18 rm ☐ – †€ 144/211 ††€ 168/288
Rest – *(dinner only) (booking essential for non-residents)* Carte €40/59
♦ 1913 Arts and Crafts house, set on the shores of Lough Caragh and surrounded by mountains. Subtle yet stylish modernisation has retained much of its original character. Smart, antique-furnished bedrooms; Garden Rooms are more traditional. Dining room offers classically based dishes with subtle modern twists.

Carrig Country House
– ℰ (066) 976 91 00 – www.carrighouse.com – *March-November*
16 rm ☐ – †€ 125/140 ††€ 150/250 – 1 suite
Rest – *(dinner only) (booking essential for non-residents)* Menu €45
♦ Victorian former hunting lodge set down a wooded drive, located on the lough shore and surrounded by mountains. Cosy country house interior with traditionally furnished guest areas. Individually decorated bedrooms boast antique furnishings. Beautiful views from the dining room; fresh, country house cooking.

CARLINGFORD (Cairlinn) – Louth – 712 N5 – pop. 623 ▌Ireland 37 D2

▶ Dublin 106 km – Dundalk 21 km
◉ Town ★
◉ Windy Gap ★, NW : 12.75 km by R 173 – Proleek Dolmen ★, SW : 14.5 km by R 173

Four Seasons
– ℰ (042) 937 35 30 – www.4seasonshotelcarlingford.ie
59 rm ☐ – †€ 69/115 ††€ 69/180
Rest – *(bar lunch Monday-Thursday)* Menu €25 (dinner) – Carte €31/38
♦ Purpose-built, town centre hotel, with large leisure centre and spa. Smartly maintained gardens boast a wrought iron pergola and lovely mountain backdrop. Well-equipped bedrooms; 'Executives' are of a good size, with separate bath and shower. Large bar leads into intimate, formal dining room with Irish menu.

↑ Beauforth House without rest
– ℰ (042) 937 38 79 – www.beauforthouse.net – *Closed 25 December*
5 rm ☐ – †€ 65/100 ††€ 100/120
♦ Modern house on the shores of the lough. Spacious lounge displays local art and old maritime charts; large, comfortable bedrooms boast water or mountain views. Welcoming owners also run a sailing school.

CARLINGFORD

 Carlingford House without rest
- ℰ (042) 937 31 18 – www.carlingfordhouse.com – Closed Christmas
5 rm ☑ – † €65 †† €90/140
♦ Early Victorian house close to the old ruined abbey; the owner was born, and has always lived, here. Smart, understated bedrooms are immaculately kept. Snug lounge and pleasant breakfast room; tasty locally smoked salmon and bacon.

CARLOW (Ceatharlach) – Carlow – **712** L9 – pop. 20 724   39 D2

▸ Dublin 80 km – Kilkenny 37 km – Wexford 75 km
ℹ College St ℰ (059) 9 13 15 54, www.carlowtourism.com
⛳ Carlow Dublin Rd, Deer Park, ℰ (059) 9 13 16 95

 Barrowville Town House without rest
Kilkenny Rd, South : 0.75 km on N 9 – ℰ (059) 914 33 24 – www.barrowville.com – Closed 24-26 December
7 rm ☑ – † €50/80 †† €90/120
♦ Attractive Georgian house located on the main road into town. Comfy, characterful drawing room with heavy fabrics, period ornaments and grand piano. Breakfast in the conservatory, overlooking the pretty rear garden. Spacious, brightly decorated bedrooms offer a good level of comfort and modern facilities.

CARNAROSS (Carn na Ros) – Meath – **712** L6 – ✉ Kells   37 D3

▸ Dublin 69 km – Cavan 43 km – Drogheda 48 km

✗✗ **Forge**
Pottlereagh, Northwest : 5.5 km by N 3 on Oldcastle rd – ℰ (046) 924 50 03 – www.theforgerestaurant.ie – Closed 24-26 and 31 December, 1 January, last week July, first week August, Sunday dinner, Monday and Tuesday
Rest – (dinner only and Sunday lunch) Menu €30 – Carte €39/46
♦ Former forge tucked away in rural isolation. Family run, traditionally styled restaurant serving tried-and-tested dishes with modern twist: ample, good value choice.

CARNE – Wexford – **712** M11   39 D3

▸ Dublin 169 km – Waterford 82 km – Wexford 21 km

🏠 **Lobster Pot**
Ballyfane – ℰ (053) 913 11 10 – Closed 25-26 December, January, Good Friday and Monday except bank holidays
Rest – Seafood – (dinner only and Sunday lunch) Carte €25/45
♦ Popular pub filled with a characterful array of memorabilia. Large menus feature tasty, home-style cooking. Fresh seafood dishes are a must try, with oysters and lobster cooked to order the specialities. No children after 5pm.

CARRICKMACROSS (Carraig Mhachaire Rois) – Monaghan   37 D2
– **712** L6 – pop. 4 387 Ireland

▸ Dublin 92 km – Dundalk 22 km
⛳ Nuremore Hotel & CC, ℰ (042) 9 66 14 38
◎ Dún a' Rí Forest Park★, SW : 8 km by R 179 – St Mochta's House★, E : 7 km by R 178 and minor road S

 Nuremore ⌂
South : 1.5 km on N 2 – ℰ (042) 966 14 38 – www.nuremore.com
72 rm ☑ – † €105/125 †† €140/180
Rest *Restaurant* – see restaurant listing
♦ Long-standing Victorian house with extensive gardens and golf course. Classical interior with formal bar and comfy lounge serving three-tiered afternoon tea. Good leisure facilities and smart pool. Peaceful bedrooms, many have rural views.

CARRICKMACROSS

XXX Restaurant – at Nuremore Hotel
South : 1.5 km on N 2 – ℘ *(042) 966 14 38 – www.nuremore.com*
Rest – *(dinner only and lunch Saturday-Sunday)* Menu € 30/40
• Traditional split-level dining room within a well-established Victorian hotel. Formally set, linen-laid tables are well-spaced and service is attentive. Menus showcase luxurious seasonal ingredients and dishes are stylishly presented.

X Courthouse
1 Monaghan St – ℘ *(042) 969 28 48 – www.courthouserestaurant.ie – Closed one week January, 25-26 December, Easter Friday, Monday (except bank holidays) and Tuesday*
Rest – Carte € 26/39 **s**
• Relaxed, rustic restaurant featuring wooden floors, exposed ceiling rafters and bare brick. Carefully prepared, flavourful dishes; good value midweek menu. Friendly efficient service.

CARRICK-ON-SHANNON (Cora Droma Rúisc) – Leitrim – 712 H6 – pop. 3 163 ▌Ireland 37 C2

▶ Dublin 156 km – Ballina 80 km – Galway 119 km – Roscommon 42 km
🛈 Visitor Information Centre The Marina ℘ (0719) 62 01 70, www.carrickonshannon.ie
⛳ Carrick-on-Shannon Woodbrook, ℘ (071) 966 70 15
◉ Town ★
◉ Lough Rynn Demesne ★

Landmark
on N 4 – ℘ *(071) 962 22 22 – www.thelandmarkhotel.com – Closed 25 December*
60 rm ⌑ – † € 90/125 †† € 130/198
Rest *Boardwalk* – Carte € 23/37
• Next to the Shannon, with a water feature in reception and water-themed pictures throughout. Traditional style bedrooms; some overlooking the river. Stylish cocktail lounges with stunning modern design. Boardwalk boasts pleasant river views.

Oarsman
Bridge St – ℘ *(071) 962 1733 – www.theoarsman.com – Closed 25-26 December, Easter Friday, Sunday and Monday*
Rest – Menu € 20/35 – Carte € 21/43
• Traditional, family-run pub filled with pottery, bygone artefacts and fishing tackle. Cooking is simple and produce, locally sourced. Comfortable restaurant area opens later in the week.

CARRIGALINE (Carraig Uí Leighin) – Cork – 712 G12 – pop. 12 835 38 B3

▶ Dublin 262 km – Cork 14 km
⛳ Fernhill, ℘ (021) 437 22 26

Carrigaline Court
Cork Rd – ℘ *(021) 485 21 00 – www.carrigcourt.com – Closed 23-27 December*
89 rm ⌑ – † € 80/140 †† € 140/220 – 2 suites
Rest *The Bistro* – *(dinner only) (meals served in bar Sunday-Thursday)*
Carte € 30/50 **s**
• Purpose-built hotel in the heart of town. Excellent leisure centre boasting a 20m pool and well-equipped events facilities. Luxurious suites and spacious, modern bedrooms with queen-sized beds. Atmospheric bar for snacks and light meals; formal restaurant has eclectic décor and offers an international menu.

CARRIGANS (An Carraigain) – Donegal – 712 J3 – pop. 191   37 C1
▶ Dublin 225 km – Donegal 66 km – Letterkenny 230 km – Sligo 124 km

⋂ **Mount Royd** without rest
– ℘ (074) 914 01 63 – www.mountroyd.com – Closed 1 week Christmas, restricted opening in winter
4 rm ⌂ – ♦ € 40 ♦♦ € 70
♦ Remotely set, creeper-clad house with well-tended gardens, lovely rear terrace and fountain. Immaculately kept throughout with snug lounge and pleasant breakfast room. Cosy bedrooms; one leading to a terrace. Tasty locally smoked salmon.

CASHEL (An Caiseal) – Galway – 712 C7 Ireland   36 A3
▶ Dublin 278 km – Galway 66 km
◉ Town ★
◉ Connemara ★★★

🏠 **Cashel House** ⚘
– ℘ (095) 31 001 – www.cashel-house-hotel.com – Closed 2 January-6 February
30 rm ⌂ – ♦ € 75/295 ♦♦ € 150/250
Rest – (bar lunch Monday-Saturday) (booking essential for non-residents)
Menu € 30/32 – Carte € 35/49
♦ Built 1840; a very comfortable and restful country house, warmly decorated with delightful gardens. General de Gaulle stayed in one of the luxurious country house rooms. Dining room, with Queen Anne style chairs, opens into elegant conservatory.

CASHEL (Caiseal) – South Tipperary – 712 I10 – pop. 2 936 Ireland   39 C2
▶ Dublin 162 km – Cork 96 km – Kilkenny 55 km – Limerick 58 km
 Heritage Centre, Town Hall, Main St ℘ (062) 6 25 11, www.cashel.ie
◉ Town ★★★ – Rock of Cashel ★★★ **AC** – Cormac's Chapel ★★ – Round Tower ★
 – Museum ★ – Cashel Palace Gardens ★ – GPA Bolton Library ★ **AC**
◉ Holy Cross Abbey ★★, N : 14.5 km by R 660 – Athassel Priory ★, W : 8 km by N 74. Caher (Castle ★★, Swiss Cottage ★), S : 18 km by N 8 – Glen of Aherlow ★, W : 21 km by N 74 and R 664

🏠 **Cashel Palace**
Main St – ℘ (062) 62 707 – www.cashel-palace.ie – Closed 23-26 December
19 rm ⌂ – ♦ € 95/130 ♦♦ € 130/234
Rest – (carvery lunch Monday-Saturday) Carte € 41/54
♦ Queen Anne house, once home to an archbishop, with pleasant gardens and path leading to the famous rock. Pillared entrance hall and high-ceilinged guest areas with ornate plasterwork and open fires. Traditional bedrooms; some in the old coach house. Characterful vaulted bar, buttery and elegant restaurant.

🏠 **Baileys of Cashel**
42 Main St – ℘ (062) 61 937 – www.baileyshotelcashel.com – Closed 23-28 December
20 rm ⌂ – ♦ € 70/80 ♦♦ € 110/120   **Rest** – Carte € 25/40
♦ Extended Georgian townhouse, used as grain store during Irish famine. Contemporary bedrooms are furnished to a high standard. Small lounge with library; bar area in basement. Restaurant with open plan kitchen serves modern European cooking.

⋂ **Aulber House** without rest
Deerpark, Golden Rd, West : 0.75 km on N 74 – ℘ (062) 63 713
– www.aulberhouse.com – March-October
12 rm ⌂ – ♦ € 50 ♦♦ € 80/100
♦ Modern house in Georgian style, within walking distance of Rock of Cashel and 13C Cistercian abbey ruins. Well-maintained gardens with wooden gazebo. Open-fired lounge, bespoke mahogany staircase and open-plan landing. Comfy bedrooms; many with king-sized beds.

CASHEL

Chez Hans
P VISA ⓪ ⓪

Rockside, Moor Ln. – ℰ (062) 61 177 – www.chezhans.net – Closed 2 weeks January, 25 December, Sunday and Monday
Rest – *(dinner only) (booking essential)* Menu € 35 (early weekday dinner) – Carte € 45/57

♦ Imposing former Synod Hall built in 1861, with stained glass lancet windows and vast, high-ceilinged inner. Carefully prepared and creatively presented dishes rely on local produce.

Cafe Hans
AC P

Rockside, Moore Lane St – ℰ (062) 63 660 – Closed 2 weeks late January, 25 December, 1 week October, Sunday and Monday
Rest – *(lunch only) (bookings not accepted)* Carte approx. € 25

♦ Just down the road from The Rock of Cashel, a vibrant, popular eatery set next to big sister 'Chez Hans' and run by the same family. Closely set tables and art-covered walls. Tasty, unfussy dishes crafted from local ingredients. Arrive early as you can't book.

CASTLEBALDWIN (Béal Átha na gCarraigíní) – Sligo – **712** G5 — **36** B2
– ✉ **Boyle (roscommon)** 🟩 Ireland

▶ Dublin 190 km – Longford 67 km – Sligo 24 km

🟢 Carrowkeel Megalithic Cemetery (≤★★), S : 4.75 km. Arigna Scenic Drive★, N : 3.25 km by N 4 - Lough Key Forest Park★ **AC**, SE : 16 km by N 4 – View of Lough Allen★, N : 14.5 km by N 4 on R 280 – Mountain Drive★, N : 9.5 km on N 4 – Boyle Abbey★ **AC**, SE : 12.75 km by N 4 - King House★, SE : 12.75 km by N 4

Cromleach Lodge 🌿
≤ 🚗 🐕 🍴 ⓦ 🅿 VISA ⓪ ⓪

Ballindoon, Southeast : 5.5 km – ℰ (071) 916 51 55 – www.cromleach.com – Closed November and Monday-Thursday December to March
57 rm ⊆ – † € 75 †† € 90/170
Rest *Moira's* – see restaurant listing

♦ Remotely located hotel in great position, affording superb views over Lough Arrow. Large, luxurious bedrooms – some modern, some classic – deluxe rooms have views and either a balcony or terrace, and are well worth the extra.

Moira's – at Cromleach Lodge Hotel
≤ 🚗 🍴 🅿 VISA ⓪ ⓪

Ballindoon, Southeast : 5.5 km – ℰ (071) 916 51 55 – www.cromleach.com – Closed November and Monday-Thursday December to March
Rest – *(closed Monday-Tuesday)* Menu € 55 (dinner) – Carte € 50/54

♦ Spacious, contemporary restaurant with views to Lough Arrow. Rear booths ideal for large groups. Fixed price menu of modern Irish cooking, with local produce to the fore.

CASTLEGREGORY (Caisleán Ghriaire) – Kerry – **712** B11 – pop. 205 — **38** A2

▶ Dublin 330 km – Dingle 24 km – Killarney 54 km

Shores Country House without rest
≤ 🚗 ✿ ⓦ 🅿 VISA ⓪ AE

Conor Pass Rd, Cappateige, Southwest : 6 km on A 560 – ℰ (066) 713 91 95 – www.shorescountryhouse.com – Closed 2 December-10 January
6 rm ⊆ – † € 45/90 †† € 60/90

♦ Modern guesthouse, beautifully set between Stradbally Mountain and a spectacular beach. Friendly owner has added a touch of fun to the place. Stylish bedrooms, some with antique beds; all with good attention to detail. Plush breakfast room. Quality furnishings.

CASTLELYONS (Caisleán Ó Liatháin) – Cork – 712 H11 – pop. 203   38 B2

▶ Dublin 219 km – Cork 30 km – Killarney 104 km – Limerick 64 km

Ballyvolane House
Southeast : 5.5 km by Midleton rd on Britway rd – ℰ (025) 36 349
– www.ballyvolanehouse.ie – Closed 24 December-4 January
6 rm ⊡ – † € 120/125 †† € 170/210   **Rest** – (dinner only) Menu € 35/55
♦ Stately 18C Italianate mansion mentioned in local legend, with lakes in parkland. Name means "place of springing heifers". Antique-filled rooms, some with Victorian baths. Dining room with silver candlesticks and balanced dishes.

CASTLEMARTYR (Baile na Martra) Cork – Cork – 712 H12   39 C3
- pop. 978

▶ Dublin 174 km – Cork 20 km – Ballincollig 25 km – Carrigaline 24 km

Castlemartyr
– ℰ (021) 464 40 50 – www.castlemartyrresort.ie – Closed
Monday-Thursday November to March
77 rm ⊡ – † € 195/230 †† € 210/260 – 26 suites
Rest *Bell Tower* – see restaurant listing
♦ Impressive 17C Georgian manor house in 220 acres, complete with lakes, castle ruins and golf course. Columned, parquet-floored hall; superb original ceiling in bar. Luxurious bedrooms boast marble bathrooms and every mod con. Stunning spa.

Bell Tower – at Castlemartyr Hotel
– ℰ (021) 464 40 50 – www.castlemartyrresort.ie – Closed Monday-Thursday
November to March
Rest – (dinner only) Menu 65 **s** – Carte € 33/60 **s**
♦ Formal hotel dining room in a grand 17C manor house that's set in 220 acres. Cooking is modern and sophisticated but with a strong classical base. Affords pleasant views out across the garden.

CASTLEPOLLARD (Baile na gCros) – Westmeath – 712 K6   37 C3
- pop. 1 004

▶ Dublin 63 km – Mullingar 13 km – Tullamore 37 km – Édenderry 36 km

Lough Bishop House
Derrynagarra, Collinstown, South : 6 km by R 394 taking L 5738 opposite church
and school after 4 km – ℰ (044) 966 13 13 – www.loughbishophouse.com
– Closed Christmas-New Year
3 rm ⊡ – † € 55/75 †† € 110   **Rest** – Menu € 30
♦ Charming 18C farmhouse on tranquil, south-facing hillside. Hospitable owners and their dogs greet you; tea and cake are served on arrival. Simple bedrooms with neat shower rooms; no TVs. Communal dining: home-cooked dishes include meats and eggs from their farm.

CASTLETOWNSHEND (Baile an Chaisleáin) – Cork – 712 E13   38 B3
- pop. 188   Ireland

▶ Dublin 346 km – Cork 95 km – Killarney 116 km

◉ Glandore★, NE : 10 km R 596 – Sherkin Island★ **AC**, W : 15 km by R 596 and R 595 and ferry

Mary Ann's
Main St – ℰ (028) 36 146 – www.westcorkweek.com/maryanns/ – Closed 9
January-1 February, Monday-Tuesday October-March and 24-26 December
Rest – (bookings not accepted) Carte € 20/42
♦ Bold red pub set up a steep street in a sleepy village. Simple rustic interior and a lovely garden with enclosed dining area. All-encompassing menus display a seafood base and Asian influences.

REPUBLIC OF IRELAND

CAVAN (An Cabhán) – Cavan – 712 J6 – pop. 7 883 ▌Ireland 37 C2

▶ Dublin 114 km – Drogheda 93 km – Enniskillen 64 km

🛈 Central Library, 1st Floor, Farnham St ℰ (049) 4 33 19 42, www.cavantourism.com

◉ Killykeen Forest Park★, W : 9.5 km by R 198

🏨 Radisson Blu Farnham Estate
*Farnham Estate, Northwest : 3.75 km
on R 198* – ℰ (049) 437 77 00 – www.farnhamestate.com
154 rm ☐ – † € 105/195 †† € 130/220 – 4 suites
Rest *Botanica* – (dinner only and Sunday lunch) Menu € 40 – Carte € 32/50
◆ Set in extensive parkland, boasting every conceivable outdoor activity and an impressive spa. Original Georgian features are combined with contemporary furnishings. Luxury bedrooms offer superb views. Traditional menus feature local seasonal ingredients.

🏨 Cavan Crystal
Dublin Rd, East : 1.5 km on N 3 – ℰ (049) 436 0600
– www.cavancrystalhotel.com – Closed 24-26 December
85 rm ☐ – † € 75/120 †† € 100/200
Rest *Opus One* – see restaurant listing
◆ Modern hotel next to – and owned by – the Cavan Crystal factory. Impressive atrium and spacious, stylish lounge-bar. Good meeting and leisure facilities. Up-to-date bedrooms in uniform designs.

🍴🍴 Opus One – at Cavan Crystal Hotel
Dublin Rd, East : 1.5 km on N 3 – ℰ (049) 436 0600
– www.cavancrystalhotel.com – Closed 24-26 December
Rest – (light lunch) Carte € 28/41
◆ Contemporary first floor restaurant in a smart hotel. Fresh, unfussy dishes at lunch; more ambitious dishes with unusual combinations and textures in the evening. Quality ingredients used in modern techniques.

at Cloverhill North : 12 km by N 3 on N 54 – ✉ Belturbet

🍴🍴 Olde Post Inn with rm
– ℰ (047) 55 555 – www.theoldepostinn.com – Closed 24-28 December and Monday including bank holidays
6 rm ☐ – † € 55/65 †† € 100/120
Rest – (dinner only and Sunday lunch) Menu € 35/56 – Carte € 41/55
◆ Keenly run former village post office; now a characterful restaurant with large rafters and exposed stone and brick. Attractive wooden conservatory. Seasonally changing menu of well presented, contemporary Irish cooking. Stylish, modern bedrooms.

CELBRIDGE – Kildare – 712 M7 – pop. 17 262 39 D1

▶ Dublin 13 km – Naas 16 km – City Centre 14 km – Rathmines 17 km

🍴🍴 La Serre with rm
The Village at Lyons, South : 4.5 km. by Ardclough rd on Newcastle rd. – ℰ (01) 630 35 00 – www.villageatlyons.com – Closed 25-30 December, Monday, Tuesday and bank holidays
14 rm ☐ – † € 180/310 †† € 180/310 – 3 suites
Rest – Menu € 30 – Carte € 55/65
◆ Charming restaurant within The Village at Lyons. Dine in the ornate 17C conservatory or rustic courtyard. Constantly evolving modern menus let quality ingredients speak for themselves. Contemporary bedrooms are set around a small lake; some have four-posters.

CLAREMORRIS (Clár Chlainne Mhuiris) – Mayo – 712 E/F6 36 B2
– pop. 2 595

▶ Dublin 149 km – Castlebar 18 km – Galway 39 km – Newbridge 41 km

McWilliam Park

Knock Rd, East : 2 km on N 60 – ℰ *(094) 937 80 00* – *www.mcwilliampark.ie*
101 rm ⊇ – ✝ € 110/130 ✝✝ € 130/170 – 2 suites
Rest – *(carvery lunch Monday-Saturday)* Menu € 21/35 **s** – Carte € 28/41 **s**

♦ Named after a local 18C landowner, this busy, purpose built hotel is located on the outskirts of town, convenient for the N17, Knock and the airport. Modern bedrooms. Stylish restaurant offers dishes made using local produce.

CLIFDEN (An Clochán) – Galway – **712** B7 – pop. 1 497 ▌Ireland — **36** A3

▶ Dublin 291 km – Ballina 124 km – Galway 79 km

ℹ Galway Rd ℰ (095) 2 11 63, www.clifden.galway-ireland.ie

◉ Connemara★★★, NE : by N 59 – Sky Road★★ (≤★★), NE : by N 59 – Connemara National Park★, NE : 1.5 km by N 59 – Killary Harbour★, NE : 35 km by N 59 – Kylemore Abbey★ **AC**, N : 18 km by N 59

Clifden Station House

– ℰ *(095) 21 699* – *www.clifdenstationhouse.com*
78 rm ⊇ – ✝ € 88/140 ✝✝ € 100/240
Rest – *(closed weekdays November-February) (bar lunch)* Menu € 30 – Carte € 30/45

♦ Purpose-built hotel on site of the old Galway-Clifden railway line, in a modern complex. Residents only kids club, leisure and wellness centre. Uniform bedrooms with good facilities. Local seafood orientated menus in restaurant. BBQs on the platform in summer.

Ardagh ⌘

Ballyconneely Rd, South : 3 km. on R 341 – ℰ *(095) 21 384*
– *www.ardaghhotel.com* – *Easter-October*
21 rm ⊇ – ✝ € 40/120 ✝✝ € 90/150
Rest – *(dinner only)* Menu € 35 – Carte € 40/65

♦ Neat hotel with modern interior, overlooking a small bay. Three lounges. Pleasant bedrooms – many with bold fabrics and colourful headboards designed by the owner; some with window seats and views. Bright restaurant affords excellent outlook; seafood a speciality.

Dolphin Beach Country House ⌘

Lower Sky Rd, West : 5.5 km. by Sky Rd – ℰ *(095) 21 204*
– *www.dolphinbeachhouse.com* – *March-October*
9 rm ⊇ – ✝ € 60/100 ✝✝ € 130/160
Rest – *(dinner only) (residents only)* Menu € 37 **s**

♦ Terracotta-coloured former farmhouse in peaceful hillside location. Mediterranean villa style interior with bright décor and red stone tiles. Good-sized bedrooms with artwork by friendly owner. Traditional home-cooked meals; wonderful bay views from dining room.

Quay House *without rest*

Beach Rd – ℰ *(095) 21 369* – *www.thequayhouse.com* – *mid-March-October*
14 rm ⊇ – ✝ € 70/110 ✝✝ € 130/150

♦ Cream-washed former harbourmaster's house and monastery, overlooking the bay. Relaxed, bohemian interior with antiques and wild animal memorabilia. Comfy, spacious bedrooms; those in the wing have kitchenettes. Homemade bread and local cheese feature at breakfast.

Sea Mist House *without rest*

– ℰ *(095) 21 441* – *www.seamisthouse.com* – *March-December, restricted opening in winter*
4 rm ⊇ – ✝ € 50/80 ✝✝ € 75/100

♦ Centrally located stone-built house with traditional lounge and pleasant gardens. Simple, modern bedrooms boast colourful fabrics and co-ordinating drapes; no TVs. Conservatory breakfast area.

CLIFDEN

⌂ **Buttermilk Lodge** without rest
Westport Rd – ℰ (095) 21 951 – www.buttermilklodge.com – Closed 25 December and January
11 rm ⌑ – ♦ € 50/75 ♦♦ € 80/100

♦ Immaculately kept guesthouse. Lounge has games, hot drinks and a real turf fire; a cow theme predominates. Homely, colour co-ordinated bedrooms. Friendly owners offer local info/packed lunches.

⌂ **Tower View** without rest
Lower Sky Rd, West : 4 km by Sky Rd – ℰ (095) 21 965 – www.towerview.clifden.com – May-September
3 rm ⌑ – ♦ € 35/45 ♦♦ € 65/70

♦ Yellow-painted house overlooking Clifden Bay. Well-priced, cosy bedrooms are spotlessly kept, with plain décor, bright fabrics and fully tiled bathrooms. All have views but no TVs.

CLOGHEEN (An Chloichín) – South Tipperary – 712 I11 – pop. 509   39 C2
▶ Dublin 122 km – Tipperary 23 km – Clonmel 21 km – Dungarvan 28 km

✕✕ **Old Convent** with rm
Mount Anglesby, Southeast : 0.5 km on R 668 (Lismore rd) – ℰ (052) 746 55 65 – www.theoldconvent.ie – Closed 24 December-31 January and Sunday-Wednesday except bank holidays
7 rm ⌑ – ♦ € 125/150 ♦♦ € 170/200
Rest – *(dinner only) (booking essential) (set menu only)* Menu € 65

♦ Home to the Sisters of Mercy for over 100 years, this converted convent retains a serene feel. Dine in the candlelit former chapel on seasonal 8 course tasting menu. Comfortable bedrooms, decorated in calming colours.

CLONAKILTY (Cloich na Coillte) – Cork – 712 F13 – pop. 4 154   38 B3
🛈 Ireland

▶ Dublin 310 km – Cork 51 km

ℹ 25 Ashe St ℰ (023) 8 83 32 26, www.clonakilty.ie

⛳ Dunmore Muckross, ℰ (023) 3 46 44

◉ West Cork Regional Museum★ AC

◉ Courtmacsherry★, E : 12 km by R 600 and R 601 – Timoleague Friary★, E : 8 km by R 600. Carbery Coast★ (Dromberg Stone Circle★, Glandore★, Castletownshend★) by N 71 and R 597

🏨 **Inchydoney Island Lodge and Spa**
South : 5.25 km by N 71 following signs for Inchydoney Beach – ℰ (023) 883 31 43 – www.inchydoneyisland.com – Closed 23-26 December
63 rm ⌑ – ♦ € 145/170 ♦♦ € 190/250 – 4 suites
Rest *Gulfstream* – see restaurant listing
Rest *Dunes Bistro* – Carte € 23/47 **s**

♦ Superbly located on a remote headland and boasting stunning views over the beach and out to sea. Contemporary bedrooms come with balconies or terraces and all you could ask for. Smart spa boasts a seawater pool. Dine in the formal restaurant or from a more accessible menu in the nautically styled bistro-bar.

✕✕ **Gulfstream** – at Inchydoney Island Lodge and Spa
South : 5.25 km by N 71 following signs for Inchydoney Beach – ℰ (023) 883 31 43 – www.inchydoneyisland.com – Closed 24-26 December
Rest – *(dinner only)* Menu € 59

♦ Formal hotel dining room located on the first floor of a vast hotel on the headland. Modern menus feature plenty of fresh local seafood. Affords superb views over the beach and out to sea.

CLONAKILTY

An Súgan with rm
41 Wolfe Tone St – ⌀ *(023) 883 3719* – *www.ansugan.com*
7 rm – †€30/60 ††€70/100
Rest – Menu €25 (dinner) – Carte €22/43
♦ Charming, personally run, salmon-pink pub with characterful dining rooms. Menus are based around daily arrivals of fresh local fish/seafood; some meat dishes also feature. Bedrooms, in the old harbourmaster's house, boast bold feature walls and flat screen TVs.

CLONEGALL (Cluain na nGall) – Carlow – 712 M9 – pop. 231   39 D2

▶ Dublin 73 km – Carlow 20 km – Kilkenny 39 km – Wexford 30 km

Sha Roe Bistro
Main St – ⌀ *(053) 937 56 36* – *Closed January, 1 week April, 1 week October, Sunday dinner, Monday and Tuesday*
Rest – (dinner only and Sunday lunch) (booking essential) Menu €34 (lunch) – Carte €32/43
♦ Rurally set restaurant with good reputation, run by an enthusiastic couple. Rustic lounge; small dining room with enormous inglenook and chef's table. Classically based menus display modern touches. Produce is local – cheese comes from the weekly farmers' market.

CLONTARF = Cluain Tarbh – Dublin – 712 N7 – see Dublin

CLOVERHILL = Droim Caiside – Cavan – 712 J5 – see Cavan

COBH (An Cóbh) – Cork – 712 H12 – pop. 11 303   Ireland   38 B3

▶ Dublin 264 km – Cork 24 km – Waterford 104 km
🛈 Ballywilliam, ⌀ (021) 81 23 99
◉ Town★ – St Colman's Cathedral★ – Lusitania Memorial★
◉ Fota Island★ (Fota House★★ **AC**, Fota Wildlife Park★ **AC**), N : 6.5 km by R 624 – Cloyne Cathedral★, SE : 24 km by R 624/5, N 25, R 630 and R 629

Knockeven House without rest
Rushbrooke, West : 2 km by R 624 – ⌀ *(021) 481 17 78*
– *www.knockevenhouse.com* – *Closed 15-26 December*
4 rm – †€65/85 ††€90/100
♦ Spacious, yellow-painted Victorian house with comfortable lounge and communal breakfast room. Traditional bedrooms feature antique furniture; flat screen TVs provide a modern touch.

CONG (Conga) – Mayo – 712 E7 – pop. 150   Ireland   36 A3

▶ Dublin 257 km – Ballina 79 km – Galway 45 km
🛈 Old Courthouse ⌀ (094) 9 54 65 42, www.congtourism.com
◉ Town★
◉ Lough Corrib★★, Ross Errilly Abbey★ (Tower ≤★) – Joyce Country★★ (Lough Nafooey★) W : by R 345

Ashford Castle
– ⌀ *(094) 954 60 03* – *www.ashford.ie*
78 rm – †€175/950 ††€175/950 – 5 suites
Rest *Cullen's at the Cottage* – see restaurant listing
Rest *George V Room* – (dinner only) (residents only) Menu €67
– Carte €49/76
♦ Hugely impressive lochside castle in formal gardens, dating from 1228. Handsome, antique-furnished guest areas. Well-appointed bedrooms display warm fabrics; some four-posters. Activities include archery, falconry and clay pigeon shooting. Elegant George V requires a jacket and tie; casual meals in Cullen's.

CONG

Lisloughrey Lodge
The Quay, Southeast : 2.25 km by R 345 off R 346 – ℰ (094) 954 54 00 – www.lisloughrey.ie – Closed January, Christmas, Monday and Tuesday
41 rm – ♦ €85/185 ♦♦ €135/225 – 9 suites
Rest *Salt* – Carte €44/51
• Georgian house in 10 acres of gardens. Guest areas boast contemporary feature walls and brushed velvet sofas. Bright, modern bedrooms have smart bathrooms and bold colour schemes; most are located in the courtyard. Three-roomed restaurant serves a modern menu.

Michaeleen's Manor without rest
Quay Rd, Southeast : 1.5 km by R 346 – ℰ (094) 954 60 89 – www.quietman-cong.com
6 rm – ♦ €50 ♦♦ €75
• Named after the lead character in the film 'The Quiet Man', filmed in the village; comfortable, brightly decorated bedrooms follow suit. Homely lounges; airy breakfast room.

Ballywarren House
East : 3.5 km on R 346 – ℰ (094) 954 69 89 – www.ballywarrenhouse.com – Closed 1 week spring and 1 week autumn
3 rm – ♦ €98/124 ♦♦ €136/148 **Rest** – Menu €45 **s**
• Passionately run by a charming couple who ensure each guest's stay is special. Open fires, galleried landing and oak staircase. Bedrooms boast luxurious linen and lovely views. Aga-cooked breakfast and tasty homemade dinners.

XX Cullen's at the Cottage – at Ashford Castle Hotel
– ℰ (094) 954 60 03 – www.ashford.ie
Rest – *(May-September)* Carte €23/51
• All-day restaurant set in a whitewashed, thatched cottage, in the grounds of an imposing restored castle. Homely inner; enjoy castle views from the outside tables. Modern, bistro-style menu.

CORK (Corcaigh) – Cork – 712 G12 – pop. 119 418 – Ireland 38 B3

▶ Dublin 248 km
✈ Cork Airport : ℰ (021) 4313131, S : 6.5 km by L 42 X
⛴ to France (Roscoff) (Brittany Ferries) weekly (14 h/16 h) – to Pembroke (Swansea Cork Ferries) 2-6 weekly (8 h 30 mn)
🛈 Grand Parade ℰ (021) 4 25 51 00, www.cork-guide.ie
⛳ Douglas, ℰ (021) 4 89 10 86
⛳ Mahon Blackrock Cloverhill, ℰ (021) 4 29 25 43
⛳ Monkstown Parkgarriffe, ℰ (021) 4 84 13 76
⛳ Little Island, ℰ (021) 4 35 34 51
◉ City★★ – Shandon Bells★★ Y, St Fin Barre's Cathedral★★ AC Z, Cork Public Museum★ X M – Grand Parade★ Z , South Mall★ Z , St Patrick Street★ Z , Crawford Art Gallery★ Y – Elizabethan Fort★ Z
◉ Dunkathel House★ AC, E : 9.25 km by N 8 and N 25 X. Fota Island★ (Fota House★★ AC, Fota Wildlife Park★ AC), E : 13 km by N 8 and N 25 X – Cobh★ (St Colman's Cathedral★, Lusitania Memorial★) SE : 24 km by N 8, N 25 and R 624 X

Plans pages 891, 892

Hayfield Manor
Perrott Ave, College Rd – ℰ (021) 484 59 00 – www.hayfieldmanor.ie
84 rm – ♦ €380 ♦♦ €380 – 4 suites   Xz
Rest *Orchids* **Rest** *Perrotts* – see restaurant listing
• Luxurious country house with wood-panelled hall, impressive staircase and antique-furnished drawing rooms – the perfect spot for afternoon tea. Plush bedrooms have plenty of extras, including putting machines. Well-equipped residents spa.

Lancaster Lodge without rest

*Lancaster Quay, Western Rd – ℰ (021) 425 11 25 – www.lancasterlodge.com
– Closed 23-28 December* Zi
48 rm – † €79/119 †† €79/138

♦ Purpose-built hotel with crisp, modern interior. Bedrooms are chintz-free, pleasingly and sparingly decorated. Largest rooms on the fourth floor; rear rooms are quieter.

Garnish House without rest

Western Rd – ℰ (021) 427 51 11 – www.garnish.ie Xr
21 rm – † €50/80 †† €75/120

♦ Justifiably proud of gourmet breakfast: 30 options include pancakes and porridge. Guests are welcomed with home-made scones in cosy rooms; those at the rear have quiet aspect.

Augustine's

*Clarion Hotel, Lapps Quay – ℰ (021) 427 93 75 – www.augustines.ie
– Closed Good Friday, 25 December, Sunday and Monday* Zu
Rest – (dinner only) Carte €36/52

♦ Smart, spacious ground floor restaurant set in corporate hotel. Modern, carefully crafted dishes made with quality seasonal produce. Formal but friendly service from uniformed staff.

Flemings with rm

*Silver Grange House, Tivoli, East : 4.5 km on N 8 – ℰ (021) 482 16 21
– www.flemingsrestaurant.ie – Closed 23-26 December* Xu
3 rm – † €75/80 †† €110
Rest – (closed Monday lunch) (booking essential) Menu €34/36
– Carte €42/57

♦ Classical cuisine, French bias; uses local produce, organically home-grown vegetables, herbs. Two dining rooms in keeping with Georgian character of house. Period furnished bedrooms.

REPUBLIC OF IRELAND

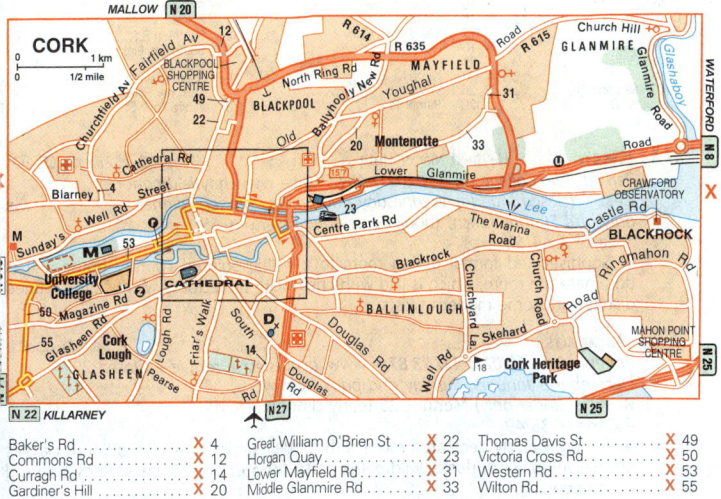

Baker's Rd	X 4	Great William O'Brien St	X 22	Thomas Davis St	X 49
Commons Rd	X 12	Horgan Quay	X 23	Victoria Cross Rd	X 50
Curragh Rd	X 14	Lower Mayfield Rd	X 31	Western Rd	X 53
Gardiner's Hill	X 20	Middle Glanmire Rd	X 33	Wilton Rd	X 55

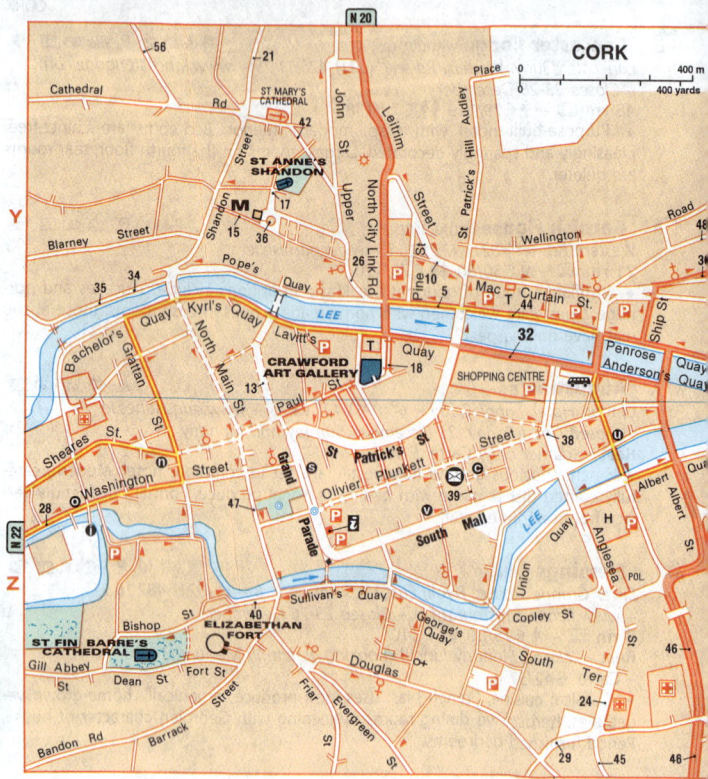

Buttermarket .... Y 36	Langford Row .... Z 29	Pembroke St .... Z
Camden Pl. .... Y 5	Lower Glanmire	Proby's Quay .... Z
Coburg St. .... Y 10	Rd. .... Y 30	Roman St. .... Z
Corn Market St .... Y 13	Merchant Quay Shopping	St Patrick's Quay .... Y
Dominic St .... Y 15	Centre .... Y	St Patrick's St. .... Y
Eason Hill .... Y 17	Merchant's Quay. .... Y 32	Southern Rd. .... Z
Emmet Pl. .... Y 18	Newsom's Quay .... Y 34	South City Link
Gerald Griffin St. .... Y 21	North Main Street .... YZ	Rd. .... Z
Infirmary Rd .... Z 24	North Mall .... Y 35	South Main St .... Y
John Redmond St .... Y 26	Olivier Plunkett St .... Z	Summer Hill .... Y
Lancaster Quay .... Z 28	Parnell Pl. .... Z 38	Wolfe Tone St .... Y

✕✕ **Orchids** – at Hayfield Manor Hotel

Perrott Ave, College Rd – ℰ *(021) 484 59 00 – www.hayfieldmanor.ie*
Rest *– (closed Monday-Wednesday and Sunday dinner) (dinner only and Sunday lunch) (booking essential)* Menu € 65
– Carte € 44/62

♦ Sophisticated formal dining room in a well-appointed country house. Pillars dominate the room, which is laid with crisp white tablecloths. Menus offer refined dishes with some modern twists.

✕✕ **Jacques**

Phoenix St – ℰ *(021) 427 73 87 – www.jacquesrestaurant.ie – Closed 25 December-3 January, Sunday and bank holidays*
Rest *– (dinner only)* Menu € 25 *(early dinner)*
– Carte € 33/49

♦ A long, warmly decorated room with modern tables on which old Irish classics are delivered. Farm ducks, wild game, fresh fish and organic vegetables are used in the cooking.

CORK

※※ Gourmandises   VISA ◎◎ AE ①
17 Cook St – ℰ (021) 425 19 59 – www.lesgourmandises.ie – Closed 1 week March, 1 week August, Sunday dinner (except bank holiday weekend) and Monday   **Zv**
Rest – French – *(dinner only and Sunday lunch) (booking essential)* Menu € 30/45
◆ Well-run restaurant with spacious, high-ceilinged interior; formerly a Turkish bath. Experienced chef produces accomplished, detailed dishes with a classical French base and original touches.

※※ Perrotts – at Hayfield Manor Hotel
Perrott Ave, College Rd – ℰ (021) 484 59 00 – www.hayfieldmanor.ie
Rest – Menu € 32 (lunch) – Carte € 40/56   **Xz**
◆ Conservatory restaurant overlooking the gardens of a luxurious country house. Smart but comfortably furnished, with adjoining wood-panelled bar. Menu offers a modern take on brasserie classics.

※ Cafe Paradiso with rm
16 Lancaster Quay, Western Rd – ℰ (021) 427 79 39 – www.cafeparadiso.ie – Closed 25-28 December   **Zo**
2 rm – † € 100 †† € 120
Rest – Vegetarian – *(dinner only and lunch Friday and Saturday) (booking essential)* Menu € 35 (dinner) – Carte € 29/47
◆ Stylish little restaurant with grey/green colour scheme, friendly service and intimate atmosphere. Extensive choice of interesting, original, vegetarian dishes which feature plenty of flavours and textures. Spacious, modern bedrooms come in bright, bold colours.

※ Fenn's Quay
5 Sheares St – ℰ (021) 427 95 27 – www.fennsquay.ie – Closed 24-27 December, 1 January, Sunday and bank holidays   **Zn**
Rest – Menu € 28 (dinner) – Carte € 31/40
◆ Modest little bistro with whitewashed brick walls, closely set tables and loyal following. Simple, flavoursome cooking offers 'tart of the day', as well as more substantial dishes at dinner.

※ Farmgate Cafe
English Market (1st floor), Princes St – ℰ (021) 427 81 34 – www.farmgate.ie – Closed Sunday and bank holidays   **Zs**
Rest – *(lunch only)* Menu € 22 – Carte € 24/29
◆ Long-standing café on 1st floor of the English Market. Small daily changing menu of food from the stalls below or from the counties of Munster; all simple, homemade and fresh.

at Cork Airport South : 6.5 km by N 27 - X – ✉ Cork

International Airport
Gate 2 – ℰ (021) 454 98 00 – www.corkinternationalairporthotel.com – Closed 23-27 December
141 rm – † € 180 †† € 180 – 4 suites
Rest *Strata* – *(closed Friday-Saturday) (carvery lunch)* Carte € 21/37 **s**
◆ Quirky hotel with aviation theme and various eateries. Decent-sized bedrooms come in Deluxe and Executive versions. The superb Pullman lounge resembles the cabin of a plane. Modern restaurant has interesting smoking terrace.

CORK AIRPORT = Aerfort Chorcai Cork – Cork – **712** G12 – see Cork

CORROFIN (Cora Finne) – Clare – 712 E9 – pop. 485 — 38 B1
▶ Dublin 228 km – Gort 24 km – Limerick 51 km

Fergus View without rest
Kilnaboy, North : 3.25 km on R 476 – ℰ *(065) 683 76 06 – www.fergusview.com – March-October*
6 rm 🖃 – † € 50/53 †† € 78
♦ Charming bay-windowed house with open-fired lounge, cosy breakfast room and country views. Bright, immaculately kept bedrooms: tiny bathrooms; no TVs. Delightful owners offer superb hospitality.

CROMANE – Kerry – 712 C11 – pop. 125 — 38 A2
▶ Dublin 201 km – Tralee 23 km – Cork 73 km – Limerick 78 km

✕✕ Jacks Coastguard
– ℰ *(066) 976 91 02 – www.jackscromane.com – Closed 7 January-9 February, Monday-Wednesday except June-October and Tuesday*
Rest – Seafood – Carte € 32/48
♦ Remotely set former coastguard station, now a bright, glitzy, split-level restaurant with panoramic windows and lovely bay views. Seafood-orientated menu offers well-presented, classic combinations. Smart bar-lounge; live piano at weekends.

CROOKHAVEN (An Cruachán) – Cork – 712 C13 – pop. 1 669 — 38 A3
▶ Dublin 373 km – Bantry 40 km – Cork 120 km

Galley Cove House without rest
West : 0.75 km on R 591 – ℰ *(028) 35 137 – www.galleycovehouse.com – Closed March 16 to October 31*
4 rm 🖃 – † € 45/55 †† € 75/90
♦ Detached house just outside the town, affording superb southerly views over the sea towards Fastnet Rock. Conservatory breakfast room and simple, pine-furnished bedrooms with bright colour schemes; all have a sea outlook. Hospitable owners.

CROSSHAVEN – Cork – 712 H12 – pop. 1 373 — 38 B3
▶ Dublin 170 km – Cork 15 km – Limerick 78 km – Galway 140 km

Cronin's
– ℰ *(021) 483 18 29 – www.croninspub.com – Closed 25 December and Good Friday*
Rest – Seafood – *(lunch only and dinner Friday-Saturday)* Carte € 15/35
♦ Classic Irish pub in the same family since 1970 and now run by the 3rd generation. Interesting artefacts and boxing memorabilia. Unfussy seafood dishes feature local produce. Limited opening in restaurant, which offers more ambitious fare.

CROSSMOLINA (Crois Mhaoilíona) – Mayo – 712 E5 – pop. 930 — 36 B2
🟩 Ireland
▶ Dublin 252 km – Ballina 10 km
◎ Errew Abbey★, SE : 9.5 km by R 315. Cáide Fields★ **AC**, N : 24 km by R 315 and R 314 W – Killala★, NE : 16 km by R 315 and minor road – Moyne Abbey★, NE : 18 km by R 115, minor road to Killala, R 314 and minor road – Rosserk Abbey★, NE : 18 km by R 115, minor road to Killala, R 314 and minor road

Enniscoe House
Castlehill, South : 3.25 km on R 315 – ℰ *(096) 31 112 – www.enniscoe.com – Closed 7 January-31 March and 1 November-27 December*
6 rm 🖃 – † € 130/150 †† € 220/260
Rest – *(dinner only) (booking essential for non-residents)* Menu € 50/56 **s**
♦ Georgian manor, overlooking Lough Conn, on Enniscoe Estate with walled garden and heritage centre. Hallway boasts original family tree; antique beds in flower-filled rooms. Home cooked country dishes served in the dining room.

DALKEY (Deilginis) – Dún Laoghaire-Rathdown – 712 N8 – pop. 8 076   39 D1
▮ Ireland

▶ Dublin 13 km – Bray 9 km
◉ Killiney Bay (≤★★), S : by coast road

✕✕ Jaipur   AC VISA ⦿ AE
21 Castle St – ✆ (01) 285 0552 – www.jaipur.ie – closed 25 December
Rest – Indian – *(dinner only and Sunday lunch)* Menu € 16 (lunch) – Carte € 27/42
♦ Central location and smart, lively, brightly coloured, modern décor. Well-spaced, linen-clad tables. Warm, friendly ambience. Contemporary Indian dishes.

DINGLE (An Daingean) – Kerry – 712 B11 – pop. 1 772 ▮ Ireland   38 A2

▶ Dublin 347 km – Killarney 82 km – Limerick 153 km
◉ Town★ – St Mary's Church★ – Diseart (stained glass★ AC)
◉ Gallarus Oratory★★, NW : 8 km by R 559 – NE : Connor Pass★★ – Kilmalkedar★, NW : 9 km by R 559. Dingle Peninsula★★ – Connor Pass★★, NE : 8 km by minor road – Stradbally Strand★★, NE : 17 km via Connor Pass – Corca Dhuibhne Regional Museum★ AC, NW : 13 km by R 559 – Blasket Islands★, W : 21 km by R 559 and ferry from Dunquin

Plan on next page

🏠 Emlagh Country House *without rest*   ≤ 🚗 |≣| & AC 🍳 ⁽¹⁾ P
– ✆ (066) 915 23 45 – www.emlaghhouse.com – 18   VISA ⦿ AE
March-October   Y**d**
10 rm ⊇ – ♦ € 90/130 ♦♦ € 180/220
♦ Built to resemble a Georgian country house, with mock period features. Personally run, it has a comfortable, relaxing feel. Large, luxurious bedrooms are colour themed around local plants and boast antique furnishings and feature beds; choose from a sea view or terrace. Homemade breads and jams at breakfast.

🏠 Castlewood House *without rest*   ≤ 🚗 |≣| & 🍳 ⁽¹⁾ P VISA ⦿
The Wood – ✆ (066) 915 27 88 – www.castlewooddingle.com – Closed 6-20
January and 6-27 December   Y**w**
12 rm ⊇ – ♦ € 55/99 ♦♦ € 99/160
♦ Well run, spacious and comfortable house. Individually decorated bedrooms; some with antique brass beds, others more contemporary. All have jacuzzi bath; most have view.

🏠 Greenmount House *without rest*   ≤ 🚗 🍳 ⁽¹⁾ P VISA ⦿
Gortonora – ✆ (066) 915 14 14 – www.greenmounthouse.ie – Closed 20-27
December   Z**c**
15 rm ⊇ – ♦ € 50/120 ♦♦ € 80/160
♦ Large, yellow painted, extended house located above the town. Two comfortable lounges and a conservatory-style breakfast room. Newest bedrooms most comfortably appointed.

🏠 Heatons   ≤ 🚗 & rm, 🍳 ⁽¹⁾ P VISA ⦿
The Wood – ✆ (066) 915 22 88 – www.heatonsdingle.com – Closed 4 January-1
February   Y**c**
16 rm ⊇ – ♦ € 49/95 ♦♦ € 70/130
Rest *Shore View* – Carte approx. € 35
♦ Large, family run house, a short walk from town and overlooking the harbour. Well-appointed lounge and conservatory breakfast room. Modern bedrooms; one with a small balcony and good views. Comprehensive breakfasts include homemade scones. Linen-laid restaurant offers concise modern menu of local ingredients.

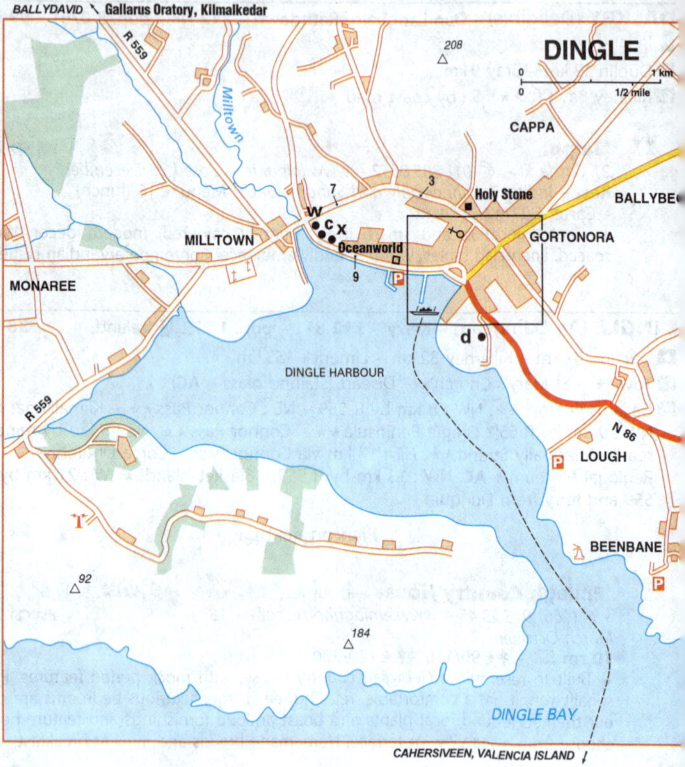

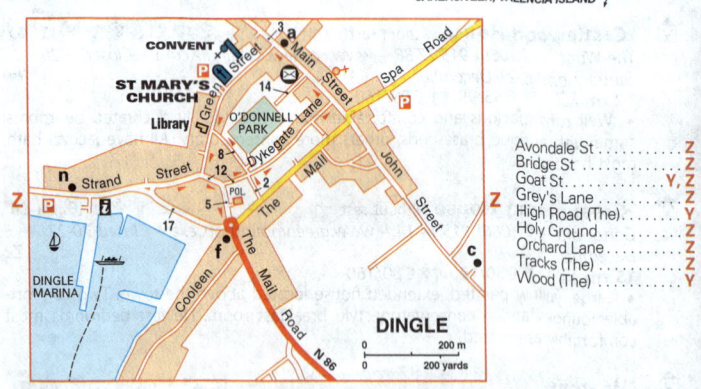

Avondale St	Z
Bridge St	Z
Goat St	Y, Z
Grey's Lane	Z
High Road (The)	Y
Holy Ground	Z
Orchard Lane	Z
Tracks (The)	Z
Wood (The)	Y

🏠 **Coastline** without rest ⇐ 🚗 📶 📱 **P** VISA 👁 💳

The Wood – ℰ (066) 915 24 94 – www.coastlinedingle.com – February-November

8 rm ☐ – † €45/55 †† €74/94　　　　　　　　　　　　　　Yx

◆ Hard to miss modern guesthouse with bright pink façade. Comfy, homely interior with lots of local info. All rooms have pleasant view; those at the front face Dingle harbour.

DINGLE

✕✕ Global Village   AK VISA ⓪ AE
Upper Main St – ℰ (066) 915 23 25 – www.globalvillagedingle.com – mid-March to mid-November **Za**
Rest – Seafood – *(dinner only) (booking essential)* Menu € 28 (early dinner) **s** – Carte € 33/52 **s**
♦ Homely restaurant with local artwork and relaxed vibe. Wide-ranging menu makes good use of seasonal, organic and home-grown produce; fantastic fresh fish dishes feature. The well-travelled owner has visited 42 different countries!

✕ Chart House   AK VISA ⓪
The Mall – ℰ (066) 915 22 55 – www.thecharthousedingle.com – Closed 2 January-12 February, 22-27 December, and Monday in low season **Zf**
Rest – *(dinner only) (booking essential)* Menu € 25/33 – Carte € 25/43
♦ Attractive stone cottage at the entrance to the town. Charming, open-plan inner with rustic flint walls, wood floors and large bar boasting stained glass dividers. Chunky wood tables and friendly, effective service. Local ingredients; meat dishes are particularly good.

✕ Out of the Blue   🍴 AK VISA ⓪
Waterside – ℰ (066) 915 08 11 – www.outoftheblue.ie – mid-March to October **Zn**
Rest – Seafood – *(dinner only and Sunday lunch) (booking essential)* Carte € 38/48
♦ Simple, brightly painted building, with a relaxing, rustic charm, located 50yds from harbour. Daily changing menu of classic fish dishes. Jolly service from a well-versed local team.

DONEGAL (Dún na nGall) – Donegal – **712** H4 – pop. 2 339 🟩 Ireland **37** C1

▶ Dublin 264 km – Londonderry 77 km – Sligo 64 km
🛬 Donegal Airport ℰ (074) 9548284
🛈 Quay St ℰ (074) 9 72 11 48, www.donegaldirect.ie
◉ Donegal Castle★ **AC**
◉ Donegal Coast★★ - Cliffs of Bunglass★★, W : 48.25 km by N 56 and R 263 – Glencolmcille Folk Village★★ **AC**, W : 53 km by N 56 and R 263 - Rossnowlagh Strand★★, S : 35.5 km by N 15 and R 231 – Trabane Strand★, W : 58 km by N 56 and R 263

🏨 Solis Lough Eske Castle ⚜   🍴 ♪ 🖥 ⓓ 🛏 Ⅰ6 ❖ & ⁽¹⁾ ♨ P
Northeast : 6.5 km by N15 (Killybegs rd) – ℰ (074)   VISA ⓪ AE ⓞ
972 51 00 – www.solisloughheskecastle.com
95 rm ☐ – † € 185/235 †† € 185/235 – 1 suite
Rest *Cedars* – see restaurant listing
♦ Beautifully restored 17C castle with many extensions, surrounded by 43 sculpture-filled acres. Fantastic spa; swimming pool overlooks an enclosed garden. Mix of contemporary and antique-furnished bedrooms, superior are worth the extra cost.

🏨 Harvey's Point ⚜   ≤ 🍴 ♪ ❖ & ⁽¹⁾ ♨ P VISA ⓪
Lough Eske, Northeast : 7.25 km. by T 27 (Killybegs rd) – ℰ (074) 972 22 08 – www.harveyspoint.com – Restricted opening in winter
66 rm ☐ – † € 198/250 †† € 198/250 – 4 suites
Rest *Restaurant* – see restaurant listing
♦ Sprawling, classical hotel in restful loughside setting, with wood-panelled rooms and leather-furnished lounge. Bedrooms in wing have high level of facilities; more traditional courtyard rooms.

DONEGAL

Ardeevin without rest
Lough Eske, Barnesmore, Northeast : 9 km by N 15 following signs for Lough Eske Drive – ℘ (074) 972 17 90 – www.members.tripod.com/ardeevin – 18 March-November
6 rm – † € 45/50 †† € 65/70
♦ Friendly, brightly painted house set in peaceful gardens and boasting beautiful views over Lough Eske; personally run by the friendly owner. Warm, pleasantly cluttered guest areas are filled with ornaments and curios. Individually designed bedrooms display quality furnishings and thoughtful extras.

Restaurant – at Harvey's Point Hotel
Lough Eske, Northeast : 7.25 km. by T 27 (Killybegs rd) – ℘ (074) 972 22 08
– www.harveyspoint.com – Closed Wednesday dinner and restricted opening November-March
Rest – Menu € 59 (dinner) – Carte lunch € 27/39
♦ Large, formal restaurant with semicircular glass side providing lovely lough views; try for a window table. Traditional cooking, local ingredients and a few international touches. Attentive, structured service.

Cedars – at Solis Lough Eske Castle Hotel
Northeast : 6.5 km by N15 (Killybegs rd) – ℘ (074) 972 51 00
– www.sollisloughskecastle.com
Rest – (dinner only and Sunday lunch) Menu € 55 – Carte € 37/70
♦ Stylish, modern grill restaurant located in a 17C castle close to the loch. Slate terrace boasts views over the lawns and woodland. Extensive grill menu features locally sourced meats and fish.

> On a tight budget? Take advantage of special prices at lunch.

DOOGORT = Dumha Goirt – Mayo – 712 B5/6 – see Achill Island

DOOLIN (Dúlainm) – Clare – 712 D8 ▮ Ireland   38 B1

▶ Dublin 275 km – Galway 69 km – Limerick 80 km

🟢 The Burren ★★ (Cliffs of Moher ★★★, Scenic Route ★★, Aillwee Cave ★ **AC** (Waterfall ★★), Poulnabrone Portal Tomb ★, Corcomroe Abbey ★, Kilfenora Crosses ★, Burren Centre ★ **AC**)

Tír Gan Éan House without rest
– ℘ (065) 707 57 26 – www.tirganean.ie – Easter to October
11 rm – † € 50/100 †† € 90/140
♦ Stylish hotel on main road into the village; part of a small holiday cottage complex. Open-plan guest areas include a comfy lounge and bar. Modern bedrooms are decorated in browns/creams and have a high level of facilities.

Cullinan's with rm
– ℘ (065) 707 41 83 – www.cullinansdoolin.com – Closed mid-December to mid-February, Sunday dinner and Wednesday
8 rm – † € 40/70 †† € 70/100
Rest – (dinner only) (booking essential) Menu € 30 (early dinner)
– Carte € 35/45
♦ Orange building in the middle of the Burren; run by a keen husband and wife team. Two walls of full length windows offer excellent views. Classical cooking uses Irish produce and portions are generous. Comfy, pine-furnished bedrooms; some overlook a small river.

DROGHEDA (Droichead Átha) – Louth – **712** M6 – pop. 35 090 **37** D3
Ireland
▶ Dublin 46 km – Dundalk 35 km
🛈 Mayoralty St ℰ (041) 9 83 70 70, www.drogheda.ie
🛈 Seapoint Termonfeckin, ℰ (041) 9 82 23 33
🛈 Towneley Hall Tullyallen, ℰ (041) 984 22 29
◉ Town★ – Drogheda Museum★ – St Laurence Gate★
◉ Monasterboice★★, N : 10.5 km by N 1 – Boyne Valley★★, on N 51
– Termonfeckin★, NE : 8 km by R 166. Newgrange★★★, W : 5 km by N 51 on N 2
– Mellifont Old Abbey★ **AC** - Knowth★

The D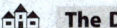
Scotch Hall, Marsh Rd. – ℰ (041) 987 77 00 – www.thed.com – Closed 23-30 December
104 rm ⌓ – † € 69/130 †† € 69/130
Rest – Menu € 27 (lunch) – Carte € 26/50

♦ Stylish hotel adjacent to shopping centre on banks of the Boyne. Modish, minimalistic interiors include two comfy bars and spacious bedrooms with a cool, clinical appeal. Popular menus in the airy dining room.

Scholars Townhouse
King St, by West St and Lawrence St turning left at Lawrence's Gate – ℰ (041) 983 54 10 – www.scholarshotel.com – Closed 25-26 December
16 rm ⌓ – † € 59/69 †† € 79/89 **Rest** – Menu € 30 – Carte € 32/62

♦ Well-run, privately owned hotel; formerly a 19C priest's house. Appealing bar and cosy lounge; smart wood panelling and ornate coving feature throughout. Comfy, well-kept bedrooms. Dine on classically based dishes under impressive mural of the Battle of Boyne.

DUBLIN

See city maps on following pages

39 D1

Dublin – pop. 2 400 437 – 712 N7 – Ireland
▶ Belfast 166 – Cork 248 – Londonderry 235
Tourist Information
Suffolk St ✆ (01) 605 77 00, www.visitdublin.com
Airport
▶ Dublin Airport : ✆ (01) 814 1111, N : 9 km by N 1 **BS**
Ferries
▬ to Holyhead (Irish Ferries) 4 daily (3 h 15 mn) – to Holyhead (Stena Line) 1-2 daily (3 h 45 mn) – to the Isle of Man (Douglas) (Isle of Man Steam Packet Co. Ltd) (2 h 45 mn/4 h 45 mn) – to Liverpool (P & O Irish Sea) (8 h)
Golf Courses
▫ Elm Park Donnybrook, Nutley House, ✆ (01) 269 34 38
▫ Milltown Lower Churchtown Rd, ✆ (01) 497 60 90
▫ Royal Dublin Dollymount North Bull Island, ✆ (01) 833 63 46

SIGHTS

In the town : City★★★ • Trinity College★★ **JY** • Old Library★★★ • Christ Church Cathedral★★ **HY** • St Patrick's Cathedral★★ **HZ** • National Museum★★ **KZ** • National Gallery★★ **KZ** • Newman House★★ **JZ** • Custom House★★ **KX** • Kilmainham Gaol Museum★★ **ATM6** • Phoenix Park★★ **AS** • National Botanic Gardens★★ **BS** • Tailors' Hall★ **HY** • City Hall★ **HY** • Temple Bar★ **HJY** • Liffey Bridge★ **JY** • Merrion Square★ **KZ** • Number Twenty-Nine★ **KZD** • Grafton Street★ **JYZ** • Powerscourt Centre★ **JY** • O'Connell Street★ **JX** • Hugh Lane Municipal Gallery of Modern Art★ **JXM4** • Bluecoat School★ **BSF** • Guinness Museum★ **BTM7**

On the outskirts : The Ben of Howth⩽★, NE : 9.5 km by R 105 **CS**
In the surrounding area : Powerscourt★★ **AC**, S : 22.5 km by N 11 and R 117 **EV** • Russborough House★★★, SW : 35.5 km by N 81 **BT**

DUBLIN

Shelbourne

27 St Stephen's Grn. ⊠ D2 – ℰ (01) 663 45 00
– www.theshelbourne.ie   JZ**c**
250 rm – † € 192/244 †† € 192/260, ⊑ €29 – 12 suites
Rest *Saddle Room* – see restaurant listing

♦ Landmark Georgian hotel with elegant guest areas, contemporary furnishings and state-of-the-art facilities. Bedrooms in original house are most characterful. High level of services and extras.

Merrion

Upper Merrion St ⊠ D2 – ℰ (01) 603 06 00
– www.merrionhotel.com   KZ**e**
133 rm – † € 460 †† € 480, ⊑ €29 – 10 suites
Rest *Cellar* – Modern – ℰ (01) 603 06 30 *(closed Saturday lunch)* Menu € 20 **s**
– Carte € 35/49 **s**
Rest *Cellar Bar* – *(closed Sunday)* Carte approx. € 34 **s**

♦ Elegant hotel boasting opulent lounges and stylish cocktail bar. Spacious bedrooms – some with original features, some more corporate in style – boast smart marble bathrooms and good facilities. Characterful barrel-ceilinged bar offers accessible menu.

Westin

Westmoreland St ⊠ D2 – ℰ (01) 645 10 00
– www.thewestindublin.com   JY**n**
153 rm – † € 399 †† € 399, ⊑ €19.95 – 10 suites
Rest *Exchange* – *(closed Sunday dinner and Monday) (dinner only and lunch Saturday-Sunday)* Carte € 25/45
Rest *Mint* – Carte € 25/50

♦ Built in 1860 as a bank; now a smart hotel set over 6 period buildings, with comfy lounges, impressive conference rooms and good facilities. Classical bedrooms boast heavy fabrics and marble bathrooms. Modern European cooking in semi-formal Exchange. Accessible menu in The Mint, a characterful room which was once the bank's vaults.

Dylan

Eastmoreland Pl ⊠ D4 – ℰ (01) 660 30 00
– www.dylan.ie – Closed 24-26 December   EU**a**
44 rm – † € 175/395 †† € 175/395, ⊑ €27
Rest – Menu € 20/40 – Carte € 40/60

♦ Modern boutique hotel with vibrant use of colour. Supremely comfortable, individually decorated bedrooms boast an opulent feel and a host of unexpected extras. French-influenced menus served in warm, stylish dining room.

Brooks

Drury St ⊠ D2 – ℰ (01) 670 40 00 – www.brookshotel.ie   JY**r**
97 rm ⊑ – † € 385 †† € 385 – 1 suite
Rest *Francesca's* – see restaurant listing

♦ Smart, boutique-style townhouse hidden down a backstreet. Traditional basement lounge and stylish bedrooms with modern artwork; executives boast fresh flowers and other homely touches. Experienced owner keeps a keen eye over proceedings.

Clarence

6-8 Wellington Quay ⊠ D2 – ℰ (01) 407 08 00
– www.theclarence.ie – Closed 25-26 December   HY**a**
44 rm – † € 109/199 †† € 159/219, ⊑ €9.50 – 5 suites
Rest *Tea Room* – see restaurant listing

♦ Attractive riverside hotel, formerly a warehouse. Stylish and well-run, with art deco reception, comfy lounge and famous domed bar. Plainly decorated, understated bedrooms; good facilities.

DUBLIN

Adelaïde Rd	BT	3
Alfie Byrne Rd	CS	5
Bath Ave	CT	9
Benburb St	BS	15
Berkeley Rd	BS	16
Botanic Rd	BS	19
Canal Rd	BT	30
Clanbrassil St	BT	40
Conyngham Rd	AS	48
Denmark St	BS	52
Donnybrook Rd	CT	54
Dorset St	BS	55
Drimnagh Rd	AT	57
Eglinton Rd	CT	63
Grand Parade	BT	72
Inchicore Rd	AT	79
Infirmary Rd	AS	81
James St	BT	84
Leeson St Upper	BT	94
Macken St	BST	99
Morehampton Rd	BT	108
Mount St Upper	BT	112
Palmerston Park	BT	123
Phibsborough Rd	BS	132
Rathmines Rd Upper	BT	135
Ringsend Rd	CT	139
St Agnes Rd	AT	141
St Alphonsus Rd	BS	144
St John's Rd West	AS	147
Sandford Rd	BT	151
Shelbourne Rd	CT	157
Shrewsbury Rd	CT	159
South Circular Rd	AS	162
Suir Rd	AT	168
Terenure Rd East	BT	172
Thomas St West	BT	174
Victoria Quay	BS	178
Western Way	BS	184
Wolfe Tone Quay	BS	195

Fitzwilliam
St Stephen's Grn. ✉ D2 – ✆ (01) 478 70 00 – www.fitzwilliamhoteldublin.com
136 rm – †€380 ††€380, ⊇ €22 – 3 suites JZd
Rest *Thornton's* – see restaurant listing
Rest *Citron* – (closed Sunday lunch) Menu €19/24 – Carte dinner €32/49

♦ Stylish U-shaped hotel set around huge roof garden – the largest in Europe. Contemporary bedrooms display striking bold colours and good facilities; half overlook garden; half, the green. Modern first floor brasserie with international menu.

Ashling
Parkgate St. ✉ D8 – ✆ (01) 677 2324 – www.ashlinghotel.ie – Closed 24-26 December BSa
225 rm – †€79/199 ††€89/340, ⊇ €14
Rest – Menu €30 – Carte €27/35

♦ Smartly refurbished hotel with sleek, modern frontage and cheery team; set close to the tram and rail links. Mix of classic and contemporary bedrooms; front rooms boast river and Guinness Brewery views. Large bar-lounge serves all-day menu. Restaurant offers carvery lunches and accessible evening à la carte.

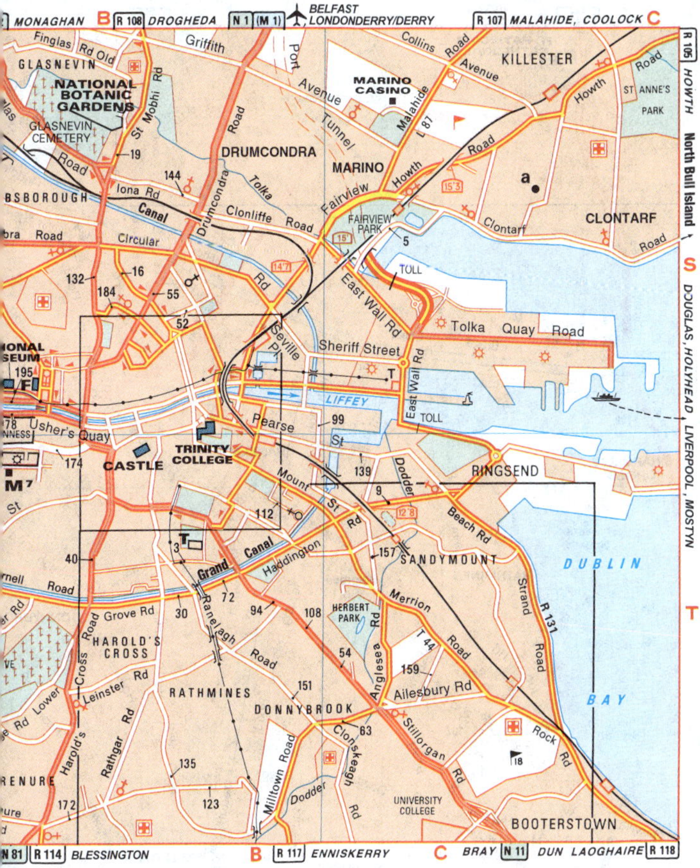

La Stampa

35-36 Dawson St ⊠ D2 – ✆ (01) 677 44 44 – www.lastampa.ie – Closed 25-26 December

36 rm – † €110/150 †† €110/150, ⊇ €14.95 – 1 suite
Rest *The Dining Room by Conrad Gallagher* – French – Menu €19 – Carte €22/76

♦ Georgian townhouse with Art Nouveau exterior and quirky, eclectic décor. Stylish guest areas and characterful spa with Far Eastern feel. Spacious bedrooms feature bespoke Asian or opulent French furnishings; the suite has a Moroccan theme. Grand dining room with interesting menu of original modern cooking.

Number 31 without rest

31 Leeson Cl. ⊠ D2 – ✆ (01) 676 50 11 – www.number31.ie
21 rm ⊇ – † €90/150 †† €175/190

♦ Unique house with retro styling, personally run by hospitable couple. Sunken lounge with open fire; quirky, comfortable bedrooms. Communal breakfast includes The Full Irish.

Ailesbury Drive . . . . FV 4	Castlewood Ave. . . . . DV 31	Harrington St . . . . DU
Baggot St Upper. . . . . EU 7	Charlemont St . . . . DU 34	Herbert Pl. . . . . EU
Beechwood Rd. . . . . EV 12	Charlotte St . . . . DU 36	Irishtown Rd . . . . FU
Beech Hill Ave. . . . . FV 10	Chelmsford Rd . . . . EV 37	Lansdowne Rd . . . . FU
Belgrave Rd . . . . DV 13	Church Ave . . . . FU 39	Lea Rd . . . . GU
Belleville Ave . . . . DV 14	Clyde Rd . . . . EFU 43	Leeson St Lower . . . . EU
Bloomfield Ave . . . . DU 18	Eastmoreland Pl. . . . . EU 61	Leinster Rd West . . . . DV
Brighton Rd . . . . DV 22	Effra Rd. . . . . DU 62	Londonbridge Rd . . . . FU
Camden St . . . . DU 28	Elgin Rd . . . . EFU 64	Maxwell Rd . . . . DV

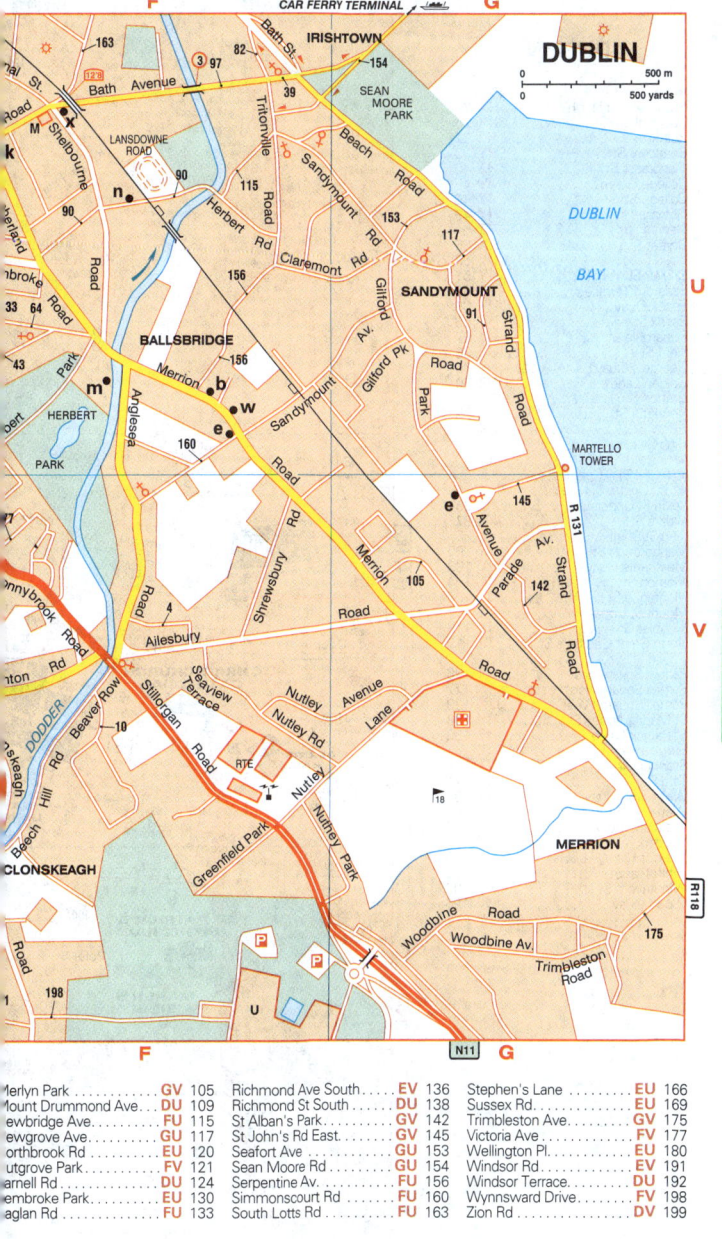

Merlyn Park	GV 105	Richmond Ave South	EV 136	Stephen's Lane	EU 166
Mount Drummond Ave	DU 109	Richmond St South	DU 138	Sussex Rd	EU 169
Newbridge Ave	FU 115	St Alban's Park	GV 142	Trimbleston Ave	GV 175
Newgrove Ave	GU 117	St John's Rd East	GV 145	Victoria Ave	FV 177
Northbrook Rd	EU 120	Seafort Ave	GU 153	Wellington Pl.	EU 180
Nutgrove Park	FV 121	Sean Moore Rd	GU 154	Windsor Rd	EV 191
Parnell Rd	DU 124	Serpentine Av.	FU 156	Windsor Terrace	DU 192
Pembroke Park	EU 130	Simmonscourt Rd	FU 160	Wynnsward Drive	FV 198
Raglan Rd	FU 133	South Lotts Rd	FU 163	Zion Rd	DV 199

905

DUBLIN

Street	Grid	No.
Anne St South	JYZ	6
Brunswick St North	HX	24
Buckingham St	KX	25
Bull Alley	HZ	27
Chancery St	HY	33
Clanbrassil St	HZ	40
College Green	JY	45
College St	JY	46
Cornmarket	HY	49
Dawson St	JYZ	
Dorset St	HX	55
Duke St	JY	58
D'Olier St	JY	51
Earlsford Terrace	JZ	60
Essex Quay	HY	65
Essex St	HY	66
Fishamble St	HY	67
Fleet St	JY	68
George's Quay	KY	69
Golden Lane	HZ	70
Grafton St	JYZ	
Henrietta St	HX	75
Henry St	JX	
High St	HY	78
Ilac Centre	HJX	
Irish Life Mall Centre	JKX	
Jervis Centre	HJX	
Kevin St Upper	HZ	85
Kildare St	JKZ	87
King St South	JZ	88
Marlborough St	JX	100
Merchants Quay	HY	103
Merrion St	KZ	104
Montague St	JZ	106
Mount St Upper	KZ	112
Nicholas St	HY	118
North Great George's St	JX	119
O'Connell St	JX	
Parnell Square East	JX	126
Parnell Square North	JX	127
Parnell Square West	HJX	129
St Mary's Abbey St	HY	148
St Patrick Close	HZ	150
Stephens Green	JZ	
Stephen St	HJY	165
Tara St	KY	171
Wellington Quay	HJY	181
Werburgh St	HY	183
Westland Row	KY	186
Westmoreland St	JY	187
Wexford St	HZ	189
Whitefriar St	HZ	190
Winetavern St	HY	193
Wood Quay	HY	196

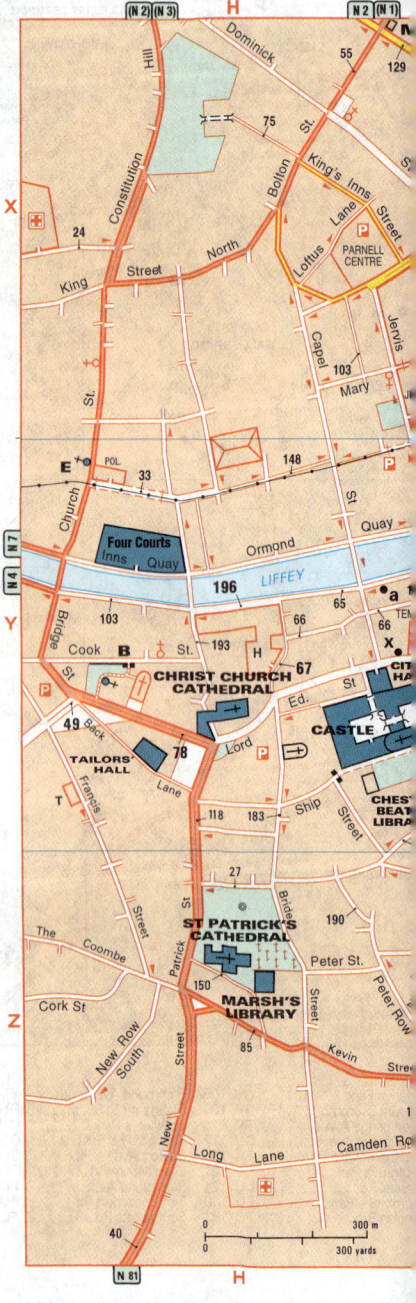

REPUBLIC OF IRELAND

906

DUBLIN

Kellys without rest
First Floor, 35 South Great Georges St ✉ *D2 –* ✆ *(01) 648 0010*
– www.kellysdublin.com   JYb
16 rm – † € 79/110 †† € 120/175

• Shabby-chic hotel set among trendy boutiques and bars, in a bustling area. Stripped paint and white emulsioned walls hung with funky artwork; airy, open-plan lounge and bar; spacious, minimalist bedrooms. Breakfast in the restaurant below.

Trinity Lodge
12 South Frederick St ✉ *D2 –* ✆ *(01) 617 09 00 – www.trinitylodge.com*
23 rm – † € 59/150 †† € 89/195, ⊇ € 7.50   JYx
Rest *Georges* – ✆ *(01) 679 70 00 (closed dinner Monday-Tuesday and Sunday)*
Carte € 20/27 **s**

• Elegant, centrally located Georgian townhouses near local landmarks. Airy, well-furnished bedrooms with good level of comfort: the larger deluxe rooms are worth asking for. Modern restaurant and popular wine bar.

Eliza Lodge
23-24 Wellington Quay ✉ *D2 –* ✆ *(01) 671 80 44 – www.elizalodge.com*
18 rm – † € 49/89 †† € 59/199, ⊇ € 9   JYu
Rest *Italian Corner* – Italian – ✆ *(01) 671 91 14 –* Carte € 24/41

• Friendly, family-owned hotel ideally situated for lively Temple Bar area. Uniform bedrooms; those at the top have the best outlook over the city and river; two have balconies. Bright restaurant serves popular Italian menus overlooking the Liffey.

Patrick Guilbaud (Guillaume Lebrun)
ॐॐ
21 Upper Merrion St ✉ *D2 –* ✆ *(01) 676 41 92*
– www.restaurantpatrickguilbaud.ie – Closed 25-26 December, 17 March, Sunday and Monday   KZe
Rest – French – Menu € 50 (lunch) – Carte € 93/149

Spec. Red king crab cannelloni, wasabi crème fraîche. Squab pigeon, sauce soubise. Granny Smith vacherin, pistachio ice cream.

• Smart, stylish and personally run restaurant within a restored and sympathetically extended Georgian house; decorated with contemporary Irish art. Accomplished and harmonious cooking, with cleverly complementing flavours and textures.

Shanahan's on the Green
119 St Stephen's Grn ✉ *D2 –* ✆ *(01) 407 09 39 – www.shanahans.ie*
– Closed Good Friday, 25-26 December and Sunday   JZp
Rest – Beef specialities – *(dinner only and lunch Friday-Saturday) (booking essential)* Menu € 45 – Carte € 45/100

• Sumptuous Georgian townhouse; upper floor window tables survey the Green. Supreme comfort enhances your enjoyment of strong seafood dishes and choice cuts of Irish beef.

Thornton's – at The Fitzwilliam Hotel
ॐ
128 St Stephen's Grn. ✉ *D2 –* ✆ *(01) 478 70 08 – www.thorntonsrestaurant.com*
– Closed 24 December dinner-5 January, Sunday, Monday except December, lunch Tuesday and Wednesday   JZd
Rest – Modern – Menu € 25/79 **s**

Spec. Bere Island king scallop with truffle mousse. Noisette of Sika deer, potato gnocchi and Valrhona sauce. Apple tarte Tatin, pressed apple terrine and cider granité.

• Elegant hotel restaurant where smart glass panels divide the room; eye-catching food photos adorn the walls. Choice of classical à la carte, or modern tasting menu displaying innovative texture and flavour combinations. Knowledgeable service.

DUBLIN

L'Ecrivain (Derry Clarke)
109A Lower Baggot St — D2 – ℰ (01) 661 19 19
– www.lecrivain.com – Closed Sunday and bank holidays   KZ**b**
Rest – Contemporary – (dinner only and lunch Thursday and Friday) (booking essential) Menu € 25/65 – Carte approx. € 86
Spec. Scallops with pork cheek and Jerusalem artichoke. Loin of veal, pumpkin and portobello mushroom. Opéra chocolate tasting plate.
♦ Three-floored, former warehouse with piano bar, whiskey-themed private dining room, mezzanine and attractive terrace. Refined cooking arrives with modern touches and contemporary presentation. Service is formal but comes with personality.

Chapter One (Ross Lewis)
The Dublin Writers Museum, 18-19 Parnell Sq — D1 – ℰ (01) 873 22 66
– www.chapteronerestaurant.com – Closed 2 weeks August, 2 weeks Christmas, Sunday, Monday and bank holidays   JX**r**
Rest – Modern – (booking essential) Menu € 38/65 **s**
Spec. Scallops with smoked bacon and spring onion, vermouth and potato mousseline. Angus rib of beef bordelaise with watercress purée, bone marrow and baby gem lettuce. Warm chocolate mousse, caramel jelly and lime ice cream.
♦ Long-established, popular restaurant in basement of historic building; contemporary lounge/bar and two smart dining rooms. Seasonal, classically-based cooking demonstrates skill and understanding. Attentive, formal service.

REPUBLIC OF IRELAND

Forty One
41 St. Stephen's Grn. — D2 – ℰ (01) 662 00 00
– www.fortyone.ie – Closed Good Friday, 25-30 December, Sunday and Monday
Rest – Modern European – (booking advisable) Menu € 28/68   KZ**x**
– Carte € 53/83
♦ Richly furnished, intimate restaurant set in an attractive, creeper-clad 18C townhouse, tucked away in a corner of St Stephen's Green. Accomplished, classical cooking uses luxurious ingredients.

Cliff Townhouse with rm
22 St. Stephen's Grn. — D2 – ℰ (01) 638 39 39
– www.theclifftownhouse.com – Closed 25-27 December and 1 January
9 rm ⌕ – † € 135/155 †† € 155/175   JZ**s**
Rest – Modern European – (booking advisable) Menu € 25/40 – Carte € 37/60
♦ Impressive Georgian townhouse overlooking the green. Large dining room with marble-topped bar and blue leather seating. Good value fixed price menus offer straightforward, classical combinations. Bedrooms display contemporary colour schemes and good comforts.

Saddle Room – at Shelbourne Hotel
27 St Stephen's Grn. — D2 – ℰ (01) 663 45 00
– www.theshelbourne.ie   JZ**c**
Rest – Grills – Menu € 26/40 – Carte € 49/63
♦ Smart restaurant with well-spaced, linen-laid tables: some are set by the window; some are in booths; and some, in glass-walled private rooms. Open kitchen specialises in seafood and steaks.

One Pico
5-6 Molesworth Pl — D2 – ℰ (01) 676 03 00
– www.onepico.com – Closed bank holidays   JZ**k**
Rest – Modern – Menu € 25 – Carte € 51/66
♦ Wide-ranging cuisine, classic and traditional by turns, always with an original, eclectic edge. Décor and service share a pleasant formality, crisp, modern and stylish.

DUBLIN

XX Locks Brasserie
1 Windsor Terr. ⊠ *D8 – ℰ (01) 420 05 55 – www.locksbrasserie.com – Closed 25 December-7 January and bank holidays* DUa
Rest – Modern European – *(dinner only and lunch Thursday-Sunday)*
Carte € 30/53

◆ Attractive, well-lit restaurant with a relaxed atmosphere and professional, engaging staff. Dining is split over two floors, with comfy banquette seating and a cocktail bar. Menu of modern European classics; well-presented dishes make use of fine ingredients.

XX Pearl Brasserie
20 Merrion St Upper ⊠ *D2 – ℰ (01) 661 35 72 – www.pearl-brasserie.com – Closed 25 December and Sunday* KZn
Rest – French – Carte € 32/58

◆ Basement restaurant with small bar-lounge and two surprisingly airy dining rooms; choose one of the stylish booths set in the old coal bunkers. Modern menus of elaborate, stylishly presented dishes and a simpler market menu. Formal service.

XX Pichet
14-15 Trinity St ⊠ *D2 – ℰ (01) 677 10 60 – www.pichetrestaurant.com – Closed 1-10 January* JYg
Rest – Modern European – *(booking advisable)* Menu € 25 – Carte € 30/50

◆ Popular brasserie with buzzy atmosphere; its long, narrow room dominated by an open-plan kitchen. Front café-cum-bar – complete with cake and pastry counter – for light snacks. Neat, flavoursome modern European cooking from good value, daily changing menus. Wines available by the glass or in a 500ml 'pichet'.

XX Dax
23 Pembroke St. Upper ⊠ *D2 – ℰ (01) 676 14 94 – www.dax.ie – Closed 1 week Easter, 2 weeks August, 10 days Christmas, Saturday lunch, Sunday, Monday*
Rest – *(booking essential)* Menu € 29/35 – Carte approx. € 79 KZc

◆ Simply furnished restaurant hidden in the basement of a Georgian terraced house not far from Fiztwilliam Square. Rustic inner with smart linen-laid tables and wine cellar. French-inspired menus include a six course 'surprise' selection.

XX Dobbin's
15 Stephen's Lane, (off Stephen's Place) off Lower Mount St ⊠ *D2 – ℰ (01) 661 95 36 – www.dobbins.ie – Closed 24 December-2 January, Saturday lunch, Sunday dinner, Mondays (except December) and bank holidays* EUs
Rest – Traditional – *(booking essential)* Menu € 23 (lunch)/25 – Carte € 38/53

◆ Smart, well-established restaurant in residential area. Small bar with booths leads to spacious, neatly laid dining room with warm, modern décor. Large menu displays international influences.

XX Tea Room – at The Clarence Hotel
6-8 Wellington Quay ⊠ *D2 – ℰ (01) 407 08 13 – Closed 25-26 December*
Rest – Modern – *(booking essential)* Menu € 15/25 HYa
– Carte € 23/42

◆ Spacious hotel restaurant, where small mezzanine level overlooks larger main room with central banquette island. Ambitious cooking displays Gallic influences. Polite, formal service.

XX Les Frères Jacques
74 Dame St ⊠ *D2 – ℰ (01) 679 4555 – www.lesfreresjacques.com – Closed 24-30 December, Saturday lunch, Sunday and bank holidays* HYx
Rest – French – Menu € 18/38 – Carte € 51/69

◆ Long-standing restaurant on narrow cobbled alley, with typical French styling and team. Classical Gallic cooking with seafood a speciality: daily fresh fish and lobster tank on display.

Pepoe's

XX

16 St Stephen's Grn. ⊠ D2 – ℰ (01) 676 31 44 – www.peploes.com – Closed Good Friday and 25-29 December   JZ**e**

Rest – Mediterranean – *(booking essential)* Menu € 25 – Carte € 36/53

♦ Well-run, atmospheric brasserie named after Scottish artist and set in former bank vault. Small bar; main room with smart mural and linen-laid tables. Extensive menu with influences from the Med.

Bleu

XX

Joshua House, Dawson St ⊠ D2 – ℰ (01) 676 70 15 – www.onepico.com – Closed 25-26 December   JZ**r**

Rest – Modern European – Menu € 21/25 – Carte € 32/43

♦ Stylish, modern eatery on a bustling street. Smart and contemporary interior, with framed mirrors a feature. The appealing, varied menu keeps its influences within Europe.

Town Bar and Grill

XX

21 Kildare St ⊠ D2 – ℰ (01) 662 4800 – www.townbarandgrill.com – Closed Good Friday, 25-27 December and bank holidays   JZ**n**

Rest – Italian influences – *(booking advisable)* Menu € 25 (lunch) – Carte € 35/58

♦ Located in the old cellar's of a famous city wine merchant. Small bar and high stools at entrance, more intimate tables to the rear. Eclectic menu of grills and bold Italian dishes, with the occasional Asian influence. Pianist at weekends.

Fallon & Byrne

XX

First Floor, 11-17 Exchequer St ⊠ D2 – ℰ (01) 472 10 00 – www.fallonandbyrne.com – Closed Good Friday, 25-26 December and Sunday dinner   JY**f**

Rest – Bistro – Menu € 25/30 – Carte € 20/44

♦ Food emporium boasting vast basement wine cellar, ground floor full of fresh quality produce, and first floor French style bistro with banquettes, mirrors and tasty bistro food.

Bang

XX

11 Merrion Row ⊠ D2 – ℰ (01) 400 42 29 – www.bangrestaurant.com – Closed first week January, Easter, Monday lunch and Sunday   KZ**a**

Rest – Modern – *(booking essential)* Menu € 25/37 – Carte € 35/45

♦ Stylish three floor restaurant displaying impressive modern art by leading Irish/international artists. Good value lunch/early evening menus; more luxurious, modern dishes on the à la carte.

Francesca's – at Brooks Hotel

XX

Drury St ⊠ D2 – ℰ (01) 670 40 00 – www.brookshotel.ie   JY**r**

Rest – Modern – *(closed to non-residents 25 December) (dinner only)* Menu € 28 – Carte € 31/51

♦ Fine dining room with an open-plan kitchen, set in a smart, boutique-style townhouse. Interesting menu offers plenty of choice and relies on local produce; good value pre-theatre selection.

Pig's Ear

X

4 Nassau St ⊠ D2 – ℰ (01) 670 38 65 – www.thepigsear.ie – Closed first week January, Sunday and bank holidays   KY**a**

Rest – Modern European – Menu € 20/25 – Carte € 33/49

♦ Split-level, bistro-style restaurant, in a Georgian city centre house with a striking pink door. Porcine-themed memorabilia features throughout. Well-priced, refined bistro cooking has French influences and relies on Irish produce. Attentive, personable service.

DUBLIN

La Maison

15 Castlemarket ⊠ D2 – ℰ (01) 672 7258 – www.lamaisonrestaurant.ie – Closed 25 December to 1 January JYc
Rest – French – *(bookings not accepted)* Menu € 26 – Carte € 25/42
♦ Appealing French bistro with light blue façade, tables on the pavement and original posters decorating the walls inside. Breton-born chef offers carefully prepared, seasonal Gallic classics at a good price, which are brought to the table by a personable team.

Rustic Stone

17 Great George's St ⊠ D2 – ℰ (01) 707 9596 – www.rusticstone.ie
Rest – Modern – Menu € 30/50 (dinner) – Carte € 22/62 JYm
♦ Split-level restaurant offering something a little bit different. Good quality ingredients are cooked simply to retain their natural flavours and menus point out the healthier options; some meats and fish arrive on a sizzling hot stone.

L'Gueuleton

1 Fade St ⊠ D2 – ℰ (01) 675 37 08 – www.lgueuleton.com – Closed 25-27 December, 1 January and Easter Friday JYd
Rest – French – *(bookings not accepted)* Carte € 32/47
♦ Rustic restaurant with beamed ceilings, Gallic furnishings and rear terrace. Interesting French menus use local, seasonal produce. Flavoursome country cooking; friendly, efficient service.

Camden Kitchen

*3a Camden Mkt, Grantham St ⊠ D8 – ℰ (01) 476 01 25
– www.camdenkitchen.ie – Closed 25-26 December, Sunday dinner and Monday*
Rest – Modern – Menu € 18 (early dinner) – Carte € 31/39 JZx
♦ Appealing bistro with canopied façade and rustic inner, set over two floors. Open kitchen serving gutsy menu of robust, modern dishes. Relaxed, friendly service from a young team.

Saba

26-28 Clarendon St ⊠ D2 – ℰ (01) 679 2000 – www.sabadublin.com – Closed Good Friday and 25-26 December JYk
Rest – Thai – Menu € 20/30 – Carte € 25/36
♦ Very trendy, buzzy Thai restaurant and cocktail bar. Simple yet stylish rooms with refectory tables in the centre and banquette seating around the walls. Fresh, clean, visual cooking from all all-Thai team who like to keep things authentic.

Port House

64a South William St ⊠ D2 – ℰ (01) 677 0298 – www.porthouse.ie – Closed 25 December JYe
Rest – Spanish – Carte € 16/43
♦ Characterful Spanish tapas bar serving a vast array of authentic, flavoursome dishes. Rustic, candlelit interior with exposed brick, semi-vaulted ceiling and tightly packed tables; small bar upstairs. Imported meats, cheeses and olives.

at Ballsbridge

Four Seasons

Simmonscourt Rd. ⊠ D4 – ℰ (01) 665 4000 – www.fourseasons.com/dublin
156 rm – ♦ € 185/289 ♦♦ € 255/329, ⊇ €29 – 40 suites FUe
Rest *Seasons* – Menu € 35 **s** – Carte € 46/65 **s**
♦ Set in grounds of the RDS arena. Elegant guest areas, state-of-the-art meeting rooms and impressive ballrooms boast ornate décor, antiques and Irish art. Spacious bedrooms; plenty of extras. Fine dining with fountain/garden views in Seasons.

DUBLIN

Herbert Park
D4 – ℰ (01) 667 2200 – www.herbertparkhotel.ie
FUm
151 rm – ♦ € 119/250 ♦♦ € 119/385, ☐ €19.50 – 2 suites
Rest *The Pavilion* – Menu € 35

♦ Contemporary hotel overlooking suburban park, with smart marble-floored reception, stylish seating areas and chic bar. Modern bedrooms display quality furnishings and marble bathrooms. Sizeable, formal restaurant offers interesting menu.

Schoolhouse
2-8 Northumberland Rd ⊠ D4 – ℰ (01) 667 5014
– www.schoolhousehotel.com – Closed 24-27 December
FUk
31 rm – ♦ € 109/129 ♦♦ € 109/159, ☐ €15
Rest *Olivier's at The Schoolhouse* – see restaurant listing
Rest *Schoolhouse Bar* – Carte € 25/50

♦ Dating back to 1861 and formerly the St Stephens Parochial School. Spacious, well-kept bedrooms – most in the extension – boast William Morris designed fabrics and locally built Macintosh-style furniture; some have half-tester beds. Busy bar with vaulted ceiling and stone fireplaces offers pub-style menus.

Merrion Hall without rest
54-56 Merrion Rd. ⊠ D4 – ℰ (01) 668 1426
– www.merrionhall.com
FUb
30 rm ☐ – ♦ € 90/159 ♦♦ € 129/399

♦ Red-brick Victorian house boasting spacious, antique-furnished guest areas with a Georgian feel. Comfortable bedrooms have a traditional edge; those to the rear are quieter.

Ariel House without rest
50-54 Lansdowne Rd ⊠ D4 – ℰ (01) 668 5512
– www.ariel-house.net – Closed 22 December-3 January
FUn
37 rm ☐ – ♦ € 69/130 ♦♦ € 79/300

♦ Personally run Victorian townhouse with comfy, traditionally styled guest areas and antique furnishings. Warmly decorated bedrooms have modern facilities and smart bathrooms; some four-posters.

Aberdeen Lodge without rest
53-55 Park Ave. ⊠ D4 – ℰ (01) 283 8155
– www.halpinsprivatehotels.com
GVe
16 rm ☐ – ♦ € 90/169 ♦♦ € 139/359

♦ Two Victorian townhouses in smart suburban setting, knocked through into one impressive hotel. Comfy lounge, warm homely atmosphere and well-equipped bedrooms – some with garden views.

Pembroke Townhouse without rest
90 Pembroke Rd ⊠ D4 – ℰ (01) 660 0277
– www.pembroketownhouse.ie – Closed 2 weeks Christmas-New Year
FUd
48 rm – ♦ € 199 ♦♦ € 310, ☐ €15

♦ Formerly three Georgian houses, now a friendly hotel with traditional styling, comfy lounge and sunny breakfast room. Bedrooms vary in shape and size: duplex rooms are the cosiest.

Glenogra House without rest
64 Merrion Rd ⊠ D4 – ℰ (01) 668 3661
– www.glenogra.com – Closed 24-27 December
FUw
13 rm ☐ – ♦ € 69/199 ♦♦ € 89/199

♦ Personally run red-brick Victorian house with informal reception, comfy lounge and homely furnishings. Simply decorated bedrooms vary in shape and size; all boast modern facilities.

DUBLIN

XX Olivier's at The Schoolhouse – at Schoolhouse Hotel
2-8 Northumberland Rd ⊠ D4 – ℰ (01) 667 5014
– www.oliviers.ie – Closed 24-27 December
FUk
Rest – *(closed Saturday lunch, Monday dinner and Sunday) (brunch Saturday and Sunday) (booking essential at dinner)* Menu € 28/40 **s**
– Carte € 39/60 **s**
♦ Formal restaurant taking pride of place in the old classroom of a former school. Original vaulted ceiling and stone fireplaces. Classical menu, written in French and English, has strong Gallic influences and showcases luxurious ingredients.

XX Bloom Brasserie
11 Upper Baggot St ⊠ D4 – ℰ (01) 668 7170
– www.bloombrasserie.ie – Closed 25 December, Sunday and bank holidays
EUx
Rest – Modern European – Menu € 25 – Carte € 25/48
♦ Sizeable basement brasserie with cool, contemporary styling, vibrant art and garden terrace. Menus offer a mix of traditional and more modern dishes; with an additional small plate selection in the evening.

ID Chop House
2 Shelbourne Rd ⊠ D4 – ℰ (1) 660 23 90
– www.thechophouse.ie
FUx
Rest – Modern European – Carte € 26/49
♦ Imposing square pub with small side terrace, dark bar and bright, airy conservatory. Relaxed lunchtime menu; more ambitious dishes in the evening, when the kitchen really comes into its own.

at Rathmines

XX Zen
89 Upper Rathmines Rd ⊠ D6 – ℰ (01) 497 94 28
– www.zenrestaurant.ie – Closed 25-27 December
DVt
Rest – Chinese – *(dinner only and Friday lunch)* Carte € 18/31
♦ Renowned family run Chinese restaurant in the unusual setting of an old church hall. Imaginative, authentic oriental cuisine with particular emphasis on spicy Sichuan dishes.

at Dublin Airport North : 10.5 km by N 1 – BS – and M 1 – ⊠ Dublin

Carlton H. Dublin Airport
Old Airport Rd., Cloughran, on R 132 Santry rd – ℰ (01) 866 7500
– www.carlton.ie/dublinairport – Closed 24-26 December
117 rm – ♦ € 89/129 ♦♦ € 89/129, ⊇ € 13.50 – 1 suite
Rest *Kittyhawks* – Menu € 18/20 **s** – Carte € 25/40 **s**
♦ Modern commercial hotel with spacious marbled reception and comfy guest areas. Uniform bedrooms display good facilities and smart bathrooms. Some rooms overlook airfield; some have balconies. Informal all-day brasserie offers popular menu.

Bewleys
Baskin Ln., East : 1.5 km on N 32 – ℰ (01) 871 1000
– www.bewleyshotels.com – Closed 25 December
466 rm – ♦ € 89/199 ♦♦ € 89/199, ⊇ € 12
Rest *The Brasserie* – Menu € 20/25 – Carte dinner € 25/60
♦ Immense eight floor hotel, ten minutes from the airport, with selection of small meeting rooms. Immaculately kept bedrooms; good value for money. Wide-ranging menu served in The Brasserie.

at Clontarf Northeast : 5.5 km by R 105 – ✉ Dublin

🏛 Clontarf Castle
Castle Ave. ✉ D3 – ✆ (01) 833 2321 – www.clontarfcastle.ie CSa
111 rm – † €79/299 †† €99/299, ☐ €10
Rest *Fahrenheit Grill* – (dinner only) Menu €25 – Carte €35/51

♦ Set in an historic castle, partly dating back to 1172. Striking medieval style entrance lobby. Modern rooms and characterful luxury suites with cutting edge facilities. Grand restaurant reminiscent of a knights' banqueting hall; local meats and seafood feature.

at Dundrum Southeast : 8 km by N 11 - CT – ✉ Dublin

XXX Harvey Nichols First Floor Restaurant
Harvey Nichols, Town Sq., Sandyford Rd ✉ D16 – ✆ (01) 291 0488
– www.harveynichols.com – Closed 25 December, Sunday dinner and Monday
Rest – Menu €25/30 – Carte €29/39

♦ Up the lift to ultra-stylish bar and plush, designer-led restaurant. Attentive, professional service. Dishes are modern, seasonal and confident with a fine dining feel.

XX Ananda
Town Sq. ✉ D14 – ✆ (01) 296 00 99 – www.anandarestarant.ie – Closed 25 December and lunch Monday-Wednesday
Rest – Indian – Menu €16 (lunch) – Carte €31/49

♦ Meaning 'bliss' in ancient Sanskrit. Stylish restaurant located in city centre arcade. Beautiful décor, attractive fretwork and gorgeous lighting. Flavourful modern Indian cuisine.

at Sandyford Southeast : 12 km by N 11 and R 112 off R 133 - CT – ✉ Dublin

🏛 Beacon
Beacon Court, Sandyford Business Region ✉ D18 – ✆ (01) 291 5000
– www.thebeacon.com – Closed 24-25 December
87 rm – † €80/300 †† €99/300, ☐ €15 – 1 suite
Rest *My Thai* – Thai – Carte €25/33 **s**

♦ Ultra-stylish hotel with uniquely quirky entrance lobby featuring a chandelier on the floor and bed with central seating! Modish bar, low-key meeting rooms, sleek bedrooms. Funky, relaxed restaurant serving authentic Asian dishes.

XX China Sichuan
The Forum, Ballymoss Rd. ✉ D18 – ✆ (01) 293 5100 – www.china-sichuan.ie
– Closed 25-31 December, Good Friday, lunch Saturday and bank holidays
Rest – Chinese – Menu €25 – Carte €25/50

♦ Established in 1979 and now run by the third generation of the family. Smart, modern interior matched by creative menus, where Irish produce is used in tasty Chinese-influenced dishes. Sichuan specialities pay homage to their heritage.

at Foxrock Southeast : 13 km by N 11 - CT – ✉ Dublin

XX Bistro One
3 Brighton Rd ✉ D18 – ✆ (01) 289 7711 – www.bistro-one.ie – Closed 25 December-3 January, Sunday and Monday
Rest – (booking essential) Menu €25 – Carte €27/35

♦ Long-standing neighbourhood restaurant; popular with the locals. Daily changing lunch and dinner menus display a mix of Irish and Mediterranean influences. Good use of local produce.

DUBLIN AIRPORT = Aerfort Bhaile Átha Cliath – Fingal – **712** N7 – see Dublin

DUNBOYNE (Dún Búinne) – Meath – **712** M7 – pop. 5 713   37 D3
▶ Dublin 17 km – Drogheda 45 km – Newbridge 54 km

Dunboyne Castle
– ℰ (01) 801 35 00 – www.dunboynecastlehotel.com
141 rm – † € 270 †† € 340 – 4 suites
Rest – (dinner only and Sunday lunch) Menu € 25 – Carte € 35/47
♦ Georgian house with vast, modern extensions and formal gardens, set in 26 acres. State-of-the-art meeting rooms with the latest conference equipment. Stylish spa and plunge pool. Spacious bedrooms boast good mod cons; some have balconies. Sizeable formal dining room offers classically based Irish dishes.

DUNCANNON (Dún Canann) – Wexford – **712** L11 – pop. 291   39 D2
I Ireland
▶ Dublin 167 km – New Ross 26 km – Waterford 48 km
◉ Fort★ **AC**
◉ Dunbrody Abbey★ **AC**, N : 9 km by R 733 – Kilmokea Gardens★ **AC**, N : 11 km by R 733 – Tintern Abbey★ **AC**, E : 8 km by R 737 and R 733. Kennedy Arboretum★ **AC**, N : 21 km by R 733

Aldridge Lodge with rm
South : 1 km by Hook Head Rd – ℰ (051) 389 116 – www.aldridgelodge.com
– Closed 3 weeks January and 24-25 December
3 rm – † € 55 †† € 90
Rest – (closed Monday and Tuesday) (dinner only) (booking essential) Menu € 39 **s**
♦ New-build house run by cheery owner. Constantly evolving menu offers tasty homemade bread and veg from the kitchen garden. Focus on good value fish and shellfish – the owner's father is a local fisherman – with some Asian and fusion influences. Simply furnished bedrooms with hot water bottles and home-baked cookies.

Sqigl
Quay Rd. – ℰ (051) 389 700 – www.sqiglrestaurant.com – Closed November-Easter and Sunday-Wednesday
Rest – (dinner only) (booking essential) Menu € 38 – Carte € 28/41
♦ Stone-built restaurant; a converted barn standing adjacent to a popular bar in this coastal village. Faux leopard skin banquettes. Modern European cuisine with amiable service.

DUNDALK (Dún Dealgan) – Louth – **712** M5/6 – pop. 35 085   37 D2
I Ireland
▶ Dublin 82 km – Drogheda 35 km
⛳ Killinbeg Killin Park, ℰ (042) 9 33 93 03
◉ Dún a' Rí Forest Park★, W : 34 km by R 178 and R 179 – Proleek Dolmen★, N : 8 km by N 1 R 173

Left Bank
43-44 Park St – ℰ (042) 933 8851 – www.leftbankdundalk.com
– Closed 25-26 December, Monday dinner and bank holidays
Rest – (closed Monday dinner) Menu € 14/22 – Carte € 20/36
♦ Well-run bistro in a busy market town. Large bar and raised dining room with tightly packed tables and booth seating; chiller cabinet offers homemade pastries and cakes to take home. All-purpose menu offer carefully prepared, hearty dishes.

DUNDALK

Crowne Plaza
*Green Park, South : 2.5 km on N 52 – ℰ (042) 939 49 00 – www.cpdundalk.ie
– Closed 25 December*
128 rm – † €55/99 †† €69/109, ⌂ €15 – 1 suite
Rest – *(bar lunch Monday-Saturday)* Menu €35 **s** – Carte €30/45 **s**
♦ Modern 14-storey hotel tower block, close to the main shopping centre, with stylish ground floor bar/lounge and good conference facilities. Uniform bedrooms boast views of surrounding countryside; ask for one higher up. Top floor restaurant offers seasonal menu of classic dishes and has superb 360° vista.

Rosemount without rest
*Dublin Rd, South : 2.5 km on R 132 – ℰ (042) 933 58 78
– www.rosemountireland.com – Closed 25 December*
6 rm ⌂ – † €40 †† €65
♦ Attractive guesthouse with flower-filled gardens; run by welcoming couple. Laura Ashley and Brown Thomas fabrics/furnishings feature throughout. Individually styled bedrooms; some with sofas and flat screen TVs. Freshly cooked breakfasts; tea and cake on arrival.

at Jenkinstown Northeast : 9 km by N 52 on R 173

Fitzpatricks
*Rockmarshall, Southeast : 1 km – ℰ (042) 937 61 93
– www.fitzpatricks-restaurant.com – Closed Good Friday, Monday September-May (except bank holidays) and 25 December*
Rest – Menu €28 – Carte approx. €33
♦ Hugely characterful pub with beautiful flower displays and intriguing memorabilia. Extensive menu of hearty, flavoursome dishes and plenty of classics; local seafood and steaks a speciality.

REPUBLIC OF IRELAND

DUNDRUM = Dún Droma – Dún Laoghaire-Rathdown – **712** N8 – see Dublin

DUNFANAGHY (Dún Fionnchaidh) – Donegal – **712** I2 – pop. 316   **37** C1
– ✉ Letterkenny ▌Ireland
▶ Dublin 277 km – Donegal 87 km – Londonderry 69 km
🛈 Dunfanaghy Letterkenny, ℰ (074) 913 63 35
◉ Horn Head Scenic Route★, N : 4 km. Doe Castle★, SE : 11.25 km by N 56 – The Rosses★, SW : 40.25 km by N 56 and R 259

Arnolds
Main St – ℰ (074) 913 62 08 – www.arnoldshotel.com – Easter-October
30 rm ⌂ – †† €130/150
Rest *Sea Scapes* – *(bar lunch)* Menu €40 – Carte €24/41
♦ Pleasant traditional coaching inn with a variety of extensions. Spacious lounge area and a charming bar with open fires. Family run with traditional bedrooms. Informal Sea Scapes serves wide-ranging menus.

Mill with rm
*Southwest : 0.75 km on N 56 – ℰ (074) 913 69 85 – www.themillrestaurant.com
– Closed mid-December to mid-March, mid-week March, April and November and part December*
6 rm ⌂ – † €70 †† €130   **Rest** – *(Closed Monday) (dinner only)* Menu €45
♦ Converted flax mill on the waterside, with lovely garden edged by reeds and great view of Mount Muckish. Homely inner with conservatory lounge and knick-knacks on display throughout. Antique-furnished dining room has a classical Georgian feel. Traditional menus showcase seasonal ingredients and fish features highly. Cosy, welcoming bedrooms come in individual designs.

DUNGARVAN (Dún Garbhán) – Waterford – 712 J11 – pop. 8 362   39 C3
🇮🇪 Ireland

▶ Dublin 190 km – Cork 71 km – Waterford 48 km

🏌 Knocknagrannagh, ℰ (058) 4 16 05

🏌 Gold Coast Ballinacourty, ℰ (058) 4 22 49

◉ East Bank (Augustinian priory, ≤★)

◎ Ringville (≤★), S : 13 km by N 25 and R 674 – Helvick Head★ (≤★), SE : 13 km by N 25 and R 674

XX Tannery with rm   AC rest, (¹) VISA ⦿ AE
10 Quay St, via Parnell St – ℰ (058) 45 420 – www.tannery.ie – Closed 2 weeks January, 25-26 December and Good Friday
14 rm – ♦ € 60/70 ♦♦ € 100/110
Rest – *(dinner only and lunch Friday and Sunday)* Menu € 30 – Carte € 37/53
♦ Long-standing restaurant in delightful coastal location, affording great views of the castle, sea and sunsets. Large conservatory, vast decked terrace and snug bar with seafaring memorabilia. Spacious dining room has dark linen cloths; classical menu features mussels and oysters from the bay. Contemporary bedrooms have gilt mirrors, plush fabrics and very comfy beds.

DUNKINEELY (Dún Cionnaola) – Donegal – 712 G4 – pop. 363   37 C1

▶ Dublin 156 km – Lifford 42 km – Sligo 53 km – Ballybofey 28 km

XX Castle Murray House with rm 🐾   ≤ 🛌 🛋 (¹) P. VISA ⦿
St John's Point, Southwest : 1.5 km by N 56 on St John's Point rd – ℰ (074) 973 70 22 – www.castlemurray.com – Closed 24-25 December, restricted opening in winter
10 rm ⌒ – ♦ € 60/70 ♦♦ € 120/130
Rest – *(closed dinner Monday-Thursday in winter) (dinner only and Sunday lunch, light lunch in summer)* Carte € 45/55
♦ In delightful, picturesque position with view of sea and sunsets from the lounges and the pleasant dining room. Good local seafood. Comfortable and contemporary styled bedrooms.

DUN LAOGHAIRE (Dún Laoghaire) – Dún Laoghaire-Rathdown   39 D1
– 712 N8 – pop. 23 857 🇮🇪 Ireland

▶ Dublin 14 km

⛴ to Holyhead (Stena Line) 4-5 daily (1 h 40 mn)

🏌 Dun Laoghaire Eglinton Park, ℰ (01) 280 39 16

◎ ≤ ★★ of Killiney Bay from coast road south of Sorrento Point

XX Rasam   VISA ⦿
1st Floor (above Eagle House pub), 18-19 Glasthule Rd – ℰ (01) 230 0600 – www.rasam.ie – Closed 25-26 December and Good Friday   e
Rest – Indian – *(dinner only)* Menu € 25 (dinner) – Carte € 40/50
♦ Located above Eagle House pub, this airy, modern, stylish restaurant shimmers with silky green wallpaper. Interesting, authentic dishes covering all regions of India.

X Alexis Bar and Grill   🛋 AC VISA ⦿
17-18 Patricks St. – ℰ (01) 280 8872 – www.alexis.ie – Closed 25 December, Good Friday, Saturday lunch and Monday   b
Rest – Menu € 16/25 – Carte € 29/44
♦ Modern bistro towards the back of town, run by an experienced owner. Simply furnished interior with tightly packed tables and buzzy vibe; sunny courtyard to the rear. Unfussy, value for money menus change daily and reflect the seasons.

DUN LAOGHAIRE

Longford Pl.	5
Marine Rd	7
Monkstown Ave	8
Monkstown Rd	9
Mount Town Upper	10
Mulgrave St.	
Pakenham Rd.	13
Patrick St.	
umberland St.	2
unleary Hill	4
eorge St.	

Cavistons

58-59 Glasthule Rd – ℰ (01) 280 9245 – www.cavistons.com – Closed 1 week Christmas, Sunday and Monday

Rest – Seafood – *(lunch only and dinner Friday and Saturday) (booking essential)* Menu € 16 *(early lunch)* – Carte € 26/45

♦ Simple, informal restaurant attached to the well-established seafood shop which specialises in finest piscine produce. Mermaid friezes and quality crustacean cuisine.

Tribes

57a Glasthule Rd – ℰ (01) 236 5971 – www.tribes.ie – Closed Good Friday and 24-26 December

Rest – *(dinner only and Sunday lunch) (booking advisable)* Menu € 24/27

♦ Personally run neighbourhood restaurant next to Cavistons. Smart, original interior harmonises seamlessly with creative modern European menus that evolve slowly over time.

DUNLAVIN (Dún Luáin) – Wicklow – 712 L8 – pop. 849   39 D2

Dublin 50 km – Kilkenny 71 km – Wexford 98 km
Rathsallagh, ℰ (045) 40 33 16

DUNLAVIN

Rathsallagh House
Southwest : 3.25 km on Grangecon rd – ℘ (045) 403 112 – www.rathsallagh.com
28 rm – † € 110/300 †† € 200/350 – 1 suite
Rest – *(dinner only and Sunday lunch , bar lunch Monday-Saturday)*
Carte € 34/50
♦ Collection of converted 18C stables and farm buildings in peaceful, rural location. Extensive grounds include a golf course; working farm to the rear. Characterful, open-fired lounges and cottagey bar. Spacious country house bedrooms with good facilities. Large formal restaurant serves classically based menu.

DUNMORE EAST (Dún Mór) – Waterford – 712 L11 – pop. 1 547   39 C2
– ✉ Waterford ▮ Ireland

▶ Dublin 174 km – Waterford 19 km
⛳ Dunmore East, ℘ (051) 38 31 51
◉ Village ★

Beach without rest
*1 Lower Village – ℘ (051) 383 316 – www.dunmorebeachguesthouse.com
– March-December*
7 rm – † € 45/60 †† € 80/90
♦ Modern house overlooking a large cove, with the beach just metres away. Inside it has an almost Mediterranean feel, with bedrooms displaying whitewashed walls and ash furniture. Superb views from conservatory lounge-cum-breakfast room.

DURRUS (Dúras) – Cork – 712 D13 – pop. 313   38 A3
▶ Dublin 338 km – Cork 90 km – Killarney 85 km

※※ Blairscove House with rm
Southwest : 1.5 km on R 591 – ℘ (027) 62 913 – www.blairscove.ie – 18 March-October
4 rm – †† € 160/260
Rest – *(closed Sunday and Monday) (dinner only) (booking essential)*
Menu € 58 **s**
♦ Charming 18C house just a stone's throw from the sea, boasting fantastic panoramic views, pretty gardens, a courtyard and lily pond. Stylish bar and large candlelit dining room with stone walls. Starters and desserts are in buffet format while the seasonal main courses are cooked on a wood-fired char-grill. Luxurious modern bedrooms are dotted about the place.

※ Good Things Café
*Ahakista Rd, West : 0.75 km on Ahakista rd – ℘ (027) 61 426
– www.thegoodthingscafe.com – Closed August - late September*
Rest – *(booking essential)* Carte € 22/48
♦ Cookery school with simple, unpretentious restaurant open for weekends in July and most Friday nights March to early December. Sit among shelves of cookery books overlooking an open kitchen. Unfussy menu offers seasonal classics with Mediterranean and Moroccan influences.

ENNISCORTHY (Inis Córthaidh) – Wexford – 712 M10 – pop. 9 538   39 D2
▮ Ireland

▶ Dublin 122 km – Kilkenny 74 km – Waterford 54 km – Wexford 24 km
ℹ Millpark Rd ℘ (0539) 23 46 99, www.enniscorthytourism.com
⛳ Knockmarshal, ℘ (053) 9 23 31 91
◉ Enniscorthy Castle ★ (County Museum ★)
◎ Ferns ★, NE : 13 km by N 11 – Mount Leinster ★, N : 27.25 km by N 11

ENNISCORTHY

Monart
The Still, Northwest : 3 km by N 11 (Dublin rd) – ℰ *(053) 923 8999*
– *www.monart.ie* – *Closed 19-27 December*
68 rm – †€112/255 ††€184/430 – 2 suites
Rest *Garden Lounge* – Carte €25/43
Rest *The Restaurant* – *(dinner only and Sunday lunch)* Menu €30/38
– Carte €39/59
• Spa resort in 100 acres; enter via the elegant Georgian house and experience various therapies in state-of-the-art treatment rooms. Bedrooms all have views; many have balconies. Enjoy lighter dishes in the Garden Lounge or out on the terrace. Formal dining in The Restaurant.

Ballinkeele House
Ballymurn, Southeast : 10 km by R 744 and Vinegar Hill rd on Curracloe rd
– ℰ *(053) 913 81 05* – *www.ballinkeele.ie* – *Closed December-January*
5 rm – †€95/105 ††€85/90 **Rest** – Menu €45 **s**
• High ceilinged, firelit lounge plus sizeable rooms with period-style furniture and countryside views add to the charm of a quiet 1840 manor, well run by experienced owners. Dining room enriched by candlelight and period oils.

Your discoveries and comments help us to improve the guide.
Please write and let us know about your experiences -
good or bad!

ENNISKERRY (Áth an Sceire) – Wicklow – **712** N8 – pop. 1 881   **39** D1
Ireland

▶ Dublin 25 km – Wicklow 32 km
▣ Powerscourt Powerscourt Estate, ℰ (01) 204 60 33
◉ Powerscourt★★ **AC** (Waterfall★★, **AC**)

Ritz Carlton
West : 1.5 km by Powerscourt rd – ℰ *(01) 274 88 88*
– *www.ritzcarlton.com*
106 rm – †€255 ††€315, ⌑ €29 – 94 suites – ††€305/365
Rest *Gordon Ramsay at Powerscourt* **Rest** *Sugar Loaf* – see restaurant listing
• Impressive curved building overlooking Sugar Loaf Mountain. Stylish guest areas, state-of-the-art conference facilities and superb spa. Luxurious bedrooms with marble bathrooms; some have balconies. Activities include archery and falconry.

XXX Gordon Ramsay at Powerscourt – at Ritz Carlton Hotel
West : 1.5 km by Powerscourt rd – ℰ *(01) 274 93 77* – *www.ritzcarlton.com*
Rest – *(dinner only and lunch Saturday-Sunday)* Carte €55/69
• Smart restaurant boasting superb mountain views and a chef's table, set in an impressive estate hotel. Classic Ramsay dishes in the main room and on the terrace; sharing boards in the wine bar.

XX Sugar Loaf – at Ritz Carlton Hotel
West : 1.5 km by Powerscourt rd – ℰ *(01) 274 88 88* – *www.ritzcarlton.com*
Rest – Carte €49/58
• Spacious Georgian-style lounge set in a smart hotel on the Powerscourt Estate. Light, airy room affords pleasant views out over Wicklow. All-day menu offers light choices and afternoon tea.

FENNOR – Waterford – **712** K11   **39** C2

▶ Dublin 115 km – Waterford 12 km – Cork 75 km – Limerick 89 km

✕ **Copper Hen**   **P** VISA ⓒ AE
Mother McHugh's Pub – ℰ (051) 330 300 – www.thecopperhen.ie – Closed 1 week January, 1 week autumn, 25-26 December, Monday-Wednesday, Sunday dinner and bank holidays
Rest – *(dinner only and Sunday lunch) (booking advisable)* Menu € 25 – Carte € 25/34
♦ Simple, likeable little restaurant above a pub, with rustic décor and a brightly coloured fireplace; set on the coast road from Tramore to Dungarven. Keenly priced menus offer hearty, unfussy classics. Owners raise their own pigs.

FETHARD (Fiodh Ard) – South Tipperary – **712** I10 – pop. 1 374   **39** C2
▮ Ireland

▶ Dublin 161 km – Cashel 16 km – Clonmel 13 km

ⓒ Cashel★★★ : Rock of Cashel★★★ **AC** (Cormac's Chapel★★, Round Tower★), Museum★ **AC**, Cashel Palace Gardens★, GPA Bolton Library★ **AC**, NW : 15 km by R 692 – Clonmel★ : County Museum★ **AC**, St Mary's Church★, S : 13 km by R 689

⌂ **Mobarnane House**   ← 🚗 🍸 ✕ ✿ **P** VISA ⓒ
North : 8 km. by Cashel rd on Ballinure rd – ℰ (052) 613 19 62 – www.mobarnanehouse.com – March-October
3 rm ⊇ – ♦ € 125 ♦♦ € 150/190
Rest – *(dinner only) (residents only)* Menu € 48 **s**
♦ Very personally run classic Georgian house with mature gardens in quiet rural setting, tastefully restored to reflect its age. Ask for a bedroom with its own sitting room. Beautiful dining room for menus agreed in advance.

FOTA ISLAND (Oileán Fhóta) – Cork – **712** H12   **38** B3

▶ Dublin 263 km – Cork 17 km – Limerick 118 km – Waterford 110 km

🏨 **Fota Island**   🚗 🍸 📺 ❄ 🛁 🎬 🎭 ⚘ rm, 🅰🅲 ✕ ¶ 🏋 **P** VISA ⓒ AE ①
– ℰ (021) 488 37 00 – www.fotaisland.ie – Closed 25-26 December
127 rm ⊇ – ♦ € 129/149 ♦♦ € 145/165 – 4 suites
Rest *Fota* – *(dinner only)* Carte € 25/41
♦ Resort hotel set within Ireland's only wildlife park. Extensive business and leisure facilities include a golf course and state-of-the-art spa. Spacious, well-appointed bedrooms; most with island views. Stylish restaurant offers modern takes on classical dishes.

FOXROCK = Carraig an tSionnaigh – Dún Laoghaire-Rathdown – **712** N7
– see Dublin

FURBOGH/FURBO (Na Forbacha) – Galway – **712** E8 – pop. 1 236   **36** A3

▶ Dublin 228 km – Galway 11 km

🏨 **Connemara Coast**   ← 🚗 📺 ❄ 🛁 ✕ ⚘ ✾ ¶ 🏋 **P** VISA ⓒ AE
– ℰ (091) 592 108 – www.sinnotthotels.com – Closed 23-27 December
141 rm ⊇ – ♦ € 130/200 ♦♦ € 178/350 – 1 suite
Rest *The Gallery* – *(bar lunch)* Menu € 40 **s** – Carte € 40/50 **s**
♦ Sprawling hotel geared to families, with super views of Galway Bay, The Burren and Aran from the spacious bedrooms. Comprehensive leisure facilities. Club for kids. Two dining options; The Gallery for adults only.

GALWAY (Gaillimh) – Galway – 712 E8 – pop. 72 414 Ireland 36 B3

▶ Dublin 217 km – Limerick 103 km – Sligo 145 km
✈ Carnmore Airport : ℰ (091) 755569, NE : 6.5 km
🛈 Discover Ireland Centre, Aras Failte, Forster St ℰ (091) 53 77 00, www.galwaytourism.ie
⛳ Galway Salthill Blackrock, ℰ (091) 52 20 33
◉ City★★ – St Nicholas' Church★ BY - Roman Catholic Cathedral★ AY – Eyre Square : Bank of Ireland Building (sword and mace★) BY
◉ NW : Lough Corrib★★. W : by boat, Aran Islands (Inishmore - Dun Aenghus★★★) BZ - Thoor Ballylee★, SE : 33.75 km by N 6 and N 18 D – Dunguaire Castle, Kinvarra★ AC, S : 25.75 km by N 6, N 18 and N 67 D – Aughnanure Castle★, NW : 25.75 km by N 59 – Oughterard★ (≤★★), NW : 29 km by N 59 - Knockmoy Abbey★, NE : 30.5 km by N 17 and N 63 D – Coole Park (Autograph Tree★), SE : 33.75 km by N 6 and N 18 D – St Mary's Cathedral, Tuam★, NE : 33.75 km by N 17 D – Loughrea (St Brendan's Cathedral★), SE : 35.5 km by N 6 D - Turoe Stone★, SE : 35.5 km by N 6 and north by R 350

Plans on following pages

REPUBLIC OF IRELAND

 Glenlo Abbey 🌿   ≤ 🚗 🔥 ⏏ 📺 ⧈ & 🏊 rm, 🍽 🐕 P VISA ⦿ AE ⦿
Bushypark, Northwest : 5.25 km on N 59 – ℰ *(091) 526 666*
– www.glenlo.com – March to December
42 rm ⚏ – 🛏 €130/200 🛏🛏 €170/400 – **4 suites**
Rest *River Room* – Menu €35 – Carte €28/54
Rest *Pullman* – *(dinner only Thursday-Sunday)* Menu €28/35 – Carte €28/54
♦ Imposing 18C grey-stone country house with impressive grounds and church/ bay views. Very comfortable lounge, leading into chapel. Spacious, traditional bedrooms. Formal restaurant boasts golf course views. Pullman, a converted railway carriage, offers modern dishes with an Asian base.

Radisson Blu   ≤ 🏠 📺 ♨ 🐕 🏋 ⧈ & 🎧 🏊 💇 🗣 🐕 🐾 VISA ⦿ AE
Lough Atalia Rd – ℰ *(091) 538 300*
– www.radissonhotelgalway.com   D**a**
259 rm ⚏ – 🛏 €175/195 🛏🛏 €550/600 – **2 suites**
Rest *Marinas* – Menu €22/40 – Carte €36/49
♦ Striking atrium leads to ultra-modern meeting facilities and very comfortable and refurbished accommodation. Higher spec rooms on the 5th floor have glass balconies. International dining; accessible, rapid lunch menu.

 G   ♨ 🏋 ⧈ & rm, 🎧 🏊 🗣 🐕 🐾 VISA ⦿ AE
Wellpark, Dublin Rd – ℰ *(091) 865 200*
– www.thehotel.ie – Closed 24-27 December   D**g**
100 rm ⚏ – 🛏 €130/320 🛏🛏 €150/320 – **1 suite**
Rest *Matz at the G* – *(dinner only and Sunday lunch)* Menu €35/55
– Carte €39/56
♦ Uber-hip boutique hotel with cutting edge design from renowned milliner Philip Treacy. Vividly assured sitting room styles; décor imbued with fashion shoot portraits. Cool, slinky bedrooms. Stunning spa. Modern Irish cooking in colourful restaurant.

Clayton   📺 ♨ 🏋 ⧈ & rm, 🎧 🏊 🗣 🐕 P VISA ⦿ AE
Ballybrit, East : 4 km on N 6 – ℰ *(091) 721 900*
– www.clayton.ie – Closed 24-27 December
196 rm ⚏ – 🛏 €99/350 🛏🛏 €120/350
Rest – *(dinner only)* Menu €35 – Carte €20/38
♦ Striking angular building on edge of city, with stylish, modern interior and bar with buffet carvery. Smart white bedrooms have a minimalistic feel, with dark wood furniture. Large first floor restaurant offers traditional menu.

Bothar Ui Eithir	BY 2	High St	BY 8	Presentation St	AY
Claddagh Bridge	AZ 3	Main Guard St	BY 9	Quay St	BZ
Corrib Shopping Centre	BY	Market St	BY 10	St Francis St	BY
Courthouse St	BZ 4	Mary St	BY 11	St Vincent's Ave	BY
Dominick St	AZ 5	Newton Smith	BY 14	Shantalla Rd	AY
Father Griffin Ave	AZ 6	New Dock St	BZ 13	Shop St	BY
Forster St	BY 7	O'Brien Bridge	AY 15	William St	BY

Ardilaun
Taylor's Hill – ℰ (091) 521 433 – www.theardilaunhotel.ie – Closed 22-26 December

120 rm – † € 79/150 †† € 99/290 – 5 suites

Rest *Camilaun* – (dinner only and Sunday lunch) Menu € 20/32 – Carte € 32/112

Rest *Blazer's Bar and Bistro* – Menu € 29 (dinner) – Carte € 20/33

♦ Georgian style country house hotel in five acres of gardens and ancient trees. Informal bar. Extensive leisure facilities. Spacious rooms; ask for one of the newer ones. Stylish, formal Camilaun. Seafood, including oysters, feature strongly in the bar-bistro.

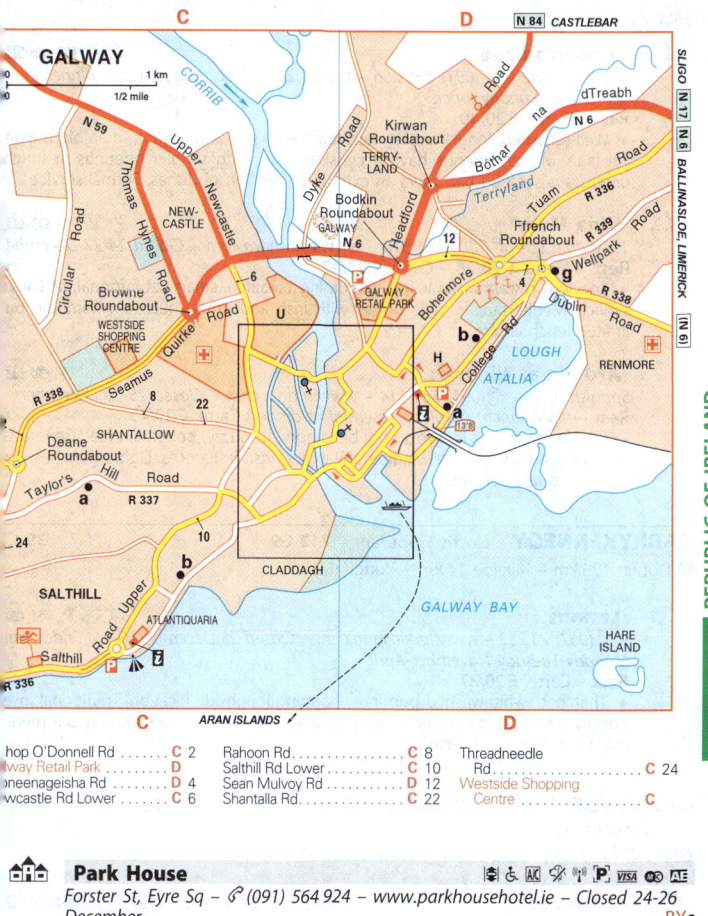

hop O'Donnell Rd	C 2	Rahoon Rd	C 8	Threadneedle Rd	C 24
way Retail Park	D	Salthill Rd Lower	C 10	Westside Shopping Centre	C
neenageisha Rd	D 4	Sean Mulvoy Rd	D 12		
wcastle Rd Lower	C 6	Shantalla Rd	C 22		

Park House

Forster St, Eyre Sq – ℰ (091) 564 924 – www.parkhousehotel.ie – Closed 24-26 December BY**c**

84 rm – † € 109/350 †† € 109/350

Rest – Menu € 42 (dinner) – Carte € 30/56

♦ Popular grey-stone hotel in city centre. Marble reception and comfy seating areas. Boss Doyle's Bar is busy and spacious. Dark wood bedrooms with rich, soft fabrics. Strong international flavours define restaurant menus.

House

Spanish Par – ℰ (091) 538 900 – www.thehousehotel.ie – Closed 24-26 December

39 rm – † € 169/199 †† € 169/199 – 1 suite BZ**e**

Rest – (bar lunch) Carte € 17/26 **s**

♦ Luxury boutique hotel, blending contemporary design with a cosy, relaxed style. Bedrooms are divided between cosy, classy and swanky. Modern menus take on a global reach; try to get a seat on the outdoor deck.

Ardawn House *without rest*

College Rd. – ℰ (091) 568 833 – www.ardawnhouse.com – Closed 20-27 December

9 rm – † € 45/90 †† € 80/160 D**b**

♦ Sample Irish hospitality at this family-run guest house. Individually decorated bedrooms and comfy lounge. Extensive breakfast menu served at linen-clad tables.

GALWAY

Kirwan's Lane
Kirwan's Lane – ℰ (091) 568 266 – Closed 25-28 December, Sunday dinner in winter and Sunday lunch
Rest – Carte € 20/40
• Well-regarded, long-standing restaurant with pleasant terrace, in an old medieval lane. Modern menus have a classical base, with simpler offerings at lunch downstairs seafood bar offers an extensive selection of dishes. Formal service.

Vina Mara
19 Middle St – ℰ (091) 561 610 – www.vinamara.com – Closed 24-27 December
Rest – Menu € 20/28 – Carte € 29/42
• Spacious restaurant in warm welcoming colours – smart yet informal; attentive service. Mediterranean style dishes with Irish and other touches. Affordable but limited lunch choice.

Ard Bia at Nimmos
Spanish Arch – ℰ (091) 561 114 – www.ardbia.com – Closed 25-26 December
Rest – (light lunch) (booking essential at dinner) Carte € 29/45
• Simple restaurant in two-storey building with buzzy, bohemian feel. Generous full-flavoured dishes have Mediterranean and Irish influences. Lighter lunches; upstairs used at weekends.

REPUBLIC OF IRELAND

GARRYKENNEDY – North Tipperary – 712 G9
▶ Dublin 176 km – Killaloe 14 km – Youghal 2 km

Larkins
– ℰ (067) 23 232 – www.larkinspub.com – Closed 25 December, Good Friday and Monday-Tuesday November-April
Rest – Carte € 20/37
• Thatched, whitewashed pub in a charming loughside location. Traditional interior plays host to folk music sessions and Irish dancers. Simple, unfussy bar menu more ambitious à la carte.

GARRYVOE (Garraí Uí Bhuaigh) – Cork – 712 H12 – pop. 560
– ✉ Castlemartyr
▶ Dublin 259 km – Cork 37 km – Waterford 100 km

Garryvoe
– ℰ (021) 464 67 18 – www.garryvoehotel.com – Closed 25 December
81 rm ⌑ – † € 74/149 †† € 74/149 – 1 suite
Rest *Samphire* **Rest** *Lighthouse Bistro* – see restaurant listing
• Modernised hotel overlooking Ballycotton Bay. Contemporary interior feature plenty of natural wood and slate. Bedrooms are spacious and comfortable – most boast balconies and sea views. A well-equipped fitness centre completes the picture.

Samphire – at Garryvoe Hotel
– ℰ (021) 464 67 18 – www.garryvoehotel.com – Closed 25 December
Rest – (dinner only and Sunday lunch) Carte € 38/50
• Formal restaurant in a modern hotel overlooking Ballycotton Bay. Menus feature meats from nearby farms and plenty of the famed local seafood that is landed on the village pier every morning.

Lighthouse Bistro – at Garryvoe Hotel
– ℰ 464 67 18 – www.garryvoehotel.com – Closed 25 December
Rest – Carte € 29/43
• Relaxed restaurant set within an up-to-date hotel and affording views out across the sea towards the Ballycotton lighthouse. Accessible menus consist largely of simply prepared pub classics.

GLASLOUGH = Glasloch – Monaghan – **712** L5 – see Monaghan

GLASSON = Glasán – Westmeath – **712** I7 – see Athlone

GLOUNTHAUNE – Cork – **712** G12 – pop. 900   **38** B3
▶ Dublin 160 km – Cork 7 km – Limerick 68 km – Galway 130 km

Rising Tide
– ✆ *(021) 435 32 33* – *www.therisingtide.ie* – *Closed Good Friday and 25 December*
Rest – Seafood – Carte € 34/48
♦ Friendly little pub in pleasant waterside village. Bright, modern interior with nautical knick-knacks and village memorabilia. Fresh, unfussy cooking; seafood plays a prominent role at dinner.

GOLEEN (An Góilín) – Cork – **712** C13   **38** A3
▶ Dublin 230 km – Cork 74 km – Killarney 67 km

Heron's Cove
The Harbour – ✆ *(028) 35 225* – *www.heronscove.com* – *Closed Christmas*
5 rm ⌂ – ♦ € 60/70 ♦♦ € 70/80
Rest – *(dinner only)* Menu € 30 – Carte € 32/49
♦ Long-standing guesthouse hidden away in a pretty location and overlooking a tiny harbour. Bedrooms are tidy and pleasantly furnished: all overlook the waterfront and most have a balcony. If you're lucky you might see herons at the water's edge.

REPUBLIC OF IRELAND

GOREY (Guaire) – Wexford – **712** N9 – pop. 7 193 🟦 Ireland   **39** D2
▶ Dublin 93 km – Waterford 88 km – Wexford 61 km
🛈 Main St ✆ *(055) 942 12 48, www.discoverireland.ie*
⛳ Courtown Kiltennel, ✆ *(055) 2 51 66*
◉ Ferns★, SW : 17.75 km by N 11

 Marlfield House
Courtown Rd, Southeast : 1.5 km on R 742 – ✆ *(053) 942 11 24*
– *www.marlfieldhouse.com* – *Closed 3 January -February*
19 rm ⌂ – ♦ € 80/190 ♦♦ € 210/250
Rest – *(dinner only and Sunday lunch)* Menu € 25/64
♦ Attractive Regency house surrounded by large informal gardens and woodland. Various stylish, classical lounges and drawing rooms with warm décor, heavy fabrics and antiques. Well-appointed bedrooms in period styles, with a good level of facilities and pleasant views over the grounds. Smart dining room and orangery offer refined, traditional dishes with modern touches.

GRAIGUENAMANAGH (Gráig na Manach) – Kilkenny – **712** L10   **39** D2
– pop. 1 376 🟦 Ireland
▶ Dublin 125 km – Kilkenny 34 km – Waterford 42 km – Wexford 26 km
◉ Duiske Abbey★★ **AC**
◉ Jerpoint Abbey★★ **AC**, W : 15 km by R 703 and N 9 – Inistioge★, SW : 8 km by minor road – Kilfane Glen and Waterfall★ **AC**, SW : 17 km by R 703 and N 9

✗ **Waterside** with rm
The Quay – ✆ *(059) 972 42 46* – *www.watersideguesthouse.com* – *Closed January and 25 December*
10 rm ⌂ – ♦ € 55/69 ♦♦ € 90/98
Rest – *(closed Monday-Thursday) (dinner only and Sunday lunch)* Carte € 25/40
♦ 1871 stone-built corn store at the foot of Brandon Hill and the Blackstairs Mountains, overlooking the River Barrow. Bright, modern bar and restaurant. Concise à la carte offers modern Irish-influenced dishes with Mediterranean touches. Simply furnished bedrooms have exposed beams and pleasant river views.

927

GREYSTONES (Na Clocha Liatha) – Wicklow – **712** N8 – pop. 14 569   39 D1
Ireland

▶ Dublin 35 km

🖥 Greystones, ℰ (01) 287 41 36

◉ Killruddery House and Gardens★ **AC**, N : 5 km by R 761
– Powerscourt★★ (Waterfall★★) **AC**, NW : 10 km by R 761, minor road, M 11 and minor road via Enniskerry. Wicklow Mountains★★

XX Chakra by Jaipur   AC VISA ©© AE
Meridan Point Centre (1st floor), Church Rd – ℰ (01) 201 72 22 – Closed 25 December
Rest – Indian – *(dinner only and Sunday lunch)* Menu € 22 (early dinner) – Carte € 27/47

♦ Red and ochre restaurant overlooked by elephant god, Ganesh, on 1st floor of modern shopping centre. Vibrant Indian cooking represents all regions; a blend of old and new.

GWEEDORE (Gaoth Dobhair) – Donegal – **712** H2   37 C1

▶ Dublin 278 km – Donegal 72 km – Letterkenny 43 km – Sligo 135 km

🏨 Gweedore Court
on N 56 – ℰ (074) 953 29 00 – www.gweedorecourthotel.ie – Closed January and 20-27 December
66 rm ⊑ – † € 69/89 †† € 69/89
Rest – *(dinner only and Sunday lunch) (bar lunch Monday-Saturday)* Menu € 35 – Carte € 19/38

♦ Rebuilt 19C house sharing grounds with a Gaelic craft centre. Spacious accommodation in classic patterns; east-facing rooms enjoy superb views of Glenreagh National Park. Classic menu matched by traditional surroundings and period-inspired décor.

HORSE AND JOCKEY (An Marcach) – North Tipperary – **712** I10   39 C2

▶ Dublin 146 km – Cashel 14 km – Thurles 9 km

🏨 Horse and Jockey
– ℰ (0504) 44 192 – www.horseandjockeyhotel.com – Closed 25 December
67 rm ⊑ – † € 80/100 †† € 100/150 – 1 suite
Rest *Silks* – Carte € 28/42 **s**

♦ Much extended hotel with stylish, state-of-the-art meeting rooms, superb spa and great gift shop. Bar full of horse racing pictures on walls. Spacious, contemporary bedrooms. Easy going dining room with traditional menus.

HOWTH (Binn Éadair) – Fingal – **712** N7 – pop. 8 186 – ✉ Dublin   39 D1
Ireland

▶ Dublin 22 km – Swords 17 km – Belfast 172 km – Cork 276 km

🖥 Deer Park Hotel Howth Castle, ℰ (01) 832 60 39

◉ The Cliffs★ (≤★)

XX Aqua   AC VISA ©© AE
1 West Pier – ℰ (01) 832 0690 – www.aqua.ie – Closed Good Friday, 25-26 December, and Monday-Tuesday in winter
Rest – Seafood – Menu € 25/30 – Carte € 36/45

♦ Glass sided, first floor restaurant in former yacht club, with super bay views. Intimate bar filled with local photos, whetting the appetite for accomplished dishes of fresh seafood. Chefs on view.

HOWTH

King Sitric with rm   ≤ AC rest, ⁞⁞ VISA ⓒ
East Pier – ℰ *(01) 832 5235 – www.kingsitric.ie – Closed 25-26 December*
8 rm ⌓ – ♦ € 145 ♦♦ € 205
Rest – Seafood – *(closed dinner Sunday, Tuesday and bank holidays) (dinner only and Sunday lunch)* Menu € 35 – Carte € 43/64

♦ Established in 1971 and one of Ireland's original seafood restaurants. Enjoy locally caught produce in first floor dining room with bay views. Modern, comfy bedrooms.

INISHMAAN = **Inis Meáin** – Galway – **712** D8 – see Aran Islands

---

INISHMORE = **Árainn** – Galway – **712** C/D8 – see Aran Islands

---

JENKINSTOWN = **Baile Sheinicín** – Louth – see Dundalk

KANTURK (Ceann Toirc) – Cork – **712** F11 – pop. 1 915 ▌ Ireland **38** B2

▶ Dublin 259 km – Cork 53 km – Killarney 50 km – Limerick 71 km
▣ Fairy Hill, ℰ (029) 5 05 34
◉ Town ★ – Castle ★

Glenlohane without rest ⌖   ≤ ♫ ♪ ♥ P VISA ⓒ AE
Southeast : 4 km. by R 580 on Cecilstown rd – ℰ *(029) 50 014*
– *www.glenlohane.com*
3 rm ⌓ – ♦ € 75 ♦♦ € 150

♦ In the family for over 250 years, a Georgian country house at the centre of wooded parkland and a working farm. Library and cosy, en suite rooms overlooking the fields.

KEEL = **An Caol** – Mayo – **712** B5/6 – see Achill Island

KENMARE (Neidín) – Kerry – **712** D12 – pop. 1 701 ▌ Ireland **38** A3

▶ Dublin 338 km – Cork 93 km – Killarney 32 km
▣ Heritage Centre ℰ (064) 664 12 33, www.kenmare.com
▣ Kenmare, ℰ (064) 4 12 91
◉ Town ★
◉ Ring of Kerry ★★ - Healy Pass ★★ (≤ ★★), SW : 30.5 km by R 571 and R 574 AY – Mountain Road to Glengarriff (≤ ★★) S : by N 71 AY - Slieve Miskish Mountains (≤ ★★), SW : 48.25 km by R 571 AY - Gougane Barra Forest Park ★★, SE : 16 km AY - Lauragh (Derreen Gardens ★ **AC**), SW : 23.5 km by R 571 AY – Allihies (Copper Mines ★), SW : 57 km by R 571 and R 575 AY – Garnish Island (≤ ★), SW : 68.5 km by R 571, R 575 and R 572 AY

Plan on next page

Park ⌖   ≤ ♫ ♪ ♥ ▨ ⓟ ♈ ♐ ♖ ☒ ♞ ♣ rm, ⁞⁞ P VISA ⓒ AE ①
– ℰ *(064) 664 12 00 – www.parkkenmare.com – Easter-October and 23 December-3 January* BY**k**
46 rm ⌓ – ♦ € 225/275 ♦♦ € 440/846
Rest *Park* – *(dinner only)* Menu € 68

♦ Substantial country house dating from 1897 and offering superb views over the bay and hills. Cosy cocktail lounge and charming drawing room filled with portraits and antiques. Tastefully furnished bedrooms boast smart marble bathrooms. Stylish, intimate spa. Linen-laid dining room; classically based dishes with a modern touch and local ingredients to the fore.

KENMARE

Back Lane	**BY** 2
Cromwell's Bridge	**AY**
Davitt's Place	**AY**
Downing's Row	**BY** 5
East Park St	**AY** 7
Finnihy Bridge	**AY**
Henry St	**AY**
Henry's Lane	**ABY** 8
Killarney Rd	**AY**
Main St	**BY**
Market St	**AY**
New St	**AY**
Old Bridge St.	**AY** 12
Railway Rd	**BY**
Rock St	**BY** 14
Shelborne St.	**BY**
The Square	**AY**

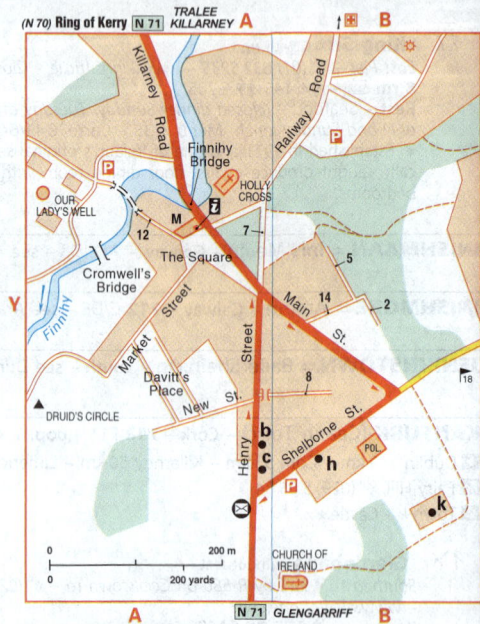

 Sheen Falls Lodge
Southeast : 2 km. by N 71 – ℰ *(064) 664 16 00*
– www.sheenfallslodge.ie – Closed January
57 rm ☐ – **†** € 310/455 **††** € 310/455 – 9 suites
Rest *La Cascade* – *(dinner only)* Carte € 60/77
♦ Luxurious hotel in an idyllic spot, where the falls drop away into the bay. Welcoming, wood-fired lobby, book-filled library and lovely airy indoor pool. Well-appointed bedrooms overlook the falls. Comprehensive service. Light lunches in cocktail bar; classical menu with a modern touch in formal restaurant.

 **Brook Lane**
Northwest : 1.5 km. by N 71 on N 70 – ℰ *(064) 664 20 77*
– www.brooklanehotel.com
22 rm ☐ – **†** € 75/90 **††** € 100/239
Rest *Casey's* – Menu € 26 (dinner) – Carte € 25/45
♦ Stylish, personally run hotel close to the town centre. Contemporary bedrooms offer a good level of comfort and range from 'Standard' to 'Luxury', the latter boasting impressive fabric headboards and designer touches. Informal bar and restaurant offer classic Irish and seafood dishes; regular live music.

 Shelburne Lodge *without rest*
East : 0.75 km. on R 569 (Cork Rd) – ℰ *(064) 664 10 13*
– www.shelburnelodge.com – 10 March to mid-November
9 rm ☐ – **†** € 75/110 **††** € 130/160
♦ Georgian farmhouse with pleasant lawns and herb garden. Antiques stylishly combined with contemporary colours and modern art. Firelit lounge and cosy rooms. Affable hosts.

KENMARE

⌂ **Sallyport House** without rest
South : 0.5 km. on N 71 – ℰ (064) 664 20 66 – www.sallyporthouse.com
– April-October
5 rm – †€ 75/85 ††€ 100/140
♦ Unassuming 1930s house hiding a charming interior packed with antiques and Irish art. Pleasant lounge with local information; breakfast, served from the characterful sideboard, features pancakes, stewed fruits and smoked salmon. Traditionally furnished bedrooms are immaculately kept and boast water views.

XX **Mulcahys**
36 Henry St – ℰ (064) 664 23 83 – Closed 25 December, Tuesday, and Monday and Wednesday October-April AYc
Rest – (dinner only) Carte € 34/49
♦ Contemporary restaurant named after its passionate, hands-on owners. Vibrant modern art, exposed stone walls and intimate candlelight. Seasonal ingredients prepared with care and a modern touch; well-judged flavours and good presentation.

XX **Lime Tree**
Shelbourne St. – ℰ (064) 664 12 25 – www.limetreerestaurant.com
– Easter-October and weekends only in winter BYh
Rest – (dinner only) Menu € 30 – Carte € 31/47
♦ Bright restaurant with exposed stone walls, open fire and country-style décor, set in a 19C former schoolhouse; modern art on display both here and in the first floor gallery. Simply laid tables with unfussy modern Irish dishes to match.

X **Packies**
Henry St – ℰ (064) 664 15 08 – Closed mid-January to mid-March and Monday
Rest – Seafood – (dinner only) (booking essential) Carte € 31/53 AYb
♦ Locally popular, personally run little place with understated rustic feel. Handwritten menu of fresh, modern Irish dishes prepared with care and super local seafood. Friendly staff.

REPUBLIC OF IRELAND

KILBRITTAIN (Cill Briotáin) – Cork – **712** F12 – pop. 185   **38** B3
▶ Dublin 289 km – Cork 38 km – Killarney 96 km

⌂ **Glen Country House** without rest
Southwest : 6.5 km. by R 600 – ℰ (023) 884 98 62 – www.glencountryhouse.com
– April-October
5 rm – †€ 65/75 ††€ 100/130
♦ Early Georgian house in 300 acres of mature parkland; the family have farmed the land for over 350 years. Comfy lounge and antique-filled breakfast room. Smart bedrooms with distant sea views.

KILCOLGAN (Cill Cholgáin) – Galway – **712** F8 – ✉ Oranmore   **36** B3
▶ Dublin 220 km – Galway 17 km

Moran's Oyster Cottage
The Weir, Northwest : 2 km. by N 18 – ℰ (091) 796 113
– www.moransoystercottage.com – Closed Good Friday and 24-26 December
Rest – Seafood – Carte € 30/60
♦ Attractive whitewashed pub with golden thatch, hidden away in a tiny hamlet – a very popular place in summer. Largely cold seafood dishes, with oysters a speciality and tasty homemade bread.

KILKENNY (Cill Chainnigh) – Kilkenny – **712** K10 – pop. 22 179 — 39 C2
🟢 Ireland

▶ Dublin 114 km – Cork 138 km – Killarney 185 km – Limerick 111 km
ℹ Shee Alms House ✆ (056) 7 75 15 00, www.kilkennytourism.ie
⛳ Glendine, ✆ (056) 776 54 00
⛳ Callan Geraldine, ✆ (056) 772 51 36
⛳ Castlecomer Drumgoole, ✆ (056) 444 11 39
◉ Town★★ – St Canice's Cathedral★★ – Kilkenny Castle and Park★★ **AC** – Black Abbey★ – Rothe House★
◉ Jerpoint Abbey★★ **AC**, S : 19.25 km by R 700 and N 9 – Kilfane Glen and Waterfall★ **AC**, S : 21 km by R 700 and N 9 – Kells Priory★, S : 12.5 km by R 697 – Dunmore Cave★ **AC**, N: 11.25 km by N 77 and N 78

Kilkenny
College Rd, Southwest : 1.25 km by Patrick St on Ormonde Rd (N76) – ✆ (056) 776 20 00 – www.hotelkilkenny.ie
138 rm ⊑ – † € 170/190 †† € 190
Rest *Taste* – Menu € 30 **s**

● Unassuming modern property just outside the city centre, with contrasting stylish, contemporary interior. Well-equipped leisure centre and smart function rooms. Funky colour schemes feature throughout. Bright bedrooms have a slightly kitsch style. Mediterranean-influenced menus in pink-hued restaurant.

Butler House without rest
15-16 Patrick St. – ✆ (056) 776 57 07 – www.butler.ie – Closed 23-29 December
12 rm ⊑ – † € 60/120 †† € 99/180 – 1 suite

● Substantial, part-Georgian house. Spacious accommodation with 1970s style furnishings – superior bow-fronted bedrooms located to the rear, overlooking neat, geometric lawned gardens.

Rosquil House without rest
Castlecomer Rd., Northwest : 1 km. – ✆ (056) 772 14 19 – www.rosquilhouse.com
7 rm ⊑ – † € 36/50 †† € 75/95

● Purpose-built guesthouse on the main road out of the city. Comfy, leather-furnished lounge filled with books and local information; linen-laid breakfast room to the rear. Simply furnished bedrooms boast flat screen TVs. Welcoming owners.

Blanchville House without rest
Dunbell, Maddoxtown, Southeast : 10 km by R 712 – ✆ (056) 772 71 97 – www.blanchville.ie – March-October
5 rm ⊑ – † € 65 †† € 120

● Large, rurally set Georgian manor house with a Peel Tower in the garden. Classical, fire-lit drawing room with heavy fabrics; traditionally styled, antique-furnished bedrooms. Tea and homemade cakes on arrival.

Fanad House without rest
Castle Rd., South : 0.75 km. on R 700 – ✆ (056) 776 41 26 – www.fanadhouse.com
12 rm ⊑ – † € 50/65 †† € 70/120

● Striking green house close to the town centre, run by a friendly owner and looking out towards the castle. Formal reception area and bright, wood-floored breakfast room. Simple, wood-furnished bedrooms come in neutral colours.

Campagne
5 The Arches, Gashouse Ln. – ✆ (056) 777 28 58 – www.campagne.ie – Closed 2 weeks January, Sunday dinner and Monday
Rest – *(dinner only and lunch Friday-Sunday) (booking advisable)* Menu € 29 (lunch and early dinner) **s** – Carte € 42/49 **s**

● Hidden close to the railway arches, away from the city centre. Crescent shaped dining room with bright contemporary art. Modern French and Irish cooking; tasty, unfussy dishes.

KILKENNY

XXX Ristorante Rinuccini
1 The Parade – ℰ (056) 776 15 75 – www.rinuccini.com – Closed 26-27 December
Rest – Italian – Carte € 30/51
♦ Named after the 17C papal nunci, this family-owned restaurant is bigger than it looks, and has long been a local favourite. Cooking is classical Italian and service is thoughtful.

XX Zuni with rm
26 Patrick St – ℰ (056) 772 39 99 – www.zuni.ie – Closed 25 December
13 rm – † € 60/90 †† € 85/150 **Rest** – Carte € 29/44
♦ Chic modern restaurant in a great city centre location. Small wood-furnished café-bar opens out into bright room with mirrored walls, leather panels and a terrace to one side. Eclectic modern menus of Irish produce and with a Mediterranean or Asian twist. Bedrooms continue the smart, contemporary theme.

KILLALOE (Cill Dalua) – Clare – 712 G9 – pop. 1 035 – Ireland   38 B2

▶ Dublin 175 km – Ennis 51 km – Limerick 21 km – Tullamore 93 km

◉ Town★ – St Flannan's Cathedral★

◉ Graves of the Leinstermen (≤★), N : 7.25 km by R 494 – Castleconnell★, S : 16 km by R 494 and R 466 – Clare Glens★, S : 24 km by R 494, R 504 and R 503. Nenagh (Castle★), NE : 19.25 km by R 496 and N 7 – Holy Island★ **AC**, N : 25.75 km by R 463 and boat from Tuamgraney

XX Cherry Tree
Lakeside, Ballina, follow signs for Lakeside Hotel – ℰ (061) 375 688
– www.cherrytreerestaurant.ie – Closed first week January, Good Friday, 25-26 December, Sunday dinner, Sunday lunch November-April and Monday
Rest – *(dinner only and Sunday lunch)* Menu € 26 – Carte € 38/45
♦ Contemporary, relaxing interior, polite staff and a wide range of original, well-sourced modern Irish dishes on offer from an open kitchen. Seasonal produce of the essence.

KILLARNEY (Cill Airne) – Kerry – 712 D11 – pop. 14 603 – Ireland   38 A2

▶ Dublin 304 km – Cork 87 km – Limerick 111 km – Waterford 180 km

✈ Kerry (Farranfore) Airport : ℰ (066) 976 4644, N : 15.25 km by N 22

🛈 Beech Rd ℰ (064) 663 16 33, www.killarney.ie

🏌 Mahoney's Point, ℰ (064) 3 10 34

◉ Town★★ – St Mary's Cathedral★ CX

◉ Killarney National Park★★★ (Muckross Friary★, Muckross House and Farms★) AZ - Gap of Dunloe★★, SW : 9.5 km by R 562 AZ – Ross Castle★ **AC**, S : 1.5 km by N 71 and minor rd – Torc Waterfall★, S : 8 km by N 71 BZ. Ring of Kerry★★ – Ladies View★★, SW : 19.25 km by N 71 BZ – Moll's Gap★, SW : 25 km by N 71 BZ

Plans pages 934, 935

🏨🏨🏨 Europe
Fossa, West : 4.75 km. by R 562 on N 72 – ℰ (064) 667 13 00
– www.theeurope.com – 10 May-8 October
181 rm – † € 182/264 †† € 230/278 – 6 suites
Rest *Panorama* **Rest** *Brasserie* – see restaurant listing
♦ Vast hotel in a superb lakeside location, boasting views over Lough Leane and Macgillycuddy's Reeks. Opulent guest areas, impressive events facilities and sublime 3-level spa. Lavishly appointed bedrooms; Lake Rooms afford the best outlook.

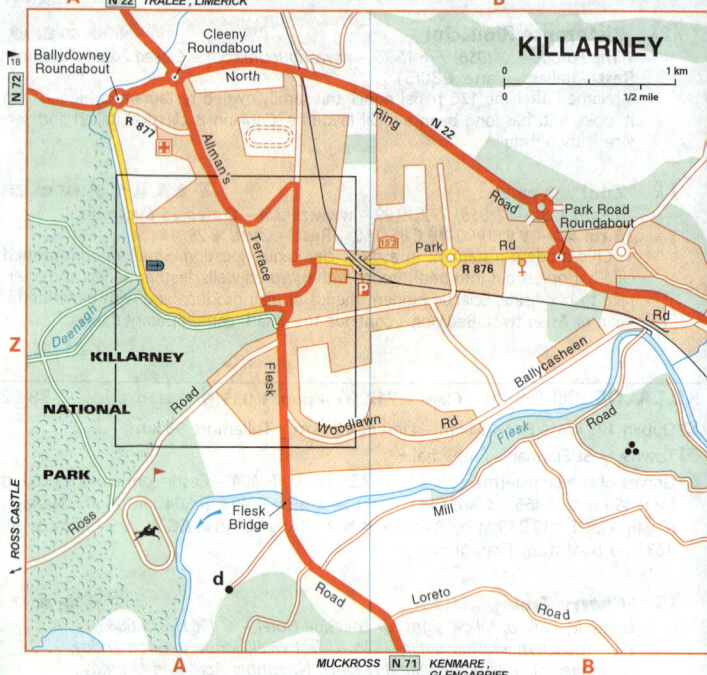

Killarney Park

- ℰ (064) 663 55 55 – www.killarneyparkhotel.ie
- Closed 24-26 December

65 rm – †€ 250/350 ††€ 250/350 – 3 suites

Rest *Park* – see restaurant listing

DXk

◆ Large, luxurious hotel run by a keen, well-versed team. Plush library and lavish drawing room; clubby wood-panelled bar for linen-laid lunches. Bedrooms range in style, mixing modern furnishings with original features and offering everything you could want. Smart spa and leisure facilities add to the appeal.

Aghadoe Heights H. and Spa

Northwest : 4.5 km. by N 22 – ℰ (064) 663 17 66
– www.aghadoeheights.com – *Weekends only January-April*

72 rm – †€ 105/160 ††€ 160/220 – 2 suites

Rest *Lake Room* – see restaurant listing

◆ Striking glass-fronted hotel in an enviable position, looking out over lakes, mountains and countryside. Luxurious interior with stylish cocktail bar, evening pianist and impressive spa. Spacious bedrooms; most have balconies or terraces.

Ross

- ℰ (064) 663 18 55 – www.theross.ie – Closed 24-26 December

29 rm – †€ 160/220 ††€ 160/275

Rest *Cellar One* – *(closed weekdays in winter) (bar lunch)* Menu € 36
– Carte € 27/50

DXb

◆ Striking modern hotel in the centre of town, overlooking the famous Killarney 'Horse and Carriages'. Contemporary bar and lounge with multi-level design. Stylish, boldly coloured bedrooms are comfortable and well-equipped. Vibrant basement restaurant with curved timbers, intimate lighting and global menu.

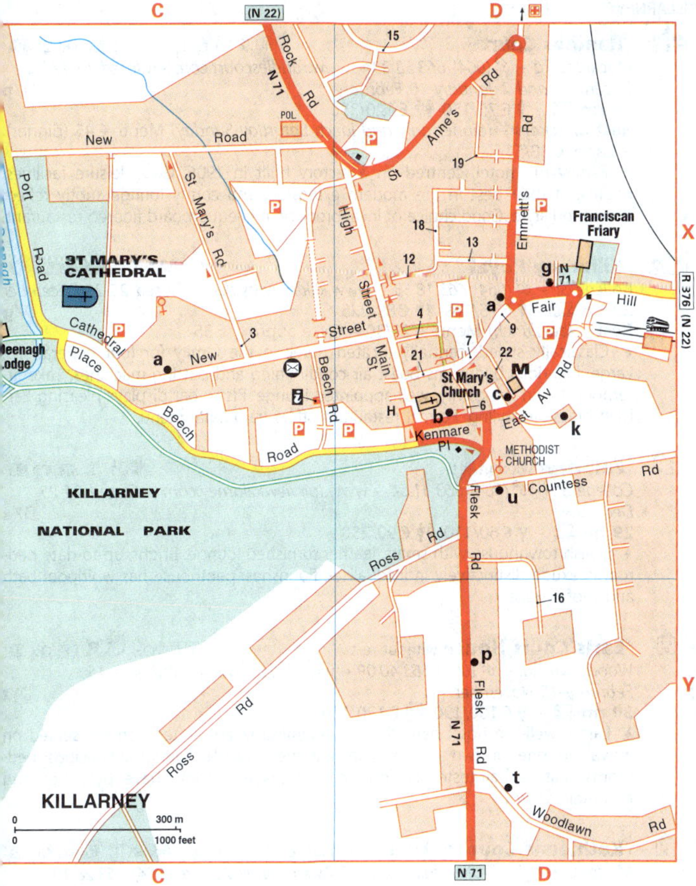

hereencael	**DX** 4	Green Lawn	**CX** 10	O'Connell's Terrace .... **DX** 18
hereen Na Goun	**CX** 3	Hillard's Lane	**DX** 12	O'Sullivan's Pl. .... **DX** 19
ewery Lane	**DX** 6	Mangerton	**DX** 13	Plunkett St .... **DX** 21
ollege Square	**DX** 7	Marian Terrace	**DX** 15	St Anthony's
ollege St	**DX** 9	Muckross Drive	**DXY** 16	Pl. .... **DX** 22

Cahernane House

Muckross Rd – ℰ (064) 663 18 95 – www.cahernane.com – *Closed December-16 March* **AZd**

37 rm – † €95/145 †† €140/190 – 1 suite

Rest *Herbert Room* – see restaurant listing

♦ Fine Victorian house built in 1877, set in a peaceful location and affording westerly mountain views. Characterful open-fired library and drawing room with stags' heads, portraits and antiques. Bedrooms range from classical to contemporary.

Fancy a last minute break?
Check hotel websites to take advantage of price promotions.

935

KILLARNEY

Randles Court
Muckross Rd – ℰ (064) 663 53 33 – www.randlescourt.com – Closed 18-27 December and 2 January-10 February DYp
75 rm ⊇ – ♦ €75/150 ♦♦ €120/350
Rest *Checkers* – *(dinner only and lunch Saturday-Sunday)* Menu €45 (dinner) – Carte €38/51

♦ Family run hotel, centred on a rectory built in 1906. Good leisure facilities. Rooms, at their best in the modern extension, and comfy lounge subtly reflect the period style. Good choice of local produce in chequerboard floored restaurant.

Killarney Royal
College St – ℰ (064) 663 18 53 – www.killarneyroyal.ie – Closed 25-26 December
29 rm ⊇ – ♦ €75/169 ♦♦ €89/225 DXg
Rest – *(bar lunch)* Menu €21/30 – Carte approx. €35

♦ Classically styled, centrally located hotel; in the family for four generations. Large, luxurious bedrooms boast air conditioning and putting machines. Take afternoon tea in the comfy, well-appointed lounge. Bistro-bar displays pleasing Parisian brasserie styling. Formal restaurant offers traditional menu.

Fairview without rest
College St. – ℰ (064) 663 41 64 – www.fairviewkillarney.com – Closed 24-25 December DXa
29 rm ⊇ – ♦ €60/110 ♦♦ €90/250

♦ Stylish townhouse with smart, leather furnished lounge. Bright, up-to-date bedrooms exude distinctively individualistic flourishes; penthouse has whirlpool bath and roof terrace.

Earls Court House without rest
Woodlawn Rd. – ℰ (064) 663 40 09 – www.killarney-earlscourt.ie – 15 February-15 November DYt
30 rm ⊇ – ♦ €100/120 ♦♦ €120/180

♦ Large, well-run hotel behind an unassuming façade. Afternoon tea served on arrival, in one of two comfortable, antique-furnished lounges. Spacious bedrooms feature half-tester or four-poster beds and some have balconies and mountain views.

Kathleens Country House without rest
Madams Height, Tralee Rd., North : 3.75 km. on N 22 – ℰ (064) 663 28 10 – www.kathleens.net – May-September
17 rm ⊇ – ♦ €55/90 ♦♦ €105/140

♦ Cosy lounge with broad, pine-backed armchairs facing an open fire and neat bedrooms in traditional patterns – an extended house run by the eponymous owner for over 20 years.

Killarney Lodge without rest
Countess Rd. – ℰ (064) 663 64 99 – www.killarneylodge.net – 10 March-October
16 rm ⊇ – ♦ €85/95 ♦♦ €100/130 DXu

♦ Modern house close to the town centre, run by a welcoming couple. Immaculately kept, well-furnished bedrooms; No.6 boasts lovely mountain views. Bright little breakfast room where homemade bread and scones feature. Afternoon tea on arrival.

Panorama – at Europe Hotel
Fossa, West : 4.75 km. by R 562 on N 72 – ℰ (064) 667 13 00 – www.theeurope.com – 10 May-8 October
Rest – *(closed Sunday dinner)* Carte €42/59

♦ Large, formal restaurant in a luxuriously appointed hotel. Panoramic windows afford superb views across the lough towards the mountains. Classical, international menu offers plenty of choice.

KILLARNEY

XXXX Park – at Killarney Park Hotel
– ℘ (064) 663 55 55 – www.killarneyparkhotel.ie
– Closed 24-26 December

DX**k**

Rest – (dinner only) Menu € 55 – Carte € 32/58

♦ Elegant fine dining restaurant boasting chandeliers, ornate cornicing and linen-laid tables, set in a luxurious hotel. Menus are distinctly classical in style. A pianist completes the picture.

XXX Lake Room – at Aghadoe Heights Hotel and Spa
Northwest : 1.5 km. by N 22 – ℘ (064) 663 17 66
– www.aghadoeheights.com – Weekends only January-April

Rest – Menu € 55 (dinner) – Carte € 45/55

♦ Set in a luxury hotel and boasting a stylish cocktail bar and lounge with evening pianist. Stunning panoramic views over the lakes and mountains. Classical dishes executed with a modern touch.

XX Cucina Italiana
17 St Anthonys Pl – ℘ (064) 662 65 75
– Closed January-February

DX**c**

Rest – Italian – (dinner only) Menu € 28 (early dinner) – Carte € 33/54

♦ Stylish, modern restaurant set over two floors, in the centre of town. Hearty, authentic Italian cooking has a strong Neapolitan feel and features plenty of daily specials. Effective service from smart Italian staff.

XX Chapter Forty
40 New St. – ℘ (064) 66 71 833 – www.chapter40.ie – Closed 24-26 December, Sunday and Monday

CX**a**

Rest – (dinner only) Menu € 25/35 – Carte € 31/48

♦ Contemporary, split-level restaurant with rich burgundy walls, polished wood floors and smart high-backed cream chairs. Visually appealing, classically based dishes are prepared with a lightness of touch; try the 'tasting plate' starter.

XX Brasserie – at Europe Hotel
Fossa, West : 4.75 km. by R 562 on N 72 – ℘ (064) 667 13 00
– www.theeurope.com – 10 May-8 October

Rest – Carte € 32/64 **s**

♦ Set within a luxurious, lakeside hotel, a modern take on a classical brasserie. Accessible all-day menu ranges from light snacks to steaks cooked on an open grill. Terrace for alfresco dining.

XX Herbert Room – at Cahernane House Hotel
Muckross Rd – ℘ (064) 663 18 95 – www.cahernane.com – 17 March-November

Rest – (closed Sunday-Monday except in summer) Menu € 35/48   AZ**d**
– Carte approx. € 30

♦ Formal hotel restaurant and atmospheric bar, set within a fine Victorian house in a pleasant rural location. Classically based dishes display some modern influences. Excellent mountain views.

at Beaufort *West : 9.75 km by N 72 off Glencar rd* – ✉ Killarney

⌂ Dunloe Castle
– ℘ (064) 664 41 11 – www.thedunloe.com – April-October

100 rm ⊑ – †€ 160/210 ††€ 180/230 – 2 suites

Rest – (light lunch) Carte € 26/63 **s**

♦ Creeper-clad modern hotel offers sizeable, well-equipped rooms and smart conference suites, not forgetting an impressive view of the Gap of Dunloe and Macgillicuddy's Reeks. Restaurant serves Irish classic dishes.

REPUBLIC OF IRELAND

KILLENARD – Laois – **712** D11 — 39 C-D1

▶ Dublin 48 km – Portlaoise 19 km – Naas 25 km – Carlow 36 km

Heritage
– ☏ (057) 864 55 00 – www.theheritage.com – Closed 20-26 December
95 rm – †€325 ††€325/550 – 3 suites
Rest *Sol Oriens* – see restaurant listing
Rest *Arlington* – *(dinner only and Sunday lunch)* Menu €45 s

♦ Vast resort hotel with plush, spacious interior. Impressive range of facilities, from huge conference centre, superb leisure club and spa to outdoor pursuits and Ballesteros-designed golf course. Beautifully furnished, sumptuous bedrooms. Traditional fine dining in Arlington and family friendly atmosphere in Italian Sol Oriens.

Sol Oriens – at Heritage Hotel
– ☏ (057) 864 55 00 – www.theheritage.com – Closed 20-26 December, Monday and Tuesday
Rest – Italian – *(dinner only)* Carte €23/42

♦ Purpose-built Italian restaurant located in the grounds of a vast resort hotel. Informal, family friendly room with open-plan kitchen. Menu offers a range of pizzas, pastas and Irish steaks.

KILMALLOCK (Cill Mocheallóg) – Limerick – **712** G10 – pop. 1 443 — 38 B2
📗 Ireland

▶ Dublin 212 km – Limerick 34 km – Tipperary 32 km

◉ Abbey★ – Collegiate Church★

◉ Lough Gur Interpretive Centre★ **AC**, N : 16 km by R 512 and minor road
– Monasteranenagh Abbey★, N : 24 km by R 512 to Holycross and minor road W

Flemingstown House
Southeast : 4 km on R 512 – ☏ (063) 98 093 – www.flemingstown.com
– February-October
5 rm – †€70 ††€120 **Rest** – *(residents only)* Carte €40/45

♦ Creeper clad, extended 19C house in centre of 200 acre working farm. The attractively decorated bedrooms boast countryside vistas and pieces of antique furniture. Satisfying homemade fare served in comfy dining room.

KINLOUGH (Cionn Locha) – Leitrim – **712** H4 – pop. 690 — 37 C2

▶ Dublin 220 km – Ballyshannon 11 km – Sligo 34 km

Courthouse with rm
Main St. – ☏ (071) 984 23 91 – www.thecourthouserest.com – Closed 1 week spring and 24-26 December
4 rm – †€35/45 ††€70/80
Rest – Italian – *(dinner only and Sunday lunch)* Menu €25 – Carte €35/45

♦ Former courthouse with stained glass entrance. Sardinian chef-owner creates extensive, seasonally changing classical menu of honest, authentic Italian dishes – including local fish/shellfish. Informal atmosphere; friendly service. Simple, good value bedrooms.

KINSALE (Cionne tSáile) – Cork – **712** G12 – pop. 4 099 📗 Ireland — 38 B3

▶ Dublin 286 km – Cork 27 km

🛈 Pier Rd ☏ (021) 4 77 22 34, www.kinsale.ie

◉ Town★★ – St Multose Church★ Y – Kinsale Regional Museum★ **AC** Y **M1**

◉ Kinsale Harbour★ (≤★ from St Catherine's Anglican Church, Charles Fort★).
Carbery Coast★, W : 61 km by R 600

938

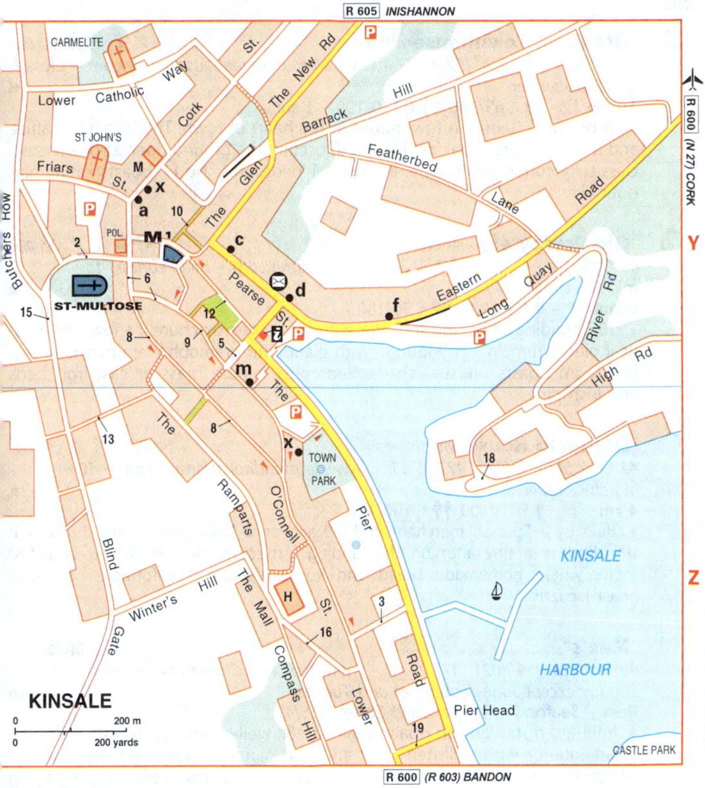

KINSALE

Church St.	Y 2	Main St.	Y 9
Denis Quay	Z 3	Market Pl.	Y 10
Emmet St	Y 5	Market Quay	Y 12
Guardwell	Y 6	Ramparts Lane	Z 13
Higher O'Connel St	YZ 8		
Rose Abbey	Y 15	St John's Hill	Z 16
Seilly Walk	Z 18	World's End	Z 19

Perryville House without rest 🚭 📶 P VISA ✱ AE
Long Quay – ☎ (021) 477 27 31 – www.perryvillehouse.com – 15 April-October
22 rm ⌑ – ♦ €120/150 ♦♦ €200/300   Yf

♦ Luxuriously appointed house in the heart of town, overlooking the harbour; named after the family that built it in 1820. Two antique-furnished drawing rooms, smart boutique and coffee shop. Tastefully styled bedrooms; 'Luxury' boast feature beds, chic bathrooms and harbour views. Comprehensive breakfasts.

Blue Haven   🛜 AC rest, 🚭 📶 ✱ VISA ✱ AE
3-4 Pearse St – ☎ (021) 477 22 09 – www.bluehavenkinsale.com – Closed 25 December   Yc
17 rm ⌑ – ♦ €65/140 ♦♦ €110/190
Rest *Fish market* – see restaurant listing
Rest *Bistro* – Menu €40 – Carte €26/47

♦ Small but well-established hotel right in the heart of town. Cosy, vibrant interior features interesting artwork. Comfortable bedrooms are named after vineyards and have a subtle contemporary edge. Chic, clubby lounge with art deco styling; adjoining all-day bistro resembles the hull of an upturned boat.

KINSALE

Old Bank Townhouse without rest
10-11 Pearse St. – ℰ (021) 477 40 75 – www.oldbankhousekinsale.com – Closed 24-25 December   Yd
16 rm – † € 65/140 †† € 110/190 – 1 suite

• Substantial Georgian townhouse in the heart of town. The local post office and a café (where breakfast is served) occupy the ground floor; above is cosy, classically furnished lounge. Traditional bedrooms; No.17 boasts great harbour views.

Old Presbytery without rest
43 Cork St. – ℰ (021) 477 20 27 – www.oldpres.com – mid-February to mid-November   Ya
9 rm – † € 70/120 †† € 90/180

• 18C building once housing priests from the nearby church; a few ecclesiastical pieces remain. Cosy lounge with piano and gramophone; upstairs breakfast room boasts unusual chairs. Bedrooms feature brass or cast iron beds and Irish pine.

Desmond House without rest
42 Cork St. – ℰ (021) 477 35 35 – www.desmondhousekinsale.com – 10 March-October   Yx
4 rm – † € 70/100 †† € 100/140

• Built by a Spanish merchant in 1780 and once belonging to the church – it still displays a tiny alter on the landing. Attractive, parquet-floored breakfast room, where homemade bread and scones feature. Comfortable bedrooms boast jacuzzis.

Max's
48 Main St. – ℰ (021) 477 24 43 – www.maxs.ie – Closed mid-December-March, Sunday except June-September and Tuesday   Zm
Rest – Seafood – *(dinner only)* Carte € 35/49

• Intimate restaurant on quaint main street; well-known by locals. Simple yet smart interior with polished floor and part-panelled walls. Unfussy, classical seafood menu offers good choice, try the 'Fresh Catches'. Efficient, engaging team.

Fish market – at Blue Haven Hotel
3-4 Pearse St – ℰ (021) 477 22 09 – www.bluehavenkinsale.com – Closed 25 December   Yc
Rest – Menu € 25/35 – Carte € 29/50

• Informal restaurant located in small, well-run hotel in the town centre. Original artwork hangs on the walls. Seafood-orientated menu specialises in fresh fish and shellfish from local waters.

Fishy Fishy Cafe
Pier Rd – ℰ (021) 470 04 15 – www.fishyfishy.ie
Rest – Seafood – *(bookings not accepted at lunch)* Carte € 33/39 **s**   Zx

• Friendly informal restaurant that's a local institution. Dine at the bar and watch the kitchen shuck oysters, in the main room amongst 'fishy' memorabilia or alfresco on the lovely terrace. Concise, all-day menus offer well-prepared, good value seafood dishes and tasty specials; owner collects the fish daily.

Toddies at The Bulman
Summercove, East : 2 km. by R 600 – ℰ (021) 477 21 31 – www.thebulman.ie – Closed 25 December, Good Friday and Sunday dinner
Rest – Carte € 25/45

• Rustic pub with nautical theme and views over Kinsale and the bay. Lunch, served in the bar, offers simple pub classics; dinner, in the more formal restaurant, presents carefully prepared, globally influenced dishes.

KINSALE

at Barrells Cross Southwest : 5.75 km on R 600 - **Z** – ✉ Kinsale

Rivermount House *without rest*
Northeast : 0.75 km. – ⌀ (021) 477 80 33 – www.rivermount.com – 16 March-October
6 rm – † € 50/90 †† € 80/90
♦ Spacious, purpose-built house overlooking the River Bandon, not far from the town. Distinctive modern style throughout, with attractive embossed wallpapers, quality furnishings and designer touches. Bedrooms display high attention to detail and boast immaculate bathrooms.

KNOCK (An Cnoc) – Mayo – 712 F6 – pop. 745 – Ireland — 36 B2

▶ Dublin 212 – Galway 74 – Westport 51
✈ Ireland West Airport, Knock : ⌀ (094) 9368100, NE : 14.5 km by N 17
🛈 Town Centre ⌀ (094) 9 38 81 93, www.discoverireland.ie
◉ Basilica of our Lady, Queen of Ireland★
◉ Museum of Country Life★★ **AC**, NW : 26 km by R 323, R 321 and N 5

Hotels see : **Cong** *SW : 58 km by N 17, R 331 R 334 and R 345*

LAHINCH (An Leacht) – Clare – 712 D9 – pop. 607 – Ireland — 38 B1

▶ Dublin 260 km – Galway 79 km – Limerick 66 km
⛳ Lahinch, ⌀ (065) 7 08 10 03
⛳ Spanish Point Miltown Malbay, ⌀ (065) 7 08 42 19
◉ Cliffs of Moher★★★ – Kilfenora (Burren Centre★ **AC**, High Crosses★), NE : 11 km by N 85 and R 481

Vaughan Lodge
Ennistymon Rd – ⌀ (065) 708 11 11 – www.vaughanlodge.ie – April-October
20 rm – † € 95/155 †† € 130/260
Rest – *(closed Sunday and Monday) (dinner only)* Carte € 34/62
♦ Stylish roadside hotel. Bright, modern interior boasts a leather-furnished lounge with flat screen TV and plenty of malts behind the bar. Smart, spacious bedrooms – in browns and creams – offer good facilities. Linen-laid dining room serves seafood-based menus.

Moy House
Southwest : 3 km on N 67 (Milltown Malbay rd) – ⌀ (065) 708 28 00
– www.moyhouse.com – March-October
8 rm – † € 145/250 †† € 225/280 – 1 suite
Rest – *(dinner only)* Menu € 55
♦ Italian-style clifftop villa, overlooking the bay. Traditional interior with a comfy drawing room, honesty bar and small library; antiques, oil paintings and heavy fabrics/drapes feature. Individually designed, classically styled bedrooms boast good extras; most have views. Friendly, attentive service. Formal dining.

LEENANE (An Líonán) – Galway – 712 C7 – ✉ Clifden – Ireland — 36 A3

▶ Dublin 278 km – Ballina 90 km – Galway 66 km
◉ Killary Harbour★
◉ Joyce Country★★ – Lough Nafooey★, SE : 10.5 km by R 336 – Aasleagh Falls★, NE : 4 km. Connemara★★★ – Lough Corrib★★, SE : 16 km by R 336 and R 345 – Doo Lough Pass★, NW : 14.5 km by N 59 and R 335

Delphi Lodge
Northwest : 13.25 km by N 59 on Louisburgh rd – ⌀ (095) 42 222
– www.delphilodge.ie
12 rm – † € 132 †† € 198/264   **Rest** – Menu € 49
♦ Georgian sporting lodge in a stunning loughside setting with extensive gardens and grounds. Haven for fishermen. Country house feel and simple bedrooms. Communal dining table: fisherman with the day's best catch sits at its head.

941

LEIGHLINBRIDGE (Leithghlinn an Droichid) Carlow – Carlow 39 D2
– **712** L9 – pop. 674

▶ Dublin 63 km – Carlow 8 km – Kilkenny 16 km – Athy 22 km

Lord Bagenal
Main St – ℰ *(059) 977 40 00* – *www.lordbagenal.com* – *Closed 25-26 December*
39 rm ⚏ – ♦ € 65/85 ♦♦ € 110/190 **Rest** – *(carving lunch)* Menu € 35
♦ Eye-catching hotel on the banks of the River Barrow; originally a coaching inn, now with vast modern extensions. Characterful bar and excellent collection of Irish art on display throughout. Up-to-date bedrooms. Traditional menus in Lord Bagenal bar and restaurant.

LETTERFRACK (Leitir Fraic) – Galway – **712** C7 Ireland 36 A3

▶ Dublin 304 km – Ballina 111 km – Galway 91 km

⊙ Connemara★★★ - Sky Road★★ (≤★★) – Connemara National Park★ – Kylemore Abbey★, E : 4.75 km by N 59

Rosleague Manor
West : 2.5 km. on N 59 – ℰ *(095) 41 101* – *www.rosleague.com*
– *mid-March-mid-November*
20 rm ⚏ – ♦ € 80/155 ♦♦ € 130/250 **Rest** – *(dinner only)* Carte € 34/44
♦ Foliage-clad country house in mature grounds, boasting excellent bay and mountain views. Spacious, antique-filled drawing rooms and wicker-furnished conservatory. Large, classically styled bedrooms with flat screen TVs. Formal dining room overlooks the gardens.

LETTERKENNY (Leitir Ceanainn) – Donegal – **712** I3 – pop. 17 586 37 C1
Ireland

▶ Dublin 241 km – Londonderry 34 km – Sligo 116 km

🛈 Neil T Blaney Rd ℰ (074) 9 12 11 60, www.letterkennyguide.com

▸ Dunfanaghy, ℰ (074) 913 63 35

⊙ Glenveagh National Park★★ (Gardens★★), NW : 19.25 km by R 250, R 251 and R 254 – Grianan of Aileach★★ (≤★★) NE : 28 km by N 13 – Church Hill (Glebe House and Gallery★ **AC**) NW : 16 km by R 250

Radisson Blu
Paddy Harte Rd – ℰ *(074) 919 44 44* – *www.radissonblu.ie/hotel-letterkenny*
114 rm ⚏ – ♦ € 55/155 ♦♦ € 89/220
Rest – *(early dinner and Sunday lunch)* Menu € 28 **s** – Carte € 25/38 **s**
♦ Corporate accommodation on the edge of town. Bedrooms are identically appointed, all are clean, modern and spacious, and 'Business Class' come with extras. Bar serves all-purpose, daily changing menu. Brasserie-style dining room offers dishes to match.

LIMERICK (Luimneach) – Limerick – **712** G9 – pop. 90 757 Ireland 38 B2

▶ Dublin 193 km – Cork 93 km

✈ Shannon Airport : ℰ (061) 712000, W : 25.75 km by N 18 Z

🛈 Arthur's Quay ℰ (061) 3 17 52 2Y, www.limericktourist.com

◉ City★★ - St Mary's Cathedral★ Y – Hunt Museum★★ **AC** Y - Georgian House★ **AC** Z – King John's Castle★ **AC** Y - Limerick Museum★ Z **M2** – John Square★ Z **20** – St John's Cathedral★ Z

⊙ Bunratty Castle★★ **AC**, W : 12 km by N 18 – Cratloe Wood (≤★) NW : 8 km by N 18 Z. Castleconnell★, E : 11.25 km by N 7 - Lough Gur Interpretive Centre★ **AC**, S : 17.75 km by R 512 and R 514 Z – Clare Glens★, E : 21 km by N 7 and R 503 Y – Monasteranenagh Abbey★, S : 21 km by N 20 Z

942

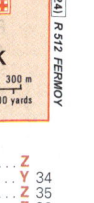

Arthur Quay............... Y 2	Grove Island Shopping	Roches St................ Z
Arthur Quay Shopping	Centre................ Y	Rutland St............... Y 34
Centre................ Y	High St................ Z 18	St Alphonsus St........... Z 35
Baal's Bridge.............. Y 4	Honan's Quay............ Y 19	St Gerard St.............. Z 36
Bank Pl.................. Y 5	John Square............. Z 20	St Lelia St............... YZ 37
Barrington St.............. Z 6	Lock Quay............... Y 21	Sarsfield St............... Y 39
Bridge St................ Y 7	Lower Cecil St............ Z 22	Sexton St North............ Y 40
Broad St................. Y 8	Lower Mallow St........... Z 23	Shannonside
Castle St................ Y 10	Mathew Bridge............ Y 24	Roundabout............ Z 41
Cathedral Pl.............. Z 12	Newtown Mahon........... Z 28	Shannon St.............. Z 42
Charlotte's Quay............ Y 13	North Circular Rd........... Y 29	South Circular Rd........... Z 43
Cruises St................ Z 15	O'Connell St.............. Z	The Crescent............. Z 14
Gerald Griffen	O'Dwyer Bridge........... Z 30	Thomond Bridge........... Y 45
St.................. Z 16	Patrick St................ YZ 32	Wickham St............... Z 47
Grattan St................ Y 17	Penniwell Rd.............. Z 33	William St................ Z

 Savoy 🛁 🏊 🕭 🛋 👥 🛎 🎵 😊 🅿 [VISA] ⦿ [AE]   Zc
Henry St. – ☎ (061) 448 700 – www.savoylimerick.com
94 rm – ♦ €99/155 ♦♦ €155/250, 🍽 €14
Rest *Market Square Brasserie* – see restaurant listing

♦ Corporate hotel named after the theatre that previously stood on the site. Spacious guest areas and bar; good-sized, uniform bedrooms with smart, modern bathrooms. Hands-on owner and his charming team provide good old-fashioned hospitality.

LIMERICK

Limerick Strand
Ennis Rd. – ℰ (061) 421 800 – www.strandlimerick.ie – Closed 25 December
184 rm – ♦ €89/179 ♦♦ €89/179, ⌂ €12 Yz
Rest *River Restaurant* – *(bar lunch)* Menu €25/27 – Carte €26/43

♦ Extensive function and leisure facilities. Modern bedrooms come in dark wood and autumnal browns and oranges; Junior suites have balconies. Terrace bar overlooks River Shannon. River Restaurant serves mix of traditional and more modern dishes.

Absolute H. & Spa
Sir Harry's Mall – ℰ (061) 463 600 – www.absolutehotel.com Ya
99 rm – ♦ €199 ♦♦ €199, ⌂ €12.50 **Rest** – Menu €17/25 – Carte €22/39

♦ Stylish, modern hotel and spa on outskirts of city centre; designed like an old mill to reflect the area's industrial heritage. Clever use of space in light-coloured bedrooms. Restaurant serves traditional menu and overlooks river.

Radisson Blu H. & Spa
Ennis Rd, Northwest : 6.5 km by N 18 – ℰ (061) 456 200
– www.radissonblu.ie/hotel-limerick
152 rm – ♦ €79/159 ♦♦ €89/169, ⌂ €10 – 2 suites
Rest *Porters* – *(buffet lunch)* Carte €28/45

♦ Modern hotel with tastefully used chrome and wood interiors. Well-equipped conference rooms and a leisure centre which includes tennis court. Smart, state-of-the-art bedrooms. Informal Porters restaurant with traditional menus.

No 1 Pery Square
Pery Sq – ℰ (061) 402 402 – www.oneperysquare.com Za
19 rm ⌂ – ♦ €89/195 ♦♦ €89/195 – 1 suite
Rest *Brasserie One* – see restaurant listing

♦ Charming, personally run house in the historic Georgian quarter of the city. Beautiful spa facility and wine shop in cellar. Well-proportioned, luxuriously appointed bedrooms.

Brasserie One – at No 1 Pery Square Hotel
Pery Sq – ℰ (061) 402 402 – www.oneperysquare.com – Closed dinner Sunday and Monday Za
Rest – Menu €25/29 – Carte €25/48

♦ Set on first floor of hotel, with well-spaced tables, Georgian-style furniture and semi-open kitchen. Tasty bistro dishes with a modern slant. Good service from a well-versed team.

Market Square Brasserie – at Savoy Hotel
Henry St. – ℰ (061) 316 311 – www.savoylimerick.com – Closed 25 December, Sunday, Monday and bank holidays Ze
Rest – *(dinner only) (booking essential)* Menu €49 – Carte €50/60

♦ Richly decorated restaurant that's relocated to the Savoy Hotel. Intimate atmosphere created by fabric-covered walls and low lighting. Modern menus offer good quality produce and a variety of textures in hearty, boldly flavoured dishes.

LISCANNOR (Lios Ceannúir) – Clare – 712 D9 – pop. 71 Ireland 38 B1

▶ Dublin 272 km – Ennistimmon 9 km – Limerick 72 km

◉ Cliffs of Moher★★★, NW : 8 km by R 478 – Kilfenora (Burren Centre★ AC, High Crosses★), NE : 18 km by R 478, N 67 and R 481

Vaughan's Anchor Inn with rm
Main St – ℰ (065) 708 15 48 – www.vaughans.ie – Closed 25 December
7 rm ⌂ – ♦ €50 ♦♦ €70 **Rest** – Seafood – Carte €28/48

♦ Lively, family-run pub in a picturesque fishing village near the Cliffs of Moher. Old favourites at lunch and more elaborate meals in the evening, with the emphasis firmly on seafood. Bedrooms boast bright local artwork, colourful throws and modern bathrooms.

LISDOONVARNA (Lios Dúin Bhearna) – Clare – 712 E8 – pop. 767 38 B1
Ireland

▶ Dublin 268 km – Galway 63 km – Limerick 75 km

The Burren★★ (Cliffs of Moher★★★, Scenic Route★★, Aillwee Cave★ **AC** (Waterfall★★), Corcomroe Abbey★, Kilfenora Crosses★)

Sheedy's Country House
– ℰ (065) 707 40 26 – www.sheedys.com – *Easter-September*
11 rm – † € 100/200 †† € 119/200
Rest – *(dinner only) (booking essential for non-residents)* Carte € 35/50
♦ Mustard-yellow house in village centre, with kitchen garden in front. Comfy library, wicker-furnished sun lounge and traditional bar. Bedrooms display plain décor with flowery fabrics and good facilities. Classical menu offered in dining room; exacting service.

Wild Honey Inn with rm
South : 0.5 km on Ennistimon rd – ℰ (065) 707 43 00 – www.wildhoneyinn.com
– Closed January-12 February, 24-26 December, and restricted opening November-December and February-April
14 rm – † € 55/60 †† € 80/90
Rest – *(closed lunch Monday and Tuesday) (bookings not accepted)*
Carte € 24/40
♦ Roadside inn close to the limestone landscape of The Burren and the Cliffs of Moher. Short, simple lunch menu; wider selection of classics at dinner. Specials best display the chef's talent and are truly satisfying. Neatly kept, simply furnished bedrooms and comfortable residents' lounge; ground floor rooms have patios.

LISMORE (Lios Mór) – Waterford – 712 I11 – pop. 1 240 39 C2
▶ Dublin 227 km – Cork 56 km – Fermoy 26 km

O'Brien Chop House
Main St – ℰ (058) 53 810 – www.obrienchophouse.ie – *Closed Monday-Tuesday except July-August, Wednesday-Thursday in low season and Sunday dinner except before bank holidays*
Rest – *(booking advisable)* Menu € 25 (weekdays) – Carte € 28/45
♦ Timeless Victorian bar leading through to a rustic restaurant with bare wooden floorboards and whitewashed walls. Very appealing, value-for-money menu offers wholesome Irish dishes, which make excellent use of locally sourced produce. Polite, friendly service.

LISTOWEL (Lios Tuathail) – Kerry – 712 D10 – pop. 4 338 **Ireland** 38 B2
▶ Dublin 270 km – Killarney 54 km – Limerick 75 km – Tralee 27 km

🛈 St John's Church ℰ (068) 2 25 90, www.listowel.ie

Ardfert★ **AC**, SW : 32 km by N 69 and minor roads via Abbeydorney – Banna Strand★, SW : 35 km by N 69 and minor roads via Abbeydorney – Carrigafoyle Castle★, N : 17 km by R 552 and minor road – Glin Castle★ **AC**, N : 24 km by N 69 – Rattoo Round Tower★, W : 19 km by R 553, R 554 and R 551

Allo's Bistro with rm
41 Church St – ℰ (068) 22 880 – *Closed Good Friday, 25-26 December, Sunday and Monday*
3 rm – † € 50/60 †† € 70/90 **Rest** – *(booking essential)* Carte € 28/40
♦ Former pub, now a simple, well-run restaurant with characterful feel. Series of homely rooms and friendly, efficient service. Wide-ranging menus rely on regional produce, with theme nights Thursdays and adventurous gourmet menu at weekends. Individually designed, antique-furnished bedrooms boast feature beds.

LONGFORD (An Longfort) – Longford – 712 I6 – pop. 8 836 37 C3

- Dublin 124 km – Drogheda 120 km – Galway 112 km – Limerick 175 km
- Market Square ℰ (043) 4 25 77, www.longfordtourism.ie

Viewmount House
Dublin Rd, Southeast : 1.5 km by R 393 – ℰ (043) 334 19 19
– www.viewmounthouse.com
14 rm ☐ – † € 50/70 †† € 100/140 – 5 suites
Rest VM – *(closed Good Friday, 25 December, Sunday dinner, Monday and Tuesday) (dinner only and Sunday lunch)* Menu € 35 (early dinner Wednesday-Thursday)/53

♦ Fine Georgian house in 4 acres, with charming period style and many original features still on display. Ornate vaulted ceiling in breakfast room; impressive staircase leads to the lounge. Bedrooms boast antique beds – opt for a duplex room. Rustic formal dining room set in the old stables; traditional menu.

MALAHIDE (Mullach Íde) – Fingal – 712 N7 – pop. 14 937 ■ Ireland 39 D1

- Dublin 14 km – Drogheda 38 km
- Beechwood The Grange, ℰ (01) 846 16 11
- Castle ★★
- Newbridge House ★ **AC**, N : 8 km by R 106, M1 and minor road

Bon Appétit (Oliver Dunne)
9 St James Ter, (1st floor) – ℰ (01) 845 0314 – www.bonappetit.ie – Closed first 2 weeks January, first 2 weeks August, and Sunday-Tuesday
Rest – Modern – *(dinner only) (booking essential)* Menu € 60
Spec. Oxtail and apricot croquette, black truffle mayonnaise and celeriac purée. Roast halibut with creamed broccoli and Morteau sausage. Raspberry tartlet with lemon curd and ginger ice cream.

♦ Set in a delightful converted Georgian terrace. Sumptuous, subtly lit bar and elegant, formal dining room with fine china and linen-laid tables. Cooking uses classic combinations and has a French accent. Efficient service, with good attention to detail.

Jaipur
5 St James Terr – ℰ (01) 845 5455 – www.jaipur.ie – Closed 25 December
Rest – Indian – *(dinner only)* Carte € 27/43

♦ Basement restaurant in terraced Georgian parade. Tasty, contemporary Indian cooking with Tandoori Jhinga (large prawns marinated in Indian spices) a speciality. Friendly, efficient service.

Brasserie at Bon Appétit
9 St James Terr., (basement) – ℰ (01) 845 0314 – www.bonappetit.ie – Closed Sunday dinner and Monday
Rest – *(dinner only and Sunday lunch) (booking essential)* Menu € 24/30
– Carte € 31/40

♦ Stylish modern restaurant in the basement of a terraced Georgian house, below the more formal 'Bon Appétit'. Largely modern dishes on the menu with a few French classics; selection of small plates in trendy bar. Pleasant, efficient service.

MALLOW (Mala) – Cork – 712 F11 – pop. 10 241 ■ Ireland 38 B2

- Dublin 240 km – Cork 34 km – Killarney 64 km – Limerick 66 km
- Ballyellis, ℰ (022) 2 11 45
- Town ★ – St James' Church ★
- Annes Grove Gardens ★, E : 17.75 km by N 72 and minor rd – Buttevant Friary ★, N : 11.25 km by N 20 – Doneraile Wildlife Park ★ **AC**, NE : 9.5 km by N 20 and R 581 – Kanturk ★ (Castle ★), W : 16 km by N 72 and R 576

MALLOW

Longueville House
West : 5.5 km by N 72 – ℰ (022) 47 156 – www.longuevillehouse.ie – Closed 25-27 December
20 rm – † € 85/150 †† € 180/190
Rest *Presidents* – (closed Monday and Tuesday) (dinner only and Sunday lunch) (booking essential) Menu € 50 (weekdays)/65
♦ Part-Georgian manor house built in William and Mary style, set in mature grounds and affording pleasant views over Dromineen Castle. Lovely oak-floored hall, superb flying staircase and stunning drawing room hung with chandeliers. Well-appointed bedrooms boast antique furniture and a high level of facilities. Grand restaurant; accomplished, elaborate French cooking.

MIDLETON (Mainistir na Corann) – Cork – **712** H12 – pop. 10 048   **39** C3

▶ Dublin 259 km – Cork 19 km – Waterford 98 km
🛈 Jameson Heritage Centre ℰ (021) 4 61 37 02, www.midletononline.com
⛳ East Cork Gortacrue, ℰ (021) 4 63 16 87
◉ Cloyne Cathedral★ **AC**, S : 8 km by R 630 and R 629

Farmgate Restaurant & Country Store
Coolbawn – ℰ (021) 463 27 71 – www.farmgate.ie – Closed 24 December-3 January, Sunday and Monday
Rest – Carte € 21/48
♦ Busy and appealingly rustic, with entrance through shop and local art on display. Market-bought produce, simply cooked; perhaps an Irish stew, some tasty squid or a freshly baked tart.

MILLSTREET = Sráid an Mhuilinn – Waterford – **712** I11 – see Cappoquin

---

MOHILL (Maothail) – Leitrim – **712** I6 – pop. 931   **37** C2

▶ Dublin 98 km – Carrick-on-Shannon 11 km – Cavan 41 km – Castlerea 44 km

Lough Rynn Castle
East : 4 km by R 201 off Drumlish rd – ℰ (071) 963 27 00 – www.loughrynn.ie
43 rm – † € 89/195 †† € 109/195
Rest *Sandstone* – Menu € 28/42
♦ 18C country house in 60 acres. Impressive interior with numerous lounges. Original features include a grand fireplace and parquet floor in the Baronial Hall. Large, well-appointed bedrooms in the house/stables. Formal dining room offers ambitious French cuisine.

MONAGHAN (Muineachán) – Monaghan – **712** L5 – pop. 6 710   **37** D2

▶ Dublin 133 km – Belfast 69 km – Drogheda 87 km – Dundalk 35 km
🛈 Clones Rd ℰ (047) 8 11 22, www.monaghantown.ie

at Glaslough Northeast : 9.5 km by N 12 on R 185 – ✉ Monaghan

Castle Leslie
Castle Leslie Estate – ℰ (047) 88 100 – www.castleleslie.com – Closed 24-26 December
20 rm – † € 203 †† € 270/320   **Rest** – (dinner only) Menu € 65
♦ Impressive castle set in 1,000 acres of parkland: home to 4th generation of the Leslie family. Ornate, comfortable, antique-furnished guest areas and individually styled bedrooms. Intimate, linen-laid dining room overlooks the lough and offers classically based menus.

MONAGHAN

Lodge at Castle Leslie Estate
– ℘ (047) 88 100 – www.castleleslie.com – *Restricted opening in winter*
28 rm – † € 128/143 †† € 170/190 – 1 suite
Rest *Snaffles* – *(dinner only)* Menu € 48 – Carte € 36/49
♦ Victorian former hunting lodge in 1,000 acres with equestrian centre. Plenty of antiques and equine-themed pictures; relaxed and informal atmosphere. Stylish and contemporary bedrooms, some with balconies. Snaffles mezzanine brasserie has open kitchen and serves Mediterranean-meets-Irish cooking.

MULLINGAR (An Muileann gCearr) – Westmeath – 712 J/K7 – pop. 18 416 ▮ Ireland 37 C3

▶ Dublin 79 km – Drogheda 58 km

🛈 Market Sq. ℘ (0449) 34 86 50, www.midirelandtourism.ie

◉ Belvedere House and Gardens★ **AC**, S : 5.5 km by N 52. Fore Abbey★, NE : 27.25 km by R 394 – Multyfarnhan Franciscan Friary★, N : 12.75 km by N 4 – Tullynally★ **AC**, N : 21 km by N 4 and R 394

Mullingar Park
Dublin Rd, East : 2.5 km on Dublin Rd (N 4) – ℘ (044) 933 7500
– www.mullingarparkhotel.com – *Closed 25-26 December*
94 rm – † € 85/160 †† € 130/250 – 1 suite
Rest – Menu € 24/30 **s** – Carte dinner € 31/47 **s**
♦ Large, contemporary hotel close to a business park and the main road to Dublin. Well-equipped, modern bedrooms in uniform style. Comprehensive leisure and spa facilities. Horseshoe bar-lounge and spacious formal dining room offering classical Irish cooking.

Marlinstown Court without rest
Dublin Rd, East : 2.5 km on Dublin Rd (N 4) – ℘ (044) 934 00 53
– www.marlinstowncourt.com – *Closed 23-27 December*
5 rm – † € 40/50 †† € 70/75
♦ Clean, tidy guesthouse close to junction with N4. Modern rear extension. Light and airy pine-floored lounge and breakfast room overlooking garden. Brightly furnished bedrooms.

MULRANNY (An Mhala Raithní) – Mayo – 712 C6 36 A2

▶ Dublin 270 km – Castlebar 35 km – Westport 29 km

Mulranny Park
on N 59 – ℘ (098) 36 000 – www.mulrannyparkhotel.ie – *Closed 7-21 January and 25-26 December*
40 rm – † € 65/105 †† € 130/160 – 21 suites
Rest *Nephin* – see restaurant listing
Rest *Waterfront Bistro* – Carte € 22/35 **s**
♦ Purpose-built business oriented hotel behind 19C façade: lovely Clew Bay views. Impressive leisure and conference facilities. Airy rooms with slightly minimalist interiors. Waterfront Bistro has informal, relaxing ambience.

XXX Nephin – at Mulranny Park Hotel
on N 59 – ℘ (098) 36 000 – www.mulrannyparkhotel.ie – *Closed 7-21 January and 25-26 December*
Rest – *(dinner only and Sunday lunch)* Menu € 39 **s** – Carte € 49/56 **s**
♦ Large, lively restaurant with fine southerly views. Modern, intricately presented cooking offers interesting combinations based around well sourced, quality ingredients.

NAAS (An Nás) – Kildare – 712 L/M8 – pop. 20 044 – Ireland — 39 D1

▶ Dublin 30 km – Kilkenny 83 km – Tullamore 85 km

🏌 Kerdiffstown Naas, ℰ (045) 87 46 44

👁 Russborough ★★★ **AC**, S : 16 km by R 410 and minor road – Castletown House ★★ **AC**, NE : 24 km by R 407 and R 403

Killashee House H. & Villa Spa
Kilcullen Rd, South : 3 km on R 448
– ℰ (045) 879 277 – www.killasheehouse.com – Closed 25-26 December
129 rm – † € 110/150 †† € 160/250 – 12 suites
Rest *Jack's* – see restaurant listing
Rest *Turners* – (dinner only Friday-Saturday) Carte € 21/44
• Impressive, part-1860s hunting lodge surrounded by vast grounds. Spacious, traditionally styled guest areas; good event facilities; superb leisure club and spa. Country house style bedrooms – those in the main house are most characterful. Elegant fine dining overlooking the garden or brasserie menu in Jack's.

Vie de Châteaux
The Harbour – ℰ (045) 888 478 – www.viedechateaux.ie – Closed 24 December-5 January, lunch Saturday-Sunday and bank holidays
Rest – French – (booking essential) Menu € 25/29 – Carte € 32/44
• Stylish, popular restaurant with open-plan kitchen and a brasserie feel. Concise, keenly priced menu moves with the seasons; mainly French dishes but with some Mediterranean influences.

Jack's – at Killashee House Hotel & Villa Spa
Kilcullen Rd, South : 3 km on R 448 – ℰ (045) 879 277 – www.killasheehouse.com – Closed 24-25 December
Rest – Menu € 19/28 – Carte € 26/38
• Informal brasserie located within an impressive Victorian hunting lodge. Contemporary, open-plan interior with white leather chairs and dark wood bar. Family friendly menu of familiar classics.

at Two Mile House Southwest : 6.5 km by R 448 – ✉

Brown Bear
– ℰ (045) 883 561 – www.thebrownbear.ie – Closed 25-30 December and 19 February-4 March
Rest – (dinner only and lunch Saturday and Sunday) Menu € 28
– Carte € 43/48
• Smart restaurant set in a small village and boasting a pubby locals bar and split-level dining room with leather furnishings and a subtle brasserie feel. Two-choice set menu or an à la carte of complex, ambitious dishes with a Gallic twist.

NAVAN (An Uaimh) – Meath – 712 L7 – pop. 24 851 – Ireland — 37 D3

▶ Dublin 48 km – Drogheda 26 km – Dundalk 51 km

🏌 Moor Park Mooretown, ℰ (046) 2 76 61

🏌 Royal Tara Bellinter, ℰ (046) 902 52 44

👁 Brú na Bóinne : Newgrange ★★★ **AC**, Knowth ★, E : 16 km by minor road to Donore – Bective Abbey ★, S : 6.5 km by R 161 – Tara ★ **AC**, S : 8 km by N 3. Kells ★ (Round Tower and High Crosses ★★, St Columba's House ★), NW : by N 3 – Trim ★ (castle ★★), SW : 12.75 km by R 161

Ma Dwyers without rest
Dublin Rd, South : 1.25 km on N 3 – ℰ (046) 907 79 92
26 rm – † € 40/50 †† € 75
• Surprisingly spacious detached house on the main road into town. Comfortable lounge and large breakfast room. Bright, up-to-date bedrooms, in uniform style, provide good value. Showers only.

NEWMARKET-ON-FERGUS (Cora Chaitlín) – Clare – 712 F7   38 B2
– pop. 1 542 Ireland

▶ Dublin 219 km – Ennis 13 km – Limerick 24 km
🏨 Dromoland Castle, ℰ (061) 36 84 44
🅖 Bunratty Castle★★ **AC**, S : 10 km by N 18 – Craggaunowen Centre★ **AC**, NE : 15 km by minor road towards Moymore – Knappogue Castle★ **AC**, NE : 12 km N 18 and minor roads via Quin – Quin Friary★ **AC**, N : 10 km by N 18 and minor road to Quin

Dromoland Castle
Northwest : 2.5 km on R 458 – ℰ (061) 368 144 – www.dromoland.ie
94 rm – † €449/878, †† €449/878, ☐ €24 – 5 suites
Rest *Earl of Thomond* – (dinner only) Menu €68
Rest *Fig Tree* – Carte €25/44

♦ Impressive 16C castle in 375 acres. Various antique-filled, country house lounges; comfy, classical bedrooms with heavy fabrics, iPod docks and flat screen TVs. Popular golf/leisure/wellness facilities. Formal fine dining in the restaurant. More casual meals in Fig Tree.

NEWPORT (Baile Uí Fhiacháin) – Mayo – 712 D6 – pop. 590   36 A2
 Ireland

▶ Dublin 264 km – Ballina 59 km – Galway 96 km
🛈 Westport ℰ (098) 2 57 11, www.mayo-ireland.ie
🅖 Burrishoole Abbey★, NW : 3.25 km by N 59 – Furnace Lough★, NW : 4.75 km by N 59. Achill Island★, W : 35 km by N 59 and R 319

Newport House
– ℰ (098) 41 222 – www.newporthouse.ie – 19 March-October
16 rm ☐ – † €115/140 †† €190/240
Rest – (dinner only) Carte €42/62 **s**

♦ Mellow ivy-clad Georgian mansion; grand staircase up to gallery and drawing room. Bedrooms in main house or courtyard; some in self-contained units ideal for families and those with dogs. Enjoy the fresh Newport estate produce used in the dishes served in the elegant dining room.

OUGHTERARD (Uachtar Ard) – Galway – 712 E7 – pop. 1 305   36 A3
 Ireland

▶ Dublin 240 km – Galway 27 km
🛈 Main Street ℰ (091) 55 28 08, www.oughterardtourism.com
🏨 Gortreevagh, ℰ (091) 55 21 31
◉ Town★
🅖 Lough Corrib★★ (Shore road - NW - ≤★★) – Aughnanure Castle★ **AC**, SE : 3.25 km by N 59

Currarevagh House
Northwest : 6.5 km on Glann rd – ℰ (091) 552 312 – www.currarevagh.com – April to mid-October
12 rm ☐ – † €80/135 †† €150/160
Rest – (dinner only) (set menu only) Menu €45

♦ Victorian manor on Lough Corrib, set in 180 acres. Period décor throughout plus much fishing memorabilia. Two lovely sitting rooms. Comfortable, well-kept bedrooms. Four course dinner menu makes good use of garden produce.

OUGHTERARD

Ross Lake House
Rosscahill, Southeast : 7.25 km by N 59 – ℰ *(091) 550 109*
– www.rosslakehotel.com – 17 March-October
12 rm – † € 105/125 †† € 150/170 – 1 suite
Rest *– (dinner only)* Menu € 45
♦ Personally run Georgian country house with attractive gardens, set in a wooded estate. Traditionally styled bedrooms; Strefens suite and Killaguile are the best. Begin the evening in the cocktail bar before dining by candlelight at smartly set, cloth-clad tables.

Railway Lodge without rest
West : 0.75 km by Costello rd taking first right onto unmarked road – ℰ *(091) 552 945 – www.railwaylodge.net*
4 rm – † € 60/70 †† € 100/110
♦ Stylish house in remote farm setting, with beautifully kept, elegantly furnished interior. Themed bedrooms boast books, stripped wood furniture and an eye for detail. Helpful owner provides good local knowledge. Homemade bread and scones; tea served on arrival.

Waterfall Lodge without rest
West : 0.75 km on N 59 – ℰ *(091) 552 168 – www.waterfalllodge.net*
6 rm – † € 50 †† € 80
♦ Heavily restored Victorian house with fishing river running through the garden. Infectiously enthusiastic owner. Sympathetically styled bedrooms with rug-covered floors and modern bathrooms; some four-posters. Pancakes, French toast and smoked salmon at breakfast.

PARKNASILLA (Páirc na Saileach) – Kerry – 712 C12 – Ireland — 38 A3

▶ Dublin 360 km – Cork 116 km – Killarney 55 km

◉ Sneem★, NW : 4 km by N 70. Ring of Kerry★★ : Derrynane National Historic Park★★, W : 25.75 km by N 70 – Staigue Fort★, W : 21 km by N 70

Parknasilla
– ℰ *(064) 667 56 00 – www.parknasillahotel.ie – April-early January*
79 rm – † € 149/199 †† € 198/240 – 4 suites
Rest *Pygmalion* – ℰ *(064) 45 122 (dinner only) (booking essential for non residents)* Carte € 42/48
♦ Grand hotel built in 1896 by The Railways, superbly set in 500 acres and overlooking Kenmare Bay. Traditional styled lounges and cocktail bar; impressive grounds and range of leisure activates. Bedrooms vary from classical to stylish and modern. Formal restaurant with portraits; menus display modern touches.

PORTLAOISE (Port Laoise) – Laois – 712 K8 – pop. 14 613 — 39 C2

▶ Dublin 88 km – Carlow 40 km – Waterford 101 km

Ivyleigh House without rest
Bank Pl, Church St – ℰ *(057) 862 20 81 – www.ivyleigh.com – Closed 25 December*
6 rm – † € 50/70 †† € 80/115
♦ Traditional listed Georgian property set in the city centre, run by a welcoming owner. Comfortable lounge and communal dining area, with antique furniture and ornaments on display throughout. Good-sized bedrooms decorated in a period style. Homemade breads, preserves, granola and muesli at breakfast.

951

PORTMAGEE (An Caladh) – Kerry – 712 A12 – pop. 375 – Ireland 38 A2

▶ Dublin 365 km – Killarney 72 km – Tralee 82 km
◉ Ring of Kerry★★

Moorings
– ℰ (066) 947 71 08 – www.moorings.ie – Closed 24-25 December
16 rm – ✝ € 60/100 ✝✝ € 90/140
Rest – (closed Monday except bank holidays) (bar lunch) Carte € 31/60
♦ Cosy, personally run hotel overlooking the harbour and bridge, and made up a series of little cottages. First floor lounge offers great views, as do some of the pleasant bedrooms; 4 and 6 boast jacuzzis. Characterful bar with music nights. Nautically themed restaurant with seafood straight from local boats.

PORTMARNOCK (Port Mearnóg) – Fingal – 712 N7 – pop. 8 979 39 D1
Ireland

▶ Dublin 8 km – Drogheda 45 km
◉ Malahide Castle★★ **AC**, N : 4 km by R 124 – Ben of Howth★, S : 8 km by R 124 – Newbridge House★ **AC**, N : 16 km by R 124, M 1 and minor road east

Portmarnock H. and Golf Links
Strand Rd – ℰ (01) 846 0611
– www.portmarnock.com – Closed 24-28 December, Sunday and Monday
138 rm – ✝ € 89/129 ✝✝ € 89/129, ⌑ €16.95 – 3 suites
Rest *Osborne Brasserie* – (closed Sunday and Monday) (dinner only)
Menu € 25 – Carte € 38/45 **s**
♦ Large golf-oriented hotel with challenging 18-hole course. Original fittings embellish characterful, semi-panelled Jamesons Bar. Very comfortable, individually styled rooms. Smart brasserie with traditional menus.

RATHDRUM – Wicklow – 712 N9 – pop. 2 235 39 D2

▶ Dublin 60 km – Wicklow 17 km – Drogheda 127 km

Bates
3 Market St – ℰ (0404) 29 988 – www.batesrestaurant.ie – (dinner only and Sunday lunch) Closed lunch September- May,25 December, 1 January and Monday
Rest – Menu € 24 (Sunday lunch)/27 – Carte € 29/51
♦ Champions local produce, with counter selling local cheese, home-cured meats and Italian staples. Various menus offer boldly flavoured dishes with Italian influences, which arrive in hearty portions.

RATHMELTON (Ráth Mealtain) – Donegal – 712 J2 – pop. 1 051 37 C1
Ireland

▶ Dublin 248 km – Donegal 59 km – Londonerry 43 km – Sligo 122 km
◉ Town★

Ardeen without rest
turning by the Village Hall – ℰ (074) 915 12 43 – www.ardeenhouse.com
– Easter-September
5 rm ⌑ – ✝ € 45/55 ✝✝ € 90
♦ Victorian house on edge of the village, with peaceful gardens and river nearby. Welcoming owner and homely, personally styled interior. Open-fired lounge with local info; polished communal breakfast table. Cosy, immaculately kept bedrooms.

RATHMINES = Ráth Maonais – Dublin – 712 N8 – see Dublin

RATHMULLAN (Ráth Maoláin) – Donegal – 712 J2 – pop. 469 — 37 C1
– ✉ Letterkenny ▮ Ireland

▶ Dublin 265 km – Londonderry 58 km – Sligo 140 km

🛈 Otway Saltpans, ☏ (074) 915 16 65

◉ Knockalla Viewpoint★, N : 12.75 km by R 247 – Rathmelton★, SW : 11.25 km by R 247

Rathmullan House
North : 0.5 mi on R 247 – ☏ *(074) 915 81 88* – *www.rathmullanhouse.com*
– *Closed 6 January-10 February, restricted opening in winter*
34 rm ☕ – ♦ € 80/175 ♦♦ € 160/250
Rest *Weeping Elm* – *(bar lunch)* Menu € 45 – Carte € 45/55

◆ Part-19C, family run country house with fine gardens, set in a secluded site on Lough Swilly. Various lounges provide pleasant spots for lunch. Stylish, individually styled bedrooms. Restaurant offers serious dinner menus taken at linen-clad tables; kitchen garden produce features.

RATHNEW = Ráth Naoi – Wicklow – 712 N8 – see Wicklow

RIVERSTOWN (Baile idir Dhá Abhainn) – Sligo – 712 G5 – pop. 310 — 36 B2

▶ Dublin 198 km – Sligo 21 km

Coopershill
– ☏ *(071) 916 51 08* – *www.coopershill.com* – *April-October*
8 rm ☕ – ♦ € 144/157 ♦♦ € 218/244
Rest – *(dinner only) (booking essential for non-residents)* Menu € 45

◆ Magnificent Georgian country house set within a 500 acre estate; home to six generations of one family. Antique-furnished communal areas and bedrooms exude charm and character. Family portraits and antique silver adorn the dining room, with much of the produce featured on the menus coming from the estate.

ROSCOMMON (Ros Comáin) – Roscommon – 712 H7 – pop. 5 017 — 36 B3
▮ Ireland

▶ Dublin 151 km – Galway 92 km – Limerick 151 km

🛈 Harrison Hall ☏ (090) 6 62 63 42, www.visitroscommon.com

⛳ Moate Park, ☏ (09066) 2 63 82

◉ Castle★

◉ Castlestrange Stone★, SW : 11.25 km by N 63 and R 362 – Strokestown★ (Famine Museum★ **AC**, Strokestown Park House★ **AC**), N : 19.25 km by N 61 and R 368 – Castlerea : Clonalis House★ **AC**, NW : 30.5 km by N 60

Abbey
on N 63 (Galway rd) – ☏ *(090) 662 62 40* – *www.abbeyhotel.ie* – *Closed 24-26 December*
50 rm ☕ – ♦ € 160/180 ♦♦ € 280/300
Rest – Menu € 35 (dinner) – Carte € 29/41

◆ Part-18C, family-run manor house with impressive castellated façade; overlooking ruins of 13C Abbey. Most characterful bedrooms in original house; some boast feature beds and roll-top baths. Good function and leisure facilities. Large bar and formal restaurant.

ROSSLARE (Ros Láir) – Wexford – 712 M11 – pop. 1 359 ▮ Ireland — 39 D2

▶ Dublin 167 km – Waterford 80 km – Wexford 19 km

🛈 Kilrane ☏ (053) 3 32 32, www.rosslare.ebookireland.com

⛳ Rosslare Strand, ☏ (053) 913 22 03

◉ Irish Agricultural Museum, Johnstowon Castle★★ **AC**, NW : 12 km by R 740, N 25 and minor road. Kilmore Quay★, SW : 24 km by R 736 and R 739 – Saltee Islands★, SW : 24 km by R 736, R 739 and ferry

ROSSLARE

Kelly's Resort
– ℘ (053) 913 21 14 – www.kellys.ie – Closed 7th December to 1st February
118 rm – ♦ €77/198 ♦♦ €154/198
Rest *La Marine* – see restaurant listing
Rest *Beaches* – Menu €25/45

♦ Started life in 1895 as a beachfront 'refreshment house', now a sprawling leisure-orientated hotel run by the 4th family generation. Various lounges, large bar and sizeable spa. Well-appointed bedrooms; the newer rooms being the largest. Formal Beaches offers exceptional wine list; Gallic-influenced bistro.

La Marine – at Kelly's Resort Hotel
– ℘ (053) 913 21 14 – www.kellys.ie – Closed 5 December - 19 February
Rest – Carte €24/36

♦ Bistro-style restaurant located within a large beachfront hotel, boasting an open-kitchen and glass-fronted wine cellar. A large zinc-topped bar from France takes centre stage, while the menu offers a selection of tasty brasserie classics.

ROSSLARE HARBOUR (Calafort Ros Láir) – Wexford – 712 N11   39 D2
– pop. 1 041

▶ Dublin 169 km – Waterford 82 km – Wexford 21 km

🚢 to France (Cherbourg and Roscoff) (Irish Ferries) (17 h/15 h) – to Fishguard (Stena Line) 1-4 daily (1 h 40 mn/3 h 30 mn) – to Pembroke (Irish Ferries) 2 daily (3 h 45 mn)

🛈 Kilrane ℘ (053) 3 32 32, www.rosslareharbour.ie

Churchtown House without rest
Tagoat, West : 4.75 km by N 25 on R 736 (Rosslare rd) – ℘ (053) 913 25 55
– www.churchtownhouse.com – April-October
6 rm – ♦ €85/110 ♦♦ €120/140

♦ Part-18C house with extension, set in a spacious, well-kept garden. Traditional country house style lounge and wood furnished breakfast room. Individually decorated bedrooms.

ROUNDSTONE (Cloch na Rón) – Galway – 712 C7 – pop. 207   36 A3
🟢 Ireland

▶ Dublin 293 km – Galway 76 km – Ennis 144 km

◉ Town ★

◉ Connemara ★★★ : Sky Road, Clifden ★★, W : 24 km by R 341 and minor road – Cashel ★, E : 15 km by R 341 – Connemara National Park ★ **AC**, N : 40 km by R 341 and N 59 – Kylemore Abbey ★ **AC**, N : 44 km by R 341 and N 59

O'Dowds
– ℘ (095) 35 809 – www.odowdsbar.com – Closed 25 December
Rest – Seafood – *(booking advisable)* Carte €22/31

♦ Busy pub in pretty harbourside town; popular with tourists and locals alike. Owned by the O'Dowd family for over 100 years, it specialises in fresh, simply cooked fish and shellfish; try the local crab. Sit in the cosy, fire-lit bar or wood-panelled restaurant.

ROUNDWOOD – Wicklow – 712 N9 – pop. 518   39 D2
▶ Dublin 25 km – Wicklow 12 km – Belfast 137 km – Limerick 144 km

Woods
Main St – ℘ (01) 281 70 78 – www.woodsbistro.ie – Closed 25 December and Monday
Rest – *(dinner only and Sunday lunch)* Menu €24/27 – Carte €29/51

♦ Stone-built property high in the Wicklow Mountains. One half is a bar, the other, a pleasant restaurant with wooden, hunting lodge style furnishings. Simple, unfussy menus provide plenty of choice; excellent homemade breads and desserts.

SANDYFORD = Áth an Ghainimh – Dún Laoghaire-Rathdown – **712** N8 – see Dublin

---

SHANAGARRY (An Seangharraí) – Cork – **712** H12 – pop. 297   **39** C3
– ✉ Midleton ▌Ireland

▶ Dublin 262 km – Cork 40 km – Waterford 103 km
◉ Cloyne Cathedral★, NW : 6.5 km by R 629

Ballymaloe House
Northwest : 2.5 km on R 629 – ✆ (021) 465 25 31
– www.ballymaloe.ie – Closed 2 weeks January and 24-26 December
30 rm – † €110/130 †† €170/250
Rest – (booking essential) Menu €37/75

♦ With pre-18C origins, this is the very essence of a country manor house. Family-run for 3 generations, it boasts numerous traditionally styled guest areas, comfy, classical bedrooms and a famed cookery school. 5 course daily menu offers local, seasonal produce.

SKERRIES (Na Sceirí) – Fingal – **712** N7 – pop. 9 535 ▌Ireland   **39** D1

▶ Dublin 30 km – Drogheda 24 km
🛈 Skerries Mills ✆ (01) 849 52 08, www.tasteofskerries.com
▨ Skerries Hacketstown, ✆ (01) 849 15 67
◉ Malahide Castle★★ **AC**, S : 23 km by R 127, M 1 and R 106 – Ben of Howth (≤★), S : 23 km by R 127, M 1 and R 106 – Newbridge House★ **AC**, S : 16 km by R 217 and minor road

Redbank House
5-7 Church St – ✆ (01) 849 1005 – www.redbank.ie – Closed 24-27 December
18 rm – † €45/75 †† €60/120   **Rest** – Menu €25 – Carte €47/55

♦ Long-standing hotel and restaurant comprising of an old bank, a butcher's and a cottage, not far from the lively harbour. Original bedrooms have a classical style; newer rooms overlook a small courtyard and are more up-to-date. Extensive, traditional menus of local seafood; wine cellar in the old bank vault.

SLANE – Meath – **712** M6 – pop. 823   **37** B3

▶ Dublin 34 km – Navan 8 km – City Centre 35 km – Craigavon 69 km

Tankardstown
Northwest : 6 km by N 51 off R 163 – ✆ (041) 982 46 21 – www.tankardstown.ie
– Closed January and 25-26 December
6 rm – † €150 †† €315 – 7 suites
Rest *Brabazon* – see restaurant listing
Rest *Bistro* – (closed Monday-Tuesday) (lunch only and Saturday dinner) Carte €25/50

♦ Fine Georgian manor house on mature country estate; extensively restored to a luxurious level. Large, antique-furnished bedrooms in the house; some with silk-lined walls. Rooms in courtyard boast kitchens. Vaulted ceilings and relaxed all-day dining in Bistro.

Brabazon – at Tankardstown Hotel
Northwest : 6 km by N 51 off R 163 – ✆ (041) 982 46 21 – www.tankardstown.ie
– Closed January and 25-26 December
Rest – (closed Monday-Tuesday) (dinner only and Sunday lunch) Carte €29/40

♦ Relaxed, rustic restaurant set in former piggery of the manor house, with modern interior, painted wooden tables and pleasant terrace overlooking the landscaped courtyard. Contemporary cooking makes use of good quality ingredients.

SLIGO (Sligeach) – Sligo – **712** G5 – pop. 19 402 ▌Ireland 36 B2

▶ Dublin 214 km – Belfast 203 km – Dundalk 170 km – Londonderry 138 km
✈ Sligo Airport, Strandhill : ℰ (071) 9168280
🛈 Temple St ℰ (071) 9 16 12 01, www.sligotourism.ie
⛳ Rosses Point, ℰ (071) 917 71 34
◉ Town★★ – Abbey★ **AC** – Model Arts and the Niland Gallery★ **AC**
◉ SE : Lough Gill★★ – Carrowmore Megalithic Cemetery★ **AC**, SW : 4.75 km – Knocknarea★ (✦★★) SW : 9.5 km by R 292. Drumcliff★, N : by N 15 – Parke's Castle★ **AC**, E : 14.5 km by R 286 – Glencar Waterfall★, NE : 14.5 km by N 16 – Creevykeel Court Cairn★, N : 25.75 km by N 15

Clarion
Clarion Rd, Northeast : 3 km by N 16 – ℰ (071) 911 90 00
– www.clarionhotelssligo.com – Closed 24-28 December
95 rm ⌑ – ♦ € 65/99 ♦♦ € 110/129 – 67 suites
Rest *Kudos* – Carte € 25/45
Rest *Sinergie* – Carte (Friday-Saturday) € 25/45
♦ Extensive Victorian building with granite façade: now the height of modernity, with excellent leisure club, impressive spacious bedrooms and a large choice of smart suites. Two former churches – now function rooms – in the grounds. Informal Asian inspired Kudos. Modern European menus at Sinergie.

Tree Tops without rest
Cleveragh Rd, South : 1.25 km by Dublin rd – ℰ (071) 916 01 60
– www.sligobandb.com – Closed 25 December and 1 January
5 rm ⌑ – ♦ € 40/52 ♦♦ € 70/76
♦ Pleasant guesthouse in residential area. Stunning collection of Irish art. Cosy public areas include small lounge and simple breakfast room. Neat, comfortable rooms.

Montmartre
Market Yard – ℰ (071) 916 99 01 – www.montmartrerestaurant.ie – Closed 9-30 January, 24-26 December, Sunday and Monday
Rest – (dinner only) Menu € 27 (early dinner)/37 – Carte € 30/48
♦ Smart, modern restaurant near cathedral with small bar at entrance and plenty of light from windows. Efficient, formal staff serve broadly influenced classic French food.

Hargadons
4/5 O'Connell St – ℰ (071) 915 3709 – www.hargadons.com
Rest – (closed Sunday) Menu € 11 (lunch) – Carte € 21/28
♦ Hugely characterful pub with sloping floors, narrow passageways, dimly lit anterooms and a lovely "Ladies' Room" complete with its own serving hatch. Cooking is warming and satisfying, offering the likes of Irish stew or bacon and cabbage.

SPANISH POINT (Rinn na Spáinneach) – Clare – **712** D9 38 B2
– ✉ Milltown Malbay

▶ Dublin 275 km – Galway 104 km – Limerick 83 km

Red Cliff Lodge
– ℰ (065) 708 57 56 – www.redclifflodge.ie – February-December
6 rm ⌑ – ♦ € 100/120 ♦♦ € 120/170   **Rest** – Carte € 33/44
♦ Thatched cottage with spacious courtyard bedrooms. Comfortable, modern lounges boast bold feature walls and antique furniture. Breakfast comes in a wicker basket delivered to your room. Informal menu of Irish produce; dine on the terrace in the warmer months.

STEPASIDE – Dún Laoghaire-Rathdown   39 D1

▶ Dublin 10 km – Dún Laoghaire 7 km – Belfast 121 km – Cork 164 km

XX Box Tree
Enniskerry Rd ⊠ D18 – ℰ (01) 205 20 25 – www.theboxtree.ie – Closed Good Friday and 25-26 December
Rest – Menu € 24/26 – Carte € 29/46

♦ Smart bistro in a small village. Daily menus offer unfussy, classically based dishes with modern presentation. Staff are eager to please and the good value wine list is well thought out. Home-grown ingredients can be exchanged for dinner.

⌂ Wild Boar
Enniskerry Rd ⊠ D18 – ℰ (01) 205 2025 – www.thewildboar.ie – Closed Good Friday and 25 December
Rest – Carte € 21/34

♦ Modern pub, unusually set beneath a small, new-build apartment block. Dining takes place in a former wine merchants shop, and ranges from breakfast and afternoon tea to filling dinners. Quality ingredients are cooked with care and passion.

STRAFFAN (Teach Srafáin) – Kildare – 712 M8 – pop. 439 ▌Ireland   39 D1

▶ Dublin 24 km – Mullingar 75 km

🏌 Naas Kerdiffstown, ℰ (045) 87 46 44

◉ Castletown House, Celbridge★ **AC**, NW : 7 km by R 406 and R 403

🏨🏨🏨 K Club
– ℰ (01) 601 72 00 – www.kclub.ie – Closed 8 January-8 February
60 rm ⊇ – † € 295/395 †† € 345/445 – 9 suites
Rest *Byerley Turk* – ℰ (01) 601 72 21 (restricted opening in winter) (dinner only and Sunday lunch) (booking essential for non-residents) Menu € 79
Rest *Legends* – ℰ (01) 601 73 10 (closed Sunday-Tuesday) Carte € 38/58
Rest *River Room* – ℰ (01) 601 72 21 (dinner only and Sunday lunch) Carte € 49/76

♦ Part early 19C country house overlooking River Liffey, with gardens, arboretum and championship golf course. Huge leisure centre. Exquisitely sumptuous rooms. Opulent food in the formal Byerley Turk. Informal Legends has views of the golf course. Accessible menu offered in the River Room.

🏨🏨 Barberstown Castle
North : 0.75 km – ℰ (01) 628 81 57 – www.barberstowncastle.ie – Closed January and 24-26 December
57 rm ⊇ – † € 150 †† € 230
Rest – (dinner only) (booking essential) (residents only Friday-Saturday) Menu € 45/55 – Carte € 24/35

♦ Whitewashed Elizabethan and Victorian house with 13C castle keep and gardens. Country house style lounges exude style. Individually decorated, very comfortable bedrooms. Dine in characterful, stone-clad keep.

TAHILLA (Tathuile) – Kerry – 712 C12 – pop. 193 ▌Ireland   38 A3

▶ Dublin 357 km – Cork 112 km – Killarney 51 km

◉ Ring of Kerry★★ – Sneem★, NW : 6.5 km by N 70

🏠 Tahilla Cove without rest
– ℰ (064) 664 52 04 – www.tahillacove.com – Easter to mid-October
9 rm ⊇ – † € 100 †† € 150

♦ Family home where the owner was brought up; great setting in a calm private cove with views over the harbour and mountains. Cosy bar and lounge with eclectic knick-knacks. Traditionally furnished bedrooms; most have patios and views.

TERMONBARRY – Roscommon – 712 I6 – pop. 518 ▌Ireland   37 C3

▶ Dublin 130 km – Galway 137 km – Roscommon 35 km – Sligo 100 km

◉ Strokestown★ (Famine Museum★ **AC**, Strokestown Park House★ **AC**), NW : by N 5

TERMONBARRY

Keenan's
– ℰ (043) 332 60 52 – www.keenans.ie – Closed 25-26 December and bank holidays
12 rm ⌒ – † € 65/75 †† € 89/110
Rest – (closed Sunday dinner) Menu € 25/35 – Carte € 26/41
♦ Modern hotel on the banks of the Shannon, with cosy residents lounge. Stylish bedrooms have flat screens and showers; some have river views; some also have balconies. Large contemporary restaurant offers à la carte menu; characterful bar serves pub classics.

THOMASTOWN (Baile Mhic Andáin) – Kilkenny – 712 K10   39 C2
– pop. 1 837 – ✉ Kilkenny ▮ Ireland
▶ Dublin 124 km – Kilkenny 17 km – Waterford 48 km – Wexford 61 km
 Jerpoint Abbey★★, SW : 3 km by N9 – Graiguenamanagh★ (Duiske Abbey★★ **AC**), E : 16 km by R 703 – Inistioge★, SE : 8 km by R 700 – Kilfane Glen and Waterfall★ **AC**, SE : 5 km by N 9

Abbey House without rest
Jerpoint Abbey, Southwest : 2 km on N 9 – ℰ (056) 772 41 66
– www.abbeyhousejerpoint.com – Closed 20-30 December
6 rm ⌒ – † € 50/75 †† € 75/85
♦ Neat inside and out, this whitewashed house in well-kept gardens offers simple but spacious rooms and pretty wood furnished breakfast room. Read up on area in lounge.

TIMOLEAGUE – Cork – 712 F13 – pop. 323   38 B3
▶ Dublin 189 – Cork 28 – Limerick 90 – Galway 151

Dillon's
Mill St. – ℰ (023) 884 63 90 – www.dillons.ie – Closed 9 January-10 February, Monday, Tuesday and dinner Wednesday October-April
Rest – Carte £ 35/45
♦ Sweet little restaurant in a small coastal village, with quarry tiled floor and pleasant courtyard. Fresh, seasonal cooking offers unfussy, traditionally based dishes. Menus evolve as new ingredients arrive; fish is from the local boats.

TOORMORE (An Tuar Mór) – Cork – 712 D13 – pop. 207 – ✉ Goleen   38 A3
▶ Dublin 355 km – Cork 109 km – Killarney 104 km

Fortview House without rest
Gurtyowen, Northeast : 2.5 km on Durrus rd (R 591) – ℰ (028) 35 324
– www.fortviewhousegoleen.com – May-September
3 rm ⌒ – † € 50 †† € 100
♦ Well-kept guesthouse just outside the village, run by bubbly owner. Built to look older than it really is, with stone walls, coir carpets and aged pine furniture providing a real country feel. Homemade breakfasts taken in the rear room overlooking the garden.

TOWER – Cork – 712 G12 – see Blarney

TRALEE (Trá Lí) – Kerry – 712 C11 – pop. 22 744 ▮ Ireland   38 A2
▶ Dublin 297 km – Killarney 32 km – Limerick 103 km
🛈 Denny St ℰ (066) 7 12 12 88, www.tralee.ie
◉ Kerry - The Kingdom★ **AC**
◉ Blennerville Windmill★ **AC**, SW : 3.25 km by N 86 – Ardfert★, NW : 8 km by R 551. Banna Strand★, NW : 12.75 km by R 551 - Crag Cave★ **AC**, W : 21 km by N 21 – Rattoo Round Tower★, N : 19.25 km by R 556

TRALEE

Grand ⓘ rest, ⌖ ⓦ ☏ ♿ VISA ⊙ AE ⓓ
Denny St – ☏ (066) 712 14 99 – www.grandhoteltralee.com – Closed 25 December
44 rm ⌂ – † €75/95 †† €130/170
Rest – Menu €25 (dinner) – Carte €27/41
♦ Opened in 1928 and located right in the heart of this bustling town. Small first floor lounge and comfy, contemporary bedrooms; those to the rear are quietest. Traditional bar, once the post office, is a popular spot, offering hearty all-day dishes. Global menu and Irish specialities in classical dining room.

Brook Manor Lodge without rest ⓘ ⌖ ⓦ P VISA ⊙
Fenit Rd, Spa, Northwest : 3.5 km by R 551 on R 558 – ☏ (066) 712 04 06
– www.brookmanorlodge.com – March-November
8 rm ⌂ – † €55/85 †† €85/110
♦ Modern purpose-built manor in meadowland looking across to the Slieve Mish mountains: good for walks and angling. Breakfast in conservatory. Immaculate bedrooms.

TRAMORE (Trá Mhór) – Waterford – 712 K11 – pop. 9 634 ⓘ Ireland 39 C2
▶ Dublin 170 km – Waterford 9 km
ⓒ Dunmore East★, E : 18 km by R 675, R 685 and R 684

Glenorney without rest ≤ ⓘ ⌖ ⓦ P VISA ⊙
Newtown, Southwest : 1.5 km by R 675 – ☏ (051) 381 056 – www.glenorney.com
– March-November
6 rm ⌂ – † €50/80 †† €80/90
♦ Smart yellow house in pretty gardens, set on the hillside, overlooking the bay. Homely lounge leads to dark wood breakfast room; book-filled sun lounge is a pleasant spot. Simply furnished bedrooms. Breakfast includes pancakes, French toast and homemade preserves.

TRIM (Baile Átha Troim) – Meath – 712 L7 – pop. 6 870 ⓘ Ireland 37 D3
▶ Dublin 43 km – Drogheda 42 km – Tullamore 69 km
ⓘ Castle St ☏ (046) 9 43 72 27, www.meathtourism.ie
ⓘ County Meath Newtownmoynagh, ☏ (046) 943 14 63
ⓞ Trim Castle★★ – Town★
ⓒ Bective Abbey★, NE : 6.5 km by R 161

Trim Castle ⓘ ♿ ⌖ ⓦ ☏ P VISA ⊙ AE
Castle St – ☏ (046) 948 30 00 – www.trimcastlehotel.com – Closed 25 December
68 rm – † €135/165 †† €150/180
Rest Jules – see restaurant listing
♦ Modern family hotel opposite the castle. Homeware shop, café, bar and restaurant. Good-sized bedrooms in contemporary hues – front rooms have the view. Discounted use of local leisure facilities; great outlook from delightful roof garden.

Highfield House without rest ⓘ ⓦ P VISA ⊙
Maudlins Rd. – ☏ (046) 943 63 86 – www.highfieldguesthouse.com – Closed 22 December-1 February
10 rm ⌂ – † €55 †† €75/80
♦ Substantial 18C stone house close to the river and castle. Well-appointed lounge and breakfast room, delightful terraced courtyard and boldly coloured bedrooms. Breakfast is comprehensive.

✕✕ Jules – at Trim Castle Hotel ⓘ P VISA ⊙ AE
Castle St – ☏ (046) 948 30 00 – www.trimcastlehotel.com – Closed 25 December
Rest – (closed Monday-Thursday) Menu €20 (lunch)/25 – Carte €25/47
♦ Set in the centre of a pleasant market town, a stylish dining room on the first floor of a modern family hotel. Open Friday and Saturday only. Good value menus of traditional European dishes.

TWO MILE HOUSE – see Naas

REPUBLIC OF IRELAND

WATERFORD (Port Láirge) – Waterford – 712 K11 – pop. 49 213

Ireland

- Dublin 154 km – Cork 117 km – Limerick 124 km
- Waterford Airport, Killowen : ℘ (051) 846600
- The Granary, The Quay, Cork Rd ℘ (051) 87 58 23, www.waterfordtourism.com
- Newrath, ℘ (051) 87 67 48
- Town★ - City Walls★ – Waterford Treasures★ **AC** Y
- Waterford Crystal★, SW : 2.5 km by N 25 Y. Duncannon★, E : 19.25 km by R 683, ferry from Passage East and R 374 (south) Z – Dunmore East★, SE : 19.25 km by R 684 Z – Tintern Abbey★, E : 21 km by R 683, ferry from Passage East, R 733 and R 734 (south) Z

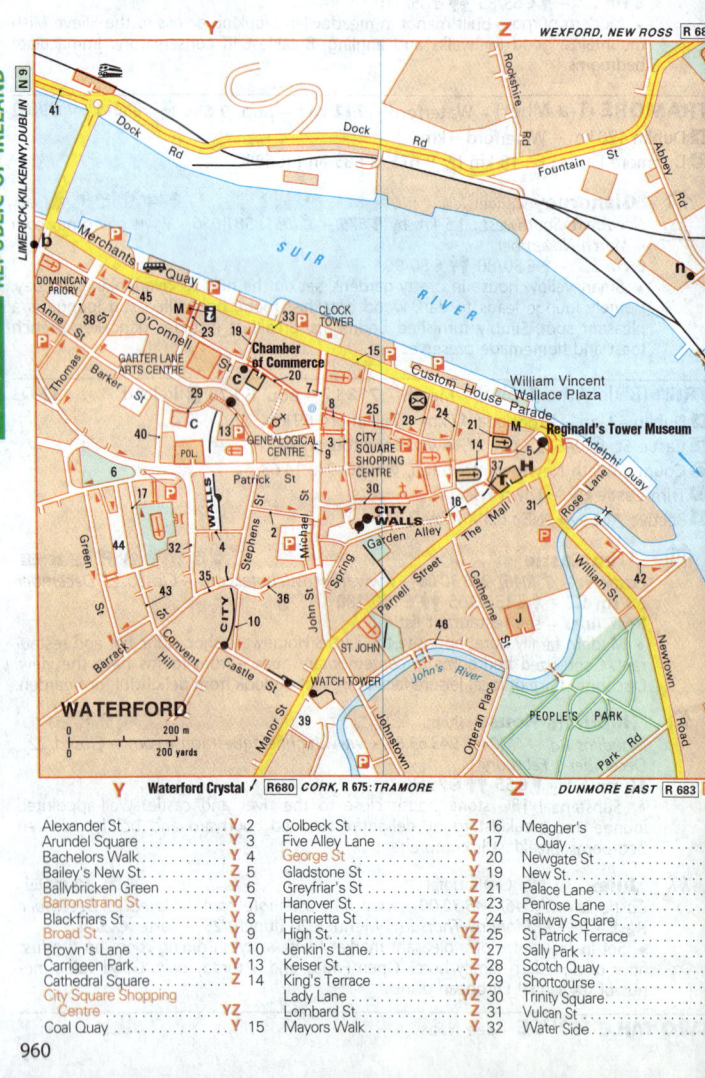

Alexander St . . . . **Y** 2	Colbeck St . . . . **Z** 16	Meagher's Quay . . . .
Arundel Square . . . . **Y** 3	Five Alley Lane . . . . **Y** 17	Newgate St . . . .
Bachelors Walk . . . . **Y** 4	George St . . . . **Y** 20	New St . . . .
Bailey's New St . . . . **Z** 5	Gladstone St . . . . **Y** 19	Palace Lane . . . .
Ballybricken Green . . . . **Y** 6	Greyfriar's St . . . . **Y** 21	Penrose Lane . . . .
Barronstrand St . . . . **Y** 7	Hanover St . . . . **Y** 23	Railway Square . . . .
Blackfriars St . . . . **Y** 8	Henrietta St . . . . **Y** 24	St Patrick Terrace . . . .
Broad St . . . . **Y** 9	High St . . . . **YZ** 25	Sally Park . . . .
Brown's Lane . . . . **Y** 10	Jenkin's Lane . . . . **Y** 27	Scotch Quay . . . .
Carrigeen Park . . . . **Y** 13	Keiser St . . . . **Z** 28	Shortcourse . . . .
Cathedral Square . . . . **Y** 14	King's Terrace . . . . **Y** 29	Trinity Square . . . .
City Square Shopping Centre . . . . **YZ**	Lady Lane . . . . **YZ** 30	Vulcan St . . . .
Coal Quay . . . . **Y** 15	Lombard St . . . . **Z** 31	Water Side . . . .
	Mayors Walk . . . . **Y** 32	

Waterford Castle H. and Golf Resort
The Island, Ballinakill, East : 4 km by R 683,
Ballinakill Rd and private ferry – ℰ *(051) 878 203*
– www.waterfordcastle.com – Closed 24-26 December and restricted opening in January
14 rm – † €110/180 †† €260/415 – 5 suites
Rest *Munster Dining Room* – see restaurant listing
♦ Attractive part-15C castle and smart lodges, set on a charming 320 acre private island in the river. Carved stone and wood-panelled hall displays antiques and old tapestries. Elegant, classical bedrooms boast characterful period bathrooms.

Athenaeum House
Christendom, Ferrybank, Northeast : 1.5 km by R 771 – ℰ *(051) 833 999*
– www.athenaeumhousehotel.com – Closed 25-26 December and January
29 rm – † €120/140 †† €150/170, ⊊ €15
Rest *Athenaeum House* – Menu €25 (dinner) – Carte €26/42   Zn
♦ In a quiet residential area, this extended Georgian house has retained some original features; elsewhere distinctly modern and stylish. Well equipped rooms exude modish charm. Eclectic mix of dishes in restaurant overlooking garden.

Fitzwilton
Bridge St – ℰ *(051) 846 900 – www.fitzwiltonhotel.ie*
– Closed 23-28 December   Yb
89 rm ⊊ – † €79/109 †† €125/159
Rest *Chez K's* – Menu €19/25 – Carte €22/45
♦ Central hotel featuring glass façade and trendy bar. Bedrooms are modern, with a good finish: some are more spacious than others; those at the back are much quieter. Contemporary restaurant offers international dishes made with Irish ingredients.

Foxmount Country House without rest
Passage East Rd, Southeast : 7.25 km by R 683, off Cheekpoint rd
– ℰ (051) 874 308 – www.foxmountcountryhouse.com
– mid March-mid November
4 rm ⊊ – † €65 †† €120
♦ Ivy-clad house, dating from the 17C, on a working farm. Wonderfully secluded and quiet yet within striking distance of Waterford. Neat, cottage-style bedrooms.

Munster Dining Room – Waterford Castle Hotel and Golf Resort
The Island, Ballinakill, East : 4 km by R 683,
Ballinakill Rd and private ferry – ℰ *(051) 878 203*
– www.waterfordcastle.com – Closed 24-26 December and restricted opening in January
Rest – *(bar lunch Monday-Saturday)* Menu €65 – Carte lunch €30/48
♦ Oak wood panelled hotel dining room boasting an ornate ceiling and evening pianist, set in a part-15C castle on an island in the river. Classically based menus fully support local producers.

La Bohème
2 George's St – ℰ *(051) 875 645 – www.labohemerestaurant.ie*
– Closed 25-27 December, Sunday, Monday and bank holidays   Yc
Rest – French – *(dinner only) (booking essential)* Menu €29 (early weekday dinner)/35 – Carte €40/56
♦ Careful restoration of this historic building has created an atmospheric, candle-lit dining room. Classic French cooking, traditionally prepared, includes daily market specials.

WESTPORT (Cathair na Mart) – Mayo – **712** D6 – pop. 5 475 — **36** A2
Ireland

▶ Dublin 262 km – Galway 80 km – Sligo 104 km

🛈 James St ℰ (098) 2 57 11, www.westporttourism.com

◉ Town★★ (Centre★) – Westport House★★ **AC**

◉ Ballintubber Abbey★, SE : 21 km by R 330. SW : Murrisk Peninsula★★ – Croagh Patrick★, W : 9.5 km by R 335 – Bunlahinch Clapper Bridge★, W : 25.75 km by R 335 - Doo Lough Pass★, W : 38.5 km by R 335 – Aasleagh Falls★, S : 35.5 km by N 59

Knockranny House H. & Spa
Castlebar Rd., Knockranny, East :1.25 km on N 5
– ℰ (098) 28 600 – www.khh.ie – Closed 24-27 December
87 rm ⊇ – †€ 110/150 ††€ 150/230 – 10 suites
Rest – (Bar lunch Monday-Saturday) Menu € 54 – Carte € 63/65

• Purpose-built hotel in elevated position, overlooking the town, mountains and bay. Furnished in contemporary yet classic style and offering excellent comforts. Large, smart bedrooms; some with marble bathrooms or four-posters. Superb spa. Formal restaurant; experienced chef and original, modern Irish dishes.

Ardmore Country House
The Quay, West : 2.5 km on R 335 – ℰ (098) 25 994
– www.ardmorecountryhouse.com – April-October
13 rm ⊇ – †€ 100/130 ††€ 100/150
Rest – (dinner only) (booking essential residents only on Sunday) Menu € 35 – Carte € 35/40

• Attractive, personally run hotel in commanding setting with views across gardens and Clew Bay. Neat, comfortable bedrooms have a sumptuous yet homely feel. Passionate chef-owner produces traditional dishes using local ingredients.

Westport Country Lodge
Aghagower, Southeast : 4 km by R 330 – ℰ (098) 56 030
– www.westportlodge.com
21 rm ⊇ – †€ 45/90 ††€ 70/140   **Rest** – Carte € 21/29

• Hotel set in 36 acres, with 9 hole pitch and putt. Rooms have big beds, flat screens and mod cons; many also have countryside views out towards Croagh Patrick. Contemporary bar and dining room. Unpretentious homemade food, with classics given a modern touch.

Augusta Lodge without rest
Golf Links Rd, North : 0.75 km by N 59 – ℰ (098) 28 900
– www.augustalodge.ie – closed 23-27 December
10 rm ⊇ – †€ 35/70 ††€ 60/90

• Family run, purpose-built guesthouse, convenient for Westport Golf Club; play the piano in the lounge while admiring the golfing memorabilia. Homely, simple bedrooms.

An Port Mór
Brewery Pl, Bridge St – ℰ (098) 26 730
– www.anportmor.com – Closed 24-26 December, Monday except July-August and bank holidays
Rest – (dinner only) Carte € 30/44

• Tucked away down a small alleyway and named after the chef's home village. Compact interior with shabby-chic, Mediterranean-style décor. Classically based menu showcases local produce in elaborate dishes; seafood specials on the blackboard.

Sheebeen

Rosbeg, West : 3 km on R 335 – ✆ (098) 26 528 – www.croninssheebeen.com
– Closed Good Friday, 25 December and lunch weekdays November-mid March
Rest – Carte € 23/42

◆ Thatched roadside pub to west of town. Cosy front bar has some tables but main dining is upstairs. Fresh, accurate cooking; go for the fresh local fish and seafood specials.

WEXFORD (Loch Garman) – Wexford – 712 M10 – pop. 18 163   39 D2
Ireland

▶ Dublin 141 km – Kilkenny 79 km – Waterford 61 km
🛈 Crescent Quay ✆ (053) 2 31 11, www.wexfordweb.com
Mulgannon, ✆ (053) 4 22 38

◉ Town★ - Main Street★ YZ - Franciscan Friary★ Z – St Iberius' Church★ Y D - Twin Churches★ Z

◉ Irish Agricultural Museum, Johnstown Castle★★ **AC**, SW : 7.25 km X – Irish National Heritage Park, Ferrycarrig★ **AC**, NW : 4 km by N 11 V – Curracloe★, NE : 8 km by R 741 and R 743 V. Kilmore Quay★, SW : 24 km by N 25 and R 739 (Saltee Islands★ - access by boat) X – Enniscorthy Castle★ (County Museum★ **AC**) N : 24 km by N 11 V

Plans pages 963, 964

WEXFORD

Whites
Abbey St – ℰ (053) 912 23 11 – www.whitesofwexford.ie
– *Closed 24-27 December*
157 rm ☕ – † € 150 †† € 250/310
Rest *Whites* – *(dinner only and carvery lunch in bar)* Menu 25
– Carte € 28/41 **s**

♦ Modern hotel built around a paved central courtyard. Spacious public area with popular meeting rooms, superb leisure facilities and very comfortable bedrooms. Internationally influenced menu served in contemporary dining room; carvery lunches in the busy bar.

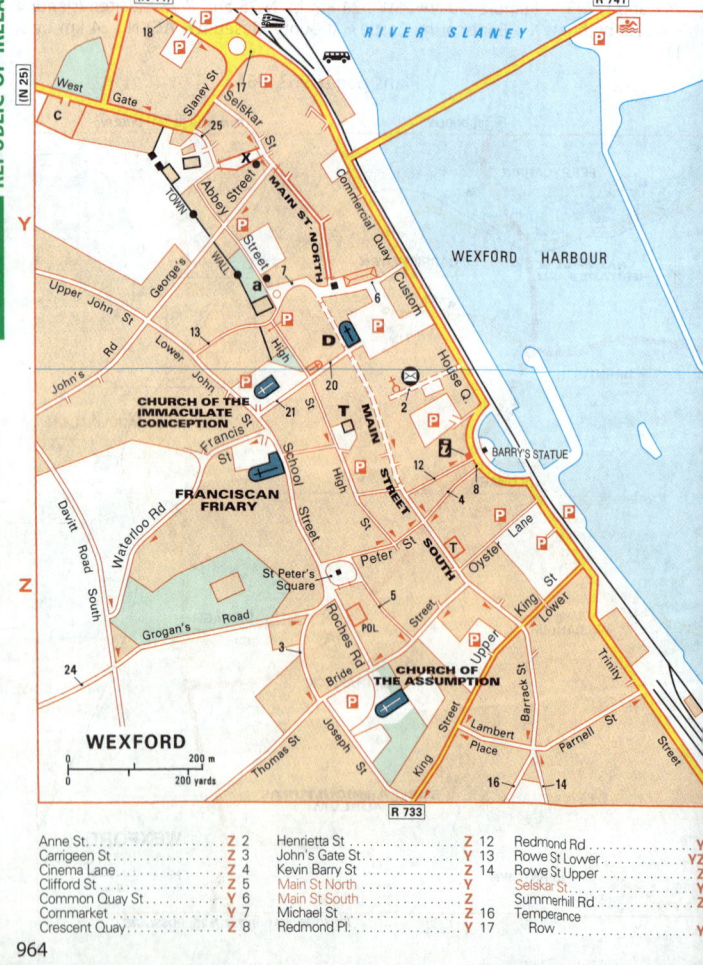

Anne St.	Z 2	Henrietta St.	Z 12	Redmond Rd.	Y
Carrigeen St.	Z 3	John's Gate St.	Y 13	Rowe St Lower	YZ
Cinema Lane	Z 4	Kevin Barry St.	Z 14	Rowe St Upper	Y
Clifford St.	Z 5	Main St North	Y	Selskar St.	Y
Common Quay St.	Y 6	Main St South	Z	Summerhill Rd.	Y
Cornmarket	Y 7	Michael St.	Z 16	Temperance	
Crescent Quay	Z 8	Redmond Pl.	Y 17	Row	Y

WEXFORD

Ferrycarrig
Ferrycarrig, Northwest : 4.5 km on N 11 – ℰ (053) 912 09 99
– www.ferrycarrighotel.ie   Va
98 rm – † € 90/135 †† € 170/250 – 4 suites
Rest *Reeds* – (booking essential at lunch) Menu € 30 (dinner) – Carte € 30/43
♦ Imposing hotel idyllically set on River Slaney and estuary. Public areas on enchanting waterfront curve. Good leisure facilities. Modern rooms with super views and balconies. Lively, informal Reeds.

Rathaspeck Manor without rest
Rathaspeck, Southwest : 6.5 km by R 730 off Murntown rd – ℰ (053) 914 16 72
– www.rathaspeckmanor.com – March-October   Xk
4 rm – † € 55/75 †† € 100/130
♦ Georgian country house with 18-hole golf course half a mile from Johnstone Castle. Period furnishings adorn the public rooms. Comfortable, spacious bedrooms.

McMenamin's Townhouse without rest
6 Glena Ter. – ℰ (053) 914 64 42 – www.wexford-bedandbreakfast.com
– January-November   Xn
4 rm – † € 55/65 †† € 90/120
♦ Homely Victorian townhouse retaining many original features. Friendly, hands-on owners. Legendary breakfasts include homemade breads, preserves, omelettes and drop scones.

Jacques Bistro
Selskar – ℰ (053) 91 23 004 – www.greenacres.ie – Closed 25-26 December, 1 January, Easter, restricted opening on Saturday and Sunday   Yx
Rest – French – Menu € 25 (weekdays) – Carte € 27/46
♦ Modern, split-level bistro with a deli and patisserie selling cheese, charcuterie, homemade pastries and breads. Well-priced French wines fill the shelves. Simple lunch menu offers salads and platters; flavoursome Gallic dishes at dinner.

WICKLOW (Cill Mhantáin) – Wicklow – **712** N9 – pop. 10 071   **39** D2
Ireland

▶ Dublin 53 km – Waterford 135 km – Wexford 108 km

🛈 Fitzwilliam Sq ℰ (0404) 6 91 17, www.visitwicklow.ie

◉ Mount Usher Gardens, Ashford★ **AC**, NW : 6.5 km by R 750 and N 11 – Devil's Glen★, NW : 12.75 km by R 750 and N 11. Glendalough★★★ (Lower Lake★★★, Upper Lake★★, Cathedral★★, Round Tower★★, St Kevin's Church★★, St Saviour's Priory★) – W : 22.5 km by R 750, N 11, R 763, R 755 and R 756 – Wicklow Mountains★★ (Wicklow Gap★★, Sally Gap★★, Avondale★, Meeting of the Waters★, Glenmacnass Waterfall★, Glenmalur★, – Loughs Tay and Dan★)

XX Black 'N' Blue Grill
Church St – ℰ (0404) 66 800 – www.blacknbluegrill.ie – Closed Monday
Rest – (dinner only and Sunday lunch) Menu € 27 **s** – Carte € 36/52 **s**
♦ Well-run, split-level, former bakery. Characterful restaurant with exposed stone, beams and an old cast iron oven; open-fired lounge in the basement. Menus fuse Mediterranean, Californian and Asian influences in tasty, well-presented dishes.

at Rathnew Northwest : 3.25 km on R 750 – ✉ Wicklow

Tinakilly House
on R 750 – ℰ (0404) 69 274 – www.tinakilly.ie
50 rm – † € 141/164 †† € 191/237 – 1 suite
Rest *Brunel* – (dinner only and Sunday lunch) Carte € 37/50
♦ Part Victorian country house with views of sea and mountains. Grand entrance hall hung with paintings. Mix of comfortable room styles, those in main house most characterful. Large dining room with rich drapes, formal service.

WICKLOW

Hunter's

Newrath Bridge, North : 1.25 km by Dublin rd on R 761 – ℰ *(0404) 40 106*
– *www.hunters.ie – Closed 24-26 and 31 December*
16 rm – † € 65/110 †† € 130/190   **Rest** – Menu € 25/45

♦ 18C former coaching inn run by the 5th generation of the same family. Traditionally styled throughout with homely lounges displaying flowery fabrics and drapes. Neat, country house style bedrooms boast sleigh beds and antique furnishings. Formal dining room offers menu of traditionally based dishes.

YOUGHAL (Eochaill) – Cork – 712 I12 – pop. 6 785 ▌Ireland   39 C3

▶ Dublin 235 km – Cork 48 km – Waterford 75 km
🛈 Market Sq ℰ (024) 2 01 70, www.youghal.ie
🏌 Knockaverry, ℰ (024) 9 27 87

👁 Town★ – St Mary's Collegiate Church★★ – Town Walls★ - Clock Gate★

🌍 Helvick Head★ (≤★), NE : 35.5 km by N 25 and R 674 – Ringville (≤★), NE : 32.25 km by N 25 and R 674 – Ardmore★ - Round Tower★
- Cathedral★ (arcade★), N : 16 km by N 25 and R 674 – Whiting Bay★, SE : 19.25 km by N 25, R 673 and the coast road

✕✕ Aherne's with rm

163 North Main St – ℰ *(024) 92 424* – *www.ahernes.com – Closed 23-27 December*
12 rm – † € 110/130 †† € 130/210
Rest – Seafood – *(bar lunch)* Menu € 25/40 – Carte € 27/51

♦ In the third generation of the family and dating back to 1910. Traditional bar, smart cocktail bar and contemporary dining room. Freshly prepared local seafood appears in tasty, unfussy dishes. Large, antique-furnished bedrooms and welcoming open-fired lounge.

REPUBLIC OF IRELAND

The MICHELIN Guide
A collection to savor!

Belgique & Luxembourg
Deutschland
España & Portugal
France
Great Britain & Ireland
Italia
Nederland
Portugal
Suisse-Schweiz-Svizzera
Main Cities of Europe

Also:

Chicago
Hokkaido
Hong Kong Macau
Kyoto Osaka Kobe
London
New York City
Paris
San Francisco
Tokyo

International Dialling Codes

Note: When making an international call, do not dial the first (0) of the city code (except for calls to Italy).

from \ to	A	B	CH	CZ	D	DK	E	FIN	F	GB	
A Austria		0032	0041	00420	0049	0045	0034	00358	0033	0044	00
B Belgium	0043		0041	00420	0049	0045	0034	00358	0033	0044	00
CH Switzerland	0043	0032		00420	0049	0045	0034	00358	0033	0044	00
CZ Czech Republic	0043	0032	0041		0049	0045	0034	00358	0033	0044	00
D Germany	0043	0032	0041	00420		0045	0034	00358	0033	0044	00
DK Denmark	0043	0032	0041	00420	0049		0034	00358	0033	0044	00
E Spain	0043	0032	0041	00420	0049	0045		00358	0033	0044	00
FIN Finland	0043	0032	0041	00420	0049	0045	0034		0033	0044	00
F France	0043	0032	0041	00420	0049	0045	0034	00358		0044	00
GB United Kingdom	0043	0032	0041	00420	0049	0045	0034	00358	0033		00
GR Greece	0043	0032	0041	00420	0049	0045	0034	00358	0033	0044	
H Hungary	0043	0032	0041	00420	0049	0045	0034	00358	0033	0044	00
I Italy	0043	0032	0041	00420	0049	0045	0034	00358	0033	0044	00
IRL Ireland	0043	0032	0041	00420	0049	0045	0034	00358	0033	0044	00
J Japan	00143	00132	00141	001420	00149	00145	00134	001358	00133	00144	00*
L Luxembourg	0043	0032	0041	00420	0049	0045	0034	00358	0033	0044	00
N Norway	0043	0032	0041	00420	0049	0045	0034	00358	0033	0044	00
NL Netherlands	0043	0032	0041	00420	0049	0045	0034	00358	0033	0044	00
PL Poland	0043	0032	0041	00420	0049	0045	0034	00358	0033	0044	00
P Portugal	0043	0032	0041	00420	0049	0045	0034	00358	0033	0044	00
RUS Russia	81043	81032	81041	810420	81049	81045	81034	810358	81033	81044	81
S Sweden	0043	0032	0041	00420	0049	0045	0034	00358	0033	0044	00
USA	01143	01132	01141	001420	01149	01145	01134	01358	01133	01144	01

*Direct dialling not possible

(H)	(I)	(IRL)	(J)	(L)	(N)	(NL)	(PL)	(P)	(RUS)	(S)	(USA)	
0036	0039	00353	0081	00352	0047	0031	0048	00351	007	0046	001	**A Austria**
0036	0039	00353	0081	00352	0047	0031	0048	00351	007	0046	001	**B Belgium**
0036	0039	00353	0081	00352	0047	0031	0048	00351	007	0046	001	**CH Switzerland**
0036	0039	00353	0081	00352	0047	0031	0048	00351	007	0046	001	**CZ Czech Republic**
0036	0039	00353	0081	00352	0047	0031	0048	00351	007	0046	001	**D Germany**
0036	0039	00353	0081	00352	0047	0031	0048	00351	007	0046	001	**DK Denmark**
0036	0039	00353	0081	00352	0047	0031	0048	00351	007	0046	001	**E Spain**
0036	0039	00353	0081	00352	0047	0031	0048	00351	007	0046	001	**FIN Finland**
0036	0039	00353	0081	00352	0047	0031	0048	00351	007	0046	001	**F France**
0036	0039	00353	0081	00352	0047	0031	0048	00351	007	0046	001	**GB United Kingdom**
0036	0039	00353	0081	00352	0047	0031	0048	00351	007	0046	001	**GR Greece**
	0039	00353	0081	00352	0047	0031	0048	00351	007	0046	001	**H Hungary**
0036		00353	0081	00352	0047	0031	0048	00351	007	0046	001	**I Italy**
0036	0039		0081	00352	0047	0031	0048	00351	007	0046	001	**IRL Ireland**
00136	00139	001353		001352	00147	00131	00148	001351	007	001146	0011	**J Japan**
0036	0039	00353	0081		0047	0031	0048	00351	007	0046	001	**L Luxembourg**
0036	0039	00353	0081	00352		0031	0048	00351	007	0046	001	**N Norway**
0036	0039	00353	0081	00352	0047		0048	00351	007	0046	001	**NL Netherlands**
0036	0039	00353	0081	00352	0047	0031		00351	007	0046	001	**PL Poland**
0036	0039	00353	0081	00352	0047	0031	048		007	0046	001	**P Portugal**
81036	81039	810353	81081	810352	*	81031	81048	810351		81046	8101	**RUS Russia**
0036	0039	00353	0081	00352	0047	0031	0048	00351	007		001	**S Sweden**
01136	01139	011353	01181	011352	01147	01131	01148	011351	0117	011146		**USA**

Index of towns

A	Page
Abberley	50
Abbotsbury	50
Aberaeron	794
Aberdeen	688
Aberdovey	794
Aberfeldy	691
Abergavenny	794
Abergele	796
Abersoch	796
Aberystwyth	797
Abingdon	50
Abinger Common	50
Abinger Hammer	51
Abriachan	691
Achill Island	864
Achiltibuie	691
Acton Green	384
Adare	864
Aldeburgh	51
Alderley Edge	51
Alderney	142
Aldfield	570
Alfriston	52
Alkham	52
Alnwick	53
Alstonefield	53
Alton	54
Altrincham	54
Alveston	623
Alyth	692
Amberley	54
Ambleside	55
Amersham	56
Ampleforth	234
Anglesey (Isle of)	797
Annahilt	856
Annbank	692
Anstey	57
Anstruther	692
Appleby	57
Applecross	693
Appledore	57
Appletreewick	58
Aran Islands	865
Arbroath	693
Archiestown	693
Archway	392
Ardhasaig	752
Ardmore	866
Arduaine	693
Arkholme	58
Arlingham	58
Armscote	58
Arnside	58
Arran (Isle of)	694
Arthurstown	866
Arundel	58
Ascog	703
Ascot	59
Asenby	633
Ash	60
Ashbourne	60
Ashburton	60
Ashford-in-the-Water	65
Ashford (Kent)	60
Ashford (Wicklow)	867
Ashprington	640
Ashwater	61
Askrigg	61
Aston Cantlow	61
Aston Rowant	61
Aston Tirrold	62
Atcham	603
Athlone	867
Attleborough	62
Auchencairn	695
Auchterarder	695
Aughrim	868
Aughton	62
Austwick	62
Aviemore	696
Avoca	869
Axminster	63
Aylesbury	63
Aylesford	63
Aylsham	63
Aynho	63
Ayot Saint Lawrence	653
Ayr	696
Aysgarth	64

B	Page
Babbacombe	639
Backwell	64
Bagenalstown	869
Bagshot	64
Bakewell	65
Bala	799
Balham	425
Ballachulish	697
Ballantrae	698
Ballater	698
Ballina	869
Ballinadee	870
Ballinasloe	870
Ballingarry	870
Ballinrobe	870
Ballintoy	842
Balloch	699
Ballsbridge	912
Ballybofey	871
Ballybunnion	871
Ballycastle	871
Ballyclare	842
Ballyconnell	871
Ballycotton	872
Ballyfarnan	872
Ballyfin	872
Ballygrant	745
Ballylickey	873
Ballyliffin	873
Ballymacarbry	873
Ballymena	842
Ballymore Eustace	874
Ballynahinch	874
Ballyvaughan	874
Balmacara	700
Balmedie	700
Balquhidder	755
Balsall Common	176
Baltimore	875
Bamburgh Castle	65
Bampton	65
Banbury	66
Banchory	700
Bandon	875
Bangor	843

975

Bansha	876	Betws-y-Coed	799	Bovey Tracey	105
Barcaldine	701	Betws-yn-Rhos	796	Bow	422
Barna	876	Beverley	78	Bowland Bridge	105
Barnard Castle	66	Beyton	131	Bowmore	745
Barnes	414	Bibury	79	Bowness-on-Windermere	669
Barnsbury	392	Biddenden	79	Box	73
Barnsley	169	Bigbury	80	Boyle	878
Barra (Isle of)	701	Bigbury-on-Sea	80	Bradfield	502
Barrasford	67	Bildeston	81	Bradford-on-Avon	105
Barrells Cross	941	Birkenhead	81	Bradwell	106
Barton-on-Sea	67	Birmingham	82	Braemar	702
Barwick	682	Birr	876	Braithwaite	258
Bashall Eaves	171	Bishop's Stortford	92	Bramfield	106
Baslow	67	Bishopstone	626	Brampford Speke	106
Bassenthwaite	68	Bishopton	701	Brampton	107
Bath	69	Blackburn	92	Brancaster Staithe	107
Battersea	425	Blackheath	414	Bray	107
Battersea Heliport	426	Blacklion	877	Bray Marina	108
Battle	74	Blackpool	93	Braye	142
Baughurst	75	Blairgowrie	702	Brearton	108
Bayswater and Maida Vale	427	Blakeney	95	Breasclete	751
Beaconsfield	75	Blandford Forum	96	Brechfa	800
Beamhurst	645	Blarney	877	Brecon	800
Beaminster	76	Bledington	621	Breedon on the Hill	109
Bearsted	479	Bletsoe	97	Brent	370
Beaufort	937	Blockley	97	Brentford	390
Beaulieu	76	Bloomsbury	371	Brentwood	109
Beaumaris	797	Bodiam	97	Bridge End	878
Beddgelert	799	Bodmin	97	Bridgend	801
Beeley	77	Boduan	829	Bridgnorth	109
Belchford	77	Bolnhurst	98	Bridport	109
Belfast	845	Bolton Abbey	98	Briggswath	659
Belford	77	Bolton-by-Bowland	98	Brighouse	110
Belgravia	430	Bonchurch	661	Brighton	110
Belper	77	Bordon Camp	99	Bristol	116
Belsize Park	371	Boreham	152	Brixton	412
Benburb	855	Boroughbridge	99	Broad Campden	166
Benenden	77	Borris	877	Broad Oak	122
Benllech	798	Boscastle	99	Broadford	777
Bepton	496	Bosham	163	Broadstairs	122
Berkhamsted	78	Boston Spa	100	Broadway	122
Bermondsey	417	Boughton Monchelsea	100	Brockenhurst	123
Bernisdale	777	Bourn	100	Brockton	506
Berwick-upon-Tweed	78	Bournemouth	101	Brodick	694
Bethnal Green	421	Bourton on the Hill	504	Bromeswell	677
Betws Garmon	799	Bourton-on-the-Water	104	Bromfield	472

Bromley	370	Caherlistrane	879	Castlelyons	885
Brora	702	Cahersiveen	879	Castlemartyr	885
Broughton Gifford	124	Callander	703	Castlepollard	885
Broughty Ferry	712	Callington	133	Castletownshend	885
Brundall	124	Callow Hill	133	Catel	142
Bruntingthorpe	125	Calne	133	Caunton	508
Brushford	191	Camber	579	Cavan	886
Bruton	125	Cambridge	133	Cawdor	704
Bryher	593	Camden	371	Celbridge	886
Buckden	125	Camden Town	374	Cemaes	798
Buckhorn Weston	125	Campile	879	Cerne Abbas	141
Buckingham	125	Campsey Ash	136	Chaddesley Corbett	259
Buckland Marsh	126	Canary Wharf	422	Chadwick End	141
Buckland Newton	126	Canonbury	393	Chagford	141
Bude	126	Canterbury	137	Chapel-en-le-Frith	151
Budleigh Salterton	127	Cappoquin	879	Charlton	162
Bunbury	127	Caragh Lake	880	Charmouth	151
Bunchrew	744	Carbis Bay	585	Chathill	53
Bundoran	878	Cardiff	803	Chatton	151
Bungay	127	Carinish	789	Cheddleton	151
Bunratty	878	Carlingford	880	Chelmsford	151
Burcombe	588	Carlisle	138	Chelsea	397
Burford	127	Carlow	881	Cheltenham	152
Burlton	128	Carlton Husthwaite	139	Cheriton Fitzpaine	156
Burnham Market	129	Carlton	495	Chester	156
Burnham-on-Crouch	129	Carlyon Bay	583	Chesterfield	160
Burnsall	129	Carmarthen	808	Chester-le-Street	160
Burpham	59	Carnaross	881	Chew Magna	160
Burray	763	Carne	881	Chichester	161
Burrington	130	Carnoustie	704	Chiddingfold	163
Burton Bradstock	110	Carradale	749	Chieveley	163
Burton-upon-Trent	130	Carrickmacross	881	Chilgrove	162
Bury	130	Carrick-on-Shannon	882	Chillaton	631
Bury St Edmunds	130	Carrigaline	882	Chillington	164
Bushey	132	Carrigans	883	Chinnor	164
Bushmills	852	Carthorpe	139	Chippenham	164
Bute (Isle of)	703	Cartmel	214	Chipping Campden	164
Buttermere	132	Cashel (Galway)	883	Chipping Norton	166
Buxhall	619	Cashel (Tipperary)	883	Chirnside	704
Buxton	132	Castlebaldwin	884	Chiswick	391
Bwlchtocyn	796	Castlebay	701	Chorley	166
		Castle Cary	140	Chorlton-cum-Hardy	489
C	**Page**	Castle Combe	140	Christchurch	167
Cadboll	785	Castle Douglas	704	Church Enstone	168
Caernarfon	801	Castle Eden	140	Church Stretton	168
Caersws	802	Castlegregory	884	Cirencester	168

977

City of London	378	Constantine Bay	543	Cutnall Green	190
City of Westminster	427	Conwy	809		
Clanfield	169	Cookham	174	**D**	**Page**
Clapham Common	412	Cookham Dean	174	Dalkeith	707
Claremorris	886	Corbridge	174	Dalkey	895
Clavering	169	Corfe Castle	175	Dalry	707
Clearwell	170	Cork	890	Dargate	207
Cleat	765	Cork Airport	893	Darley	179
Cleeve Hill	156	Cornhill-on-Tweed	175	Darley Abbey	186
Clent	170	Corrofin	894	Darlington	179
Clerkenwell	393	Corse Lawn	633	Dartmouth	180
Cley-next-the-Sea	95	Corton Denham	176	Dartmouth Park	375
Clifden	887	Cotebrook	627	Datchworth	182
Clifton	545	Coventry	176	Daventry	182
Clipsham	170	Coverack	176	Daylesford	620
Clitheroe	170	Cowbridge	810	Deal	183
Clogheen	888	Cowley	176	Deddington	183
Clonakilty	888	Cowshill	176	Dedham	183
Clonegall	889	Crackington Haven	177	Deganwy	820
Clontarf	915	Cranbrook	177	Denham	184
Clovelly	171	Crayke	193	Derby	184
Cloverhill	886	Criccieth	811	Devizes	186
Clun	171	Crickhowell	811	Didsbury	488
Clynnog-Fawr	809	Cricklade	178	Dingle	895
Cobh	889	Crieff	706	Dingwall	708
Cockermouth	171	Crinan	706	Ditcheat	186
Cockleford	172	Crockerton	648	Ditchling	186
Coggeshall	172	Croft-on-Tees	179	Doddington	187
Coleraine	852	Cromane	894	Dogmersfield	187
Colerne	74	Crookhaven	894	Dolfor	812
Coln St Aldwyns	172	Cropston	178	Dolgellau	812
Colonsay (Isle of)	705	Cross Ash	795	Donaghadee	853
Colston Bassett	173	Crossgates	816	Doncaster	187
Coltishall	173	Crosshaven	894	Donegal	897
Colton	626	Crossmolina	894	Donhead St Andrew	187
Colwall Stone	218	Crosthwaite	255	Doogort	864
Colwyn Bay	809	Crouch End	388	Doolin	898
Colyford	173	Croydon	383	Dorchester	187
Combe Hay	74	Crudwell	480	Dornoch	708
Comber	852	Crumlin	853	Dorridge	188
Comrie	705	Cuckfield	178	Douglas	481
Coneythorpe	265	Cuddington	178	Dounby	763
Cong	889	Culloden	744	Dover	188
Congleton	173	Cupar	707	Downpatrick	853
Connel	705	Currie	725	Downton	475
Constable Burton	277	Cury	235	Drewsteignton	190

978

Drogheda	899	East Garston	193	Exton	203
Droitwich	190	East Grinstead	193		
Droxford	190	East Haddon	194	**F**	**Page**
Drumbeg	708	East Hoathly	194	Fairford	203
Drumnadrochit	708	East Sheen	417	Fairlie	727
Dry Doddington	216	East Witton	194	Falmouth	204
Dublin	900	Eastbourne	194	Far Sawrey	231
Dublin Airport	914	East Chiltington	277	Farnborough	206
Duisdalemore	778	East End	475	Farnborough	370
Dulverton	190	Eastgate	196	Farnham	96
Dumfries	709	East Hendred	647	Farningham	206
Dunbar	710	East Kennett	491	Faversham	207
Dunblane	710	East Lavant	162	Felingwm Uchaf	808
Dunboyne	916	Easton (Devon)	142	Felixkirk	633
Duncannon	916	Easton (Somerset)	652	Fennor	922
Dundalk	916	Easton on The Hill	196	Fermain Bay	142
Dundee	711	Ebrington	166	Fernhurst	207
Dundrum (Down)	854	Eccleston	197	Ferrensby	265
Dundrum (Dublin)	915	Eckington (Derbs)	197	Fethard	922
Dunfanaghy	917	Eckington	548	Finsbury	395
Dungannon	854	Eddleston	766	Fionnphort	727
Dungarvan	918	Edinbane	778	Fishguard	813
Dunkeld	712	Edinburgh	714	Flaunden	207
Dunkineely	918	Edington	197	Fletching	208
Dun Laoghaire	918	Ednam	746	Flodigarry	778
Dunlavin	919	Egham	197	Folkestone	208
Dunmore East	920	Eldersfield	198	Fordingbridge	208
Dunoon	713	Elgin	726	Forest Green	208
Dunster	191	Elie	726	Forest Row	209
Dunvegan	778	Elland	198	Forgandenny	768
Durham	191	Eltisley	198	Forres	727
Durness	713	Elton	198	Fort Augustus	728
Duror	713	Ely	198	Fort William	728
Durrus	920	Emsworth	199	Fortingall	691
Dyke	728	Enniscorthy	920	Fortis Green	389
		Enniskerry	921	Forton	210
E	**Page**	Enniskillen	855	Fortrose	729
Ealing (Borough of)	383	Epsom	199	Fota Island	922
Ealing	384	Eriska (Isle of)	727	Fotheringhay	534
Earl's Court	405	Ermington	200	Fowey	210
Earl Stonham	193	Ettington	200	Foxrock	915
Earsham	127	Eurocentral	739	Freathy	497
Easingwold	193	Euston	375	Fressingfield	211
East Aberthaw	813	Evershot	200	Frilsham	681
East Chisenbury	193	Exeter	201	Friston	51
East Dulwich	413	Exford	203	Frithsden	235

979

Fritton	211	Great Malvern	218	Haringey	388
Froggatt	211	Great Missenden	220	Harlaxton	215
Frome	211	Great Totham	220	Harlech	813
Fulham	386	Great Wolford	220	Harome	233
Fuller Street	212	Great Yarmouth	220	Harray	763
Fulmer	212	Great Gonerby	215	Harris (Isle of)	752
Funtington	163	Great Milton	539	Harrogate	225
Furbo	922	Great Whittington	175	Harrow	389
Fyfield	539	Green Island	146	Harrow on the Hill	389
		Greenwich	384	Hartington	227

G	Page
Galgorm	842
Galson	752
Galway	923
Garrykennedy	926
Garryvoe	926
Gateshead	212
Gattonside	756
George Green	213
Gerrards Cross	213
Gillingham	213
Gittisham	243
Glasgow	730
Glaslough	947
Glasson	868
Glendevon	739
Glenkindie	740
Glenrothes	740
Glounthaune	927
Godshill	661
Golant	211
Goldsborough	659
Goleen	927
Gorey (Channel Islands)	145
Gorey (Wexford)	927
Goring	213
Gorran Haven	214
Goveton	260
Graiguenamanagh	927
Grange-over-Sands	214
Grantham	215
Grantown-on-Spey	740
Grasmere	216
Grassington	217
Great Dunmow	217
Great Easton	218

Greetham	221	Hartland	227
Gresford	837	Harwell	227
Greta Bridge	66	Harwich	228
Greystones	928	Hastings and St. Leonards	228
Grimston	260	Hatch Beauchamp	630
Grindleton	171	Hatfield Heath	230
Grinshill	602	Hatfield Peverel	230
Groeslon	802	Hathersage	230
Grouville	146	Hatton Garden	376
Gruline	758	Haverfordwest	813
Guarlford	218	Hawes	230
Guernsey	142	Hawkshead	230
Guildford	221	Hawnby	231
Guildtown	768	Haworth	231
Gullane	741	Haydon Bridge	240
Gulval	547	Hayling Island	232
Gweedore	928	Hay-on-Wye	814
Gwernymynydd	824	Haywards Heath	232
		Headlam	180

H	
Hackney (Borough of)	385
Hackney	385
Hadleigh	223
Hadley	190
Halford	223
Halfway Bridge	551
Halifax	223
Haltwhistle	223
Hamble-le-Rice	608
Hambleton	531
Hammersmith	387
Hammersmith and Fulham	386
Hampstead	375
Hampton in Arden	224
Hampton Poyle	224

Heathrow Airport	390
Hebden Bridge	232
Heddon on the Wall	232
Hedley on the Hill	232
Helmsley	233
Helperby	234
Helston	234
Hemel Hempstead	235
Hemingford Grey	248
Henfield	235
Henlade	630
Henley	496
Henley-in-Arden	236
Henley-on-Thames	236
Hepworth	242
Hereford	237
Herm	145

Herne Bay	238	Howey	817	**J**	Page	
Herstmonceux	238	Howth	928	Jedburgh	745	
Hessle	261	Hoxton	385	Jenkinstown	917	
Hetton	605	Huddersfield	246	Jersey	145	
Hexham	239	Hullbridge	247	Jevington	196	
Heytesbury	648	Hunningham	247			
High Crosby	138	Hunsdon	247	**K**	Page	
Highbury	396	Hunstanton	247	Kanturk	929	
Highclere	240	Huntingdon	248	Keel	864	
Highcliffe	240	Hunworth	248	Kegworth	254	
Higher Burwardsley	628	Hurley	249	Kelsale	254	
Highgate	389	Hurstbourne Tarrant	249	Kelso	746	
Hillingdon	390	Hurstpierpoint	249	Kelvedon	255	
Hillsborough	856	Hurworth-on-Tees	179	Kendal	255	
Hindon	241	Hutton-le-Hole	249	Kenilworth	255	
Hindringham	241	Hutton Magna	67	Kenmare	929	
Hintlesham	253	Hyde Park and Knightsbridge	432	Kenmore	746	
Hinton St George	241			Kennington	413	
Histon	136			Kensal Green	370	
Hitchin	241	**I**	Page	Kensington	405	
Hockley Heath	241	Icklesham	250	Kensington and Chelsea	397	
Holbeach	242	Iden Green	250	Kenton	203	
Holborn	376	Ilfracombe	250	Kerne Bridge	573	
Holford	242	Ilkley	250	Kessingland	256	
Holkham	242	Ilmington	251	Keswick	256	
Holmfirth	242	Ingham	251	Kettlesing	227	
Holt (Wilts)	106	Ingleton	251	Kettlewell	258	
Holt (Norfolk)	243	Ingliston	725	Kew	415	
Holton	243	Inishmaan	866	Keyston	258	
Holywood	856	Inishmore	865	Kibworth Beauchamp	258	
Honiton	243	Innerleithen	741	Kibworth Harcourt	259	
Hook	243	Invergarry	741	Kidderminster	259	
Hope	244	Inverkeilor	742	Kilberry	749	
Horley	244	Invermoriston	742	Kilbrittain	931	
Horncastle	244	Inverness	742	Kilchrenan	747	
Horndon on the Hill	245	Ipswich	251	Kilcolgan	931	
Horningsea	136	Irby	253	Kildrummy	747	
Horningsham	648	Iron Bridge	253	Kilham	259	
Horn's Cross	245	Islay (Isle of)	744	Kilkenny	932	
Horringer	132	Islington (Borough of)	392	Killaloe	933	
Horse and Jockey	928	Islington	396	Killarney	933	
Horsham	245	Itteringham	254	Killenard	938	
Hough-on-the-Hill	215	Ivychurch	254	Killiecrankie	770	
Hounslow	390	Ixworth	131	Killinchy	857	
Hove	115			Kilmallock	938	
Hoveringham	246					

981

Kinclaven	748	Laleston	801	Lismore	945
Kingairloch	748	Lambeth	412	Lisnaskea	858
Kingham	259	Lambourn Woodlands	266	Listowel	945
King's Cross	397	Lamlash	695	Little Bedwyn	491
King's Lynn	260	Lamphey	828	Little Bollington	54
Kingsbridge	260	Lancaster	266	Little Budworth	627
Kingskerswell	261	Langar	266	Little Eccleston	280
Kings Mills	143	Langass	789	Little Langford	590
Kingston Bagpuize	539	Langho	93	Little Marlow	493
Kingston upon Hull	261	Langport	267	Little Petherick	542
Kingston upon Thames	412	Langthwaite	568	Little Thetford	199
Kingswear	181	Lapworth	267	Little Wilbraham	136
Kington	261	Larne	858	Littlehampton	280
Kingussie	748	Laskill	231	Liverpool	281
Kinlough	938	Lastingham	267	Lizard	288
Kinsale	938	Lavenham	267	Llanarmon Dyffryn Ceiriog	815
Kintillo	768	Lawhitton Rural	268	Llandderfel	815
Kintyre (Peninsula)	749	Ledbury	268	Llanddewi Skirrid	795
Kirkbean	749	Leeds	269	Llandeilo	815
Kirkby Fleetham	263	Leenane	941	Llandenny	835
Kirkby Lonsdale	263	Leicester	273	Llandovery	816
Kirkby Stephen	263	Leighlinbridge	942	Llandrillo	816
Kirkbymoorside	264	Leigh-on-Sea	276	Llandrindod Wells	816
Kirkcudbright	749	Leith	724	Llandudno	817
Kirkmichael	750	Lerwick	776	Llandwrog	802
Kirknewton	725	Letcombe Regis	647	Llandyrnog	820
Kirkwall	764	Letterfrack	942	Llanelltyd	812
Kirkwhelpington	264	Letterkenny	942	Llanerchymedd	798
Kirk Yetholm	750	Levington	276	Llan Ffestiniog	820
Kirtlington	264	Levisham	551	Llanfihangel	821
Knaresborough	264	Lewdown	276	Llanfihangel-y-Creuddyn	821
Knighton	814	Lewes	276	Llanfyllin	821
Knock	941	Lewis (Isle of)	751	Llangammarch Wells	821
Knowstone	607	Lewisham	414	Llangollen	821
Knutsford	265	Lewiston	753	Llangrannog	822
Kylesku	750	Leyburn	277	Llangybi	836
Kynaston	268	Lichfield	277	Llanllawddog	808
		Lifton	278	Llanover	796
L	**Page**	Limavady	858	Llanrhidian	834
La Haule	150	Limehouse	423	Llansanffraid Glan Conwy	810
La Pulente	150	Limerick	942	Llanuwchllyn	822
Lach Dennis	265	Lincoln	278	Llanwrtyd Wells	822
Lacock	266	Linlithgow	754	Llyswen	823
Lahinch	941	Liscannor	944	Loans	788
Lairg	751	Lisdoonvarna	945		
Lake Vyrnwy	815	Liskeard	279		

Lochaline	754	Lytham St Anne's	476	Merton	414	
Lochearnhead	755			Mevagissey	495	
Lochinver	755	**M**	**Page**	Mickleham	165	
Lochmaddy	789			Middleham	495	
Lochranza	695	Machynlleth	823	Middleton-in-Teesdale	495	
London	291	Madingley	136	Midhurst	496	
Londonderry	859	Maenporth	206	Mid Lavant	162	
Long Compton	467	Maghera	860	Midleton	947	
Long Crendon	467	Maiden Bradley	477	Midsomer Norton	496	
Long Melford	467	Maidencombe	639	Milfield	497	
Long Sutton	467	Maidenhead	477	Milford-on-Sea	497	
Longford	946	Maidensgrove	479	Millbrook	497	
Longhorsley	504	Maidstone	479	Millstreet	880	
Longridge	468	Mainland (Shetland Islands)	776	Milstead	497	
Longstock	615	Mainland (Orkney Islands)	763	Milton Abbot	631	
Longtown	468	Malahide	946	Milton Keynes	497	
Looe	468	Mallow	946	Minehead	501	
Lorton	172	Malmesbury	479	Minster Lovell	502	
Loughborough	469	Malpas	481	Minster Lovell	674	
Louth	469	Maltby	481	Mistley	502	
Lovington	140	Malvern Wells	218	Mitton	658	
Low Fell	213	Man (Isle of)	481	Mobberley	265	
Lower Peover	265	Manchester	483	Moffat	756	
Lower Shiplake	237	Mansfield	489	Mohill	947	
Lower Vobster	469	Marazion	490	Mold	823	
Lower Froyle	54	Marcham	50	Monaghan	947	
Lower Hardres	138	Margate	490	Monks Eleigh	503	
Lower Oddington	620	Market Drayton	491	Monkton Combe	74	
Lower Slaughter	104	Marlborough	491	Monmouth	824	
Lower Swell	621	Marldon	492	Montgomery	824	
Lowestoft	470	Marlow	492	Montrose	757	
Low Row	568	Marple	493	Morecambe	503	
Ludford	470	Marsden	493	Moretonhampstead	503	
Ludlow	470	Marston Meysey	493	Moreton-in-Marsh	504	
Lupton	263	Martinhoe	476	Morpeth	504	
Luton	473	Marton	494	Morston	96	
Luxborough	473	Masham	494	Morton	505	
Lyddington	644	Matfen	494	Moulsford	505	
Lydford	473	Mawgan Porth	518	Moulton	505	
Lyme Regis	473	Mayfair	433	Mousehole	505	
Lymington	474	Medbourne	494	Much Hadham	506	
Lymm	475	Mellor	93	Much Wenlock	506	
Lyndhurst	475	Melrose	756	Muir of Ord	758	
Lynmouth	476	Melton Mowbray	495	Mull (Isle of)	758	
Lynton	475	Memus	756	Mullingar	948	
Lytham	477	Menai Bridge	798	Mulranny	948	

Murcott	506	North Kilworth	520	Pateley Bridge	543
Muthill	706	North Lopham	520	Patrick Brompton	544
		North Molton	521	Pattiswick	172
N	**Page**	North Queensferry	761	Paulerspury	640
Naas	949	North Uist	789	Paxford	166
Nailsworth	507	North Walsham	521	Peat Inn	765
Nairn	759	Northallerton	521	Peebles	765
Nantgaredig	808	Northampton	521	Pembroke	827
Nantwich	507	Northaw	523	Penarth	808
Nant-Y-Derry	796	Northleach	523	Penmachno	800
Narberth	825	Norton St Philip	523	Penn	544
Navan	949	Norwich	523	Penrith	544
Nether Burrow	507	Noss Mayo	526	Penzance	545
Nether Westcote	621	Nottingham	526	Perranuthnoe	490
Netley Marsh	609	Nuneaton	530	Pershore	548
New Milton	507			Perth	766
New Romney	508	**O**	**Page**	Peterborough	548
Newark-on-Trent	508	Oakham	530	Petersfield	550
Newbiggin	545	Oaksey	531	Petworth	550
Newbury	508	Oare	207	Pickering	551
Newby Bridge	511	Oban	761	Pickhill	552
Newcastle	860	Oborne	600	Pierowall	765
Newcastle upon Tyne	512	Ockley	531	Pillerton Priors	552
Newick	517	Offchurch	576	Pinner	389
Newmarket on Fergus	950	Old Burghclere	532	Pitlochry	769
Newport (Newport)	825	Old Radnor	827	Plockton	771
Newport (Pembrokeshire)	826	Old Warden	532	Plumtree	530
Newport (Mayo)	950	Oldham	532	Plymouth	552
Newport Pagnell	518	Oldstead	532	Plympton St Maurice	555
Newquay	518	Olton	606	Polperro	555
Newton Longville	518	Ombersley	533	Pontdolgoch	802
Newton Poppleford	604	Onich	762	Ponteland	517
Newton Stewart	760	Orford	533	Poole	556
Newton-on-Ouse	685	Orpington	370	Pooley Bridge	643
Newtown	827	Osmotherley	533	Porlock	557
Newtownards	860	Oswestry	533	Port Appin	771
Nigg	785	Oughterard	950	Port Charlotte	745
Niton	661	Oundle	534	Port Ellen	745
Nomansland	519	Oxford	534	Port Erin	482
North Bay	701	Oxhill	540	Porthcawl	828
North Berwick	761			Portinscale	258
North Bovey	519	**P**	**Page**	Portlaoise	951
North Charlton	53	Padstow	540	Portmagee	952
North Hinksey	539	Painswick	543	Portmahomack	771
North Kensington	408	Parkmill	833	Portpatrick	771
		Parknasilla	951	Port Sunlight	558

Portgate	558
Porthleven	558
Portmarnock	952
Portmeirion	828
Portree	779
Portrush	861
Port Saint Mary	482
Portscatho	558
Portsmouth	559
Portstewart	861
Postbridge	562
Potterne	186
Powerstock	562
Prestbury	562
Preston	562
Preston Candover	563
Prestwich	489
Primrose Hill	377
Pulham Market	563
Purton	563
Putney	426
Pwllgloyw	801
Pwllheli	828

Q	Page
Queen's Park	370

R	Page
Radnage	618
Rainham	563
Ramsbottom	564
Ramsey	482
Ramsgate	564
Ramsgill-in-Nidderdale	544
Rannoch Station	772
Ratagan	772
Rathdrum	952
Rathmelton	952
Rathmines	914
Rathmullan	953
Rathnew	965
Ravenstonedale	264
Rayleigh	564
Reading	564
Redditch	567
Redford	496

Reed	567
Reeth	568
Regent's Park and Marylebone	444
Reigate	568
Retford	569
Rhoscolyn	798
Rhos-on-Sea	809
Rhydycroesau	534
Rhyl	829
Richmond (London)	415
Richmond (N. Yorks)	569
Richmond-upon-Thames	414
Ringwood	569
Ripley (N. Yorks)	569
Ripley (Surrey)	570
Ripon	570
Rishworth	611
Riverstown	953
Roade	571
Rochdale	571
Rock	571
Rockbeare	203
Rockfield	824
Roecliffe	99
Rogate	572
Romaldkirk	67
Romsey	572
Roscommon	953
Rosslare	953
Rosslare Harbour	954
Ross-on-Wye	573
Rothbury	573
Roundstone	954
Roundwood	954
Rowde	186
Rowen	810
Rowhook	246
Rowsley	574
Royal Leamington Spa	574
Royal Tunbridge Wells	576
Rozel Bay	146
Runswick Bay	578
Rushlake Green	578
Ruthin	829
Rye	578

S	Page
Saffron Walden	579
St Albans	580
Saint Andrews	772
Saint Asaph	830
St Austell	582
St Blazey	583
Newtown Saint Boswells	774
Saint Clears	830
Saint David's	830
Saint Fillans	775
Saint George	831
St Ives	583
St Keverne	585
St Mawes	586
Saint Monans	775
St Osyth	586
St Anne's	477
St Aubin	147
St Brelades Bay	147
St Helier	148
St Hilary	490
St James's	451
St Kew	646
St Margaret's at Cliffe	189
St Margaret's Hope	764
St Martin	143
St Martin's	593
St Mary's	593
St Merryn	543
St Pancras	377
St Peter Port	143
St Saviour (Guernsey)	145
St Saviour (Jersey)	150
Salcombe	587
Sale	588
Salisbury	588
Sandford-on-Thames	539
Sandiway	590
Sandsend	659
Sandwich	590
Sandyford	915
Sandypark	141
Sanquhar	775
Sapperton	169

Sark	150	Sidmouth	603	Spittal of Glenshee	781
Saundersfoot	831	Sinnington	552	Sprigg's Alley	164
Sawdon	592	Sissinghurst	177	Staddle Bridge	521
Scalasaig	705	Sittingbourne	604	Stadhampton	612
Scalpay	752	Sizergh	255	Stafford	612
Scarborough	591	Skenfrith	832	Staines	612
Scarista	753	Skerries	955	Stamford	613
Scawton	234	Skipton	604	Standish	614
Scilly (Isles of)	593	Skirling	777	Stanley	769
Scourie	775	Skye (Isle of)	777	Stansted Mountfitchet	614
Scrabster	787	Slaley	240	Stanton	614
Scunthorpe	594	Slane	955	Stanton St Quintin	164
Seaham	595	Slapton	605	Stapleford	530
Seahouses	595	Sleat	779	Stathern	495
Seasalter	660	Sligo	956	Staverton (Northants)	182
Seaview	661	Snainton	605	Staverton (Devon)	614
Seer Green	75	Snape	605	Stepaside	957
Seion	802	Snettisham	606	Stevenston	781
Sennybridge	832	Soar Mill Cove	587	Stilton	615
Settle	595	Soho	454	Stirling	782
Shaftesbury	595	Solihull	606	St Issey	543
Shaldon	596	Somerton	606	Stockbridge	615
Shanagarry	955	Sonning	567	Stockport	615
Shanklin	662	Sorn	780	Stockwell	413
Shedfield	596	South Brent	607	Stoke-by-Nayland	616
Sheffield	597	South Croydon	383	Stoke Poges	617
Shefford	600	South Dalton	79	Stoke Holy Cross	525
Shelley	247	South Kensington	409	Stokenchurch	618
Shepherd's Bush	388	South Molton	607	Stoke-on-Trent	616
Sherborne	600	South Rauceby	607	Stokesley	618
Shere	222	Southampton	607	Ston Easton	618
Sheringham	600	Southbank	413	Stonehall Common	680
Sherwood Business Park	530	Southend-on-Sea	610	Stonehaven	783
Shieldaig	777	Southfields	427	Stornoway	752
Shilton	176	Southport	610	Storrington	619
Shinfield	567	Southrop	611	Stowmarket	619
Shiplake Cross	237	Southwark (Borough of)	417	Stow-on-the-Wold	619
Shipley	601	Southwark	419	Strachur	783
Shoreditch	386	Southwold	611	Straffan	957
Shottle	77	Sowerby Bridge	611	Strand and Covent Garden	460
Shrewsbury	601	Spanish Point	956	Stratford-upon-Avon	621
Shrewton	603	Sparsholt	666	Strathpeffer	784
Shurdington	156	Spean Bridge	780	Strathyre	784
Sibford Gower	66	Speen	612	Strete	181
Sidford	604	Speldhurst	578	Stretton	130
Sidlesham	163	Spitalfields	423	Stromness	765

986

Strontian	784	Tetbury	632	Troutbeck	670
Struan	779	Tewkesbury	632	Trowbridge	640
Stuckton	208	Thirsk	633	Trumpet	268
Studland	624	Thomastown	958	Truro	641
Summercourt	624	Thornbury	633	Tuddenham	642
Summerhouse	180	Thornham	248	Tufnell Park	378
Sunbury	624	Thornhill	786	Turnberry	788
Sunningdale	624	Thornton	95	Turners Hill	642
Sunniside	624	Thunder Bridge	246	Twickenham	417
Surbiton	412	Thundersley	564	Two Bridges	642
Sutton (Borough of)	421	Thursford Green	634	Two Mile House	949
Sutton	421	Thurso	786	Tynemouth	642
Sutton Coldfield	625	Tickton	79		
Sutton Courtenay	625	Tighnabruaich	787	**U**	**Page**
Sutton Gault	199	Tillington	551	Uckfield	643
Sutton-on-the-Forest	625	Tilston	481	Udny Green	789
Swansea	832	Timoleague	958	Ufford	643
Swettenham	625	Tintinhull	634	Ullapool	790
Swinbrook	128	Tiroran	758	Ullswater	643
Swindon	626	Titchwell	634	Ulverston	643
Swinton	784	Titley	261	Upper Oddington	620
Swiss Cottage	377	Tobermory	759	Upper Slaughter	105
		Tollard Royal	635	Upper Woodford	590
T	**Page**	Tongue	787	Uppingham	644
Tadcaster	626	Toormore	958	Upton Scudamore	648
Tahilla	957	Toot Baldon	539	Urmston	644
Tain	785	Topsham	635	Usk	835
Talmine	785	Torquay	635	Uttoxeter	645
Talsarnau	835	Torridon	787		
Tangmere	162	Totford	639	**V**	**Page**
Taplow	626	Totley	600	Valley	798
Tarbert	753	Totnes	639	Veensgarth	776
Tarbet	786	Towcester	640	Ventnor	662
Tarporley	627	Tower	877	Veryan	645
Tarr Steps	627	Tower Hamlets	421	Victoria	463
Tattenhall	627	Tralee	958	Virginstow	645
Taunton	628	Tramore	959		
Tavistock	630	Trebetherick	572	**W**	**Page**
Tayvallich	786	Tregrehan	582	Waddesdon	645
Teangue	780	Trelowarren	235	Wadebridge	646
Teddington	416	Tremeirchion	835	Walberswick	646
Teffont Magna	589	Tresco	594	Walford	573
Teignmouth	631	Trim	959	Walkerburn	790
Temple Sowerby	545	Triscombe	630	Wallingford	646
Tenterden	631	Troon	788	Wandsworth (Borough of)	425
Termonbarry	957	Trotton	496		

Wandsworth	427	Weston-super-Mare	656	Wiveton	96
Wantage	646	Wexford	963	Woburn	674
Wapping	424	Weybridge	657	Woking	675
Wareham	647	Weymouth	657	Wold Newton	675
Waren Mill	65	Whalley	658	Wolf's Castle	836
Warkworth	647	Whepstead	131	Wolvercote	540
Warminster	648	Whitby	658	Wolverhampton	675
Warrenpoint	861	Whitebrook	824	Wooburn	76
Wartling	239	Whitechapel	424	Woodbridge	676
Warwick	648	Whitehaven	659	Woodhouse Eaves	469
Waterford	960	Whitewell	660	Woodstock	677
Watergate Bay	518	Whitstable	660	Woofferton	472
Watermillock	643	Whitton	836	Woolacombe	678
Waterstein	780	Wick	790	Wooler	678
Watford	650	Wickham	660	Woolhope	678
Watton	651	Wicklow	965	Woolsthorpe by Belvoir	215
Wellingham	651	Wighill	626	Wootton Bridge	662
Wellington	651	Wight (Isle of)	661	Worcester	679
Wells	651	Wighton	652	Worcester Park	421
Wells-next-the-Sea	652	Willesden Green	370	Worfield	109
Welwyn	652	Willian	663	Worksop	680
Welwyn Garden City	653	Wimbledon	414	Wormit	791
Wentbridge	653	Wimborne Minster	663	Worth	183
West Bagborough	630	Wimborne St Giles	663	Wrexham	836
West Didsbury	489	Winchcombe	664	Wrightington Bar	614
West End	654	Winchelsea	664	Wye	680
West Hampstead	378	Winchester	664	Wymondham	680
West Hoathly	654	Windermere	667	Wyton	248
West Kirby	654	Windlesham	671		
West Malling	654	Windsor	671		
West Meon	655	Wineham	236	**Y**	
Weston under Wetherley	576	Winforton	238	Yarm	681
		Winsford	673	Yarmouth	663
Weston Subedge	166	Winster	670	Yattendon	681
West-Overton	655	Winston	673	Yeovil	681
Westport	962	Winterbourne Steepleton	188	York	682
Westray (Isle of)	765			Youghal	966
West Tanfield	655	Winteringham	673		
West Witton	655	Wiswell	171		
Westfield	655	Witherslack	674	**Z**	
Westleton	655	Witney	674	Zennor	685

Major hotel groups

Central reservation telephone numbers

ACCOR HOTELS (NOVOTEL)	0871 6630624
DE VERE HOTELS PLC	0845 3752808
DOYLE COLLECTION	0870 9072222
HILTON HOTELS	08705 515151
HOLIDAY INN & CROWNE PLAZA WORLDWIDE	0800 40 50 60 *(Freephone)*
HYATT HOTELS WORLDWIDE	0845 8881234
INTERCONTINENTAL HOTELS	0800 0289387 *(Freephone)*
MACDONALD HOTELS PLC	08457 585593
MARRIOTT HOTELS	00800 1927 1927 *(Freephone)*
MILLENNIUM & COPTHORNE HOTELS PLC	0845 3020001
RADISSON HOTELS WORLDWIDE	0800 374411 *(Freephone)*
SHERATON HOTELS & RESORTS WORLDWIDE	0800 353535 *(Freephone)*

Maps
Regional maps of listed towns

Map Key
Places with at least one

- •   hotel or restaurant
- ✿   starred establishment
- 🙂   « Bib Gourmand » restaurant
- 🛏   « Bib Hotel »
- ✗   particularly pleasant restaurant
- 🍺   particularly pleasant pub
- 🏠   particularly pleasant hotel
- ⛺   particularly pleasant guesthouse
- 🤫   particularly quiet hotel

Distances in miles

(except for the Republic of Ireland: km). The distance is given from each town to other nearby towns and to the capital of each region as grouped in the guide. To avoid excessive repetition some distances have only been quoted once – you may therefore have to look under both town headings.
The distances quoted are not necessarily the shortest but have been based on the roads which afford the best driving conditions and are therefore the most practical.

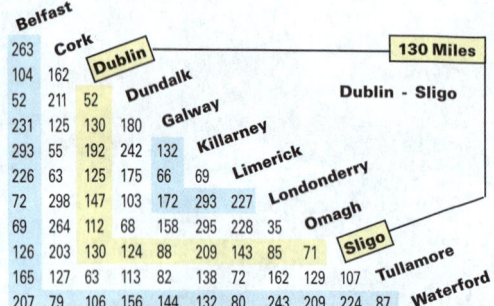

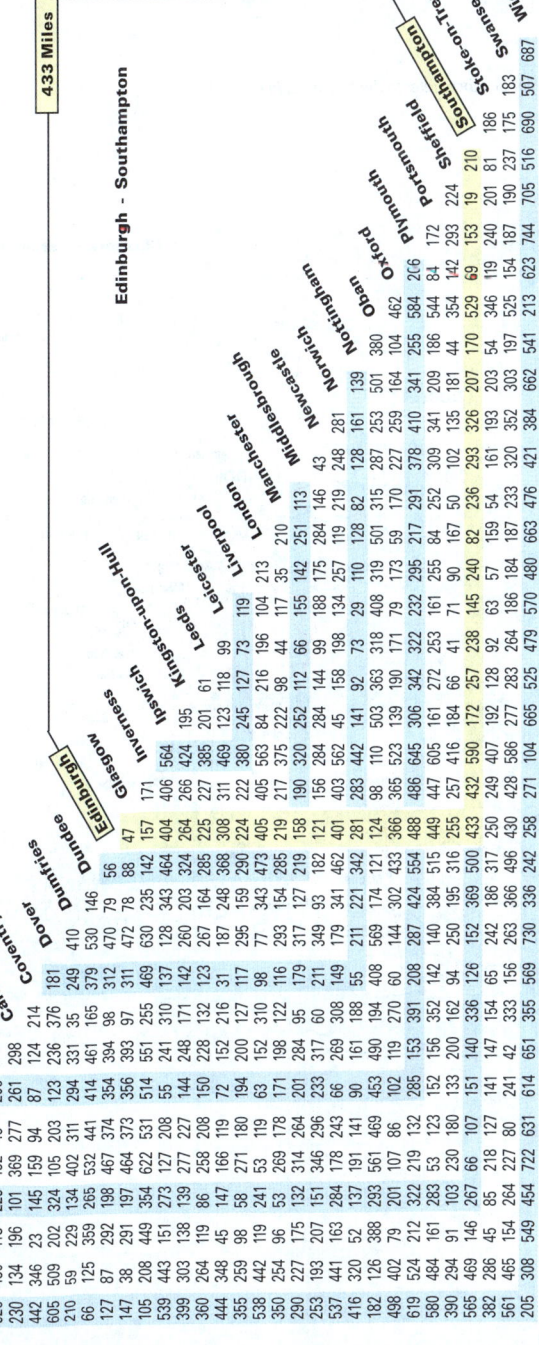

231	455	399	336	304	**Amsterdam**	667	693	834	937	541	**Lyon**
1017	1043	1184	1287	891	**Barcelona**	1165	1191	1333	1436	1040	**Madrid**
665	690	832	935	539	**Basel**	1495	1521	1663	1766	1370	**Málaga**
773	799	941	724	648	**Berlin**	861	887	1028	1132	736	**Marseille**
725	750	892	995	599	**Bern**	874	900	1042	1145	749	**Milano**
735	760	902	1005	609	**Bordeaux**	798	824	965	1069	673	**München**
1059	1085	1227	1330	934	**Bratislava**	563	589	731	834	274	**Nantes**
1492	1518	1660	1763	1367	**Brindisi**	1787	1813	1955	2058	1662	**Palermo**
319	345	486	590	194	**Bruxelles-Brussel**	369	395	536	640	244	**Paris**
161	156	329	448	86	**Cherbourg**	1360	1386	1527	1631	1234	**Porto**
637	663	804	907	511	**Clermont-Ferrand**	879	905	1047	1150	754	**Praha**
440	466	608	711	315	**Düsseldorf**	1240	1266	1407	1510	1114	**Roma**
566	591	733	836	440	**Frankfurt am Main**	879	905	1046	1149	753	**San Sebastián**
703	729	870	974	578	**Genève**	580	605	747	850	454	**Strasbourg**
509	691	677	605	540	**Hamburg**	794	820	962	1065	669	**Toulouse**
701	883	868	796	731	**København**	1229	1255	1397	1500	1104	**Valencia**
264	290	431	535	139	**Lille**	1119	1144	1286	1070	993	**Warszawa**
1455	1481	1623	1726	1330	**Lisboa**	1006	1032	1174	1277	881	**Wien**
452	478	619	722	326	**Luxembourg**	1117	1143	1285	1388	992	**Zagreb**

Birmingham   Cardiff   Dublin   Glasgow   London

Cornwall, Devon, Isles of Scilly

1

BRI

Isles of Scilly

- Bryher
- Tresco
- St. Martin's
- St. Mary's

- Clov...
- Hartland
- Bude
- Crackington Haven
- Boscastle
- **Rock**
- Padstow
- St. Issey
- Wadebridge
- Mawgan Porth
- Watergate Bay
- Newquay
- Bodmin
- Summercourt
- St Blazey
- Tregrehan
- Golant
- Liskea...
- St. Austell
- Fowey
- Looe
- Polperro
- Zennor
- St. Ives
- Mevagissey
- Marazion
- Veryan
- Gorran Haven
- Penzance
- St. Hilary
- Portscatho
- Perranuthnoe
- St. Mawes
- Mousehole
- Porthleven
- Helston
- Falmouth
- Truro
- Cury
- St. Keverne
- Coverack
- Lizard

CORNWAL...

The MICHELIN Guide
A collection to savor!

Belgique & Luxembourg
Deutschland
España & Portugal
France
Great Britain & Ireland
Italia
Nederland
Portugal
Suisse-Schweiz-Svizzera
Main Cities of Europe

Also:

Chicago
Hokkaido
Hong Kong Macau
Kyoto Osaka Kobe
London
New York City
Paris
San Francisco
Tokyo

Channel Islands 5

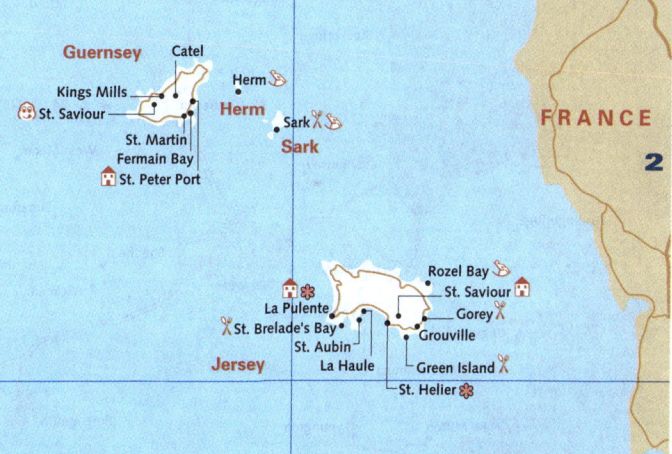

ENGLISH CHANNEL
LA MANCHE

Alderney
Braye

Cherbourg-Octeville

Guernsey
Catel
Kings Mills
St. Saviour
St. Martin
Fermain Bay
St. Peter Port

Herm
Herm

Sark
Sark

FRANCE

Rozel Bay
St. Saviour
La Pulente
Gorey
St. Brelade's Bay
Grouville
St. Aubin
La Haule
Green Island
Jersey
St. Helier

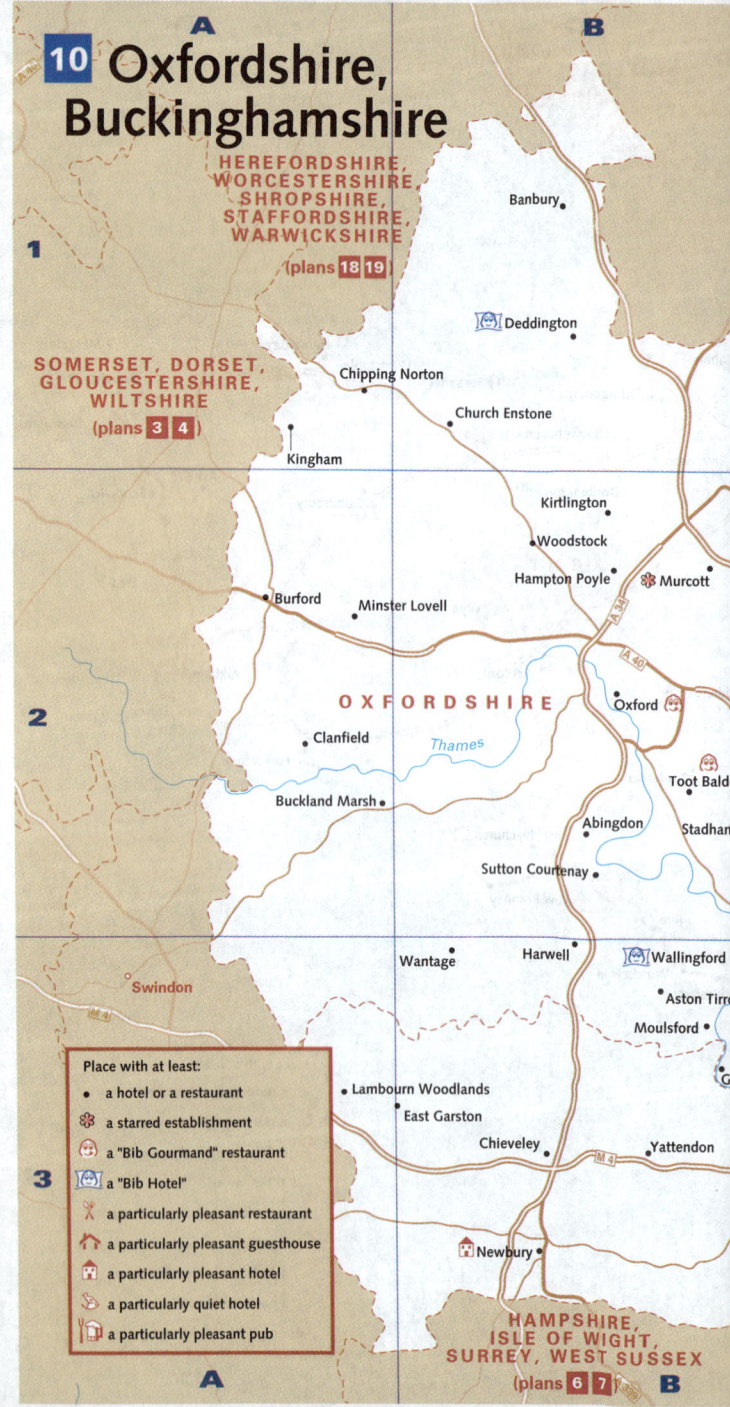

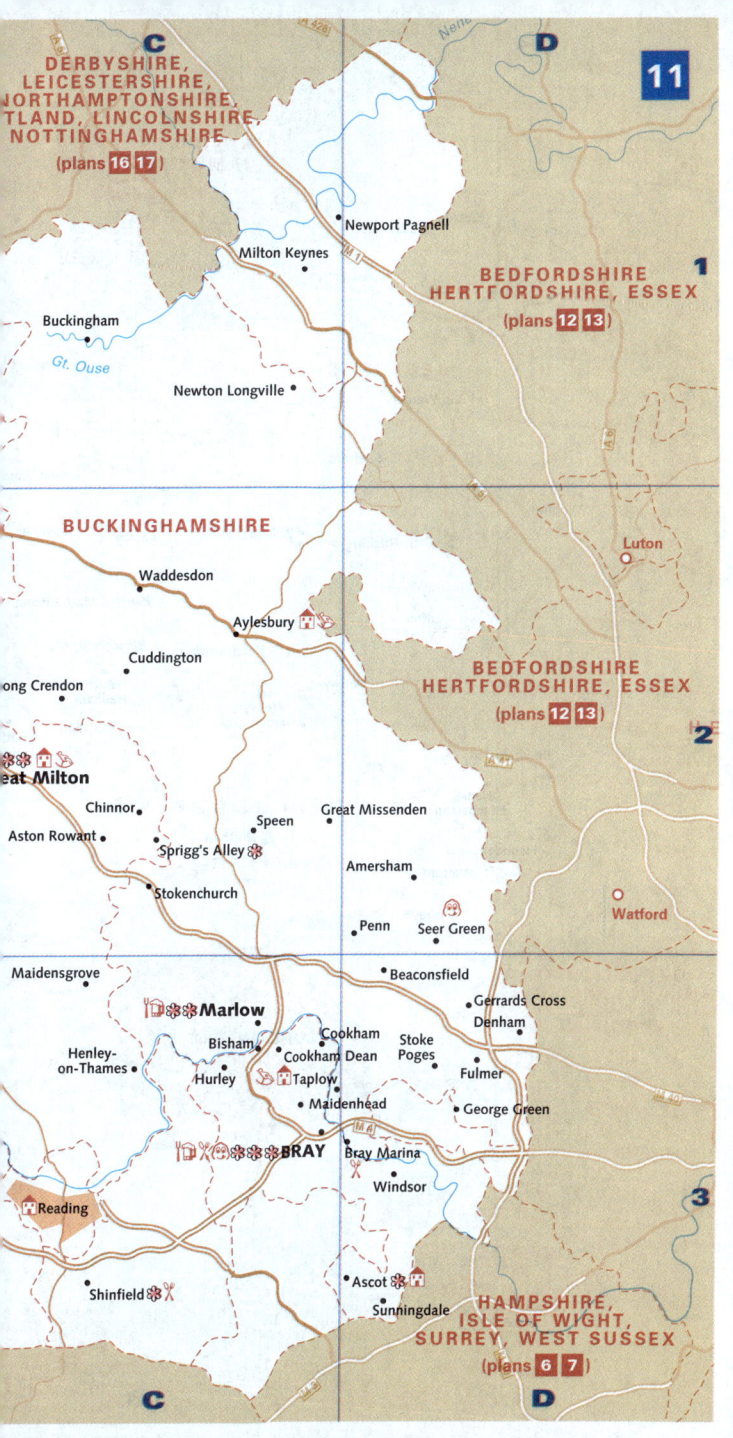

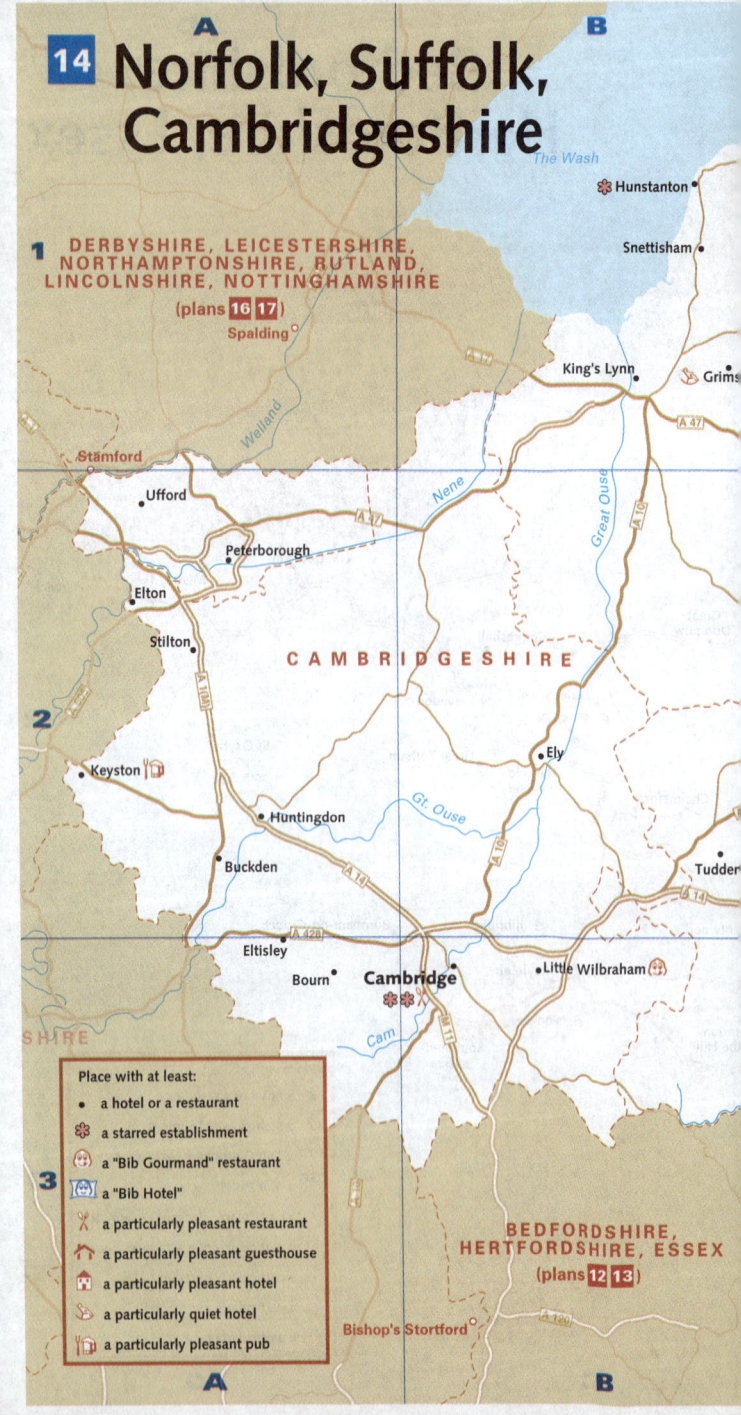

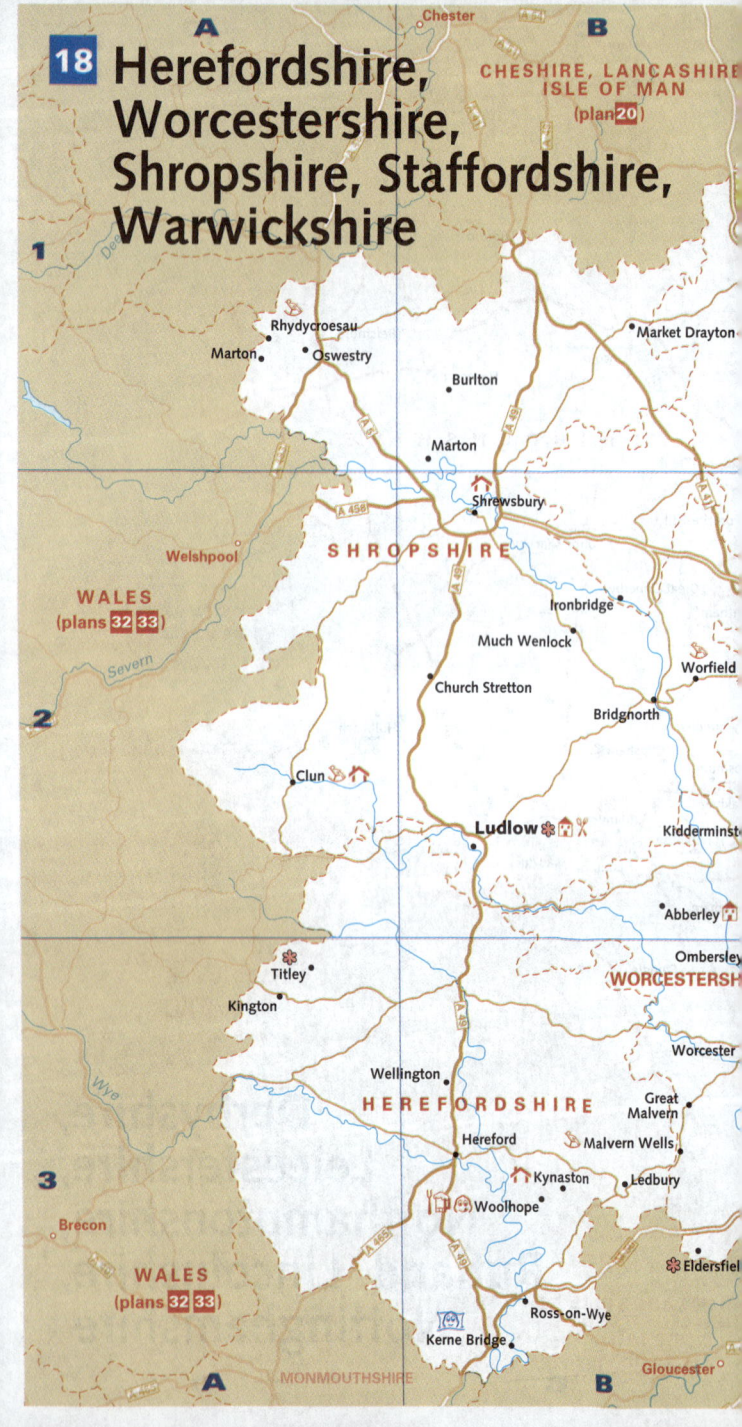

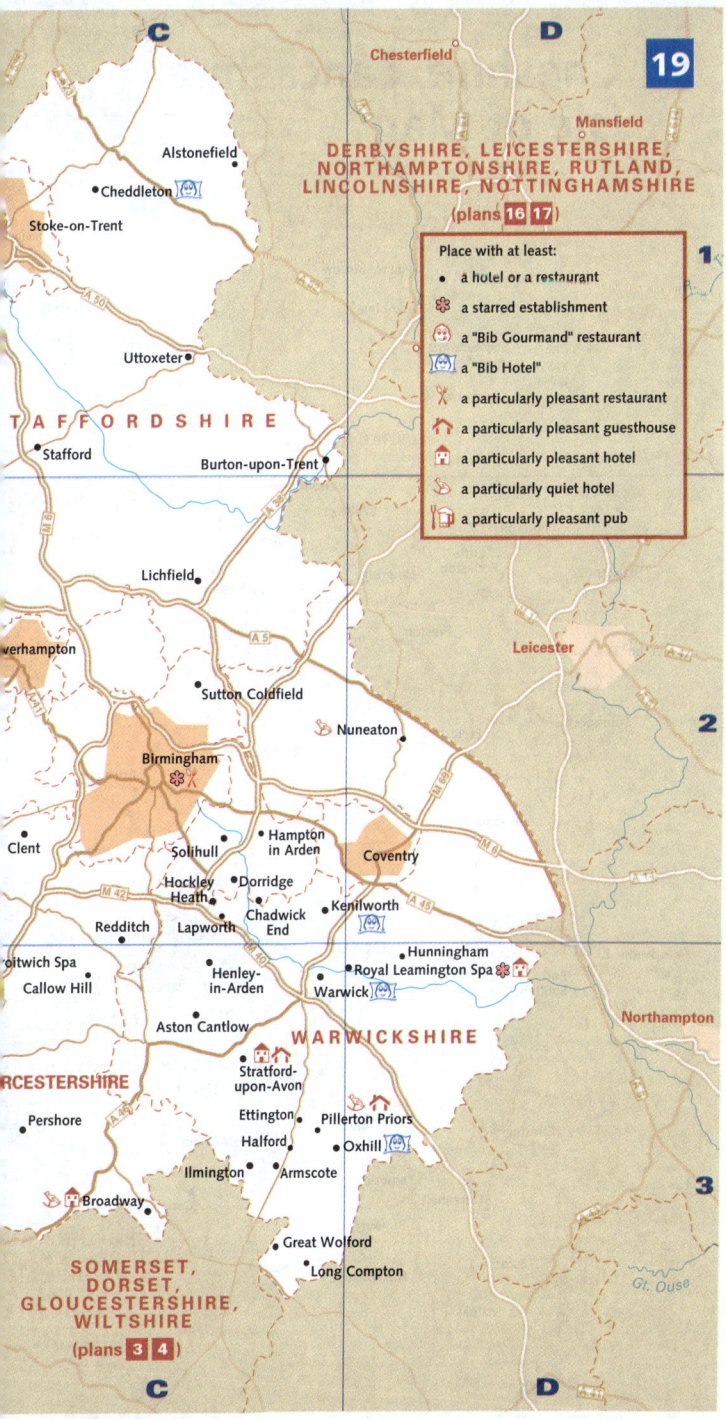

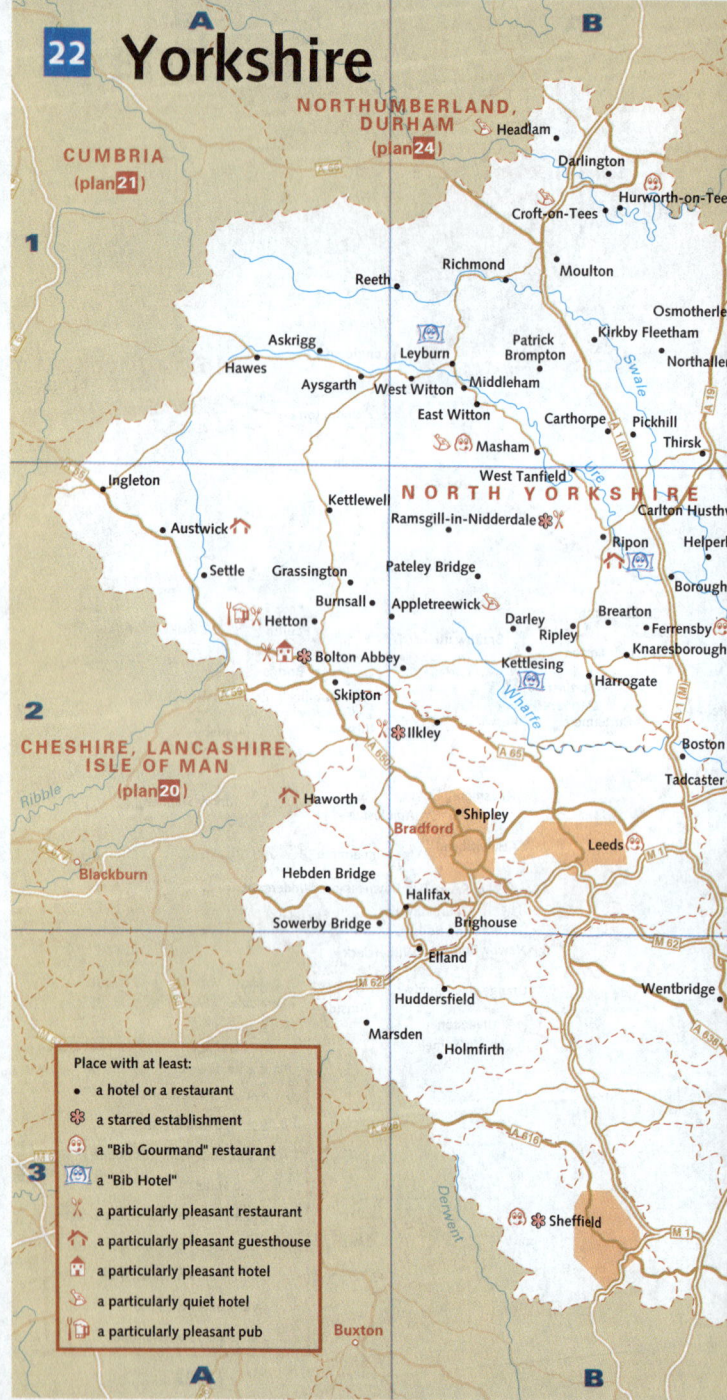

Shetland & Orkney 31

SHETLAND ISLANDS

- Unst
- Yell
- St. Magnus Bay
- Muckle Roe
- Papa Stour
- Whalsay
- Mainland
- Veensgarth
- Bressay
- Lerwick
- Foula

ORKNEY ISLANDS

- Westray
- Pierowall
- The North Sound
- North Ronaldsay
- Cleat
- Westray Firth
- Sanday
- Eday
- Stronsay
- Mainland
- Dounby
- Stronsay Firth
- Shapinsay
- Harray
- Kirkwall
- Stromness
- Scapa Flow
- Hoy
- Burray
- St Margaret's Hope
- South Ronaldsay
- Cleat
- Pentland Firth

HIGHLAND & THE ISLANDS (plans 29 30)

- Thurso
- Wick

Place with at least:
- • a hotel or a restaurant
- ✽ a starred establishment
- 😊 a "Bib Gourmand" restaurant
- 🏠 a "Bib Hotel"
- ✕ a particularly pleasant restaurant
- ⌂ a particularly pleasant guesthouse
- 🏠 a particularly pleasant hotel
- ⌇ a particularly quiet hotel
- 🍺 a particularly pleasant pub

36 Republic of Ireland